Barnaby Rogerson

Morocco

Cadogan Guides are published by
Cadogan Books plc
27–29 Berwick Street, London W1V 3RF, UK
e-mail: guides@cadogan.demon.co.uk

Distributed in North America by
The Globe Pequot Press
6 Business Park Road, PO Box 833, Old Saybrook, Connecticut 06475–0833

Book and cover design by Animage
Cover photographs by Alex Robinson
Maps © Cadogan Guides, drawn by Map Creation Ltd

Series Editor: Rachel Fielding
Editor: Nick Rider
Indexing: Dorothy Frame
Production: Rupert Wheeler/Production Services
Mac Help: Adrian McLaughlin

A catalogue record for this book is available from the British Library
ISBN 1-86011-043-6

The author and publishers have made every effort to ensure the accuracy of the information in this book at the time of going to press. However, they cannot accept any responsibility for any loss, injury or inconvenience resulting from the use of information contained in this guide.

Please help us to keep this guide up to date: We would be delighted to receive any comments concerning existing entries or omissions in this guide. All contributors will be acknowledged in the next edition and writers of the best letters will receive a copy of the Cadogan Guide of their choice.

Printed and bound in Great Britain by Redwood Books Ltd.

To Michael Scott who would have understood that I would first see Molly at Tangier.

About the Author

Barnaby Rogerson was conceived on a yacht and born in Dunfermline. He first fell in love with the idea of Morocco aged nine, standing before Delacroix's *Arab Tax* in Washington D.C.'s National Gallery. He first visited Morocco when he was 16, on an errand to buy fresh vegetables for his mother at the market in Tetouan. He has been going back ever since, but over the last twenty-one years has also found time to restore garden temples, lay pebble floors in grottoes and write a history of North Africa.

Acknowledgements

One of the great joys of preparing this third edition has been to travel with Rose Baring and Molly Rogerson in continual, sweaty proximity for two months seeing places I thought I knew well completely anew. Another has been to realize the depths of my ignorance and tap the expertise of various friends. I would particularly like to thank Fi Lowry for improving the section on birds, Johnny Bell for that on flora, David Flower on music, Annie Bell on cooking and Rose Baring on language, in which I remain in a shameful state of ignorance. I have also leant on the much greater expertise of various organizations, particularly Annie Austin at CLM, Simon Ames at GB Airways, Chris Lawrence of Best of Morocco, Mr Jouad of Always Rent a Car, Madame Gunnel Nejjar of Salam Hotels and Mr Ali el Kasmi of the Moroccan Tourist Board.

Among the dozens who have walked or talked Morocco with me in the last three years I would particularly like to thank Rebecca Nicholson, Anthony and Charlotte Rowe, June Baxter, Christopher Gibbs, Moulay el Kebir of the magic market at Marrakech, Bouhrazen Hassan of the mountains, Barry Stern of the Kabah at Tangier, William Bickerdike of the British Council at Rabat, Nicky and Susanna Johnstone, Max Lawrence of Marrakech and Tarhazoute, Haj Elbas Mimoun, Jamal Atbir Eddine of Immouzèr-des-Ida-Outanane, Mohammed Jebbour of Missour, Hassan Cheradi, the enthusiastic new director of the Dar Jamaï museum in Meknès, Si Mohammed, archaeologist, teacher and director of the Tangier museum and Mohammed Choukri of the centre for Alaouite research in Rissani.

Letters received from readers are an unexpected offshoot of guide-book writing. The adventures of Martin Wright of the Seychelles, Lia Belles of Mallorca, Kitty Odell and Sir Timothy Harford have all been read with great interest, as have the improvements suggested by Helen Gane, RF Mellor, William Plowden, Peter Hinwood and Alan Balchin. I was also delighted to see that the Cadogan Guide to Morocco was acknowledged by Carol Malt as the inspiration for her latest historical novel.

Amongst the many who labour away tirelessly at the editing and production of guidebooks at the Cadogan Books office in the steamy heart of Soho I would like to thank Rachel Fielding and Nick Rider who have edited this edition, and Linda McQueen who has attempted to keep everything in order, everybody sane and endlessly helped me find my cursor without once losing her cool.

Contents

Travel 1–14

Practical A–Z 15–40

History 41–58

The Southern Oasis Valleys 449–504

Agadir, the Sous Valley and the Anti-Atlas 505–60

The Western Sahara 561–78

Islamic and Moroccan Terms and Language 579–85

Further Reading 586–8

Index 589–96

Maps

Introduction

If travel is a search for lost paradise, the Muslim Kingdom of Morocco is large and mysterious enough to infinitely prolong the quest. It has an exoticism all of its own, created by the conflicting influences that have washed against this northwestern corner of Africa. Whatever your experience of the latin temper of southern Europeans, the heady lifestyle of Morocco is more dramatic. From the moment you land adventure assails you. In simple transactions, like buying a kilo of oranges, there is unexpected drama, humour and competitive gamesmanship. The sun is always shining somewhere in Morocco, and from March to October it is difficult to avoid. Travelling from the cool peaks of the Atlas mountains to the baking heat of a Saharan oasis, or from the city of Marrakech to a beach, is cheap and easy. You can fly, drive, take the train, or share the tempo of local life by packing into a communal taxi or bus.

It is not only the sites of Morocco—the Roman ruins, the ancient cities, mountain kasbahs and elegant Islamic monuments—but also the everyday way of life that lingers in the memory: breakfasts of fresh coffee and *croissants*; the heavy odour of virgin olive oil; and the pyramids of fruit, vegetables and nuts which are so fresh and pure they seem like a new species altogether.

Morocco is a land fit for the jinn, full of extremes to reflect the changing whims and petulant egotism of proud spirits—high mountain chains, desert plains, long rivers, lush secluded valleys, broken wooded hills and undulating farmland. South from Tangier are the rich but flat and largely treeless agricultural provinces of the Rharb, Chaouia and Doukkala, punctuated by large coastal cities such as Kénitra, Rabat, Casablanca and Safi. East from Tangier the Rif mountains run along the Mediterranean coast of Morocco like a northern rampart against Europe. They reach their peak at Jbel Tidiquin, above the *kif*-growing centre of Ketama, and decline as they approach the Algerian border. To their south, fertile plains surround Fès and Meknès, and a thin strip of low land to the east—the Taza Gap—separates the highlanders of the Rif from those of the Middle Atlas. Beyond the citadel of Taza this brief gap in the mountains opens out into the wide eastern desert, the plains of Jel and the Rekkam.The Middle Atlas is an amorphous mountainous mass, a vast irregular limestone plateau whose ancient rounded summits dominate much of central Morocco. Three great rivers, the Sebou, the Moulouya and the Oum er Rbia, drain its forested slopes. To the south rises the much more intensely dramatic mountain range of the High Atlas, which extends east from the

Atlantic coast for 700km (430 miles) and exceeds 4,000m (13,000ft) at the summit of Jbel Toubkal. The northern face shelters innumerable mountain valleys, wooded heights drained by fast flowing streams that create lush basins of fertility around the cities of Beni Mellal and Marrakech. The southern slopes of the mountains face the Sahara and, though dramatically denuded, collect whatever rain falls and direct it south to create for 100km (60 miles) the astonishing oasis valleys of the pre-Sahara. The palm-shaded valleys of the Dadès, Drâa, Rhéris and Ziz, overlooked by traditional settlements and in total contrast to the sunbaked arid mountains, create some of the most enduring and potent images of Moroccan travel. The Anti-Atlas range, next to the Atlantic seaboard, rises a clear 100km (60 miles) south of the High Atlas across the verdant Sous Valley, though at its eastern end the massifs of Siroua and Sarhro merge their twisted barren slopes with those of the High Atlas. South of the last oasis villages of the Anti-Atlas the flat wasteland of the Western Sahara stretches immutably south; a harsh landscape that shows a 1000km (600 mile) face of savage cliffs to the Atlantic, broken by beaches at Tarfaya, Laâyoune and Dakhla.

Moroccan landscape and the country's regional cultures are all extraordinarily diverse, but ultimately it is its people that prove most fascinating. In any one Moroccan there may lurk a turbulent and diverse ancestry: of slaves brought across the Saharan wastes to serve as concubines or warriors; of Andalusian refugees who came from the ancient Muslim and Jewish cities of southern Spain, and of Bedouin Arabs from the tribes that fought their way along the North African shore. All these peoples have mingled with the indigenous Berbers, who have continuously occupied the land since the Stone Age. The ruler of Morocco, King Hassan II, shares these influences, as well as being a direct descendant of the prophet Mohammed. He explains the peculiar temperament of his country by likening it to the desert palm: rooted in Africa, watered by Islam, and rustled by the winds of Europe.

It is a mistake to move too quickly around Morocco. Far too many visitors visit a city, suffer all the initial hassle and leave before they are relaxed enough to explore beyond the well-trodden list of major tourist sites. The frenetic energy, noisy animation, odours and ceaseless babble of the Moroccan street initially threaten to overwhelm a visitor. In Morocco, however, do as the Moroccans do. Take things slowly, and catch the afternoon siesta in order to be fresh for the evening paseo. A certain wry but friendly sense of humour is all that is needed to cope with the anarchic but addictive lifestyle.

If you want an ideal introduction to Morocco, a suggested itinerary might begin with a flight to Agadir, which you would leave quickly to stay a night or two at the delicious hilltop village of Immouzèr-des-Ida-Outanane, amid waterfalls, banana plantations and palm groves, before travelling east to the walled city of Taroudannt. From there you could cross the High Atlas at the Tizi-n-Test pass on your way to Marrakech. After a few days in this great city, move west again to the coast at the charming town of Essaouira, before moving down the southern coast to the desert gateway of Tiznit, on your way to a last few days' walking in the magnificent valleys of the Anti Atlas around Tafraoute.

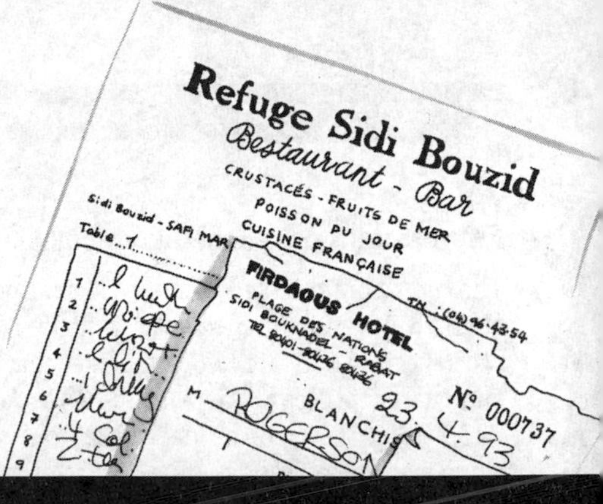
Refuge Sidi Bouzid
Restaurant - Bar
CRUSTACÉS - FRUITS DE MER
POISSON DU JOUR
CUISINE FRANÇAISE
FIRDAOUS HOTEL
PLAGE DES NATIONS
SIDI BOUKNADEL - RABAT
Nº 000737
royal air maroc

Travel

Getting There

By Air

From Britain on a Scheduled Flight

The most comfortable and most efficient way to travel between Britain and Morocco (and often, in the end, the cheapest) is with one of the scheduled flights to Tangier, Casablanca or Marrakech. There are two companies that run regular, year-round flights between Britain and Morocco: **Royal Air Maroc** (**RAM**) and **GB Airways**. Prices can vary from around £250 to £350 return, depending on season. Peak periods for prices are around Christmas/New Year and over the Easter holiday season.

RAM fly from Heathrow (from Terminal Two, using the Air France lobby at the far right end, from the main entrance, of this otherwise crammed building). They fly to Tangier on Tuesday, Wednesday and Saturday at 17.15, arriving 19.00, and on Fridays at 22.20, arriving 00.05. There are flights to Casablanca every day of the week. The Tuesday, Wednesday and Saturday flights go via Tangier (with a 45-minute wait there), and having left Heathrow at 17.15 arrive in Casablanca at 20.35. Monday, Friday and Sunday flights are direct, leaving Heathrow at 17.40 and arriving 19.50, while the Thursday flight alone leaves at 19.05 and arrives at 21.00. There are no direct flights to Marrakech, but it is easy to make a connection at Casablanca's Mohammed V airport, the hub of RAM internal services to regional airports such as Agadir, Fès, Marrakech, Ouarzazate, Oujda and Laâyoune.

To make a reservation use a local travel agent or inquire directly from the RAM office at 205 Regent Street, London W1R 7DE, ✆ (0171) 439 4361, 📠 (0171) 287 0127.

GB Airways (half-owned by British Airways and half by the Gibraltar-based Bland Group) operates a fleet of Boeing 737s out of Gatwick and Heathrow. The current schedule offers one flight a week to Tangier (BA 6924) leaving Heathrow at 15.45 and stopping in Gibraltar before arriving at 18.45. For Casablanca there is a daily direct service leaving Heathrow at 17.10 (Saturdays only at 16.05), and they also have a twice weekly direct flight to Marrakech, leaving Gatwick at 08.45 on Tuesday morning and 09.15 on Fridays.

For GB-British Airways flight information, call ✆ 0990-444000 (a 24 hour, part automated answering service) or ✆ 0345-222111 for a direct sales line.

From Britain on a Chartered Flight

Seats on charter flights are supposed to be sold as part of an inclusive package holiday, but un-booked seats are routinely sold at a discount. Flights can sometimes be picked up very cheaply, although you will need to fit in with whatever a company has to offer in terms of availability, destinations, fixed return dates, departure times and unfashionable departure airports. In recent years political events (the Kuwait war and Algerian insurrection) have had an adverse effect on the British package holiday market to Morocco. There are fewer charter flights (especially to Agadir) and fewer bargains. Check prices and availability from any of the independent bucket-shop ads in the back pages of *Time Out, Private Eye, The Sunday Times* and the *Observer*, or ring the Air Travel Advisory Bureau, ✆ (0171) 636 5000, which can give you a short list of some of the most competitive bucket shops to ring for prices.

In times of heavy demand when there is not a seat to be found it can also be useful to bear in mind an alternative route, which is to pick up one of the many cheap charter flights to Malaga or Almeria in southern Spain. You can then catch one of the ferries (detailed below) or the three times a week RAM Malaga—Casablanca flight

From Ireland

There are no direct scheduled flights from Ireland but **Sunway Travel**, Blackrock, Dublin 6, ✆ (01) 288 6828 arranges direct charter flights from Dublin to Agadir in southern Morocco throughout the year. An off-season flight can usually be picked up for around IR£200, or around £300 with accomodation. If calling from Britain the Irish code is 00353.

From France

Paris has by far the best air connections with Morocco of anywhere in Europe. The routes are shared equally between Air France and Royal Air Maroc. There are 30 flights a week to Casablanca, 12 to Marrakech and half a dozen each to Agadir, Oujda, Tangier, Fès and Rabat. From provincial cities such as Toulouse, Strasbourg, Nice, Marseille, Lyon and Bordeaux there are at least twice-weekly flights direct to Casablanca.

To check timetables and prices in Britain call Air France on ✆ (0181) 759-2311 for recorded information, or visit or call their London office at Colet Court, Hammersmith Road, London W6, ✆ (0181) 742 6600

From Other European Destinations

Royal Air Maroc runs regular services to the principal Moroccan airports (Casablanca, Tangier, Marrakech and Agadir) from Brussels, Amsterdam, Dusseldorf, Frankfurt, Geneva and Madrid. There are also direct weekly flights to and from Copenhagen, Lisbon, Strasbourg, Stockholm, Vienna, Zurich, Milan and Munich.

From North America

There are a variety of ways of crossing the Atlantic to Morocco. The easiest is to book yourself onto the direct twice-weekly **RAM** (Royal Air Maroc) flight from JFK airport in New York to Casablanca, or the weekly flight from Montreal to Casablanca. Check availability well in advance, as not all the advertised flights actually run. In New York inquire from the RAM office, ✆ (212) 750 6071, 📠 212-980-7924; in Montreal the RAM office is on ✆ 285 19 37 and ✆ 285 14 35. Both flights currently depart around 8.30pm and arrive in Morocco just after 7am. An APEX return currently costs around US $1,000, depending on season. People under 24 can get a ten per cent reduction by buying directly from these offices.

The second option is to make a two-stage flight with one of the national European airlines with services to Morocco such as Air France, KLM, Lufthansa, British Airways or Iberia. They have the advantage of a wide variety of North American departure points, if you don't live near New York or Montreal. The disadvantage is having to change planes and wait in a European transit lounge for the connection to Morocco. APEX returns from the East Coast can usually be picked up for around $650–$800, from the West, for around $900–$1,100.

The third option is to hunt for a bargain flight across the Atlantic to London or Paris (return ticket prices can be anything from $200 to $800) and then pick up on the cheap travel offers available in these European cities. Financially this only works well if you have friends or family to stay with, or want a few days in Europe. A London or Paris hotel bill could distort this route into a false economy. There are hundreds of transatlantic flight options—ring around budget travel agents that advertise in Sunday papers, especially the *New York Times.*

To keep these initial enquiries cheap, here is a selection of toll-free numbers: British Airways ✆ 1 800 247 2747; Air France ✆ 1 800 237 2747; Iberia ✆ 1 800 722 4642; RAM ✆ 1 800 892 6726; and Virgin Atlantic ✆ 1 800 862 8621.

From Australia and New Zealand

There are no direct flights from Australasia to Morocco. The nearest thing available is either the Singapore to Casablanca connection operated by Royal Jordanian Airways, or Royal Air Maroc's Dubai to Casablanca flight, but as this already involves one change you might as well visit those sad, grey-coloured cousins in London and pick up a connection from there. It usually works out cheaper.

By Sea

There are no ferries from Britain or northern Europe to Morocco, though there is a good choice of routes once you reach the shores of the western Mediterranean. Outside of the peak six weeks from late July to early September, it is usually possible to pick up tickets for a vehicle crossing at ferry ports without too much of a wait. If you wish to make a firm booking in advance there is an efficient British travel agent, **Southern Ferries** at 179 Piccadilly, London W1V 9DB, ✆ (0171) 491 4968, @ (0171) 491 3502, who can make all the arrangements necessary or just advise you as to the times, price and frequency of this year's sailings.

Though the thought of travelling to Morocco by boat, gently shedding the shores of Europe for those of Africa, is undeniably appealing, it also has its disadvantages. Some of Morocco's most sophisticated and aggressive hasslers wait outside the port gates in Tangier to pounce on new arrivals.

From France

The car ferry *Marrakech* sails from **Sète**, near Montpellier, three times a week in summer and once a week over the winter, and takes 39 hours to arrive in Tangier. This is a popular passage from France but an odd route to take from Britain. Tickets (a return adult fare costs around $405/£270) are available from the SNCM offices at 4 Quai d'Alger in Sète, or through their British agents, Southern Ferries (*see* above).

From Spain

The ten-hour trip from **Almería to Melilla** is covered by five sailings a week in the summer and three in winter. Boats depart at 1pm from Almeria and at 11pm from Melilla. Tickets can be bought from the port gates or their British agents Southern Ferries (*see* above).

Ferries run daily throughout the summer for the 8hr trip from **Málaga to Melilla**, and in the winter there are five sailings a week. Boats depart from Malaga at 1pm and at 11pm from Melilla. Two boats a week travel from **Málaga to Tangier**, a 5hr sail, throughout the year. In Málaga buy tickets from Limadet, Muelle Heredia 8, or Trasmediterranea, Calle Juan Diaz 4, or book ahead through Southern Ferries (*see* above).

The ferries from **Algeciras to Tangier or the Spanish enclave of Ceuta** offer by far the quickest, cheapest and most popular connection to Morocco. Of the two choices of destination, the sailing to Ceuta is temptingly cheaper and quicker, but the lack of public transport and delays at the border crossing can sometimes make this a false economy. Unless you want to visit Ceuta it is better, even with a car, to go to Tangier. All ferry tickets can be bought at the port gates at Recinto del Puerto in Algeciras, or in advance from Southern Ferries (*see* above). In high season there are 12 one-and-a-half-hour crossings to Ceuta a day, and three or four crossings to Tangier (two and a half hours). The frequency drops to eight (Ceuta) and one or two (Tangier) in the winter.

hydrofoil routes

Hydrofoils offer quick, noisy, passenger-only crossings. There is not much view, and no passing breeze as you are usually confined inside the aircraft-like interior. They do not run in rough weather and do not operate on Sundays, but the tickets (which are all around $30/£20 for a single) are only about a third more expensive than for a conventional ferry.

Transtour of **Algeciras**, © (956) 665200, run at least four half-hour crossings daily to **Ceuta** throughout the year, the cheapest and most reliable hydrofoil crossing of the Straits of Gibraltar. They also run a daily one-hour service to **Tangier** from March to September. In high summer a service also sometimes runs to **Mdiq**,, a port on the 'Côte du Rif'.

The celebrated steamer SS *Mons Calpe* which ran from **Gibraltar to Tangier** is no longer in operation. Its place has been taken by a twice-weekly hydrofoil, which takes an hour and a half. In the summer months there is a also a weekly boat to Mdiq. Timetable details and tickets are obtained from **Seagle Ltd**, 9B St George's Lane, Gibraltar, © 76763/71415.

The route from **Tarifa to Tangier**—shortest of them all—is very liable to cancellation if the on-off situation of the last five years is anything to go by. At the time of writing, **Transtour** provides hydrofoil crossings five days a week.

By Rail

From Britain via France and Spain

The train remains the most civilized way to travel. As my great-grandmother was fond of declaring, if God had meant us to fly he would never have given us the railway. A conventional return ticket from London to Algeciras in Spain will cost about $420/£280, with perhaps $75/£50 extra to pay in supplements for couchettes and fast trains in Spain. If you decide to leave London after breakfast on a Thursday, a Eurostar train through the Channel Tunnel will have you in the Gare du Nord in Paris by early afternoon (or early evening, if you take the cheaper ferry train via Dover). You then need to cross Paris to the Gare d'Austerlitz for the 22.58 to Irun on the Spanish border. Arriving at 07.40, you leave at 08.15 to arrive in Madrid at 14.56. You can then have the afternoon and evening on the town before catching the 23.00 night train, which takes you into Algeciras by 9.30am on Saturday morning.

For information and reservations on all of these services in Britain call International Travel at Victoria Station, © 0990-848848.

If you are over 26 the discount **Inter-Rail Pass**, which provides unlimited rail travel for a variable period of between 15 days and three months (but is only available to European citizens) is a waste of money for this trip, as it excludes France, Spain and Morocco. If you are under 26, it works for these vital countries, but you will still have to pay extra supplements for ferries and sleepers. The similar **Eurail pass** is designed for the use of non-European citizens who are not resident in Europe for more than six months. It offers unlimited rail travel in 17 European nations, but again excludes Morocco. There are also supplements to pay for ferries, sleepers and the first and last leg of travel. A two-month pass for someone under 26 costs around $930/£620, and would not be of any use for a Moroccan-based trip. They are available from many travel agents.

By Bus

From **Britain** there is a regular thrice-weekly service (Monday, Tuesday and Wednesday at 10pm) from London's Victoria Coach Station for the two-day journey to Tangier. A return ticket from Eurolines at 52 Grosvenor Gardens, London SW1W 0AU, © (0171) 730 8235, currently costs just $255/£170, a single $135/£90. From **France**, if you make your own to Paris, there is a Euroline coach that leaves from Porte de la Villette station on Mon, Wed, Fri and Sat for Tangier, from where the same route continues down through Rabat, Casablanca, Marrakech and Agadir, to terminate finally in Tiznit. For reservations call Eurolines at Porte de la Villette, © (01) 40 38 93 93 or (01) 42 05 12 10.

By Car

It is possible with two drivers and very little rest to get from England to Tangier in two days, although four or five days would allow you to enjoy something other than fast driving. To effect a smooth entrance into Morocco with a car, it is best to have your paperwork well organized, with documents under one name and one address. You should have **Green Card Insurance** for the journey through Europe, your **Vehicle Registration Document** and your **Driving Licence**. The pink EC driving licence is recognized in Morocco, although the more impressive International Driving Licence (available from the RAC or AA, or the AAA in the US) with its seal, passport photograph and French translation is preferred. At the customs post you must buy **Moroccan Frontier Insurance**, which is about $75/£50 for the maximum permitted visit of three months. This is a bureaucratic 'third party' requirement, which whatever the paper might actually claim is unlikely to provide any reimbursement in the event of an accident. For working insurance you will need to take out separate cover. In the UK, fire and theft insurance can be arranged with the Norwich Union for a month but no British company is yet prepared to give comprehensive cover for any longer period. If you are bringing a **caravan** (trailer), you will need an International Customs Carnet.

There is a full range of ferries connecting the various channel ports of France and England. The most useful are the night crossings to Le Havre, Caen or Cherbourg. Arriving in these ports in the early morning you can cross France during that day, to stay in the Pyrenean foothills that night. Crossing Spain can be done at a more leisurely pace, perhaps with a stop at Segovia before concentrating on the splendours of Moorish Andalusia in Granada, Cordoba or Seville.

There is a twice-weekly ferry from Plymouth to Santander (no sailings in January), but it is an expensive and tedious voyage. Ferry cafés compare badly in expense, entertainment and quality with the roadside restaurants of France and Spain.

Travel Agents and Specialist Holidays

Travel Agents

There are two **British** travel agents who specialize in arranging holidays to Morocco for the independent traveller. They can arrange flexible flight plans (flying into one city and coming out of another) fix good rates for a hire car, organize riding, walking, fishing, or shooting holidays, and drivers, as well as recommend restaurants or the hire of a villa. The first step in any planned holiday is to look through their annual brochures.

Annie Austin has presided over **Creative Leisure Management** (CLM) for 23 years and has an exhaustive and intimate knowledge of the country, in part learnt in the seven years when she ran a hotel in Salé. CLM are now based in the heart of London's West End at 1st Floor, 69 Knightsbridge, London SW1X 7RA, ✆ (0171) 235 0123/2110, @ (0171) 235 3851.

Chris Lawrence has managed **Best of Morocco** at Seend Park, Seend, Wiltshire SN12 6NZ, ✆ (01380) 828533, @ (01380) 828630, since 1967. He is aided by a branch at 17 Nottingham Street, London W1M 3RD, ✆ (0171) 487 4224, @ (0171) 487 4010, and an office in Marrakech. His son Max works fulltime in Morocco, but has branched out of general travel to take advantage of Morocco's growing popularity as a film and photo-shoot location.

Both CLM and Best of Morocco act as British agents for **Atlas Sahara Trek** (AST), a well-established Moroccan–French agency that is run by Bernard Fabry and based in Marrakech. They can set up week-long hiking, rafting and camel-riding trips anywhere that you wish to go in the Moroccan south.

Even if you are travelling from **North America or Australasia**, it may be worth making special arrangements you require via a specialist agent in the UK, since there are more of them there. **STA Travel** have branches in the USA, Canada, New Zealand, Australia and Britain. They are an experienced firm well placed to give advice on connecting flights and can also book you in with one of the British-based specialist operators detailed in this section.

In Australasia: STA Auckland at 10 High Street, ✆ (9) 3099723; STA Melbourne at 256 Flinders Street, ✆ (03) 347 4711; STA Sydney at 1 Lee Street, (02) 281 9866.

In the USA: STA Los Angeles, 7204 Melrose Avenue, CA 90046, ✆ (213) 934 8722; STA San Francisco, 116 Geary Street, Suite 702, CA 94108, ✆ (415) 391 8407; STA Boston, 273 Newbury Street, MA 02116, ✆ (617) 266 6014; STA New York, 48 East 11th Street, NY 10003, ✆ (212) 477 7166.

To check up on your travel plans, or pick up tickets while in London there are two STA offices at 74 and 86 Old Brompton Road, SW7 3LQ and 117 Euston Road, London NW1 2SX; for North American inquiries ✆ (0171) 937 9971, for European inquiries ✆ (0171) 937 9921, for Africa ✆ (0171) 465 0486, for rest of world ✆ (0171) 937 9962.

In North America you could also ring the **Moroccan Tourist Board**, who will send you their current list of approved travel agents which at the moment includes the New York firms **Les Soleil**, ✆ (212) 308 4249; **Marsans**, ✆ (212) 239 3880 and **RAM tours**, ✆ 1 800 344 6726. In Virginia you can call **Morocco Travel** toll-free on ✆ 1 800 428 5550; in the Mid West there is **Maupintour**, ✆ 1 800 255 6162; and on the West Coast there is **ATC**, ✆ 1 800 227 9747.

Andante A Wiltshire-based agency specializing in historical and archaeological tours who do an annual ten day trip through the Imperial cities and classical ruins, as well as a five day investigation of Marrakech and the High Atlas. ✆ (01980) 610555, ℻ (01980) 610002.

Discover Four trekking trips a year into the Atlas mountains and sub-Sahara. Timbers, Oxted Road, Godstone, Surrey RA9 8AD, ✆ (01883) 744392, ℻ (01883) 744913.

Dragoman Four-wheel-drive journeys of 5–10 weeks that follow the old caravan and existing nomadic routes through the Sahara. Camp Green, Kenton, Debenham, Suffolk IP14 6LA, ✆ (01728) 861133.

Encounter Overland 15-day tours of Morocco from May–Sept, starting from Málaga. 267 Old Brompton Road, London SW5 9JA, ✆ (0171) 370 6845, ℻ (0171) 244 9737

Explore Worldwide Small-group walking treks in the High Atlas and in the southern massifs of Jbel Sarhro and Jbel Siroua; also Imperial Cities and desert tour. 1 Frederick Street, Aldershot, Hampshire GU11 1LQ, ✆ (01252) 319448.

Exodus A well-established company that arranges jeep tours of southern Morocco, and also walking expeditions into the High and Anti Atlas mountains. 9 Weir Road, London SW12 0LT, ✆ (0181) 675 5550, ℻ (0181) 673 0779.

Field Studies Council Overseas A special botanist's tour is organised annually, in late March. Preston Mountford, Shrewsbury, Shropshire SY4 1HW, ✆ (01794) 850164.

Golf International Golfing holidays based around the courses at Tangier, Rabat and Mohammedia. International House, Priestley Way, Staples Corner, London NW2 7AW, ✆ (0181) 450 6671.

Ramblers Holidays Walking holidays in the foothills of the High Atlas, starting from Marrakech. Box 34, Welwyn Garden City, Hertfordshire AL8 6PQ, ✆ (01707) 331133.

Martin Randall arranges an annual trip in late October, with a strong architectural and historical bias, that follows the old caravan route of the Saharan gold trade from Tangier to Sijilmassa and back to Marrakech. Contact 10 Barley Mow Passage, Chiswick, London W4 4PH, ✆ (0181) 742 3355, ℻ (0181) 742 1066.

Naturetrek A 10-day birdwatching tour of southern Morocco in mid January. Chautara, Bighton, Hampshire SO24 9RB, ✆ (01962) 733051.

Saga Holidays Holidays for the over-60s in Marrakech and Agadir. Middleburg Square, Folkestone, Kent CT20 1AZ, ✆ (0800) 300500.

Sherpa Expeditions Week and two-week-long treks in the Jbel Sarhro. 131A Heston Road, Hounslow, Middlesex, TW5 0RD, ✆ (0181) 577 2717.

Topdeck Five or seven-week tours through Spain, Portugal, Morocco, Algeria, Tunisia and Italy; a whistle-stop cultural skirmish that is popular with non-European students and Australians. 131 Earls Court Road, London SW5 9RH, ✆ (0171) 244 8641.

Guerba Expeditions Two-week jeep tours in the Anti-Atlas or the High Atlas/Oasis Valleys. 101 Eden Vale Road, Westbury, Wiltshire BA13 3QX, ✆ (01373) 858956.

General Agencies

Other recommended travel agencies that know Morocco and are used to arranging flights and car hire and are accustomed to making multiple hotel bookings to suit individual requirements include such major names as—

Abercrombie and Kent Sloane Square House, Holbein Place, London SW1W 8NS, ✆ (0171) 730 9600, 📠 (0171) 730-9376.

Cadogan Travel Cadogan House, 9–10 Portland Street, Southampton, Hampshire, SO9 1ZP, ✆ (01703) 332661 (which has no connection with Cadogan Books).

CV Travel 43 Cadogan Street, London SW3 2PR, ✆ 0171 581 0851, 📠 (0171) 584 5229.

Hayes and Jarvis 152 King Street, London W6 0QU, ✆ (0181) 748 0088, 📠 (0181) 741 0299.

Steppes East Castle Eaton, Cricklade, Wiltshire, SN6 6JU, ✆ (01285) 810267, 📠 (01285) 810693

Entry Formalities

A valid Australian, British, Irish, Canadian, New Zealand or United States passport allows you to enter Morocco. A small 90-day entrance visa is then stamped into your passport. Temporary British Visitors passports are not accepted. As a retaliation for Benelux restrictions on Moroccan migrant workers, Dutch and Belgian passport holders have to apply for a visa in advance which is valid for only one month.

Whether arriving by air or sea you will need to have filled in a form (a *fiche*) with personal details as you approach the immigration desk. This is perfectly straightforward, providing you avoid any flowery prose beside 'purpose of visit' and humbly write 'tourism'. If you are a journalist or spy you should pretend to have another profession while on holiday in Morocco. If you are, or could be mistaken as a hippy, and are coming off the boat into Morocco it is worth tidying yourself up. If for some reason your hair, dress and jewellery has excited the enmity of an immigration officer, then in extremis there is nothing to stop you trying a different boat and/or port on another day.

Extending Your Stay

For extending a visit beyond 90 days you are officially required to report to a *gendarmerie* headquarters. In practice even these officials counsel against entering the labyinthine world of Moroccan bureaucracy and recommend a simple day trip across the border to either Ceuta, Gibraltar, Algeciras or Melilla in order to collect a fresh 90-day entrance stamp.

Customs

The usual duty-free allowances mean that many people start their trip with an extra bag, a shin-bruising thing in clanking, garish bright yellow. Unless you are a confirmed whisky drinker, forget all the duty-free hype and stick to Moroccan products while you're there.

Cars, sporting guns and expensive electronic equipment (which generally means professional still and video camera equipment) can be imported into the country duty-free for 90 days.

The details will be entered into your passport on arrival and will be checked off as you leave. If you cannot produce evidence of their theft (police documentation) you will be presumed to have sold them and charged a punitive duty. There is no way around this; even if you have written your car off on some obscure mountain road you will eventually find yourself having to fetch the wreck and tow it on to the ferry.

Customs officers routinely check bags as you arrive and depart. They are generally courteous and correct with foreigners. Moroccan emigrant workers returning home are careful to include some tempting item at the top of their bag, a small bottle of scent or tin of tea that might take their fancy.

Currency

Make certain that in addition to any credit cards or travellers cheques, you have enough liquid cash in a major currency on you to cover the first couple of days of your trip.

The Moroccan currency is the **dirham** (dh). It is not one of the world's hard currencies (those with rates of exchange fixed by the fast-dealing world of international markets). The dirham's exchange rate is fixed by the Moroccan government at an artificially high rate. In order to maintain this the exportation of currency is strictly forbidden, and so it is not possible to acquire dirhams outside the country. There is no black market, although shopkeepers are often happy enough to accept dollars and major European currencies.

There is usually an exchange booth open at seaports and airports on arrival. Should you arrive at night or outside conventional hours you may find them closed and that it is impossible to cash Travellers' Cheques or Eurocheques at all until the next day, let alone a credit card, so it's best to be armed with cash as well. Local taxi drivers, again, will be only too happy to accept dollars, francs, pounds and just about any other European currency, but try not to accept wildly excessive charging, even after a long flight (*see* below *By Taxi*).

Before **leaving** try to use up any Moroccan dirhams you may have already exchanged, as currency checks are carried out at passport and customs control at departure points. You will only be allowed to change back half of any amount you are carrying in excess of about 10dh, and the rest will be confiscated outright, with no compensation offered.

Getting Around

Distance chart (in kms) between principal cities, by road.

	Agadir	**Casa**	**Fès**	**G'mim**	**M'kech**	**Oujda**	**Rabat**	**Tangier**
Agadir	—	490	739	199	256	1082	608	860
Casablanca	490	—	290	689	234	633	92	370
Fès	739	290	—	938	483	343	198	307
Guelmim	199	689	938	—	465	1281	807	1059
Marrakech	256	234	483	465	—	826	326	604
Oujda	1082	633	343	1281	826	—	541	604
Rabat	608	92	198	807	326	541	—	278
Tangier	860	370	307	1059	604	604	278	—

By Air

There are plenty of Royal Air Maroc (RAM) internal flights between the principal cities of Morocco, although the timetables shift constantly. Contact the nearest RAM office for details. To give you a rough idea of prices, it currently costs about $90/£60 to fly from Tangier to Agadir. All RAM return flights need to be confirmed three days before departure, and there is a 25 per cent discount for students and under-26-year-olds.

To fly between the principal cities of Morocco would negate the very real pleasure of travelling through the countryside. However, an internal flight makes much more sense as a quick return back from a distant town, such as Al Hoceima or Oujda in the east of the country, or Laâyoune and Dakhla deep down in the Western Sahara.

By Rail

Travel by train whenever possible. The Moroccan state railway, the ONCF, manages the difficult trick of being both colourful and efficient. It runs over 1,700km (1,000 miles) of line on two axes, from Tangier to Marrakech and Casablanca to Oujda. Both of these long routes have a **sleeper service**, but otherwise daytime travel is divided between first, second and a very basic *économique* class. A second-class ticket is not much more than a bus fare, although the air conditioning and less cramped seating of first class makes it especially attractive in summer. A bar and restaurant operate on the major connections and there are cafés, newsstands and left-luggage kiosks at most stations. Only lockable luggage is accepted, but nearby cafés can often be persuaded to look after shopping and backpacks. The railway stations are handsome colonial buildings, placed off a major avenue on the edge of the French-built new towns. The recent establishment of the elegant chain of Moussafir hotels beside many of the principal stations has also greatly improved the convenience of rail travel.

For details of prices and daily departures (which are modified but not radically changed from year to year) look under 'Getting Around' in the relevant sections of the guide.

People under 26 can travel with InterRail cards in Morocco. Those of us over 26 but still passionate about rail travel can however buy a *Carte Fidelité* from the ONCF, which entitles you to a 50 per cent reduction on second-class tickets for twelve journeys. These can then be topped up with a supplement to allow you to travel first class.

By Bus

Morocco is well served by buses, which apart from being a quick, cheap and convenient way across the country are a pleasure in themselves. Musicians, beggars and vendors collect around bus stops throughout the country and often wander down the aisle before departure. There is an undoubted camaraderie of travel, and buses are one of the best places in which to meet some of the vast majority of unhustling Moroccans, a relaxing place to gather unbiased information, exchange oranges or cigarettes, enjoy unusually frank discussions and perhaps collect an invitation to tea. All those who dismiss the internal combustion engine as an unromantic form of travel cannot have taken a night bus in Morocco, stopped at a lone café for a bowl of soup under the stars, paused beside a smoking row of kebab stalls lit up by a chain of lights, or joined the queue that obediently follows the conductor to drink from a favourite hillside spring in the early morning light.

There is a barrage of bus companies that all enjoy some level of state or provincial funding. Whenever possible (and it usually is), travel by **CTM**, which runs an efficient national network. They have a regular schedule of departures, numbered seats with sufficient leg-room, and a secure baggage check-in system that issues tallied receipts. They are only slightly more expensive than local firms. In some cities, such as Casablanca, they have their own depot; in others such as Tangier and Marrakech they share the central bus depot with a lively assortment of rival firms. Above CTM in speed and comfort is **ONCF,** the state railway bus company, which runs express coaches connecting cities like Agadir, Tetouan, Nador, Beni-Mellal and Laâyoune to the railway system. Tickets are up to 50 per cent more, but as buses are so cheap anyway they are still well worth buying. Local bus firms tend to run older, slower buses that stop more frequently and only leave when they are full. This can add to your education and entertainment but drastically increase the presumed length of a journey.

The bus companies are increasingly being brought together in one terminal or neighbourhood of each city. This makes buying tickets in advance for popular inter-city routes an easy and effortless procedure. Even if companies still run separate depots or, as in Agadir, a series of adjacent booths overlooking a dusty square, check out the travel situation for yourself as soon as you have deposited your bags. Hotel porters, guides and tourist offices cannot ultimately be relied upon, while guide-books can get out of date surprisingly quickly. It is customary to pay 1 or 2dh for each item of baggage stored on the roof, but not for the use of the side lockers.

By Taxi

Travelling by 'place' in a ***grand taxi***, usually a big, battered Mercedes, should work out only a few dirhams more than a bus ride. At specific collection spots, which are mentioned throughout the guide, taxi drivers shout out their destination; if there are none going in your direction ask around. However, as six passengers are packed into a white diesel Mercedes before the taxi will leave, this method of travel has the advantage of speed but not always of comfort. In this enforced proximity it is, however, quite easy to ape the bulk of the passengers and fall fast asleep for most of the trip. *Grands taxis* only travel on routes where they can be sure of picking up a full load, typically from one town to the next. For a long distance you will have to leapfrog along a chain of *grand taxi* routes.

For more **individual destinations** you will have to bargain a price for the journey or employ the taxi for the whole day. Though much more than a 'place', when compared to hiring a car it appears reasonable enough.

Petits taxis are limited to three passengers and the city limits. Except in Fès, Casablanca and Rabat the meters seldom seem to function. The going rate for locals is around 3dh per person for a short city ride, but for tourists the sky can be the limit. Arabic, charm or conviction is required to get the price down to the reasonable level of 5–10dh per person for the usually quite short journey required from a bus/train station to a central hotel. Do not be afraid to ask for a price in advance, ideally with a door open before taking a seat, for pricing discussions at the end of a journey have a habit of becoming more vociferous and less successful.

Do not take up the offers of **unlicensed cars** operating as taxis whatever the price. Even if they are perfectly honest with you, their manoeuvres to avoid the attention of the police on the main roads can make for an exasperatingly slow journey.

By Car

Driving on the near-empty Moroccan country roads is a treat in itself, provided you bear a few warnings in mind. Remember, of course, to drive on the right-hand side. Following the French system vehicles coming from the right have priority, so give way to cars coming on to a roundabout. Watch out for trucks on narrow roads, as they will expect you to move out of the way. Beware of patches of gravel on the hairpin bends of mountain roads, which can have the same effect as ice. Though comparatively empty of cars, Moroccan roads seldom lack wayside fruit stalls, dogs, drifting livestock, cyclists and children. In the cool of the night there is also often quite a stream of quiet horsedrawn traffic, walkers and cyclists which requires especial vigilance. I saw two children killed on a bridge in the confused light of dusk by a careless lorry driver. The roadside was quickly filled with ululating village women, and angry farmers rushed in from the fields armed with hoes and forks to demand instant justice. Fortunately, the police were at hand. Be careful.

On the open roads there is a **speed limit** of 100km (62 miles) an hour, though few drivers seem to respect it. In the Western Sahara the police posts take an almost positive pleasure in informing you of speeds that in the more hidebound Anglo-Saxon world would make you lose your licence. The usual urban speed limit of 40km (25 miles) an hour should be adhered to whenever there is the slightest evidence of inhabitation.

Driving in cities becomes especially confusing, with streams of mopeds and cyclists weaving through the traffic. It is often better to find a hotel, park and then forget your car. Wherever you leave your car, always appoint a guardian. Hotels, restaurants and city streets often have their own *gardien de voiture,* identified by a brass badge, who will accept 2dh for each guarding session. In the countryside, try and appoint a child. Hire-cars are very easy to break into (a well-directed backward thump will open the locked front window of any Renault 4), and batteries and spare wheels are mobile and useful trading items.

Petrol/gasoline is roughly the same price as in Britain (about twice as much as in the US) and stations are reasonably well distributed. Not all the petrol gauges are totally reliable so it is advisable to keep topping the tank up whenever possible, or buy a plastic canister to make an emergency reserve. Moroccan mechanics are among some of the more resourceful and innovative in the world. I have witnessed in stunned admiration a clutch plate being carved out of an old Bedford truck and fitted into an Alfa Romeo, although if you are driving a Renault, Peugeot or Land Rover there should be no lack of orthodox spare parts.

car hire

Buses, though admirably friendly, keep you on well-established routes. In practice, despite the best of intentions, you often end up whizzing from one tourist feature to another. By hiring a car you can picnic, find lone places to swim, and explore empty sites and the magnificent and hospitable countryside of Morocco.

Each city section of the guide includes a full list of car-hire firms. It is worth shopping around, and also finding out whether you can return the car to another depot. Even the big agencies are often prepared to drop prices or do deals in tune with the season and demand. The various offices are usually found in close proximity to each other on the major avenue of a city's New Town. The two specialist travel agents listed on p.7, CLM and Best of Morocco, can organize flexible car-hire that often works out cheaper than anything you can arrange directly, and is certainly more convenient. They can have a car delivered to a hotel or awaiting you at an airport, which can be dropped off later somewhere else.

As a basic indication, a Renault 4 (which is the cheapest, most universal and often the most useful vehicle in Morocco) can be hired from a reputable dealer for around 3400dh ($360/£240) for four days, which includes all taxes, full insurance and unlimited mileage. At the top end of the rentals, a Land Rover can be hired from around 8000dh ($855/£570) a week, but book in advance to be certain of getting one. Before receiving a car you should check the brakes, insurance documentation, and that it has a working jack and a spare tyre.

The minimum rental period is usually one day. You will need to be over 21 (usually 25 for Land Rovers) and to have held a full driving licence for a year. A deposit, usually around 2500dh, is accepted by most agencies through credit cards. Hire includes third-party, fire and theft insurance, although the latter only applies for the total theft of the car and not for any missing parts. There are often optional personal insurance policies, and you might hire an extra spare tyre and accident coverage if you are planning on any dirt-track driving.

By Bicycle, Moped and Donkey

Moroccan enthusiasm for any sport extends to cyclists, who can expect a welcome and consistent interest wherever they go. If you are thinking of bringing your own bicycle to Morocco, the **Cyclists' Touring Club**, Cotterell House, 69 Meadrow, Godalming, Surrey GU7 3HS, © (01483) 417217, can provide invaluable information on flight transport and insurance, as well as suggesting some routes.

Ask about bicycle, moped or donkey hire from hotel porters, who usually know much more about this shifting pattern of trade than the tourist offices. A day's bicycle hire will cost around 50dh. You can if you wish buy a donkey or mule for around 600dh, but rental works out at about 10dh an hour.

Disabled Travellers

Neither the pavements of the New Town boulevards of Moroccan cities nor the narrow, packed streets of medinas are particularly suitable for visitors in wheelchairs. To set against the many stairs, few ramps and virtually complete absence of adapted toilets there is, however, the very willing and unflappable attitude to be found in Morocco. You will seldom be short of a pair of extra hands in need, though as with any Westerner, tips or at least cigarettes should be offered around. Do not let the difficulties put you off. Some of the most enthusiastic accounts of North Africa I have heard have come from friends who use wheelchairs. If you are in need of encouragement, read Quentin Crewe's *In Search of the Sahara*, a book full of possibilities and adventures.

Practical A–Z

Bargaining

This is a necessary art that is fully enjoyed and understood in Morocco. For a foreign traveller, transport, hotel and restaurant prices are all fixed. It is only in the purchase of local crafts (and the odd taxi ride) that your bargaining skills will be required. A visit to a museum to remind yourself of what quality you are aspiring to, and to a state-run *Ensemble Artisanal* for the maximum price is a good start: you will be helpless unless you have a firm and confident idea of the price you should be paying.

It is good tactics, and in the highest order of gamesmanship, to greet the shopkeeper, shake his hand and praise his colourful display of goods before he does. Look at some items other than what you are actually interested in first, and have a friend act out the negative, mean and unenthusiastic role. Accept as many cups of tea as you are offered but delay for as long as possible the mention of your first price, praising the goods but looking sad, wistful and tearful in turn at the impossible prices. Once you have named your price be obstinate, and watch out for the skilfully-deployed ratchet gambit by which he gradually drops his price in exchange for a gradual rise in yours.

There are three rules: Never bargain for something you don't want, don't hurry, and even if you think you have just made a great financial coup, praise your opponent for his ruthless hard bargaining and great skill.

Beggars and Alms

Keep and collect all loose change from cafés for alms and tips. A dirham is considered generous in a country where 3dh an hour is still a reasonable labouring wage. Any more than that and you will be presumed not to recognize the value of money and possibly be asked for more. On the giving of alms, the Koran gives the most excellent advice. The Prophet Mohammed was questioned: 'What shall we bestow in alms?' to which he replied, 'What you can spare—for thus God instructs that you might think more deeply. . . but if you turn away from them, while you yourself yet hope for help from God, at least speak to them in a kindly manner.'

Children

Children are much more of an advantage than an impediment to travelling in Morocco. Next to speaking Maghrebi Arabic or converting to Islam, they form the most enduring bridge between cultures. They cause a drastic reduction in hassle and can be relied upon to look effortlessly stoical during bargaining sessions and (unless they are absolute monsters) improve your relationship with the staff of a restaurant, café or hotel. Hotels are usually happy to provide extra mattresses in a room or a cot usually without any extra charge.

Children's tastes should be taken into account when planning trips for they tend to be easily bored by architecture and museums but more than usually excited by snakes, minerals, working potteries, horse-drawn carriage rides, camels, donkeys, mules, mills and running water. The one thing you must always bear in mind, even on the most sheltered beach, is the strong undertow off the Atlantic coast.

Wide straw hats can be bought locally as necessary protection against the sun, and packets of nuts, raisins, sultanas, dates and other dried fruit can be carried around in a raffia bag for snacks. Sterilized *Ecremé* milk can be bought in litre cartons, but should be consumed quickly once opened. Throughout Morocco it is also possible to buy small plastic sacks of fresh milk for 2.5dh which have their date stamped in one corner. However, no matter how attentive you are about mineral water and peeling fruit it is very likely that your child will be hit by an attack of diarrhoea in the first week or two in Morocco. Try not to panic, and feed them lots of bananas.

Climate

The Tourist Board promises 350 days of sunshine a year, and as hotels and restaurants remain open all year round, any month is a good time to visit Morocco. There are, however, seasonal variations to take into account when planning the shape of your holiday. Also, during the 1990s Morocco, like much of the world, has witnessed a more erratic climate.

From November to February there is the possibility of rain, and you will find the beach-resorts distinctly off-season. This is the prime period to visit the oasis valleys of the Sahara, Agadir, Taroudannt and the Western Sahara, which are all bearably hot and comparatively green in these months. February sees Tafraoute and the Anti-Atlas at their best, although rain is still a possibility.

March, April and May are reliably but not cripplingly hot, and the countryside, with its fast ripening harvest and busy rural souks, is at its most interesting. This is a good period for a general tour of the country.

June, July and August are the hottest and busiest tourist months, but there is little activity in evidence on the part of the locals during the heat of the day. The farmland is baked dry and most schools, offices and industries have stopped work. The nation is on holiday, if not at the beach. These months do have most of the *moussems* (religious festivals). The High and Middle Atlas mountains are at their most accessible and attractive now.

September and October witness a slight but welcome reduction in temperature and in the crowds. Olives and dates are ripening, and these two months make another fine period for a general exploration of the country.

average daily temperatures °C (°F)

Morocco has been defined as a cold country with a hot sun. The monthly averages given here hide an often dramatic range in temperatures through each day. Even in the mid-summer months a sweater may be useful against evening coastal breezes, the cool of the mountain peaks and the desert nights. At the very least it can be moulded into a pillow for long bus journeys.

	Jan	**April**	**June**	**Aug**	**Oct**	**Dec**
Agadir	21 (69)	24 (75)	26 (78)	26 (79)	26 (78)	21 (69)
Al Hoceima	16 (61)	19 (67)	26 (78)	29 (85)	23 (74)	17 (63)
Casablanca	17 (63)	20 (68)	24 (75)	27 (81)	25 (77)	18 (64)
Essaouira	18 (64)	19 (66)	20 (68)	21 (70)	21 (70)	19 (66)
Fès	16 (61)	22 (72)	31 (88)	36 (97)	28 (81)	16 (61)

	Jan	April	June	Aug	Oct	Dec
Marrakech	19 (66)	26 (79)	33 (91)	38 (101)	28 (82)	16 (61)
Meknès	15 (59)	21 (70)	29 (84)	34 (93)	26 (79)	16 (61)
Ouarzazate	17 (63)	27 (80)	36 (96)	38 (100)	27 (80)	17 (62)
Rabat	17 (63)	21 (70)	25 (77)	28 (82)	25 (77)	18 (64)
Tangier	15 (59)	19 (66)	25 (77)	28 (82)	23 (73)	16 (61)
Taroudannt	22 (72)	27 (81)	32 (90)	38 (100)	32 (90)	22 (72)
Safi	18 (64)	22 (72)	27 (81)	30 (86)	26 (79)	19 (66)
Zagora	21 (69)	30 (86)	39 (102)	41 (106)	30 (86)	21 (70)

Electricity and Gas

The standard European current of 220 volts AC has now largely replaced the 110 volt AC system. You will need **two-pin flat plugs** to fit Moroccan sockets, and if you have any US or Canadian 110-volt appliances you will also need a current transformer.

On or off the grid, cooking, heating and lighting is largely dependent on charcoal or gas. The ubiquitous blue gas bottles fitted with a ceramic hob are subsidized by the government as one of the principal necessities of the poor.

Embassies and Consulates

Casablanca:

British Commercial Consulate: 60 Blvd d'Anfa (0) 221653

US Consulate: 8 Blvd Moulay Youssef (0) 361588

Rabat:

British Embassy: 17 Blvd de la Tour Hassan (07) 20905

Canadian Embassy: 13 Rue Joafar Assadik, Agdal (07) 71375

US Embassy: 2 Av. de Marrakech (07) 62265

Tangier:

British Consulate: 9 Rue Amérique du Sud (09) 35895

The former American legation in Tangier has been preserved as a historic monument, but is no longer a consular office. Australia, Ireland and New Zealand all have arrangements for their citizens to be represented in Morocco by British diplomatic staff.

Food and Drink

Morocco has a distinctive, varied and very attractive national cuisine, with dishes from simple to sophisticated that make great and imaginative use of Mediterranean produce. Whatever your budget, try to eat in a good Moroccan restaurant at least once during your stay, and accept any genuine invitation to a share in a family meal. Eating, for all but the rich,

French-influenced merchant class, is a home-based family affair. In a country of high unemployment the shared family meal of couscous, usually enlivened by a few chunks of steamed meat and vegetables, is the one great source of sustenance for the day.

traditional dishes

One of the most striking features of Moroccan cooking is the quality and freshness of the ingredients. Produce comes from a land without pesticides, fattening sheds, chemicals, hormones or preservatives. Animals are slaughtered just hours before they are eaten, and not even goats' hooves or heads are left to waste. The meat you are offered will generally be mutton, not lamb. Market vegetables will have been gathered that morning. Spices, herbs, fresh fruit, nuts and dried fruit have an invigorating vitality and a freshness that seems completely removed from the packaged and imported products available in much of Europe and North America.

To encourage you here are explanations of some of the most common and popular Moroccan traditional dishes (for details of Arab and French pronunciation, *see* the language section at the back of this book):

Harira: a thick soup of chick peas, lentils and haricot beans often flavoured with mutton or chicken, lemon and tarragon.

Brochettes: grilled kebabs of mutton, liver and fat.

Kefta: spicy meatballs made of minced mutton and offal, often served piping hot in a rich sauce with an egg.

Pastilla/Bastilla: a pie made up of mutiple layers of flaky pastry filled with finely-chopped pigeon meat, eggs, almonds and spices. Chicken or fish may sometimes be used instead of the pigeon.

Tagine: With couscous the most universal of Moroccan dishes, a slowly simmered stew, cooked in its own juices in an earthenware bowl with a distinctive conical lid. The ***tagine*** provides a basis for a whole galaxy of ingredients, spices and styles. The most popular variants found on most menus are: *tagine de viande*, mutton stew cooked with vegetables, or served alone with prunes; *tagine de poisson*, usually bream or sardines, cooked with tomatoes and herbs; *tagine de lapin*, rabbit stew; and *tagine de poulet aux olives et citron*, a delicious dish of chicken cooked with lemon and olives, the lemon giving a delicious bitter touch to the meat.

Mechoui: a lamb roasted whole on a spit or baked in a special oven. This delicate and fragrant meat, far removed from the usual mutton, is eaten with bread. It is, however, an elaborate luxury which is often only available if ordered well in advance.

Couscous: made from flour that is half-baked then ground to form semolina-like grains. A perfectly prepared couscous is laboriously cooked in a succession of steamings and oilings that allow each grain to cook while retaining a distinct granular texture. Couscous served outside of a home or a good restaurant is unlikely to be found at its best. It is usually accompanied by *sept légumes,* seven steamed vegetables with the odd lump of mutton. It can also be served as a pudding with sugar, cinnamon and rich warmed goat's milk.

Cornes de gazelle: croissant-like pastries filled with honey and almonds.

Exceptions aside, there are four basic categories of public eating-places: the **café**, the **café-restaurant**, the **New Town restaurant** and the **Moorish palace**.

All the more conspicuous **cafés** are male social centres that might serve a cake or croissant with mint tea or coffee, but seldom anything more substantial. It is usually quite acceptable to consume something from a nearby pâtisserie at a café table. The smarter pâtisseries may have their own tables, and serve fruit juices, ice creams and delicious cakes. They are one of the few places where you will regularly see the two sexes happily mix in a public place. Rural cafés serve *tagines* on market days, but can usually be persuaded to run up an omelette and salad at any time.

Café-restaurants serve the freshest and by far the cheapest food in town. There will usually be a choice of salads, vegetables, soups, grilled meats and cold puddings. Their clients are principally travellers and workers away from home who are deprived of their customary meal. Café-restaurants usually do not have a license to serve alcoholic drinks and are fairly functional, and in short are not places to dawdle away an evening with wine and chatter. They are easy to sniff out and are excellent for a quickly consumed lunch or supper, eaten while perched on a shared bench. They are often clustered in a row along a street in such a way that it is useless to make distinctions, or suggest an exact address or telephone number.

New Town restaurants: for a neat tablecloth, wine, a menu and regular opening hours you will usually have to go to a French, Spanish or Italian -influenced restaurant in the modern port or New Town areas of a city. On the Atlantic coast of Morocco (where they attract the local business and adminstrative class and serve freshly caught seafood) these restaurants can be very good and yet remain reasonably priced. Inland, unless you go very expensive they tend to become increasingly dependent on the tourist trade and frequently suffer from a corresponding blandness.

Moorish palaces: there are a number of 19th-century merchant palaces in the medinas of Fès, Meknès, Tangier and Marrakech that have been converted into restaurants. Traditional Moroccan cooking is served in a sumptious Moorish interior; most, though, have drinks licenses. It is rare to have this kind of evening without hearing local music or suffering some belly-dancing entertainment, and you won't be surprised to find that such places are almost entirely filled by tourists. Nevertheless, even thouhg they are often expensive and boisterous they are also some of the few places where you can sample the more sophisticated and opulent dishes of Moroccan cuisine. If you are saving up for one grand meal, make it in Marrakech, which is where the best and most genuinely opulent examples of this kind of restaurant are to be found.

restaurant price categories

The **price categories** used for restaurants throughout the book are per head for a full meal without drinks:

expensive	over 300dh (£20/$30)
moderate	between 300dh (£20/$30) and 150dh (£10/$15)
cheap	under 150dh (£10/$15)

The cost of a bottle of **local wine** in most restaurants is around 90dh.

The principal drink of Morocco is **mint tea**. This is green or gunpowder tea flavoured with a few sprigs of mint and saturated with sugar. It is almost repulsively sweet when you first taste it. You will be offered glasses of mint tea in every house or shop you visit, and it is expected that a guest drinks at least three glasses of tea before departing. Enjoying mint tea becomes a vital social grace and, with luck, before long you may begin to appreciate this invigorating and thirst-quenching drink. Before tea was brought to Morocco (it was first imported by British merchants in the 19th century; they also later created the distinctive Moroccan teapot, first manufactured in Manchester, by giving the Yemeni coffee pot a fat bottom), hot infusions of sweet mint, verbena and wormwood were popular. These are still occasionally added to green tea.

Morocco is a Muslim nation. There is a law that prohibits Moroccan Muslims from buying bottles of alcohol—though this is not strictly enforced outside of Ramadan. This ban does not apply to visitors and, curiously, it is in any case legal for Muslim Moroccans to drink at bars, which are found discreetly tucked behind closed doors in the New Town areas, never in the medinas, which are generally no-alcohol zones. Due to the actual wording of the Koran, which specifically mentions wine when counselling against alcohol abuse, Moroccans tend to consume **grain-based drinks** such as *'spéciale flag'* beer, *anis* or whisky, but seldom touch wine in public. Away from the big coastal cities or principal tourist destinations drinking is confined to the bars of just a few hotels. In all but a few of the very smartest hotels it is impossible to drink wine, either by the glass or the bottle, outside of the structure of a meal. In which case, if you really must have a drink, order a plate of prawns or a *salade niçoise* to act as tapas and justify the wine.

You can order Moroccan **wine** to drink with your meal in licensed restaurants. Wine for lunch-time picnics can be also bought from a few selected grocery shops in larger towns and cities (mentioned in the guide). Despite Islamic prohibitions wine is produced in Morocco in three regions: Berkane, Meknès and Boulâouane. You might find the Moroccan reds rather strong and heavy to drink without something to nibble at: they are at their best when accompanying a rich spiced meat *tagine*. Due to the problem of keeping a white or a rosé cool while travelling reds are also much better suited for picnics, and don't seem to mind being shaken around in the boot of a car or bus for several hundred kilometres. The principal reds are Toulal, Rabbi Jacob, Beni Snassen, Père Antoine, Le Châtelain, Valpierre, Les Trois Domaines, Amazir Beni M'Tir and Cabernet Président. If you have a choice, you might try the last two mentioned in this list first.

The best of the Moroccan whites is Special Coquillages, and after that Valpierre Blanc de Blanc, which is dry and not too astringent. They are at their best when accompanying fish or a plate of shellfish at a meal on the coast. The rosé wines, Gris de Boulâouane and Oustalet, are delightful at any time of the day, especially when chilled, and provide one of the basic sensory backdrops to a Moroccan holiday.

The universal multi-national colas are naturally available throughout the country, but a recommended **non-alcoholic** choice is freshly-squeezed orange juice (*orange pressé*), which is often served enlivened with a little grapefruit or lemon. This is available in hotels and cafés in most towns.

Guides

Official guides of the highest (national) grade can be hired from Tourist Offices for 150dh (£10/$15) for a half-day and 250dh for a full day. The same prices are charged by mountain guides. Local guides charge 120dh the halfday, 150 dh the full day. They are all well-trained in history and anecdotes, fluent in most languages, and trustworthy.

Alternatively, if you have just arrived in a city and not yet found your way to your hotel, let alone the tourist office, you will not find it difficult to find yourself an unofficial guide. In fact, there will most probably be a profusion of them offering their services and asking where you want to go as soon as you appear on the street.

Dealing with the attention of unwanted urban guides is one of the recurring problems of travelling in Morocco. The discordant cries of hustlers just as you arrive fresh in a town or at the medina gates can be irritating. Accept this, though, as a facet of Moroccan life. There is certainly no easy way to avoid it short of jumping in a taxi and hiding in a hotel. Use your energy not to avoid these guides, but to select the most appealing. As in all situations of life the eyes are the true mirror of the soul, and there is no point in having a conversation with anybody while they wear dark glasses.

A little humility is also an asset. On your first visit to a large and strange town, some help in finding your hotel or a taxi will very probably actually be useful. The aggression with which many visitors cold-shoulder themselves through potential helpers and then later bemusedly consult their imported maps and guide books is a faintly ridiculous, but a curious and revealing, insight into Western attitudes. Meet the problem in a Moroccan manner, and deploy qualities of charm and enthusiasm. Enjoy the human skills required in choosing the friendliest character from a group. Greet him with a *salaam* and a handshake, praise the weather and his town and tell him how delighted you are at last to be here. If need be, check out your character judgement over a cup of tea. Tell him exactly where you want to go and what you intend to give, which however rich you are should never be more than 10dh.

A guide's natural interest lies in directing you to the medina. For in the confusing labyrinth of medina avenues you become more dependent on him, and this is also where lurk the bazaars, where he can earn commissions (fixed at a traditional five per cent, which can win your guide a comparative fortune) and additional kudos with his neighbours. Be aware of this, and if need be, hold out a visit to a bazaar as a carrot at the end of the day. You will soon find out that the habitat of the hustling guide is almost entirely confined to bus stops and medina gates. Marrakech, Fès, Tangier and particularly Tetouan have hustling reputations. But in all these cities, when you know your way around (and show an increasing lack of interest in bazaars) you will find yourself increasingly left alone. As a corollary to this, try not to pack too many large cities into a short itinerary.

When you feel annoyed, run over a few relevant facts. An unskilled labouring wage in Morocco is 3dh an hour. The chances of getting even that in a country of 25 per cent employment, with over half the population under 21 years-old, is low, and competition is heavy. Even a European unemployment dole converts into an enviable quantity of dirhams. Under those conditions might you not try your luck at skimming off a few dirhams from often arrogant and unfriendly foreigners? A wise old woman told me that the street kids of Tangier reminded her of nothing so much as her youth in Edinburgh.

Hammams

A *hammam* is a public steam bath which, before the advent of showers and private bathrooms, was one of the great urban centres of Moroccan life. Some of them are a little bit run-down from their days of glory at the turn of this century, but they survive throughout this arid country as a working institution. Apart from in those in tourist hotels, male nudity is taboo and the sexes are strictly divided, either by different opening hours (usually for women in the daylight hours, with men in the evening) or by a completely different set of chambers. The *hammams* of Morocco are rarely as elaborate as the great domed, multi-chambered marble-clad structures of Ottoman Turkey, though they will usually have an entrance lobby, a changing room and a double set of doors into the steam room. Here you can gently steam, wash yourself from taps, basins or black plastic buckets or for an extra charge you can be rigorously scrubbed, massaged and expertly manipulated. In an interesting inversion of street etiquette women often bathe with just the skimpiest pants or completely naked, and remove hair from the most intimate parts of their body, while men are very strict about wearing either a cotton wrap or swimming trunks and wash their genitals privately facing the wall.

Several *hammams* are listed in the text, but by inquiring from your hotel you can find many others that are happy to accept foreign visitors. A minority of establishments, usually those directly attached to a mosque, do not like the presence of *Rumi*, as Christian tourists with only the slenderest relationship to Orthodox Byzantium are still called.

Health

No **immunizations** are officially required to enter Morocco. For peace of mind, though, you should be up-to-date on your typhoid, cholera, tetanus and polio protection, and you might talk to your doctor about the pros and cons of a hepatitis jab. In the far south, anti-malarial pills are sometimes advised during the summer, though these can cause various side-effects and are famously unpleasant. Bilharzia worms lurk in some of the oasis streams and still pools south of the High Atlas, though I have swum and waded through many with no ill effects—yet. **Tap water** is quite safe north of Marrakech, though you may prefer to drink from the ubiquitous bottles of Sidi Ali and Sidi Harazem mineral water. It is considered by connoisseurs to be amongst the best mineral water in the world.

All-eventualities private **travel insurance** covering you for medical emergencies as well as theft need not be expensive and is the best protection against any serious health problems. If you have private health insurance you may already be covered—check the fine print. Moroccan **pharmacies** are usually knowledgeable, sympathetic and well stocked, and can often recommend a French-speaking doctor. They sell contraceptives, including the pill, but tampons, soap, shampoo and toilet paper are often easier to find in a general store. Even the most basic travel kit should include a good supply of painkillers and some proprietary medicine, such as Imodium, for rapid diarrhoea relief. Tom Owen Edmunds, a very experienced travel photographer, carries a stock of seemingly innocuous things which can be put to emergency medical use. A tampon can become a dressing for a wound, condoms can be used for carrying water and chewing gum a replacement for a missing tooth filling. Medical addresses for most big cities are given in the guide. The larger package-tour hotels often have a medical specialist. In an emergency, dial **15** for medical help, or **19** for the police.

Holidays and Festivals

The principal secular and religious holidays are observed by government offices, banks, post offices, public covered-markets and some shops. Tourist restaurants and hotels continue in operation, though sometimes with delays entailed by a much-diminished staff. On the days before a holiday there will be extra pressure on transport and hotel space, particularly in the principal cities.

national holidays

1 Jan: New Year's Day

3 Mar: Feast of the Throne—celebrated with a conspicuous amount of bunting, processions, public feasts and music

1 May: Labour Day

9 July: King Hassan II's birthday

14 Aug: Allegiance Day

6 Nov: Day of the Green March

18 Nov: Independence Day

Muslim holidays

These are based on a lunar calendar, which loses 11 days a year (or 12 in a leap year) against the Gregorian Calendar.

The great event of the Islamic year is the fasting month of **Ramadan** (*which will begin in late December in 1998 and 1999*). To be in Morocco in one of the great cities during Ramadan is a fascinating experience, but it is not a good time to travel around the country. Ramadan, the ninth month of the Islamic lunar year, is the Muslim equivalent of Lent. The fast has remained a great institution in Islam and is cherished as an act that binds the whole nation, indeed the entire Muslim community, together in a month of asceticism. For all except the sick, travellers, children and pregnant women, Ramadan involves abstaining from food, sex, drink and cigarettes during the hours of daylight. It is an ancient custom, one that was in full force when the Prophet Mohammed was a child in Mecca, when this holy month was a time when a general truce reigned over Arabia and the demands of vengeance and tribal animosity were put aside. Non-Muslims are not involved, but you will find most cafés, bars and licensed grocers firmly closed. It is insensitive to smoke, eat or drink in public during Ramadan. It can be more rewarding to join Ramadan quietly as a volunteer, sharing the exuberance at dusk when the daily fast ends with a bowl of harira soup, and the café-restaurants fill up with customers and music. A spirit of relief breaks out across the nation and continues deep into the night. The 26th night of Ramadan, 'holy night' (when the first verse of the Koran was first delivered to the Prophet Mohammed) is particularly magical, with young children paraded in glittering costumes in an endless promenade.

The feast of **Aid es Seghir** celebrates the end of the month of Ramadan, when the new moon is sited. A few months later **Aid el Kebir** commemorates Abraham's sacrifice of a ram instead of his son, and is a great excuse for family reunions. The week before Aid el Kebir is colourful, as the streets are full of thousands of rams being led around on leashes like honoured members of the family. After the excitement of public prayers and the sacrifice on the morning of the Aid, the Festival is mostly celebrated indoors. Shops, souks and some museums are closed for the week. Three weeks later is **Moharran** (or **Achoura**) the feast of the Muslim New Year, when almond cakes are baked, drums are beaten and gifts given to children and the poor. The fourth principal holiday is **Mouloud**, the prophet's birthday, celebrated with presents for children and firecrackers on the street. In particular, there is a *moussem* (religious festival) at **Zaouia-Moulay-Brahim** in the High Atlas, a candle procession at **Salé** and the Aissawa *moussem* at **Meknès**.

moussems and festivals

Moussems and *ammougars* (the Berber version) were originally annual pilgrimages to the tomb of a Saint, but the words are now used for any festival, although most do still have religious roots. There are hundreds of local festivals throughout Morocco that celebrate a saint in either a day (or a week-long) trading fair, with some feasting, dancing, religious music and *fantasia* display. In mood they are not dissimilar from an especially animated rural souk, and so for the vast majority of visitors may be only of passing interest. Even the major festival dates are impossible to predict accurately. Some depend on the harvest, the lunar cycle, the Muslim religious year, the national tourist office or the diary of the regional governor. You will have to ask the tourist office or a major local hotel for more accurate information, though even they are unlikely to know more than two months in advance.

The most rewarding festivals for a foreigner are the week long **Folk Music** festival staged in **Marrakech**, usually in June); the week-long **Festival of Sacred Music** at **Fès**, usually at the end of May or beginning of June; the **acrobat** festival held at the zaouia of **Sidi Ahmed ou Moussa**, near **Tiznit**, in August, the ***Fantasia*** festival held at Moulay Abdullah near **El-Jadida** in August; the week-long **Festival of African Music** held in **Agadir** in September; and the week-long High Atlas tribal **marriage fair** at **Imilchil** in September.

Of the two-day-long harvest festivals the most photogenic and reliable are the **almond blossom festival** held at **Tafraoute** in February, the **rose festival** held at **El Kelaâ-M'gouna** in the Dades oasis valley in May, the **horse fair** at **Tissa** in the begiining of October, and the **Date festival** in **Erfoud** towarrds the end of October.

Houses to Rent

The interlinked British and American expatriate community in Morocco has for the last century or so been concentrated in Tangier and Asilah. If you wanted to rent, or borrow a house in the country in the past, this was the place to go. This is still true today, and currently there are two splendid places in the area available for letting. The old **Tangier** house of David Herbert, the famous doyen of the city's expatriate social life, which started life as the hermitage of a Muslim saint but is now equipped with a very English interior and a delightfully exuberant garden, is now owned by Noureddine, ✆ (09) 335846, his Moroccan companion of many years, who lets out it to visitors.

In the same 'mountain quarter' but on a different scale of grandeur is **Dar Sinclair**, built in the 1930s by the architect Jack Sinclair and now owned by his granddaughter Tessa Wheeler. It enjoys a fine view of the city and bay of Tangier, and has a large steeply-sloping garden and a pool embellished with a Moroccan caidal tent. The house also offers a large

Moroccan sitting room, a library (used by such past literary tenants as Gavin Young and Nicholas Shakespeare), a dining room, a verandah and four bedrooms. It is cared for by Abdul Latif and his wife Fatima, who live in an adjoining cottage, while if you want more bedrooms it is possible to rent the neighbouring house as well. Depending on season prices range from £800/$1500 to £2,000/$3000 per month. Tessa Wheeler, née Codrington, can be contacted in London on ✆ 0171 622 3895, or in Kent on ✆ 01227-730221.

In **Essaouira** art dealer Jane Lovelace rents out one floor of her medina house for £120/$180 a week, and for a bigger group it can be combined with her studio at £70/$105.

In **Marrakech** Nigel Toft, an eminent authority on International Law, rents out his charming traditional Riad (with three rooms on each of the two floors that overlook the courtyard) in the medina for £250/$375 a week. For further details write to 8, Cape Yard, London E1 9JU orcall ✆ 0171 480 7995. In La Palmeraie there is the **Deux Tours** (Douar Abiad) complex, with 24 rooms in six finely-decorated houses each with their own patio and pool. They can be booked through **Best of Morocco** (*see* p.7), who also handle Gilles Bentallamy's garden villa between two kasbahs in the village of **Oumnast**.

In **Taroudannt** the educational tour company **Naturally Morocco Ltd** have a small environmental and cultural studies centre within the walls of the city where they rent out two large apartments which can be used in conjunction with the conference facilities, library and roof terrace. For further details write to the company in Wales at Parc y Berllan, Ffynnonddrain, Camarthen, Wales SA31 1TY, or call ✆ 01267 230523, 📠 01267 233279.

An educational tour company has a centre for walking/study courses in the modern hilltop **Kasbah du Toubkal** outside **Imlil** in the Toubkal National Park in the High Atlas. Costs are based on groups of ten, with a ten-day tour under £400/$600 per person. Details: Discover, Timbers, Oxted Road, Godstone, Surrey RH9 8AD, ✆ 018837 44392, 📠 018837 44913.

Outside **Ouarzazate** in the villa area beside the golf course that overlooks the lake you can rent the spacious **Kasbah du Lac**, which can sleep up to 10 people in its 4 double bedrooms and 2 single rooms. The house is arranged as four separate buildings, joined together by a walled garden, and comes with the services of a cook, maid and gardener. There is also a pool and a long lakeside terrace on which to lounge. Further details from **Best of Morocco**.

Kif

In 1840 Hooker and Ball remarked that 'the use of tobacco for smoking appears to be unknown in Morocco while kif, prepared from the chopped leaves of common hemp is almost universally employed for that purpose both by Moors and Berbers.'

The Rif mountains grow some of the best common hemp (*Cannabis indica)* in the world. In the Ketama region its cultivation is legal (with 81,000 hectares, or 200,000 acres, currently planted) until another crop can be found that will grow as well on these denuded hills. The hemp (also known as marijuana) is planted in February and harvested in June. To collect their rich stores of pollen, plants are shaken inside a gauze-lined hut. The sticky mass is then kneaded into cakes. This resin is sold by farmers to the gangs who deal in the riskier but more profitable smuggling trade to Europe. The cut leaves and flowers are preferred by locals for their gentler aromatic smoke, which is inhaled from a thin pipe with a disposable pottery head. The flowers and seeds can also be made into *majoun,* an edible fudge.

In the north of the country discreet possession and use is, in practice, tolerated and the police concentrate their activities on monitoring the big traders. The Moroccan law framed in 1954 is, however, quite explicit. Possession, purchase and transportation is illegal, the minimum penalty is three months imprisonment and a 2,400dh fine, the maximum, five years and a 240,000dh fine with the confiscation of any camouflage and transport involved.

Visitors who wish to smoke Moroccan kif can reduce the risk of receiving these penalties by buying small quantities for their own use, preferably not in Tangier or Tetouan, and by not travelling with any in their possession. As elsewhere, dealers also double as police informers. It would be foolish and quite misguided to attempt to smuggle kif. Smuggling is an extremely intricate, big business which does not tolerate amateurs. While possession of small quantities of kif in Spain is now legal, in Algeria you can be imprisoned for life for this offence.

About a dozen British and twenty Americans are arrested for drug-related offences each year in Morocco. Consuls are unsympathetic but professional, and try to visit within a week of imprisonment, every three months whilst on remand, and twice a year during imprisonment. The current penalties run on a rough quantity-tariff: a girl hitching from Ketama to Chechaouèn with half a kilo strapped to her thigh was given a month in prison and fined; a New Zealand pilot caught loading a light aeroplane got five years and the full fine.

On a note of caution, all the shake-down stories and alarmingly heavy tales of hassle that I have heard in the last twenty years all involve kif. Never smoke somewhere or with someone that makes you the slightest bit uneasy. It is a recognized aspect of the drug that as well as inducing laughter and an apparently increased perception, it can also cause mild paranoia.

Maps

Despite the great care spent over city maps in this guide, the medinas will often remain a maze to you for the first few visits. The free coloured tourist-leaflets and the beautifully produced *Editions Gauthey* maps to Tangier, Rabat–Salé, Casablanca, Agadir, Marrakech and Meknès are however a great help in getting to know the general street pattern.

There are a large number of national road maps to choose from. Bear in mind that any map that marks a border or even a difference in scale between Morocco and the Western Sahara is liable to be confiscated. Kümmerly and Frey (1:100,000), Michelin sheet 169 (1:100,000), Hildebrand (1:900,000), and Reise und Verkehrsverlag (1:800,000) all publish full-colour maps, useful for advance planning. Road conditions do change and most maps contain one or two inaccuracies. The most accurate road maps are the large-scale (1:400,000) *Maroc, Carte Routière,* published by Editions Marcus, Paris, on sale throughout Morocco for 30dh a sheet, though they lack the clarity of full colour and are fragile. Moroccan official survey sheets of the High Atlas (1:50,000) are available in Imlil, the central base for High Atlas climbing.

In Britain the Moroccan Atlas survey sheets, some French-language walking guides and a wide variety of other regional maps can be obtained from Stanford's Map Centre, Long Acre, Covent Garden, London WC2, © (0171) 836 1321. For specialist information for walking, *Guide Collomb: Atlas Mountains* is available from West Col Productions, Goring, Reading, Berks. The Royal Geographical Society, Kensington Gore, London SW7 2AR, © (0171) 589 5466, has an Expeditionary Advisory Service which runs weekend courses and can point you towards old reports and maps.

In the USA try either the Traveller's Bookstore at 22 West 52nd St, New York, NY 10011, ✆ (212) 664 0995, or The Complete Traveller Bookstore at 199 Madison Avenue, New York, NY 10016, ✆ (212) 688 9007. They also have a branch in San Francisco at 3207 Fillmore Street, CA 92123.

Media

English-language **newspapers** are available throughout the year in Tangier and Agadir, and less reliably in Marrakech. French newspapers are more widespread and cost about half the price. The daily official French-language paper, *Le Matin du Sahara*, is worth buying, though its coverage, and certainly its opinion, seldom changes. Morocco remains a good place to shed your paper habit and pick up tuning into the World Service direct from Bush House on 9.41 and 5.975mhz—31.88 and 50.21m.

There is little temptation, apart from being caught in a rainstorm, to visit a **cinema** in Morocco. If you do find yourself inside (tickets are around 10dh), you could become more fascinated with the audience than the film. The different cultural attitudes to humour, violence and romance always make fascinating study.

Money

The Moroccan currency is the **dirham**, which fluctuates between 12 and 15 to the pound and 7 and 10 to the US dollar. It is divided into 100 units, which are officially called *centimes* but are occasionally and confusingly referred to as *francs*, *pesetas* or *reales*. The denominations of notes are 200, 100, 50 and 10. There are silver-coloured coins worth 5, 2 and 1 dirham and brass ones worth 50, 20, 10 and 5 centimes.

There are active restrictions against exporting dirhams from the country, although you can usually buy Moroccan money in Malaga, Algeciras or Gibraltar. There are no black market rates, though tourist bazaars and carpet shops may be persuaded to accept dollars and European currencies. Keep your **currency exchange slips**, for at the departure point when you leave the country you will only be allowed to change back up to half what you can prove to have changed in the first place.

You should bring enough liquid cash to cover the first couple of days in Morocco. Passports are required for most transactions. For those with a European bank account, **Eurocheques** are perhaps the most useful way to carry the bulk of your holiday money; they are widely accepted in banks and are cashed without commission. Each cheque can be cashed for a maximum of 2000dh, about £150/$225. They come in books of ten with a cheque guarantee card, and are available from all major European banks. Order them well in advance of your trip. Standard international **travellers' cheques** in dollars or main European currencies are also easily exchanged in banks, as are **International Girocheques**, which are on sale at your local post office and can be cashed in Moroccan post offices. Major international **credit cards** such as Visa and Mastercard are accepted in the smarter hotels and restaurants and a great many shops in the bazaars, though in the latter they might try and charge you the credit agency's six per cent handling fee.

Moroccan **banks** display a wide range of tempting stickers on their windows but often don't match up to all their advertisements. There is usually one bank in every town that operates some form of foreign exchange desk, though you will usually save time by heading directly for either the Banque Marocaine du Commerce Exterieur (**BMCE**) or the Banque Credit du Maroc (**BCM**) which both take cards, travellers' cheques, Eurocheques, and of course cash.

Opening Hours

Opening hours of **banks** vary depending on their location and the time of year. In the winter they should be open at least 8.30–11.30am and 3–4pm, Mon–Fri; in the summer and during the month of Ramadan 8.30am–2pm is a likely minimum. Banking hours are usually longer in resorts and big cities. **Post offices** (once known as **PTT** but now relabelled **La Poste**) are open Mon–Fri 8am–3pm in winter; and 8am–12pm and 3–6pm in the summer. They sell stamps and can cash International Girocheques and receive *poste restante/* general delivery mail, although an established hotel usually makes a safer and more accessible address.

Museums are not well signposted nor do they sell the postcards, brochures, catalogues and reproductions that are part of the museum experience elsewhere. **They also decide their own opening hours**, so please treat the information given in this guide as an informed opinion, not an absolute authority. In general they are open 9am–12pm and 3–6pm through the week, but will usually be closed on **Tuesday** and sometimes on Friday afternoons as well as on all major national and religious holidays. Also, the lunch break can sometimes spread over most of the afternoon. Custodians of national monuments cannot be identified by any official cap, uniform or badge, but only by their possession of a book of entrance tickets. In short, do not be haunty with unshaven, shabbily-dressed, sleepy looking individuals who are in the vicinity of a museum or monument, if you wish to gain entrance. **Medersas** follow the same schedule, but sometimes will be closed for the whole of Friday.

Packing

A photocopy of the first four pages of your passport may come in handy if you mislay it for any reason. A corkscrew and a sharp knife are vital for picnics and peeling fruit. An alarm clock is useful for those early-morning bus departures. A suction bath plug will be needed in a surprising number of hotels, while a good lighter, a few candles and a torch are basic tools for exploring caves and simple hotels at night. On average, at least half of any holidaying group will be struck by a violent purge that might strike anytime anywhere. By packing a roll of soft toilet paper and a packet of Imodium and Nurofen you can earn undying gratitude.

To ease your passage around the country, buy a stock of presents (like those that you might fill a Christmas stocking with, and especially pens) for local children who have shown you around a village, put you on the right path or guarded your car. Anything with a football motif is usually eagerly received. My mother has travelled for years with a bag filled with goodies, ranging from 'improving' notebooks and small sets of coloured pens, to more hazardous items such as whistles and water pistols that should only be given on departure.

Although shorts and swimwear are perfectly acceptable on the beach and in your hotel, you should not wear them anywhere else. Trousers and a short-sleeved shirt are acceptable; women wishing to appear respectable should pack a long skirt and a full shirt.

Photography

'Why destroy the present for an unsatisfactory image of the past in the future?'

Cameras are the symbol of the 20th century tourist driven by a mania to record, to move on, before you have the time to understand. Photographs give the illusion that one has the time to study these things later at greater depth. Even if you have the time for only the slightest sketch of a building or a landscape, it will imprint the image more vividly than a whole reel of film. As a means of preserving images of wild flowers without picking them and of wild animals without killing them, however, they are entirely on the side of the angels. The two invaluable tips I have been given by a professional are to photograph at dusk and never put your subject in the centre of the frame.

Films can be bought and developed in most large towns. Excluding anything remotely military, you are free to photograph anything architectural. Do not photograph anybody, least of all a rural woman, without permission. Be prepared to tip for photographing animals or people at a tariff that can range from 1–5dh. Most museums forbid flash and operate a partial restrictive policy, like that which forbids photographs of the bronzes in the Rabat Archaeological Museum or anything in the archaeological gallery of Tangier's Dar el Makhzen Museum. This only seems to make sense as an opportunity for tips.

Police

The Moroccan police-force is modelled on the French, and is divided into two forces—the *Gendarmerie* and the *Sûreté*. The Gendarmerie live under semi-military discipline, wear khaki serge and green berets and carry batons. They cover both cities and the countryside with a regular grid of barracks, and could be compared to a mixture of a county constabulary and a reserve regiment. The Sûreté are the grey-uniformed and armed police who patrol the roads and the cities, and to whom robberies of tourist will normally be reported to obtain a declaration for insurance purposes. They are more directly concerned with crime and law enforcement and are considered, as in France, more street-wise, sophisticated and corrupt; commonly referred to as 'Ali Baba and the forty....'.

Grey customs officers may be seen, particularly on the northern coast, trying to control the flow of electrical goods smuggled in from Ceuta and Melilla, and kif being smuggled out. Prison officers wear blue. Firemen wear blue with red piping and might be seen trying to sell their calendars to unwary motorists, particularly on the road south of Tangier. The army, by comparison, look rather underdressed in their plain lovat-green uniform.

Sexual Attitudes

'Abd as Slam, Malika's husband, is young and handsome. Like most young Moroccan men in Tangier, he dreams of finding a rich Christian woman who will take him to Europe or the States and make him a rich man' (*The House of Si Abd Allah*, Henry Munson).

Moroccans traditionally have an uncomplicated attitude to sex—chauvinist to women and liberal to men—but a great respect for outward forms and standards of dress. Homosexuality is neither scandalous nor unusual and is socially treated not so much as a condition but as a mere matter of personal taste. 'In the towns and among the Arabic-speaking mountaineers of northern Morocco, where pederasty is exceedingly prevalent, it is practically regarded with indifference...' (*Ritual and Belief in Morocco,* Edward Westermarck). The Koran cautions against celibacy: 'As to the monastic life they invented it themselves . . . many of them were perverse'. Against the confusion of Jewish or Christian sexual guilt, the Koran freely acknowledges sexual appetite: 'Your wives are your field, go in therefore to your field as you will but do first some act for your soul's good', and is only mildly disapproving of homosexuality—'come ye to men, instead of women lustfully? Ye are indeed a people given up to excess.'

AIDS awareness is very slight and public education and posters on the spread of the HIV virus have been low key and unspecific. As yet, only the King has managed to break through the general reluctance to air these matters publicly, and given a few general talks on television. The bulk of the population continues to think of it as a disease that affects rich, white Europeans and Americans but that has no power over the Arab nation. Moroccans also tend to think of themselves as immeasurably more virile and potent than Western men. However chaste your intentions, why not pack some condoms beside the sun oil and romantic fiction.

women

In general Moroccan men conceive of mature women in three guises: the mother whom they adore, the wife in whose modest conduct rests all the honour of her husband, and all other women, who are potential objects of their desire. This is particularly true of all women who show themselves in the public domain of the streets and the cafés, let alone in bars and restaurants. Western women (especially in view of their power to bestow a foreign passport on the father of their children) are all near-automatically placed in the third category to a greater or lesser degree.

Morocco subsequently tends to divide women travellers between those who couldn't cope and those who loved it. Dig a little deeper and you will often find that the former went alone or with another woman, and had never been to a Muslim country before. Of course there are single women who have holidayed happily in Morocco, but they tend to have a proven track-record as independent travellers. If in doubt, err on the cautious side. There's no point in having a miserable trip, and no stigma attached to not feeling comfortable in a country where the men tend to see white women as possible lays and have little respect for them. If you do travel with a man, the most irritating thing will be the way in which any decision will be instantly referred to him by Moroccans. The easiest way to cope if you're alone is to play one of the stereotyped but recognizably 'less available' roles: the wife, the mother, the intellectual or the sportsperson. Unfortunately there are no easy ways to deal with a hand where you don't want it, but being soberly dressed will make you less of a target. Be open and straightforward, and don't be embarrassed to yell loudly at the man, in any language. He'll understand, and suffer the indignity of a public reproval. A sharp slap, satisfying as it might be, only seems to make things worse. In some of the larger towns it is not advisable for single females, or even female couples, to stay in the cheapest medina hotels.

On a more upbeat note I once came across a mixed group of six Australian girls who were travelling with six male High School students that they had met up with in Tangier. The girls could take the Moroccan boys into the tourist zones where they would not otherwise have been welcome, while the girls were both protected, entertained and introduced to aspects of Moroccan domestic life which they would otherwise never have seen. I felt very envious.

For a sense of sorority go to the local women's *hammam.* Laughter and curious communication, if not outright friendship, will result. By way of reading matter, any of the studies of women and sexual politics by Fatima Mernissi make compelling if depressing reading. It is much, much more difficult for them than one can possibly imagine. As Fatima Mernissi has observed, 'The conception of the woman as a lust-driven animal that must be kept under lock and key is one of the sickest and most disgusting aspects of Arab culture.' So is the sad record of male divorce and the neglect of their responsibilities as a father, though this has much more to do with poverty and lack of opportunity than any cultural determinant.

Shopping

Arab cities were designed with the **souk** or market at the centre of the community. Islam has none of the Christian anxiety about mixing trade and worship. The streets around a grand mosque are usually the busiest and the richest and are known as the ***kissaria.*** The outer walls of mosques are commonly obscured by workshops and stalls whose rent helps pay for the upkeep of the building. A new zaouia (religious college) or mosque was often the initial impetus that coalesced a trading community into existence. On Fridays you will notice a marked reduction in trade as the merchants shut up shop for noon prayers.

Moroccan crafts remain active and have recovered from the exodus of more than 250,000 Moroccan Jews, who were among the most skilled craftsmen in the country. The Jews were particularly prominent in jewellery, tailoring, weaving and non-ferrous metalwork. All large towns maintain a government-run craft centre called an **Ensemble Artisanal**, where traditional trades are taught and products exhibited for sale. Tourism greatly assists the craft economy, and it has been assessed that a fifth of any visitor's expenditure is on crafts.

A visit to a typical contemporary Moroccan home reveals a subtle difference in taste from the 'typically Moroccan' souvenirs of the souks. Rich embroidered cloth (covering cushions and day beds), nylon blankets and masses of deep carved wood are dominant. The tiled floors are rarely covered by carpets. Ceramics tend not to be Islamic in decoration but plain glazed earthenware or a Chinese pattern for grand occasions. The radio, TV or tape recorder will be conspicuous and you notice the complete absence of any pictures (other than an obligatory photo of a Moroccan football team, the King and a calligraphic Koranic blessing). It is chiefly in the traditional embroidered kaftans worn by women, the low tables and all the impedimenta of a tea ceremony that the tourist bazaar taste and the domestic economy coincide.

blankets

The souks are all well stocked with loose-weave large brown and white blankets that make excellent bed covers. In the far south you will come across brilliant patterns of tie-dyed cotton for the women's enveloping *haiks* and the enormous, many-coloured thick blankets of the Sahara region. Two of these can completely line a nomad tent and provide excellent protection against the bitter nights.

carpets

Only buy for your pleasure. Moroccan carpets are not an investment and you can only expect to recoup a fraction of the price by selling back to a dealer abroad. While a Persian carpet may have between 150 and 1200 knots a square inch, a Moroccan version of the traditional Persian prayer rug (often woven in **Rabat**) rarely exceeds 50. Their ability to age, and increase in value, is therefore correspondingly reduced. Also, the dyes used in Morocco are almost all aniline now, and can produce harsh single colours with few tones. Do not, however, be discouraged from visiting the great carpet bazaars in Tetouan, Fès, Meknès, Rabat and Marrakech. These are often housed in magnificent interiors, and the merchants will offer you tea while they display their still wonderfully-tempting wares.

The ***Hanbel*** or ***Arerbal*** (the Moroccan version of the familiar Turkish Kilim) is woven, not knotted, though a rich pattern of embroidery can sometimes confuse this distinction. On the ground they have an even shorter life than carpets, but they are more flexible and can be used as hangings and throws, and can look especially lavish for picnics or as covers for day-beds or dining-room tables. They should be much cheaper than carpets, with which they share many designs as well as the traditional nomadic production areas. All the more interesting ones are produced in the Middle or High Atlas, or at least to the traditional patterns that were developed in these tribal regions.

The Berber tribes of the Middle Atlas plateau dominate the weaving tradition of Morocco. Travelling inland from Rabat southeast towards Midelt you will successively pass through or near the main weaving tribal zones: the **Zemmour** (centred around Khemisset), **Zaér** (centred around Rommani), **Zaïane** (covering the area around Khénifra, Moulay Bouâzza and Mrirt), **Beni-M'tir** (around El-Hajeb and Azrou) and **Beni-Mguild**, the old territory of which stretched between Azrou and Midelt. There is a basic similarity in both texture and design throughout this large interlinked region. In their raw state at local markets they are as likely to be found woven for a practical purpose and made up as saddlebags, belts, waistcoats, sacks, wall hangings, tent divisions, decorative hangings or cushions, than as convenient lengths for your floor. A warm red wool, which used to be made from the madder root, provides the basic background against which the finely-executed details are picked out in bright white cotton and black. Today, with the use of chemical dyes widespread, there are innumerable colour variations. The designs, however, remain entirely geometric and generally rely on bands of plain colour alternating with richly worked bands of lozenges, diamond grids and elaborate crosses. A good weaver will brook no repetition in design and create a dazzling kilim full of movement, colour and elegantly executed detail. A less inspired version can look static, lifeless and repetitive. The most elegant and hard-wearing kilims, which rarely come up for sale, are often so heavy with sequins that the pattern is all but obscured. These are woven specifically for the weaver's wedding, and afterwards are hung up in her house, or tent, as a decorative hanging. On the weaver's death they are used as a cover for her corpse, the sequins glistening in the dusk for the last time as she is borne up to a hillside cemetery.

Another, smaller area of weaving is in the High Atlas mountains. These simple, dignified *hanbels* are known as **Glaoua**, after the Berber dynasty from Telouèt. They have a similar pattern of banded plain and decorated stripes, although they usually have no colour and are woven from plain undyed black and white wool. In the area to the south of the High Atlas and Jebel Siroua (often referred to as **Aït Ouaouzguite**) these plain *hanbels* are worked over with an extra layer of knotted carpet work; examples are sold in the towns of Tazenakht, Agdz and Ouarzazate. In addition, a full range of colours can be used to accompany the dominant saffron hue to create a rich depth of pile, geometric design and colour. There are in addition some more straightforward carpets with pale green geometric designs worked onto a saffron field. In this area will also be found brighly-coloured tent bands loosely based on the magnificent tradition of weaving ornate coloured borders into the local white woolen cloth.

A third area of weaving is found among the Arab tribes who are settled along the banks of the river Tensift between Marrakech and the Atlantic. This can be referred to under such specific tribal identities as **Oulad Bou Sbaa** ,**Chiadma**, **Ahmar** and **Rehamna**, or under a regional appelation such as Boujad or Tensift. They are best known for their carpets, typically very long with a thick almost crude tufted pile and dominated by warm colours such as red or purple, with an almost abstract floating pattern of geometric designs.

You will also see in many of the carpet bazzars the so-called 'message rugs' with their bright colours and vivid row of pictograms such as camels, women and goats. These are popular trading items (of a size well suited for a childrens bedroom) but are not an indigenous Moroccan tradition, since they originated in southern Tunisia, in the region around the desert town of Gafsa.

ceramics

Pottery plates or large fruit bowls, particularly the traditional geometric designs of blue on white—glazed, plain or tinted green—translate well and seldom look out of place back home. The old ceramic centres of Morocco were Fès, Meknès and Tetouan, joined by Safi in the late 18th century. Today most of the pottery on sale in Morocco is made in either Safi or Fès. Good basic earthenware pots are also made in such typical Berber areas as the Ourika Valley, Et-Tleta-de-Oued-Laou, Amizmiz and Zaouia-Moulay-Brahim as well as on the western edge of Marrakech. Tamegroute in the southern Draa produces a rough, green, glazed ware identical in look (if not in quality) with the medieval wares of North Africa.

clothing

The city souks are full of the distinctive clothing of the Maghreb: ***gandouras*** (collarless cotton smocks), ***burnous*** (woollen cloaks with hoods), ***kaftans*** (cotton 'nightshirts' for daytime with embroidered necks) and ***jellabas*** (full-length woollen tunics with hoods). Though they're vital for dressing up, you need conviction to wear them well in Morocco. Back home a gandoura can serve as an admirable nightgown, a burnous is excellent as an outdoor cloak and a jellaba works well as a warm housecoat. Straw hats are useful in the summer, but no one should encourage any further manufacture by buying a hateful nylon **fez**. There are felt ones to be found, or lambs'-wool 'Nehru' hats.

jewellery

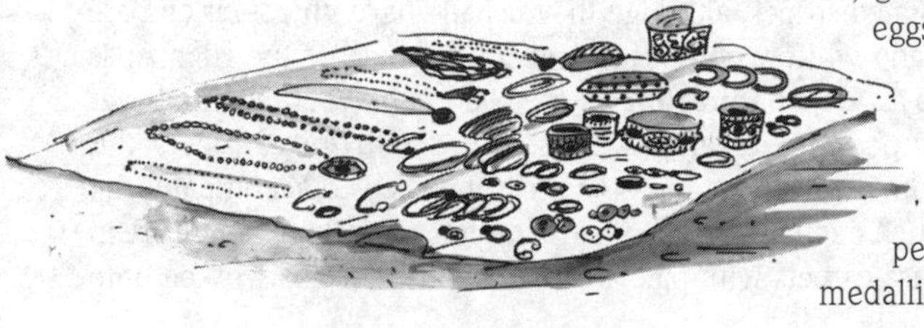

It's still possible to find good pieces of traditional Moroccan jewellery, although you will have to hunt for it, and know your prices in advance. The opportunities for self adornment are innumerable: silver crosses based on the traditional designs of the Tuareg and other Saharan tribes, green and yellow enamelled silver eggs from Tiznit, thick silver bracelets, a cascade of bangles, pairs of ornate triangular brooches linked by a chain, golden hand of fatima pendants, pierced coins, necklace medallions, small hanging boxes for miniature Korans or an Islamic prayer, or a thick rope of amber or cornelian beads interspaced with silver arrow heads. As well as all this there are the sumptuous necessities of a modern Moroccan marriage: golden tiaras, belts, bracelets, earrings, and rings studded with emeralds and brilliants. Moroccan jewellers are an entirely courteous but comparatively restrained breed of salesmen. Even so, one sometimes returns with something that looks just too 'tribal' back home. Many an aunt and niece have become the surprised beneficiaries of Berber pieces that the buyer found impossible to wear.

leather

The distinctive Moroccan **slippers**, the pointed and trodden-heeled ***babouches***, are immediately useful. They are for men and come in grey, white and yellow. You can also hunt for a softer chamois leather version in a much larger field of colours. The heavily embroidered and gilded versions are supposedly for women, but tend to have little flexibility or much use except for a dinner party.

Gilt-embroidered **belts** can be easily absorbed into western dress. They look better and more amusingly ostentatious the shabbier the trousers they support. Check when buying, however, that the leather isn't cardboard, that it has been stitched, not just glued, and that the buckle is strong enough.

Stamped and gilded red and ochre **portfolio-wallets** come in a range of sizes. They are generally made of fine leather and make admirable cases for letters, documents, bills you have no wish to pay or as a detachable binding for a book. The complete desk-sets found in many leather shops (a blotter, envelope stand and desk-size portfolio) are also usually of a high quality. If you have time, ask for a favourite book to be Morocco bound.

metal

There is a mass of decorated brass plates and silver-coloured implements in every bazaar. Candlesticks, mirrors, trays, pestles, incense burners, cake stands and ornate kettles attached to bowls (for the washing of hands before a meal) can be acquired before you even realized you had a need. The distinctive silver-coloured Moroccan teapot is the most attractive single item. The weak hinge of the lid and the failure of the insulating joints on the handle seem to be universal faults. Handkerchiefs are used for pouring and bent nails secure the lid throughout Morocco.

minerals

For under a pound/$1.50 you can pick up superb pieces of Sahara rose, amethyst and goniatites from the High Atlas and the Ziz valley. There are plenty of stalls selling 400-million year old minerals on the roadsides of the High Atlas passes, and also in Midelt, Marrakech and especially Erfoud.

spices

Moroccan spices, principally cumin, *harissa* (hot pepper), paprika, ginger, saffron, cinnamon and bunches of fresh mint, coriander and parsley create the most colourful displays in the souk. The intriguing displays of the apothecary and cosmetic stalls are often found close by, selling blocks of silvery antimony, kohl—ground antimony for the eyes, henna—in leaf or powder, *ghassol*—a brown mud for washing, *snib* for stopping shaving cuts, cochineal, porcupine quills, tooth-cleaning twigs, incense and dried Dadès roses.

wood

The skilled carvers and joiners of Essaouira work upon odiferous thuja wood to create some of the most attractive and durable items that you can acquire in Morocco. Inlaid chessboards, backgammon sets, polished boxes and carved jars can be bought directly from the craftsmen. Watch out for the hinges which are invariably shoddy, and hunt around for boxes which have snugly fitting lids. It is not a new trade, for the Romans were mad about thuja wood and spent fortunes on tables with knots and colouration that must have been in pleasing harmony with their liking for marble.

Sports

fishing

The streams and lakes of the Middle and High Atlas provide opportunities to catch a small local trout called *farios* and some imported rainbow. This could provide a few days distraction, but is unlikely to make the basis of a holiday for a keen fisherman. The season starts on 31 March. Bring all your own fly-fishing equipment. Information is available from Roger Chaban's *La Pêche au Maroc*, Editions Alpha. Fishing permits can be obtained from Administration des Eaux et Forêts, 11 Rue Reveil, Rabat.

Coarse fishing is a more popular sport. The natural lakes around Ifrane and the Bin-el-Ouidane, Moulay Youssef (east of Marrakech), Idriss (east of Fès), Ouel el Makhazine (east of Ksar-el-Kebir), and El Kansera (west of Meknès) reservoirs are stocked with bass, perch and pike. Permits, official seasons, lists of approved reservoirs and lakes can be obtained from the Ministry of Forest and Water in Rabat. No permit is required to fish anywhere from Morocco's enormous coast line where mackerel, bream, sea bass, red mullet or *loup de mer* (sea perch) can be caught from boat or line.

golf

Tangier has an 18-hole golf course 3km from the city overlooking the bay. Rabat has a 45-hole course at Dar es Salaam, 14km south of the city, set in an undulating area of cork woods (closed on Mondays, green fee 120dh). Mohammedia has an 18-hole golf course beside the sea. Marrakech has an 18-hole golf course 4km from the city. The Agadir course, placed halfway between Inezgane and Aït Melloul is extending its 9 holes to 18. The Casablanca course has 9 holes, and is found in the middle of the race track. Cabo Negro has a 9-hole course and so does Meknès, but this course, situated in part of the old royal palace, is only accessible to serving army officers and their friends. A new course is currently being created just east of Ouarzazate while another has recently been opened outside El Jadida. For precise information on a Moroccan golfing holiday, contact the specialist travel agents listed on p.7–9 or the Moroccan Royal Golf Federation at 2 Rue Moulay Slimane, Rabat.

hill walking and mountain climbing

The established centres for the major mountains are **Imlil** for the Toubkal area of the High Atlas; the **Aït Bou Guemès** Valley for the Central High Atlas, **El-Kelaâ-M'Gouna** for Jbel Sarhro, **Boumalne Dadès** for the High Atlas gorges, **Taliouine** for Jbel Siroua, **Tafraoute** for the Anti-Atlas, **Immouzer-des-Ida-Outanane** for the western High Atlas and **Midelt** for the Middle Atlas. The Ministry of Tourism has recently set up a Central Office of Information for the Mountains (CIM) and the *Grande Traversée des Atlas Marocains* (GTAM), a network of approved mountain guides, porters, village accommodation and hillside refuges. The full brochure of prices, addresses and itineraries can be acquired from CIM, Ministère du Tourisme, 1 Rue Oujda, Rabat, © (07) 701280/760915. Alternatively you could look through the hiking expeditions run by the specialist British travel agents listed on p.8–9. There is nothing to stop you hill walking throughout the country, and a number of less visited peaks within range of a comfortable hotel are suggested in the text.

riding

La Roseraie hotel at Ouirgane and the Rose du Dadès hotel in El-Kelâa-des-Mgouna both run riding stables that offer anything from a simple half day's ride to a week's expedition, complete with mule-borne tents. Both hotels can be booked with a riding itinerary arranged through the travel agents recommended on p.7.

shooting

Sochatour at 72 Boulevard Zerktouni, Casablanca, © (02) 314694, organizes shooting holidays for foreigners. They run sporting estates, organize suitable hotels, provide dogs and keepers, and arrange for a temporary shooting licence and importing your guns. On offer are snipe, turtle doves, duck, pheasant, pigeon, quail and wild boar from forests near Tangier, Agadir and Marrakech, and particularly the 120,000-hectare preserve around Arbaoua. The snipe, duck and pheasant season is from Oct to March; turtle doves from May–June; partridge from Oct-Jan; and driven wild boar from Oct to mid-Feb.

skiing

Mischliffen, between Ifrane and Azrou in the Middle Atlas, and Oukaïmeden in the High Atlas are the principal resorts. Snow can be found between November and March —see these two areas of the guide for details.

swimming and water sports

The principal beaches for summer water sports are Agadir, Tangier, Mdiq-Cabo Negro, Asilah, Mohammedia, Oualidia, Essaouira and El-Jadida, where donkey-rides, water-skiing, sailboarding, pedaloes, or paragliding can all be found. When swimming on the Atlantic coast, be constantly aware of the powerful undertow.

Study Resources

The Society for Moroccan Studies operates out of SOAS (School of Oriental and African Studies) at Thornhaugh Street, Russell Square, London WC1H 0XG. They publish a journal and arrange half a dozen lectures for an annual membership fee of £15.

Another key academic address in Britain is the Maghreb Bookshop at 45 Burton Street, London WC1, © (0171) 388 1840, run by Mohammed Ben Madani. It not only stocks rare and out-of-print editions but is also the hospitable nerve-centre of the *Maghreb Review*, a scholarly quarterly review of North African affairs in French and English.

The British-Moroccan Society at 35 Westminster Bridge Road, London SE1 7JB, © (0171) 401 8146, is a more social affair dominated by ex-members of the Foreign Office. The society publishes an annual newsletter, arranges a drinks party at the House of Lords in the spring and a dinner party in a grand hotel in November, and sponsors an annual art exhibition.

Telephones

The central post office of any large town or city will normally have a separate international telephone room where an operator at the central desk sets up international calls, which are taken in a row of airless cabins. These telephone rooms often operate longer opening hours than the post office itself, and though generally filled with a long queue, are much cheaper than phoning from a hotel. Estimate around 15dh a minute to Europe and 50dh a minute across the Atlantic. In addition some post offices have recently been equipped with a line of international phone booths outside the building which are operated by coins or charge cards, which can be bought at post office counters. Deregulation of the telephone system has combined with satellite technology and the demands of Morocco's large expatriate population to encourage a real explosion of private telephone companies in most of the cities and towns, and calling may become easier in future.

For international calls first dial 00, then when you hear a tone, add the country code (44 for Britain, 353 for the Irish Republic, 1 for Canada and the USA, 61 for Australia, 31 for the Netherlands),and then the local code and number, leaving out the initial 0 in area codes that have them. If you ask a friend to call you back, the country code for Morocco is 212.

The Moroccan telephone system has been completely overhauled in the last few years. All the former five-figure numbers have been promoted to six figures with the simple addition of another numeral. The country has been divided up in eight code-districts: (02) Casablanca, (03) Settat, (04) Marrakech and Safi, (05) Meknès and Fès, (06) Oujda and Sefrou, (07) Rabat, Salé and Kénitra, (08) Agadir and southern Morocco, and (09) Tangier and Tetouan. However, some out-of-the-way villages remain outside this system, and hotels and other places in these areas can still only be called through the operator.

It would not be fair to pretend that everything is quite so simple and straightforward as this basic outline might suggest. In practice, Moroccan telephone numbers are constantly being changed, there is no authoritative listing of numbers in any part of the country and, although we have double checked the numbers given in this guide some of them will near-inevitably already be obsolete. When communicating with a hotel try to use a fax wherever possible, as this will allow you to keep a receipt of the agreed booking.

Time

Morocco keeps Greenwich Mean Time throughout the year, so when Britain goes into summer-time Morocco appears to be one hour behind.

Tipping

Be frequent but concise with your tips. Service charges and tax are added on to most restaurant and hotel bills, but a waiter will expect another 5dh a head. For helping you park a car and watching over it, 2dh is standard throughout Morocco. Anything between 1 and 10dh is the going rate for photographs of camels, water carriers and snake charmers, depending on how keen you appear to be. Museum attendants also like the odd dirham or two or three extra, as do barmen, café waiters, hairdressers, hotel porters, bus luggage porters and petrol-pump attendants. Taxi drivers,however, are not customarily tipped on top of the fare.

Toilets

There is no need to feel embarrassed about asking to use a lavatory, for unlike the staff in London pubs no waiter or barman would dream of refusing a passer-by in need. Afterwards you could stop and order a drink, a simple coffee or Fanta, and leave an extra tip in grateful thanks. Most classified hotels and large restaurants are equipped with Anglo-Saxon flush bowls, though water supplies and efficient drainage can be variable, particularly in summer. It is a wasteful system for a nation grappling with the recurring problems of drought, and has been established largely for the benefit of tourists. Urban cafés and houses have a crouch hole and no paper, but a tap for washing your left hand and an old tin for sluicing. There are no public lavatories, although in tanneries you will see urinals that collect up urine for use later in curing the hides.

Tourist Offices

The Moroccan National Tourist Board, the ONMT, and French-styled Syndicats d'Initiatives are found in every city and even in most small towns of Morocco. They are useful as a source of official guides, glossy handouts, hotels, the dates of local festivals, the location of rural souks and the odd local map. They are seldom informative about local history, but very keen on the regular run of tourist sites, bazaars and large hotels.

Before you depart for Morocco one visit to a local office of the Moroccan Tourist Board can stock you up with the full range of handouts. There is a useful booklet of all the classified hotels, a collection of package tour prices, a sheet with the year's maximum hotel prices and half a dozen regional leaflets. In London look in at 205 Regent Street, W1, © (0171) 437 0073/74, in Paris at 161 Rue Saint Honoré, Place du Théâtre Français, © 42 60 63 50, in New York at 20 East 46th Street, 5th floor, Suite 503, NY 10017, © (212) 557 2520, and in Toronto at 2 Carlton Street, suite 1803, Toronto, M5B 1K2.

Where to Stay

One of the great joys of travelling in Morocco is the range and variety of hotels. You will intensify your enjoyment of the country if you switch freely between the most spartan and the most lavish accommodation. One night might be spent beside a bus station in preparation for a dawn departure, a second gazing at the stars in a place without running water or electricity, and a third wallowing in a luxurious oriental dream.

It is rare to find any Moroccan hotel, of whatever standard, without clean bedrooms. Bare stone floors will receive a daily wash and beds are made up with freshly laundered cotton sheets. The twin curses of the 20th-century traveller, nylon bedding and a synthetic fitted carpet ornamented with cigarette burns, are rarely found in Morocco. Reliable supplies of bath water can be more problematical. Rationing has begun in some resorts, while even the grandest hotels can have their off-days, though moderately priced hotels and above can usually be relied upon.

In the body of the guide there is a complete price range of hotels to choose from in each city and town. Small hotels with character, gardens, fires in winter, a resident owner-manager and large double beds have been preferred.

The official Moroccan star classifications for hotels are not reproduced in this guide, as they are not necessarily a reliable indication of the relative expense of comfort level of a hotel, and can be seriously confusing, especially in the middle ranges. As in many countries they are based on a fairly arbitrary list of potential facilities (whether or not a hotel has a separate reception desk, a lift and so on) more than price. It can work out that a small two-star can be a good deal more comfortable and attractive than a four-star, or that a four-star can be cheaper than a three.

Instead, the classification used in the guide is simply based on prices, although this can still hide an enormous flexibility depending on room size, position, season and your bargaining ability. It is only possible to bargain down the published rates by fax (℻) or by telephone in advance, as once you have arrived in the lobby looking desperate the game is over.

hotel price categories

The price categories used throughout the guide for a night for a double room are:

luxury	over £100/$150
expensive	between £50–£100/$75–$150
moderate	between £20–£50/$30–$75
inexpensive	below £20/$30
cheap	£10/$15 or under

campsites

It is not advisable, or legal, to camp except in an official campsite, though in the mountain valleys it is often possible to come to some short-term arrangement with a farmer or a café.

The best campsites in Morocco tend to be on the coast. The beach camps at Asilah, Moulay-Bousselham, Ech-Chiahna, Oualidia, Kédima, Tarhazoute, Sidi-Rbat and Kalah Iris are all delightful. Going inland the campsites at Meknès, Volubilis, Ifrane, Tinerhir, Zagora and Meski all have some special charm though there are many others that are perfectly adequate. Be prepared, particularly in Fès, Rabat, Tangier and Marrakech, to sacrifice scruples and spend one or two nights in a hotel. Sleeping on a hotel roof can be almost as cheap and romantic as camping. Prices vary but if you plan in terms of 5dh per person, plus 5dh per tent, plus 5dh per vehicle (15dh for a caravan or camper) you will not be far out.

youth hostels

There are youth hostels at:

Asni—40 beds	Azrou—40 beds
Casablanca—80 beds	Fès—60 beds
Meknès—50 beds	Chechaouèn—30 beds
Marrakech—89 beds	

They are uniformly clean and spartan, and charge around £2/$3 a night.

History

Morocco was long known in the Muslim world as *maghreb el Aksa*, the land of the furthest west. It was literally considered to be on the edge of the world, a place notorious for its powerful magicians and demon-like jinn. It is a country with an intense, almost insular, awareness of itself. In a sense it is an island, encircled by the seas of the Atlantic, the Mediterranean and the sand-sea of the Sahara. The land is further defended by four great mountain ranges (the Rif, Middle Atlas, High Atlas and Anti-Atlas) that run like vast ramparts across its breadth, breaking up the area's geographical unity and providing a secure mountainous refuge for the indigenous people, the Berbers, against both invaders and any central power. The Berber tribes of the mountains have remained in occupation of the land ever since the invention of agriculture.

Moroccan history is essentially the tale of a conservative society which has managed to triumph against all attempts at conquest. At the same time it has happily absorbed technical and spiritual innovations from the various foreign cultures that have tried to dominate the country. The first great change was from 1,000 BC, when Phoenician traders brought settled agriculture and urban civilization to Morocco. The second came in the 8th century AD when the cavalry armies of the Muslim Caliphate brought Islam, Arabic and the advanced culture of the Near East. Aristotle was being translated in the court of the rulers of Morocco when Oxford was still a muddy unlettered village. Arab military rule lasted only a few decades, but the spiritual and social message took deep root. All subsequent rulers of Morocco were only legitimate for as long as they championed Islam, either as reformers or as military protectors.

The third great revolution has been in the twentieth century when the French, albeit for the selfish motives of a European power, implanted the scientific and medical advances of the Industrial Revolution in Morocco. Morocco's identity has been likened by King Hassan to the desert palm: rooted in Africa, watered by Islam and rustled by the winds of Europe.

To *c.*150 BC: Berber Roots

Evidence of the camp fires and tool-making of the wandering bands of *Homo erectus*, who first crossed the Sahara to North Africa about a million years ago, have been discovered in the coastal sand dunes around Rabat and Casablanca. It was not until 10,000 BC that the melt waters of the last Ice Age separated North Africa from southern Europe, and the original inhabitants of both shores are of similar racial stock. The Neolithic Revolution, with the invention of both agriculture and stock breeding, reached the inhabitants of Morocco by about 3000 BC. It transformed the small bands of hunter-gatherers living in the area into communities of agriculturalists or nomads, and vastly increased the population. Stone circles in northern Morocco, such as that at **M'Soura** from around 1800 BC, prove that local tribes had strong contacts with the Megalithic culture of the Atlantic coast of Europe. There is also evidence of an ivory trade between the Tangier region and Spain. At about this time we can begin to speak of the indigenous population of North Africa, who spoke a language of the Hamitic family related to ancient Egyptian, as Berber (from the Greek for 'barbarian'). The men were devoted to war, polygamous and allowed their women to do most of the agricultural labour. The horse, first bred in North Africa in this period, and the donkey were greatly prized, while in the savannah plains the chariot became a dominant element in war. A brief wet period allowed the Berber tribes to expand into the Sahara, an event recorded in cave paintings showing dreadlocked cattle herders fleeing before conquering charioteers.

The Berbers enter the written history of the Mediterranean world via the trading settlements of the **Phoenicians**. By about 1100 BC these merchants from the coast of Syria had established a network of harbours along the North African shore which allowed them access to Cornish tin, Spanish silver and Saharan gold. The Phoenicians had a good eye for a harbour, and the shore of Morocco is dotted with their trading stations, such as Rusaadir (Melilla), Tingis (Tangier), Lixus (Larache), Sala Colonia (Rabat), Tit (Moulay-Abdallah) and Mogador (Essaouira). As well as their lucrative trade in metals and precious oils the Phoenicians developed a more humdrum 'country trade' in corn, oil, fish, dyes, timber and ivory. These trading colonies were responsible for the diffusion of new skills to the tribes of the North African coast. The pottery wheel, an alphabet, improved weaving techniques, the art of masonry, new crops, arboriculture, iron and metal work were all Phoenician gifts to the Berbers of Morocco.

*c.*150 BC–AD 429: Roman Influence

Effective dominion over the Phoenician colonies passed in the 5th century BC to Carthage, and with the defeat of Carthage in the second century BC to Rome. The Romans exercised a loose protectorate over the extensive kingdom of **Mauretania**, which covered both Morocco and eastern Algeria. Mauretania remained an area of Phoenician culture (recalled by the Libyo-Berber script that can be seen carved on stones in the sub-Saharan region) and was ruled from the two capitals of Volubilis (in central Morocco) and Cherchel (in the centre of Algeria). Roman influence increased from 25 BC under Juba II, a Mauretanian prince who had been educated in the household of the Caesars in Rome.

The gradual absorption of Mauretania into the Empire was reversed by a widespread revolt in AD 42 which it took an army of four legions over three years to subdue. In AD 44, the Emperor Claudius officially annexed Mauretania, but the fierce resistance of the tribes left the Moroccan portion of the old kingdom much reduced in size. The frontier of Roman Morocco, known as the province of **Mauretania Tingitania**, extended just south of Sala Colonia (Rabat) and just east of Volubilis. There was no secure road east to Roman Algeria, whose western frontier reached Oujda and the river Moulouya.

The Romans' authority was continuously challenged by the Berber tribes, but within their frontiers they built upon the trade and settlement patterns of the Phoenician period to create a small but prosperous and civilized province. In addition to the magnificent ruins of the capital **Volubilis**, their achievement is witnessed by lesser sites such as Lixus, Cotta, Banasa, Thamusida, Sala Colonia and Tamuda. As part of the reorganization of the Empire in the reign of Emperor Diocletian (285–305) the frontier was withdrawn to a defensive line between Tamuda (Tetouan) and Lixus (Larache). Volubilis was abandoned, but the two port cities of Tangier and Ceuta were protected. These remained under Roman rule until 429.

429–704: Vandals and Byzantines

An army of the Germanic Vandals, led by Gesneric, invaded North Africa from Spain in 429, landing at Tangier. Although they were relatively few in number their rule in North Africa lasted a century, until their defeat in 535 by the Byzantine general Belisarius. The Byzantines installed governors at Ceuta and Tangier, who remained dominant figures in local politics until the Arab invasion two centuries later.

704–740: The Arab Conquest

The Arab conquest brought Islam to Morocco: a religion, a social code, a system of law and a new language that were to provide the central identity of all future Moroccan states. Its introduction was due not to peaceful missionaries but to Arab cavalry armies despatched by the caliphs, the political heirs of the Prophet. Within 25 years of Mohammed's death the first three caliphs had conquered an empire that stretched across Syria, Mesopotamia, Persia, Egypt and Libya. The Arab advance along the North African coast was delayed by a succession dispute, but in 682 **Uqba ben Nafi** made his famous raid. Partly a dazzling conquest, partly a missionary voyage of discovery, this is a cherished episode in Moroccan history, but the facts have long since been wrapped up in legend. The tale records that Uqba defeated a joint Berber and Byzantine army, was welcomed by Count Julian into Tangier, accepted the submission of Volubilis and went on to conquer the Haouz, the Drâa valley and the Sous. Arriving at the Atlantic he rode deep into the surf declaring, 'O God, I take you to witness that there is no ford here. If there was I would cross it.' This was all to no avail, for on his return east Uqba was ambushed and killed by an old adversary.

The Arab conquest of Morocco did not begin in earnest until 704, when Musa ben Nasser arrived at Kairouan in Tunisia to take up his appointment as commander of the western Arab army. Between 705 and 710 he advanced rapidly westward, content to accept the nominal conversion of towns and tribes which he enforced by establishing garrisons, notably at Tangier, Tlemcen and Sijilmassa. His aim was to secure Morocco in order to be able to proceed with the conquest of Spain. The prospect of an invasion of rich, plunderable Spanish provinces brought thousands of Berber warriors flocking to the Arab banners. In 711 an advance guard of 7000 under the command of the governor of Tangier **Tariq** crossed the straits, first landing at what came to be known as Jbel Tariq, or Gibraltar. He was welcomed by many among the Christian and Jewish population of Spain as a deliverer from the harsh rule of the Germanic Visigoths. In one day's work at the battle of the Barbate River, Tariq destroyed the Visigothic army. Muslim armies quickly occupied Spain, and the Arab advance into Western Europe was not checked until Charles Martel stood firm at Poitiers in 732.

In 740 a mutiny among the Berbers in the Arab garrison at Tangier lit a chain of rebellions that swept right through North Africa. Though the caliphate sent a succession of Arab armies, these were only able to reconquer Tunisia. Morocco, having absorbed the message of Islam, returned to its customary independence.

740–1042: The Spread of Islam

For a while northwest Morocco found unity under **Moulay Idriss**, a kinsman of the Prophet who had fled civil war in Arabia. The tribes of central Morocco accepted him as a holy man and arbitrator. His son **Idriss II** established a unitary state based around a small army and the new settlement of Fès, which Moulay Idriss had founded in 799. Within a few decades it had grown into an influential city, filled with skilled craftsmen and noble Arab warriors who fled there from civil war in Spain and revolution in Tunisia. Fès became the cultural, political and economic centre of Morocco, from where Arabic language, religious knowledge and technical innovations spread into the rest of the country.

The political authority of Idriss II was lost when his kingdom was divided between nine sons on his death in 828. The various Idrissid princes soon fell under the influence of powerful neighbouring dynasties, such as the Shiite Fatimids of Tunisia and the Omayyads of Spain, who controlled many of the chief ports and towns of Morocco throughout the 10th and11th centuries. This period also witnessed the gradual conversion of the Berber tribes of the interior by missionaries and warriors, many of whom claimed descent from the Idrissid princes. Idrissid ancestry is still a mark of prestige in Morocco, while the process of conversion is remembered in hundreds of different local folk tales that recall trials of power between Muslim holy men and diabolic magicians.

1042–1147: The Almoravids

In the middle of the 11th century there was no Morocco, just a confused patchwork of half-converted Berber tribes, Arab trading cities, foreign garrisons and petty principalities. The Almoravids created Morocco. Their conquests welded the civilized northwest of the country to a vast Berber and Saharan hinterland and created a common identity. The Almoravid Empire marks a historical threshold, just as the Norman Conquest, which occurred in the same period, does for England.

The Almoravids were not a foreign power but a simple confederation of Berber tribes from the Western Sahara who had been united by **Ibn Yaasin**, a charismatic holy man from the Sous valley. Determined to impose a pure Islamic state, he launched his crusade from the desert in 1042. A generation later, in 1070, the young Almoravid general **Youssef ben Tachfine** established Marrakech as their advance northern base and principal city. By the 1080s he controlled central Morocco and Fès. In 1086 he landed in Spain at the invitation of the embattled Muslim states. He promptly defeated the Christians, but then proceeded to absorb the 26 principalities of Spain into his Empire. At its height the Almoravid Empire stretched from Spain to West Africa and from the Atlantic to eastern Algeria.

The empire sought to be the ideal Islamic state. The ruling class of princes and tribal emirs were deposed, and all taxes not sanctioned in the Koran were abolished. Islamic law according to the Malekite tradition was imposed upon society. Almoravid generals subdued even the remotest hill tribes, built stone castles on the summits of mountains (which can still be seen at **Zagora** and **Jbel Amergou**) to enforce their authority and encircled cities in protective walls. After the conquest of Spain, skilled craftsmen were brought over to build and decorate mosques, fountains and public bathhouses. Talented Andalusian secretaries, employed in the court, brought increased literacy and the Maghrebi script to the country. The Almoravid sultans also made a practice of consulting the doctors of Islamic law in order to seek their approval before making any major decision, even in matters of war. This council, the *ulema*, remained a central feature of the Moroccan state. The sultans sought recognition from the caliphs of Baghdad for their title *Amir al Muslimin* (Commander of the Muslims), which aptly expresses their championship of orthodox Islam.

There was a dark side to Almoravid rule. The great flowering of Andalusian mysticism, poetry and intellectual inquiry seen in the previous two centuries was suppressed. Their insistence on collecting only Koranic taxes left them short of revenue, made up for by extortion. Their narrow puritanism led to the persecution of Jewish communities and the extermination of the last Christians in Morocco.

Ali ben Youssef succeeded in 1107. He completed the conquest of Muslim Spain and his generals advanced the frontier by adding Lisbon and the Balearics to the empire. Ali reigned for 37 years and was responsible for the great building projects of the Almoravids: the grand mosque of Tlemcen (in Algeria), the Karaouiyne Mosque in Fès and the Ben Youssef Mosque and Koubba Ba'Adiyn in Marrakech. His sons, though, lost control to a rival Berber dynasty the Almohads, who stormed Marrakech in 1147 and killed Ishaq, the last Almoravid sultan.

1147–1248: The Almohads

Medieval Morocco reached its zenith of confidence and achievement under the Almohad Empire, whose rule extended over Spain, Morocco, Algeria and western Libya. The Almohads had much in common with the Almoravids. They too were a confederation of Berber tribes (though from the High Atlas not the Western Sahara) that had been united by the zeal of a charismatic holy man, **Ibn Tumert**, and led to final victory by his more pragmatically minded successor, **Abdel Moumen**, whose descendants inherited the Empire. An Almohad fleet dominated the waters of the western Mediterranean, and the monumental architecture of this period still dominates the cities of Morocco, such as the Hassan minaret and Oudaïa gate in Rabat and the Aguenaou gate and Koutoubia minaret in their major centre, Marrakech. The regional capitals at Taza, Tlemcen, Tunis and Seville were also adorned, and great philosophers such as Averroes enjoyed the friendship of the sultan.

The Empire's first important reverse came in 1212, when the Spanish Christians inflicted a crushing defeat on it at Las Navas de Tolosa. It was a blow from which Muslim interests in Spain never fully recovered. Ferdinand III of Castile captured Córdoba in 1235 and Seville in 1248, leaving only the mountainous kingdom of Granada under its own independent Nasrid dynasty. Remorselessly, the empire contracted. In Tunisia an Almohad governor established the Hafsid dynasty, whilst western Algeria fell to a Berber tribe, the Ziyanids, who ruled from Tlemcen. In 1248 an Almohad sultan died whilst on campaign against the Ziyanids. His leaderless army was betrayed and then massacred on the eastern plains of Morocco by the Beni-Merin tribe. The Beni-Merin chieftain then promptly seized control of Fès (the chief city of the north) and founded the Merenid dynasty. However, it was not until 1276, when the last Almohad sultan was killed in the High Atlas, that the Merenids controlled the south of the country as well, and could feel secure on the throne of Morocco.

1248–1554: The Merenids

The rule of the Merenid sultans is recalled by a series of dazzling architectural compositions. The ruins of the Chellah necropolis at Rabat, the sumptuous *medersas* that can be seen in Fès, Salé and Meknès, as well as numerous mosques, fountains and *fondouqs* scattered throughout the towns and cities of Morocco reveal the exquisite taste and wealth of this period. Merenid power and creativity was at its glorious peak during the reign of **Abou Hassan** (1331–51) and his son **Abou Inan** (1351–58). A series of ambitious campaigns seemed on the point of recovering the old territory of the Almohad Empire in North Africa, while the glittering new *medersas* (university colleges) helped train a new generation of loyal officials to serve in **Fès Jdid** (New Fès), the separate and defensible royal city that they founded to the west of old Fès. Literary figures such as the great historian Ibn Khaldoun and Ibn Batuta (the Muslim Marco Polo) received the enlightened patronage of the court.

By the beginning of the 15th century it was a very different story. The Merenid state fell into the hands of a corrupt cabal of viziers, financiers and generals. Against a background of economic decline the Portuguese and Spanish gradually seized control of most of the Moroccan ports, starting with the sack of Ceuta in 1419. By the mid-16th century the Portuguese cavalry controlled the Atlantic coast and had begun to penetrate deep into the interior. Marrakech and Fès were defended only with the military assistance of the Ottoman Turks, who had already seized control of Tunisia and Algeria.

1554–1668: The Saadians and the Battle of the Three Kings

From this point of apparent hopelessness Morocco unexpectedly recovered. The Saadians, an influential family from the Drâa oasis valley, led the fight against the Portuguese and made themselves rulers of southern Morocco in the process. By 1542, their success in expelling the Portuguese from Agadir, Safi and Azemmour had brought them the support necessary to dethrone the old dynasty which, surrounded by Turkish guards, hung on to power in Fès.

The true turning-point in Saadian power came in 1578, when they destroyed a Portuguese invasion led by the youthful King Sebastian at the battle of Ksar-el-Kebir. This is also known as the 'Battle of the Three Kings', since the reigning sultan, Sebastian and his treacherous Moroccan royal ally all died during the battle.

The throne passed to **Ahmed el Mansour**, 'the victorious' (1578–1603) who further increased his prestige and wealth by seizing control of the goldfields of West Africa. Ahmed el Mansour remodelled the state along the lines of Ottoman Turkey. External trade was encouraged and with the revenue from customs duties he was able to fund a professional army, recruited from Andalusian exiles, Christian renegades and Turks, that was untarnished by tribal loyalties. He gave audiences from behind a screen and introduced the scarlet parasol that is still a distinguishing mark of a Moroccan sultan's sovereignty, and built the palace of El Badia in Marrakech to be the magnificent ceremonial heart of his court. Provincial leaders were enticed away from local politics to the glittering life of the capital. His rule was that of an enlightened despot: in the words of the chroniclers, 'he sweetened his absolute power with much clemency'. In Marrakech the magnificent ruins of El Badia, the serene elegance of the Ben Youssef Medersa and the glittering opulence of the Saadian Tombs survive to give a suggestion of this near-fabulous period of history.

In 1603 a vicious **succession war** between the Saadian princes shattered the prosperity of the state. For much of the 17th century the Saadian sultans were mere shadows locked in their Marrakech palaces while real authority was exercised by a jumble of petty powers that included the pirate republic of Rabat–Salé and four rival dynasties of sheiks who controlled the Berber tribes in the Western Rif, Middle Atlas, High Atlas and Anti-Atlas.

1668–1727: The First Alaouite Sultans, Moulay Rachid and Moulay Ismaïl

The Alaouite prince **Moulay Rachid**, from an Arab holy family long resident in the oasis of Tafilalt, succeeded in seizing the throne in 1668. His family still holds it to this day.

During the 54-year reign of his younger brother **Moulay Ismaïl** (1672–1727) the Portuguese were expelled from their fortresses on the Atlantic coast, the English were driven out of Tangier, and the Turks pushed back on the eastern frontier to the line of the present border with Algeria. Morocco is filled with evidence of the constructive nature of his reign. He founded towns, built bridges, ports and forts, and secured the safety of roads. He encouraged trade and reformed religious life, purging unorthodox cults but restoring shrines and mosques.

Moulay Ismaïl deliberately neglected the existing capitals of Fès and Marrakech with their rebellious citizens and built up **Meknès** to be the new administrative and ceremonial centre of the nation. Meknès was also the headquarters of the sultan's negro slave army of 150,000 men, which functioned as both a corps of engineers and the brutal instrument of his authoritarian regime. There were a number of bloody campaigns against the mountain tribes and frequent instances of despotic tyranny. The sultan's proudest boast was that he had made Morocco safe enough for a woman or a Jew laden down with jewellery to travel across the breadth of the country without being troubled.

1727–1822: Decline and Isolationism

A vicious period of **civil war** followed Moulay Ismaïl's death as the slave regiments championed a swift-changing variety of his heirs. None of his descendants could hope to equal the power of Moulay Ismaïl. They ruled as much by consensus and arbitration as by decree. The authority of the government was restricted to the fertile coast, river valleys and towns—the 'Bled el Makhzen', the 'land of government'. The dry plains and mountains were known as the 'Bled-es-Siba', ('land of dissidence'), where the tribes respected only the spiritual authority of the sultan and had no time for his tax-gatherers and ministers.

Sidi Mohammed (1757–90) was one of the most astute sultans of the period, beloved by the towns for his firm but fair rule and by the nation at large for his expulsion of the Portuguese from El-Jadida. He maximized government revenue by concentrating the export trade at **Essaouira** which he built up into the elegant town it is today. He also played a clever game with the European nations and kept their influence at a minimum by a quick-footed policy of encouraging competition between them. His son, **Moulay Sliman** (1792–1822), changed to the ultimately disastrous policy of isolationism, attempting to seal Muslim Morocco from any contact with Europe. His foreign policy was dominated by suspicion of all the Christian powers and a particular loathing for the French Revolution. Despite being offered Ceuta and Melilla he refused to recognize the upstart Bonaparte as king of Spain. All exports were banned, a 50 per cent duty imposed on imports, and European consuls were confined to Tangier in an attempt to keep outside influence firmly at bay.

1822–1904: The Growth of European Influence

Moulay Sliman ignored the claims of his inadequate sons and nominated his nephew, **Abder Rahman** (1822–59) to succeed him on the throne. It was during his reign that Morocco felt the full force of the growing power of France. The sultan had provided some support for the Algerian tribes during the French invasion of Algeria. This policy was shattered in 1843 when a Moroccan army was destroyed at the Battle of Isly (outside Oujda) and the ports of Tangier and Essaouira were bombarded. The tribes' reaction to these humiliating national defeats was to rise in widespread revolt against the sultan.

Suddenly aware of his nation's military vulnerability, the sultan played on the strong and traditional **Anglo–French rivalry**. He made approaches to the British, who were interested in opening up Morocco to their traders and obsessed by keeping the Straits of Gibraltar open for their shipping. As a corollary of British diplomatic support against the French, the 1856 **Treaty of Tangier** removed all the sultan's restrictions on trade except his monopoly on tobacco and arms. It instituted a flat 10 per cent customs rate and introduced consular courts and privileges which soon deprived the sultan of any control over his nation's trade. Spain as well as France soon became envious of British influence. In 1859, as the sultan lay dying, a Spanish army advanced from Ceuta to defeat a tribal army and occupy the city of Tetouan. The tribes rose again in revolt against their defeated government, and British protection was revealed to be a false and illusory hope.

Abder Rahman's son Sidi Mohammed (**Mohammed IV**, 1859–73) was faced with a problematic inheritance. The Spanish demanded a crippling indemnity of 100 million pesetas before they would leave Tetouan; a pretender to the throne appeared in the Rif; and the Rehamna tribe pillaged Marrakech. The Spanish left Tetouan in 1862, paid off by a British loan which required the surrender of customs revenue and its administration by the British and Spanish. Internal dissidence was subdued by 1864.

The unhappy start to the reign was followed by a remorseless growth in European influence. By 1900 there were over 10,000 European residents in the country. Foreign consuls in the ports of Tangier and Casablanca organized lighthouses, port works, sanitary services and a national postal service, increasingly supplanting the sultan's sovereignty. The consular privileges of the treaty of 1856 put European merchants and their many Moroccan agents beyond the law of the sultan. As a graphic illustration of this trend, between 1844 and 1873 the national currency lost 90% of its value. Trade was conducted in the French five franc coin.

Sultan **Moulay Hassan** (1873–94) attempted the almost impossible task of modernizing Morocco while keeping the nation's independence. On his accession in 1873, he began a programme of **reform and modernization**. Whilst instituting his reforms, however, he still had to maintain central authority through the traditional system of annual military campaigns. The students he dispatched to Europe to learn the latest medical and engineering skills returned unable to cope with the political realities of their homeland.

The sultan attempted to stabilize the currency by minting the Koranically approved *riyal* in Paris. It was of such quality that it was hoarded or smuggled abroad. At the Conference of Madrid in 1880 he attempted to limit the ruinous extent of consular privileges, and a limit was set of two agents per country in each port. No European power except Britain respected these terms. Military reforms proved just as difficult. When the European powers blocked his schemes, he wisely balanced their influence: there was a French military mission, a British chief of staff ('Caid' Maclean), the German Krupp firm was given contracts for coastal defence, and the Italians built and ran a munitions factory at Fès. Moulay Hassan exhausted himself in the service of his country, reasserting order and personally dispensing justice in regions that had not seen an official of the sultan for a hundred years. He died while on campaign in 1894.

His two sons presided over the last stormy decade of Moroccan independence. Useless Western products were enthusiastically acquired, their purchase financed through ruinous foreign loans. **Abdul Aziz** (1894–1908), surrounded by a court composed of European adventurers, unscrupulous salesmen and doctors, became alienated from his traditional advisers and political realities. Meanwhile the tribal chiefs and *caids* (magistrates) appointed by Moulay Hassan, notably in the High Atlas mountains, expanded their power in the vacuum created by the disordered central government.

1904–36: The Imposition of French Rule

It is doubtful whether any ruler could have successfully resisted the anarchy created by the advance of French power in Morocco at this time. In exchange for a free hand in Morocco the French had begun to negotiate a series of bargains with the other colonial powers. Spain was offered territory in northern and southern Morocco, Italy a free hand over Libya; while the French agreed to recognize Britain's rule over Cyprus, Egypt and the Sudan, with the additional promise that Tangier would remain a demilitarized zone.

French control was tightened in 1904 when Abdul Aziz accepted a loan of 50 million francs from a consortium of French banks. In 1906 the Conference of Algeciras ratified the various secret negotiations that had been taking place between the Europeans over the future of Morocco. The French army had slowly been occupying oases on the eastern frontier since 1900, but in 1907 the lynching of a few Europeans in Marrakech and Casablanca gave them the excuse for direct intervention. Oujda was occupied in the east and 3000 French troops were promptly landed at Casablanca. The 'Moroccan Crises' of 1905 and 1911, when Imperial Germany sought to gain influence in Morocco, only spurred the French into more aggressive action, to deny access to the country to their greatest rival.

Sultan **Moulay Hafid** (1908–12), faced with simultaneous French and Spanish invasions and internal rebellions, accepted the inevitable and signed the **Treaty of Fès** (1912) which established colonial rule over Morocco. The nation was carved up into Spanish and French spheres of influence: the French took everything of value, leaving only bare bones for their rivals. The **Spanish protectorate** consisted of Ifni (an enclave in the Anti-Atlas), a stretch of desert south of the Drâa valley, and the mountainous Rif coast of northern Morocco.

The French takeover of Morocco was not entirely unopposed. Two weeks after the Treaty of Fès was signed revolution broke out in Fès, eighty Europeans were lynched and the walls were manned. In the south El Hiba,'the Blue Sultan', raised the black banners of revolt and marched up from the Sahara with a tribal force of 12,000. French artillery and machine guns, though, did for them both and by September Marrakech had been occupied.

The colonial regime soon became critically short of manpower, as the stormclouds of the First World War became apparent. Deals were struck with the Glaoui brothers, a pair of ex-government ministers from the Berber High Atlas, who were armed and encouraged to build up a private army to secure the south. Taroudannt was taken in May 1913 without the use of a single French soldier. The first French resident general, Marshal Lyautey, was able to hold central Morocco with a skeleton military presence. The Rif, Middle Atlas and the areas south of the High Atlas remained beyond his control until reinforcements in 1921 allowed the conquest to proceed. It was not completed until 1936.

It was in the rugged Eastern Rif, in the Spanish zone, that the colonial powers encountered the most serious military resistance. The rebel leader **Abdel Krim** defeated a Spanish army in July 1921. It took several years and a full-scale combined Franco-Spanish campaign under the command of Marshal Pétain to subdue him.

Tangier was left as a demilitarized zone. A constitution in 1923 provided the international city of Tangier with a ruling council of consuls, a small house of representatives and the *mendoub*, the representative of the sultan. In practice French and Spanish officials dominated the administration, the Italians gave the best parties, and the British created some beautiful gardens.

1912–56: The Achievements of the French Protectorate

Peace, with the end of tribal pillage and administrative extortion, led to a rapid growth in population and trade. In 1921 Morocco had a population of three million. After only thirty years of French rule this had risen to 8 million.

Apart from military conquest and administration the Protectorate's chief concern was to develop Morocco's agricultural and mineral wealth. French banks financed major public works, ports, dams, roads and railways, and the government attracted capitalist investment into mining and agriculture by a tempting package of low taxes, cheap labour and land.

By 1953 irrigation, expropriation and purchase had created one million hectares of cultivable land under French ownership concentrated in the fertile coastal zones. In 1951 there were 325,000 Europeans in the country, including a rich controlling minority of 5000 and a subclass of 80,000 'poor whites'. An impressive infrastructure of roads, railways, ports, administrative centres and dams was developed to provide water and power for the settlers and facilitate the economic exploitation of the country. Hospitals, schools and hotels were also built, for the use of settlers and a tiny minority of the traditional Moroccan ruling class of *caids*, merchants and sheiks. Even by Independence in 1956 less than 15 per cent of the Moroccan population had received any sort of education.

The Second World War

Morocco was involved in the events of the Second World War as a Protectorate of France. After the conquest of France by Nazi Germany in 1940 her overseas possessions passed under the control of Marshal Pétain's Vichy regime. Pétain strove to maintain a degree of neutrality, but a series of British/Free-French attacks soon pushed Vichy into a tacit alliance with Germany. After the entry of the USA into the war many of Pétain's generals in North Africa began to enter into covert discussions with the Allies, and in November 1942 a British-American force stumbled ashore in the Casablanca landings that 'liberated' Morocco. It was a near farce: the soldiers were all horribly seasick and the whole thing had been arranged in advance by secret negotiations. Morocco was promptly placed under the Free French administration of de Gaulle, and in January 1943 Roosevelt and Churchill met in the country for the Casablanca Conference. In a meeting with Sultan Mohammed V the American president gave private encouragement that the post-war era would bring a return of sovereignty to Morocco.

By the end of the war, also, there were 300,000 Moroccans under arms. They formed a very substantial portion of the French forces that fought alongside the Allies in Italy and then in France itself after the collapse of the Pétain regime in 1942. It was the Moroccan 4th

Mountain Division that in May 1944 broke the Gustav Line. The Moroccan 2nd Division captured Monte Pantano in 1943 and, transferred to France, also won great respect for crossing the Rhine under heavy fire on 31 March 1945.

1947–56: The Struggle for Independence

Though there was no immediate political evidence for it, the Second World War saw a transformation in the relationship between France and Morocco. France had been humiliated, whilst Moroccan forces had contributed to the liberation of Europe. The European colonial powers had been replaced by the anti-colonial world leadership of America and Russia. India and Egypt, which both rapidly achieved independence at the end of the war, pointed the way for Morocco.

Mohammed V had been chosen by the French in 1927 to succeed his father for his apparent docility. He proved to have an unexpectedly strong character and enjoyed the moral high ground against a series of unimaginative generals who served as Residents. The sultan resisted all of Vichy France's anti-semitic measures and refused to receive a single German officer, and while 200,000 French Jews died in Nazi concentration camps he protected all 300,000 of his Jewish subjects. By 1953 the sultan was so clearly identified with the popular demand for independence that the French authorities deposed him and exiled him to Madagascar. By the summer of 1955 the campaign of civil disobedience for the sultan's return had escalated into widespread violence and the French were threatened by an incipient armed rebellion. The situation in Algeria, where the FLN revolt had erupted in 1954, helped concentrate their minds. The French decided to quit Morocco (and Tunisia) with good grace in order to concentrate on holding on to Algeria. The Spanish and the 'international protectors' of Tangier were forced to follow suit. In November 1955 Mohammed V returned to a tumultous popular reception, and by March 1956 the French had formally recognized Moroccan independence.

1956–61: King Mohammed V

Upon Independence the sultan restyled himself as King Mohammed V to emphasize his position as a modern constitutional monarch removed from the practices of the pre-1912 regime. In the euphoric first years of independence a national government established schools, universities and newspapers, and elected regional assemblies. The Sufi brotherhoods, many of whom had become involved in pro-French politics, were reformed, orthodoxy and public morality reaffirmed, and massive public work schemes launched. In the early burst of nationalist enthusiasm labour battalions absorbed unemployment and created some lasting monuments, such as the Route de l'Unité road across the Rif which joined the road systems of the hitherto separate French and Spanish Protectorates.

For all this wave of modernization Mohammed V was quietly determined that the monarchy should always remain the controlling force in national politics. The Istaqlal, the sole national party, which had played a central role in the struggle for independence, was seen to pose a potential threat. It dominated the first cabinet, although Mohammed V insisted on retaining control over the army and the Ministry of the Interior. By 1959 the left wing of the Istaqlal under Ben Barka had broken away to form the UNFP (Union Nationale des Forces Populaires) and ranged themselves in a socialist alliance with the UMT labour union; the centrist rump of Istaqlal then established their own union, the UGTM. The rural Berber hinterland, meanwhile, remained suspicious of the urban Istaqlal, and with discreet support from the King a new and conservative party, the Mouvement Populaire, was formed.

Crown Prince Hassan was given the task of creating a royal army. Units of the Liberation Army were absorbed within this new force which by recruiting experienced veterans of French service soon rose to 30,000 men. In 1958 and 1959 rebellions in the Rif, the Saharan oases and the Middle Atlas tested the army's discipline and efficiency. The more radical and militant members of the Liberation Army were meanwhile directed south to the unofficial siege of the Spanish enclave of Ifni and the struggle to gain control over the Western Sahara.

1961–1975: The Early Years of King Hassan II

In February 1961, at the height of his powers, King Mohammed V died and was succeeded by his son, Hassan II, who remains firmly in power today. The new king excluded the socalist UNFP from government by forming a cabinet from the Mouvement Populaire and Istaqlal in June 1961. In December 1962 a referendum was held to give popular approval to Morocco's **first democratic constitution**. The UNFP called for a boycott, but this failed due to lack of support from the labour unions. The new king, having won the referendum, no longer felt the need for Istaqlal support, and sacked its members from his cabinet.

The **first parliamentary elections** were held in March 1963. The ministries of Agriculture and the Interior assisted the electoral victory of the FDIC, a royal coalition headed by the Mouvement Populaire. Istaqlal was strongest in the older cities and successful farming areas like Tadla, Doukkala and the Rharb; UNFP in the new cities of the coast: Rabat, Casablanca and Agadir, and throughout the Sous Valley. The Mouvement Populaire's greatest support came from Marrakech and the Berber hinterland as well as Oujda, Taza and Nador.

The socialist UNFP increasingly identified itself with the Arab republics of Egypt and Algeria, which its supporters publicly cited as role models for Morocco. The local elections of July 1963, and the conspicuous but fixed FDIC victory of an 85% vote encouraged the UNFP to think in terms of revolutionary change. The King responded by arresting over 130 UNFP militants on treason charges later in the month. Ben Barka, the leader of the UNFP, fled to Paris and widened the political breach by calling on the Moroccan army not to resist Algeria in the border war fought in the Sahara during the winter of 1963.

The first parliament was a failure. In two years of existence, it passed only three minor bills. A three-year plan drawn up in 1964 was aborted as the planners had failed to consult the Finance Ministry. A short-lived liberal party was formed around disgruntled technocrats appalled by the jobbery and factional intrigue that dominated the parliament.

The **student and worker riots** of Casablanca in March 1965 encouraged the King to dissolve parliament in June and rule directly, though he retained most of the parliamentary cabinet. Ben Barka was assassinated in Paris that August, in a plot that was traced back to the Moroccan Ministry of the Interior. The King, in an adroit political move, then borrowed a popular UNFP issue and initiated the **nationalization of foreign businesses and farms**.

By August 1970 a new constitution was prepared and approved in a national referendum that gave the King increased influence over parliament. Istaqlal and the UNFP boycotted the elections, with the result that the parliament was made up of loyalist placemen. As a result of this narrowing of the field of power there were two **coups d'état**. A group of senior army officers had grown disgusted at the scale of corruption in government and the extent of patronage and client networks. In the coup of Skhirate in July 1971 they attempted to purge the King of his existing advisers, who were to be replaced by a puritanical reforming military council; in 1972 there was another failed coup when the King's aeroplane was ambushed by Air Force jets but was saved by a quick talking pilot. Investigations traced the plot back to General Oufkir, the widely feared Minister of the Interior. The following year, in March 1973, bands of armed men crossed the border from Algeria in the hope of sparking off a popular rising. It never got off the ground, but the public trial was used to accuse some of the left-wing opposition of treasonable rebellion.

1975–88: The Green March and Economic Reform

If the first 14 years of King Hassan's reign earned him the nickname of the 'Great Survivor', his later period of rule allows him to be considered the 'Unifier'. In 1975 the King orchestrated a march of 350,000 civilians south to reintegrate the Spanish colony of Rio de Oro (Western Sahara) into greater Morocco. This 'Green March' buried the political problems of the past in a surge of nationalism. It was a brilliantly timed political gamble which caught the Spanish government paralysed by the lingering death of General Franco. The resulting **war** against a group of the Saharan tribes, united under the **Polisario** movement for independence in Western Sahara, prolonged the mood of national unity. Libya and Algeria supported the Polisario, but this 'revolutionary' alliance led to firm backing for Morocco from both Saudi Arabia and the United States.

After a shaky start the war has now been militarily won. A methodical system of well-patrolled sand walls, begun in 1981 and completed in 1987, has excluded the Polisario fighters from all but the frontier fringes of the province. This policy of practical action was matched by a 'hearts and minds' programme that sought to win over the Saharan population with new housing and development schemes. The enhanced pay, equipment and prestige afforded to the army has kept it loyal to the King. Meanwhile the Polisario, locked up in their refugee camps around the Algerian town of Tindouf, gradually lost the support of their hosts. In 1989 a UN-sponsored **ceasefire** was agreed and King Hassan met with Polisario leaders for talks in Marrakech. His hand was further strengthened in 1992 when the foreign minister of the Polisario defected to Morocco and the Algerian government seemed to renounce the idea of an independent Western Sahara. Ever since the ceasefire there has been talk of a UN-monitored referendum, but the question of who is eligible to vote will be decisive.

The enormous cost of the war, an estimated $1 billion a year, added to Morocco's already grave **economic problems**. Strikes in 1979 led to the arrest of activists, but wages were increased to keep abreast of the annual 10 per cent inflation rate. The political temper had been heated by these strikes and later that year teachers and students demonstrated against the presence of the deposed Shah of Iran, who had sought refuge with the King.

By June 1981, the situation had been aggravated by a succession of bad harvests that increased basic food prices just when the IMF insisted that the state subsidy on food must be reduced. A day-long demonstration against the IMF cuts degenerated into looting and rioting. The police restored order after many casualties, and some of the organizers of the original demonstration were prosecuted.

Local elections were held in June 1983, but the scale of the royalist victory suggested heavy-handed electoral influence. Parliamentary elections were subsequently cancelled and the King assumed **emergency powers** in October, though again he skilfully checked criticism by assembling a cabinet from a broad spectrum of political parties. In January 1984 the events of 1981 were repeated as the IMF insisted on further heavy cuts in subsidies in exchange for vital loans. **Riots** broke out throughout Morocco. The King withdrew the cuts in question, but at the same time heavy police action against rioters and political dissidents put 2000 men behind bars.

The state of emergency lasted only six months and by the summer of 1984 a new parliament had been elected which produced a moderate government committed to economic reform. There was much work to be done. The internal tax situation was in an anarchic state, with all the big earners such as tourism, agriculture and property speculation enjoying an official tax holiday. The state phosphate industry that bestrides the domestic economy ran at a paper 'loss', while a flourishing black market, covering much the same ground, turned over an estimated $5 billion a year.

The IMF provided the **new reforming administration** of Morocco with a series of loans to restructure its industry and gradually create something approaching a free market. Though there is still much to be done a bold start has been made in creating an open stock exchange, statutory accounting for businesses, VAT, independent management, cuts in the top-heavy civil service, and some accountability in the state phosphate monopoly. A policy of privatization, initiated in 1989, has already disposed of some of the enormous state sector, although as in many such schemes elsewhere it is the small profitable concerns that are easy to sell off while the monolithic loss-makers remain. These reforms have attracted an increasing amount of foreign investment and there are now over 1,000 foreign companies in operation, mostly concentrated around the tourist, part-assembly and textile trades, which look to the EU as their natural market.

Though the man in the street is much more concerned with Morocco's relations with the rest of the Arab-speaking world, it is the **European Union** that is the country's vital trading partner. The rejection of the 'Muslim applications' of both Morocco and Turkey to join the EU during the 1990s has allowed a more pragmatic spirit to be introduced into later negotiations for a free trade agreement between Morocco and the Union. Of the EU countries, relations with the old colonial powers of **France** and **Spain** remain dominant. Over 40 per cent of Morocco's imports come from France and Spain, and also the bulk of her invisible earnings through tourism and guest workers. Both countries have proved generous suppliers of government loans, technical assistance and arms. Despite the nationalization of foreign-owned land and businesses in the seventies, both France and Spain have a substantial stake in the Moroccan economy, for French and Spanish banks hold influential shareholdings in Morocco's own chain of commercial banks. The Spanish territories of Ceuta and Melilla are not yet a major issue of confrontation, although it is easy to imagine they could become a tempting nationalist diversion in any future period of popular unrest.

The connection with France remains very strong. Thousands of young Moroccans finish their education in a French university, and there are still thousands of skilled French technicians, teachers and governmental experts employed by the government of Morocco. French and Moroccan troops have even performed joint operations, such as the 'policing' of Zaire in

1979. **US support and aid** throughout the Polisario war has drawn Morocco quite firmly into the Western camp. Bases have been put at the disposal of American rapid deployment forces and Voice of America relay stations have been established.

1989 to the Present: Maghreb Unity, the Gulf War and After

In June 1988 several decades of mutual hostility between Morocco and Algeria were ended with the restoration of full diplomatic ties. This was followed in the spring of 1989 by the **Maghrebi Union Treaty** between all the countries of northwest Africa—Libya, Tunisia, Algeria, Morocco and Mauritania. This surprising turn of events had as much to do with the economic difficulties of Algeria and Libya and mutual anxiety at the growth of an isolationist Europe as the common culture of the Maghreb. This block of nations is known as UMA (Union de Maghreb Arabe), which has pleasing associations with the Arabic word *umma*, which refers to the wider community of Islam. The alliance did not have any dramatic consequences, but for a time allowed an easing of border controls that permitted Morocco and Tunisia to sell food to net importers like Libya and Algeria. However, the collapse of Algeria since 1992 into ferocious violence between the established FLN regime and army and the Islamic fundamentalists of the FIS has led the Moroccan government once again to seal the Algerian border, undoubtedly motivated to a considerable extent by concern to head off any contagion of fundamentalism within its own territory.

There was no display of Maghreb unity during the Gulf War of 1991. King Hassan rode the conflict with consummate skill. His early pledge to send Moroccan troops to join the alliance forces put him in good standing with all those powers—the USA, Saudi Arabia, the Gulf States and Western Europe—on whom Morocco is dependent for loans and investment. Faced with massive popular demonstrations in favour of Saddam Hussein he was forced to back down from his original strong pro-Alliance stance, but in the aftermath of the war Morocco did not suffer the sudden withdrawal of aid that affected so many Arab states.

The 1993 elections to parliament produced few surprises and confirmed the King's control of the political life of the country. The Moroccan parliament is neither sovereign nor democratic, but nor is it entirely servile. Political parties are free to address social and economic issues but criticism of the King, the constitution, and the desert war are effectively forbidden. The press operates within the same parameters but despite these limitations remains one of the liveliest of any Arab or African nation. There are a number of political prisoners, and Amnesty International has produced a series of reports of human rights abuses in Morocco. When the political life of a nation has involved coups, foreign plots and a long war the boundaries between treason and a loyal opposition are not always clear-cut. A recent indication that the wind of change may continue to blow in a reforming direction is the conviction of the Chief of the Casablanca Police. Though his crimes, which involved decades of murder and sexual abuse, were truly monstrous, never before has someone so powerful been exposed to public trial for a non-political offence.

No one can be certain of the future. From the past you learn that Islam, anarchy, regional loyalties and nationalism are consistent if contradictory features of Moroccan history. But it seems clear that only a strong man can rule a nation of such triumphant individualists.

The Moroccan Economy

Farming is the most important element in the economy. Despite its rapidly growing population, Morocco remains almost self sufficient after a good harvest, when the land yields about 4 million tons of wheat and 3 million tons of barley. More than 40 per cent of the population works on the land, producing cereals and root crops from 8 million hectares as well as grazing animals over a vastly more extensive area. Excluding beasts of burden like mules, donkeys, horses and camels, the nation's livestock numbers 18 million sheep, 6 million goats and 3.5 million cattle. Exportable agricultural goods such as sugar, citrus fruits, early vegetables and potatoes are principally produced by a few large well-irrigated estates established by the French in the Haouz Plain around Marrakech and the Rharb.

Industry is concentrated on the Atlantic coast around Casablanca, Rabat and Kénitra. It employs about 15 per cent of the population and is principally involved with the processing of the country's enormous **phosphate** deposits and its **agricultural products** (such as olive oil, flour, milk, fish, fruit and vegetables). A second tier of industry includes cement works, tyre and textile factories. **Traditional crafts**, such as hand weaving, leather work, metalwork, pottery and carpet making are still broadly distributed among traditional towns and cities. **Mining and construction** employ another 15 per cent of the population, with lower numbers of workers absorbed by running the tourist industry, utilities and government services. **Unemployment** is officially placed at 11 per cent, but this would appear to be mere wishful thinking.

Customs duties, as throughout most of Morocco's history, provide the bulk of state revenue. Foreign exchange comes from three major sources: $1bn in receipts from over a million migrant workers, $610m from tourism, and $480m from phosphates. These figures help fill the 20-billion dirham gap in the balance of trade. The export of fruit and vegetables to Europe is a lesser earner and this market has been severely threatened since the entry of the similar Mediterranean agricultural economies of Spain, Portugal and Greece into the EU in the 1980s. Fishing, though still a small earner of foreign cash, has been an area of continuous growth for several years. Morocco now lands over 500,000 tonnes a year, largely composed of the world's largest sardine catch.

An unlikely but valuable national resource is King Hassan's friendship with the royal families of Saudi Arabia and the Gulf States. Generous loans, help in rescheduling debts, a daily 'allowance' of 50,000 barrels of oil and outright gifts have propped up the Moroccan economy on numerous occasions. In 1985, for instance, US$250m suddenly appeared in the ledgers of the foreign currency reserves when all other sources were known to be exhausted. Over-ambitious central planning, government waste, inefficient tax collection, a bungled attempt to quadruple the world phosphate price and the desert war have pushed the load of **foreign debt** perilously high. In 1993 it stood at $23 billion, which would seem to be an almost impossibly high burden. At current rates of exchange it is larger than the entire annual domestic economy (estimated at 106 billion dh—just over $10 billion) and without international relief would require more than 60 per cent of the value of all exports from Morocco just to pay the interest on the debt! In recent years the state's annual deficit has been reduced to 6 per cent of revenue but this, though commendable, still results in steady additions to the total debt every year.

Problems

The major issue in Moroccan politics would appear to be to democratize the country and yet maintain the stability, peace and unity afforded by the enlightened autocracy of King Hassan. Too many of the country's intellectuals and entrepreneurs remain outside the system of local and national government, while too many of the influential merchants and industrialists remain outside the system of law and tax-gathering. Without frightening them out of the country, revenue must yet be raised from this small but immensely prosperous class. This could then be spent on much needed social and educational aid for the 60 per cent of the nation who live below the poverty line.

The economy has seen a steady annual growth of 2.4 per cent a year, but this achievement is constantly undermined by the equally **fast-growing population**. From 8 million in 1952 it has now grown to more than 27 million. Over half the population of Morocco are under 20, and the majority of this age group are unemployed, with 60 per cent illiterate. There has yet to be any evidence that the population growth rate is slowing down. Family planning is still restricted to the small professional urban class: in any case, popular myth considers it a Western-funded plot to restrict the size of the Arab nation. Population growth is accompanied by a shift from the conservative society of the countryside to the radical identity of the shantytowns, which house more than 20 per cent of the urban population. Whichever way you look at things, this augurs future political stress.

Despite the dramatic and terrifying events in neighbouring Algeria, **Muslim fundamentalism** does not seem to have emerged as a difficulty in Morocco, although (typically) the Rif may yet prove to be an exception. The old role of the sultan as the Commander of the Faithful has been carefully retained by King Hassan. Morocco has never witnessed a split between the *ulema*, the Islamic hierarchy, and a determinedly secular government as so many other Arab states have. The daily TV weather report provides an example of the natural religious conservatism of Morocco and the opportunities for consensus. The predictions of the weather were at first considered impious by the *ulema*, but once the announcer started to add enough *insha' Allah*'s (if God wills it) there was no further complaint. As an indication of relative political strengths, the chief fundamentalist newspaper, *al Jamaa*, has a print run of 3000, which compares badly with the 70,000 copies of the establishment *Le Matin du Sahara*, the 50,000 copies of *Al Alam*, the Istaqlal paper, and the 17,000 daily sale of the left-wing USFP paper, *Al Muharmir*.

Moroccan Themes

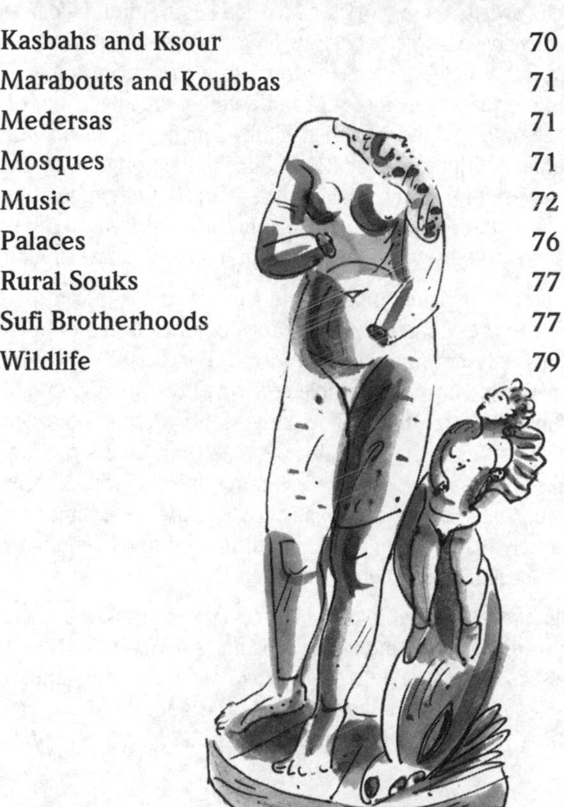

Architecture

As Muslims and Christians approach books from different ends, so do they architecture. This is less of a philosophical division and more to do with a difference in climate. Islamic architecture aims to enclose space, to create a sheltered garden from a wilderness. Architectural decoration, of pavilions, fountains, raised paths and pools, is reserved for the interior of this enclosure. European traditions are the complete reverse. Gardens emanate from outside the house, decoration is reserved for the exterior of a structure, and the interior has more to do with a collection of rooms isolated from the environment than any feeling of a defined space.

In architectural detail both Christendom and Islam share the same classical influences, though it is interesting that Islam has more fully identified itself with the domes and arches of Christian Byzantium whilst Europe continually reaches back for its references to the earliest pagan temples of Greece. Muslim architects in North Africa rejected horizontal beams early on and began experimenting with **horseshoe arches**. They also moved away from using columns as a central structure and developed rectangular piers to support their arches. **Columns** that freely borrowed their capitals from classical, Egyptian and Persian styles were increasingly used as mere decoration. Often combined in pairs, they flank a window frame or define the edge of a horseshoe arch, or appear so ornate and thin as to be almost free-standing beside the load-bearing pier of an arch. In short, the column becomes vestigial. In Andalusia and its artistic colony of North Africa all attention is focused on the horseshoe arch. This was developed into a pervading, almost obsessive regional theme. The **tracery** of the interlocking arch is ubiquitous: rising from walls to support domes, or in serried ranks to support the roof of every major mosque, and defining the lowest tier of every interior courtyard. The squinches, the awkward corners left by a dome, are filled by **muqurnas** which can appear like disordered dripping stalactites, though in their origin they are highly ordered tiers of arches. The surface of the arch itself is next adorned, with circular half lobes, tracery and muqurnas. By the 19th century the style had become debased; to see it with its early confidence and elegance you must visit the monuments of the Almoravids, Almohads and Merenids.

The construction of the port-town of Essaouira in the late 18th century by a Christian architect in the service of the Moroccan Sultan provides a first taste of the **Neo-Moorish** style of architecture. This only became widespread in the late 1920s, when the French colonial administration began to construct a whole new infrastructure of post offices, railway stations, judicial and administrative offices. The New-Moorish style took elements of Morocco's medieval heritage and used them, totally divorced from their structural relevance, as mere decorative details and façades for otherwise entirely Western buildings.It was an inversion of the whole historical development of Islamic architecture, yet seems to work well. So far the style remains largely restricted to public buildings and hotels, though some newer housing developments are beginning to incorporate its repertoire.

Further reading: *Islamic Monuments in Morocco*, R. B. Parker (Baraka Press, USA); *Art of Islam, Language and Meaning* and *Moorish Culture in Spain*, both by Titus Burkhardt; *The Splendours of Islamic Calligraphy*, Abdelkebir Khatabi and Mohammed Sigilmassa (Thames & Hudson, 1976); *Islamic Ornamental Design*, Claude Hurbert (Faber & Faber, 1980); *Pattern in Islamic Art*, D. Wade (London, 1976); *Zillij: the Art of Moroccan Ceramics*, Salma Damluji (Garnet).

Moorish Decorative Arts

Morocco has an active tradition of decorative art which was first developed in Moorish Spain. This rich heritage combines geometric, floral and calligraphic themes in a distinctive style that also remains true to the mainstream traditions of Islam. Throughout the country you will find dazzling examples of decorative art carved into stone, cedar and plaster; painted on tiles, furniture, ceilings and ceramics; or assembled in tile mosaics.

Islamic art draws attention away from the real world to one of pure form. Titus Burkhardt defined Islamic art as the way to ennoble matter by means of geometric and floral patterns which, united by calligraphic forms, embody the word of God as revealed in the Koran. Of these forms of decoration only the calligraphic can be considered an Islamic invention, though the way all are combined is distinctively Islamic. Decorative themes from architecture provide many of the motifs for the lesser arts of ceramics, cabinet-making, embroidery and carpet-making.

Geometric decoration presents a direct analogy to spiritual truths, for both direct attention away from the confusing patterns of the world to find hidden cores of meaning. From the muddled three dimensions of the physical world geometry creates a clearly defined two-dimensional order. But beyond the ordered geometric patterns a single hidden point rules the kaleidoscopic images of the surface. Thus all relates to the one, just as on the Day of Judgement all that has been created will return to the single entity of the Creator. Time, space, angles, planes, lines will collapse in on themselves and the physical universe will return to the One. There is no God but the one God.

Islam also inherited earlier Semitic religious traditions that saw sacred art as having an essentially geometric and mathematical nature. Many familiar Islamic geometric patterns were borrowed from Egypt and Syria. Representational art was a dangerous distraction that could degenerate into graven images and paganism, but numbers and figures were seen as symbols that defined a perfect world, created by the single Creator. Islam also absorbed the Platonic and Pythagorean respect for the divine harmony of **geometry and mathematics**. Numbers and shapes in the Pythagorean and Cabbalistic tradition were connected to mystical properties: a pyramid with its six sides represented fire; a tetrahedron air; a cube earth; and an icosahedron water. The result was a detailed symbolic vocabulary which allowed hidden abstractions to be built into a pattern. The infinite repetition of geometrical patterns, the lattices, interlaces, overlays and borders, is also the perfect aesthetic accompaniment to the human ritual of Islam, the endless chanting of single phrases, the recurring ritual of daily prayer and the repetitious nature of the Koranic verses themselves.

According to the Koran every artist on the Day of Judgement will be challenged to breathe life into his work and on failing will be condemned. The **floral art** of Persia and Rome was not considered to fall under this interdict, and was eagerly borrowed by the first Muslim conquerors. Floral motifs—acanthus, peonies, tulips, roses, pine cones, vine leaves, pomegranates and palmettes—are also a constant reminder to the faithful of the rewards of paradise, for the Koran is full of references to the overhanging trees and fruits in heaven. The symmetry of flowers and seed pods also reveals the geometric hand of the Creator.

Many Muslims believe that Arabic is the **divine language** and that their language did not exist before the prophet Mohammed received the first verses of the Koran. Archaeological evidence, though, shows that written Arabic developed from the Nabato–Aramaic script, which was itself a successor to Phoenician. The earliest Arabic inscription was found near Aleppo and has been dated to AD 512. There appear to have been four distinct Arabic scripts before the Islamic era. A reform by the Caliph Abdel Malik (685–705) established the **two schools of calligraphy** that exist today. These are **Kufic**, an angular, solid, hieratic script suitable for carving and ornamental texts, and **cursive**, a rounded flowing script (sometimes referred to as *Nashki*), suitable for everyday use.

This reform did not check the continual development of scripts, which continued evolving until the spread of printing. Among the more characteristic is the graceful Persian *Taliq;* the variant cursive of *Rihani*; *Tughra*, the cryptic Tartar lettering; the thick, stout *Riqa* script of the Turks; *Sayaquit*, the secret script of the Seljuk clerks; and the opulent *Diwani* of the Ottoman court. *Ghober* script allowed for letters to be carried by pigeon post and could only be read with a magnifying glass, whilst the different tones of *Manachir* could indicate reprimand or satisfaction before even the first letter had been read.

Up to the 12th century Morocco remained dominated by the old **cursive script of Kairouan**, in Tunisia. This was replaced by the distinctive **Maghrebi script** which had been developed in Andalusia, and preserved an ancient synthesis of Kufic and cursive. Abdelkebir Khatabi and Mohammed Sijilmassa in *The Splendours of Islamic Calligraphy* describe it as 'Virile and generous with angular outlines, both horizontal and vertical well emphasized and accompanied by large cursives open at the top.' Maghrebi script was written in black with ink prepared from scorched wool taken from a sheep's stomach. The official standard pen was composed of 24 donkey hairs, though dried reed was a common substitute. A red copper pen was used for marriage documents, a silver or stork beak pen for a special friend and a pomegranate sliver was used for an enemy.

Cursive and Maghrebi can be found in architectural decoration, though a plain Kufic or floral Kufic are much more common. Beyond their own attraction, horizontal bands of script are often used to bind different sections of materials and decoration together, as the Koran binds the community of Islam.

Flowers, Trees and Gardens

The Prophet said: 'If the end of the world happens while one of you is holding a palm tree that you are about to plant, do not get up before having planted it, if possible.' Such an appreciation of the value of plants, so gently put, informs the Moroccan attitude towards the care and cultivation of their own plots, and the land is filled with the exuberance and beauty of plants which flourish under the clear skies of the Maghreb.

The progression from a Mediterranean to a desert ecology occurs in a diagonal belt across the country. Water-supply rather than latitude is the key to plant identification. To the east the desert virtually reaches the Mediterranean whilst in the south, around Marrakech and Béni-Mellal, irrigation allows groves of olive, orange and cypress trees to flourish. Plant growth ceases from June to August and begins properly with the rains in October. Some species flower throughout the winter but most perennials peak in March and April.

The real beauty of Moroccan flowers and trees lies not within the courtyards of the harems, but all around you, and all year round, on city streets, in the countryside, on the coast and in the mountains. **Flowering trees** along the boulevards, almost all imported from South America, decorate the streets from January onwards. The early yellow pom-poms of mimosas give way in April to the delicate blossoms of the coral tree (*Erythrina caffra*) and the pink calodendrum. May sees the jacaranda trees reveal their flowers of indescribable blue, and in June the delicate tracery of Jerusalem thorn (*Parkinsonia*) is lit up by an eruption of yellow flowers. The handsome evergreen leaves of figs and magnolias provide shade during the summer months; in December the extraordinary *Montanoa bipinnitifida* blazes with huge white daisies. Over the walls of the swanky out-of-town villas tumble hedges of bougainvillea, jasmine, passion flower, podranea, solanum, honeysuckle and roses, with the powerful fragrance of *Cestrum parqui*, charmingly known as *galant de nuit* in French, filling the June night air. And everywhere, of course, are palm trees, stretching up to the sky, providing a vertical counterpoint to the horizontalism of much of the urban architecture.

Out in the countryside the tall flower spikes of the century plant (*Agave Americana*), produced only once in a lifetime as the plant's swansong, dominate the flat landscape. Along the roads miles of poplars are pollarded for charcoal and timber, despite their presumed original purpose of providing shade. In **spring meadows** iris, asphodel, orchids, marigolds, lupins, crocus, snowflakes (*Leucojum*), thistles and sea holly abound. The clear blue flowers of larkspur, used in the ceremonial garlands of Egyptian mummies and undimmed 3000 years later when the tombs were opened, still overcome the dust of Moroccan roads and roundabouts in early summer. The sickly fragrance of *Datura* (angels' trumpets) is everywhere in villages and towns. It has been used as a (dangerous) hallucinogen since ancient times. The Greek doctor Theophrastus prescribed: 'If 3/20 of an ounce is given, the patient becomes sportive and thinks himself a fine fellow... four times the dose, he is killed.'

Cytisus battandieri (Moroccan or pineapple broom), indigenous to the Atlas Mountains, bursts with golden pineapple-scented flowers in April. In the summer mint and oleander flourish in an otherwise parched landscape. Fresh mint for tea is in demand year-round throughout Morocco, and that cultivated outside Meknès is most esteemed. Oleander produces a blast of colour on the dry river beds. Legend has it that the first plant grew from Fatima's tears when she discovered that her husband Ali had taken a second wife, and the leaves are still unbearably bitter, although useful as a cure for scabies. In the northern hills the scrubland of the **maquis** shelters cistus, lavender, fennel, rocket and wormwood; also rosemary, which is surprisingly seldom used in cooking, but has traditionally been used for fragrant self-flagellation after a *hammam*.

Along the **coast**, countless Mediterranean pines clothe the hillsides, with the strange silhouettes of *Araucaria heterophylla*, the Norfolk Island Pine, punctuating the slopes like some child's drawing of a South Sea Island Christmas tree. Along the Mediterranean coast, purple and pink stocks grow wild, perfuming the evening air, and there is a reddish-lilac candytuft, *Iberis gibraltarica*, that is native to Morocco. Along the Atlantic coast bright blue sea squills are collected and made into rat-poison. The ferocious cactus *Euphorbia regis-jubae*, named after King Juba II of Mauretania and his doctor Euphorbius, can be found in the hills from Safi to Tiznit. The king, who married the daughter of Cleopatra and Mark Anthony, wrote learned treatises in Greek on philosophy and botany, among them works on the medicinal uses of opium and euphorbia; a medicinal gum, used as an emetic and a purgative, was extracted from the latter. The king's bronze head may be admired in the Archaeological Museum in Rabat.

It is in the **river valleys of the Atlas Mountains** that you will find a paradise on earth, a remote Garden of Eden. The Atlas cedar crowns the mountains, with oak, cypresses and juniper lower down; wild flowers dot the valleys at all times of the year (though February–April is the very best season), and poplars and willows flash in the sun along the banks of noisy rivers. On terraced hillsides the inducement of the Prophet that all who cultivate plants for the nourishment of man, bird or beast shall be rewarded by God is taken up by the Berbers, and the lushness and abundance is hard to believe after the arid dust of Marrakech or the desert. Walnut and chestnut march up the valleys, and the neat rectangles of crops on the smallholdings are shaded by olive, almond, fig and pomegranate. Village houses are submerged beneath grapevines, and the communal watercourse halfway up the hillside is diverted through a simple complex of sluices to irrigate plums, apples, oranges, lemons, grapefruit and loquat.

In the souks the musty smell of boxes and bowls turned from **thuja wood** from the Atlas fills every woodworker's shop. An ancient tree, esteemed by classical writers from Homer to St. John, thuja is still much sought-after. Its convoluted grain patterns of knots, spirals and veins are identified as tiger-, panther- and peacock-eyes by the cognoscenti, who prefer wood the colour of wine mixed with honey. Cicero paid one million *sesterces* for a thuja table, and Pliny mentioned the tree, 'which has given rise to the mania for fine tables, an extravagance with which women reproach the men when they complain of their vast outlay upon pearls.'

The **argan tree**, *Argania sideroxylon*, is unique to Morocco and only grows in a 100km radius of the **Sous Valley**. It flowers in June and the fruit ripens in March, when, by a cunning piece of husbandry, sheep and cattle are herded under, or (more often) goats are left to climb into, the trees to eat the green fruit that they find so delectable. The indigestible inner nut is regurgitated or excreted, depending on the animal, and is collected by the villagers who process the nut to extract an oil used for lamps, cooking and making soap. The preparation of the oil is complicated; used in its virgin state it is said to promote leprosy.

Roses figure highly in Moroccan agriculture and horticulture. Rose bushes surround the pisé walls of Marrakech, and the mass production of roses for export is big business in the **Dadès Valley**, providing the florists of Paris with fine long-stemmed, sweet smelling blooms. The ancient damask rose *trigintipetala* is grown on a massive scale in Dadès, and is known as *beldi* in Arabic and *rose de Mgouna* in French. Cultivated for the distillation of rose-water and used as a handwash by Muslims, it is grown in hedgerow-like strips. In late April and early May the harvest is celebrated with a festival at El Kelaâ M'Gouna.

Traditional enclosed **Moorish gardens** aim to create a harmony of audible flowing water and restful shade thrown from elegant trees, typically laurel, cypress and olive. Roses, violets, jasmine, hollyhocks and blossoming fruit trees were traditionally planted chiefly for their scent. Modern gardens borrow some of these themes but are often dominated by 19th century imports like Australian mimosa, Brazilian bougainvillea and the 'boulevard palm' from the Canary Isles. A tour of traditional gardens in Morocco would include the Chella and the kasbah in Rabat, the Dar Batha and Palais Jamaï Hotel in Fès, the Dar el Makhzen in

Tangier, the Dar Jamaï Museum in Meknès and conclude with the Mamounia Hotel, the Ménara and the vast Aguedal Gardens in Marrakech. The latter, more agriculture than horticulture, is still a living exponent of the tradition. The rhythm of the walks radiating from the massive central basins through acre upon acre of olive and orange grove lends a calm, reflective solitude all the more striking in its proximity to the bustling streets of the city.

Of the botanical gardens, Yves St Laurent's celebrated haven the Majorelle Garden in Marrakech is a collection of spiky plants rather than a garden, and any tranquillity is shattered from 9am onwards by the whistlestop busloads. The Jardins Exotiques at Bouknadel outside Rabat are much more extensive and overgrown, and less visited.

Islam

Allah is a noun which can be translated as 'the divinity' or 'the only and true God'. Islam literally means 'submission' or obedience to the divinity. The **Koran** means 'the recitation'—the announcement of the word of God to **Mohammed** via the archangel Gabriel. This at its simplest is the Muslim religion: recognition of and obedience to the single divinity whose will is clearly stated in the Koran.

The Prophet Mohammed is not considered divine but a mere human mouthpiece for divine will. There is no veneration for a single historical act in the life of Mohammed, in contrast to Christianity where the moral teaching of Christ can be obscured by his miraculous birth, crucifixion and resurrection. Nor does Islam encourage any hopeless if heroic attempt to imitate the perfect life of a Christ-figure. Instead it establishes a moral code that it is possible for the entire community to follow and which assures salvation for those who honestly attempt to obey and damnation for those who ignore it or fail. It is acknowledged that man is deeply flawed, but great trust and hope is placed in the all-compassionate and mercifulGod.

Islam is not considered a new religion but a reformation of the ancient monotheistic worship of Abraham. The teachings of Mohammed presented an opportunity for the squabbling Christian and Jewish sects to unite on the common basics of belief. Moses, St John the Baptist and Christ are honoured in the Koran as prophets, but although Christ's birth is seen as miraculous he is not considered to be the son of God. Such a sub-division of divine power is regarded as impossible in monotheistic Islam, although a kind carpet-seller sympathetically suggested to me that if Christians could believe that Christ was filled with the breath of God rather than being his son there would be little disagreement between the two faiths. Towards the end of his life Mohammed realized the impossibility of converting all Christians and Jews. The direction of prayer was changed from Jerusalem to Mecca, and while he still instructed his followers to respect the '**peoples of the book**' his views hardened. From the tolerant words of his early teaching, 'Will you dispute with us about God? When he is our Lord and your Lord! We have our words and you have your words but we are sincerely his', the Prophet progresses to, 'O believers! Take not the Jews or Christians as friends.'

The Prophet Mohammed

Born in Mecca in 570, the young Mohammed was left an orphan and brought up by a succession of relatives from the influential Koreisch clan. As a young man he served as agent for Chadjilla, a wealthy widow fifteen years his senior, whom he later married. Mecca was he centre of pagan Arab spiritual life, and Mohammed and his wife joined the circle of **Hanyfs**, puritan seekers after enlightenment. The Hanyf venerated the religion of Abraham and were familiar with Jewish, Christian and Persian doctrines. These influences are repeatedly acknowledged in the Koran: 'Nothing has been said to thee which has not been said of old by apostles before' and, 'Every people has had its own apostle'. Mohammed received his first revelation in 610, fifteen years after his marriage, when he was 40 years old. The archangel Gabriel appeared to him in a cave outside Mecca that he used frequently for prayer and meditation. He was at first doubtful about the revelations but, encouraged by his wife, risked ridicule and shared the word of God. His ardent monotheism and criticism of the pagan worship centred on Mecca won some followers but even more enemies. Eventually the protection of his clan proved inadequate, and to avoid assassination he fled to the city of Medina on 15 June 622, which is taken as the start of the **Hegira**, the Muslim era.

Mohammed was welcomed to the oasis of Yathrib (thereafter known as Medina el Nabi—city of the Prophet) and invited to become its arbitrator, the learned figure who decided disputes within the community. There he established a theocratic state, and ironed out practical moral and legal codes for his community and the practice of prayer. From Medina he waged a defensive war on the Meccans and gradually subdued the surrounding Jewish and pagan tribes. By 630, two years before his death, his authority extended over all Arabia, and he proved magniminous in victory. His enemies were pardoned and loaded with gifts (the booty of the war) while the Prophet returned to his simple house alongside the first mosque, built from palm trunks and canes.

The divisions within the Muslim world originated over the succession to the Prophet's leadership. **Shiites** believe in the claims of Ali (his cousin) to have succeeded Mohammed, while the **Sunni** accept the legitimacy of the first three caliphs. Sects like the **Ismailis**, **Druze** and **Kharijites** all have their own beliefs on what the rightful succession should have been.

The Koran

'The recitation' was first dictated to the illiterate Mohammed by the archangel Gabriel in his cave above Mecca. More verses were revealed to the Prophet in succeeding years, and memorized and then written down by his followers. The Caliph Othman established the first written version eighteen years after the death of Mohammed, in 650. Its 114 unequal chapters, the **suras**, containing 6211 verses, were assembled carefully but in order of length, which has given the Koran a chronologically haphazard order. The suras have names, but these, 'The Cow', 'The Bee', 'The Ant', have no significance other than as a memory aid. There are four main themes: the worship of Allah; the Day of Judgement with the division between heaven and hell; stories of earlier prophets; and proclamations and social laws. A collection of the Prophet's sayings and traditions remembered by his companions was also assembled, but despite great efforts there is no definitive edition of this **Hadith**. In Morocco the *caids* follow the **Malekite tradition**, one of the four schools of orthodox Islamic law.

The Five Pillars of Islam

The Prophet codified the religious life of his community into the **five pillars of Islam**: daily prayer, the pilgrimage to Mecca, the fast of Ramadan, the giving of alms, and acceptance that there is no other divinity but God.

There were originally only three daily prayers, but sometime after the Prophet's death this was increased to five. The first is known as *Moghreb* and is said four minutes after sunset; *Eshe* is said when it is quite dark, *Soobh Fegr* at dawn, *Dooh* at noon, just after the sun has passed its zenith; and *Asr* midway between noon and sunset. At each mosque a muezzin announces prayers by calling, 'God is great. I testify that there is no God but God. I testify that Mohammed is his prophet. Come to prayer, come to security. God is great.' For *Soobh Fegr*, the dawn prayer, an extra inducement, 'Prayer is better than sleep', is added.

Alone or in a mosque the believer ritually **purifies himself** by washing with water or sand (this ritual purification was standard practice in all religions of the Near East, including early Christianity). Then turning to Mecca the believer stands with hands held up and open to proclaim that Allah is great. He then lowers his hands and recites the *fatiha* prayer still standing: 'Praise be to God, Lord of the worlds, the compassionate, the merciful, king of the day of judgement, thee do we worship and your aid do we seek. Guide us on the straight path, the path of those on whom you have bestowed your grace, not the path of those who incur thy anger nor of those who have gone astray.' The believer bows with hands on knees and completes a full prostration. Kneeling up again he recites the *chahada*, a prayer for the Prophet. The **three positions of prayer** have a symbolic meaning: standing distinguishes the rational man from an animal, bowing represents the act of a servant to his master, and prostration abandonment to the will of God. On Fridays the noonday prayer is only recited in the grand or licensed mosque. This is followed by a sermon, the *khutba*, given from the steps of the pulpit-like *minbar* (with the throne and higher steps left symbolically empty).

In some of the grand mosques there are specific doors for the use of women. These lead to areas screened off from the sight of men, often at the side or the back of the prayer hall. This is however the exception. In most of Morocco the mosque is a completely male preserve, and women pray at home or in the prayer halls that surround *koubbas*, the shrines of the saints (*see* p.71 'Marabouts and Koubbas').

The **pilgrimage to Mecca** was an annual monthly event centuries before the Islamic era. Mohammed acknowledged the Kaaba shrine as the ancient altar built by the son of Abraham (which incorporates a holy meteorite in its walls), and a specific Islamic calendar of events was imposed on a cleaned-up verison of the old rituals in 630. For a poor man it could be the journey of a lifetime, and in the past it was restricted to the healthy and wealthy, who granted their marriage partners a temporary divorce in case they should never return from the hazards of the journey. On their return to their community they were greeted with the proud title of *hajji*. The distance of Mecca from Morocco (750 days by caravan for the complete trip) increased the attraction of local shrines. Towns such as Moulay-Idriss claimed that five pilgrimages there equalled the trip to Mecca.

The **fast of Ramadan**, during the daylight hours of the ninth month of the Muslim year, commemorates Mohammed's spiritual practices before the Koran was first revealed to him. The night of the 26th day of the fast which commemorates the first recitation is known as the night of power, and is filled with processions while the heavens are opened to hear the prayers of the faithful. It was specifically based on existing Arabian custom and Christian and Jewish spiritual practices such as Lent. The **giving of alms** is a continual duty for the Muslim. The *zahir*, or 'fortieth', tax originated out of this obligation and was the foundation of all direct taxation in the Islamic world.

Jewish Morocco

The late 1990s have witnessed a minor renaisssance in Jewish Morocco, as Moroccan Jews who emigrated en masse to Israel have begun to return to visit the land of their forefathers. On a mountain road I was told by a Jewish pilgrim that there are two great holy places in the world where heaven and earth are in the closest and most occasionally violent proximity. First is the land of Palestine, but after that there is only Morocco. Tombs, cemeteries and synagogues have been restored on the back of this growing pilgrimage trade, which coincides with a new assertiveness by the Sephardic community within Israel. May is the busiest month, when there is a general pilgrimage to the koubbas of the great Jewish saints of Morocco such as Rabbi Amrane, buried in the Rif above Ouezzane, or Rabbi David O'Mouchy, whose koubba is amongst the stone fields of the High Atlas, 10 miles north of the village of Agouim. A second season is in October.

Jews first came to Morocco in the ships of the Phoenicians, for they provided a skilled labour force experienced in the working of inland mines. Initially they were concentrated in southern Spain, but gradually became a ubiquitous presence in all the Semitic-speaking ports established by the Phoenician traders along the North African coast. A tradition records that this scattered community sent tribute to King Solomon to assist in the construction of the first temple. Archaeological evidence is scant, though Hebrew gravestones have been found in the excavations of the Romano-Punic capital of Volubilis. The community was greatly strengthened by refugees fleeing the destruction of Judea in the reign of the Emperor Vespasian (69–79) and again in Hadrian's time (113–138), as well as following the failed Jewish revolt in Cyrenaica, in the east of present-day Libya.

The 'Dark Ages' following the fall of Rome are the unchronicled golden period of Jewish activity in Morocco, when missionaries converted whole Berber tribes and communities were established in every corner of the country, from its mountain summits to tidal estuaries and furthermost oases. When Moulay Idriss first reached Morocco in the 8th century the Jewish-dominated city of Sefrou, in alliance with the Meknassa tribe, was a key political force. As Islam triumphed Jews were marginalised from political life, but established a key position in trade, metalwork, jewellery and similar crafts. During the Merenid period the first walled ghettoes (the *Mellah*) evolved from out of the traditional Jewish quarters of cities to facilitate the protection, self-government and efficient taxation of this wealthy community. In the cities Jews were ruled by their own Caids and judged and taxed by their own officials, while in the countryside Jewish villages placed themselves under the protection of the local military power. A second great wave of Jewish settlement occurred after the fall of Granada in 1492, when the sophisticated urban Jews of Andalusia, the heirs of intellectual figures of world importance such as Maimonides, were expelled from Spain and settled in such cities as Fès, Tetouan, Azzemour and Rabat. In music, speech, dress, cuisine and architecture these refugees had much more in common with their fellow Moors (Muslim Andalusians) than with the so-called Berber Jews, and this division remains today.

Jews were seen as a vital resource of the state and often held the most important financial posts in the administration, although when the Merenid Sultan Abdul Haqq tried to appoint a Jewish Grand Vizier he met widespread popular resistance. The ongoing distrust between Muslim Moroccans and the Christian Europeans, fomented by centuries of war and piracy, also meant that the Jews were in constant demand as middlemen by both antagonists. The Alaouite Sultans in particular leant heavily on Jewish expertise. It was they who established the large and important Jewish community in Tangier, mostly recruited from the old community in nearby Tetouan, as well as those in Essaouira and Casablanca, most of whom were originally from Azzemour.

In the period of French dominance, European-based Jewish charities were quick to pour funds into Morocco for the education of the community. This effort was so successful that the native Moroccan Jews began to be co-opted into the settler community, though this never reached the level of assimilation (mixed with outbursts of anti-semitism from the French *pied noir*) seen in Algeria and Tunisia.

During the Second World War, King Mohammed V protected the 300,000 Moroccan Jews from the horrors that overtook their brethren in France and the rest of Europe. Nevertheless, although the Moroccan Jews had always enjoyed royal favour and formed one of the world's oldest-established Jewish communities, they remained apart from the majority community, and with the rise of nationalism under the Protectorate they were frequently regarded by other Moroccans as a privileged, semi-Europeanized group who had identified themselves too closely with the French and Spanish colonizers. The events of the Holocaust followed by the establishment of the State of Israel in 1947 galvanized attitudes and Jewish opinion. Emigration to Israel began immediately after the state's foundation, and the trickle of the late forties turned into a flood after the Suez crisis of 1956 led to a wave of anti-Jewish feeling throughut the Arab world. By 1967 this mass migration was all but complete, although the thread has not been completely broken. Around 8000 Jews remain in Morocco today, and Moroccan Jews, even after they have settled in Israel, are allowed to keep their Moroccan passports. King Hassan has sought to use the bridge afforded by this community (especially when represented by such a figure as Moshe Dayan) in attempts to intervene in the turbulent waters of the Middle East.

Throughout this guide you will find information on accessible Jewish cemeteries and the location of the old Mellah quarters. If you wish to try and make personal contact with the surviving communities, the following are useful contact numbers. **Agadir**: try Simon Levy, ✆ (08) 842141, or the community office, ✆ (08) 840091, 📠 822268: **Casablanca**: the city retains 25 synagogues, and the Council of Moroccan Jewish communities is on Rue Abbon Abdullah, ✆ (02) 270976, 📠 266953: **Essaouira**: speak to either Meyer Cohen or Simon Look at 22 or 29 Rue des Siaghines; **Fès**: Mme Danielle Mamane in the boutique of the Palais Jamai hotel can field enquiries; **Marrakech**: Henri Cadoch, ✆ (04) 448754: **Meknès**: Community Centre at 5 Rue de Ghana, ✆ (05) 521968; **Rabat** Community Centre at 9 Rue Ismail, ✆ (07) 724504; **Safi**: there are two synagogues on Rue du R'bat, as well as the glittering complex of Sidi Ouled Ben Zmirou Besseba, to the south of the Medina walls; the Community centre is at 1 Rue Boussouni; **Tangier**: a number of synagogues survive in the old city; contact Abraham Azancot at the Community Centre at 1 Rue de la Liberte, ✆ (09) 931633 or 921024; **Tetouan**: the Community Centre at 16 Rue Moulay Abbas stands beside two synagogues in the Mellah quarter of this venerable city. Across the straits from Tetouan in British **Gibraltar** there is a lively and hospitable 600-strong Jewish community with an 18th-century synagogue (Shar Hashamayim), a lovely old cemetery and a centre at 10 Bomb House Lane, ✆ 72606, 📠 40487.

Kasbahs and Ksour

A Moroccan **kasbah** (or Qasaba) can be a fortified manorhouse, the citadel of a city, an isolated government garrison or a tribal fort. A key to its definition is not so much its scale as its purpose, for a Kasbah should be the domain of a ruler, be he Sultan, governor or just a tribal chieftain. Most of the ancient cities of Morocco retain a large portion of their outer walls, but the kasbah (the government citadel containing palace, barracks, prison, arsenal and treasury) has too often decayed beyond recognition. Tangier, Safi, Rabat and Chechaouèn provide honourable and accessible exceptions. The finest government kasbahs were built by **Moulay Ismaïl** in the 17th century, and can also be seen outside the great cities at Kasba-Tadla, Boulâouane, Mehdiya, Kasba-Hamidouch and Agouraï. The walls of Essaouira are in even better condition, for they were built on the best European principles in the 18th century. Other towns on the coast have older defences dating from the Portuguese occupation: Ksar es Seghir, Asilah, Azemmour, El-Jadida and Safi are the best preserved. They are not always described as a kasbah, for there is a parallel military terminology which refers to these fortifications by names such as *Mahalla* (a fortified marching camp), *Rabat* (or *R'bat*), meaning both a castle and a fortified base for the holy war, *Hisn*, 'stronghold' and *Bordj* (or *Burj*), a 'tower'.

The rise in power of the High Atlas *caids* and particularly the Glaoui tribe has left the southern region of Morocco studded with decaying kasbahs from which they administered their feudal domain. **Glaoui kasbahs** can still be seen at Telouèt, Tazzerte, Tioute, Taliouine, Tinerhir, Tiffoultoute and Tamdaght. At their best these fuse the dazzling variety of traditional Berber battlemented exteriors with finely proportioned interiors that drew on Andalusian palaces for their inspiration.

The Berber hill tribes were more capable of defending themselves than oasis or valley dwellers. They could afford to live in smaller family units, but stored their corn in communal stone-built hill-top fortresses which are known as an **agadir** (plural *igoudar*), *igherm* or *tighremt*, depending on which Berber dialect region they are in. There are many of these well distributed around the valleys south of the High Atlas, and there are some fine examples in the Anti-Atlas.

The sub-Saharan region and the oasis valleys are studded with the fortified villages of cultivators. A **ksar** (also spelt *qsar* or *qusur*) was traditionally administered by a council of headmen who strove to remain independent of the influence of the surrounding nomadic tribes and chieftains. *Ksour* (the plural of ksar) were constructed out of stone or pisé (packed and baked mud), and date palms were used for the internal timbers and wattle. The use of palm trunks set a natural limit to the internal dimensions of a ksar. The rooms and passages have harmonious proportions, but are often dark, airless, and infested with insects. Ksars are attractive chiefly for their brick or pisé **decorated towers**. As the interior could be the product of any culture in the last two or three thousand years, they have an ageless sense of stimulating mystery. Each oasis system has its own distinctive style, which gives off flickering references to Egypt, Mesopotamia, Tyre, Mycenae or Gothic Christendom. They may last for a few generations, but it is rare for a pisé ksar to survive for more than two hundred years. The disintegrating pisé reveals little to archaeologists and, though widely spread throughout Saharan Africa, their origins and architectural inspiration are unknown.

Marabouts and Koubbas

Throughout the cities, towns, villages and countryside of Morocco you will observe the ***koubbas***, the domed tombs of marabouts—Muslim holy men. They are a striking feature of the Moroccan landscape and can range from a simple whitewashed, earth-walled hut to an opulent chamber covered by a green-tiled pyramid roof. The marabout's tomb may be obscure, half ruined and forgotten, or stand at the centre of a great city surrounded by a maze of outer courtyards around which stand dependent mosques, markets, *hammams*, schools and charitable institutions. As well as the size of the shrine, the nature of the holy man can vary. The venerated Lalla or Sidi could be a reforming sultan, a fearless warrior of the *jihad*, a Sufi master, the near legendary ancestor of a tribe, the founder of a city, a pious protector of the poor, a learned arbitrator, or an Islamic identity for an old pagan deity of the mountain, river, forest or field. The one thing they have in common is *baraka*, which means both an enhanced spiritual standing and the power to benefit a pilgrim with a blessing.

The koubba and the marabout's tomb is often the centre of spiritual life for the women of the area, as well as functioning as an asylum and a charitable centre. In the countryside it may also be the site of a weekly market or an annual *moussem*. These *moussems* may officially be held in the honour of the saint but they also function as exuberant secular festivals, popular social events, trade fairs and marriage markets.

Medersas

The earliest residential religious college in the Islamic world, or *medersa*, was built in Persia in the 9th century. Medersas were not built in Morocco until the 13th century, under the patronage of the Merenid sultans. Until then teaching took place in the courts of a mosque or in the houses of learned men. The earliest surviving Moroccan medersa, the **Seffarine** in Fès from 1280, clearly shows the origin of this religious college in the town house of a lecturer. Later medersas drew more heavily on Andalusian decoration and the architectural developments of Cairo, though the basic plan of an open-air court surrounded by an upper storey of student lodgings and leading to a prayer hall remains consistent. Marrakech, Salé and Meknès each have a medersa that is open to the public, and Fès has three.

Mosques

All mosques in Morocco are closed to non-Muslims, though you are free to admire the exterior details such as gates and minarets. Mosque literally means the place of prostration. At its simplest it can be an open air space with a small niche, the **mihrab**, that indicates the direction of prayer towards Mecca. These mosques are known as **msalla** and can be seen outside the walls of Marrakech and Fès where they are used during festivals. The next stage in the development of the mosque can still be seen in use in poorer rural areas. A wall is built to enclose the prayer area and the mihrab extrudes, to appear like a white sugar-loaf. It is only a small further development to roof over the **prayer hall**, leaving an open-air court, the **sahn**, exposed at the opposite end to the prayer niche. The sahn or an adjoining building could be equipped with basins or a fountain for the **ritual washing** enjoined in the Koran.

Byzantine influence from Syria was strong in the construction of the cathedrals of Islam, the first **grand mosques**. The tendency to embellish the central aisle of the mosque with arches, pillars and domes strongly echoes the nave of a church. That characteristic Islamic feature, the **minaret**, was initially developed from the short towers that used to define a Byzantine churchyard. The first Muslim architects also borrowed from previous religious practice and elaborated the mihrab into a cave-like half dome, upon which the two declarations of faith were carved, whilst the exterior of the niche was covered by an arch and flanked by two columns.

The walls and floors of Moroccan mosques are kept free of architectural decoration. The white pillars and arches may carry some simple carving, but there is seldom any colour beyond the hip-height reed matting pinned along the walls and the carpets on the floor. Decoration is reserved for elaborate **chandeliers** and the pulpit-like **minbar**. The original minbar, used by the Prophet for his lectures at Medina, had six steps. He used a lower step in order to leave the throne symbolically empty. More steps were added by his successors to allow them to sit further from the throne, and so make clear their lesser spiritual authority.

The only substantial traditional mosque that a non-Muslim may enter in Morocco is also one of the oldest. The half-ruined **Tin-Mal Mosque** in the High Atlas was built by the Almohads in the 12th century. It is contemporary with the great achievements of Moroccan architecture, the **Koutoubia** of **Marrakech**, the **grand mosque** of **Taza** and the **Hassan Tower** of **Rabat**. The minarets of the Koutoubia and Hassan led to the creation of a characteristic style. Moroccan mosques all echo these two tall, square towers, which should be capped with a lantern that is exactly a fifth the size of the tower.

In contrast the new **Grand Mosque of Hassan II** in **Casablanca** has fortunately broken with tradition and offers conducted tours of the interior. This system, which allows non-Muslims to meet an intelligent and sympathetic believer who can dispel centuries of European obscurantism during the tour, would be worth extending elsewhere.

Music

The cry of the muezzin, summoning the faithful to prayer, is the most distinctive, universal and haunting sound in Morocco. In a large city like Fès or Marrakech the principal mosque has the honour of initiating the call, which is then picked up and echoed by dozens of lesser mosques. It is most impressive in the comparative quiet and diffused light of the early morning and evening, when it mocks the daytime bustle of the secular world.

Travelling through Morocco you will automatically be exposed to the music of the country as you sit scrunched up in a *grand taxi* or bus. Few cafés would feel complete without the sound of a radio, cassette player or television, while at country markets, festivals and urban squares like the Jemaa el Fna in Marrakech there is always live music. No market, however small, is complete without at least one cassette stall selling a colourful assortment of their own 45-minute recordings. These barrows carry a broad selection, ranging from Egyptian singers such as the great Ulm Khaltoum, West Indian reggae and some major Western bands to the home-grown stars of *chaabi*, Moroccan popular music.

The centre for today's Moroccan music industry is Casablanca, where the main contemporary pop influence—Algerian Rai music—is most common. Moroccan Rai stars such as Cheb Khader and Chaba Zahounia and their Algerian counterparts create the most prominent sounds on today's urban soundtrack. In most cases they replace traditional instruments with electric and digitalized equivalents, but in their inspiration still draw heavily on a rich seam of Arab and indigenous musical traditions.

You will win instant street kudos by asking for a tape by any of the big Moroccan names such as El Hussein Slaoui, Lafkih Laomri, Nass el Ghiwane, Abselam Cherkaoui, Lhaj Amar Ouahraouch, Lem Chaleb, Jil Jalala or Muluk el Hwa.

Berber Music

The music of the Berber people is of ancient origin and inextricably linked with movement and dance. It is an astonishing example of the tenacity of an oral heritage which preserves a combination of dance, poetry and drama that could almost come from pre-Homeric Greece. There are musical differences between the three main dialect regions of Berber speech, the Tariffit of northern Morocco, the Tamazight of the Middle Atlas and the Tashelhit, or Chleuh, of the south. There is also a division between the music of the villagers and that produced by travelling musicians.

In **village music** (variously known as *ahaidous*, *ahidus* or *ahouach*) flutes, drums, rhythmic hand-clapping and large choruses predominate. The choruses, composed of long lines or circles of men and women, dance around the musicians as they perform. Soloists, known as *inshaden*, sometimes supported by two accompanists or by the sound of their own violin, improvise lyrics within the basic framework of these distinctive choral chants. As well as there being a difference in dialect, the music of southern Morocco is quite distinct as it is based on the pentatonic scale (like that of West Africa), while the other two regions use seven notes. Until this century traditional village music remained largely unknown to a wider audience, as it was considered improper to perform outside the tribal region or to seek any financial gain. Fortunately folk festivals and recordings have changed this.

Traditionally, **travelling musicians**, usually groups of four, were led by a singer-poet, supported by a violin, tambourine and flute. He sang of heroic qualities, such as martial bravery and impossible love, into which he skilfully wove gossip and topical references to local politics, as well as flattering or chiding his hosts for their hospitality. These troupes bore a striking resemblance to the bards of Celtic Europe, and medieval troubadours of France. At the turn of the century they began to add female vocalists to the line-up, whose job was to echo the poetic refrain and to dance. These groups were increasingly based in the new urban centres of the coast, and replaced the older tribal tradition. Today's professional performers (male *shioukh*, female *shikat*) form a near-hereditary guild, and enjoy the kind of celebrity and notoriety that touring actors in the West experienced a hundred years ago. The groups are known as *ameziaren*, though in southern Morocco they can be referred to as *rwais*.

Two groups of particular eminence are the Jajouka and Daqqa. The Jajouka are known for their 1969 recordings with the Rolling Stones. They are a unique caste of musicians from the Jebala foothills in the western Rif, who perform on *ghaita, lira, guenbri* and drums to create a pagan ritual music that invokes the gods of fecundity and energies in a way similar to the ancient rites of Pan. The Daqqa of Marrakech perform a ritual dance for the religious festival of Achura, accompanied by percussionists playing the tar drums and *n'far* trumpeters.

Further listening: *Brian Jones presents the Pan Pipers of Jajouka* (Rolling Stone, London); *Berberes du Maroc*—from the far south (Le Chant du Monde, Paris); *Anthologie des Rwâyes*

(4 CD Sous Berber collection, La Maison des Cultures du Monde); *Najat Aatabou*: Goul el Hak el Mout Kayna (Blue Silver); *Najat Aatabou: The Voice of the Atlas* (GlobeStyle); *Master Musicians of Jajouka: Apocalypse across the Sky* (Axiom); *Bachir Attar: The Next Dream* (CMP); *Medium Atlas Range: Sacred and Profane Music* (Ocora); *Marrakech Festival* (Playasound); *Maroc: Chants et Danses* (Chants du Monde); *Mohamed Rouicha: Ellil Ellil* (Sonodisc); *Mohamed Rouicha: Ch'hal Bkit Ala Alli Habit* (Sonodisc); *Lyrichord*, 141 Perry Street, New York, NY 10014, publish a good selection including Rwais from the High Atlas and a collection of sufi Music; *Festival de Marrakech, Folklore National du Maroc* in 2 vols; *Rais Lhaj Aomar Ouahrouch—Musique Tachelait* (Ocora).

Al-Ala: the Classical Music of Andalus

The classical music of all the Maghreb countries is firmly based on the heritage of Moorish Spain. It is a lyrical and instrumental repertoire that has been elaborated over the last 200 years from verses written during the 700-year Muslim occupation of Spain, but which in turn had their origins in ancient Baghdad. The original reconstruction of these venerable verses was made in Morocco towards the end of the 18th century by Al-Hayek, under the enthusiastic patronage of two sultans, Mohammed ben Abdellah and Moulay Sliman. He completed his work in 1799, and the resulting manuscript provided the basis for the three collections of the modern repertoire, each based on a particular oral history and dynastic memory.

Of the original repertoire of 24 symphonies or *nuba* only eleven have even partly survived, though even this fragment takes some 90 hours to be sung right through. Each *nuba* is based on a specific mode that reflected one of the hours of the day, and is divided into five main rhythmic phases: the prelude *(mizan)*, broad *(muwassa)*, increased *(mahzuz)*, quick *(inshad)* and fast *(insiraf)*. Each *nuba* simultaneously passes through five tempo changes: *al bacit, al qaim wa nsif, btayhi, darj* and *quddam*. The sung poetry in the *nuba* is based on a corpus of classical Andalusian verse and later additions in similar tone and style.

Al-Ala is associated with the urban middle class, particularly from those cities that benefited from Andalusian refugees. In Morocco it is performed by extensive orchestras that use the lute, two-string viol, tambourine, vertically played European violin, as well as clay and skin drums. As well as the three big orchestras in Casablanca, Rabat and Fès there are others from Tetouan, Tangier and Oujda. The latter follows the traditions of Algeria and performs the *gharnati*, believed to be the specific heritage of Granada. Going even further east other variations include *malouf*, played in Constantine, Tunisia and Libya, while a distant cousin called *moshahat Andalusia* can be found in Egypt, Syria and the Lebanon. A further offshoot of Andalus is preserved by the Sephardic Jews of Morocco, who added liturgical singing in the form of psalmodies and responsorial anthems to the common tradition.

These days Al-Ala is in healthy condition. There are conservatories in all the major cities, the complete *nuba* are available on a number of recordings, academics are currently notating all the varieties and the Moroccan Royal Academy has commissioned a definitive edition of Al-Hayek's original manuscript.

Further listening: The complete Nuba repertoire has been recorded and is being issued in several CDs (over several years) by La Maison des Cultures du Monde, Paris. For other recordings of Andalusian music see also *Fes Orchestra: Classical Music of the Andalusian Magreb* (Ocora); *Ustad Massano Tazi: Classical Andalusian Music from Fès* (Ocora);

Orchestre de Meknès: Musique Andalouse Marocaine (Sonodisc); Orchestre de Fès: Irabbi Lward (Sonodisc), and for a crossover between the music of Muslim Andalus and the flamenco of Spanish Andalusia, *El Lebrijano and Orquesta Andalusi de Tanger*, Encuentros (GlobeStyle).

Gnaoua

The word Gnaoua refers to both a spiritual brotherhood (originally based around communities of negro slaves), a musical troupe and a style of music closely related to that produced in West African countries such as Mali and Senegal. It is strikingly distinctive, whether you concentrate on the music (usually produced by drums, castanets and a distinctive long necked flute), the characteristically African beat or the cowrie shell caps of the whirling Gnaoua dancers, and is a confirmed favourite with tourists, whether in their hotels or the Jemaa el Fna square in Marrakech. It has always had a public aspect, for the Gnaoua were employed to exorcise evil spirits and built up a variety of acts that include *l'fraja,* the show, designed to entertain crowds.

Gnaoua is at its most impressive at a *lila,* an all-night ritual held on religious feast days where the great Islamic saints and prophets as well as the spirit world are invoked while dancers take turns to swirl to the point of exhaustion and possession. In such trances they will bang their heads on the stone flagging, eat glass and cut themselves with knives, all without apparently inflicting damage. The instruments used are iron castanets, a big t'bal drum and a large bass-gimbri lute with a camel-neck skin stretched over a walnut body.

Further listening (Gnaoua and Sufi): *Mustafa Baqbou* (World Circuit); *Hadra of the Gnawa of Essaouira* (Ocora); *Gnawa Music of Marrakesh*: Night Spirit Masters (Axiom).

Arabic Song: Guedra, Melhun and B'Sat

In the Saharan provinces south of the Anti-Atlas mountains, the Hassani Arabic dialect became dominant in the 13th century. The most famous musical song-dance of this region is ***guedra***, the erotic, swaying dance of the Saharan women, performed on their knees, and which shares many of the West African influences of Gnaoua spirit music. There is also the more light-hearted tradition of ***b'sat***. This developed as an annual festival of popular theatre, one in which music and lyrics were inextricably mixed into the farcical shows of the actor–storytellers. These shows are very popular in festivals, such as Aid el Kebir, and can often be seen at the Jemaa el Fna in Marrakech. As well as for their musical background, they are being examined with renewed interest as a source of indigenous drama for local television and theatre.

Melhun represents a much more polished and literate tradition, as indicated by alternative names for the style which translate as 'the gift' or 'the inspiration'. It is believed to have derived from the pure Arabic poetry of Andalusia, which was first converted into a popular strophic verse sometime in the 12th century, before being transformed into a rhythmic formula at the time of Merenid rule. Each song would begin with an instrumental prelude that was then followed by short, sung verses marked by choral and instrumental refrains; a gradual, accelerated rhythm marked the end. The songs' subject matter was the many themes made familiar in the Sufi-inspired medieval poetry of Andalusia, images and ideas such as the beloved, wine, gardens, sunset and night, and could be taken at a popular level or understood as metaphors for a spiritual quest. There was also a tradition of satire (known as *lahjou, ashaht* or *addaq)* which could be combined with prophecy *(jofriat)* to bring a strong political content to the songs.

The Jebala region has developed its own ***toqtoqa*** music from Andalusian strains for the lascivious boy dancers of these hills of the northwestern Rif.

Sufi Music

All Morocco's rich musical heritage was used by the Sufi brotherhoods in the composition of ritual chants and dances. These have a spiritual goal which is directed at the performers, not the audience, and may extend over many hours before reaching their sudden conclusion. It is a form of music that is inaccessible to the non-initiate, let alone a non-Muslim, but remains a vital force and influence in the lives of many of Morocco's leading musicians. The Derkaoua, Hamadasha and Aïssoua are three of the most influential brotherhoods, though their influence has necessarily taken a second place to that of the Gnaoua. Instruments generally used are a simple oboe, cymbals and a variety of clay and skin drums.

Musical Instruments

Percussion instruments: *Bendir*—round wooden frame drum sometimes with snare; *Deff*—square wooden frame drum; *T'bal*—large wooden round drum played with sticks and hung round the neck; *Daadouh, guedra, harazi, darbouka, goual, taarija, tbila*—clay and skin drums in descending order of size; *Karkabus/qarqaba*—iron castanets; *Naqus, nuiqsat and handqa*—all two-inch iron castanets; *Tar*—tambourine.

Stringed instruments: *Ud*—lute, usually the six-course Egyptian-style, round backed version; *Kamanja*—the Western violin, but played vertically on the knee; *Rbab*—the two-string viol, with a bow that is a short iron arc holding strands of horsehair; *Guenbri/gimbri*—the most popular lute, a sound box made of the shell of a turtle, covered with goat skin with one or three strings along its neck. The body of a treble *guenbri* is customarily pear shaped, the bass rectangular, and that with a round-backed body with six or three strings is known as a *lotar* or a *soussi guenbri*, and used to be distinctive to southern Morocco; *Hajouj* or *sentir*—large bass *guenbri* with a rectangular walnut body covered with camel-neck skin and goat gut strings; *Swisdi*:—small two-string lute; *Kanum*—Arabic zither or psaltery with 26 triple courses.

Wind instruments: *Awwadat*—metal pipe, played like a straight flute; *Lira/Gasba*—flutes; *Nai/nira*—Arab bamboo flute; *Rita/ghaita*—super oboe-like flute with double-reeded mouthpiece, used by snake charmers; *N'far*—one note processional trumpet, of copper.

Palaces

The Roman ruins of **Volubilis** contain a number of palatial houses that correspond in design with the lesser palaces of later Muslim rulers. Moroccan palaces have an inconspicuous exterior and a covered hall that leads to a central open-air court. Around the walls of this court are arranged four public reception rooms or **pavilions**. The **women's quarters** are secluded from this male preserve and were known as the forbidden, the *harem* court. This arrangement of courts could be endlessly repeated or expanded in scale. The entire complex was known as the *dar* and a suite of rooms around a court a *bayt*. The *méchouar* was a space outside the immediate palace confines but within the outer walls where a ruler could review military parades or receive selected portions of the populace.

The oldest accessible palace in Morocco is the ruined 16th-century **El Badia** in **Marrakech**. Of the palaces built in the 17th century by Sultan Moulay Ismail, the **Dar el Makhzen** in **Tangier** and the **Oudaïa** in **Rabat** are well-preserved and open to the public; both now house museums. Meknès, for all its past glory, gives little insight into palace architecture. Of the royal palaces built in the 19th century, only the **Dar Batha** in **Fès** is accessible, as it has also been turned into a museum. There are however a number of lesser viziers' palaces that have survived from this period and are open to the public: the **Palais Jamaï Hotel** in Fès, the **Dar Jamaï Museum** in Meknès, the **Bahia** and the **Dar Si Saïd** in Marrakech.

Rural Souks

The endless pattern of tribal feuds mitigated against any one tribe being happy at either attending a market deep in the territory of their rival or hosting a market full of potential enemies in their central village. Souks were therefore established on tribal borders, usually beside some distinctive feature: a spring, cult tree or koubba (shrine). The most successful were sited on the division between pastoral and agrarian areas, allowing the two separate communities to trade surpluses of milk, wool and meat for grain, oil and fruit. The site of a souk was often completely deserted apart for the actual day of the market. It would be named after the day of trading, possibly combined with the name of the region, a local saint or dominant tribe to distinguish it from others. Souk el Had is 'the first or Sunday market', Souk el Tnine, 'the second—Monday', el Tleta, 'the third—Tuesday', el Arba, 'the fourth—Wednesday', el Khemis 'the fifth—Thursday'. There are no rural souks held on Friday; Es Sebt, 'the seven', is the Saturday market.

In these more settled times souks have become a natural focus for local administration and permanent traders, although rural souks that exist for only the day of trading can still be found throughout Morocco.

Sufi Brotherhoods

Alongside the formal practice of Islam there has always been a parallel tradition of Sufi mysticism. A Sufi attempts to go beyond mere obedience to Islamic law and reach for experience of God in this life. Ali, cousin and son-in-law of the Prophet and the militant hero of early Islam, is considered to be the originator of this mystical approach to Islam and the first Sufi. Traditions record that Ali received the secrets of the mystical life, which were considered too dangerous to be written down and revealed to the unprepared mass of mankind. They are reserved for initiates who must first make themselves capable and prove themselves worthy of receiving this body of inherited verbal instruction.

The mystical discipline has been passed down through the generations in a human chain of masters, each of whom trained his disciples to succeed him. Sufi brotherhoods arose as aspirants gathered around a celebrated mystic who evolved into the master, or sheikh, of the community. Branches obedient to the teaching of a popular master might be formed throughout the Muslim world; as new brotherhoods formed they were all proud to be links in this one chain of spiritual succession.

The first Moroccan Sufi master was **Sidi Harazem** of Fès, whose name now features on a popular brand of mineral water. He was succeeded in the tradition by two great scholars of the 12th century. **Abu Medyan of Tlemcen**, who died in 1198, and **Abdessalam ben Mchich**, who died in 1228, are central to the brotherhoods of north-west Africa (the latter is also known as the master of Jbel Alam, and is the patron saint of the Jebala region of Morocco). These influential masters combined the teaching of Sidi Harazem with that of the great eastern masters, Al Jilani of Baghdad and Al Ghazzali. The life of a Sufi was not always easy or safe. The 12th-century Almoravid sultan, Ali ben Youssef, burnt all Al Ghazzali's books and sentenced to death any Muslim found reading them.

Despite the fervent opposition of the 'fundamentalist' Almoravid and Almohad dynasties, the brotherhoods survived underground. Their spiritual heir was **Abou el Hassan Ali ech Chadhili**, who died in 1258 and from whose teachings arose 15 separate Sufi brotherhoods, many of which survive today. **Al Jazuli**, who taught and wrote in Fès *The Manifest Proofs of Piety*, was a continuation of this tradition. After his death in 1465 there was another explosion of brotherhoods, who all considered themselves his heirs.

The Sufi brotherhoods, whatever the exact pattern of their spiritual regime, all owe total obedience to a sheikh, their master. Most brotherhoods practise asceticism, and include charitable works and teaching among their activities. Initiates use spiritual tools in their search for *wajd*—ecstatic experience of the divine—including *hizb*—recitation, *dikr*—prolonged recitation, *sama*—music, *raqs* and *hadra*—dancing, and *tamzig*—the tearing of clothes. For an outsider the most common Sufi trait is indifference to the concerns of the world. This trend was developed by the **Aïssoua** and **Hamadasha brotherhoods** into self-mutilation to show indifference to pain, while the more off-beat practised the prolonged contemplation of a beautiful young man, an ephebe, who was believed to embody the divine.

Influential Brotherhoods

The **Chadhilia** was founded by Abou el Hassan Ali ech Chadhili, who is considered to have been born in the Rhomara region of the Rif coast. Before his death in 1258 he established a college near Chechaouèn, from where the brotherhood spread.

The **Jazuliya** was founded by Al Jazuli (Sidi Mohammed ben Sliman al Jazuli), the respected Sufi teacher from the Jazula tribe of the Sous valley who was poisoned in Fès in 1465. The Al Shawyal brotherhood carried his body around the country as a focus for dissidence against the Fès-based Wattasid Sultans, before finally burying it in Afughal in Haha province. The brotherhood later put all its energies behind the Saadian Sherifs, and 62 years after its burial the body of the Sidi was transferred in honour to the shrine at Marrakech, where it still lies.

The **Aïssoua** was founded in the 16th century by Sidi Mohammed ben Aissa, who despite numerous legends died before the rule of Moulay Ismail, but was buried at Meknès. Their spiritual practices were dramatic, as were those of the **Hamadasha**, founded in the 18th century by Sidi Ali ben Hamdasha, buried in the village of Beni-Rachid in the Jbel Zerhoun. Also based on Jbel Zerhoun are the **Dghuglia**, founded by Sidi Ahmed Dghughli, originally a Hamadasha brother, who is buried in the neighbouring village of Beni-Ouared.

The **Derkawa/Derkaoua** was founded by Moulay al Arbi al Darkawi (1760–1820) of an Idrissid family of the Beni Zerwal tribe, from just north of Fès. A calm and studious boy, he moved from his village to Fès where he encountered the teaching of Moulay Abderrahman el Anirami (also known as Jamal el Fassi), who had a zaouia in the city's R'mia quarter. His master gave him his blessing on his deathbed in 1779. Al Arbi's most important centre for teaching was the Al Ingrisi zaouia near the Algerian town of Maskara, where his teachings were recorded by Sidi Buziyyan, but an equally important source are the collected letters (*rasa'il*) to his disciples. He was imprisoned by the ultra-orthodox Sultan Moulay Sliman and died in southern Morocco, but was buried in his home territory, at Bu Berih. The brotherhood's gentle spiritual chants (*soma*), invocations (*dhikr*) and dance rituals (*imara*), alongside Koranic recitations and an emphasis on holy poverty, humility and the footsore way of the desert pilgrim won it widespread popularity throughout Morocco, Algeria and the Sahara.

Tijaniyya was founded by Ahmed al Tijani (1737–1815) who first founded a college in Algeria in 1781, but whose successors moved to Fès to avoid Christian rule. Its original influences were the teachings of the 14th-century Ottoman Khalwatiya brotherhood. The sheikhs claimed to enjoy ecstatic communication with the Prophet, but remained strongly orthodox and loyal to the sultans. It was a brotherhood for courtiers and intellectuals.

The **Naciri** revitalized the zaouia (spiritual school) of Tamegroute in the Drâa Valley, and laid great emphasis on education and orthodox knowledge of the Koran.

The **Taibia** was an influential brotherhood amongst the northern tribes of Morocco and Algeria in the 19th century; their master ruled from Ouezzane.

The **Kittania** was founded by an Idrissid master, Sidi Mohammed bel Kheir el Kittani. The sect grew in influence throughout the 19th century, and a Kittani master claimed the throne in 1911. His defeat and execution by Moulay Hafid led the brotherhood to side strongly with the French, in order to pursue a vendetta against the Alaouites.

Of lesser orthodoxy were the **Rma** brotherhood for soldiers and the **Gnaoua** (see p. 75), still widely admired for its music and occult powers. The Gnaoua claim spiritual descent from the Ethiopian Bilal, whose melodious voice first sounded the muezzin call from the Prophet's mosque at Medina.

Wildlife

Even the most distant and desolate wilderness landscape is likely to be a seasonal grazing ground for a village or nomadic herd. By day you are more likely to find herds of goat, sheep and camel than wild beasts but it is possible, even without entering the guarded sporting and forestry reserves of the Administration des Eaux et Forêts, to spot wild boar, Barbary apes, a range of mountain cats, the ubiquitous red fox and the smaller desert fox with its bat-like ears. Most of these can only be seen at dawn, dusk or briefly caught in a car's headlights by night. This is particularly true of the sub-Sahara, where small numbers of edmi gazelle, jackal and addax antelope survive enthusiastic hunting.

If you sleep anywhere near water you will be serenaded by a chorus of frogs and toads. In the daytime their identity can usually be patched together from squashed bodies on the roadside, and may include the Berber toad, green toad, green frog, western marsh frog and Mauritanian toad. Without even moving from a café chair it is possible to spot and photograph a variety of insect-hunting lizards. The Moorish gecko, Spanish wall lizard and chameleon all seem particularly tolerant of the presence of humans. The species of the mountains and deserts are harder to spot, although patches of sand will often be dotted with the winding tracks of the spiny-tailed sand lizard, the Algerian sand lizard and the Berber skink, or 'sandfish'.

The mouflon or wild mountain sheep, from which all the world's varieties of sheep derive, is indigenous to North Africa. Early Moroccan rock carvings, of a sun set between the twin horns of a sheep, and Egyptian records hint that the cult of Amon, the horned-god of the sun and the herds, originated in the Maghreb. The people of this area may also have first perfected the practice of nomadic herding. Dominant tribes sometimes maintained sacred herds that acted as their standard or totem. The horse was a late arrival to Morocco (from *c.*1600 BC, while the Arabian camel was not successfully bred in the Moroccan Sahara until about AD 600. Nomads and herdsmen still recognize the sacred animals of a herd such as the *Saiba*—the chief mother, the *Bahira*—the eleventh calf, and the *Hami*—the senior stallion. In a widespread custom that extends throughout Africa and Arabia, a sacrificial calf is designated from birth and left free to graze over any field or boundary. Dedicated to a saint or spirit, it is sacrificed at their shrine and then consumed at the communal feast.

further reading on wildlife

Flowers of the Mediterranean, Oleg Polunin and Anthony Huxley (Chatto and Windus)—the classic well-thumbed travelling companion.

A Field Guide to the Mammals of Africa, T Haltenorth and H Diller (Collins, London).

Rough Guide to Mediterranean Wildlife, Peter Raine—fine general coverage plus a detailed country chapter.

Birdlife

Birds are easily the most impressive of Morocco's wildlife. There is a large number of resident species, and dazzling and vastly varied concentrations of migrant flocks, which generally come to Africa for the mild winter from October to March and fly across the Mediterranean for the European summer.

Birds of Power

The swift, swallow and crag martin are respected as birds inspired by Allah to protect the harvest and remove noxious insects and reptiles. They can be seen in showy evening flights above the rooftops of cities such as Fès and Marrakech. The stork is Morocco's other great holy bird, and there are numerous legends to explain their constant attitude of prayer and symbolic prostration whenever they rest. Hospitals were established in Fès and Marrakech to care for injured birds, where they could recover or die peacefully in protected enclosures.

The striped hoopoe is conspicuous during its migration but is trapped by Moroccans, for its heart and feathers are powerful charms against evil spirits. The barn owl, a permanent resident, is recognized to be the clairvoyant ally of the Devil. The owl cries out the name of a fore-doomed individual who can only escape by cursing the owl with its own hidden name. Even a normal owl cry has the power to kill a child unless there is someone to spit and curse as they fly overhead. The Tangier raven is also viewed with suspicion, and always lays its eggs on 21 April. Killing a raven soothes the evil eye whilst a raven's liver, tongue, brain and heart are made into useful antidotes.

Surprising Disguises

Take a moment to look more closely at the Moroccan versions of familiar birds. Sparrows turn out to be mainly of the Spanish race (with rich chestnut heads and a pronounced black bib) and occasionally rock sparrows (with smartly striped heads); chaffinches are most exotic with slate-blue heads, olive-green backs and salmon-pink underparts. The starling is not *vulgaris* but *unicolor*, which is to say spotless. Magpies sport a neat tear-shaped mark behind the eye in brilliant turquoise blue.

Birds Easily Seen

Crested larks are common along roadsides; buntings (corn, cirl, rock and house) are easily seen on top of walls and telephone wires; pigeons turn out to be turtle doves or rock doves with bright white rumps; glorious blue rollers and smart ginger, black and white hoopoes are widespread summer visitors; summer evenings are filled with the screeching and aerial displays of swifts and pallid swifts; herds of cattle are invariably accompanied by a few white cattle egrets; and common bulbuls sing delightfully from every bush in gardens and parks.

Moroccan Specialities

Certain bird species now so rare as to be threatened with extinction but which still occur in Morocco are the bald ibis (tiny numbers of which have been seen at the mouth of the river Sous and Massa); the slender-billed curlew, with just a few records for the last decade from the marshes and lagoons along the coast of northwest Morocco; and bustards (Houbara, Arabian and great), which have almost been hunted out of the desert and southern steppes. Visiting birders will have better chances of tracking down desert specialities such as the sand-grouses (Lichtenstein's, crowned, spotted, black-bellied and pin tailed); raptors such as the black-shouldered kite, tawny eagle, Barbary falcon, dark-chanting goshawk (mainly found on the inland plateaux) and Eleonar's falcon (breeding on sea-cliffs and the pair of rocky islets off Essaouira); crested coots (resident on lakes in the Middle Atlas), Audouin's gulls (both breeding and wintering along the Mediterranean coast); the African marsh owl (at Merdja Lerge); fulvous babblers (gregarious and easy to find); black-headed bush shrike (common but very hard to find lurking in thick scrub); and Levaillant's woodpecker, an endemic green woodpecker found in mature woodland in the Rif and Middle Atlas.

Hot Spots for Birdlife

Tangier: March to May and August to October witness a remarkable concentration of migrating birds. Depending on wind direction and strength, enormous numbers of birds (120,000 honey buzzards, for example) will be passing up the east or west side of the Tangier peninsula. If weather conditions are unfavourable great concentrations of raptors in particular can be found congregated in the forest to the west of Tangier.

The Northwest Atlantic Coast: Lagoons here include the internationally important reserve of Moulay-Bousselham, also known as Merdja Lerge, and the Lac de Sidi Bourhaba; both contain a splendidly rich array of birds throughout the year. Large numbers of wintering birds, such as 1000 greater flamingos, 30,000 ducks, 50,000 waders (including the very rare slender-billed curlew) inhabit the lagoons from November to March. Summer breeding birds include collared pratincoles, red-necked nightjars, fan-tailed warblers and crested coots. The lagoons also host a vast array of passage migrants—practically everything that winters in Africa and breeds in Northern Europe can be seen here in spring and autumn.

The Sous Valley: This area, rich with citrus plantations, also has a relict habitat, the Argana Forest, which is the place to track down stone curlews, Moussier's redstart, black-headed bush shrike and raptors such as the tawny eagle, the dark-chanting goshawk, the long-legged buzzard and the golden-booted and Bonelli's eagles.

The High Atlas Mountains and Dadès Gorge: The lammergeier, the largest of the old world vultures, can be seen here soaring among the high cliffs of the spectacular Dadès Gorge. Other birds to be seen in this area include crag martins, blue rock thrushes, black wheatears, trumpeter finches, rock sparrows and the elusive crimson-winged finch.

The Tafilalt: This area contains the true desert specialities: hoopoe lark, thick-billed lark, cream-coloured courser, lanner falcon, the pale North African race of the eagle owl, the sand-grouses and the desert, mourning and white-crowned black wheatears.

The Sous and Massa Rivers: Immediately south of the river Sous the mud and sandbanks provide roosts for large numbers of waders, gulls and terns. On a good day you might be able to spot white storks; spoonbills; avocet; ruddy shelduck; Mediterranean, slender billed and Audouin's gulls and gull-billed caspians; Royal, lesser crested, whiskered and white-winged black terns. The mouth of the river Massa forms a large lake backed by huge dunes, a biological reserve of major importance with year-round birding. Exceptional rarities like the bald ibis still appear very occasionally. There are very large numbers of wintering duck, large gull and tern roosts, breeding species such as Barbary partridge, brown-throated sand martins, Moussier's redstart, fan-tailed warblers and passage migrants such as great spotted cookoe, hoopoes, red-rumped swallows, spoonbills, spotted and Baillon's crakes and bee-eaters.

further information and contact addresses

The best field guide is *Birds of the Middle East and North Africa* by Hollom, Porter, Christensen and Willis (published by Poyser), used in conjunction with *Birds of Britain, Europe, North Africa and the Middle East* by Heinzel, Fitter and Parslow (published by Collins). For comprehensive site information, there is an excellent 70-page booklet, *A Birdwatcher's Guide to Morocco* by Patrick and Fedora Bergler (published by Bird Watchers' Guides, Prion Ltd, 21 Roundhouse Drive, Perry, Cambridgeshire PE18 0DJ).

Bird records of your sightings should be sent to the Institut Scientifique, Charia Ibn Batouta, BP 703, Agdal, Rabat or to Patrick and Fedora Bergier, 4 Avenue Folco de Baroncelli, 13210 Saint Rémy de Provence, France.

If you have the good fortune to see either the bald ibis or slender billed curlew be very careful not to disturb them and report your sightings to Birdlife International, 32 Cambridge Road, Girton, Cambridge CB3 0PJ. These records could be of paramount importance as both these species are close to extinction.

Tangier, the Rif and the Mediterranean

The Rif mountains rise immediately south of the Mediterranean coast of Morocco and run parallel to the shore. They are the dominant physical feature of the region, and have either reduced the coast to a narrow fringe of land or over-awed its beaches with lines of menacing cliffs. The Rifs are central to national history, for they have protected and isolated the distinctive culture of Central Morocco from mainstream Mediterranean civilization. The coast is littered with the history of failed colonial settlements and the fortresses of maritime powers from every age. Even today Spain still maintains five sovereign settlements on the Rif coast: the two accessible ports of Ceuta and Melilla, the two inaccessible islets of Peñón de Velez de la Gomera and Peñón de Alhucemas, and the empty Chafarine islands.

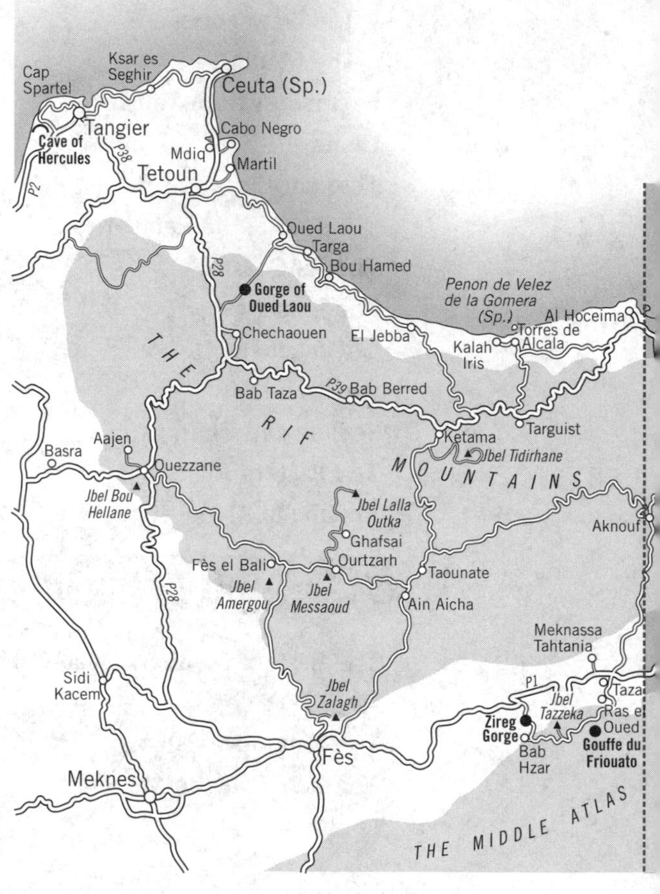

The barrier formed by the Rifs against the Mediterranean is not just physical. The mountains are inhabited by some of the most independent and intransigent of all the peoples of North Africa. These tribes have occupied the mountains since Neolithic times. They developed their own Berber dialect, known as Tariffit or Zenata, and a rich body of traditional music and beliefs. There is an ancient division between the people of the eastern and western mountains. The latter, known as the Jebala, were historically distinguished from the eastern tribes by their acceptance of homosexuality and *kif* (marijuana) and their use of the Arabic language.

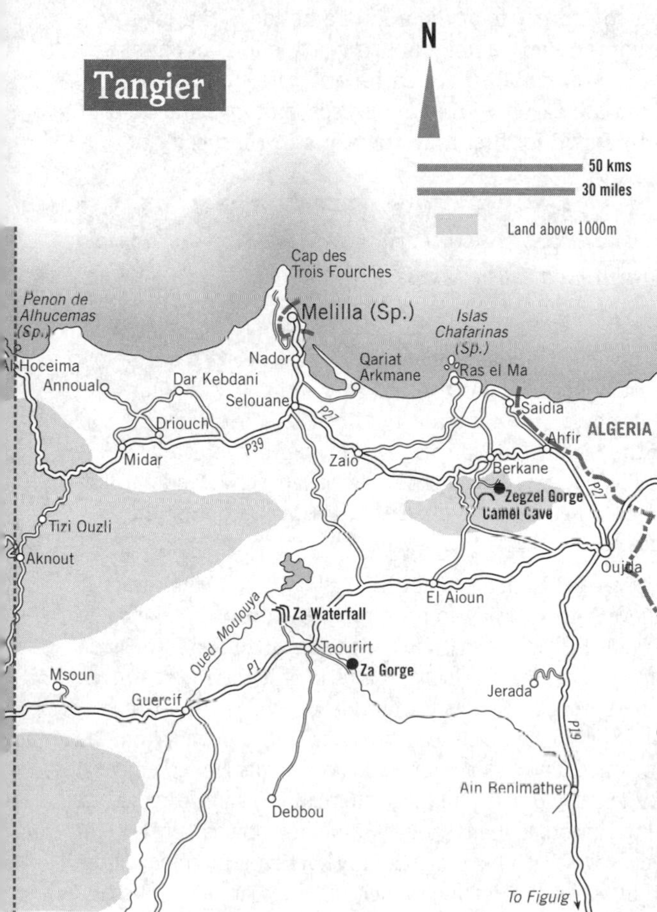

Only the strongest sultans have been able to conquer the Rif, where it was a deadly insult to assert that 'your father died in his bed'. This bellicose tradition was immortalized in the Rif rising of 1921–6. The tribes of the eastern mountains, led by Abdel Krim, almost succeeded in driving both France and Spain out of Morocco. The dissident nature of the region is still strong. On independence, when the rest of the country would have happily died for the national hero, King Mohammed V, the women of Tizi Ouzli refused even to come out of their houses to sing a welcome. Two years later the Rif were in revolt, but were crushed in the campaign of February 1959, when the present King led an army of 20,000 into the hills. It is still one of the poorest and most troublesome regions in the country. The northern cities are usually the first to flare up in any urban unrest, while the eastern mountains, due to 'business'—the semi-tolerated traffic in marijuana—are close to being a no-go area.

In the heart of the Jebala mountain region is the old, compact and beautiful Andalusian town of Chechaouèn, its streets still filled with craftsmen. This is the customary goal for travel in the region, a friendly and accessible stop on your way south. The two northern cities of Tangier and Tetouan, despite their sophistication, monuments and equable climate, share an evil reputation with travellers. Countless first-time visitors to Morocco, fleeced or hassled by 'guides' the minute they get off bus or ferry, leave before they have become accustomed to the initial shock of the street culture. Their idiosyncratic street life and beautiful buildings, countryside and beaches are often easier to appreciate at the end of a holiday. The city of Oujda on the Algerian border, and its neighbouring attractions of Saïdia beach and the Beni-Snassen mountains, are easier and safer to approach from Fès. The road across the eastern Rif is the preserve of *kif* bandits; it's exciting, but not recommended for first-time travellers in Morocco.

Tangier

That African perdition called Tangier.

Mark Twain

Tangier is the oldest continually inhabited city in Morocco. It sprawls over a series of low hills that overlook a wide sandy bay halfway along the narrow straits of Gibraltar. The medina, the old walled city with its dense mass of narrow twisting alleys, overlooks the port area. To the south and west of the medina are spread the 20th-century streets of a fast expanding northern city overlooked by an assortment of Christian spires and Muslim minarets that bear witness to its confused past. To the east of the port, fronting the long sandy bay, stretches a line of large beach hotels.

It is the Straits of Gibraltar that have made Tangier. They have always had a vital strategic role, for they command both the easiest crossing from Europe to North Africa and the western entrance to the Mediterranean. Tangier has always been a prize and has passed under the control of a litany of empires. For the first half of this century it was too controversial a possession for any one of the European powers to control, so it was an International City, ruled and misruled by a council of foreign consuls. It was during this period, from the twenties to the late fifties, that it earned its legendary reputation for sexual and commercial licence. The Tangier of political exiles, homosexual brothels, international banks, smugglers, spies, arms and dirty deals so lovingly recorded in film and literature has now largely gone. It is now a mass passenger port, a package beach resort and a burgeoning northern city struggling for a manufacturing role, but it has also retained much of its old artistic and social glamour. One should be thankful that it remains a tolerant place where cultures continue to mix, but never completely blend. The more you travel in Morocco the more you begin to appreciate the compact centre of Tangier where you can live a truly urban existence amongst cafés, bars, art galleries, libraries and museums. The long hot days can be broken by day trips out to beaches and quiet restaurants, returning back in time to join the evening *paseo.*

Hercules and Anteus

In the stormy waters of the Straits, where seven currents follow their own course at different levels of the ocean, the god of the sea mated with the goddess of the earth. This coupling of Poseidon and Gaia in due course produced the giant Anteus, who was married to Tingis, a beautiful North African nymph. Anteus, who remained invulnerable whilst his feet remained in contact with his mother—the earth—made a nuisance of himself by challenging any traveller to a wrestling match, which invariably led to their death. When he challenged

Hercules, however, Anteus had finally met his match. Hercules succeeded in catching the giant off-guard, lifted him from the earth and broke his back. The giant's vast corpse was buried under Charf hill, which can be seen on the south-eastern edge of Tangier where it remains a popular burial place. Hercules celebrated his victory with the widowed nymph Tingis, who nine months later gave birth to the boy Sophix. In order to safeguard his son's inheritance, Hercules decided to pull Africa and Spain apart. Gibraltar and Jbel Musa were his hand-grips, and have ever after been known as the twin pillars of Hercules. Sophix then ruled over a land protected by the sea, and named his city 'Tingis' in honour of his mother.

History

The Traders' Port—750 BC–706 AD

To the west of the present medina there is a sea cliff studded with the rock-carved tombs of Phoenician merchants. They first established the port of Tingis here around the 8th century BC, a day's journey south from the important city of Gades (Cádiz). All the Phoenician ports in the area came under Roman control after the destruction of Carthage in 146 BC. Roman Tingis was granted the privileged status of *colonia*, allowing for virtual self-government within the empire.It remained undisturbed by the fate of the province to its south and accepted the passing inconvenience of Vandal conquest in AD 429, and Byzantine reconquest in AD 533.

The Garrison City—AD 706–740

The first Arab missionary army that ventured into Morocco, in AD 682, was a mere expeditionary force that was content to parley with the governor of the walled city of Tangier. A second much greater force, under the command of the redoubtable Musa ben Nasser, seized control of the city in AD 706. Musa appointed one of his Berber military slaves, Tariq, as governor of Tangier while he returned to the regional headquarters of the Arab Caliphate in Tunisia. Tangier was of paramount importance in this period, for it was one of the only two military garrisons established in Morocco (the other one was in the Tafilalt, on the edge of the Sahara). In 711 Tariq led a small expedition force of 7,000 across the straits to Spain. Tariq's small Berber army achieved the lightning conquest of Spain, but the rewards of victory were reserved for the Arab ruling class. The smouldering dissatisfaction with Arab rule was exacerbated in 740 when a new governor of Tangier gave orders that Berber regiments should be tattooed for easy identification. The revolt of the Berber garrison at Tangier rapidly swept across North Africa to end the brief period of direct rule by the Caliphate.

A Pawn of Empires

Though both shores of the Straits of Gibraltar were Muslim in the medieval period, there was a constant jockeying for position. Control of Tangier passed like a symbolic orb among the Islamic dynasties of Spain and North Africa. By the 15th century the Portuguese, moved both by a crusading spirit and a desire to win a slice of the profitable Saharan trade, had begun to seize control of the Moroccan ports. Tangier fell to them in 1471, but it became only a sterile garrison town removed and isolated from the commercial life of the interior. In 1661, Portugal gave the city to the English as part of the dowry that went with Catherine of Braganza when she married King Charles II, together with Bombay.

English rule was an unmitigated disaster. The garrison was penned within the walls by a continuous Moroccan siege that completely isolated the port, which had been improved at great expense, from any trade. The troops went unpaid while administrators, such as the diarist Samuel Pepys, lined their pockets. The town's Jewish population was expelled, and both Catholic and Muslim holy places desecrated, before the English decided to quit in 1685. They spurned negotiations, including a Portuguese offer to buy Tangier back, and sailed away like some barbarian fleet from an empty, burnt-out ruin.

Sultan Moulay Ismaïl immediately ordered the rebuilding of Tangier. All the city's important monuments, such as the kasbah and the grand mosque, date from this period. The farmland around the town, which had been an empty war zone ever since the Portuguese occupation, was given to Rifi soldiers. They bore a hereditary obligation to protect Tangier and came into the town to pray and sell their crops in the markets that sprang up around the walls.

An International City

In 1810 Tangier was a small market town of 5000, but during the rest of the century it gradually spread beyond its walls as European merchants made increasing use of it as an important trading centre. Most of Morocco's diplomatic life was concentrated in Tangier before the colonial period. The financiers, foreign consuls and their delegated native agents, backed up by the presence of naval squadrons, soon grew into a controlling influence.

Soon after the French took over most of Morocco in 1912, they moved the focus of maritime trade, diplomacy and finance south to Rabat and Casablanca. The British, worried about the security of Gibraltar, had insisted that Tangier should remain neutral. It was not until 1923 that this anomalous situation was tidied up, and an international authority established for the city and 140 square miles of the surrounding country. Spanish and French political influence was predominant; the Italians gave the best parties; and the British occupied themselves with gardens and a rigid social hierarchy. The lack of regulations attracted a variety of otherwise illegal financial services. It was, however, the combination of sexual licence, drugs, political exiles, spies, smugglers, cheap living and eccentric expatriates which gave the International City its peculiar reputation. Poor Spanish conscripts, eager for any way to make money, and the innate respect for homosexuality among some of the Arabic speaking hill tribes, fuelled its popularity as a gay resort which over the years attracted such figures as Oscar Wilde, Joe Orton, Truman Capote and Ronnie Kray. The life of the international city has been reflected in a rich literature (*see* Further Reading). The light, life and oriental backdrop also attracted such eminent artists as Eugène Delacroix, Henri Matisse and Francis Bacon.

Tangier was reunited with Morocco on 29 October 1956, and within a few years the banks had moved to Geneva and the more outrageous gay bars had been closed down. Today, the city's population has grown to 300,000 and the local economy is based on the twin pillars of migrant work in Europe and tourism.

Getting Around

by air

Tangier's **airport**, Boukhalef-Souahel, is 15km southwest of the town off the P2 coast road to Rabat. A taxi ride to the centre of town will cost around 120dh. There is no direct bus connection. Tickets and timetables are available from the Royal Air Maroc office at 1 Place de France, ✆ (09) 935501 and 935503, 📠 (09) 932681; Air France is also represented by RAM. The GB Airways office is at 83 rue de la Liberté, ✆ (09) 935877, 📠 (09) 933112.

by sea

The **ferry** journey from Spain takes over two hours; in high summer there are six boats a day in each direction (leaving from Algeciras between 9.30am and 8pm, from Tangier between 7.30am and 7pm) but in winter there are only two. Until the turn of the century ferry passengers were carried ashore on the naked shoulders of a native stevedore. Now alas gang planks are always used. All ferries dock beside the tall ferry terminal building, which contains a bureau de change and a railway ticket office, while the small hydrofoil terminal is close by. There is a small railway station, Gare du Port, inside the port area, but only about half the trains use it. Unless there is a train just about to leave it is much better to use the town station, Gare de Ville, which is just outside the port gates. It is also more lively and has a left luggage kiosk where you can leave your luggage whilst viewing the street life from one of the neighbouring cafés and bars. Just before the port gates you should come across a taxi rank; unless you are feeling very mean or confident, take one and avoid the ugly barrage of hustlers waiting for new arrivals at the port gates.

Departing: Allow an hour or more for boarding, even though the boats are invariably late; the near anarchy of acquiring an immigration departure form, getting it and your passport stamped and then going through customs does eventually sort itself out–but only if you allow enough time. **Ferry tickets** can be bought at any of the travel agents around town, at the port gate or direct from Limadet, the main agent. Their office is at 13 Rue du Prince Moulay Abdullah, ✆ (09) 931142 or 932913.

The **hydrofoil** is quicker than conventional ferries, taking just under an hour. It is for passengers only and only costs about 30 per cent more. There are, however, disadvantages. Timetables, ownership and routes of the boats are constantly changing, but this is nothing compared to the irritation of buying a ticket and then finding that all seats have subsequently been taken by a tour group. They do not run in bad weather, are often out of service in winter, and also you can't see much out of the window. At present there are daily services to and from Algeciras, a near-daily connection to Tarifa and a twice-weekly link with Gibraltar. Transtour, who currently run the Tarifa/Gibraltar hydrofoil, have offices at 4 Rue Jabha Al Ouatania, ✆ (09) 934004.

by rail

The station is just 50m beyond the port gates, ✆ (09) 931201. Trains are the obvious, efficient and easy way to travel further on, unless you are heading east towards Tetouan and Chechaouèn. For Casablanca and Rabat, there are four trains a day, of which the last two continue on to Marrakech. There are also four trains that call at Meknès, Fès and Oujda. The last trains of the day to both Marrakech and Oujda are night trains for which you will need to buy an additional sleeper ticket. The left luggage office at the station will only accept bags with a secure lock, which in practice seldom means a backpack.

by bus

All bus companies now use the smart new terminal, ✆ (09) 946940, on the south-east edge of town off the Rabat/Tetouan roundabout at the end of the Rue de Fès, which is further identified by the tapering illuminated minaret of the Syrian Mosque. It is a dull 2km walk from the centre of town but an easy 5–10dh ride in a taxi. There are plenty of departures to southern destinations, but apart from towns like Larache which are off the rail network, the major usefulness of buses is for getting to Tetouan and Chechaouèn. There is a bus to Tetouan (1hr away) about every half hour, about half a dozen daily departures for Chechaouèn (2–3hrs) via Tetouan, about half a dozen to Asilah (30mins–1hr) which go on to Larache (90mins) and about four each to Ceuta (2hrs), Meknès (5hrs), Ouezzane (4hrs) and Fès (6hrs).

Local **city buses** leave from the top of the Grand Socco but are not of much use to a tourist. Bourghaz, a private company, runs a minibus service from the port gate to the new bus station and in summer runs trips out to Cape Spartel-Cave of Hercules.

by car and taxi

For a place, squeezed in among five other passengers, in a black or cream coloured Mercedes ***grand taxi*** to Tetouan, Asilah or Ceuta, use the *grand taxi* park recently established beside the bus station at the end of the Rue de Fès.

For more individual destinations you can usually find a *grand taxi* in either the Grand Socco, the port gate or at a rank on Rue de Hollande (Zankat Hollanda). You will have to negotiate a rate, though a single trip to the Atlantic beaches to the east of town should cost around 70dh for a whole car load. The blue *petits taxis*, which can carry three passengers anywhere within city limits, are generally busier and more elusive but can again be found at the port gates, on Blvd Pasteur/Mohammed V and the Grand Socco. They should charge around 5dh per person for an average city trip but the meters seldom operate. Fares officially double after 9pm.

Car hire: All the car rental offices are in the new town in or around Av Mohammed V. The established agencies include Europcar at 87 Av Mohammed V, ✆ (09) 938271; Hertz at 36 Av Mohammed V, ✆ (09) 933322; Budget at 7 Av du Prince Moulay Abdellah, ✆ (09) 937994; Avis at 54 Blvd Pasteur, ✆ (09) 933031. These companies also have booths at the airport. The best places to park in the centre of town are on the medina side of the Grand Socco or on any of the streets off Av Mohammed V. Pay a flat fee of 2dh to the street guardian. For a longer stay use the underground car park of the Tanjah Flandria hotel.

For **bicycle and motorbike** hire try Mesbahi at 7 Rue Ibn Tachfine, off Av des FAR, ✆ (09) 940974.

Garages: For Peugeots go to 37, Rue Quevedo, ✆ (09) 935093; for Renaults to Tanjah Auto, 2 Av de Rabat, ✆ (09) 936938.

Orientation

You can happily walk around all of central Tangier and have no need for a bus or taxi. If you are just passing through the city you will find taxis, boats, trains and cafés

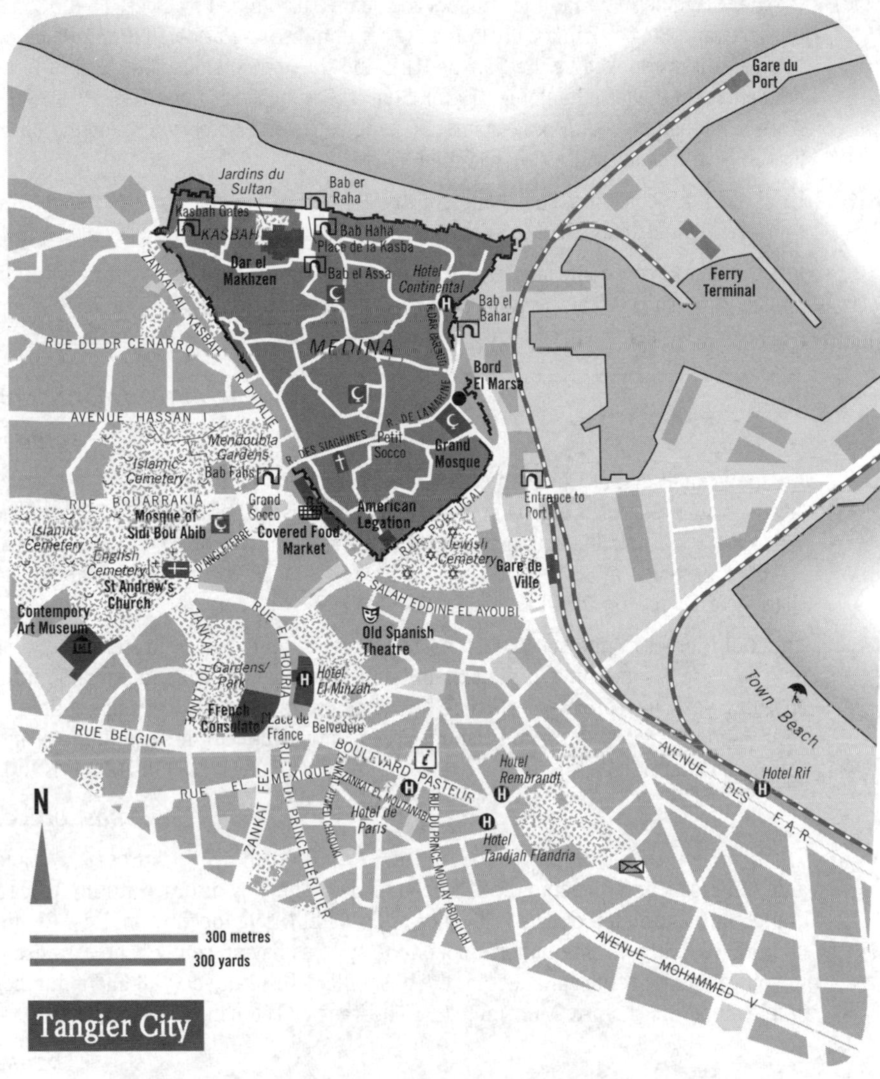

all waiting for you just beyond the port gates. The bus terminal also used to be here but has moved to the southeast edge of town. The two streets on the right as you walk out of the port, Rue (or Zankat) Portugal and Rue Salah Eddine el Ayoubi, both lead steeply uphill to the Grand Socco, an open circular space surrounded by taxis and local buses. This dusty space, overlooked by the entrances to a number of covered markets as well as an equally dusty old cinema, is the centre of town.

On its north side, gates lead into the medina, the old walled town, which contains a warren of narrow lanes. It is easy enough, however, to follow the broad, bazaar-lined

Rue des Siaghines down to the Petit Socco square, surrounded by cafés. To the south of the Grand Socco, Zankat El Houria twists uphill to the also-café-lined Place de France, still overlooked by the Café de Paris and the French Consulate. East of Place de France, on the left, the Boulevard (or Charih) Pasteur turns imperceptibly into the Avenue Mohammed V. Most restaurants, bars, banks and hotels will be found on or just off Blvd Pasteur and Av Mohammed V.

Parallel to the coastline, south and southwest of the medina, rise the hills of the smart residential areas, the Montagne and the Marshan.

Just to make things confusing, **street names are signposted interchangeably** in French, Spanish or Arabic, as Rue, Calle or Zankat respectively. Many colonial names have officially been changed to Arabic, but street usage often remains unaffected.

Tourist Information

guides

As a newcomer do not expect to be left alone to explore the town. Accept this fact in advance, hire a taxi, an official guide or select a pleasant unofficial 'student guide'. There are 115 multilingual trained guides who can be hired from the tourist office at 29 Blvd Pasteur, ✆ (09) 948661, or from the Association of Guides above Le Claridge café, also on Blvd Pasteur, ✆ (09) 931372.

Think of Moroccan unofficial guides as cats, independent souls who stick around as long as there is something in it for them (usually a flat 5 per cent commission from anything you buy), often entertaining but totally unreliable and very susceptible to your mood. They will spit and shout if you are rude but love politeness and mannered charm, which is indeed a rare commodity amongst the bulk of tourists.

post offices

The main post office, ✆ (09) 935657, is at 33 Av Mohammed V (European, Arabic and American newspapers are on sale outside). There is also a centrally placed branch at the junction of Zankat Belgica and Rue el Msala (open Mon–Fri 8.30am-noon, 2.30-6.30pm). International telephone systems have recently been privatised, so you can no longer telephone from the post office. Instead, you will find a number of telephone shops on Av Mohammed V. The Tangier-Tetouan code is (09).

banks

There is a full cast of banks stretched along Boulevard Pasteur and its extension Avenue Mohammed V. **BMCE**, usually the most broad-ranging in its services, and **Crédit du Maroc** are on Blvd Pasteur, while **SGMB**, **Banque Populaire** and **Banque du Maroc** are at 58, 76 and 78 Av Mohammed V.

health and emergencies

Among the large choice of chemists around Av Mohammed V is the **Pharmacie Pasteur** on Place de France, ✆ (09) 934242. There is also a 24-hour chemist at 22 Rue de Fès, ✆ (09) 932619. Dr Joseph Hirt at 8 Rue Sorolla, ✆ (09) 931268, is an English-speaking doctor used to making hotel calls. In an emergency head for the

Croissant Rouge on Rue el Mansour Dahbi, where you will find someone who speaks English 24 hours a day, or the Spanish Hospital, ✆ (09) 931018. The emergency ambulance number is ✆ 15; for the Police station, on Rue Salah Eddine, call ✆ 19.

consulates

The **British Consulate** is at 41 Av Mohammed V, ✆ (09) 941557; the **US Consulate** has closed. The **German** consulate is at 47 Av Hassan II, ✆ (09) 938700; **Italy** at 37 Rue Assad ibn-al-Farrat, ✆ (09) 936997, the **Netherlands** at 47 Av Hassan II, ✆ (09) 931245, **Sweden** at 31 Av Prince Heritier, ✆ (09) 938730.

The New Town

The Grand Socco

At the heart of Tangier, just outside the walls of the old town but by no means part of the new, sits the large open circular space of the Grand Socco. Blue buses pull in noisily beneath the cinema, taxis queue by the central patch of grass and cars attempt to push their way through the chattering crowds. Grill kitchens, stalls and cafés ring the space. Storms of angry shouts or laughter break out from the cafés, usually over nothing more substantial than the loss of a few bottle-top game counters. A slender minaret to the southwest of the Grand Socco is entirely decorated with rich coloured mosaic. This is the Mosque of Sidi Bou Abib, a valuable landmark by which to find the souks that ring the Grand Socco.

Tangier still follows the ancient plan of the Roman city. The Grand Socco has always been an open market space outside the walls, surrounded now as then by cemeteries and markets. Its official name is the Place du 9 Avril 1947, celebrating a speech made here by King Mohammed V which marked the beginning of the ten-year struggle for independence.

Grand Socco Souks

The country surrounding Tangier uses the city as a permanent souk. The market ladies with distinctive broad hats, red striped cloth and blankets folded around their waists come into town to trade throughout the week, and are especially busy on Thursdays and Sundays. The Rue Salah Eddine el Ayoubi, running to the port, is lined with stalls and entrances to internal covered markets. The entrance to the **clothing market** is opposite the shop at 41 Rue Salah Eddine. The smarter covered **food market** is found through the medina gate from the Grand Socco—first right through the archway. A chaotic covered souk exists beside the minaret of Sidi Bou Abib, where old clothes, chickens, car radios and herbs are for sale.

The Mendoubia

Off the north side of the Grand Socco a gate leads to the old offices of the Mendoubia, set in their own park (now renamed the Jardins du Tribunal du Sadad). The *mendoub* was the representative of the sultan in the independent city of Tangier, a job that was held by two generations of royal cousins. If the low green door at the gateway is open, enquire politely from the guardian if it is possible to visit. The interior courtyard is dominated by an enormous 800-year-old banyan tree. Beyond the residence, partly occupied by the Justice Department, there is a brand new terrace built around the monument to commemorate

Sultan Mohammed V's 1947 speech. Flowers are interspaced among a fine collection of bronze European cannons that overlook the rest of this deliciously overgrown and neglected garden right in the centre of town. In the background you may catch the sound of the steady thud of rubber stamps from the legal offices.

The English Church

Looking at the minaret of Sidi Bou Abib from the centre of the Grand Socco, the cross of St George can be seen flying from the Anglican church of St Andrew, to its left. The church and its shady quiet **graveyard** are entered from the Zankat Angleterra. Across from the church are a number of stalls that sell striped Berber cloth and Islamic red or black embroidered scarves. The caretaker Mustapha Cherqui will open the church to visitors (please leave a donation) and point out the Lord's prayer, carved in Arabic above the chancel.

The graveyard is full of stones that commemorate a past era of British influence in Tangier and Morocco. Look out for the one dedicated to Walter Harris, the flamboyant journalist, travel writer and intimate of the bandit Raissouli who had a house both in the kasbah and out towards Cape Malabata. Sir John Drummond-Hay, a British consul in the 19th century, was a close friend of Sultan Moulay Hassan and worked throughout his life to maintain the independence of Morocco. Sir John secured the appointment of Harry Maclean in 1877 as chief of staff to train a modern army for the sultan and his son. Maclean was happy to transfer from Gibraltar, for he was under a cloud due to an affair with his superior officer's wife. He became a flamboyant figure in Moroccan society, with his personal bagpiper and a mounted bodyguard dressed in burnouses of Maclean tartan. 'Caid' Maclean's tombstone can be found here, while his portrait dominates the bar of the El Minzah Hotel.

Most romantic is the story of Emily, the Sherifa of Wazzan. She came out to Tangier at the beginning of this century as the companion of Mrs Perdicaris, whose husband was one of the first American hostages to become an international cause. The powerful hereditary saint, the Sherif of Wazzan (Ouezzane), fell in love with Emily one morning as he rode by and spied her singing and combing her hair on the seaside balcony of the Villa Perdicaris. They were married by Sir John (who was full of misgivings) in a Christian service, had children and perhaps just as inevitably separated. Emily, however, stayed on in Tangier, running a free inoculation clinic and dispensing vast quantities of sweets to children until her death. One of her sons in due course inherited the mantle of Sherif.

Tangier Gallery of Contemporary Art

Open Wed-Mon 9am–12.30pm, 3–6.30pm; closed Tues; adm.

Further up Zankat Angleterra there is a covered fountain, decorated in the full Moorish taste. This was raised in memory of Sir John Drummond-Hay's successor in the Consulate, and son-in-law, William Kirby-Green. On the opposite side of the road is the gatehouse of the old British Consulate. This handsome old house, approached through its garden, has been converted into the Tangier Gallery of Contemporary Art (Musée d'Art Contemporain de Tanger), © (09) 938436. It is the first such public museum in Morocco and is a happy testimony to Tangier's role as a cultural gateway between Europe and the Maghreb. Several dozen works from Morocco's first generation of artists to have taken up the Western habit of painting on canvas are on permanent display in the six downstairs rooms. Their techniques might be borrowed, but the vision is quite separate from that of Western artists who have painted in Morocco. Foreign artists have tended to focus on recording the exhilaratingly different landscape, vegetation, people and street life, when they are not totally absorbed in a painterly obsession with the qualities of North African light.

In contrast, the canvases of Fatima Hassani show a glamorized spiritual world as viewed by the women of Morocco. Bright textile-derived images are set in domestic situations, with fields of bright colour defined in black. Mohammed Hamidi draws upon the imagery of his native sub-Sahara, and religious symbolism. His initially vivid colours are toned down by a thick dust-like application of varnish. Chabia Tallal, 'the Dubuffet of Morocco' creates naive figures from oil and acrylic with broad brush strokes and finger smears. His palette dominated by reds and blues, his images have a haunting power belying their apparent simplicity.

New Town Boulevards

If you continue up Zankat Angleterra you will reach Zankat Belgica. Turn left to reach the **Ensemble Artisanal** (*see* p. 105 Shopping), or continue down the Zankat Belgica to the Place de France for coffee at the Café de Paris, a prime observation post for taking in the absorbing and diverse stream of Tangier life: holidaying homosexuals, turbanned Berber farmers, students, beggars, burned package tourists, elegant European residents, portly businessmen who could be Jewish, Soussi, Fassi or Spanish, veiled women and young street Arabs who like your sugar lumps. Its tables have witnessed a legendary parade of resident intellectuals, political exiles, spies and smugglers. Captain Zoondab may be seen quietly smoking at one table in his fez and white burnous. Now the retired doyen of the tourist guides, as a boy he ran messages between Gordon Curney, the British gun-runner, and Abdel Krim, the leader of the Rif rebellion. The broad Boulevard Pasteur to the east of Place de France, with its row of bronze cannons, has a fine view over the port and the old town.

Returning to the Grand Socco down Zankat El Houria, the imposing French Consulate is on the left. A little way past it is **Galerie Delacroix,** © (09) 941054, one of the best places in Morocco to find exhibitions of contemporary art. The gallery, in which most exhibits are for sale, is run by Georges Bousquet and also holds lectures, film shows and readings, and promotes visits by drama companies. A few doors down are the separate **Galerie Tindouf**, its windows filled with elegant glass and ceramics, and the **Bazaar Tindouf**, which overflows with books, postcards, kilim cushions, odd treasures and cascades of turn-of-the-century junk. The twin shops, directly opposite the El Minzah hotel, are Tangier institutions that have furnished (and then a generation later cleared away) the oriental excesses of many an expatriate villa. Their intriguing interiors are among the most restful and interesting places in Tangier. Prices are high, but both shops have good stock and there is absolutely no sales pressure. Attempts to bargain are skilfully deflected by a wonderfully perplexed look.

The American Legation

Open Mon, Wed, Thurs, 10am–1pm, 3–5pm or by appointment, © (09) 935317.

Although the American Legation at 8 Zankat d'Amerique is actually within the walls of the old city, it is almost impossible to find by yourself once you are in the medina. The only reliable way to approach it is to walk down Zankat Salah Eddine el Ayoubi from the Grand Socco, turn up Zankat Portugal (left at the first crossroads) and then left up a flight of steps to enter the medina through an archway. The shaded gate of the Legation is a few metres further on the left, under a covered arch.

The Legation was established here in 1821 on the edge of the *mellah*, the despised Jewish quarter of town, as a gift from Sultan Moulay Sliman. It now extends over both sides of the alley, connected by an overhead arch.

Inside, Marguerite McBey has created a permanent art collection on the ground floor that contains a charming mixture of Moroccan and Western artists who have worked in Tangier. There are sketches, prints, watercolours and oils. She has also lent the fine portraits that can be seen upstairs, executed by her late husband, James McBey, the vigorous self-taught Aberdonian engraver-painter who produced much of his finest work in Morocco.

The first floor contains a range of elegantly furnished 19th-century New England-style rooms that overlook a series of courtyards. These house an extensive collection of old engravings, prints and maps of Tangier as well as the correspondence between the sultan and George Washington. The government of Morocco was the first to recognize the independence of the USA, but a closer study of the letters reveals that the subject they primarily debate is the amount of gold and silver America is to pay in order to buy immunity from Moroccan corsairs. The Legation has also made a niche for itself as a reference library for university students, a working lending library for English readers and a research centre for scholars.

Leaving the Legation it is surprisingly easy to thread your way down through the back streets of the *mellah* to the Petit Socco—but for some reason it doesn't work in the other direction. Alternatively you can leave the way you came. Almost directly opposite the Legation gateway, on Zankat Portugal, is the entrance to the extensive enclosed **Jewish graveyard**. There is a buzzer by the grey gates and the guardians will usually allow interested visitors to explore this wilderness of carved flat stones, ringed with cypress trees: a half-overgrown oasis of silence in this town of ceaseless movement. It is easier if you are, or at least pretend to be, Jewish; but whatever your religion, leave a tip as you depart. As you rejoin Rue Salah Eddine, a street almost opposite leads up towards the **Old Spanish theatre** with its dilapidated façade of Andalusian tiles bravely awaiting a long-delayed audience.

The Medina

There is an enormous and innocent fascination in blindly exploring a Moroccan medina. Its confusing landscape of dark tunnels, worn staircases, twisting narrowing alleys, old secretive closed doorways, veiled women and aggressive youths is like some dream or nightmare sequence from adolescence. Tangier's medina follows the ancient Roman city plan. The medina walls mark the line of the Roman defences, the kasbah is on the old fort, the grand mosque rises on the site of a temple to Neptune and the Petit Socco covers the forum area.

Rue des Siaghines

If you pass through the right-hand of the two medina arches leading out of the Grand Socco, you will find yourself on the busiest and widest market street of the medina, thickly lined with the major tourist bazaars. This is the Rue des Siaghines, the silversmith's street, though there is little to justify that name today. Off to the right, two alleyways lead into the *mellah*, the **old Jewish quarter**, where there are over ten synagogues, the most impressive of which are the old Nahom Temple and the Ribby Tahya Temple. Back on Rue des Siaghines you pass a locked **Spanish Catholic church** complete with a bronze dome on your right. It was supposedly established on the site of the old Franciscan mission, where five of the brethren were slaughtered by the Muslims in the course of their preaching ministry. St Francis on hearing their fate cursed the city, *O Tingis! Tingis, O dementia Tingis, illusa civitas* ('Oh Tangier! Tangier, oh mad Tangier, foolish citizens…').

The Petit Socco

At the end of the Rue des Siaghines lies the Petit Socco. In the days of the international city this was the centre for male prostitution, boy brothels, and pornographic film shows. Rooms in the adjacent streets could be rented by the half-hour. It still retains a furtive, slightly conspiratorial air, a place where you can readily imagine the shadowy figures of Camille Saint-Saëns, William Burroughs, Jean Genet, Jack Kerouac and Allen Ginsberg. The central café remains open throughout the night, and is a delightful place to play backgammon or ludo and sip glasses of *café au lait* after a tour of the night clubs and bars.

The Petit Socco is a convenient and recognizable place from which to explore the rest of the medina. There are two routes suggested. The first route takes you past the grand mosque and down to the port gate. The second takes you up to the kasbah quarter.

The Grand Mosque

If you walk across the Petit Socco square there are two alleys at the east end, Rue de la Marine and Rue de la Poste, which both skirt the grand mosque (forbidden to non-Muslims) and then descend through the old area of the tanneries back to the port gates below the medina. Take the left of these two, Rue de la Marine, which passes a fountain in front of the grand mosque. The bulk of the mosque is hidden by shop fronts but the impressive gates, its green and white minaret and acreage of green tiled roof can be seen. It was built by Moulay Ismaïl over the ruins of a Portuguese cathedral, itself raised on the foundations of an earlier mosque built over a Roman temple. Opposite the mosque you can see the gates of a **medersa** founded by the Merenids in the 14th century. Inevitably, it was destroyed by the English, but rebuilt in the 18th century by Sultan Sidi Mohammed and restored in this century as a school by Mohammed V.

After the mosque you reach a terrace overlooking the port, built on top of the **Bordj el Marsa**, the port battery, which contains two cannons supplied by W. G. Armstrong of Newcastle and was constructed on the orders of Sultan Moulay Hassan in 1882. Just to the south of this bastion stands the port gate, originally the main entrance into the medina.

Coming off the terrace, turn right along Rue Dar Baroud, which takes you past the Hôtel Continental where you can have mint tea in the tranquil faded grandeur of its hall. Another reward for the inquisitive explorer is the Café Makima, a hidden Moroccan local tearoom which overlooks the sea walls (just follow Rue Dar Baroud to the little Place de l'Arsenal, then follow Rue Zaitouna and Rue Bouhacin to the end).

The Kasbah Quarter

The easiest way to approach the kasbah quarter is to stay outside the medina walls. From the Grand Socco follow Rue d'Italie, lined with aged colonial balconies, street stalls and the tables of the Café des Colonnes. Continue up the steep Zankat al Kasbah to the kasbah gate, then follow the tarmac road, Rue Riad Sultan, to enter the open square in front of the Dar el Makhzen museum.

A more satisfactory approach is from the Petit Socco. Take the first narrow left turning after the Rue des Siaghines, the dark shop-lined Rue des Chrétiens, which after about 150m joins Rue Ben Raisul, which climbs up past an ornamental fountain on your left before reaching the stairs to **Bab el Assa**, the gate of watchfulness. This open gateway leads directly into the pebble-paved square (known as the Méchouar or Place de la Kasba) before the Dar el Makhzen (Government House).

The kasbah quarter, which is the highest part of the medina, has been the preserve of palaces and castles for thousands of years. Roman governors, Byzantine counts, Arab princes and Portuguese crusaders all succeeded in possessing this citadel. When they left Tangier in 1685, the English destroyed the ancient medieval fortress (which they knew as York Castle) with fire, gunpowder and pickaxes. What you see now was built by Sultan Moulay Ismaïl and his pacha in the late 17th century.

In the late 19th century British remittance men, like the writers Walter Harris and Richard Hughes, built oriental palaces for themselves here behind innocuous pisé walls. A continuous gallery of exquisites have settled, danced, dined and debauched here ever since. One such decadent fed his cats from tins of caviar and bankrupted himself entertaining the sister of the king. Barbara Hutton gave her silk underwear away to the people in the street after a day of use, employed Saharan nomads as doormen, and in moments of boredom distributed money to her guests in order to persuade them to leave.

The Méchouar—Place de la Kasba

In the Méchouar, also known as the Place de la Kasba, the area that is immediately around the Bab el Assa was the site for the public execution of government business. Here the pacha would marshal troops before issuing out of the town on campaign, here he would publicly receive the zankat tax, judge the accused and order the immediate punishment of the guilty. A flight of steps leads up to the cool triple-bayed audience hall, the Dar ech Chera. This was connected by an interior passage to the neighbouring prison, with its barred windows, which stands immediately to the right. No one was sentenced to imprisonment here, as the jail was used simply for holding the accused before trial, and debtors until their families paid up. The entrance to the palace-museum is up the alley to the left, above which rises the octagonal minaret of the kasbah mosque.

On the seaward length of outer wall of the square a gate, the **Bab er Raha**, leads to a terrace with a fine view over the Straits. A rough path allows you to follow the sea walls of the medina from the outside. In addition, a cascade of rubbish flows from the houses of the medina down the sea cliffs to create the perfect odour to give a complete impression of a medieval walled city. The port compound is securely fenced, so that ultimately you will have to retrace your steps.

Dar el Makhzen

Open Wed-Mon 9.30am–1pm, 3–6.00pm; closed Tues; adm, © (09) 932097.

The 17th-century palace built by Sultan Moulay Ismaïl and embellished by his pacha and successors now houses a museum. It was last used as a palace in 1912 by Moulay Hafid, his four wives and sixty concubines, who stayed here while a larger palace was built to the west of the city. Accommodation was cramped and the ex-sultan was forced to use the gatehouse, where he played cards with his European friends and carried on with his scholarly research into the Sufi Tijaniyya brotherhood.

As in most museums in Morocco, the actual structure of the palace vies with the exhibits for your attention. The **Bit el Mâl**, the treasury hall, holds immense strongboxes and—in symbolic juxtaposition—the enclosed sedan-chair with which virgin brides would be transported from the house of their father to that of their husband. The private apartments are arranged around an **interior courtyard**. The different forms of decoration—deep carved floral motifs on dark stained cedar doors, *zellij* tile work, plaster carved with rich calligraphic forms of Koranic verse—all compete for attention. Only the baroque details on the carved marble capitals add a jarring note, indicating the work of Italian rather than local craftsmen.

The **portable arts of Morocco** are triumphantly displayed in salons off this interior courtyard. Each room displays a different collection: musical instruments, swords and rifles, leatherwork, fine embroidery, wrought iron, the more delicate incised and damascened metal ware, kilims and carpets. The pottery collection illustrates all the different styles of the artisans of Meknès, Safi, Tamegroute and Fès, pointing up the manner in which the hues of green, blue and yellow in the tradition of floral ceramic decoration contrast with the more austere obsessive blue and white of the geometric tradition. The room devoted to the products of Fès is the natural climax of the exhibition, where the illuminated and beautifully bound Korans deserve special attention.

The **Archaeological Museum** is down a passage off the inner courtyard. The mosaic of Venus and the copies of the bronze busts recovered from Roman Volubilis are the most striking exhibits—the originals can be seen in Rabat. There are also a number of objects recovered from the classical sites of Lixus, Banasa, Thamusida, Tamuda, Cotta, and Sala Colonia, and a map illustrating the extent of the Roman province. Upstairs there are four rooms devoted to Morocco's prehistory, with displays of coins, ceramic shards, flintwork and a number of excavated funerary remains.

The Sultan's Garden

The walls of the Dar el Makhzen enclose a beautiful, mature Andalucian garden. There is a formal shrubbery, with constant delightful changes of light, odour and colour that contrast strongly with the monochrome details of Phoenician graves. Orange, canary palm and lemon trees provide shade whilst at dusk datura and jacaranda fill the garden with a rich heady perfume. On the northern side of the garden there are craft halls that are sometimes filled with carpet-makers. As you leave the garden you pass the entrance to the Détroit Restaurant, founded by Brion Gysin. This was once the last word in chic, but has long since become more reminiscent of a cross-Channel ferry. It is seldom open for meals but offers tea, a fine selection of Moorish pastries and a good view over the Straits of Gibraltar.

The Marshan

If you leave the medina by the kasbah gate you can walk west, parallel to the coast, along Rue Assad Ibn Farrat towards the Marshan, once a smart residential district up on the sea cliff but now gently ageing. You will pass the football stadium on your left, the centre of Tangier life for the one o'clock Sunday match and surrounded the rest of week with informal games played in the dusty shade of eucalyptus trees. Opposite, on the right, Rue Haffa leads to an open green space overlooking the sea. Here there are a number of superbly sited **Phoenician rock-cut tombs**, which point due east through the Pillars of Hercules.

Palais Mendoub (Forbes Museum)

Previously open Fri-Wed 10am–5pm; closed Thurs, free, tips accepted.

On one corner of the Marshan's main square is the Palais Mendoub, the 1920s palace of the sultan's representative in International Tangier, which was bought and restored by the American publisher Malcolm Forbes. He filled it with a large but slightly bizarre collection of Western militaria and **military miniatures**, featuring battles such as the Somme, Waterloo and Dien Bien Phu. Of more immediate relevance to Morocco are the displays on the battle of Tankodibo against the African kingdom of Songhai in 1591, when the Saadian Sultan Ahmed el Mansour had his army cross the Sahara to capture the gold mines, the Battle of the Three Kings in 1578, when the Portuguese invasion of Morocco by King Sebastian was defeated, and the Green March of 1975, when King Hassan II recovered the Spanish-held Western Sahara. However, the museum has sometimes been closed in recent years when the collection has been lent to exhibitions abroad, and its long-term future is in question, so you may or may not find it open. Even if it is closed, the exterior of the house is impressive, and the gardens, with immaculate terraces descending to the sea, offer spectacular views.

The road to the left of the museum, Rue Shakespeare (Mohammed Tazi), passes two large 19th-century mansions before it eventually deteriorates into a track that takes you to the healing sands of the Jews' Beach (*see* p.107 'Excursions from Tangier'). Almost opposite the museum is the **Palais Marshan**, now a conference hall but originally planned to hold the parliament of International Tangier.

The empty plinth that stands by the football stadium used to support an impressive bronze monument to the traveller **Ibn Batuta** (1304–77), the Muslim Marco Polo. He was born in Tangier, trained in Islamic law, and travelled all over the Islamic world and beyond, from China to Timbuktu. Sadly, some of Tangier's present citizens stole the statue one night.

Charih Hassan II will take you back to the central Zankat Belgica, passing on your left the sanctuary **tomb of Tangier's patron saint**, Sidi Bou Araquiza, and then on the left the Catholic **cathedral** with its inverted minaret spire. Beyond can be seen the massive, high and inelegant minaret of the Kuwaiti Mosque.

The Seafront

At midday the **port** and the baking expanse of heated tarmac and dock sheds are not much of an attraction. At dusk or dawn it can be interesting to wander through the port gates and watch the fishing boats preparing to sail or landing their catch. Just inside the port gates on the right is the **Tangier Yacht Club**, which though theoretically members-only is usually quite welcoming to any reasonably dressed and affable visitor.

The **beach** stretches east of the port, bordered by the railway line and the ugly silhouettes of large, modern beach hotels. Though it provides sheltered and safe swimming it is usually worth the effort of travelling to any of the less crowded beaches further east or to the west of Tangier (see p. 107 'Excursions from Tangier').

Swimming or **playing football** on the beach is free to all, although a local law forbids changing or wearing heavy clothing on the beach. This is thought to have been designed to exclude traditionally dressed Muslim women from the seafront. Walking east beyond the line of bars, clubs, restaurants and changing-rooms you enter a soliciting ground made famous in the diaries of Joe Orton, though the Miami Beach, Macumba and Windmill Club bars might be just as efficient. The Windmill has a nightly cabaret in the summer, and the beach after dark can have some unusual human tableaux. By day an efficient police and first aid post opposite Les Almohades Hotel discourages such activities.

Where to Stay

There are at least 50 hotels and *pensions* scattered throughout Tangier, but advance booking is still advisable in high season.

luxury

El Minzah, ✆ (09) 935885, ✉ (09) 934546, at 85 Zankat El Houria is one of the most celebrated hotels in Morocco. It is a solid building standing right in the centre of Tangier, although its extent has been cunningly hidden from the street. The interior is ranged around a cool Moorish courtyard with gardens tucked in a broad crescent to the east. It has a swimming pool, tennis court, two restaurants and a bar, so that even if you can't afford one of the 100 rooms the charm of the place can still be enjoyed for the price of a judiciously sipped drink.

Le Mirage, ✆ (09) 333331, ✉ (09) 333492, situated on the cliffs above the Caves of Hercules some 20 minutes from the city centre, is a luxurious new complex of 21 bungalows set in an extensive garden. Life centres on the swimming pool which, like the rest of the hotel, looks out onto the rolling Atlantic surf

expensive

Since the demise of the Grand Hôtel Villa de France, which now stands empty in its gardens above the Grand Socco awaiting development by its Iraqi owner, there is no immediate first choice among the upper-mid-range hotels. The beach-front **Rif** at 152 Avenue des FAR, ✆ (09) 941731/77/66, ✉ (09) 941794, has the advantage of good views from the bedrooms, a *hammam* and a pool with a grotto cascade tucked into the tight back garden. The **Rembrandt**, ✆ (09) 937870–2, has a good central position, on the corner of Blvd Pasteur and Av Mohammed V, and has a pool and a popular bar. The **Tanjah Flandria** at 6 Av Mohammed V, ✆ (09) 933279, ✉ (09) 934347, has been renovated to a high state of efficiency and boasts a roof top pool, *hammam*, disco, art gallery—you name it.

moderate

The **Continental** at 36 Rue Dar Baroud, ✆ (09) 931024, ℻ (09) 931143, is a distinguished 19th-century hotel tucked away on the edge of the medina overlooking the port. It has no bar or restaurant but gives you the welcome feel of staying in a well-furnished house, and has a splendid view over the harbour from its terrace. If you book in advance, ask for a room with a harbour view and see if either nos. 108 or 208 are spare. The entrance can be approached by car or taxi by following the road to the west of the Port Gate which zig-zags up a narrowing road to Rue Dar Baroud. A more functional alternative would be the **Africa** at 17 Rue Moussa Ibn Noussair (Zankat El Moutanabi), ✆ (09) 935511, which has a bar, restaurant and roof-top pool and is just a street south of Blvd Pasteur.

inexpensive

There is a large selection of hotels opposite the train station and port gates on the palm lined beachfront avenue variously known as Charih Espagna or Av des F.A.R. There is also a row of pensions along Zankat Salah Eddine el Ayoubi which have an unwelcome reputation for charging well over the odds at peak times or when faced with a desperate-looking new arrival. You will be much better off in the **Biarritz** at 102 Av des FAR, ✆ (09) 932473. The **Valencia** at 72, ✆ (09) 930770, and the **Cecil** at 112, ✆ (09) 931087, charge more of a premium for their useful position.

There are also a number of useful addresses tucked away in the new town streets. The **De Paris** at 42 Charih Pasteur, ✆ (09) 931877, the **Lutetia** at 3 Rue du Prince Moulay Abdellah (Rue C. Goya), ✆ (09) 931866, and **El Muniria** on Rue Magellan, ✆ (09) 935337, are all small functional places right at the heart of things. The Muniria has the distinction that it housed William Burroughs in room 9 while he wrote *The Naked Lunch*.

cheap (in the medina)

The pensions around the Petit Socco, in the heart of the medina, are some of the most characterful places in Tangier. Many have big, well-proportioned bedrooms with large beds and shuttered balconies overlooking the cafés. Some of them once served as brothels, but are now perfectly secure and proper. Choose from the **Mauretania**, 2 Rue de la Kasbah (Rue des Chrétiens), ✆ (09) 934677, or at no. 8 the **Pension Becerra**, ✆ (09) 932369, with the **Fuentes** at no. 9, ✆ (09) 934469, above the first-floor café. There is also a good selection along Rue de la Poste, which leads off east from the Petit Socco, including the **Palace Hotel** at no. 2, ✆ (09) 936128, and the **Pension Marhaba** at no. 14, ✆ (09) 938802. The **Olid** and the **Mamora** Hotels at no. 12 and no. 19 are also fine but a bit above this price range.

camping

The campsites are all too far out of town—the **Miramonte**, ✆ (09) 937133 is on the Marshan plateau 3km to the west of the port; the **Tingis**, ✆ (09) 940191, 6km to the east, is to be avoided, and **Camp Robinson** is 8km west, ✆ (09) 938765, in the holiday complex around the Caves of Hercules. A cheap central pension is really much more practical. If you want to camp, Asilah is a much better base.

Eating Out

There is no need to eat in your hotel. There are a number of well-established New Town restaurants, mostly found along the streets just off from Blvd Pasteur, that serve fresh fish and a variety of French, Italian and Spanish dishes. The licensed restaurants serving Moroccan food tend to include tourist-oriented floor shows that can vary from appetite-destroying belly dancing to the soothing repetitive melodies of Moroccan traditional music. As ever in Morocco, some of the freshest and certainly the cheapest food can be found in the café-restaurants on the edge of the medina.

expensive

The El Minzah Hotel at 85 Zankat El Houria (Rue de la Liberté), © (09) 935885, has two separate restaurants. The **El Erz** serves a wide range of European dishes, which tend towards the bland, but it has an extensive wine list. It is more rewarding to book a low table in the opulent hall of the **El Korsan**, which serves traditional Moroccan food of the highest quality. If you are looking for a more low-key evening you can take a table at the brasserie-style **Patio Wine Bar** in the courtyard.

Belying its Spanish name the **Restaurant Las Conchas** at 30 Rue Ahmed Chaouki, © (09) 931643, serves the best French food in town, and you would be wise to reserve a table in advance.

moderate (new town restaurants)

The **San Remo** at 15 Rue Ahmed Chaouki (Rue Murillo), © (09) 938451, is a clean, simple, reasonably cheap and popular Italian restaurant. Try the house speciality of dressed crab or the lasagne, followed by their chocolate gâteau. They also have a new property across the road, which offers take-away pizza. The **Nautilius**, © (09) 936454, is at 9 Zankat Khalid Ibn Oualid (Rue Velazquez), and is a small and deservedly popular restaurant run by Rachid Temsamani. Try the peanut soup, followed by their choice of fish; if you arrive early, or they are booked up, you can pop into **L'Ibis** bar-restaurant at no. 6 for a pre-dinner drink. In the same area is **Negresco**, 20 Zankat El Mexique, © (09) 938097, which has a tapas bar next door, and specializes in seafood and paellas.

La Grenouille, © (09) 936242 (closed Mon), is a French restaurant on Rue Rembrandt, off Blvd Pasteur, which serves a three-course menu with wine by the carafe; **Le Provençal**, Rue Fernando de Portugal, © (09) 937471, is another place to find good French cooking. **Romero** at 12 Rue du Prince Moulay Abdellah (Rue C. Goya), © (09) 932277, specializes in Spanish seafood dishes, with an excellent house paella, and delicious seafood is also found at **Restaurant Populaire Saveur**, 2 escalier Waller Local, just down the road from the El Minzah Hotel, © (09) 336326.

Guitta's at 110, Zankat Sidi Bou Abib, © (09) 937333, is one of Tangier's surviving institutions from the international era, tucked away rather reclusively in a villa. Their fairly straightforward menu of soups, salads and grills gives way to a traditional English lunch on Sunday.

moderate (Moroccan cuisine)

Raihani's, 10 Zankat Ahmed Chaouki, ✆ (09) 934866, just opposite the cannon terrace on Blvd Pasteur, is the best of the bunch. It serves good Moroccan food in a calm interior—try their *tagine de poisson* washed down with a bottle of Boulaouane.

Damascus at 2 Rue du Prince Moulay Abdellah (Rue C. Goya), ✆ (09) 934730, is furnished in a garish confusion of carved plaster, cushions and coloured lights and offers floor shows to accompany its *bastilla* and *tagine*. If you want still more of an Orientalist–*Arabian Nights* flavour you could try the **Mamounia Palace**, ✆ (09) 932277, perched above the Rue des Siaghines as you head towards the Petit Socco. If you can get a table overlooking the street this will more than make up for the slightly perfunctory set menu. The **Marhaba**, 67 Place Ahannar, ✆ (09) 937643, serves excellent Moroccan food in its wonderfully over-furnished Moorish hall, all to the intoxicating strains of traditional Moroccan music.

The **Tricka** restaurant, 11 Rue Ben Raisul, is an exceptional place, open for lunch and dinner. The simple furniture is arranged around a high internal courtyard, and there is an elaborate selection of pictures on its walls. It occupies a traditional house in the heart of the medina, has a Moroccan menu that makes enthusiastic use of local spices, and they can send out for some wine given warning. A further advantage, and one that will allow it to maintain its special identity, is that it is tucked away in the heart of the medina on the alley that connects the Petit Socco to the kasbah.

cheap café-restaurants

One of the most entertaining places to eat in Tangier is in one of the eight cafés that line the medina side of the Grand Socco, at tables behind the grills or up the steep staircases that lead to secretive dining rooms above. Salads, grilled or fried vegetables, meat and fish are available at about 10–25dh a head.

In the heart of the medina on the Petit Socco, the **Restaurant Ahlen**, 8 Rue des Postes, is run with considerable panache by its moustachioed *patron*. Steaming *harira* and freshly roasted chickens are the stock in trade.

cafés

Tangier is famous for its café society and there is no better place to watch the evening promenade than one of the tables around the Place de France, either at the **Café de Paris** or, across the street, the **Café de France** and the **Semiramis**. They are also excellent places to while away the midday heat with a book. You cannot overdress; locals are all impeccably turned out. The best shoe-shine in Tangier, and information service, is provided by Laarbi Ouezzani who once ran a bar in Aberdeen for three years, and now works from the Café de Paris. Further down Blvd Pasteur you will find the **Metropole**, conveniently close to the delicious eats available at **Le Petit Prince** patisserie. **La Colombe**, opposite the Rembrandt Hotel on Av Mohammed V, has a good selection of cakes including the gazelle horn of pastry stuffed with honey and almonds, the most famous Moroccan pâtisserie speciality. For a really long mooch over a favourite book, though, there is only one place, the **Haifa Café**, overlooking the sea on the west side of the city behind the Palais Mendoub.

In the medina, the place to head for is the **Café Tingis**, on the left as you enter the Petit Socco, to savour the well-worn grace of the waiters providing mint tea or *café au lait* on its narrow terrace. From the café on the first floor of the Hotel Fuentes, though, you will get a calmer view of the busy square.

bars

The **Caid's Bar** in the El Minzah Hotel is a well known international gathering point. Prices are high, but you can loll around in its deep leathery atmosphere and contemplate the portrait of Harry Caid Maclean. Considerably down market from this is the tapas bar **Juana de Arco**, on Zankat Allal Ibn Abdellah, which is something of a meeting place for Tangier's Moroccan literary and artistic community. **Dean's Bar**, the watering place of Hemingway and Errol Flynn, still functions, although socially it plummeted after Dean died from a cocaine overdose in 1963. You will find it at 2 Rue d'Amérique-du-Sud. Now run by Brahim, it retains its secretive air, photographs of the famous and polished brass bars. Other useful New Town bars include the **Panama** at 17 Av Mohammed V; **Bar le Bourse** at 8 Rue Mexique, and **Bar Lisbo** at 7 Rue El Jarraoui.

The Pub at 4 Rue Soroya, ✆ (09) 934789, is near the Tanjah Flandria hotel. Despite, or perhaps because of, its name and English decoration it is a popular place with both visitors and Moroccans. Beneath William Burrough's old haunt the El Muniria hotel is the **Tanger Inn** at 1 Rue Magellan, ✆ (09) 935337. It's run by ex-guardsman John Sutcliffe, whose book *The Unknown Pilgrim* is on sale at the bar, and open till 2am.

There are also a lot of bar-restaurants along Avenue des FAR beside the beach, which are only open in summer. If you want to eat rather than just mix, the **Nautilius** is probably the best, although the expatriate haunt **Emma's BBC Bar** has a great following amongst devotees of English home cooking. The summer-only bars along the beachfront also include such celebrated gay cruising grounds as the **Miami Beach**, ✆ (09) 943401 and the **Windmill**, ✆ (09) 940907.

All the package hotels have their own bars, which are usually well worth avoiding. The bars in the large hotels in the new town, such as the Rif, Tanjah Flandria and Rembrandt can, however, draw in a more varied clientele.

Shopping

Ignore the general tendency to rubbish the shopping in Tangier; there are some well-stocked bazaars along the principal thoroughfares of the medina, the Rue des Siaghines, Rue des Chrétiens and Rue Almanzor. The problem with shopping in Tangier, indeed in any major Moroccan city, is that other tourists, fresh off the boat or plane, have often been persuaded to pay spectacular prices. You may have to spend more time than usual establishing your rational credentials and bargaining down to a sensible price.

Contemporary art and original craft work can be seen in the American Legation, the Tangier Gallery of Contemporary Art and Galerie Delacroix, but (except for occasional exhibitions) cannot be purchased. Fortunately a couple of commercial art galleries have recently been established. **Boutique Majid**, 66 rue des Chrétiens, contains a wonderful collection of art and craft from all over the world, selected by its owner Abdelmajid El Fenni. The **Tanjah Flandria Art Gallery** is behind the hotel of the same name–the entrance to its first-floor showrooms is on Rue Ibn Rochd, © (09) 933000. Another showroom for art and crafts is the **Volubilis** at 6 Sidi Boukoiya in the Kasbah district (closed Mon), and the **Bazaar Tindouf** (*see* p.95) often has treasures among its very varied stock.

As well as in the souks more traditional Moroccan craft work can be found at Tangier's **Ensemble Artisanal**, © (09) 933100, on Zankat Belgica. Traditional crafts are also taught here, and the fixed-price showrooms will give you an idea of the maximum price you should pay for an article when bargaining in the souks. The chipping of coloured tiles to create the pieces for *zellij* mosaics is fascinating to watch. There is also the book-binding service run from a stall by Mohammed Lymouri, which is patronized by foreign embassies and government ministries in Rabat. He charges from 100 to 200dh a volume to 'Morocco bind' a book, although you will need to give him a few days' notice.

The **Madini Perfumerie** at 14 Rue Sebou in the medina, accessible from Rue d'Italie or the Petit Socco, is a great treat, a shop rich in coloured liquids. Its shelves are laden with heavy bottles containing over 60 different scents, some made to recipes held secret by generations of the Madini family.

The **Epicerie Marhaba** at 45 Av Mohammed V, just west of Hôtel Rembrandt, or the **Spanish grocery** at 63 Zankat Hollanda are two of a fair number of **grocers** in the new town that sell wine, spirits and beer. If you want to **assemble a picnic**, the central courtyard **market**, nicknamed the 'bourgeois market', three streets down Zankat Fès if you are going south from the Place de France, is ideal. Also a good place to find fresh foods is the covered market off the **Grand Socco**.

Thanks to its long literary connections Tangier is a city where it's easy to find international reading matter. The **Librairie des Colonnes**, 54 Boulevard Pasteur, has an excellent range of relevant **English and French literature**, Moroccan history and books on a wide variety of Islamic and related topics. It enjoys a central position in the literary world of Tangier and is decorated with a series of photographic portraits of local figures.

Sports

There is an 18-hole **golf course** nearby, the Country Club de Boubanah. **Horse riding** is available at Club de l'Etrier at Boubanah and **tennis** at a club on Zankat Belgica. Tangier beach is safe for **swimming** and is also a venue for friendly **football** matches.

Entertainment and Nightlife

Tangier's nightlife is concentrated on a group of streets just south of Charih Pasteur; principally Zankat El Mexique/Zankat El Moutanabi (Rue Sanlúcar) and Rue du Prince Moulay Abdellah (Rue C. Goya).

Scotts is the simplest and most famous club on Zankat El Moutanabi. The walls, decorated with Stuart Church's homoerotic pictures of young Moroccan boys in Highland uniform, set the mood for this club, which embraces a friendly mix of homosexual and heterosexual couples. Nearby there are a string of more conventional disco clubs, such as **Churchill, Rancho Bar** and **Gospel**. The **Koutoubia Palace** is the only one to charge an admission ticket. It hosts a variety of cabaret turns: belly dancers, fire eaters and dance troupes, which alternate with live bands in a capacious hall with ugly plastic seats and two busy bars.

Rue du Prince Moulay Abdellah (Rue C. Goya) has a further selection of clubs that include the **Borsalino**, ✆ (09) 943163, guarded by a bouncer dressed as a Chicago gangster. This is the 'smartest' of the clubs, with a white interior designed to contrast well with a blazer. Also along this street, at no. 11, ✆ (09) 935564 is the **Morocco Palace** where live Moroccan bands and cabaret turns perform until about 1am, and may be followed by a couple of hours of dancing. Nearby is the **Ranch Club**, a wonderfully seedy place where the bouncer has a double role as a lead singer in one of the local bands. The club is full of hostesses who urge visitors to be generous and drink more quickly in magnificently stereotypical style, while the elegant dark lady behind the bar consumes gin in a flash and tidies the ashtrays by spilling their contents on the floor. Prices and entertainment are endlessly variable.

Many hotels also have discos. One of the best is **La Palace Disco**, entrance on Rue Ibn Rochd, in the Hôtel Tanjah Flandria. Others include the **Ali Baba** at the Chellah hotel, 49 Rue Allal ben Abdullah, the **Up 2000** on top of Les Almohades hotel, ✆ (09) 940431, and **Aladin's Club** on top of the Solazur Hotel on Av des FAR.

Festivals

The Palais Marshan is the seat of many national and international conferences: a **music festival** is held in Tangier in July, and an **International Week** and the ***moussem* of Dar Zhirou** in September. The social season culminates in early September, the month of public festivals when the small international Tangier expatriate community is boosted by those who harbour a quiet wish to join them.

Excursions from Tangier

West to Cape Spartel, the Caves of Hercules and Cotta

Leave the city centre and follow Zankat Belgica for the road west to Cape Spartel. Three km on, the Oued el Ihoud, the Jews' river, divides the city outskirts from the garden suburb of **La Montagne**. The central tree-shaded space at the foot of La Montagne hill becomes an animated vegetable and clothes market on Sunday mornings. A dirt track to the right of this rustic forum passes below the Miramonte campsite to lead down to the small **Jews' Beach** where there is a café-restaurant run by Sidi Mustapha. The beach was named after the first landing place of the Jewish refugees who had been expelled from Spain due to the harsh religious and racial laws of the Catholic monarchs. The hot sands in the summer are a recognized cure against gout and rheumatism. In 1930, the beach was invaded by a large army of lobsters, but they have not since returned.

A road leads up the hill of La Montagne past the villas lived in by such British painters as Sir John Lavery and James McBey. La Montagne used to be dense scrubland, a refuge from where *mujaheddin*, holy warriors, harassed the infidel Portuguese and English who held the port of Tangier from the 15th to the 17th century. It was transformed into an exclusive English expatriate community from the turn of this century and now, lot by lot, is slowly returning to affluent Moroccans. Where the tarmac ends, a stone-paved cliff walk continues the 11km to the lighthouse at Cape Spartel.

The road to Cape Spartel skirts below La Montagne to pass the English-inspired People's Dispensary for Sick Animals which has a farm, a clinic and an expanding animal graveyard. The road then climbs up past heavily guarded and meticulously maintained villa-palaces of the King of Morocco, to which his deposed great uncles, the Sultans Abdul Aziz and Moulay Hafid, retired. Ravenscraig, the old villa of the British consul Sir John Drummond-Hay, is also now the property of King Hassan. The last wild lion of the region was seen from a terrace here in 1859. The celebrated English artist George Stubbs painted more than 50 pictures of a lion attacking a horse, and is supposed to have been given his obsession with the subject by witnessing an actual incident on the north Moroccan coast. The last immense palace on the right is one built recently for King Fahd of Saudi Arabia.

Continuing through these wooded hills you pass a number of tracks that lead to fine views over the straits of Gibraltar. That from the **Perdicaris Belvedere**, which is surrounded by a mature forest of Aleppo pine, is the most popular. This is where the Greek-American millionaire Perdicaris built a villa from where he was kidnapped by Raissouli (*see* p.169). The lighthouse at **Cape Spartel**, 14km from central Tangier, is built on the far northwestern corner of Africa, known to the ancients as the Cape of vines. This is a fine position from which to watch the flocks of migrating birds that travel to Europe in late March/early April and return south to Africa in October. The lighthouse is not open to the public but you can sometimes catch a glimpse of its Moorish interior courtyard—a delightful space of worn brick paving with a central schist menhir which supports a giant conch of cascading flowers and a little fountain. The nearby café is open all year round.

Travelling south from the lighthouse you pass three sandy bays separated by rock outcrops before you reach the Robinson tourist village that has developed around the **Caves of Hercules**. From the car park, concrete steps lead down to a ticket booth, which offers the opportunity to buy a woolly hat and employ a multilingual guide in addition to buying your ticket. Schist millstones have been quarried from the cave for centuries, and the incised lines high up in the cavern roof give the fanciful impression of a giant scallop shell. The sea picturesquely thunders into a turbulent cleft carved into a lower cave whilst on the cliff edge a number of blow holes produce dramatic blasts of water during a heavy swell. Until independence these caves were the haunt of prostitutes who practised their trade in the dark recesses. Customers were escorted by a guide with a lantern who discreetly extinguished the light once a choice had been made. This is no longer a feature of a tour of the caves, although prostitution may have been a very ancient tradition here. In the 1920s a pre-Neolithic gallery of hundreds of ritual phalluses was discovered in one of the more secluded sea caves.

A short 5-minute walk south from the caves takes you to the **Roman site of Cotta**, a small area of stone ruins just above the beach. A guide will appear from the neighbouring cottage and show you around this mixture of villa and Roman industrial complex, with its baths,

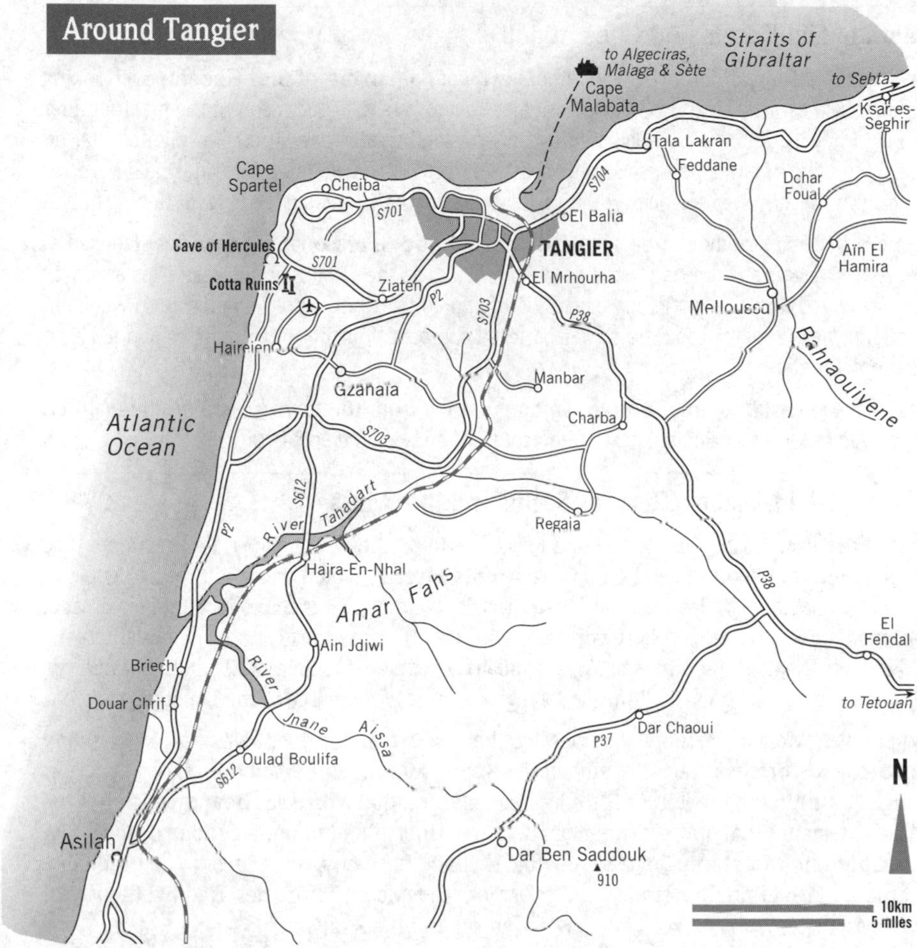

Around Tangier

temple shrine, oil press and central courtyard lined with vats that were used for processing and storing oil and the other products of the town. Like many of the classical sites on the Moroccan coast, Cotta specialized in the manufacture of the rancid sauce made from fish guts, Garum, that was so beloved of the Romans.

Where to Stay and Eating Out

The largest bay south of the Cape Spartel lighthouse is bordered by the **Café Restaurant Sol**, © (09) 931548, which can provide a moderately-priced lunch of fish and salad washed down with wine, but tends to serve dank coffee. A much better bet is the restaurant of the new **Le Mirage** hotel, © (09) 333331, which dominates the cliff above the Caves of Hercules (*see* p.101).

South to Sidi Kacem and Chez Abdou

Just south of Tangier Airport is the windblown coastal **shrine of Sidi Kacem**, overlooking the brackish estuary that also bears his name. Kacem was the fourth son of the great founder of Fès, Idriss II, but was so disgusted by his brothers' rivalry over their inheritance that he retired to a life of pious poverty on this coast. An important three-day festival is held here, on or around the summer solstice, when young brides bathe in the surf to assure their fertility.

A more hedonistic day can be spent at **Chez Abdou**, a reasonably expensive licensed al fresco fish restaurant that is tucked above the beach in the Diplomatic Forest. This area was once reserved for the pig-sticking parties of foreign consuls but is now popular with weekend picnic parties. Look out for the rather battered signpost pointing out the drive about 17km south of Tangier.

The walled coastal town of **Asilah**, an hour's drive from the town centre on the main P2 road to Rabat, is the principal destination south of Tangier (*see* pp.166–71).

East to Cape Malabata, Ksar-es-Seghir and Jbel Musa

East of the city, pass along the bay of Tangier, avoiding the new holiday developments. The Club Mediterranée occupies the grounds of **Villa Harris**, which was a gift to the people of Tangier but is now alas inaccessible. Walter Harris, London *Times* correspondent in Morocco, designed an elegant garden here complete with oriental gatehouse and ornamental towers. This Moorish fantasy, and his homosexual affairs, occupied so much of his time that his wife left him, though she only cited the gardening as grounds for divorce in the London courts.

Where the Melaleh estuary emerges by the sea are the ruined walls of an outlying **Portuguese fortress**, recently embellished with some rusting cannon. Eight km out of Tangier a turning to the left leads to the clean and tranquil **Murissat beach** which has the Mar-Bel restaurant and a few summer café-restaurants. One km on, a curious Gothic folly, the **Château Malabata**, appears on the skyline. It is now inhabited by a hospitable Moroccan farmer and his family, and the track leads down to the deserted lighthouse on Cape Malabata, with an excellent view of Tangier and the Straits.

The S704 coast road passes by many attractive and deserted beaches, rarely without a complement of beached fishing boats. If you examine the coast carefully you can spot customs men on look-out from ex-Spanish pill boxes. They were first built to halt the smuggling of arms to the Rif army of Abdel Krim in the 1920s.

Ksar-es-Seghir is 37km east of Tangier, where a ruined fortified town sits in a bay encroached by dunes and bordered to the west by the estuary of the river el Ksar. A wharf erected on this estuary provides a base for a few fishing boats. The **Caribou**, a popular fish restaurant, and the basic café-hotel **Tarik ibn Ziad** can be found beside the road which overlooks the ruins. The town was first fortified by the Merenids in the 13th century when it was known as Ksar al Majaz, the castle of the crossing, for this is the traditional site of Tariq's embarkation for the conquest of Spain. The remains of a mosque and *hammam* have been excavated from beneath the debris left by the Portuguese occupation of 1458–1550.

The road continues another 12km along the coast, with a turning to the little-visited lighthouse and beach at **Cape Cires** marking the beginning of the ascent up the flanks of Jbel

Musa. This mountain is a conspicuous feature on the eastern horizon from Tangier, its peak (842m high) often obscured in a wreath of clouds. It is the northerly extension of the line of mountains, the Haouz, that runs along the coast between Ceuta and Tetouan. Jbel Musa is one of the two Pillars of Hercules that guards the entrance to the Mediterranean. There is an old belief that a natural tunnel travels under the sea to connect Gibraltar to Jbel Musa. They do indeed have certain connections: geologically Gibraltar is a piece of Africa, and the Barbary apes and partridges there are curiously found to breed nowhere else in Europe. Both mountains have caves high up on their flanks where Mesolithic remains have been discovered. Migrating birds of prey use the thermal winds from both peaks to climb to a sufficient height to make a safe crossing of the Straits.

The old Arab port of **Ben Youch** (Balyounesh), which is also thought to have been one of the ports used for the Muslim conquest of Spain in the 8th century, lies at the foot of the mountain. The narrow tarmac road that snakes 7km down to the village has become dangerously eroded. Perched above the small beach with its grey fishing boats stands a half-ruined tower, all that remains of a Merenid palace that was built on this dramatic cliff edge and which tapped the local mineral springs to fill an extensive bath complex. From the main road there is a splendid view over Ceuta as you drop down to Fnideq, the dusty Moroccan frontier town that sits at the end of the Tetouan coast road.

Ceuta

Ceuta (Sebta) is one of the five Spanish enclaves in Morocco and has been held against an almost continuous siege—passive for long periods, at other times more violent—since 1580. It occupies the narrow spit of land lying to the east of Jbel Musa, a fiercely contested peninsula that guards the shortest crossing between Africa and Europe. For six centuries the cross and the sword have been dominant in Ceuta, symbolized by massive stone-dressed walls protected by a sea moat and the gloomy baroque interior of the cathedral. The present is represented by serried rows of ugly apartment blocks to the west and a town full of duty-free Indian shops selling cigarettes, alcohol, electrical goods and gaudy knicknacks to be smuggled across the border into Morocco.

Like Melilla, Ceuta only really makes sense as an arrival or departure point. The delays at the border crossing can add anything between ten minutes and an hour to a day visit there from Morocco. For all its seediness, though, it is a curious historical survival that can easily consume half a day. Also, its baroque churches appear particularly striking after a couple of weeks peering at the exteriors of Moroccan mosques.

The Seven Sleepers

The name Ceuta is derived from *septem*, in reference to the ancient myth of the seven sleepers. It was here that seven brothers hid from the persecution of the Roman Emperor Decius and miraculously fell asleep for 200 years, waking only when Christianity had become the official religion. The story is corroborated by a verse of the Koran, and throughout the Muslim world there are dozens of rival locations. A local variation also has Ceuta as the site of Calypso's lair, where she held Odysseus in ravishing enchantment for seven years.

History

Like practically all the good harbours along the North African shore, Ceuta was founded by the Phoenicians. It was a prosperous port throughout the classical era and became one of the chief naval bases of the late Roman and Byzantine Empires. Indeed it was the last Byzantine governor, the legendary Count Julian of Ceuta, who is considered to have welcomed Uqba ben Nafi, the first Arab conqueror. He is also said, a generation later, to have plotted the Muslim invasion of Spain in revenge for a dishonour done to his daughter by the Visigothic king. Whatever the truth of Ceuta's role, the town grew in splendour in the early Islamic period to become one of the leading centres of the region. Both El Idrissi, the celebrated geographer, and Sidi Bel Abbès, the philanthropic missionary whose memory is still cherished in Marrakech, were born here. Descriptions from the 14th century speak of its harbours packed with shipping and its streets filled with fine mosques, colleges and palatial town houses.

Disaster struck in 1415 when King John of Portugal fell on Ceuta with 200 ships and an army of 50,000 men. He knighted his four young sons amidst the carnage and smoking ruins of the once great city. The fortress passed to Spain when Philip II acquired Portugal in 1580. It has been the object of innumerable sieges, and many a sultan has won acceptance from his people by attempting to recapture it. Even at times when there was not a formal siege, the tribes of the surrounding Anjera hills have continually sniped away at the garrison.

Ceuta was the springboard for Franco's nationalist army to enter Spain in the Civil War of 1936, but since Moroccan Independence in 1956 time has hung heavily on the fortress. It is still garrisoned by bored Spanish conscripts.

Getting Around

The customs can be very thorough on both sides of the border. The Spanish are looking out for kif, the Moroccans for cheap duty-free goods from Ceuta, while a cluster of market-ladies play a grandmother's-footsteps war of attrition with the customs men in their efforts to get across the line to sell their goods on the other side. The Moroccan customs can also be keen on books, and may confiscate all books and maps of Morocco that do not show the Western Sahara as an integral portion of the nation and to the same scale. Other kinds of literature can also be considered suspicious. I have lost *M'hashish* by Mohammed Mrabet which was thought disreputable, and a book on Sufi mysticism whose title, *Islam, the way of submission*, caused great consternation.

by sea

You can buy **ferry** tickets for Algeciras or Melilla from the Transmediterranea office, © (56) 515476, on Muelle Cañonero Dato (the port road that leads to the ferry pier), or direct from the port building (Islena de Navegación), © (56) 518340. There are at least half a dozen boats a day Mon–Fri between 8.30am and 10.30pm, while on Sundays five boats depart from 8.30am–9pm, so there is usually not much of a wait.

The **hydrofoil**, however, can be booked up; details of departures and prices are available from the office at 6 Muelle Cañonero Dato, © (56) 516041.

by road

To cross by **car** into Morocco you will need a green insurance card, a vehicle registration document and a passport, and you will have to fill in an immigration form for the car and each passenger. The paperwork is not complicated, but knowing which window is in operation is more demanding. Fortunately there is a cluster of porters who for a small fee of $1 will help you sort it out. Crossing from Morocco into Ceuta you will also have to attest that you are travelling with no dirhams. There is a Citroen garage on the Muelle Cañonero Dato, a Fiat garage at 2 Av Marina Española and a Peugeot one at 20 Av Marina Española. Fill up with petrol, which is 40 per cent cheaper in Ceuta than in Morocco.

A **taxi** or the no. 7 Spanish **bus** from the Plaza de la Constitución can take you to and from the border village of Fnideq, 3km from the port. At Fnideq there is a rank of *grand taxis* that ply the 38km to Tetouan ($2 per place) and you might also find cars going direct to Tangier and Chechaouèn. If not, go to Tetouan first and carry on from there. The long-distance Spanish bus station is on the southern coast road just west of Foso de San Felipe, and has periodic coaches to Al Hoceima, Casablanca and Nador. It is usually quicker and more reliable to taxi directly down to the Tetouan bus station, which has many more services.

Tourist Information

The **tourist office** is on Muelle Cañonero Dato, ✆ (56) 509496, by the ferry pier, and can provide a complete list of pensions. The **Banco de España** is found on the Plaza de España and **Banco Popular Español** on the Paseo del Revellín. The US and Britain do not have consuls here but France and Belgium have a joint office at 47 Muelle Cañonero Dato, ✆ (56) 515741. There is a Moroccan **Banque Populaire** and an exchange booth on the Moroccan side of the border.

To **telephone** between Ceuta and Morocco involves making an international call. To call Ceuta from Morocco, dial the Spanish code of 0034, followed by 56 for Ceuta; to call Morocco from Ceuta, dial 07 followed by 212 for Morocco and the Moroccan area code, omitting the first zero in the code where there is one.

The Museum and the Plaza de Africa

Open Mon–Sat 9am–1pm, 4–6pm; Sun and holidays 10am–2pm .

Directly in front of the port is the small **Archaeological Museum** (Museo Municipal), surrounded by an Argentinian garden. Its door is protected by two 16th-century bronze cannons bearing the Portuguese royal arms. Inside is a collection of Neolithic, Punic, classical and medieval pottery shards. The star of the collection is a decorated Roman white marble sarcophagus. Outside is the entrance to the tunnels built in the 16th and 17th centuries to provide shelter from bombardments and storage for fresh water and provisions.

The **ramparts** are impressive. The massive inner walls with their angular battlements draped in bougainvillea look their best as you cross the Foso de San Felipe. Built in 1530 with the aid of Portuguese crusading orders, the battlements and twin towers guard a number of tranquil shaded gardens.

The **Plaza de Africa**, the formal centre of the town, is immediately behind these defences. This in the 14th century was the central souk for the Muslim city, and was lined with medersas and palaces. The **church of Our Lady of Africa** (Nuestra Señora de Africa) occupies the site of the old grand mosque. She is Ceuta's patron saint, and in 1744 was given authority over the town by the despairing Governor Pedro de Vargas when it was ravaged by the plague, which she promptly dispelled. King John I of Portugal had invested his first governor of Ceuta with an olive branch, and in an annual ceremony this is now presented by the current governor to the 16th-century image of the Virgin. The church is a baroque extravaganza of the early 18th century. The **cathedral** is directly opposite. It was built over the grand mosque in the 15th century, but was refurbished in line with baroque taste in 1729; it is decorated with the heraldic emblems of the various bishops of Ceuta and several immense gloomy oil paintings on the life of Christ. These are unexceptionable if you have just arrived by ferry from Spain, but have a strong impact if you have spent some time in Muslim Morocco.

In the middle of the Plaza is a **monument to the Spanish invasion** of Morocco in 1859, when General O'Donnell led an army of 25,000 out of Ceuta to do battle in the heights above Tetouan. Over 1300 of them died, but a victory Mass was sung in the grand mosque of Tetouan the next day.

To Monte Hacho

To the east the old town rambles up towards the low, fortress-crowned summit of Monte Hacho. Walking along the **Gran Vía** with its central gardens leads you past the **town hall**, decorated with panels by Mariano Bertuchi extolling the grave duties of colonialism. Just south of the **Plaza de la Constitución–Plaza Rafael Gilbert**, on the seafront, is the **Museo de la Legión** (*open Sat, Sun only, 11am–2pm, 4–6pm; adm*). This is stuffed full of militaria that recalls the extraordinary career of the *Tercio*, the Spanish Foreign Legion, and their bloody campaigns in the Rif, Sahara and as the spearhead of Franco's army in the Spanish Civil War.

Further east, in the Plaza Ramos, is the **church of San Francisco** where rests the body of the young King Sebastian of Portugal, killed as he invaded Morocco in 1578 at the battle of Ksar-el-Kebir or Alcazarquivir (see pp.177–9). His body was returned to Philip II of Spain free of charge by the Saadian Sultan Ahmed el Mansour. Sebastian became the focus of a 16th- and 17th-century quasi-nationalist cult in Portugal which believed he would be reborn to lead the country to renewed glory. Still further east, on the left, you can visit another church, **Nuestra Señora de Los Remedios**, built in 1716 and housing a prominent memorial to the Spanish struggle against Napoleon.

The old town dwindles as you come closer to **Monte Hacho** but the Avenida Marina Española, the north coast road, allows you to take a pleasant stroll right around the peninsula with views of the ferries entering the port and the distant prospect of Gibraltar. Possible halting points include the coastal cemetery, the lighthouse, and the remains of an old Portuguese fort, before you reach the turning that climbs up underneath the walls of Fort Hacho to the viewpoint by the **Ermita de San Antonio** and a statue to Franco. In the fort there is another military museum (the Museo Militar del Castillo del Desnarigado) that is again only open at weekends, 10am–2pm, 4–6pm.

Where to Stay

Unless you have forged an unusual love for Ceuta there is no need to stay a night; Tangier is only 75km away and Tetouan 38km. Hotels are surprisingly expensive for what they offer, and are often booked up by families visiting their soldier sons.

expensive

The **Gran Hôtel La Muralla** on Plaza de Africa, ✆ (56) 514940, ℻ (56) 514947, is the smartest address in Ceuta. It has 83 bedrooms, a bar, the renowned La Torre restaurant and a night club open on Saturday nights. If this is full, the **Ulises Hotel** at 5 Calle Camoens, ✆ (56) 514540, is comfortable and well placed in the centre of the old town streets.

moderate

Dropping down in price there is the **Africa** opposite the ferry terminal at 9 Muelle Cañonero Dato, ✆ (56) 509467, and two similar small, comfortable hotels at no. 23 and no. 6 on the Avenida Reyes Católicos, the **Miramar**, ✆ (56) 514146, and the **Skol**, ✆ (56) 514161.

inexpensive

Try for rooms in the **Pensión La Perla**, ✆ (56) 515828, or the **Pensión Los Angeles**, ✆ (56) 513892, both of which are on Calle Real.

Eating Out

For seafood, go to **Casa Fernando**, ✆ (56) 514082, out on the Benzu beach-front at the cleaner northwestern corner of Ceuta, which has a particularly good reputation. For a passing snack use the **Delphin Verde**, which is easy to find, just opposite the ferry pier on Muelle Cañonero Dato.

Nightlife

For evening tapas in traditional Spanish style you could call in on any of a number of bars in the old town, such as **Regina** on Calle Independencia. The **Pub Bo Go** on Calle Cervantes has been recommended as a late night bar, while in the summer months there are several discos open for the season, at **Calle Real**, the **Bogoteca**, and the **Coconut** on Carretera del Jaral, and out at the **Ermita de San Antonio** on Monte Hacho.

Festivals

There is a carnival in February, and processions during Easter Week; another religious *fiesta* at the Ermita de San Antonio on 13 July; a procession of fishing boats on 16 July to celebrate Our Lady of Mount Carmel; and the festival of Our Lady of Africa on 5 August.

The Coast from Ceuta to Tetouan

The line of the Haouz mountains runs parallel to the shore, its fierce silhouettes graphically representing the old predatory power of the Anjera hill tribe. Superb Mediterranean beaches continue for 40km in an almost unbroken line from the Moroccan border at Fnideq to Martil, the old corsair port of Tetouan. Moroccan families come to camp along sections of this beach every summer to escape the heat of the cities. Large hotels have recently been built beside two brand new marinas, an upgraded golf course and the waterslides of the Blue Lagoon Aquapark. This rather amorphous beach strip is increasingly known as Smir-Restinga and unless you come on a package deal would seem to have little attraction.

The village of **Fnideq** is on the edge of the *cordon sanitaire* that surrounds the frontier around Ceuta, so it stands at a polite 2km back from the custom posts. It is a rough place filled with mechanic's workshops, cafés and heavily draped market ladies on smuggling missions. A new hotel, the **Sebta** on Blvd Mohammed V, © (09) 976140, might make a distinctively different base for exploring both Ceuta and the surrounding beaches.

If you stop anywhere let it be at **Mdiq**, a small coastal village that is halfway to becoming a resort. The Mdiq fishing harbour built out from the Ras Tarf hill is lined with wooden fishing boats which can be seen in every stage of construction along the carpenters' quay. Peregrine falcons nest in the cliffs above. The fish café-restaurant in the harbour is the most interesting place for lunch; if you are intending to stay, the **Hotel Playa** at 31 Boulevard Lalla Nouzha, © (09) 975166, is charming and reasonably priced.

The other side of the hill from Mdiq, 2km by road, is **Cabo Negro beach**. It has the finest stretch of sand in the area, and is dominated, but fortunately not yet owned, by the **Club Mediterranée Yasmina**. Beside it is the ugly but enjoyable **Hotel [illegible] Marou**, © (09) 978176/18. Just off the beach is the restaurant **Al Khayma**, with Moroccan meals served [illegible] a Moorish interior. **La Ferma**, a few kilometres inland, is [illegible] expensive, an old house admirably converted into a restaurant [illegible] little crowded in the evening. Here you can also hire horses.

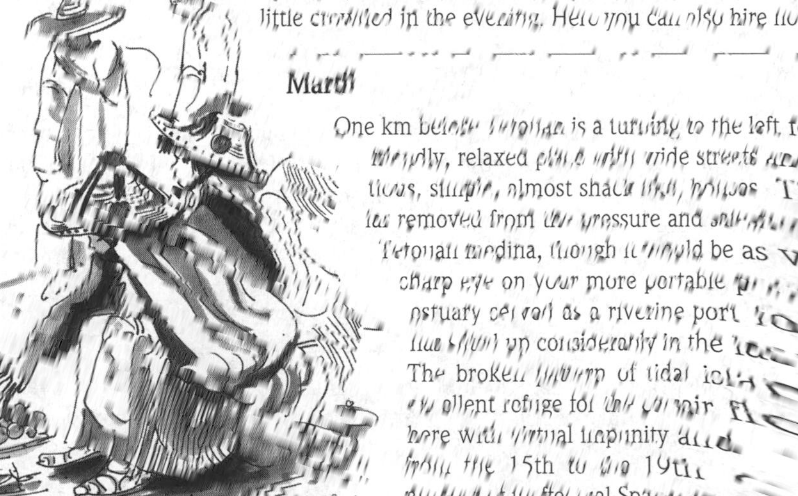

Martil

One km before Tetouan is a turning to the left, fo[illegible] friendly, relaxed place with wide streets and [illegible] tions, simple, almost shack-like, houses. Th[illegible] far removed from the pressure and [illegible] Tetouan medina, though it would be as w[illegible] sharp eye on your more portable p[illegible] estuary served as a riverine port fo[illegible] has silted up considerably in the [illegible] The broken pattern of tidal isl[illegible] excellent refuge for the corsair fl[illegible] here with virtual impunity and [illegible] from the 15th to the 19th [illegible] [illegible] Spanish [illegible] stone [illegible]

Where to Stay

Unless you have forged an unusual love for Ceuta there is no need to stay a night; Tangier is only 75km away and Tetouan 38km. Hotels are surprisingly expensive for what they offer, and are often booked up by families visiting their soldier sons.

expensive

The **Gran Hôtel La Muralla** on Plaza de Africa, ✆ (56) 514940, ℻ (56) 514947, is the smartest address in Ceuta. It has 83 bedrooms, a bar, the renowned La Torre restaurant and a night club open on Saturday nights. If this is full, the **Ulises Hotel** at 5 Calle Camoens, ✆ (56) 514540, is comfortable and well placed in the centre of the old town streets.

moderate

Dropping down in price there is the **Africa** opposite the ferry terminal at 9 Muelle Cañonero Dato, ✆ (56) 509467, and two similar small, comfortable hotels at no. 23 and no. 6 on the Avenida Reyes Católicos, the **Miramar**, ✆ (56) 514146, and the **Skol**, ✆ (56) 514161.

inexpensive

Try for rooms in the **Pensión La Perla**, ✆ (56) 515828, or the **Pensión Los Angeles**, ✆ (56) 513892, both of which are on Calle Real.

Eating Out

For seafood, go to **Casa Fernando**, ✆ (56) 514082, out on the Benzu beach front at the cleaner northwestern corner of Ceuta, which has a particularly good reputation. For a passing snack use the **Delphin Verde**, which is easy to find, just opposite the ferry pier on Muelle Cañonero Dato.

Nightlife

For evening tapas in traditional Spanish style you could call in on any of a number of bars in the old town, such as **Regina** on Calle Independencia. The **Pub Bo Go** on Calle Cervantes has been recommended as a late night bar, while in the summer months there are several discos open for the season, at **Calle Real**, the **Bogoteca**, and the **Coconut** on Carretera del Jaral, and out at the **Ermita de San Antonio** on Monte Hacho.

Festivals

There is a carnival in February, and processions during Easter Week; another religious *fiesta* at the Ermita de San Antonio on 13 July; a procession of fishing boats on 16 July to celebrate Our Lady of Mount Carmel; and the festival of Our Lady of Africa on 5 August.

The Coast from Ceuta to Tetouan

The line of the Haouz mountains runs parallel to the shore, its fierce silhouettes graphically representing the old predatory power of the Anjera hill tribe. Superb Mediterranean beaches continue for 40km in an almost unbroken line from the Moroccan border at Fnideq to Martil, the old corsair port of Tetouan. Moroccan families come to camp along sections of this beach every summer to escape the heat of the cities. Large hotels have recently been built beside two brand new marinas, an upgraded golf course and the waterslides of the Blue Lagoon 'Aquaparc'. This rather amorphous beach strip is increasingly known as Smir-Restinga, and unless you're on a package deal would seem to have little attraction.

The village of **Fnideq** is on the edge of the *cordon sanitaire* that surrounds the frontier around Ceuta, so it stands at a polite 2km back from the custom posts. It is a rough place filled with mechanic's workshops, cafés and heavily draped market ladies on smuggling missions. A new hotel, the **Sebta** on Blvd Mohammed V, ✆ (09) 976140, might make a distinctively different base for exploring both Ceuta and the surrounding beaches.

If you stop anywhere let it be at **Mdiq**, a small coastal village that is halfway to becoming a resort. The Mdiq fishing harbour built out from the Ras Tarf hill is lined with wooden fishing boats which can be seen in every stage of construction along the carpenters' quay. Peregrine falcons nest in the cliffs above. The fish café-restaurant in the harbour is the most interesting place for lunch; if you are intending to stay, the **Hotel Playa** at 31 Boulevard Lalla Nouzha, ✆ (09) 975166, is inviting and reasonably priced.

The other side of the hill from Mdiq, 2km by road, is **Cabo Negro beach**. It has the finest stretch of sand in the area, and is dominated, but fortunately not yet owned, by the **Club Mediterranée Yasmina**. Beside it is the ugly but enjoyable **Hôtel Petit Merou**, ✆ (09) 978176/18. Just off the beach is the restaurant **Al Khayma**, with Moroccan meals served in a Moorish interior. **La Ferma**, a few kilometres inland, is more expensive, an old house admirably converted into a restaurant but a little crowded in the evening. Here you can also hire horses.

Martil

One km before Tetouan is a turning to the left for Martil, a friendly, relaxed place with wide streets and unpretentious, simple, almost shack-like, houses. The tempo is far removed from the pressure and salesmanship of the Tetouan medina, though it would be as well to keep a sharp eye on your more portable possessions. This estuary served as a riverine port for Tetouan but has silted up considerably in the last few centuries. The broken pattern of tidal islands provided an excellent refuge for the corsair fleets that operated here with virtual impunity and almost continually from the 15th to the 19th centuries despite a number of ineffectual Spanish blockades. The small stone 18th-century kasbah that can be seen in the centre of the town was built to protect a fleet of 30 well-armed oared galleys that could nip out and seize any merchant ship unlucky enough to be caught becalmed in the tricky waters of the Straits of Gibraltar.

Where to Stay and Eating Out

On the town's main drag, Rue Moulay Hassan, you will find the **Etoile de la Mer**, © (09) 979058, which has its own café-restaurant and a reliable water supply for its thirty bedrooms. Nearby is the **El Bahia**, © (09) 979215, a family-run licensed fish restaurant with a good line in charcoal-grilled fish brochettes. Both the **Café-Restaurant Avenida**, 100 Av de Tetouan, and **Restaurant de Grenada**, 58 Av de Tetouan, serve excellent food at reasonable prices as well. If you're looking for real budget accommodation, the **Hôtel Rabat** and the **Pension Rif** by the bus station charge under $8 for a room and are both pleasantly social places.

Festivals

The traditional **water *moussem*** of the Ansara used to be held on the other side of the estuary from the town, below the mound and koubba of Sidi Abdussalam al Bahr on 13 August. It has now been transferred to Martil and is held in July in a more secular vein.

Tetouan

Tetouanis claim that they are the true heirs of the Andalusian civilization and affectionately call their city 'the daughter of Granada'. Architecturally the Hispanic influence is dominant throughout the city, for Tetouan was first built by Muslim refugees from Spain in the 15th century, and then many years later was enlarged by the Spanish government in the early years of the 20th century to become the official capital of their protectorate of Northern Morocco. Its medina is one of the most fascinating and absorbing in the country, a delightful warren of detail even if it is not always free from a tinge of alarm for the newcomer. The modern Spanish new town complements this old Andalusian medina. The ostentatious grandeur of the tall and formal official buildings, constructed on a rational, regular grid of wide, straight and Iberian-looking streets, contrasts well with the eclectic and very individual disorder of the medina.

Beneath this civilized veneer Tetouan is also very much part of the Berber hinterland. It has a dramatic position on the north-western edge of the Rif. The densely-packed dirty white city falls from the slopes of Jbel Dersa to dominate the green valley of the Martil, and is overlooked by improbably folded and majestic mountains to both the north and south. Tetouan is a Berber word which can variously be translated as: 'the eyes', 'the springs', 'the edges of water' or 'the female wild boar'. The last has a certain ironic appeal for a Muslim city, and as a warning to visitors. Tetouan shares the dissident mentality of the Rif tribes and has a reputation for harbouring the most assertive and aggressive tourist hustlers as well as some rather crude pickpockets. It can consequently make a frustrating start to a holiday but is a rewarding city once you adjust to Moroccan street life.

History

On the empty southern side of the Martil valley a hillock is crowned with the remains of Tamuda, Roman Tetouan. These ruins have more of the air of a fortified marching camp than a civil city, and they do not seem to have been occupied for more than three centuries. This was not the first settlement to stand here, for the Romans had themselves destroyed the Phoenician–Berber town during their conquest of Morocco in AD 42.

A Merenid kasbah stood here in the 14th century, but as a city, Tetouan's foundation dates to 1484 when a group of citizens, led by the nobleman al-Mandari, left Granada just a few years before their city fell to the Catholics. An alliance with the independent princes of Chechaouèn, a growing flood of skilled refugees from Andalucia, and the profits from piracy assured the rapid growth of Tetouan. It soon became one of the largest cities in the land, an oasis of refined urban living and skilled craftsmen producing silk, ceramics, fine metalwork, intricate embroideries and painted chests.

The Pirate Queen

Fatima bint Ali Rashid began her political career when she was married to al-Mandari, the distinguished founder of Tetouan. She assisted her increasingly blind husband in the town's administration and helped usher in the city's most prosperous period. In 1512, after the death of her husband, the 20-year-old Fatima became the Hakima, the governess of the corsairs feared throughout every Christian coast. Though she had her own resources she could also count on the support of some powerful friends like Ibrahim, the Emir of Chechaouèn, who was her brother, and the sultan at Fès, her second husband. Fatima was also an enthusiastic ally of the Ottoman Turks and even sailed to their advance base, Velez de la Gomera, to offer supplies to the pirate fleet of Barbarossa. Nor did she allow the military struggle against Catholic Spain to betray the intellectual traditions of Granada. The Dutch savant Nicholas Kleinatz fled from intolerance in his own country and received the protection and patronage of her court. This extraordinary and talented woman ruled Tetouan for 33 years before her son in law, Hamad al Hassan, ended her rule in a palace coup in 1542. She was politely escorted back to her home town of Chechaouèn, where she lived a life of piety and scholarship for another 20 years.

The city walls had to be manned not just against the Spanish, but against the predatory ambitions of the tribal warlords of the Rif. It was the Spanish who in the end proved the greatest threat. In 1859 a Spanish army marched out from Ceuta and fought a bloody battle in the hills which gave them possession of the city. They only left a year later after they had extracted a fortune in 'reparations' from the sultan. They returned in 1912, and made the city the headquarters of the Spanish Protectorate of Northern Morocco. Apart from a series of grand public buildings, and the odd cement and brick works, the colonial period achieved little of economic value. However, the relatively hands-off nature of Spanish rule did help the city maintain its strong cultural traditions. Its intellectuals were at the forefront of the early Moroccan independence movement, but it now largely stands aside from the political structure. It has however retained a strong position in the artistic life of the nation, with a respected university, art school and classical Andalucian orchestra.

Getting Around

by air

Martil Airport, also known as Sania R'mel, ✆ (09) 971233, is 6km out from the city. It has regular RAM connections to Casablanca, Al Hoceima and Rabat and is being prepared for charter flights to the beach. The RAM office, for tickets and information, is at 5 Rue Mohammed V, ✆ (09) 961260, 961610 or 961577.

by rail

There was once a railway line between Ceuta and Tetouan, but the Spanish took it away with them in 1956. However, the ONCF booking office on Av Achrai Mai, facing the Avenida cinema by Place A Hadala, sells tickets which include a ride in the ONCF coach to the nearest station at Souk Tnine-de-Sidi-el-Yamani about halfway between Asilah and Larache.

by bus

Travelling by bus to and from Tetouan is quick and convenient. All buses, CTM and private companies, arrive in the central covered station at the junction of Av Hassan II and Rue Sidi Mandri, ✆ (09) 966263. The ticket booths are in the hall up the stairs. There are hourly services for Tangier (90mins away) and the Ceuta border post of Fnideq (30mins). Chechaouèn is a two-hour trip with at least half a dozen departures a day, and there are about four departures for Fès (9hrs) and Meknès (8hrs). For Rabat you might consider travelling to Tangier to catch the train, although there are two daily bus departures for the eight-hour journey.

In the summer the beaches to the north are served by an efficient and cheap shuttle service that leaves just downhill from Av Hassan II, behind the distinctive green and white old railway terminal. There are three buses a day to Et-Tleta-de-Oued-Laou and the more tempting beaches of the east coast.

by taxi

Taxis assemble on Rue Moulay El Abbas, just to the west of the bus station and along Rue Al Jazaer as it skirts the new walled car park set below the medina. There is a continual shuttle of taxis offering a place to Tangier ($2–2.50 per place) or to Fnideq on the Ceuta border ($1.50-2). You should also be able to find a place to Chechaouèn or Et-Tleta-de-Oued-Laou, though you will have to wait longer for the car to fill up.

Tourist Information

The **tourist office** is just down from Place Mulay el Mehdi at 30 Rue Mohammed V, ✆ (09) 961915/16 (closed Sat, Sun). The **post office** is on the Place Mulay el Mehdi and is open Mon–Fri, 8.30–noon and 2.30–6.30pm, and Sat 8.30–12pm.

The **Banque du Maroc** is at no. 7 and the **BMCI** at no. 18 Rue Sidi Mandri. There is an after-hours currency exchange at the **BMCE** on Place Mulay el Mehdi.

dealing with guides

Tetouan has a deserved reputation for being a difficult city to visit, particularly in high summer. The university is closed, the beaches open and the student hostels overflowing with eager young men persistently pushing their claims to be your guide. New arrivals will be met at the bus station and at the edge of the medina. It is in the nature of the country: rather than indignantly resisting, spend your energies trying to choose someone you can vaguely trust, or employ an official guide from the tourist office. This only applies for the medina; a visit to the Archaeological or Folk Museum is easily made and trouble-free. Without wishing to sound discouraging, do be on your guard against the town's skillful pickpockets.

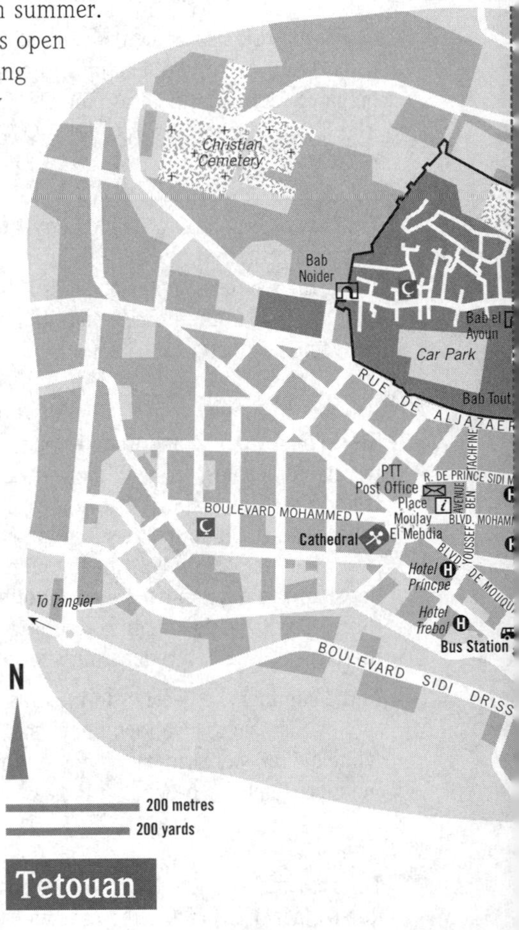

Place Hassan II

This has always been the centre of urban life, the focal market and place of assembly contained, in the past, within the old circuit of the walled medina. Its character was drastically altered in 1988 when the formal Spanish Andalucian garden in the centre was swept away and replaced by the present wide sweep of paved Islamic design, incidentally built by Italians.

The north side of the square is occupied by the Ministry of Justice, while the east is dominated by the new Royal Palace. The square now has four towering, free-standing minarets, floodlit at night. A large area in front of the palace is often roped off. It is still too early to see what long-term effect this will have on the surrounding cafés and pension balconies: it's highly likely that the kif smoke and the cries of boys selling smuggled cigarettes will remain.

The *Mellah*

To the south of the Place Hassan II there are two entrances to the *mellah*, or **Jewish quarter**—the Rue de la Luneta or the Rue al Qods, which is just to the right of the Bab er Rouah. This quarter, also known as the Kouds, has tall, square buildings, a regular grid street pattern and dark painted iron balconies with ornate window grills, all of which distinguish it from the Muslim medina. The original 15th-century Jewish quarter is less easy to distinguish;

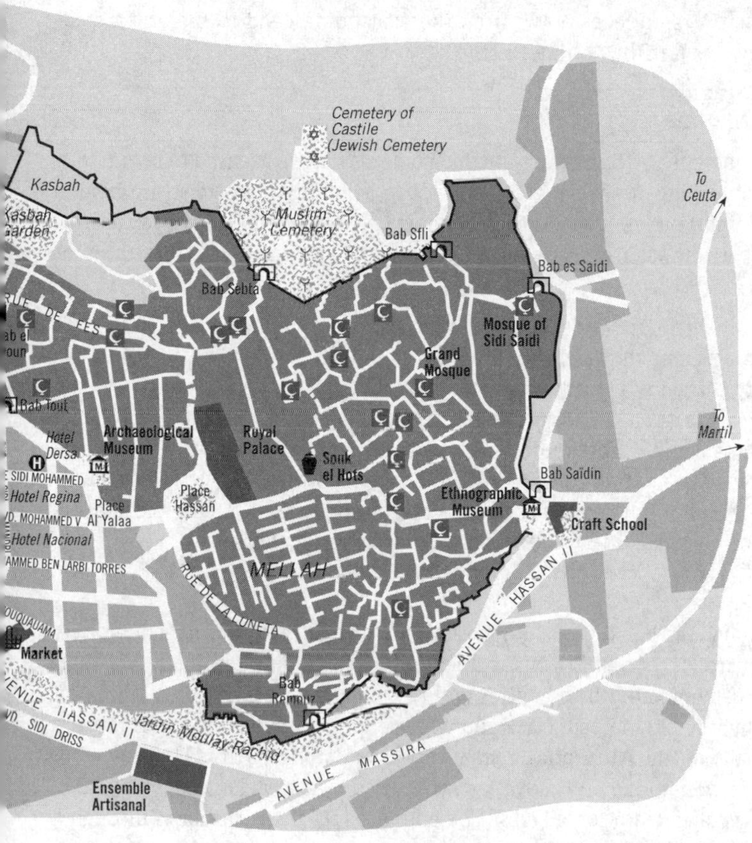

it is in the cramped streets that surround the Grand Mosque. The community exchanged this in 1807, during the reign of Moulay Sliman, for the present larger site to the south. Three synagogues can be found, one at 12 Zankat Florida, and the Ben Dayan Temple and the Grand Synagogue on Zankat Benguali. A fountain installed in 1908 on the right of the Rue al Qods in honour of Israel has had its inscription obscured by whitewash. The Arab-Israeli wars forced the majority of Jews to leave Morocco for Israel or South America. Moshe Dayan, the distinguished general and archaeologist, was from a prominent old Tetouan family, and the former chief minister of Gibraltar, Sir Joshua Hassan, came from another family of the *mellah*. General Franco and his wife were befriended by Jews when they lived in the Tetouan medina; in thanks he supposedly issued Spanish passports to Sephardic Jews during the war to save them from his Nazi allies. Sephardic Jews were socially much in demand during the Spanish protectorate as they had retained the language of 15th-century Spanish Jews, *Ladino*, which was much appreciated by 20th-century Spanish conquerors.

For the skilled street navigator it is possible to follow the Rue de la Luneta to its end and then turn right for the **mosque** by the Bab Remouz. Walking out through the gate from the narrow shady streets of the *mellah* to the glaring view of the coast around Martil makes a fine dramatic contrast. A ramp leads down from the walls to descend to the ornamental rampart gardens known as **Jardin Moulay Rachid**.

The Heart of the Medina

The old city contains more than 50 mosques of which only eleven are licensed to hold Friday prayers. The meanest-looking doors can give entrance to delightful high courtyard houses with each floor holding four elegant traditional rooms. The worn paving, cooled with buckets of fresh water drawn from private wells, shows evidence of the centuries of occupation.

The **Bab er Rouah**, the gate of winds, at the eastern corner of the Place Hassan II leads straight on to the main medina thoroughfare, the Rue Ach Ahmed Torrès. By keeping to this broad street, recently shaded with handsome slats, you can pass across the medina to the east gate, the **Bab El Okla**, which leads to the Ethnographic Museum and the Craft School of Traditional Arts (*see* below). This route will take you over the hidden *mazmoras*, the underground slave pens that in 1648 still housed 690 Christians who were allowed by day to visit their wives who lived in huts on the surface. A Spanish priest excavated the chambers this century and found a well, a chapel and an oratory for the resident priest.

Souk El Hots

Take the first left through the Bab er Rouah, opposite a mosque, to reach this delightful, tree-shaded, intimate square. The Souk El Hots is lined with stalls selling terracotta pots and glazed ceramics but is dominated by a central group of dignified Berber ladies selling an impressive range of their traditional red, black and white striped cloth. Behind the square are the 15th-century walls of the **Alcazaba**, a small brick and stone fortress; the tower of homage is in the northwest corner. It is now partly occupied by a weaving cooperative that produces fine black woollen cloth for jellabas. The entrance into the Alcazaba is through a modern passageway beside the octagonal minaret of the mosque and its associated baths.

The left passage from the Souk El Hots takes you in 25m to another irregular medina square, the **Guersa El Kebira**, furnished in its northern corner with a fountain. It was once a great garden, but is now a dusty open-air market where you will have a second opportunity to buy the distinctive striped blanket, the *fouta*, of the Jebala mountain women. This *fouta* is worn as an outer skirt over the folded brown blanket worn around the waist that gives the women of the Rif such a stout profile. In this sunbaked court the slumped sleeping figures of the women can blend imperceptibly with their wares.

Place de l'Usáa

Behind the Guersa is a pretty little area, known as the Place de l'Usáa, really more of a thoroughfare than a square, ringed with whitewashed houses and heavy decorated doors. The Place is easily reached from the right-hand corner of the Guersa. Vines provide shade and a café allows you to pause and examine the procession of medina life: stubble-faced hill farmers in thick jellabas; women from the mountains in their broad pompom hats; street kids hiding alert eyes behind dark glasses; and graceful aged figures in clean white linen crowned with a fez, perhaps the last of a long line of scholars from Andalucia.

Souk el Foki

The central commercial area of the medina is north from these small squares. The wood carvers, coppersmiths, leather workers and cobblers are found along or in *fondouqs* off the Rue El Jarrazin, which leads up to the **Bab M'Kabar** (Bab Ceuta). The Souk el Foki is just off this alley. It is bordered to the north by two mosques, the first of which is the **sanctuary of Sidi Ali** where snack shops, spice stalls and wood carvers collect.

From the Souk el Foki a left turn opposite the fountain leads down the twisting Rue de Mexuar and takes you under arches and buttresses to pass the richer stalls—the tailors, embroiderers, jewellers, and arrays of decorated slippers—and back to the Place Hassan II.

Rue de Fès

Alternatively, continue west along the Zankat Fès, a bustling straight alley that passes through the Trancats and Ayun quarters out through the **Bab Noider** (Bab Fès). Vegetables and kitchen equipment predominate on this route, with intriguing low dark alleys disappearing off to left and right. You pass a number of mosques: **Sidi Ben Messaoud** with its carved stalactite portal; the **Ayun Mosque** by the fountain; and the tiled **sanctuary of Sidi Ahmed en Naji**. The stalls sell little to attract the tourist and it is subsequently a pleasant, carefree street, busy with local trade.

A Tour of the Ramparts

The present extent of the walls contains fragments of 15th-century Andalusian work that followed the Merenid foundations. Most of the ramparts, though, date from the 17th century, when the corsairs were in full operation and the war against the Spanish in Ceuta was being waged by Moulay Ismaïl's general Pacha Ahmed er Riffi from his base at Tetouan.

On Rue Mohammed V, just before it enters Place Hassan II, is the triangular **Place Al Yalàa** where a cannon captured by the corsairs, dated 1607, has been placed below a fragment of wall. The zaouia of Abdul Qader Jilen can be seen opposite.

The line of city wall can next be admired by walking down to the ring road, Avenue Hassan II, just below the bus station. Opposite the Ensemble Artisanal (*see* p. 127 'Shopping'), the **Jardin of Moulay Rachid** runs beneath the walls, the formal seats, fish pools, palm-lined promenades and café chairs occasionally offering a splendid view of Jbel Rhorgez. A ramp leads up to the **Bab Remouz** and the *mellah*. Continuing along the road below the walls to the right, in an anti-clockwise direction, you pass the Suika quarter to reach the **Bab El Okla**.

The **Craft School** (Ecole de Métiers d'Arts Traditionnels) is opposite the Bab El Okla (*open during term time 9am–12pm, 3–5pm, closed Fri and Sun; adm*). Do not miss the opportunity to be taken on a short tour around this Moorish craft centre, curiously built by the Spanish in the 1930s. The splendid tiled entrance hall of the main block hides a display hall filled with a fine selection of ancient and modern pieces. Around the gardens at the back of the main block are arranged the carpentry, pottery, carving and painting workshops. The making of mosaic wall tiles, or *zellij*, is the most fascinating demonstration. In Tetouan the wet clay is cut to shape and then fired and glazed before being fitted face down into the pattern and sealed in portable segments with mortar. The Fès style used elsewhere in Morocco is to cut the mosaic pieces after firing from plain square tiles.

Within the crenellated gates just on the left is the entrance to the **Folk Museum** (Musée Ethnographique) where an Arabic plaque proclaims, 'in the name of God the merciful and compassionate, the triumphant, the consolidator...' (*open Wed, Thurs, Fri 8.30am–12pm, 2.30–6pm, Sat 8.30am–12pm; no photographs; adm*). There is a beautiful collection in the upstairs rooms of Andalusian Jewish and Islamic **embroidery**, with a dazzling display of sumptuous trousseaus and rooms prepared for the rich traditional marriage ceremonies. The exhibition of a countryman's house downstairs with its simple loom producing striped cloth illustrates the large gulf between the rural tribal culture and that of the sophisticated urban merchants. There is also a Moroccan kitchen and a display of armaments and embroidered saddles. One of the most dramatic features is when the curator theatrically throws open a door to the sunbaked terrace: the darkened interior full of rich secretive female clothing suddenly gives way to a panorama of sunlight and mountains.

Of less interest is the **Brishka Palace**, a well-signposted 19th-century Muslim merchant's house which now sells carpets.

On to the **Bab Saïdia** where, a short distance inside the gate, is the elegant **mosque of Sidi Saïdi**. A fountain plays opposite and water also flows below the elaborate tracery decoration of the minaret. The entrance to the mosque, forbidden to non-Muslims, is from the decorated covered arch to the side. It was built in 1738 by the Pacha Ahmed er Riffi, and incorporates the 13th-century shrine of the saint Sidi Saïdi, who lived from 1227–1254. This saint's main claim to fame was that he killed the assassin of Moulay Abdessalam of Jbel Alam. On his death he was buried in the empty ground of Tetouan, and a koubba was raised above his grave during the foundation of the city some thirty years later.

The **Bab Sfli** (Bab el Jiaf) is the 'gate of evil odours'—possibly a reference to the tanning vats which used to be just inside the town walls. It re-earned its name in the 19th century when rotting bodies piled up against the gate in a failed siege of the town by mountain tribesmen.

The walls are clearly defined here, as a cemetery extends to cover the rising ground above the town. To the northwest is the **Cemetery of Castile**, one of the largest Sephardic burial grounds in the world. The upper area houses tombs from the 15th century with the sex of the dead symbolically indicated on the stone carvings. Holy men can be distinguished by an urn decorated with books. The tomb of Jacob Benmalka, the cabbalist, is still visited, and a meteorite that protected a Cohen grave from desecration is still whitewashed and spotted with wax from votive candles. In the **Muslim cemetery** beside the walls a large modern tomb simultaneously honours both the 15th-century Andalusian founder of Tetouan and Abdul Khaleq al Torres, who established an early nationalist cell here in 1932.

Just inside the **Bab M'Kabar** (the cemetery gate), also known as the Bab Ceuta, are the elaborate portals of the Harraquiza zaouia of the Derkaoua Sufis, which was built in 1828 over the tomb of a celebrated master. Walking by on a Friday you may overhear arm-linked ritual chanting or a faint whisper of the theological discussions held within.

Further on, you can clamber up past the walls of the **kasbah**, which is still garrisoned and consequently inaccessible. Immediately to the left after the kasbah, up a dirt track, are the ruined **ornamental gardens** below the military whitewashed walls, their flaking Andalusian tiles and monuments framed by palm trees. There is a superb view from here over the roofs of white Tetouan, down to the river and the surrounding mountains. Youths play football in the dust, and old friends puff on a tranquil pipe in the shade amongst the elaborate ruins of the Spanish garrison's formal promenade.

Steep steps from the gardens can take you down into Zankat Fès in the medina, or you can retrace your steps to continue west around the Catholic cemeteries, whose despoiled tombs are surrounded by a wall of elegant dark cypress. This route will bring you to **Bab Noider** (the threshing gate), also known as the Bab Fès. It is guarded on the right by the hexagonal **Shorfa's Tower**, while to the left is the town's **electrical souk**. A long stretch of recently repaired wall alongside the Rue Al Jazaer brings you to the **Bab Tout** (Bab Tangier), the old mulberry gate. Until the 20th century Tetouan was a walled city ringed to the south and the east by a patchwork of orange groves and mulberry trees for the local silk industry. Then the tightly packed medina truly deserved the nickname *hamari il baidha*, the white dove. Just to the right of the Bab Tout is an ornamental fountain built by an 18th-century governor who re-established the full extent of the city walls, which had been levelled after one of Tetouan's rebellions

Archaeological Museum

Open Wed–Mon 9am–12pm, 2–6pm; closed Tues and holidays; adm.

This small museum (the Musée Archéologique), on the left as you walk from Bab Tout to the Place Hassan II, is an ideally cool and tranquil finale to a tour of Tetouan. The shaded, well-kept **garden**, with two classical mosaics from Lixus and littered with a complete assortment of Roman amphorae, Punic stelae, carved Libyan script and Jewish and Iberian gravestones, is its greatest attraction.

The museum rooms have a suitably dusty aura. In the entrance hall there are two mosaics: the three Graces with the four seasons in corner medallions; and the more animated scene of Bacchus being led in triumph on his mule by two naked supporters. In the first room there is a fine prehistoric rock carving of a bison taken from Es-Semara in the Western Sahara. The model of the M'Soura stone circle before the desecration of the excavation may prompt your interest (the real one is off the Tetouan to Larache road). The second room has a fine head of Oceanus amongst the bronzes and four further mosaics, two of which star Venus discovering Adonis, on your left, and being discovered asleep by Mars in her turn. The upper floor has bits and bobs from excavations at Ksar-es-Seghir, Tamuda and various Punic graves. The large tribal and antiquities map is really more absorbing.

The **Tamuda Excavations** are just 4km out of Tetouan on the road to Chechaouèn. They could make a wonderful picnic site but are unlikely to appeal to those not already excited by the late Roman period. As you cross the river Martil they occupy the hill immediately to your left. The rectangular circuit of town walls, and a number of gates, villas, streets and public buildings are easily identifiable amongst the goat-grazed weeds.

Where to Stay

There are a large number of elegant old balconied pensions scattered through the town and in particular around the Place Hassan II. On a first visit to Tetouan, though, it's advisable to steer clear of these places and stay in one of the older and more secure hotels in the Spanish-built New Town.

expensive

The **Safir** on Route de Sebta (Av Kennedy), ✆ (09) 970144, ℻ (09) 970692, is a standard 100-room package hotel with pool, restaurant and night club. It is 3km out of town on the road north to Ceuta; dull, but efficient accommodation. Cheaper and more friendly is the **Hotel Chams**, on Av. Abdeljalak-Torres (route de Ceuta), ✆ (09) 990901–6, ℻ (09) 990907.

cheap

The **Hôtel Dersa**, ✆ (09) 966729, on Rue de Prince Sidi Mohammed (Rue General Franco) is a massive but attractive hotel. There is an elegant hall beside a large sitting room, and a subterranean room decorated in the imperial operatic style which serves as a popular late night bar. The Dersa has 74 spacious rooms and a restaurant. The **Hôtel Nacional** at 8 Rue Mohammed ben Larbi Torres, ✆ (09) 963290, is another distinguished and ageing hotel, arranged around a cool tiled central courtyard where there is a calm café. If both of these are booked up there are a number of other perfectly adequate places. Try the **Regina** at 8 Rue Sidi Mandri, ✆ (09) 962113, which has 58 rooms and restaurant, or the **Trebol** at 3 Rue Yacoub el Mansour, ✆ (09) 962093, a small, simple and comfortable hotel just above the bus station (sometimes noisy, so try to get a room which doesn't look over the road). The **Hôtel Principe**, which has a downstairs café, is just beyond the Trebol at 20 Youseff-ibn-Tachfine, ✆ (09) 962794/5.

Eating Out

Sadly the **Zerhoun**, 7 Rue Mohammed ben Larbi Torres, ✆ (09) 966661, well-known as Tetouan's smartest restaurant, is currently closed, and may remain so for some time. Try instead the **Palace Bouhlal**, ✆ (09) 974419, beside the great mosque, which occupies a wonderful old palace. The **Saigon** on Rue Mohammed V, despite its name, has a Spanish/Moroccan menu with quick, cheap and largely unexciting food—salads, fish, paella and omelettes. The restaurant **Granada**, a little-known, attractively lit place on Place Al Yalàa, has a certain charm, and there is a surprisingly elegant but nameless café supplemented by a grill restaurant established in the car park off Rue

Al Jazaer, which has a very good view of the medina. There is also the **Café Moderne** on 1 Pasaje Achaach, between Rue Mohammed ben Larbi V and Avenue Mohammed Torres, a busy, cheerful, cheap local place that serves *tagines* but has no licence for alcohol.

Shopping

The enclosed **fish and vegetable market** is right beside the bus station. There is a fine **library** maintained by the Ministry of Culture on Avenue Mohammed V, and a **bookshop** on the same avenue with a good stock of Spanish and French books including Robert Aspinon's initiation into the Berber dialects, written when he was a *Lt-Col. des Affaires Musulmans.* The **Ensemble Artisanal** on Av Hassan I houses an extensive but lifeless display of fixed-price crafts, in an ugly modern building.

The Rif Coast

The S608 road from Tetouan to El Jebha is a thrilling 125km journey on an exhilarating twisting coastal hill track that passes above desolate cliff-fringed sandy beaches, pebbled bays with beached fishing boats and across the beds of five mountain streams. The farmers and fishermen of the coast (also known as Rhomara, or Ghomara, country) are generally welcoming and easy-going. 'Business', the kif industry, is much in evidence and smugglers' tales can be heard in every café, though there is none of the hard sell to visitors and outright banditry of the Ketama highlands.

As you first approach the sea, a dirt track on your left provides a 20-minute walk to the **koubba of Sidi Absullam al Bahr**. The tomb stands on the site of an old trading post, the tell, a mound of ruins, contains the foundations of a Punic temple and is still used as a cemetery. A salt marsh estuary extends inland and the white houses of Martil can be seen on the opposite bank. A pillbox below the koubba is now an observation post for the customs men.

On 13 August, the herds of the Beni-Madan tribe used to receive their ritual washing in the sea here, surrounded by boats of musicians and dense crowds singing from the shore. The siren Lamna was appealed to for the fertility and protection of the herd. At night the music around the fires was *zazuka*, an ancient Punic relic now almost completely forgotten. This pagan ritual was stopped in the early reforming years after Independence, and the funds that had been collected to preserve the *moussem* were given over to the founding of a **Koranic school**, shaded with bamboos, where you can hear children chanting lines of the Koran as the waves break on the beach.

The road passes a scattering of villas and the Alanana campsite before climbing around a number of small fishing bays and toiling up the surrounding cliffs on a dramatic and fascinating 44km journey to the long beach and fertile open valley of Et-Tleta-de-Oued-Laou.

Et-Tleta-de-Oued-Laou

This village is strung along part of the beach that follows a delightful, wide and empty bay. Fishing boats are beached on the shingle and in summer half a dozen café-restaurants open directly on to the beach.

The octagonal **mosque** has each face encased in different ceramic tiles and vies for your attention with the false-castellated **Spanish barracks**, which now houses the *gendarmerie*. A feature of the Rhomara coast are the rival twin villages that flank each fertile valley. The eastern Et-Tleta-de-Oued-Laou has a smart new café and a number of stalls selling well stewed and spiced fish *tagines*. The weekly Saturday market is held at an inland site equidistant from the two villages.

Two km beyond the western village a right turn takes you along a tarmac road to Chechaouèn past the **Laou Gorge**. As you approach the gorge the road follows along a continuous gravel landslide which falls down to the riverbanks. The cool muddy water of the river has polished smooth great grey and white boulders on its bed. On the other bank an immense golden cliff decorated with occasional remnants of stalactites looms up and hints at a past existence as a subterranean gorge. A hydro scheme further upstream restrains the seasonal excesses of the river, forming the lake which you pass before joining the P28 10km north of Chechaouèn.

Where to Stay and Eating Out

There are two cheap places to stay, either at the **Restaurant Hôtel Layyoune** or its neighbour the **Hôtel-Café Et-Tleta-de-Oued-Laou**. Both places can produce fresh fish *tagine*, vegetables, salads and fruit, though off-season the Et-Tleta-de-Oued-Laou is more likely to be open than the Layyoune. The **Camping Laou** is a secure site just a little inland from the beach, beside the road.

Targa

Another 17km to the east is Targa, a striking village of traditional houses set in the folds of hills and facing two conspicuous outcrops of venerated black stone. The nearest rock is crowned by a stone fort, and both contain whitewashed caves and are associated with the lively saints' cults of Targa. The old, low, brick-built **mosque** was built in the 13th century and has witnessed frequent reversals of fortune. Andalusian refugees reinforced the port in the 15th century, when it was a large enough corsair base for Diego López de Siquira to attack in 1494, capturing 300 slaves and sinking 25 small ships; the following year he returned with 70 galleons.

Nowadays Targa has only one café and a grocery shop to tempt the visitor. The fortifications on the hill are largely the work of the Spanish protectorate, and are now used by the Beni-Ziat tribe for sorting out the kif harvest. The local *moussem* is well worth witnessing if you are staying nearby on 15 July.

Steha and Bou-Ahmed

Beyond Targa are a number of cliff-fringed beaches of black sand—tranquil, exquisite wastelands. Eighteen kilometres beyond is the valley of the river Bouhia, with the two villages of Steha and Bou-Ahmed (their souk is on Tuesday). Steha is the new administrative centre, with an efficient seasonal campsite, a vet and the *gendarmerie*; Bou-Ahmed is the old village of the Beni Bouzra tribe, with charming fragments of paving and architectural detail from a grander past. Further along, by the river, **M'Tr**, there are tantalizing views of El-Jebha.

El-Jebha

The town, 52km beyond Bou-Ahmed, is a striking Spanish blue and white creation neatly arranged on a grid plan and overlooked by the surrounding forested mountains. The bleak hill to the east is decorated with Spanish defences and the **koubba of Sidi Yahia el Uardani**, which overlooks the harbour. There is a charming cliff-fringed turquoise bay on the other side. By negotiating with a fishing boat it is possible to be taken to the bays of **Teknint**, **Si Mektor** or on to **Hamed Saidi**, the central village of the Mestassa tribe. El-Jebha is still off the beaten track and it will be presumed that you have come here on business. The *gendarmerie* faces the harbour, there are a number of cafés, some basic provision shops, a decaying Spanish square, a few fish grills and a garage. Even the bandits, easily recognizable by their leather jackets and large fast cars, are reasonably friendly.

Getting Around

The **fish souk** is on Tuesday morning, a good day for taxis or lifts in lorries to Tetouan, and a reliable **bus** leaves at about noon for the 7-hour ride to Tetouan; a less dependable service connects with Chechaouèn and Tetouan on alternate days. It is a memorable journey: goats travel with the baggage and farmers clasp baskets of lightly salted fish destined for the hills. The moment the bus has departed, sweet-smelling smoke from a dozen pipes calms the passengers. The drivers always stop for a refreshing drink at a mountain spring and a snack at Et-Tleta-de-Oued-Laou.

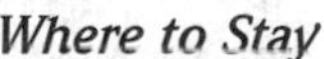

Where to Stay

In summer some of the cafés may let roof space or the odd room but otherwise it is the **Petit** or the **Grand Hôtel**. The **Grand** is opposite the harbour to the right of the police station, with three adjoining rooms packed with beds equipped with some grey blankets and sometimes a bottle of water. The **Petit Hôtel** is less comfortable.

South of El-Jebha

A badly pot-holed tarmac track, the 8500, at a small risk takes you up and inland through a splendid panorama of Rif mountains. The track is narrow and its coils, holes and hidden bends demand careful driving on the 61km climb from sea level to the 1500m of the Ketama road. On Saturdays a **souk** is held at Es Sebt, and there is a Monday market at Souk Tnine d'Uxgan; both these hamlets are directly along the road.

There are also two dirt tracks for the adventurous. One follows the west bank of the Ouringa river to the Sunday **souk** of El Had, 8km before the Ketama road. Another passes through a separate Es Sebt, with a Saturday **souk**, about 10km from El-Jebha, to re-emerge at Bab Berred.

The Jebala

The Jebala is one of the most idiosyncratic districts of Morocco. It has an almost Alpine grandeur, against which nestle valleys of sacred Islamic monasteries, walled medieval towns and xenophobic tribes. It was populated by shifting coalitions of fiercely independent mountain tribes. The tribes are of Berber ethnic origin but Arabic-speaking, as they learnt the language in the armies of the Muslim monarchs of Spain. Though obedient to the spiritual authority of the Sultan they were led by their own highly literate dynasties of holy lineage, like that of Ouezzane, Jbel Alam and Si Raisuli. Nor has the Jebala's sense of mystery ended at the end of the 20th century. In the early 1970s the Rolling Stones recorded some albums with a caste of Jebala musicians known as the Jajouka, whose haunting music summons back goat-legged, horny Pan to the hills.

Tetouan to Chechaouèn

The direct inland route from Tetouan to Chechaouèn along the P28 runs through mountain scenery of growing splendour. The shifting views over this 60km journey are the main attraction, although there are a number of rural markets just off the road. On Tuesdays there is a market at **Tleta-des-Beni-Yder-Cherki**, 16km west, along the S602; and on Wednesdays there is one at **Souk-el-Arba-des-Beni-Hassan**, which is just 3km west of the main road, on a signposted turning. The Beni Hassan still use the Tamazight Berber dialect, unlike their neighbours. They were for long the most powerful and militant tribe of the area and the backbone of the 8th century Khajarite revolt that overthrew Arab rule. Khajarite imams remained in control of the region until an Almohad sultan destroyed the heresy in the 12th century, in a four-year campaign.

Chechaouèn

Chechaouèn (also spelt Chaouen, Xaouen or Chefchaouèn), 'the horns', is one of the most beautiful towns of Morocco and hangs like a crescent from high twin mountains. The medina, a mass of red tiled roofs, crisp whitewashed walls and elegant architectural details, is a precious 15th-century relic from the Muslim civilization of Andalusia. The cemetery immediately above the town creates a fine contrast between the wilderness of graves and the tightly packed medina. Surrounded on all points of the compass by the Jebala mountains, this compact town is a popular but still friendly destination.

History

Chechaouèn was founded in 1471 as a fortress for the faith, a secure mountain citadel from which to assault the growing power of Portugal. It was established by a native Idrissid prince, Sherif Moulay Ali bin Rachid, but largely settled by the flood of skilled Andalusian refugees that were fleeing from the Catholic conquest of the old Muslim kingdom of Granada. The Andalusians were responsible for the rapid and elegant growth of the town while the Sherif and his heirs ruled over much of northern Morocco. The Idrissid Emirate of Chechaouèn, Tetouan and Targa was recognized by the sultans in Fès until both were swept away by the Saadian dynasty in the mid-16th century. The last emir escaped and died a pilgrim at Mecca.

The tradition of enmity toward Christians was fiercely maintained over the centuries. Before the arrival of Spanish troops in 1920 only three Christians had even seen the town: the intrepid French ascetic and traveller Charles de Foucauld saw the walls for an hour disguised as a rabbi in 1883; Walter Harris, the flamboyant Tangier-based reporter for *The Times* saw the town in 1889; and William Summers, an American missionary, made it to Chechaouèn and was poisoned here in 1892.

On 15 October 1920 Chechaouèn was occupied by a Spanish column after token resistance from the town, which was then controlled by the bandit Raissouli's sixth cousin, thrice removed. The Chechaouèn Jews, with little regard for the history of their race, welcomed the Spanish troops as liberators. To the amazement of their conquerors they still spoke in the pure accent of 15th-century Andalusia, and shouted to the bemused Spanish, *'Viva Isabella!'*, praising the Castilian queen who had expelled their ancestors from Spain. The advance of Abdel Krim's army during the Rif rising forced the Spanish to withdraw from the town in 1924, in a long, bitterly fought retreat to Tetouan that left 14,000 dead. The Rif soldiers entered the gates of Chechaouèn and showed their respect by marching in bare feet. The Spanish army returned in 1926, but finally left in 1956 on Independence. The Andalusian garden at the centre of Place Mohammed V, the Catholic church and Pepe's Bar are their finest memorials.

Getting Around

CTM coaches, private line buses and *grand taxis* all use different sections of the market area immediately below Av Hassan II and the Bab el Ain gate to the medina.

The half a dozen or so daily **buses** from Tetouan provide the most useful connection with Chechaouèn. There are currently three coaches daily from the town to Fès or Meknès (a 5–7hr ride), although these are sometimes fully booked up and it is worth buying tickets well in advance. There are two buses a day for Al Hoceima, an 8hr ride, which would take you through Ketama, although an equally exhilarating journey is the 7hr twice-weekly bus to El-Jebha. There is also a daily dawn bus (leaving at around 5am) that runs down to the sea at Et-Tleta-de-Oued-Laou, a one-and-a-half hour journey.

Finding a place in a ***grand taxi*** to Tetouan or Quezzane is usually never a problem. If you can fill up a taxi you could charter one to Fès for between $40-$50.

Tourist Information

The **tourist office** is just off Place Mohammed V. It is open sometimes in the summer, but is of little or no use. The **post office** is on Charih Hassan II. The **Banque Populaire** and **BMCE** both operate branches on Charih Hassan II.

Uta el Hammam

On a first visit or by car or taxi it is easier to reach the **Place Uta el Hammam** by the Rue Tarik Ibn Ziad, the continuation of Avenue Hassan II that climbs uphill around the medina walls. The small open area in front of the Chaouen-Parador Hôtel (the Place El Maghzen) is a parking area. From here the tower of the kasbah can be seen to your left and the central square at the heart of the medina, the Uta el Hammam, opens out before you. Pass a couple of stalls selling minerals and fossils to enter this delightful cobbled area surrounded by cafés and the cheaper pensions. The cafés are at certain times of the year equipped with perforated tin cones to protect the sweet mint tea from the vociferous and determined local bees. The various types of honey from the mountains provide an almost complete pharmacy—the honey produced from bees feeding on a red button berry, for instance, is a cure for diabetes. Franco was supplied throughout his life with marjoram honey from Chechaouèn.

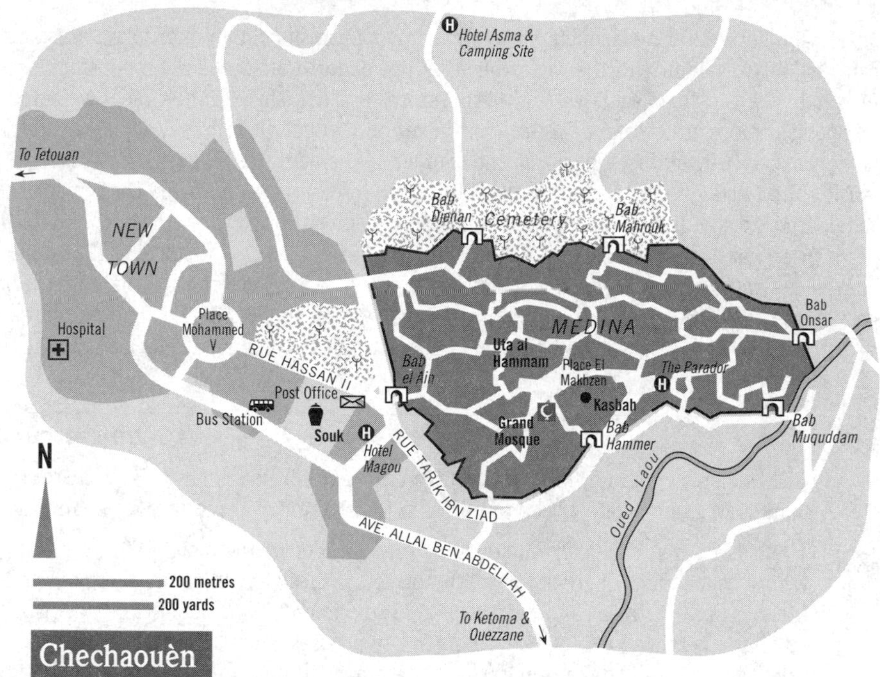

The upper rooms of the cafés are frequented by kif smokers, the odd hippy, and students studying in the shade. A few boys sell cannabis resin to visitors, but locals prefer to smoke the cut and dried leaves. The experienced kif smoker dips his long wooden pipe into a leather pouch, packs the herb tightly into the small clay head and takes three puffs before blowing the glowing residue out on to the floor with accustomed skill and ease. Next door to the Kasbah Restaurant is a *fondouq* used on souk days by farmers for their donkeys and mules; the first floor provides overnight accommodation for the men. Behind Lehsen's Café is the 15th-century ***hammam***, a Moorish bath which male tourists are welcome to use.

Slave boys were still being openly sold in the medina markets of Chechaouèn until 1937, and the hill tribes of the Jebala have always been open about their sexual affairs. Edward Westermarck, who collected local proverbs from these hills from 1910 to 1930, records that intercourse for three days in succession with an ass was then considered a cure for gonorrhoea, with a black dog, a permanent safeguard against imprisonment; whilst boys abused she-asses in order to make their penis grow. The nearest he comes to a moral comment is, *'Nakeh z'zwamel kaiwarrat d'damel', 'Intercourse with boy prostitutes produces boils'.*

The Grand Mosque

Opposite the cafés is the Grand Mosque, easily recognizable with its octagonal minaret. This was one of the first buildings erected by the Sherif Moulay Ali bin Rashid, though it was restored in the 17th and 18th centuries. Next door there is the smaller portal of a 16th-century **medersa**, founded by the last Emir of Chechaouèn, but it is not currently open to visitors. The alley that separates the mosque from the kasbah leads down to a zaouia and school where Fatima bint Ali Rashid, the 'governess' of the corsairs, is buried.

The Kasbah

Open Wed–Mon 9am–1pm, 3–6.30pm; closed Tues; adm.

The conspicuous **Tower of Homage** dates from the 15th century, but the distinctive pisé walls of the kasbah date from a restoration ordered by Sultan Moulay Ismaïl. Feel free to clamber along the battlements. The interior contains a pleasant pattern of cobbles and gardens while a small folk museum (Musée Ethnographique) and Andalusian study centre has been established in the old apartments (*separate adm*). In the opposite corner of the kasbah you may visit the dungeons over which Abdel Krim presided after he expelled the Spanish in 1921, but to which he returned as a prisoner five years later after the suppression of the Rif rebellion. Traditions record that in the northwest corner, where some cellars have been exposed, a 15th-century tunnel used to lead out of the walls to the site of the present Parador Hotel. The last emir used this route to escape from the Saadian siege in 1562.

The Medina

The medina is small and friendly enough for you to explore leisurely at your own pace from the Uta el Hammam. It provides an endless range of fascinating vistas with the accent on individual decoration. The steep pitched red tile roofs are an architectural memory of Granada, where the roofs had to be capable of supporting a heavy fall of snow. The houses also retain the Andalucian motif of horseshoe double windows, shielded by eyebrows of ceramic tiles and protected and decorated by twisted metal grilles. The walls of the houses are painted with contrasting shades of electric blue and pure whitewash, which flows out to demarcate part of the alley.

Elaborate fountains play, the smell of fresh bread wafts from a local bakery, artisans ask you in for a smoke and to admire their work, whilst areas of pebble and stone mosaic reflect and complement the traditional and intricately carved wooden window frames.

The Walls

The walls are best appreciated by walking in the cemetery, above the town. With the aid of a guide it is easy to identify the **Bab Mamluk**, the mountain gate, surrounded by 500-year-old olive trees. The **Bab es Souk** is the only gate that retains its architectural decoration.

Walks and Swimming

The stream that supplies the town with excellent cool clear water, the **Ras el Ma**, flows down from the high valley between Jbel Meggou, 1616m and Jbel Tisouka, 2050m, the two horns of Chechaouèn. A spacious shaded café surrounded by concrete terraces sits beside the collecting pool for the spring-water, which can be reached by walking uphill through medina streets from the northeast corner of the Place El Maghzen. Nearby is the **tomb of Sidi Abdallah Habti**, who died in 1555.

A scrambling walk allows you to follow the stream uphill for 3km to its source, where it emerges through the rocks. This has been traced back through numerous caves and reportedly snakes some 4km underground to the east. Looking out from the spring, the horizon of mountains is fringed with cedars.

Walks up the surrounding mountains may allow you to see or meet hyenas, wild boars, red cobras, golden eagles, kites, buzzards, Barbary apes and partridges. Alternatively you can join the dirt track that leads back to the town via the Asma Hotel, providing you with excellent bird's-eye views of the medina. A shorter stroll would take you beyond the Ras el Ma spring up to the **fake Spanish-built 'mosque'** on the hill above. This viewpoint folly has a steep spiral staircase within the minaret: there is a fine view from the roof. Watch out where you put your feet—there are turds about.

The river Laou has a number of **swimmable pools** which can be approached from the main P28 road which runs parallel. It is easily accessible by taxi or car. Alternatively take the road to the coast, a 42km drive that passes the Laou Gorge before reaching the coastal fishing village of Et-Tleta-de-Oued-Laou (*see* p.127).

Where to Stay

Chechaouèn is a small but popular destination, and as beds can be in short supply most of the town's hotels are listed here.

expensive

The **Asma Hotel**, ✆ (09) 987158, looks an unforgivable intrusion on the historic skyline of the town. The architect and the interior designer should certainly feel ashamed, for the hotel occupies the exact site of the old Husu Abdul Hamid fort. However, it has a pool, efficient plumbing and a magnificent view of the town. The **Parador-Hôtel de Chaouen** on Place El Maghzen, ✆ (09) 986136 and 986324, @ (09) 987033, has a pool, bar, restaurant, 37 bedrooms and the best position in town. There's also the 'mosque'-folly built by the Spaniards on the hill opposite to add a final touch to the view.

inexpensive

The one two-star hotel in town is the **Magou** at 23 Rue Moulay Idriss, ✆ (09) 986275. Just above the souk and below the medina, it is a comfortable but unexceptional place. The **Hôtel Rif**, 29 Rue Tarik Ibn Ziad, ✆ (09) 986982, is run by a genial manager who has covered the furniture with his own painted floral designs and serves a good three-course dinner. The nearby **Hôtel Salam** at 39 Rue Tarik Ibn Ziad, ✆ (09) 986239, is equally popular, with meals served either in the salon or on the roof terrace.

Two good modern places are a short distance away from the old town but conveniently close to the souk square/bus stop: the **Hôtel Bonsai** at 12 Rue Sidi Srif, ✆ (09) 986980, and the aptly named **Hôtel Panorama** at 33 Rue Moulay Abder Rahman Chrif, ✆ (09) 986615.

cheap

The medina pensions are intimate places that often occupy an old courtyard house. They are easily the most distinctive form of accommodation and are popular throughout the year, much beloved by serious kif smokers as well as earnestly friendly backpacking students. They are all easily found in the streets around the Uta el Hammam, and in the rare event of no helping guide at hand they are well signposted. Best of all is **Pension Casa Hassan**, 22 Rue Targhi, ✆ (09) 986153, with its magnificent Moroccan interior and warm fire in winter. You may have to try them all before finding a room; ask for **Pension Rachidia** or **Pension Batouta** on Rue Sidi Boukhancha, ✆ (09) 986044. **Pension Moritania** is at 15 Rue Kadi Alami, ✆ (09) 986184, with communal dormitories awash with music and international camaraderie. **Pension Andaluz** at 1 Rue Sidi Salem, ✆ (09) 986034, has clean individual rooms; **Pension Castellane**, 4 Rue Sidi Ahmed Bouhali, ✆ (09) 986295, is beside the men's *hammam*. **Pension Cordoba** is beside the Tissemal café-restaurant on Rue Granada, **Pension Valencia** is on Rue Hassan I, ✆ (09) 986088, **Pension Znika** is on the street of that name, ✆ (09) 986024, and the **Pension Knancha** is at 57 Rue Lala el Hora, ✆ (09) 986879—25m into the medina from Bab el Ain gate.

Eating Out

For a formal meal with a bottle of wine you will have to go to either the **Hôtel Asma**, the **Parador** or the **Magou**. The **Restaurant Kasba** is the best of the several café-restaurants on Uta el Hammam, though up in the medina streets there is the **Granada Restaurant** beside the Pension Valencia and the **Tissemal Restaurant** near the Pension Cordoba. The **Pension Casa Hassan** also offers excellent Moroccan cooking. None of the medina places serves alcohol. For a cheap evening drink, head down to the **Restaurant-Bar Omo Rabi**, ✆ (09) 986180, next door to the travel agent on Rue Tarik Ibn Ziad, which is licensed to sell beer and can serve wine with a meal.

Shopping

The town has two market days, on Monday and Thursday, when large groups of **vegetable stalls** appear in the courtyards below the Hôtel Magou. The main shopping thoroughfare for **woollen cloth, carpets** and **worked leather** is the street that leads downhill from the Uta el Hammam to Charih Hassan II. Chechaouèn is nationally famous for its looms which weave from mountain wool the striped Rif cloth, jellabas and blankets. Threads spun by the tailors' apprentices crisscross the narrow streets in an endless game of cat's cradle.

Festivals

Chechaouèn nurtures a long memory and a number of saints' tombs. The biggest and most accessible *moussem* is that of **Sidi Alla el Hadj** on 9 August. The ***moussem* of Abdessalam ben Mchich**, held at the saints shrine in the hills (equidistant from Tetouan and Chechaouèn) around the summer solstice, draws together all the tribes of the Jebala. This saint, who died in 1188, was one of the main sources of the mystical tradition in Morocco. Every Jebala bridegroom places himself under the saint's protection on his marriage day. He is also known as the master of Jbel Alam, for he lies buried on this mountain in a grave open to the air. One of the secrets of the bandit Raissouli's power (*see* p.169) was his descent from this great figure, strengthened by a ceremony where he made the tribes swear loyalty to his leadership in a mass oath taken up on the high slopes of Jbel Alam on the night of a full moon.

From Chechaouèn to Ouezzane

The P28 takes you 60km on a twisting mountain road through the heart of the Jebala hill country. The crossing of the river Loukkos provides a good excuse for a stop. The old Franco-Spanish frontier post just by the bridge has been converted into a covered roadside **souk** busy with café-restaurants, and a waterfall on the right provides a pleasant, cool picnic site. Beside the road there are a number of decorated fountains, originally established for mule trains but now occasionally used for overnight parking by camper vans. On Saturday morning there is a **souk** just to the west of the road at Es Sebt, which could be worth a visit.

Ouezzane

Ouezzane (Wazzan) has kept its aura of a highland sanctuary. There are delightfully few concessions to the tourist and it remains a calmly prosperous provincial town famous for its olive oil and its holy dynasty of *sherifs*. If you can arrive here on Thursday morning you will find Ouezzane full of mountain farmers drawn to the busy **souk**, and the artisan shops in the medina will be at their busiest and most accessible.

History

Ouezzane is a comparatively recent creation. The distinguished Idrissid *sherif* Moulay Abdullah ben Brahim settled here in 1727 and established the first Taibia Sufi brotherhood. Before his arrival Ouezzane was known as **Dechra Jbel er-Rihan**, the village on the mountain of myrtles. The *sherif* gave moral direction to the tribes and instructed them in the Sufi mysticism of the Taibia brotherhood. His prestige as the heir to one of the senior lines of descent from Idriss II and hence from the Prophet, the spread of the Taibia brotherhood throughout the whole of North Africa, and the lack of a strong government in this period catapulted the *sherif* and his heirs into a position of great influence.

By the early 19th century the *sherifs* of Ouezzane enjoyed the respect of all the tribes of the Rif and the Jebala. Typically, it was the family of the *sherif*, not the sultan, who led the hill tribes to the defence of Tetouan during the Spanish invasion of 1859. In the maze of bitter tribal rivalries their impartial arbitration and declarations of peace were of great value. Many tribes voluntarily contributed a tithe in order to share the *baraka*, the blessing or holy luck of the *sherifs*. The *sherifs* used these gifts to feed travellers, protect widows and orphans and act as patron to craftsmen, students and scholars. The sultans in Fès governed through requests to the *sherifs* and employed members of the *sherif's* family in high positions at their court. The proud boast of Ouezzane was, 'No sultan for us; without us no Sultan.'

Sherif Si Absellam caused great scandal at the end of the 19th century by divorcing his three wives to marry an English girl, Emily Keene, whom he had met riding outside Tangier. Far from converting to Islam, she insisted on an Anglican marriage. The *sherif* explained his wife's difficult religious attitude to his relations with a parable. He would pour sugar on the floor and watch ants arrive from each corner. All have attained the mountain and achieved sweetness: such is the case with Muslims, Jews and Christians in their search for the one God.

This kind, tolerant man eventually fell victim to his family's madness: he developed a paranoid fear of assassination and a craving for alcohol (good Muslims claimed that champagne turned to milk in his mouth). He also fell under the damaging influence of the French consul Ordega, who used the *sherif* as a front to acquire vast land holdings and mineral rights for the French Compagnie Marocaine. Within a few decades the Ouezzane family had lost most of its power and influence, although they retained great status throughout the French protectorate. The present line of *sherifs* are descended from the children of Emily and Si.

Getting Around

Ouezzane is 60km south of Chechaouèn and 135km north of Meknès. There are half a dozen daily **buses** that stop at Ouezzane on the regular Chechaouèn to Fès and Meknès runs. The bus station is just below the Place de l'Indépendance on the Rue de la Marche Verte. On Thursdays in particular, there are any number of places available in ***grands taxis*** going towards Chechaouèn, Meknès or Fès, and west to Souk-el-Arba-du-Rharb.

Orientation

The large triangular space at the foot of the medina, the Place de l'Indépendance, is the heart of the town, where the Thursday **souk** assembles. All three roads to Ouezzane naturally lead to this square, where there are hotels, cafés and a branch of the Banque Populaire. To the east of the square is the Place du Marché, and to the west is the Avenue Mohammed V. There is a municipal **swimming pool**, open in the summer months, which is in one corner of the sports area on the south side of Avenue Hassan II.

The Medina

The town climbs uphill from the Place de l'Indépendance—an enchanting, intriguing network of cobbled streets, shop fronts, arched buttresses and aged town houses decorated with tiled eaves which it is easy and entertaining to explore. Ouezzane is a provincial town that remains a craft and marketing centre for the hinterland of surrounding mountain villages. It has no tourist-oriented bazaars, but a profusion of artisan stalls—with all the usual crafts, weavers' looms, tailors, cobblers and smiths,and the local speciality, painted furniture.

From the Place de l'Indépendance turn left past the Grand Hotel café to climb up the Rue Abdellah ben Lamlih which leads to the centre of the souks, the triangular Place Bir Inzarane. Take the left turn, the Rue Haddadine, below the mosque of Moulay Abdallah Chérif, opposite which is the covered **blacksmiths' souk** (*souk des forgerons*). Here you can find the Café Bellevue, its stone pillars now enlivened by an unmissable layer of gay new paint. It has a wonderful, uncommercial atmosphere and a fine view of the folding landscape of mountains from its high terrace. Immediately below the café, the blacksmiths create a soothing pattern of hammer blows.

Continue on, keeping right and passing through an arch into the broad Rue de la Zaouia. This internal space is dominated by the octagonal minaret of the **mosque of the Taibia brotherhood** (*mosquée S'Ma des Zaouia*), built by Sherif Moulay Ali; it has a wistful appeal—the fading green faïence tiles enclosed by a bas relief of intricate stone arches are graceful even in decay. The surrounding buildings, old pilgrim lodgings and apartments, are deteriorating at a faster rate, and the formal gates to the *sherif's* palace look particularly precarious. The towers of the old sanctuary palace are often used by nesting hawks who teach their young to kill above the confused roof tops of the medina.

Around Ouezzane

Jbel-Bou-Hellal provides a fabulous view of the town and the mountainous country from its summit of 609m. You can walk up to it through the medina alleys and out through the olive groves, or drive—take the road for Fès and turn right 50m after the public gardens and modern church for the climb up the mountain slope. There is a viewing platform about 400m from the end of the tarmac.

To the west of Ouezzane on the P23, a turning to the right, the 2635, will take you 9km to the pretty village of **Azjen**. Here, in a **koubba**, lies buried the celebrated 18th-century Jewish rabbi, Amrane, famous for his arcane knowledge and magical powers.

Where to Stay and Eating Out

There are no officially classified hotels in Ouezzane but it is easy to find a bed in one of the half-dozen small, cheap, simple places that are grouped below the conspicuous square clock tower on the Place de l'Indépendance. The **Marhaba**, the **Horloge** and **El Elam** all have one or two rooms with balconies over the square. If they are full there is also the **Grand Hôtel** (in name only) and the **Hôtel de Poste**, just off the square on Avenue Mohammed V. Opposite the Poste is a *hammam* associated with the mosque which travellers are welcome to use.

The Place holds practically all the café-restaurants in town, offering the ubiquitous menu of fresh salads, kebabs and *brochettes.* Eat early, as most of the cafés close early in a town ungeared to tourist requirements.

Shopping

Ouezzane's reputation for skilled craft work is reflected in two state-run **Ensembles Artisanaux**, open 8am–7pm. One faces the Place de l'Indépendence and the other is on the Avenue Hassan II, the Fès road, just before the Lalla Amina square.

Sefiane and Cheraga

The Sefiane and Cheraga are two neighbouring administrative regions on the upper reaches of the Sebou and Ouerrha river valleys. They do not recall any specific tribal identity; before the Protectorate this area was inhabited by clans of Arabic-speaking herdsmen. It is an area of undulating open hills that remains completely rural and traditional. It stands between the gaunt mountains of the Rif and the big central cities of Fès and Meknès, virtually untouched by tourism and with no hotels or restaurants. For the more intrepid traveller it has a number of interesting corners, such as Basra, Fès-el-Bali, the fortress on Jbel Amergou and the summit view from Lalla-Outka.

About 33km west of Ouezzane on the P23 Rabat road there is a small village of corrugated iron-roofed farms enveloped in their individual hedges of prickly pear, encircled by ancient stone betowered city walls. These once enclosed the great city of **Basra**, founded by Idriss II in the 9th century as a sister to Fès. The walls, which were raised in the 10th century, are a testament to its size, but by the 16th century Basra was caught up in the war between the Portuguese on the coast and the hill tribes, and reduced to ruin.

In the opposite direction, about 70km southeast of Ouezzane on the beautiful, if very windy, P26, is the sprawling farming settlement of **Fès-el-Bali**, Old Fès. This was an 11th-century Almoravid foundation. Sections of the red pisé walls can still be traced amongst the village paddocks and one of the farm boys may show you the surviving Almoravid ***hammam***, a remarkably Roman-looking rectangular building decorated with marble and a fountain. The proud city of the Taouda tribe did not survive long after their Almoravid patrons fell from power—their old tribal enemies on the Rhomara coast fell upon the town and slaughtered all the inhabitants.

About 11km on from Fès-el-Bali (81km southeast of Ouezzane on the Fès road) is the small roadside village of **Et Tnie**, a minor marketplace of the Fichtala tribe. The **zaouia of Moulay Bouchta** is only 1km east of the market, up a track. This saint and his equally venerated daughter, Aicha, are appealed to for rain and honoured in a lively *moussem* in September which attracts competing bands of local musicians. Overlooking the shrine is the outcrop of **Jbel Amergou** whose summit is crowned with a stone fortress, a rare survival from the Almoravid period. On the hour-and-a-half walk to the peak from the village you pass through a secluded mountain-top village, an idyllic cluster of thatched houses beside a mosque and spring. The **11th-century stone fortress**, built to guard the eastern approaches to Fès-el-Bali, is in surprisingly good condition: the perimeter wall studded with a dozen towers is complete and the arched entrance gate still stands proud. The interior is divided by

a central keep into two extensive courts with water tanks in the eastern half. The view from the walls takes in the wide sweep of the Ouerrha valley and the new dam that is being built to control the river's flow.

To the east of Jbel Amergou is the village of **Ourtzarh** (about 18km along the S304 from the junction below the mountain), positioned by a river junction and overlooked by the heights of Jbel Messaoud. Though there is a wonderful view from this 835m high mountain, it is the summit of **Jbel Lalla-Outka**, at 1595m, that attracts greater attention. From Ourtzarh take the tarmac road 14km north to Rhafsai (Ghafsai), which celebrates its olive harvest with a festival in December. From here a good track climbs for 37km, passing through the hamlets of **Souk el Had** and **Tamesnite** to swing up the side of the mountain and approach the summit and its breathtaking view over the Rif mountains from the south.

The view northwest partly overlooks the reclusive territory of the Beni Ahmed tribe. Traditions believed them 'to have a secret city, so hidden that no one may ever see it, and marvellous parchments written in a strange language ... it may be that there is something, for there are *ulema* among the Beni Ahmed who never learnt their wisdom at the schools.' (*El Raissouli*, Rosita Forbes). A linguist investigated these persistent rumours in the late 1940s, but he cut short his work after his female informant died suddenly in a shooting accident.

The Eastern Rif

The Rif Mountains east of Chechaouèn cannot compete with the beautiful forested peaks of the Jebala. They do, however, have a solemn grandeur entirely in keeping with the notorious bellicosity of the local tribes. The eastern Rif has its own rewards, but do not attempt to explore this area on your first trip to Morocco.

Chechaouèn to Ketama

Driving east from Chechaouèn you soon enter **kif country**, which, if not necessarily dangerous for the visitor, is a place where prudence is always a good idea, and you are advised to read through this section before deciding whether to take the road or not. It can be genuinely hair-raising. The turning east to Ketama from the Chechaouèn to Ouezzane road is a favourite police checkpoint, but it is not until you reach **Bab-Taza**, about 20km along, that you enter the real area of 'kif business'. Bab-Taza, which has a ruined Spanish fort and a café-restaurant, is also the traditional frontier between the people of the Jebala, the western Rif, and the Rifis proper who inhabit the eastern Rif. After the village of Bab-Taza the road follows the mountain crests and exposes you to an intermittent line of kif salesmen. Small boys will hiss 'Shit!' at you and perform a crumbling mime with their thumb and fingers, or a smoker's drag, anywhere along the next 135km of road.

Cheferat, 15km east of Bab Taza, has for half the year a spectacular cleft spring. Cold mountain water rushes spouting out from the cliff as if Moses had just tapped the rock with his staff. The water is directed into fast-flowing channels and spun around an intriguing central corkscrew whirlpool to draw the water under itself on to another level. Other attractions of the village, are its two cafés, on the right-hand side of the road going east, which serve good snack lunches.

Before the town of **Bab-Berred** you pass below the disturbed foothills, scree slopes and cavern-strewn face of **Jbel Tisserine**. There is a basic **café-hotel** at Bab-Berred which you might conceivably need to stay at since it's the last stopping-place before the cedar forests beyond the Bab-Besen pass and the area of really serious aggressive salesmanship. Cars are frequently sandwiched by vans on this exhilarating mountain-top drive to enable great lumps of marijuana resin to be offered for sale. Headlights flash from woodland clearings, and urgent hand-signals insist that you stop. Do not be tempted to dawdle in admiration of the mountains and the cedar forests. Stop for no one, however innocent the situation appears to be: travellers' tales of extortion, theft and enforced sales of kilos of marijuana are true, and common enough.

After the thrill of the mountain scenery and the heady aroma of bandit country the little roadside junction village of **Ketama** is slightly disappointing. Large *gendarmerie* barracks line the approaches and pine woods enclose the few buildings. The cone shaped mass of **Jbel Tidiquin**, 2448m high, dominates the horizon to the east, its peak capped in snow throughout much of the year. It is the sacred mountain of the Rif, where in former times bulls were sacrificed on the summer and winter solstices. Local tradition also states that Noah landed the Ark on this peak.

Ketama was a popular hill-walking and cross-country skiing centre during the Protectorate. Nowadays it is no longer a resort but an internationally recognized marketplace for marijuana. This grows naturally throughout Morocco, but the hill farmers of the Rif specialize in the cultivation of it as a cash crop in their high, isolated valleys (*see* p.26 'Kif'). The terrain and the tradition of tribal dissidence are remarkably similar to those found in other great marijuana-producing areas of the world: Lebanon, Afghanistan and Mexico. The distribution of the product, sales and smuggling to Europe are handled by rival gangs whose activities are broadly tolerated by a government fully aware of the region's poverty and explosive history. It is so influential and rewarding a trade that in the Rif the word 'business' is now synonymous with kif. An outsider attempting to enter into this highly competitive market will inevitably be sold out by the dealers to their friends in the customs, police or *gendarmerie*. Despite this, every year about a dozen British people and similar numbers of other Europeans try to set in motion schemes that involve light planes, frogmen, yachts and cross-country marches. The jail sentences are served in Morocco.

This all gives a certain prurient vicarious excitement to the first hour in Ketama. It is unadventurous but wise to refuse politely any invitations to visit a neighbouring farm. Throughout your stay you will be ceaselessly offered enormous quantities of kif at bargain prices. A strict no-smoking policy will allow you to keep your judgement unimpaired. If Ketama sounds undesirable, though, it remains useful as a bus connection, and has the one efficient hotel between Chechaouèn and Al Hoceima.

Where to Stay

Maroc-Tourist run the **Hôtel Tidighine,** © Ketama 16 (call via PTT or phone offices), which is the one expensive sanctuary from business in Ketama. This has a tennis court, swimming pool, a bar and restaurant, with 68 largely empty and unused bedrooms. The porter nodded his head in sadness at my innocent request for a mountain guide with a mule.

For a tighter budget the **Café-Hôtel Saada** or the **California** on the road to Fès can offer you a cheap room for a night.

La Route de l'Unité

The road south to Fès, the S302 or Route de L'Unité, is one of the most exhaustingly dramatic and thrilling mountain roads in Morocco. It was cut out of the mountains in the first heady years of Independence in the late 1950s, linking the Spanish protectorate of the north coast to central Morocco. Voluntary labour battalions mixed together hill tribes and city dwellers in units that absorbed potential dissidents and gave education in the new nationalism and ideas of Islamic reform.

Nine km out of Ketama is **Tleta-Ketama**, a hamlet with a few cafés and a market on Tuesdays. The most useful track up which to approach **Jbel Tidiquin** is 500m south of this hamlet. Continuing along the Route de l'Unité through wooded hills, forested slopes and pretty waterfalls you come after about 10km to the first of a succession of magnificent mountain panoramas. Possibly the most dramatic portion of the road is that around the village of **Souk-el-Had-de-Ikauen**, the Sunday marketplace of the Ikauen tribe. The views remain compelling the whole 40km down to **Taounate**, a large modern town which has its market day on Friday and a festival in September. If you are passing this way in August or October you should check out **Tissa**, another 40km further south, which celebrates the *moussem* of the 15th-century saint Mohammed ben Lahcen and an accompanying horse fair with some spectacular equine demonstrations. From there, it's a final 35km through the eastern Cheraga hills down to Fès.

Ketama to Al Hoceima

East of Ketama the cedar and pine forests soon give way to a much more austere, bleak landscape. The eastern hills of the Rif are stark, rounded slopes stained with shades of red. The soil looks dangerously bleached and the slopes are bare of any woods. The houses are square blocks set alone in the hard-worked ground, without any sheltering gardens or shade trees. The Rif breeds heroes, not flowers. The fields have to be constantly cleared of crops of stones, and in this landscape feuds begin to look like a form of relaxation.

About 12km east of Ketama look out for the northern turning that can take you down a rough tarmac road, the 8500, 60km to El-Jebha (*see* p.129). It is an exhilarating twisting drive which you take at some risk to your sump. There is a mechanic at El-Jebha; the nearest tow trucks are in Tetouan.

Thirty-seven km east of Ketama a left turn, the 8501, takes you 30km down to the coast through the territory of the Beni Bu Frah tribe. The village of **Bni-Boufrah**, 5km inland from the sea, has two shops and a post office with a telephone. **Torres-de-Alcalá** is a small white-washed village beside a river a few hundred metres inland from the coast. A track leads to a pebble beach with three fishermen's huts, beached boats and a single basic café. On a hill above, the remaining towers of a fortress survey the emptiness and serenity.

From Torres-de-Alcalá a bad dirt road travels east to the site of the old Muslim port of Badis, which faces the **Peñón de Velez de la Gomera**, a tiny offshore island still in the possession of Spain. The Peñon is just visible without travelling along this road. It can be recognized by the white tower that crowns this improbably steep island, but is so overshadowed by the surrounding folds of the mountain massif of Bokkoyas on the mainland that it takes time to separate it out from the background. It appears so hopelessly quixotic, so outrageously useless a possession that it can hardly figure as an insult to Moroccan sovereignty, more of a glorious Spanish absurdity.

Badis was one of the principal trading ports for Fès in the Middle Ages. The installation of the Spanish on the island in 1508 began a rapid decline in trade. In 1522 it became a corsair base where Bou Hassoun, a prince of the old dynasty, created a formidable fighting machine from a mixture of professional Turks, Andalusian refugees and local tribesmen. He became a threat to both the Spanish and the new Saadian dynasty, who secretly conspired together to destroy this mutual enemy. In 1564 Philip II's fleet descended on the town. Nothing remains, even though the Spanish still garrison the Peñon opposite, and during the Protectorate used it as a secure prison.

Kalah Iris, 4km west of Torres-de-Alcalá, is a stunningly beautiful length of beach broken by a central spit that connects an island to the shore where fishermen moor their boats. Another island sits offshore and the whole area is sealed from the hinterland by enclosing cliffs. A charming **campsite** with bungalows for rent as well as pitches for tents is run by Ahmed Hmeddach, planted with mimosas and open throughout the year. A fish restaurant functions during part of the summer and a café throughout the year, providing the generator is in action. Each year there seem to be fewer visitors to this picturesque, tranquil beach.

Targuist, 42km east of Ketama on the P39, is just east of the area of kif business. The surrounding Ghis plateau is cultivated with groves of olives, almonds and walnuts which are traded in the **souk** on Saturdays, though the café-restaurants are open and busy throughout the week. It is a strong, wind-blown, regular featured town which is proud to be have been the last refuge of Abdel Krim before he surrendered to the French forces in 1926. There are a number of cheap, basic hotels in the centre. The cheapest, providing you don't mind sharing your washing water from an old oil barrel with other guests, is the **Hôtel Chaab** at 14 Calle Hassan II. A *hammam* for washing can be found just off the central roundabout, the Calle Sahat Rifal. Sixty-five kilometres on from Targuist you pass through the village of **Youssef ou Ali**, which was originally the chief village of the powerful Beni Ouriaghel tribe, and the home of Abdel Krim.

Al Hoceima

Al Hoceima was built by the Spanish (who called it Villa Sanjurjo) in 1926 immediately after they had suppressed the Rif rebellion. It was deliberately sited in the midst of the Beni Ouriaghel lands so that a Spanish garrison could keep a close watch over the tribe that was at the heart of the rebellion. It is now a confident, hospitable town with a population of 40,000, but little apparently in common with its harsh hinterland. Even the mosque doors are set wide open and the streets are largely hassle-free. White houses cascade down the hill with few architectural embellishments to form neat, long avenues that reach down towards, but never manage to overlook, the bay. The small, attractive but well-populated area of beach is confined by two massive sea cliffs, and the Hôtel Quemado takes up the area of falling ground that connects town to beach. The **Place du Rif** is the centre of town life, lined with cheap cafés and hotels. There is a small fishing port to the west and a camping beach to the east. The massive central block of the old Spanish residency has now usefully been transformed into a school and cultural centre.

Getting Around

by air

The Côte du Rif airport is at Charif al Idrissi, © (09) 982063 and 982005. There are regular RAM flights to Casablanca, Marrakech and several other parts of the country, and European charter flights also arrive here.

by bus or taxi

Buses leave from Place du Rif—check with the tourist office for departure times, which can change with the season. Usually there are two a day going west for Tetouan via Chechaouèn (a 10–hour journey), daily buses heading south for Taza and Fès (12hrs), and several east to Nador and Oujda. ***Grands taxis*** also leave from the Place du Rif, with places regularly offered west for Chechaouèn or east to Nador/Melilla.

Tourist Information

The helpful tourist office, ready with leaflets, a town map and lists of pensions and local souks, is on Avenue Tariq Ibn Ziad, © (09) 982830, and is open Mon–Sat 8.30am–12pm, 2–6pm. There is a **Banque Populaire** at 47 Avenue Mohammed V. The town **souk** is held on Tuesdays.

The Beaches and the Peñón

To the east of Al Hoceima is the relatively fertile bay of **Alhucemas** fed by the rivers Rhis and Nekor. The beach stretches along most of the bay, a tranquil area in delightful contrast to the crowded town beach. The **Peñón de Alhucemas**, another tiny offshore island that has been in the possession of Spain for centuries, is capped with a church and tower. At night, dressed with lights, it looks like some visiting liner at anchor in the bay.

Where to Stay

expensive

The three big hotels, **Maghreb el Jadida**, **Mohammed V** (currently closed for repairs) and **Quemado** are all run by Maroc Tourist as an interchangeable beach front unit for the packaged tours that fly into the local airport. Within this bracket the Maghreb El-Jadida, © (09) 982504, at 56 Av Mohammed V, is the best.

inexpensive

The independent traveller has a choice between the **National** at 23 Rue de Tetouan, © (09) 982431, **Hôtel Karim** at 27 Charif Hassan II, © (09) 982184, or the **Marrakech** at 21 Rue Abdellah Hamou, © (09) 980325. The Karim has got the most facilities and is the largest, with 50 rooms, while the National with 16 rooms and the Marrakech with nine are more intimate. The National is particularly welcoming to its guests.

cheap

All the cheaper unclassified hotels are clustered around the Place du Rif where the CTM buses arrive, and can be relied upon to have clean beds but dubious water supplies. The **Café-Hôtel Florido**, 40 Sahat Rif, © (09) 982235 is the most immediately visible of these, decorated with the truncated star of David, the emblem of Abdel Krim's Republic of the Rif. If it's full there is also the **Afrique** on Rue de Tahnaout, © (09) 983065, the **Nord** on Rue Imzouren, © (09) 983079, and the **Hôtel Saada** which is opposite a Sufi lodge. The Saada can seem a little rough, but the delightful Madame Fatima who runs it makes up for it.

camping

A seasonal camping site, **El Jamil**, © (09) 984026, is a 500m walk east down from the town to a pleasant little bay directly opening on to its own beach with fine views looking over the Rif mountains.

Eating Out

The Quemado, Maghreb El Jadida and Karim hotels all have bars and restaurants that serve alcohol. Near to the National is the **Café Tamsamaon** on Calle Al Amir Moulay Abdulah, which can feed you on salads and *brochettes*, and the **Café Marhaba** on the Place du Rif is the busiest in this competitive area, serving grilled chicken, meat and salads—cheap and cheerful. There is a cluster of fish restaurants on the port, the best of which is **Le Karim**, with its terrace overlooking the activity.

Battlefields of the Rif—Al Hoceima to Nador

The modern-looking village of **Beni-Bou-Ayach**, about 11km beyond the airport turning on the P39, was once the capital of the medieval **Emirate of Nokour**. The Emirate had been founded in 709, in the first decade of Arab conquest. It survived the Khajarite revolt and remained an oasis of orthodox Islam and Arab culture that prospered from the old Saharan trade with Spain. It survived for 350 years until the Almoravid sultan, Youssef ben Tachfine, descended like a desert wind to destroy its fortresses and incorporate the area into his Empire of Morocco. Various European trading powers tried to revive Beni-Bou-Ayach as a trading station but the flickering war between the Spanish (who garrisoned the Peñón de Alhucemas in 1673) and the Rif tribes effectively closed the area to merchants.

About 42km east from Al Hoceima you cross over the river Nekor (Nokour). A turning immediately on your right, the 8505, twists 5km west to the kasbah of **El-Arba-Taourit**, a dark red magenta fort on a dramatic outcrop overlooking the riverbed. The kasbah is entirely Spanish in construction, but was an ancient seat of power. The Merenids built a key fortress here during their long battle to wrest supremacy from the Almohad dynasty during the 13th century. Beyond the kasbah a track leads up towards **Jbel Hammane**, where the Beni Ouriaghel tribe made their last stand in 1926 against the combined Franco-Spanish forces massed against them.

The village of **Talamight** has the Taza café-hotel where you can stop for a coffee and contemplate driving across the narrow, twisting Tizi-Ouzli pass over the Aleppo-pine-covered summits of the Rif, passing through Aknoul on the way south to Taza. Just 13km beyond the turning look out for the dirt track to the north that leads to the hot springs of **Aïn Chiffa** where you can take a natural *hammam*.

Midar, 102km east of Al Hoceima, only comes alive for a passing visitor at the Wednesday souk, though like Driouch and Monte Arouit, further east, it has café-restaurants and basic hotels for those wanting to explore the untouched **Annoual** hinterland.

This was the area that saw the original dramatic success of the 1920s Rif rising. It was not a set battle but a confusion of individual engagements. In a series of preparatory raids, Abdel Krim established that the Spanish forces were of poor calibre and their supply lines over-stretched. By 17 July 1921 he had organized all the tribes to launch a simultaneous attack on the Spanish posts which, individually overwhelmed, were unable to support each other. By 9 August Monte Arouit, the last Spanish fort outside Melilla, had fallen. An army of 18,000 had been destroyed in what became known as the Rout of Annoual. The few prisoners that survived the appalling rituals of tribal vengeance were sold back to Spain in the next year.

Fortunately it is difficult to imagine the massacres that took place here, where young Spanish conscripts were impaled on their barbed-wire posts and raped with bayonets. Annoual is a comparatively fertile place with a small river gorge. If you turn north on the 8105, just before Tiztoutine, you will pass a couple of old Spanish watchtowers at the wadi crossings between **Kandoussi** and **Dar-Kebdani**. The latter has a crumbling fort in the middle of the village.

Selouane, the village at the Oujda–Al Hoceima–Melilla road junction, is enthusiastically hailed in the national press as the iron town of Morocco. The skyline is indeed ugly with pylons but so far only two factories, run by Sonisaid, have located here. It is, however, well worth a stop. The kasbah, off a side road to the north beside the lone crossroads café central, overlooks the grimy banks of a wadi which can occasionally fill to form a pretty moat. It was built by Moulay Ismaïl on the site of an old fortress and reinforced in 1859 when it was feared that the Spanish might invade from Melilla, though as it turned out they attacked Tetouan from Ceuta. It was used, from 1902 to 1909, as the headquarters of the Rogui Bou

Hamara, a pretender to the throne who came close to seizing Fès from the Alaouite Sultans. He is supposed to have buried his treasure here but never revealed its location despite the determined interrogation of Sultan Moulay Hafid. The castellated compound is now partly occupied by some squatter families and used as a secure grain store. After your tour of the kasbah have a meal at the **Restaurant Brabo**, ✆ (09) 609033, at 110 Avenue Mohammed V, which has been enthusiastically recommended. North of Selouane you leave the dry hills and enter the efficiently irrigated coastal plain filled with fields of sugar cane, olives, corn and waving stands of bamboo.

The Eastern Mediterranean Coast and the Border

Nador

The city of Nador is not a tourist destination, but as the border into Spanish Melilla can be unpredictable you may find yourself needing to stay a night here.

Nador is the creation of post-Independence planners, and now houses 120,000 citizens. Though Melilla is only 15km north, the newly independent Morocco wished to create a Mediterranean port free from Spanish control. A new urban centre would also attract industry to the north and absorb the surplus and potentially dissident population of the Rif. These calculations were based on the assumed mineral wealth of the Rif mountains, which has since proved to be something of an illusion. There is only a little low grade iron ore outside Selouane, coal from Oujda and local agricultural produce to export through the port. Nor has Nador fulfilled its industrial expectations. In common with most of the north, it increasingly feels neglected by the central government. There is a long tradition of Rif dissidence to which Nador has added its own footnote of occasional political violence in the last few decades.

Getting Around

Some maps continue to show ferry services between Nador and Ibiza and Sète, but these are no longer in operation.

by rail

There is no train station at Nador but the ONCF run connecting coaches from their office on Avenue Sidi Mohammed to the nearest station at Taourirt (about 100km south of Nador, on the Oujda–Fès line) where you can pick up connections to Oujda, Taza, Fès, Rabat, *et al.*

by bus or taxi

CTM **buses** use the station by the prominent town hall at the inland end of Avenue Mohammed V. There are four departures daily for Al Hoceima (4hrs), two for Fès, Taza and Casablanca, and about a dozen for Oujda. There are also private bus companies that mostly operate from the lagoon end of Avenue des FAR, which is where you will also find the ***grand taxi*** ranks, particularly useful for the short hop to the border with Melilla.

Tourist Information

There is a **Banque Populaire** on Rue de la Ligue Arabe, and a **BMCE** on the corner of Avenue Ibn Rochd and Avenue Youssef ben Tachfine.

Nador Town

Nador is designed on a grid plan, and falls off from low hills to face east across a saltwater lagoon, the Sebkha bou Areq. The whitewashed houses with their details picked out in blue and green look pleasant enough, and the central avenues are elegantly lined with palms. The Avenue Corniche runs along the shoreline and in its centre is the conspicuous **Club Café**, set on stilts in the lagoon, where you can while away an hour or two over coffee and cakes. The lagoon water does not look very inviting or safe to swim in. The vegetable and fish markets on the way into town on either side of Av des FAR and the two-storey 'Grand Souk' near the waterfront between Av des FAR and Av Youssef ben Tachfine are better distractions.

Above the new town as you leave on the main road to Melilla is a ruined **Spanish fortress**. Guarded by a charming sentry-box with tiled benches, the walled compound contains barrack blocks still wearing their decorated corniches and areas of glazed tile work. The friendly squatters who live there make a picturesque, rather bizarre scene with turkeys, goats and chickens milling around the military debris where once only majors and colonels ruled.

Around Nador

Twenty kilometres east of the town on the 8101 through the coastal agricultural plain are the beach, campsite and restaurant of **Kariet-Arkmane** (Qariat Arkmane). They face out on to the Mediterranean, avoiding the mud and dubious water of the lagoon. The restaurant has a deserved reputation for fish and scallops and is popular with Spaniards from Melilla. The **campsite**, Karia Plage, charges under 10dh for a tent, person and car. Kariet-Arkmane is the only approach to the long spit of sand dunes that encloses the lagoon, with a **wilderness of reeds and birds** to explore on foot. The **coast road east** to the small fishing port of Ras-el-Ma (*see* p.153) runs beneath the Kebdana hills and makes a wonderfully tranquil 40km drive.

North of Nador, before you reach the port installations of **Beni-Enzar**, you pass a turning west to Farknana village which can take you above Spanish Melilla to explore the peninsula. The road to **Cap des Trois Fourches**, guarded by a pair of lighthouses, is tarmacked for half the way, with fine views but no sandy beaches. Tucked into the southwestern corner of the peninsula is the **shrine of Sidi-Messaoud**. This commemorates the saintly hero of this region who alone was trusted by the tribes and the European powers to negotiate the release of those captured by the pirates who were active along this coast deep into the 19th century.

Where to Stay

Nador is not a thrilling town and if you decide to stay a night it might be worthwhile taking a reasonably comfortable hotel.

expensive

The **Hôtel Rif** on the Avenue Youssef ben Tachfine, ✆ (06) 606535, is run by Maroc Tourist and has that permanent air of waiting for the group party that never seems to arrive. It does however partly overhang the lagoon and has the only swimming pool in town. It has a bar and restaurant, although the kitchen closes early, so get there before 8pm.

moderate

There is a much larger choice of mid-priced hotels, which pick up a surprising amount of custom from holidaying expatriate workers and businessmen. The **Mansour Ed Dahabi**, ✆ (06) 606583, at 101 Rue de Marrakech has its own restaurant and bar, which makes it the first choice. Opposite the Rif on the corner of Youssef ben Tachfine and Moulay Abdellah is the **Hôtel Mediterranée**, ✆ (06) 606611; more pleasant is the **Hôtel Khalid**, ✆ (06) 606726, at 129 Avenue des FAR.

inexpensive

The **Annoual**, ✆ (06) 606669, is a 30-bedroom hotel with its own café-restaurant at 16 Rue 20 Hay Khattabi, off Av Hassan II close to the private bus station.

Eating Out

Aside from the drinks-licensed restaurants in the Rif and Mansour Ed Dahabi, there are good, and much cheaper unlicensed restaurants around. **Romero's** is near the Rif hotel at 50 Av Youssef ben Tachfine; the **Al Mahatta** restaurant at 38 Av Abbas Mohammed Akkad, off Av des FAR, ✆ (06) 602777, is a busy place well used to feeding travellers off the buses at any hour of the day. If you have a car or a taxi fare you could also head out to Selouane or Kariet-Arkmane.

Melilla

The North African port of Melilla is memorably unattractive. No one should miss the opportunity of sampling this miasma of damp sea mist, rubbish-strewn waters and military barracks. Quixotic hopelessness has long had a grip on this ancient fortress and turn-of-the-century harbour town. It has been in the possession of Spain since 1497, and is considered by Madrid, at least, to be sovereign Spanish territory. The border is open, and Melilla makes an unusual point of entry into Morocco. It is linked by government-subsidized ferries to the two Spanish ports of Málaga and Almeria, but this is still an expensive way to bring a car or motorcycle to Morocco. The Moroccan customs and immigration officers, never the speediest operators, can offer masterful demonstrations of bureaucratic delay. Allow anything from ten minutes to two hours for your passport, green card, registration document, immigration form and currency form to be approved. The customs are on the look out for kif and migrant workers being smuggled into Spain and duty-free goods being shifted into Morocco. Cars hired in Morocco are not permitted to cross the border.

History

The sheltered bay to the south of the citadel promontory has always proved attractive to merchants. The Phoenicians first established the city of Rusadir here, and a full catalogue of invaders have in turn despoiled and revived the port: Romans, Vandals, Byzantines,

Visigoths, Arabs, Omayyads, Idrissids, Almoravids, Almohads and Merenids. During Merenid rule traders from the city states of Europe berthed at Melilla to acquire the fruits of the Saharan caravan trade. Melilla or Mlilya means 'the white' in Arabic, which the Berber tribes translated into their own dialect as 'Tamlit'.

In 1494 the Berber hill tribes rebelled against the Wattasid *caid* of Melilla and expelled him. Two Castilian captains who were trading off the coast found Melilla temporarily undefended and returned quickly to alert their king. In 1497 Pedro Estopiñón was dispatched with part of Columbus' second fleet to seize the town. A few years later its Muslim inhabitants were forcibly ordered to convert to Christianity, and the Inquisition arrived to monitor these newly-baptised believers. This led to an exodus of the original population, most of whom took refuge in Tetouan.

The Rif tribes, periodically assisted by a sultan, were never able to recapture the fortress but nor were the Spanish capable of extending their rule beyond the city walls. As a result a desultory border war flickered on for centuries. This intensified when Spanish engineers, extending the walls, demolished the holy tomb of Sidi Auriach in 1893. The most famous casualty of this border war was General Margallo, who was shot by one of his own lieutenants for being too conciliatory. The peace negotiations in Madrid were complicated when the Moroccan ambassador was assaulted at court by General Fuentes.

The cycle of ambushes and raids continued to escalate, and the Rif rebellion of 1921 to 1926 can be seen as the last and greatest stage of the Melilla border war. Abdel Krim acknowledged that his one great regret was in not seizing Melilla in the aftermath of the rout of Annoual. During the Spanish Protectorate Melilla enjoyed a brief relevance and prosperity due to its having been united with the hinterland for the first time since 1497, but after the end of the Protectorate in 1956 it returned to its isolated fortress mentality.

Despite its proud walls Melilla does not have a Castilian identity, and its declining population includes a polyglot mixture of trading nations. Jewish, Hindu Indian, Romany Gypsy and Genoese families leaven the predominant brew of Andalusian and Moroccan citizens. Local parliamentary representatives have long striven for an autonomous city-state (as has British Gibraltar), which could operate as a tax haven and repeat the boom years of Tangier when it functioned as an international city.

Getting Around

by air

Iberia has frequent flights between the Melilla airstrip (✆ 689948) and Málaga. Tickets can be bought at the Iberia office at 2 Cándido Lobera, ✆ 681507.

by sea

Apart from on Sundays, there is always at least one ferry sailing daily to Spain on either the *Albatros* or the *Canguro*, to Málaga (a 10hr crossing) or Almería (8hrs). Buy ferry tickets directly from **Compañía Transmediterranea**, 1 Calle General Marina, ✆ 681993; if you are travelling near the peak times of Easter and late August you should book ahead.

by bus or taxi

On the Spanish side of the frontier there is a regular shuttle every 15 minutes from the border post along the coast road to the central Plaza de España. On the Moroccan side of the frontier there is a local bus to Nador at least every hour as well as a *grand taxi* rank. Further connections await at Nador.

Tourist Information

The **Spanish tourist office** is at 20 Calle del General Aizpura, © 684204, and is open Mon–Fri 9am–2pm, 4–6pm, and Sat 10am–noon. The **post office** is on Calle Pablo Vallescá, the **Banco Central** at 1 Calle Ejército Español, © 681790, and **Banco de España** on the Plaza de Espana, © 682190. There are also **currency exchange booths** on both sides of the frontier (cash only), and though the exportation of Moroccan currency is illegal, in practice dirhams and pesetas are accepted in both Nador and Melilla.

To **telephone** Melilla from Morocco you must make an international call, dialling 0034 for Spain followed by 52, the Melilla area code. To call Morocco from Melilla, dial 07 for international, followed by 212 for Morocco and the area code, omitting the initial zero where the code has one.

The Town

The circular central garden of the **Plaza de España**, faced on its east side by 1930s government offices, divides the regular avenues of the turn-of-the-century new town from the more interesting alleys of the old citadel. The Avenida del Rey Juan Carlos I is the most animated of these broad streets and the centre of the shopping district. Due west of the Plaza de España stretches the regular, palm-lined pavement of the Parque Hernández, which comes alive for the evening *paseo.* Turn left at the far west end of the Plaza to stroll 150m down to the town's bull ring.

The Citadel

The citadel (*Ciudad Antigua*), a rocky acropolis still enclosed within 16th-century walls and almost entirely surrounded by the sea, is of much greater interest. From the harbour road, Avenida del General Macias, climb up the steps to enter the citadel through the marine gatehouse and twist through the dank passageway to enter the interior Plaza de la Maestranza. The tiny **chapel of Santiago** (St James the apostle, the patron of the Spanish crusaders) is ahead, whilst another passage to your left leads to an **elaborately carved gateway** filled with the arms of Charles V, the Holy Roman Emperor and King of Spain who nearly died on a disastrous crusader expedition on the North African shore. The gateway overlooks a dirty gully of the Mediterranean and leads into a dank barracks annexe.

Returning back to the Plaza de la Maestranza, walk up beside the battlements to the **Baluarte de la Concepción** bastion and the **Town Museum** (Museo Municipal; *open 9am–1pm, 4–6pm; closed Mon and Fri; adm*). Its weathered stone interior houses old weapons, a selection of archaeological finds, some prehistoric carved stones from the Western Sahara, and some placards that favourably compare Melilla's long Spanish history with the brief timespan of the USA. The **church of La Concepción**, just below the bastion, is usually kept locked, though the Baroque furnishings of the interior and the overblown gilt statue of the Virgin and Child as Our Lady of Victory (Nuestra Señora de la Victoria) repay a visit. Continue on around the sea-eroded battlements taking in the breeze and harbour views to leave the citadel at its southermost corner through the Túnel de Florentina, which pops you down by the ferry terminal.

Where to Stay

A tour of Melilla with a meal can occupy three hours, and few visitors find they need to stay a night. Compared to Morocco the hotels are expensive and rooms can be surprisingly hard to find. In season they are often full, and out of season, closed up.

expensive

The smartest hotel is undoubtedly the **Parador Don Pedro de Estopiñón**, © 684940, on Avenida de Cándido Lobera, to the north of the post office across the Lobera park. It has a garden, the only hotel pool in Melilla, and a bar and restaurant. However it is fairly lifeless and within earshot of the listless chants of prisoners in the jail. Dropping down in price a bit there is the **Hôtel Rusadir San Miguel** at 5 Calle Pablo Vallescá, © 681240, which has a bar and restaurant.

moderate

The following half dozen addresses are simple pension-style lodging-houses, though with some period charm from the high ceilings and family management. The **Miramar** is well placed to catch passing trade on the port front, Avenida de General Macias, © 683642, while the **Hostal España**, © 684645 and **Hostal Avenida**, © 684949, are both found along the central Avenida del Rey Juan Carlos I. The **Cazaza** is at no. 6, © 684648, and the **Nacional** at no. 10 Avenida Primo de Rivera, © 684540. The **Parque** is at 15 Avenida General Marina, © 682143, and the small **Hôtel Rioja** is at 6 Ejército Español, © 682709.

Eating Out

In the summer and weekends head straight up to the citadel where you will find the **Barbacoa La Muralla**, a terrace bar and traditional Spanish restaurant, right beside the Florentina tunnel. It has a fine view over the harbour and after dinner you can take a stroll around the ramparts or pop into the Peña Francisco flamenco nightclub. For a calmer and slightly cheaper evening in the citadel, eat at **Casa El Marco,** which is in Calle San Miguel just off Plaza de la Maestranza.

The **Metropol** café-bar overlooking the Plaza de España is the traditional place to take a drink, accompanied by some tapas, as you watch the world stroll by. Other tapas bars can be found in the town centre, especially along Calle Castelar, which has both the **Bodega Madrid** and the **Casa de Comidas** at no. 9.

Festivals

There is a procession of penitents during Easter Week, a Spanish festival in July; and our Lady of Victory at the end of September.

The Moulouya Estuary

The river Moulouya is born near Khénifra in the mountainous centre of Morocco and then flows northeast to drain all the southern slopes of the vast range of the Middle Atlas before emptying out into the Mediterranean. Its narrow fertile valley is in striking contrast to the arid plains of the Gareb and the Jel to the west of the river. This natural boundary was continually fought over by rival empires and the valley lands preyed upon by surrounding nomadic tribes.

Zaïo, 25km east of Selouane, is now on the edge of this rich irrigated zone. It appears strikingly rich and green in comparison to the scorched, treeless landscape of the eastern Rif. A thin tarmac road, the 8100, travels north from Zaïo, winding beside the river and overlooked to the west by the harsh contours of the Kebdana mountains. At its end, 49km from Zaio is the Mediterranean fishing village of **Ras-el-Ma** (Ras Kebdani), tucked just to the east of the lighthouse on the headland. It is a pleasant, listless place with a grid of white and blue houses around a market square where you can eat fresh sardines and red mullet at the **Café-Restaurant du Port**. East of town a fine sandy beach, still quite empty of development, runs along to the estuary mouth.

The Moulouya Estuary teems with **bird life** and in the summer there is a scattering of tents camped happily along the shore looking out towards the **Islas Chafarinas**. These islands were seized in 1848, and comprise the most eastern of the five Spanish possessions on the North African coast. They are inaccessible from Morocco and only used by a handful of visiting Spanish fishing crews. Their threatened tourist development has fortunately not yet occurred, and there are plans afoot to declare them a nature reserve. Internationally endangered species including monk seals, slender-billed curlews and Audouin's gulls all breed on the islands.

Saïdia

On the eastern side of the Moulouya Estuary stretches the 10km sandy beach of Saïdia. The one-street town of Saïdia is a seasonal beach resort, a motley collection of chalets, sports areas, three campsites and four hotels. It has however the relaxed, raffish air of all Moroccan holiday towns—the hotel bars are busy, music and laughter are almost continuous and there is no 'business' or bazaar touts. For those who prefer solitude the **long beach** (easily accessible from the 5013 coast road) is fringed by a natural bird preserve of marsh and broken woodland and makes an enticing sanctuary—a paradise for bird-watching or sunbathing.

Immediately to the east of the town is the Algerian frontier, and though the border posts had until recently been open for several years it has always been well guarded by both nations, with pillboxes and watchtowers. The **kasbah**, a recently restored, large, square enclosure, was built by Sultan Moulay Hassan in the late 19th century to deter further erosion of his borders by the French. The interior is occupied by villagers and in summer is enlivened by cafés and musicians. A pleasant area of mature trees surrounds the walls providing welcome midday shade—a popular place for family picnics and the Sunday market.

Getting Around

Buses and ***grands taxis*** leave regularly for the 60km trip from Oujda to Saïdia, arriving beside the Kasbah. Sunday is the busiest day because of the souk. Driving to Saïdia **from the west** take either of the two roads north from Berkane, a rapidly expanding agricultural centre, where the wines of Beni-Snassen are grown.

Where to Stay and Eating Out

Saïdia is a popular local beach resort, buzzing in the three months of high summer (when rooms are difficult to come by), but apart from some weekend trade it's pretty listless for the rest of the year.

inexpensive

The **Hôtel Hannour**, Place du 20 Août, © (06) 615115, is best known for its night-club, bar and restaurant. The nine rooms are usually booked well in advance. The **Al Kalaa**, © (06) 615123, is just inland from the conspicuous corner Blue Bar which faces the sports square and sea front, and is a safer bet. Its restaurant only functions in the summer, but it also has a bar, and with 33 bedrooms there is a better chance of finding a room there. The cheapest of Saïdia's three hotels is the **Select** at Boulevard de la Moulouya, © (06) 615110, which has 18 rooms and a bar. There is also the **Hôtel Sherif**, behind the kasbah, a boisterous place with a bar and cabaret which, like the Hannour, has not really got its heart in accommodation.

campsites

There are three official campsites, although the **Camping du Site** is reserved for families. Just east is the **Camping Caravaning Al Mansour**; the less fussy **Camping Tours** is behind the sports arena.

The Beni-Snassen Mountains

Between Saïdia and Berkane stretches a fertile coastal plain, fed by the Triffa irrigation canal. South of Berkane, away from this industrious, tractor-strewn landscape is the more striking scenery of the Beni-Snassen Mountains. The Beni-Snassen are a sedentary Berber tribe, related to the Rif hill tribes, who successfully defended themselves from destructive Arab nomadic invasions in their mountains. These mountains are accessible by car or taxi and make an interesting day's exploration from Berkane, Oujda or Saïdia. There are seven roads that enter the region, providing a number of possible mountain-track drives.

Along the Oujda to Berkane mountain road, the S403, is the high village of **Taforalt**, a small faded hill resort which does however still have a café and a traditional **souk** on Wednesdays. One km to the south of Taforalt there is a fine view on clear days over the Moulouya Valley to the sea. A tarmac road turns east from here into the mountains. One km on your right is the **Grotte des Pigeons** where three small streams trickle down a hillside leaving a number of calciferous deposits. The actual cave system has been wired off due to the apparently endless excavations amongst the Palaeolithic remains. The last report was published at Casablanca in 1962 by D. Ferembach.

The **Camel Cave** (Grotte de Chameau) is a further 8km east along a pleasant wooded tarmac road. An unobtrusive turning to the right takes you to a cliff face where there are two entrances to the cave system across a small stream. You will need a strong torch for each person. The long entrance passage is easily navigated but the great stalagmite halls, multiple paths and potentially dangerous holes require a certain caution. Narrowing tunnels lead deeper underground and grow noticeably hotter. It is quite easy to lose one's way for short periods, for the caves are wonderfully free of any organization, tickets or lighting systems. A hot-water stream flows out from the depths and a camel-shaped stalagmite near the entrance enjoys a reputation for curing sterility. Boys bicycle up to the caves for picnics and it is not unusual to hear discordant strains of Moroccan music coming up at you from the echoing passages. Candles and torches throw weird shadows and dancing silhouettes against the powerful, looming stalactite walls. Outside the caves the hot stream flows into a number of deep pools where you can bathe.

The entrance to the **Zegzel Gorge** is 1km beyond the Camel Cave turning. The cultivated orchards and terraces of the valley floor contrast with the violent, bare cliff faces dotted with intriguing caves. A difficult mountain track can be attempted that follows the gorge east, rejoining the main Oujda to Saïdia road in 50km. The safer and equally interesting road, a left turn at the Gorge entrance, follows the river Zegzel 12km down to Berkane.

Oujda

Oujda, 'The City of Fear', the easternmost city of Morocco, is in fact a calm and easy place in which to arrive and stay. Despite its long history, it is a pre-eminently modern town—a 20th-century city of half a million, quietly prosperous from agriculture and the coal mines of Jerada. The medina is still at the centre of the city, partly enclosed by 12th-century Almohad walls, and can be explored in an hour.

Whatever direction you have travelled from—Figuig, Hoceima or Taza—the long hot journey can be comfortably broken at Oujda, with side-trips to the beach at Saïdia or the Beni-Snassen Mountains.

History

Before the Arab invasions of the 7th century this area was a settled agricultural community. The Roman town of Marnia, part of the province of Mauretania Caesariensis—modern Algeria—has been discovered nearby. Roman rule was an isolated era of peace for a region since dominated by border wars and rivalry between the nomadic tribes of the eastern plains.

Oujda was founded in 994 by Ziri Ibn Attia, the leader of an aggressive nomadic Berber tribe, to be the commanding citadel for his domination of the eastern plains. Ziri, who prided himself on his Islamic orthodoxy and Arab speech, was succeeded by a different but like-minded dynasty of Berber nomad chiefs. The Emirs of the Magrawa nomads ruled the east from Oujda for 80 years, their authority extending far south to Sijilmassa before the Almoravid Youssef ben Tachfine destroyed their rule in 1070.

The Almohads captured Oujda in 1206 from its Almoravid governor and ordered the construction of the present extent of the city walls. The Almohad Empire extended far to the east to modern Libya, and Oujda was for once in its existence removed from any disputed frontier. The decay of the Almohad dynasty ushered in centuries of wars, where a fast-changing cast of conquerors aptly earnt Oujda the title of the 'City of Fear'. The 14th and 15th centuries saw this shifting pattern of allegiances at its most unstable, bloody and unpredictable, for the ruling dynasties of Morocco and Algeria both originated from nomadic Berber tribes from the eastern plains around Oujda. The bitter rivalry between the Merenids of Morocco and the Ziyanids of Algeria was reflected in a continuous struggle for possession of Oujda, Tlemcen and Sijilmassa.

This pattern of border war has continued ever since, though there have been changes in the cast. The Turks, advancing from Algiers, were opposed by virtually every active sultan of the Saadian and Alaouite dynasties, but from 1727 Oujda was held by an Ottoman garrison for a hundred years. The French replaced the Turks in Algeria after 1830 and continued the history of this smouldering frontier. There were significant border wars in 1844 and 1857, prior to the Moroccan conquest of Oujda in 1907, the same year that the French first landed troops at Casablanca.

During the Algerian struggle for Independence this border zone was a key area of activity. After the French left the border saga continued with rivalry between the newly independent states of Algeria and Morocco. The armed clashes of the sixties were replaced by a slowly improving understanding which culminated in 1989 in the Maghrebi Union Treaty. However, recent events in Algeria have caused sufficient concern in Morocco for the government once again to close the entire border.

Getting Around

by air

The Oujda-Angads Airport, © (06) 683261, is 15km north of the city, off the P27 road to Saïdia. There is a regular schedule of flights via Casablanca. The Air France and RAM offices are in the Oujda Hotel on Avenue Mohammed V, © (06) 683963.

by rail

The railway station is conspicuously aligned on the city's central avenue, the Rue Ez Zerktouni, © (06) 682701, which leads directly east to the medina. There are three to five daily trains to Taza (3½hrs), from where there are trains on to Fès (6hrs). On Saturday nights, a train departs on the 8hr journey south to Bouârfa, from where there are bus connections to Figuig or Er-Rachidia.

by bus or taxi

The CTM and other **bus** companies all now use the Oued Nachef depot, a 10min walk from the railway station: turn right along Boulevard Hassan el Oukili, and right at the junction to cross the bridge over the river Nachef. There are six buses daily to Saïdia (80mins); six to Berkane (1hr); three to Casablanca; two to Fès (try and catch the 5am departure); four to Nador; and one to Midelt. The most epic bus ride is the 7hr, 370km journey south across the desert plateau of the Rekkam to Figuig oasis.

Grands taxis can be found at the train station or by the town hall (Hôtel de Ville). They take 2–3hrs to Taza or Nador, and under an hour to Saïdia.

Tourist Information

Practically all your administrative needs can be met on the streets around Place du 16 Aout 1953. The **tourist office**, © 689089, is here on the corner of Avenue Mohammed V. It is unusually helpful and hands out a city map in addition to the usual glossy leaflet.

The **post office** is on Avenue Mohammed V just north of the town hall. The **BMCE** bank is at 93 Avenue Mohammed V and the **Banque Populaire** at 34 Boulevard Mohammed Derfoui.

The conspicuous **Catholic church** on the Place El Amira Lala Nezha, off the Avenue Mohammed V, celebrates mass in a side chapel at 6.30pm on Saturday and 9am on Sunday morning. The French priest draws upon the Koran, perhaps inspired by the ecumenical influence of the local shrine to Sidi-Yahya/John the Baptist.

The Almohad Walls

Leave the central Place du 16 Août 1953 and follow the broad Rue de Marrakech to the Place du Maroc. Surrounded by stalls, this is an animated, twinkling area of gas lights in the evening, busy with departing local blue buses. Halfway along the Rue de Marrakech you will have noticed the **Bab Ouled Amrane**, the gateway that gives access to the old **Jewish quarter** (the *mellah*) of the medina. South of the Place du Maroc on the Avenue des Marchés there is a long covered area of **vegetable and clothes souks** below the city walls. The **Bab Sidi Abd el Ouahab** is the best-preserved of the medina's gates, a high, imposing, battlemented entrance flanked by towers. This 'gate of the heads' was where the grim relics of decapitated criminals and rebels were displayed transfixed on poles until the early 20th century. Even without this display it remains the most bustling area of the city, best appreciated at dusk when the café-restaurants come to life and musicians and acrobats often entertain the crowds. Immediately within the gate, in a wide central space, are three dusty, frenetic markets, overlooked by the battlemented walls and the tombs of local saints.

Continuing outside the walls again, a pleasant, shady flower- and tree-filled park faces the entire and most impressive extent of walls on the southern side of the medina. The entrance to this **Parc Lala Meriem** is along the Rue Maghrib el Arabi, where there is a local **folk museum** (Musée Ethnographique), a familiar display of clothes and crafts (*open Wed–Mon 8.30am–12pm, 2.30–6pm; closed Tues; adm*). The gateway at the end of the park leads directly to the **grand mosque,** while the next gate, **Bab Sidi Aissa**, allows you to wind along the Rue El Ouahda, passing below the high towers of the still functioning **catholic church** to rejoin the Avenue Mohammed V.

The Medina

The medina can be entered halfway along your walk around the walls at the **Bab Sidi Abd el Ouahab** or from the Place du 16 Août 1953. Take the corner street from the square, Boulevard Ramdane el Gadhi, and turn left on to the Rue El Mazouzi that takes you straight into the **Souk el Màa**, the water market dominated by the minaret of the **mosque of Sidi Oqba**. Here is the **Tlat Skaki fountain**, its three niches covered in mosaic. Water from the fountain is free; what is sold in the Souk el Màa are rights to so many hours of water from the irrigation canals, the price of which is affected by wild caprices of climate, season and speculation.

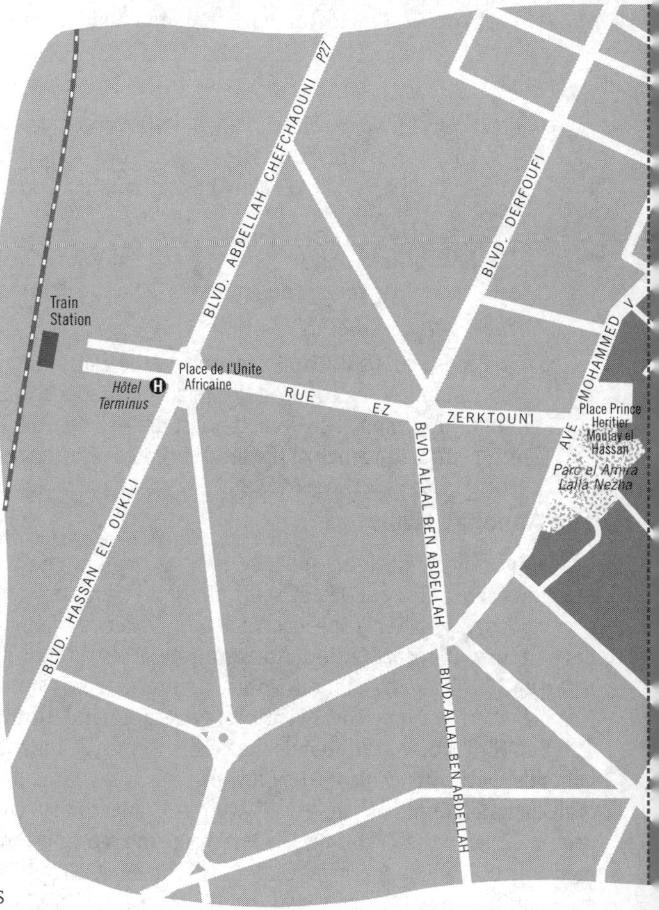

Pass into the **Souk ez Zeràa** and then turn left to enter a chain of small market spaces—the **Kissaria**. Here arcades enclose the more expensive shops rich with gold embroidery, a fountain court, and then a square with the **Khayattine zaouia**, full of cloth merchants. After this, a right turn takes you to the **Place El Attarine**, the tree-shaded centre of the souks decorated with a central fountain and koubba. From there Rue Chadli leads east past innumerable craft stalls to the large covered market just inside the **Bab Sidi Abd el Ouahab**.

Prominent gates on the southern side of the Place El Attarine lead to the **grand mosque** with its associated **medersa**. Both closed to non-Muslims, they were built by the Merenid Sultan Abou Yacqub at the end of the 13th century. A passage allows you patiently to trace the outer walls, diving under occasional arches to face the main entrance where a fountain plays in the dusty square. On your right facing the mosque is the old **kasbah quarter**, the former residence of the pachas of the province and their machinery of government.

The Shrine of Sidi-Yahya

The shrine of Sidi-Yahya has been venerated by all three Peoples of the Book, for it is considered to be the tomb of St John the Baptist (a prophet for Jews as well as Christians and Muslims), where the actual body, or Salome's dancing prize of his head, is buried—the tradi-

tions do not relate which. The enticing grove of baobab and palm trees watered from sacred springs is approached by a 6km (once ceremonial) road that runs east from the medina. The expansion of the town has not dealt too kindly with this retreat; the approach is now through twisting suburban roads and some municipal planner has been let loose to add a profusion of pavements, paths and parking zones around the sanctuary. A taxi can run you out for a few dirhams—the walk or drive is not inspiring.

The stream still snakes through the groves of trees and there is seldom a shortage of pilgrims visiting the various koubbas, lighting candles, praying, washing in the water (a cure for rheumatism), or tying fragments of cloth to the trees or sanctuary grilles.

In the past the grove attracted hermits—Jewish, Christian and Muslim holy men who camped in poverty under the trees hoping to be possessed by the same spirit that animated St John. One of their **hermitages**, once occupied by Sidi bel Abbès, one of the seven patron saints of Marrakech, is still preserved and venerated. Another cave has been named **Ghar el Houriyat**, the grotto of the houris, those handmaidens that wait in paradise beside cool, shaded streams for the believers, but who look disappointingly Scandinavian in contemporary Islamic popular prints. The true origins of the shrine are likely to lie in pre-Islamic beliefs that venerated sacred springs as centres of divine fertility—sanctuaries for poetry and worship, such as Mecca was with its zemzem spring when Mohammed was a boy. You can camp or picnic here in the shade, wash in the stream, and buy candles, holy trinkets and snacks from the stalls.

Where to Stay

expensive

Stay at the **Terminus Hotel,** ✆ (06) 683211, if you can afford to. Near the station on Place de l'Unité Africaine, it is the ideal reward after a hot journey. It has a fine pool, an abundant garden, efficient plumbing and a good restaurant. The best hotel in Morocco east of Fès, and the bar is a rendezvous for all species of travellers.

moderate

Dropping down in price, but keeping bar, restaurant and pool, your best choice is the **Hotel Moussafir**, also on Place de l'Unité Africaine, ✆ (06) 688202. With this chain you know you will get comfort and value. There is also the **Al Massira Salam**, ✆ (06) 685600/1/2, on Rue Maghreb el Arabi, part of the equally reliable Salam chain. Also in this price bracket, and useful for their bars and restaurants even if you are not staying, are the new **Concorde** on Avenue Mohammed V, ✆ (06) 682328 and the **Mamounia** at 12 Rue el Madina el Mounard, ✆ (06) 690072.

inexpensive

The **Hôtel Simon** at 1 Rue Tarik Ibn Ziad, ✆ (06) 686303/4 was the first French colonial hotel to open in Morocco, in 1910, and remains the best value in Oujda. It is conveniently placed on the edge of the medina with 40 rooms, car parking, a bar and a restaurant. The **Afrah** at 15 Rue Tafna (one street south of Place du 16 Aout 1953) ✆ (06) 683365, is a useful alternative address with a good view from its upstairs café. The **Royal** at 13 Rue Ez Zerktouni, ✆ (06) 682284, is a well-established place with a central position and 50 bedrooms. The **Lutetia**, a fifties colonial edifice at 44 Boulevard Hassan el Loukili, ✆ (06) 683365, is conveniently close to the station and a choice of bars.

cheap

For the medina enthusiast, the new **Hôtel du 16 Août 1953**, ✆ (06) 684197, on a crossroads on the Rue de Marrakech has scrupulously clean rooms from which you can watch the street life and showers. If full, the **Majestic** at 8 Rue Neggai, ✆ (06) 682948, makes a useful standby.

Eating Out

moderate

Besides the Terminus Hotel there are a number of reliable restaurants at hand. Choose from **El Bahia**, Rue Ez Zerktouni, ✆ (06) 683731, the **Brasserie de France**, 87–89 Avenue Mohammed V, ✆ (06) 683801, or **La Mamounia**, Rue Madina el Mounara, ✆ (06) 684072 (which specializes in traditional Moroccan cooking). The **Dauphin** fish restaurant, 38 Rue de Berkane, ✆ (06) 686145, is the best the town has to offer.

cheap

There are a number of **open-air stalls** around Bab Sidi Abd el Ouahab where you can piece together a satisfyingly composite meal of snails, soup, grilled meat, nuts and fruit from a number of vendors. There are also smaller selections of grill barrows at the medina end of Rue Ez Zerktouni, in the Place du Maroc and in the Place du 16 Aout 1953—they all do grilled kebabs and spicy sausage sandwiches. For breakfast head straight for the **Café des Pyramides** beside the Royal Hotel on Rue Ez Zerktouni. Among the many tucked away **bars**, the **Anciens Combattants** and **Jour et Nuit** are both easily accessible—close by the Lutetia hotel.

Shopping

Local crafts are displayed at fixed prices (which are handy for comparison with other shops and stalls) at the **Ensemble Artisanal** and the **Maison de l'Artisanat** on Boulevard Alla ben Abdellah. The city is large enough to maintain an almost continuous level of market activity throughout the week, though Sunday and Wednesday are the traditional **souk** days, with extra vegetable, cloth and flea markets springing up in the suburbs.

Festivals

Sidi Yahya, the pre-eminent saint of Oujda, has two *moussems*, one in the high summer, usually August, and another in September. They are a riot of colour and celebration and should not be missed.

The Algerian Border

Because of the state of virtual civil war in Algeria since 1992 the Moroccan–Algerian border crossing is now completely closed, after a brief period following the signing of the 1989 Maghrebi Union Treaty when cross-frontier traffic was able to move relatively freely. If this situation changes, you can bet that procedures will be at least fairly similar to what they had been since 1989. Completing the exit and entrance forms on either side if you were travelling by foot was quite quick, although drivers with a car needed to allow several hours for the customs of both countries.

Citizens of Australia, Canada, Ireland, Great Britain, New Zealand, the Netherlands and the USA were all required to have a visa to enter Algeria. Although there is an Algerian consulate in Oujda (at 11 Boulevard Bir Anzarane, © (06) 683676), their usual practice was to send documents and applications on to Rabat and wait for them to be returned, so it was actually much better and quicker for travellers to go to the Algerian Embassy in Rabat themselves. Every traveller was obliged to buy 1000 Algerian dinars (about $130) at the government rate in Algeria, which is about a quarter of what you can get on the black market. It was really more like a transit tax.

To get to the border, when the crossings were open there were occasional local buses and a more reliable shuttle of *grand taxis* (5dh a place) from Oujda to the border, and from there to Tlemcen on the Algerian side.

South to Figuig Oasis

Staying within Morocco, another journey that can be made from Oujda is the 268km trip south to **Bouârfa**, at the junction of the Figuig road, across the barren plain of the Rekkam. To go with the thrill of a desert crossing there is an almost unnerving absence of traffic; the heat and direct sunlight, even in winter, can be exhausting. The earliest possible departure by bus is advisable and if you are going by car a night drive through the astonishingly cool, clear sky, with the desert lit by the moon and stars is an attractive alternative. There are basic café-hotels at Aïn Benimathar, Tendrara and Bouârfa.

Guenfouda, a small dusty railhead 28km south of Oujda, has a Saturday **souk**. Beyond is the Jerada mountain pass (1150m), which is just before the mine crossroads. To the west a road leads to the coal mines of **Jerada–Hassi-Blal**, which have been in production since 1952 and now send 700,000 tonnes a year north to the port at Nador. To the east are the mines of **Sidi Bou Beker**. Tthe reserves of lead and silver here have been almost worked out, but large deposits of zinc still await extraction.

Aïn Benimathar, 83km from Oujda, is the ancient central market of the Mathar nomads and now, due to irrigation, is a sparkling 5km-long oasis valley. Their **souk** is held on Mondays and a number of old **kasbahs** survive in the village—two date from before the 19th century, a venerable age for buildings that seldom long outlive their creator. It was this settlement that Lyautey, then commander of Algeria's western frontier, captured in 1904 as part of his aggressive forward policy. His political masters had forbidden such an advance but by renaming Aïn Benimathar as Berguent he successfully fooled his superiors in Paris, who searched their maps in vain for such a town. Four km to the west along the S330 is the oasis of **Ras-El-Aïn**, a spring beside the river Za watercourse. Eighteen kilometres downstream, though seldom flowing, is a waterfall, with a larger fall another 10km beyond that.

Tendrara, 198km from Oujda, is an isolated desert administrative post. The **souk** of the nomadic Beni Guil tribe is held here on Thursdays. Sixty-two km further on, you descend through a cleft in black hills to arrive at **Bouârfa**, where the P19 goes east to Figuig, and the P32 west to Er-Rachidia.

The Atlantic Coast

The Atlantic coast was known by the French as 'Maroc Utile'—useful Morocco. The industrial, commercial and political heartland of the country is concentrated in the three neighbouring coastal cities of Kénitra, Rabat and Casablanca, and the fertile coastal provinces of the Rharb, Chaouïa and Doukkala have long been prized as the grain-bowl of the nation.

This coast has also served as the frontier of Morocco. Phoenician traders first brought the higher arts of agriculture and civilization to Morocco through a chain of trading colonies established along the shore. The earliest settlements looked to Gades (Cádiz) as their mother city, but in the 5th century BC the Carthaginian Admiral Hanno, returning from an exploration of West Africa, established six new towns along the coast to control the gold trade. The Roman province of Mauretania Tingitania, with virtually all its towns by the sea and no eastward land connection to the rest of North Africa, scarcely altered this pattern of coastal development.

The long, destructive relationship between Morocco and Europe was fought out on the Atlantic shore. Centuries of raids, invasions and occupations deprived Morocco of the full use of one of its most important assets. Viking raids in the 10th century were continued by the Normans, whose destructive crusading impulse was inherited by Castile and Portugal. The destruction of King Sebastian's Portuguese army at Ksar-el-Kebir marked a turning point in Morocco's fierce defence of her coast. Over the 17th and 18th centuries the remaining Portuguese and Spanish Atlantic fortresses were recaptured, and Muslim pirates took the war back into Christian territory. By the early 19th century, this cycle of aggression was replaced by a boom in trade, and merchants and foreign consuls settled in Essaouira, Safi, Rabat and Casablanca. Once more the cupidity of Europe was excited, though this time it was France that acted as the aggressor. French troops first swarmed ashore in 1907 at Casablanca, and from 1912 the Protectorate implanted the industrial revolution upon the Moroccan coast. It has taken a firm but fortunately idiosyncratic root.

For a visitor the comparatively prosperous and western-influenced Atlantic coast serves as an excellent bridge to the more striking and aggressive culture of the interior. No visitor should miss a day in the metropolis of Casablanca, although the smaller towns are likely to prove more attractive. The perfect blend of architecture, beach, night life, fine cooking and historical monuments is a highly personal choice. Journeying south along the coast you can afford to be selective, picking a route that might include picturesque Asilah, ruined Lixus and Spanish Larache, the beach of Moulay-Bousselham, the monuments of Rabat, the medina of Salé, the lagoon of Oualidia and the potteries of Safi and conclude with the finest town of all, Essaouira. In the background in all of them is the raw smell of iodine from the pounding waves of the Atlantic surf, locked in an endless

The Atlantic Coast from Tangier to Agadir

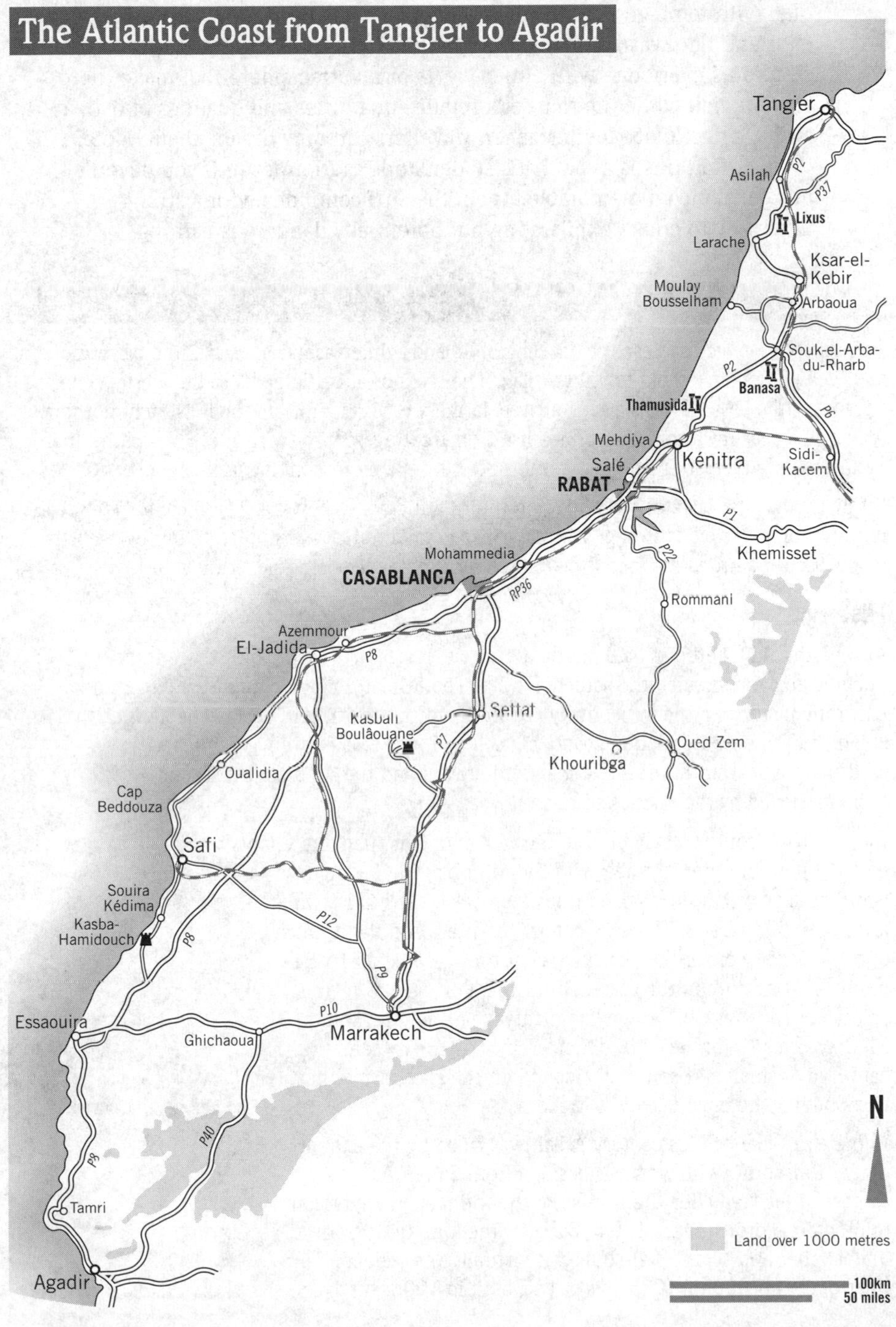

duel with tomb-girt headlands, shepherd-watched meadows defended by cliffs and tide washed sands. Dotted along this coast is a succession of fish-resturants every one with either views or an atmosphere that make them exceptional, while the rich sea provides quantities and qualities of fish, at such a price, that Mediterranean travellers can only dream about. Note, though, that this is a sea that also demands caution, even if you haven't just consumed a memorable lunch: the surf combines with a strong undertow to create exhilarating but potentially dangerous bathing.

Asilah

Portuguese defences enclose the dazzling blue- and whitewashed houses of the picturesque and well-photographed old town of Asilah. The sea laps at battlements to the west, while at the foot of the eastern walls a souk attracts farmers who ride in from the hills each morning. Asilah is a seaside resort that prides itself on treating visitors with more sympathy than Tangier. It is a pleasant restful place, but suffers from a corresponding lack of energy.

If this is your first taste of swimming on the Atlantic coast, beware. The breakers are great fun but the undertow is strong; several years ago my brother and I much to our own excitement rescued a drowning man from the waves, who never even said thank you.

History

Asilah, the first harbour of the Atlantic coast, was founded in the 8th century BC by Phoenicians, who named the settlement Zili. The Roman Emperor Augustus deported its entire population in the 1st century AD and filled the town with more reliable Iberian colonists. The new foundation governed itself and in the succeeding centuries weathered the political storms of the Roman withdrawal and the Arab conquest, only to be destroyed by the Vikings around the year 900.

By the 14th century, Asilah had revived and Christian merchants berthed here in order to trade with the interior. The Portuguese so valued the port that they seized it for themselves in 1471 with an armada of 477 vessels. This was bitterly resented, and the fortified port of Asilah was for the next two centuries a constant battleground. In 1589 control passed from the Portuguese to the Spanish, who held the town for eighty years before Sultan Moulay Ismaïl stormed the defences in 1691. He sent the captured Spanish garrison in chains to join the slave army that was building the imperial city of Meknès.

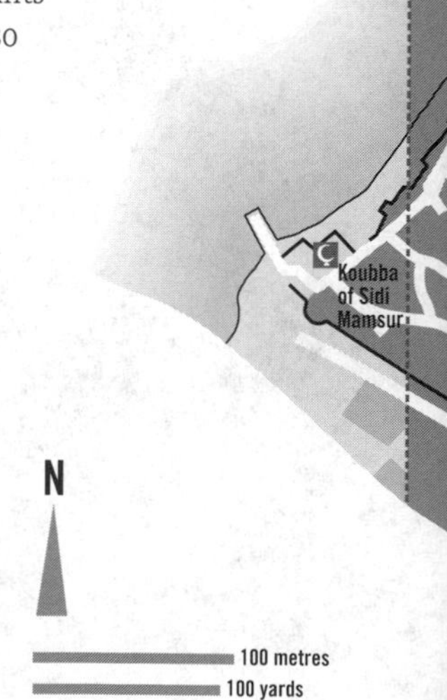

In the early years of this century Asilah was ruled by the extraordinary **Raissouli**, who won this position from Sultan Abdul Aziz as part of his terms for the release of the kidnapped American millionaire Perdicaris in 1904. Bandit, freedom-fighter, saint, philosopher and tyrant, Raissouli was virtually the independent ruler of the north until 1925. His palace, built in 1906, survives.

Getting Around

by rail

The train station is 2km north of the town, where the beachside campsites are clustered. It is only 45 minutes to Tangier on one of the half-dozen trains each day.

by bus

The bus journey from Tangier takes an hour, with seven possible departures between 7am and 7pm. You are dropped at the small triangular Place Mohammed V which leaves you with a 200m walk down to Place Zelaka, in front of the main gate into the medina. There are five buses a day south to Larache.

by car and taxi

Asilah is 46km south of Tangier off the main P2 road running south to Rabat. Taxis from the train station to the town centre should charge 5dh, a place in a ***grand taxi*** to or from Tangier is 20dh and on to Larache around 10dh.

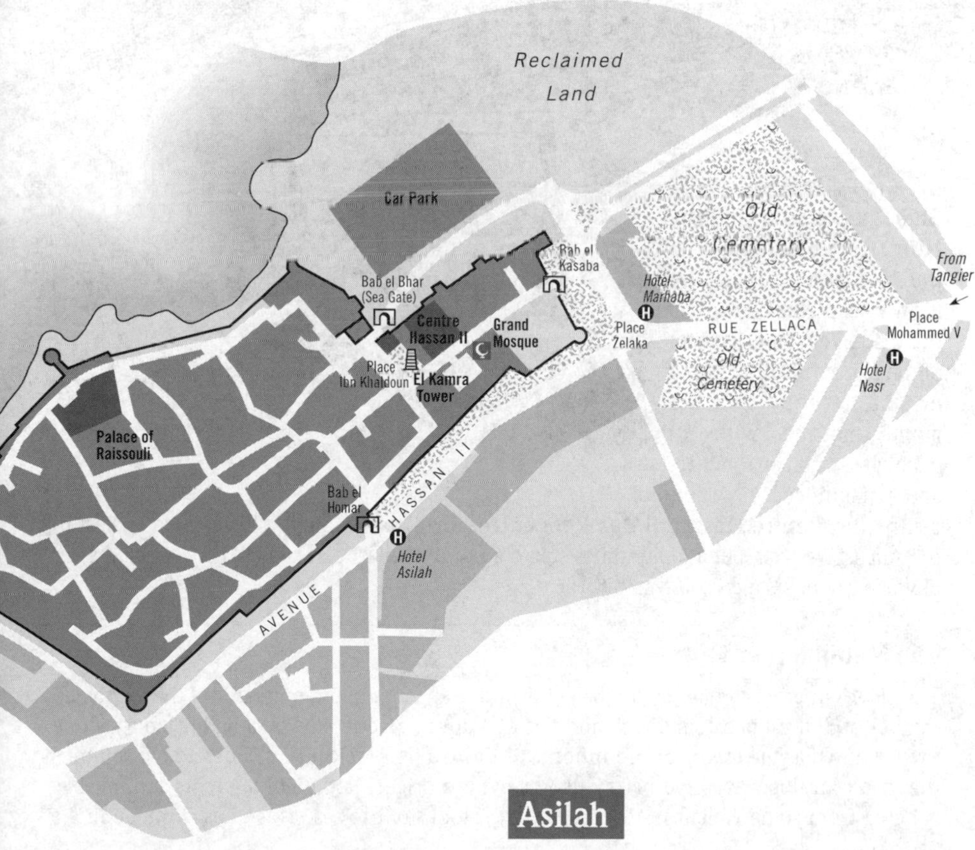

Asilah

Outside the Walls

The Spanish built a harmonious new town beside the medina, from which a slowly evolving new harbour and beaches extend northwards along the coast. The main avenue of the new town, Avenue Mohammed V, houses the bank, the police station and a chemist. It leads past corner cafés and the tower of the (closed) church down the Rue Abdel Moumen ben Ali to **Place Zelaka**. The Zelaka is a quiet but pretty enough square—a couple of café-restaurants look onto the walls of the old town, where a koubba and some poetry carved in stone nestle in the garden shade.

The 16th-century **Portuguese ramparts** of Asilah are of attractively worn yellow stone. They were built in two years by the great military architect Botacca, after a prolonged Moroccan siege had virtually breached the earlier defences. He punctured the walls with

three gates: **Bab el Bhar**, the old sea gate, **Bab Homar**, the land gate, and the **Bab Kasaba**. The latter leads from Place Zelaka directly into the old government quarter of the town, now dominated by the recently enlarged grand mosque with its distinctive octagonal minaret and a magnificent new cultural centre (the **Centre Hassan II des Rencontres Internationales**). This is at its busiest in the August Festival, but at other times stages a number of art exhibitions, concerts and sales of work among its tiled courtyards.

The Medina

The old town proper begins by the Bab el Bahr at the continuous courtyards of the combined squares of Sidi Ali ben Hamdouch and Ibn Khaldoum, overlooked by a high, slender stone tower known as the **tower of the moon**, **'El Kamra'** in Arabic. The slender gothic columns that flank an upper window betray its Portuguese origins, although lately its summit has suffered from some violent restoration work. It looks out to sea, as well as commanding a useful field of fire around the sea gate below it. The open square is usually filled with the children of Asilah: kicking a football, following a tourist or employed in twisting long lines of thread for the fine embroidery of the town's tailors.

From the square stroll down to the sea wall. A few fishing boats still bob on their buoys. The old Portuguese breakwater provided partial but picturesque protection against the Atlantic surf until 1987, when a new more extensive harbour took its place. Work is still continuing on this new port, which remains a desultory wilderness of unemployed reclamation land.

Halfway along the seafront stands the **Palace of Raissouli**, the 'House of Tears', built with forced labour and an extra burden of taxation so that it was completed within a year—but it is beautiful. Raissouli himself declared, 'In my life I have been little loved and much hated, but above all I have been feared.' The palace partly hangs over the sea walls, and has an upper gallery of arches with a view of Cape Spartel on a clear day. You approach the main block along a covered way which, originally, had a row of prisons on the left and a long shaded seat for petitioners on the right. This passageway leads into an interior courtyard with the house on one side and an audience chamber on the other. The palace is used for the August Festival and not open to the public, though if you catch the eye of the custodian try and persuade him to give you a quick tour. The two stages of rooms, built around a great court with an Italian fountain, a floor of black and white marble and walls in familiar Moorish style with faience mosaic, sculpted plaster and carved wood, are cool and attractive.

The Bandit Governor

Raissouli is described in the works of Walter Harris, whom he once kidnapped, and in Rosita Forbes's biography, *The Sultans of the Mountains*. Both writers are far too sympathetic, for they shared a taste for strong leaders in the heroic mould, which in Rosita's case extended to a brief affair with Mussolini.

Raissouli was however an undeniably remarkable man, with a rich grain of charm, humour and erudition to mask his ambition. He was the heir of a saintly dynasty, a *sherif* trained in Islamic law, but was by turns a bandit, philosopher, freedom-fighter and merciless tyrant. The wise Sultan Moulay Hassan seems to have seen through the charm, and had the young bandit Raissouli locked up on the Isle of Mogador; his sons were neither so wise nor so able, and Raissouli was released in a general amnesty. He soon launched upon a career of kidnapping. The seizure and eventual release of 'Caid' Maclean, Walter Harris and the Greek-American millionaire Perdicaris brought him the attention of the world press, a fortune and the governorship of Asilah.

By 1906 Raissouli was at the height of his powers, deep into the intrigues that swirled around in the last few years before the Protectorate. By 1911 he was the acknowledged leader of all the tribes of north-west Morocco. He at first welcomed the new Spanish government as a possible means to extend his power, but later fought two bitter guerrilla wars against them before negotiating his retirement, with a handsome pension, to his mountain palace of Tazrut deep in the Jebala hills. Raissouli refused to join Abdel Krim's Rif rebellion in the 1920s. Some have considered this the action of a man refusing to break his word to the Spaniards, while

others see it as mere envy at the success of the tribes of the Eastern Rif. His neutrality was crucial in allowing the Spanish a safe haven in the west, but in January 1925 he was kidnapped by Abdel Krim's commandos. He died in captivity a few weeks later.

The August **cultural festival** is held at the palace with poetry, music and painting competitions. Asilah is fortunate as its parliamentary representative has also been Minister of Culture, and created a **horse festival** in the town to follow the two weeks of culture.

Beyond the palace continue along the ramparts, the sea view largely obscured by houses, towards the corner bastion and pier, which overlooks a courtyard cemetery filled with neatly tiled tombs aligned towards Mecca. Traditions record that these were Andalusian *mujaheddin*, holy warriors, who died in the corsair war against the Christian powers and in the capture of the Asilah fortress. Their graves are guarded by the **koubba of Sidi Mamsur**, painted a gorgeous bruised bluish whitewash. The pier also gives a good prospect of the town's sea walls overhung by the House of Tears, a view reproduced in thousands of photographs as well as by Matisse in his sketchbook.

As you return through the medina you will notice the many striking **murals** that decorate its walls. These have been created as a gift to the town by artists in thanks for the August festival. New works are painted each year, often over previous designs, giving an interesting contrast between these modernist geometric forms and the medina's traditional pattern of life. A walk from the cemetery to the Bab Homar takes you past many of these murals, and two communal bakery ovens. There are a few tourist bazaars which will be part of the itinerary of any guide, but the medina is an easy place in which to walk, well used to visitors.

The **Bab Homar** is the central land gate, decorated with the faded royal arms of Alfonso V of Portugal. The **souk** is clustered here below the outer walls in the partial but welcome shade of ramparts and gardens. Across the road, opposite the battlements, are gateways leading to two large courtyards where masses of donkeys are tethered by the farmers who come in from the hills to sell their vegetables. In addition to the daily vegetable market, on Thursdays baskets and wicker-work are piled up for sale near the **koubba of Sidi Al Arbi**. The saint had a reputation for healing the mentally ill, who were chained by an iron collar to a tree near the saint's tomb. Exposure to the saint's *baraka* was thought to drive away the jinn who had possessed the victim.

Old coins and belt buckles are sold opposite the Bab Homar, and Av Hassan II leads up to a long line of artisan shops making goods for the locals. The fish market is held most mornings by the nearby old Spanish church.

Where to Stay

moderate

Hotel Al Khaima, ✆ (09) 417428, @ (09) 417566, is about 2km north of Asilah beside the road to Tangier, a large modern motel-like place with garden, pool, tennis courts, bar and restaurant. However, the new **Hotel Zelis**,10 Av Mansour Eddahabi, ✆ (09) 417069, is much closer to the centre of things.

inexpensive

The **Hôtel Oued El Makhazine** on Av de Melilla, ✆ (09) 417090, ℻ (09) 417500, is well-placed in the town centre, with 29 rooms, a bar and a view over the sea. There are also two small but slightly more expensive two-star hotels: the **Mansour**, ✆ (09) 417390, ℻ (09) 417533, at 49 Av Mohammed V has only eight rooms; **L'Oasis**, ✆ (09) 417186 at 8 Place des Nations Unies occupies an old colonial house and has a bar and restaurant. If all of these are full another decent alternative is the **Sahara**, located at 9 Rue Tarfaya.

cheap

The **Hôtel Asilah**, ✆ (09) 417286, at 79 Av Hassan II has several basic rooms, and some on the second floor have a good view overlooking the battlements and the souk. The **Marhaba**, ✆ (09) 417144, at 9 Rue Zelaka (on the right as you walk down Av Mohammed V towards the ramparts), has a calm friendly atmosphere with plenty of cool tiles and a good central location. The **Nasr** on Place Mohammed V is very basic, cheap, and well placed for catching that early morning bus.

Asilah is better known for its seaside **campsites**, spread out along the beach to the north of the town. **Camping As-Saada** and **Camping Echrigui** are the closest to town, which has to be an advantage. There is little to choose between them, though at both the atmosphere can be a little intense and over-organized with discos, barbecues and displays. **Camping Sahara**, the cheapest and most basic, is generally less crowded and a bit more laid-back.

Eating Out

moderate

The **Place Zelaka** is still an irresistible place to sit but standards have slipped downhill in the past few years. You can, however, still enjoy a cold beer, fried fish and salad at **Chez Pepe/El Oceano**, ✆ (09) 417395. Other eating opportunities exist along the harbour front, Rue Moulay Hassan ben Mehdi, at either **Casa García**, the **Du Pont** or **El Espignon**.

cheap

There are a number of good snack-cafés in the souk stalls below the ramparts, but in the evening the pavement cafés along Av Mohammed V are better places to find the life of the town. The **Restaurant Medina**, opposite the El Hamra tower, also makes a convenient place for a mint tea or light lunch.

In the evening you can check out the bars in the **Al Khaima** and **L'Oasis** hotels, and the well advertised discos that operate in larger campsites such as the **Safari**. For a calmer evening stroll past the local cafés strung along Av Mohammed V and Av Hassan II, where musicians sometimes interrupt the interminable games of cards.

M'Soura (The Holy Place)

> *For in these stones is a mystery, and a healing virtue against many ailments. Giants of old did carry them from the furthest ends of Africa and did set them up*
>
> Merlin in Geoffrey of Monmouth's *History of Britain.*

At **M'Soura**, 15km south of Asilah, there is an important **neolithic stone circle**. Leave Asilah on the main Rabat road, then take the inland road (P37) for Tetouan and turn first left after crossing the railway line on to a 4km loop road to the village of Souk-Tnine-de-Sidi-el-Yamani. Here you should ask for a guide, as the site is 5km northeast over a confusion of dirt and sandy tracks. It is watched over by Afdil Abdu-Hamid, who keeps a log of visitors.

The central tumulus, now severely scarred by the unfilled excavation work, is thought to be the tomb of an early Mauretanian king which was inserted in the centre of a much older stone circle. This was originally composed of 167 stones, of no uniformity but all hammered and polished by hand. They were arranged in a perfect ellipse, which made frequent use of the Pythagorean right-angle and conforms to Professor Thorn's megalithic yard of 0.830 metres in its construction. Of the 400 stone circles in Brittany and the British Isles there are only 30 with a perfect ellipse, and there are no other elliptical stone circles anywhere else in the world. The east-west alignment of the ellipse marks the path of the setting sun of the equinoxes, the first day of spring and the first of autumn. This curious conformity hints at an ancient cultural link with Atlantic Europe somewhere between 1600 and 2000 BC. To the north and northwest of the circle are at least three separate outer groups of stones, as well as an artificially filled level earth platform.

Lixus

The ruins of this ancient city of the sun ('Makom Shemseh' to the Phoenicians) are scattered over a hill that overlooks the wide meanders of the river Loukos as it flows out through a salt marsh to the sea. The site is quite accessible, less than 5km north of Larache beside the main road from Asilah and Tangier. This was one of the Phoenicians' first and most successful settlements in Morocco, though practically all the visible remains are from the Roman era, when Lixus was at the height of its prosperity. *Garum*, a peculiar, highly spiced, almost rancid fish sauce was manufactured here. A staple of Roman cookery, it was a profitable export, and the tuna fish from which it was made appeared on Lixus' coinage. Diocletian withdrew imperial administration from the area at the end of the 3rd century AD, but Lixus continued some form of existence in later centuries, as Arabic coins excavated here attest.

The **port buildings** would have been to the east of the road. This may seem strange, but in this period the sea penetrated much further up the estuary almost to surround the city—indeed Pliny records that Lixus was an island. The vats of the garum factory and port store houses are beside the road on the west side, just before the signposted turning for Plage Rasmanal, the Larache beach. There are no set opening times (or entry charges); the guardian of the site, El Moukhtar, who lives with his family and chickens on the hillside, will just appear and lead you up the path to the theatre. The theatre in Lixus had one of the largest orchestra pits known, at 33m in diameter even wider than that in Athens. Tastes

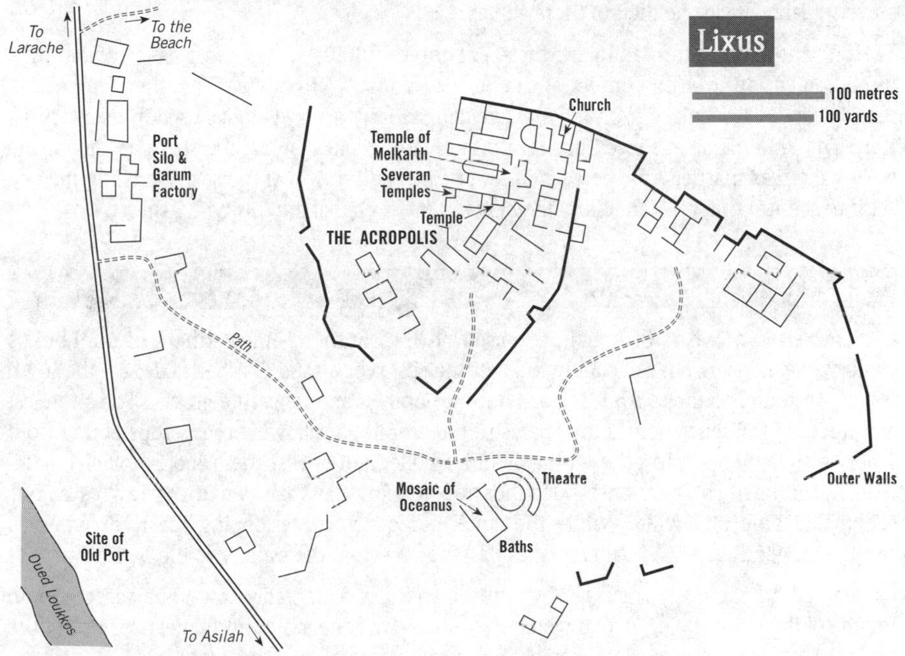

changed, and when the theatre was converted into an **amphitheatre**, the orchestra was made into an arena for fights with wild beasts, with a 4m-high wall to protect the audience.

In front of the theatre are the remains of a **public bath**, built by the Severian dynasty (of Phoenician–North African origin) in the early 3rd century AD. Large portions of painted plaster survive around the semi-circular vestibule, and the floor of the tepidarium includes a **mosaic** of the head of the sea god Oceanus, an angry figure whose wild hair is entwined with the claws and feet of a lobster. The path then climbs up through the ruins of what was once a rich quarter of **villas**, though the single upstanding monument is the apse from a Roman temple. The mosaics found around here—Helios, Mars and Rhea, the three Graces and Venus with Adonis—are all exhibited at the Archaeological Museum in Tetouan, with some bronze statuettes. The **perimeter walls** of Lixus can be traced far out to the north and date from the 4th century BC, while the walls immediately left of the theatre, largely from the 4th century AD, guard the **acropolis**, the summit of which once held at least eight temples.

The **temple ruins** include buildings of different dates spanning over 1000 years—Phoenician, Roman and Muslim—and their individual elements are now difficult to untangle. Excavations carried out have so far identified a cistern in the side tower, the forum, and an early mosque, shaded by three olive trees. The Temple of Melkarth has been cut in half by the perimeter wall, and now only a broad apse survives from its days of glory. Here the God was served by barefoot priests clad in unsewn linen who maintained a fire altar unpolluted by bloody sacrifice. The Phoenician god Melkarth is better known to the world as Hercules. The Loukos valley was long identified with the garden of the Hesperides, where golden apples were guarded by a dragon and the daughters of the giant Atlas. Hercules' eleventh labour was the theft of these apples.

To the southeast of this landmark there are three buildings, two temples sandwiching a public office, built on the orders of the Severi dynasty. Directly east another Phoenician temple can be recognized from the massive and skilfully dressed stones used in its construction. The Phoenicians believed in the supreme beneficent God El, the sun and king of the west, who was married to Asherat, mother of earth and queen of the sea. Watching the sun set into the Atlantic you can follow the benign El as he sinks into his wife Asherat.

Larache

Larache, also known as El Araïch, is poised on the southern embankment of the Loukos estuary, meandering out reluctantly to meet the sea over a sand bar. Sea cliffs seal the town to the west, and to the south it spreads out into orange and tangerine groves. The strongest architectural influence here is the Spanish Protectorate, a relatively prosperous period from 1911 to 1956 that left Larache with a dignified collection of Hispano–Moorish official buildings and hotels. The new post-Independence housing has maintained the town's colour scheme of blue and white, while the small old quarter overlooking the river wharves survives in good repair. A boat taxi takes passengers across the estuary to the beach.

Larache is comparatively neglected by tourists, and it is remarkably easy to be accepted into the life of the town. Being able to watch the sun set into the sea from the nearby ruins of the Phoenician temple at Lixus is reason enough to stay here at least one night.

History

Larache was founded during the Arab conquest of Morocco in the early 8th century and named after one of its heroes, 'El Araïch' ('The White') Beni Arous—a pure Muslim city on the opposite bank from infidel Lixus. The twin cities co-existed for several hundred years, but by the 11th century the great Andalusian geographer El Bekri only lists El Araïch. Larache was the principal port of the entire Atlantic coast before a Spanish fleet destroyed the town in 1471. The Portuguese established a castle here in 1489, but only held it for a year. A few years later a native kasbah was acting as base for a large fleet of corsair galleys manned by crews of Andalusian refugees, European renegades and Turkish soldiers of fortune. The sand bar in the estuary kept the European deep-keeled galleons at a safe distance. This vital naval base was sold to King Philip II of Spain in 1610, an act that did much to discredit the Saadian dynasty. Sultan Moulay Ismaïl recaptured it in 1689 and it continued to harbour the sleek corsair craft until the 19th century. In 1911 the Spanish occupied Larache and made it one of the three provincial capitals of the Spanish Protectorate of Northern Morocco.

Getting Around and Tourist Information

Buses and ***grands taxis*** leave frequently for Tangier or Rabat, and several travel inland to Fès. The bus station is just 300m from Place de la Libération on Rue Mohammed ben Abdellah. The no. 4 bus leaves from the port every 20 minutes for the 7km land route to the beach on the opposite side of the estuary, passing the

Lixus ruins on the way. There is also a boat taxi from the fishermen's wharf that makes for a more romantic crossing to the beach, where there are cabins, summer camping and cafés grilling fish. In Larache the **Banque Populaire** and the **post office** are both found on the Av Mohammed V.

The New Town

Avenue Mohammed V leads off from the Tangier–Rabat road to the heart of the town. This graceful avenue, decorated with gardens, leads to the **Place de la Libération**, surrounded by cafés and hotels that congregate in an elegant and very Spanish plaza around a central tiled fountain. The **town market**, a splendid turreted affair, is down the third turning to your left if you enter the Place from Av Mohammed V.

The Place opens out towards the coast, which is capped by **Avenue Moulay Ismaïl**, a long garden balcony that overlooks the surf and cliffs. The esplanade leads south up to a lighthouse, past the ruins of the **Spanish jail** and the active Moroccan one with daily queues of women bringing parcels of food to their relations. This vaguely disturbing walk past shanties and cliff faces dotted with long bamboo fishing lines is a fitting start for the pilgrimage to the **grave of Jean Genet**, the great French post-war novelist and playwright, in the Spanish graveyard to the south of Larache. He was a frequent resident of both Larache and Tangier, both towns enhanced by compounds of imprisoned men. His last boyfriend, Mohammed, accidentally killed himself with Genet's gift of a fast car days after the author died.

To the north, the esplanade sweeps below the **fortress of Kebibat** to curve down to the fishermen's wharf, where you can catch the boat taxi across to the beach for 1dh. The beach offers the best view of the fortress, now a gaunt ruin. It was refurbished by the Spanish as a military hospital for casualties of the Rif rising, but now the tile and plaster decoration mixes with mounds of waste that cascade down from the high terrace to the gardens below.

The Medina

From Place de la Libération, the **Bab el Khemis**, an impressive arch of aged bricks and tiles lined with swallows' nests, leads to the **souk** and the old pre-Spanish town. The atmosphere immediately changes as you step from the leisurely café life of the Place to the souk in the heart of the medina. The souk is a long cobbled courtyard, lined with aged galleries: small artisan stalls compete with Berber market ladies for attention, and though the souk is most active on Thursday it is an area of perpetual animation. Just past the Bab el Khemis you'll find the greatest density of cafés selling mint tea and brochettes. An old fountain at the far end of the souk flows beneath the long arch of the **Bab Kasbah**.

Kasbah de la Cigogne

The Rue Moulay el Mehdi leads, twisting and turning, out of the medina to an esplanade, Place de Makhzen, on top of the old battlements that offers a fine view over the sinuous Loukos river. Behind and partly covered by a sprawling garden are the higher ramparts of the triangular Kasbah (or Château) de la Cigogne. It attracts a number of tales. One claims it was a Moorish fort built by the Saadian Sultan Ahmed el Mansour to hold the Portuguese prisoners taken in the Battle of the Three Kings in 1578 while he arranged profitable ransoms from their families; another records that it is the remains of a star-shaped artillery bastion built by Philip II of Spain to sweep the estuary; a third that it was built by Spanish prisoners after the fall of the town during the reign of Moulay Ismaïl.

Archaeological Museum

The smaller stone-built bastion nearer the estuary looks and is a Christian **fort**. It was so thoroughly restored at the beginning of this century that it is best seen as a monument to all the Iberian occupations of 1489–91, 1610–89 and 1911–57 than as surviving from any particular period. It is decorated with the arms of Charles V, which the Spanish brought to Larache to give the place a better look. The building now houses the Archaeological Museum (Musée Archéologique, *open Wed–Mon 9am–12pm, 3–5.30pm, closed Tues*). It is a slightly uninspiring collection of cast copies and lesser items from the digs at Lixus, but there are some decent figures of Zeus and Bacchus and some pleasant geometric mosaics.

Opposite the museum is a whimsical **Andalusian palace** built in 1915, a fitting exterior for the **National Conservatoire of Music** which maintains uncorrupted the musical heritage of the Andalusian princely courts, and teaches the modern guitar.

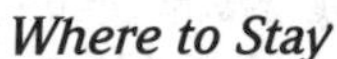

Where to Stay

Since visitors tend just to pass through there is rarely a problem finding a bed in Larache. There is a scattering of pensions and hotels around Place de la Libération and Av Mohammed V.

moderate

The **Hôtel Riad**, ✆ (09) 912626, ℻ (09) 912629, is at 88 Rue Mohammed ben Abdallah, a street leading off the Place. It is the former house of the Duchess of Guise, set in a mature and delightful garden, and has a calm atmosphere with dignified and attentive uniformed staff, a pool, a bar, a restaurant and 24 rooms.

inexpensive

The **Hôtel Espana**, ✆ (09) 913195, ℻ (09) 915628, has recently been renovated and, with balconies overlooking the square, makes a great place to stay. It is large cool and echoing, on the corner of the Place and Av Hassan II.

cheap

The **Hotel Cervantes**, 3 Rue Tarik-Ibnou-Ziad, ✆ 910874, has clean rooms on the second floor with views of the sea or overlooking the Place. The **Pension Amal**, ✆ (09) 912788, and **Es-Saada**, ✆ (09) 913641, are found on or just off Rue Abdallah ben Yasin about 120m from the Place. The cheapest rooms are in the **Hôtel Atlas**, just inside the medina through the Bab Khemis.

The bar-restaurant **Flora** runs a campsite in summer, one km out of Larache on the road south to Rabat, and every year a semi-official Moroccan campsite is established on the beach.

Eating Out

The **Riad Hotel** bar and restaurant stand aloof from the rest of town, but still come within the moderate price category. In the same range, the **Restaurant Cara Bonita** at 1 Place de la Libération also serves delicious seafood prepared with flair.

Of the cheaper-range choices, the **Café Central**, also known as **El Pozo**, is the most resolutely Spanish of the café-bars around the Place, run as a delightful rearguard of the Protectorate with polished bar and tapas. The **Café Koutoubia** and **Café Lixus**, also on the Place, can produce a three-course dinner with fresh fish, as can the **Café-Restaurant Oscare**, on the corner of the Place and Av Mohammed V. There are some conspiratorial café-restaurants just inside the medina through the Bab Khemis, situated in holes in the wall. They all will serve you a delightful range of salads and fish for a few dirhams.

Festivals

There are three local *moussems*, but like most genuine Muslim celebrations they do not correspond to any fixed date in the Christian calendar. The festival of **Moulay Abdelkader Jilali** and that of **Lalla Menama** are held in June and that of **Sidi Allal ben Ahmed** sometime during the spring.

The Rharb

The western coastal plain of the Rharb (or Al-Gharb) is one of the most fertile areas of Morocco, well irrigated by the sluggish waters of the Loukos and Sebou rivers. Though the land is rich and well worked, with large wooded reserves and undisturbed estuaries, it never rises far above the merely attractive. The hotels in Arbaoua, by the beach in Moulay-Bousselham or at Plage des Nations make excellent centres from which to explore this region, so long as you have your own vehicle or make frequent use of a taxi. The Rharb contains several places of interest—Ksar-el-Kebir, Moulay-Bousselham, the Roman ruins of Banasa and Thamusida, Mehdiya-Plage, Plage des Nations and the Bouknadel Gardens—which, while in no one's top ten, more than make up for it by the total lack of other tourists.

Ksar-el-Kebir

Ksar-el-Kebir (also known by its old Spanish name of Alcazarquivir) is only 36km south-east from Larache. The road passes along the fertile Loukos valley, where the lush upper slopes are covered by great orange, tangerine and lemon groves. Until this century a sacred forest stood between the two towns which was left totally undisturbed by plough or herdsmen. Here the sick were cured under the branches of the holy trees, and many lepers used to camp, hoping to lose their sores.

Ksar-el-Kebir is bypassed by the main Tangier to Rabat highway and the modern town, punctuated by tall sugar and flour mills, has gravitated towards the railway station, where the huge **Sunday market** is held. The old town does however show evidence of a dignified urban past fuelled over centuries by cultured Andalusian refugees. A guide, necessarily an amateur in this non-tourist town, is required if you are to navigate the medina streets and find its sanctuaries, mosques and courtyards.

History

The old town stands on the site of the Roman settlement of Oppidum Novum, and seems to have functioned as a natural marketplace continuously throughout history. It was enclosed in walls by the Almohads in the 12th century and embellished by the Merenids, but entered its period of greatest importance once the Iberian powers began to seize control of the nearby ports. Ksar-el-Kebir became both a great fortress of the faith and a secure refuge for those driven from the Atlantic coast. The obliteration of the Portuguese invasion of 1578 in a great battle just outside the town ironically began the slow erosion of its importance. In the succession struggle of the mid-17th century, following the collapse of Saadian authority, it was the headquarters of the dashing General Ghailane, who aspired to seize the throne. The town revolted during the reign of Moulay Ismaïl, who once he had crushed the dissidents decided to level the walls, since the Portuguese were no longer considered a threat. The town was an easy victim during recurring periods of anarchy, and rapidly declined. Its fortunes have been modestly restored during the peace of this century. In the Protectorate period, when it was officially called Alcazarquivir, it was an important Spanish garrison town.

Getting Around and Tourist Information

Rail (six trains daily north to Tangier, four east to Meknès and Fès and four south to Rabat-Casablanca), **bus** and ***grand taxi*** connections are all by the Sunday marketplace. Walk down from the station, past a number of cafés and the only hotel (the cheap **Andaluz**) to reach the Place Granada and the gate on your left, the Bab el Oued, which gives entrance to the medina.

The Medina

Ask to be shown the 18th-century **Fondouq es Soltan**, which stands near to the Mosque of Sidi Mohammed with its distinctive octagonal minaret. The grand mosque was built by the Almohad Sultan Yaacoub el Mansour in the 12th century, at the same time that he enclosed the town in walls and gave it its name of Ksar-el-Kebir—the great enclosure. It has recently suffered a glittering and very enthusiastic restoration. Beside the mosque is a Merenid medersa and the koubba of Sidi Dais, the pious ruler of Cadiz who gave up his high position in Spain for a devout life in Morocco. Amongst the mass of shrines and small mosques you could also ask to be shown the weavers and tanners at work and, by the cemeteries, the eight sided tower of Sidi Ben Abbase, who is venerated by both Jews and Muslims.

The Battle of the Three Kings

The **battlefield** of Alcazarquivir is 12km north of Ksar, by the railway station at Makhazen, where the victory is commemorated every year on 5 August. The Portuguese boy-king Sebastian led a 20,000-strong army out from Asilah to seize Ksar-el-Kebir on his way to Fès in 1578. The Saadian Sultan Abdel Malik positioned his own force of 50,000 between the

Makhazen and Ouarour streams, with artillery on the high ground and his Andalusian troops to the fore. In a bitterly contested battle, in which Abdel Malik, Sebastian and the latter's treacherous Moroccan ally all died, the Moroccans annihilated the Portuguese, largely due to the resilience of the Andalusian infantry and the ferocity of the cavalry drawn from the Middle Atlas tribes. This victory effectively preserved Moroccan independence for three centuries, for it not only ended Portuguese colonial ambitions (Portugal, kingless, was actually absorbed by Spain for 60 years), but impressed two other potential predators—the Hapsburgs of Spain and the Ottoman Turks.

Arbaoua and Souk-el-Arba-du-Rharb

Almost exactly halfway between Tangier and Rabat, 11km south of Ksar-el-Kebir, **Arbaoua** is the site of the old frontier between the French and Spanish Protectorates. The group of French-built lodges, campsite and hotel on a wooded hill just off the main highway form a purpose-built base for hunting in the 35,000-hectare game reserve that stretches along the rough coastal strip between Larache and Moulay Bousselham.

Souk-el-Arba-du-Rharb, the Wednesday market of the Rharb, is an unpretentious local market and transport centre complete with banks, a number of licensed restaurants, cheap café-restaurants and a couple of hotels. Local buses and *grand taxis* depart from here for Moulay Bousselham, 36km to the west and Ouezzane (*see* pp.136–9) 53km to the east, as well as to Sidi-Kacem, on the way to Meknès, and Kénitra/Rabat.

Where to Stay

The **Route de France** hotel, © (09) 90 26 29, in Arbaoua is a piece of the French Alps transported to North Africa, furnished with wood and hunting trophies throughout. It has 13 large, comfortable bedrooms, a bar and a restaurant that serves up wild game in season. The campsite is open all year and is well-shaded by fir trees.

In Souk-el-Arba-du-Rharb there is the inexpensive **Hotel Du Gharb,** © (07) 902441, on the main road, which has three dozen rooms, a bar and restaurant.

Moulay-Bousselham

This small seaside resort, about 35km west of the main road and reachable from Ksar-el-Kebir or Souk-el-Arba, is entirely surrounded by unblemished countryside, but also the sanctuary for an important annual pilgrimage. Sandy cliffs ring beaches on both sides of the one-street village, strung above a sea-filled lagoon. A large brackish lake, the **Merdja Lerga**, is separated from the sea by a spit of settled sand. The original Phoenician trading-post here, Mulechala, was known to Pliny the Elder and survived intact at least into the 12th century. It was then fortified to provide a secure port for the inland city of Basra, whose fate it apparently shared. There are traces of an **old fort** on the rising ground to the north of the town.

The simple avenue of the village is lined with a row of half a dozen simple fish restaurants, all under a continuous arcade which faces the new **mosque**. This mosque partly hides the view of a delightful family of **seven maraboutic shrines** that dip down the slope towards the sea. The modern name of the town comes from the marabout Moulay Bousselham, literally 'the saint in a cloak'. He was an Egyptian, Abou Said, a pantheistic Sufi who fled from orthodox persecution to take refuge in Morocco, where he died in 951 and was buried by the seashore. On the other side of the lagoon a single shrine looks in danger of being engulfed by the cascading sand of a towering dune.

For a centre of Muslim pilgrimage the town shelters some surprising local beliefs. The **tomb of Joseph, the son of Aristotle**, is venerated in a cave near to that of **Bou el Kornien**, the two-horned man. Bou el Kornien is an apocalyptic figure in Islamic mythology, who confined the terrifying anarchic giants on the edge of the civilized world, the tribes of Gog and Magog, behind walls of iron. He is often associated with Iskender, Alexander the Great, who was frequently depicted on coins in his manifestation as the son of Zeus–Baal–Ammon, the ram-horned supreme deity, for Alexander after the siege of Tyre visited the Berber oracle of Ammon at Shiwa in the Sahara, where he was received as the son of the god. Some strength is added to this local interpretation in that Alexander's tutor was Aristotle. In the cave where Bou el Kornien is venerated, a sacred stalactite secretes a salty, milky fluid which is sucked for good luck by devotees.

The shores of the **lagoon**, a protected wildlife reserve, provide more innocent amusement for bird watchers. Ask for Idriss at the 'Sable d'Or', who can organize boat trips. Just a few kilometres south of the lagoon the **hill of Nador** (watchtower) has a fine view over the surrounding plain. Inland, due east of Moulay-Bousselham, rises the spine of a **sacred hill**, littered with rock-cut and stone-framed tombs of the late Neolithic and Phoenician periods. It can be reached by walking south from Lalla-Mimouna, a village halfway between Moulay-Bousselham and Arbaoua.

Where to Stay and Eating Out

There are two places to stay in Moulay-Bousselham, both moderately priced. The **Lagona**, © (07) 432603, is a comfortable motel-like place with 30 bedrooms that overlooks the lagoon. It has the only bar, licensed restaurant and swimming pool in town. Downstairs there is a disco club with a television/video room off the open-plan central lounge, which can mean that it gets a bit crowded at times. There is in addition, in summer, a family-run pension, the **Villanova Club**, on the seafront strip of bourgeois villas. The **campsite** is one of the most delightful in Morocco. It is right down by the edge of the lagoon, with fishing boats beached up to its perimeter fence. The sites have been carefully arranged so that you are screened and shaded by the many trees (the mosquitoes, though, are hell in summer).

Festivals and Sports

The **pilgrimage** to Moulay-Bousselham takes place in late June or July, when the space by the petrol station is transformed into a holiday town. Bulls and sheep are sacrificed and eaten amid much general music and festivity. A quieter *moussem* occurs in September for **Sidi Ahmed ben Mansour**. Throughout the summer the beach-chalets are full of prosperous Moroccan families on holiday. The lake is full of boats as it has a great reputation for **fishing**, while the sea here is one of the most celebrated places for **scuba diving** and **spear-gun fishing** in Atlantic Morocco. On the lake **boats** can be hired and there is a flamingo trip regularly touted. As everywhere on the coast, the sea provides exhilarating but dangerous surf, and warning flags and lifeguards are deployed here every summer.

Roman Banasa and Thamusida

Between Souk-el-Arba-du-Rharb and Kénitra are the excavated traces of two Roman towns, **Banasa** and **Thamusida**. They are both tranquil, reclusive sites, difficult to reach without a car and best enjoyed with a good supporting picnic.

Banasa

Turn left 3km south of Souk-Tleta-du-Rharb, cross the river Sebou and then turn left again for another 3km. Look out for a faded sign on the left indicating the farm track for Banasa. A cluster of cypress trees on the brow of a hill and a scattering of marabout shrines (including that of Sidi Abou el Jenoune, 'the Master of Jinn') indicate that you have reached the surrounding ruins of the baths, forum and temples of the city of Banasa, pleasantly sited above the high banks of the Sebou.

The city of Julia Valentina Banasa has been excavated to reveal three distinct pre-Roman layers that date back to before the 3rd century BC. The present visible remains and the typical, regular Roman street pattern date from the enlargement of Banasa into a colony ordered by Octavian before he became the Emperor Augustus in 27 BC. A circuit of walls, defended by towers and over five feet thick, was built in the beginning of the 3rd century AD, and there are traces of an army camp to the west. It was overwhelmed by the Baquates tribe in 280 AD, during the era of decline when Rome endured nearly 30 soldier-emperors in as many years. A partial restoration of Roman authority in North Africa was achieved by Diocletian's co-Emperor Maximian a few years later, but Banasa was left in ruins and was never rebuilt.

The custodian, Hmida Nouar (who speaks French), lives by the ruins and will show you around the main features. The **forum**, the public square of the town, is easily recognizable as it retains its 3rd century paving stones. To its southern end is the three-chambered state shrine on a high terrace, the **capitol**, dedicated to the triad of Olympian gods, Jupiter, Juno and Minerva, and rebuilt in the 2nd century AD. Opposite the temple is the **basilica** with its vaulted round arch, where justice was dispensed in public. South of the forum are a number of rooms that were almost certainly municipal offices.

There are five sets of **public baths** in Banasa. The large western baths are approached by crossing the old main street, which would have had the major shops, factories and houses ranged along its pavements. A hoard of 457 coins was found by archaeologists here, hidden in a baker's oven. The central hall of these baths, the under-floor heating system and the cold plunge pool, at the end on your right, are all quite distinctive.

The little western baths, the 'baths of the nymphs', are nearby at a lower level, overlooked by a well that is still in active use. The entrance floor is covered in a herringbone grid of worn bricks, and the wall paintings in the intimate octagonal fountain pool are still visible, framed beneath their conch-like apses. The hot rooms have geometric mosaic fragments, and parts where village boys still wash with water drawn from the nearby well: a continuity of use that briefly brings these dry stones sparkling back into life. Walking towards the river from here will bring you past the market baths.

Pliny the Elder recorded that the Rharb was infested with elephants. An inscription from the Emperor Caracalla confirms this, thanking the town for a gift of elephants and cancelling any back tax owed to the imperial chancery. Archaeologists have discovered an elephant head carved from blue schist with marble tusks. There is also evidence that the Egyptian goddess Isis had a temple here.

Thamusida

The ruins of Thamusida are another 50km further south, and 5km west of the P2 road. About 13km north of Kénitra (on the old P2 road, not the new motorway) stop at the Tamuzida Café in the low-lying village of Souk el Khemis. Having ordered a coffee, ask to be shown the view from the roof, from where the koubba of Sidi Ahmed, crowning the ruins flanked by half a dozen palms, can be clearly seen. Having taken a siting of this crucial landmark you then head west along the sandy farm tracks for about 2.5km before the white dome reappears on your horizon. Beware of the mud, for after the slightest touch of rain the tracks turn into a quagmire.

Thamusida, like Banasa, stands on the banks of the river Sebou. It began life as a settlement of the Mauretanian kings, which was destroyed by Claudius' legions when they put down the rebellion of AD 42. The present excavations have been intended to uncover the 2nd century Roman town, which during the reign of the Emperor Marcus Aurelius was enclosed within a circuit of walls and defended by a permanent garrison. These defences worked well for over a hundred years, but by 280 Thamusida, again like its neighbour Banasa, seems to have been overwhelmed by the Baquates.

The koubba of Sidi Ahmed provides the best view of the excavations, ranged over a gentle elevation of land above the slow-moving Sebou. Upstream, the smart new motorway bridge provides an effective contrast to the simple wooden fishing boats that work the sluggish waters of the river, also fished by a variety of raptors. In spring the site is transformed into a delightful meadow, but for the rest of the year only doum, the dwarf palm, provides contrast to the sunbaked stones, covered each year by the river with a new coat of silt.

Between the koubba and the river is the square walled enclosure of the 165m by 135m Roman army camp. In the centre stands the **praetorium**, the headquarters, with its piazza overlooked by the remains of a sanctuary approached up a flight of stairs. Here the military standard would be kept, and the local gods and the personification of military discipline worshipped. The west face of the camp coincides with the town walls, and so its entrance, the **praetorian gate**, was strongly defended. In the other direction from the camp (towards a conspicuous clump of eucalyptus trees), you can follow the main street of the town as it approached the east gate. Heading down from here towards the riverbank you pass the foundations of a square temple and the 'Dallage' villa, before reaching the remains of the riverside **docks** beside which stretch extensive but confusing remains of the **town baths**. Scattered about the site are a number of millstones, and the ground is flecked with terracotta sherds. This is considered locally a place of ill omen, populated by snakes and large spiders

Kénitra and Mehdiya

It is possible to pass through the broad central avenue of **Kénitra** and have few regrets at not stopping. It's a sprawling modern city and port that was founded by the French in 1913, on the site of a humble fort. It was later named Port Lyautey after the charismatic first French Governor, and today with Rabat and Casablanca forms the essential triangle of industrial Morocco. It used to have quite a busy nightlife, fuelled by a US military base. The GIs and airmen have long gone but there are enough businessmen to keep bars, restaurants and local bands busy in the town's several hotels. Banks are found at 363 and 365 Av Mohammed V, the central street where the Post Office and the CTM bus station are also situated. The railway station (frequent connections both north and south) is to the south of the town.

Mehdiya

About 11km south of Kénitra, off the unpromising and busy road to Rabat, a turning to the west takes you through the **Lac de Sidi Bourhaba nature reserve** established along the Sebou estuary. The lake is a wonderful place for bird-watching, and Sidi Bourhaba sits alone in his koubba, like St Francis preaching to the birds, disturbed only by a *moussem* in August. It is a favourite haunt of raptors; in particular marsh harriers and the small white streaked black-shouldered kite, which looks faintly like an osprey. A campsite and nature reserve information centre have been established on the east bank of the lake. From the reserve the road twists down to the beach resort village of **Mehdiya-Plage**. It is a very Moroccan resort that bustles with promenade activity in the three-month summer season.

The only site of any interest is **Mehdiya Kasbah**, which overlooks the estuary near the Restaurant Belle Vue. The gates are protected by two flanking castellated towers that were erected by Sultan Moulay Ismaïl. Stairs lead up the left-hand turret for a fine view of the large interior compound of the fortress; you can also walk past the 17th-century rustic **mosque** through the ornate brick arch to the **Governor's Palace**. Dark subterranean passages give way to sudden pools of light, illuminating a brick-paved courtyard filled with branches of figs. Stairways lead up to bare balconies that provide odd vistas of buildings, barracks, cisterns and storehouses that are now deserted and full of weeds, but were once occupied by Moulay Ismaïl's regiments of black soldiers. An old gun platform overlooks the estuary—seven rusting ships' cannon are still in place.

Pirates and Admirals

Mehdiya Kasbah has a turbulent history typical of the Atlantic coast. It was first founded by the Carthaginians, who settled a colony at the strategic mouth of the navigable Sebou river. In the early Islamic period it was known as 'El Mamora'—the populous—, surrounded then as now by forests. It was a natural site for the shipyards of the Almohad sultans, but the navy had decayed by the end of the 14th century, and only an unarmed zaouia marked the kasbah hill. In June 1515 King Manuel of Portugal sailed a fleet of 200 ships up the river. Two thousand cavalry were landed to protect the army of soldier-workmen, who hastily erected a timber stockade on the river bank. The Wattasid Sultan waited a month before springing his trap. The fort was isolated by a screen of 30,000 horsemen and a river battery cut off naval support, while his five *pasamuras* (wall-smashers) pounded the fort from the kasbah hilltop. Manuel was forced to order a withdrawal. The Moroccans waited until the final moment of evacuation, with the Portuguese barges massed in the river, before opening fire: half the Portuguese force was destroyed and 52 cannons captured, in a victory that briefly seemed to promise the Wattasid dynasty new hope. Later in the 16th century Mehdiya became a great corsair base, used by such *rais* as Mainwaring, an enterprising English privateer who worked in turn for all the major pirate bosses, the Bey of Tunis, the Duke of Tuscany, the Venetian Republic and the Sultan of Morocco. From Mehdiya he preyed on all shipping, selling his victims according to their religion and race in the slave-markets of Villefranche, Fès, Leghorn or Algiers, before retiring from this profitable enterprise to a respectable life in England as landlord, naval officer and MP. His timing was impeccable, for just a few years later a Spanish fleet destroyed the corsair ships in the raid of 1610. They returned in 1614 and fortified the kasbah. There they remained for 50 years until they were expelled by Moulay Ismaïl's general Ali er Riffi, the 'caesar of the north'. The existing palace, gate and mosque all date from the 17th century rebuilding of the kasbah that followed this reconquest. To celebrate this second great Moroccan victory at Mamora the kasbah was renamed El Mahdia, 'the delivered one', the origin of modern Mehdiya.

The Kasbah of Mehdiya last witnessed military action in the American landings of 1942. In the one dashing gesture of this muddled campaign two trim destroyers, the Bernadou and the Cole, swept up the estuary on the morning of 8 November, raked the harbour with machine-gun fire and landed marines on the quay with their feet dry.

Where to Stay and Eating Out

In Kénitra the **Assam**, ✆ (07) 378628, on Route de Tanger, the **Safir**, ✆ (07) 371922/3, on Place Administrative and **Mamora**, ✆ (07) 371310 on Av Hassan II are all busy business hotels. If you want or need to stay a night here it's usually better (and cheaper) to choose one of the two decent two-stars, **La Rotonde** at 60 Av Mohammed Diouri, ✆ (07) 371402 or the **Ambassy**, ✆ (07) 362926, at 20 Av Hassan II.

In Mehdiya-Plage, as well as the beach café decorated with stills from Casablanca, there is the delightful **Hôtel Atlantique**, ✆ 116 (through the operator), a raffish, intriguing place that comes to life after dinner and buzzes with exuberant Moroccan music until 3am or 4am. The singers are of such outstanding character, intensity, size and determination that they broaden your appreciation of Moroccan women overnight. The audience can also be entertaining: I was lucky enough to observe the arrival of the local chief of police, an enormous man-of-respect immaculately covered in a double-breasted suit who, having had his hand kissed by anyone who ought to, sat sipping a sticky green cordial for hours and watched the singers with an almost proprietorial interest. Be careful of the bars, which tend to sag if you lean too heavily on them, and you may also have to keep a watch on the bar prices.

You can have dinner on the hotel verandah looking towards the sea, or at the seafront **Restaurant-Café Dauphine**. Better still, drive up the estuary to the **Restaurant Belle Vue**, © (07) 388366/388006 (which serves alcohol), now run by 'Charlot', who really appreciates his food. Here you can watch the sun set over the water while licking the garlicky juices of fried prawns off your fingers. Ask what is freshest on the day.

Bouknadel and Plage des Nations

It's nine km from the Mehdiya turning and a one km drive off the Kénitra–Rabat highway to the most attractive and tranquil beach on this area of coast—the **Plage des Nations**. Its name is due to its status as a haunt of Rabat's diplomatic community, and it still retains a certain cachet, with the expensive **Hôtel Firdaous** sitting perfectly alone on the Atlantic shore. Its unchanged late-sixties interior is beginning to look rather classic. All the rooms face the sea, there are two pools, two restaurants, bars and a piano, and the staff are friendly to day visitors who may use the facilities for a small charge. The beach is open to all and a few cafés are established here in summer. To get to the beach from Salé, there is a no 28 bus that leaves about every 20 minutes from Bab Mrisa and drops you beside the road for the beach or gardens. A place in a *grand taxi* will cost around 10dh, and take you right to the beach.

The **Jardins Exotiques** *(open daily 9am–6.30pm, adm)*, with their tattered signpost, are on the west side of the road 8km after the Plage des Nations turning, and 12km from Rabat. Even if you are not wild about plants, the cool, shaded, intimate bamboo benches, the flowers, smells and tranquillity make this a whimsical and restful place. The gardens were created by the ingenious horticulturist and ecologist M. François in the 1950s, and held over 1500 species at their peak. His verse thoughts on ecological principles and his love for Morocco are found at the entrance, before a mass of hibiscus and red-hot pokers. It originally contained a zoo and an aquarium but these cages are thankfully now empty, leaving a delightfully profuse series of gardens inhabited by birds, turtles and frogs. The site extends in a long, thin belt of four hectares between the road and the coastal dunes. There are three sections: an indigenous collection of Moroccan flora; a formal Islamic Andalusian garden; and a collection of exotica from all over the world. The lush ecosystems of America, Japan, China, the Pacific, the Caribbean and southeast Asia have all been skilfully recreated in delightful confusion on this dry, sandy coastal plain. The network of bamboo bridges, stone walkways, root passages, ruined temples and pagodas is magnificently eclectic, definitely bizarre and saved from being kitsch by rapid weathering and luxurious overgrowth. There are special coloured and timed routes of three-quarters or one hour, but it's hard to imagine that anybody would allow themselves to be organized in such a way. Leaving the gardens, on the way into Rabat you will pass a number of nurseries, as well as local sculptors hacking the bright yellow sandstone into architectural embellishments.

Rabat–Salé

Rabat has been the political capital of Morocco since 1912. It wears the well-ordered urban architecture of the 20th century: broad tree-lined avenues, a central park, apartment blocks and suburban quarters for the Ministries, officialdom and foreign diplomats. The conurbation now has a population of over a million and an impressive air of activity by day. Brisk men armed with briefcases stride to their appointments along the avenues of the city centre. The main streets are lined with newsagents, book shops, cinemas and cafés, but this familiar core of a modern capital city also contains striking monuments from the past.

The twin cities of Rabat and Salé, on opposite banks of the Bou Regreg estuary, have a long history. Rabat, the city on the southern bank, has known greater extremes of fortune, while its northern twin has had a steadier but less glamorous history. Half an hour's walk from the city centre, Salé is now really a suburb of Rabat, but retains its own traditional identity.

The 12th-century city walls still dominate 20th-century Rabat. The more intimate achievements of the Merenid dynasty can be found in the 13th-century medina of Salé and in Rabat's royal necropolis—the walled garden of the Chellah. The Rabat kasbah, in its strategic position above the estuary, has been at the heart of the city's long Islamic history. It has a celebrated Almohad gate, an Andalusian urban interior and a garden palace from the 17th century now transformed into a delightful museum. For rarer insights into the Phoenician and classical achievements there are the Archaeology Museum and the ruins of Sala Colonia inside the Chellah walls, to reward you with haunting views and art of the highest order.

History

All the civilizations of Morocco have been drawn to the safe harbour of the estuary of the Bou Regreg, where the river has cut access to the sea through a forbidding line of Atlantic cliffs. For Rabat the wheel of fortune has in 2500 years twice turned to elevate it as an imperial capital, and twice as a maritime trading power; in between these glories it has been reduced to a humble village.

Ancient Sala Colonia and the Orthodox *Rabat*

Like Tangier and other cities of the Moroccan coast Rabat was first Phoenician, then Roman. It was the southernmost urban centre of the Roman province, and, as Sala Colonia, given the privileges of a *colonia* or self-governing city by Trajan. Though Roman rule was withdrawn in the 3rd century it remained a trading centre, identifying with the Muslim Kharijite heresy in the mid-8th century. Protected by the powerful Berber Berghouata confederacy it survived until the 10th century, when a garrison of orthodox Arabs established a *Rabat*, a religious community of warriors, on the site of the present kasbah. The Almoravids took up the struggle against the heretic Berghouata and lost their first two leaders to it, but their deaths were avenged by Youssef ben Tachfine, celebrated founder of the Almoravid Empire.

The Imperial Capital

The first Almohad sultans, in the 12th century, found the site useful as a combined military and naval base, but it was not until the reign of Yaacoub el Mansour, the third Sultan, that it was decided to turn Rabat into an imperial capital. He raised the vast grand mosque of Hassan, the series of impressive gateways, and built the enormous and still surviving extent of city walls for his *Rabat el Fath*, the Rabat of Victory. Work stopped the day Yaacoub died; his successors neglected this empty but magnificent encampment on the Atlantic coast, and chose to rule from Seville or Marrakech. The Almohad walls of Rabat were only to be fully occupied in the 20th century. In the 14th century the Merenid sultans with their exquisite

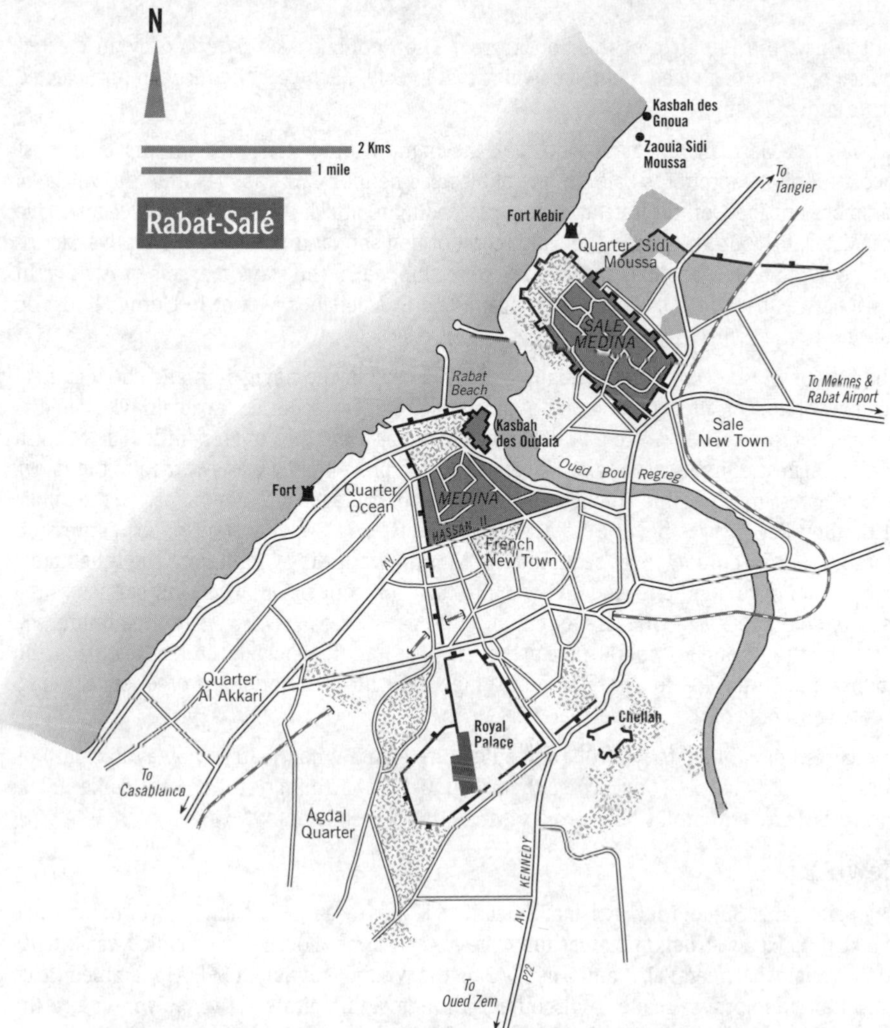

taste selected the backdrop of the near-empty city as the site for their royal necropolis. They enclosed the Roman ruins of Sala Colonia in high walls pierced by a magnificent gate that hid a complex of fine gardens, delicate mosques and sanctuaries, the Chellah. Commercial life was then concentrated in Salé—for Leo Africanus, who passed through Rabat in 1500, reported that it sheltered a scattering of a mere hundred houses.

The Pirate Republic

Recovery came in the early 17th century when Muslim refugees, expelled from Andalusia by Philip III of Spain, were offered the empty city of Rabat by the Saadian Sultan Zaidan. Because the original Almohad walls enclosed far too large an area the Andalusians built the dividing wall that still separates the medina from the new town. The principal business of Rabat and its sister city of Salé then became organized piracy, and due to the collapse of Saadian authority from 1627 the two cities were able to establish themselves as an independent entity, the Republic of the Bou Regreg. The Republic was governed by an elected council or *divan* of sixteen members, which met in Salé. Each year the *divan* in turn elected a *caid* and an admiral.

Jan Jansz, a German renegade who took the name Murad Reis, was the first and most successful pirate admiral of Salé. In one of his raids he took 237 captives from the village of Baltimore outside Cork in Ireland, before proceeding to attack fishing fleets off Iceland. Five years later, in 1636, he raided the south coast of England, and then sent his captives across France by land to Marseille, where they were shipped to the slave markets of Algiers. In 1640 he was back in northern waters again, and St Michael's Mount in Cornwall lost 60 villagers to the 'Sallee Rovers'.

The European renegades were usually employed only in the navigation and the technical handling of the corsair ships. It was the Andalusian refugees under their captain who acted as the fighting force. They spoke a lingua franca that was a mixture of French, Italian, Spanish and Portuguese. On return to Salé, 10 per cent of the prize money was awarded to the *divan*, which increasingly became an oligarchy of successful captains and merchants. The Republic of the Bou Regreg was never a homogeneous entity, and only constant external pressure from the European powers at sea and rival Muslim warlords by land kept the inhabitants from pursuing faction fights and civil wars to their full conclusion. The sand bar across the estuary and the savage cliffs prevented any European fleet from seriously threatening the pirate craft, although a subtle mixture of bombardment, blockade and bribes from the English and Dutch led to the release of some slaves and a variety of 'protection' arrangements with some of the European powers.

The golden days of anarchy, profit and adventure ended when Sultan Moulay Rachid took possession of Rabat in 1666. The sultan assumed a controlling 60 per cent stake in the corsair business and profits nose-dived for the other shareholders.

New Rabat

The period after Sultan Moulay Ismaïl's death in 1727 saw a rapid decline in Moroccan trade and widespread destruction by warring heirs to the throne. Locally this conflict was intensified by rivalry between Rabat and Salé. During the wise rule of Sultan Sidi Mohammed (from 1757) an attempt was made to discourage the remaining pirate activity, even before the French bombardment of Rabat in 1765. After this attack the Sultan allowed a French consul to settle in Rabat, established a new administrative palace on its present site—safely out of range of European cannon—and encouraged the town to develop its now renowned carpet trade, as well as building two new mosques and laying out a park. Unofficial coastal piracy and wrecking continued, though, until the navy of the Austrian Empire took savage revenge for the loss of one ship in 1829 by shelling all the coastal cities of Morocco.

Rabat enjoyed reasonable prosperity as one of the towns under the firm control of the government during the 19th century, though it was increasingly superseded as a trading centre by Casablanca, with its large harbour. Its future was radically altered in 1912 by France who, wary of the old cities of the interior, selected Rabat as the new political centre for the administration of the country. The fiction that the French Resident administered Morocco for the sultan was vigorously maintained, and Sultan Moulay Youssef was duly installed in the palace of Rabat.

French rule from 1912 to 1956, while rapidly developing a glittering new town, made few changes to the traditional pattern of life in the old city. The Protectorate was a colonial regime interested in ruling a conquered Islamic nation with the minimum of expense. This necessarily involved ruling through traditional power structures, and avoiding any unnecessary social, moral or political interference. As part of this policy the native quarters were left as sanctums of traditional custom, while separate modern quarters for Europeans were built outside them. This policy, defensible on aesthetic grounds as well as that of convenient security, was initiated in Rabat by the first French Resident Marshal Lyautey.

After Independence Mohammed V and his son, the present King Hassan II, developed the palace of Rabat from a mere symbol into the actual seat of national authority.

Rabat

Modern Rabat, with the French New Town and Royal Palace, sprawls inland between the medieval Muslim city and the Merenid Chellah, the original site of Roman Sala Colonia.

Getting Around

by air

International flights use Casablanca rather than Rabat's own small airport. Half a dozen buses a day leave from outside the Hotel Terminus by the central train station on Av Mohammed V direct to Casablanca's Mohammed V International Airport. It also possible to get there with a change of trains at Casablanca. Taxis are an expensive option, but 400dh isn't that much if you are about to miss a flight. The RAM ticket office, © (07) 709710, is opposite the train station on Av Mohammed V and open Mon–Sat 8.30am–12.15pm, 2.30–7pm. Air France have an office here at 281 Av Mohammed V, © (07) 707066.

by rail

Travelling by train to and from Rabat is recommended: no more expensive than buses, punctual, reliable, and it takes you straight to the city centre. The elegant white Rabat Ville station, complete with cafés, lockers, electronic departure boards and newsstands, is at the intersection of Av Mohammed V and Av Moulay Youssef. Other nearby stations include Rabat Agdal, 2km southwest of the centre, and Rabat-Salé, the other side of the estuary. There are frequent (almost hourly) departures for Casablanca (50mins on the direct, 90mins on the stop-a-lot), five daily trains for Meknes, Fès and points east, four for Asilah and Tangier, seven for Marrakech via Casablanca, two for the five-hour trip to Safi and just one for El-Jadida. There is a café-restaurant and baggage lockers in the station.

by bus

Local buses can be picked up on Av Hassan II. No. 17 heads south for Temara beach, the 6 or 12 take you to the Bab Fès at Salé. Nos. 1, 2 and 4 go south along Av Allal ben Abdallah; for Chellah, get off at Bab Zaer, where you pass through the outer walls. No. 30 runs from the centre to the main bus depot at Place Zerktouni, which is otherwise a tedious 2km walk along Av Hassan II from the Bab Al Had (ticket 3dh, or *petit taxi* for 10dh). At the depot it is worth getting a CTM ticket at booths 14 or 15. Other services have elastic departure routines and Arabic timetables. CTM services from Rabat include Marrakech and Ouezzane, three buses a day; Tangier, Fès and Meknes four departures; Tetouan and Azrou two; and there are buses to Casablanca every two hours.

by car and taxi

Petits taxis, which normally keep to their meters, are found next to the train station, along Av Hassan II and opposite the Kasbah. *Grands taxis* for crossing over to Salé or long-haul destinations are found along Av Hassan II. For a place to Casablanca, or the beaches of Skhirat, Témara or Bouknadel (Plage des Nations), go to the taxi rank outside the bus depot at Place Zerktouni. It's a quicker, more pleasant trip which should cost you only a few dirhams more than the bus ticket.

Driving in Rabat's one-way system is confusing. It is easier to park your car along Av Hassan II and walk. **Car hire** agencies in the city are Avis, 7 Zankat (Rue) Abou Faris El Marini, © (07) 767959; Hertz, 291 Av. Mohammed V, © (07) 769227; and InterRent-Europcar on Place Mohammed V, © (07) 704416.

Orientation

Rabat and Salé have spread enormously in recent decades, but all the places of interest remain in walking distance of each other. Rabat itself could hardly be more convenient for the traveller. Av Hassan II conveniently divides the medina from the new city: to the east it leads to the Pont Moulay Hassan, the bridge across the Bou Regreg to Salé, and to the west (having passed through the Almohad walls) it takes you to the main bus station and the road to Casablanca. Av Hassan II is crossed by Av Mohammed V, which leads you north right through the medina or south, as Av Yacoub al Mansour, past the Royal Palace to the Chellah.

The pavements of Av Mohammed V are the heart of the city, and here you can find the impressive exteriors of the post office, the train station and the major banks. Cinemas, cafés, hotels and restaurants are also all concentrated on this boulevard or on the side streets that connect it to the parallel Av Allal ben Abdallah to the east.

Tourist Information

The **tourist office** is on Rue Patrice Lumumba, © (07) 773272, in the New Town. The central PTT or **post office** is on Av Mohammed V at the junction with Rue Soekarno, and open Mon–Fri 8.30am–12pm, 2pm–6.45pm. As elsewhere in Morocco, international telephone calls are best made from the numerous private booths. Central **banks** include the BMCE at 260 Av Mohammed V and at the train station; Banque Populaire at 64 Av Allal Ben Abdallah; and Banque du Maroc at 277 Av Mohammed V.

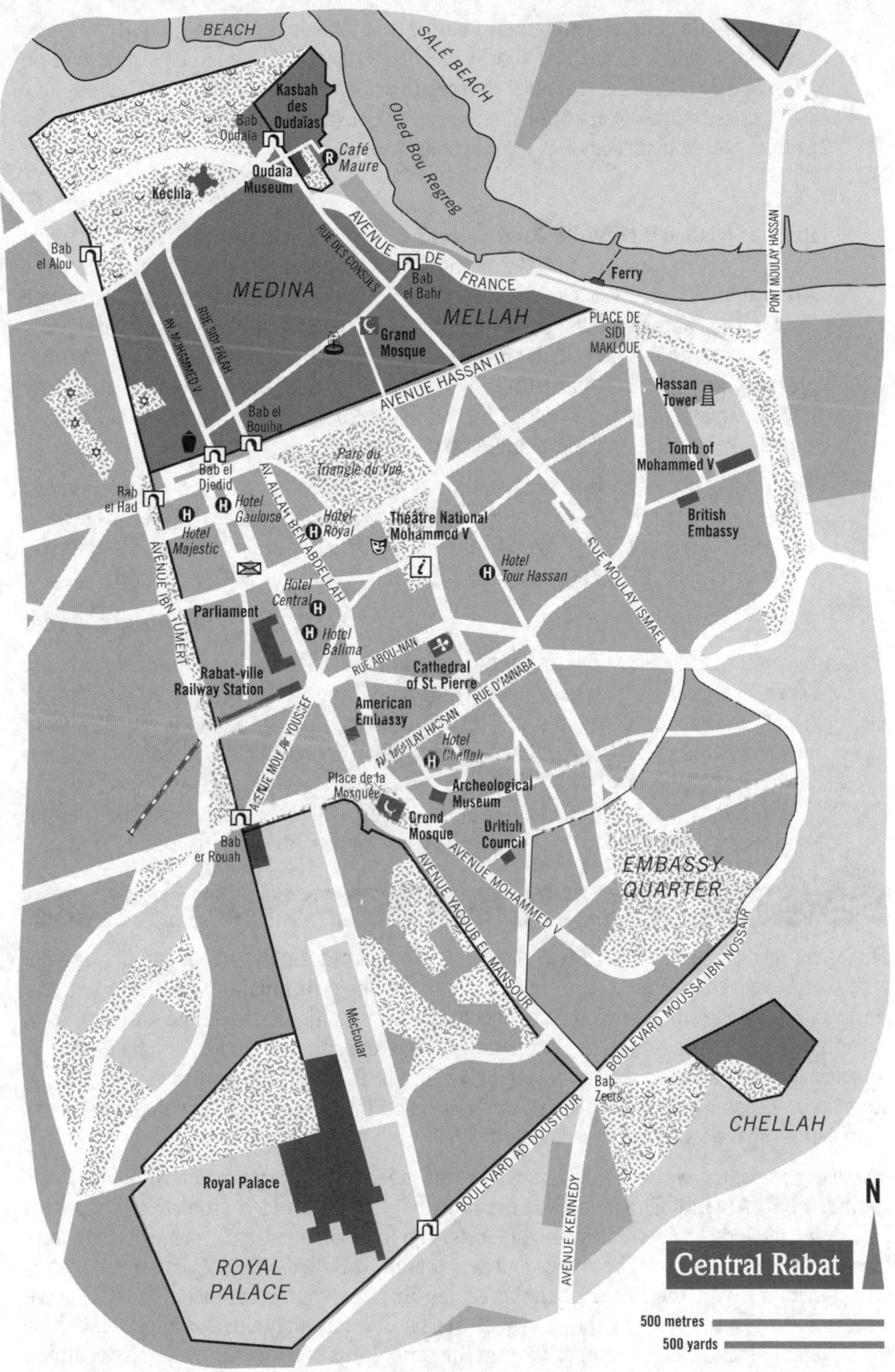
BEACH
SALÉ BEACH
Kasbah des Oudaïas
Bab Oudaïa
Café Maure
Oudaïa Museum
Kechla
Oued Bou Regreg
Bab el Alou
AVENUE DE FRANCE
RUE DES CONSULS
Bab el Bahr
Ferry
PONT MOULAY HASSAN
MEDINA
MELLAH
PLACE DE SIDI MAKLOUF
RUE SIDI FALAH
AV. MOHAMMED V
Grand Mosque
AVENUE HASSAN II
Hassan Tower
Bab el Bouiba
Tomb of Mohammed V
Parc du Triangle du Vue
Bab el Djedid
Bab el Had
Hotel Majestic
Hotel Gauloise
Hotel Royal
AV. ALLAH BEN ABDELLAH
Théâtre National Mohammed V
British Embassy
AVENUE IBN TUMERT
Hotel Tour Hassan
RUE MOULAY ISMAEL
Hotel Central
Parliament
Hotel Balima
RUE ABOU-NAN
Cathedral of St. Pierre
Rabat-ville Railway Station
RUE D'ANNABA
American Embassy
AV. MOULAY HASSAN
Hotel Chellah
AVENUE MOULAY YOUSSEF
Place de la Mosquée
Archeological Museum
Grand Mosque
British Council
Bab er Rouah
AVENUE MOHAMMED V
EMBASSY QUARTER
AVENUE YACOUB EL MANSOUR
BOULEVARD MOUSSA IBN NOSSAIR
Méchouar
Bab Zeers
CHELLAH
BOULEVARD AD DOUSTOUR
Royal Palace
AVENUE KENNEDY
ROYAL PALACE
N
Central Rabat
500 metres
500 yards

There is a late-hour **pharmacy** on Rue Moulay Sliman as well as the Pharmacie de Chellahh on Place de Melilla, ✆ (07) 724723. Others are listed in newspapers or on ✆ (07) 726150. The **Hospital Avicienne**, on Av. Ibn Sina, offers emergency medical assistance. Dial 15 for fire or medical **emergency** services, and 19 for the **police**, whose main station is on Rue Soekarno.

embassies and consulates

British, **Irish** and **New Zealand** citizens all use the **British Embassy** on 17 Blvd de la Tour Hassan, ✆ (07) 720905. The **Canadian Embassy**, also used by **Australians**, is on 13 Jaafar As Sadik, ✆ (07) 672880. Other national offices include the **United States** on 2 Av de Marrakech, ✆ (07) 762265, **Netherlands** at 40 Rue de Tunis, ✆ (07) 733512, **Denmark** at 4 Rue de Khemisset, ✆ (07) 767986, **Norway** at 13 Zankat Joafar Es-Sadik, Agdal, ✆ (07) 771375, **Sweden** at 150 Av John Kennedy, ✆ (07) 754440, **Finland** at 16 Rue de Khemisset, ✆ (07) 762352, and **Germany** at 7 Zankat Madnine, ✆ (07) 709662.

The Consulates of neighbouring countries that issue visas include **Mauretania** at 9 Rue Taza, ✆ (07) 756817 (though their office in Paris is more reliable), **Algeria** at 10 Zankat Azrou, ✆ (07) 767668, (though the frontier is now closed) and **Tunisia** on Av de Fès, ✆ (07) 730636. **Spain** is at 3 Rue Madnine, ✆ (07) 707600.

religious services

In addition to the large number of mosques in Rabat, open to Muslims only, there are several churches and synagogues. Synagogue Talmud Torah is at 9 Rue Moulay Ismaïl, Synagogue Berdugo is at El Aloul Buenos, Rue dar El Beida. For details of services ✆ (07) 725404. For details of services in the Catholic Cathedral of St Peter in the new town, ✆ (07) 722301, for the Church of St Francis of Assisi, ✆ (07) 724380, for the Church of St Peter in the Agdal, ✆ (07) 770450. French Protestant services are conducted at the Temple, 44 Av Allal ben Abdallah, ✆ (07) 723848.

The Medina

The Rabat medina was built by the Moriscos, those Spanish inhabitants of Muslim descent who were expelled by Philip III in 1607. They built the **Andalusian wall** (*Rempart des Andalous*), a long rampart reinforced by rectangular towers that enclosed the northerly fortifiable portion from the excessive 5km perimeter wall constructed in the Almohad era. The Andalusian wall stands on the north side of Av Hassan II, its flat top furnished with narrow gun slits in keeping with its 17th-century origins and in contrast to the comparatively gay crenellations that decorate the medieval Almohad walls to the west.

Two gates pierce the western Almohad wall of the medina: the northern Bab Al Alou and the southern **Bab Al Had**. The latter was the principal entrance and is protected by a pair of protruding five-sided towers cut with gun ports. The handsome entrance gate is formed from three superimposed horseshoe arches and was rebuilt by Sultan Moulay Sliman in 1814. It was decorated with the heads of the executed until early this century. Since the hole punched through the walls by the nearby Av Hassan II it has functioned as an entrance into the vegetable market that stretches beyond this gate. In its shadow, a row of clerks armed with typewriters sit ready to assist the less literate through the formal paths of bureaucracy. Around the market are ranged all the cheaper pensions, as well as a tempting assortment of grill cafés that provide some of the best cooking in the city.

Just behind the bustling market area with its artisan's stalls, bazaars and intimate little cafés are the tranquil residential quarters of an Andalusian town. Houses of stone are barred by old stained and rivetted doors, their walls half plastered and painted with lime with details picked out in azure or ochre yellow. Each quarter has a local mosque for daily prayers, a communal bakery, a fountain and usually a bath-house. Its ordered 17th-century Andalusian foundation has given the medina a regulated street pattern. It is easy to explore, in contrast to the tortuous mystery of the medieval medinas in Tangier or Fès.

Beginning in the southwest, at the crossing of the Rue Souika and Rue Sidi Fatah, is the **mosque of Sultan Moulay Sliman**, which he founded in 1812. Further along Rue Souika, past intriguing displays of domestic goods—mostly bolts of cloth and kitchen ware—is the **grand mosque**, entirely rebuilt in the late 19th century, although it was founded by the Merenids. Opposite the mosque, on the right-hand side of the road that leads down to the Bab Chellahh, there is a 14th-century **fountain** that is the sole surviving remnant of the Merenid mosque: the three broken arches with their fading decoration were placed here around 1370. They now provide an impressive façade for an Arab and Islamic bookshop.

The market booths around a grand mosque traditionally hold more expensive merchandise (their rents help in the upkeep of the mosque). The covered **Souk es Sebat** was once a famous centre for Morocco work, the intricate gold-stamped leatherwork which can still be found amongst the glittering array of embroidered slippers, filigree belts and ornamental hats. There are a number of specialist courtyards off the main market. A reconstructed arch marks the end of the Souk es Sebat and leads into Rue des Consuls. Across this medina thoroughfare, a street passes through a small square colonized by fishermen and cheap grill cafés to twist down past pavements dressed with the pathetic objects of the flea market and pop out through the low walls of the **Bab el Bahr**, the old port gate, to meet the thundering traffic on the coastal highway. From this gate an alley leads south up to the **shrine of Lalla Qadiya**, where returning pilgrims from Mecca spend their first night home in prayer. Here a charming trader has set up a tea shop in the street which has a fine view up the estuary. If you follow this alley you will head into the old *mellah* (Jewish quarter), while a short walk upstream along the main road takes you to the boat crossing to Salé.

Rue des Consuls

This is where the larger carpet dealers and bazaars are found. Between the French bombardment of 1765 and the Protectorate of 1912, all European consuls and merchants were obliged to live on this street. No. 62 was the house of the consul Louis Chenier, father of the celebrated French poet André Chenier. There is a series of splendid old *fondouqs* , No. 109, the Fondouq ben Aicha, being the grandest; No. 93 is the narrow Tailleurs' Courtyard; No. 141 the Kissariat Moline; No. 31–2 is the Fondouq Ben Aïssa; and at No. 232 Rue Souka there is Fondouq Daouia.

A right-hand turn on to the main coast road, Rue Tarik Al Marsa, takes you to the **National Artisan Museum** (Musée National de l'Artisanat: *open 9am–12pm, 3–6pm; closed Tues;*

adm) with a display of traditional crafts in two old shops. On the other side of the road, arranged around a modern courtyard and beside a private beach club, is the **Ensemble Artisanal**, which can be useful for carpet-pricing research; their own prices are fixed high.

Souk el Ghezel

At the end of the Rue des Consuls in front of the kasbah is the Souk el Ghezel, now no more than a tree-shaded car park with a whitewashed koubba at its heart. This was the wool market for the carpetweavers of Rabat, a space that was also convenient for the auction of Christian captives from the 16th to the 18th centuries, when speculation over the size of the eventual ransom played a large role in the bidding. The wool market hasn't moved far; it can be found about 150yds to the west, spread down half of the length of Blvd Al Alou. The shops in this area are home to the best joiners, wood carvers and painters in the medina, as well as to a number of profusely stocked antique-bazaars.

The square whitewashed **Kechla**, also known as Château Neuf, was built by Sultan Moulay Rachid in the 17th century to keep a check on the Andalusian population of the kasbah and medina and has served as a prison, slave pen, arsenal and garrison in its day. It is surrounded by an extensive Muslim cemetery; these hug the coast in both Salé and Rabat. An underground tunnel connects the Kechla to the kasbah, but neither this secret entrance nor the Kechla fortress itself is open.

The cemetery is enlivened once a year by the ***moussem*** of Lalla Kasba, when young girls pray for help in finding a good husband. At the west end of the boulevard is a collection of shops such as Himmi's, which can provide everything on hire for the great day: tents fit for *caids*, vast couscous pots, and a fantastic assortment of bridal litters that range from traditional painted boxes to peacock and conch-shell floats formed from glittering glass.

Rue Sidi Fatah

There is no need to carry on west to the Bab Al Alou, it is not one of the city's great gateways. About 150m down the Rue Sidi Fatah, near the mosque el Qoubba, are the 'new' baths, *hammam* el Jedid, a 14th-century Merenid building whose income is partly devoted to the maintenance of the Merenid tombs at Chellah. Further down Rue Sidi Fatah a splendid high porch shelters the gates to the mosque and tomb of Moulay Mekki, an18th-century saint. The painted geometric design of the porch includes wreaths of flowers, a very rare detail in the strictly image-less religious art of Morocco. It hints at Ottoman influence and has now faded into a charmingly harmonious fusion of light blue and green. The mosque's elegant octagonal minaret is decorated with small arches and stalactites under the windows. Beyond it there is also the **zaouia of Sidi ben Aissa**, on the right before the Rue Souika.

The *Mellah*

This, the old Jewish quarter of the medina, can be entered through its own gate in the Andalusian wall, opposite Place du Mellah. After 50m a right turn off Rue Ouqqasa (the southern continuation of Rue des Consuls) leads to the central passage of the *mellah* with its many dead-end alleys extending off from both sides. The *mellah* is now very low-rent, when

it has not crumbled completely and the cramped, claustrophobic atmosphere is intensified by the street vegetable and meat stalls with their accumulated refuse.

Somewhere within this area are over a dozen synagogues, all now closed, some carefully locked and preserved, some the haunt of squatters. It is not though a particularly old *mellah*; the Jews of Rabat were constantly being moved around by different sultans, and this cramped but defensible quarter was only allocated to the community by Moulay Sliman in 1808. At the far extremity of the *mellah* is the **mausoleum of Sidi Makhlouf**, a Jew who converted to Islam. He was venerated for his piety and spectacular miracles, not least of which was parting the waters of the Bou Regreg to enable a student, stranded in Salé, to visit him.

The Oudaïa Kasbah

The Kasbah of the Oudaïas is at the heart of the military history of Rabat. This was the site of the original *rabat* from which generations of cavalry issued out to bring the heretic Berber tribes into obedience to successive sultans. It has also been a government bastion against a recurring enemy that came to destroy by sea. Garrisons of Almoravid, Almohad, Merenid, Andalusian and Alaouite troops have stood on guard here ready to repel raiding fleets, which from the Vikings of the 11th century through to the marines of 20th-century France have all come from Western Europe.

The kasbah walls are subsequently ten feet thick and thirty feet high. Built by the Almohads, they have been constantly reinforced, most noticeably by the Andalusian refugees and the Alaouite Sultans in the 17th and 18th centuries.

The name Oudaïa is a comparatively recent innovation. The Oudaïas were one of the bedouin Arab tribes that entered southern Morocco in the 13th century. They became clients of the Alaouite sherifs from the Tafilalt, and were an important source of strength in the meteoric rise of Moulay Rachid to the throne. Moulay Ismaïl sent part of the tribe to the Rabat kasbah to keep an eye on the Andalusians and to campaign against the Zaer, a truculent Berber hill tribe.

The Bab Oudaïa

The approach to the Oudaïa Gate is up a broad stairway from the Souk el Ghezel to the kasbah. The gate was constructed in the late 12th century by the Almohad Sultan Yaacoub el Mansour. Though capable of defence it has an obvious ceremonial purpose and this side of the kasbah is not a first line of defence; the city walls screen the land to the west and the coast to the north. Instead, the Oudaïa Gate overlooks the medina, and formed the entrance to the original Almohad palace complex in the kasbah. The sultan's gate had a role in Moorish society not far removed from an ancient forum. Here petitioners would wait, assemblies and meetings take place and justice be seen to be dispensed.

The Oudaïa Gate is one of the accepted masterpieces of Moorish architecture. The puritanism and self-confidence of the Almohad creed, rather than restricting artistic expression, encouraged a triumphant return to first principles. The powerful impression that you receive from the gate is not achieved by either great size, expensive materials or lavish decoration but by an instinctive sense of balance, proportion and inner tension. At one level you have the simple, clear, strong form of a horseshoe arch cut through a stone wall and flanked by two rectangular towers. At a second level the veneer of exuberant decoration seems to float out from the stone in an abstraction of pure form. The traditional Islamic decorative design has been cut into the same strong ochre-rose stone as the gatehouse, the bold cut reliefs casting dark, contrasting shadows against the evening glow of burnt gold. Two bands surmount a false circular arch with the corner spaces balanced by two stylized scallop-shell palmettes surrounded by bevelled serpentine forms. The false outer arch is decorated with a distinctive band of *darj w ktarf*, that ubiquitous leaf-like profile of interlocking arches. The superior bands each continue the shell motif, one with a calligraphic layer and the upper band with a shell-studded relief line of stalactite arches.

The genius of the whole is in the subtle relation of decoration to form. The decorative arch discreetly indicates with its diffuse edge the circumference of a circle whose diameter is exactly half the width of the square formed by the top lintel that includes the two flanking towers. A few minutes spent absorbing this tension, pursuing the clean form defined by the decorative skin, is to enter into a form of meditation.

The **gatehouse** is composed of two halls with the inner gate set at a right angle to its more celebrated brother. It is often used for exhibitions and may at other times be closed, but at such times an arch to the right gives entrance to the kasbah. The Oudaïa Gate is one of the few spots in Rabat where young men importune you to be your guide. This must be a hard task, as the kasbah is small, safe and easy to find your way around in.

Inside the Kasbah

The kasbah interior is a delightful whitewashed Andalusian village built by the refugees from Hornachos, who also fortified the roof of the gatehouse in their feud with their fellow Andalusian refugees in the medina. The central street, the Rue Jemaa, passes the **kasbah mosque**, La Jamaa el Atiq, founded by Abdel Moumen in 1150 and the oldest in Rabat. The minaret was restored in 1700 and the mosque repaired by Ahmed el Inglizi, an English renegade who worked for Sultan Sidi Mohammed (1757–90). Further on is the **semaphore terrace** (*plate-forme du sémaphore*), a signal station that now provides an intriguing view over the entrance to the Bou Regreg estuary and across to Salé. A storehouse on the right built by the mad Sultan Moulay el Yazid at the end of the 18th century now houses a **carpet factory**. Below the platform there are further defensive walls and a round tower refortified in 1776 by Sidi Mohammed after the French bombardment. The chief defence of Rabat–Salé remained the estuary sand bar, which sealed the harbour from any deep-keeled sailing vessels. The Atlantic swell, the savage cliffs and outlying rocks made naval bombardments in the age of sail a difficult operation.

It is possible to climb down to the batteries where you will find the **Le Coulille** bar *(closes at 8pm in summer)* in the Borj des Suboefis, © (07) 738844. It no longer serves food, but you can consume cold beer on the terrace or in the kilim-strewn bar. The beach below is sandy and although it can become quite crowded in summer the Atlantic current keeps the water reasonably clean and provides some gentle surfing.

The Palace Museum of Oudaïa and the Andalusian Garden

Open Wed–Mon 8.30am–12pm, 3–6pm, closed Tues and national holidays, adm museum, garden free.

The Palace Museum, which is ranged in an assortment of rooms around the Andalusian Garden, can be approached from either of two archways below the Oudaïa gate and also from the kasbah. Rue Bazzo, the second turning on the right from the central Rue Jemaa in the kasbah, takes you downhill by a beautiful twisting path to the museum. You pass by the **Café Maure**, enclosed in a secretive terrace between the museum garden and the estuary ramparts. It is a delightful place, with tiled benches and rush mats, where you can sip a restful mint tea and consume plates of sticky cakes.

Sultan Moulay Ismaïl built this palace between 1672 and 1694. It is a walled enclosure within the kasbah area, the delightful garden it contains cut through by a number of traditional pebble-paved paths. The museum is housed in two rooms on the west side of the garden as well as in the **palace apartments**. At the heart of the palace stands a cool courtyard paved in terracotta and green tiles, filled by the sound of a central marble fountain gently trickling into a basin. This is enclosed within a whitewashed arcade to form a heavenly vision of Moorish taste.

The two raised alcoves on each side have been used to display the two traditions of ceramic design. On one side there are pots painted in pale green, yellow and washed blue, their basic geometric patterns enlivened with floral motifs. On the other side the pure blue on white design sticks to a sterner geometric scheme of interconnecting circles and stars. The latter is sometimes considered to have come exclusively from Fès, the former from coastal towns like Rabat, Tetouan and Safi. In fact they both seem to have come from Andalusia, and to have coexisted in every urban centre of pottery production. Glazed coloured ceramic tiles (seen in *zellij* mosaics throughout Morocco) date from the 13th century, while the tradition of painted pottery seems to have been created by the influx of skilled Andalusian refugees in the late 15th century.

The reception room overlooking the garden has been furnished in the traditional style with a cascade of colours from the carpets, embroidered cushions, curtain hangings—the rich reds with purple, and greens with gold beloved by Moroccan women. You may recognize the four distinctive marble capitals of the columns which are copied from those in the 14th-century Attarine medersa in Fès. To the east a passage leads to the two domed chambers of the *hammam*, their marble floors lit by small glass skylights set into the dome. The former kitchen area beyond, used for occasional exhibitions, leads back into the gardens.

The two galleries on the west side of the garden contain the best collection of Moroccan crafts in the country. There is enough here to keep you busily sketching for hours: costumes, armour, jewellery, pottery and musical instruments of the different tribal groups of Morocco are all displayed and labelled in slightly dusty glass cases amongst blown-up photographs. Aside from the blue robes of the Saharan tribes, the star of the collection is a black tent of the Middle Atlas nomads, complete with all its woven blankets, kilims and cooking pots. Folk art rather than fine art, the simple geometric decoration of the pottery from the Berber tribes seems closer to the warrior culture of Greece in 800 BC than the urban Moroccan tradition, while the jewellery throws up strong analogies with the torcs and brooches of Celtic Britain.

The Hassan Mosque

Open daily 8am–dusk, adm free; daily guard ceremony at 5pm.

For eight centuries the unfinished Hassan Tower has loomed above Rabat. It is the minaret of the Almohad grand mosque, the truncated pillars of which stretch out in a great rectangular field below. The mosque had fallen into disrepair and was a bramble-covered ruin when Leo Africanus visited Rabat in 1500, but it was not until the great earthquake of 1755 (the same one that shattered Lisbon) that the arches and pillars of the mosque were thrown down. More recently, on the southern edge of the site a white **mausoleum, mosque and library** has been built on a raised terrace to the memory of King Mohammed V.

The Hassan Tower

Poised on the high escarpment above the river the tower looks particularly magnificent as you approach Rabat by the bridge from Salé. It has great solidity, a lordly purpose and, in its unfinished state, a noble flaw that does not distract from the beauty of its proportions or the decoration of boldly carved tracery.

The tower was built between 1195 and 1199 by the Almohad Sultan Yaacoub el Mansour as the centrally-aligned northern pivot of his grand mosque. It was to be the conclusion of a building programme that included the Koutoubia in Marrakech and the Giralda in Seville. The floor of the mosque was raised and levelled from the surrounding ground so that the tower has two heights; 50m from the natural level of ground on its north wall and 44m from the raised mosque floor of the southern wall. Each face of the tower is different, with a subtle movement of relief arches and interlaced decoration that is based on two classic designs brought to Almohad Morocco from the sophisticated culture of Andalusia. Inside, a ramp rather than a staircase ascends through six chambers that become more ornately decorated the further you climb. This ramp deliberately echoes the Samarra Mosque in Iraq, which was acknowledged to be the biggest in the world. It was built in AD 850 and allowed the caliph to ride up to the summit on horseback on an external ascending ramp and call his army to Friday prayers.

Behind the tower there is a staircase that leads down to a tomb for the unknown warrior, and a small additional mosque dedicated jointly to all the many previous ruling dynasties of Morocco.

The Mosque Ruins

The ruins of the Hassan Mosque and that of Samarra in Iraq are still among the largest in the world. Yaacoub el Mansour, who ruled over the entire western half of Islam, with an empire that stretched from Spain to Libya, deliberately attempted to build a mosque that would vie with the finest efforts of the great cities of the East. The rectangular plan of the mosque measures 183m by 139m, and was crossed by a forest of aisles: 21 longitudinal spans and 28 laterals that multiply into 312 marble columns and 112 stouter arch-bearing pillars. Three arcaded courts open to the sky broke this massive roofline. The open court nearest the tower, the *sahn* or washing area, had rows of fountains that played into marble basins and were fed from eleven huge cisterns hidden beneath the floor. There were four doors in this north wall and six on the eastern and western sides. The central 'nave' leading up to the mihrab was designed to be significantly wider, to draw the worshippers' attention to the direction for prayer. It is difficult now to imagine the splendour of the interior, by ignoring the irritating modern paving and transforming the truncated remnants into the shifting vistas of columns, flooded with arcaded pools of harsh sunlight and the mass of genuflecting warriors that filled it for just a few years.

The Mausoleum

King Mohammed V's tomb has a traditional and distinctive green-tiled pyramidal roof capped with a triplet of golden spheres. A broad ornate staircase leads up to it from the southern end of the old mosque. Royal guards in scarlet with a white burnous patrol the arcade of Italian white marble, with its four arches leading to the balcony of the royal koubba. The sarcophagus is a block of white onyx from the mountains of the Hindu Kush set in a sea of polished black marble. A scholar mutters verses from the Koran in one corner, or dozes. Heraldic banners from all the provinces and towns of Morocco are suspended in serried ranks under the balcony and a bronze chandelier, which weighs one ton, hangs from the roof. The decoration of the ascending ceiling must be the last word in gilded ornate. The king's sarcophagus has been accompanied by that of his youngest son, the genial Prince Moulay Abdullah, since his death in 1983.

The mausoleum was designed by a Vietnamese architect, Vo Toan, and finished in 1971, and aesthetically must be considered something of a disaster. It is impressive only in the lavish use of luxurious materials, which expresses the Moroccan people's great regard for the king who led them in their struggle for Independence. He has already assumed an almost holy status, and it is traditional in Morocco that the interiors of saints' shrines should be decorated as richly as a community can afford.

On a lower level of the terrace a mosque has been constructed, its three handsome doors and mihrab arranged on the same axis as the ancient mosque. The colonnade of finely sculpted white marble from Carrara stands atop a library dedicated to every aspect of the reigning Alaouite dynasty.

The New Town

The Boulevards

The major French-designed public buildings of Rabat are all found along or around the Avenue Mohammed V, the grand boulevard that connects the medina with the royal palace. Their architecture combines Egyptian, classical and Moorish elements to create an impression of order and stability. The PTT ministerial building contains a small **postal museum**, mainly a stamp collection, which is open during office hours. Rue al Mansour ad Dahbi leads off to the **Theatre Mohammed V** opposite which is the **Triangle de Vue**, a pleasant, restful urban garden created in 1920. The northern corner contains the walls of a ruined 18th-century mosque and a number of tombs.

Further down Avenue Mohammed V is the terracotta-coloured and U-shaped **parliament building** (Chambre des Représentants). Opposite the station Rue Abou-nan leads to Place Sahat al Golan and the striking Catholic **Cathedral of Saint Pierre**. Two palisade-like towers emerge from a totally white nave; the windows and lintels have been decorated with geometric shapes in brick in a deliberately Islamic borrowing.

The Walls and the Bab er Rouah

The **Almohad wall** encloses the kasbah, medina, palace and new town in a surviving 5km length of wall with five city gates surviving in some form; the Bab Al Alou, Bab Al Had, Bab er Rouah, Bab Makhzen and Bab Zaers. The section between the Bab Al Had and the Bab er Rouah on Rue Ibn Tumert provides a pleasant one km walk; the ochre battlements are decorated with flowering plants and clusters of palm trees.

The Bab er Rouah, the gate of the winds, was built in the same era as the Oudaïa Gate, and is the only true surviving Almohad structure that is comparable with it. Set above Place An Nasr, isolated from the traffic flow, the two massive surrounding stone bastions still allow you to envisage its central defensive role. The stone carving in this exposed position is still carefully balanced and controlled with a ring of concentric engaged arches rippling out from the gate and enclosed by an ancient scroll of the Koran in Kufic script. The eastern face of the gate has an even lighter cut of stone with a delicate bed of floral and vegetable tracery supporting a palmette. The blend of elegant fantasy, tension of design and the gate's purpose in defence are reinforced by the interior chambers. Four rooms with elegant cupolas inevitably force visitors into a series of dizzying turns. The rooms are open periodically for exhibitions and for the moment are as close to a national gallery of art there is in Morocco. If they are open at all the hours will be 8.30am–12pm, 2–8pm.

Going bakc into the city from the gate you face the **As Sounna Grand Mosque**, the minaret of which dominates the skyline of the new town. It was built by Sidi Mohammed in the 18th century and has been the victim of frequent restorations.

The Royal Palace

The southeastern corner of the Almohad defences was selected as the site for a new palace in the 18th century, and a park was enclosed behind the grand mosque. Constantly altered and improved, the palace has been almost entirely rebuilt by the present king who has also extended the grounds behind the main block to include a private golf course enclosed by a new stretch of the city wall. Many of the chief offices of state are housed within the walls and it is very much a working palace. You can go into the grounds, but don't wander off the central avenue.

Through the ornamental northern gate, on the left, is the **Lycée Moulay Youssef** and a small suburb for past and present employees of the king. On the right are the stables, an exercise paddock and the princes' school, and then the open ***méchouar***, or assembly place. The building on the right is the Ministry of the Habous (responsible for religious foundations). The outer wings of the main block contain the house of the president of the council and cabinet offices. A mosque, the supreme court, an oratory and the central **mausoleum of Moulay Hassan** coexist with the various royal apartments. The three large windows in the distinctive tower occasionally frame the king in his dressing gown. The queen mother has her apartment just to the south, next to the kitchen wing with its separate access to the Blvd Ad Doustour. The **mosque** on the left, **Ahl Fas**, is used for the official Friday royal prayers when the king as *imam* rides the short distance from the palace in a carriage and returns riding on a horse, his brow shaded from the sun by a crimson parasol of state. This procession, a weekly ritual for past sultans, is now rarely performed, and the 12.30pm cavalcade will be advertised well in advance.

The southern gate leads into the Blvd Ad Doustour. If you turn left, the southern Almohad wall leads to Bab Zaer, from where you can return to the new town or take the turning right to go into the Chellah.

The Archaeological Museum (Musée Archéologique)

Open Wed–Mon 9–11.30am, 2.30–5.30pm; closed Tues, adm.

This small but excellent museum is the major attraction of the new town. To reach it, take the Rue Moulay Abdul Al Aziz from the As Sounna Grand Mosque and turn right on to Rue al Brihi. The museum is the low, modern building on the corner.

The **central hall** contains a large marble statue that was discovered at Sala and has been identified with King Juba II or his son Ptolemy. The handsome marble torso beside it was recovered from Volubilis and considered to be from the 2nd century AD. Around the walls are the results of the excavations at the microlithic site of Taforalt, and Neolithic child burials from Skhirate and Harhoura from about 4000 BC.

The **first floor** has a chronological collection of artifacts extracted from Sala Colonia, in four cases. The first contains bronze fragments of sculptures, a little bust of Juba II, an ivory cylinder with four carved scenes and a representation of Apollo; the second ceramic shards and coins from the excavations; the third funerary objects from the classical period; and the fourth objects from Islamic Chellah. The next exhibits demonstrate the often-overlooked survival of the classical sites into recent history with Christian and Jewish cult objects, and relics of Islamic occupation up to the 14th century.

Recent archaeological digs reflected in the museum have concentrated on old Islamic sites. Finds from two towns opposite the Spanish coast, Ksar-es-Seghir and Balyounesh (between

Tangier and Ceuta), show the high state of Islamic civilization that these foundations of Ommayad Córdoba enjoyed from the 10th century. There is also pottery from Sijilmassa, from the 8th century, and fragments from the medieval sugar mill at Chichaoua (between Marrakech and Essaouira). Going back down to the central hall, a small open-air courtyard on one side is lined with a random selection of carved stones from different epochs.

The greatest treasures of the museum are its **bronzes**, displayed in a special side hall (*no photography allowed*). The finest pieces are the 1st century AD **bust of Cato the younger**, probably modelled from the death mask of the orator who preferred to die free under the republic than live under an emperor, and the **bust of the young Berber man** with his hair bound by a fillet, another sculpture thought to be King Juba II, who married Cleopatra Selene, daughter of Anthony and Cleopatra.

The **Lustral Dionysius** is a superb full-length statue, a Roman copy of the original carved by the Greek master Praxiteles. The fisherman casting his net and the rider with his missing leg are further 1st or 2nd century Roman works. The bronze guard dog from Volubilis was discovered in 1916, and probably made during the reign of Hadrian in the 2nd century.

In the glass cases further small bronzes can be seen—a horse and rider from Volubilis, a snake discovered in Banasa, a head of Oceanus from Lixus and figurines of Eros and Bacchus. There are fine marble heads of Diana and of a Berber youth. In the extensive collection of classical objects the military diploma given by the Emperor Domitian on 9 January to the cavalryman Domitius and found at Banasa adds a striking personal touch.

Five Phoenician standing stones are on show, their crude symbolic carving looking out of place in this treasure-house of humanistic art. They do however convey the Semitic devotion to an abstract divinity, which has been a much stronger influence in Morocco than the buried remnants of Greece and Rome. One of them was discovered in the ancient mound of the temple the Romans equated with Saturn at Volubilis.

Chellah

Open daily from dawn to dusk; adm.

One of the most beautiful of the many striking historical ruins in Morocco, Chellah is not distinguished architecturally, but has a wistful, almost tangible atmosphere of antiquity. The walled enclosure has bred strange beliefs—such as those of the buried treasure of Sultan Yaacoub, guarded by a prince of the Jinn, and of a fleeting visit from the prophet Mohammed—but the factual narrative is fanciful enough.

Freshwater springs flow out from this hill less than 500m from the brackish estuary of the Bou Regreg, and human settlement probably always clustered on this slope even before the Phoenicians founded Sala. This city, after a millennium of existence, was reduced to a ruined mound in the 10th century. It continued to be used as a revered burial ground, however, until the Merenid Sultans enclosed it for the use of their own dead in 1320. Now their shrines are also reduced to picturesque ruin, and Roman Sala Colonia has been re-exposed by excavation. A lush growth of jungle garden is firmly established beside the path that leads down to the sacred spring, the Merenid tombs and along to the corner tower that looks over the meandering turns of the Bou Regreg river.

The Walls

The Merenid Sultan Uthman, 1308–31, began the walls, which were finished by his successor Abou Hassan in 1339 and further embellished by Abou Inan, 1351–58. The Zippoun Berber tribe were appointed as the hereditary protectors of Chellah, a duty which they continued for centuries after the fall of the dynasty.

The simple arch of the gate is enclosed by half-octagonal towers, their lean, twisted battlements supported by a delicate tracery of dripping stalactites. The square platforms for these outrageous gothic towers use a honeycomb-patterned stone for the shift to the octagonal shaft. The Kufic script on the gate reads, 'I take refuge in Allah, against Satan, the stoned one', a useful invocation for the biers of dead sultans to pass under. The gate enforces a double twist before you enter the Chellah through a more orthodox Islamic horseshoe arch decorated with flanking shell motifs. On the left there is a café inside a disused guard-house, and street-sellers and snake-charmers sometimes gather here.

A stairway descends steeply through the well-watered, luxuriant gardens, a confused mass of palm, bamboo, banana, hibiscus, fig and the drooping handkerchief leaves of the datura.

The Roman Ruins

To the left are the excavations of the Roman city, which have still not been opened for inspection. They occupy the northern half of the enclosure and border the necropolis. The site consists of a main thoroughfare, the Decumanus Maximus, connecting the forum to the capitol, plus the foundations of a triple triumphal arch, shops, a terrace, small sanctuaries and a whole range of sumptuous baths.

The Sacred Pool

A group of koubbas surrounds a walled pool. Stubs of gutted candles can be found within; the venerated saints, though wrapped in Islamic green shrouds and familiar whitewashed shrines, belong to pre-Islamic cults of great antiquity. The pool is surrounded by old brick vaults and drains out through a gravel stream that runs through an enclosing grove of drooping banana plants. Sacred black eels swim up to lurk in shaded recesses of the pool: infertile women peel boiled eggs (sold by two boys who sleep on the floor of the shrine above) to offer to them. The scene is so strongly archetypal, such a graphic pagan survival in the shadow of ruined cities and royal tombs that you instinctively check twice to discover if you are dreaming. That barren women should offer eggs, the universal symbol of fertility, to be devoured by phallic eels as emissaries of an ancient deity calls any visitor to compose a few lines of verse.

The Merenid Sanctuary

The sanctuary is easily recognized: its two minarets, of the mosque and zaouia, are invariably topped with a ponderously balanced pair of storks adding to their nest. Enter into the *sahn*, the small introductory courtyard, and proceed into the ruined **prayer hall** built by Abou Yusuf. The **mihrab** is straight ahead, by the four columns of the pillared **mosque**. The ruined minaret is conspicuous to your right, near a pool. Pass either side of the mihrab to enter the necropolis.

Leo Africanus counted thirty-two Merenid graves here in 1500, but the number that can be distinguished today is very much less. The grave of the 'Black Sultan', Abou Hassan, lies against the outer wall to the right, within a koubba decorated with arches and tracery. The facing koubba is that of Sultan Yacaub, the 'Commander of the Jinn'.

The **tomb of Shams ed Douna**, 'The Light of Dawn', can be seen in the southeast corner (bottom left as you stand by the mihrab) under a recess. Her long tombstone has been carved with verses celebrating the magnificence of her funeral. A Christian convert to Islam, she was a concubine of Abou Hassan and mother of Abou Inan, who eventually deposed his father. Abou Hassan was chased into the High Atlas and died an exile in the winter of the following year, 1352, but was buried decently, as you can see, in the Chellah.

The sanctuary also contained a **zaouia**, a religious college, which though damaged is in a better state than the mosque. The minaret is on the left, with the wash basins and latrines directly below. The court lined with cells faces a central rectangular pool with two sunken white marble shells for water jets that drained into the pool. The bases of the thin white marble columns can be seen with some surviving mosaic tilework. A much smaller prayer hall faces the mihrab, with its passage behind that allowed pilgrims to make the seven circuits that was believed by some to be equal to the pilgrimage to Mecca.

The beautiful soft red glow of the sanctuary wall shields a tranquil and formal **garden** formed by a double line of orange trees with the plots fed with water from the sacred spring. From here you can look out over the walls to inspect tidy and fertile vegetable plots.

Where to Stay

Bedrooms fill up quickly throughout the year in Rabat and it is advisable to find a room early in the day or book in advance. Rabat is an easy city to walk around and so there is no need to buy the protective shelter of a hotel. Anywhere clean and central should do for all but the fussiest travellers.

luxury

The **Farah Safir**, ✆ (07) 734747, @ (07) 722155, has everything you could ask for from a modern, international, luxury hotel and has a superb position on Place Sidi Maklouf, overlooking the estuary, medina and the tower of Hassan. The popular **La Tour Hassan**, ✆ (07) 732535, @ (07) 725408,at 26 Av Abderrahman is closed for restoration. A good new alternative in the same range is the **Dawleez** across the river in Salé (*see* below, p. 214).

expensive

The **Chellah**, 2 Rue d'Ifni, ✆ (07) 701051, @ (07) 706354, is a comfortable but unexceptional hotel near the grand mosque and the Archaeological Museum, with a good restaurant, Le Kanoun grill. It and the **Bélère**, ✆ (07) 709689, @ (07) 709801, at 33 Av Moulay Youssef are favourite locations for tour-groups.

moderate

There is a good selection of moderately-priced hotels that get most of their business from locals, not tourists. All have bars and restaurants. Good choices are the bustling

Chellah: The Merenid Tombs

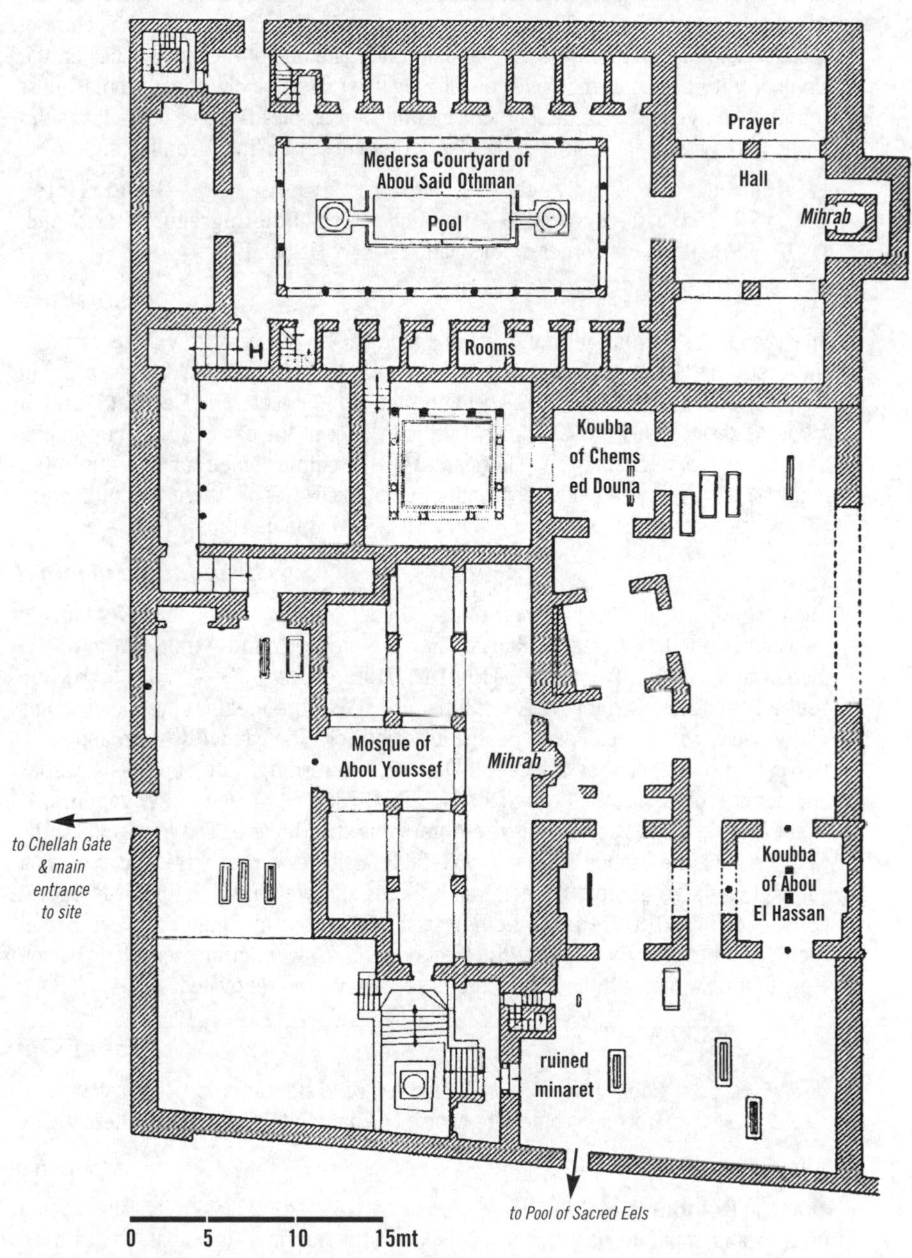

Terminus, very near the railway station at 384 Av Mohammed V, © (07) 700616, or the fading grandeur of the **Balima**, © (07) 708625, directly opposite the Parliament on Av Mohammed V and Rue de Jakarta. Once the smartest hotel in town it now has an aged interior, but retains all its external dignity, and is usually one of the last in Rabat to fill up. The foyer and café gardens are still at the centre of Rabat social life, and for twice the standard rate, take one of the faded suites on the top floor with balconies that give an alarming view over the city. These rooms must be full of the ghosts of caids, French senators and assorted power politicians who stayed here while petitioning the Resident or his successors the Alaouite kings.

Two smaller and slightly cheaper personal favourites are **Grand Hotel**, © (07) 727285, at 19 Rue Patrice Lumumba and the **Bou-Regreg** (ex Rex) Hotel, © (07) 724110, on the corner of Rue Nador and Av Hassan II.

inexpensive

The two most comfortable and amusing hotels in the new town are also the cheapest. The **Hôtel Majestic** on 121 Av Hassan II, © (07) 722997, has a piano in the foyer, faded furniture and an ageing poster of the Kaaba. The **Central Hotel** at 2 Rue Al Basra, © (07) 707356, fills up slightly later in the day and is run by an efficient but remorseless matron. There are 34 large comfortable rooms in this hotel, immediately to the left of the prominent Balima Hotel. If these are full, other addresses include the **Gaulois**, © (07) 723022, at 1 Rue de Hims.

cheap (in the medina)

There is no particular charm, short of the perennial bonus of economy, in staying in unclassified medina hotels in Rabat. They are mostly found within 200m of the market area by the Bab el Had. **Hôtel Marrakech**, © (07) 727703, at 10 Rue Sebbahi (the third turning off Rue Mohammed V in the medina) has clean rooms with towels, with a small extra charge for a shower. The gaudy **El Alam** and indifferent **Regina** are nearby if it is full. The second turning, Rue Souk Semara, has another nest of hotels, the **France** © (07) 723457, at no. 46 and the **Voyageurs**, © (07) 723720, at no. 8, as well as the **Algers** and **du Marché**. The Voyageurs is the best run, but the France might be preferable as it has a roof terrace as well as a surprisingly large number of small dank rooms and well-used double beds. **Hôtel Darna**, © (07) 736787, is on the northern edge of the medina at 24 Blvd Bab el Alou. It's the most expensive in this category but has a wonderfully secluded position close to the Kasbah and the beach, and has recently been renovated.

Eating Out

Rabat is not a city famed for its restaurants but if you have the money and something worth celebrating there are a few alternatives.

expensive

The **Koutoubia** at 2 Rue Pierre Parent, © (07) 720125, with its gaily painted interior and separate bar, is one of the oldest restaurants in Rabat. It has been accused of living off its reputation but can still throw some memorable evenings. For traditional Moroccan cooking the best evening is to be had at the **Dinarjat**, 6 Rue Belgnaoui, © (07) 704239 or 722342, opposite the Oudaia Kasbah. From the car park on Ave. El-Alou, a flunky will lead you deep into the medina. Abandon yourself to the mystery, and take plenty of cash. Two restaurants vie for laurels over the best seafood in town, **Le Goéland**, 9 Rue Moulay Ali Cherif, © (07) 768885 and **Le Vert Galant** in the quartier Agdal, © (07) 774247. If you would rather eat your fish overlooking the sea, try the very popular **Restaurant de la Plage**, © (07) 707586 or 723148, on the beach opposite the Oudaia Kasbah, or **Restaurant La Caravelle** on a terrace in the kasbah itself, © (07) 733876.

For those in search of music with their meal, the three singers who perform in **Zerda,** 7 Rue Patrice Lumumba, © (07) 730912, provide something for most tastes, from Simon and Garfunkel to traditional Moroccan music.

moderate

The greatest concentration of bistro-like French restaurants licensed to serve alcohol is just south of the train station on or off Av Moulay Youssef. If you choose the *menu du jour* this can work out very reasonably at around 50dh, though you can obviously spend much more. Choose from the **Restaurant Brasserie Français** at 3 Av Moulay Youssef with its downstairs bar and upstairs restaurant; **Café-Restaurant de la Paix** at no. 1, or just around the corner on Rue Hattim the **Restaurant La Clef**, © (07) 701972, above the bar Marocain et Français. Excellent crêpes are served at **Au Crép'uscule**, 10 Zankhat Laghouat, © (07) 732438.

For Italian or Spanish food pop behind the Balima Hotel to eat pizza and pasta at **La Mamma** at 1 Rue de Tanta, © (07) 707329 or paella and tapas at **La Bamba** at no. 3. A more exotic experience (for Morocco) can be found at the **Yucatan**, 7 Rue Al Osquofiah (formerly Rue de L'Evêche), © (07) 720557, which provides fairly standard Mexican dishes.

There is one good place to eat reasonably cheap Moroccan food and drink alcohol at the same time—**Saadi** on 87 Av Allal ben Abdallah, © (07) 769903. Despite its history and grand demeanour the **Balima Hotel** provides food that's filling but only very ordinary, so unless you are a bulk consumer, it's best to be satisfied with just sipping a drink in the courtyard.

cheap

As ever in Morocco, some of the most rewarding eating is to be found not in a formal restaurant but in the cheap café-restaurants scattered around the market area in from the Bab el Had. These you can sniff out for yourself, but there are in addition a few specific café-restaurants nearby that are worth finding.

The **El Bahia** is built into the Andalusian walls of the medina, approached along Av Hassan II, halfway between the entrances to Rue Sidi Fatah and Av Mohammed V. Take the cheap fixed menu or order a chicken or kefta tagine in the upstairs Moorish dining room or in the courtyard. The **CTM café**, on the corner of Zankat Bayreuth and Av Hassan II, stays open late, serving good cheap Moroccan food on tables around the animated oblong bar. The caged birds, when in the mood, can produce extraordinary volumes of sound.

cafés and bars

No visit to Rabat is complete without a visit to the **Café Maure**, tucked between the Oudaïa Palace museum and the estuary. Amongst the cafés strung along Av. Mohammed V, **Le Petit Poucet** rates highly, and an evening spent 'people watching' in the café and bar of the **Balima Hotel** remains one of the city's chief entertainments.

Just behind the Balima on Rue Tanta there is a more intense drinking scene in either the **Baghdad Bar** or **La Dolce Vita**. The glass-fronted lobby of the **Terminus Hotel** is another good observation post for street life. Just up from here, along Av Moulay Youssef, there are a string of busy bars: that of the d'Orsay Hotel as well as the ground floor of restaurants such as the Français, de la Paix and Marocain et Français. On Place des Alaouites, opposite the train station and beneath the 'Siemens' sign, there is the wood-lined **Henry's Bar**, with next door the elliptical hall of the Italian Restaurant—which has long since become another café-bar, lined with cliched views of a dozen great cities.

Shopping

The shops and stalls of the medina hold all the traditional **Moroccan crafts** for sale—the best streets are Rue des Consuls and the Souk es Sebat. **Flowers** are sold in the market in the medina, and in a square on Av Moulay Hassan. Sunday is the busiest day for the **vegetable market** in the medina.

As befits a capital city the New Town is conspicuous for its large number of **bookshops**. There are two English-language bookshops—one American at 4 Rue Tanger, with a good shelf on Islam and Morocco, and one English at 7 Rue Ayamama, with a similiar stock supplemented by some second-hand shelves. There also two useful English-speaking cultural centres in Rabat: the **George Washington Library** at 35 Avenue Fas has American papers and journals available in its lounge; the **British Council** at 36 Rue Tanger, © (07) 760836, also operate a small library and reading room (*open Tues–Fri 9.30am–12pm, 2.30–5.45pm, and Mon afternoon*). **French–Moroccan phrase books** are available from the bookshop at 38 Av Allal ben Abdallah. The train station newsstand usually has a good selection of **international newspapers and magazines** in English, French and other languages, normally a day after publication.

There are only a handful of **galleries** in Morocco that show the works of contemporary artists. The pre-eminent dealer and exhibitor of these is **L'Atelier** run by Mme Demasier, who has drawn an impressive range of pan-Arab and Islamic art to her elegant gallery at 16 Rue Annaba, © (07) 722668. The **Gallery Marsam** deals purely in prints, but has a good stock of fine limited editions which enables you to see the work of many of Morocco's leading artists (6 Rue Oskofiah, © (07) 709257). **Antiquités Lyre**, 38 Av. Mohammed V, and **Galerie le Mamoir**, 7 Rue Baitlahm, have the same management and one or two good things amongst piles of international junk. The prolific French painter of Moroccan scenes, Henri Pilot, can often be seen at work in one or the other gallery.

Sports and Activities

The Royal Dar es Salaam **golf club**, a quarter-of-an-hour's drive from central Rabat, is one of the world's top 50 golf courses. The 45-hole complex was designed by Robert Trent Jones on a 1000-acre woodland site. Four hundred groundsmen maintain three courses: the 9-hole green course, the 18-hole blue, and the red, an 18-hole championship course for those with at least a handicap of 18. There are also two **tennis courts**, a **swimming pool** and a luxurious clubhouse where you can eat a three-course lunch with wine for under 140dh.

Entertainment and Nightlife

The **Théâtre National Mohammed V** on Rue Cairo is the home of one of Morocco's three classical orchestras that conserve the traditions of Andalusia. It also puts on a range of visiting Arab stars and western **classical orchestras**. French, American and good quality Maghrebi films can be seen at the **Cinema Martignan** on Av Mohammed V and at **Salle du 7ème Art** on Av Allal ben Abdallah. American films are shown in the same building as the American bookshop (4 Rue Tanger), but check with the shop for the schedule.

The distinctive feature of Rabat's street life is that the city has a mad flurry of paseo life at dusk but begins to close down at 8 in the evening and is shut by 10. As in other new and earnest political capitals, such as Ottawa, Canberra and Washington, the demand for sleazy joints and raffish bars does not seem to be strong amongst the administrators of government.

Dancing and floor-shows are however staged in the Queens Club at the **Tour Hassan Hôtel** (open from 10.30pm; adm) and in Club Five of the **Farah Safir Hotel**. The singer Ziad Abdine performs there from 0pm 1am practically every evening except Sunday. There is a distinctively down-market disco at the back of the Balima, **L'Arc en Ciel**, as well as the conspiratorial **Baghdad nightclub** which has belly-dancing shows after ten o'clock, though they are not as exciting as its black-studded door promises. The Place de Melilla-Av Patrice Lumumba, on the eastern corner of the Parc du Triangle de Vue above Av Hassan II, is another area for music-bars and discos, such as **Jefferson's** and **Biba's**.

Festivals

In August there is the ***moussem*** of Dar Zhirou and the ***fête des cires*** on Mouloud in Salé. Rabat also sometimes hosts a two-week film festival in December, below the law courts in the new town.

Salé

Salé has long maintained a separate identity from Rabat. Its great period of prosperity was under the Merenid sultans, who rebuilt the walls, constructed the medersa, a medical school, the Mrini Mosque, the Nossak Zaouia and an aqueduct. These achievements of the 14th century still seem to express the spirit of the town.

History

The very name of Salé proclaims a past different from that of its neighbour. Local traditions assert that the citizens of the ancient city of Sala Colonia settled the headland of Salé after their venerable home had been destroyed by the orthodox *rabat* garrison in what is now known as the Oudaïa Kasbah of Rabat. Salé grew into a prosperous port city, until one terrible night Alfonso X of Castile descended like a wolf on the fold, attacking during the feast night of Aid es Seghir in 1260. The booty the Castilians captured was immense, the city was sacked and most of its citizens were killed or enslaved. Abou Yusuf Yacqub, the brother of the founder of the Merenid dynasty, hurried to the rescue of the city and reached Salé in one heroic day's ride from Taza. He was too late to rescue the city but succeeded in expelling the raiders, and in an emotional scene vowed to rebuild it. His actions helped establish the Merenids as credible rulers of Morocco, and Salé subsequently became a cornerstone of Merenid pride.

The sacked city was rebuilt with an energy and elegance which still marks its identity. While Rabat shrank to a village raided by the Portuguese in the 16th century, Salé according to Leo Africanus had 'all the ornaments, qualities and conditions necessary to make a city civil, and this in such perfection that it was visited by several generations of Christian merchants'.

Old Salé maintained a troubled supremacy over the Andalusian settlements in Rabat in the dazzling days of the pirate Republic of the Bou Regreg from 1629–66, but then stagnated. The Alaouite sultans who came to power from1668 preferred to live and build in Rabat.

Getting Around

There is hardly anywhere to stay in Salé, so most visitors base themselves in Rabat. A fishing boat will take you from the wharf below the Rabat medina across the Bou Regreg for a dirham. The Jaich el Malaki, also known by its old name of Avenue de la Plage, leads straight up from the Salé wharf to the medina through the Bab bou Haja. Walking across the bridge you will arrive at the Bab Mrisa, while a *grand taxi* (*petits taxis* are restricted to either Rabat or Salé) or bus (nos. 6 and 10 ply the route from Rabat's Avenue Hassan II) will drop you further along at the Bab Fès.

The Medina

Three streets, Boulevard Touil, Rue de la Grande Mosquée and the central Rue Souika/ Kechachin provide sinuous crossings of the length of the old town, an under-visited network of twisting and irregular streets. They wind past the white façades of houses that have little ornamentation other than strongly reinforced doors. The medina is entirely enclosed by walls and roughly rectangular in shape, 800m wide and 1500m long; the northern coastal third is occupied by a large cemetery. Outside the walls Salé has grown greatly to the north and west, in a fairly dismal style, since Independence.

Bab Mrisa

This unmistakable massive arch is flanked by two elegant towers and decorated with floral tracery and sculpted inscriptions. It was built by Sultan Abou Yusuf Yacqub between 1260 and 1270, after the Castilian sacking of the city, in a similar style to the Almohad gates of

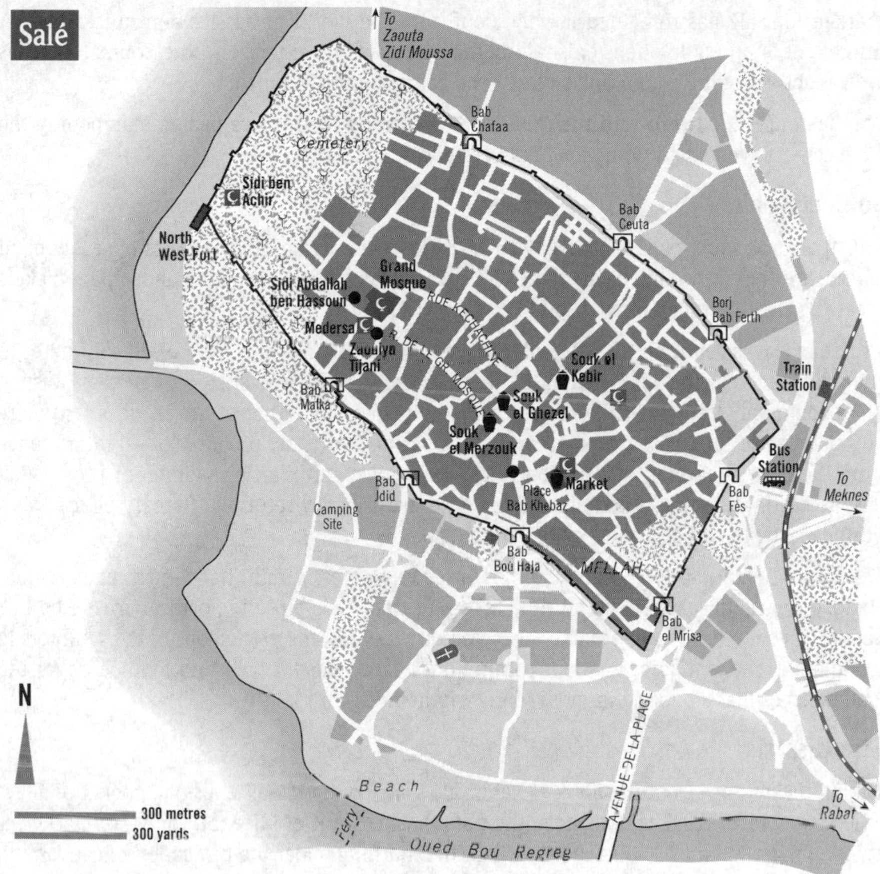

Rabat. A reinforced canal led from the estuary through this water-gate into a basin within the city walls. Here the fleet moored in complete safety, surrounded by arsenals and dockyards.

The *Mellah*

The Jews were given this area after the canal had become hopelessly silted. They were moved again, over the road to the north, when Moulay Ismaïl required this corner for a garrison of Abids, but expanded back again before the exodus after Independence. The two neighbouring gates with restored and elegant battlements, the Bab el Mellah, allow you to drive through the *mellah* into the middle of town.

The Souks

The **Bab Fès** is a natural point of entrance with taxis, train and bus station clustered outside it. Stalls of grilled kebabs, and tables full of nuts, sweets and fruit are clustered in and around the portals. There is a health centre immediately on the left through the gate, and the second left turning after it, Rue Dar Reghai, takes you in a natural flow of pedestrians to the heart of the town. The stalls along the way are full of products for the local rather than the tourist market, for Salé has remained largely aloof from the world of hassles and quick sales. A number of tempting kitchens exist along this street and its extension, Rue Souika. Here, as well as absorbing the colour and sounds, you can also taste the medina.

On the right is the **tomb and mosque of Sidi Ahmed Hadji**, a respected marabout of the 17th century, venerated with gifts of tall green candles.

Souk el Kébir

This triangular souk, partly shaded by trees, is the main market in Salé. Piles of secondhand clothes are sorted through at the back whilst carpenters, leather-workers and slipper-makers create a delightful cacophony of sound and activity.

Christian slaves captured by the 'Sallee Rovers' of Rabat and Salé were often sold here. In spite of the many salacious-Orientalist tales that have circulated ever since, Christian women were commonly treated with a certain care and respect. Whether or not these rules where always adhered to is of course another matter, but in theory any proof of sexual interference from the captors gave automatic liberty to the captive, and married women or those who, despite beatings, refused to embrace Islam were occasionally returned. Barbary piracy was a business activity, which had its code of conduct.

To the left of the Souk el Kebir, just before some gates, a right-hand turn leads to Rue Haddadine, the blacksmiths' and tinkers' street that leads directly north to cross Rue Bab Sebta. To your left Rue Kechachine takes you on west past the workshops of the sculptors in wood and stone, and joiners' shops turning out headboards for beds and footboards for the wall benches that are found in most Moroccan homes.

The Kissaria

Taking the left turn from the Souk el Kebir takes you to the Kissaria, a small pocket of alleys where the most skilled artisans have their stalls. The **Souk el Ghezel**, the wool market, is an open space lined by shops where early in the morning under the protection of canvas and a few trees bales of wool are weighed from tripod stands and gently haggled over.

The adjacent **Souk el Merzouk** is the quarter for the tailors, cloth merchants and embroiderers, whose young assistants create long trails of twisting silk. After the fountain on the right, look out for the door of the **Fondouq Askour**, the hospital and school founded by the Merenid Sultan Abou Inan in the 14th century. The courtyard is functional but the door is covered in a cascade of carved stalactites.

The Medersa and Grand Mosque

The main mosque is 300m on down Rue de la Grande Mosquée. Tailors' shops with their array of kaftans give way to the larger walled houses of the merchants, decorated with their Andalusian, rather classically proportioned doorways. A charming small whitewashed square has stairs leading up to the grand mosque and on the left, just past an 18th-century fountain, a gate into the medersa. The mosque was built in the reign of the Almohad Abou Yaacoub Youssef (1163–84). The clear lines of the doorways and the simple elegance of the carving contrast with the gates of the Merenid medersa built by the Black Sultan, Abou Hassan, in 1341 (*open; ask for the custodian; adm*). Here there is rich cedar and plaster carving, vivid paintwork and an overhanging roof over the arch. The building is much smaller than the great medersas of Fès though the details are as lavish and exciting. In the central court a gallery of columns, decorated with contrasting designs and coloured faïence mosaics, leads your eye up to the area of delicately carved cream plaster that gives way to the crowning walls and hanging gallery of sombre carved cedar. The prayer hall has a finely painted ceiling and the **mihrab** has some fine carved decoration. The courtyard is designed to sit in rather than pace around. A few minutes can be spent spotting the recurring motifs of Islamic decoration drawn entirely from the natural world—flowers, fruit and shells. These are found at every level and worked into each material by bands of the cursive Arabic script of the Koran.

The foundation stone introduces the one distracting secular tone, 'Look at my admirable portal, rejoice in my chosen company, in the remarkable style of my construction and my marvellous interior. The workers here have accomplished an artful creation with the beauty of youth . . .' Arabic poetry does not always translate well. The courtyard pillars would perhaps present a more serene interior if their distracting decoration were removed. Two galleries of cells can be explored, and do not miss the opportunity to get out on the roof with its view over the rooftops of the Salé medina across the estuary to Rabat.

The Zaouia of Sidi Abdallah ben Hassoun

Through an arcade just to the left of the grand mosque is the door of the **zaouia of Sidi Ahmed el Tijani** decorated with geometric mosaics and carved plaster. At the back of the mosque is the **zaouia of Sidi Abdallah ben Hassoun**. A window allows you to look into the mausoleum which was rebuilt in the 19th century. Each year on the afternoon of Mouloud, the prophet Mohammed's birthday, a collection of large candles and complicated wax lanterns is escorted through the town in a great procession guarded by the guild of boatmen dressed as Turks or corsairs, and the saint's descendants and devotees carrying filigree and silk-decorated candles. The entire retinue deposit their offerings at the shrine where they remain until the new year. Sixteen days later Sidi Abdallah, Salé's patron saint, is venerated by all the religious brotherhoods, who sing chants, psalms and mystical exercises in his honour. Sidi Abdallah came from the south of Morocco but moved to Salé in order to avoid the distractions of tribal politics. He was respected during his lifetime and attracted many pupils before his death in 1604. The Sidi was adopted by sailors and travellers, who continue to visit the shrine for auguries to indicate the safety of their voyage.

The Cemetery

The cemetery extends west from Sidi Abdallah's shrine and a dirt track winds out across the large expanse of graves to the northwest fort, **Borj Nord-Ouest**, an 18th-century redoubt containing a number of bronze English and Spanish cannon. At the end of the bastion there is a good view across the estuary to Rabat. The track passes a number of simple whitewashed koubbas. The **shrine** nearest the fort is that of **Sidi ben Achir**, an Andalusian scholar and mystic who died in 1362. He has a great reputation for curing the sick and the mad, and in 1846 Sultan Abder Rahman built a series of lodgings for pilgrims to stay as they await their cure. The reputation of the saint has not diminished, particularly among women. The old ladies will be upset if you walk too close, perhaps for your own benefit as the saint also has the power to wreck Christian ships along this coast.

Sidi Moussa ed-Doukkali

The cliffs along the coast at Salé do indeed look evil to shipping; the Boulevard Circulaire that runs along the edge of the cemetery takes you out through the Bab Chafaa, from where the road continues above the sea. Patient men with long bamboo fishing poles perch above these high and dangerous cliffs.

A 3km walk beside the shore will take you to the **koubba of Sidi Moussa ed-Doukkali**, which Moulay Ismaïl carefully restored. This Sidi is greatly beloved by the poor, who hold an enormous celebration in August in his honour. He voluntarily chose an ascetic life, grubbing along this shore for edible roots and sorting driftwood and debris to sell in order to buy fresh bread for the poor. He was also a skilled magician and humbled the arrogant rich by miraculously flying to Mecca each year for the pilgrimage. Today, the shore is lined with refuse while shantytowns extend inland from the road, a fitting environment for the Sidi to continue his work.

The Gnaoua Kasbah

Just beyond is the kasbah of the Gnaoua, a pisé fortress built by Moulay Ismaïl to house his Abid troops, black Africans from Guinea as the name still proclaims. The wind and the salt spray have etched weird patterns into the walls, and graffiti left by the Abid regiments or renegades with their captives can still be seen etched into the less eroded sections.

Oulja Pottery

A rich deposit of clay has been discovered recently on the northern bank of the Bou Regreg estuary and there are now two dozen kilns at work in the pottery hamlet of Oulja, a 2km *petit taxi* ride from Salé. Though Rabat–Salé was a pottery producing centre in the 17th, 18th and 19th centuries nothing has been made on a wheel here for over a century. This new craft centre follows some of the traditional influences that can be seen in the Oudaïa Palace museum, as well as striking out in new directions.

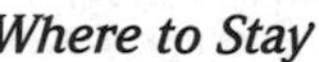

Where to Stay

If you have your own good reasons for staying in Salé rather than Rabat, the new **Dawleez Hotel**, © (07) 883278, looks out across the river to the Hassan Tower and is good value. Ask for a room which is not disturbed by the popular Piano Bar. The only other choice is **L'Hôtel des Saadians**, on Place Bab Khebaz.

Above Salé beach is the ***camping municipal*** that serves both it and Rabat. This was once a pleasant place to be, shaded by woodland and close to the wharf, but has been moved a little further north to a bleak open area immediately below the graveyard, surrounded by a 2m wall. The beach can be near-overwhelmed with detritus.

The Chaouïa Coast between Rabat and Casablanca

The Chaouia is a flat coastal plain that stretches between Rabat and Casablanca. Partly covered by belts of woodland, the land rises slowly inland, interrupted by river valleys farmed by smallholders. Even before the construction of the railway and the now-three separate main roads (S222, P1 and RP36 motorway) that run down this coast it was not an especially beautiful area, but for anyone living and/or working in Morocco its quiet hotels, calm fish-restaurants and easily accessible beaches have long provided a welcome escape from the bustle and heat of the great cities. If, on the other hand, you are on your first visit to the country you may be forgiven for giving this area a miss and gazing blankly out of the window at the passing landscape.

Témara-Plage

Only 16km south of Rabat on the S222 coast road is Témara-Plage (served by the no 7 bus or *grands taxis*), a strip of beach and rocky coves. A holiday atmosphere keeps the bar and nightclub life going, compared to Rabat, late into the night. This is concentrated in the central asphalted area, with **La Baraka** restaurant, © (07) 741346, the **Casino Témara** and **Al Khaima** restaurant as the hubs of activity. The 'casino', actually a promenaders' café, has a few basic rooms. The beach is lined with several streets of holiday villas for Rabat's more prosperous citizens. The **Hôtel la Feloque,** © (07) 744559, appeals to this more affluent community with its 'country club'-like tone. It has its own beach area and pool, and the Sables d'Or restaurant provides an excellent seafood meal, although a good dinner here will not leave much change out of $40 a head. A disco-nightclub operates in summer.

South on the P1

Heading south on the slightly inland P1 route, 11km from Rabat is **Témara Zoo** (*open daily 10am to dusk; adm*). It opened in 1973, and there are plans to fill up the 50-hectare site with 1800 caged animals. The unnatural mass of caged eagles is a sad sight, though the budgies and mallards are enjoying something of a population explosion and some storks have even voluntarily nested on a suitable tower within the zoo garden. The chief attraction is the semi-circle of caged great cats and bears. Insane-looking beasts lie either asleep in the corner or restlessly pace against the bars. Only one lion seems to have resigned himself to a life of imprisoned ease, and imitates the zoo-keepers by sunbathing on his back.

Témara Town is 5km further south, and is served by the 17 bus from Rabat. It contains an old kasbah, restored by Moulay Ismaïl to house a branch of the Oudaïa tribe who served as one of the principal cavalry regiments of the Alaouite dynasty. Now, appropriately enough, it houses the Royal Cavalry School. The pretty little mosque of Sidi Lahcen was built by Sultan Abdul Aziz in 1900. An even greater attraction on the southern edge of town is **Auberge Le Provençal,** © (07) 741111, acknowledged to be one of the best, and most expensive, places to eat in the region. If you just want a drink you can pop into the nearby Pergola bar.

Six km south of Témara on the P1, a right turn in the village of Aïn Attig leads 2km south to the ruins of the **Dchira Kasbah**, built by the great Almohad Sultan Abdel Moumen in the 12th century. It was a rectangular fortress studded with 16 towers. The principal western gateway, the mosque, keep and rock-cut cisterns can all be identified. It guards the source of the Ghebboula stream, which was diverted along an aqueduct to bring clean water to Rabat. The fortress was probably thrown up as a legacy of the last Almohad campaign against the Berghouata tribal confederacy, which was finally humbled in 1149.

Témara Forest

A circular drive of more than 160km will take you through the finest scenery of the area, along little-frequented forest roads, past rural souks and saints' shrines; it is ideally finished with a swim and a meal in Témara. You will need to set out by car or taxi in the morning with a picnic. Leave Rabat by the Bab Zaers gate, and head along the P22 road to **Rommani**, 33km inland, past the river Korifla gorge and pleasantly wooded low hills. Rommani hosts a **souk** on Wednesdays that attracts the surrounding Ouled Khalifa tribe. There is also a big festival held here in September at the koubba of Sidi Bou Amar. From Rommani head west, along the S106, towards **Sidi-Bettache**, crossing another gorge cut by the river Korifla on the way. The village of Sidi-Bettache has grown around the marabout's tomb that stood on the old Almohad road from Rabat to Marrakech. From here a right turn on to the S208 takes you for 33km through parts of Témara Forest. Perched above the crossing of the riverbed of the Yquem is one of the major **souks** (held on Tuesdays) of the Zaër tribe, **Sidi-Yahya-des-Zaër**. The saint's tomb is surrounded by a sacred grove of aloes. From here it is 11km through more of the Témara Forest to the town of Témara (*see* above).

Ech-Chiahna

Ech-Chiahna, a coastal resort 23km from Rabat, is a favourite stopping place for European travellers. Between the road and the sea is the expensive **Club Hôtel La Kasbah**, ✆ (07) 749116, which offers a lot of facilities such as pool, *hammam*, solarium, riding and all manner of ball games, arranged and largely filled by the French tour agency Fram. The neighbouring **Rose Marie** campsite, with 75 places, is also run by the hotel and consequently well-organized and equipped, ✆ (07) 742307.

On the other side of the road from the beach is the cheap-range **Auberge Cambusias**, ✆ (07) 749149, and a larger, slightly chaotic campsite, where you cannot hear the waves for the guttural cries from competitive holiday tennis tournaments.

Skhirate-Plage

This resort is 31km from Rabat and reached by turnings off the S222, P1 or RP 36. If coming by train, you will find the station is at the inland village of Skhirate (Sunday souk), which leaves you with a 4km walk to the coast. Skhirate-Plage is another definitely upmarket resort, the site of the King's summer palace. This was the scene of dramatic political events in July 1971, when General Mohammed Medbuh attempted a palace coup using the impressionable military cadets under his command. A large number of guests, gathered together for King Hassan's birthday party, were killed before order was restored by the personal magnetism of the King and the accidental death of the general, shot by one of his cadets.

A turning by the south end of the palace takes you to the moderately expensive **Amphitrite Hôtel**, ✆ (07) 742236, @ (07) 742317, the most tranquil place to stay on this stretch of coast.

It has 36 rooms, bar, restaurant, private beach, pools with vivid murals on the walls, and occasional art exhibitions. In summer rooms are also available at the **Auberge Potinière**.

Further south along the coast roads, between Skhirate-Plage and Mohammedia, there are several turnings down to **campsites** at the downmarket summer resorts of **Bouznika** (also known as Dahomey Plage), **Essanoubar** and **Mansouria** (also known as Itilal).

Mohammedia

Mohammedia does a surprising double act. It is on the one hand the centre of Morocco's oil business, with a refinery and an oil terminal on the western side of town, and on the other a swish summer beach resort with a 3km seafront promenade, casino, racecourse, a pretty kasbah quarter, a yacht marina and a terrific golf course. The yellow sands of the beach have so far remained untouched by pollution from the oil tankers, and from June to September the town is full of families from Casablanca on holiday. The beach gets emptier and more enticing the further north you travel. If you are a golfer looking for a relaxed resort without tourists and a strongly Moroccan flavour, Mohammedia is made for you. For most other visitors it fits in well as a day-trip to the beach out from Casablanca.

Though the oil terminal was only opened in 1960 Mohammedia has a long history as a port. It was known as Fedala to the medieval merchants of Europe. Their common trading pitch was taken over by the Portuguese, who briefly occupied the place at the turn of the 15th century. Local opposition soon forced them out though they have left a memorial—the kasbah looks indigenous enough but was actually built by the Portuguese. It has been restored in recent years and now contains a pretty residential quarter whose neat pavements and window boxes are at happy variance with the usual medina street scene.

Getting Around

Mohammedia is 28km north of Casablanca on the S111 coast road, but is most easily approached by train, from Rabat or Casablanca. The station looks out over a small square on Av Hassan II which is also used by taxis and buses. This is directly behind the kasbah, and a 500m walk north along Av Abderrahmane Sarghini and Blvd Moulay Youssef will lead you directly down to the beach and the Samir hotel.

The **Banque Populaire** is on Av Hassan II and **cars can be hired** from Auto-location Firdaous on Rue Farhat Hachad, © (03) 322086. Locally made cane furniture is for sale by the far side of the Christian cemetery, on the coast road north of town.

Where to Stay and Eating Out

The luxurious **Miramar Hôtel**, © (03) 312433, @ (03) 324613, stands just back from the beach at the western, port end of town, between Av Moulay Ismaïl and the Rue de Fès. It is a large complex with pool, bar, casino, ranch night-club, golf, riding and water sports. About 600m to the east along the beachfront you will also find the expensive **Samir Hôtel**, © (03) 310773, @ (03) 323330, at 34 Blvd Moulay Youssef. There is also the reasonably-priced **Hôtel Argana**, © (03) 320308, about 150m northeast of the Kasbah along Av des FAR.

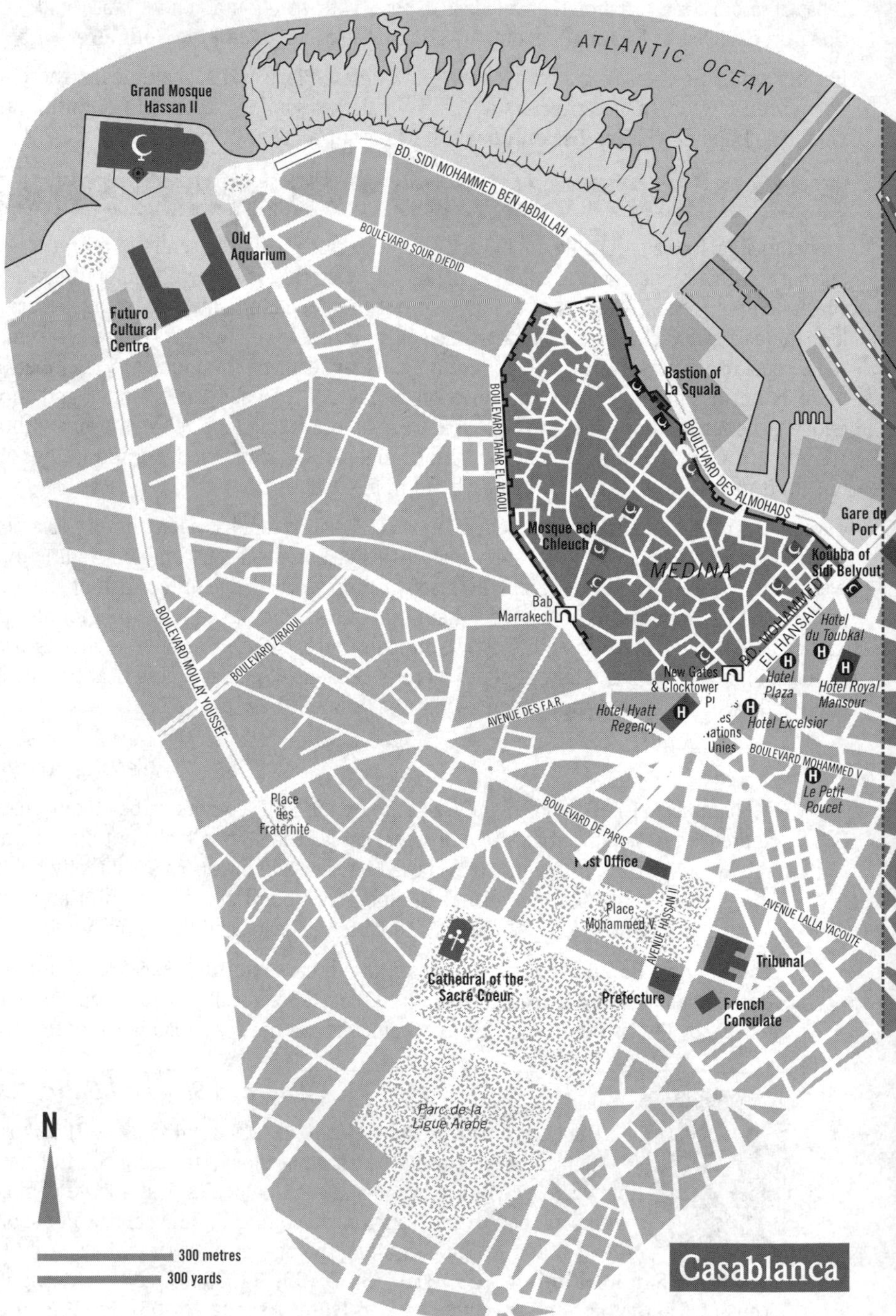
ATLANTIC OCEAN
Grand Mosque Hassan II
Old Aquarium
Futuro Cultural Centre
BD. SIDI MOHAMMED BEN ABDALLAH
BOULEVARD SOUR DJEDID
BOULEVARD TAHAR EL ALAOUI
Bastion of La Squala
BOULEVARD DES ALMOHADS
Gare du Port
Mosque ech Chleuch
MEDINA
Koubba of Sidi Belyout
Bab Marrakech
BD. MOHAMMED EL HANSALI
Hotel du Toubkal
New Gates & Clocktower
Hotel Plaza
Hotel Royal Mansour
Hotel Hyatt Regency
Hotel Excelsior
Nations Unies
BOULEVARD MOHAMMED V
Le Petit Poucet
BOULEVARD ZIRAOUI
BOULEVARD MOULAY YOUSSEF
AVENUE DES F.A.R.
Place des Fraternité
BOULEVARD DE PARIS
Post Office
Place Mohammed V
AVENUE HASSAN II
AVENUE LALLA YACOUTE
Tribunal
Cathedral of the Sacré Coeur
Prefecture
French Consulate
Parc de la Ligue Arabe
N
300 metres
300 yards
Casablanca

The cheaper **Hôtel Ennasr**, © (03) 322373, the **Hôtel des Voyageurs** and the **Hôtel Castel**, © (03) 324107, all face the Kasbah along Av Abderrahmane Sarghini. **Camping Loran**, © (03) 322957, is on the coast road 2km east out of town, open all year and in a good position above the sea. There are a few bungalows available, which in summer might be preferable to a hotel room in town. **Les Sablettes**, a motel with restaurant, is at the far eastern end of the coast road with a beach caught between two rocky outcrops that provide good snorkelling and a lagoon ideal for bird spotting at dusk.

The best restaurants are congregated at the west end of town near the port. **Restaurant du Port** (formerly known as Chez Irene), naturally by the harbour at 1 Rue du Port, © (03) 322466, is easily the most famous place to eat in town. Here you can gorge on fresh fish simply grilled on charcoal in the garden courtyard. Equally popular are the **Sans Pareil**, © (03) 322855, on Rue Farhat Hached and the **Frégate**, Rue Oued-Zem, © (03) 324447.

Casablanca

This city is a surprise for those who have been fed with picturesque images of Marrakech and Fès. For here is a modern city, with a skyline dominated by towering office blocks and sprawling suburbs ringed in the approved metropolitan style by a motorway ringroad. The streets are jammed with cars and the five-storey apartment block is the dominant housing motif. The pavements are filled with elegant besuited figures and women dressed in international styles such as you would find in any southern European city.

Casablanca dominates the national economy: it is the chief port, the financial, industrial, commercial and manufacturing centre of the kingdom. This has all been achieved within this century—from a town of 20,000 in 1900, the Casablanca conurbation is now home to 3,500,000. In North Africa, only Cairo can compete with Casa in growth, verve and vibrancy, but it is this city facing out to the Atlantic that seems the more oriented to the international pattern of trade and sympathetic to Western influences. At times, as you cruise down a palm fringed car-packed boulevard to catch glimpses of the sun setting in a western ocean, you could be mistaken for thinking yourself in California.

The French administration must be credited with much of this achievement. They carefully planned the new Atlantic face of Morocco in their own image, while allowing the xenophobic cities of the interior to wither into mere historical monuments. The fusion of cultures, Moroccan and French, seems so complete and intricate here that one can easily forget that the battle for independence was chiefly fought on the streets of Casablanca. Morocco's future national and political growth is inextricably linked with the actions of Casablanca. It is a child of the industrial revolution with many of the traditional problems of that transformation—great divisions in wealth and problems in structuring health and housing for a mushrooming city. This is the only place in Morocco where it's possible to talk in terms of class awareness, and to foresee a time when a larger political role is forcefully demanded by its citizens.

Nothing to Do With *Casablanca*

No scene of the film *Casablanca* was shot in Morocco, nor does the finished film bear much relation to the city of the past or the present. The film was released in the winter of 1942 and was lucky to gain from the enormous free publicity generated by the Casablanca landings and the Allied conference here. It was also fortunate in a last minute change of cast: Ronald Reagan and Ann Sheridan were replaced by Humphrey Bogart and Ingrid Bergman, and as an inspired afterthought the director Michael Curtiz added Dooley Wilson singing 'As Time Goes By'.

If Casa is a source of fascination to the political observer and speculation for the businessman it has tended to be dismissed by far too many travellers. It is, however, a remarkably easy city to get around and stands astride all the national transport systems. Though you are unlikely to centre a holiday here, you are more than likely to pass through. There is no need to rush for the next connection; a pleasant day can be spent taking a taxi out to the vast new Mosque of Hassan II, or a stroll through the grand streets of the French-built new town and the stone arcades of the suburban Nouvelle Medina, Morocco's most elegant and hassle-free souk. No one with an eye for colour or street theatre should miss a stroll through the packed streets of the medina (the old quarter) in the evening. It is true that as a mere 18th-century construction it cannot stand comparison with any of the medieval cities, but if you have spent any time in Morocco there is an almost unearthly satisfaction in walking through a medina without so much as a whiff of a bazaar, carpet shop or a guide. Casa also has some fabulous fish-restaurants, while its humbler bars and cafes offer the opportunity to dive through the external distractions of tourism and meet some of the people of Morocco on common ground. My abiding image of the city is of two old women walking hand in hand down a street, one typically French, one unmistakably Moroccan. This could and should happen anywhere, but only in Casablanca did it feel commonplace.

History

The smart western residential suburb, Anfa, was the site of a Phoenician trading station founded in the 6th century BC. It became the capital of the great Berghouata confederacy of Berber tribes who, under the banner of the Khajarite heresy, resisted the authority of the early Islamic states. The Almohad Sultan Abdel Moumen finally broke the resistance of the Berghouata and destroyed Anfa in 1149. The port remained in use for the export of corn, but by the 15th century it also housed a flotilla of corsairs who raided the Portuguese coast so effectively that the Kings of Portugal were forced to send an armada of 50 ships against this threat in 1468, and again in 1515.

In 1575 the Portuguese commander of El-Jadida closed the corsair base for ever by building a fort at Anfa which also served to guard the northern approach road to El-Jadida. This citadel remained in European hands until the Lisbon earthquake of 1755 shattered both the walls of Anfa and the treasury of Portugal.

Sultan Sidi Mohammed reclaimed Anfa, and built the present medina to the east of the ruins in 1770. The walls, fortifications and grand mosque of the medina all date from this period. From the previous era only the Portuguese name for their fort, *Casa Branca*, white house, remained in use, although strangely it would be neither the Arabic translation, *Dar el-Beida*, nor the French equivalent of *Maison-Blanche* but the Spanish version, *Casa Blanca*, that would pass into general usage.

Sultan Moulay Sliman closed the port as part of his policy of isolating Morocco from Europe, but it was reopened by his successor in 1830. The tempo of trade increased with exports of wool and corn to Britain, whose merchants sold tea, teapots, clothes and paraffin candles through the city in return. In 1907 the town exploded in anger against the predominant influence of the Europeans and nine French port workers were killed in the streets. This, however, furnished a useful pretext for the subsequent landings by the French army in Morocco. The energetic French Resident-Governor from 1912 to 1925, Marshal Lyautey, began the process of urban planning and port extension that soon produced its own tempo of commercial dynamism and growth. Morocco's mercantile élite from Fès were quick to move to the coast, and join in the colonial city's development and property boom.

A generation later the new city was at the forefront of agitation against French colonial rule. It still is the centre of contemporary political protest. In Western minds it is linked to three rather spurious events—the landings, the conference and the film. The Casablanca landings of November 1942 had no military significance as the result had already been pre-arranged between the supposed opponents, the American and Vichy French generals. Seasick American troops were in fact landed with great confusion at Safi, Mehdiya and Fédala (Mohammedia), but not Casablanca. The Casablanca conference was held two months later in January 1943. It had no significance for Morocco; Roosevelt and Churchill spent their days planning the invasion of Sicily from a suburban villa in Anfa.

Getting Around

by air

All international and most domestic flights use the Airport Mohammed V, 30km out of town on the main P7 route to Marrakech. By far the easiest way to get there is on the direct train link that takes you from either the Port or Voyageurs railway stations in Casablanca to the main airport concourse in half an hour. There are 12 trains a day, running from 6am. CTM also run a connecting **bus** service that takes you direct from the airport to the central CTM station. In addition there is a *grand-taxi* rank, though the taxi fare, at around 200dh, compares badly with a train ticket of 35dh.

Most airlines offices are on the central Av. des FAR: Air France, © (02) 294040 is at no. 15; RAM, © (02) 311122 is at no. 44. GB—British Airways is on the 6th floor of the Tour Atlas building at 57 Place Zellaqa, © (02) 491870.

by rail

Arriving by train you can get off at the port station, **Casa Gare du Port**, or **Casa Gare des Voyageurs**. The Port station is admirably sited by the main coast road and fronts on to Blvd Houphouët-Boigny (formerly Blvd Mohammed el Hansali, and still shown as such on many maps), which leads 500m straight to Place des Nations Unies (formerly Place Mohammed V). This is the hub of the city and of its major avenues, as well as the main entrance to the medina. Gare des Voyageurs leaves you with a half-hour walk or a taxi ride into the centre of town. However, if you are picking up an early connection in the morning, the moderately priced Moussafir Hotel (*see* p. 229), just beside the Gare des Voyageurs, makes a very useful base.

Most, but not all, trains to Rabat (1hr) leave from Gare du Port. There are 18 a day between 6.50am and 8.30pm, including seven that stop at Mohammedia (20mins) and two slow trains that stop at Bouznika and Skhirate. For Tangier (about 6hrs) there are five trains a day from one or other of the stations. There are four trains daily from Gare des Voyageurs to Fès—usually a 5-hr journey but slightly longer if you have to change at Sidi Kacem. Three of these continue east to Taza and Oujda. All trains south to Marrakech (3–5 hrs) leave from Gare des Voyageurs. There are eight a day. South along the coast to Azzemour and El-Jadida there are two trains a day, leaving from Gare des Voyageurs and arriving about one-and-a-half hours later. There are also two trains to Safi, leaving Gare des Voyageurs and arriving 4–5hrs later. If you are leaving for the airport there is an effecient direct train route running throughout the day that takes 45 minutes.

by bus

Travelling from Casablanca by bus, there is no need to stray beyond the efficient CTM service. The CTM station with its café and separate luggage check-in is on Rue Vidal, which runs parallel to and between the central thoroughfares of Av des F.A.R. and Rue Allal ben Abdallah. There are 11 buses a day for Rabat (100mins), two for Tangier (6–7hrs), one for Agadir (10hrs) and three a day for El-Jadida (2hrs), Essaouira (6–7hrs) and Marrakech (4hrs).

by car and taxi

Walking around the city centre is one of the major charms of Casablanca. It is only worth catching a taxi for a trip out to the Great Mosque of Hassan II, the coastal resort of Aïn Diab, the Nouvelle Médina or the Gare des Voyageurs. *Petits taxis* can be caught on Place Mohammed V and the Av des F.A.R. They usually have meters, but often have them switched off. The fare, per person, for Aïn Diab should be around 20dh, 10dh for the Gare or the medina.

If at all possible try not to **drive** in Casablanca, which has few street signs, competitive traffic, packs of scooter riders and the normal indomitable Moroccan pedestrians who maintain a courageous indifference to cars. The ringroad is, however, well signposted and provides an efficient bypass. **Car hire**: There is absolutely no need to hire a car while in the Casablanca-Rabat area. Only hire once you are ready to leave; by following the coast road along to Aïn Diab there is an easy and pretty way out of town. It is usually possible to return the car out-of-town at Mohammed V airport. The best rates, and excellent service, are from Always Rent-a-Car, who have an office at the airport, ✆ and 📠 (02) 538186, and on the 3rd floor of 46 Av Moulay Hassan I, ✆ (02) 225960. 📠 (02) 225658. Of the bigger international agencies, you will find Avis at 19 Av des F.A.R., ✆ (02) 311135, Europcar-InterRent at Tour des Habous, 44 Av des F.A.R., ✆ (02) 313737, Hertz at 30 Av des F.A.R., ✆ (02) 312223, and Inter-Voyages at 4 Av des F.A.R., ✆ (02) 222250.

Tourist Information

The **tourist board (ONMT)** is at 55 Rue Omar Slaoui, ✆ (02) 271177, and the **tourist office** at 98 Blvd Mohammed V, ✆ (02) 221524. Both dispense city maps and booklets.

The **post office** at the junction of Blvd de Paris and Av Hassan II is open Mon–Fri, 8.30am–12.00pm. There is a smaller branch at 116 Av. Mohammed V. There are plenty of **banks**: Banque Populaire, 101 Blvd Mohammed Zerktouni, BMCI, 26 Place Mohammed V, and SGMB, 2 Av des FAR are some of the most convenient.

Emergencies: dial 19 for Police, 15 for ambulance. A **24-hour chemist** can be found on Place Oued el Makhazine. **Doctors** can be recommended by hotels, the Croissant Rouge, ✆ (02) 340914, or through the Médecins de garde, ✆ (02) 252521. The **British Consulate** is at 43 Blvd d'Anfa, ✆ (02) 221653 or 223185.

Religious services: There are as many mosques in Casablanca as there are days in the year, but these are only open to Muslims. There is an Anglican Church (all welcome) at 24 Rue Guedj, ✆ (02) 365104, which usually has its service at 11.15am Sun. There is also a French Protestant Church at 33 Rue d'Azila, ✆ (02) 301922 and half a dozen Catholic Churches. Largest and most central is Notre Dame de Lourdes, ✆ (02) 220852, on Place de l'Europe, where Mass is celebrated on Sunday at 10am and 7pm. Amongst the Synagogues in use there is Tehila le David on Blvd du 11 Janvier, Temple Beth-El at 67 Rue Verlet-Hanus and a couple along Rue de Lusitania.

Exploring the City

A few years ago King Hassan II swapped the names of the two principal centres of the city, Place Mohammed V and Place des Nations Unies, around. This change is still by no means recognized by every citizen, taxi driver, directory or map-maker. It's as well to be aware of the potential misunderstandings this can lead to, and at the risk of things becoming over-bracketed, but in an attempt to minimize confusion, both are used in this guide.

Place des Nations Unies (old Place Mohammed V) is a swirl of traffic overlooked by the Hyatt Regency Hotel on one side and the reconstructed medina gate plus colonial clock tower on the other. It is the central point for two introductory strolls: north, through and around the medina; and south to look at the formal public buildings arranged around Place Mohammed V (formerly Place des Nations Unies) and the Parc de la Ligue Arabe.

Before tackling either of these worthy objectives have a gentle saunter down through the heart of the old French colonial new town. The 500m length of Blvd Mohammed V is lined with some delightful art deco apartments and hotels, as are the two parallel streets, Rue Allal ben Abdallah and Av Houmane el Fetouaki. The **market** square, a splendid Moorish courtyard, is your principal objective. The arcaded interior is lined with a dazzling display of the full range of Moroccan fruit, vegetables, meat, shellfish and flowers. It is a wonderful vision of the freshest and ripest products of the land, with one or two tourist stalls for visitors. The surrounding streets have a large choice of bars, cafés and licensed restaurants. On the way back, stop to have a coffee in the cool arcade, or a drink in the unreconstructed twenties interior of the **Petit Poucet** at 86 Blvd Mohammed V. This is the ideal place to imagine the lost world of French North Africa immortalized by Albert Camus. It was the favourite haunt of Antoine de Saint-Exupéry, the pioneer poet of flight and philosopher of aviation. Though better known for *The Little Prince*, his classic work *Wind, Sand and Stars* is partly based on the heroic days of flying mail across the Western Sahara.

The Old Town (Ancienne Médina)

There is an enormous and continual charm in exploring the medina of Casablanca, where the crumbling 18th, 19th and early 20th century houses conjure up an almost Neapolitan vision of street animation. The early evening is the best time to explore, noon and mid afternoon the worst. Due to the late date of its construction, though, it is relatively easy to pick your own route through the streets, which are comparatively wide, well labelled and without the labryinthine intensity of Fez or Marrakech. It is also quite without carpet-shops and bazaars (which are all neatly laid out by the southern exterior wall, along ex-Blvd Mohammed el-Hansali), and so is empty of guides and multilingual commission men. Instead the narrow streets are packed with street stalls with exuberant displays of vegetables, fruit, groceries, cooked food, massed tupperware and clothes. Those with an eye for architecture will notice that the handsome proportions of La Squala bastion and the principal mosques have affinities with the pared-down Moorish-classicism of Essaouira. This is no accident, for Casablanca and Essaouria are brood sisters that were both constructed during the enlightened reign of Sultan Sidi Mohammed.

The old Jewish quarter, the ***Mellah***, stood just to the north of Place des Nations Unies (old Place Mohammed V). A dusty car park a few years ago, the old back entrance to the medina here has now been completely reconstructed with an ornamental colonial clock-tower (the third in a succession of such towers to stand here) in front of the elegant walls and a gate worthy of Anfa's Almohad period. The area behind it is filled with an open-air market selling T-shirts and tourist bric-à-brac as well as freshly squeezed orange juice. A mosque at the back of the market marks the **Rue Jemaa ech Chleuh**, a reasonably broad thoroughfare that neatly bisects the medina and can lead you right out to the triangular garden at the northern end. From here Blvd Sour Jdid provides a grand kilometre-long approach avenue to the beckoning mass of the grand mosque.

An alternative walk is to skirt right around the medina quarter. The road behind the Hyatt Regency, Blvd Tahar el Alaoui, leads you on a 2km circuit of the **old walls**. The defences now look somewhat bedraggled, but contrast well with the streams of traffic in this modern city. A couple of hundred metres north of the Hyatt is the **Bab Marrakech**, sometimes called the Bab Jdid (the new gate). At the north end of the medina, turn right on to Blvd Sour Jdid, past a triangular park (often dominated by dusty footballers) and then right on to the busy Blvd des Almohades, between the medina walls and the port. Walk beneath the walls of the18th-century **bastion of La Squala** and continue for another 100 metres, then take the road that winds up into the medina and then a right turn to reach the **koubba of Sidi Allal el-Kairaouni** and the pleasant garden cafe that gives access to the bastion. This prominent artillery terrace is dominated by a handsome gatehouse, from where the battery commander once directed the range and elevation of cannon fire that last opposed a European fleet in the mid-19th century. Today there are only four cast-iron cannon, their muzzles pointing towards the rattling masts of the yacht harbour, while on either side the white houses of Casa stand suspended above the sand-yellow city walls. The postern gate, which once led directly to the old port but now gives access to the wallside gardens, is usually locked.

Retrace your steps to the Blvd des Almohades and continuing on for another 50m you will reach another breach in the ramparts that leads directly past another handsome 18th-century mosque into the square of Sidi Bou Smara. The first alley on the left, forking left at the next turning leads to the **koubba of the Sidi** surrounded by a small cemetery, a charming corner of the medina shaded by fig trees, quietly removed from the frenetic street life and used by a drifting population of dossers. A wider arcaded alley leads on to the **grand mosque** built by Sidi Mohammed in celebration of his recovery of Anfa from the Portuguese. Carrying on along this route will lead you back to the Place des Nations Unies (old Place Mohammed V), or you could retrace your steps and continue the circuit along the Blvd des Almohades. Opposite the Port station sits the **koubba of the marabout Sidi Belyout** (a name derived from Abou el Louyou, 'father of the lions', the title of a great commander of a *jihad*), set reclusively amid a stand of trees within white-washed walls. Non-Muslims are not allowed to enter, but you can peer through the gateway and admire the constant succession of Casa babies brought by their mothers to pay their respects to one of the principal patrons of the city. From there continue up Blvd Houphouët-Boigny (formerly Blvd Mohammed el Hansali), with a line of bazaars on the medina side making a classic contrast with the towering modern edifices on the other. The Plaza hotel building, capped by a white tower, stands like a memorial to the Casa of the 1950s. Return to Place des Nations Unies (old Place Mohammed V) and take a sharp right to find Le Don Quichotte café-bar, on the corner.

Place Mohammed V (old Place des Nations Unies)

Heading south from Place des Nations Unies the broad Av Hassan II leads towards Place Mohammed V, which was formerly the Place des Nations Unies, the dry administrative heart of Casablanca. In the 1920s Henri Prost and Robert Marrast were employed as the architects for most of the official buildings that surround the square. They helped define the neo-Moorish style of French colonial architecture, which remains very influential. They took details hitherto reserved for the interior of a Moorish house and used them to create an impressive monumental exterior. Behind the traditional decorative elements—the green tiled roofs, horseshoe-arch arcades, interior courtyards and the free use of *zellij* mosaic—the functional subdivision of the building into corridors and offices followed Western traditions.

The central fountain operates on Fridays and weekends; to its east rises the mass of the **Palais de Justice** or Tribunal. Next door, tucked into the corner is the **French Consulate** with a statue of Marshal Lyautey to the fore, neatly protected by a high fence. The **Préfecture** to the south is easily recognizable with its famous modernist clock tower striking a jarring note amid the principles of the neo-Moorish style. The post office and the Banque du Maroc sit very solidly on the northern face of the square.

To the south of the Place stretches the flat expanse of the **Parc de la Ligue Arabe**, cut through with neat promenades and containing a number of elegant cafés such as La Pergola du Parc, in the half-shade along Blvd Moulay Youssef. On the western edge is the School of Fine Arts, across the street from the old **Cathédrale du Sacré Coeur**, designed by Paul Tornon in 1930. The ferro-concrete nave washed with a creamy yellow is being converted by the municipality into a cultural centre. It is a striking structure, the exterior dominated by three rows of descending buttresses and gargoyles. The long narrow apertures are filled with a geometric arrangement of glass that deliberately recalls the marquetry and *zellij* mosaic traditional to a religious building in Morocco.

At the far southern end of this wooded park is the inner ring road, the Blvd Mohammed Zerktouni. About 600 metres to the east, heading left as you leave the park, is the still-functioning church of **Notre-Dame de Lourdes**, finished in 1956. The interior is hung with some fine tapestries that illustrate the doctrine of the Immaculate Conception and the appearance of the Virgin at Lourdes. The borders have been picked out in blue and red in an intentionally Moroccan scheme, though figurative religious art is of course completely removed from the practice of Morocco.

The Nouvelle Médina or Quartier Habous

Created as a showpiece of colonial paternalism, this new quarter for Muslims was built to the southeast of the then European city centre. It was directly modelled on the surviving 18th-century quarters of Casablanca, and on the elegant town of Essaouira to the south. A few of the inhabitants of the shantytown slums were transferred to these elegant narrow streets, with wider connecting roads lined with stone arcades. The Nouvelle Médina now has Casablanca's largest concentration of bazaars and craft shops. It is the cleanest, most ordered **souk** in Morocco, lacking vitality but with a fine selection of all the national crafts. The most attractive arcades are in the area north of the railway and south of Blvd Victor Hugo. The high walls of the **royal palace**, which enclose a secretive and elegant garden, line the boulevard to the north. A street surmounted by three picturesque arches leads to Place Moulay Youssef, with a central garden and a mosque built by the present king's grandfather in 1938. Two arcaded and arched streets on the left of the square lead to the larger Place de la Mosquée, with well-kept shaded gardens and the **mosque of Mohammed V** on its south side. To the north are the imposingly high outer walls of the **Mahakma du Pacha**, the combined residence of the Pasha of Casablanca and tribunal of the Islamic courts, finished in 1952 by the French. It is for the moment closed to visitors, which is a pity, as the interior is a maze of courts decorated in traditional Moorish style with carved plaster and wood.

A bridge, the **Sidi Jdid**, leads south across the railway line to the main residential area of Nouvelle Médina. The vegetable and spice market of the **quartier Balilida** is off the Rue du Rharb, a delightfully animated court full of the competing colours and odours of the souk. A terrace that runs parallel to the market above, the Rue Taroudannt, contains the stalls of herbalists and enchanters. Hedgehogs and turtles are sold live, and there are curtains of dried animal and bird skins from which to make charms and love potions. Madame Chrifa Dukkalia, who runs one of the stalls, will tell your fortune from her pack of henna-stained cards. The small cones of green dried leaves from the henna tree are sold as the base for the henna paste used throughout Morocco for decorating hands and feet, and for invigorating and dyeing hair.

The Port

The 400m tree-lined Blvd Houphouët-Boigny (another city feature that has been renamed, formerly Blvd Mohammed el Hansali) provides a pleasant walk down from Place des Nations Unies (Place Mohammed V) to the port area. On the other side of the busy multi-lane coast road the Blvd des Almohades stands Centre 2000, just before the Gare du Port. This is a 1990s shopping mall which, though not exactly what you come to Morocco to see, does contain a number of pizza bars and restaurants.

The nearest dock to the road is the one used by the fishing fleet, after which comes the area dedicated to liners and yachts before the three commercial piers and a great extension that is being finished to the east which will double the size of the port, already the fourth busiest in Africa. The export of phosphates dominates the activity of the port; vegetables and fruit are also despatched to Europe, and corn, wood, sugar, oil and manufactured goods imported. A walk along the harbour breakwater of Moulay Youssef quickly reveals the need for swimming pools in Casablanca. A mass of weathered, disturbingly sharp bedrock extends hundreds of metres out to sea from the beach at low tide. The sewage from a city the size of Casa, and the Atlantic currents, should discourage even an eel from swimming here.

The Grand Mosque of Hassan II

The 200m-high minaret of this vast new mosque—the second largest in the world, surpassed only by that in Mecca—floats above the skyline of Casablanca, the sun glancing off its façade of pale marble and glazed tile and from the three gilded balls at its summit. The tower is offset from the enormous rectangular 22-acre prayer hall, three times the size of St Paul's Cathedral. The glimmering interior, a palatial expanse of polished marble floor, granite columns, carved stone and plaster Moorish arches with more than 70 cedar-panelled cupolas, is lit by vast Venetian chandeliers of pale green crystal. The roof is richly carved, painted and gilded and the size of a football pitch, but can slide open automatically to flood the hall with sunlight. As well as the cool marble ablution fountains beneath the prayer hall, on important feast days the water rill in the middle of the mosque flows as well. A mezzanine level, wrapped in a carved wooden screen, seems to float on a floor of coloured tiles and provides a reserved area for female worshippers.

Perhaps the most astonishing aspect of the mosque is its position. It has been built out from the natural shoreline on a reclaimed embankment. This is in deliberate fulfillment of a Koranic verse, 'the throne of God was built on the water'. It is also a careful piece of symbolism, the wedding of late 20th-century Morocco to its new but ever-more influential Atlantic identity. Moroccan culture has long been concentrated in the cities of the interior and has virtually ignored the Atlantic coast, still littered with the monumental evidence of medieval invaders, colonists and foreign merchants. For a long time the Arabs felt insecure about the Atlantic, a coastline that was the final refuge of weak tribes driven from the good grazing of the interior. Only the most desperate stooped to the dishonourable occupation of living from the sea. This vast mosque is an attempt to correct a long cultural imbalance, its towering minaret a beacon to draw the faithful seawards.

It is one of the King's most extraordinary, extravagant but ultimately successful building projects. Its cost has been estimated at £500/$750 million, entirely funded by donations from the people of Morocco, as the ubiquitous certificates displayed in every café, hotel, shop and home proudly attest. The square opposite is being enclosed by an arcade of shops and cafés that will eventually incorporate a cultural complex with a museum, school and medersa. As well as the existing approaches there is to be a new processional avenue opened to the west of the medina. It will be interesting to see if this will eventually shift the focus of the city, for at the moment the area around the Mosque remains determinedly low-rent. This is the only working mosque in Morocco open to non-Muslims, but at a price (currently 100dh). There are four escorted tours a day, in the mornings, everyday except Fridays.

Aïn Diab

Two km west of the grand mosque, Aïn Diab is a coastal resort of little attraction to most non-Moroccan or Arab travellers, apart from perhaps visiting businessmen. The bars, the bathing clubs and the mixing of both sexes in a public area with fewer clothes on than normal has a fascination for less sophisticated Moroccans that it is difficult to share. The shore is lined with a number of enclosed clubs that seem to have taken their inspiration from Club Med: an exclusive members-only policy (though as a foreign visitor you will often be welcomed in), swimming pools, concrete flooring, continual music and constant hearty ball games comes close to a vision of purgatory. There are a number of serviceable but unexciting upmarket hotels, by far the best of which is the **Riad Salam**, which puts on a truly splendid buffet lunch. A new **Saudi Palace**, with an associated library and mosque, has been built above the hotel. The area is popular with wealthy holidaymakers from the Gulf States, who while remaining in a Muslim country can luxuriate in the greater freedoms of Morocco, particularly its wine, women, song and boys, denied them by their own puritanical laws.

Sidi-Abd-er-Rahmane

Three km west beyond Ain Diab the striking **shrine of Sidi-Abd-er-Rahmane** squats atop a rocky outcrop surrounded by pounding surf. The cluster of whitewashed shrines and sanctuary lodgings entirely occupies the headland—almost an island—linked to the mainland only by a sandy connecting strip that is covered by the advancing tide. It is a holy site much frequented by pilgrims in hope of a cure from Sidi-Abd-er-Rahmane, a medieval mystic originally from Baghdad. He has shown special concern for the nervous and mentally ill. Non-Muslims, especially those bearing cameras, are not welcome at the shrine. Stay on shore. At dusk you can watch the sun being swallowed by the Atlantic: as the whitewashed tombs are flecked with the dying red rays it seems certain that man has worshipped here or watched in awe since the dawn of consciousness. Remains of *Homo erectus*, the first user of fire, have been found in the nearby quarries.

A pleasant windswept stretch of sandy beach with two small settlements and campsites, at **Dar-Bouâzza** and **Tamaris-Plage/Hajra Kahla**, is 10km further, at a signposted right turn off the S130. This road is a slower but more entertaining route than the inland P8, through **Bir Jdid**, only of interest on Thursday for its **souk**. The roads rejoin at Azemmour.

Where to Stay

Casablanca has a number of moderately-priced hotels, solidly built during the Protectorate, which are concentrated in the city centre. They have spacious, comfortable bedrooms and are largely undamaged by improvements. There is not much interest or economy to be enjoyed by staying in the medina. If this is your first night in Morocco, give yourself a bit of extra comfort while you slowly adjust.

luxury

If you are inextricably wedded to getting the best on offer, you might as well stay in the **Hyatt Regency**, ✆ (02) 261234, ℻ (02) 220180, which stands behind soundproof windows right in the centre on Place des Nations Unies (ex Mohammed V). There are in addition several other luxury hotels along Av des FAR, of which the **Royal Mansour** at no. 27, ✆ (02) 313011, 312112, ℻ (02) 312583, is currently rated the best with its opulent polished-marble interior, pseudo-Moorish style and swanky doormen.

expensive

The **Hotel Toubkal**, ✆ (02) 311414, ℻ (02) 312287/311146, at 9 Rue Sidi Belyout (2nd left off Av des FAR from Place des Nations Unies and directly opposite the Royal Mansour) has an unexceptional exterior but reveals itself to be a model of calm efficiency within. With just 68 rooms, some with trelliswork balconies, it is a more intimate alternative to the vast hotels and less than half the price. There is also a small bar, a restaurant and a popular night-club within the building.

moderate

The **Moussafir**, ✆ (02) 401984, ℻ (02) 400799, is just beside the Gare des Voyageurs on Blvd Bahmad. Though away from the centre of town it is part of an efficient and attractive national chain and has its own garden, bar and restaurant. In the city centre similar facilities are offered by the rather older **Plaza**, ✆ (02) 297822 at 18 Blvd Houphouët-Boigny (ex Mohammed el Hansali), the tree-lined street leading from the Gare du Port.

cheap

For something dignified, colonial and dead central, with a comfortable touch of shabbyness, head for the **Excelsior**, ✆ (02) 200048/200263, at 2 Rue el Amraoui Brahim (ex-Rue Nolly), which looks onto Place des Nations Unies, or the small **Hotel de Foucauld**, ✆ (02) 222666 at 52 Rue Araïbi Jilali (ex-Rue de Foucauld).

Eating Out

expensive

Casablanca has the reputation of having some of the best cooking in Morocco, led by André Halbert's celebrated **Restaurant A Ma Bretagne**, ✆ (02) 362112/397979, fax (02) 944155, generally considered to be the best French restaurant in Africa. It occupies an unusual modernist building with a stunning outlook over the sea that includes an oblique view of the headland shrine of Sidi Abd-er-Rahmane, a 10km taxi ride from the city centre near Aïn Diab (closed Sun). Prices are worthy of a *Maître Cuisinier de France*, but remain a bargain by European standards. The sort of delicacy to expect might be fillets of sole with a cream and oyster sauce, the fish lightly steamed in a *couscoussier* while a fish stock is reduced to its concentrated essence. Cream, oysters and butter are added to the stock and gently spooned over the delicate fish.

Dropping down the price scale there are three more good French seafood restaurants clustered on El Hank, 'The Lighthouse', a rocky peninsula on the road to Aïn Diab. Choose from **Le Cabestan**, ✆ (02) 391190; **Au Petit Rocher**, ✆ (02) 395748, or **La Mer**, ✆ (02) 363315, which all have an international following. La Mer was the Casablanca restaurant always favoured by Valéry Giscard d'Estaing when he visited Morocco as President of France. If you prefer not to make a trip out of town then right in the centre of Casablanca at 133 Rue Allal ben Abdallah there is the **Brasserie Bavaroise**, ✆ (02) 311760/443299, which also serves excellent classic French food.

moderate

For a reasonably-priced French fish restaurant go into the port past the customs post to **Le Port de Pêche**, ✆ (02) 318561, a tranquil place where you can sip sangría while you decide what fish to choose and how it is to be cooked. Better still, head for the bustling, friendly atmosphere of the **Taverne du Dauphin**, ✆ (02) 221200/277979, at 115 Blvd Houphouët-Boigny. Fish seldom tastes this good, particularly the grilled prawns. For more French cooking head for **La Braserade**, ✆ (02) 298428 (closed Mon) at 68 Rue el Araar (ex Gay-Lussac), or carry on to the nearby Spanish place **La Corrida**, ✆ (02) 278155, at no. 59 (closed Sun).

For a traditional evening of Moroccan cooking both **Al Mounia**, ✆ (02) 222669 (closed Sun), at 95 Rue du Prince Moualy Abdullah and **Imilchil**, ✆ (02) 220999 at 27 Rue Vizir Tazi are reliably decorative and not too expensive. The food in the Al Mounia is probably the best Moroccan fare in town.

La Lombardie, ✆ (02) 265685, at 201 Blvd Rahal el Meskini is the first choice for an Italian restaurant, though **La Mama**, ✆ (02) 391558, out on the corner of Blvd de la Corniche and Blvd Biarritz near Aïn Diab has live music most nights. The Lebanese cooking at **Le Beyrouth**, 7 Rue Karachi, ✆ (02) 308798, is very popular.

cheap

For a considerably less extravagant night out try **L'Etoile Marocaine** at 107 Rue Allal Ben Abdallah, ✆ (02) 314100, a small restaurant decorated in the Moorish taste and serving traditional food(but no alcohol) at a reasonable price.

Le Petit Poucet at 86 Blvd Mohammed V, © (02) 275420, was one of the smartest centres of urban life in Casablanca before the Second World War. It has a reasonably priced restaurant, but for a cheaper evening use the snack bar next door. Another good cheap address on this street, unlicensed to serve alcohol, is **Le Buffet** at no. 99. Of the cheap snack-bars around the market, the **Brasserie Sphinx** a block south on Av. Houmane el Fetouaki on the corner opposite Rue Ibn Batouta, is one of the most spacious and tranquil.

pâtisseries and glaciers

The most famous Moroccan patisserie in Casablanca is **Bennis** at 2 Rue Fikh el Gabbas. Along Blvd Mohammed V you will find **Trianon** at no. 37 and **La Normande** at no. 213. Blvd du 11 Janvier boasts the two finest ice-cream shops, **Glacier Gloria** and **L'Igloo**, where the most exotic combinations of fruit, sherbets, ice creams, whipped cream, flavoured milks, juices, teas and coffees can be ordered. The Boulevard is just east of Place Mohammed V (old Place des Nations Unies).

Shopping

Though there are a number of large **bazaars** to the east of Place des Nations Unies (Mohammed V), but they are rather drab and dusty places. The market off Blvd Mohammed V and the streets of the Nouvelle Médina make a much more memorable shopping trip: for antiques and decorative pieces get a taxi to **Le Riad des Antiquaires** on the corner of Av Lalla Yacout and Rue Mustapha el-Maami. The stands around the Place des Nations Unies and in the Hyatt Regency Hotel sell **English papers**. There are two English-language **bookshops**, at 27 Rue Mouttaker Abdelkader and 1 Place de la Fraternité, and an engaging second-hand bookshop for old and rare books on Morocco, **Le Bibliophile**, at 16 Rue des Eperviers.

There are a number of well-established commercial **art galleries** in Casa that have exhibitions of Moroccan artists, decorative art from other Islamic countries and works from France and Belgium: **Galerie d'Art Moderne** at 5 Rue Manaziz, the **Galerie Alif** at 46 Rue Omar Slaoui and **Galerie Bassamat** at 2 Rue Pierre Curie.

Sports and Activities

The chief sports in Casablanca, the businessman's city, are inevitably **golf** and **tennis**. The Royal Golf d'Anfa shares the race track, which has races on Sundays. The club (the Hippodrome, Anfa, © (02) 361026) is usually welcoming to visiting players and boasts an 18 and a nine-hole course. There is also a course at Mohammedia. Tennis courts are at the major clubs: Tennis USM at Parc de la Ligue Arabe, © (02) 275429, and Tennis Romandie, Blvd de Libye, © (02) 361640.

Riding can be arranged at Club Bayard, Anfa, © (02) 272581, and the Club d'Etrier, quartier des Stades, © (02) 253771, and **racing** takes place at the Hippodrome in Anfa on some Sundays, as advertised.

Water sports are constricted by the fierce Atlantic surf and rocky coast. **Swimming** is generally restricted to large saltwater concrete pools along the coast towards Aïn Diab or the beach at Mohammedia. There are both **sailing and rowing clubs** which occasionally function from jetties in the port.

Entertainment and Nightlife

The **Theatre Mohammed V** is on Av des FAR. Despite its reverence for story-tellers, Morocco does not have any tradition of theatre. The hall is used for concerts and visiting productions. The shows are widely advertised, and usually televised.

Casablanca enjoyed a brief notoriety as the sex-change capital of the world, but the surgeons from the West have returned home to practise their art in their own, now legal clinics. The city retains a reputation for sophisticated commercial sex-shows, but this idea seems no more than a continuation of a Victorian 'Oriental' obsession.

A real night in Casablanca might begin and end on Boulevard Houphouët-Boigny (ex Mohammed el Hansali). Start at **Don Quichotte** at no. 6, moving on to the **American Bar** at no 49 before finishing at **La Fontaine** at no. 133. The Fontaine has live music for its belly dancers, who can be quite direct in their demands for tips, while the barflies and bar hostesses have expensive and unquenchable thirsts. Another equally expensive but more reputable evening could be spent having dinner and listening to live music in the **Alcazar Club** at no.170 or in the nightclub of the **Hotel Toubkal**. The clubs get more international in their tastes as you move away from the port into the glamorous world of Aïn Diab. To dress for an evening here, drop the Jack Kerouac lonely traveller look for the evening and arrange to have your white trousers and silk jacket spotlessly clean and pressed. Most of the well-established disco/night-clubs such as **Le Balcon 33** and **Le Tube** are on the left of the Blvd de La Corniche (the Aïn Diab coast road) as you swing past the Riad Salam hotel. If while in Aïn Diab you still can't quite shake Bogart and Rick's Bar out of your mind stop off for either a drink or a meal at **Tio Pepe**, ✆ (02) 360189 (on the right just before the traffic lights as the coast road heads inland after the Aïn Diab strip), which retains its undisturbed late 40's interior

Festivals

Casablanca only really comes alive as a city if you approach it with schemes for the import or export of goods, skills or franchises. Festivals are almost all commercial: the leather and textile fair in February, the international fair in April, a building fair in July and craftsmen's *moussem* later that month. International summits and African or Mediterranean sports competitions also feature, and there is a car race in April.

Business Addresses and Cultural Centres

The British Chamber of Commerce for Morocco, with 52 years of experience, is at 291 Blvd Mohammed V, ✆ (02) 303760, and the American Chamber in the Hotel Mansour, Av des FAR, ✆ (02) 313011. The Chambre de Commerce et d'Industrie de Casablanca is at 98 Blvd Mohammed V, ✆ (02) 221431, and the Chambre de Commerce Internationale on 4 Rue de Rhone, ✆ (02) 309716.

The Churchill Club, 1 Rue Mediterranée, ✆ (02) 367280, maintains an English-speaking rule in its premises in the heart of Francophone Africa, a surprisingly popular place for Moroccan businessmen in which to practise their new language skills. Dar America at 10 Place Bel Air, © 221460, is the only English-speaking cultural centre in Casablanca. The British Council is located in Rabat (*see* p.208).

South from Casablanca

The coastal region receives enough rainfall to support a large population of farmers, which in the 19th century were the bedrock of the nation. The loyal peasants of the region filled the sultan's granaries with corn, and his regiments with men. The immediate hinterland of Casablanca is known as Chaouïa, while the Doukkala region runs between El-Jadida and Safi. Inland from these farming regions stretches an arid plain that only two generations ago was the territory of the Rehamna nomads (*see* pp.411–2). It is still sometimes known as *Pays de Rehamna*, though *Plateau des Phosphates* better expresses its key role in the national economy. The mines of Khouribga, Youssoufia and Ben Guerir extract millions of tonnes of phosphate-rich rock: the spoil heaps of the mines flicker like pyramid mirages in the plain, but though impressive in scale they are ugly in detail.

Casablanca to Marrakech

The P7 road from Casablanca and Marrakech crosses the phosphate plain with determination. The one feature of interest off this road is the **Boulâouane Kasbah**, one of the least visited but most impressive of all the royal kasbahs of Morocco. Unless you are very determined it is only approachable if you have your own transport. To get there make for Settat, on the P7, and take the S105 for El-Jadida as you enter the town. At Boulâouane, 50km from Settat, turn left on to the S124 for Sidi-Bennour and then shortly afterwards left again onto the S128, then (feeling rather dizzy with all these directions) turn left again onto a long drive through pinewoods to reach the kasbah.

Sultan Moulay Ismaïl built this fortress in 1710, on a spit of land wrapped in one of the more serpentine coils of the great, slow-moving Oum er Rbia river. The kasbah is protected on three sides by the natural moat of the muddy waters of the river, and overlooks the flat agricultural plain at the boundaries of the three provinces of Chaouïa, Doukkala and Rehamna.

The land **gate**, decorated with scallops, its wooden gates still in position, is in fine condition. An inscription records its noble founder and the date. Through the gatehouse chamber is a large enclosed courtyard. To the left is the abandoned **mosque**, which you may enter, and a minaret which can be climbed for a fine view of the encircling walls and the meanders of the river. The tarnished tomb of Sidi Mansana is in the northeast corner, and a hole reveals an underground chamber near the wall. The **palace courtyard** and tower are opposite, to the right of the gatehouse. Details of the paved mosaic floor can be made out and some plasterwork survives on the stone walls. Broken and diminished fragments of white marble bear witness to what was once a delicate pillared courtyard. The *hammam* is in the southern corner. Beyond the palace walls an open tunnel descends beneath the fortress's curtain walls to appear in an external bastion. Two thick walls enclose this passage, which descends a steep slope to the remains of a hexagonal tower. The twin walls continue their progress down to the river to provide a secure wharf on the Oum er Rbia. Another low doorway has been cut through the curtain wall to lead out to a natural terrace, where there is a tomb of a holy man partly underground.

Returning inside the walls, look out for the air vents of the underground chambers. Four out of the original six vaulted chambers survive and can be entered. One is used by a barn owl that nests in a hole that connects with one of the battlemented towers. Old garrison quarters can be traced around the remaining areas of the curtain wall. A complete circuit can be made of the **battlements**, which provide excellent, potentially predatory, views of the surrounding countryside. An arch leads to the village, stranded on the far reaches of the promontory.

Stopping Places

Travelling directly from Casablanca to Marrakech there are two possibilities for a stop to break the journey. There is a restaurant just north of the village of **Mechra-Benâbbou**, 114km south of Casa, and on the southern edge of the village a wood by the banks of the Oum er Rbia makes a pleasantly shaded picnic site. **Sidi-Bou-Othmane** (197km from Casa, 40km from Marrakech) which stands on the ridge of the bleak Jbilet hills, has a Monday souk, two koubbas shaded by jujube trees and several café-restaurants, including the **Auberge La Lorraine**. It was here, in 1912, that Colonel Mangin fought the tribal army of El Hiba, the Blue Sultan, who had marched up from the Sahara to throw the French out of Morocco. Mangin's small force was armed with machine guns and howitzers, and having destroyed El Hiba's army he rushed quickly to Marrakech and succeeded in rescuing the seven French hostages being held there before the end of the day.

Azemmour

On the coast road 83km south of Casablanca, Azemmour is the least visited of all Morocco's medieval Atlantic towns, with few provisions for tourists and a welcome air of unhurried grace and ease. It is only 16km north of El-Jadida, and if visited at all tends to be taken in as an excursion from there. The old Portuguese walled town presents a striking view as you cross one of the three bridges that span the river Oum er Rbia, 'the mother of spring', to approach Azemmour. The white walls of the medina houses rise up directly from the river-bank, and seem to bleed their colour down into the remains of the riverine fortifications.

Azemmour was an ancient river port, known as Azama. Its Portuguese walls have long outlasted their creators, who ruled here for less then 30 years. The town was occupied by the Portuguese in 1510 but, alarmed by the fall of their fortress at Agadir in 1541, they abandoned it to concentrate their forces at El-Jadida. The presence of that Portuguese garrison town, as well as that at Anfa (Casablanca), hindered Azemmour's development until the Christian enemy was finally expelled in the 18th century.

Getting There

Azemmour is easily reached from El-Jadida, only 16km away, by bus (every half hour) or *grand taxi*. There are also buses from Casablanca to El-Jadida which pass through Azemmour.

The Medina

The aged red walls of the **medina** are an impressive site, partly covered in cascades of bougainvillea and punctuated with impressive and very European-looking defensive towers.

There are three land and two river gates, overlooking the mud-red waters of the Oum er Rbia. The northern gate has a stairway to the right which allows you to climb up to the battlements and look down upon the old ***mellah*** (Jewish quarter). Since the great exodus of Jews from Morocco in the fifties the *mellah* is only half occupied by newcomers, and many of the houses are falling into ruin. Such an aerial view of the internal layout of a medina, with its connecting alleys, has a distinctly prurient fascination. The medina was rebuilt after the Portuguese left in 1541, and is a totally Moroccan creation.

The battlements lead round to the **Dar el Baroud**, the crumbling remains of the central Portuguese fortress, with its central, dark, pillared chamber boasting a decaying gothic window. It has been described as the arsenal but is now used quite frequently for shitting. Whistle or hum as you explore if you wish to avoid potential embarrassment, not that Moroccans seem particularly ashamed at performing so natural a function in an ancient monument. Near the west gate is the small **synagogue of Rabbi Abraham Moul'niss**, which is locked; the key is kept at the tourist office.

A tarmac road leaves the Place du Souk for the 2km drive north to the **beach**. Alternatively, a path leads from below the northwestern tower, with its gothic fringe of battlements like an inverted crown, and passes through the old raised carved stone tombs of the Jewish cemetery, now completely overgrown, and on through the scrubland that borders the estuary to reach the beach. The Atlantic, though rough, is a safer bet than swimming in the river, which has an even more treacherous reputation and a disturbing colour and consistency. The sandy beach, fringed by dunes and woodland, continues on to El-Jadida. Here there is the **koubba of Sidi Ouadoud** surrounded by a few chalets, and the pool complex of **Haouzia**, largely used by railway workers in the summer.

Where to Stay and Eating Out

Restaurants and accommodation tend to be pretty basic. There are three main cafés. The **Café de l'Atlantique** is a pavilion conspicuously set in the central public garden; the slightly more raffish **Café el Manzah** has an upstairs room with a fine view of the walls; and the **Café de la Victoire** is ideal for breakfast since it is next door to the single (cheap) hotel in town. This is the first-floor **Hôtel la Victoire** at 308 Av Mohammed V, run in a relaxed and amiable manner by Rochdi Larbi. Alternatively, there is a **tourist office** at 141 Av Mohammed V, just past the pharmacy, that will know if anybody in the medina is interested in taking lodgers.

The café-restaurants and couscous kitchens face the northwest corner of the Portuguese walls, where the bougainvillea is at its thickest. If you desperately want a drink with your meal, the promising-looking **Restaurant La Perle**, at Haouzia beach, signposted from the centre of town, is the only possibility. Unfortunately all promise fades when you see the shabby, be-curtained interior and smell the institutional food. Order something simple if you must.

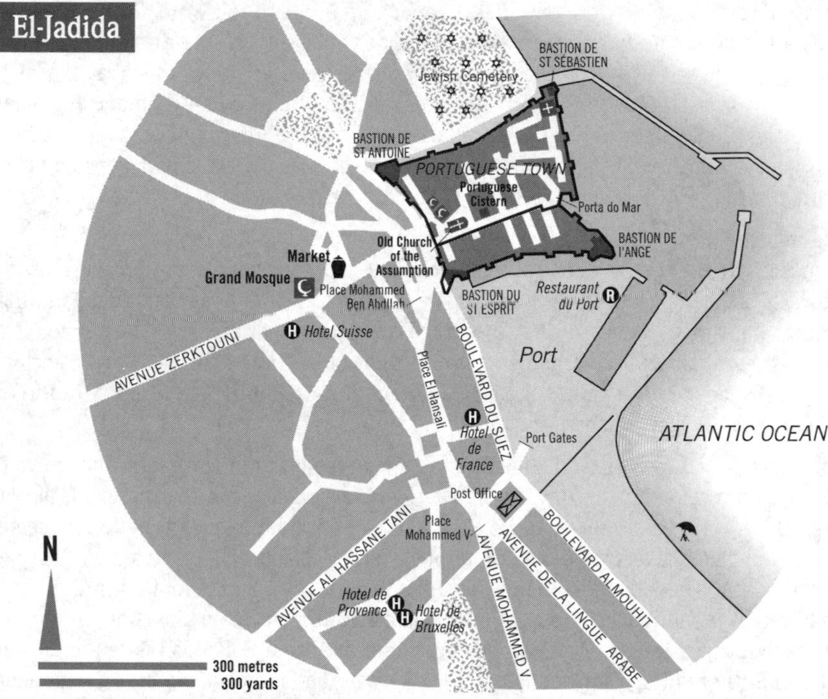

El-Jadida

El-Jadida is both the administrative centre for the agricultural province of Doukkala and a summer resort for the young people of Casablanca and Marrakech. The general social relaxations and freedoms of a holiday town make it a good place to meet Moroccans as equals. The evening sea breezes and trouble-free population can be a refreshing contrast to the summer heat and hassle of the cities of the interior. Out of season, however, El-Jadida wears the same slightly injured air as Le Touquet in October.

The 18th-century Portuguese citadel is at the heart of the town. Within the sea-moated walls there is a small but complete town that contains El-Jadida's most distinctive site, the celebrated Portuguese Cistern. Around the citadel are the neat avenues of the French-built new town. Post-Independence development proceeds inland, where a large but handsome domed mosque now breaks the skyline. The 16km-long sandy beach east of the town is lined by an elegant boulevard that gives way to a wilderness of dunes and a forested nature reserve.

History

El-Jadida is entirely the creation of the Portuguese, who built a fort here in 1502. Four years later this was greatly expanded to the present dimensions, and the new town christened Mazagan. It withstood the furious siege of the Saadians in 1562, and resisted all further assaults until it fell to Sultan Sidi Mohammed in 1769. A new Muslim quarter was built landward of the citadel, which remained an empty shell until Sultan Abder Rahman repopulated the old Portuguese streets in the early 19th century by transplanting some of the Jews from Azemmour to Mazagan, which he renamed 'the new one'—El-Jadida. The town's trade revived in the late 19th century, and the French Protectorate gave El-Jadida a new identity as an administrative centre and summer beach resort.

Getting Around

by rail

There are two trains a day that travel to El-Jadida from Rabat-Casablanca and back, one in the early morning, the other in the evening. The station is 2km from the centre of town beside the main road to Safi, but is well served by *petits taxis.*

by bus

The bus station is on Av Mohammmed V, a 15-minute walk or a *petit taxi* ride from the central Place Mohammed V. There are at least three buses a day to Casablanca (2hrs 30mins), two to Rabat (4hrs), three to Safi (2hrs 30mins), two to Essaouira (8hrs), one to Oualidia (90mins) and at least nine to Marrakech (3hrs 30min).

Orientation and Tourist Information

El-Jadida is an easy town to understand. The active centre is arranged along Place El Hansali, between the Portuguese city and Place Mohammed V—hotels, cafés and restaurants are all within a few minutes' walking distance from each other. The **souk**, which offers some fine Moroccan slippers, kaftans and teapots, is concentrated along Rue Zerktouni, and a lively vegetable and meat souk is held every Wednesday below the new lighthouse, when the surrounding farmers ride into town to trade.

Place Mohammed V is ringed with neo-Moorish public buildings: a theatre, the Hôtel de Ville, the **bank** and the **post office** (open Mon–Fri 8am–12pm, 3–6.30pm). The **tourist office** on Av Ibn Khaldoun is staffed by two charming girls who give out the usual brochures and answer enquiries (Mon–Fri only). The **hospital** is on Rue Sidi Bouzid, on the southern edge of town, but given a choice head for the **Clinique El-Jadida**, on Rue de Tunis. There is an after-hours pharmacy on Av de la Ligue Arabe.

The Portuguese Town (Cité Portugaise)

The Portuguese garrison escaped the siege of Sidi Mohammed in 1769 by sea. Historical records say they dynamited the city and trapped the triumphant besiegers in the resulting inferno, which is strange, for architecturally the city is an almost perfect survivor of its period that has attracted a number of film directors. Of the five Italian-designed bastions four survive, and it was probably this missing tower that was blown up by the departing Portuguese. The city remained a deserted ghost town until the whole enclosure was transformed into a *mellah* in 1815. As trade grew through the century European merchants joined the Jewish community within the walls, while the Muslim farmers of the Doukkala preferred to settle outside in tents or adobe huts. The departure of the Jews in the 1960s has left the Portuguese town feeling like a historical monument rather than a living community.

The west-facing walls overlooking **Place Sidi Mohammed ben Abdellah** are the most picturesque. This landward section was almost completely levelled during the 18th century Moroccan siege that took the town. After its capture the walls were quickly restored, but with nothing of the breadth and solidity of the remaining three Portuguese sections. These are built to the 18th-century requirements of a European siege, with a sloping glacis, casemates, cannon portals and rampways for the rapid deployment of artillery.

The city is approached through twin gates facing Place Sidi Mohammed ben Abdellah. The left gate leads to the Praca do Terreiro, which is dominated by religious buildings. The **grand mosque** on the left is decorated with an odd pentagonal minaret, for it was formed by converting the old lighthouse to sacred purposes. The **Church of the Assumption** on the right, once the centre for the sumptuous ceremonies of the Roman church, is now a cultural centre and therefore usually shut. The alley to the left of the gate, the Rue do Arco, leads to the **bastion of St Antony**, while turning to the right you meet the main axis of the citadel, Rue Mohammed al Hachmi Bahbah. A recent restoration, commissioned by the Portuguese ambassador, has given cobbles back to the streets and a new ochre render to many of the buildings. It has also cut away later excrescences to define the old citadel-barracks that stands plumb at the centre of the town. This remains unlived in, and you can take the stairway in the northern corner to reach the dilapidated parade ground on the roof. The famous cistern, which occupies the western basement of the citadel, has a separate entrance.

The Portuguese Cistern (Citerne Portugaise)

Open daily 9am–1pm, 3–7pm; adm.

The 'cistern' is halfway along Rue Mohammed al Hachmi Bahbah, on the left going towards the sea. This chamber was built in the 16th century as the arsenal of the citadel, and also served as a fencing school before being converted into a water cistern. The vast underground room is an astonishing site—a flooded cathedral crypt lit up by a bolt of African sun—and was used by Orson Welles in his film of *Othello*, the noble Moor.

The brickwork of the ceiling is held fast by groins of stone that fan out in a regular confusion of vaults from rows of square-dressed pillars interspersed with more delicate Tuscan columns. The vaulting is linked to the walls and the floor is a serene level surface of worn herring-bone brick. This is flooded with a few inches of water to create a graceful architectural reflection. For into the centre of the chamber sunlight streams, in almost tangible force, through a skylight. The sunlight has dressed a few of the pillars in an oozing green lichen that throws an extra element of colour into the reflection.

The entrance room of the cistern has a model of the city, and an adjacent room contains two broken cannon and a number of Portuguese inscriptions.

Porta do Mar and the Bastions

Rue Mohammed al Hachmi Bahbah continues to the sea gate, Porta do Mar, through which the last Portuguese governor departed for the awaiting evacuation fleet. The wide arch, still screened by an iron grille, is protected by flanking bastions. A communal bakery exists within the walls, wafting out gorgeous scents of baking dough.

A gate to the right of this bastion allows you to climb up to the **bastion de l'Ange** (the Angel). There are two other gates to the battlements at the **bastions of the Holy Spirit** (St-

Esprit) and **St Antony**; if they are locked (they seldom are these days) and no one appears, ask the guardian at the cistern for the key.

The Bastion de l'Ange gives a fine view of the harbour and town, its walls lined with bronze European cannon. These are not necessarily captured spoils of war, for obsolete but still impressive cannons proved to be popular gifts from 19th-century consuls anxious to win concessions from the sultan. In the company of a young, agile guide you can walk along the battlemented walls around three-quarters of the city. The views and the odd scrambling climb are rewarding along the whole length. At the **bastion of St Sebastian** you may be shown the 'old prison compound' and the 'tribunal of the Inquisition' by enthusiastic guides. The prison is just a casemate, where shot and powder was safely stored in the depths of the ramparts, while the austere courthouse is in fact an early 19th-century synagogue, as the surviving Star of David testifies. It would have been inconceivable to have allowed anything to be built on the summit of the walls if you were expecting a siege. From here you can see an extensive Hebrew cemetery outside the walls, while inside there is the northwest corner of the town, which contains the best examples of Portuguese stone and ironwork decoration on its houses, and is the most inhabited section of old El-Jadida. There is also a chapel built by the Spanish here, for on the death of the young King Sebastian at Ksar-el-Kebir in 1578 the entire Portuguese Empire passed in inheritance to his cousin, King Philip II of Spain.

The Port

The jetty provides a pleasant view of the sea walls by day, and at night the lights of the town flicker in reflection across the waves. It was largely rebuilt by German prisoners of war. The **lighthouse of Sidi Bouafi** is to the southeast of the town on a rise of land that affords views down to Cape Blanc. The 57m high tower was built in 1916, and the guardian will sometimes show you around.

The Beach

To the east of the port area a formal promenade, lined with half a dozen cafés, introduces a visitor to the beach. It stretches on for miles, and gets rapidly more deserted and delightful the further you travel, while a wrecked ship torn in two is a useful reminder of the power of the Atlantic surf. This ship was registered in Cyprus with an international crew and had been working its way up from Sierra Leone with a cargo of forest woods, which have ended up decorating many a house in El-Jadida. The roadside is also decorated with dredged and washed-up anchors and buoys. Opposite is a racecourse and the stables of the national stud. A left turn as the main road heads inland for Azemmour will take you beside the dunes, a deserted beach on your left and a wilderness of wildlife and birds on your right.

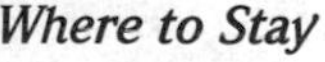

Where to Stay

El Jadida is easily accessible from both Marrakech and Casablanca, and rooms can be in short supply during weekends and the summer months from June to September. It is usually well worth booking a room in advance.

expensive

If you are a mad keen golfer, you might enjoy the **Royal Golf Hotel**, 7 km north of town on the road to Azzemour, © (03) 354141/8, @ (03) 353473. However, if you don't swing a club the place might seem forlorn and isolated. It is partly used by Club Med. There is also a pair of beachfront hotels just east of Parc Mohammed V in the town itself. The art deco **Mara Hôtel**, © (03) 344170, and the more spacious grounds of the **Doukkala Salam** are both entered from Av de la Ligue Arabe. They should in principle make excellent bases for a relaxing beach holiday, but though both have a full complement of facilities (pools, tennis courts, bar, disco and restaurant) there is something not quite right. Perhaps they stand on an unpropitious site and have been cursed.

moderate

Le Palais Andalous, © (03) 343745, @ (03) 352115, on Blvd Docteur de Lanouy is a more attractive proposition. To get to it take Rue Zerktouni from the Portuguese walls, and turn left onto Rue Pasteur at the mosque on the junction with Av Moulay Idriss. Turn right at the sign saying 'Laboratoire Jorf', and the hotel is just up on the right. Since it is a little hard to find,this hotel in a converted palace is frequently underused. On the ground floor cool dining and sitting rooms lead off from the vast central courtyard, a riot of *zellij* mosaic. The bedrooms are arranged off a balcony above the courtyard on the first floor, and are profusely tiled. All the hallmarks of 19th-century Moroccan palace decoration, including incised plaster and painted cedar ceilings, can be admired throughout the hotel. The beds are big, and high enough to require steps, which have thoughtfully been fitted. There is a bar, but sadly the restaurant is not up to much.

inexpensive

There are three small, clean, functional hotels in the new town which all have spacious double bedrooms with balconies. The **Suisse**, © (03) 342816 is at 145 Blvd Zertouni; **De Bruxelles**, © (03) 342072 at 40 Rue Ibn Khaldoun, and **De Provence**, © (03) 342347/344112, @ (03) 352115, at 42 Av Fquih M'hamed Er Rafi. The Provence has a licensed restaurant, and is everybody's favourite. For a long time it was managed by an Englishman who with the genius of his race filled this corner of Morocco with the slightly camp gentility of Brighton. Today his Moroccan partner continues to maintain the old traditions, and you can still have mint tea in your room or in the front lounge.

cheap

Of the cheap hotels by the port the long-established El-Jadida and De Port have slipped down in the estimation of most visitors. The eccentric double entrance to the **De France-Maghreb Hotel**, © (03) 342181, remains the first place to look. The hotel can be entered on one corner of Place el Hansali or down a side street, at 16 Rue Lecoul. Of the other cheaper options, the best hotel to go for is the **Bordeaux**, © (03) 354117, at 47 Rue Moulay Ahmed Tahiri. Communal showers on each floor serve clean rooms arranged around an internal courtyard.

The **Camping International** on Av des Nations Unies is a very, perhaps too, well-organized site, with its own pool, bar and restaurant. It is well-positioned on the edge of town, opposite the hotel school and just above the beach.

Eating Out

moderate

The **Restaurant du Port**, inside the harbour area itself, gives you the best view of the Portuguese citadel walls, lapped by the sea and surrounded by bobbing fishing boats. To find it go through the harbour gates, pass pavilion one and at the far end of the long dock building is this fish-restaurant (which has a drinks license). The smartly-decorated **Restaurant El Khaima** is by the camping site on Av des Nations Unies. It offers a combination of local fish and seafood and Italian cooking beneath a domed roof in an oval dining room, and also has an attractive garden terrace and bar attached.

Restaurant le Tit, at 2 Av de la Ligue Arabe, which runs parallel to the beach, offers cheerful service and a good selection of wine; avoid their fish soup, though, which is appalling. The food is better at the **Restaurant Ali Baba**, © (03) 341622, nearby on the same road. The dining room of the **De Provence** hotel (see above) has a French-based menu, a good selection of local wines and a calm atmosphere.

cheap

Amongst the cheap no-alcohol alternatives on and around Place el Hansali there is the **Tchikito**, just off the Place on Rue Mohammed Smiha, which serves only fish, **Cherazad** at no. 3 and **La Broche** at no. 46.

cafés

The café **Hammanat** in the middle of the shore-front promenade is an excellent people-watching centre. There are several busy cafés lining Place Mohammed V and Place el Hansali, of which the new-ish **Café Bahia** has regrettable modern tiles but delicious cakes. There is also the cool **La Portugaise**, almost opposite the entrance to the cisterns in the old town.

The Ancient City of Tit

The hamlet of **Sidi-Bouzid** is 5km southwest of El-Jadida along the old coast road, which twists past a clutch of summer bungalows, the **Auberge Beau Soleil**, a campsite and two roadside fish restaurants, **Le Refuge** and **Le Requin Bleu**. The actual beach, a broad cove filled by a sweep of pure golden sand overlooked by the Sidi's koubba, is delightful.

Six km further southwest, 11km from El-Jadida on the main S121 road which here runs slightly inland from the coast, is **Moulay-Abdallah**, a small farming and fishing village built within the walls of the ancient city of **Tit**. The ramparts which face the sea have been heavily restored, and every autumn (usually the third week in September) the walls are briefly filled by a tent city which assembles to celebrate the *moussem* of Moulay-Abdallah. Both the Almoravid and Almohad empires garrisoned and adorned this holy town, which became an important centre of Islamic orthodoxy in the struggle against the heretical Berber kingdoms of the coast—the Berghouata and Doukkala. It was not the Berber tribes, though, but the threat of Viking raids that caused the Almohad Sultan Abdel Moumen to build the city walls, and indeed it was the threat from the sea that caused Tit to be abandoned four centuries later. A Wattasid sultan, Mohammed el Bertougali, moved the entire population to a village near Fès rather than have them pay tribute to the Portuguese. Since El-Jadida remained in Portuguese hands until the late 18th century, the mosques and houses of Tit crumbled to leave only the minarets and a few doorways surviving, though the **shrine of Moulay-Abdallah**, as the centre for the annual *moussem*, remained in continuous use by the surrounding tribes. Tit remained deserted until this century when the present scattered population of farmers and fishermen moved in, occupying less than a tenth of the area used when it was last inhabited in the 16th century.

The whitewashed domes and green-tiled roof of the zaouia of Moulay-Abdallah are beside a **minaret** that was built by Abdel Moumen in the 12th century. This is all that remains of the Almohad mosque. The recessed mouldings and window carvings have been compared to the greater and more elaborate towers built by his son and grandson, the El Hassan at Rabat and the Koutoubia at Marrakech. The walls have recently been cleaned and the missing lantern top has been replaced. Few tourists venture here, and (except during the festival) no one seems to mind you strolling around the exterior of the shrine.

Hidden by the rising ground from the road is the sole surviving **Almoravid minaret** in Morocco. The Almohad Empire destroyed most of the buildings of the preceding dynasty which they had fought such a long and bitter struggle to overthrow. Here however the tower has endured, though there is no longer any trace of its accompanying mosque. The tower is strongly built from thin courses of stone, and the high, arched windows have a characteristic simplicity. As you walk closer, admire the inset panels, the carved stone arches and supporting pillars that delicately frame the alternating double and single windows. The richest form of decoration and arch is reserved for the single window. Some of the nearby farm buildings and barns for livestock boast fine carved stone doors from the 16th century.

On to Oualidia

Another six km on, in perfect contrast to ancient Tit, is the brand new gleaming chemical complex of **Port de Jorf-Lasfar**, built since the 1980s beyond the lighthouse of Cape Blanc. Japanese and Spanish capital helped build this, the fabulous world of Moroccan Phosphates III & IV, which will take the strain off the present plants at Safi and Casablanca. To add to the intricate confusion of chimneys, gantries and conveyors there is a petrol refinery, a port and a little fishing harbour. There is a café-restaurant used by visiting businessmen which has a good view over the large but empty harbour. A human touch is added by shepherds who, quite unconcerned, continue to graze their flocks right up to the perimeter fence.

A few kilometres beyond Jorf stands the **Restaurant Le Relais**, © (03) 345498, sandwiched between road and crashing surf. This is a delightful, sybaritic world of its own. In winter there are two wood fires burning and a well-stocked bar. From May to August the six bedrooms are opened for guests on full board. The dining room has an invigorating view of sea-smashed rocks and a small sandy beach where you can bask or snorkel whilst preparing yourself for another excellent meal of crayfish, lobster, oysters, mussels or other shellfish.

The coastal road to Oualidia passes along a sandy plain for the next 60km. An almost continuous lagoon shelters behind the natural sea wall. The area is given over to the cultivation of oysters and intensive strips of market gardening in and out of greenhouses, while salt is also extracted from the brackish lagoon in evaporation pans. Some 16 km after Le Relais, the **Villa La Brise**, © (03) 346917, offers an equally idiosyncratic stop. Also with 6 bedrooms, it has a terrace above the lagoon where you can opt for seafood or a langorous sundowner.

Oualidia

Oualidia is one of the least exploited beach resorts of Morocco. It is a quiet village of a place that falls in a scattering of houses, bourgeois summer villas and hotels down a hill towards a sandy inland lagoon, filled by the sea which roars in through two breaches in the coastal rock wall. In the summer wind surfers and fishing boats can be hired from the beach, and a local **souk** is held beside the road every Saturday. Oualidia is appreciated by families from Marrakech for its gentle charms—safe bathing, good service, a quiet welcome and delicious food—which, though, have never appealed to the bulk of foreign visitors.

One of the last Saadian sultans, El Oualid, built a kasbah here in 1634 in order to defend the lagoon port of Oualidia, which had become his only secure access to the sea. It was a measure of his desperation that he so valued Oualidia as a port, and he employed a Dutch engineer to widen the lagoon entrance with explosives. Only one of the **walls of the Saadian kasbah** survives beside the road. The tower staircase remains intact, and leads up to the upper gallery, where some rusting cannon still protrude between the crennelations. The kasbah mosque is a restoration, as is the arch, though a fine Saadian gateway survives just down the hill, its carving best appreciated from the seaward side. It remained in declining though continuous use into the 18th century, for it was from this little-watched port that the Cornish renegade Thomas Pellow escaped from the service of Sultan Moulay Ismaïl and returned home on board an Irish merchantman.

The present king's father, Mohammed V, built his summer **villa** below the kasbah, directly facing one of the sea entrances into the lagoon. The walls of the royal villa were built the same colour as the golden sand of the lagoon, with details picked out in green. Though still officially royal property you can sometimes cautiously explore its two compounds and deteriorating walls, but at other times a whistle will be blown and a finger wagged at you.

Getting Around

The CTM bus stop is on the coastal side of the road by the petrol station and opposite the local stalls. There is a daily bus from El-Jadida and twice daily buses from Safi and Marrakech. A road slips down the terrace a little further west that will take you to the lagoon beach and past the hotels and campsite on the way.

Where to Stay and Eating Out

inexpensive

The **Auberge de la Lagune**, © (03) 346477, is approached from the main road. It is the oldest establishment here, with a wonderful view from its terrace, a dozen rooms with sea views, powerful hot showers and the busiest local bar. The dining room is large and cool, with a terrace overlooking the lagoon where you can have breakfast. It is however used by passing tour groups and the service has subsequently become a bit surly.

Halfway down the hill from the main road is the totally delightful **Hippocampe**, ✆ (03) 366108, @ (03) 366461. It has a spacious (licensed) dining room where you can consume plates of fresh seafood and local oysters before tottering down a terrace of steps and slipping into the lagoon. There are several clean cabins with portholes arranged around a small but profuse flower garden full of roses, and a separate pool area. The original *patron* got involved in a smuggling ring, and was executed after a celebrated trial revealed a string of murders. The present owners, a charming Rabati and his Lebanese wife, have a less complicated attitude to business, and at weekends preside over a hotel that can appear to be half-filled by their own urbane friends.

cheap

Further down the road you will find the **Motel à L'Araignée Gourmande**, ✆ (03) 366144/366447, which has clean rooms and a 20m walk across golden sand for your morning swim. The restaurant overlooking the lagoon serves a veritable feast of seafood for next to nothing. Order *le festival de coquillage*, and prepare for the seafood marathon of your life, including such rarities as sea anemonies.

Opposite is the seasonal campsite **Sables d'Or**, and at the end of the road the more ambitious **Chems** complex just below the dunes; this has spaces for tents and caravans, bungalows for rent and its own bar and restaurant.

Inland from Oualidia

If you are spending a few days at Oualidia, have your own transport and fancy a ride in the country you might take the road inland, the S1336 (turn opposite the Oualidia kasbah), which in just over 20km passes the kasbah of **Tnine-Gharbia** (or Tnine-Rharbia). The journey is more important than the destination, for the kasbah is a vast semi-ruined enclosure of pisé walls built to house the sultans' armies as the various levies assembled here on this old crossroads on the routes from Safi to Azzemour and Oualidia to Marrakech. Today there are just fields and a few cottages where once regiments wheeled past in review.

Tribes and Regiments

At the summit of the Moroccan military heirachy were the Hashm, the foundation tribes of a dynasty, who were assisted by the Jaysh, the military or government tribes such as the Oudaïa who were exempted taxes and given certain privilieges. These groups effectively formed the standing army, garrisoned in the principal cities. In such places as Kasbah Tnine-Gharbia they would be joined by the Mutaqila, volunteer tribal cavalry, who ranked above the Mutatawwia, the seasonal volunteers, while lastly came the Hushud, the conscripts. They would all be gathered together for an offical muster, the Ard, before being informed whether there was a Haraka (campaign) planned for the year. This might involve nothing more than a march around the province collecting the customary gifts and taxes. Before the army moved off the government secretaries worked to try and impose the official Muslim military hierarchy upon the tribal and conscript assembly. The basic unit was the tent of 8 soldiers, an *aqda*, commanded by a *Nazir*, above which all formations were formed from multiples of five. Five *aqda* formed a *bend* of forty men under an *Arif*. In their turn five *bend* made a *liwa*, a company of 200 men under a *Naqib*. Five such companies made an *alam*, a regiment of a thousand men under a *Caid*. Five *alam* made a *raya*, an army of 5,000 men, under an *Amir*.

As you wander across the fields watch out for holes in the ground, which can drop you down into any of the old underground cisterns used for storing grain for the army. If you have a few hours to spare (and just a few words of Arabic) you could also allow yourself be taken by the village boys to visit the house of the Islamic school master, who has ornamented his roof top terrace with unusual animated stones, maintains a small museum of junk to rival my own collection and uses inlaid bone and metal to illustrate some chosen Koranic texts.

Oualidia to Safi

Beyond Oualidia on the road south to Safi the intensive pattern of cultivation recedes and the lagoon wall disappears. The road becomes more dramatic, passing along high sea cliffs, through arid grazing where a number of sandy trails lead down to totally deserted sandy beaches. **Cap Beddouza**, 33km from Oualidia and 23km from Safi, is one of the most beautiful of these—a last great wide expanse of golden beach before the lighthouse at Beddouza. A **koubba**, with waves breaking at the foot of its walls, has been built on an exposed rocky outcrop in the midst of the sand. The lighthouse is protected by charming green and white mock fortifications, and the hamlet spread out below includes the **Auberge Cap el Bedouza**, with a fine view of the sea. The Auberge has a few basic rooms in its terraced courtyard and a cavernous bar. They can provide a quick grill with chips, or if you have some time in hand the kitchen may be able to prepare you a delicious fish *tagine*.

Touali Mohammed's Cap Beddouza Fish Tagine

I dined at the Auberge Cap el Bedouza with the *Independent* cookery writer, Annie Bell, who persuaded the chef to disclose the secret of this dish.

6 tablespoons olive oil
25 strands saffron, 1 dessertspoon paprika and 1 dessertspoon of cumin, all ground
1 tablespoon tomato purée
1 large clove garlic, minced
1 onion, halved and sliced
2 green peppers
12 oz manicrop potatoes
3 lb grey mullet, cleaned and gutted
1 lb marmande tomatoes

1 lemon
3 fl oz white wine
salt, pepper

Preheat the oven to 200° C. Grey mullet is an underrated fish, firm and fleshy and not unlike sea bass. You will require a flameproof casserole long enough to hold the fish. Heat 4 tablespoons of the oil in this, when it is very hot add the spices and immediately turn the heat down low; moments later add the tomato purée, onion and garlic and cook for 2–3 minutes; add the peppers and cook for another few minutes until the vegetables soften, stirring all the time. Distribute this mixture evenly over the base of the casserole. Peel and thinly slice the potatoes and lay them on top of the vegetable mixture. Place the fish on top. Thickly slice the tomatoes and lemon and arrange on top of the fish and vegetables—first the tomato, then the lemon. Season and pour over the wine and remaining olive oil. Cover with foil, or a lid, and bake for 30 minutes. Remove foil or lid and cook for another 20 minutes. Discard the lemon, fillet the fish, and serve with the vegetables to one side and the sauce spooned over the fish.

A turning to the right just beyond the lighthouse leads down to the beach. Cap Beddouza is identified as Cape Soloeis, where the Carthaginian admiral Hanno dedicated an altar to the god of the sea in the 5th century BC on his voyage to discover the gold trade of Guinea. In his day the coast was covered in trees and there were numerous elephants bathing in a lagoon. The altar has disappeared, but if you let your spirit wander it is easy to find a suitable spot. Directly below the lighthouse the sea cliffs and caves begin, and a puckered, sea-battered rock lets in an arm of fuming water. Natural rock arches and overhanging cliffs provide pleasant bowers for Poseidon and his Nereids to sport. There is an old burial ground nearby, beside a small, almost subterranean **mosque** with carved pillars that have been cut from the living rock. The mihrab emerges from the mosque like a pillar of salt.

A broken row of street lights stretches a little way along this beach, and though there is no established site, this is an obviously attractive area in which to camp.

From Cap Beddouza to Safi the coast is a savage cliff face. There are only two accessible beaches, Sidi-Bouzid, just above Safi, and **Lalla-Fatna**, halfway there. Turn right by the Lalla-Fatna **café** for a 2km hairpin descent to the beach through a boulder-strewn landslip. In the summer a café is manned beside the small car park. If you plan to pitch a tent or park overnight here, watch out for the tides. The beach has a strong atmosphere, for it is entirely enclosed by dramatic cliffs with seams of quartz that reflect the setting sun. A *moussem* is held here in the last few days before Ramadan.

Five km before Safi the remains of a Portuguese bastion, **Fort Nador**, can just be recognized beside the cliffs. Further along the cliff edge is a **shrine** to the marabout **Sidi-Bouzid**. Nearby is the **Refuge**, © (04) 464354 (*see* p.252), where the dining room and bar enjoy a spectacular view over Safi, which may look deceptively close but is a 4km walk away. A road descends from this small group of buildings to swing down past a long shaded café, with another superb and wind-cooled prospect of the town and port. The surrounding pine woods are a popular weekend picnic spot. The road continues down to the rocks, a good area for

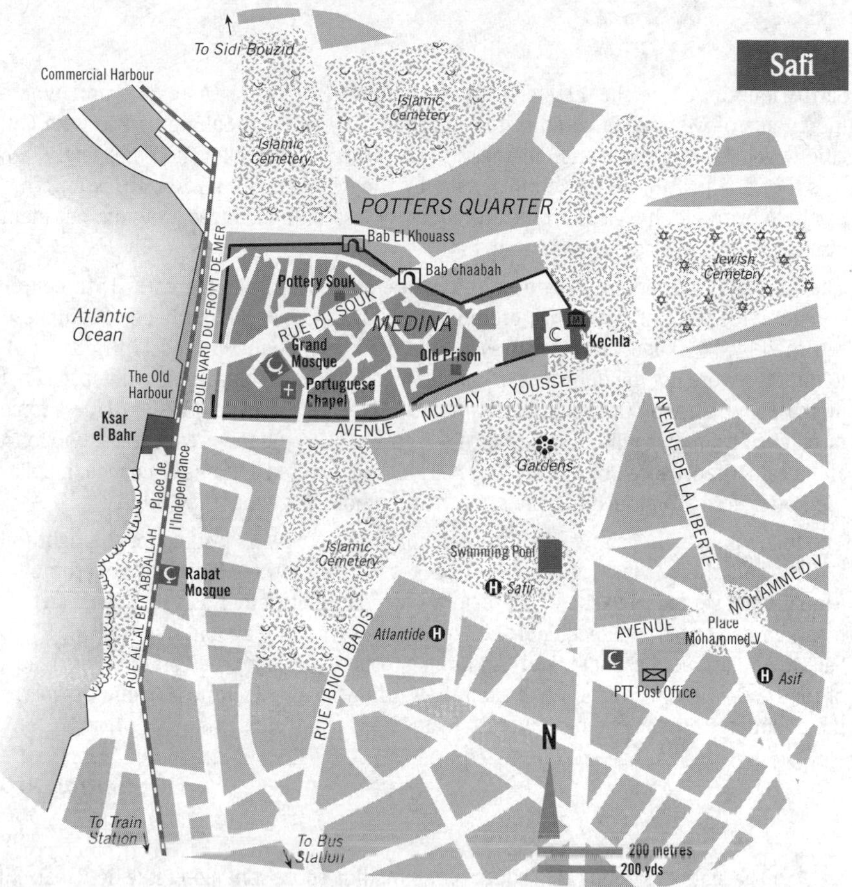

snorkeling and the nearest clean sea bathing if you are staying at Safi. A kilometre closer to Safi is the only campsite in the area, the ***camping municipal***, which is open throughout the year and has an attractive site shaded by trees and its own pool, bar and shop.

Safi

A successful, industrious town, Safi has never appealed to many tourists. The medina is consequently an easygoing and attractive place in which to walk, and you often have the sites (city walls, potteries, Portuguese chapel and fortress, and the Kechla fortress which now houses the national ceramic museum) entirely to yourself. The sardine-packing industry and the phosphate plant are to the south of the town, which makes that area an uninviting place to swim, but there are excellent beaches within 30km both north and south of the town.

An element of quixotic romance was added to this working-man's town in 1969–70 when Thor Heyerdahl sailed *Ra I* and *Ra II* from Safi to prove that it was possible that ancient Egypt could have influenced the development of civilization in Central America. Ptolemy does at least record that Safi might have been the ancient Phoenician trading centre of Mysokaras.

History

Safi is mentioned by the 11th-century geographer El Bekri as Asfi, as a port where the merchants of Marrakech could sell the products of the trans-Saharan trade with Guinea, chiefly gold, slaves and ostrich feathers. In the 14th century a fortified monastery, a *rabat*, was founded just to the south of the port by the Merenid Sultan Abou Hassan. This was partly to overawe the Mediterranean traders, whose influence was growing, but mainly to discipline the Jbel Hadid to the south.

The European traders proved to be the greater threat, and in the early 15th century all contact with the Christians was prohibited and the port was closed. The Portuguese had returned by 1450 and their consul was soon deeply embedded in local intrigues, but they found they were not the only ones to dabble in politics, and, threatened by the pacha of Safi's increasing reliance on the Spanish, decided to strike quickly. In 1508 a Portuguese force was dispatched from Essaouira to seize Safi. They embellished the town with walls, two fortresses and a cathedral. The fall of Agadir, however, in 1541 caused a dramatic change in policy and the Portuguese abandoned Safi the same year, demolishing what they could.

The following centuries saw the European commercial powers jostling for the right to trade at Safi, and the pacha of the port was a key figure in the Moroccan government. Sidi Mohammed served as pacha of Safi before succeeding his father as sultan, although during his reign he caused the decline of the port by concentrating all external trade at Essaouira. Safi now relies on phosphates and fish for its prosperity, as a journey on the coast road south of the town will testify. The smell from the sardine-packing factories is unmistakable, while the pollution from the chemical works creates spectacular sunsets.

Getting Around

by rail

The station is about 2km south of the medina shorefront along Rue de Rabat/Rue du Caid Sidi Abderrahman, © (04) 463375/462408, but well served by *petits taxis*. The railway travels up to the phosphate mines of Ben Guerir to connect with the main Casablanca to Marrakech track. There are two rather slow trains a day, to and from Casablanca and Rabat. Change at Ben Guerir for Marrakech.

by bus

Travelling by bus is cheaper, quicker and easier. The new bus terminal is however, like the train station, on the southern edge of town, about 1.5km from the medina. It's worth getting a *petit taxi* from there to your hotel or to Place de l'Indépendance. There are four buses a day to Marrakech (3hr 30 min), three to El-Jadida (under 2hrs direct but another 40mins if via Oualidia) and two to Essaouira (6hrs).

Local buses leave from Place de l'Indépendance by the post office, with hourly services along the coast both north and south. Catch the no. 10 or no. 15 for Lalla Fatna and Cap Beddouza, or look out for the summer buses south to Souira Kédima.

by car

With a car, park between the medina and the sea on Blvd du Front de Mer. Cars can be **hired** from Safi Voyages (Europcar) on Place de l'Indépendence, © (04) 462935.

Tourist Information

The **tourist office** is on Av Moulay Youssef, © (04) 462145. The three **banks**, the BMCE, BMCI and Banque Populaire, are in the three main squares; Place de l'Indépendance, Place Ibnou Sina and Place Mohammed V, also the site of the main **post office**. There is a French Consulate on Rue Chaouki, and a **Catholic church** at 16 Rue Chechaouèn, with Mass on Saturdays at 7pm and Sundays at 11am.

The New Town

Place de l'Indépendance is the animated centre of the town. To the south is Rue de Rabat–Rue du Caid Sidi Abder Rahman, lined with shops and cafés, and the direct route to Souira Kédima. The coastal road, the right exit from the place looking south, passes an elegant cliff promenade with a busy café. Further on a small mosque on the right is all that's left of the *rabat* founded in the 14th century by the Merenids. Beyond it there is a **koubba** raised over the grave of **Sidi Abou Mohammed Salih**, the patron saint of Safi, which has an associated zaouia attached.

Ksar el Bahr

Open Mon–Fri 8am–12pm, 2–4pm; adm.

This stone fortress, also known as the Château de la Mer, was built by the Portuguese in the 16th century to guard the old harbour. It was the governor's residence during their 40 years of rule and was used by visiting sultans until the late 18th century. A saint's tomb is hidden down a dark passage off the large, square, paved interior. The old prison is at the foot of the tower, where a spiral staircase leads up to the summit for a fine view over the medina. A ramp leads from the central court to a firing platform that commands the sea approaches, and is lined with a medley of European cannon. The southwest bastion provides a fine commanding vista of the sea and the surrounding cliffs.

The Medina

This, the oldest part of Safi, is roughly triangular in shape tapering inland to a summit crowned by the **Kechla**, the citadel. The **walls** of the old town are complete on the landward sides and surrounded by open gardens and weed-infested cemeteries. Beyond the north wall potters have traditionally settled, beside the stream that runs down to the sea. To the north of the main, seaward, entrance to the medina there used to be a line of functional but impressively elegant line of 18th-century custom sheds, built outside the city walls for the use of European merchants, but these have sadly been demolished, only within the last ten years, to give a clear view of the walls.

The central street of the medina is aptly known as **Rue du Souk**, for it is one continuous market place. It is nevertheless an easy place to wander around in, since it handles goods above all for the local market—hence there's not a tourist bazaar or potential guide in sight. Entering from the seaward side, an alley on the right, Rue du Cadi Ayad (enticingly labelled *Passage touristique et Toilette*) leads past the great outer walls of the **grand mosque**. A hundred metres further on the left is the entrance to the **Portuguese Chapel** *(theoretically open 9am–12pm, 3–6pm, but often closed)*, which is in fact the choir, all that remains of the gothic cathedral of Safi built by the Portuguese in 1519. Cool and dark, decorated with a number of symbolic bosses, the roof looms above you. The central stone boss of the arms of Portugal is surrounded by a ring of eight. The world as divided between Spain and Portugal by the Borgia pope is easily recognizable, as are the keys of St Peter, an episcopal mitre with two croziers, and the arms of the crusading order of St James. Continue on down the shadowy stone street hung with buttresses and arches to emerge into full daylight through a gate in the outer wall.

The Kechla and the National Ceramic Museum

Open Wed–Mon 9am–12pm, 2–4pm; closed Tues; adm.

From Place de l'Indépendance, a walk up Av Moulay Youssef past battlements, a cemetery, the ornate koubba of the **Ouled ben Zmirou Besseba** Jewish saints and part of a park leads to a traffic junction, off which is the entrance to the Kechla. The two unequal crenellated round towers were built by the Portuguese in the 16th century. The offices of the governor were moved up here from the Ksar el Bahr in the 18th century, and a courtyard, garden, towers and new apartments constructed within. At the entrance are two cannon cast in The Hague for the sultan. In the centre of the internal courtyard is a **koubba** shaded by two overhanging trees. A broad Andalusian pavement leads up to the summit of the large round tower lined with British cannon and fitted with a *garderobe*. The high white towers, roofed in green tiles, are open and offer excellent views of the fishing fleet, sea fortress, potteries and the medina. The old courtyard jail and mosque can be seen immediately below, though the inmates have been moved to the gaol at El-Jadida.

The collection of the **National Ceramic Museum** is divided into two sections. The Safi-made pottery is arranged in a long corridor on the southern side of the Kechla, while the older wares made in Fès and Meknès are housed in the elegant rooms around the green paved courtyard built by Sidi Mohammed in the 18th century. Safi is a relative newcomer to the traditional pottery centres, for although earthenware has been produced here since time immemorial its present status is due to the arrival of master potters from Fès and Meknès, who migrated towards this rich new seam of clay in the 18th century. It was given a further fillip when the Algerian master Lamalli settled here in 1918, and set about teaching all the unbroken traditions of the Maghreb. The most striking aspect of the display is his success, for there is a strong sense of continuity, in shape, pattern, colour and design, from pieces made centuries ago down to the pottery that can be seen being produced today just 300m away.

Potters' Quarter (Quartier des Potiers)

You can cut across the park around the Kechla to visit the Quartier des Potiers. Scattered around a valley that is still quarried for clay, the potters of Safi are a large and well-established guild whose kilns and workshops stretch deep inland. The delightful confusion of potteries are arranged on terraces littered with shards. The puffing beehive kilns, fired with tamarisk brushwood and covered with palm leaves, are the same as they have been for centuries.

Great lorry-loads of wood are delivered, tanks of wet clay stand ready, while the shovelled clay is kneaded and cleaned of impurities elsewhere before being worked on wheels in subterranean sheds, sun-dried, stacked, fired, painted, glazed and fired again. Stacks of tiles, drums, plates and bowls are sold in bulk to wholesalers who distribute them around the country. The relatively low temperature of the kilns restricts production to relatively thick earthenware, which for longevity, delicacy and price can never compete with the thinner 'porcelains' that can only be achieved with carefully controlled high temperatures.

A training school and market square lined with booths has been established just above the café by the Bab Châabah. An excitingly full range of local pottery is exhibited here to be freely handled and gently bargained over. Prices are seldom lower elsewhere, the range never so extensive. No one should leave Safi without encumbering their baggage with a few pots. The traditional polychrome or blue-on-white decorations with tracery or geometric patterns are perennial favourites. The range has recently been greatly expanded by the use of metal rims and a variety of coloured glazes, such as burnt yellow, thin blue and glassy green. These glazes can be particularly attractive when set over a plain complementary colour.

Bab Châabah takes you back to Rue du Souk, or you can continue outside the walls through the Bab Khouas and visit the fishing harbour. Home to over 200 boats, Safi is one of the busiest sardine ports in the world, landing over 40,000 tonnes of fish a year. The commercial port further north is still being extended and mostly handles the export of phosphates.

Where to Stay

expensive

The **Safir**, ✆ (04) 464299, is at the seaward end of Av Zerktouni, about 500m west of Place Mohammed V, and has a splendid position tucked into a corner of the public gardens with a view over the medina. To find it, take Av Mohammed V uphill from the Kechla roundabout until you reach the new mosque, where you turn right. It has plenty of facilities such as a pool, bar and restaurant, but like many such large hotels it is geared to the group trade, and feels very sad whenever there is no-one else there.

moderate

The **Atlantide**, ✆ (04) 462160, sits 150m south of the Safir on Rue Chaouki. The directions to it are the same as for the Safir, but carry on beyond it for another 200m. The Atlantide has 50 rooms, a restaurant, an extensive but run-down garden, a bar and a certain dignity, with its octagonal columned hall and dilapidated grand piano. The bar acts as a local clubhouse in the evening while lunch is dominated by the phosphate company. Apart from breakfast, eat elsewhere.

inexpensive

The **Assif**, ✆ (04) 622311, (04) 621862 on Av de la Liberté (just 50m south of Place Mohammed V) has rather tied up the passing trade. It is an immaculately clean, tidy place with 30 bedrooms simply furnished with wood and local weaving. The ground floor is occupied by a café and good but unlicensed restaurant. Picnics can be acquired in the concrete hangar of a covered market just to the east. If it is full, go to the **Anis**, ✆ (04) 463078, on Rue de la Falaise.

cheap

There are a number of cheap hotels in the medina which are all found off the central Rue du Souk or facing out to sea by the iron railings of the port. **L'Avenir**, © (04) 462657, has a café downstairs and some rooms with a sea view. The **Hôtel de Paris**, © (04) 462149, is arranged around a cool central courtyard, with a fading poster of a panther and some worn chairs.

Eating Out

expensive/moderate

Once you have consumed a bottle of chilled rosé and a plate of *crevettes provençales* followed by a *plateau de fruits de mer* while watching the port lights from the terrace of **Le Refuge**, © (04) 464354 at Sidi-Bouzid (4km north on the coast road, *see* p.246), it is difficult to imagine any better way to spend your first evening at Safi. If you're here for a second night try **La Trattoria Chez L'Italienne**, 2 Route de L'Aouinate, © (04) 620959 (closed Sun), an excellent Italian restaurant just 300m north of Bab Khouas on the Sidi-Bouzid road. People travel hundreds of kilometres to eat in Safi.

cheap

The cheaper fish grills and cafés are all clustered around the entrance to Rue du Souk or along Place de l'Indépendance opposite the Ksar el Bahr. It isn't hard to sniff out your own place, but two well-established favourites are the **Restaurant Calypso**, in a courtyard garden off the Place, which provides a fine three-course lunch of fish, salad and fruit at a very good price, and **El Bahia**, which has an à la carte dining room perched upstairs from the ground-floor café. A fairly new addition, the **Gegène** restaurant and bar just uphill from the **De Safi** café, has also been recommended. Other cheap no-alcohol places in the new town include the Asif hotel and **Le Poulet d'Or**, at 65 Av Mohammed V.

Shopping

Safi is not a tourist destination and the prices asked for the bold geometric **carpets** for sale in one or two of the shops in the new town can be encouraging. The price, and to a lesser extent the choice, of ceramics is also excellent. The **souk** is held on Mondays. The covered food market is in the new town, by the intersection of Av de la Liberté and Av Moulay Ismaïl, about 100m southeast of Place Mohammed V.

Sports and Activities

Ask at the stud farm on the way out to Essaouira if you are interested in **horse-riding**. **Tennis** is available on Rue Marceau. **Swimming** is best at Sidi-Bouzid, Lalla-Fatna or Cap Beddouza to the north, or in summer time in the municipal pool in the park south of the Kechla.

Souira Kédima

The coast road 6537, having passed the last effusions of the phosphate plant, leads in 33km to the dune-girt beach of Souira Kédima. Halfway there a turning towards the sea takes you to the **Shrine of Jorf-el-Yhoudi**, the Jews' fort.

Souira Kédima, sometimes spelt Quadima, was mentioned by the geographer El Bekri as 'the old enclosure', which refers to the *rabat* of Agouz, an Almoravid bastion that stood here. There are no longer any remains of it visible, although there is a substantial square Portuguese fort of Agouz, built in 1521 but abandoned only four years later. It is a sturdy rectangle 40m by 25m, with a round tower in the southeast corner. Fishermen formerly made use of the courtyard as their camp, but today they are housed in a functional rectangular barracks arranged around a mosque, with store cupboards, dormitories, workshops, a bakery and a terraced café. Much of the time their small boats are beached in a delightful confusion of colours and nets on the shore. A little further on there is an encampment of holiday bungalows, a campsite and the **Echabba** Restaurant, where you can have fresh grilled fish and *tagines* served on a bamboo-canopied terrace. It only functions in high summer, when it becomes Safi's beach club.

Kasba-Hamidouch

A few kilometres after Souira Kémida a recently-built road crosses the river Tensift. Just before the third white concrete milestone beyond the bridge (nearly 3km on) there is a dirt track with sandy patches that takes you towards a plantation of blue gum trees that camouflage the extensive walls of Kasba-Hamidouch. The kasbah was built by Sultan Moulay Ismaïl in the 17th century just above the river, which once flowed into the moat surrounding the crumbling remants of the central keep. This fortress is offset from the northeast corner of a much larger enclosure, a vast extent of mud walls, topped by disintegrating parapets and guarded by a number of toppling towers. The deserted site is now also guarded by dozens of hawks and storks, which nest in the crumbling walls.

Jbel Hadid

Until recently Souira Kédima and Kasba-Hamidouch could only be reached by a dead-end road from Safi. Now, however, the 6611 road continues south through the undisturbed countryside of the Regrada directly to Essaouira. It's a wonderful drive, past fields laboriously cleared of rock and enclosed in drystone walls, hamlets built from drystone and thatch, and the hitherto remote shrines of the Jbel Hadid. The whitewashed shrine of **Moulay-Bouzerktoun** (about 30km north of Essaouira), perched above the beach amidst sand dunes and surrounded by a few low village buildings, has a particularly serene air.

The Seven Saints of Regrada

The Regrada are Chleuh Berbers who speak the Tachelait dialect. They have always lived on the Jbel Hadid, the 'iron mountain', a network of hard limestone hills partly covered in low woods and dense maquis that is still populated with jackals, wild boar and mountain fox. It stretches south from the

N
300 metres
300 yards
Essaouira
Bastion Nord
Sqala de la Ville
Sqala de la Kasbah
RUE LAATOUJ
Town Museum
RUE SIDI MOHAMMED BEN ABDALLAH
SOUK
SOUK
Hotel Riad Al-Madina
RUE EL ATTARIN
AVENUE DE L'ISTIQLAL
MEDINA
Grand Mosque
RUE D'AGADIR
RUE DE LA SQALA
Place Moulay Hassan
OLD KASBAH QUARTER
Place Chaouni
Clock-tower
NEW KASBAH QUARTER
Hotel Villa Maroc
AVENUE OQBA BEN NAFIL
RUE DU CAIRE
Galerie Frédéric Damgaard
Bab es Sebaa
Orson Welles Square
Customs
Chalet de la Plage
Hotel des Iles
BOULEVARD MOHAMMED V
Sqala du Port
Marine Gate
Customs Gate
Entrance to harbour
Fish grill-cafés
Chez Sam

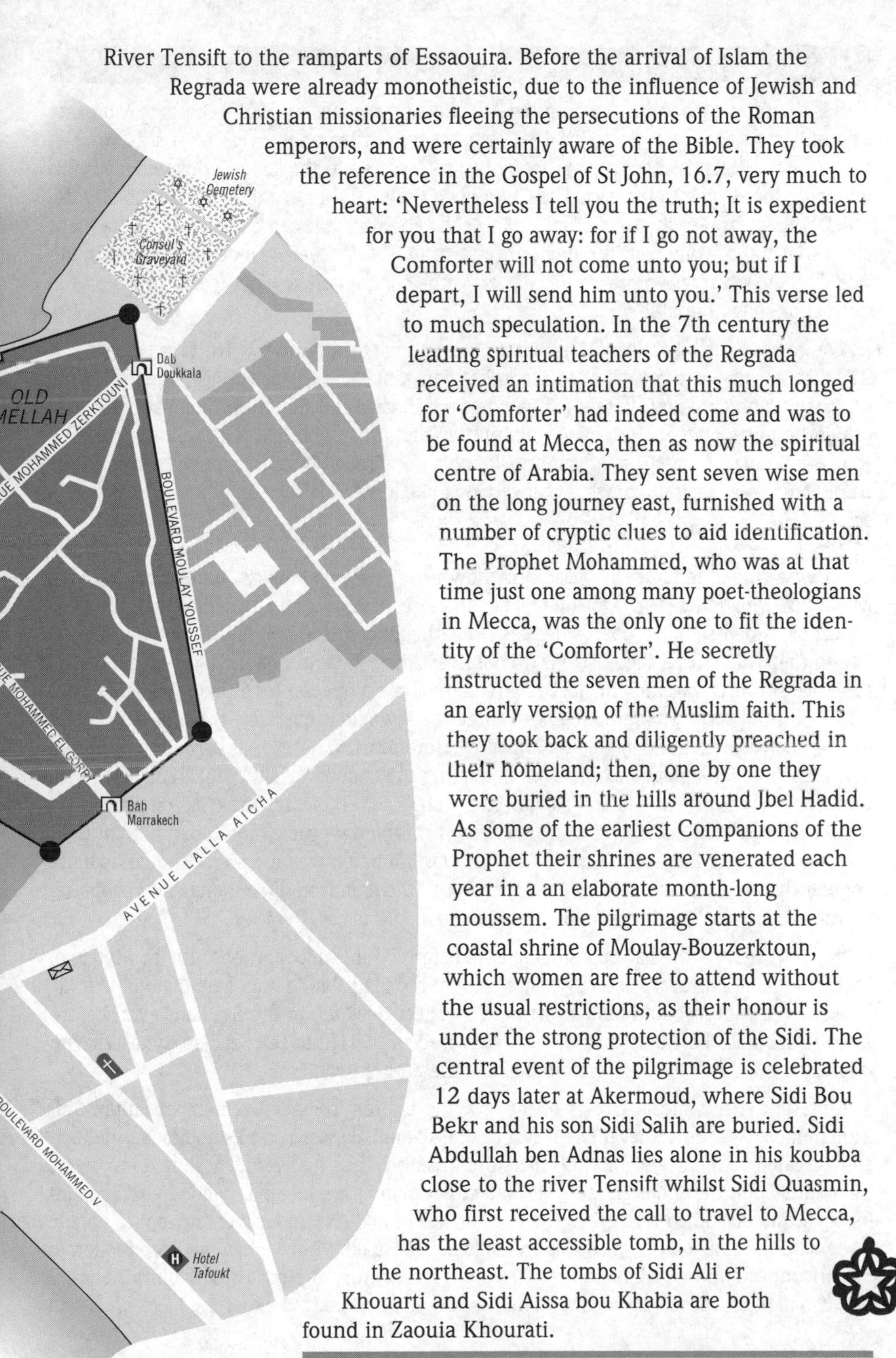

River Tensift to the ramparts of Essaouira. Before the arrival of Islam the Regrada were already monotheistic, due to the influence of Jewish and Christian missionaries fleeing the persecutions of the Roman emperors, and were certainly aware of the Bible. They took the reference in the Gospel of St John, 16.7, very much to heart: 'Nevertheless I tell you the truth; It is expedient for you that I go away: for if I go not away, the Comforter will not come unto you; but if I depart, I will send him unto you.' This verse led to much speculation. In the 7th century the leading spiritual teachers of the Regrada received an intimation that this much longed for 'Comforter' had indeed come and was to be found at Mecca, then as now the spiritual centre of Arabia. They sent seven wise men on the long journey east, furnished with a number of cryptic clues to aid identification. The Prophet Mohammed, who was at that time just one among many poet-theologians in Mecca, was the only one to fit the identity of the 'Comforter'. He secretly instructed the seven men of the Regrada in an early version of the Muslim faith. This they took back and diligently preached in their homeland; then, one by one they were buried in the hills around Jbel Hadid. As some of the earliest Companions of the Prophet their shrines are venerated each year in a an elaborate month-long moussem. The pilgrimage starts at the coastal shrine of Moulay-Bouzerktoun, which women are free to attend without the usual restrictions, as their honour is under the strong protection of the Sidi. The central event of the pilgrimage is celebrated 12 days later at Akermoud, where Sidi Bou Bekr and his son Sidi Salih are buried. Sidi Abdullah ben Adnas lies alone in his koubba close to the river Tensift whilst Sidi Quasmin, who first received the call to travel to Mecca, has the least accessible tomb, in the hills to the northeast. The tombs of Sidi Ali er Khouarti and Sidi Aissa bou Khabia are both found in Zaouia Khourati.

Essaouira

This is the most enchanting town on the Atlantic, and perhaps on all the coasts of Morocco. The old town and port, encircled by 18th-century battlements, overlook a scattering of barren, wave-worn islands. A great sandy bay sweeps out to the south, while wooded hills dominate the skyline to the east. The old parts of the town, the medina, the kasbah and the *mellah*, fully express the exoticism of Morocco. The dark alleys are broken with frequent arches, and the women of the town are mysteriously concealed under their enveloping *haiks.* At dusk the call to prayer echoes across the silhouetted skyline unchallenged by the distracting sound of traffic.

Essaouira has a remarkably equable climate: the average temperature is 18° C in January and 22° C in August. The coastal wind is another constant—the town will never appeal to the mass suntanning market. Rooms are easy to find all year and the mixed population of fishermen, farmers, craftsmen, tourists and multilingual urban youths coexist effortlessly. The town's potential for hassle, after you have found a hotel room, is small, though hashish might be offered in a conspiratorial whisper if you look like a potential consumer.

History

Es-saouira, 'the little ramparts', has been known over the millennia as Amougdoul, Migdol, Mogdoul, Mogdoura and Mogador. The offshore isles are still collectively known as Mogador, a name that probably derives from the Phoenician *migdol*, a look-out tower. Phoenician sailors used these islands from at least the 7th century BC, while archaeological evidence suggests that the principal villa remained in occupation for a thousand years from 500 BC to 500 AD. Though there is no evidence it would seem likely that this was a base for the silent barter trade in gold described by Herodotus. The excavations also confirmed that a sizeable settlement specialized in extracting the famous Tyrian purple, crimson to us, from shellfish during King Juba II's reign. King Juba's son, Ptolemy, was wearing just such a purple when the circus crowds at Lyon cheered this young prince more heartily than their own monarch, the Emperor Caligula. Caligula was infuriated that any prince should be more popular than himself and had his cousin Ptolemy (the grandson of Anthony and Cleopatra) murdered, driving Morocco into full rebellion against Rome.

In the 11th century the bay opposite the islands formed the chief port of southern Morocco. King Manuel of Portugal seized Essaouira early in his campaign to dominate the whole trade and coast of Morocco and built a fort here in 1506. This fell to the Saadians even before Agadir, the main Portuguese base, was recovered in 1541, but the Saadian dynasty (who originated from the far south) preferred to use the port of Agadir.

The present shape and character of the town is entirely the achievement of Sultan Sidi Mohammed. Agadir had never been loyal to the Alaouite dynasty, and Essaouira was deliberately created to replace it. In 1760 the sultan used his captive French architect-engineer, Théodore Cournut, to design the walls and street plan of the medina, which helps account for their unaccustomed regularity. The Jews of Agadir and Azzemour were invited to handle trade with the Christians, which was dramatically boosted by Sidi Mohammed's reduction of import duties and free-trade policies. By the 19th century the port of Essaouira handled nearly half of Morocco's trade: importing Manchester cottons and exporting bales of ostrich feathers, almonds, gum arabic, ebony, ivory and dried camel skins. The commercial connection with Britain was strong, and tea was first imported to Morocco through this port, a drink which, with the addition of mint and French-imported sugar, took the nation by storm. The distinctive Moroccan teapot was first manufactured in Manchester by creating a fusion from the existing Andalusian and Yemeni patterns.

The port was also the home of a flourishing and only partly clandestine trade in arms. The Berber *caids* of the High Atlas, the Arab tribes of the plains, and sheiks from the Sahara all had their commercial agents at Essaouira who purchased arms and munitions and also presided over ransom negotiations. By the turn of the century the local Berber chieftains had grown predominant, while other trade had all but withered away. In 1906 a Berber chief from the Haha, Caid Anflous, brushed aside the government garrison, rode into the town at the back of 200 horsemen and efficiently looted the medina. An apocryphal story records that six years later on a windswept day Marshal Lyautey inspected the empty streets of the dispirited town. He rode away confirmed in his plans to create the new commercial centre of Morocco around Casablanca and Kénitra. Since then an assorted group of artists, windsurfers and hippies have put up with its damp winds and fallen in love with the town, though only such cultural heroes as Orson Welles, Jimi Hendrix and Cat Stevens (who, as Yusuf Islam, still comes here frequently) are remembered much.

Getting Around

by bus

All buses use the new bus station, plonked in some drab pot-holed streets about a 1.5km walk from Bab Doukkala on the northern edge of the medina. Walking towards the conspicuous town walls from the bus station is relatively easy, though if there is a *petit taxi* around (anywhere in town should be under 10dh), take it. For a dawn departure *petits taxis* can be more elusive. Walking to the bus station from Bab Doukkala, take the first right and second left, then continue along for 500m until you reach an assortment of cafés and the different booths of the bus companies, including CTM. There are at least four departures a day to Casablanca (7hr journey by one of the two CTM night buses, 9hrs by private line), plus six to Marrakech (4hr), six to Agadir (4hrs), two to Safi (6hrs) and two to El-Jadida (8hrs).

The ONCF operate a connecting service to the nearest **railway** station, which is in Marrakech. Their coach leaves from outside the Hotel des Isles at 6.30am in time to meet the nine o'clock train to Casablanca. Tickets and any timetable changes can be obtained from the reception desk of the hotel.

by car and taxi

Arriving by car the main approach to the town, the coastal Av Mohammed V, leads directly to the car park (10dh a day) that stands between the port and Place Moulay el Hassan and the old town.

Petits taxis can usually be found at a rank by the clocktower on Av de L'Istiqlal, at the bus station or along the beach road. ***Grands taxis*** operate from the bus station but will usually be happy to deposit arrivals on the open square between the port and the medina. They mostly serve routes to nearby inland market towns, but you should be able to charter a full car to Agadir or Marrakech for around 300dh.

Orientation and Tourist Information

Once you have arrived there is no need for any transport. Essaouira is an easy, relaxing place to walk around and explore, although it is worth fixing the general layout in your mind. From the broad square between the port and the walled town there are two entrances. The arched gateway leads to a straight thoroughfare known successively as Av Oqba ben Nafia–Av de l'Istiqlal–Av Mohammed Zerktouni. This arcaded way, lined with courtyards, is the souk and main shopping street of the town, and leads directly to the Bab Doukkala on the northern end of the medina.

To the north of the square between the port and the walled town is Place Prince Moulay el Hassan. This is the social hub of the town for visitors, lined with cafés, restaurants, a few cheap hotels and the Banque Populaire.

The **tourist office** is in a shed in the square between the medina and the port. It is not often open, but has a beautiful wooden model of the northern ramparts. There are leaflets, but not another scrap of information.

The **post office** is on Av. Lalla Aicha, the avenue which encircles the town walls just east of the Hotel des Isles. It is open from 8am–6pm, but there is little need to go there, as you can make **phone calls** from Jack's Kiosk on Place Moulay el Hassan and buy **stamps** from the kiosk below the clock tower on Av Oqba ben Nafia. There are four **banks** around or just outside Place Moulay el Hassan; the BMCE, Banque Populaire, BCM and Credit du Maroc.

The Port

The harbour is guarded by the L-shaped **Skala du Port**, the port bastion, where two castellated towers and great banks of cannon once commanded the northern and westerly approaches. Two land gates still control entrance to the enclosed quays of the harbour. Do not be put off by the guards standing around by these gates: despite appearances you are perfectly free to join the rest of the town and take a leisurely stroll through the docks, in order to admire the massed nets, flag-fluttering floats and busy decks of the fishing boats. The sardine fishing fleet, the third largest in Morocco, provides a great spectacle of activity in the early morning or after dusk. The southern edge of the quay is occupied by ship builders, working on a line of emerging wooden hulls that illustrate every stage of the fascinating process of construction.

Just beyond the customs gatehouse a new fish-restaurant has been built, **Le Coquillage** or Restaurant du Port Essaouira, with exterior walls ornamented with swirling rococo designs in a dozen different shells among which swim mosaic fish. Do not ruin the effect by going inside, for the dining room is devoted to the passing coach trade. Just beyond it is a double alley of open-air seafood grills, which cook throughout the year and compete relentlessly with each other for every chance at some passing business. It is as well to settle a price amicably in advance before taking your place on one of the blue benches. Gulls cry overhead, and a gentle sea breeze wafts away the tempting odours of roasting sardines and crabs.

The main entrance to the harbour is through the **Porte de la Marine**, which you may occasionally find shut. It is one of the town's most famous structures. Its 18th-century architect, Cournut, achieved an equable fusion of traditions—details from a classical gateway combine with the green-tiled pyramid roof of a koubba. It is, like most of the town, a forerunner of 20th-century neo-Moorish public architecture, achieved at a time when Morocco was assertively independent. The three crescents of the Moroccan navy, a device borrowed from the Ottoman Turks, stand proudly carved into the limestone by an inscription that records that the gate was erected by Sultan Sidi Mohammed in 1769, year 1184 of the Hegira.

The Town

The best place to get the flavour of Essaouira is **Place Moulay el Hassan**. The square is lined with elegant, tall white houses picked out in blue that help give it a tranquil and intimate atmosphere. The cafés seem to break down the strongest reserve, while the travellers who have arrived for a day but stayed for a few weeks are quick to offer an exchange of books or some tedious but well meaning advice. Avoid their solicitations by arming yourself with an elegant little booklet on Islamic mysticism that can be acquired across the Place at Jack's Kiosk. Do not ignore the beggars, like most of the other tourists, but befriend them immediately with a silver coin. They are a feature of the place, and there is nothing more rewarding than earning their salute in the morning rather than trying (ineffectually) to avoid their unremitting attention. The impressive doorway on the right of the square, no 17, once led into the law court, but now serves an indoor basketball court. In the evening the empty square between Port and Place becomes alive with colourful kaftans, as the inhabitants outnumber tourists for the paseo.

Skala de la Ville

There are three alleys to the left of Place Moulay el Hassan, looking towards the town. Any of these will lead you through the shade of high tenements, past fine carved stone doorways and under connecting arches to the town battlements, the Skala de la Ville, and the round tower of the north bastion. A 200m terrace is lined with bronze cannon, most of them cast for Philip II and Philip III of Spain. The crenellated walls look out over a rocky shore to the Atlantic and the outlying islets.

The Woodcarvers' Souk

In the casemates and pebble-paved courtyards below the bastion and tower some of the skilled joiners and carvers of Essaouira have their workshops. The root boles of thuja trees can be seen piled at the doorways, where young apprentices work on the less skilled tasks. The rich, resinous smell of the wood is a great attraction and the craftsmen are usually happy to demonstrate their skills. Thuja wood has a rich chestnut colour; the root bole *racine de thuja* provides a rich confusion of knots, while the trunk *tige de thuja* has a plainer, striped grain. Acacia and ebony are both dark woods that are contrasted very successfully with the light pale wood of the lemon-tree. Shells, mother of pearl, strips of silver and copper are also inserted to create astonishingly inlaid tables, chests and cabinets. Essaouira also has the best selection of trays, chessboards, dice cups, thuja boxes and backgammon sets. Similar work seen in other cities is likely to have come from Essaouira, and be more expensive. You should bargain in the bazaars, but the cooperatives in town and the casemate workshops have less time for negotiations and generally offer a reasonable first price. Any hinges and locks should be examined carefully—skill with wood is seldom matched with much love for metalwork.

The Museum

Open Wed–Mon 8.30–12pm, 2.30–6pm ; closed Tues; adm.

The ethnography museum of Sidi Mohammed Ben Abdallah is found on the southern side of Rue Laâlouj, the street which leads from the Skala de la Ville back to the centre of town. Originally constructed in the early 19th-century as the town house of a pacha, it was transformed into the town hall during the French Protectorate, with the unfortunate addition of a monolithic central staircase that now completely dominates the central courtyard. The museum has recently been overhauled and extended, to become a delightful repository for the traditional crafts, textiles, carpets, clothing, jewelry and weapons of the region, as well as of some early maps, engravings and sketches of the town. The notes beside the exhibits are self-explanatory and concise, especially those concerned with the origin of the different musical instruments and their close relationship with the Sufi brotherhoods. The director also has an admirable collection of literature in his office which is available to those who wish to pursue any further interest. The effects of tourism are not always negative, for in the past five years the museum has produced over half a dozen publications (mostly in French) to feed the inquisitive minds of its visitors.

Past the museum, at the central crossroads, the Rue Mohammed ben Abdallah leads up through the medina into the dark, secretive passages of the *mellah*, the old Jewish quarter, and then out into the main street just before the Bab Doukkala.

The Medina Thoroughfare

From the main square outside the port, the high red archway with its green tiled roof (sometimes used to house exhibitions of art) leads to the old ***méchouar***, now the tree-lined Av Oqba ben Nafia. This attractive broad avenue was originally an assembly place, where the garrison paraded and processions were marshalled. The rectangular area of tall housing to the east is the new kasbah, for the old kasbah area around the Place Moulay el Hassan proved inadequate and in the 19th century a new quarter was constructed for government offices, many of which are still housed here. Avenue du Caire leads from the old *méchouar* to the strongly guarded Bab Sebaa. The triangular patch of open ground just to the south of the gate has recently been named **Orson Welles Square** and provided with a plaque to commemorate that fantastic polymath who was producer, director and principal actor of the film *Othello*, which was mainly shot here in 1949. Though his financial backers deserted him he won the affection of the town, who for a mere 2dh a day each provided him with all the craftsmen and extras he wanted, while everyone was fed on sardines.

The east side of Av Oqba ben Nafia is lined with hotels and a growing number of art galleries, led by **Galerie d'Art Frederic Damgaard**. The fortified west side of the Avenue (the city walls, before the construction of the new kasbah) is dominated by a distinctive clocktower beneath which is an archway leading into the small kilim-lined and cafe-overlooked Place Chefchaouni. Pass under the second archway (occupied by Damgaard's framing workshop) to twist past more intriguingly furnished bazaars and inviting cafés before passing beneath the old kasbah and returning to Place Moulay el Hassan.

Alternatively, take the archway at the northern end of Av Oqba ben Nafia, which leads to the civil area of the old town and the central thoroughfare of **Avenue de l'Istiqlal**. It is here that you notice how far south you have come. The women of the town are well covered in *haiks*, great drapes of brown or white cotton or wool with which they obscure their figures while on the streets, leaving only a pair of dazzling brown eyes glinting through a fold. To the right, on the east side, rises the minaret of the **grand mosque**, its spacious prayer-hall mostly tucked out of sight. The 200m-long avenue is largely devoted to kitchen and hardware stalls, piled high beneath the green-tiled overhang and framed by blue shutters.

The heart of the town's trading is reached at the central crossroads. The central souk area, known as **Souk Jdid**, lined with an arcade of short stone arches, is enclosed by twin gate ways. Off to the west are courtyards housing fish, chicken and spice markets. To the east the *fondouqs* house old metalware and other second-hand goods; jellabas and kilims; as well as the densely packed network of jewellers' booths. North of these souks, Avenue de l'Istiqlal, now lined with a blue-tiled arcade, becomes devoted to the vegetable and grocery trade.

The Consuls' Graveyard and the Jewish Cemetery

Out through the Bab Doukkala the small area immediately on the left has been designated the Place des Artistes, and has 24 kiosks where students can sell their work directly to the public in the summer season. Just beyond, at the seaward corner, a tattered gateway leads to the enclosed Christian cemetery. A bustle of assorted European consuls, doctors and priests lies buried here. These include two figures from the diffuse world of English literary-consuls. R. N. L. Johnston produced *Fadma* in 1906, a fervent poem of devotion dedicated to the Mother Goddess which he pretended to have translated from the Chleuh poet and mystic Sidi Hammo. C. A. Payton, his 19th century predecessor, was a stout white-bearded man from Scarborough who flooded the pages of the *Field* for 16 years with descriptions of his fishing expeditions around Essaouira under the pen-name 'Sarcelle'.

A much larger Jewish cemetery borders this graveyard to the north, and you can sometimes get to it through a small door in the far corner. Schist blocks with their symbolic carvings and Hebraic script lie apparently haphazard over the tightly-packed compound. The Jews of Essaouira were always the chosen intermediaries between the Moors of the interior and European merchants. The Jewish community consequently developed enduring relationships with various trading firms and a cosmopolitan scattering of kin. Benjamin Disraeli is one of the most celebrated of these, for his father Isaac, author of *Curiosities of Literature*, lived for a few years as a child in the *mellah* of Mogador.

Leslie Hore-Belisha, who served as both Home Secretary and War Minister in Britain in the 1930s, was the third-generation descendant of a Mogador-Manchester trader who settled in England. Seeking to impress, a visitor to the town informed the Belishas who still lived in the *mellah* of their cousin's great status. To which they glibly replied, glancing briefly up from their holy books, that yes they had heard that young Leslie was for the moment high in the counsels of a northern city. Nicholas Shakespeare has recently tracked the old Hore-Belisha (Horeb-Elisha) house in the *mellah* down to 56 Rue el Mellah. The entire Jewish community, once 9,000 strong, has now left their old quarter, the first wave in 1948, the few remaining following in 1967. In the words of a local shopkeeper, 'One day we woke up and they were gone.'

Berber Souk

The Berber market keeps to the coastal fringe of Essaouira but otherwise has to move slowly north as the town grows. An uninspiring walk past new houses and the large leather factory brings you to the compound where vegetables, charcoal, old and new clothes are sold to a bustling crowd on Thursdays and Sundays.

The Beach

The beach to the south of the town, protected from the full force of the Atlantic surf and current, is one of the safer bays on this coast in which to swim. The area nearest the town is often occupied by football games and piles of seaweed, but as you walk out further towards the **ruined fort** the sand gets cleaner and the beach emptier. This ruin is for once not a Portuguese relic but a remnant of Sultan Sidi Mohammed's defence system. Built on a rocky promontory, the fortress's compact walls have split but not disintegrated, despite being washed daily by the incoming tide.

Back from the beach and screened slightly by the dunes is the town's stumpy lighthouse, built beside the koubba of one of the town's patron saints, **Sidi M'gdoul**. There is a story about the origin of this saint which claims that he was a Scottish merchant called McDougall who saw the error of his hard-hearted ways, and having converted to Islam settled down in a hermitage on the shore to help the poor of the town. The more historically minded will recall that Essaouira used to be known by its old Carthaginian title of Migdol, which gives the saint an even more venerable link to another widely-scattered trading nation.

Diabat

A walk inland from the fort, along the estuary of the river Ksob, will take you across the fallen bridge to the straggling village of Diabat. A right turn about 7km south along the Agadir road could also bring you here by car.

The villagers of Diabat still seem to maintain a noticeably cold air to visitors, for Diabat is notorious for a multiple beach murder in the late sixties. This brought a climactic end to the hippie settlement that had grown up along the beach in the wake of Jimi Hendrix, whose drug consumption, sexual energy and death set standards which few have been able to follow. He had attempted to buy Diabat in order to secure the future of the encampment. Yusuf Islam, formerly Cat Stevens, spends his summers in Essaouira today , but his orthodox Muslim lifestyle attracts much less of a cult following.

Beside the road is the ruined compound of an old tanning factory, with engineering equipment supplied by Huxham & Brown of Exeter quietly rusting away. Towards the shore from the factory and now besieged by dunes and shrubbery is the palace built in the 18th century by Sultan Sidi Mohammed, the **Dar Soltane Mahdounia**. A pavilion can be seen in the centre surrounded by the walls of a square keep, decorated with low towers on each corner. The eastern tower can be entered through a low tunnel; the room it leads to still retains some of its mosaic flooring and a thin strip of plaster carved with Koranic verses on the wall. A small balcony with three arches that used to overlook the port now surveys a prospect of encroaching dunes and a wall of vegetation.

The **Auberge Tangaro**, off the Diabat approach road, is a delightful sanctuary where you can buy fresh-squeezed orange juice and sit on the sunbaked terrace listening to the rattle of the wind pump. Seven km further south a dirt track will take you to **Cap Sim**, with its windswept dunes, empty sands and fine view of Essaouira.

The Isles of Mogador

These half-dozen islands are periodically closed to visitors, but in the last few years have been accessible to those prepared to go to *Province*, the modern administrative headquarters guarded by gendarmes and set back from the coast road in Essaouira. Armed with your passport you can then respectfully wait upon an official and within an hour or two receive written authorisation for a visit on the following day. It is then a comparatively easy matter for your permit to be double-checked by the port authorities, so that the fishing boat you charter from the harbour can be seen to have life jackets. The last but most crucial detail is to bargain ferociously over the price before you put so much as a foot into the boat. I tried to insist on 50dh, but ended up paying 200dh.

The islands are covered in a low stunted maquis, so take stout shoes. There is a small harbour on the largest island, the **Ile d'Essaouira**, where fishing boats can dock and your papers can be checked by the resident custodian who protects this island nature reserve. The gulls hardly need his help, for they protect their territory themselves by diving at human visitors and regaling them with shit bombs. Your boatman-guide will take you on a tour of the island with its ruined mosque, five artillery bastions and cunningly contrived and still intact rain-fed water cisterns. In the centre of the island is the grim high-walled enclosure of the open-air prison compound, entered through a series of five diminishing gateways. Raissouli (*see* p.169) was imprisoned here for four years, originally shackled by his neck to a

sunbaked wall. He made two failed escape attempts and killed several guards, but with the governor's assistance was granted a pardon on the death of Sultan Moulay Hassan. It is a chilling journey even in the company of a chatty boatman, but nothing can prepare you for the flagpost hill, a rabbit-strewn sandy eminence still littered with the human bones of half buried prisoners. There is little above-ground evidence of the Punic and Roman villa and its associated dyeworks, apart from a scattering of broken amphorae, some half-filled ditches and spoil heaps along the landward facing shore of the island. If you are having trouble identifying it ask to be shown the area where the French dug to discover gold, the local interpretation of the archaeological dig. The shoreline is as busy as a James Bond film with scuba-divers, though these are neither smugglers nor secret agents but fishermen, gathering seaweed into adapted inner tubes of truck tyres.

It is not normally possible to land on **Dzint Faranan**, the smaller of the two islands, unless the sea is very calm, but from a nearby cliff face on the larger island you can observe some spectacular caves on its northern shore, a tide-washed inner lagoon and the feeding activities of that most elegant and rare bird of prey the Eleonora's falcon, dining off young pigeon squabs and gull chicks.

Where to Stay

expensive

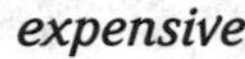

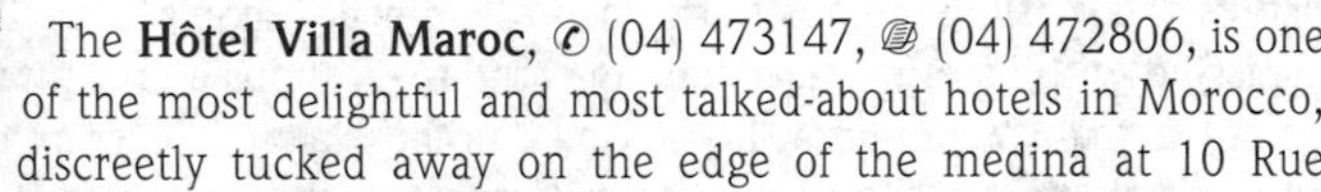

The **Hôtel Villa Maroc**, ✆ (04) 473147, ✉ (04) 472806, is one of the most delightful and most talked-about hotels in Morocco, discreetly tucked away on the edge of the medina at 10 Rue Abdellah Ben Yacine—to find it go through the archway beside the clock on Av Oqba ben Nafia, turn left and walk down beside the wall for about 60m. It has the intriguingly confusing interior of a traditional house, but one which now proudly displays a scattering of exquisitely furnished sitting rooms lit by fires, and two-dozen bedrooms arranged around a pair of interior courtyards. Breakfast can be taken on the roof terrace or in your room, while dinner (which should be booked in advance) is served at tables tucked around the courtyards. The interior, a fusion of bold Greek colours with a disciplined selection of Moroccan crafts, is a showpiece that has already appeared as background in dozens of fashion shoots. It is usually essential to book in advance, and to be safe you should reserve a room two months ahead, although in practice a last-minute cancellation may often leave a room or two free

If you simply want a pool, reliable plumbing and a sense of spacious ease you will be better off in the **Hôtel des Iles**, ✆ (04) 472329. This well-established hotel stands in a prime position at the northern end of Blvd Mohammed V between the beach and the medina walls. It has 40 bungalows arranged around a garden and swimming pool courtyard, with bar and restaurant nearby in the sturdy pre-war roadside block.

moderate

The **Auberge Tangaro**, ✆ (04) 4784784 direct or (04) 4785735 for its representative in town, is another of Morocco's stunning hotels and its reclusive position, 8km out of town off the road south to Diabat, will always keeps the bulk of tourists and tour groups away. Its charm is based in a calm white-washed simplicity, with a rustic terrace shaded by trees, clad by creepers and overshadowed by a creaking wind-pump. There are just 18 sets of rooms—many suites with two bedrooms—to go with a shared sitting room with a brick fireplace, and bright blue-painted cane chairs on the terrace. Prices are based on a half pension rate; dinner is served in an austere but stylish cool dark cube with a cafe-like tiled floor, and ochre walls atmospherically lit by eighteen brass candlesticks.

The old hotel du Pasha used to be *the* hotel in town as its guest list of distinguished visitors proudly proclaims. After a long period of closure it has resurfaced as the **Hotel Riad Al Madina** at 9 Rue Attarine, © (04) 475727, @ 475727, with 27 bedrooms around a splendidly-restored 18th-century courtyard. There is no licenced bar but the hotel has a fine view from the terrace and, though the decorator responsible for the renovation has tried much too hard to make an effect at times, especially in the bedrooms, the staff are cheerful and willing.

The **Hôtel Tafouket**, © (04) 472504, is on the southern end of town along Blvd Mohammed V, a fair distance from the medina but ideally placed for the sea and sand. Do not let the slightly unpromising exterior put you off. This 40-room hotel is run with a rare blend of efficiency and hospitality. It has its own bar, a good restaurant and faces the beach.

inexpensive

There are five good reasonably priced hotels to choose from. The **Sahara**, © (04) 472292, and **Al Mechouar**, © (04) 472018, are comfortable, slightly humdrum places but easy to find on Av Oqba ben Nafia. The latter is smaller and has its own bar and restaurant, and is generally preferable. For more medina-atmosphere try the **Tafraout**, © (04) 472902, on 7 Rue de Marrakech, or better still **Des Remparts**, © (04) 472508. This is perhaps the dampest and least efficient of the five but is nevertheless a friendly place in which to stay, run by El Houcienne and his son Mustapha. Thirty rooms are arranged around a three-storey interior courtyard. The roof provides a spectacular view perched above the ramparts, and a possible sunbathing spot if you can find a corner out of the wind. It is at 18 Rue Ibn Rochd, the entrance of which is in the far left hand corner (looking inland) of the Place Moulay el Hassan, where you will also smell a bakery in the morning on the opposite side of the street. Deep in the heart of the medina is the **Residence El Mehdi**, © (04) 475943, at 15 Rue Sidi Abdesmith. It's a suprisingly modern place with televisions in every bedroom, a central courtyard with a parrot, a restaurant and the sort of cleanliness and domestic calm which you normally associate with a house, not a hotel.

cheap

The **Hôtel du Beau Rivage**, © (04) 472925, above the **Café de France** in the Place Moulay el Hassan is easily the best option in this bracket: clean, scrupulously honest, and some rooms have a sea view while some overlook the Place. If this is full try the **Hôtel du Tourisme**, © (04) 472075, on Rue Mohammed ben Messaoud. It is perched on the medina walls and offers clean simple rooms, cold water and cats. The **Pension Smara**, © (04) 472334, at 26 Rue de la Skala is another good standby, though a somewhat bossy management offsets some of the charm of the view.

Eating Out

moderate

Chez Sam, ✆ (04) 476513, also known as the 'Restaurant du Port de Peche', is at the far end of the port, a delightful clapper-built restaurant overlooking the harbour and the fishing fleet that at first appears to be a stranded boat-house. Its location, and a reputation for seriously fresh fish, are enough to guarantee a continuous flow of customers. Beware of the combination of low ceilings and walls clad with photos of movie stars who have dined here, which can combine to catch you a suprising blow on the head. The service is famously erratic, so get a good view or plenty to drink so as not to get frustrated. Once you have dined here there is a danger that you may never wish to go elsewhere.

Chalet de la Plage, ✆ (04) 472158, at 1 Blvd Mohammed V, stands on the seafront opposite the Hôtel des Iles, with a terrace directly washed by the tide. It serves alcohol and has a seafood menu and a range of cheaper local dishes. At lunchtime it can be rather over-busy with passing day-trippers, but is less crowded in the evening. The terrace makes a memorable place for a drink at sundown, while the separate local back-bar is occasionally enlivened by live music. Further along the beach front there is the also-licensed restaurant of the **Hôtel Tafouket**, which has cheaper set menus but a more sophisticated à la carte.

On the southern edge of Place Moulay el Hassan is the restaurant **El Khaima**, which serves wholesome filling meals in its over-the-top dining room. Though its kitchen cannot hope to rival some of the smaller cheaper places nearby it has the distinct advantage of serving wine and staying open much later.

You can also dine in the courtyard of **Dar Loubane**, ✆ (04) 476296, a beautiful 18th-century palace furnished with modern orientalist pictures, Mogador memorabilia, some intriguing junk, a fountain and the patrons' beautiful dogs. It is licensed, and the competent menu embraces both French and Moroccan cooking. It's at 24 Rue de Rif, just a few yards from the clocktower arch in the centre of the old town.

cheap

There are four restaurants (none of which serves alcohol) that offer good cheap Moroccan food in and around Place Moulay el Hassan. The **Essalam** provides one of the cheapest and most perfunctory meals with its bargain rates for the set three courses. The café-restaurant **Bab Lachour**, also on the Place, is only slightly more expensive, but more calm. You can eat outside on the café terrace, or upstairs in a first-floor dining room. On the east side of the Place is another series of cafés that includes **Toufiks Restaurant** and **Café L'Horloge**. Toufiks serves a delicious vegetable tagine and freshly-squeezed orange juice in its kilim- and mat-strewn interior; L'Horloge occupies an old synagogue.

The **Riad**, 18 Rue Zayane, in the heart of the medina but well signposted, serves local dishes in imaginative menus amid a tranquil traditional atmosphere. A meal could start with harara, courgette and argan oil salad, then *tagine* with potato soufflé. The Manager, Azriguine el Mostapha, is a charming, informative man.

There are also the outdoor tables of the fish grill-stalls in the Port to remember, as well as a number of good, simple cafés in the larger streets of the medina that serve freshly-fried fish, meatballs and kebabs with a selection of well-spiced and seasoned salads, as well as fish tagines. The largest and best-known of these, known variously as **Chez Sefrani** or **Mustafa's**, is on the corner of Rue Zayane and Rue Sidi Mohammed Ben Abdallah.

cafês and pâtisseries

Aside from the **Café de France** on Place Moulay el Hassan there is the **Petit Algue** on the beach front, which is however outshone by **Chez Driss** at 10 Rue Al Hajalli, an exceptional place founded in 1925 and run by father and son. You can breakfast at one of the tables, and try to exercise self-control with their fresh pastries.

bars

Drinking in Essaouira is confined to restaurants and hotels. In the latter there is a good range in style from the heavily embroidered tent-bar of the **Hôtel des Iles** and functional efficiency of the **Tafouket** down to the cavernous back bar of **Al Mechouar** on Av Oqba ben Nafia, inhabited by almost exclusively beer-drinking locals.

Shopping

In any walk around town you will naturally get exposed to a vast quantity of carved thuja wood, artistically draped kilims, locally knitted thick sweaters, locally made grass slippers, *haiks* and jewellery.

Books, newspapers, an international telephone and fax service and stamps can all be found at **Jack's Kiosk**, 1 Place Moulay el Hassan, ✆ (04) 475538, 📠 476901. Second-hand books, antiquities and much informed talk can be found at **Galerie Aida**, ✆ (04) 476290, at 2 rue de la Skala (walking away from the cafés on Place Moulay el Hassan, take the first right) run by Joseph Sebag, an English speaking ex-habitué of Manhattan and a scion of the famous Sephardic-Jewish family of philanthropists. On this same alley there is also the **No Work** surfer's boutique and a well-stocked and not outrageously-priced carpet-shop.

For pictures your first port of call should be **Galerie d'Art Frederic Damgaard**, ✆ (04) 784446, 📠 472857, on Av Oqba ibn Nafia, which shows the work of local artists, has collaborated in a number of art-books and organises foreign exhibitions. Some major pieces can be priced around $2,000, but the inscrutable Danish dealer is no money snob for there are also folios of unframed student pieces scattered around the gallery and his framing shop in Place Chefchaouèn.

East from Essaouira to Marrakech

There is little over which to delay this journey, though the initial scenery climbing up from the coast through forested hills is pleasant enough. The **koubba of Sidi Amoughal**, the town saint, is just before the main road south to Agadir. Thirty-five km east of Essaouira is the village of **Tleta-Henchane**, 1km off the road, which has a **souk** on Tuesdays. Forty km further on is the shrine and village of **Sidi-Mokhtar**, which has a **souk** each Wednesday.

Chichaoua, just over half way to Marrakech, is the obvious place to stop for a coffee or a *tagine*. It has a **souk** on Sundays and a carpet cooperative with shop attached. For the distinctive history behind this town and its carpets, *see* the *Arab Tribes of the Plain*, p.399.

Haha Province

South of Essaouira lies the province of Haha and the most beautiful portion of the Atlantic coast of Morocco. Rough hills scarred with gorges fall down to the coast. A line of forbidding, high cliffs, that occasionally parts to reveal isolated beaches, seals the land from the sea. The mountainsides are covered in argan woods, trees that grow nowhere else in the world but cling tenaciously enough to these slopes. Goats climb the trees in order to pick the fruit, an initially astonishing and improbable sight. This is often enthusiastically pointed out by children wishing to earn tips from photographers, while their fathers sell bottles of argan oil. Gentler surprises are revealed with the emergence of cultivated valleys from the wilderness of secretive hamlets and agadirs on the barren hills.

The main road to Agadir, the P8, follows a delightful twisting course that has to be repaired each year after the rains rush off the peaks of the High Atlas and wash away part of the road. A large number of dirt tracks of very variable condition extend away from the road deep into the hill country, and offer excellent opportunities to explore the rural Berber hinterland for those with a robust car.

Haha is one of the strongholds of the Berber language. The Tachelait dialect is still widely spoken, and off the main road little French or even Arabic is understood. The indigenous tribes long held a reputation for skilful farming and commerce. Leo Africanus, who travelled through the region in the 15th century, commented on the large number of provincial towns with more than 6000 inhabitants that were scattered across the region. He was the last to be able to comment on this prosperity, for the autonomy of the province was soon to be broken by the Merenid sultans in Fès. They dispatched part of the fierce Bedouin Arab Maql tribe to settle on the plains just to the north, from where they broke the independence and prosperity of the Haha in a series of murderous raids. Despotic governors were sent to rule the land, supported by nomad cavalry. The savagery and corruption of local government in Haha became notorious. A British botanical expedition in the last century heard tales of a governor who punished those who resisted his exactions with the 'leather glove'. The victim had quicklime tightly bound into the palm of his hand which was then soaked in water. When the bindings were removed a few weeks later, only a tattered stump would be revealed.

Eventually a popular rising was planned by all the tribes, but the resourceful governor escaped with 22 mules laden with treasure. He found safe refuge with his friend the *caid* of Chichaoua, and was canny enough to promptly present half his wealth to the sultan. He was permitted to retain the rest, which enabled him to live in great splendour at Marrakech. His kasbah in Haha was of course pillaged after his escape and two of his nephews, long missing, were found entombed in the walls. He had made thoughtful provision that they should not be the last of his victims, for his store of honey was laced with arsenic, and the rebels' victory feast in his hall ended with terrible scenes of mass agony and death. The rebellion spread and the tribes, not for the first or the last time, descended on the rich walled town of Essaouira. In 1847 the sultan, as well as depatching a *harka* or army to burn the land, used his spiritual authority to *sokhta*, solemnly curse, the fertility of the Haha tribes. The tribes sued for peace in the customary manner. Bullocks were sacrificed before the outer gates of the sultan's palace, their front legs cut away so that the animals poured out their lifeblood in a position of stooped supplication on behalf of their masters.

Sidi-Kaouki

A right turn off the P8 about 20km south of Essaouira on to the tarmac road 6604 leads in 11km to the **shrine of Sidi-Kaouki**. Set on the shoreline of a bay, the beach strewn with sea-washed roots and driftwood, the sanctuary is totally encased in a number of bare apartments, all with their own eccentric pattern of sea terraces and fragile stairways. Smoke from driftwood fires has soot-stained the interiors, in contrast to the outer whitewashed walls. A new mosque has also been built, with a surrounding scattering of low dry-stone cottages. At night the shrine is scanned by the rotating light from Cap Sim, and the white walls flash out into the night. There is a popular pilgrimage to the shrine every year in mid-August, for the saint has a reputation for curing the sterility of women. Throughout the year both men and women make lonely pilgrimages and supplications to the saint.

Just south of the shrine and set back from this perfect surfing beach is the newly-constructed **Residence Le Kaouki**, which has several almost monastic single bedrooms. There is a sitting room with a fire and shaded seating outside, shared toilets on each floor and showers on the ground floor. The food is fresh, and excellent. If the hotel is full, the Sidi-Kaouki community can also offer a neighbour who rents rooms, another who rents out horses for rides along the beach, and the café-restaurant **Chez Omar**. There is no direct telephone line, and so bookings for Le Kaouki are taken through the Villa Maroc in Essaouira, ✆ (04) 473147, @ (04) 472806.

Around Smimou

Forty km south is **Smimou**, an unobtrusive town with a pretty, arcaded main street. There are some old working saltworks just outside the town. For a trip inland turn east up the 6606 for 17km to reach **Souk-et-Tnine-Imi-n-Tlit**; the market is on Mondays. The kasbah of **Allal-bou-Fenzi** is 32km further southeast on the 6606, and up a 2km dirt track. The locked keep still stands within the outer wall with its round towers. An old Renault is garaged by the studded wooden doors of the gatehouse. It is the silence and the chance to picnic beside the magnificent view over the hills to the south and west that draws visitors up to this kasbah. The neighbouring village, **Sebt-des-Aïnt-Daoud**, has a souk on Saturdays for the mountain tribe of the Aïnt Daoud. For the truly determined four-wheel driver a track of sorts continues across the mountains to rejoin the P40 Agadir to Marrakech road.

Four km beyond Smimou a dirt track, 6633, to the east (signposted for Souk-et-Tnine-Imi-n-Tlit) climbs up through a landscape of red earth dominated by argan and thuja trees to an especially fine view from **Jbel Amsittene**. A right at the first turning and a left at the second should get you after 16km of twisting road to the foot of the 905m summit. The complete all round view of the Haha, with the High Atlas peaks to the east and the sea to the west, is well worth the effort of climbing to this modest height. Beside the viewing tower dwells the beekeeping guardian, one of those courteous tranquil mountaineers you should remember if you are ever tempted to make wild unflattering generalizations about Moroccans.

Tamanar and Beyond

Sixty-eight km from Essaouira is **Tamanar**, the local administrative centre. There is a **souk** here on Thursdays, and some tempting *tagines* simmering by the roadside. The **Hôtel Etoile du Sud** has basic cheap rooms and makes a convenient stop for coffee, orange juice or a full meal. The Wednesday market at **Arba-des-Ida-ou-Trhouma** is off the road to the east; the turning is 10km south of Tamanar.

Six km further on the P8 a right turn onto a narrow tarmac road leads 20km to **Point Imessouane**, a remote fishing village which is being remade by the Japanese in cast concrete. It is supposedly a gift but no doubt has some tie-in with fishing policy, UN votes and Morocco's rich fishing banks. High season for the fishermen is at the end of summer, when the *tassergal*, a fine fish that can weigh 14 lbs, migrates past this coast. On the sandy beach west of the new port you find a scattering of camper vans as well as a highly organized surfing camp.

Just above the village is the **Berber Auberge**, with a dramatic sea view from its terrace. You can eat and sleep cheaply here in one of the few beds, though most people seem to arrive in a VW van. There is a small strip of sandy beach and rocks you can dive from. It's a popular base for surfers and wind surfers, with its comparatively sheltered cliff-lined bay to the east.

Tamri

One hundred and seventeen km south of Essaouira the road swings around the riverbed at the village of **Tamri**. Bananas are planted in the estuary and sold at the roadside in season, while hallucinogenic euphorbia grows wild on the surrounding hills. The river is partly supplied from the waterfall at Imouzzèr-des-Ida-Outanane (*see* pp.521–2), one of the network of three river valleys that extend east to form the heartland of the Ida Outanane tribe (historically separate from the Haha).

A small beach can be reached along a turning to the right just as you leave the estuary. There is a strong undertow here, for Cape Rhir (Ghir) is only about 17km away. **Amesnaz**, the first safe swimming beach of the Paradise Plage coast, is 30km south of Tamri. This area north of Agadir is covered on pp.520–3.

Meknès and Fès

The heart of Morocco is the plain of Saïss, and upon this plain sit the two Imperial cities of Meknès and Fès. They are the twin pulsating valves that have for centuries fed the sophisticated Arab urban culture of the country, largely derived from Moorish Spain, into the rest of the nation. The Saïss Plain is low and fertile enough to support an urban population, yet is secured from external enemies by the Rif and Middle Atlas mountains that almost entirely enclose it.

The first independent Muslim kingdom of Morocco was established here, upon the shell of the old Roman capital of Volubilis, by a great-grandson of the Prophet Mohammed, Moulay Idriss, at the end of the 8th century AD. The Idrissid state that was created by his son, Idriss II, stands at the core of Moroccan national identity. Idrissid Morocco declined as a political power after a mere century of rule, but it left behind a new city—Fès—where Islam, law, literacy, art, industry and skilled crafts had a safe refuge. The citizens of Fès, the *Fassi*, became an urbane upper-middle class that were sufficient unto themselves. They paid lip-service to the current powers, but kept their true loyalty for the fallen Idrissid dynasty. In the heart of the city of Fès stands the ornate tomb of Idriss II, who to be put in an Anglo-Saxon context must be compared to some fallen Arthur descended from the family of Christ, to whom many of the chief citizens can proudly trace their genealogical descent.

For all their pride and insularity the *Fassi* yet provided a vital pool of skills that were at the disposal of the Almoravids, the Almohads, and any dynasty that could unite the disparate regions of Morocco. Fès is most imperishably linked, though, with the Merenids, who through the 13th and 14th centuries presided over the most prosperous period of the city's history, as well as choosing it to be their capital. There was no love lost between the sultans and the *Fassi*, however, despite the plethora of Merenid buildings in the city. The former dwelt in a separate walled enclosure, the palace city of Fès el Jdid, where all the instruments of government were located.

One of the greatest Moroccan sultans, Moulay Ismaïl, turned his back on the pre-eminence of Fès in the 17th century and attempted to create a new centre for the nation. He built a vast new Imperial City beside the old medieval walled town of Meknès, but within a generation his Herculean building projects had been reduced to the ruins that still strike awe today.

The 20th century saw a gradual shift of the national economy from the interior to the Atlantic coast. Meknès and Fès have long since been eclipsed by the new political and commercial capitals of Rabat and Casablanca, but for a visitor their past glories are one of the central goals of travel in Morocco.

Meknès, Fès and Around

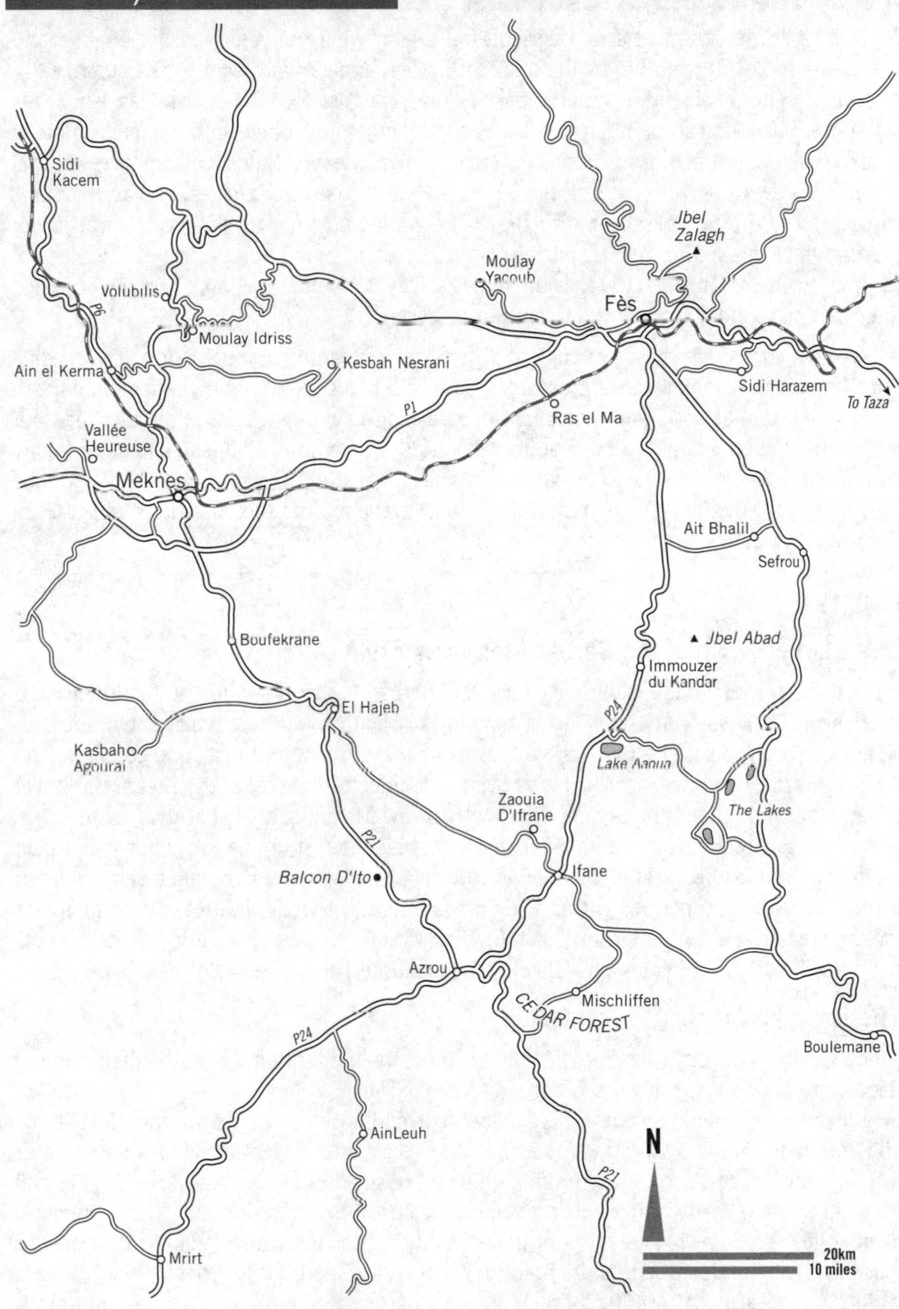

Meknès

Meknès is at the centre of a rich agricultural region where olives, grain, vegetables and grapes are successfully grown by the thick-set Berber farmers who seem to characterize this region. Despite its splendid imperial past as the capital city of Sultan Moulay Ismaïl, its present population of around half a million, an army base and a university, it remains more of a large Berber town than a cosmopolitan urban centre. Meknès is divided into three distinct areas. The new town with its neat, French-built, tree-lined avenues, cafés, bars and hotels is to the east of the Boufekrane river valley. The walled medina, its skyline a confusion of green, white and gold minarets, perches on the western hill. To the south of the medina, through the Bab Mansour, stretches the Imperial City, a bewildering, only partially occupied enclosure surrounded by over 25km of massive pisé walls.

A three-day stay in Meknès is enough to visit all the conventional tourist sites. The medina with its souk, Dar Jamaï palace museum, Bou Inania Medersa, mosques, ornamental gates, koubba of Sidi Aïssa and hidden corners can easily consume a day. Behind the Bab Mansour within the Imperial City are the Koubbet pavilion, the underground 'slave pens', Moulay Ismaïl's mausoleum, the Dar el Ma and the Aguedal Tank, which require a 5km walk to be fully seen and experienced. On a third day, a taxi circuit around the outer forts and walls of the Imperial City could be the prelude to visiting Volubilis and Moulay Idriss.

History

The Market Town of the Berber Meknassa Tribe

The origins of Meknès are exclusively local and Berber, in direct contrast to the foreign and Arab birth of Fès. The city originated as a hill-top kasbah that won renown as one of the principal bases of the Khajarite Berbers, who overthrew the rule of the first Arab conquerors in AD 741. By the 10th century it had grown into the principal market of the Meknassa Berber tribe, which dominated the region. The power of the Meknassa was shattered by the great Almoravid general Youssef ben Tachfine in 1069, when he first united the country, but their name survived in the town of Meknès. It was rebuilt on a generous scale a century later, during the Almohad period, within a rigid square grid of walls. Its neat street plan was focused around the central mosque; Bab El Jdid is a survivor from this period. A later reconstruction under the Merenids is recalled by the exquisite 14th-century Bou Inania Medersa.

The Imperial City of Moulay Ismaïl

A new period in the city's fortunes dawned in 1666 when the ruling Alaouite sultan, Moulay Rachid, appointed his younger brother, one Moulay Ismaïl, to be its governor. He proved to be a loyal and efficient servant who happily involved himself in administration, local trade and the tilling of his own land. After the early, accidental death of his brother in 1672 Moulay Ismaïl succeeded to the throne, which he retained until his death in 1727. Fès and Marrakech were both embroiled in rebellions against the young monarch, who therefore decided to create a new capital out of the loyal city of Meknès. The existing walled medina was left largely undisturbed, and a brand new Imperial City built just beyond its southern walls. A slave army of 50,000 Berbers and Europeans was employed on the enormous project. Dozens of palaces were built for Moulay Ismaïl's court, for his 500 concubines and four wives, and his few favoured children (out of the 800 he sired); gardens, parks, ponds and pavilions were built, improved, knocked down and constantly replaced within the confines of the massive external walls.

The Imperial City also served as the headquarters and garrison for a standing force of 25,000 Abids, the disciplined black slave army which the sultan employed to impose his arbitrary rule. Vast storehouses, stables, exercise fields, enclosures for allied nomadic cavalry and armouries enabled the sultan to dispatch a force quickly at the first sign of dissidence.

Moulay Ismaïl has been presented to history (mostly through the accounts of ex-slaves, missionaries and the snubbed literate population of Fès) as a megalomaniac tyrant. Though his rule was certainly arbitrary, his achievements were sound. He humbled the wild mountain tribes, recaptured Tangier, Mehdiya, Larache and Asilah from foreign powers, and rebuilt mosques, shrines, bridges, kasbahs and whole towns. He attempted to reassert orthodoxy in the confused, cult-ridden life of the country, and was the last sultan to treat the European powers as equals. His offer for the hand of Louis XIV's illegitimate daughter, Marie Anne de Bourbon, should be seen as an overture for an alliance with France against Spain, while in his letters to King James II of England you can read his sound and disinterested advice, arguing in favour of Protestantism.

The Imperial City did not, however, long outlast its founder: the Abid slave regiments grew reckless and greedy without the stern hand of their master, and deposed a succession of his sons. The Lisbon earthquake of 1755 shattered the palace compounds and while his son Moulay Abdullah and grandson Sidi Mohammed (1757–90) altered and maintained portions of Meknès, they increasingly returned the business of government to either Fès or Marrakech. It was the French who revived Meknès, for like the great sultan they appreciated the city's strategic position and made it their central army base, building a new town across the river for their regiments.

Getting There

by rail

The main train station is on Av de la Basse, © (05) 520017, just off Av des FAR, the Fès road. Turn left at the entrance and the centre of the new town is a 1km walk east, or you could get off at the Meknès el Amir Abdelkader station (ex Lafayette) on Rue Alger, closer to the centre. There are plenty of trains in all directions: eight a day west to Rabat (2–3hrs) and Casablanca (4–5hrs), from where you can pick up a Marrakech connection; at least eight a day east through to Fès (50mins) and on to Taza (2hrs) and Oujda (6hrs,) and five north to Asilah and Tangier (6hrs) with a possible change of trains at Sidi Slimane or Sidi Kacem.

by bus

There are two bus terminals. The most useful and efficient is the CTM coach station at 47 Av Mohammed V, at the junction with Av des FAR in the new town. There are almost hourly departures to Fès (50mins) and at least three departures a day to Rabat (4hrs). Going north there are two to Tangier (7hrs), two to Ouezzane (4hrs) and one to Chechaouèn (6hrs). Heading south there are four to Azrou (90mins), one to Beni Mellal (6hrs)/Marrakech (9hrs) and one to Midelt (6hrs)/ Er-Rachidia (9hrs).

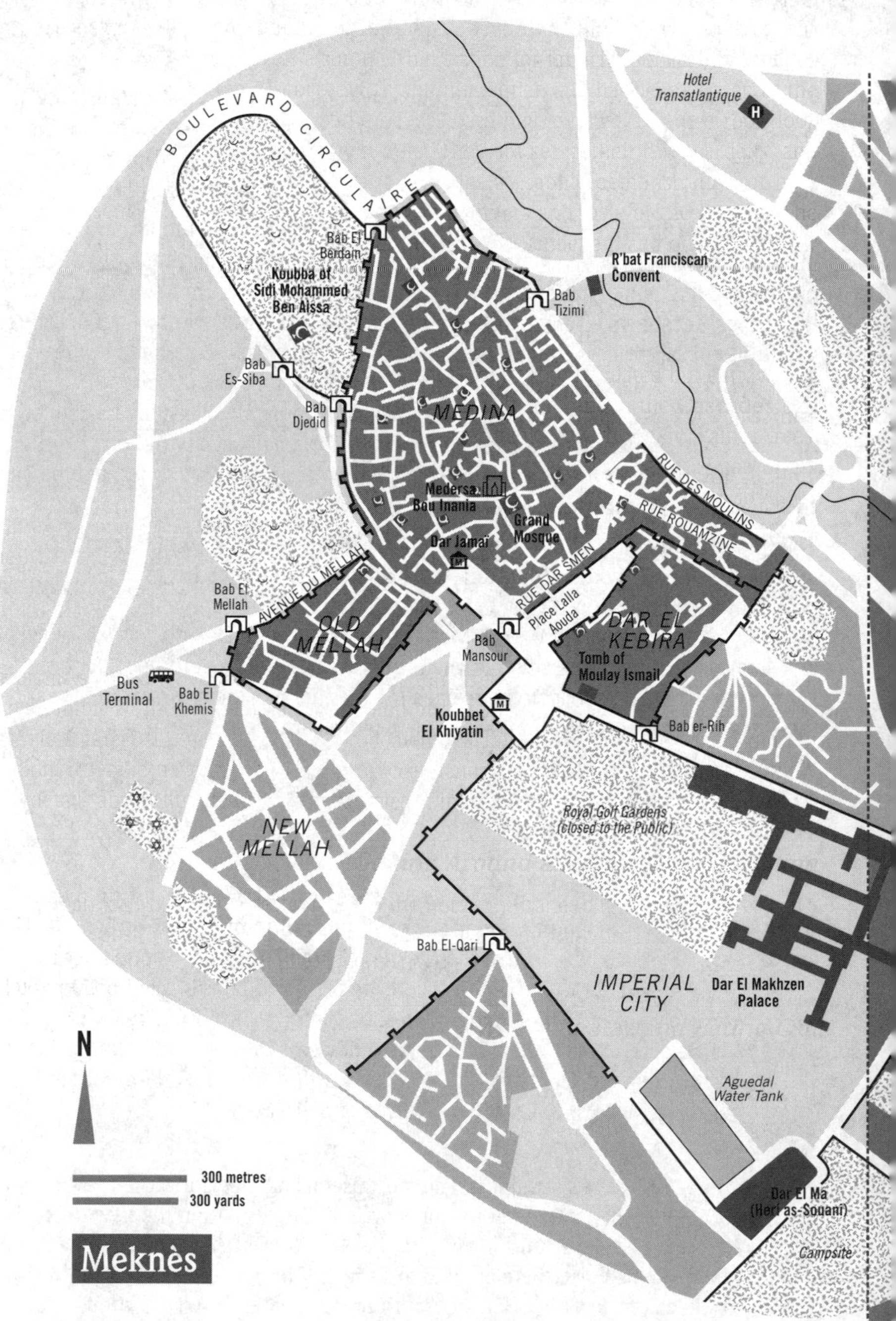
BOULEVARD CIRCULAIRE
Hotel Transatlantique
Bab El Berdaïn
Koubba of Sidi Mohammed Ben Aissa
R'bat Franciscan Convent
Bab Tizimi
Bab Es-Siba
Bab Djedid
MEDINA
Medersa Bou Inania
Grand Mosque
Dar Jamaï
RUE DES MOULINS
RUE ROUAMZINE
RUE DAR SMEN
AVENUE DU MELLAH
Bab El Mellah
OLD MELLAH
Place Lalla Aouda
Bab Mansour
DAR EL KEBIRA
Tomb of Moulay Ismail
Bus Terminal
Bab El Khemis
Koubbet El Khiyatin
Bab er-Rih
Royal Golf Gardens (closed to the Public)
NEW MELLAH
Bab El-Qari
IMPERIAL CITY
Dar El Makhzen Palace
Aguedal Water Tank
Dar El Ma (Heri as-Souani)
Campsite
N
300 metres
300 yards
Meknès

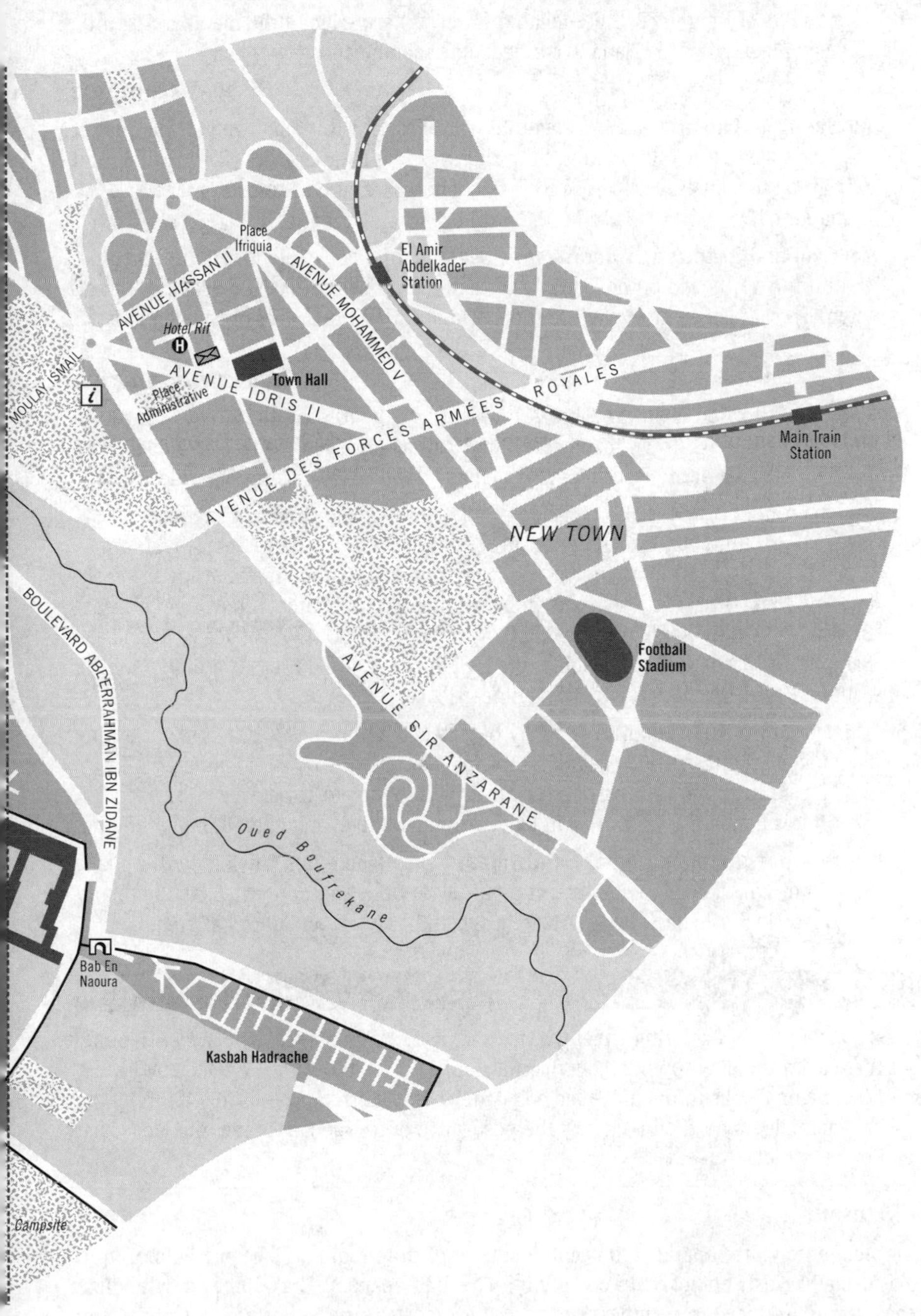
Place Ifriquia
El Amir Abdelkader Station
AVENUE HASSAN II
AVENUE MOHAMMED V
Hotel Rif
MOULAY ISMAIL
Town Hall
Place Administrative
AVENUE IDRIS II
AVENUE DES FORCES ARMÉES ROYALES
Main Train Station
NEW TOWN
Football Stadium
BOULEVARD ABDERRAHMAN IBN ZIDANE
AVENUE BIR ANZARANE
Oued Boufrekane
Bab En Naoura
Kasbah Hadrache
Campsite

Other private coach companies and local buses use the new consolidated terminal outside Bab el Khemis/Bab El Mellah on the western edge of the medina. A shuttle service of buses, nos. 5, 7 and 9, connects the medina and new town.

by car and taxi

All the major **car-hire** agencies operate from Fès, but this small gap in the market has been filled by two local firms: Stop Car at 3 Rue Essaouira, © (05) 525061, and Zeit at 4 Rue Antsirebe, © (05) 525918. There is a good Renault garage at 4 Av Mohammed V, tel (05) 521144.

You will find ***grands*** and ***petits taxis*** just west of Place el Hédime in the medina, and on the north side of the Place Administrative, beside the post office, in the new town. They are of most use for the short 40min/20dh hop to Fès or Moulay Idriss.

Tourist Information

The **tourist office** is on the Place Administrative, © (05) 524426. They distribute the usual attractive town map leaflets and can arrange for the hire of guides. The building is south of the Place on the Esplanade de la Foire, inside a big yellow gate.

The main **post office** is also on Place Administrative, and there is a sub-office in the medina on Rue Dar Smen. Both are open Mon–Fri, 8am–2pm in summer, 8.30am–12pm, 2.30–6pm in winter. Telephone calls can be made inside the main building (8am–9pm) or from some international phone booths in the street outside. **Banks** in the new town are the BMCE, © (05) 520352, at 98 Av des FAR, and the Banque du Maroc at 33 Av Mohammed V. In the medina there is a branch of the Banque Populaire along Rue Dar Smen near Place el Hédime.

The Moulay Ismaïl **Hospital** is on Av des FAR, © (05) 522806. Normal working hours for chemists such as Pharmacie Central on Av Mohammed V are 8.30am–8.30pm. An **after-hours chemist**, Pharmacie d'Urgence de Nuit, © (05) 522664, is beside the Town Hall in Place Administrative, and open 8.30pm-8.30am.

There are two French Catholic **churches**, Notre Dame des Oliviers by the Place Poereiam, which celebrates Mass on Saturday at 6pm and Sunday at 10.30am, and the Chapelle St Michael, Rue el Merzch, which has Mass on Sunday at 7pm.

The Medina

The best place to begin exploring either the medina or the Imperial City is Place el Hédime. To get there from the new town, follow the main road across the valley, Av Moulay Ismaïl, to enter the medina walls through the Bab bou Ameir. Then turn right to climb 400m up the busy Rue Rouamzine, and then go left by the post office onto Rue Dar Smen; the Place is at the end of this street.

Bab Mansour

This monumental gate separates the central square of the medina, Place el Hédime, from Moulay Ismaïl's vast, enclosed Imperial city. The Bab Mansour has come to symbolize Meknès: it is reproduced in countless books, articles, postcards and posters. It is difficult to see it at its best during the day, for the sun shines into your eyes from the east and leaves the gate in shadow. The softer evening light picks out the details, but even then the gate appears ponderous and over-decorated, and the relief too bold. The pillars, a mixture of Ionic and Corinthian columns torn from the classical ruins of Volubilis, appear empty gestures that distract from the overall harmony. It succeeds as architecture in a way that the sultan might have been content with: powerful, looming, appearing obsessively strong and rigid, its top panel of carved Koranic script a reminder of the strong Muslim orthodoxy of the Alaouite dynasty. The less obtrusive but altogether more agreeable gate to the right looking from the square, the **Bab Jema en Nouar**, was built in the same period; it now leads to a school housed in an old mosque and the gate apartments. Both gates were designed by Moulay Ismaïl's court architect, the renegade Christian known as Mansour el Aleuj, and completed in 1732 during the reign of the great sultan's son, Moulay Abdullah.

Place el Hédime

This square was only created in the mid-17th century by Moulay Ismaïl, who required a grand entrance before the Imperial City, the traditional area in an Islamic city for the public execution of justice, the issuing of proclamations, the jostle of petitions, the emergence of the royal procession to the grand mosque and the distribution of charity. In modern times it degenerated into a dusty car park, but a few years ago it was transformed once again into an elegant public space complete with new fountains. These are in pleasing harmony with the original 17th-century **enclosed fountain** (on the far side of the square), with its dazzling glimmer of *zellij* mosaic circles.

A **food market** runs along the south side of the square, screened by a long row of barbers and pottery shops. It is a wonderful place to gather a picnic: choosing from the glistening cones of flavoured olives, pats of goat's cheese, prime fruit and fresh vegetables from the farms that surround Meknès. Here even the dates look polished. At the northwest corner of the square an alley leads directly to the grand mosque, passing on the left a 14th-century town house, the *'Maison Merenide'*, which has been turned into a tourist bazaar.

Dar Jamaï Museum

Open Wed–Mon 9am–12 noon, 3–6pm; closed Tues; adm; © (05) 530863.

The Dar Jamaï is a 19th-century vizier's palace that now houses a collection of Moroccan arts and crafts (the Musée Régional d'Ethnographie). Like every Moroccan museum, it is a disordered presentation of often-undated Andalusian-influenced products from urban craftsmen together with the traditional crafts of the Berber tribes of the Middle Atlas.

The palace is an attractive, calm building, and the worn ceramic floors and graceful patina of age greatly contribute to your enjoyment of the exhibits. It belonged to the same brothers who built the Palais Jamaï in Fès. They were powerful officials in the court of Sultan Moulay Hassan, descended from one of the Arab tribes that had taken service under the Alaouite sultans, the Oulad Jamaï, and become hereditary servants of the government. At the centre of the museum is a mature **Andalusian garden**, well planted with shrubs and often buzzing with birds.

The Dar Jamaï has an unobtrusive entrance off the bustling Place el Hédime. The contrast as you enter through the cool, dark, twisting entrance passage emphasizes the domestic sanctity of an enclosed Moroccan house. Along this passage are some examples of Andalusian painted wall tiles, their foliate patterns familiar from woodcarvings but rarely seen in this form in Morocco. Even more surprising is the small collection of miniature paintings, all of which were produced here in Meknès.

In the few rooms off the central garden you can see the silk banner used by Sultan Moulay Hassan for his campaigns, dated 1874–87 in the Gregorian calendar, and a small display of brilliantly bound, compact Korans. The collection of elaborate keys is entertaining, and the other items of wrought ironwork, splendid door bosses and supporting hinges show how much the Gothic borrowed from the Moorish taste.

The **vizier's reception room** upstairs is fully furnished, and a useful antidote to the false impression of Moorish domestic style given by the serene interiors of medersas and empty palaces. For here there is a riot of familiar 19th-century clutter—coloured glass, debased workmanship, painted wood and conflicting plasterwork. The display of 19th-century Fès and Meknès ware is more pleasing: these **ceramics** have a gentler line, and warmer, more fluid shapes than seen in today's merely capable, rigid geometricism. The contrast with rural domestic pottery is always strong; though geometric in intent, the gourd-like shapes of the vessels and the black lines on red show Berber design at its most primitive and conservative.

The collection of **Berber jewellery** makes for an interesting comparison with that offered in today's souks, although the universal style of much native Islamic jewellery holds few surprises. The metalwork has a solidity that one hardly expects today, for these were collections of disposable wealth, while nowadays jewellery concentrates on display. For more on this see Jean Besancenot's highly informative *Bijoux Arabes et Berbères du Maroc* (Ed de la Cigogne, Casablanca); he reckons that traditionally workmanship used to add less than 25 per cent to the metal's value.

There is a fine mixed collection of Moroccan **carpets and kilims** from the indigenous Berber tribes of the High and Middle Atlas. The tendency was to produce woven and embroidered kilims rather than a true knotted carpet. The carpet collection also clearly shows why few Moroccan carpets have survived from any period further back than the 19th century: the large, thinly spaced knots tied to inadequate backing will not last more than a century unless the carpets have been used as wall hangings. Consequently, the admirably warm and simple diamond lozenge original designs are difficult to find today. The Zayan/Zaian carpet is a good example of this, while opposite the carpet from Aït-Bousba shows the origins of the pictogram, or 'message carpet', though it is splendidly random and primitive compared with the over-busy pattern-book designs found in today's bazaars. All the kilims here show a natural restraint in embroidery, with designs based on harmonious stripes of colour, interspaced with geometric lozenges, diamonds and triangles. The products from Zemmour and the Beni Mguild tribal confederation are most attractive, and are still being created.

The Bab Berrima and the *Mellah*

Back in Place el Hédime and facing the Dar Jamaï again, turn left in front of the museum and walk down Rue Sekakine. In 200m you reach Bab Berrima, a busy junction of streets. On the right is the site of the Berrima Kasbah that once defended this section of the medina, although now you can see only a **17th-century gate** and portions of the medina **perimeter wall**.

On the left, the long and comparatively wide Av du Mellah, lined with cloth merchants and tailors, extends downhill. Moulay Ismaïl attracted a large Jewish community to Meknès and built a separate *mellah* quarter in 1682, a square enclave projecting from the medina and securely enclosed behind its own wall, pierced by three gates, and governed by Caid Ali, an English renegade. The great sultan was under the firm influence of his treasurer, the Jewish financier Joseph Maimaran, who was succeeded by his son Abraham on his death in 1685. The Jewish community were later moved even further downhill, into the new *mellah* outside the walls, and Sultan Sidi Mohammed built the **Bab Berrima Mosque** in the 18th century for this increasingly Muslim district of the city. The exterior of the mosque can be seen by twisting through the gate passage on your right, where there are a couple of delicious hole-in-the wall grill-cafés.

Bab el Jdid and the Koubba of Sidi Aïssa

A 300m walk from the Bab Berrima along Souk Bezzarin on the outside of the medina wall—a local shopping street which is a mass display of Tupperware, kitchenware and jeans—will take you to the brick-built Bab el Jdid. This translates as the new gate, somewhat contrarily since it is the oldest gate in Meknès—with arched vaults dating from the 12th-century Almohad city. In front of the Bab el Jdid there is a good selection of grill-cafés, and a row of tent-makers will probably be busy in their shops cutting canvas and sewing awnings together on their pedal-operated Singers.

Beyond the Bab el Jdid, keep to your right the wall that surrounds the vast cemetery of Sidi Aïssa and follow it to the Bab es Siba, the gate of dissidence, just beyond which an avenue on the right leads up to the distinctive green-tiled pyramid roof that covers the venerated tomb of Sidi Mohammed ben Aïssa, built by the Sultan Sidi Mohammed (1757–90). You should not approach too closely, nor wander through the cemetery, which is decorated with the domed tombs of many revered Islamic saints. A mosque and various courts are attached to the shrine, for Sidi Aïssa was the founder of the important religious brotherhood of the Aïssoua, whose influence has spread throughout North Africa. Partly suppressed in the early reforming years of Independence, this ecstatic mystical sect has revived in recent years.

Beyond the shrine, on the left, city and country meet in a shantytown of corrugated stalls. Shafts of spectacular light flicker over the dark piles of vegetables, and the chicken, pigeon and dove salesmen work amid cages of live birds.

The Medina Souks

If, on the other hand, you enter the old town through the Bab el Jdid, a right turn will lead you to the Souk Seraria, the **blacksmith's souk**, populated by an assortment of knife-grinders, charcoal salesmen and tool-makers. On the left you can enter the sultan's *fondouq*, a delightful 18th-century brick courtyard established for the use of armourers.

As the street narrows you enter the centre of the **jewellery trade**. A right turn lets you out by the Bab Berrima, a left turn brings you into the covered **Souk Khiatine el Najarine**, the central thoroughfare of the medina, lined with the shops of metalworkers, tinkers and carpenters. You soon pass on the right the **Najarine** ('the carpenters') **mosque**, which follows a 12th-century Almohad plan even though the visible work is all 18th-century restoration. Beyond the mosque, again on the right, is the **Dlala Kissaria**, one of a number of interior courts lined with carpet and kilim booths that stock the products of the Middle Atlas tribes. It is one of the easiest and most accessible places in which to bargain for kilims—there is a good range of stock and the merchants are jovial.

A right turn by the Kissaria can take you down the old dyers' street passing the **Sebbarine Mosque** on your left to re-emerge in Place el Hédime by the Dar Jamaï museum.

If you continue along the main covered thoroughfare, known at this point as **Rue Sebat**, you will enter the richest and most tourist-oriented area of the souk. A hundred metres further on your right are the ornately decorated gates of the **grand mosque**. The mosque is at the heart of the medina, and has five elaborate entrances; it occupies the same area as the 11th-century Almoravid grand mosque, replaced by the Almohads and then again in the 13th century by the Merenids.

Medersa Bou Inania

Open Mon–Fri, 9am–5pm July–Aug; 8.30am–12pm, 3–6pm rest of the year; adm.

The medersa is directly opposite the grand mosque; its entrance is below a cupola in the main street, and protected by enormous bronze decorated doors. It was begun by Sultan Abou Hassan, creator of the Salé medersa, but finished by and named after Sultan Abou Inan, who reigned from 1351–58.

The entrance passage leads through a gate in a cedar screen with the Barakat Mohammed symbol carved above, which could be translated as 'the chance for faith'. The tall, rectangular court paved with black and white marble squares surrounds a central pool.

A band of *zellij* mosaic runs beneath bands of Koranic script that are carried upwards by all the decorative materials—carved plaster, glazed tile, marble and carved cedar all conspire together to carry the word of God. Around three sides of the court runs a gallery above which are two storeys of students' rooms. The solid, angular pillars of the gallery are saved from stolidity by columns that reach up towards the tiled cornice, and restrain the tracery design of the plaster walls. The fourth side of the courtyard opens into a spacious prayer-hall tiled in green and yellow, with a carved peacock fan set above the mihrab.

The beauty and sophistication of the Arabic script entwined in the decoration can mislead modern visitors on the depth of the education that was undertaken in a medersa. There was little emphasis on formal literacy: generations of students simply learned to recite the classical Arabic poetry of the Koran. Even centuries ago the language of the Moroccan street, Maghrebi Arabic, not to mention the three Berber dialects, was already far removed from the language of 7th-century Mecca.

The communal life of the *tolba*, the student reciters, is revealed in the ground-floor washroom with its long shared sink, although the upstairs rooms include an individual and very European-looking WC. Do not miss the view from the roof across the green-tiled grand mosque and prominent minarets of the medina. The double lancet windows of the Touta minaret can be seen almost due west, with the minarets of the Ahmed Chebli and Sidi Kadour el Alaoui mosques to its right.

Leaving the medersa, the rich clothes shops and bazaars of the Kissaria stretch ahead, but a sharp right turn beside the grand mosque will take you down Rue Sabab Socha, passing on the left the **Medersa Filala**, built by Moulay Ismaïl in the 17th century. This is a smaller and cruder version of the Bou Inania, and is not open to the public. From there a right turn down Rue es Zemmour will eventually return you after a few twists and bends to Rue Dar Smen and Place el Hédime.

The Northern Medina

The districts of the northern medina remain unseen by most visitors, protected by their confusing labyrinth of streets. This area is easier to approach from the northern gate, the Bab Berdaine. If you're starting from Place el Hédime, walk through the medina towards the new town and out through the Bab bou Ameir, then turn left along Rue des Moulins outside the city walls. Below in the valley of the Boufekrane are the extensive El Haboul **public gardens**, with formal paths, shaded benches, a zoo and an open-air theatre. There are also two club **swimming pools**, both of which charge entrance fees—a smaller, quieter, more expensive one surrounded by grass, and a larger pool with a diving platform that's surrounded by orange trees. At the far end of the gardens are the recently restored battlements of **Bab Tizimi**.

Opposite Bab Tizimi is the **R'bat**, the convent of the Franciscan sisters who run a school for Muslim girls. Ring the bell on the small left-hand door and a sister may appear to show you the echoing chapel and a selection of embroidered work for sale. The convent is built over the site of Moulay Ismaïl's gunpowder mill, prudently built outside the medina and far away from the Imperial City.

You can go through the Tizimi gate to walk beside the battlemented walls and then dip out again to approach the 17th-century **Bab Berdaine**, the saddlers' gate, at the northern end of the medina, from the outside. The decorative bands seem to flaunt the power of its two great flanking towers. The best way to approach it is to climb up from the potters' district, down by the Boufekrane. The extent of the gate is slowly revealed as you ascend the hill feeling tired and suitably submissive.

Through the gate is a long inner compound, Place Berdaine, with facing you at the opposite, south end of the square the clean and admirably unadorned stonework of the **Berdaine Mosque**. From here, beginning on Rue Zaouia Naceria and continuing onto Rue Soulka, you can walk down the length of the northern medina, admiring the undisturbed nature of most of the city, with each set of workshops, *hammam*, bakery and mosque delineating a separate 'parish'. Halfway down, about 600m from Bab Berdaine, a left turn down the narrow Rue Knout will bring you to the exterior of the **koubba of Moulay Ahmed el Ouezzani**, which was the open-air sanctuary of this famous ascetic who lived here from 1917 until his death in 1933.

Further down the central thoroughfare, which bears a number of different names along its length, you pass the **El Mansour Palace**, on Rue Karmouni, a richly decorated 19th-century merchant's house with an interior that's partly hung with the trappings of a tourist bazaar. In the medina you will probably also see signs for the **Zitouna** restaurant (*see* p.289), which has a slightly institutional aroma and caters heavily for group tours, but.is also established in a fascinating medina town house

The Imperial City

I have built these buildings—let those who can destroy them.

Sultan Moulay Ismaïl

We have never seen anything equal to it, neither among the modern buildings nor among the ancient.

Temim, a 17th-century French ambassador

The extent and past grandeur of the Imperial City can best be appreciated in a 5km walk broken halfway at the café at **Heri es Souani**. Most of the city is in ruins and has been built over by village communities, and the royal palace is not open to the public. The little pavilion of Koubbet el Khiyatin, the nearby underground store rooms, Moulay Ismaïl's mausoleum, the Dar el Ma and the Aguedal Tank are the highlights of the Imperial City, though inevitably the abiding image left at the end of the day is of a bewildering series of massive walls.

Dar Kebira

The first thing you come to through the Bab Mansour is the large Place Lalla Aouda, the formal processional square of the old Dar Kebira or enclosed palace quarter, which like the Place el Hédime has been recently renovated with fountains and newly-planted trees. None of the palaces has survived, though, and it is now just another residential area of the city.

The Dar Kebira was finished in 1677 and opened by the sultan, who sacrificed a wolf under the full moon at midnight and set its head above the gateway to the palace. According to the chronicler ez-Zayyani, the Dar Kebira contained 24 separate palace compounds, gardens and barracks, and two mosques. Most of these were destroyed by the sultan's son Moulay Abdullah, and the mosques alone have survived. Called the **Lalla Aouda** and **Chaouia**, they face the square, where only eunuchs were permitted to make the call to prayer. The palace museum in the Oudaïa Kasbah at Rabat was also originally built as a palace by Moulay Ismaïl, and gives some indication of the varied splendours of the Dar Kebira. It would have been decorated with columns extracted from Volubilis, and ornamentation looted from the great Saadian palace of El Badia at Marrakech.

Comparisons with the palace of Moulay Ismaïl's great contemporary, Louis XIV, continue to be made. However Versailles, with its radial axes of parkland, its draughty uncomfortable interiors and the exterior splendour of its façade can hardly be further removed from Moulay Ismaïl's secretive, heavily enclosed pavilion gardens. The sultan could not have begun Meknès in any spirit of competition with the French—he is known to have started work ten years before he received the first reports of Versailles. In any case he is much more likely to have looked east to Ottoman Istanbul for his exemplar. What Meknès and Versailles share is a roughly equal consumption of material and human lives.

Koubbet el Khiyatin

If you go through the Bab Filala at the southwest corner of Place Lalla Aouda, you will find yourself in a small square that has the pavilion of Koubbet el Khiyatin in the far right corner. This was an audience chamber used for the reception of foreign ambassadors and the interminable bargaining over the ransom of slaves. The decorated carvings on the walls endlessly repeat in Kufic script, *All jell*—glory to God.

Beside the Koubbet is the entrance to the '**prison of the Christians**', a misleading title for a massive vaulted underground network of storerooms, an impressive and mysterious acreage of damp stone lit by skylights. Intriguing bricked-up passages disappear to other decayed sections of the old underground city of cellars.

The Christian slaves of Meknès were actually never housed here; at first they lived under the 24 arches of a now-vanished bridge, a dozen for the Spanish, the rest shared between French, English and Portuguese. After the fall of Larache, 1700 more Spaniards joined the community and some disused tanneries were converted into a distinct European quarter. The slaves had four holidays a year; at Easter, Christmas, the nativity of St John the Baptist and that of the Virgin Mary, and were ministered to by Franciscan missionaries. These priests were free to travel throughout Morocco (corsairs were forbidden by the sultan to capture Franciscans), and they collected a tax on brandy sales and gambling from their charges.

The right-hand arch of the two ahead leads to the exclusive, walled and guarded **Royal Golf Club**, which has been created out of the central palace garden. Moulay Ismaïl kept a delightful menagerie in this garden: four wild asses from Guinea ran wild, two white dromedaries allowed themselves to be washed in soap every morning and wounded storks were cared for. Royal Arabian horses that had completed the pilgrimage to Mecca remained unridden and free for the rest of their lives; beads and scrolls from the holy city hung from their necks and any criminal was assured of sanctuary if such a horse allowed him to approach. On its death, each horse was reverently buried in shrouds and a koubba raised over its tomb.

Moulay Ismaïl's Mausoleum

Open Mon–Fri 9am–5pm July–Aug, 8.30am–12 noon Sept–June, 3–6pm; adm.

Through the left-hand arch, opposite half a dozen bazaars, is the long white mausoleum of Moulay Ismaïl. The actual prayer-hall of the mosque remains closed to non-Muslims, but the tomb can be approached providing you are respectfully dressed and tip the guardian. The sanctuary was completely restored by King Mohammed V in 1959. As you progress through the three admirably austere courtyards with serene tiled floors and walls you progressively shed the distractions and the noise of the outside world. The rectangle of blue sky framed by the high walls itself works as a form of meditation on the absolute. At the central fountain court remove your shoes, and enter through the door on the left into a lavishly gilded and decorated Moorish hall with a high-vaulted ceiling capped by a pyramidal koubba. From here you may look on to the marble tomb of the great sultan, flanked by two clocks, the gift of Louis XIV, but do not advance into the room which is used by pious pilgrims for prayers.

Dar el Makhzen

Beyond the mausoleum is the **Bab er Reth**, the gate of winds, which opens onto a kilometre-long passage below a stretch of massive double walls. The Sultan used to ride along this road in a chariot drawn by his plump concubines. The harem had a precarious status, for Sultan Moulay Ismaïl cared for few of his children and even less for his concubines (most of his adult sons were exiled to the oasis of the Tafilalt). His official wives were, however, forceful characters. Moulay Ismaïl's first wife, Zidana, who was black, was a fearsome witch who was even allowed out of the harem when escorted by a suitable chaperone. Her ally was his third wife, the English sultana. She had been captured in 1688, aged 15, en route to Barbados with her mother. Moulay Ismaïl returned this surprised mother-in-law to England with presents and a letter for the king.

The wall on the left of the passage is the exterior, defendable perimeter of the Imperial city; that on the right defines a particular palace enclosure, the enormous **Dar el Makhzen** or chief palace of the sultan, which was finished in 1697 and refurbished by Moulay Hassan in the late 19th century. The eastern portion of the original palace now forms the **Royal Palace of Hassan II**. A right turn at the end of this long walk, below the Water Fort, **Bordj el Ma**, will take you into the ***méchouar***, a colonnaded space where rulers could receive the ovations of their people. The gate on the right is the guarded main entrance to the palace, whilst a stroll to the left, through an enclosed hamlet clustered around a mosque and out through a gate, will allow you to admire the extent and width of the outer walls. To the east, stretching inside these walls is the **Kasbah Hadrach**, the old barracks of the Bukharis, the crack guards regiment of the sultan's black slave army. This old kasbah quarter is protected by two gates, Bab en Nouar and Bab Lalla Khadra, next to the mosque of that name.

Beyond the *méchouar*, an **arboretum** has been established in the pavilioned **Jardins de l'Ecole d'Horticulture** (Ben Halima Park) on the left of the road, while on the right a squatter village nestles beside the royal palace in the ruins of the **Kasbah Bab Merrah**. Storks nest on decaying pisé buttresses and towers, a few cows graze in a paddock that once held a delicate pavilion, and a young cripple shelters in a cardboard hut decorated with pseudo-erotic pictures cut from advertisements in the Western press. Broken faïence tiles are unearthed as the foundations for a new breeze-block wall are dug in the half-shadow of vast soot-blackened arched chambers.

Dar el Ma

A further 500m walk beside the pisé walls that partly hide these areas will bring you to the Dar el Ma, also known as Heri es Souani. This is the most accessible and impressive remnant of the Imperial City, a massive warehouse where silos held provisions for the court and standing army. Nowadays there is a café selling coffee and cold drinks, surrounded by a garden of olive trees happily growing on the massive roof. From here you can see miles of walls, modern villages and ruins stretching in every direction, surrounded by open farmland enclosed in turn by distant mountains. To the south a campsite, racecourse, arboretum, military academy and two schools partly fill the enormous enclosed area of the old Aguedal gardens. To the west stretch the 4 hectares of the **Aguedal Tank** (Bassin de l'Aguedal), constructed by Moulay Ismaïl to supply water for the palace gardens and orchards and now often surrounded by picnicking families. Inside the Dar el Ma there are impressive arched chambers and cascades of creepers hanging illuminated from skylights in the roof. In two of the corners, round chambers surround a well where water could be drawn up 50m by machinery worked by circulating mules. A large, roofless area of vaulted rooms—15 rows of 21 broken arches—extends southwest, partly overgrown with fennel, to create a famously impressive vista. It is thought to have been used as a stable, where some of the Sultan's horses were housed in the cool shade.

Dar el Beida

Southeast of Dar el Ma is the palace and mosque of Dar el Beida, an elegant arrangement of tiled towers, pavilions and gardens built by Sultan Sidi Mohammed at the end of the 18th century. King Mohammed V created the military academy here after Independence and, though you can admire the exterior, the inner arcaded court and gardens are inaccessible.

Heri el Mansour

South of the academy, still enclosed by the Imperial perimeter wall, is the modern settlement of Sidi Ayad and below that the battlement district of Heri el Mansour. Within is the 18th-century **mosque of Er Rouah**, the mosque of the stables, built by Sidi Mohammed in 1790, with its own attached medersa. To the left of the mosque, down the central street, are the immense walls of the Heri el Mansour, now usually closed to visitors. This was considered the chief glory of the Imperial City, a vast, beautifully appointed arcaded stable that reputedly held over 12000 cavalry horses and was fed by its own aqueduct. The roof has long since fallen, and it is now an enclosed wilderness of worn pillars, broken tiles, acacia scrub and arches. Above the stables on the elevated platform created by their roof the sultan laid out a formal Andalusian garden, its ornate paths studded with dozens of delicate pavilions that formed the el Mansour palace. Poised above the southern turreted and battlemented outer wall, this was the most splendid and fanciful of the sultan's creations. From here he could review the assembled masses of his tribal cavalry.

As the Dar el Beida and Heri el Mansour are currently inaccessible, most visitors are content to walk beside the Aguedal Tank back towards the medina from the Heri es Souani. At the far end of the tank a left turn brings you into the Beni M'Hammed district, and a right turn along the central avenue takes you out of this modern settlement through the **Bab el Kari**. Below this gate is one of the most impressive stretches of external wall, the 'wall of riches', the battlemented and towered defences of which stretch in an unbroken line a kilometre southwest to the **Bordj el Mers**. A road leads from this gate across empty ground west to the new *mellah*, while a right turn climbs up past a taxi rank towards the medina. A left turn along the Blvd As Salam will take you to the most beautiful gate in Meknès, the towered **Bab Lakhmis**, or you could continue uphill and go through the **Bab Zine el Abadine** to re-enter Place el Hédime.

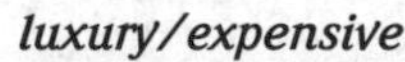

Where to Stay

luxury/expensive

The **Transatlantique**, ✆ (05) 525050(–4), @ 520057, on Rue El Meriniyine, has a superb view across the Oued Boufekrane to the skyline of Meknès' medina. The 120 bedrooms are divided between two sections; the traditional rooms in the old portion of the hotel are the same price but of much greater character. It also has two pools, a bar, two restaurants and a tennis court, and a good buffet lunch is served by the pool; for dinner, it's worth reserving a table in the Moroccan restaurant. Don't be put off by the staff's lack of response to telephone calls, for it's worth checking out room availability here in person despite what they say.

At a less extravagant level, the **Rif,** ✆ (05) 522591, ℻ 524428, on Rue d'Accra is an unexceptionable, rather worn but pleasant hotel in the centre of the new town with a popular bar, the Bahia nightclub and two restaurants.

moderate

Dropping down just a notch in scale and location there are three clean and engaging old hotels in the new town each with around 30 bedrooms and their own bars and restaurants, the **Palace,** ✆ (05) 511260, at 11 Rue de Ghana, the **Volubulis,** ✆ (05) 525082, at 45 Av des FAR and the **Majestic,** ✆ (05) 520307, ℻ 527427, at 19 Av Mohammed V. Also worth considering are two recent additions to the Meknès stable, **Bab Mansour,** ✆ (05) 525239, ℻ 528395, at 38 Rue Emir Abdelkader, and direectly opposite at no. 27 the **Hotel Akouas,** ✆ (05) 515967, ℻ 5159944, both firmly directed at prosperous local businessmen.

inexpensive

There are three comfortable one-star hotels in the new town still within walking distance of the CTM bus station and the two railway stations. The **Continental,** ✆ (05) 525086, at 92 Av des FAR is a fine hotel with wide corridors, large bedrooms and an elegant staircase with a fish tank on its banister. The **Excelsior,** ✆ (05) 521900, at 57 Av des FAR has 37 tidy rooms, and the **Touring,** ✆ (05) 522351, is found nearby at 34 Av Allal ben Abdellah.

cheap (in the medina)

There are a number of budget hotels in the medina, found along Rue Dar Smen and Rue Rouamzine. The **Maroc Hotel,** ✆ (05) 530075, at 103 Rue Benbrahim, just off Rue Rouamzine, is by far the best and often the cheapest of these. If it's full the **Regina,** ✆ (05) 530280, at 19 Rue Dar Smen is a perfectly acceptable alternative and also offers free use of its cold showers.

There is a good campsite in the middle of the Imperial City, in a pleasant meadow next to the Heri es Souani arsenal and Aguedal tank. The **Camping Aguedal/Jnane Ben Hlima,** ✆ (05) 530712, is open all the year and has a kitchen, restaurant, hot showers and a shop.

Eating Out

expensive

The **Al-Ismaili** Moroccan restaurant at the **Hôtel Transatlantique** (*see* above) needs to be booked in advance. It can produce a memorable evening,, with some of the best food, service, music and view in Meknès.

moderate

The French-influenced restaurants licensed to serve alcohol are all in the new town, most of them along or just off Av Hassan II. **La Coupole,** ✆ (05) 522483, on the corner of Rue du Ghana and Av Hassan II, is one of the oldest addresses in town, with a capable, reasonably priced Moroccan-French menu and calm, dignified service. Going up in price a bit, **Le Dauphin** on Av de Paris, © (05) 523423, is the only place in the city to serve consistently fresh fish, and has the sense to put the passing group trade in a separate dining room. For classic, rich, meat-based French cooking head for **La Case**, © 524019, at 8 Blvd Moulay Youssef (closed Mon).

For Moroccan cooking chosen from a menu there is the **Annexe de Metropolis**, © (05) 525668, at 11 rue Sherif-Idrissi, near the covered market just north of the Av Hassan II/Av Mohammed V junction. For a more palatial traditional Moroccan evening you will have to head out of the new town to the medina. Just in from Bab Tizimi at 44 Jamaa Zitouna is the **Restaurant Zitouna,** © 530281, which occupies a traditional 19th century Moroccan house. Pop in at lunchtime and it will be filled by coach groups, so it's best to reserve a table in the tranquillity of the evening—possibly armed with your own bottle of wine, for it has no licence.

cheap

In the new town, for a filling bargain meal head straight for the **Novelty Restaurant,** © (05) 522156, at 12 Rue. de Paris. Alternatively, on Rue Atlas there are two good addresses, **Pizzeria Le Four** and directly across the road the **Restaurant Montana,** © (05) 520968, which runs a close second to the Novelty and has the advantage of a drinks licence. In the medina there are some delightful café-restaurants by the Bab Berrima and Bab Jdid that are well placed for a quick lunch, and a good selection along Rue Dar Smen and Rue Rouamzine. The **Café Bab Mansour**, on the Place almost opposite its namesake, is particularly good; you can eat couscous and salad here and sip tea until midnight.

bars

The bars of Meknès are casual places dominated by locals of both sexes openly drinking. This is comparatively unusual for Morocco, and at times you can almost forget you are a foreigner. Of the hotels that have bars, the **Transatlantique** is calm to the point of quiet. Instead, pop into the plush red interior of the **Rif Hotel** in the centre of town, the **Bab Mansour** or the **Akouas.** All three of these hotels support nightclubs where you can listen to contemporary Arab music from around 8–10pm.

For a more lively drinking spree you could leave the comparative protection of a hotel and set off on a tour of **Roi de la Bière**, **Jour et Nuit** and the **Du Trésor**, which are all along Av Mohammed V, the latter at no. 33. On Av Hassan II at no. 3 there is **Bar Vox Brasserie**, at no 11 the **Bar de Centre** and at no. 24 the **Bar American**. There is also the **Novelty Bar** at 12 Rue de Marseilles, near to which at no. 6 a tranquil pastis-sipping atmosphere can be found at **La Caravelle**.

Sports

There are two club **pools** and **tennis** and **basketball courts** in the Lahboul park below the El Haboul gardens, © (05) 520415. There is an efficient *Hammam* in the new town (open 7am–9pm) with separate male and female sections, at 4 Rue Patrice Lumumba off Av Hassan II.

Entertainment and Nightlife

The **Hacienda**, © (05) 521092 is a taxi ride away, outside the centre of town but well signposted off the road to Fès. It has a country club-like atmosphere and is usually filled with well-groomed urban youth out on a spree, with its disco night club, occasional live bands, charcoal grills and outdoor terrace.

The **Bar Continental**, on the corner of Av des FAR and Av Hassan II beside the hotel of the same name, is decidedly low-rent in comparison, with a series of three dark bars run by a team of strong Berber women. Almost opposite is the **Café Français Club de Nuit** at no. 73 Av des FAR, where the bar closes half an hour after midnight. A door down from this bar is the cellar **Cabaret Oriental**, a Moroccan nightclub where live local bands play each night until 3am.

Festivals

A *Fantasia* festival is held in the Imperial City in September, the same month as the *moussem* of Moulay Idriss and Sidi Bouzelm. The Aïssoua celebrate at Mouloud, and a week later the Hamadasha and Dghughlia sects in Jbel Zerhoun.

Around Meknès

South

The **kasbah of Agouraï** is a 35km drive south from Meknès on the 3065 road. This beautiful rectangular fortress was built by Moulay Ismaïl in the early 18th century as the chief base for his regiment of Spanish renegades. It has five towers on each side, and the pisé walls have mellowed into a range of pink and ochre colours. Two small cannons still protect the entrance, while storks roost on the walls. The kasbah is packed full of low white houses, a conglomeration touched with shades of green and blue within which you find a gently ageing mosque with a faïence fountain in front. Water cascades throughout the kasbah from stand-pipes, and below the outer walls a washing souk has established itself on the lower slope. The graveyard above the village is dominated by the **koubba of Sidi Said l'Hakusi**. The village has now spread far beyond the kasbah: it has a souk on Thursdays, and a *hammam*. On the north edge of the village, beside the Meknès road, is the **El Ghazail** café.

East

East of Meknès only **El Ghor** is likely to delay your journey across the 60km of flat farmland before you reach Fès. It is, however, something of a quest to find this impressive and ancient funerary monument in the middle of the featureless agricultural plain. Take the 3110 out of Meknès, then turn left onto the 3109. On your right, just before a bridge with a metal handrail, a track leads to a circular mound surrounded by two complete circular bands of well-dressed stone. This architectural tumulus was raised by some great Berber king sometime in the 7th century AD. Elements of its construction suggest familiarity with Roman measurements. There was once an altar on the east side that was lit up by the first light of dawn, so perhaps this evocative, mysterious site was linked with sun worship. Like the celebrated tomb of Queen Tin Hinan, the legendary ancestress of the Tuareg of Algeria, this site offers us tantalizing evidence of the complex Berber society that existed in the so-called Dark Age between the Roman and Islamic periods.

West

Going west of Meknès on the P1 road to Rabat–Salé there are three places of sufficient interest to merit a stop: an old garden, a lake and a weekly market.

The dilapidated **Vallée Heureuse** gardens are just 11km out of Meknès. They were created by a French prison governor, Bagnon, as therapy for his inmates. Just before the turning to Sidi Slimane there is an unmistakable stone and shell-decorated archway through which a track leads to the water gardens, overlooked by the huts of the rural poor. In their working heyday they must have been quite excessively prissy but now, in partial ruin and covered in cascades of wild roses, brambles, broken palms and wild figs against a background of olives, the gardens have a Fragonard sumptuousness. A waterfall flows over limestone stalagmites to contrast with the wreck of the stone boat island and the ruins of a boating pond. In the summer a café operates on the terrace from a shack obscured by foliage.

The journey west to Rabat is a pleasant enough drive through 100km of farmland and woods of cork, holm oak and eucalyptus that comprise the Mamora Forest. The uninspiring French-built town of **Khémisset**, complete with defunct church, is 46km from Meknès. It was built as a focal settlement for the hitherto nomadic Zemmour tribe, but is only of interest for its Tuesday market. The Zemmour have one of the richest weaving traditions of all the Middle Atlas tribes, and their distinctive kilims, carpets and *argtil* are still to be found in the market. It is also known for woodcarvings, available on other days as well at the Ensemble Artisanal.

Carpets for the Earth

Argtils are only created in the rural areas of the Middle Atlas. They are woven from a combination of wool and fronds made from the leaves of dwarf palm trees. Colour and decoration is all achieved by the wool, which is usually dyed the distinctive madder-red of the Zemmour, though this dominant shade of red is often balanced by black and white. The patterns are based on the traditional Zemmour repertoire of narrow bands of recurring geometric designs, chiefly diamonds, triangles and zigzags, set against plain backgrounds. Modern versions of the argtil have excess fronds left loose on the underside for added insulation. They were designed for rough use—the name translates as carpets for the earth—and served as mere underlay for the better kilims or carpets.

Fifteen kilometres south of Khémisset, along the S106, is a freshwater lake, the **Dayèt-er-Roumi** (the lake of the Christians), surrounded by gentle hills. It is an idyllic pastoral spot where you can fish, swim, picnic, camp or eat at the café that opens in the summer months. The two faces of Morocco are perfectly expressed by a clutch of bourgeois summer villas and the drifting flocks of semi-nomadic shepherds that are attracted to the lake's edge.

If you want to go further afield in your quest for local crafts, especially textiles, you could check out the Friday souk held by the koubba of **Sidi Bettache** (9km along the road to Maaziz from the lake), while on Thursdays there is a souk at **Khemis-de-Sidi-Yahya** and on Wednesdays one at **Tiflèt** on the main Rabat road. Tiflèt is known for its woven pompom hats, which are held out on poles for the admiration of passing traffic throughout the week.

Where to Stay and Eating Out

Apart from the summer campsite at the Lake the only place to go in the area is the inexpensive **Diouri Hotel**, ✆ (07) 552645, in Khémisset, on Av Mohammed V opposite a colonial church at the Fès end of town. It is a functional, place that has 15 bedrooms and its own café-restaurant.

Moulay Idriss, Volubilis and the Jbel Zerhoun

About 30km north of Meknès stand the twin sites of Islamic Moulay Idriss and Roman Volubilis, just 4km apart on the edge of the limestone, olive-covered hills of Jbel Zerhoun.

Getting Around

From the dusty square to the west of Place el Hédime in Meknès ***grands taxis*** charge 10dh for a place to Moulay Idriss, and **buses** only 4dh. There is a bus with more frequent services on Saturdays for the **souk**. By **car** it's 10km along the P6, then right onto the P28 for 14 km. There are two narrow right turns into the town; the second one takes you to the car park. Volubilis is 4km away off a loop road, the 3312, to the left of the P28.

Moulay Idriss

Moulay Idriss is the principal and most famous of the villages on Jbel Zerhoun. It is a national pilgrimage site as it holds the tomb of Moulay Idriss, the holy founder of the first indigenous Islamic kingdom of Morocco. As an indication of its high status it is governed by its own pacha, and is home to the *caid* of the whole Zerhoun region. It is an astonishingly dramatic site. The two distinct quarters of the town, Tasga and Khiber, are piled up, around and between two massive exposed outcrops of volcanic stone. The landscape around the town—hills where ordered olive groves alternate with rough forests—is in harmony with the spiritual atmosphere, for the Jbel Zerhoun is a centre both of orthodoxy and ecstatic cults.

The First Idrissids

The tomb of Moulay Idriss ibn Abdulla, 'el Akhbar'—the great—is the venerated heart of the town. He was a sherif, a kinsman of the prophet, and fled to Morocco from Arabia to escape the slaughter ordered by the Abbasid caliphs, who had destroyed his family at the fateful battle of Fakh in ad 786. Accompanied only by his loyal slave Rashid, he journeyed through Egypt and headed west to escape from the area of Abbasid rule. He had arrived at Volubilis (known as Walila in this period) by 788, when he was welcomed by the prominent Arab Auroba tribe as their imam. He was assassinated by a secret agent of the Abbasid caliph in May 791, but the posthumous birth of a male heir in August, from a local Berber concubine, allowed his holy dynasty to continue. The slave Rashid exercised authority until he himself was assassinated (this time by an agent of the Aghlabid dynasty of Tunisia) at which time the 11-year-old-Idriss II was proclaimed leader in the mosque at Volubulis. Idriss II later went on to greatly expand his authority and found the city of Fès, in which he was buried. The tombs of both father and son were rediscovered in the 15th century, in the Merenid period, after centuries of neglect. It was a period when Morocco was threatened by strong external enemies and these new shrines helped provide a focus for a politically expedient orthodox nationalist cult. The present town and sanctuary of Moulay Idriss is mostly 18th-century, for Moulay Ismaïl piously and sympathetically restored the shrine, including some of the pillars from Volubilis. The entire town was closed to Jews and Christians until 1912.

Your first experience of the holy town is likely to be of a busy and dusty bus and car park. Above and ahead a line of stalls leads to the triangular wedge of souks that points towards the sanctuary **mosque of Moulay Idriss**. To the right of the sanctuary stretches the Tasga quarter of the town; the higher Khiber quarter is to the left. The souk stalls are lined with eyebrows of green tiles that contrast well with the rising white mass of the double village beyond. Curious woven reed plates, rosaries, golden scarves, grilled food, religious trinkets and embroidered cloth are displayed for the pilgrims; as you near the sanctuary masses of coloured nougat and enormous green candles predominate. An unmistakable wooden bar halts non-Muslims before the outermost courtyard, while within stretches a whole complex of halls, fountains for washing, prayer-halls and the holy tomb of Morocco's first legitimate Islamic ruler. Pilgrims are allowed to stay in the courtyards, but in summer the chants and collective enthusiasm seldom allow much sleep. To the right of the sanctuary entrance is the royal guesthouse, to the left the offices of the *Habous*, the ministry that administers religious endowments. Most of the olive groves in the region are leased annually by the *Habous* to farmers, the rents being used to maintain the shrine, mosque and schools.

If you go back to the bus park and follow the tarmac road up a steep hill, turn right past the post office and climb some stone steps, you will come to a famous cylindrical minaret encased in blue and white Koranic script, built in 1939 from stone and faïence. Later the path splits under the shadow of a great vine, and there is an excellent view down onto the glazed roofs and white courts of the secretive sanctuary of Moulay Idriss. Both paths lead downhill towards the sanctuary **souk**. The **medina** is small enough to allow you to wander freely along its erratic climbing alleys, their secrecy interrupted by surprising views, lone cafés and a generally friendly populace.

Just above the river is a complete, round, open-air **Roman bath**, the stones worn by use. It's still connected to a hot sulphur spring that oozes up through healing mud, and is particularly good for rheumatism. Further on, a **bridge** built by Moulay Ismaïl spans the river Khoumane; on the other side a path climbs up past a few cottages, deteriorating rapidly into a goat track. Scrambling up this slope of rocky undergrowth you reach a ruined 18th-century **pavilion** with a fine view over the back of the twin rocks and houses of the Tasga and Khiber quarters.

Festivals

The massive national festival is held in September. Five visits to the festival used to be considered, by locals at least, to equal a pilgrimage to Mecca.

The Villages of Jbel Zerhoun

The Jbel Zerhoun region is a 100-square-mile network of limestone hills through which emerge dark metamorphic extrusions. The hills rise abruptly north of the plain of Saïss, separating it, and its twin cities of Fès and Meknès, from the fertile ploughland of the Cheraga that borders the Sebou valley. The central, forested summit of Jbel Zerhoun is 1118m high. The lower foothills are covered in orchards and olive groves that are cultivated by a string of villages; these mountain settlements have a tradition of self-sufficiency and piety intensified by the idiosyncratic spiritual life of the Hamadasha and Dghuglia brotherhoods. The villages on the northern hills speak the Berber Tariffit dialect of the Rif, while the southern villagers speak the Tamazight dialect of the Berbers of the Sahara and Middle Atlas.

Many of the villages are still enclosed by stone kasbah walls that shelter the cottages, minareted mosque and zaouia found in each of them. The Homeric dignity of a life spent with olive trees and flocks on the rough hills seems stamped in the mood of the villages. The back road through Moulay Idriss, the S306, takes in some superb views on its way to join the main Ouezzane to Fès road at Nzala-des-Beni-Ammar.

An even more distinctive area of the Zerhoun is accessible along the S323, an unobtrusive tarmac road that turns off the P28 some 7km south of Moulay Idriss. This road takes you past the hamlet of Beni Jennad, 2km after which a right turn leads up to the village of **Beni-Rachid**. Beni-Rachid holds the tomb of Sidi Ali ben Hamdasha, the founder of the mystical Hamadasha brotherhood, who died in 1722. Sidi Ali was strongly influenced by the teachings of Sidi Mohammed Bu'abid ech Cherki, who founded the maraboutic dynasty whose shrines can be seen in the Middle Atlas town of Boujad. The Hamadasha brotherhood used the intoxication of dance and repetitive music to achieve a state of mystical ecstasy in which they became insensitive to cuts and heavy blows. Their festival is held here seven days after Mouloud, although the more notorious mutilatory aspects of the cult have been outlawed. Sidi Ali's tomb, covered by a green cupola, is in the centre of the long shrine building just above the therapeutic bath and basin of Aïn-Kebir.

The dank grotto of Aisha Qadisha, a powerful and malevolent female spirit, is 100m east of this shrine. Aisha Qadisha is widely feared throughout Morocco. She appears at dusk looking dazzlingly attractive and seduces men on little frequented streets and then leads them away to their doom. She can be recognized by her cloven hoofs and, like all jinn, is terrified of iron. The entrance to the grotto is difficult to spot as it is overhung by a large cult fig tree. A barefoot saint, Sidi Hazlyan, is also buried in Beni-Rachid, in the southeast corner under a yellow and white minaret. He was the ascetic and uxorious brother of Sidi Ali, from whom about half the village claim descent. There is in addition a third koubba in the village, a plain white affair that marks the grave of Sidi Musa. Village traditions credit *Caid* Bel Shaqur with the construction of the kasbah wall; however this same *caid* later overreached his authority by demanding the first night with every bride. He was subsequently flogged to death by the irate men of Beni-Rachid.

The pretty stone-walled village of **El-Merhasiyne** is 6km further along the road. Here there is a turning which cuts over the forested hills below Jbel Zerhoun to take you straight into Moulay Idriss. If you continue along the S323 you will reach the village of **Moussaoua** in about 4km. A conspicuous green pyramid shrine at the centre of the village covers the grave of Sidi Ahmed Dghughli, a disciple of Sidi Ali who went on to establish the allied Dghuglia brotherhood. The tarmac track stops here and a rough dirt track heads up for some 10km to a left turn to the well-preserved **kasbah of Nesrani**, perched on the crest of a hill, which enjoys a spectacular view to the south.

Volubilis

Open daily from dawn to dusk; 20dh adm.

The gorgeous ruins of the Roman city of Volubilis, ancient capital of the province of Mauretania Tingitania, sits below the escarpment of Jbel Zerhoun. At dusk it is a magical place and though I have now trod through the stones for twenty years I am constantly surprised by its delicate, melancholic beauty. It is the finest archaeological site in Morocco and fully equal to any of the more famous Roman North African ruins that can be seen in Tunisia, Algeria and Libya. Its most distinctive feature is an astonishingly well preserved basilica, though the complete triumphal arch, the columns of a Capitoline temple and a dazzling series of mosaic floored villas are equally memorable. A ruthless tourist on a guided tour can see these within an hour; the more interested visitor will only be torn away by the descent of dusk. It is an exposed, largely shadeless site, so try and avoid the midday sun. It is at its best in the morning or evening, when the sun gives a warmer colour to the stones.

History

The physical remains of Volubilis, like so many of the great Roman sites in North Africa, largely date from the golden period of the empire. This stretched from the reign of Trajan to the end of the Severi dynasty (of North African origin)—AD 97–235. The city has, however, a richer and more complex history that symbolically unites the two great Middle Eastern cultures that have had a fundamental influence on Morocco: the Phoenicians and the Arabs.

Excavations into the mound of ruins at its centre hint at a past that extends back into a Neolithic culture that came early under Phoenician influence, as ruins found here of an old temple to Baal attest. This inland market town covered 15 hectares in the 3rd century BC, but had already trebled in size before the first Roman official set foot here in AD 24, when it became the western capital of Juba II of Mauretania. Juba, though of North African blood, was a Roman client-king educated in the household of the Emperor Augustus. His wife was not some native princess but Cleopatra Silene, the child of Mark Anthony and Cleopatra. He became increasingly dependent on Roman support to govern his kingdom, so that in all practical matters it was absorbed into the empire long before Claudius' formal annexation in AD 45. The city stayed loyal to Rome through the testing years of Aedemeon's revolt in northern Morocco (roughly contemporary with that of Boadicea in Britain) and was rewarded with grants of citizenship, a ten-year tax holiday and confirmation of its role as capital. A succession of procurators ruled Mauretania Tingitania from here for the next 250 years.

Volubilis was also the centre of a rich agricultural region (over 50 villas have been found in the immediate area) which exported corn, wild beasts and oil to the coast. It was, however, on the vulnerable southeastern edge of the province, and was defended by a ring of five forts at the modern hamlets of Sidi Said, Bled el Gaada, Sidi Moussa, Tocolosida and Aïn Schkor. There was no road east to the city of Oujda, then ruled as part of Mauretania Caesarensis (Roman western Algeria), for the sternly independent Baquates tribe occupied the area around Fès and Taza. Increased frontier tension at the end of the 2nd century is evident in the decision during the reign of the Emperor Marcus Aurelius to construct a 2.5km circuit of city walls, pierced by eight gates and buttressed by forty towers. This period also witnessed the peak of prosperity, with a population estimated at over 20,000. The near collapse of central government by the end of the period of military anarchy (235–284), when over 30 generals had seized control of the Imperial throne in a debilitating succession of coups, resulted in the fall of the city to tribal attack in around 280, a disaster evidenced by the hidden caches of coins and bronze statuary found by archaeologists beneath some of Volubilis' villas. This partial collapse of the frontier (Banasa and Thamusida had also fallen at this time) was confirmed during the reign of the Emperor Diocletian (284–305), for although a Roman army was based in Tangier in the 290's under the command of a co-Emperor, it was decided that it was too expensive to undertake the reconquest of much of Morocco. The province was reduced to just the northern hub of the ports of Lixus-Tangier and Ceuta, and henceforth governed as if it was part of Spain.

After the initial trauma of the sack a reduced form of urban life seems to have continued in Volubulis, boosted by refugees escaping the heavy taxes and persecutions of the late Roman Empire. Records from the Arab conquest speak of an independent trading community, now known as Oualila, ruled by a council of Christian tribal chiefs. It was to this city that Moulay Idriss fled at the end of the 8th century, and where his son Idriss II was first proclaimed Imam. Idriss II's foundation of Fès deliberately removed the capital from this ancient town with its traditions of oligarchy and religious pluralism. The new capital quickly drained the old of vitality, and by the 11th century Volubilis was a magnificent but deserted shell.

The city was only reduced to ruin in the 18th century by Moulay Ismaïl's architects, who used its stones to build the Imperial City of Meknès, and by the Lisbon earthquake of 1755. Fortunately an English antiquarian, John Windus, had sketched the site in 1722. These drawings were of great use to the French archaeologists who began work here in 1915, their digging assisted by Marshal Lyautey's loan of thousands of German prisoners of war.

The Site Entrance

The arch by the ticket office is the old southeast gate of the Roman city. There is an open-air collection of sculpture and inscriptions next to the office, and a shaded café which sometimes serves lunch.

The Olive Presses

From here a path leads across a largely unexcavated area of the city to cross a stream, the river Fertassa. Beyond this stream, on the left, squats the first of many classical stone olive presses with their associated drains, storage and separation tanks. The recent construction of a replica press here is a delightful addition to understanding the site.

The extraction of olive oil was of primary importance to Volubilis, as it still is to the villages of Jbel Zerhoun, where techniques have remained unchanged. The olive flesh and stones are

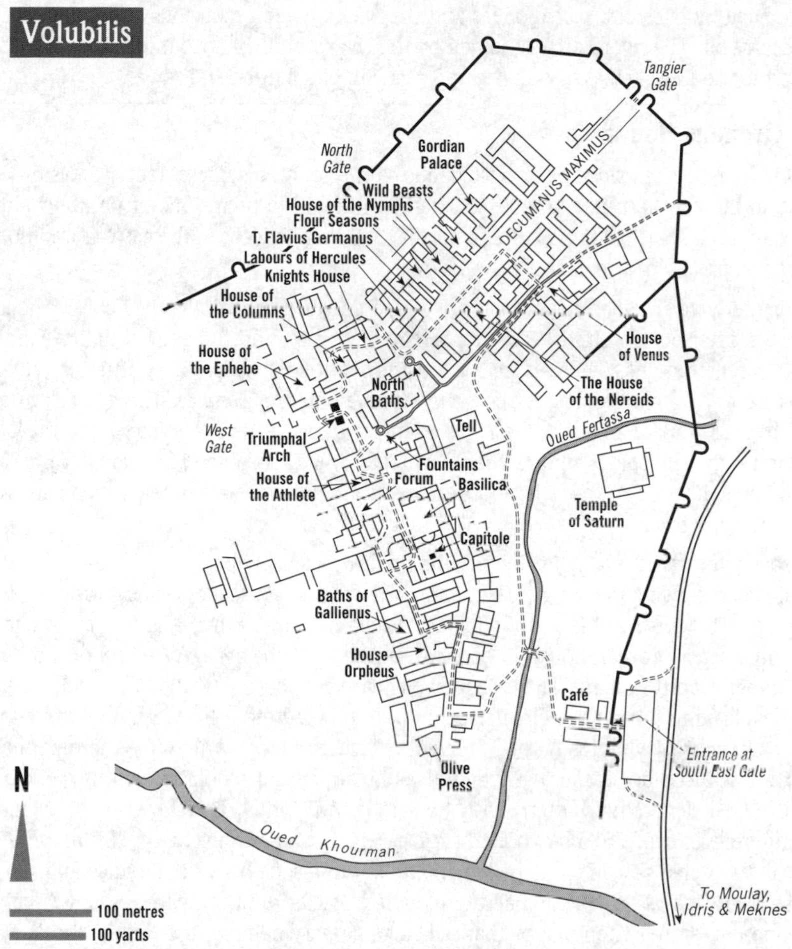

first crushed by a large millstone, then shovelled into woven grass-reed sacks that look like a deflated tyre. These are then packed on top of each other on a pole (or poles) and compressed by a heavy cross beam which is gradually tightened. Liquid oozes out from the sacks and is caught by a circular drain which feeds off into a number of tanks where the oil, watery fluids and solid vegetable matter separate naturally. It is an easy matter to add more water and float the olive oil off into jars for export or domestic use.

Olive oil was an essential part of ancient urban life: it was a basic ingredient of cooking; used for bathing and medicines; and was the preferred fuel for lamps. The residue from the presses was all used up—it was either fed to livestock, or the dried cakes were used as fuel to power the bathhouses. Throughout the city you will find that even the grandest houses had their own olive press. Commerce and manufacture were forbidden to the Roman senatorial class but anything remotely agricultural, even making bricks, could be done to your heart's content without losing status. It is refreshing to imagine this grand provincial capital surrounded by piles of crushed olives and the back doors of mansions reeking of discarded black tarry oil. The river Fertassa, joined by the river Khoumane from Moulay Idriss, flowed outside the southern city walls and served as a combined moat and sewer.

The Orpheus House

The Orpheus House stands by a conspicuous clump of three cypress trees. This is the largest house in the southern part of the city, named like all the mansions of Volubilis after the subject of their principal mosaic. It is a palatial building divided, in the eastern tradition, into public and private quarters, each with its own entrance.

The first, private entrance leads to a room with a **dolphin mosaic** on the floor. The diamond lozenges, interlocking circles and airy curls which surround the central figure echo traditional carpet designs. There is also a **kitchen** with its niche for statuettes and lamps dedicated to the household gods, the *genius*, the *lar* and the *penates*. The *genius* can be best thought of as a guardian angel, the *lar* as a representative of dead ancestors, and the *penates* as twin benevolent spirits who stopped food and drink going off and looked after the sanctity of the family hearth. To the right of the kitchen is an intimate and simple paved bath with its adjacent boiler room.

The second entrance leads directly into the **atrium**, a lavish open-air court decorated with a mosaic floor showing the sea goddess Amphitrite pulled by a seahorse and surrounded by sea creatures. The courtyard is surrounded by the main living rooms, a similar arrangement to contemporary Moroccan houses. The large southern room, the ***triclinium*** or dining room has a **magnificent mosaic**. The U-shaped plain area of flooring would have been covered by couches, leaving the central circular panel free to be admired from a number of angles. It shows Orpheus playing his harp, encircled by a ring of trees which like the mammals and birds, are seduced by his music—even the sphinx and griffins look tranquil. It is enclosed by a disciplined decorative pattern with two delightful infills that show a pair of mallards feeding from an urn, and a pair of Barbary partridges at a bird table. Orpheus (amongst other musical triumphs) descended to hell in an attempt to rescue his wife Eurydice and, 'so to the music of his strings he sang and all the bloodless spirits wept to hear; . . . and Sisyphus sat rapt upon his stone. Then first by that sad singing overwhelmed, the Furies' cheeks it's said were wet with tears' (Ovid).

Next door, to the left of the path lie the ruins of the **Gallienus Baths**, an extensive *hammam*, notable now only for one section of broken and faded mosaic amongst a series of gaping holes. These public baths were redecorated by order of the Emperor Gallienus (AD 260–68), which turned them into the most lavish in the whole city. Gallienus is otherwise known for his military reforms. He divided the army between reserve forces and highly trained mounted regiments, who could rush to any trouble on the border.

The Forum, Basilica and Capitoline Temple

Passing another smaller public bath on the right the path climbs a flight of steps to enter the paved public square of the city, the forum. This formal centre was usually ringed with market courtyards, official temples and the offices of civic government. On the west side the *macellum*, a small butcher's souk, has been identified. Archaeologists have also discovered that it was built over a number of ancient temples. The south face of the forum is dominated by the long arcaded outer wall of the **basilica**, the Roman courthouse, which was completed in the early 3rd century AD. It is one of the finest examples in North Africa of one of the most determinedly Roman of all civic buildings. The walls are substantial enough for the original shape of the building to be easily imagined, though you will have to fill the central nave with two double rows of columns. These ran down the entire interior length to frame the two apses at either end of the building. In the centre of each of the two apses would sit a presiding Roman magistrate, usually the governor and his deputy, surrounded by his legal staff and secretaries. The administration of justice was a very public affair, and the citizens of Volubilis would freely wander in and out from the forum to listen to part of a case, view a prominent litigant or assess the character of a new Roman official. The plan of the building may recall to mind that of a church; rightly so, for the first state-built churches of the 4th century took the basilica, not the existing religious architecture of the temples, as their direct model. In front of the basilica stand various plinths that bore monuments to commemorate officials, generals and emperors.

The raised **capitoline temple** with its elegant Corinthian columns stands to the right of the basilica. Now very obvious, it would have been less so when the area was enclosed in an arcaded courtyard. Within this enclosed court an altar can be seen from which thirteen steps advance up to the terrace of the Capitoline temple. This, like the ancient temple in Rome, was dedicated to the trinity of gods, to Jupiter, Juno and Minerva. There were two classes of Roman gods, those who protected the state and those who protected the family. The Capitoline triad were the chief divinities of the state. A council would assemble below the Capitol to declare war, generals appeared before setting out to battle, and after victory they would return here to offer crowns of gold and booty. Juno and Minerva, like the Virgin Mary, were appealed to on all manner of occasions, but in their Capitoline role they watched over the health and population of the whole province.

At sunset the view through these pillars east to Moulay Idriss is triumphantly photogenic. This would have been the usual orientation for a temple, but instead it stares mysteriously at the back of the Basilica.

The **House of the Athlete**, labelled *'Maison au Desultor'*, stands at the northwest corner of the forum. It contains a crude mosaic of a sportsman who has won a cup for vaulting over a grey horse. Beyond this stand the ruins of some fashionable shops and opposite, on the right, is one of two public fountains that surround the ruins of the city's third and largest public bath, which covered an area of 1500 square metres. This, the **north bath**, and the fountains were probably built on the orders of the Emperor Hadrian, and fed by an aqueduct that channelled fresh spring water from the Zerhoun hills.

Triumphal Arch

The path now leads across the principal avenue to the magnificent triumphal arch, raised in AD 217 by the governor Marcus Aurelius Sebastenus in honour of the Emperor Caracalla and his mother Julia Domna, whose defaced medallion bust can be seen on the right. Julia Domna, a Syrian intellectual and a princess in her own right, accompanied her husband the Emperor Septimius Severus on his campaign in Britain in 208–11, where she became known as the 'mother of the camp'. After Septimius' death at York she was later the unhappy witness of the fratricidal murder of her son Geta, who had tried to take refuge in his mother's lap from his brother and co-Emperor Caracalla's murderous rage. For all this, the family may have been genuinely popular in Volubilis, for they were North African by origin and had achieved a remarkable legal reform by extending Roman citizenship to all provincials. By the time the arch was finished, however, they had already both been murdered by an usurper. The Arch remains an impressive monument, built from local Zerhoun stone and with little evidence of the reconstruction by French archaeologists in 1933. It was originally capped with a bronze six-horse chariot and nymphs that cascaded water into carved marble bowls below. It carried an inscription which thanked the province for this symbol of loyalty and remitted all outstanding debts to the Imperial exchequer, though there was a broad hint that the emperor would be happy to accept a free gift of soldiers and elephants.

From the arch the broad **Decumanus Maximus** leads to the Tangier gate. This central street was faced with a columned arcade which would have been lined by small shops and craft stalls. Tucked discreetly behind this screen were the large residences of officials, landlords and merchants. Just south of the arch is a house that is sometimes pointed out to visitors as a brothel due to a penis carved onto a stone lintel that now stands alone in a room.

The Grand Houses

The **Ephebe House**, named after the fine bronze head found here (now in the Archaeological Museum in Rabat), is immediately north of the arch. It has an impressive interior courtyard with a central pool, around which are arranged public rooms ornamented with mosaics. The most elegant of them, second on your right, has Bacchus being drawn in his chariot by leopards. On the north side of the house there is an old mausoleum which seems to have been incorporated into the house as a cellar. Next door to the west is the **House of Columns**, which sports a circular pool in the atrium, beds of geraniums and a famous spiral, fluted column which was carved in the early 3rd century AD.

At a back dining-room in the next door house, known as the *Maison au Cavalier*—the **Knight's House**—there is a mosaic of a lascivious Bacchus, aided by Eros, discovering Ariadne, neglected by Theseus, asleep on the shore at Naxos. The figures are crude but the god's prurient eyes are alive and the flesh glistens with colour. Ariadne subsequently bore Bacchus six children, and her bridal chaplet was placed in the stars, where it forms the Corona Borealis or Cretan Crown.

Next along, staying on the left of the road, is the **Labours of Hercules House**, named after the crude mosaic found in the dining room. Here, in oval frames, are strip-cartoon images from the life of Hercules—as a child strangling snakes; the capture of Cerberus; the Cretan Bull; cleaning the Augean stables; the Stymphalian birds, wrestling with Antaeus, the Erymanthian boar, the Lernean hydra, Hippolyta's girdle; and slaying the Nemean lion. It is thought the mosaic might have been made in the reign of the Emperor Commodus, who had a Hercules obsession, but Hercules was always a popular hero in Morocco due to his identification with the Phoenician Melkarth and the number of his achievements that occurred here. Another room has Jupiter and his boyfriend Ganymede in the centre, with the four seasons depicted in the corners. There are the usual private quarters behind the public rooms, with bath and frescoed panels painted to imitate marble. The arches in front of the house provided space for eight shops. The house was originally entered from a side street, guarded by a porter's lodge.

Beyond the Labours of Hercules House is a row of five smaller but still grand houses. The first held an inscription that has identified it as the **house of T. Flavius Germanus**; the second has a well preserved and amusing mosaic of Dionysis and the four seasons; the third, marked by one crude pillar, is known as the **Bathing Nymphs House** (*Maison des Bains des Nymphes*) after a mosaic which shows three nymphs undressing and dancing beside the Hippocrene spring, overlooked by Pegasus, an ancient cult tree, and a horned wild-man (presumably Acteon half-metamorphosed into a deer). Directly behind this house is the north gate, which opens out into the extensive western cemetery, while opposite, across the street, is the **Nereids House**. If the restorations have been completed the poolside mosaic here is well worth a look, as is the disturbing mosaic of four wild beasts—a bull-baiting scene, a lion, a lioness and a leopard eating heads.

Back on the left-hand side of the main street, beyond the smaller houses, is the **Gordian Palace**. With its imposing exterior of a dozen Ionic columns, this is believed to have been the governor's residence, rebuilt during the reign of Gordian III, AD 238–44. Two houses were combined to give a total of 74 rooms, including courtyards with pools and bath-houses. Inscriptions found in the palace record a series of agreements between the Roman governor and the chief of the Baquates tribe. The frequency of new treaties in the 3rd century suggests a troubled frontier. The last pact, made just a few years before the fall of the city, refers wishfully to a *'Foederata et ducturna pax'*, a federated and lasting peace. To those in the know the wording of the treaty which treated the Baquates kingdom almost as an equal entity to the Roman Empire must have spelt trouble. Though the palace is strong in atmosphere, its decoration is restricted to a few columns and some simple geometric mosaics.

A single cypress tree about 100m east of the Decumanus Maximus marks the **Venus House**. Renowned for its mosaics, this was also where the superb bronze busts of Juba II and Cato (now in the Rabat museum) were discovered, buried in a protective bed of sand. The house is currently undergoing stabilization and is not accessible to the public, although a platform has been built to one side to allow a good view of the two most famous mosaics

The currently-closed central courtyard has an 'I' shaped pool, decorated with a damaged mosaic of a series of racing chariots drawn by rival teams of peacocks, geese and ducks, which includes accurate period details of a hippodrome. The large dining room straight ahead used to house the mosaic of Venus being carried through the waves that is now displayed in the Tangier museum. From the raised platform one can see the naked Hylos captured by nymphs, a colourful composition dominated by rippling muscles and erotic curves; the two side panels show scenes of guilty *erotes* being chastised. Hylos was an Argonaut who joined Jason's crew as the darling squire of Hercules. He went ashore but was seized by two nymphs, Dryope and Pegae, who dragged him away to live with them in an underwater grotto. The next-door mosaic shows chaste Diana with a nymph surprised by Acteon at her bath, her bow hanging from the branches of a cult tree. Acteon is already sprouting horns, for the goddess, in revenge for being surprised, changed him into a stag, and he was then chased and devoured by his own hounds.

Returning back to the forum you get a brief look at pre-Roman Volubilis as you pass an ancient mound composed of fragments of past temples and burial chambers. Across the river Fertassa are the foundations of the **Temple of 'Saturn'**, where over 600 carved stone offerings have been discovered. This was established centuries before the Roman period as the Phoenician temple of Baal, a Semitic horned male deity of the mountains and streams, whose rites and worship continued unchanged under the Roman label of Saturn.

Where to Stay

Moulay Idriss has fortunately been kept quite free of hotels and non-Muslims are not officially permitted to stay in the town. Outside the great September festival, though, it can be possible to find families who rent rooms; ask around in local cafés or try the cedar-lintelled house of Sidi Fridolla, first right at the wooden bar prohibiting entry to the sanctuary, then first left and knock at the red door of no. 24.

Three kilometres north of Moulay-Idriss along the P28 is the recently-built **Volubulis** hotel, © (05) 544408, fax (05) 544369, postal address BP20, Moulay Idriss, Zerhoun, par Meknès, Morocco. In the expensive price range, it is a large complex specifically designed for sudden influxes of coach-born parties, but has a wonderful view over the Roman ruins from its terraces, plus a bar, a serviceable restaurant and helpful staff.

Otherwise, but much cheaper, there is just the campsite **Refuge Zerhoun**, well signposted and just uphill from the hotel with a few basic rooms to rent around the central café-block. Be warned however that the dogs of the Zerhoun hills keep up an almost continuous nocturnal howl.

Eating Out

This area is almost perfect for a picnic, taken either in the olive groves of Jbel Zerhoun or by the tree-shaded, ruin-skirted Oued Khoumane stream that trickles just south of Volubilis. Provisions can be bought in Moulay Idriss or Meknès. Aside from the café inside the Volubilis site entrance, the café-restaurants in Moulay Idriss and the licensed restaurant at the Volubilis hotel, there is one exceptional local address:

The **Baraka de Zerhoun**, © (05) 544184, is on the left of the tarmac hill road that climbs directly through Moulay Idriss, at 22 Aïn Smen-Khiber. It is a delightful, recently-opened but traditional restaurant that offers meals that can consist of bowls of local Zerhoun olives, freshly-made butter, an excellent spiced vegetable salad and local *tagine*. It is run by two women in white, Benfares Soad and Tahrzouti Amina, has no drinks license and is moderately priced.

Fès

Fès, where all is Eden, or a wilderness.

Anon

Fès is the most complete Islamic medieval city in the world. Its history has for a thousand years also been the history of Morocco's political, commercial and intellectual life, even though it is now superseded by the modern cities of Rabat and Casablanca, and to some extent by its own new town, built by the French after 1912.

Fès was founded in the 9th century as the capital of the Idrissid state, the first Muslim kingdom of Morocco. A century later the Idrissid dynasty had declined, but the city they had established survived. Fès grew in wealth and remained the acknowledged religious and cultural centre of Morocco, despite the establishment of new administrative capitals at Marrakech and then Rabat. Its golden period of wealth, fame and prosperity was in the 13th and 14th centuries under the Merenid sultans. Much has perished in the long decline from this period, and it is chiefly the old mosques, tombs and religious colleges that have survived, respected by each dynasty, every mutinous regiment and pillaging tribe. The medersas are open to non-Muslims, but the rest of the vast heritage of religious architecture remains inaccessible. Visitors are left to concentrate on the street pattern, the style of life, the sounds and odours, which remain triumphantly unchanged.

The city has a population of half a million and is divided into three parts. **Fès-el-Bali** (Old Fès) is the enigmatic and fiercely Muslim medina, a maze of hidden quarters, *fondouqs*, medersas and mosques with narrow streets that remain inaccessible to cars. **Fès Jdid** (New Fès) is the 13th century Imperial city to the west of the medina, which is still dominated by the royal palace and the *mellah*, the old Jewish ghetto. The French-built **New Town** is even further to the west, a separate entity with wide avenues and new developments which would be without interest but for its cafés, hotels, restaurants, and convenience.

History

Foundation Legend

Idriss II inherited his father's kingdom at his posthumous birth in 791. It was centred on the two existing cities of Christian Volubilis and Jewish Sefrou. He and his loyal regent Rashid decided to create a specifically Muslim city, and one day while travelling between the two cities they rested halfway, at the Ras el Ma spring. The boy Idriss followed it downstream to discover a wide, well-watered valley fringed with hills. Greatly encouraged by this gorgeous vista, and the prophetic welcome of an aged holy man, they decided to establish a settlement on the right bank of the river that year, in 799. During the excavation for the foundation walls a golden axe, a *fas*, was unearthed. This fateful discovery helped settle the form of the human sacrifice required if each gateway of the new city were to be protected by a resident spirit, a tradition that was widespread in many parts of the world. A pair of Persian exiles, or *Fars*, were buried alive at each gate, and the city was known as Fès and its citizens as Fassi.

Idrissid Fès, 799–1075

Idriss II ruled his kingdom from a walled city on the left (north) bank of the valley which contained his El Aliya palace and barracks for his 500-strong Arab guard. This bare nucleus of a city was soon flooded with refugees from the turbulent politics of the more prosperous and Arabized Muslim states of Spain and Tunisia. In 818 a civil war in Andalusia drove 8000 refugees to Fès, who were presented with the empty right (north) bank by Idriss II. Seven years later another tide of refugees fled a revolution in the holy city of Kairouan and were given land on the left bank. This settlement pattern remained for the next 250 years. Fès-el-Andalous and Fès-el-Karaouiyne were two quite separate cities that faced each other across the riverbed, each enclosed in its own walls. The Andalusians were considered to have the prettiest women and the men were considered strong, brave, handsome and good farmers, but also just a little dull. The Kairouan men were considered more elegant, better educated but a bit over-partial to the luxuries of life. What they both shared was a strong Arab identity and an urban, literate, technical and intellectual culture far in advance of any mere Berber tribe. It was as if a fortified Manhattan were suddenly placed in the middle of the prairies.

Idriss II died in 828 and his tomb became the focus of the city's pride and identity, as it is today. His kingdom was divided amongst his squabbling sons, but the ruler of Fès was accepted as first among equals. During his grandson Yahya's reign the two grand mosques of Andalous and Karaouiyne were founded to give graphic evidence of the settlements' prosperity. In 917 Fès fell under the control of the Shiite Fatimid Empire, expanding west from its core territory of Tunisia. In 930 the Ommayad Caliphate of Cordoba took over, and ruled the city through a governor for over a century.

The Almoravid and Almohad Period, 1075–1248

In 1075 the Almoravid leader Youssef ben Tachfine captured Fès, just five years before he succeeded in crushing all resistance and uniting Morocco for the first time. The Fassis could not at first accept these unsophisticated Berbers from the Sahara, but they soon learned to benefit from their firm rule. Though Marrakech was the political capital, Fès was better suited to act as the commercial hub of an empire that stretched from West Africa to the Pyrenees. The Almoravids dismantled the divisive twin walls and erected a single circuit to protect both districts. The endless bickering over river rights ended, for the Almoravids came from the desert and knew all about the efficient collection and distribution of water. Clean mountain springs were tapped and a network of pipes, sewers and mills prepared the ground for future expansion.

Water was also the tool by which the Almohads, based in Taza, at last seized control of Fès in 1146 after a long siege. Abdel Moumen built a dam upstream in order to collect a great head of water which he suddenly released; the resulting flood washed the walls around the valley clean away. The Almohads then marched in and demolished the remaining walls, declaring that 'only justice and the sword shall be our ramparts'. They also demolished any traces of Almoravid rule, on the flimsy basis that the architectural decoration of the previous dynasty had been impious. Later Sultans ignored these early declarations and constructed a massive new perimeter wall. This still defines the extent of Fès-el-Bali, and some gateways and large sections, particularly to the north, are still in place.

Merenid Fès, 1248–1465

Abou Yahya, the chief of the Beni Merin tribe, captured Fès in 1248, the year that he had treacherously massacred the leaderless Almohad army. So important had the city now become that this date is taken to be the start of his reign as the first Merenid sultan. Though the period of Merenid rule was to prove the glittering zenith of the city's fortune, the Fassis never took to this dynasty, mere Berber chiefs of a nomad tribe from the eastern plains. They frequently rebelled against their new rulers, and in truth no dynasty has been able to win the city's affection away from the original Idrissid line, from whom many of the chief Fassi families proudly trace their descent. Abou Yusuf Yacqub, the second Merenid sultan, reigned from 1259 to 1286 and firmly established Fès as the capital of Morocco. He did not however feel secure enough to dwell amongst his citizens. On 21 March 1276 he started work on Fès Jdid, 'New Fès', enclosing it in a double wall 750m away from the turbulent politics of Fès-el-

Bali. It was known officially as *El Medinat el Baida*, 'the white city', and a portion of the river Fès served as a moat for its outer walls, crowned with crenellations and reinforced by square towers. The white city held the court and palace of the sultans, the mint, baths, markets, three mosques—the Grand, the Red and the Flower—an aqueduct and separate quarters for the sultan's mercenary guard. Sultan Abou Yusuf Yacqub was the first Moroccan ruler to build a medersa, a residential college for religious education. It was an archetype which his successors developed and embellished into one of the great glories of Fès.

In 1438 the barracks were enlarged and converted into the first separate Jewish quarter in Morocco. Wealthy Jewish merchants had long been convenient targets in urban unrest, and by placing them within the protection of the royal city the Merenids bound this community, useful for its many skills and taxable wealth, to their service. One of the more disagreeable services was the preservation of the heads of the executed, in salt, before they were displayed on gates. The word for salt, *mellah*, soon became synonymous with a Jewish quarter.

The Decline of Fès after 1465

In 1465 the last Merenid sultan, Abdul Haqq, was dragged through the streets of Fès-el-Bali before having his throat cut like a sacrificial goat. A council of Idrissid *sherifs* had planned this bold insurrection, and they succeeded in ruling a republic for seven years. This political experiment was finished by the Wattasids, the hereditary viziers of the Merenids, who marched into Fès at the head of an army. Wattasid authority over the next century was slowly reduced to Fès itself, as the Portuguese seized control of the coast while tribal dynasties fought over the rest. An earthquake shattered the town in 1522, and the Saadians, a dynasty from southern Morocco, occupied Fès 19 years later. They made no secret of their preference for Marrakech, and their only constructive action was to build two artillery forts with which to intimidate the city. In 1666 Fès welcomed the first Alaouite sultan, Moulay Rachid, as a liberator, and he responded in kind by building another medersa here. This *rapprochement* was quickly reversed; Sultan Moulay Ismaïl detested the city and did everything in his power to humble Fès and vaunt Meknès. Most of the later Alaouite sultans tended to alternate between Fès and Marrakech, and it was not until the reign of Sultan Moulay Hassan (1873–94) that decay was decisively checked. He built three administrative palaces that physically and symbolically united Fès Jdid and Fès-el-Bali, and most of the substantial Fassi merchant houses date from his reign.

The grip of the European powers strengthened after Moulay Hassan's death and on 30 March 1912 Sultan Moulay Hafid was forced by the French to sign the Treaty of Fès, which established the French Protectorate. The city reacted violently to the surrender of national sovereignty and on 17 April the European population were hounded through the medina streets and lynched—over 80 mutilated bodies were stacked up before the palace gates. The sultan's army joined the rebellion and manned the city walls, but the following day a French force marched from Meknès and first shelled and then occupied the subdued city.

Sultan Moulay Hafid was removed to Rabat, where the government of Morocco has since remained, and Casablanca became the still-unrivalled mercantile metropolis. The French built an ordered new town of regular avenues well to the west of the old city to house the European population in comfort and safety. Fès-el-Bali is now a unique medieval survivor, fallen far from grace but remaining one of the most distinctive cities of the world.

Getting There

by air

The Fès-Saïss airport, © (05) 624800/624712, is 11km due south off the P24 road to Immouzer. Internal flights include a daily flight to Casablanca, a twice-weekly service to Agadir and Marrakech and useful weekly connections to Er Rachidia, Tangier and Oujda. Of the international flights there is a three-times-a-week connection to London (via Casablanca or Tangier). Royal Air Maroc have an office at 54 Av Hassan II, © (05) 625516, reservations (05) 620457, as well as a booth at the airport, © (05) 624712/652161. The airport bus, no. 16, leaves from Place Mohammed V, or pay 30dh for your own taxi, 5dh for a place in a *grand taxi*.

by rail

Travel by train whenever possible, trust no published schedule and buy your ticket and a seat reservation early and directly from the main station, which is located off the Av des Almohades on the northern edge of the new town, © (05) 622043. There are nine trains a day to Meknes (1hr), eight trains a day to Casablanca (8hrs), two north for Tangier (6.5hrs), one east to Oujda and two south to Marrakech (8hrs) including a recently-established sleeper connection. A taxi ride, in a licensed cab with meter on, from the station to any centrally-placed Fès hotel will be under 10dh.

by bus

Bus travel into and out of Fès can be slightly confusing as there are three bus stations. The busiest and most convenient is the new terminal just north of Fès-el-Bali's Bab Mahrouk gate. This has replaced the old mess of garages (still marked on some maps) around Place Baghdadi and Bab Bou Jeloud. It has its own café, and is well served by *petits taxis*. The CTM have began to use this terminal, as well as continuing with their own station in the heart of the New Town on Blvd Mohammed V, © (05) 622043. If you wish to head east (to Taza or Oujda) or north into the Rif there is also a local bus station by Bab Ftouh on the southeast edge of Fès-el-Bali. The most frequent bus connections are west to Meknès (50mins), Rabat (4–6hrs) and Casablanca (8hrs), with at least twice-daily connections to Tangier (6hrs), Tetouan (8hrs), Nador (8hrs), Marrakech, Er Rachidia via Midelt, and the Middle Atlas towns of Sefrou, Immouzer, Azrou and Ifrane

Tourist Information

The two principal **tourist offices** are in the new town: in the western corner of Place de la Résistance at the end of Av Hassan II, © (05) 623460, and the Syndicat d'Initiative (SI), on the east side of Place Mohammed V on Av Mohammed es Slaoui, © (05) 624769. However, most useful for the visitor is the SI booth (open 8am–7pm Mon–Sat) beside Bab Bou Jeloud in Fès-el-Bali, where official guides, with their official gold medallion and working outfit of white cotton jellaba, red fez and dark glasses, can be hired.

Banks are mostly in the new town. The BMCE on Place Mohammed V offers the most useful range of services, but there is also the BMCI at 10 Rue Assela, Banque Populaire and Crédit du Maroc on Av Mohammed V. In the heart of Fès-el-Bali there is a branch of Crédit du Maroc uphill from the Cherratin Medersa for currency exchanges. All large hotels will change money and travellers' cheques for guests.

The **post office** is in the new town at the corner of Av Hassan II and Blvd Mohammed V, and open Mon–Fri in summer from 8am–2pm, winter 8.30am–12 noon, 2.30–6pm, stamps sold on Saturdays from 8–11am. The telephone section, which is open until 9pm, has its own side entrance when the rest of the building has closed up. Other branches are found at Place de l'Atlas, and Place Batha in Fès Jdid.

Emergencies: The central **police** station is on Av Mohammed V, © 19. There is an **all-night pharmacy**, © (05) 623380, in the new town on Blvd Moulay Youssef by the Place de la Résistance. In the daytime there are dozens of chemists open in the new town, and also one by the Bab Ftouh in Fès-el-Bali.

There is a **French consulate** on Av Abou Obeida Ibn Jarrah. The **Catholic Church** of St Francis on Av Mohammed es Slaoui in the new town has Mass on Saturday at 6.30pm, and Sunday at 10.30am.

Getting Around

by bus

Fès is one of the few Moroccan cities where local buses can be of real use to a visiting tourist. The route numbers are marked on the sides, not on the back or front as you might expect. The **no. 1** bus runs between Place des Alaouites (the southwest end of Fès Jdid) and Dar Batha (at the western end of Fès-el-Bali), **no. 3** goes between Place des Alaouites and Place de la Résistance (in the northeast corner of the new town), **no. 9** from Place de la Résistance to Dar Batha, **no. 10** runs from Bab Guissa (the centrally placed northern gate to Fès-el-Bali) to Place des Alaouites, **no. 18** from the Place de la Résistance east via Bab Jdid to Bab Ftouh (the southeast gate of Fès-el-Bali), and **no. 19** from the train station to Place des Alaouites.

by taxi

Fès's red ***petits taxis*** use their meters and are therefore delightfully cheap and trouble-free. Taxi fares increase by 50 per cent after dusk or 9pm, whichever is earliest. In the new town you should be able to find taxis on Avenue Hassan II (especially around the crossing with Blvd Mohammed V), at Place Mohammed V, the train station and in Rue des Normandes, off Blvd Mohammed V, which is a *grands taxis* park. In Fès Jdid try the Place des Alaouites, while in Fès-el-Bali they can usually be hailed outside all the principal transport gates; Place Baghdadi (between Bab Bou Jeloud and Bab Mahbrouk), the northern Bab Guissa, southern Bab er Rsif, south east Bab Ftouh and Dar Batha-Place Istiqlal (just south of the Bab Bou Jeloud). ***Grands taxis*** can be found at Place Baghdadi (for a place to Meknès), Bab Jamai,-Bab Guissa and Bab Ftouh (for a place to Taza) in Fès-el-Bali. The rank on Rue des Normandes just off Blvd Mohammed V in the new town is one of the most useful and covers the destinations south of the city; Sefrou, Azrou, Ifrane and Immouzer.

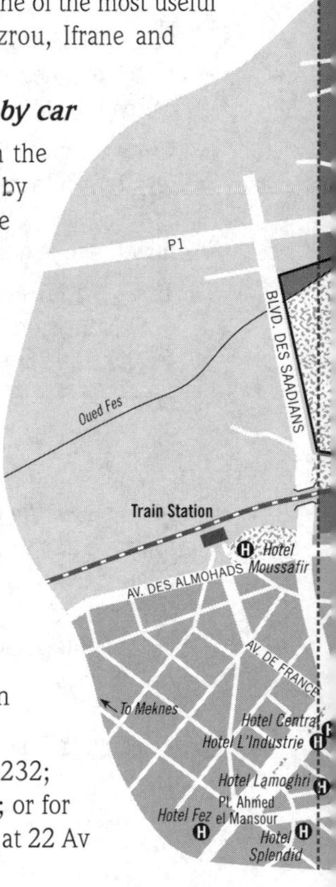

by car

A car is a hindrance in Fès. If you drive into the city from the west or south you will invariably find yourself escorted by motorbike-born 'guides'. There is absolutely no way to shake them off (apart from revealing a deep knowledge of the city in colloquial Maghrebi), but treat them as a convenience, for they can lead you directly to your chosen hotel. It is as well also to be aware, though, that they are aiming for the greater prize of taking you round the medina and earning a commission from the bazaars and carpet shops. Once in Fès, get your hotel receptionist to recommend a secure parking place, then completely empty your car and forget about it.

A car is however, a great advantage in exploring the Middle Atlas or the hills to the north. For **car hire** ask at reception in big hotels or go directly to such agencies as Avis at 23 Rue de la Liberte, © (05) 622790 or 50 Blvd Chefchaouni, © (05) 626746, or Europcar- at 41 Av Hassan II, © (05) 626545.

Garages: for Renault service, 26 Rue Soudan, © (05) 622232; for Fiat, Auto Maroc, on Av Mohammed V, © (05) 623435; or for problems with all makes of car try the Méchanique Générale at 22 Av Cameroun.

A Tour of the Ramparts

Before leaving Fès try to witness dusk from the hills. Flame-coloured light plays on the ochre walls and flickers finally over the high minarets. The sky is full of pigeons and swallows enjoying the evening flight; smoke from thousands of kitchens lifts off from the medina. Then you are hit by the call to prayer.

A 15km circuit around the outer walls by taxi makes an excellent introduction to the city. The surrounding hills, particularly at Bordj Sud and by the Merenid tombs, all provide magnificent views over Fès-el-Bali.

Fès Jdid

Starting from the Place de la Résistance in the New Town, take the southern exit, for Taza, which descends into the river Zitoun valley. The outer walls of Fès Jdid rise to your left, enclosing the *mellah* and the Jewish necropolis, which is entered through the Bab Jiaf.

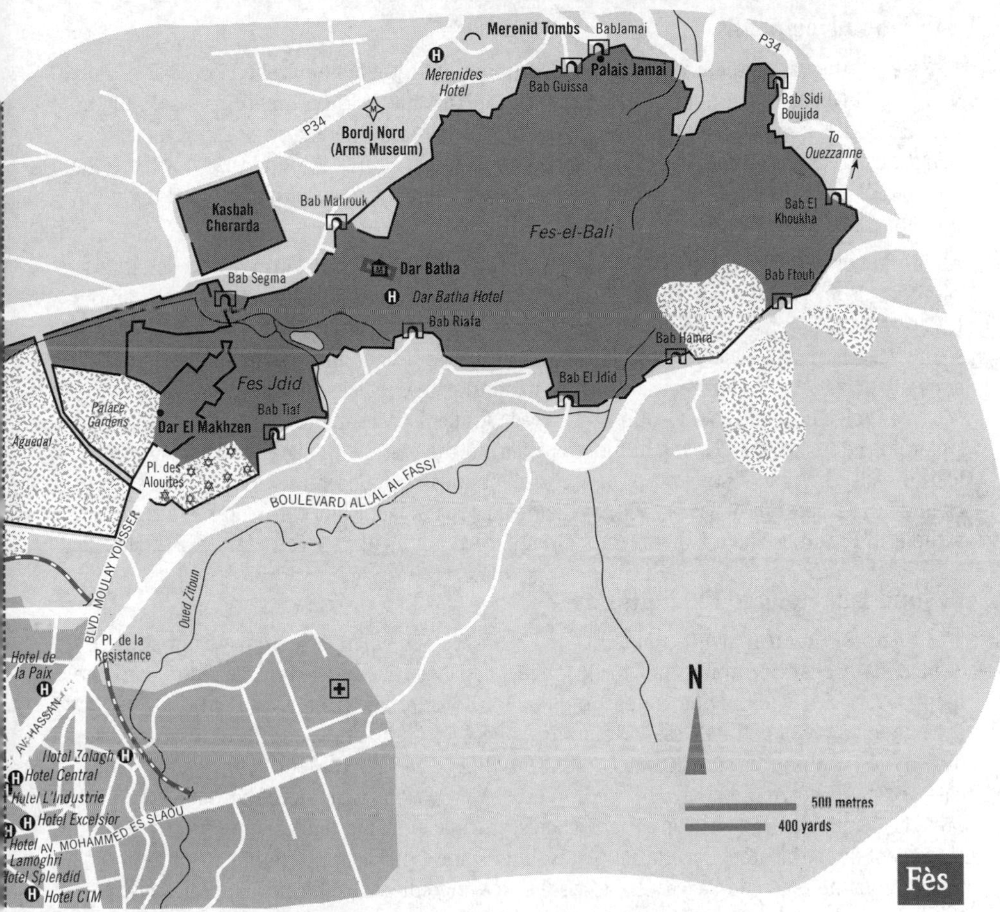

Schools and hospitals cluster around the Bab Jebala/Bab Riafa which leads to the area that Moulay Hassan developed in the 19th century to unite Fès-el-Bali and Fès Jdid. An electrical sub-station on your right marks the site of an old aqueduct; opposite is the Bab el Hadid. Below the walls a great artesian fountain ensures that there is a patch of bright green grass around the splash pool. Near here are the discreet walls of the American Fondouk, a charitable hospital for animals. As the road swings closer to the walls you pass Bab Jdid, which provides direct bus and taxi access into the heart of the medina.

Bordj Sud

Crossing over the river Boufekrane here the approach track to Bordj Sud can be seen to your right. This fort was built by Portuguese prisoners of the Saadian Sultan Ahmed el Mansour (1578–1609) as part of a system that was designed as much to intimidate the Fassis as to defend them. The fort is partly in ruins now, but it would have had a good field of fire over the Andalous and Karaouiyne districts that rise either side of the now-invisible river Fès.

Bab Ftouh Necropolis

Pass below the vast cemetery of Bab Ftouh studded with the whitewashed koubbas of holy men—non-Muslims are not usually welcome on this hill. All the great professors of the University of Karaouiyne are buried here and on the summit there is an open-air mosque, a *msalla*, used for the great feasts of Aid el Kebir and Aid es Seghir. Around the *msalla* are the koubbas of the Sebatou Rijal, the anonymous seven saints who, according to local tradition, brought Islam to Morocco.

At the lower eastern corner of the cemetery is a koubba to **Sidi Harazem**. He came to Morocco from Arabia and before retiring to a life of poverty and silence taught at the Karaouiyne Mosque. He was so skilful a debater that he silenced the most agnostic and sophistic of jinn, and has become the patron of Koranic studies and students in general. The ancient festival of Sidi Harazem takes place in spring; an equivalent of the European Lord of Misrule is elected, and processes up to the great Andalous Mosque to officiate as the student sultan for Friday prayers. Now a humorous affair, in the past it was a great occasion for political unrest. The final resting-place of the Sidi's bones is a contentious issue: they are not claimed to lie here but in Marrakech, or the nearby spa of Sidi-Harazem. Below the cemetery is the **Bab Ftouh**, to the left of which behind the walls stretches the cemetery of Bab Hamra.

Beyond Bab Ftouh to the Potteries

The **Potters' Quarter**, with its distinctive chimneys belching black smoke from kilns still fuelled by orchard prunings and dried olive pressings, has been moved away from the medina and is now found one km east of Bab Ftouh just off the main Taza road. Turn left by the blue-tiled tower of the Boissons Talounite café: a left turn at the next dirt crossroads leads directly to the **Poterie Fakh-Khari**, ✆ (05) 649322, well geared to receiving visitors with a café and two showroom shops. In the compound you can watch apprentices kneeding the raw clay, skilled potters working it on wheels, the stacking and unstacking of furnaces and schools of fluent painters decorating plates, bowls and hotel ashtrays, while in other rooms teams of young boys cut glazed tiles to be the raw ingredient for the *zellij* mosaics made by the master craftsmen. There is no admission charge, prices are not bad and there can be an encouraging murmur of business from designers and exporters commissioning special pieces.

Otherwise, continue east of Bab Ftouh to pass the eastern gate, Bab Khouka. An extensive suburb has here sprawled out beyond the old city to obscure most of the eastern walls. The next gate, **Bab Sidi Bou Jida**, is named after the koubba of that saint which is on your right. He can be compared to St Jude, the patron saint of lost causes, and is greatly favoured by students before exams and women before marriage. Across the river Fès there is a new tiled auction yard outside the walls. The smells and sights here are intense: trucks unload raw, bloody skins direct from butchers and slaughterhouses. The great wet bundles are forked over by specialists, bought, packed on to mules and sent down into the medina for the first stage in the long tanning process.

The Jamaï

Next is the **Bab Jamaï**, which leads in to the luxurious Palais Jamaï Hotel. This incorporates a few rooms and a magnificent Andalusian garden that belonged to a distinguished Fassi family, the Ulad Jamaï, which had a tradition of government service. The Jamaï brothers, Haj Amaati and Si Mohammed Soreir, served Sultan Moulay Hassan as Grand Vizier and Minister of War. After the death of their master they fell victim to the jealousy of the child-Sultan Abdul Aziz's Turkish mother and her ally the half-black chamberlain, Bou Ahmed. They were imprisoned in Tetouan, their property forfeit and their families persecuted. Haj Amaati died in prison but remained chained to his brother (in high summer) for eleven days. Si Mohammed survived the ordeal but was only released after fourteen years. On his deathbed he requested that 'my chains and fetters are to be put back upon my limbs. I desire to appear before God…that I might appeal to Him for the justice my sultan refused me.'

The Vista and the Merenid Tombs

The next gate after the Bab Jamaï is the 13th-century Almohad **Bab Guissa**, above which the road climbs up through the cemetery hill of the same name. Beside the turning down to the ugly Merenides Hotel a long, wide garden terrace has been established which allows locals as well as rich tourists to enjoy this unsurpassed view over Fès-el-Bali. As you join the colourful mass of kaftans billowing in the breeze of the evening paseo, you see below, tucked behind its ribbon of ancient wall virtually the complete extent of the Karaouiyne district. The zaouia of Idriss II is immediately recognizable by its high, green-tiled pyramid roof and accompanying tall minaret. Just to the left, and lower, a great expanse of green tiles marks the Karaouiyne Mosque, with its whitewashed minaret. This is crowned with a dome, not the usual Moroccan lantern, faithfully echoing the grand mosque at Kairouan, in Tunisia, founded by Uqba ben Nafi in 683. A lower, conventional minaret can be seen to the right: this is the Trumpeter's tower from which the end of the fast of Ramadan is announced. The city below remains defined by its 12th-century walls, the intense urban network in heady contrast to the hillside olive groves that overlook the medina to the north and south.

The actual tombs can only be reached by taking a goat track from the road. Most visitors seem content to enjoy them at a distance, surrounded by a crumbling mass of ruined walls, old quarries, caves and the odd melancholic figure. The tombs were originally established within the extensive walls of an old Merenid kasbah that defended this hilltop. Below it but outside the city walls was the medieval leper colony. The prominent arched cube among the tombs was once covered with a green-tiled pyramid roof, while a marble-columned interior court held a simple stone tomb carved with an elegant epitaph in a sea of coloured *zellij* mosaic. In the 14th century this patchwork of enclosed hilltop tombs must have equalled Rabat's Chellah in elegance. Now it is all dust. Well might Alexander have wept at the tomb of Cyrus, the greatest of all the great Persian Kings, when he saw that his mausoleum was neglected and covered in dust and rubbish less than a century after his death.

Bordj Nord

Open Wed–Mon 9am–12 noon, 1–6pm; closed Tues; adm.

Below the garden terrace viewpoint a series of neat paths take you down to the star-shaped Bordj Nord. Built in 1582, this was the second of the Saadian fortresses designed as much to cover the city with a threatening field of fire as protect it. A century and a half later, in the Alaouite period, the elegant lance-shaped corner redoubts were added; in 1964 the weapons collection from the Dar Batha museum was moved here to form a separate **Museum of**

Arms (Musée d'Armes). A walk around the cool dark vaults and casements of this immaculately preserved old artillery fortress, however, is worth the price of the ticket by itself. The collection takes you through the whole history of armaments, with cases of prehistoric Stone tools, Bronze and Iron Age weapons, casts of rare medieval European devices and a comprehensive display of 18th, 19th and 20th century weapons.

For a foreign visitor it is the vast array of Moroccan weapons stacked in an imposing mass in the three rear casements and which date from the 16th to the 20th centuries that is most rewarding. They show clearly how far the souvenir swords in the bazaars have evolved from the original very serviceable military sabres with their characteristic 'snake-head' wooden handles and chased-steel hand-guards. This is also true of the daggers, with a practical grip given by their bone, metal and leather handles and the very slight curve of their blades. The *fusils Marocains* with their almost 2m-long barrels (made in Fez, Tetouan or Taghzout) alone live up to one's exotic expectations, with some of their stocks and powder-horn accessories so encrusted with carved ivory, raw coral and silver and gold that they become male jewellery. For the historian the two bronze cannon at the exit provide crucial evidence of Morocco's industrial sophistication in the 16th century, and the self-sufficiency that allowed her to keep both the Portuguese and the Ottoman Empire at bay. The Arabic inscription on the damaged cannon reads 'made on the order of [Sultan] al-Walid ibn Zaydan in 1044 H' (1634 AD), while that on the vast 4.5m-long bronze cannon reads 'made by el Haj el Ghourg on the order of el Ghalib', the Saadian Sultan who ruled from 1557–74.

Cherarda Kasbah

The fort overlooks the extensive square-walled Cherarda Kasbah, protected by towers and surrounded on almost all sides by a cemetery. It was built by Moulay Rachid in 1670 to house tribes in the Sultan's service, notably the Oudaïa and Cherarda cavalry. It is now divided into hospital and university buildings and is therefore closed to tourists.

At the end of the long kasbah wall the **Bab Segma**, with a single remaining 14th-century octagonal tower, separates the kasbah from Fès Jdid. A kilometre of wall runs west from here to enclose the royal park and palace, and then a left turn before the sports park follows another monumental kilometre stretch of royal wall to arrive back at Place de la Résistance.

Fès Jdid

Though the most famous sites are in Fès-el-Bali, a walk through the simple street plan of Fès Jdid and a visit to the Dar Batha museum make a good preparation for the heady and confusing alleys of the old town.

Place des Alaouites

From the Place de la Résistance in the new town, Blvd Moulay Youssef leads directly to the Place des Alaouites, a kilometre away; or you can hop on the no. 3 bus. This main entrance to the palace was created by King Hassan II between 1969 and 1971, as the ceremonial guard and great gates proclaim. On occasion this entire square is covered in a patchwork of carpets brought out by Fassis to honour some official guest. The gleaming brass doors were manufactured in the medina in 1971, and are kept clean by being rubbed with lemons.

The Royal Palace

Christopher Kininmonth, in *The Traveller's Guide to Morocco*, writes that, 'I believe this to be the finest single sight Morocco has to offer; one of the wonders of the world.'

The royal palace, the Dar el Makhzen, occupies half of Fès Jdid and covers over 80 hectares. Within its walls is an inaccessible city that holds 700 years of pavilions, squares, gardens and palaces. It includes a mosque, the koubba of Sidi Mejaed, and a medersa built by the Merenid Sultan Abou Said Othman in 1320. Sidi Mohammed built the Dar Ayad el Kebira palace in the 18th century; Moulay Hassan the present royal apartments in 1880; and in 1980 another palace was added, the Dar el Bahia, for the Arab summit held the next year.

The *Mellah*

The Grand Rue du Mellah runs from Place des Alaouites through the whole *mellah* district. The Jewish community had to walk barefoot within the three royal cities (Marrakech, Fès and Meknès), and before a mosque, but by the 18th century the Fassi Jews had acquired the right to wear sea-rush socks outside the *mellah.* There are now few Jews left, but a legacy of jewellers' shops, brocade, balconies, small windows with their tracery of iron grille work and an air of business gives the quarter something of its old distinctive atmosphere. Tiny side streets lead off into a labyrinth of covered passages, underground workshops and timbered houses. By heading south you can eventually find your way to the Jewish cemetery, a great walled enclosure of whitewashed inscribed stones. You will need a guide to find the two former synagogues, the **Serfati** and the **Fassiyn**, one now a house, the other a bazaar.

Bab Smarine

As you approach the distinctive, crenellated, high gate of the Bab Smarine, restored in 1924, you pass through the glittering displays of the **jewellers' souk**. The Bab Smarine used to separate the *mellah* from the Muslim quarter, and before that marked the southern entrance of the city. Immediately beyond the arch is a covered food market which was established in an old granary built by the Merenid sultans. From the gate the Grand Rue de Fès-Jdid, lined with stalls and cafés, runs due north through the city to the outer walls. Along the way, on the right, is the **Hamra**, the red, and then the **Beida**, the white, **Mosques**, built in the 13th century by the creator of Fès Jdid, Sultan Abou Yusuf Yacqub. The alleys to the left stop at the perimeter wall of the palace, beneath which is the pretty **mosque of Al Azhar**, built by Sultan Abou Inan in the 14th century, with a fine sculpted gate. The street opens out to form a small walled square known as the Petit Méchouar, under which the river Fès flows and in which is a gleaming back entrance to the royal palace

Quartier Moulay Abdullah

A small arch to the left in the Petit Méchouar is the only entrance into the Moulay Abdullah district. This area is almost entirely enclosed by high walls and was chosen by the French as the *quartier réservé*, the red-light district, but there is little remaining evidence of those days. Wandering through this calm residential area you soon pass the entrance of the **grand mosque**, built in just three years (1273–76) by Sultan Abou Yusuf Yacqub. Sultan Abou Inan was buried here in 1358, and a koubba raised above his tomb beside the mosque. The main street leads in 200m to the other **mosque** of the district, with a conspicuous, slender minaret, built in the 18th century by Sultan **Moulay Abdullah**. The mosque has become a principal Alaouite tomb, full of the graves of princes and two sultans including Moulay Youssef, 1912–27, King Hassan II's grandfather.

Petit and Old Méchouar

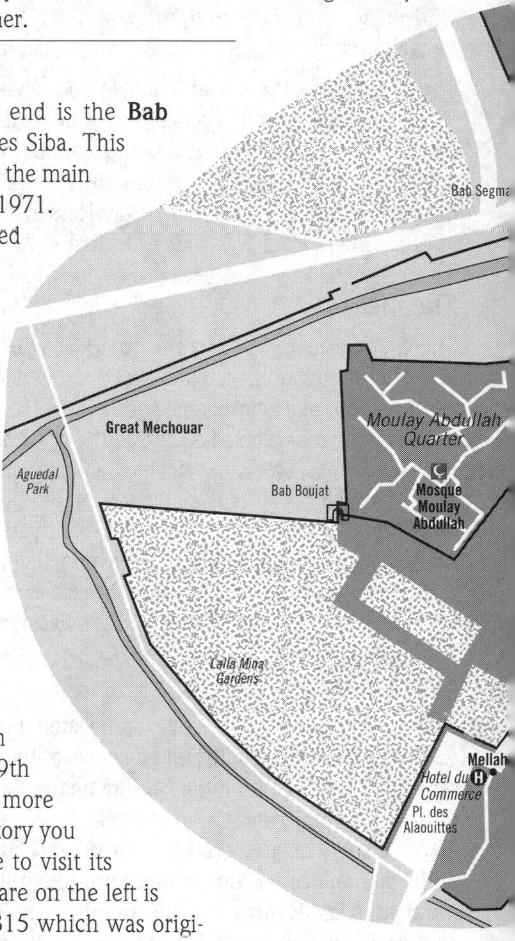

Back in the Petit Méchouar, at the north end is the **Bab Dekakène**, sometimes known as the Bab es Siba. This massive, triple-arched Merenid gate served as the main entrance into the city and royal palace until 1971. Ferdinand, prince of Portugal, was imprisoned for six years in this gate. He had surrendered himself as hostage to allow his army to escape after a disastrous attempt to seize Tangier in 1437; his brothers refused to return Ceuta to the sultan in exchange for his release. On Ferdinand's death his naked body was hung from the gate, pierced through the heels like a butchered goat, where it swung for four days. His corpse was then gutted, stuffed with straw and put on show for a further 29 years.

On the far side of the arches there is the larger, walled **Vieux Méchouar**. On the left is the *Makina*, the old royal ordnance factory, built and run by the Italian 'Campionario Di Spolette' in the late 19th century. Although it now holds nothing more offensive than an export-oriented carpet factory you will need permission from the tourist office to visit its huge vaulted halls. At the far end of the square on the left is the **Bab Segma**, a Merenid gate built in 1315 which was originally flanked by a pair of distinctive octagonal arches, like the gate to the Chellah in Rabat, although only one tower now survives. The smaller gate, the **Bab es Smen**, built in the 19th century, is the one that is used nowadays.

Bou Jeloud and the Gardens

The Avenue des Français leads due east from the Petit Méchouar 600m to the **Bab Bou Jeloud**, the main point of entry to Fès-el-Bali. For 500 years this area was a wasteland, caught between the cities of Fès Jdid and Fès-el-Bali. It was developed in the 19th century by Moulay Hassan into the three palace gardens of Dar Batha, Bou Jeloud and Dar Beida. The old Bou Jeloud Palace, symbolically, was entered from either Fès Jdid or Fès-el-Bali. Only one of these palaces, the Dar Batha, is open, and now houses the **Museum of the Arts and Traditions of Fès**. Otherwise the area remains dominated by high walls that hide gardens, palaces and pavilions, while less attractive administrative buildings are left exposed.

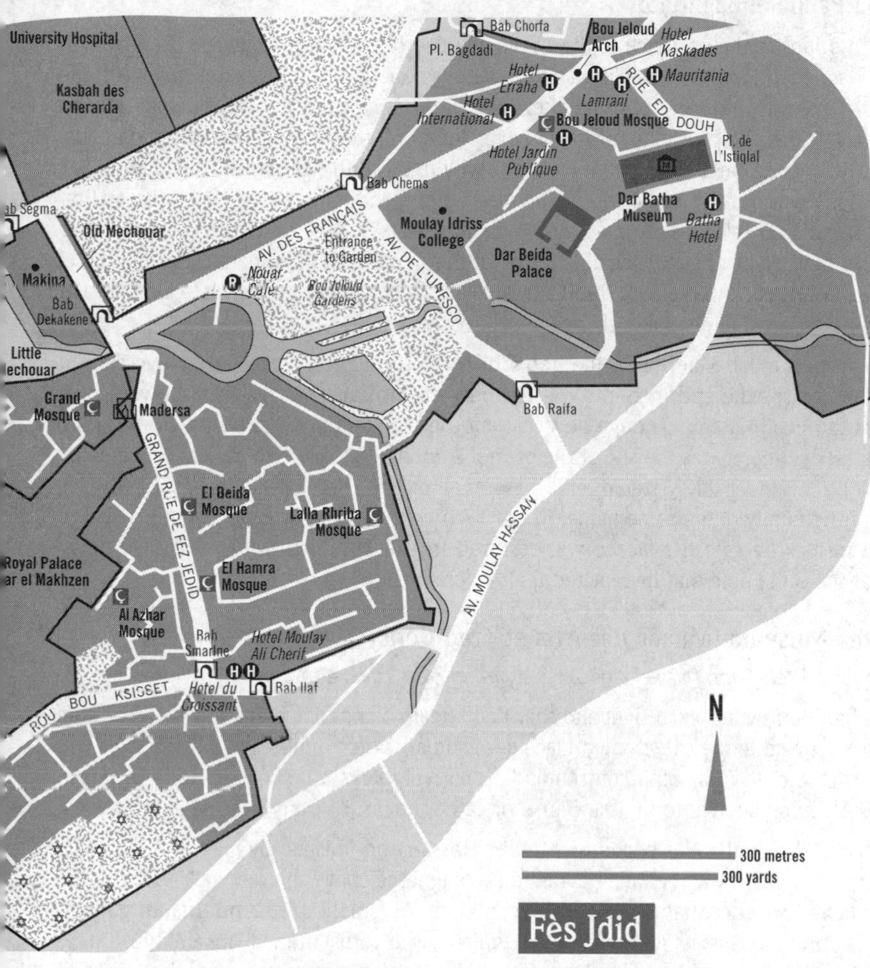

There is an entrance just east of the Petit Méchouar to the **Jardins de Bou Jeloud**, a delightful park with palm-shaded formal walks, cut through with ornamental watercourses that feed the round but slightly disappointing pond. The most famous and restful corner of the garden (also accessible directly from the road) is **La Nouria** café, which overlooks a mill race and its namesake waterwheel. This wooden watermill is sadly stuck solid, but it recalls a time when all the backstreet workshops of Fès were powered by dozens of such gently moaning creatures. Just outside the back door of the café is the pitch of a photographer, who continues to make use of an old box apparatus complete with cape and tripod.

Halfway along Avenue des Français toward Fès-el-Bali is a crossroads. To the left is the keyhole arch of **Bab Chems**, to the right the Avenue de l'UNESCO divides the public Bou Jeloud gardens from the walled park, pavilions and palace of **Dar Beida**, now occupied by a school, the Lycée Moulay Idriss, and so not open to visitors.

Place du Pacha el Baghdadi

A left turn opposite the entrance to the Lycée Moulay Idriss will take you to the Place du Pacha el Baghdadi. Buses waiting for passengers now no longer take over this dusty triangle of land, where nut, fruit and cake hawkers and *petit taxis* collect. At dusk small groups gather around the odd musician, or haggle over temporary displays of secondhand goods, particularly on the side of the square by the solid-looking **Bab Mahrouk**, the 'gate of the burned'. This was built in 1214 by an Almohad sultan, Mohammed en Nasir. It was first known as the Bab ech Cheria, the gate of justice, as this was the execution square. It received its new name after El Obeidi, a leader of the heretical Rif Rhomara tribe, and Ibn el Khatib, a harmless 14th-century intellectual, were burnt alive here. This was a savage punishment designed to deny any chance of resurrection.

To the right of the Bab Mahrouk is the **Bab Chorfa**, a strong gate protected by two elegant towers that guards the entrance into the **Kasbah en Nouar**, the kasbah of flowers, also known as the Filali Kasbah. Though now just another residential district with a busy, stall-lined central avenue, it was the site of the central Almohad fortress, which was occupied by the pacha of Fès under the Merenids and then renamed the Filali Kasbah to honour Moulay Rachid, of the family of the same name, in the 17th century. The original mosque is just to the right inside the gate. Its façade was restored in the 18th century by Sultan Moulay Sliman, at the same time that he repaired the battlements.

Dar Batha Museum (Musée des Arts et Traditions)

Open Wed–Mon 9am–12 noon, 3–6pm; closed Tues; adm.

Through Bab Bou Jeloud, turn right and then right again along the comparatively broad Rue Ed Douh for 100m to the café-fronted Place de l'Istiqlal, where another right turn takes you to the entrance of the Dar Batha museum. Alternatively, take a taxi or the no. 1 bus from Place des Alaouites straight to the Dar Batha, or catch the no. 18 from Place de la Résistance.

The palace of Dar Batha was begun by Moulay Hassan and finished by his son Abdul Aziz (1894–1909). A range of green-tiled pyramid roofs emerge above the red walls to cover the apartments and galleries that now house the exhibits. An amply-sized **Andalusian garden** extends within the walls, its grid of blue and white raised paths interlocking amid lush trees and swathes of shrub and bamboo. It's a delightful place, the tranquillity of the enclosed garden appealing as much as the exhibits. In September and May concerts of Andalusian music are held here.

Inside, the cases of exhibits follow no particular scheme: astrolabes, Middle Atlas carpets, stamps, illustrated Korans, pens, Berber jewellery, embroidery, guns, rural pots, coins from either the Idrissids or Alaouites are interspersed with blue geometric ware from Fès. The corner rooms contain the larger pieces of carved cedar, plaster or stone that have been recovered from restorations and excavations of Fassi tombs, mosques and medersas, some of them dated to the Merenid and Saadian dynasties. As ever in Morocco, the achievements of urban Andalusian culture appear timeless, as objects from the 10th to the 20th centuries have so much in common. The true contrast is with products from the Berber tribes, even ones as close to Fès as Jbel Zerhoun or the Rif. Fès' past role as an oasis of technical skill and literate culture for the nation is well revealed by this charming jumble of exhibits.

Fès-el-Bali

The three major accessible sites of Fès-el-Bali—the Bou Inania Medersa, Attarine Medersa and the tanneries—can be seen in half a day. The lesser medersas, the exteriors of the ancient mosques, the hidden bakeries, *hammams*, *fondouqs*, workshops and alleys of the medina could take weeks to find—to understand the city fully you have to have been born a Fassi. Fès exists on trade, and to arrive at the medina with the intention not to buy anything is to miss out on the central life of the city. But, see all you wish before making the rounds of the bazaars. Then you can savour the ritual of commerce without impatience, delight in the gift of mint tea, the opulent decoration of the large bazaars, and the loquacious salesmanship.

Guides

Arriving at the medina, usually at the Bab Bou Jeloud, accept the need for a guide for at least your first half-day. He can show you intimate parts of the old city where an unescorted foreigner would not be welcome. Official, gold badge and fez-wearing guides can be found at the tourist office, the Syndicat d'Initiative on Place Mohammed V in the New Town, and often at the SI booth by the Bab Bou Jeloud gate. These official guides are a professional body but their talk and itineraries can become uninspiring through repetition. Unofficial guides charge less and may try harder to please, although their routes are often given an erratic twist as they try to avoid the police, since they are illegal—but that remains their problem, not yours.

The Golden Age of Fès

At the beginning of the 14th century Fès-el-Bali had a population of 125,000. None of the houses was permitted to touch the city walls, which were lined with gardens and cemeteries and pierced by eight gates. Within the medina there were 785 mosques, 372 flour mills, 135 bakers' ovens, 93 public baths, 467 *fondouqs* and 80 fountains. Outside the walls potteries, olive oil presses, sawmills, weavers' workshops, tanneries and smithies collected in three industrial zones around Bab Guissa, Bab Ftouh and along the riverbanks.

The medina was divided into 18 districts which each had a headman agreed upon by the chief residents. The *caid*, a magistrate learned in Koranic law, judged civil cases, with a deputy who specialized in marriage and divorce suits. There were 35 secretaries and accountants on the *caid's* staff helping to supervise the financing of pious foundations, hospitals and baths. The *caid* also acted as rector of the university and censor of intellectual life. The various medersas lodged 2000 students in Fès while they pursued their studies in the University of Karaouiyne. Lectures were given in the grand mosques after morning prayers; the university library was housed behind the mihrab of the Karaouiyne Mosque, and the courts of the various medersas or the houses of professors were used for smaller teaching groups.

There was a hospital for the sick without family, and a leprosarium outside the ramparts housed lepers in isolation. The *muhtasib*, the prefect of manners, kept surveillance over the baths, the honesty of exchanges, weights, and measures, and organized a weekly inspection of prostitutes by physicians.

There were 150 guilds each under the protection of a patron saint, such as Sidi Mohammed Ibn Attab for the shoemakers and Sidi Mimum for the potters. Numerically the corporation of weavers was dominant—500 workshops employed almost 20,000 workers— but the most powerful corporation was that of the semi-official water and drainage technicians. They and the water jurists alone understood the labyrinthine pipe system—the chief wonder of Fès. It filled fountains, public baths and mosque pools, drove 400 mills, and then 'the river doth disperse itself into manifold channels insinuating itself unto every street and member thereof to pass through countless conduits into sinks and gutters.'

Above the urban hierarchy, the sultan appointed a pacha as governor of the city. He occupied the Almohad fortress at the western end of the medina, held enormous power and directly ran the police, criminal trials and ordered executions.

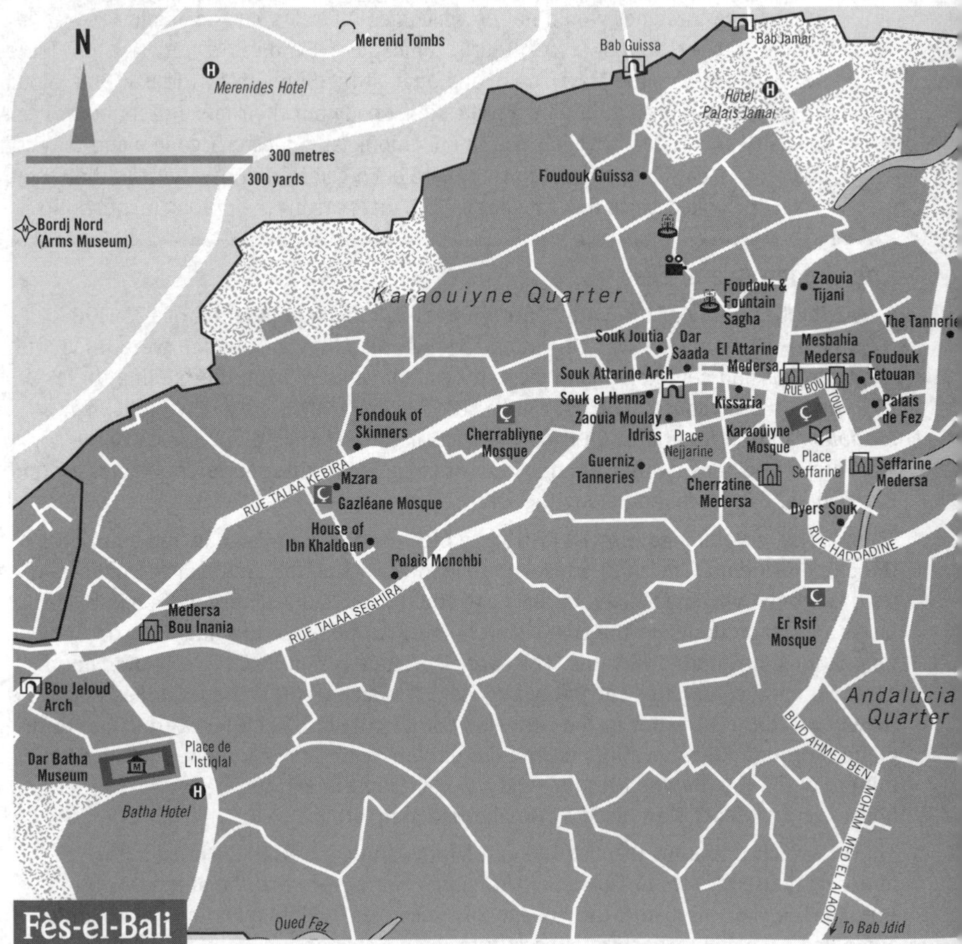

The Karaouiyne Quarter

The square in front of the main city gate is a bustling throng of cafés, cheap hotels, taxis, buses, bemused tourists and confident young guides. Originally it was the site of another Almohad kasbah, itself built over the ruins of an Almoravid fort which had defended this exposed western edge of the city. Some of the kasbah foundations were found recently during building work on ground just to the west of the Bou Jeloud Mosque.

The famous Bou Jeloud triple arch was built in 1913 by the French beside an earlier gate, just a year after they had occupied Fès. It served as a recognizable border between the native quarter of the medina and the administrative districts and resident-general's palace that were established in the Dar Batha and Dar Beida in the first years of the Protectorate. The gate frames the minarets of the **Sidi Lezzaz Mosque** and **Bou Inania Medersa**. The gold and blue tracery decoration represents Fès 'the blue'; the gold-green on the far side is for Islam.

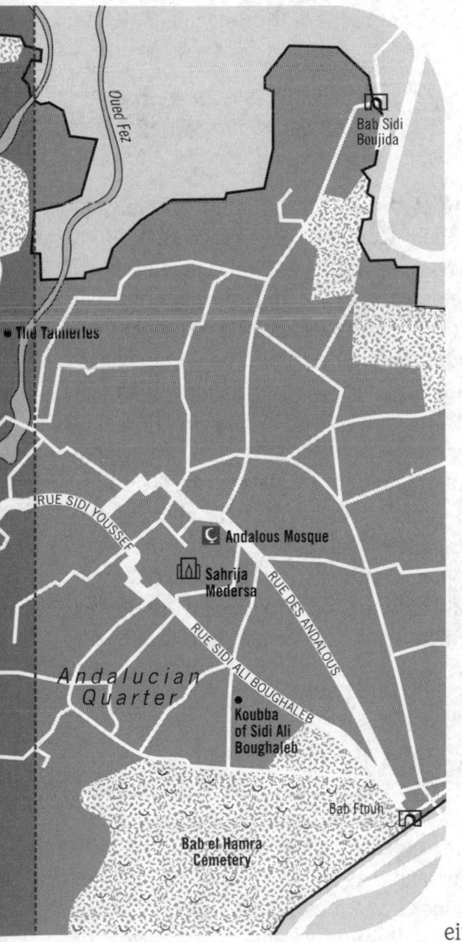

Beyond the arch is an area lined by a few cheap hotels, food stalls and café restaurants while straight ahead is the **Kissariat Serrajine**, a small courtyard lined with a glittering array of stalls selling embroidered leather, slippers and silverware. The medina's two major arteries appear here: Rue Talaa Kebira is down the narrow turning to the left, while Rue Talaa Seghira is to the right. They run roughly parallel to each other in a bow-shaped way, and are both lined with stalls, shops and bazaars. Periodically covered by arches and slats of bamboo, they meet in the confused web of narrow streets known as the Kissaria.

Bou Inania Medersa

Open daily 8am–6pm except Fri am, though you may be asked to leave during hours of prayer; adm.

Taking Rue Talaa Kebira, which passes to the left of the two minarets, you approach the Medersa of Bou Inania 100m on your right under a covered archway and opposite an area of scaffolding. The Bou Inania Medersa is the finest and largest in Fès. The prayer-hall is in active use, which saves the spirit of the place from disappearing under the flow of visitors. The entrance hall has a stalactite-domed roof; to the left is a room for the faithful to wash their feet. The main open-air court, paved in marble with a round, central pool, is surrounded by a carved cedar screen. There is a lecture hall at either side and a large prayer-hall at the end, across a marble-moated portion of the river Fès. The prayer-hall should not be entered by a non-Muslim, but it is fine to look at its mihrab, columned hall and minbar. The elegant **minaret** is clearly visible above the cedar lintelled and green tiled roof. Access to the roofs is currently closed, due to repairs, but it has an exciting view over neighbouring roof tops and a barrage of minarets.

The Bou Inania Medersa is an expression of the Spanish Moorish style, a direct importation of 14th-century Andalusian techniques to Morocco. All the materials—the *zellij* mosaic, the plaster, marble and cedar—carry a range of patterns, in excellent condition, that threaten to overwhelm the architecture. But the geometric swirls hide a single point; the detail of the floral patterns illustrates a divine symmetry; and even the array of stalactites breaks down into an ordered span of interlocking arches. The cedar screen with its delicate weave of knots and stars seems to simplify into two dimensions, and invites a further reduction to the one-dimensional, single point. All can be seen as witness to the one God, while the bands of Kufic calligraphy which bind the decoration contain lines from the Koran. For a Muslim the Koran represents the direct instructions of God as dictated by the angel Gabriel to Mohammed:

> *'Read in the name of thy Lord thy creator; who created man from a drop of blood. Read, thy Lord is most bountiful, who taught by means of the pen, taught man what he knew not.'*

Medersas were residential colleges for the learning of the Koran, but they seldom had adequate provision made for the maintenance of their students. In practice they often became finishing schools for the children of the privileged. This had an obvious political function, for the Merenid sultans could counter regional loyalties and divisive spiritual brotherhoods by educating future *caids, cadis* and tribal chiefs near their side and within a state-approved orthodoxy. A little of this political dimension has crept into the Bou Inania. It was built by Sultan Abou Inan between 1350 and 1357 on an area of wastelandset apart and so removed from the independent spirit of the Karaouiyne University, which feared his intentions. This powerful sovereign (who had deposed his own father) strove energetically to enhance his new foundation and supercede the traditional university. The medersa's sumptuous proportions and decoration were deliberately designed to eclipse its rival, although the sultan is remembered for his famously aestheticist response when presented with the costs: 'What is beautiful cannot be expensive at any price; what is enthralling is never too costly.' It is no surprise that several lines praising Abou Inan and his munificent generosity have crept into the decoration of the main court, while the dedication stone declares him caliph, the successor to the Prophet.

Clock and Sahn

Opposite the medersa gate on the left is a mass of scaffolding. This hides, high up on a carved lintel of cedar, a dilapidated row of thirteen windows with a few brass bowls on the sills and the odd surviving water spout. This is known as the water-clock, though no description has survived and no satisfactory explanation of its working has been devised. It is subsequently considered to have been the work of a magician Rabbi, and was finished in 1357 in time for the medersa's inauguration. It may not have been a clock but a musical instrument of timed jets of tinkling water on brass, in celebration of the building, inside which is the *sahn,* or courtyard for washing, of the medersa. Male tourists used to be able to enter this working portion of the medersa complex, and admire the court with its central marble basin, stone closets and impressive flow of water. It is now closed, hopefully in order to repair its rich but precarious geometric plaster and cedar carving.

Rue Talaa Kebira

Further down the street is the **zaouia of Sidi Ahmed Tijani**, one of the two Fassi lodges of this widespread Sufi brotherhood. The street continues downhill into the intensity of the medina—a confusion of bazaars, bakeries, grill cafés, zellij-decorated fountains and the furnaces of *hammams* stoked with a graceful routine of hand thrown wood shavings. The heavily-loaded mules of the hereditary Guir Valley porters pause for no man. Listen for *'Balak!'*, the muleteers' look-out cry, or run the risk of being knocked off your feet. The rich odours of olive oil, fresh mint, cedar shavings, leather, fat burnt on charcoal, kif, mule dung and human urine swirl around to mix with the sounds of chanting from a Koranic nursery school, running water, hooves and the overlying babble of business. Buy fresh-squeezed orange juice, sweet cakes, fresh bread, or fried potato cakes to add another layer of sensual enjoyment.

As you begin to climb uphill you pass a row of blacksmiths and beyond this, on the left, is an old **Merenid prison**, just like any other *fondouq* except for its noticeably heavier arches and colonnades where the prisoners would be chained. It is now the market for the butter and honey wholesalers, who can weigh you out a Tupperware pot full of strong-tasting Moroccan butter. On the right, just before the **Gazléane Mosque**, an alley marked by a plaque leads to the house where Ibn Khaldoun (1332–1406), the great historian and sociologist, lived. Just beyond this turning is the **M'Zara of Moulay Idriss**, a monument that commemorates the place where the founder rested and envisaged the future city. On the left is the **Derb bou Haj Mosque**, and just beyond that the **skinners' fondouq** *(fondouq des peaussiers)*, the yard where wet hides are scraped clean of fat and tissue. Some of the near-transparent, vellum-like finished products are then fitted here to ceramic drums and wooden tambourines. After this there is a distinctive fountain on the right opposite which is the oldest *hammam* in Fès.

Cobblers' stalls increasingly dominate the street with their displays of slippers, and the second mosque on the right is called the **Chérabliyn**, the slipper-makers'. This was founded by the Merenid Sultan Abou Hassan, 1331–51, though only the minaret is original—which is all, apart from the gate, that a non-Muslim can see. Beyond the mosque there are a number of bazaars and then the **Souk Aïn Allou** area, where the fine leather workers trade; their distinctive gold-stamped and decorated book-binding is still known as Morocco work, or *maroquinerie.*

Souk Attarine Gate

Beyond the Souk Aïn Allou look out for a modest gateway across the road marked by a rusty 'Souk Attarine' sign. The gate stands before a busy crossroad of paths and is as landmark. It can be used as a starting point for short walks to the **Henna Souk**, to **Place Nejjarine** and to the zaouia of **Moulay Idriss II**, before heading further along the main street to the **Attarine** medersa and the great **Karaouiyne Mosque**.

Henna Souk & Sidi Frej Maristan

Just before the Souk Attarine gate take the right turn and then ten paces later take the first left to bring you into the Souk au Henné, an intimate triangular place under the dappled shade of an old poplar tree. Here henna paste, hessian sacks of henna leaves, silvery blocks of antimony, rhassoul and dark, powdered kohl are weighed out and sold. More alarming is the display of the dried skins of lizards, snakes and small predators, with hutches of live hedgehogs and terrapins for the preparation of magical pastes, aphrodisiacs and love potions. All the stall holders are happy to explain the use of their various products and can put you in touch with the local women who specialize in the creation of the rich geometric patterns with which hands and feet are decorated with henna.

On the far side of the little place stands a normal-looking trading fondouk which occupies the site of the **Sidi Frej Maristan**, a mental asylum built in the reign of the Merenid Sultan Yacqub (1286–1307). A plaque on the wall proudly records this early example of enlightened medical care, and that Leo Africanus worked here as a doctor for a while. The Sidi Frej charitable foundation was also famous for running another hospital which nursed sick cranes and storks back to health, and respectfully buried these holy birds when they died.

Place Nejjarine

Take the second right turn down a narrow alley before the Souk Attarine gate, and after 25 paces turn right again to walk down a vine-covered alley lined with workshops to approach Place Nejjarine (the place of the carpenters), which has been recently restored to its old splendour. This is another of the medina's intimate places, which can be appreciated *en-passant* or at your ease in one of the small cafés. An elegant drinking fountain plays here into a basin of mosaic tiles, and cedar beams support a green-tiled canopy. On a weekday morning the carpenters can be found at work off any of the surrounding streets, adzing away at a twisted trunk, for instance, to carve a light, strong plough. The 18th-century **Nejjarine Fondouq** dominates the Place, with a great imposing ornamental gateway standing behind the fountain to frame one of the classic pictorial images of the city. The gate is rarely open, although there are plans to open the interior up as a working fondouk, which will restore access to this high and elegant courtyard with its colonnaded floors. This *fondouq* had, for a Christian, the pleasant combination of lodging theological students and carpenters.

If you take the alley beside the fondouk you will be heading towards the smell of the Guerniz tanneries, which are just before the Sidi Moussa Mosque. These are the oldest of the three **Fès tanneries**; tradition has it they were established by Idriss II.

Moulay Idriss II Zaouia

Non-Muslims are not allowed into the sanctuary here, but you can get an excellent view of the interior from the edge of the women's gate.

Take the right turn just beyond (east of) the Souk Attarine gate, and after about 80 paces you will pass under a gate. Bear left, up through a street dedicated to the selling of nougat, for 19 paces before turning left (having ducked beneath the wooden bar that hangs across the alley), from where it is about 70 paces along a street dedicated to selling votive candles and trinkets to the best view into the zaouia of Moulay Idriss II. Within the darkened sanctuary the tomb can be seen heavily draped in a rich embroidered velvet cloth, the *ksaoua*, and surrounded by baroque brass, flickering coloured candles, glittering lamps, offerings, European clocks and praying women. It is strikingly similar to a saint's shrine in Spain, Naples, Sicily or Greece, and around the corner of the sanctuary a hole lined by well-worn copper allows the devotees to touch the tomb. As well as being the patron saint of the city, he is especially appealed to by boys before circumcision and women before giving birth.

It is not known if the reforming Almoravids or Almohads suppressed the cult, but Idriss II's tomb was re-identified during Merenid rule, in 1307, after an uncorrupted body was unearthed here. The present zaouia was constructed in 1437, but it was the Wattasid dynasty (1472–1554) that developed it into a major cult centre. Throughout August the numerous guilds of the city still go in procession to the tomb and offer decorative gifts, animal sacrifices, religious chants and *nubas* of classical Andalusian music before starting their festivals. In the 18th century Moulay Ismaïl restored the shrine, and until the 19th century it was hung with contracts by which the various towns and tribes tried to establish the exact terms upon which they accepted the rule of each new sultan. The right of sanctuary, *horm*, is still respected, and Sultan Abdul Aziz appalled the Fassis when he arrested the murderer of a European who had taken shelter beside the tomb.

The Kissaria

The Souk Attarine is also the 'spice sellers' gate that marks the entrance to the Kissaria, the dense network of traditionally expensive shops on an irregular criss-crossing grid of alleys and tiny shop-filled squares that cluster at the heart of the medina. This is a sublime area for shopping, a world away from the piles of tack in the enormous tourist bazzars, with each proprietor sitting in his own small booth with everything within reach. It fortunately remains an area dedicated to local needs, fine cloth, silk threads, jewellery, clothes, hats and blankets, and at night the whole kissaria is locked.

On your first visit stay close to the main street. About 35 paces along the street (on your left) is the welcoming interior of the Dar Saada café-restaurant; while another 40 paces brings you past a quiet cul de sac alley (on your right) with a fine view of the minaret of the zaouia of Moulay Idriss.

Attarine Medersa

Open daily 9am–12noon, 2–6pm, except Fri am; adm.

A hundred metres (225 paces) past the Souk Attarine arch, on the left just as you enter a vaulted and confusingly busy crossroads, are the distinctive bronze doors of the Attarine

Medersa. Built by Sultan Abou Said Othman in 1322–25 within a confined space, it does not have the grandeur of the slightly later Bou Inania, but is a finer, more delicate structure. It is at least as rich in its *zellij*, plaster and wood decoration, but with a lighter architectural touch emphasized by reflecting pairs of arches seemingly supported by thin stone pillars.

The plan is familiar: an entrance hall with stairs to the upper floors where there are 60 rooms for students and a central fountain court with a prayer-hall beyond. There are no lecture halls, as in the later Bou Inania, as the Attarine was designed as an addition to the Karaouiyne University, not a rival. You may enter the prayer-hall; the **mihrab** is to the right, flanked by pillars and lit by coloured glass windows. A bronze chandelier hangs from the cedar ceiling, inscribed with the name of the founder and details of the medersa's construction.

Two hundred metres north of the medersa is the **zaouia of Sidi Ahmed Tijani**, the main lodge of this influential Sufi brotherhood founded by Sidi Mohammed Tijani in Algeria in the 18th century. Persecuted by the Turks, he fled to Fès. The brotherhood was a great ally of the Alaouite sultans, aiding them in religious reforms; when Moulay Hafid retired to Tangier in 1912 he wrote a scholarly work in praise of the order.

The Karaouiyne Mosque

It is perhaps appropriate that this grand mosque at the heart of Fès and Moroccan culture should remain such an elusive building. Its outer walls are so encrusted with shops and houses that its shape is lost, while the four main gates offer intriguing but baffling vistas of a succession of pure white colonnades and simple rush matting with a woven red design. They occasionally frame a turbanned lecturer sitting cross-legged against a far wall.

First built in 859 by Fatima bint Mohammed ben Feheri, a prosperous refugee from Kairouan, the mosque was improved by a Fatimid governor in 933 and enlarged by Abd er Rahman III, governor of the Omayyad Caliph of Cordoba, in 956. Rebuilt by the Almoravid Sultan Ali ben Youssef from 1135 to 1143, it was finished a few years before the dynasty fell.

It is a rectangular space sufficient for 20,000 to say their prayers simultaneously. The roof is upheld by spacious round-topped arches supported on sixteen arcades of twenty-one spans. An open-air court, the *sahn*, of four spans' width, is at the opposite end from the mihrab. Within this open court the Almohads placed a marble basin and the Saadian Sultan Abdullah el Ghalib added two flanking pavilions modelled on those of the Lion court in the Alhambra at Granada. The chief glory of the mosque remains the central aisle that leads up from the centre of the court to the mihrab. This is embellished with increasingly elaborate floral and Kufic script carved into the plaster as you advance, while the domes that span the arches are raised higher and higher as they approach the Mihrab and are ribbed or vaulted with bold stalactite decoration. The carving is in mint condition, as it was covered by the Almohads two years after they were finished and only revealed in the restorations of 1950. Other treasures, hidden from view, are a bronze chandelier from 1203, a minbar or pulpit of precious woods and inlaid ivory from Cordoba, and one of the richest libraries of the Islamic world.

A Rooftop View of the Mosque

The best view of the mosque available to a non-Muslim is that from the roof of the **Palais de Fès** restaurant and carpet shop (*see* p.331), which has a wonderful, multi-level terraced café on its rooftop and very elegant toilets. To find it (at 16 Rue Boutoil-Karaouiyne), follow the alley that skirts around the Great Mosque. On your way, depending on which gates are open (ten of the 14 gates are opened on Fridays), you can see into the *sahn* and the main body of the mosque, but never as far as the central decorated aisle or the domes. On your left you will pass the locked door of the **Mesbahia Medersa**, closed for restoration. It was built in 1346 by Sultan Abou Hassan, and nicknamed *'er rokham'*, the marble, due to his lavish use of the stone; the central white marble basin was brought over from a mosque in Algeciras.

Having turned the corner you pass on your left the **fondouq of the Tetouanis** *(Fondouq Tétaounine)*, a fine 14th-century Merenid court used by Andalusian merchants from Tetouan, which you are welcome to enter as there is a small carpet shop within. There is a less grand *fondouq* a few doors below and then the Palais de Fès, from where you can sip mint tea, gulp mineral water and recover your strength as you enjoy the stunning view over the vast acreage of the mosque's green-tiled roof. The tall, distant minaret is that of the Moulay Idriss Zaouia, while the lantern-less minaret on the grand mosque is the Trumpeter, from which Ramadan is announced; the nearest is the 10th-century white domed minaret that echoes the grand mosque of Kairouan, Tunisia. The mosque's internal court, the *sahn*, with flanking twin pavilions and dazzling blue and white floor, is also partly overlooked.

Place Seffarine

By the southeastern corner of the mosque, the direction of the mihrab and prayer, is the Place Seffarine, shaded by fig trees. It has a pleasant fountain and is full of metalworkers tapping away at an impressive range of pots and kettles, including some really gigantic ones. This, like the Souk Attarine arch, is a recognizable centre from which to explore this end of the medina: the **Seffarine Medersa** and the dyers' souk; the **Cherratine Medersa**; or the **tanneries** and the **Medersa es Sahrija** beside the grand mosque of the Andalusian quarter.

The Library and University of Karaouiyne

The great library of the University is stored in the white walls between the Place and the mihrab, to which there is no entry. Considering the physical state of the city, the library has survived well. It boasts a 9th-century manuscript Koran and an original manuscript of Averroës–Ibn Rachid amongst its 30,000 precious volumes.

An Ancient Centre of Learning

The Karaouiyne University is one of the oldest in the world, dating from AD 850. Its origins lie in the teaching of the Koran in the mosque, just as Christian universities coalesced out of monastery and cathedral schools. Allied subjects like grammar, theology and Koranic law were taught in informal lectures, with an accent on verbal memory rather than debate or written papers. It is claimed that Pope Sylvester II learnt mathematics at Fès a century before Bologna, the first European university, was established. In the 14th century 2000 students, *tolba*, dwelt in the various medersas to be instructed by the *ulemas*, the doctors and professors. Ibn Rachid, Ibn Khaldoun, Leo Africanus and Ibn Batuta all participated in the intellectual milieu of Fès. In 1963 the university was 'nationalized', having been the single source of higher education until then. Departments were dispersed to the new town, and faculties established in Rabat, Tetouan and Marrakech.

Seffarine Medersa

A doorway on one side of the Place Seffarine gives entry to the Seffarine Medersa. This remains in use, occupied by Islamic students, who are often happy to show a few affable visitors around (tips accepted), but is normally closed to groups and brusquer tourists. It was established by Sultan Abou Yusuf Yacqub, the founder of Fès Jdid, in 1280. It was the first medersa in Morocco, and follows the design of a Fassi house, since professors used to lecture in their home when not using the mosque. Medersas had long been established in Egypt, Syria and Iraq, but with the additional gift of a library the sultan showed that he too was interested in education. The rooms and small pool arranged around the irregular courtyard have a simple domestic elegance, but the dilapidated central prayer-hall (offset from the irregular medersa courtyard) shows signs of the extravagance that would be unleashed in the Attarine medersa 25 years later. It is good to see a medersa in use, the plain mattresses, heaps of books and notes and the normal squalor of student life adding a vital missing ingredient to empty tourist-thronged halls. It's hardly possible to tire of medina views, and the medersa roof has an intriguing outlook over the river mills, houses and bridges.

Dyers' Souk

Continue on past the Medersa door and drop down into the dyers' souk, the Souk Sabbighin or Souk des Teinturiers, which is on the riverbank to the right of the bridge. The swatches of bright coloured wool draped over the street to dry are a perennially photogenic sight. The vats of dye and the grave, grey-clothed vat masters are more disturbing. If you are with a guide, ask to be shown the riverside mill where seeds and minerals are crushed to extract the raw dyes. The millers wade through the thick pungent waters of the stream, raking aside mounds of garbage in order to direct enough water into the workings of the mill—a vision of mingled squalor, rancid steaming waters and skilled medieval use of water power.

Cherratine Medersa

Standing before the library at the top of Place Seffarine, turn left and walk along Rue Haddadine (lined with displays of teapots, kitchenware and jewellery), for about 90 paces and then turn right up Rue Cherratine. Walk for about 130 paces, and having passed the **Dar Sekka bazaar**, once a mint, you will reach the twin bronze doors of the Cherratine Medersa, a dilapidated but delightfully unvisited corner of the city. It is an extensive complex built by the first Alaouite sultan, Moulay Rachid, in 1670 to celebrate his reunification of Morocco. From the bronze doors on the street an ornamental passageway leads directly into the calm, quiet order of the spacious interior courtyard with its central pool. One side opens directly into a high-vaulted mosque, the orientation of which allows the whole courtyard to be treated as a *sahn*. No windows break the severity of the walls: instead, the residential blocks, each looking into its own lightwell, have been cunningly placed off the three corners, approached through passages. The fourth corner houses the ablutions courtyard, which is the only one in Morocco to remain in exuberant working order, with a fountain by the entrance and water-filled pool in the central courtyard, around which are ranged seven L-shaped closets. For its combination of privacy without prudery, functionally inspired decoration mixed with a touch of grandeur it is exemplary. It is no wonder that the Victorian closet makers looked to the East for their inspiration

Beyond the medersa there is a pretty triangular square, **Place Chemaïne**, where dried fruit is sold, and beyond that the kissaria begins with several shops that specialize in lambswool hats and embroidered fezzes.

The Tanneries

The **Chouara** or Dabbaghin is the largest of the three ancient tanneries in Fès. It is on a terrace above the river Fès, a well beaten 200m walk along Rue el Mechattine from the northeast corner of Place Seffarine. The powerful, distinctive smell is enough to guide you. Once there boys will take you to terraces and courts where you can see the operations without being too much in the way. There is a rush of guilt as you attempt to stifle your initial nausea and notice that you are part of a stream of foreigners who arrive, look repulsed, take photographs, tip and leave. The honeycomb of vats, their assorted colours, processes and levels have an endless fascination. The neighbouring roofs and hills are flecked with drying skins, a tone down in colour from the livid vats of saffron, poppy, indigo, mint and antimony. The scantily dressed tanners are born to their trade and appear like so many human storks, their long elegant legs working through the pools, bobbing down to worry a skin and then striding off to wash at the fresh-water standing pipes.

The tanneries are worked by a mesh of specialist and cooperative guilds with their own hierarchies of apprentices, craftsmen and master craftsmen. A whole range of processes are undertaken here: fresh animal skins are treated and pounded in alternating liquid and solid vats of urine and pigeon shit; they are then scraped, wet dyed, scraped, and perhaps dry dyed before being trimmed and sorted for auction.

Out of the Medina

From Place Seffarine a short walk downhill through the Dyers' souk (avoiding the narrow bridge across the river into the Andalous side of the old city) and a right turn in the twisting street should drop you down into the sunbaked tarmac space overlooked by the green-tiled minaret of the **Er Rsif** mosque. No cars or coaches are allowed to park here to make room for local buses and *petit taxis*, which provide a quick means of leaving the medina.

Alternatively, retrace your path going uphill from the Souk Attarine arch towards the Bou Jeloud Gate, or if you have the energy explore a different section of the old city by walking uphill to the Bab Guissa and Bab Jamai.

From Souk Attarine Arch to Bab Guissa and Bab Jamaï

A turn north off the Souk Ain Allou, just after the Attarine arch and 15m before the conspicuous Dar Saada restaurant, will take you into the **souk Joutia**, the market for salt, eggs and fish. The Rue Hormis runs roughly north from this souk towards Bab Guissa. About 40m beyond the Joutia and 20m to the right of the street is an 18th-century *fondouq* and fountain, the central square of the **Es Sagha** district, which used to be a great haunt of jewellers. The elegant carved plaster and cedar colonnades of the *fondouq Sagha* are now one of the centres of the wool trade: raw spun wool is stored here, auctioned off and brought back from the dyers in bright coloured batches to be sold to weavers and carpet-makers.

Back on Rue Hormis, bear left and climb uphill past a cinema, a local social centre that's surrounded by cheap grills and cafés. Off from here is another henna and spice market, the

Place Achabin. Snaking further uphill you should pass a fountain on your left to enter the area around *Fondouq el Yhoudi* or Guissa. If you come here in the morning there will be a distinctive aroma of cedar wood and singed hooves from the workshops of farriers, joiners and wood-turners. Ask to be shown the original **Fondouq el Yhoudi**, high up on the left, where Jewish merchants were based in the 13th century before the Merenids moved them to Fès Jdid. Replaced several times since then, the *fondouq* is now used for the sorting, grading and auctioning of tanned and dyed skins.

Below the **Bab Guissa** gate is a complex of three buildings, a 14th-century mortuary chamber and a 19th-century mosque and medersa, none of which are open to non-Muslims. To the right of Bab Guissa are the more elaborate Bab Jamaï and Bab Ferdaous, where you can find a no. 10 bus to speed you back to the Place des Alaouites on the western edge of Fès Jdid, or a taxi to take you to the new town or on a tour of the ramparts.

The Andalusian Quarter

This half of Fès-el-Bali is a quieter, residential area; it has the Sahrija Medersa, no bazaars, lots of local shops and, as a direct consequence of there being hardly any tourists, a much friendlier and more courteous population. It is likely to stay that way, for the quarters' great historical centre stands on the summit of a hill and has even by Moroccan standards a particulary elusive Great Mosque (*Jemma el Kebir*, to a local). To get to it, or to the partial view from the side doors, there are two main approaches. From the Chouara tanneries cross the conspicuous **Pont de Beïne el Mdoun**, the bridge of the two cities, into the Andalusian Quarter and then follow the Rue Seffah for about 500m as it climbs the hill. Alternatively, cross the oued Fès at the smaller **Sidi el-Aouad** bridge (by the Er Rsif square), which is just off the Dyer's souk–Rue des Teinturiers below Place Seffarine. From here it is probably easiest to keep to the fairly level Rue Nekhaline for about 300m, until you turn right onto the Rue Seffah and trudge uphill.

Andalusian Grand Mosque

One of the best views of the mosque is from a side gate that looks straight across the elegant *sahn* courtyard towards the white minaret, capped with a stumpy dome. It was first built by Meriem, the equally pious sister of Fatima, the founder of the Karaouiyne Mosque, but was largely rebuilt by the Almohad Sultan Mohammed en Nasir in the 13th century. The Merenids gave it a fountain and built two nearby medersas for students. They presented an entire library to the mosque in 1415, but this never developed into a separate university.

Sahrija Medersa

This medersa 'of the pool' lies southwest of the grand mosque. It was built by Abou Hassan between 1321 and 1323, while he was still heir to the throne. When he became sultan he built another in the Karaouiyne Quarter, the Mesbahia medersa, and commissioned others at Taza, Meknès and Salé. The Sahrija, which remains in partial use for the accommodation of Islamic students, is theoretically open to the public every day of the year (except Fridays) from 8am–6pm, but in practice it is often locked up outside university terms. It is a dilapidated but enchanting jewel of the period, with a simple but harmonious plan. A rectangular pool fed from a marble bowl surrounded by a worn grid of tiled drainage rills dominates the centre of the small courtyard, with splendid carved plaster, cedar walls and *zellij* mosaics touched with the true serenity of age. On the outer face of the the prayer hall you can still see the hinges of those typical Moorish hanging gates which would later become associated more with secular than with sacred buildings. The prayer hall, with simple coffered ceiling and comparatively austere central mihrab, retains a venerable dignity. On two sides of the courtyard, behind wooden grilles, are the students' rooms, four of which have windows that overlook the pool. On my last visit the medersa kept up with the proud traditions of its past by offering free accommodation to students drawn from a huge hinterland: Chad, Niger, Algeria, Mali… You are free, at your own risk, to explore the roof, but there is no view from there of either the Andalusian mosque or the other, inaccessible, Merenid medersa in this quarter, the **medersa el Oued** (the river), which is sometimes known as **es Sebbayin**, the seven, as the seven approved styles for the chanting of the Koran were taught here.

Instead of retracing your steps, you could also continue south from the Grand Mosque/Medersa al Sahrija out of the medina down Rue Sidi Ali Boughaleb. The **koubba** of this saint is on the right just at the beginning of the cemetery. The saint is not actually buried here, but the shrine remains an important popular cult centre. The ill and the mad surround the koubba on Tuesday nights, and wait for the saint to appear in their dreams and suggest a cure. The **cemetery of Bab Hamra** on the right should not be entered by non-Muslims and has a local reputation as the resort of black magicians. At **Bab Ftouh** you can find a taxi to get around the ramparts or take a no. 18 bus back into the new town.

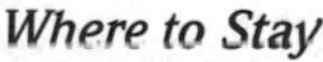

Where to Stay

Whatever your budget, stay as close as you can to the heady medieval sights, odours and sounds of the medina for as long as you can. Fès repays familiarity with a dramatic drop in hassle.

luxury/expensive

Fès has many luxurious hotels with immense marble foyers, big bedrooms and magnificent pools, but they are all tucked away in the New Town suburbs, while to stay in the Merenides hotel overlooking the old city is to make oneself complicit in the architectural rape of Fès' millenial skyline. On the other hand the **Palais Jamaï**, ✆ (05) 634331, ✉ 635096, just in from Bab Guissa, though it has fallen back from the high standards of the past, still has by far the best position and all the cachet. It is the only grand hotel from which you can walk straight out into the medina streets

The Palais Jamaï was established in 1930 in the enclosed 19th-century palace of a Fassi Vizier. Its position just within the medina ramparts of Bab Jamaï, its extraordinary tiled Andalusian garden, enormous heated pool, tiled *hammam* and Moroccan restaurant make it an exceptional place to explore the city from. It is featured in many novels, not least Paul Bowles' *The Spider's House*.

moderate

The **Batha Hotel**, ✆ (05) 741077/638267, ✉ 741078, occupies an even better position than the Palais Jamaï, beside the Batha museum on the edge of Fès-el-Bali just above the small but animated Place de l'Istiqlal. Its address is listed as Rue de l'UNESCO, but it is actually at the junction of Av de la Liberté and Rue ed Douh by Place de l'Istiqlal. The recently-constructed double row of tiled bedrooms surround a long open courtyard, and there are fountains, a small but welcome pool and a licensed restaurant and bar in the old block, which once functioned as a British consulate. Book in advance to avoid being squeezed out by tour groups.

Hotel Mousaffir, ✆ (05) 651902, 📠 651909, is on Av des Almohades just beside the train station on the northern edge of the New Town. It is part of a well-designed national chain of beside-the-station hotels that all have efficiently-plumbed bedrooms, pools, bars, licensed restaurants and garden areas. Despite it having 83 rooms, it can rapidly get filled up, and is worth booking ahead.

The **Zalagh**, ✆ (05) 932234, 📠 651495, is at 10 Rue Mohamed Diouri, a quiet suburban street which turns off Blvd Abdellah Chefchaouni just 200m south of Place de la Résistance. A 60's hotel, on the edge of the New Town with a pleasant view over the Oued Zitoun to the Mellah and Fès Jdid, it has recently been given a total renovation and a brand-new pool. It also has 70 rooms, a restaurant and a bar that's popular with locals.

Another useful hotel in this range, right in the middle of the New Town, is the 40-bedroom **De La Paix**, ✆ (05) 625072, 📠 626880, at 44 Av Hassan II.

inexpensive

First choice would be the **Grand**, ✆ (05) 625511/932026, on Blvd Abdallah Chefchaouni, a large 80-room old colonial hotel at the southern end of this New Town boulevard, overlooking the gardens of Place Mohammed V. If it's full, try the **Mounia** at 60 Rue Asilah,✆ (05) 624838,📠 650773.

Other well-established hotels with restaurants in the centre of the New Town include **Lamdaghri**, ✆ (05) 620310, at 10 Rue Abbas Masaadi, **Olympic**, ✆ (05) 622403, on Blvd Mohammed V and **Amor**, ✆ (05) 622724, at 31 Rue Arabie Saoudite.

cheap (New Town)

Among the several clean, functional small hotels with some character are the 34-room **Central**, ✆ (05) 622333, at 50 Rue Brahim Roudani off Blvd Mohammed V, the **Excelsior**, ✆ (05) 655602, at 107, Rue Larbi el Kaghat as it meets Blvd Mohammed V, and the **Kairouan**, ✆ (05) 623590, at 84 Rue du Soudan (ex d'Espagne).

cheap (Medina)

There are half a dozen very basic hotels around the Bab Bou Jeloud. Busy and with unreliable water supplies, but much quieter since the departure of the bus station, their attraction is their proximity to the main entrance to Fès-el-Bali and the evening café life. In order of preference: **Hôtel du Jardin Public** ✆ (05) 633086, at 153 Kasbah Bou Jeloud—up a small alley and immediately south of the Bou Jeloud mosque; **Hotel Kaskade**, ✆ (05) 633991 at 26 Rue Serajine (and its neighbour the **Mauretania** at no. 14, which is a last resort), just through the Bou Jeloud gate, with wide double beds and an old *hammam* on the second floor. **Hotel Erraha**, ✆ (05) 633226, is tucked away above the two-corner café and entered from a side alley. On the opposite (north side) of the Bou Jeloud square is the **National**, ✆ (05) 633248.

The **Lamrani**, © (05) 634411, is deeper into the medina on the Talaa Seghira, just before the Bou Inania Medersa..

Outside Fès

It may be worth bearing in mind a couple of alternatives just outside Fès, which can be useful if you need a respite from the city. The moderately-priced **Hotel Fadoua**, © (05) 694050, stands in the centre of the spa of Moulay Yâcoub, 20km northwest of Fès, and has been recommended. The mini resort of Aïn Chkef, 6km south of the city, has the **Reda**, © (05) 640978, with its own pool and restaurant. It can be reached off the P24 to Immouzer and then on the S315, or with the no. 14 bus from Place de Florence, on Av Hassan II in the centre of the New Town.

Eating Out

In the daytime, eat in the Medina, but in the evening hop into a taxi and explore some of the variety of restaurants in the New Town.

In the Medina

expensive

The only exception to this rule is the **Palais Jamaï Hotel**, © (05) 634331, which maintains the **Al Fassia** Moroccan restaurant, above the hotel's Andalusian garden in a hall of this former palace. It is watched over by a splendidly imposing head waiter, and most evenings your meal is accompanied by the sounds of classical Andalusian music played by a traditional quintet.

moderate

Dropping down a rank in style there are two more Moroccan restaurants very near the Palais Jamaï that also serve traditional food amid palatial 19th-century interiors and have licences to serve alcohol, but can be dominated by tour groups and belly dancing shows to the detriment of their cooking. **Restaurant Firdaous** is just inside the medina through the Bab Guissa at 10 Rue Jenifour, © (05) 634343 (turn right as you approach the Palais Jamaï gates), while for **Les Remparts**, © (05) 637415, at 2 Arset Jiar, turn left in front of the hotel gates.

For a grand lunch in the medina most visitors and groups stop at either the **Dar Saada**, © (05) 633343, or the **Palais de Fès**, © (05) 634707, a pair of opulent turn-of-the-century mansions that double up as carpet bazaars. The Palais has by the far the best view from its rooftop terrace as it stands just east of the grand mosque of Karaouiyne at 16 Rue Boutouil-Karaouiyne (*see* p.324), but the **Dar Saada**,in the heart of the medina's richest shopping district at 21 Souk el Attarine, has a licence to serve alcohol. Both are closed in the evening.

The **Palais M'Nebhi**, © (05) 633893, is one of the best and most reclusive addresses in Fès. It is about 450m east of the Bou Jeloud gate on the north side of Rue Talaa Seghira. It occupies a beautiful palace built by the famous Menehbi family that was later used by Marshal Lyautey, and also a language school. The current *patron*, Haj Sentissi, provides the best couscous in the medina, which you can eat in the Fès or Meknès salons, at either end of the vast courtyard. It is normally only open for lunch, but has been known to reopen for favoured customers in the evening.

cheap

In the medina there are many tiny hole-in-the-wall grill-kitchens and café-restaurants. Rue Hormis, deep in the heart of Fès-el-Bali, has the best selection of them, which are found by turning left just before the Souk Attarine gate, coming from Bou Jeloud.

In the area just in from Bab Bou Jeloud there is a good choice of restaurants that are used to feeding budget-conscious backpackers. The **Bouayed** at 26 Rue Serrajine or the **Des Jeunes** at no. 16, © (05) 634975, are both just in from the gate, stay open late, and are clean, quick and honest. Other recommended places in this area include **La Baraka** at 33 Rue Talaa Seghira, and the **Tariana** at no. 25.

In the New Town

expensive

The **Restaurant El Ambra**, 47 Route d'Immouzer, © (05) 641687,is one of a half-dozen relatively new places that have opened up in the smart quarter of Fassi suburban mansions beside the road to Immouzer. Many are purposely designed for grand marriage and circumcision celebrations; El Ambra is the quietest of them, but still sumptuous enough.

moderate

Chez Vittorio, © (05) 624730 is found just south of Av Mohammed es Slaoui a block east of Place Mohammed V at 21 Rue Brahim-Redani, sometimes known as Rue Nador. It is a small, efficiently run Italian restaurant, though both staff and the customers are predominately and animatedly Moroccan. You can choose pasta, pizza or meat dishes from the menu, while picking over some antipasti as you sip your wine. They prefer to be paid in cash.

Le Nautilus is on the lower floor of the Hotel de la Paix at 44 Av Hassan II, © (05) 625072. It's an efficient place with a good kitchen and a mixed menu (try prawn pil-pil followed by pastilla), only slightly let down by its basement location. Nearby, the **Roi de la Bière** at 59 Blvd Mohammed V, © (05) 625324, is another delightfully aged but dignified place that serves a very reasonable three-course à la carte meal.

La Cheminée, © (05) 624902, stands on the avenue that leads directly out of the train station, at 6 Av Lalla-Asmae. It offers a simple but effective selection from its *menu du jour*, and the calm unruffled service found in places that do their own thing and do it well.

Bars and Cafés

There are few places as relaxing as a table by the waterwheel at the **Nouria** café, © (05) 625422. El Idrissi Hamid, a courteous, English-speaking musician, is the current *patron* of this famous establishment beside Fès Jdid's Bou Jeloud gardens.

A welcome addition is the **Mirador**, 1 Dhar Lakhmiss, © (05) 645623, beside the new square and garden terrace built above Bordj Nord and the Merenid tombs. It has a delicious array of cakes, ice creams and cappuccino to accompany the superb view.

Along the great thoroughfares of the New Town, such as Av Hassan II (especially around Place de Florence), Blvd Mohammed V and Av Mohammed es Slaoui you will find a whole range of cafés. If you are looking for some French colonial vibes, head straight for Place Mohammed V, where you will find the **Café de la Renaissance**, **Le Cristal** and **Café du Centre** (which can all serve alcohol).

Bars in the New Town are mostly concentrated along Av Mohammed es Slaoui, but unless you are a very seasoned male traveller the mass of beer-drinking men packed within can be too great a challenge. The more cloistered bars found in the major hotels are really your only option. A tour of these would include the **Palais Jamaï** (in order to stroll around its garden), the **Bahia** in Fès Jdid and the **Zalagh**.

Shopping

Fès positively bursts at the seams with ceramics, carpets, metalwork, leather, drums, tambourines, shoes and belts that it enthusiastically offers to every visitor. If you are looking for something a bit special try **Mohammed ben Abdeljalil**'s shop at 35 Rue Talaa Seghira. Do not be content with his street-side stall but ask to be shown the rooms behind, which are laden down with objet d'arts.

There are a couple of **bookshops** that stock English titles, as well as the newsstands found in the big hotels. **The English Bookshop**, 68 Av Hassan II, has the largest range, but the **Librairie du Centre** at 134 Blvd Mohammed V and the **Hôtel de Fès**, Av des FAR, are also worth a look. Newspapers are sold at all these shops and along Blvd Mohammed V. For **picnics**, the central market is off Blvd Mohammed V, just across the street from the Café Zanzibar.

Sports

Riding is possible from the Club Equestre Moulay Idriss, © (05) 623438, at the race-course. **Swimming** is possible in summer at the crowded municipal pool near the Stadium off the Av des Sports (adm), or at the **campsite**, © (05) 641537.

A mixed ***hammam,*** with attendant masseur, operates in the Palais Jamaï Hotel. Alternatively, use the *hammam* Aturki in the medina for 5dh; turn right through Bab Bou Jeloud on to Rue Talaa Seghira and then right, first door under the covered arch.

Entertainment and Nightlife

Although it hardly counts as a night on the town you could watch the music show and historical illuminations that cover 12 centuries in 45 minutes and are staged at Bordj Sud every night at 9.30pm. For information, call the Bordj, ©(05) 629371, or Apt 65, Place de Florence, © (05) 931893 (adm).

There are disco/night clubs in the **Palais Jamaï**, **Les Merenides**, **Jnane Fès, Sofia** and **Zalagh** hotels, though none can be enthusiastically recommended.

Festivals

The students' moussem of Sidi Harazem is held at the end of April, and the two major city festivals of Moulay Idriss II and Sidi Ahmed el Bernoussi are both in September.

For the last few years a **festival of sacred music** has been held in Fès around the end of May and beginning of June, with two or three concerts daily for a week in the garden of the Dar Batha museum, the Old Méchouar or the governors' palace.

Musicians from all over the world may perform as well as Jewish, Muslim and Christian musicians from Spain and Morocco who share the common inspiration of Andalusia. The French Consulate (33 Rue el Bahrain, ✆ (05) 623921) also has a cultural section that organizes a variety of exhibitions and events through the year.

Around Fès: Moulay-Yâkoub, Sidi-Harazem and Jbel Zalagh

Moulay-Yâkoub is just 20km northwest of the city, across gently rolling hills. It is a pleasant holiday resort, a favourite sketching-ground of Maghrebi artists and much loved by Moroccan families, who can all indulge in some quiet hypochondria there. It's built on terraces above a hot sulphurous spring which fills a series of natural *hammams* and enclosed pools. In the past it enjoyed a reputation as a haunt of prostitutes and a cure for venereal disease; now the waters are modestly only claimed to cure 'renal and urinary' diseases. There is a small admission charge for the warm sulphurous pool and for the *hammam*, which has separate enclosures for men and women. Swimming trunks are worn in the baths; souk stalls sell a selection of these as well as soap, beads, towels and candles. You can eat at a number of cafés or at the **Restaurant Merhaba**, just above the baths. Opposite the village is the rounded hill of Lalla Chafer, with a few pine trees growing on its slope. Walking up the hill to the café on the summit is all part of the cure, while lower down the hill an all-new spa has been constructed in the last few years. There are half a dozen *pensions* in the village, the best of which is the **Lamrani**, as well as the three-star **Fadoua** (*see* p.331).

Sidi-Harazem is 15km east of Fès-el-Bali, approached off either the P1 to Taza or the P20 to Sefrou. It is a ubiquitous name in Morocco, due to the bottled mineral water sold throughout the country. The spa was known as Hammam Khaoulan until Sultan Moulay Rachid moved the bones of Sidi Harazem here from Marrakech in the 17th century. So now the *moussem* of this great national saint is held in April around three rival tombs; at this spa, at Fès and at Marrakech. The 17th-century koubba and its small adjacent *hammam* are pleasant enough. They were built by Moulay Rachid, who used to relax away the cares of state and his own furious tension here: it took the court masseur three hours to get the sultan to release his grip on his sword after a battle. However, the bottling plant, a four-star health hotel and an ugly expanse of concrete terracing for the use of the public has smothered the charm of the place. It is still a place of popular piety, full in the summer season with trinket sellers, musicians, café-restaurants and proud family groups out for a picnic. The snaking stream of 35°C hot, manganese-rich water is full of bodies taking the cure and women washing clothes.

If you are travelling with children break your sightseeing with a trip out to **Les Trois Sources**, ✆ (05) 606523, just 4km from the centre of Fès on the P24 road south to Immouzer, where there are three swimming pools are watched by lifeguards, together with a playground, table-tennis and billiards tables as well as a range of organised activities and a dancefloor and restaurant.

Another choice for a day-trip is to take the P26 due north of Fès-el-Bali. The view from the road as it snakes up the hill is already a good enough reason for the drive, but the point of the journey is the healthy ascent up to the 900m summit of **Jbel Zalagh**, with its fine views east towards the Idriss I Dam. The track up to the summit begins about 7km north from Fès on the right-hand side of the road, about 1km before the koubba of Sidi Ahmed el Bernoussi.

The Middle Atlas

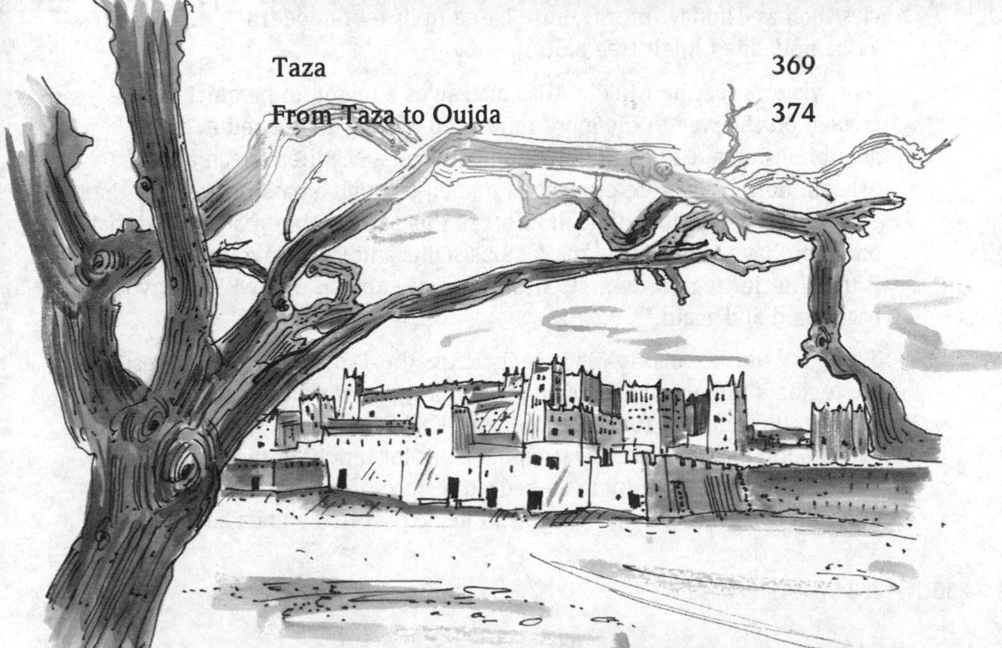

South from the great cities of Fès and Meknès there is a continuous thread of towns where the agricultural lowlands of the Saïss Plain first meet the limestone uplands of the Middle Atlas mountain range. These towns have acted throughout their long history as both markets and border posts, fortified against the nomadic Berber tribes of the highlands. Taza and Sefrou are the oldest and most elegant of them, and are surrounded by a striking and little-visited hinterland.

The Middle Atlas mountain region itself is in total contrast to the sophisticated Moorish culture of the nearby cities of Meknès and Fès. It is still essentially a pastoral space, a high, partially forested plateau that has always been the realm of Berber nomadic tribes, principally the Beni-Mguild of the cedar forests, the Zaïane and the Aït-Serri. It boasts no distinguished architecture or ancient areas of settlement. The neo-colonial hill stations—Imouzzèr-Kandar, Ifrane and Azrou—provide a refreshing change in atmosphere and pace from the frenetic, humid street life of the old cities, but apart from a well established tour of cedar forests, ski runs and lakes, have little interest in themselves. The Middle Atlas landscape is at its most rewarding in the higher, distant and more remote regions, such as the source of the Oum er Rbia, the El Abid Gorge and the Ouzoud Falls. For the moderately adventurous hill walker the Middle Atlas is an unexploited haven of peaks, hidden valleys, kasbahs, lakes and high mountain passes. They can be explored from hotels in the principal highland towns or with specialized local agencies such as Timnay Inter-Culture based in its own modern kasbah outside Midelt (*see* p.366).

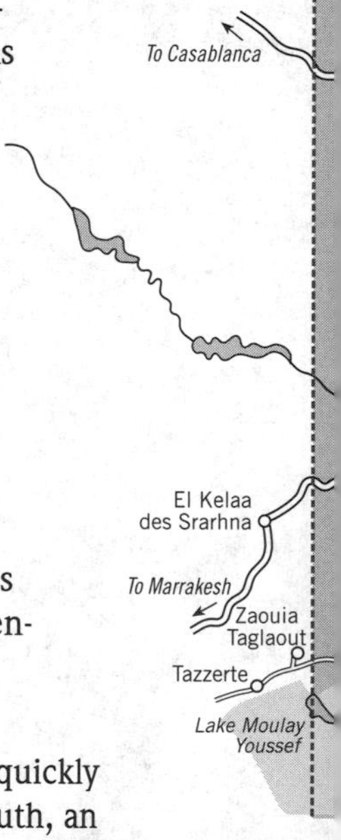

Most visitors see the Middle Atlas plateau as a region to be quickly crossed on the way to the more renowned regions to the south, an amorphous area, a zone of transition between a Mediterranean and a Saharan flora. It is more often seen framed through a passing window than explored in detail. It is difficult to break this pattern, but rest assured that once you have explored all the famous sights and far corners of Morocco it is this interior region, with its strong Berber culture, that will draw you back again and again.

Travelling on the road to Marrakech across the Tadla Plain, an interest in the region's tumultuous warring history brings rewarding insights to the initially unpromising towns of Khénifra, Kasba Tadla and Boujad. If you are just looking for a convenient stopping point for lunch, without moving off the main road, use the hibiscus-hedged terrace of the France by the Khenifra barracks. Taza guards the strategic pass that stands between the

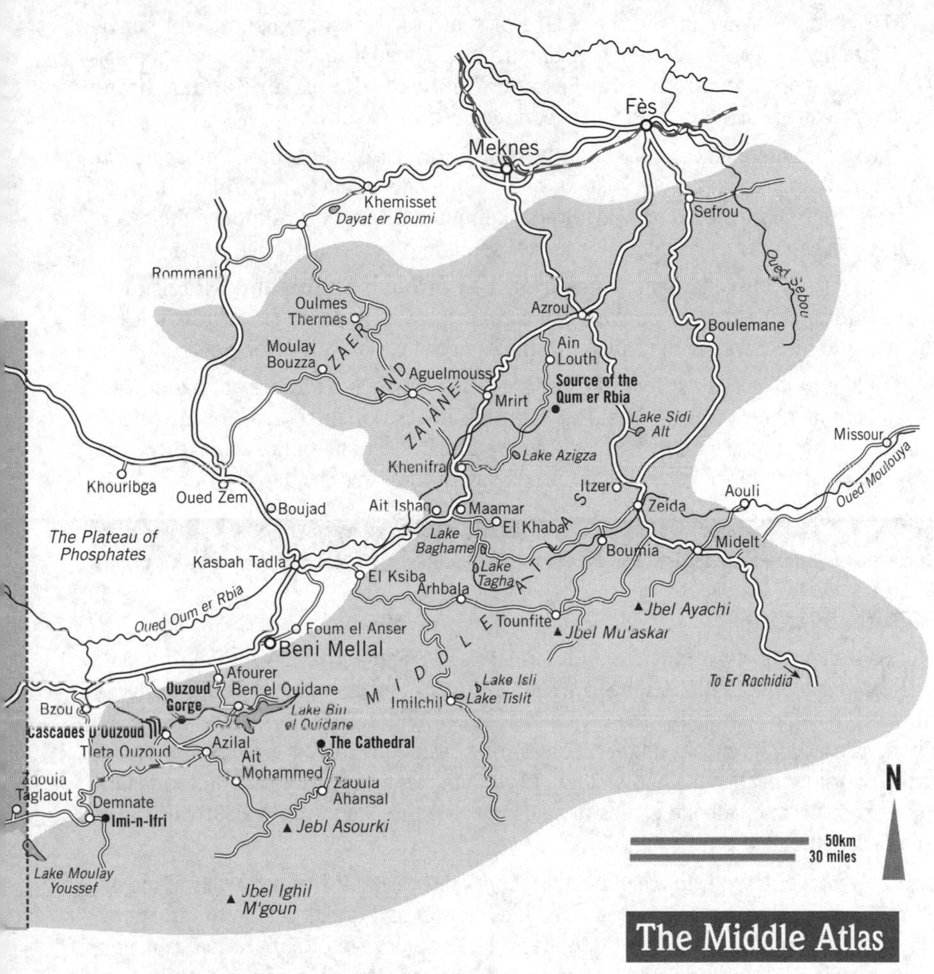

The Middle Atlas

hills of the Rif to the north and those of the Middle Atlas to the south. To its east stretches the arid, little-populated Plain of Jel which, like the eastern border city of Oujda, has been much fought over by invaders.

Though it leads to a pleasant Mediterranean beach at Saïdia, and the cave-studded Beni-Snassen hills just outside Oujda (*see* pp.154–161, in the Tangier, the Rif and the Mediterranean chapter), this whole area has received very few visitors, even before the recent closure of the Algerian frontier cut down at a stroke its still limited passing traffic. It does, therefore, the traveller who likes to get away from the crowd.

Finding Your Way Around This Chapter

This chapter covers an enormous area of central Morocco, which has for convenience been organized into five distinct routes. The first route is the most popular, the well worn trail **South from Fès and Meknès to Imouzzèr-Kandar, Ifrane and Azrou**, with a tour of the lakes and the Forêt de Cèdres.

The second route takes you on **South from Azrou to Béni-Mellal**, with some side trips to the hills, lakes, river, markets and monuments of the Middle Atlas. The third route, from **Béni-Mellal to Marrakech**, continues this journey, although the best of this area can only be seen by taking roads south into the Central High Atlas.

The fourth route takes you **South from Fès through Sefrou and Midelt to Er Rachidia**, along the old caravan trail across the Middle Atlas. This is the quickest and most direct way to the Sahara, with some good opportunities for walks en route.

The fifth route goes **East from Fès towards the eastern frontier**. Apart from Taza and the neighbouring Jbel Tazzeka Park this area is not strictly part of the Middle Atlas, although the journey towards Oujda and the Algerian frontier across the battle-scarred eastern plain fits well into the general mood of this chapter.

Route 1: South to Imouzzèr-Kandar, Ifrane and Azrou

Imouzzèr-Kandar

This hilltop settlement sits on the first substantial rise in land above the agricultural plain south of Fès. It is a modest place, ranged around the main road and perched on the edge of the limestone plateau that marks the beginning of the Middle Atlas. In summer this open town with its park and twin bathing lakes shaded by deciduous trees is a refreshing change from the exhausting heat, smell and vitality of Fès. It makes a popular escape from the city, and its relaxed bar- and café-life comes to a head for the three-day **Apple Festival** held in July to celebrate the harvest.

Although this market town is in an ancient location, built beside the ruined walls of the old kasbah of the Aït-Seghrouchen, its square red-tiled houses and hotels belong to the French colonial period. A **souk** is held every Monday inside the decayed **kasbah**, its walls now barely discernible. Within this muddled compound, entered through a double archway just left of the town's conspicuous mosque, are a few surviving examples of the **underground houses** that once characterized this region. Subterranean homes are difficult to appreciate without becoming insufferably nosy, and you might content yourself with a brief glance at the entrances to the pair down a short passageway to the right of the kasbah gate.

The **Massif du Kandar** is a much admired range of hills just outside the town. Take the 4620 track east from Imouzzèr and 5km later turn north (left), to approach (in another 5km) the summit of Jbel Abad, where a viewing tower at 1706m offers a splendid view south over the Saïss Plain, backed by distant mountain ranges.

Another excursion out from town is to the river Cheggag and the Aïn Chifa spring, a verdant oasis in summer made all the more tempting by a pool of fresh spring water. The turning to it is 8km north of Imouzzèr, along route 4633 as it heads west.

Where to Stay and Eating Out

The moderately priced **Royal Hotel**, © (05) 663080, is on Boulevard Mohammed V. It is functional, with a good position by the dammed-up pond at the back of the town, and has its own bar and restaurant.

The best place to stay and eat is the reasonably priced **Des Truites**, © (05) 663002, also on Boulevard Mohammed V. It is a small family-run hotel with just 17 simple rooms, a popular bar and a restaurant where wholesome meals are served in the evening. It is raised on a terrace and has no sign post, and so can be surprisingly difficult to spot. Coming from Fès, it is one of the first houses you pass, up on your left as the road climbs the last corner before reaching the town. If it is full try **La Chambotte**, © (05) 663374, on the opposite side of the Boulevard from the Royal, another small, friendly place, but much easier to find in the heart of the town.

The Lake Tour

About 9km south of Imouzzèr-Kandar and 16km north of Ifrane, on the P24, a signposted turning to the east leads directly to **Dayèt (Lake) Aaoua**. It is a long, attractive sheet of water, a natural depression formed from dissolving limestone, its banks fringed with mixed woodland and surrounded by rounded low hills. The lake has undoubted appeal for anyone enduring the long summer in a Moroccan city, though it obviously has less appeal for a Western visitor eagerly seeking the desert and some Islamic sensations. You can stay, drink, eat or rent boats at the excellent **Chalet du Lac**, © (05) 663197/663270. The redoubtable Madame who ran the place for decades finally relinquished her duties in the spring of 1997, and has gone to her grave. It is hoped that her spirit remains, to assure the future of this small corner of *Maroc Française*. Note that the hotel tends to be firmly closed up outside meal times, from noon to 2.30pm and from 7–9.30pm.

Continue along the same road beyond the hotel to reach (in 16km) the P20, the main Fès to Midelt road. Turn right here (heading south) and then about 2km later turn right again. This track passes by the banks of the tinted **Dayèt Afourgah**, which drains through a cavern in the limestone into the quite separate crater lake of **Dayèt Iffer**, a little way to the west, where the water appears filtered and cooler. From there turn left onto another, still tarmacked, track which in 5km reaches **Dayèt Ifrah**, a great circular bowl of water in the middle of a natural depression. Around the lake's edge horses are often pastured and nomads gather in their black tents to water their herds, and two rival hamlets exist on either side of the lake, each with its own mosque.

About 5km further along this dirt track you arrive at **Dayèt Hachlaf**, though it is no longer much of a lake—more of a marsh watered by a spring. It sits at the foot of the **Vallée des Roches**. The hill to the west, the double peak of Lalla Mimouna, is named after a holy woman hermit who died after being raped by the jinn of the woods. The right-hand track (in bad condition) passes through the weather-sculpted rock forms thought to be jinn petrified by avenging angels until the Day of Judgement; the track rejoins the road at Dayèt Aaoua. The left-hand track, route 3325, is much easier and passes a large circle of carved stones before meeting the road to Ifrane.

Ifrane

This town was established in 1929 as a summer hill station for French colonial officials, and is today a favourite resort of the Moroccan rich and influential, and has been chosen as the site of a new university. The well-built stone houses with high-pitched, red-tiled roofs look prim and self-satisfied behind their green shutters. They are set in their own gardens, and many are named after French flowers. Ifrane provides a graphic demonstration of how strongly the present ruling class have absorbed the manners and taste of the French. The skyline is dominated on one side by the bulk of the Hôtel Mischlieffen, and on the other by the King's new palace, a Gothic château with yellow walls and a green roof. The 'season' is from June to September, plus a brief flurry of activity during the winter when the King comes to ski or walk and his court comes too, occupying every bed in town.

Below the King's palace a network of illuminated paths follow the regulated but extravagant meanders of the river Tizguit, which flows down to the west of Ifrane as the **Cascades des Vierges**. It is undeniably pretty and the serpentine river banks, overhung by walnut trees, come close to the Muslim ideal of paradise, as revealed in the innumerable cheap prints found in cafés and hotel bedrooms throughout the land. A minor tarmac road, the S309 to El Hajeb, allows you to follow the river down to **Zaouia d'Ifrane**. This is an unpretentious settlement, a scattering of huts spread around the mosque, koubba and associated buildings. The limestone caves along the river's length were a favourite refuge for ascetics living in holy poverty, removed from the wicked temporal cities of the plain. Several of their tombs can be found by following the rough track below the zaouia, while upstream the shaded bank is a popular picnic spot. King Mohammed V, anxious to correct the spread of unorthodox cults, made an example of the area around Ifrane and ordered the destruction of the numerous koubbas. Fortunately this example, though obediently acknowledged by his people, did not set a fashion. It would have deprived the Moroccan landscape of one of its most delightfully inventive details and obliterated myriad examples of indigenous architecture.

Getting Around and Tourist Information

There are cafés, bars and restaurants in the hotels in Ifrane, but no bank. Buses leave from the post office, with at least half a dozen a day heading north to Fès and south to Azrou, rising to about eight a day in summer.

Where to Stay and Eating Out

For a passing visit stay in Azrou or Imouzzèr rather than Ifrane, which is expensive for what you get and tends to be either empty or fully booked. For those who like the place, the choice is between three hotels, all of them usefully placed for a meal or a passing drink as they have bars and licensed restaurants. At the top of the range is the large and very expensive **Hôtel Mischliffen,** ✆ (05) 566607, with over 100 bedrooms, a fine viewing terrace, pool and all mod cons. Down a scale or two in price is the recently opened **Hotel Tilleuls,** ✆ (05) 566558, with the **Grand Hotel,** ✆ (05) 566203, on Avenue de la Marche Verte, offering a reasonably priced evening in a monument to mock-Alpine taste with a dark interior heavy with a mass of brown painted and varnished wood.

The **Perce-Neige Hôtel**, © (05) 566404, on Rue des Asphodèles, may be listed in some guides but has been taken over by the state petrol company. It was a joyless place and is no loss. There is however a good **campsite**, a large and well shaded paddock on the eastern edge of town beside the Meknès road.

Sports

Skiing is possible anytime between December and March. The snowfall is not nearly predictable enough to plan a holiday around but most years there will be a good couple of weeks' skiing. There are short runs and ski lifts at Mischliffen and Jbel Hebri, equidistant from Ifrane and Azrou. Ski equipment can be hired in Ifrane from **Café-Restaurant Chamonix** while the ski-club at Mischliffen sells passes to the lifts and has a café-restaurant.

Forêt de Cèdres

Though large acreages of Morocco's natural forests have been felled to make sleepers for the national railway system, magnificent stretches still exist, and a 52km circuit around Ifrane provides an easy and stimulating introduction. If you leave Ifrane on the S309, heading east, you will pass through an area of inferior pine woods and treeless plateau before the right turn to the S3206. As the road climbs the **Tizi-n-Tretten** pass you enter the right altitude for magnificent cedars. The groves tend to be isolated on rises in the land, further emphasizing their height in contrast to the surrounding pastures. At the summit of the pass (1934m) there is a fine view south to the distant peaks of the Middle Atlas. The road passes close to the local 'hills' of Jbel Mischliffen (2036m) and Jbel Hebri (2104m), old volcanoes that have risen above this forested mountain plateau. A few ski lifts have been planted on their slopes.

A right turn after Jbel Hebri will take you onto the P21 to Azrou. A few kilometres later there is a track on the right—route 3387, marked *Cèdre Gouraud*—that winds for 5km through a spectacular belt of the forest. Sunlight pierces through the branches, the track shifts to thread through the massive trunks and the resinous red bark emits a delicious odour. The track leads down to the P24 Azrou to Ifrane road, where there are fine views of the plateau and the rounded volcanic outcrops to the north.

Azrou

Azrou is a Berber town of 45,000 people, caught between steep wooded hills and facing a distinctive puckered volcanic outcrop. From this the town gets its name, for *Azrou* translates as 'rock' in the local Berber dialect. Sultan Moulay Ismaïl built a kasbah here to guard this strategic market town on the crossroads of the routes from Fès to Marrakech and from Meknès to the Tafilalt. There is little trace of it, but the rock remains unaltered except for the frequent change of clothes laid out to dry on its flanks, and a splendid new grand mosque.

By the late 19th century Azrou had fallen outside the pale of government control and into the hands of the Beni-Mguild, a powerful Berber tribal confederation that had originated in the Sahara. The French, after they had subdued the Middle Atlas, recruited Berber highlanders to serve in their administration and educated them at the *Collège Berbère* they established in Azrou. The college carefully stressed the difference between Berbers and

Arabs, but this clumsy colonial attempt to divide and rule had little permanent effect, though the influence of the 'Azrou graduates' is still particularly strong in the army. The college still survives, though its post-Independence name of 'Tariq ibn Ziad' now recalls the ancient partnership of Berber and Arab as they conquered Spain under the flag of Islam.

As an old market town of the once nomadic Beni-Mguild, Azrou has a tradition of weaving and craftsmanship. Among the mass of everyday goods it is often possible to come across newly-woven kilims and natural wool blankets. Outside the Tuesday **souk** these can be found for sale at the **Ensemble Artisanal**, a school that maintains traditional patterns, creates new designs and is experimenting with figurative tapestries. It also has a stone and wood-carving section. The quality of pieces on sale is good, and prices are fixed. The Ensemble is below the rock on the left, and open 8.30–12pm, 2.30–6pm, Mon–Sat.

Getting Around and Tourist Information

There are four **buses** a day to Meknès (67km), seven to Fès (77km). Fès buses stop at Ifrane and Imouzzèr. Four Marrakech buses pass through daily but may be fully booked from Fès or Meknès. There are often seats free on the daily Er Rachidia bus.

Buses and ***grands taxis*** depart from the mosque that stands in the large triangular space that opens out above the rock, Place Hassan II. Immediately above this is Place Mohammed V, a pleasant, small square fronted by cafés with green glazed tiles flashing in the sunlight. Here you will find the Banque Populaire, BMCI, post office, cafés and shops, while the cheaper hotels are found in neighbouring Place Souikia.

Where to Stay

expensive

The **Auberge Amros**, © (05) 562005, formerly just a roadside restaurant about 7km out on the Meknès road, has been converted into a four-star hotel. It is principally directed at the weekend trade from the cities, and apart from the pool and innumerable storks' nests there is little reason to stop at this monstrous red-tiled mansion without a view.

moderate

The **Panorama**, © (05) 562010, @ 561804, is an efficiently-run, friendly place with a fire in the sitting room, 39 rooms, a bar and a restaurant that produces nourishing home cooking. Although it is tucked away in the eastern corner of the town, 500m up from the centre, it is a natural base from which to explore the area

inexpensive/cheap

The inexpensive **Cèdres** on Place Mohammed V, © (05) 562326, stands right in the centre of the town and also has its own café and restaurant, though with just nine rooms it can get filled up very quickly.

The cheapest basic rooms can be found behind Place Mohammed V in Place Saouikia, in either the **Hôtel Salaam**, **Beauséjour**, **Atlas** or **Ziz**. Try the Beauséjour first—it has fine views from its balcony and roof terrace.

Eating Out

Apart from the bars and licensed restaurants listed in the hotels listed above, there is **Le Relais Forestier** on Place Mohammed V, an immaculately clean little restaurant where you can eat a cheap lunch freshly prepared by Madame Idijer, and listen to her Minerva Radio.

South from Meknès to Azrou

The roadside village of **Boufekrane** is 17km southeast of Meknès on the P21 to Azrou. It is lined with a tempting row of grill cafes, and just above the modern village are the ruins of an 18th-century government kasbah.

El-Hajeb is 12km further south, perched on a limestone terrace. It is in an ideal geographical position for a traditional market town, on the neutral ground between the pastoral land of the nomadic Berber Beni-M'Tir tribe to the south and the farmed land of the Saïss Plain. A souk is held here on Mondays. The walls of a large kasbah, last restored by Sultan Moulay Hassan at the end of the 19th century, still stand proud beside the road. On the sultan's death the *caid* of the Beni-M'Tir, Hammou el Hassan, occupied the kasbah. He had under his command less than 2000 horsemen, but played a very active if malicious role in the turbulent political life of Morocco. He encouraged the ill-fated Moulay Cherif El Kittani to claim the throne in 1909, but his candidate was whipped to death by the soldiers of Sultan Moulay Hafid. Not the least bit discouraged, he fielded two separate candidates in May 1911; they also died horribly, but the *caid* survived to make his submission to the French in 1913.

Cafés cluster around the municipal garden and there is a **campsite** by the road, a pleasant place from which to explore the limestone escarpments to the east and west which conceal a number of caves, rock pools and springs.

The **Balcon d'Ito/Belveder Tigrigra** is just 17km before Azrou. This is a natural terrace, a cliff escarpment that drops away from the road at 1500m and provides a wonderful panorama over a massive depression full of the eroded stacks of ancient volcanoes, through which the river Tigrigra flows.

Southeast from Azrou to Midelt

The cedar forests extend south of Azrou for about 15km, trailing off after the conspicuous volcanic cone of Jbel Hebri. After a further 16km south on the P21 road through pine woods and decayed cedars you reach the hamlet of **Timahdite** at 1815m, and then pass through a confused terrain of old volcanic activity where craters have filled to form small lakes.

The hamlet of **Bekrit**, 48km from Azrou, marks the far edge of the forest and the beginning of a pastoral landscape that is dotted with nomad tents in the summer. A left turn 4km later leads to the **lake of Sidi-Ali**, a beautiful, long stretch of water, full of fish and one of the favoured summer watering points for the Beni-Mguild nomads.

Ten kilometres on is the **Col du Zad**, which at 2178m divides the catchments of the three great rivers of Morocco. If you were a rain drop falling to the north you would flow down the river Sebou into the Atlantic at Mehdiya-Plage; falling to the south or east you would drift down the river Moulouya out into the Mediterranean at Saïdia beach; and landing to the west you would join the Oum er Rbia and flow into the Atlantic ocean at Azemmour.

After the hamlet of **Aït-Oufella** there is a right turn 4km south that leads to **Itzer**, a worthwhile diversion on Mondays and Thursdays for its important **souk**, which in the lawless past was held under the ksar and patronage of the saintly family of Sidi Boumoussa. From Itzer the road passes through **Boulôjoul** (after the Sefrou junction) and **Zeïda**, a manganese mine by the Khénifra junction, before reaching Midelt, 125km from Azrou (*see* pp.365–8).

Route 2: South from Azrou to Béni-Mellal

This route takes you past Middle Atlas towns such as Khénifra and Kasba Tadla which only 70 years ago were battlegrounds and major prizes in a tumultuous struggle. The tale of their lone fortresses, ambitious governors and clouds of nomadic tribal cavalry reads like a fabulous episode of medieval history. Some of the most interesting country is way off from the main road, so there are some suggested side trips.

Azrou to Khénifra

The P24 from Azrou to Khénifra runs across an uninspiring stretch of Middle Atlas plateau. Eleven km from Azrou, the village of **Assaka-n-Tatsa** has a **souk** on Sundays. **Mrirt**, halfway between Azrou and Khénifra, is the biggest settlement of the region; a lead mine operates in the hills just west of the town. Mrirt has a well-attended **souk** on Thursdays where you may find distinctive kilims covered with a mass of sequin embroidery. To the east of Mrirt, a road leads in 11km to **El-Hammam**, the central village of the Aït-Segougou tribe, who enjoy a reputation for weaving fine carpets. Finding the nomadic weavers is more difficult; rough tracks fan out from El-Hammam to a number of small settlements with only periodic markets that fluctuate with the movement of the herds. About 9km before Khenifra you pass through the village of **El-Bordj**, named after the gaunt 17th-century tower of dark stone that guards the bridge across the Oum er Rbia.

The Source of the Oum er Rbia

A slower but greatly preferable alternative route from Azrou to Khénifra goes through the territory of the Beni-Mguild tribe, a land of cedar forests, Alpine meadows and mountain streams. It is a spectacularly beautiful journey which allows you to explore or camp at the source of the Oum er Rbia river and Lake Azigza. Note, though, that there are no cafés, buses, hotels or petrol pumps between Aïn-Leuh and Khénifra, and the road can often be blocked by snow in the winter.

Turn left 19km west of Azrou off the P24 on to the S303, and travel 13km to **Aïn-Leuh**. Alternatively you could head south from Azrou for 3km on the P21 before turning right on the 3398, a track that passes through 24km of cedar forest punctuated by magnificent views to the north before also arriving at Aïn-Leuh. This is an old souk of the Beni-Mguild tribe that was adopted as an administrative centre by Sultan Moulay Ismaïl in the 18th century, and later by the French. The steep-roofed 1920s Alpine houses spill down from the heights to the brown houses and terraced gardens that surround the market. The **souk** for the Beni Mguild is officially held on Mondays and Thursdays, but trade can continue all week.

Climbing beyond the village, hill-top promontories crowned with rich dark stands of towering cedar give way to clear, natural meadows of grazing land. Mountain huts, their walls of wooden boards pierced by stove pipes, interchange with the broad sweep of the brown-black *khaïma* tents, contrasting styles that perfectly reflect the need of each season.

The Source

Thirty-two km from Aïn-Leuh on the S303 (43km from Azrou) you cross two bridges; a track on the left just past the second leads directly to a large pool. It is full of entangling weeds and on its far side the cavorting force of the river threatens to drag any swimmer away to his doom. The trickling stream on the right, fed by a tranquil round pool, is one of the three salt springs you pass before reaching the main torrential cascade of the river, its banks overhung with trees. Springs just above the river level gush great volumes of water which noisily rush out, enraged and foaming, from hidden limestone caverns and miles of natural tunnels. A few minutes' walk upstream brings you to the main waterfall, which drops into a smooth round red bowl carved from the great cliff face that looms up above, Jbel Sang. The bluff on your right gives a good prospect back over both falls and cascades. There are over 40 springs in the immediate area and you can continue upstream to discover a series of smaller secretive falls and pools that stretch back 15km into the mountains.

About 12km south of the source a signposted tarmac road leads to **Aguelmane Azigza**. This lake, introduced by a great Alpine meadow, is partly enclosed by limestone hills dressed in dense cedar forest. A fairly recent rock fall on the opposite cliff face has cleared a path through the forested slope and left a deep ravined cleft. Back on the road, the 3485, a slow descent gradually sheds the cedars and then pines to enter the farmed red soils of Khénifra, 30km to the west of Azigza.

Khénifra

This extensive market town stretches along both banks of the Oum er Rbia, surrounded by the folding hills of the Middle Atlas. The houses of Khénifra are painted a deep red, with their doors and windows picked out in green, mirroring the region's fierce red soil and bright spring vegetation.

It is the centre of an immense mountainous pastoral region. Horses and mules remain in constant daily use, and the cavalcades that ride in from the hills to attend the souks provide a memorable spectacle. The town is also well placed for an exploration of the Zaïane mountains to the west or the source of the Oum er Rbia to the east.

Until the 17th century Khénifra was a fortified enclosure where one of the dominant and turbulent Zaïane hill tribes wintered their herds. Sultan Moulay Ismaïl recognized its strategic location, and spanned the river Oum er Rbia with a bridge that was guarded by a government kasbah, while a walled enclosure served as a caravanserai for passing merchants and provided the nucleus around which the town grew.

Getting Around and Tourist Information

Khénifra is 160km from Fès, 82km from Azrou, 129km north of Béni-Mellal and 300km from Marrakech, and is well served by buses plying the Fès–Marrakech route. The BMCE bank has a branch at 13 Boulevard Mohammed V.

The weekly **livestock market** is held below the bus station on the Kasba Tadla and Marrakech road. There are separate corrals for the auction of cows, sheep, goats, mules and horses, with *fondouqs* to hold the mounts of the travelling farmers. The busiest souk is held on Sundays, with a smaller one on Wednesdays.

Caid Hammou of Khénifra

In the late 19th century Sultan Moulay Hassan recognized a tribal chief of the Zaïane tribes, Moha ou Hammou ez Zaiani, as the *caid* of Khénifra. Moha ou Hammou ruled vigorously and established markets, baths, a mosque and *fondouqs* in Khénifra. He gained in authority and ambition during the weak rule of Abdul Aziz, and asserted himself as a tribal warlord, his cavalry squadrons preying on caravans and raiding up to the walls of Meknès in the years that preceded direct conflict with the French. However by November 1914 Hammou had been forced back on his mountain capital by an advancing French column. Khénifra was stormed with the loss of 600 lives, but the undaunted Hammou continued a guerrilla campaign against the French garrison, which for years could only be supplied by convoys protected by armoured cars. The resistance diminished after Hammou died in battle, attempting to raise a general rebellion against France in 1921.

The modern extent of the town dwarfs the scant relics from the 18th century. Moulay Ismaïl's bridge remains astride the river overlooked by two stone corner towers that are all that remain of the old government kasbah. This area is used by taxis, but the view across the riverbed to the medina with its old mosque and zaouia is rewarding and in the evening, when the shops are open, is the perfect place for a stroll. There are several pleasant gardens and public spaces in the town. A pretty terraced garden leads down from the hotel restaurants to the river bank, and a racetrack can be found beside the road south of town.

Where to Stay and Eating Out

expensive

The **Hammou Azzayani** hotel, © (05) 586020, is up in the hillside new town. An international, 60-bedroom place, it can appear rather forlornly empty, but has a bar, restaurant and pool

inexpensive

By the river a road leads up to the garrison gates of the FAR depot, whose sentries wear a ceremonial uniform of a rather fetching green turban, red cloth belts and baggy, lightly striped trousers. Here you find the liveliest corner of Khénifra, and the **Hotel France**, © (05) 586114, which has a spacious downstairs dining room, a hibiscus-fringed terrace and alongside a bar and an *Alimentation Générale.*

Zaïane Highlands

This rugged area of mountains, with no peak exceeding 1600m, is a westerly extension of the Middle Atlas. It is a land sharply cut by a number of steep valleys lined by small streams that collect to drain into the Atlantic through the river Bou Regreg, which flows out between Salé and Rabat. The region has always been dominated by the Zaïane Berber confederation, and in particular by the mounted nomadic clans whose herds of cattle, sheep and goats are moved up from the lowland pastures into the central highlands for the summer. There are separate souks for the summer and winter in the southern region.

Passing through this landscape, with its fleeting glimpses of moving herds and distant tents, reinforces the interest of the local souks. The people still rely on horses, mules and asses for transport, and every highland souk is a pageant of riders. At the head of the hierarchy of elegance are those who own a horse, cavaliers astride a tooled leather, high-pommelled saddle with bucket stirrups, elaborate trappings and reins. A step below is the more common sight of a strong docile mule ridden on ancient, well-worn kilim saddle bags and controlled by a simple rein of rope. At the bottom of the scale of dignity are the owners of donkeys, sitting side-saddle on straw panniers, or well back to avoid strain on the ass's spine. The cavalcades that depart into the hills, hooded cloaks trailing along the spine of their mounts after the trading, eating and gossip of the souk is over, make an intensely romantic image.

Local buses travel to the souks but otherwise this region can only satisfactorily be explored by car, mule or motorbike. The crossroad **souk of Aguelmouss** is 34km northwest of Khénifra along the 2516, set in the centre of a wide plain. The souk is held on Saturday mornings, a delightful, transitory affair, and there are four bedrooms available at the café, where you can also begin negotiations for the rent of a horse. A right turn at the Aguelmouss crossroads will take you back to **Mrirt** on the P24 (*see* p.344). A left turn on the other hand takes you in 42km to the town of **Moulay-Bouâzza**, the spiritual heart of the Zaïane. Moulay-Bouâzza was one of Morocco's great mystical instructors; he developed Sufi doctrines here before his death in 1176. His tomb and accompanying mosque were restored by Moulay Ismaïl in the 17th century. There are a couple of cafés near the mosque. You can get the best view of this tightly packed red settlement, clustering around a tomb in the fold of the hills, by travelling up the one-way road to the administrative 'Cercle'. The road from Moulay-Bouâzza to Oued-Zem, 60km southwest on the S131, passes through the most beautiful scenery of the region—volcanic plugs rise up from the forested valleys and hills to create an entrancing, broken, wilderness scenery.

Continuing north from Aguelmouss along the 2516, in 8km there is a ford across the river Marrout in the middle of a plain dominated by granite tors. Massed blocks are piled securely on each outcrop, the natural vents used as chimneys for the rude shelters of passing shepherds. Fine clay is washed from these hills into kaolin pipes, which have always been eagerly sought and dug up to sell to the potters of Fès and Meknès.

The small settlement of Oulmès is reached in 18 km, and 4km beyond this hamlet there is a left turn for **Tarmilate/Oulmès-les-Thermes** which is a bottling plant, a hotel and a few houses at the centre of a pleasant wooded limestone plateau. Oulmès mineral water and Sidi Ali sparkling water are extracted and bottled here to be sold throughout Morocco. Rich in carbonate, calcium, magnesium, bicarbonate of soda and, according to the label, 'radioactive' they assist intestinal, hepatitis, anaemia and arthritis sufferers. A very thin twisting road, now closed to traffic, descends in 2km to the hot water springs of Lalla Haya at the foot of the valley, where the mineral water emerges at 43°C. The bottling plant jeeps can take you down on a tour for 70dh and the surrounding hills of the plateau are dotted with caves, wooded groves and streams which can be explored in walks from the hotel. The moderately priced **Oulmès Hotel**, ✆ (07) 552353, is an interestingly remote and unusual holiday base.

It is closed from July to August but reopens for the September shooting season. There are some well preserved wild boar heads in the hall, and a small store of local woodcarvings. It has a restaurant, bar and a lift.

El-Harcha, 17km northwest of Oulmès, is at the heart of a scrubland and forest reserve still partly populated by wild boar and panthers. The road skirts the foot of Jbel Mouchchene, which at 1086m gives an extensive view over the Zaïane mountains and the lowland region to the west. **Tiddas**, the administrative centre for the Zemmour tribe is 20km on; it has a **souk** on Mondays, and a *moussem* is held in September around the shrine of Sidi Abd el Hadj, a great gathering point for Berber horsemen. **Mâaziz**, at the confluence of the rivers Tanoubert and Bou Regreg, is on the far side of the highlands, where they meet the plains, and has a **souk** on Sundays.

Khénifra to Midelt

This route has a dramatic mountain climb for the first third of the distance before it reaches the bleak Middle Atlas plateau. It can be blocked by snow any time from December to February. Leaving Khénifra on the P24 south to Kasba Tadla a small road to your left, 17km out of town, leads in 16km to the village of **El Kebab**, where there is a **souk** on Mondays that is well attended by skilled craftsmen of the local Ichkern tribe. It was here that Father Albert Lefont, who had previously spent several months with the ascetic Charles de Foucauld in the wilderness of the central Sahara, established himself as a doctor from 1928 to 1959. He wrote his *Dictionnaire de psychologie linguistique* in a hermitage which still survives above the village. To find it, have a cup of coffee or the usual tea in the central **Café Le Jardin** by the *Caid*'s offices, then walk along the road towards the rocky bluff. At the new mosque turn right to go up a stone path, and at the end of this alley you will find a red cross above the doorway to the hermitage, within which you will find its garden, library and, still, resident Christian fundamentalist.

Returning 8km back towards Khénifra a left turn takes you straight on to the P33 Midelt road to pass the village of **Azrou-n'Aït-Lahcem** and the lake of **Aguel Baghane**. Another lake, the **Aguel Tegha**, is hidden high up to the south; its tranquil surface provides the suitably secretive source of the river Moulouya, which flows northeast to the Algerian frontier. After Aguel Baghane the road climbs to the Tanout-ou-Fillali-pass, which at 2070m marks a distinct change in landscape. The rolling Alpine meadows of the foothills are now replaced by the windswept mountainous plateau of the Middle Atlas, broken by outcrops of granite boulders and high peaks looming to the south.

The journey could be broken at a café in one of the few villages beside the road. **Arhbalou-n-Serdane** is 18km from the pass, **Sidi Tiar/Tamaroute** 9km beyond that and **Boumia**, the largest of these settlements, is a further 18km east, 3km off the road. Boumia has a **souk** on Thursdays. A tarmac track extends 34km south from Boumia to **Tounfite**, a small administrative post for the Aït-Yaha tribe, built below the Jbel Masker peak. Besides three **ksour**, it boasts a basic café. It is an unusual entrance to the mountainous hinterland. A rough track travels due west below the peaks of Jbel Oujjit (2781m) and Jbel Toujjit (2690m) to reconnect with the El-Ksiba tarmac road 40km later. Another track leads east of Tounfite to swing around the slopes of Jbel Masker and then south up a mountain valley full of inhabited pisé **ksour** belonging to the Aït-Yaha, the most noticeable of which, **Ksar Agoudim**, is 18km from Tounfite. Beyond Agoudim the road deteriorates fairly rapidly as you cross the Atlantic–Mediterranean watershed and enter cedar-forested mountain slopes. A third alternative from Tounfite is to travel back along the road to Boumia for 13km and take a track to the east, which leads in 12km to a fine **group of ksour** which guard the upstream entrance to the river Ansegmir gorges.

Returning to the main road there is only the **Zeïda manganese mine**, 18km east of Boumia on the junction with the P21 Meknès road, before Midelt (another 30km south).

Khénifra to Kasba Tadla

Southwest from Khénifra, the red soil of the town fades into yellow as you enter an area of intensive olive cultivation. The P24 road runs below a limestone escarpment, crossing small streams fed by mountain springs. A succession of small village presses sell their own olive oil. These communities have a long tradition of sanctity and are often grouped around active zaouia. The great maraboutic dynasties of Djila and Boujad that once ruled this region originated from such humble foundations.

Twenty-three km south of Khénifra you pass through the village of **Es Sebt**, whose neighbouring settlement of **Maamar**, inland to the south, guards the ruins of the military kasbah of the maraboutic dynasty of Djila. The Djila were poised in the 17th century to succeed the Saadians. Their authority extended over Rabat, Fès and Meknès, but their power was shattered in a few years by Moulay Rachid, and by 1668 their zaouia lay in ruins. Shortly beyond here, after a brick factory you reach the Midelt turning and the roadside **Hôtel TransAtlas**, ✆ 30 through the Khénifra post office. It has a circular red courtyard, bedrooms that face inwards towards a swimming pool, and a detached roadside air, bar and constant television, making for a surprisingly mid-West, motel-like atmosphere.

The village of **Zaouia des Aït-Ischak** is 6km beyond, a few kilometres west of the road. This was one of the first centres of the Djila brotherhood that grew into a recognized centre of scholarship. The future Sultan Moulay Rachid was sent here as a young manto study, and to escape the fate of his father, the saintly Moulay Ali Cherif, who had fallen prisoner. Here he learnt theology and absorbed the tactics of his future enemy and knowledge of their geography and political weaknesses. An arch remaining from the mausoleum of **Sidi Bou Beker**, a Djilan sheikh, can be found surrounded by the ruins of a mosque on the edge of the village.

In another 26km, past Ouaoumana and Dechra-el-Oued, is the larger village of **Zaouia-ech-Cheïkh**. There are a few basic hotels beside the road south of the village, the best of which is the **Hôtel-Café Rif**, while near the central bus stop area there are a number of cafés under the shade of white arcades where good *tagines* are served for lunch. **Souks** are held here on Wednesdays and Saturdays.

El-Ksiba

Twenty-two km before Kasba Tadla a turning south off the main road leads in 7km to **El-Ksiba**, most charming of this string of villages, 1100m up at the entrance to a forested mountain valley and surrounded by orchards and groves of apricots, olives and oranges. Until the 19th century El-Ksiba was just the central souk of the Aït-Serri tribe. Sultan Moulay Hassan, in order to restrain the influence of his capable but ambitious *caid* of Khénifra, made a local chief, Moha ou Said, the *caid* of El-Ksiba, an equal power in the region. Caid Moha ruled over 5000 families and, with subsidies from the sultan, built the kasbah of Saarif at El-Ksiba. This has not survived, but the **Sunday souk** is still a central rendezvous for the hinterland settlements. A pretty mosque flanked by two zaouias is also found at the top of the village, above a neat garden of rosemary hedges and roses. Beside this is a café, beneath which arcaded stalls sell fruit and grilled snacks. Peugeot taxis group around the petrol station and you can browse through the book and nut shops, and through collections of wicker baskets, sandals, gumboots and old radios.

On the way out of the village there is a rushing mountain stream and to the left a semi-circle of official buildings, the *gendarmerie*, post office and the **Hôtel Henry IV** , © (03) 415002, which has a bar, restaurant, courtyard parking and a pleasantly aged but clean interior.

South from the village route 1901 enters a narrow valley full of toy-like wooden bungalows and glades of poplar and silver birch, with a stream-fed swimming pool and a basic campsite.

The Atlas Crossing and Imilchil

Though El-Ksiba is pretty enough, its chief attraction is as an access point for the **Imilchil September marriage fair** and the adventurous crossing of the Atlas mountains to **Tinerhir**. The crossing is often closed during the winter months (November to April) and is challenging even when the snow has melted: there is no hotel, bank or petrol along the 220km of rough mountain tracks between El-Ksiba and Tinerhir. It is an exhilarating journey, although scenically this treeless belt of high plateau cannot compare with the accessible foothills at either end. In summer, with patience and a tent, it is possible partly to walk and to buy lifts for some of the way in the infrequent trucks that ply this route.

The first 40km of the road to Imilchil are tarmacked. Three km from El-Ksiba the road climbs the Tizi-n-Aït-Ouirra pass to reach the Drent valley, continuing through twisting hills and forested slopes for 30km to the Tizi-n-Ifar pass. Seven km after this pass a turn south at the village of **Tizi-n-Isly** puts you on the mountain road, 1903, for Imilchil. Lake Tislit and the Tassert Ksar at Imilchil are 61km south of the crossing of the river Ouirine.

Every year the Atlas tribes congregate at Imilchil for a grand *moussem* in the second or third week of September (The date is arranged on a lunar calendar and changes each year). This is the famous **marriage festival** of the Aït-Haddidou tribe, where young men and women from different clans can briefly meet before the business of negotiating dowries begins in earnest. Some of the hazards of an impulsive choice are checked by the ease and frequency of divorce. The festival is well attended, not least by camera-happy tourists who stay in 'caidal tents' arranged each year by the Salaam hotel chain. Otherwise you can join the nomadic encampments along the dung-infested shores of the saline lakes of Tislit and Iseli and enjoy the unrivalled opportunity of admiring the clothes, jewellery, dance, music and artefacts of the Berber hill tribes who form a transient city of tens of thousands. From Imilchil the worst section of the Atlas crossing awaits; the most common route is to take one of the tracks that pass through **Takkat**, **Timariyne** and **Agoudal**. Then on to **Aït-Hani** along route 3445, which crosses the Tizi-Tirherhouzine pass at 2706m. From Aït-Hani route 3483 goes down to **Tamtattouchte** and follows the river Todra through the Todra Gorge to Tinerhir (*see* pp.479–83)

In Revenge for Djila

The province of Tadla, a plateau irrigated by the Oum er Rbia, has always been a much fought-over and prized possession. The Djila, a local marabоutic dynasty, led the Tadla tribes in the 17th century and seemed capable of succeeding to the Saadian throne. These halcyon days were ended by the first Alaouite sultan, Moulay Rachid, who destroyed the Djilan army and sacked their capital on 24 June 1668. Frustrated in their bid for political power, the Tadla tribes maintained a long feud against the Alaouite sultans.

Moulay Rachid's brother, Moulay Ismaïl, was equal to the challenge. He established a line of fortresses to hold the Tadla plain and keep the road to Marrakech open. An Abid regiment was placed in the new kasbah of Tadla on the banks of the Oum er Rbia and rival regiments of cavalry garrisoned at Kasbah Adeksane and Aït Ishak. In 1700 he unified the command and appointed a son, Ahmed er Debhi, pacha of Tadla Province. Ahmed was also trusted with the command of another 3000 Abids, and he enlarged Kasba Tadla to create a provincial capital.

This pacification did not long outlast the reign of Moulay Ismaïl and in the 19th century two government armies were defeated in battle by coalitions of Middle Atlas tribes. Moulay Sliman's army was trapped in the Serrou Gorge in 1818 and destroyed in a night attack. The sultan was captured and feasted for three days before being firmly but respectfully escorted back to Fès. Moulay Hassan secured order in the plain but even this capable sovereign could not secure the mountain valleys, and a vizier lost an entire army trapped in the Boutferda Gorge in 1885. The French occupied Kasba Tadla in 1913, but suffered a rare defeat at El Herri in 1914 before they subdued the Tadla tribes in a campaign lasting from 1915 to 1917.

Kasba Tadla

The training camp to the west of the modern town of Kasba Tadla maintains the military history of the town. It is now a pleasant place of trees and gardens that surround the severe and noble beauty of the 18th-century kasbah. Steep crenellated walls drop down from the kasbah almost to meet the river. Within these 18th-century walls a village community exists among the old storehouses and barracks, and a shop has colonized the kasbah gate. One of the two mosques is in a high state of ruin, and the Dar el Makhzen—Governor's palace—is filled with squatters. On the town side of the kasbah wall a park has been created, and a road below the walls leads down to the river beside more terraced gardens, market arcades and the battlemented minaret of the mosque. Moulay Ismaïl's bridge of ten arches still carries traffic across the Oum er Rbia, the height of which is now controlled by a small dam. A small square fort holds the slight ground on the other bank.

Getting Around and Tourist Information

There are four buses a day that do the one-hour trip from Kasba Tadla to Béni-Mellal, and three for the 20min ride to El Ksiba. The **souk** is held on Mondays.

Where to Stay

The **Bellevue Hôtel**, ✆ (03) 418733 (expensive), stands beside the main P24 Fès–Marrakech road just north of Tadla town. It has an ornately carved plaster lobby, 40 bedrooms with large modern bathrooms, a bar, pool and licensed restaurant.

There are a also couple of cheap-range hotels with character in Tadla, all within listening distance of the bus stop. The basic **Hôtel Restaurant des Alliés**, 38 Avenue Mohammmed V, ✆ (03) 418172, is the most comfortable, and if this is full try the **Hôtel Atlas** at 46 Boulevard El Majjata Obad.

Boujad

Boujad is just off the P13 road, a 24km taxi ride north of Tadla. About 22km further on the road divides for Casablanca or Rabat, at the mining town of Oued-Zem.

This region west of the fertile Tadla plain has been long dominated by the Seguibat and Beni-Meskin nomadic tribes. On the edge of this semi-desert stands the holy town of **Boujad**, awash with mosques, koubbas and zaouias. In the 19th century it was the most important town in the whole central region of Morocco between Meknès and Marrakech, a holy town equal to Ouezzane or Moulay Idriss, although now it is merely one of a string of provincial markets that functions after the growing seasons of March and September, and home to a population of 15000.

In the 16th century, Sidi Mohammed Bu'Abid ech Cherki, known as the patron of Tadla and the master of horsemen, established a zaouia here. He was a celebrated Sufi mystic who died in 1600, and his descendants were respected by the surrounding tribes for possessing the power of giving the *baraka* blessing. The agglomeration of sanctuaries, colleges and storehouses became the accepted capital for the surrounding nomadic tribes after the authority of Kasba Tadla decayed. The saintly dynasty of Boujad arbitrated disputes and acted as an intermediary for the tribes in their relations with the sultan's government. Sultan Sidi Mohammed destroyed the power of the zaouia and razed the town in 1785; most of Boujad dates from subsequent rebuilding.

The centre of the town, the Place du Marché, is a vast paved area surrounded by trees and the outer arcades of the white houses of the medina. It's possible to stay and/or eat in Boujad, at the basic **Café-Hotel Essalyn** in one corner of the Place. The **zaouia**, southwest of the town, was rebuilt in the mid-19th century after the death of Sultan Sidi Mohammed, and is surrounded by houses still occupied by descendants of the Sidi Mohammed ech Cherki. The **souk** is no longer held in the centre of town but beside the main road on Wednesdays and Thursdays.

The old town that surrounds the Place du Marché is encrusted with tombs of the saintly dynasty. The largest **shrine** is that of **Sidi Othman** where a number of courts give on to the koubba raised above the tomb. This you can enter for a fee and in the company of a guide, and if you manifest great interest and many tips it is often possible to enter a few others.

Ask to be shown the **sanctuaries of Sidi Abd el Kader Ziz** and **El Hibi** in the Beni-Meskin district. The **mosque of Sidi Slimane** is in the el Kedrin; from the corner of the Place du Marché by the Hotel Essalyn, turn left and left again by the bridge and you will find yourself passing beneath the great square minaret and lantern of the mosque.

Various shrines, and a single palm tree, are found along the yellow stone path that snakes its way through the El Kedrin quarter. The **mosque and tomb of Sheik Sidi Mohammed Bu'abid ech Cherki** with its tall lantern minaret is entered through a pyramid arch. The shrine has a *hammam* beside it and holds an inner courtyard lodge for men and women pilgrims, two of whom have been honoured by burial in the inner court. By day the outer court is full of pilgrims resting against the walls, the air full of the music of songbirds. The **koubba of Sidi el Maati** is within its own courtyard, with an old fig tree also full of birds. The **shrine of Sidi Larbi** is covered by two green domes. Opposite a little mosque on Rue Sidi Salah is the **tomb of Sidi Salah**, with a courtyard full of practical aids: two palm trees provide shade and there is a room for women to henna their hair, and a well for washing.

Just out of Boujad on the road north to Oued-Zem there is a spectacular array of five white koubbas on a hill which include the **tombs of Sidi Abdesalam** and **Lalla Hania**. Just before Oued-Zem a tarmac road, the S131, leads through the distinctive scenery of the Zaïane highlands to arrive at **Moulay-Bouâzza**, from where you could continue round through Aguelmouss to Khénifra (*see* p.345–7).

Kasba Tadla to Béni-Mellal

The direct road, the P24, has no distractions for the 30km between Tadla and Béni Mellal. If you take the slower road to the east there are a number of rewarding old villages which sit at the spring line of a limestone escarpment, surrounded by olive orchards. Just south of Tadla, turn left off the P24 on route 1662 for 18km to the village of **Tarhzirt**. Protected by a disintegrating kasbah, this ancient settlement is split in two by a gorge, its low houses hugging the ascending slopes while the stream runs clear between them. **Zaouia Fichtala** is 5km south of Tarhzirt on route 1674 to Béni-Mellal. This quiet hamlet was once known as Tefza, and the Saadians made it the capital of Tadla Province to commemorate the destruction of a Wattasid army and the capture of their sultan here in 1536. **Foum-el-Anser/Aït-Said**, framed by limestone cliffs, is split in two by a small gorge fed by half a dozen springs. The village, only 10km from Béni-Mellal, is surrounded by caves decorated with fantastic rocks, believed to be miners petrified by a jinn who guards the secret mineral wealth of the hills.

Route 3: West to Marrakech and the Central High Atlas

The direct route west from Béni-Mellal to Marrakech, the P24, runs across an arid plain, and is a largely colourless journey apart from some irrigated orchard estates and, for the first 70km, a view of the Atlas foothills. The mountains to the south are a conjunction of the otherwise separate Middle Atlas and High Atlas mountain ranges. This area goes under a host of variant names, though within the hiking fraternity it is increasingly referred to as the Central High Atlas. South, off the main highway, a number of roads tempt you to head into this mountainous region. The Bzou Waterfall, the el Abid Gorge, the Ouzoud Falls, Demnate, Imi-n-Ifri and Tazzerte can all be reached by car in an easy day trip from a hotel in either Béni-Mellal or Marrakech. If the gaunt magnificence of this mountain region is to your taste, you may wish to plan a more adventurous foray. La Cathédrale rocks, Zaouia-Ahanesal, the hidden valley of the Aït Bou Guemés, and a traverse of Ighil M'Goun south to the sub-Sahara are some of the more rewarding targets for mountain treks. For your first couple of trips you should use one of the specialist expedition agencies, listed on pp.8–9.

Béni-Mellal

The Tadla Plain is littered with the previous capitals of this valuable but turbulent province. Béni-Mellal is the current seat of power, a rapidly expanding largely modern city of a quarter of a million, prospering from the electricity and irrigation water that the Bin-el-Ouidane dam provides. Groves of olives and oranges extend around the city to form an oasis in the sun-scorched plain. The houses of Béni-Mellal rise up the limestone slope to the Aisserdoun spring, above which the conspicuous Borj Râs el Aïn crowns a prominent bluff.

Getting Around

The **bus station** is now in a smart new terminal on the edge of town, on the bypass road from Khénifra to Marrakech. There are at least half a dozen buses a day to Marrakech (6hrs), three to Fès (8–9hrs) and four to Demnate (3hrs). There is a daily ONCF coach at 6.36am that connects up with the **rail** network at Khouribga station, in the mining town about 90km north north-west of Béni-Mellal. The most efficient **garage** in town is the Belkhoya, on Boulevard Mohammed V.

Tourist Information

There are three **banks** in Béni-Mellal, the BMCE on Av. Mohammed V, the BMCI at 87 Rue de Marrakech and the Banque Populaire on Boulevard Mohammed V.

The Town and the Aïn-Asserdoun Spring

The oldest, central portion of the town lies within the walls of the **Kasbah Bel Kush**, built during the reign of Moulay Ismaïl. Scattered fragments of walls and gates can be found among the houses, alleys and shops that surround the central rectangular medina square, the arcaded Place de la Liberté, where the clothing bazaars and cheap hotels are found. Neither the French new town, the medina or Béni-Mellal's post-Independence housing have any great distinction. It is however a relaxed, friendly place that makes a pleasant stop between the challenging cities of Fès and Marrakech.

A signposted tourist route climbs above the town to the **Aïn-Asserdoun spring**. This is a welcome sight; cool, fresh water flows through a series of contrived cascades and meanders, and out through an ornamental public park into the olive groves. From Aïn-Asserdoun a tarmac road climbs one km to the **Borj Ras el Aïn**. The best view of it is from a distance, for this stone fortress has been heavily restored and is now surrounded by a tarmac car park. The view from the terrace over Béni-Mellal is fine, but climbing the restored staircases of the corner towers can be a nauseous experience as they are usually covered in shit.

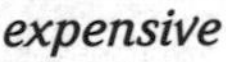

Where to Stay and Eating Out

expensive

The **Al Bassatine**, ✆ (03) 482247, 📠 486806, is tucked away in an orange grove just west of the town—100m on the left travelling out on the Fkih ben Salah road from the town centre. It has 60 bedrooms, a pool, waiters in green plush and gold embroidery and continues its culinary traditions from the days when it was just a restaurant. If this is full there are also two neighbouring and indistinguishable four-star hotels just beside the road to Marrakech that are used by coach tours. The **Chems**, ✆ (03) 483460, and **Ouzoud**, ✆ (03) 483752, both have pools, tennis courts, restaurants, bars and fine views of the mountains.

inexpensive

The **Auberge du Vieux Moulin**, ✆ (03) 482788, at the Tadla end of Boulevard Mohammed V remains the first choice for passing travellers. It's an old colonial hotel with a bar, a decent restaurant, 10 rooms and a worn, comfortable interior. If that is full then try the **De Paris**, ✆ (03) 482245, which also has a bar and restaurant and is situated uphill from the Vieux Moulin on Rue Hay Ibn Syna. Failing that there is the **Gharnata**, a modern comfortable hotel at the heart of the new town on Boulevard Mohammed V, ✆ (03) 483482, which has 14 rooms, a bar and a functional but uninspiring restaurant.

cheap

The cheap hotels in the barely discernible medina quarter are not very appealing. The arcaded **Hôtel El Fath** at 15 Place de la Liberté is one of the best, with a courtyard surrounded by two floors of rooms and good views from its roof terrace.

Local Souks

About 11km west of Béni-Mellal on the P24, turn south at the hamlet of Oulad-Moussa and travel a couple of kilometres to **Oulad-M'barek**. This village has the **Restaurant Assaisse**, planted in the middle of a garden, which is good for a mint tea if not necessarily for its group-oriented meals. **Timoulilt** is 6km beyond Oulad M'barek on a passable but deteriorating road. It has its **souk** on Mondays, and was the chief village of the N'Oumalou tribe, one of the component clans of the great Berber Aït-Atta confederation. The N'Oumalou were the northernmost vanguard of the Aït-Atta, whose homeland is south of the High Atlas. In their progress they were closely following the route of the Beni-Mguild, another Berber Saharan tribe who fought their way north to richer grazing lands.

Beyond Timoulilt there is a road which climbs over the Tizi-n-Ghenim pass at 1802m to **Ouaouizarht**, another market town and pilgrimage centre. From Ouaouizarht a tarmac road takes on you for another 15km beside the lake to the Bin-el-Ouidane Dam, where you can lunch (*see* 'The Ouzoud Falls', p.344), return to the Marrakech road, or continue along the Mid Atlas plateau.

Back on the Marrakech road, 23km from Béni-Mellal, a right turn leads in 16km to the busy Saturday souk held at **Souk-es-Sebt-des-Oulad-Nemâa**.

Aït-Attab and the el Abid Gorge

The distinctive sugar factory at **Khemis-des-Oulad-Ayad**, 46km from Béni-Mellal, marks the left turn for the **el Abid Gorge**. A thin, twisting tarmac road winds up to cross the Atlas foothills at 1000m and provides tremendous views back over the plain. Passing through an area of scrub wilderness, you descend into a Berber mountain valley that appears completely content in its isolation, the surrounding hilltops and their cleared area of land crowned by inhabited square-towered kasbahs. The road leads directly to Aït-Attab, the small central village of the valley with three cafés, pretty yellow arcades and a **souk** on Wednesdays. From Aït-Attab a dirt track leads west to the green-tiled **tomb of Moulay-Aïssa Ben Idriss**, where a *moussem* is held on 24 March. Aïssa, one of the sons of Idriss II, died fighting the Aït-Attab tribe of this valley, who were finally converted to Islam only after Aïssa's death, when each spring a whirlwind emerged from his grave and destroyed the crops of the valley. Reduced to starvation, the Aït-Attab took the advice of a holy man, converted to Islam and built a tomb over Aïssa's grave which they honoured each spring with a *moussem.*

A new tarmac road leads 7km from Aït-Attab to just short of the gorge entrance. This is a remarkable dark, high, narrow wall of stone through which the river flows down towards the Ouzoud Falls. It is a wonderfully impressive and isolated canyon; the only sound that interrupts the gurgling water and singing birds is likely to be the echoing call of a goatherd gathering together his flock. High up above the entrance to the gorge is a deserted **kasbah**, an excellent place in which to camp, though Berber farmers of this valley are often hospitable to the few travellers. A dirt track continues across the river by a metal bridge and then twists uphill in 20km to the Ouzoud Waterfall (*see* 'The Ouzoud Falls' below).

On to Marrakech

Back on the Marrakech road, **Pont d'Imdahane** is 72km from Béni-Mellal. It is a traditional junction point where the police often man a checkpoint, with **cafés** around its dusty square that prepare simmering *tagines*, grilled kebabs and oranges for the passing traffic. A turn south beyond the bridge on route 1810 leads in 11km to the village and **waterfall** at **Bzou**. Turn left into the village, opposite a café, and follow the road to a dirt square. Then bear right, drawn by the sound of water, to find a clear pool fed by a spring. Two channels drain the pool in a series of natural falls, and then the river Tamla disappears into a scrub wilderness.

Back on the main road to Marrakech you pass through **El Kelaâ des Sraghna**, a large modern town of 40,000 overlooked by the sterile black volcanic Jbilet Hills that stretch west to shield Marrakech from the baked wind of the Bahira Plain. El Kelaâ was enclosed within kasbah walls only a few decades ago and traditional **souks** are held here on Fridays and Sundays. Thirty km south, the large village of **Tamelelt** has a **souk** on Tuesdays, and in a further 50km you approach the outlying irrigated gardens and palm groves of Marrakech.

The Ouzoud Falls

The *Cascades d'Ouzoud* are one of the more memorable, mysterious and unexploited sites of Morocco, though they may be familiar from hundreds of Tourist Board posters. They are only a 20km walk from the el Abid Gorge (*see* above), but are usually approached from Béni-Mellal via the Bin-el-Oudiane Dam. Getting to the falls without a car is not too much of a problem. There are daily buses from both Béni-Mellal (1–2hrs) and Marrakech (5–6hrs) to the town of Azilal, where you can charter a taxi for around 45–60dh, or in high summer you might find a place in a *grand taxi* for around 10dh.

A right turn 20km out of Béni-Mellal, the S508, leads in 6km to **Afourèr**, which is dominated by the hydro-electric plant powered by the Bin-el-Ouidane Dam perched high in the hills above you. To the left before the village is the roadside **Hôtel Tazarhoute,** ✆ (03) 440201, which has a pool, bar and restaurant. It is expensive but can make a useful stop for a drink, meal and swim. Behind the village you climb the hill in a series of dramatic hairpin bends. The view back is dangerously distracting, but a terrace has been built at one of the best viewing points, 12km from Afourèr. The Tadla plain is spread out below, the lush irrigated estates of orange and olive groves looking like oases in the denuded expanse.

A canyon has been cut through these arid mountains by the river el Abid, the waters of which are collected by two streams that extend 200km east, draining the scarred plateau caught between the peaks of the Middle and High Atlas. Ruined stone agadirs dot the canyon summits as you approach the concave vault of the **Bin-el-Ouidane Dam**. A slip road leads down to the **Auberge du Lac** hotel and a **campsite**. They have a superb position beside the slow, wide river, looking up at the dam and across to cave entrances in the limestone wall on the opposite bank. Swimming is officially prohibited. The lakeside area is administered as a military region, for the road passes along the top of the dam, 300m wide and with 130m high walls holding back over a billion cubic metres of water which are used to irrigate the Tadla Plain and produce most of Morocco's electricity—a tempting target for any terrorist.

Beyond the dam to the south there is 26km of Atlas plateau, a bleak but farmed expanse punctuated by pisé kasbahs, before the town of **Azilal**, an uninspiring administrative post at 1360m that straggles, wind-blown and dusty, along the road. There is a **souk** held here on Thursdays and the basic **Hôtel-Restaurant Tahanouton** on the edge of the town, which is a useful base for an approach to Bou Guemès (*see* below).

Twenty km from Azilal along the Demnate road (S508) is **Aït-Taguella**, a scattered collection of hill-top agadirs surrounded by almond trees and patches of cultivation. Just beyond, a right turn leads for 16km through similar scenery to the hamlet of **Et Tleta-Ouzoud**, some three houses poised above the **Ouzoud Falls**. It's a friendly, undeveloped place, expanding in summer as visitors are seduced into camping here for a week, though rooms and meals are available throughout the year. Barbary apes come down from the hills, there is no electric light, only candles, and nearby an immense quantity of cool, refreshing falling water.

The falls consist of several streams that plummet 100m into a pool, the water thundering past a rich mixture of vegetation and oozing rock while the spray sunlight forms a shifting rainbow in the sunlight. The immediate plunge pool has dangerous currents but you can swim in any of the ones strung out below. This rich, natural site set deep in the Atlas and fringed by massive, glowering low hills at night has a universal pantheistic appeal, a perpetual celebration of the unadorned earth.

From here you could contemplate a 20km walk upstream to the **el Abid Gorges** (*see* above), or paddle through the river pools downstream for a while, or take the 20km old track (the 1814), now impassable for vehicles, that leads across country to Azilal, passing the **Akka-n-Tisekht**, an impressive devil's punchbowl enclosed by tortured cliffs.

Where to Stay

At Bin-el-Ouidane the superbly-located **Auberge du Lac**, ✆ (through the post office), Bin-el-Ouidane 5, is open throughout the year. It has a few bedrooms that open onto two separate terraces, a cavernous bar and a restaurant. The hotel is full of local hunting and fishing scenes, and half a dozen pointers lounge around. The nearby campsite is open only in summer.

At Et Tleta-Ouzoud, you can camp under a vine terrace by the river bank above the falls, to the right of the car park through an arch, or you can rent an elegant verandah café room that sleeps four from Thami Abassi, who cooks omelettes, prepares salads and *tagines* to order. Alternatively, stay at **Mohammed's**, to the left of the large central house, where half a dozen rooms surround a little orange tree in a courtyard. In summer you can also camp at the bamboo **Café Ouzade**, beside the path on the way to the falls, or another of its seasonal rivals. All are cheap and equally delightful.

Exploring the Central High Atlas: Expedition to Aït Bou Guemès and Zaouia-Ahanesal

It is possible to visit the hidden valley of the Aït Bou Guemès in the summer by foot, mule or four-wheel-drive. On your first trip, go with a specialist trekking service such as the Marrakech-based Atlas Sahara Trek (see p.7). They know these mountains like the back of their hand, employ locals and run their own auberge, built in the indigenous style of the valley, one of the most serene and beautiful of all the Berber mountain valleys of Morocco.

The 1807 to **Aït-Mehammed**, 20km south of Azilal, is tarmacked, but beyond there is 30km more of twisting mountain track, usually inaccessible from November to February, up to the lower slopes of Jbel Azourki (3690m). This track divides below the peak: to the right it descends west over 30km into the beautiful, isolated valley of Aït Bou Guemès. The barren stone of the mountain slopes gives way to terraced garden fields and pastures watered by twisting mountain streams shaded by nut trees. The length of the valley is overlooked by a series of interlinked hamlets, all composed of the traditional earth-built kasbah houses of the Aït-Isha tribe. Two prominent, cone-shaped hills rise above the valley, one crowned by the empty but only partially ruined **Igherm (Agadir) Takhida Aït-Ziri**, the other by the circular **koubba of Si Moussa**. The saint has long been renowned in the valley, but his cult may yet spread further afield. A Belgian woman, who had exhausted all the scientific cures of the West, gave birth to a child nine months after making her supplication to the Sidi. The chief village is Tabant, also known as **El Had**, for it hosts a market on Sundays. If you haven't got your own transport this is a key destination, as it is possible to get a lift here from Land-Rover taxis that operate out of Aït-Mehammed three days a week, especially on Sunday mornings.

Dotted throughout the valley are various Gîte d'Etape signposts. This new and admirable national scheme indicates the houses of mountain guides, muleteers and simple bed-and-breakfast type accommodation in village houses. There is a lifetime of walking in the surrounding hills, hidden gorges, mountain streams and valleys. Some of the more popular routes head south to the sacred snow-covered peak of **M'Goun**, 4071m (one of the great summits of the High Atlas) while others go east to **Lake Izourar**, around which the nomadic Aït-Haddidou tribe assemble each summer to find water and grazing for their herds.

Northeast lies **Zaouia-Ahanesal**. Leaving the valley, continue east at the junction, along track 1807 for 28km to reach the zaouia, crossing the Tizi-n-Ilissi pass (2650m), where there are some fossilized tree trunks. The zaouia is built around a koubba at the head of a valley dotted with small villages and beautifully decorated kasbahs of the saintly Ihansalen clan. This community is celebrated in Ernest Gellner's classic anthropological study, *Saints of the Atlas*. The Ihansalen consider themselves descendants of a 16th-century saint, an ally of Dada Atta who established the Aït-Atta confederacy. At the focal point of the four largest and aggressive tribes of the central High Atlas, the zaouia presided over the many local disputes, the focus of a republic where 'anarchy was mitigated by holiness'. The zaouia also handled negotiations with the sultan; they sent a delegation to Moulay Hassan when he attempted to resolve the disputes of the tribes from his court established at Tafilalt. North of Zaouia-Ahanesal an arduous 40km mountain walk leads to a famous rock formation known as **la Cathédrale**, across the valley from the **ksar of Tilougguite**.

Demnate and Imi-n-Ifri

Back on the main Azilal road (S508) it is 22km west from the turning to the Ouzoud Falls to **Tananmt**, an administrative post established by the French on a hill with a fine view of three massive peaks 50km to the south. Counting from the west, there is Jbel Ghat (3825m), then Ighil M'Goun (4071m) and Jbel Azourki (3690m). Just south of Tanannt there is a **waterfall** on the river Tainit.

Demnate, off the main road 26km south of Tanannt, is a town still largely contained within its crenellated pisé walls. It is sited on the high edge of an intensively cultivated, fertile valley lined with massed olive groves that make it appear conspicuously green. Above Demnate begin the bleak or only partially forested slopes of the Atlas highland plateau.

The town's **kasbah** was held by a succession of *caids* from the Glaoui clan. Abdelmalek was the most celebrated of these; he was a boy of great beauty and bravery, the favourite son of Madani, the ruthless and able founder of Glaoui power. His early death, aged 17, in a tribal skirmish is credited with breaking his father's heart. The kasbah was on a nearby hill, around which the French erected the administrative offices of the 'Cercle'. The Sunday **souk** is an animated, picturesque affair held by the town's old storage tanks.

A tarmac road twists east of Demnate 6km to **Imi-n-Ifri**, an astonishing **natural bridge** over which the road passes and under which a stream flows. The riverbed is full of washed boulders and its steep bank and the bridge are liberally decorated with limestone deposits. The bleak, isolated mountain slopes, crests of distant snow, pine forests and freak wafts of mist and cloud give the bridge a strange, malignant atmosphere. Half-an-hour's walk upstream is a grotto, where animals are sacrificed to the spirit of the spring at a festival held on the 14th day after Aid el Kebir. The spirit destroyed an evil jinn who was fond of attacking the women of Demnate. The body of the jinn materialized on his death but instantly rotted and was consumed by hideous caterpillars that metamorphosed into crows. These birds attempt to disrupt the annual sacrifice, and their defiant shrieks can be heard throughout the year echoing over the valleys and hills. Various good gravel roads are being extended beyond the bridge, and there is even a plan to push these all the way up to the Bou Guemès valley. The signposted road to **Tifni**, first right and then second left, crosses some spectacular gorges before climbing the Tizi-n'Outfi at 2150 m.

The Demnate olive groves stretch 15km west of the town to include the pleasant village of **El-Arba**, which has its **souk** on Wednesdays and an imposing **kasbah** away on the high land to the south. A turn south at a crossroads 16km from Demnate leads in 12km to the **Aït-Aadel Lake/Moulay Youssef Dam**. The lake teems with black bass, and in the summer there are boats for hire to fishermen. Turning north at these crossroads leads to the **Zaouia-Taglaout**, a regional branch of the great Naciri college of Tamegroute on the Drâa. This zaouia restored a much older water system in the early 18th century, which was improved upon in 1840 and then further embellished in 1971 to create the Aït-Aadel Lake.

Where to Stay

There are three very basic and cheap hotels if you have to stay a night at Demnate: the **Iminfri**, the **Fetouka** and the **Zakovia**. They are on the main street just inside the triple-arched gates of the town.

Tazzerte

Ten km west of the dam crossroads on the 6206 road is the village of Tazzerte, dominated by four massive decaying kasbahs built by the Glaoui clan. The village is divided by an olive-shaded irrigation ditch. There is a mosque in each half, but all four kasbahs are in the eastern section overlooked by the brown hilltop **koubba of Sidi Mohammed Mustafa**. This koubba contains a sacred black stone in a niche, kissed by pilgrims who leave offerings of money or barley. This grain impregnated with the saint's holiness is made into couscous, which is eaten over the grave on the saint's anniversary. The women of the village also tie clothing and hair onto the bushes around the shrine in promise of an offering should the fragment blow free, enabling their prayer to be granted.

Arriving at the village you will be taken to see the guardian of the kasbahs, a venerable, slightly crippled gentleman who used to be one of the Glaoui's shepherds and who delegates a tour to one of his sons. The strong outer walls of the ***caid's*** **kasbah**, the smallest detached four square building at the far west, were built by Madani el Glaoui, 1866–1918, who reached his pinnacle of power as Grand Vizier and Minister of War to Sultan Moulay Hafid in 1909. The vast extent of the neighbouring **palace Kasbah** is the work of his younger brother Thami el Glaoui, 1879–1956, who led the clan after his brother's death and established an empire within an Empire, ruling and subduing the troublesome south for the French as the feared pacha of Marrakech. Stout towers and walls enclose a large garden adjacent to the courtyard shell of the kasbah, where the white plastered walls enclose a half acre of rubble. The controlled decoration of windows and cornices and the traceable proportions of the rooms hint at its past elegance.

East of Thami's palace is the high double-arcaded court of **Si Hammou's Kasbah**; the graceful, controlled horseshoe arches directly support columns with lotus capitals linked by a decayed cedar balcony. The towered staircase is quite unsafe, and the view from the top among battlements, storks and hawks' nests precarious but memorable. Si Hammou ben Mohammed was the xenophobic nephew of Thami, and a ferocious tribal warlord who maintained his embarrassing hatred for the French but remained *caid* of the High Atlas kasbah of Telouèt until his death. Hammou married Madani's daughter, Lalla Hamina, and the high standard of internal decoration is likely to have been commissioned by their son Abdallah, a favourite of Thami, who adopted him on his father's death. This kasbah was occupied as late as 1966, while the others fell empty soon after the pacha's death in 1956, when King Mohammed V banished the most guilty members of the clan from Morocco.

The least impressive of the four is **Si Omar's Kasbah**, built by a son of Madani whose other responsibilities at Demnate and at Taliouine must have left him little time at Tazzerte.

A **souk** is held at Tazzerte on Mondays, though this takes second place to that of **Sidi-Rahhal**, 7km west of Tazzerte on the 6117, which has the busiest local souk on Fridays, as well as a zaouia, a café and a garage. The **tomb of Sidi-Rahhal**, credited with great magical powers—flying on carpets is just one from the long catalogue of his skills—is respected by Jews and Muslims alike. The Sidi has a *moussem* in August by his tomb, which is 2km to the west near the bridge over the river Rdat. There are two turnings off the main road beyond Sidi-Rahhal for **Aït-Ourir**, which has a big **souk** on Tuesdays, before you reach the main P24 road 17km outside Marrakech.

Route 4: South from Fès to Sefrou, Midelt and Er Rachidia

The road south from Fès to Er Rachidia follows the *trik es soltan*, the old caravan trail. This route was followed by the caravans that brought precious goods up from the Tafilalt, which for 1000 years was one of the principal ports of the trans-Saharan trade. It is the quickest route to the southern oasis valleys of Morocco and also the least travelled of the routes across the Middle Atlas plateau. Even if you have no intention of following this road, Sefrou, an ancient walled town, is well worth a visit. It is the setting for two outstanding books about Morocco, *Reflections on Fieldwork in Morocco* by Paul Rabinow, an American anthropologist unburdening his heart in his search for a Moroccan friend he could trust, and *Mimoun*, a haunting novel by the Spaniard Rafael Chirbes about the alienation and destruction awaiting Europeans who attempt to live apart from their compatriots among Moroccans.

Sefrou

The ancient walled town of Sefrou is just 30km south of Fès on the P20. Sefrou stands on the border between the fertile Saïss Plain and the limestone plateau of the Middle Atlas. This prime position allowed the pastoral tribes to the south and the sedentary agriculturists to the north to meet and trade in mutual security. Numerous springs flow from the base of the plateau to water the surrounding gardens and cherry orchards of the region. The walled medina remains at the heart of this prosperous town of 45,000, its alleys twisting either side of the steep banked river Aggaï, which is occasionally spanned by an elegant bridge.

History

Sefrou is an ancient town whose Berber population was converted to Judaism by missionaries perhaps even before the fall of Jerusalem in AD 71. Moulay Idriss I is recorded to have lived for three years outside Sefrou at a ksar called Habarnoa (between 787–792), while he converted the town and its surrounding tribes to Islam. Firmly established astride the *trik es soltan*, the town prospered from the Saharan trade in the 12th century. The Bedouin Arab invasions of the 13th century endangered Jewish communities to the east and on the borders of the Sahara, and refugees from the Tafilalt and Algeria settled in Sefrou to establish an influential Jewish community who, however, have all emigrated in the last three decades.

The town has returned to its old ways as a regional market that supports a flourishing artisan community; the **souk** is held on Thursdays. The **cherry harvest** is celebrated in June with several memorable days of music, dance and feasting. The patron saint of the town, Sidi Lahcen Lyoussi, is venerated with a ***moussem*** in August.

Getting Around

There are at least three **buses** a day that travel the 30km between Fès and Sefrou. Buses leave Fès from Bab Bou Jeloud and arrive at the main entrance to the Sefrou medina, Bab Lamkam. There are three buses south from Sefrou to Midelt (5hrs) and Er Rachidia (8hrs) but they start in Fès and are occasionally fully booked.

Grands Taxis offer a quick communication route between Fès and Sefrou, with ranks at Bab Ftouh in Fès-el-Bali or on Boulevard des Normands between Place de l'Atlas and Boulevard Mohammed V in the new town of Fès.

Tourist Information

The tourist office is on Boulevard Hassan II beside the Aggaï bridge, © (05) 660380. The post office, BMCE and Banque Populaire are all on Boulevard Mohammed V.

The Medina

The crenellated ochre pisé walls of the city have been continuously restored, although there are a few sections that survive from the 18th century. Nine gates pierce the ramparts: five enter the medina, and four the old *mellah* on the south bank of the river Aggaï. Four bridges connect the two districts.

Opposite the bus station on Place Moulay Hassan there is a busy garden café, a fountain and two gates, the **Bab Taksebt** and the **Bab M'Kam**. The Bab M'Kam, on the left, leads past the **Echebbah Mosque** above the riverbank and past a wall plaque indicating the height of the 1950 flood, which drowned 30 people in the medina. Continuing on the north bank, the street leads past the zaouia and **tomb of Sidi Lahcen Lyoussi**, Sefrou's 18th-century patron saint, to enter the **souks**, a network of streets lined with green booths where skilled tailors, embroiderers, cobblers and carpenters practise their trade before your eyes. One of the city's three ***fondouqs*** can be found behind the souk, its central courtyard packed with farmers' donkeys on market day. The **grand mosque of El Kebir** was restored by Sultan Moulay Hassan in the 19th century, its white arcades and minaret perched on a terrace above the riverbank (but closed to non-Muslims).

The bridge in front of the mosque looks out over pine and fig trees growing out from the high riverbanks and down over trails of decorative rubbish and hanging fragments of cloth. The mixture of water and effluent flows down over worn rocks to fertilize the lower gardens. Across the bridge is the ***mellah***, the distinctive Jewish quarter with its more regular streets, angular buildings and brown balconies. The white café immediately to the left of the bridge is a regular gathering spot for war veterans. From here the Rue du Marché continues through the *mellah*, past a covered market on your left to the Bab Merba, outside which the

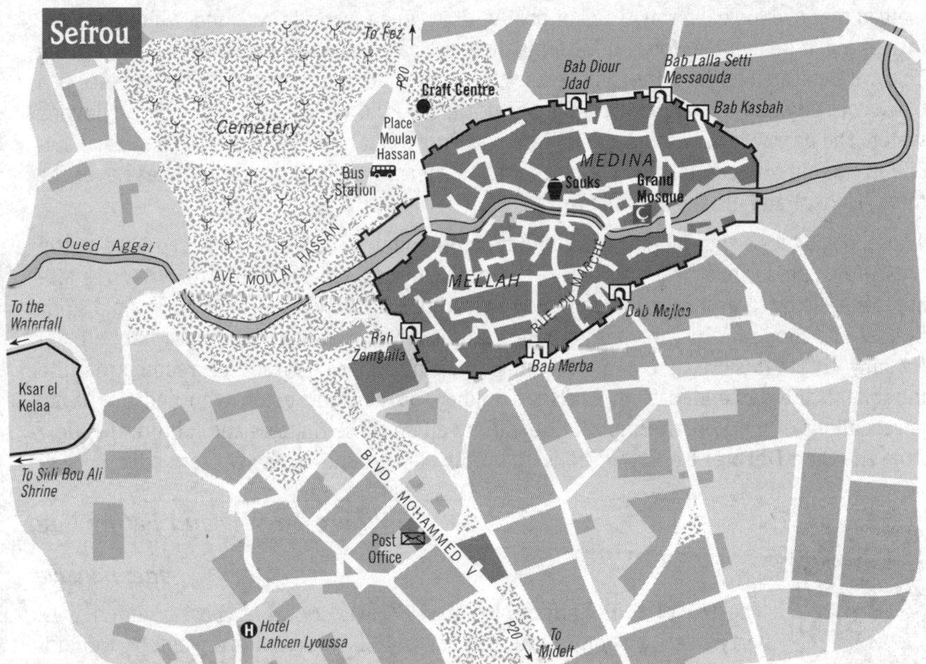

Thursday souk used traditionally to be held (it now takes place beside the road on the outskirts of town). A less conspicuous entrance west of Bab Merba passes the largest *hammam*, the **Essalam baths**, and by twisting through narrow dark alleys you can cross another bridge and return to Place Moulay Hassan through the Bab Taksebt.

Below the crenellated walls in a small garden just to the north of Place Moulay Hassan is the **Ensemble Artisanal**, full of leatherwork, pottery, ironwork and the distinctive embroidered textiles of Sefrou. It is open from Monday to Saturday. Just opposite, and immediately to the west of the medina, there is a pleasant, shaded public park running along both banks of the river, with a swimming pool.

Three Walks from the Medina

Walking west from the park you pass the twin gates that guard the entrance to the separate walled **Ksar El Kelâa**. To the right a road follows the river upstream for 1km, passing numerous **caves**, some of which were venerated as **tombs of holy men** by both Jews and Muslims. The caves are known as Kef el Moumen or Kef el Yhoudi, according to your religious affiliation. The enduring myth of the grotto of the seven sleepers (told at Ceuta) has a local version, and there is another tradition that the prophet Daniel is buried here. The **waterfall** at the end of this road is dramatic in winter but its glory has otherwise been diminished by the work of a local pumping station. It is however possible to paddle in the rock pool and enjoy an alfresco shower before consuming a beer from the nearby hotel bar.

Taking the left turn in front of Ksar El Kelâa puts you on the steep road that climbs up in 2km to the **shrine of Sidi bou Srhine**, in a spectacular position on the edge of the limestone plateau that overlooks Sefrou. The koubba, with its green pyramid roof and white outbuildings, is much-frequented; for non-Muslims there is a café and some trinket stalls. The **spring** below is dedicated to the saint Lalla Rekia who is propitiated each year with the sacrifice of a black cock, a white hen and a black billy goat, the blood of which is mixed with the flowing water. The nearby fort, known to the French as Prioux but now called Sidi Ali ben Zaïane, is still in use but you can take the track that skirts beneath it for another fine **view** over the town, gardens and distant mountains.

Those looking for a slightly longer walk, 8km cross-country there and back, can head northwest from the shrines over the hill to the neighbouring village of **Bhalil**, which is also approachable by car from a turning off the Fès road. It is a pretty place, a mixture of old stone houses and modern blue and white buildings ranged around a central mountain stream (usually dry) that is criss crossed with small, elegant bridges. A tradition records that the inhabitants are descended from Christian soldiers of the 2nd Legion who fled the pagan percecutions of the Roman Empire. You can dwell on these matters and admire the view from the **Café Derb el Kebir**, which is up on the high ground on the western edge.

Where To Stay and Eating Out

inexpensive

The **Hôtel Sidi Lahcen Lyoussi**, © (05) 660497, has a garden with cherry trees, a pool, restaurant, bar and 22 rooms. It is a friendly, tranquil place, the ideal base for exploring the area, and just a 200m walk east from the prominent post office on Boulevard Mohammed V, the main Fès to Midelt road.

cheap

The **Café Lafarine**, a secluded house surrounded by a garden just north of the medina on the road to Fès, rents rooms, and the **Cascades Hotel** by the Oued Aggaï falls has five rooms that overlook the river and beer for sale at the bar. You can also drink at the bar-café **La Poste**, next to the post office on Boulevard Mohammed V.

Above the town beside the shrine of Sidi Bou Ali Srhine there is a hotel-café which has a few rooms. The **campsite**, © (05) 6733440, is also beside the road to the shrine. It has a fabulous view, is well shaded by trees and is equipped with a cool underground cellar.

South of Sefrou

Just outside the town is the **koubba of Sidi Youssef**, on a summit that guards a nearby spring. Along the road heading south are circular towers where crushed limestone is burnt to be sold throughout Morocco for lime. The village of **Annoceur**, on the left 24km from Sefrou at 1345m, marks the final limits of the irrigated lands; south of here only a few areas of orchard cultivation break an immense arid pastoral plain. A classical inscription was discovered 3km east of Annoceur in 1960; this created a flurry of excitement as historians reassessed the extent of Roman rule, but it is now thought to have been dropped by a passing caravan that was carrying antiquities from Volubilis to decorate a palace in the Tafilalt. Three km beyond the Annoceur turning is a right turn for **Dayèt (Lake) Aaoua**, and 2km further south, the dirt track for **Dayèt Afourgah** and **Dayèt Iffer** suggested in 'The Lake Tour' (*see* p.339). Once you have crossed the Tizi-Abekhnanes pass at 1769m, the right turn on route S309 to join the tour of the Forêt de Cèdres (*see* p.341) is only 9km further south.

The scattering of red-roofed houses at the old French administrative post of **Boulemane** is 76km south of Sefrou. It is in a dramatic position 1700m up the Recifa Gorge, at the foot of Jbel Tichchoukt and surrounded on almost all sides by cliff bluffs and scree slopes. There are two garages in Boulemane and the café-restaurant **Essada** with its central stove pipe, as it can be as cold here in winter as it becomes hot in summer.

South of Boulemane you can also take a long and obscure foray along the dead-end road to **Imouzzèr-des-Marmoucha**, 55km east at the foot of Jbel bou Iblane. The road takes you past the **Ifkern Ksar** on the river Sebou, and the **Aït-Makhlouf Ksar** of the Marmoucha tribe poised below Jbel Issouka. Imouzzèr-des-Marmoucha (1639m) is the central village of the Marmoucha hill tribe of shepherds. A track from Imouzzèr climbs for 30km to **Talzemt,** an old French army post where a ski lift is reportedly still operating.

The main road south crosses a high desert plain (up to 2000m) for 70km before rejoining the Meknès–Midelt road, the P21, near Boulôjoul (*see* p.344).

Midelt

This sprawling roadside market town is set in the centre of the Middle Atlas plateau at an elevation of 1500m. It has a windswept, almost forlorn air, though it is home to a population of around 16000. At the turn of the century Midelt was just a lone ksar outside the central market of the Berber Aït-Idzeg tribe. The French when they advanced into the Middle Atlas established a garrison beside this ksar, which has since been built over, leaving an initially commonplace atmosphere of a garrison town dominated by colonial red-tiled chalets and telegraph lines. Midelt is, however, well placed to break a journey and explore the Middle Atlas hinterland. It is 192km from Meknès, 154km from Er-Rachidia and has hotels, cafés, garages, a Banque Populaire and a souk. The town has a reputation as a friendly and useful base for walking to the surrounding ksour or driving into the mountains. The horizon to the south is dominated by the peaks of Jbel Ayachi, 'the mother of the waters'.

The big **market** of the area is still held on the northeastern edge of the town, on Sundays. On other days if you are looking for Middle Atlas kilims, carpets, minerals and fossils you will be well served in the **Souk Djedid**, a pair of courtyards just to the west of Avenue Mohammed V in the centre of town, opposite the bus station. Look in at **Moha Oulfkih**'s booth at no. 26 Souk Djedid, for good-quality kilims, cushions and djellabas. Another centre for local weaving and embroidery is **Kasbah Meriem** (*Atelier de Tissage*), a craft school for local girls run by Franciscan sisters just west of the town. To find it take the 3418 road, sign-posted for Jaffar and Tattiouine; the convent is on your left as you climb out from the valley. You can see the girls at work and buy samples of their production.

The Aït-Idzeg Tribe–the Children of Jbel Ayachi

Before the French pacification, the Aït-Idzeg were a sedentary tribe of about a thousand extended families that occupied the high slopes of Jbel Ayachi. In a time-honoured pattern they were threatened by tribes from the south of the Atlas, in particular by the Aït-Atta who each summer drove their herds from the Sahara up into the Atlas mountains. Each year they moved further north and stayed longer until portions of the tribe became firmly established in the Middle Atlas. The Aït-Idzeg, who were on the front line of this creeping threat, joined the Aït-Yafalman confederation of tribes that continually opposed the Aït-Atta.

A number of the Aït-Idzeg ksour survive along the valley floor both to the north and south of Midelt, and can easily be reached in a 40-minute walk. There are spectacular, shifting views of the tightly confined earth walls of these fortified hamlets, neatly terraced fields and small orchards, that hardly show above the surface of the denuded plain. Ksar Pilo, one of the most picturesque, is 9km south of the town, off the road to Tattiouine.

Where To Stay, Eating Out and Expeditions

moderate

The **Hôtel El Ayachi**, © (05) 582161, is on Rue d'Agadir on the southern edge of town. It is enclosed by its own garden, surrounded by tiled chalets and has 28 rooms, a bar and restaurant.

On the main road south of town is the **Kasbah Asma** hotel, © (05) 583945, third in a chain of three family hotels that are models of Moroccan private enterprise. The roadside Kasbah has a cool spacious hall, exuberantly furnished dining rooms and two dozen bedrooms upstairs. Surrounded by a vibrant array of rose beds and with a pool in construction at the back, it makes an ideal place to stop off whether overnight or for lunch or dinner.

inexpensive

About 20km north of Midelt standing just back from the road is the **Timnay Inter-Culture** centre, © (05) 583434, a mock kasbah which has a quadruple identity as a village shop, licenced restaurant, café, campsite and motel, with a river-filled pool. It is also a centre for expeditions into this section of the eastern High Atlas, ranging from a day trip up to the Cirque Jaffar by jeep with plenty of walking and time to savour lunch prepared in a mountain hut, to trips into the villages of the upper Taarart valley, Tadroute canyon and Arougou via the cedar forest of Tiz-n-Warou or a week long march across the breadth of the Atlas. The centre take genuine pleasure and great trouble in arranging contacts and cross overs between the Berber culture and that of visitors, handling them with considerable subtlety. This is no accident, as the centre is inspired by Youssef Ait Lemkadem, a local scholar and Professor who is equally at home in Paris, Rabat or Timnay.

cheap

The **Hôtel Mimlal**, © (05) 582266, has seven rooms, sells beer and wine at the bar and has a dining room. It is on the left as you enter the town from the north, and keeps up a raffish, boozy atmosphere. The **Hôtel Roi de la Bière**, © (05) 582675, is in the centre of town on the corner of Avenue Hassan II and Avenue des FAR, with 10 cool rooms but, despite its name, no bar.

Trips Around Midelt: the Cirque de Jaffar, Jebel Ayachi and Aouli

The rough tracks to the west of Midelt that lead towards Jbel Ayachi are more suitable for four-wheel-drives than standard cars. On your first trip into the mountains it's best to hire a guide (from any of the bigger hotels, or the Timnay Centre) to lead you on the Jaffar circuit, which makes an excellent introduction to the region's fauna.

Route 3426, which turns off the P21 some 15km north of Midelt, climbs through heavily-cultivated river valleys dotted with yellow adobe houses and ordered apple orchards. North of these valleys stretches a belt of wheat cultivation, as you approach the grazing grounds of low hills scattered with stunted evergreen oaks distorted by years of firewood pruning. Then, once over a brow of land you enter an Alpine-like valley overlooked by rocky peaks and the few remaining proud cedars. Follow the track west, past a line of stone and adobe shepherds' cottages, to enter the fabulous limestone gorge of the **Cirque de Jaffar**, hung with trees, crows and hawks and with the washed stones of the dry river bed marking a sinuous, narrow path through the mountain that returns you to the foothills east of the tomb of Sidi Jaffar.

Your next, and more testing expedition, is to be driven 15km south to Tattiouine, where mules and guides can be found to lead you on all or part of the 20km walk from the spring above the village along the Ikkis valley to ascend the 3737m summit of **Jbel Ayachi**.

The **mines and gorge of Aouli** are 25km northeast of Midelt on the tarmac S317. After 12km the road dips down to run within the gorge carved out of the plateau by the waters of the river Moulouya. The dark holes of old mine workings gape enticingly from the gorge walls. Copper and silver were extracted from this region until 1979; now the machinery, bridges, catwalks, great metal flood doors and housing for some of the 3000 workers stands neglected and empty. The gorge has returned into the possession of goatherds and fishermen.

South from Midelt to Er Rachidia

Only 30km south from Midelt you cross the watershed of the Atlas at the pass of the camel, the **Tizi-n-Tagalm/Talrhent**, which reaches 1907 m. There is a distinctive transition from the northern forested face of the mountain range to the desiccated south-facing slopes. The climate, vegetation and culture south of the pass is Saharan. Settlement is restricted to fortified villages along the valleys, the dry riverbeds of which cover a network of *khennegs* (underground irrigation channels) that feed the small gardens with water. The ksour of this mountain region are occupied by the Aït-Idzeg tribe, while the dry slopes and plateau are grazed by the Aït-Haddidou, a fierce nomadic tribe who were

a vital part of the Aït-Yafalman confederation. The Aït-Haddidou, distinguished by their cohesion, their costume and their particularism, were notorious raiders who descended from their secure mountain valleys to pillage caravans from the lower slopes of the Middle Atlas to deep in the Sahara.

The road which follows the *trik es soltan* route from the Tafilalt to Fès is pockmarked with kasbahs, ksour, caravanserai and French Foreign Legion forts to protect farmers, merchants and isolated garrisons from these raiders, whose chiefs only surrendered to France a few years before the Second World War.

Twelve km downhill is **Nzala**, where there is an eight-towered Foreign Legion fort to add to the succession of half-empty disintegrating ksour and caravanserai. Six km further south is the substantial **ksar Aït-Kherrou** of the Aït-Idzeg that guards the entrance of the gorge of the river Nzala, beyond which there is a water-hole known as the fountain of Aïn Chroub ou Hrob, which translates as 'drink and run'.

Seventy-five km south of Midelt a turn to the west leads in 3km down to the village of **Rich** beside the banks of the Ziz at the centre of a dry mountain plain. To the south is the dramatic face of Jbel bou-Hamid, its slopes appearing golden in the evening light. A central garden of pine trees stands at the entrance of the village, where a collection of battlemented stalls sell snacks to travellers. The village comes alive for the **Sunday souk**, the southernmost market of the Aït-Idzeg tribe, and there are two basic **hotels** overlooking the souk compound.

About 7km south of Rich the **ksour** of the Aït-Krojmane tribe guard a crossing of the river Ziz. A turning to the east here leads to an attractive **string of ksour** along the valley, their yellow walls punctured by the high arcaded arches, terraces and windows of mountain architecture, unlike the blank exteriors to be met further south.

The main road follows the Ziz as it snakes gently down through the dusty mountain plain, which does little to prepare you for the drama of the **Ziz Gorge** as you descend south. After the **Legionnaire's Tunnel** you pass beneath vast bleak gold and red cliffs that hem in the two beautiful oasis-style **kasbahs** of Ifri and Amzouf to provide you with one of Morocco's most awesome vistas. At the foot of the gorge the river is caught by the Hassan Addakhil Aït Dam to form a muddy lake. The dam was finished in 1971 and built from the revenue of a special tax on sugar. Below the lake there are a large number of modern military installations, as well as a line of riverine kasbahs, that stretch beside the road on its 16km descent to Er Rachidia, so do not try to photograph this area. For Er Rachidia *see* p.484.

Route 5: East from Fès towards the Eastern Frontier

The ancient fortress town of Taza is 120km east from Fès along the P1 highway. If you are driving and looking for a stop, the village of **Sidi Abdeljelil** is the traditional place. It is almost exactly halfway, at the eastern edge of the Idriss I Dam, and has a number of tempting roadside grill-cafes. About 15km further to the east look out for the bridge over the Bouhellou which marks the site of the most easterly Roman frontier fort, established deep into the territory of the independent Baquates tribe, who were the great power in this region in classical times. The **Touahar Pass**, just 17km west of Taza, provides some fine views of the forested highlands of Tazzeka to the south of the road, before you descend along the valley of the river el Abiod to reach Taza.

Taza

This ancient city-fortress, poised on a high outcrop of limestone, has a turbulent history. It controls the Taza Gap, a narrow valley that separates the Rif from the Middle Atlas and divides the eastern nomadic steppe from the farmed lands of the west. From its high, ageing battlements you can survey the surrounding landscape and then explore the dark, busy souk that runs straight through the medina.

On lower ground to the east of the medina the French built a grid-pattern of streets in 1920 which recent development has extended. Today the two districts of the town are still physically apart, divided by an olive grove and a 3km walk. As the seat of the provincial governor and the region's central market, Taza has a certain bustle, and the quiet charm of the town has fortunately been left unaffected by mass tourism.

History

Taza is the key to Morocco. It has been used as an alternative capital by three successive dynasties during their struggle for power. The first Almohad sultan, Abdel Moumen, ruled his fledgling empire from Taza for 20 years before he seized complete control of Morocco. The Beni-Merin tribal chiefs held the town for 25 years before they could destroy the last Almohads and rule as sultans. The first of the Alaouites, Moulay Rachid, selected the town to be his military headquarters in 1666 and, in a series of lightning campaigns, destroyed the armies of half a dozen rivals. In 1902 the Rogui (the pretender) Bou Hamara proclaimed himself sultan at Taza and several times seemed on the point of repeating history before he was finally taken prisoner in 1912.

Taza, though vital in the struggle for power, has proved less useful afterwards and so has repeatedly risen in importance during war and declined in peace. Its monuments have also had to survive the batterings inflicted on a border fortress. From its first foundation (like Meknès it was founded by the Meknassa, a powerful Berber tribe which after the successful Khajarite revolt of 741 controlled much of central Morocco), it has also had to serve as the border fortress of last resort. It has been fortified against a succession of threats from the east: the Fatimids in the 10th century; the Ziyanids in the 13th and 14th centuries; the Ottoman Turks from the 15th to 18th centuries; and the French, in Algeria, throughout most of the 19th century. The French finally occupied Taza in 1914 and established a large garrison here which was used in the long conquest of the Middle Atlas and Rif tribes. Active campaigning continued until 1934, but the barracks were converted into the nucleus of the present new town after 1920. The French garrison witnessed a few more months of fighting when the Rif tribes and the Liberation Army reopened a guerrilla campaign in 1956. After Independence the region has known a rare era of peace, though confused revolts in the Rif in 1958 and the Middle Atlas in 1959, and an army mutiny in 1974, have reasserted its strategic importance.

Getting Around

by rail

There is a daily train daily going east to Oujda (3–4hrs), and west to Fès (2hrs) and Meknès, with the possibility of changing at Sidi Kacem or Sidi Slimane to put you on the line for Rabat, Tangier and Casablanca.

by bus

All buses stop at the train station, though CTM coaches officially start from the Place de L'Indépendance. There is a daily bus to Oujda (3–4hrs), three for Fès (2hrs 30mins), two for Nador (5hrs) and two for Al Hoceima (4–5hrs). Local buses go directly from the train station to the medina, or you can ride in a *petit taxi* for 10dh.

by car and taxi

Taza is 120km from Fès and 223km from Oujda. There is a regular ***grand taxi*** run west from Taza to Fès (1hr 30mins) and east to Oujda (2hrs 30mins). The new town is full of mechanics' shops, and the central garage is on Place de l'Indépendance.

Tourist Information

The **post office** is by Place de l'Indépendance in the New Town, on the corner of Rue Allal ben Abdallah and Mouassa Ibn Noussair, and open from Monday to Friday. There are two **banks**, the Banque Populaire on Rue Anoual and the BMCE at 24 Av Mohammed V. The **tourist office** is at 56 Av Mohammed V, open from Monday to Friday, and there is a useful private agency, Taza Tours, also on Av Mohammed V, ✆ (05) 672005. The ***moussem*** of Sidi Zerrouk is held in September.

Orientation

Taza is a town on three levels; Roadside, New Town and Medina. At the very bottom by the main road is the train station; at the top of the New Town, a half-hour walk away, is the Place de l'Indépendance; and at the entrance to the medina is the Place Moulay Hassan. The medina has everything of interest in Taza, the Place de l'Indépendance has the bars, cafés, hotels, banks and post office, while the train station, ✆ (05) 672005, is the transport hub of the town.

Old Taza

Avenue Moulay Youssef leads from the new town to a roundabout at the foot of the medina, from where a long staircase climbs up through the Bab Jemaa to Place Moulay Hassan. Arriving by bus or car you sweep beyond this, up in a wide arc around the outer lower walls, where to the left you may catch a glimpse of the **koubba of Sidi Aissa**, on the road to the campsite, where Sultan Abou Inan built a lodge and a zaouia for poor students in the 14th century. Taza's chief attraction should be the magnificent Almohad grand mosque but this is, of course, closed to non-Muslims. The **medina** consequently has no outstanding attraction, but is a pleasant and unhassling place, and small and friendly enough to explore at random.

The Southern Ramparts

The ramparts which wrap Taza in 3km of walls follow the 12th-century Almohad defences, although successive restorations undertaken by Merenid, Saadian and Alaouite sultans mean that the surviving structure has a confusing variety of dates. The main road into the medina, as opposed to the Bab Jemaa steps, enters through the **Bab el Guebour**, a breach in the southern ramparts. On the right is the palace of the pacha or governor, behind which is the 25m **El Bastion**, a brick-built artillery fortress constructed by the Saadian Sultan Ahmed el

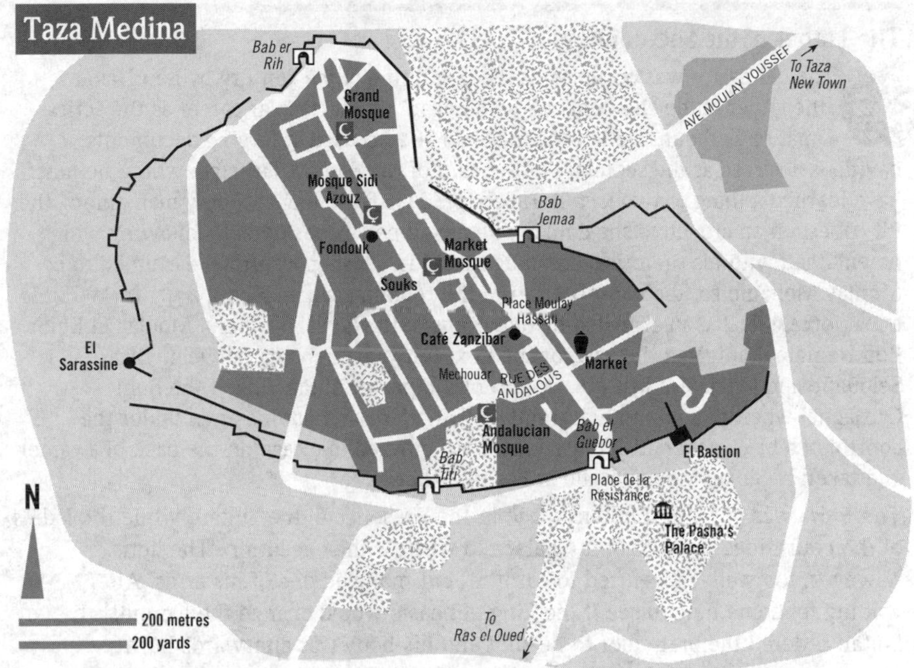

Mansour against the Turkish threat. Inside the 3m thick bastion walls some 16th-century graffiti of ships can be seen, carved by the Portuguese prisoners captured at the battle of Ksar-el-Kebir. During the restoration of the Bastion in 1916 the entrance to the Kifan el Khomari cave was discovered beneath here, revealing Paleolithic finds from the Mousterian culture.

Two hundred and fifty metres to the left of the Bab el Guebour entrance is the surviving 12th-century gate of the **Bab Titi**. Twice that distance again away to the west is the imposing circular Almohad tower known as **El Sarrasine**, which stands guard over the western corner of the medina plateau.

Once you have crossed inside the ramparts Rue Bab el Guebour leads from the gate directly to the Place Moulay Hassan, the main hub of the old town. Cars, buses and taxis park here; the covered food market is to the east and the souks to the west, and the street life is best watched from a table at the Café Zanzibar.

Méchouar

On the left on Rue Bab el Gebour, before Place Moulay Hassan, there is a mosque and a fountain at the corner of the Rue des Andalous. This twisting alley, crossed by arches and buttresses, leads to the walled and gated *méchouar*, a formal space established next to the old governor's palace and the **Andalusian Mosque**. The Mosque, which retains its 12th-century Almohad minaret, is largely hidden from view but a courtyard to the west allows a discreet examination. There is a delightful public lavatory with a garden courtyard on the right as you enter the *méchouar*, from where you can ask directions for the hidden and decaying 18th-century governor's palace, tucked in behind the mosque.

The Father of the She-donkey

The old palace was occupied at the beginning of the century by Bou Hamara, 'the father of the she-donkey', who began his spectacular career as the scribe Omar ez Zerhoun. He left Meknès in 1901 accused of forging documents, having last served as the secretary of the *caid* of the Beni-M'Tir tribe, where he must have learned a thing or two (*see* El-Hajeb, p.331). Travelling as a holy man among the Rif tribes, on an attractive she-donkey, he developed a considerable following which he enlarged with his rhetorical and magical skills. As support grew he claimed to be Moulay Mohammed, the elder brother of the reigning sultan, Abdul Aziz. In 1902 his tribal force defeated an army led by one of the sultan's real brothers, Moulay el Kebir. Bou Hamara dominated the east for the next ten years, moving between Taza, Selouane and Oujda. He lost the support of the powerful Rif tribe of the Beni Ouriaghel when he sold mineral rights to Christians and put his army under the control of a black general. Captured, he was confined in a cage on the back of a camel and taken to Sultan Moulay Hafid at Fès in 1912.

There 'he was put into the lions' cage in the presence of the Sultan, while the ladies of the court lined the roof of the palace to witness the execution. The lions, however, too well fed, refused to eat him, but mangled one of his arms. After waiting for some time to see if the king of beasts would change their minds, the Sultan ordered the pretender to be shot and his body was afterwards burnt . . . terrible as was his end, Bou Hamara himself had been guilty of every kind of atrocity, and had regularly burnt, after sprinkling them with petroleum, any of the sultan's soldiers that he had been able to capture during his campaigns' (Walter Harris, Morocco That Was).

The Souk

Beyond the *méchouar* a central street, under a variety of names, leads straight through the medina. On the left is the entrance to a small but reportedly charming **medersa**, built by the Merenid Sultan Abou Hassan in the early 14th century and currently closed. The neighbouring secondary school has some elegant carved cedar and tilework in its courtyard. The road narrows as you enter the covered souk quarter, passing the **shrine of Sidi Ali er Derrar** before you reach the **Jemaa es Souk**, the market Mosque, which, if you can get a view of it, has a curious minaret with a tower wider than its base. A web of alleys to the left of the mosque make up the ***kissaria***. The products of the souk are entirely for local trade, and the medina is delightfully free of salesmen and tourist bazaars. It's worth hunting for local basketwork, braided mats and carpets made by the Beni-Ouaraïn hill tribe. Look out for the mint tea café in a *fondouq* at no. 53 on the main street, and the grain market courtyard.

The 12th-century **mosque and shrine of Sidi Azouz** (the patron of Taza) on the left marks the transition from the souk to a richer residential district, its quiet houses guarded by heavy doors and ornate grilles on the windows.

The Grand Mosque

The central aisle of the grand mosque is aligned with the street, but the great clean area of high white wall punctured by a number of green-tiled, decorated gates is firmly closed to non-Muslims. Alleys to the right and left allow you to admire the extent of the mosque and thread your way out to the ramparts. It was founded by Abdel Moumen in 1135 and built to the same plan as the Almohad mosques at Tin-Mal, in the High Atlas, and the Koutoubia in Marrakech. The Merenids adorned the interior—Charles Terrasse's detailed study, *La grande mosquée de Taza* (1943) shows the finely carved stucco panels of the dome, the ivory inlaid minbar, and an enormous bronze chandelier.

Bab er Rih

The Bab er Rih, the gate of the winds, at the north end of the medina is a 12th-century Almohad bastion with a fine view of the surrounding mountains. Squat huts hug the edge of the fortress, and clearly defined garden plots extend east to the olive groves. To the west Moulay Rachid built a palace, the **Dar el Makhzen**, of which there is little trace; only the view and the cool winds remain unchanged. If you turn right here and walk around beside the ramparts you will come back to Place Moulay Hassan.

Where To Stay

moderate

The **Friouato Hôtel**, © (05) 672593, on Av de la Gare is an isolated modern concrete hotel situated off the avenue linking the New Town to the medina, set in its own garden. It has good facilities such as a pool, tennis court, bar and restaurant, and 58 rooms.

inexpensive/cheap

The **Grand Hôtel du Dauphin**, © (05) 673567, is the best place to stay, an old and comfortable hotel with balconied bedrooms that overlook the Place de l'Indépendance in the New Town. It has a sweeping staircase, an ancient switchboard, an enclosed pinewood bar, 26 rooms and a restaurant.

If the Grand is full there is a reasonable and cheaper alternative also on the Place, the **Hôtel de la Poste**, © (05) 672589. Just outside the medina, amid the arcades of Place Moulay Hassan is the cheap **Etoile**, © (05) 270179, with a few rooms arranged around a traditional inner courtyard.

Eating Out

The streets of the Taza New Town have more bars than restaurants, and the town actually has more of a reputation for beer than food. There are a few grill cafés in the medina concentrated around Place Moulay Hassan, and in the New Town the cheaper cafés, such as the **Majestic**, at no 26, are found along or just off Blvd Mohammed V. For a more formal meal with wine, head for the **Grand Hotel du Dauphin**.

Jbel Tazzeka

The forested highlands of Jbel Tazzeka, which stand to the southwest of Taza, are one of the two great national parks of Morocco. A 76km drive through these hills on the S311 can make an exhilarating approach to, or day trip from, Taza.

Turn off the main P1 road from Fès at the village of **Sidi-Abdallah-des-Rhiata**, from where the road climbs up through the **Zireg Gorge**. The cliffs are often patrolled by circling raptors and buzzards, while the small riverbed can occasionally be glimpsed below. Beyond the Saturday market of Es-Sebt and the neighbouring village of Bab-Azhar lie the forested hills. The road twists up to climb through a wilderness of pine, cedar, holm oak and cork to the **Bab-Taka pass** at 1540m. Just before the summit of the pass a rough track heads north for 7km towards the **summit of Jbel Tazzeka** (1980m), though the radio aerial at the peak destroys some of the grandeur of this celebrated view over rippling forested slopes.

About 8km beyond the pass you reach **Bab-Bou-Idir**, a superbly positioned, decaying colonial hill station that enjoys a liberating view. Down from Bab-Bou-Idir you pass the damaged entrances to a number of old lead mines before reaching the serene depression of **Daïa Chiker**. This punchbowl of pasture was formed by the slow attrition of limestone by thousands of years of rain. Two small lakes appear seasonally, the furthest draining into the Chiker cave system, a potholer's heaven of subterranean tunnels and caverns.

A signposted turning off the main road leads up to the **Friouato Hole** (*Gouffre de Friouato*) which has an admission charge. A huge number of irregular steps lead down a tunnel into an enormous 180m deep subterranean bowl. This is lit by a 30m wide cleft in the rocks, through which sunlight streams to pick out one moss-covered rock wall. The increasingly erratic staircase descends down the scree slope to the bottom of the bowl. This is quite impressive enough, though with a torch you can descend further to view caverns with oozing stalagmite and stalactite forms. The narrowing tunnel and steps descend to where the water level fluctuates, and most amateurs are relieved to halt by the silt deposits which are warm, dank and dark enough for most tastes.

Below the Daïa Chiker is the **Sidi-Mejbeur Pass** (1198m), which frames a memorable **view** down over Taza, triumphantly revealing its strategic position. The **Ras-el-Oued Falls** have been dry for several years, though the empty riverbed is shaded by the twisted trunks of some beautiful old cork trees. At the summit of the falls is a terrace **café**, with a fine view over the olive groves to the city.

From Taza to Oujda

From Taza a desert plain extends to the eastern city of Oujda. This bleak expanse is broken by a scattering of eucalyptus groves and a few dusty towns. A defenceless area that stretches between the two citadel cities, it has been a natural battleground and most travellers still hurry across it, leaving the few places of interest—Msoun, Gouttitir, Debdou, the Za canyon and Za Gorge and Falls—largely undisturbed. Msoun is only 28km east of Taza but all the other sights can be explored from Taourirt, which has a couple of basic hotels.

The **kasbah of Msoun** commands the ground to the north of the road and the approach to the ford across the river Msoun. This secure compound was built by Sultan Moulay Ismaïl in the 18th century. Each side is protected by four turrets that stud a battlemented wall, and even the wooden gates are still in place. Within the walls are some olive trees and the dusty hamlet of the Haoura tribe, a semi-nomadic group of shepherds who are absent from their kasbah home for most of the year. It is a strange but attractive place that houses a complete community and has a shop, post office, school, mosque and tea room, and a view south to the peak of Jbel Ouarirth. A great battle was fought here in AD 933. The Berber Meknassa tribe, who held Taza under the suzerainty of the Idrissids, were destroyed by an army of the Shiite Fatimid Empire, which during the following century succeeded in uniting all of North Africa under its rule.

Guercif, 36km east of Msoun, is a village at the centre of an oasis of agricultural lands irrigated by the rivers Melloulou and Moulouya. The surrounding orchards and gardens provide welcome shade for a picnic, but the village has small appeal and the listed campsite even less. From Guercif a road follows the Moulouya Valley, the least-visited oasis valley of Morocco, southwest to Midelt.

The Birth of a Dynasty

In the 12th century the Moulouya Valley was controlled by the Beni-Merin, an ethnically Berber but Arabic-speaking nomadic tribe of the eastern plain. They were periodically employed as cavalry by the Almohad sultans in their wars of conquest, and developed an increasing taste for the power and wealth that could only be won in warfare. In 1248 an Almohad army retreated from Algeria after their Sultan, es Said, had been killed. This demoralized force was escorted across the Eastern plain by Beni-Merin scouts, who treacherously led them to a difficult crossing of the Moulouya. The Almohad army was massacred as it struggled across the swollen river. After this ruthless act the reputation of the Beni-Merin chiefs grew greatly. Taza and the eastern plain fell instantly into their power, to be followed by the great city of Fès, which they ruled as the Merenid sultans.

Between Guercif and Taourirt look out for a left turn to **Gouttitir**. It is a hamlet only a kilometre from the road, established beside a natural hot-water mineral spring. Men have use of this natural *hammam*, hidden from immediate view by the deep bed of the stream, until dusk when it becomes the women's property. The **Café Sidi Chaffi** with its enormous spacious hall and cool arcades echoes to almost continuous reggae. Haffid can rent you a hut and fix up a light meal.

Taourirt Kasbah is crowned by radio aerials, for it is in active use by the Moroccan Army who value its commanding view of the Za river crossing. Its most active period was after 1295, when it became a Merenid base against the Ziyanids of Tlemcen. By the central crossroads there are four grill cafés to the south and half a dozen cafés that serve breakfast. There are too a couple of hotels, of which **El Mansour**, © (06) 694003, is the best. It is to the left of the road south to Debdou. A busy local **souk** is held by the crossroads on Sundays, with lesser business on Saturday and Thursday mornings.

Za Gorge, Debdou and Za Falls

A road from the central crossroads, marked 'Beni Koulal', follows the river south of town almost to the entrance of the dramatic Za Gorge. Do not accelerate past the bollards: the road ends in a lethal cliff drop. A dirt track next to the koubba and cult tree of Sidi Mazark allows you to walk to the gorge.

A 53km drive south of Taourirt through the land of the Haoura nomads, the desert plain of the Sedjaa de Tafrate, will take you to the hillside village of **Debdou**, surrounded by orchards and woods. The Beni-Merin controlled this kasbah before they fought their way to the throne. Elevated to higher concerns, in the 15th century they gave the kasbah to some cousins, the Beni-Ouatta, who as the Wattasid hereditary grand viziers were destined eventually to succeed the Merenids to the throne. Typically it was their old neighbours in Debdou, the Beni Urtajjin, that proved themselves implacably opposed to Wattasid rule. The kasbah was later occupied by the Berber-speaking Haoura, who had not yet developed similar political aspirations. South of Debdou a tarmac road climbs through forested hills towards the **El-Ateuf Kasbah** and a mosque built by Caid Goarich.

If you leave the main road 6km west of Taourirt and travel north, downstream towards the Mohammed V Reservoir, the **Za Falls** are 9km along the road. Pass the buildings of the colonial farm and the distinctive white koubba, and about 1km further a dirt track to the right leads to the falls. A delightful cascade of water falls over the hard pebble conglomerate into a large and swimmable bowl below complete with gravel beds, caves and drying rocks. The river valley makes a pleasant, unconventional camping ground.

El-Aïoun

The town of El-Aïoun, which has a souk on Tuesdays, is 49km east of Taourirt. El-Aïoun was founded by Moulay Ismaïl, who built a kasbah here in 1679. He had made a practice of recruiting the Berber Beni-Snassen tribe into his army but found it convenient to guarantee their obedience by having a garrison within striking distance of their mountain homeland. Sultan Moulay Hassan restored the kasbah in 1876 at the same time that he reinforced those at Selouane and Saïdia against the growing threat of French expansion from Algeria. A zaouia of Sheikh Bou Amama (1840–1908) was also welcomed here, as this Sufi brotherhood increasingly devoted itself to resistance against the French. Just to the south of the town is a cemetery where many martyrs of this resistance lie buried with koubbas raised over the most celebrated *mujaheddin*. On the western edge of town, above the railway station, is the **kasbah** which survives in good condition. Four turrets guard each wall, while a restored mosque and souks cluster around the battlements.

The Battle of Isly

About 50km east of El-Aïoun, just south of the modern road, a Moroccan army was destroyed by the French at the Battle of Isly. The leader of the Algerian resistance, the Emir Abdel Kader, had retreated into Morocco in 1843 and had been joined outside Oujda by thousands of Moroccan volunteers and the army of Sultan Abder Rahman. The French General Bugéaud, ignoring both the border and the declared pacific intentions of the sultan, boldly advanced into Morocco. On 13 August 1844 he attacked the combined Moroccan–Algerian army on the banks of the river Isly. The river was dry in this midsummer month, but it flowed blood that day for 6km downstream into Oujda.

For Oujda and the frontier, *see* pp.155–61.

Marrakech

Marrakech the Red is the heart that beats an African identity into the complex soul of Morocco. The city walls, overlooked by the Koutoubia minaret, are framed against the towering blue wall of the High Atlas mountains. From outside the city promises much, but at first it may seem to contain nothing more than a vast transitory souk. The Jemaa el Fna, the celebrated square at the centre of the medina, is full of visiting farmers (when not dominated in the harsh daylight hours by bewildered looking tourists). It is strikingly African compared with the Atlantic character of Casablanca, and the intensely Arab attitude of Fès; yet it is not some desert border town but a city with a long and proud record as an imperial capital.

The Phoenicians, Romans, Arabs and Idrissids ruled over a mere portion of Morocco, a patchwork of hills and the northern Atlantic coast. The Empire of Morocco was first created not by any of these distinguished, alien powers, but by a Berber tribe from the depths of the Western Sahara. They were the first to forge a Moroccan identity by linking a vast continental hinterland to the civilized lands of the northwest. Marrakech was the Berber capital, a city where they embraced Islam and an urban culture on their own terms. Here they brought together, like heraldic symbols of the future state, palm trees from the desert and craftsmen from Andalucia.

Marrakech has retained its aura of African exoticism, while its guaranteed dry heat, the heady atmosphere of its souk, its celebrated monuments, and the nearby High Atlas mountain valleys have a universal appeal. It is a fascinating city, the central objective of most visitors to Morocco, but be aware that you will not be alone: Marrakech is, alongside Agadir, Morocco's chief tourist destination. It is also undeniably demanding. As always in Morocco, take things slowly and do not try to rush your way through its precious store of monuments. Marrakech has stood for a thousand years, has now endured generations of star-struck travellers, and its thick-lidded eyes will not be stirred by much. I was rather shocked to hear a Moroccan (admittedly from Casablanca) denounce it as a 'city of thieves and prostitutes without either religion or honour'. This was, however, in response to exceptional circumstances, for he had just been publicly propositioned in the full heat of midday by a drunk old glue-sniffing prostitute who I had once taken out to lunch.

History

1062–1147: Foundation and Empire

Archaeologists have found that the site of Marrakech has been almost continually occupied since Neolithic times, but the modern city has its origins in an Almoravid garrison town of the 11th century. In 1062 Abu Bekr, an early commander of the Almoravids, threw up a wall of thorn bushes to protect his camp and built a fortress amid his tented army, the Ksar el Hajar, the tower of stone. Nine years later he appointed his young cousin, Youssef ben

Tachfine, to command this new post. The meteoric conquest of Morocco and Spain by Youssef ben Tachfine from this base marks the true foundation of both the city and the Almoravid Empire. Marrakech's position on the border of three agricultural regions meant that it soon eclipsed the older towns of Aghmat and Nfis to become the main market for the farmers of the Tensift valley, the nomadic pastoralists of the plains and the Masmuda Atlas tribes. It still has that feel to this day.

It was Youssef ben Tachfine's son and successor, Ali ben Youssef, who built the great circuit of walls, two large mosques, palaces and fountains which were all superbly decorated by Andalusian carvers. As in Fès, the Almoravids brought the technology of desert survival and used it to improve the city's seasonal water supply. Long *khettera* (pipes) were built to carry water underground from the High Atlas mountains to the houses and gardens of Marrakech.

1147–1269: The Capital City of the Almohad Empire

After decades of warfare between the Almoravid Sultans and the Almohads, whose headquarters were tucked up in the High Atlas mountains, the walled city of Marrakech finally fell in 1147. The Almohads deliberately demolished any evidence of the previous dynasty and remade the city in their own image. It did, however, remain the capital city of a great empire, and the monumental buildings of this period—the Koutoubia Mosque, the El Mansour Mosque, the Bab Aguenaou—still dominate the city. Almohad princes ruled on in Marrakech decades after the rest of their empire had fallen into the hands of rival dynasties. Like the Almoravids before them, they were fated to die defending the walls of the city, which were finally breached by the Merenids in 1269.

1269–1524: A Decaying City

Under the Merenid Sultans (1248–1465) Morocco was ruled from Fes and Marrakech stagnated into a provincial town. By the early years of the 16th century even this comparative prosperity had ended. Portuguese cavalry raided up to the walls of the city, Ottoman Turks were poised to advance from the east, and the authority of the central government, threatened by dozens of rival dynasties, had shrunk to the area around Fès. In 1524 the dilapidated city welcomed the rule of Mohammed ech Cheikh, forceful founder of the Saadian dynasty, whose power was based on the tribes of the south. Using Marrakech as his base, Mohammed ech Cheikh succeeded in subduing the rest of country. He was murdered in a High Atlas valley by an Ottoman assassination squad. The governor of Marrakech promptly ordered the murder of six of his sons, to clear the succession for Abdullah el Ghalib.

1524–1668: The Golden Capital of the Saadians

The reigns of Abdullah el Ghalib and his half-brother Ahmed el Mansour, the victorious (also known as *El Dehbi*, the golden) witnessed a magnificent revival in the prosperity of Marrakech. Abdullah founded the *mellah;* rebuilt the kasbah and the Ben Youssef Mosque and Medersa; and built a hospital and the new Mouassine Mosque. Ahmed built the incomparable El Badia Palace and the Saadian Tombs, and sprinkled the city with fountains, *fondouqs*, libraries and *hammams*.

The prosperity of Marrakech in these centuries was partly based on a thriving trade in sugar, saltpetre, cotton and silk. The city became the collection and transit point for the produce of the Sahara and sub-Sahara—slaves, gold, ivory, gum arabic and ostrich feathers—which was then exported through the Atlantic ports.

1668–1912: Alaouite Marrakech, the Twin Capital

The vicious civil wars of the late 17th and early 18th centuries, in which Marrakech was repeatedly besieged and plundered, were a disaster from which it never entirely recovered. Sultan Moulay Ismaïl (1672–1727) restored the religious shrines of the city but decided to rule from a new capital in Meknès. Later Alaouite sultans attempted to check the city's continued decline by alternating government between Fès and Marrakech, and many of its finest buildings date from the 18th and 19th centuries. The comparative order and prosperity of Moulay Hassan's reign (1873–94) is revealed in the large number of opulent merchants' houses and the palaces of the Bahia and Dar Si Saïd, built by viziers during the minority of his son, Abdul Aziz.

But the city remained pitifully backward. At the turn of the 20th century there were no wind or steam mills in the city, and trade depended on pack animals being safely escorted past the Rehamna tribe to Essaouira.

The 20th Century

Growing European influence was bitterly resented, and this reaction culminated in the lynching of a French resident, a Dr Mauchamp, after he attached an aerial to his roof in 1907. Personal resentment against Dr Mauchamp was intense, from both native healers and city traders, who were infuriated that with his aerial the doctor could discover prices in Essaouira days before they could. The city mob for their part were convinced the aerial was a sorcerer's device, for it was well known on the streets, and with some truth, that Mauchamp had great knowledge of the occult. It proved to be one of several incidents which provided the excuse for the French landings in Casablanca in the same year. Five years later the French army occupied the city, having destroyed the tribal army of El Hiba, the Blue Sultan, at Sidi-Bou-Othmane.

Marrakech became an important centre of French influence in the south, though its old predominance was deliberately shattered with the location of the new commercial centre at Casablanca. In Marrakech the French built a new town, 'Guéliz', to the west of the old city, its ordered avenues and quiet leafy suburbs overlooked by their enormous army

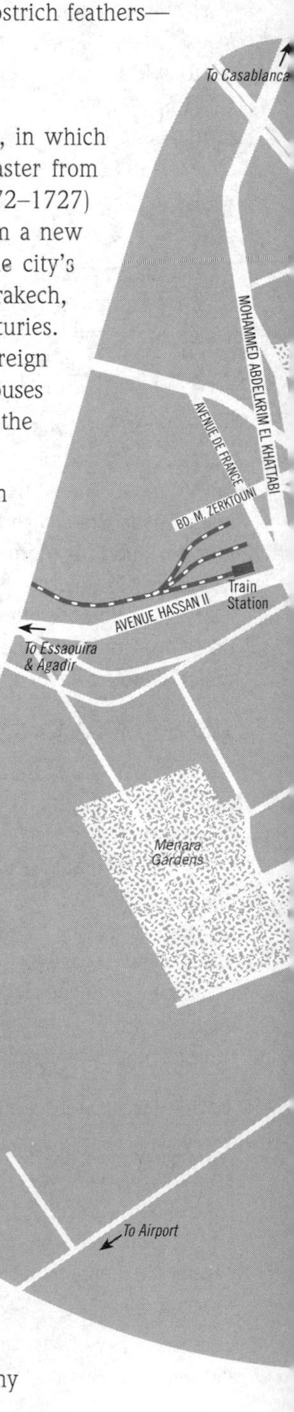

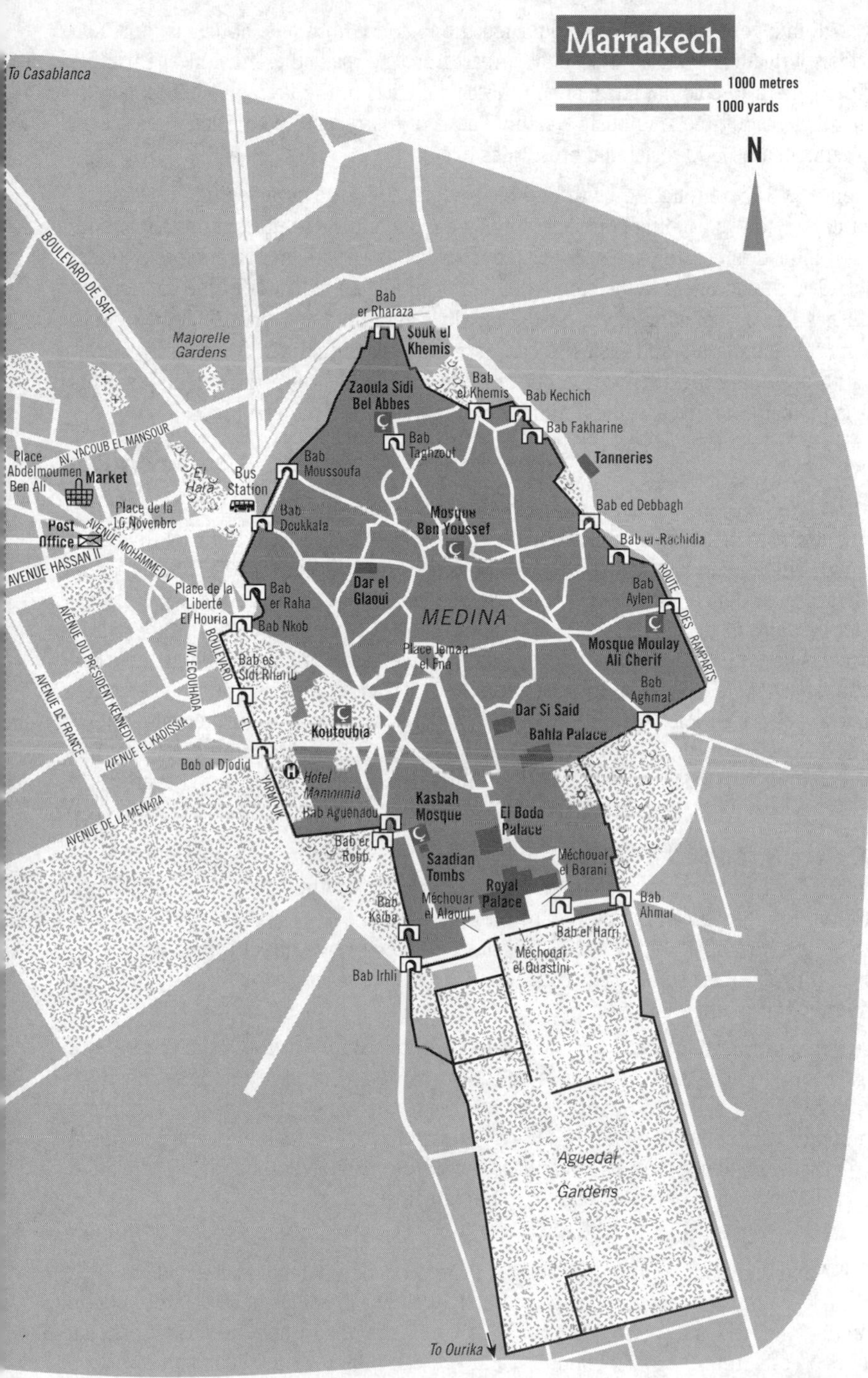
Marrakech
1000 metres
1000 yards
N
To Casablanca
BOULEVARD DE SAFI
Majorelle Gardens
AV. YACOUB EL MANSOUR
Place Abdelmoumen Ben Ali
Market
El Hara
Bus Station
Place de la 16 Novembre
Post Office
AVENUE MOHAMMED V
AVENUE HASSAN II
Bab er Rharaza
Souk el Khemis
Zaoula Sidi Bel Abbes
Bab el Khemis
Bab Kechich
Bab Fakharine
Bab Taghzout
Bab Moussoufa
Tanneries
Bab Doukkala
Mosque Ben Youssef
Bab ed Debbagh
Bab er-Rachidia
ROUTE DES REMPARTS
Bab Aylen
Place de la Liberté El Houria
Bab er Raha
Dar el Glaoui
MEDINA
Bab Nkob
Mosque Moulay Ali Cherif
AVENUE DU PRESIDENT KENNEDY
AV. ECOUHADA
BOULEVARD EL YARMOUK
Bab es Sidi Rharib
Place Jemaa el Fna
Bab Aghmat
AVENUE DE FRANCE
Dar Si Said
Koutoubia
Bahia Palace
AVENUE EL KADISSIA
Bab el Djedid
Hotel Mamounia
Kasbah Mosque
El Bedi Palace
Bab Aguenaou
AVENUE DE LA MENARA
Bab er Robb
Saadian Tombs
Méchouar el Barani
Royal Palace
Bab Ksiba
Méchouar el Alaoui
Bab Ahmar
Bab el Harri
Méchouar el Quastini
Bab Irhli
Aguedal Gardens
To Ourika

barracks. Within a generation they had adorned the region with roads, hotels, pylons, railroads, schools, irrigation works and hospitals. Apart from the roads these technical advances were for the benefit of colonial farmers and the caidal allies of the French. Their chief ally was Si Thami el Glaoui, the fabulously wealthy Pacha of Marrakech, who ruled a medina in which an estimated 20,000 registered prostitutes lived.

Independence in 1956 brought a swift and bloody end to his corrupt regime. Marrakech today houses a rapidly expanding population of half a million. It is the most important administrative and industrial centre of the south, and earns valuable foreign currency as a tourist destination. The spread of car ownership, while an encouraging indicator of the distribution of wealth, has had a damaging effect on the air. It is very doubtful that today you could follow Churchill's example and visit the city as a cure for bronchitis. Marrakech is still, though, a natural market place, with a cultural life that recalls both the splendour of its periods as an imperial capital and the traditions of its rural Berber hinterland.

Getting Around

by air

The Marrakech–Menara international airport, © (04) 447862, is 5km southwest of town. There is, theoretically, a bus to the city every half hour, no. 11, but it is not always in evidence. There are *grand* and *petit taxi* ranks at the airport were drivers can be quite extravagant in their demands, though 50dh is usually considered an acceptable tourist rate (*see below* 'by taxi'). As well as international flights there is a regular schedule of internal RAM services to Casablanca, four a week to Ouarzazate, one a week to Er Rachidia, and two a week to Fès and Tangier. Further information and prices are available from the RAM office at 197 Av Mohammed V, © (04) 436205. Return tickets should be reconfirmed here a day or two before departure.

by rail

The station, © (04) 447947, is off Av Hassan II, a five-minute walk west from Place du 16 Novembre on Av Mohammed V. Four trains a day travel north to Casablanca (4hrs) where you can connect with trains to Rabat, Fès, Meknès and Oujda, and there is a new direct service to Fez at 9am. There are two direct trains to Tangier, including an overnighter with couchettes. These are worth booking early, and the journey is best undertaken with a picnic.

Arriving in Marrakech you are certain to be met by touts as you leave the station. Take only official taxis, though even these can be expensive enough, and their meters seldom function. About 10–15dh is the going rate for most *petit taxi* journeys around the city, but to obtain this price you will have to exhibit an enviable level of calm self-confidence (*see also below* 'by taxi'). Alternatively, catch a no. 3 or a no. 8 local bus, which connect the station to the Jemaa el Fna.

by bus

CTM and other bus companies all depart from the modern depot just outside the Bab Doukkala on Place Mouarabiten. It is usually well worth going ahead of your luggage and buying tickets a day in advance. Take your time to sort out the various alternatives on sale from the kiosk windows, and you can mull over the final details of your travel plans in the station's garden-café. As ever, travel by CTM whenever possible.

Going **west** (into the area covered by the **Atlantic Coast** chapter) there are currently around seven buses a day to El-Jadida (3–4hrs), six to Essaouira (3–5hrs), four to Safi (3–4hrs), eight to Rabat (5–6hrs) and almost hourly departures for Casablanca (4hrs).

Going **east** (the area of the **Middle Atlas** chapter) there are three to Fès (11hrs), nine to Beni-Mellal (3hrs), four to Demnate (3hrs), and four to Azrou (5–6hrs).

Heading **south** across the High Atlas there are five for Inezgane-Agadir (3–4hrs), four to Ouarzazate (4–5hrs), two to Zagora (11hrs) and two to Taroudannt (8–9hrs), which includes the dawn departure across the Tizi-n-Test.

If you are heading for the **High Atlas** itself you should go to the dusty area just outside the Bab er Rob gate, where the local buses and *grands taxis* that ply the routes to the Ourika valley, Asni, Moulay Brahim and Amizmiz collect.

Local buses depart from Rue Moulay Ismaïl, beside the triangular garden at the southern end of the Jemaa el Fna. No. **1** goes right along Av Mohammed V to below the Guéliz hill, **2** passes the Bab Doukalla bus station, the **3** (and **14**) head along Av Mohammed V and Av Hassan II to the train station, **4** along Av Mohammed V and then on to the El-Jadida road, **5** on to the Beni-Mellal road (useful for Souk el Khemis), **6** to the Quartier Industriel (and the youth hostel), **7** to Av Hassan II and further northwest, **8** along Av Mohammed V and Av Hassan II, **10** to Bab Doukkala and the Safi road, and the elusive no. **11** to the airport via the Menara gardens.

by taxi

Petits taxis are found along the length of Av Mohammed V, by the covered market in the new town, by the bus station, train station and by the Jemaa el Fna. Bargaining for taxis is part of Marrakech life. When driven to distraction remember that you have it expensive but easy, for locals are often habitually ignored in favour of tourists and their fares. While all this is not without its irritation it also has its quiet rewards, since you gradually reduce your fares as you grow in confidence, though you will never be able to compete with Marrakechi women and their forceful cries of '*Wahd dirham*' (one dirham) as they leap aboard. Prices fluctuate in tune with your desperation, destination and charm. Negotiate in advance, with the taxi-door open but before taking your seat or loading on any luggage. The standard fare for any *petit taxi* trip for a tourist should be between 10–20dh. Good luck.

Grands taxis are found in the Jemaa el Fna, outside the Post Office in the new town, by the bus station and by the Bab er Rob, where a place to the Ourika valley should cost 20dh. As a group you might want to hire a taxi for a day in Ourika or up the Tizi-n-Test, for which you will have to pay between 150dh and 300dh.

by car

You will not need a car in the city until it is time to leave. There are plenty of **car-hire** firms in Marrakech. The smaller companies can offer cheaper deals, but this is often reflected in the condition of their cars and their legal contracts. One misadventure that ended up with a protracted two-day negotiation at a police station has given me a bias towards the mainstream operators. The more reputable companies include **Avis** at 137 Av Mohammed V, © (04) 433727, **Europcar-InterRent** at 63 Blvd

Zerqtouni, ✆ (04) 431228, **Hertz** at 154 Av Mohammed V, ✆ (04) 434680, and especially the English-speaking team at **Always**, Complex Kawkab, Centre Guéliz, ✆ (04) 446797, fax 430938, who will deliver the car to your hotel.

Parking: You can park anywhere off the Av Mohammed V in the new town, in any big hotel, or at the Jemaa el Fna in front of the Foucauld Hotel. There is also a car park in an old covered bus depot immediately beside the CTM Hotel.

Car parts are available from Union Pièces Autos, 18 Blvd Mansour Eddahbi, ✆ (04) 431790 or the Centre Européen de l'Automobile, 18 Blvd Moulay Rachid, ✆ (04) 434527

Garages: Ourika, the main Fiat agent, is at 66 Av Mohammed V, ✆ (04) 430155, and the Renault dealer Tazi is on Rue Bab Agnaou, ✆ (04) 422339.

Bicycle and moped hire: Bicycles can be rented from the Foucauld Hotel, ✆ (04) 445499, on Av. El Mouahidine in the southern corner of the Jemaa el Fna, and mopeds from the **Peugeot garage** at 225 Av Mohammed V, as well as from two places out on the Casablanca road, **Marrakech Motos** at 31 Blvd El-Khattabi, ✆ (04) 448359, and **Adoul Abdallah** at 14 Blvd El-Khattabi, ✆ (04) 432238.

by carriage

For a horse-drawn carriage that seats five, 60dh an hour is a price to aspire to, but it may be easier to settle one overall price for a tour of the ramparts and gardens. In the last few years the carriages have been equipped with a municipally-approved list of maximum prices, which is an aid but not a conclusive element in the bargaining process. I usually end up paying 120dh for a rampart tour, and with just one or two suggestions leave the route up to the driver.

On one trip, when my birthday coincided with the feast of Achoura, this rather hackneyed tourist excursion yet proved to be one of the most enchanting journeys of my life. We set off before dusk with both of the kerosene side lamps lit, and drove for hours passing mosques with their silent queues of seated paupers waiting for the traditional festival charity, and through unknown back streets thronged with young children beating their festival drums, demanding presents and dancing around bonfires that scattered wild shadows on the glowing red walls. When it came to paying the driver had lowered his price (perhaps because the back wheel came off twice), but we then doubled it as our two-year-old daughter, who had sat mesmerised with delight on the driving bench, had clearly fallen in love with both the ancient driver and his horse.

Tourist Information

The **tourist office** is at Place Abdelmoumen ben Ali on Av Mohammed V, ✆ (04) 448889, and the *Syndicat d'Initiative* at 176 Av Mohammed V, ✆ (04) 434797. Both are open Mon–Fri 8.30am–12pm, 3–6pm, and give away familiar free leaflets with maps and lists of hotels and arrange the hire of guides, but do not provide much else.

The main **post office** is halfway along Av Mohammed V at the major junction of Place du 16 Novembre, and open Mon–Sat 8am–2pm. There is a **telephone** section tucked into the right-hand side of the building with a separate entrance for after-hours service that stays open until 9pm. There is a good sub-post office housed in the prominent neo-Moorish public building on the southern side of the Jemaa el Fna. This is open Mon–Fri 8am–2pm, and also has a telephone section as well as a line of card-operated booths on its west wall. In addition there has been a recent explosion in private telephone kiosks linked up to satellite systems.

Banks: The BMCE, as ever, is first choice for banking services. Their main branch is in the new town at 144 Av Mohammed V, © (04) 431948, and is open for currency exchange Mon–Fri 8am–8pm. In the old town there is a selection of banks just south of the Jemaa el Fna on Rue Bab Agnaou which include a *bureau de change* booth run by Banque Populaire, as well as branches of Crédit du Maroc and SGMB, while there is a BMCI branch on nearby Rue Moulay Ismaïl.

There are ***hammams*** throughout the medina. There are a couple on Rue Zitoun el Kedim that are used to accepting Europeans, but the most magnificent interior is undoubtedly at Hammam Dar el Bacha on Rue Fatime Zohra, with both male and female sections. In the New Town the Hammam Salama on Blvd Safi (behind the petrol station near the Majorelle garden) has been recommended, though the Hammam in the basement of the Tichka Hotel wins an even more loyal following for it employs one of the city's most skilful masseurs.

emergencies

For the **police**, at the Rue Ibn Hanbal station, dial 19; for **fire**, at the Rue Khalid ben Oualid, dial 16.

Dial 15 for an **ambulance** or use the private ambulance service that operates from 10 Rue Fatima Zohra, © (04) 443724. There are two large **hospitals**; Hôpital Ibn Tofail on Rue Abdel Ouahab Derraq, © (04) 448011, and Hôpital Avenzoar on Rue Sidi Mimoun, © (04) 422793.

There is an **all-night pharmacy** on Rue Khalid Ben Oualid, the *Pharmacie de Nuit*, © (04) 430415, and an enormous selection open during normal shopping hours. The Bab Ftouh Pharmacie on Jemaa el Fna, © (04) 422678, or the *Pharmacie Centrale*, © (04) 430151, at 166 Av Mohammed V are among the most usefully placed.

Among the English-speaking **physicians** in the city there is the well established Dr Perez, © (04) 431030, at 169 Av Mohammed V and Dr Hamid Mansouri, © (04) 430754, on Rue Sebou. English-speaking **dentists** include Dr Gaillères at 112 Av Mohammed V and Dr Hamid Laraqui, © (04) 433216, at 203 Av Mohammed V.

Orientation

Marrakech is an easy city in which to orientate yourself. The straight central street of the new town, Av Mohammed V, runs with the Koutoubia minaret, which is just west of the Jemaa el Fna, as its focus. The areas around Av Mohammed V and the Jemaa el Fna support most of the offices, hotels, cafés and banks.

The minaret of the Koutoubia Mosque and the Jemaa el Fna are the dominant images in the medina of Marrakech. Even if you avoid all other conventional tourist sites, and explore only the most reclusive quarters of the medina, these two will remain at the centre of your experience of Marrakech.

The Koutoubia

The **minaret of the Koutoubia Mosque** appears at its most elegant from a great distance. Approaching Marrakech from the High Atlas, the tower rises magnificently above the barely perceptible city, and you can begin to understand the veneration in which it is held locally. The interior of the mosque (and minaret) are of course closed to non-Muslims. In the last few years the dusty wasteland that surrounds it has slowly been converted into a tidy garden, while the surrounding ruins—of the earlier mosque and elements from the Almoravid palace—have been exposed, stabilized and are being turned into an accessible terrace.

This wasteland was once the centre of the city. The Almoravid Sultan Ali ben Youssef rebuilt his father's mosque and added a new palace to the south, on the site of the present Koutoubia, but these buildings were both razed to the ground when the Almohads captured Marrakech in 1147. Abdel Moumen, the Almohad Sultan, immediately started on the construction of a new mosque, but the work was pushed forward too quickly. It was found wanting, among other faults incorrectly aligned to Mecca, and was dismantled soon after its completion. The sole remaining trace of it before the current excavations was a stumpy little minaret that survived into the 19th century. Undeterred by this first failure, Abdel Moumen ordered a fresh start. This, the Koutoubia, followed the same plan, though it was slightly wider with an interior dominated by a forest of horseshoe arches resting on solid square pillars decorated by pairs of pilasters. Five domes rise along the high, wide central aisle to focus attention on the mihrab prayer niche. At the opposite end the open air *Sahn* courtyard, the place for ritual ablutions, also served as the customary place for lectures on the Koran and Islamic law before the construction of medersas in the 13th century.

Due to the vagaries of the site, the minaret was positioned in the northeast corner of the mosque, and was only completed in the reign of Abdel Moumen's grandson Sultan Yaacoub el Mansour, one of the world's greatest architectural patrons, also responsible for the Giralda tower in Seville and the Hassan tower in Rabat. From its 12m by 12m base it rises to almost 70m. It was built from an internal ramp that climbs between its double walls. This connects six rooms that increase in delicate ornamentation as they ascend. Each side of the minaret has a different decorative scheme, and the boldly carved lancet

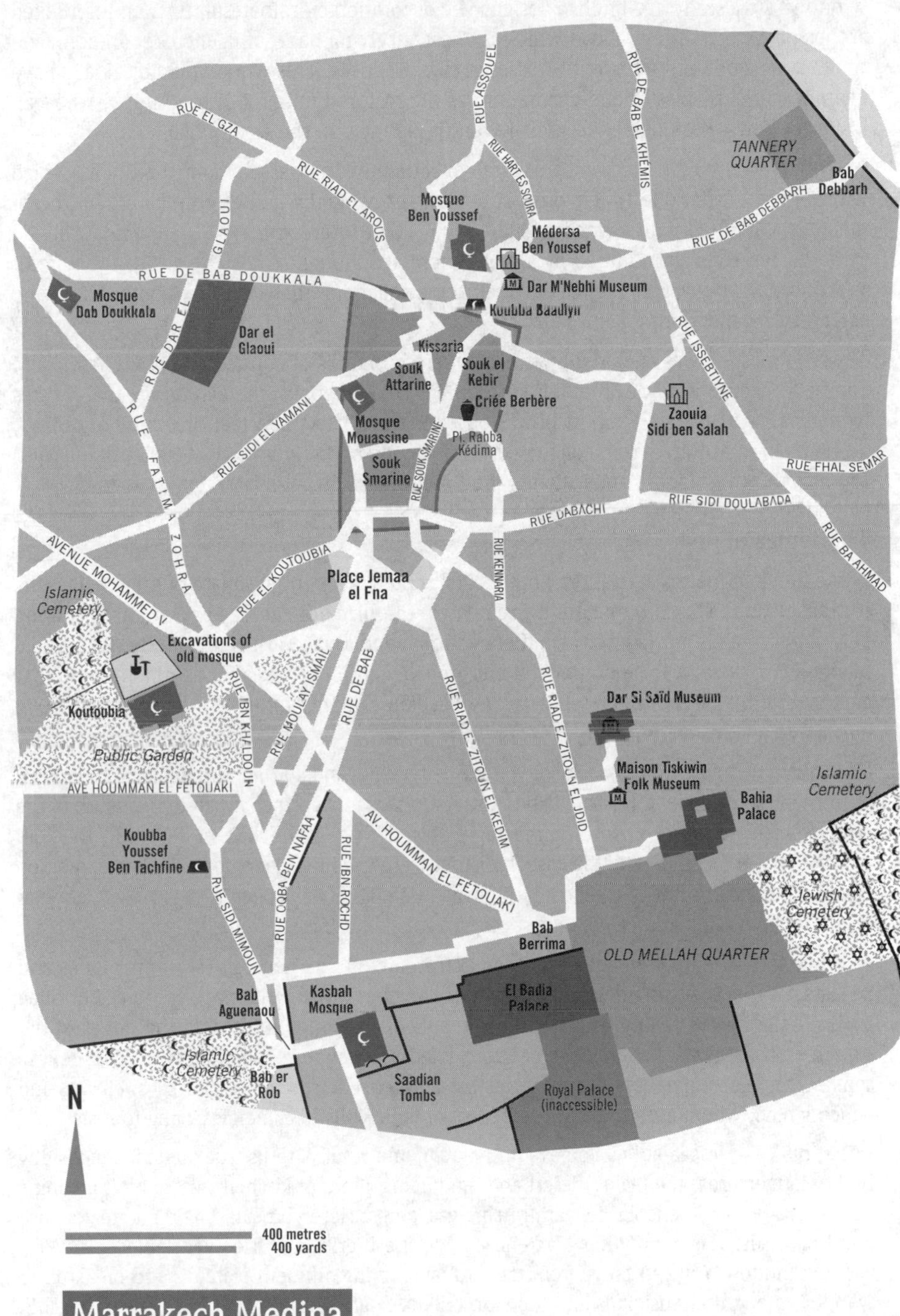
RUE EL GZA
RUE ASSOUEL
RUE DE BAB EL KHÉMIS
TANNERY QUARTER
Bab Debbarh
RUE DE BAB DEBBARH
RUE HART ES SOURA
RUE RIAD EL AROUS
GLAOUI
Mosque Ben Youssef
Médersa Ben Youssef
RUE DE BAB DOUKKALA
Mosque Bab Doukkala
RUE DAR EL
Dar el Glaoui
Dar M'Nebhi Museum
Koubba Baadiyn
Kissaria
Souk Attarine
Souk el Kebir
RUE ISSEBTIYNE
Zaouia Sidi ben Salah
Criée Berbère
Mosque Mouassine
RUE SIDI EL YAMANI
Pl. Rahba Kédima
RUE SOUK SMARINE
Souk Smarine
RUE FHAL SEMAR
RUE SIDI DOULABADA
RUE DABACHI
RUE FAT'MA ZOHRA
AVENUE MOHAMMED V
RUE EL KOUTOUBIA
Place Jemaa el Fna
RUE KENNARIA
RUE BA AHMAD
Islamic Cemetery
Excavations of old mosque
RUE IBN KHALDOUN
RUE MOULAY ISMAIL
RUE DE BAB
RUE RIAD EZ ZITOUN EL KEDIM
RUE RIAD EZ ZITOUN EL JDID
Dar Si Saïd Museum
Koutoubia
Public Garden
AVE HOUMMAN EL FETOUAKI
Maison Tiskiwin Folk Museum
Islamic Cemetery
Bahia Palace
Koubba Youssef Ben Tachfine
RUE OQBA BEN NAFAA
RUE IBN ROCHD
AV. HOUMMAN EL FÉTOUAKI
RUE SIDI MIMOUN
Jewish Cemetery
Bab Berrima
OLD MELLAH QUARTER
Bab Aguenaou
Kasbah Mosque
El Badia Palace
Islamic Cemetery
Bab er Rob
Saadian Tombs
Royal Palace (inaccessible)
N
400 metres
400 yards
Marrakech Medina

windows are a study in Almohad design. The decoration culminates in the rich interlinked arches of the top storey, above which is a last surviving band of faïence decoration. The rough stonework of the tower decreases in size as it rises. This work would originally have been obscured by plaster and decoration, as the restored minaret of the Almohad Kasbah Mosque shows. Fortunately no similar work is planned on the Koutoubia.

Above the tattered faïence band a decorative battlement frames the domed minaret, which was built in a strict one to five proportion to the tower, the golden rule for all Maghrebi minarets. On the summit a wooden gallows flies a blue or green prayer flag on Friday, beside three golden balls surmounted by a tear. These are thought to be the gift of the wife of Yaacoub el Mansour, who melted down all her jewellery for the globes in penance for having eaten three grapes during Ramadan.

The new mosque was enclosed by streets where hundreds of copyists, scribes, binders and booksellers kept stalls. It is from this surrounding souk of books, the *kutubiyyin*, that it takes its name. For its inauguration in 1158 Abdel Moumen had a spectacular trophy to display, for he had just acquired from conquered Córdoba one of the four original copies of the third Caliph Othman's official compilation of the Koran. From these all later texts descend.

The Jemaa el Fna

Three hundred metres east of the Koutoubia lies the great central square of the medina, the **Jemaa el Fna**. This is popularly translated as 'the place of the dead', a suitably chilling phrase which adds a mysterious whiff of exoticism and savage justice to an otherwise undeniably lively place. A less entertaining but probably correct translation is 'the mosque that came to nothing'—a sly reference to the Saadian Sultan Ahmed el Mansour's abortive attempt to build a mosque here.

The square has always been at the centre of medina life, and started as the formal *méchouar* in front of the Almoravid Kasbah. When the Almohads moved the kasbah to the south of the city, official processions were increasingly staged there—the Bab er Rob and the Bab Aguenaou at the entrance to the kasbah district were used for executions and the exhibition of the salted heads. But in essence the Jemaa el Fna has always been as it is now, a popular forum for entertainment, celebration, riots, gossip and business.

At dawn it is an empty wedge of tarmac, surrounded by parked cars, shuttered cafés and bazaars, an area of no architectural interest. As the morning progresses a perimeter is formed by lines of barrows selling nuts and freshly squeezed orange juice, and the edges of the square erupt in a sea of shops. The centre is filled by a random and changing assortment of snake-charmers, storytellers, acrobats, dentists, water-sellers, scribes, monkeys, clowns and dancing boys, who during the day direct most of their skills to camera-carrying tourists.

But at dusk the Jemaa el Fna comes into its own, and returns to its true audience of visiting Berber farmers from the plains, desert and mountains. Lines of kitchens set up their groaning tables, braziers and benches beneath hissing gas lamps. Here you can dine on a great assortment of salads, vats of brewing goat's-head soup, fresh grilled or fried vegetables, chickens, fish and mutton. You can move from table to table trying different platefuls and break off to wander among the musicians and the storytellers. Sharp young street kids hiss 'Hashish!', veiled women offer trinkets, or sit beckoning by their stock of woven baskets and woolly hats. Blind beggars cry 'Allah!' as they extend a bowl or fix you with one accusing, rheumy eye. Innocent looking children with beguiling almond eyes solicit, or try rather clumsily to pick your pockets. From worn tarot cards, the waddle of sacred doves, ink dots, cast bones or your palm, incidents from a possible future will be divined by hunched figures perched on low stools, surrounded by the instruments of their trade. As the evening progresses the crowds thin, the kitchens close, and small knots of musicians are left, surrounded by a crouching audience furtively smoking from their pipes.

This is the time to seek out powerful music influenced by the spiritual brotherhoods: the Aïssoua, Derkaoua, Hamadasha and Gnaoua, freed from the irrelevancies of a tourist audience. The repetitive, rhythmical music produced on drums, flutes, crude violins and *guenbris* (long, few-stringed guitars), is far removed from light entertainment. Shuffling dancers are animated by a spirit that plays upon piety and continence at one moment and sends lewd, erotic displays in the next breath.

The Jemaa el Fna is a rich but undeniably exhausting carnival. It encapsulates much of the fascination of Morocco: the difference, colour and energy of its alien culture, compounded by a rarely diminished sensation of being a stranger on the edge of any understanding. If you haven't found a nearby hotel bedroom, there are a number of cafés that surround the place where you can rest and watch in comparative serenity, and stock up on loose change.

The Medina Souk

Beyond the northern edge of the Jemaa el Fna stretches the great souk of Marrakech. It is a triumphant, labyrinthine marketplace, a glittering display of all the traditional arts and regional crafts of Morocco, grouped together by trade in separate but interlinked streets and courtyards. Compared with the woodcarvers' areas in Essaouira or the souks of Fès it has relatively few workshops, though there are turners, carpenters, weavers and tailors to be found.

The souk is not best appreciated at the tail-end of a bemusing and exhausting tour. It should be dipped into; chosen areas gently explored and discovered at different hours of the day. The traditional trading period is in the morning, but the hours before dusk are the busiest for traffic, both human and motorized, when the souk becomes so packed that the crowds of people seem to sway and move in unison.

For your first visit employ a guide to show you the main streets and features. Then, armed with a little knowledge of the street pattern, you can afford to explore—the earlier in the morning the better.

Rue Souk Smarine

Along the northern edge of the Jemaa el Fna a range of bazaars and the Ouessabine Mosque hide the main, arched entrance to the principal street, the Rue Souk Smarine. Here, before entering the souk proper, you can find a pottery and a spice market. The whole area is often obscured by shifting displays of clothing laid out on canvas. These pavement vendors are constantly on the look-out for police; they operate against an echoing soundtrack of bird whistles and hustling calls.

Rue Souk Smarine is, however, easy enough to identify. It is broad, well paved and shaded from the sun by a high trellis cover. Commercially, it is dominated by the cloth merchants, whose shelves groan under the weight of hundreds of bolts of bright silks and embroidered cloth for kaftans. Interspersed amongst the cloth merchants are tailors, who have been joined by a number of upmarket bazaars with halls stacked full of carpets half-hidden behind gleaming gates of brass, and who accept all manner of credit cards.

Rahba Kédima

About 150m along Rue Souk Smarine two right turns lead into the Rahba Kédima, the old corn market. Until the 19th century, it was forbidden to export grain, as it was considered immoral to profit by feeding Christians to the discomfort of poor Muslims. This open courtyard usually has a few vegetable stalls at its far end, but is dominated by spice and jewellery stalls. The latter are hung with amber necklaces which are often synthetic. The strange hanging curtains of dried eagles, mountain foxes, hedgehogs, snakes, porcupines, lizards and unnamed grim relics in pots are real enough, however. These ingredients are used in the concoction of love potions, stimulants and aphrodisiacs—a balancing form of female magic which helps to correct the many male-dominated features of Moroccan life. The trinity of Maghrebi cosmetics are very prominently displayed: silvery blocks of antimony which are ground into kohl—a powder which both outlines the eyelids and stimulates an attractive watery sheen that protects eyes from soot and dust; henna in all its variety—green leaves, powder or ready-made pastes for dying hair, and for the intricate decorative tattooing of hands, face and feet which you may have noticed; and pottery saucers of cochineal, which is used as a rouge. Also look out for sacks of dried Dadès roses, a deliciously fragrant and cheap pot pourri.

On the right as you enter the Rahba Kédima is the **Souk Larzal**, where wool is auctioned in the morning to spinners and dyers. Next on the right is the pungent **Souk Btana** of the leather trade, where raw sheep- and goat-skins are sorted, dried on the rooftops and sold to the tannery guilds.

La Criée Berbère

Halfway along the north side of the Rahba Kédima an entrance leads to the narrow Criée Berbère, a tight, enclosed space lined with displays of kilims, kilim cushions, kilim waistcoats, carpets and woollen burnouses. Most trading here is done from the shops, but auctions of goods are often held in the morning and evening. Moroccan auctions are distinctive affairs: the sellers walk around with odd composite bundles of stock, shouting the current price in the hope of attracting a larger one. Nothing seems to get sold very quickly.

This auction square was used before 1912 for the sale of slaves, at dusk on Wednesdays, Thursdays and Fridays. These auctions were only for the disposal of stock at the lower end of the domestic market, as influential clients would expect private and advance viewing. Galla women were considered the most attractive but girls of the Hausa country fetched the best prices as they were considered more cheerful and neater. In the 1840s about 4000 slaves were sold in Morocco each year, but by 1870 there was such a glut that prices dropped below $3. Even before then the common rate was two slaves for a camel and 10 for a horse.

A left turn from here leads you past a selection of turtleshell bellows to the main street, or you can retrace your steps to Rue Souk Smarine.

The Kissaria

Just past the Rahba Kédima turning Rue Souk Smarine splits into the **Souk el Kebir** (on the right) and the **Souk Attarin** (to the left). The Souk el Kebir passes a jewellers' alley on the right, before the alleys of the Kissaria open up on your left. The Kissaria is traditionally the heart of a souk, and in Marrakech specializes in clothes, with stalls selling modern western clothes, traditional cotton *gandoras*, woven blankets and arrays of western-influenced open-necked kaftans for women. Further along Souk el Kebir are the aromatic stalls and small courtyards of the carpenters and wood-turners who make wooden screens and book holders. On the right hand side, after an arch labelled Souk des Sacochiers, a skilled craftsman makes elaborate embroidered saddles and all the trappings of an Arab cavalier. Almost opposite at 127 Souk Chkaria, craftsmen will Morocco-bind a favourite book for you, although covers for video cassettes are more in demand.

If you bear left at the far end of the souk, you will find yourself in **Souk Cherratin**, a collection of alleys with a few leather, wood and metal craft stalls. This will lead you round to the left into the long **Souk des Babouches**, a delightful street of tightly packed stalls selling yellow, grey and white slippers and the more exotic gilded velvet. The Kissaria alleys are now on your left. At the end of the slipper souk, a right turn takes you west towards the famous **Souk des Teinturiers**, the alley used by the dyers. Here, cascades of brightly dyed wool dry from the terrace above, a memorable and striking sight. To the right of this alley is the coppersmiths' souk, more carpenters, a courtyard used for selling olive oil and beyond that the **Souk Haddadine**, the blacksmith's souk, which is surrounded by charcoal-sellers.

Returning back to the Souk des Teinturiers you pass a shop selling unpressed felt hats and genuine fezzes before reaching the **Mouassine Fountain** on your left. A left turn past the Mouassine Mosque takes you down the wider and uncomplicated Rue Mouassine, lined with cloth, carpet and tourist bazaars, which brings you back to the Jemaa el Fna.

Ben Youssef Medersa, Koubba Ba'Adiyn & Dar M'Nebhi

There are three monuments open to non-Muslims in the medina: the Saadian Ben Youssef Medersa, the Almoravid Koubba Ba'Adiyn (also spelt el Baroudiyn) and the recently-opened private Museum housed in the 19th-century Dar M'Nebhi palace. The Medersa and the

Koubba are two of the finest buildings in Marrakech, some would say in all Morocco, and no visit, however short, should exclude these architectural treasures. They are relatively easy to find as they are both associated with the Ben Youssef Mosque, just to the north of the souk.

From the Jemaa el Fna head up the main souk artery, the Rue Souk Smarine/Souk el Kebir for 450m, turn left at the far Y-junction and then right under an arch and left again along a broader street to reach an open square, the Place Ben Youssef. This is usually occupied by at least one football game, while the mosque walls are draped with long, spinning strands of tailors' silk. The entrance to the koubba is behind the wall on your left, the museum is on the right, and the medersa down the alley to the right of the mosque.

The Ben Youssef Mosque

Above the square rises the green-tiled roof and minaret of the Ben Youssef Mosque. A mosque was first built here by the Almoravid Sultan Ali ben Youssef in the 12th century, as the central mosque of the medina. It was then twice as large as the present building. The Saadian Sultan Abdullah el Ghalib attempted to make Ben Youssef the most popular and esteemed mosque in Marrakech. By this time it was in ruins, and he had to rebuild it entirely, along with the neighbouring medersa, and to cap his work he presented it with a large library. The mosque, however, did not survive the well-intentioned improvements of his successors. What you now see dates entirely from the early 19th century, when an ancient and beautifully carved Almoravid fountain was also destroyed.

The Koubba Ba'Adiyn (Kobbat El Mourabitine, Kobba El Baroudiyine)

When this building was rediscovered in its sunken position in 1948, French art historian Gaston Deverdun exclaimed that 'the art of Islam has never exceeded the splendour of this extraordinary dome'. The koubba is all that remains to hint at the glory of 12th-century Almoravid Marrakech. It is a small pavilion covering a shallow ritual washing pool in the outer courtyard of the mosque, and is still surrounded by brick cisterns and latrines that once enclosed it in the centre of a courtyard. However, it introduces many of the shapes that become so familiar in later Islamic architecture.

The plan itself is simple enough: a rectangular two-storey domed structure pierced by arches. At ground level a pair of scalloped arches face each other; there are twin horseshoe arches on the longer sides. These silhouettes are repeated in the rows of three and five inset window arches on the upper storey, where scallop and horseshoe have been joined by an impaled turban motif. A decorative battlement frames the dome, which is decorated with a band of interlocking arches and surmounted by a series of diminishing seven-pointed stars.

Standing inside you look up into a dome of astonishingly bold, confident, solid yet supremely elegant and disciplined carving. The remains of a Kufic frieze announcing its creator, Ali ben Youssef, can just be made out. Above this rests an octagonal arched dome, its interlaced scallop arches infilled with rich foliate carving upon which hang shell-shaped palmettes. The corner squinches are framed by *muqurnas*, elegant spanning arches that in later centuries degenerated to appear like dripping stalagmites. The *muqurnas* ring a seven-pointed star that frames an eight-podded dome, which in turn echoes the triumphant, deep carving of the central cupola.

Both the exterior and interior carvings play with the strong African sun to create pools of dark shadow and contrasting patches of light. It shows up well the confident architectural origins of the Spanish Moorish style. The gradual debasement of this style into a mere veneer of decoration can be seen progressively at the medersa, the Saadian Tombs, the Dar M'Nebhi, and finally in the modern hotels of Marrakech.

The Dar M'Nebhi (Musée Privé de Marrakech)

Open daily except holidays 9am–12.30pm, 3–6.30pm; adm; © (04) 390911.

This opulent turn-of-the-century palace has recently been converted into a museum owned by a charitable foundation, supported by an American-style Association of (rich) Friends. Its exhibits are mainly items on loan from state museums or rarely-seen pieces drawn from Moroccan private collections.

The Fortunes of the Menehbi

The M'Nebhi (Menebha) family no longer possess either of the great palaces in Fès and Marrakech that bear their name. They are descended from a clan from among the Arab nomad tribes that held a privileged military position, and were settled by the Alaouite Sultans on the good grazing ground between Marrakech and Essaouira. The family rose to a great position at the turn of the century, when one of the most promising young cavalry officers in Sultan Moulay Hassan's army, El Mehdi bel Arbi El Menebhi. rose to become Minister for War to the boy Sultan Abdul Aziz. As was customary, this Menehbi made a great fortune from his position and elevated his least talented nephews and sons to various official positions. After Moulay Hafid replaced his brother on the throne M"nebhi arranged for his transfer to Tangier, where he served as the *Mendoub*, the Sultan's representative. His charm, erudition, bubbly wit and hospitality endeared him to the foreign community and especially to the British, who showered him with honours including a knighthood while he attended the coronations of three kings at Westminster Abbey. Even as an old man, seated on a comely mule, he was delighted to escort his guests out to picnics and pig-sticking parties in the woods around Tangier. On one such expedition, when things were on the point of getting ugly, the old minister plucked a lance from a neighbour and deftly swivelled in his saddle to transfix the maddened boar so that nine inches of spear protruded on the farther side.The startled onlookers were left wondering what he had been like in his prime.

The heart of the museum is the enormous internal courtyard, in which three marble fountains play beneath the subdued light that filters through the modern steel and stretched canvas roof. Exhibits on show in the rooms alongside include two vast plates, one imported from Andalusia, the other from the Saharan oasis of Tafilalt; a circumcision kaftan; an 18th-century painted dowry coffer from the Rif; a sumptuous red velvet- and gold-embroidered Jewish wedding dress, and Lucine Vola's collection of textiles. The latter includes two fine Glaoua *hanbels*, but is richest in Beni Yacoub and Aït Ouaouzguite work. These two tribal regions on the southern slopes of the High Atlas have specialized in producing restrained bands of brightly coloured embroidery on cream white woolen *haiks*, though the work currently on sale in the south has long since fallen from these high standards.

In a secondary courtyard there is a small collection of modern Moroccan art, of much greater interest than the orientalist imagery culled from French and British magazines that is also on show. There is a fine example of Hassan el Glaoui's work, with his view of a royal procession centred around the mounted figure of the Sultan with his crimson parasol. An artist of much greater influence is Farid Belkahia, who has looked to Saharan-derived imagery and traditional designs painted on leatherwork and drums for his parchment-like canvases. Another key figure, Fatima Hassani, is also represented here. Her poster-bright colours (taken from traditional embroidery), henna-like decorative details and her concentration on depicting, and glorifying, feminine-dominated spaces have touched upon a rich new artistic vein. Other pictures include Jacques Azema's disturbingly iconic view of three boys in a *hammam*, Ben Haim's powerful portrait of a lady in red and yellow, and Mohammed Ben Allal's picture of a basket-weaver at dusk

The palace's toilets are also a wonderful feature, and on your way out (passing some press photographs of the great and the good at the royal opening) look out for two large pale green tiles with a central rivetment hole. These 11th-century tiles were once fixed to wooden batons at the summit of the Koutoubia minaret, and so are among the oldest known examples of Morocco's long tradition of *zellij* tiling. Their celadon-like colouring and simplicity of form provide a tantalising insight into a lost world of colour. It is all too easy to see the Almoravids and Almohads in an austere stone-like monotone, in the same way that we mistakenly visualise the Normans and Romans.

Ben Youssef Medersa

Open Tue–Sun 8am–12pm, 2.30–6pm; closed Mon and Fri am; adm.

This was founded by the philanthropic Merenid Sultan Abou Hassan in the 14th century as part of an educational programme that established Koranic colleges in Fès, Taza, Salé, Meknès and Marrakech. In 1564 it was replaced by the Saadian Sultan Abdullah el Ghalib, who ordered the building of the largest medersa in Morocco, a feat which was completed in under a year. It was part of his ambition to make the Ben Youssef Mosque a rival intellectual centre to Fès. Dedicatory inscriptions to the sultan can be seen on the lintel of the entrance gate and along the prayer-hall.

You may have to knock at the inconspicuous door to the right of the covered arch to enter. A long twisting passage then leads to the entrance hall, a secretive Marrakechi feature not found in any Merenid medersa (they have proud portals and direct entrances). From the hall, stairs lead up to over a hundred plain wooden rooms where students lived, each sharing small courtyard skylights. This is another distinctive feature, for earlier medersas used windows overlooking the central courtyard to provide a central decorative theme.

The open **courtyard**, a great interior space of peace and silence, centres on a marble basin and is flanked by two galleries of solid pillars. Directly opposite is the entrance to the prayer hall. The richness of decorative detail never disturbs the graceful simplicity of the plan. An initial height of *zellij* mosaic is broken by two bands of tile and plaster carved with Koranic inscriptions, which lead up into the ornate plaster and cedar carving. The courtyard has a distinctive unhurried harmony, a grandeur touched with an element of severity not found in the more intimate Merenid medersas.

The **prayer-hall** is divided into three aisles by four marble columns, and a further four enhance the arched mihrab which carries the two traditional inscriptions of the Muslim declaration of faith.

Go upstairs to see the students' rooms arranged around internal lightwells, their sparse dignity enlivened by the elaborate details of the carved wood balconies and turned window frames. The students (known as *tolba*, or reciters) were allowed to lodge here for six years whilst they memorized the Koran and studied the commentaries and laws. In the summer they wandered through the country, begging, listening to marabouts and reciting their verses throughout the night at rural festivals.

A Walk Past the Lesser Monuments in the Northern Medina

North of the medersa stretches the great bulk of the medina, without souks, bazaars, guides or many tourists. Modern houses have for the most part replaced the pisé buildings, but the streets retain their labyrinthine design and you can wander freely through this living maze, catching glimpses of old *fondouqs*, mosques, *hammams* and bakeries. The route outlined here take you past the notable sights of the area, and will give you a feel for this less-explored section of the medina. You can, however, only look at the monuments in this area of the medina from the outside, unless you are a Muslim. It is a long walk: if you are short on time or energy, leave it for another visit.

Turn right from the Ben Youssef Medersa, and then left down a covered passage. As you re-emerge into daylight you face a crossroads where Rue Baroudienne joins Rue Amesfah. Both these streets are lined with a number of elegant 16th and 17th-century ***fondouqs***, which are still very much in use as craftmen's and tradesmen's courtyards. They are well worth a discreet look inside.

Turn right up Rue Assouel, passing several more *fondouqs*, the most elegant of which is beside the monumental decorated fountain on the left, the **Echrob ou Chouf**, which translates as 'drink and admire'. A left turn by the fountain, up Rue Diar Saboun, takes you into Rue de Bab Tarhzout, which is often half-filled by a souk of secondhand clothes.

In medieval times the **Bab Tarhzout** marked the northern edge of the city, but in the 18th century Sultan Sidi Mohammed extended the walls to include the zaouia suburb of Sidi Bel Abbès, one of the seven saints of Marrakech, within the city.

Zaouia of Sidi Bel Abbès

The direct approach to the shrine is through an arch lined with an expensive and elaborate arcade of jewellers. The zaouia, mosque and tombs are forbidden to non-Muslims, but by going to the left or the right of the main entrance you can get impressive views into the extensive complex and of the great pyramidal shrine.

The zaouia rose beside the grave of the Sidi in the cemetery of Sidi Marwan, which at that time was just to the north of the city walls. The existing buildings are the work of the 18th-century Alaouite Sultan Sidi Mohammed, who apart from extending the city walls and rebuilding the entire shrine complex added a further gift of a medersa courtyard with two flights of horseshoe arches.

Es-Sebti, the Seven Saints of Marrakech

Combinations of seven saints or seven sleepers reach back beyond Islam and Christianity to an older universal myth, and in Morocco Ceuta, Jbel Hadid, Fès and Marrakech all share in this common tradition. In the 18th century, Sultan Moulay Ismaïl removed various unorthodox Berber aspects of the annual celebration of Marrakech's *es-Sebti*, and at the same time he rebuilt the sanctuaries of the historical, orthodox saints. A new week-long *moussem* was established, which began at the shrine of Sidi Lyad, moved on to Sidi Youssef ben Ali, Sidi Abd el Aziz, Sidi el-Ghawzani, Sidi es Suhayi and Sidi ben Slimane al Jazuli before culminating at the major shrine of the city, that of Sidi Bel Abbès.

Sidi Bel Abbès, 1130–1205, was born in Ceuta but moved south to establish a hermitage outside Marrakech. His learning, moral sermons, miracles and ascetic lifestyle gained him a widespread popular following. The Almohad Sultan Yaacoub el Mansour invited him into the city and presented him with buildings and funds to carry on his good works. Centred on his shrine, these continue today: city merchants support the zaouia in running a number of schools and hostels, and in feeding the blind each evening. A number of potent legends still circulate in the city—that Christians venerate Sidi Bel Abbès as St Augustine, for instance, and that he haunts the minaret of the Koutoubia each night until he is certain that all the blind have been fed.

The Zaouia of Sidi ben Slimane al Jazuli

Turning back through Bab Tarhzout, a right turn takes you past the covered Souk el Mjadlia and out below the Zaouia of Sidi ben Slimane al Jazuli, another of the seven patron saints of Marrakech. Its distinctive green pyramid roof and neighbouring mosque can be seen from alleys to the north and south of the zaouia, but the street beside it is closed to non-Muslims.

Sidi ben Slimane al Jazuli was one of the great Sufi mystics of Morocco, whose followers went on to found important religious institutions throughout the country. Al Jazuli's book, *The Manifest Proofs of Piety*, remains a seminal mystical text. As well as being famed as a spiritual teacher, he was a leading figure in the struggle against Portugal and his embalmed body would became a powerful totem in the *jihad*. Buried at Afugal in Haha province for a few decades, his body was brought to Marrakech by the Saadians in 1523. Six Saadian princes were murdered shortly afterwards in a palace coup. They were buried together beneath a single koubba beside Al Jazuli's shrine, giving a further bizarre resonance to the legend of the seven.

Walk down to a dusty crossroads square below the zaouia. Ahead and to your right you will see the minaret of the Sidi Bou Ameur Mosque. Turn left when below the minaret to walk down Rue Dar el Glaoui.

The Dar el Glaoui

At the junction between Rue Dar el Glaoui and Rue de Bab Doukkala is the massive bulk of the Dar el Glaoui, the palace of Si Thami el Glaoui, Pacha of Marrakech, which was built in the early years of this century. Unfortunately, its magnificent interior remains firmly closed to visitors and is in use as a Trade Union headquarters.

Dar el Glaoui was a place of legendary hospitality which from the 1920s to 1950s entertained an international social élite including Roosevelt, Churchill and Patton. Beautiful Berber girls or boys, opium or marijuana, Lafitte or Latour were offered to guests with the freedom and nonchalance with which other Moroccan houses offer a glass of mint tea. Compliant European females could rely on a parting gift of emeralds, and society figures fought for the chance to have been the Pacha's friend for a night. But behind the pampering of sophisticated guests lay French 'loans', illicit taxes, bribery, blackmail and protection rackets, and it was common knowledge that the thousands of Marrakech prostitutes had the Pacha as their ultimate pimp.

Only hours after the Pacha's death in 1956 a crowd broke into the Dar el Glaoui. Such was their hatred for the Pacha, who had allied himself so closely to the French colonists, that they preferred to destroy rather than loot the palace and even the cars were smashed and set on fire. The mob then had their vengeance on the traitorous henchmen and officials of the Pacha, who were hunted through the streets of the medina. They were treated like the cars: beaten, stripped and then burnt alive on the rubbish dump outside the Bab Doukkala. It is said that King Mohammed V would not eat for seven days when he heard of this brutality, even though the men killed had been his bitterest enemies.

From the Dar el Glaoui you can walk due west along Rue de Bab Doukkala, which runs towards the gate of that name, to look at the **Bab Doukkala Mosque**, on your left. This was built in 1558 by Lalla Messaouda, daughter of a *caid* of Ouarzazate, wife of a sultan and a redoubtable mother. While in exile in Istanbul she educated her two sons, later to be the great Saadian sultans Abdel Malik and Ahmed el Mansour. All that can be seen by non-Muslims is the slender elegant minaret to the northeast of the mosque and the elegant **Sidi el Hassan Fountain**, named after one of the founding professors of the medersa that used to be attached to the mosque.

Returning back to the Dar el Glaoui, walk east for 300m until you reach the prominent crossroads with Rue Mouassine. Just up the street to the left is the **mosque and shrine of Sidi Abdel Aziz**, another Sufi follower of the teachings of Al Jazuli, who died at Marrakech in 1508 and has entered the pantheon of the seven saints. While on this crossroads look out for the gates to half a dozen *fondouqs*, some of which may be open. Try 192 or 149 Rue Mouassin, which will reveal courtyards surrounded by galleries supported by high simple pillars and graceful cedar beams.

The Mouassine Mosque

South from the crossroads, 150m down Rue Mouassine, is the Mouassine Mosque, a monumental building established by the Saadian Sultan Abdullah el Ghalib in 1560, complete with baths, medersa and exterior fountain. The mosque has an equivocal local reputation. It is named after a prestigious local *shorfa* family, but during the building of the foundations a 14th-century Jewish plague cemetery was unearthed. This is considered to have reduced the sanctity of the site, and rumours of a curse released in disturbing the grave of a cabbalistic rabbi began to circulate. The mosque is largely hidden from non-Muslims by the surrounding buildings, and unfortunately the gates and stumpy minaret give little indication of the reported magnificence inside.

The impressive triple-bayed **Mouassine Fountain** with its ornate portico is in a small square to the left of the mosque. In the far corner of the square, beside a large vine growing up the wall, is the door to the secretive **Café Maur Abouid**. Built over a bridge, it has a wonderful view from its sunbaked roof. Glimpses of tranquil courtyards and hidden koubbas show how much of the city remains hidden, even here in the heart of the medina. The café is draped with vines and cats, and dotted with an assortment of aged benches and photographs.

Walking beneath this bridge you enter the Kissaria at the heart of the souk, but by continuing down the bazaar-lined Rue Mouassine you resurface at the western corner of the Jemaa el Fna.

Monuments of Imperial Marrakech—South of Jemaa el Fna

The Marrakech of the sultans has grown up since the 12th century in what is now the southern area of the medina. Here, the Almohads first established their kasbah, palaces, barracks and a royal mosque. Successor dynasties continued to develop the southern district into an imperial city, but in a typically Moroccan way paid scant regard to the achievements of their predecessors. The Royal Palace of King Hassan II—not open to the public—therefore stands on ground that has seen a dazzling succession of pavilions, courts and gardens.

The glories of imperial Marrakech include the massive and very impressive ruins of the 16th-century Saadian El Badia Palace, which contrast perfectly in their state of decay with the Saadian Tombs, which have survived completely intact from the same period. Apart from exploring two 19th-century viziers' palaces, the Bahia and the Dar Si Saïd, you can also lose yourself in the dark alleys of Marrakech's ancient Jewish quarter, the *mellah*.

To get to imperial Marrakech from the Jemaa el Fna, walk south down the café-lined Rue de Bab Aguenaou to a crossroads dominated by the Tazi Hotel. To your right is the Place Youssef ben Tachfine. This Almoravid sultan's original tomb was destroyed by the Almohads, but Youssef's cult revived and this traditional Berber holy place was consecrated to his memory by the Merenids in the 14th century. The symbolic tomb in the **koubba** is left open to the sky, the only dome that the spirit of this desert warrior will accept.

Returning to the Tazi Hotel, a walk down Rue Oqba ben Nafaa takes you 600m south. The intermittent wall on your left is not an old city wall but marks out the inner city, the kasbah quarter of sultans, the imperial city.

Bab Aguenaou

The official entrance into the kasbah lay through the Bab Aguenaou. You will find this distinctive carved gate on the left at the end of Rue Oqba ben Nafaa just before the outer Bab er Rob, where a potters' souk, taxis and local buses collect. Aguenaou is a Berber word that translates as 'the mute ram without horns'. A less prosaic but more logical translation names it the Guinea Gate—the southern gate leading to black Africa, the homeland of the sultans' guards. It was built on Sultan Yaacoub el Mansour's orders in 1185, and has added prestige as one of the few stone structures in this city of pink pisé. It is carved from local 'blue' Guéliz stone which is still being quarried to the north of Marrakech. The semi-circular frieze has been delicately cut but is surprisingly assertive and strong.

The Kasbah Mosque

Passing through this gate you approach the Kasbah Mosque. It was finished in 1190 by Sultan Yaacoub el Mansour. The long white exterior wall is capped with decorative battlements and for once left free of encrusted buildings to give an indication of its impressive extent. Neither the wall nor the recently restored but well proportioned minaret on the northwest corner, however, give much indication of its age.

The Merenids added a famous medersa to the Almohad mosque, but this was destroyed in a gunpowder explosion in 1569. The Saadian Sultan Abdullah el Ghalib restored the damaged mosque, which has been touched up every two hundred years since, by Sidi Mohammed in the 18th century and recently by Hassan II. For a Muslim the principal approach is through the great domed north gate which looks across the extensive open sahn court to the domed mihrab flanked by four Omayyad columns of jasper. Beside the mihrab a door leads to the enclosed garden courtyard of the 16th-century royal necropolis—the Saadian Tombs.

The Saadian Tombs

Open daily 8am–12pm, 2–6pm; adm, visits are often in the company of a portly guide, tips accepted.

The tombs are one of the most visited sites in Morocco, so in order to recapture some sense of serenity and isolation try to avoid the coach tours—go either early in the morning or in late afternoon. A tight, thin passage to the south of the mosque was cut through the protective Saadian walls in 1917 for the use of non-Muslims. Coming through it you enter an ancient rectangular enclosed garden, planted with trees, cascading shrubs and rosemary hedges. This is the ancient cemetery of the *shorfa*, the descendants of the prophet, which had been in use for centuries before any Saadians arrived in Marrakech. The identity of most of the open-air mosaic graves is lost but a Merenid sultan, Abou Hassan, was buried here in 1351, to be followed by the first Saadian sultan, Mohammed ech Cheikh, in 1557, in a tomb covered by a simple koubba. The existing koubbas were all built by Mohammed ech Cheikh's third ruling son, Ahmed el Mansour, in two stages. First he built a pavilion around his father's simple tomb, where he also buried his mother, Lalla Messaouda, in 1591. Later he built the hall of twelve columns to be his own mausoleum, and attached to it a prayer hall. The extraordinary interiors of both koubbas can be examined from their thresholds.

The prayer-hall is the first hall on your left as you enter; it extends south of Ahmed el Mansour's tomb. Four clean pillars support elegant high horseshoe arches which, with the skylight, divide the roof space into eight rectangles. The decorated mihrab niche can be seen to your left. Although it has the most pleasing dark, simple sepulchral quality of them all, this was never intended as a tomb. It contains, however, a plethora of them, mostly the resting places of Alaouite princes from the 18th century. There is a sad little nest just to the left of the mihrab where half a dozen plague victims, the children of Sultan Sidi Mohammed, were buried between 1756–77. The large tomb to the right, surrounded by a wooden balustrade, is one of the many tombs that are claimed to be that of the Black Sultan, the Merenid Abou Hassan. He is also thought to be buried in the hall of three niches, at the back of the Saadian Tombs, and at the Chellah in Rabat.

The Hall of Twelve Columns is the central mausoleum of Ahmed el Mansour. The three central tombs are surrounded by a colonnade of twelve decorated marble pillars. The upper plasterwork is so intensely carved as to appear like gilded lace. The dome is even more fantastically rich, and prolonged inspection induces an almost physical sense of nausea. Decoration has overwhelmed form to produce a heady mystery, a pointillist scattering of reflected gilded light and depth that verges on a spiritual unworldliness. It is with relief that you concentrate on the layer of white script interwoven with black flowers, the lower area of *zellij* mosaic and the clean sober tombs at ground level. The central tomb is of course that of Ahmed el Mansour, who died in 1603. To his right is his son and successor Zaidan, who died in 1628, and to his left that of his grandson Mohammed ech Cheikh II, who died in 1655. There are 33 other tombs of Saadian princelings, although only 15 are identifiable by their inscriptions. Immediately behind the tomb of Ahmed el Mansour is an inscription commemorating his father.

Through this magnificence a small darkened room can be glimpsed to the right, known as the **Hall of Three Niches**. An inscription in the middle niche commemorates Ahmed el Mansour's elder half-brother, the great building sultan of Marrakech, Abdullah el Ghalib. The large tomb at the back is the aforementioned alternative tomb of the Black Sultan, Abou Hassan, who died an exile in the High Atlas in 1351.

Crossing over unidentified *shorfa* tombs, the passage that leads into the Kasbah Mosque is on the left. This used to be covered by another dome but now the three sheiks' tombs are left open to the elements.

Ahmed el Mansour enclosed an original koubba with an outer decorative shell and in the process created an extra hall, the **Second Koubba**, which is overlooked by two ornate loggias. The loggias' slim white marble pillars bear a lintel of carved cedar that supports the green tiled roof. The inner koubba is decorated with stalactites and contains four tombs. Ahmed el Mansour's mother, Lalla Messaouda, is buried in a niche next to the wall on the right, beneath a commemorative inscription. The tomb to her left is that of the Sultan Abdullah el Ghalib, to his left that of Sultan Mohammed ech Cheikh, who died in 1557. The final tomb is that of the mad Alaouite Sultan Moulay el Yazid, who reigned for three years before his death in 1792. The main hall, where a number of Saadian and a few 18th-century Alaouite princes are buried, is refreshingly clear of decoration other than the tranquil patterns of *zellij* mosaic.

To find the El Badia Palace from the Saadian Tombs, return to Bab Aguenaou, turn right and retrace your route back up Rue Oqba ben Nafaa for about 150m and then turn right again onto Av Houmman el Fétouaki. After about 600m you will arrive in the dusty square known as the **Souk du Mellah**, where oranges, fruits and olives are often sold. From the Souk du Mellah pass through one of two gates to the right into the Place des Ferblantiers, a large rectangular *fondouq* where metalworkers can be seen at work. Among other unusual processes, strips of unused Safi canning metal are cut to make intricate brass lanterns. Passing through the southern gate, the Bab Berrima, you enter a double-walled space familiar to anyone who has tramped the imperial city of Meknès. The outer wall divides the imperial kasbah district from the civil medina; the massive wall further south, decorated by storks' nests, encloses the El Badia Palace.

El Badia, the Incomparable

Open daily except holidays 9am–12 noon, 2.30–6.30pm; adm.

The palace was started in 1578, five months after the Battle of the Three Kings put enormous wealth from Portuguese ransoms and captured booty into the hands of Ahmed el Mansour, 'the victorious'. Efficient management of the Sous sugar trade and the capture of Timbuktu in 1598 added to this wealth, and el Mansour became known by the honorific *el Dehbi*, 'the golden'. He employed the finest craftsmen in the world, and Montaigne, on his travels in Italy, saw sculptors carving marble pillars of extreme height and delicacy for the palace.

Entering the palace, now in ruins, through a series of crumbling walls, you find yourself in a massive empty rectangular courtyard. It is crossed by a rigid grid of paths which lead to a central pool, 90m long with an island, and flank four sunken gardens. The paths were actually raised to allow room for a great vaulted underground water system. The four sunken gardens would have been planted with sweet-smelling flowers: roses, violets, jasmine, acacia and hollyhocks, and with orange trees and tall cypresses, palms and olives for shade. A Moorish garden drew its chief glory from the arrangements of trees and running water, and flowers were almost entirely prized for their scent.

In the centre of each of the four massive walls pavilions were built, flanked by smaller pools and fountains. The largest of these was known as **Koubba el Hamsiniya**, the pavilion of fifty pillars. Opposite it stood the crystal pavilion, to the north was the green hall and to the south 'the Hayzouran', named after the sultan's favourite wife, who was black.

In his book *Black Sultan*, Wilfrid Blunt describes

> *walls and ceilings encrusted with gold from Timbuktu . . . gaily decorated boats to entertain the King and his guests in the cooler hours of the evening . . . . Its vast halls were filled with fountains, and in looking-glass ceilings far overhead the fish appeared to swim, reflected from the cool waters of marble basins. There was a domed hall where golden stars set on a blue ground gave the appearance of the heavens themselves. Long fish ponds between the alleys ended in grottoes and arbours.*

In the southeastern corner of the courtyard, a gate now leads to a smaller series of yards and cellars. In the shadow of the present royal palace, this is an intriguing area where you can see the slave pens, old potteries and baking ovens. These ruins only constitute the ceremonial court of the palace however; el Mansour's private apartments for himself, four wives, dozens of concubines, children and ministers extended to the south and west.

El Badia, an almost impious borrowing of one of the 99 names of God, was finished in 1603 only a few months before the death of its creator. Descriptions of the celebratory feasts and inaugural gifts are of almost unsurpassable splendour. During a lull in one of the festivals, the ageing sultan asked his fool for a compliment on the palace, to which was returned the famous reply that 'it would make a fine ruin'. Before the century was out, in 1696, Moulay Ismaïl fulfilled this prophecy by stripping the palace bare in order to embellish Meknès, a process that took twelve years.

The *Mellah*

From the Bab Berrima, Rue Berrima runs east of the El Badia outer walls, past intriguing dark entrances, into the heart of the *mellah.* You eventually emerge, after 600m, in a *méchouar* outside the present royal palace, where the walls and guards are distinctly off-putting.

Some hundred years after it occurred in most of the other cities of Morocco, the Jews of Marrakech were moved into a *mellah* in 1558 on the orders of the Saadian Sultan Abdullah el Ghalib. The sultan created a secure quarter for them beside the royal palace, protected by walls and entered through only two gates. They were a talented community of traders, metalsmiths, bankers and linguists, a useful and valuable asset for the sultans, who have seldom shared the anti-Jewish feelings of their subjects. The community was governed by an *ulema,* a council of rabbis, ruled by a separate *caid,* and maintained its own cemetery, gardens, souks and fountains.

For some time the Jews prospered as middlemen between Moroccan Muslims and Christian merchants, but were recurrently accused by the populace of spying whenever there was a war. This antagonism grew with the strength of Portugal in the 15th and 16th centuries. Where learned rabbis had once been invited to lecture in mosques, it became accepted practice that if a Jew strayed into a mosque he was given the choice of immediate conversion or being burnt alive. They had to remove their hats and shoes when walking past a mosque, and in a royal city were forbidden to wear any shoes at all outside their own quarter.

But within the *mellah* walls the community grew into one of the most populous and over-crowded in Morocco. Before 1936 there were 16,000 Jews living here, but with the foundation of Israel in 1948 and the Suez crisis in 1956 the community disintegrated, either moving to more tolerant Casablanca or emigrating.

Only a handful of Jews are left here, but the distinctive tall, cramped houses cut by low but regular narrow streets remain. Within the quarter, mostly to the north, the traditional Jewish specialist trades of jewellery, textiles and tailoring remain. At the centre of the quarter is the small **Place Souweka**, with its fountain. If you are interested in visiting the **old synagogues** which have now been converted into houses and shops, you should find a young guide here or ask advice from the Jewish–American hostel in the *mellah.* On the eastern edge of the *mellah* is an extensive Jewish cemetery separated from the larger Muslim one by the city's outer wall. Until recently it was a wilderness of shrubs and mating dogs, but now it is kept secure and the tombs are frequently whitewashed.

The Bahia Palace

Open officially daily 8.30am–12 noon, 2.30–6pm; adm; in practice often closed.

From the Place des Ferblantiers, which stands just before the El Badia Palace, the Avenue Houmman el Fétouaki heads north and then east to the long garden entrance of the palace ahead. If you manage to get into the palace, you will find it a perfect contrast to the vast sunbaked simplicity of El Badia. The Bahia, 'the brilliant', contains a series of paved court-yards, dark interior reception halls and Andalusian gardens, built by two generations of 19th-century grand viziers.

Si Mousa was vizier to Sultan Sidi Mohammed ben Abderahmane (1859–73), and his son, Ba Ahmed, served Sultan Moulay Hassan and became the powerful regent of the child-sultan Abdul Aziz. Their choice of architecture was highly traditional, and as father and son gradually amassed over eight hectares of the city they created a maze of passages, connecting doors, courtyards, gardens and pavilions. However, fortunes created by a sultan's officials always return to their master eventually. Ba Ahmed was exceptional in having been able to enjoy his father's inheritance and his own wealth until the hour of his death, for a provincial *caid* or pacha in Morocco could expect to be squeezed of his ill-gotten gains any time after just a decade in office. Not until Ba Ahmed lay dying did the sultan's guards quietly replace the viziers at the doors of the Bahia palace. Before the corpse had grown cold, they had stripped the palace of all portable possessions, and a few days later nothing remained but the great empty building as it is seen today.

The oriental complexity of plan, the locked side doors, beckoning passages and the ghosts of French and Moroccan courtiers (it was lived in by the resident-generals after 1912 and is still used on occasions by the Royal Family) give it an undeniable charm. The guided tour will take you through a dazzling series of reception halls with their great panelled Moorish ceilings of carved, painted and gilded wood. It is, though, the low empty range of the extensive concubines' courtyard, the garden courtyard and the courtyard of the four official wives that provide some of the most powerful, enduring and melancholic images of this palace. It is impossible not to feel sympathy for the imprisoned women that once inhabited this gilded cage, even though they themselves no doubt felt protected, pampered and privileged.

The Dar Si Saïd (Museum of Moroccan Arts and Crafts)

Open Sat–Mon, Wed–Thur 9–11.45am, 2.30-5.45pm, Fri 9–11.30am, 3–5.45pm; closed Tues; adm.

From the gates of the Bahia Palace turn right up Rue Riad ez Zitoun el Jdid and then right again opposite a mosque to find this secluded museum. Si Saïd was the idiot brother of Ba Ahmed, though they shared the same slave mother and powerful vizier father. He held a number of court posts as extra sinecures for his brother, whose palace communicated with the Dar Si Saïd by an underground tunnel. The Dar Si Saïd is more modest and attractive in plan than the Bahia, and greater attention has been paid to the detailed decorative work. Worthy of attention in its own right as a town palace, it also houses an important collection of the decorative arts of southern Morocco.

The entrance passage of the museum (Musée des Arts Marocains), lined with doors rescued from the decaying kasbahs of southern Morocco, leads to a magnificent marble fountain bowl carved for Abdelmalik ben Abi, grand vizier to the Omayyad Caliph of Cordoba Hisham II. It was carried away from Spain by the Almoravid Sultan Ali ben Youssef to embellish the Marrakech mosque that bears his name. The figurative carving (on the sides a central imperial eagle is seemingly supported by two mountain goats, with a pair of apes on the outspread wings) would not have survived the fundamentalist cleansing of the Almohad period, and it was fortunate to have lain buried in ruins until discovered by excavations in 1926. You also pass a curious old fairground machine on your way to the delightful courtyard, with green and white pavement, fountain and central pavilion almost lost among bird-filled trees.

In the long room to the left is an uplifting display of the many Berber jewellery traditions of southern Morocco; the gorgeous fibules and green and yellow enamel eggs of Tiznit, the red stones set in dark silver from the Western High Atlas, the elaborate filigree from Jebel Siroua, the black-on-silver repoussé designs from the Tafilalt oasis and thick bracelets from Jebel Bani. On the other side of the courtyard there is male jewellery, as worked into ornamental daggers, powder horns and long-barrelled flintlocks. The two smaller rooms are dedicated to ceramics; one housing the traditional yellow, green and blue decorated wares produced in the great centres (Safi, Marrakech and Fès, and also the traditional green slipware of Tamegroute), while the other is filled with different examples of the local red wares produced in the country and the mountains.

The **collection of carpets** includes many of the best examples you will find in southern Morocco. Several are on view in the magniifcent upstairs apartment. Stylistically they are divided between Berber and Arab. Those produced by the Arab tribes of the plain are sometimes collectively known as Tensift, or individually identified as Rehamna, Oulad Bou Sbaa, Chiadma, Ahmar or Boujad. Typically they are very long and narrow (to fit the dimensions of a tent, or the interior of a Kasbah), and dominated by fields of madder red and purple with an almost abstract use of geometric designs floating in and out of scale with each other. By way of a contrast those carpets and *hanbels* (similar to kilims) produced by Berber tribes such as the Glaoui of the High Atlas and the Aït-Ouaouizarht of the Jebel Siroua region are set against a predominately black and white background with details worked in gold, yellow, red and blue. They are both more ordered and more colourful, though once again they use an entirely geometric repertoire of patterns. The figurative shapes, those brightly-coloured strip pictograms so beloved of the bazaars are not indigenous to Morocco, even though their influence was already apparent in the 19th century. They come instead from southern Tunisia, and in particular the Gafsa region.

The collection concludes with some ornate and sometimes beautiful pieces of local **carved cedar**—heavy dark doors, the delightful doors within painted Moorish gates, turned window frames and screens, among them some 16th-century Saadian work recovered from El Badia palace.

Maison Tiskiwin (Bert Flint Museum)

Open 8.30am–1pm, adm; if you turn up on Saturday at noon you might be lucky enough to get a personal tour from the proprietor, otherwise you will be left to the tender mercies of his bored housekeeper.

The entrance to this private museum, at 8 Rue de la Bahia, is reasonably easy to miss as it is overshadowed by the group of three bazaars immediately in front of the Dar Si Saïd Museum. It houses another collection of Moroccan decorative art, put together by the Dutch anthropologist Bert Flint during three decades of field work in Morocco. The house, ranged around a traditional Moorish courtyard, is itself reason enough for a visit. The exhibits offer an overview of the traditional material culture of Morocco. Unless you are already familiar with the material, or Moroccan museums, you might find the labelling rather sketchy. The highlight of the collection is the Zemmour room, with its dense collection of Middle Atlas weaving on floor and walls forming a bit of textile heaven for the nomad-dreaming but urban-bound visitor. The vivid patterns on the leatherwork he has collected from around the various Sahara regions are enough to fuel a sketchbook with dozens of derivative designs. The exit from the museum rooms goes through the kitchen courtyard with its orange tree, and you are meant to pass quickly through the private rooms which are, however, equally intriguing. You might have to pinch yourself to prevent the feeling of having strayed into a design magazine article as you take in the faultless blending of traditional High Atlas weaving and bold modern carpets.

A Tour of the Ramparts

The pisé walls of Marrakech respond with a dazzling range of colours to different degrees of light. They glow with changing hues of pink, ochre, gold and brown against the startling backdrop of High Atlas peaks and clear blue sky. Stretches of the walls wind through places defined by a wilderness of dusty graves; elsewhere they are overhung by rustling palms or interrupted by frantic streams of traffic. Elsewhere again they are found decorated with drying skins, sheltering a souk or a passing flock, or enclosing the processional court of the palace of a king. The walls are a shifting pattern of colour and life, at once both monotonously extensive and the city's richest aesthetic treat.

Alarmed by the growing Almohad threat from Tin-Mal, the Almoravid Sultan Ali ben Youssef decided to protect Marrakech with walls in 1126. He asked his generals for tactical advice and consulted his astrologers for an auspicious date to start work on them. Within a year a 10km circuit of 9m high walls, defended by 200 towers and pierced by twenty gates, had been built. This has been constantly repaired and occasionally expanded but still substantially follows the 12th-century plan.

A 16km walk around the city walls of Marrakech would be arduous at any time of the year. Travelling in the morning by horse-drawn cab, bicycle, moped or taxi is a much more pleasurable alternative. The trip can be broken at Bab El Khemis for the souk, and Bab Debbarh, for a look at the tanneries, but the rest of the gates are likely to be only of passing interest. A circuit of the walls would ideally end with a leisurely afternoon picnic in the Ménara or Aguedal gardens.

Leave from the Jemaa el Fna, where horse cabs, taxis and bicycles are easy to find, and take the Av Mohammed V, passing the town hall on your right and the orange-tree shaded park of Moulay Hassan opposite. Crossing through the line of the city walls at the Bab Nkob breach follow the walls round to the right, passing the double crenellated towers of the Bab Larissa in the corner to approach the Bab Doukkala.

Bab Doukkala

The massive but unequal towers of this Almoravid gate are now isolated to the left of the modern entrance to the medina. If the doors are open, go in to examine its dark, twisting defensive passages. The gates guarded the road to Doukkala, the fertile coastal region between El-Jadida and Safi inhabited by Arabic-speaking Berber tribes who were considered to be among the more loyal and dependable subjects of the sultan. Just within the gate, to the right, are the impressive modern green-tiled law courts.

The area outside the gates, despite being used by a busy and modern bus station and passing fairs, retains a melancholy air. To the south of the bus station is the cemetery and **koubba of Sidi Bennour**, which belonged to the El Hara, the old leper colony.

Pass two small gates, Bab Boutouil and Bab Moussoufa, to reach the **palm grove of Sidi Bel Abbès**. Inside the walls here is the zaouia of Sidi Bel Abbès; despite the fact that he was the venerated patron saint of Marrakech, his zaouia was in a suburb outside the city until the walls were extended in the 18th century.

Souk and Bab El Khemis

The northern end of the medina has spilled beyond the walls around the Souk El Khemis, the Thursday market. Fruit and vegetables are sold throughout the week here, though livestock trading is still concentrated on Thursdays.

From the souk enclosure a road passes between the cemetery of Sidi Ahmed Ez Zaouia and a lunar landscape of baked mud and refuse to approach the old Almoravid Fès gate which when rebuilt became known as Bab El Khemis. Just before the gate on the left is the **Koubba of Sidi el Barbouchi**, the saint of the slippers, and straight through the gate within the walls is the **zaouia of the Derkaoua Sufi brotherhood**. The road to the left leads to a series of yards where scrap, broken machinery and bruised food are traded by the most impoverished on the grounds of the old Christian cemetery. It is a powerful, disturbing place, threatening only through its misery. It was at the centre of an insurrection in January 1904. A revolutionary mob led by the cobblers' guild marched under black flags to the cemetery and there exhumed the graves of Christian missionaries. The skulls were impaled to serve as standards that led the mob in its assault on the money-lenders in the *mellah*, the merchants in the souk and the kasbah of the pacha.

Returning outside the city follow the road south beside a magnificent stretch of wall and an extensive cemetery through which snakes the dry bank of the river Issil. The cemetery is often flecked with the bright colours of drying skins as you approach Bab Debbarh, the tanners' gate.

Bab Debbarh

The entrance to the tanners' quarter is beneath the ancient Almoravid towers of Bab Debbarh, through a twisting three-chambered entrance passage. By one of the gate-towers there is a door to the precarious roof which, if open, provides the best view over the tanneries. If the gate is closed there will be no difficulty in finding a young guide to give a quick tour of the tannery vats. They are at their busiest and least pungent in the morning.

Continue south, past Bab Rachidia, to reach **Bab Ailen**, a strong portal named after a Berber tribe that inhabited land to the east. In 1130 an Almohad army descended from the High Atlas to besiege the city. They concentrated their assault on this gate, but were driven off by Almoravid cavalry who sallied out from the neighbouring gates. Just within the gate is the minaret and extensive shrine of the **Qadi Ayad Mosque**. This was built by Sultan Moulay Rachid in the 17th century to hold the tomb of Moulay Ali ech Cherif, the holy ancestor of the Alaouite dynasty. Two later sultans, Moulay Sliman (1792–1822) and Mohammed IV (1859–1873), chose to be buried here beside him.

The Southern Ramparts

The angle in the southeast corner of the walls is filled by the enormous **cemetery of Bab Rhemat**. To the east stretches a modern suburb, and a green-tiled koubba peeks over the houses to your right. This shrine covers the grave of a 12th-century saint, Sidi Youssef ben Ali, who is remembered for his great piety—he continued to praise and thank God even for the gift of leprosy that killed him. The twin towers of the **Bab Rhemat/Aghmat** were betrayed by a Christian regiment in the service of the Almoravid sultans, who opened the gate to the Almohads in 1147. If you pass under the gate here and continue a kilometre into the medina along Rue Ba Ahmad you can see the exterior of the **zaouia of Sidi ben Salah**, its carved minaret inset with green tiles rising above a jumble of roofs, arches, passages and gates. This complex was built in the 14th century by the Merenid Sultan Abou Said Othman.

Continuing outside the city walls, pass beside the cemetery wall to reach the **Bab Ahmar**, which was rebuilt by Sultan Sidi Mohammed in the 18th century. The gate was reserved for the use of the sultan on the feast of Mouloud. The area inside the gates used to house the barracks of the Bouakher regiment of black soldiers, who had a religious cult based around a jujube tree that grew from the gate. To the south three km of walls enclose the Aguedal, the private gardens of the sultan.

Pass through the Bab Ahmar to enter a number of processional squares or ***méchouars*** to the south of the royal palace. From **Méchouar Barastani** pass through the gate of the winds, the Bab er Rih, to go into the smaller **Mechouar El Ouastani**. In the southwest corner a double wall allows private communication between the palace and the Aguedal. The Bab El Arhdar, just before this on the left, may be left open for the use of the public. Beyond is the great **Méchouar des Alaouites**. The **pavilion of Essaouira** in the middle of the southern wall and an artillery magazine in the corner were both built by Sidi Mohammed in the 18th century. The pavilion was used for diplomatic receptions, parades and for reviewing *Fantasia* displays. Pass out through the city walls at **Bab Irhli** and turn left.

The **koubba of Sidi Amara** is just south of here, on the right, and eight hundred metres further on is the **Sqallet el Mrabit**. This elegant ramped fortress was built by Sidi Mohammed in the 18th century to house a mobile squadron from the 600-strong regiment of cavalry he kept permanently posted to defend against the Rehamna tribe. Beyond it you can see the white mihrab of the **msalla**, an open-air mosque used during religious festivals.

Just north of Bab Irhli, the **Bab Ksiba** leads to the Derb Chtouka district, once the site of an Almohad fortress. In the 19th century this was still a government kasbah, occupied by the Mokhazines who guarded the sultan's prison.

Bab er Rob, Bab Aguenaou and the New Town

After extending the city to the south in the 12th century the Almohads were left with a potentially vulnerable angle in the southwestern wall, which they protected by building the Bab er Rob. *Grands taxis* collect up passengers and local buses stop here, and there is a **souk** for cheap pottery and fruit extending around the gate which is named after raisin juice, perhaps a memory of an old dried-fruit market or a morbid reference to the executed heads that in former times were displayed from the battlements. Just inside the Bab er Rob is the most elegant gate in Marrakech, the Bab Aguenaou. This carved stone arch led from the medina to the imperial city.

To the west of the Bab er Rob the walls are hidden by the **cemetery of Sidi es Soheili**, another of the seven saints of Marrakech, whose koubba is beside the cemetery gate, Bab ech Charia.After a detour around the outside of the cemetery you will eventually reach the long wall that contains the garden of the Mamounia Hotel, the entrance of which is just inside the next gate, the Bab Jdid. North of this gate is the **Bab Makhzen**, which used to form a direct entrance to the 12th-century Almoravid kasbah and today is still reserved for the use of the king. This is no inconvenience, as the **Bab Sidi Rharib**, just 200m north, will lead you just as directly back to Av Mohammed V, with the main streets of the New Town to the left and the Jemaa el Fna and the medina to the right.

Alternatively, if you are in no hurry, instead of returning towards the medina here you could head in the other direction from Bab Sidi Rharib into the **New Town** and wind your way through the **Hivernage**, a tranquil French-laid-out garden suburb of villas—and a substantial number of hotels—with the casino at its centre. After a day spent in the medina and the souk its avenues can seem quite bizarrely quiet. There are also some recent buildings in the New Town that toy with the New-Carthage style, a fusion of traditional Moorish and Saharan styles spiked with the odd detail from Egypt and Tunisia, that might be of interest. In particular, look for the recent work of the Tunisian-born French architect Charles Bocarra, responsible for the design of the much talked about Tichka Hotel (see below) and the opulent Les Deux Tours villa (available for rent through 'The Best of Morocco' agency) in the Palmeraie quarter as well as the great mass of the Marrakech Opera, which now dominates the junction of Av de France and Av Hassan II, near the railway station.

The Gardens of Marrakech

You cannot expect to be able to visit the gardens of Marrakech alone. The Ménara and the Majorelle are both well established ports of call on coach trips around the city's sights. Do not let this discourage you: there is no better way of sheltering from the afternoon heat and hassle of Marrakech than by picnicking in the Aguedal or the Ménara. The main market on Av Mohammed V in the New Town sells everything you need: wicker baskets, wine, cheese, fresh bread, pâté and a bewildering selection of olives, nuts and fresh fruit.

The Aguedal

These gardens were established in the 12th century by the Almohad Sultan Abdel Moumen. Two enormous tanks were built and filled by pipes that tapped the Ourika stream. By the 18th century, however, the walls had decayed, the water had been diverted and tribesmen grazed the orchards. The present garden is the creation of Sultan Abder Rahman (1822–59), who reclaimed the water rights and rebuilt the walls, although his successors still had to keep a constant guard against tribesmen, especially the nomadic Rehamna, who enjoyed nothing more than raiding the sultan's garden.

In the 19th century a succession of pavilions were built in the gardens, most notably the **Dar el Beïda** provided for the harem of Moulay Hassan. However the garden's primary purpose was always to be an efficient and very profitable private agricultural estate. Two visitors from Kew who saw it in 1840 estimated that its 40 acres gave the sultan produce worth at least £20,000 each year.

When the Royal Family is not resident in Marrakech visitors are allowed to go down through the orchards to the 200m square main tank, the Sahraj el Hana, or pool of health. The pavilion of **Dar el Hana** is beside the tank. You can still enjoy its tranquil rooftop view south to the Atlas peaks, and then join the knots of Moroccan families picnicking under the shade of the surrounding trees. On the far side the ruins of a gunpowder factory are being turned into a waterfront palace.

From the roof of the Dar el Hana you might in 1873 have witnessed the death of the Sultan Mohammed IV, who drowned while boating with his son on the tank. A forlorn, almost wistful, acceptance of fate is beautifully expressed in the official epitaph: 'He departed this life, in a water tank, in the expectation of something better to come.'

He was not the only sultan to die in the Aguedal Gardens. On 9 April 1672, after the feast of Aid el Kebir, Sultan Moulay Rachid took out a spirited horse to gallop away his ennui through the orange groves of the Aguedal. In the morning, the court poets sang, 'The tree's branch did not break the skull of our *imam* out of cruelty; nor from ingratitude, unmindful of the duties of friendship. It was out of jealousy of his slender figure, for envy is to be found even among trees.'

The Ménara

The Ménara is 2km west of Bab Jdid. It is an agricultural estate of irrigated olive orchards and gardens that have been planted around a massive water tank. Like the one in the Aguedal, the tank was built by the Almohads in the 12th century, but what you now see was established in the 19th century by the Alaouites. Mohammed IV replaced the outer walls, refurbished the tank and built the green-tiled pavilion in 1869 to replace a ruined Saadian one. There is a a wonderful, tranquil view over the great expanse of water from its open, balconied first floor (if you can arrive independently of the constant stream of coaches). Away from the pavilion and the click of cameras you can enjoy a quiet picnic by the basin or in the orchard, looking towards the mountains. Any spare bread can be used to feed the enormous carp, which will churn up a small frenzy of turbulent waters with their gaping wide mouths as they descend on leftovers.

Majorelle Garden

Open daily 8am–12 noon, 3–7pm summer; 8am–12 noon, 2–5pm winter; no children; adm.

The Majorelle is a privately-owned botanical garden off a side street in the New Town north-west of the medina opposite the wholesale market on Av Yaacoub el Mansour. It was created by two generations of French artists, Jacques and Louis Majorelle, and is now owned by the couturier Yves Saint-Laurent (who was born in Algeria). It is an immaculately manicured walled garden full of pavilions, paths and rills painted a bright Mediterranean blue that snake through an admirably lush botanical collection, especially strong in cacti. The Majorelles' old studio has been turned into a small museum (*separate admission charge; closed Mon*), which displays the present owner's idiosyncratic collection of Maghrebi decorative art: carpets, ceramics, textiles, woodwork and jewellery, as well as offering a gallery filled with some of Majorelle's original canvases.

The Mamounia Garden

This lush formal garden with its central pavilion was established in the 18th century by Pasha Mamoun, governor of Fès, and was later bequeathed to the Sultan. It then served as the crown prince's residence, and was occasionally lent to visiting diplomats, until the era of French rule when it was turned into a luxury hotel. The hotel's charm was drastically reduced by its 1986 renovation, and somewhere in its marble halls there should be installed a constant video of the old interior as preserved in Hitchcock's 1956 film *The Man who Knew Too Much*. The 300m sweeping wall of bougainvillea and the quiet, undisturbed half-dozen regular plots of olive and palm trees are supposedly reserved for residents. Ignore this restriction, though it is as well to dress up a bit and buy a cup of coffee on the terrace.

The Palm Grove (La Palmeraie)

Follow the Fès road east for a kilometre past the Souk el Khemis, then take a signposted left turn for an 8km drive through the palm grove to the north of the city. The Almoravids are credited with planting this grove, but palms in Marrakech are useful only for wood, shade and desert imagery, for they are too far north ever to bear fruit. Olives or oranges would be a more useful crop, and the palm grove has a deserved aura of neglect. The pisé walls, fragments of irrigation systems and barren palms might be entertaining if you are not travelling further south, but the area has increasingly become colonized by smart villas, time-share holiday homes, and hotels.

Around Marrakech

To the south of Marrakech the valleys and peaks of the High Atlas beckon, and to the east is the gathering mass of the Central High Atlas. Heading north and west from the city the arid and comparatively flat landscape cannot hope to compete in grandeur. It does however have its own spirit, and there are plenty of roadside cafés and rural souks at which to break the journey. There is also the poetry of Arab tribal names and a recent vivid history with which to entertain yourself.

West of Marrakech there are a couple of dusty **souks** off the main road by the bridge over the river Nfiss, and on the banks of the river Tensift. The names, **Tnine des Oudaya, Sebt-des-Aït-Imour** and **Sidi-Chickèr** recall the Arab tribes, the Oudaïa, the Aït-Imour and the Oulad-Sidi-Chickèr, who were settled here on the Rehamna's best land by Sultan Abder Rahman in 1862. The Oudaïa were one of the most loyal components of the Alaouite army, and were placed by the sultans in a number of key fortresses such as Fès Jdid, the Oudaïa Kasbah of Rabat and Temara Kasbah. For Chichaoua and the road between Marrakech and Essaouira, *see* pp.267–8 and p.426.

The Arab Tribes of the Plain

Before the 12th century only a tiny minority of Arabs lived among the Moroccan Berbers, concentrated in the city of Fès. Large-scale Arab migration into North Africa began in 1050 when two impoverished Bedouin confederacies, the Hillal and Sulaim, entered Egypt from the Arabian desert. They advanced west with their herds and families, destroying the ancient cities and farmland of the North African shore. The 14th-century Arab historian Ibn Khaldoun was referring to these tribes when he wrote that 'the Arabs are incapable of good government and bring the desert with them'.

Though seldom a unified force, the Arab tribes could field an army of 50,000 warriors, and their success drew other impoverished tribes from Arabia to follow in their wake. The Arabs were first defeated by the Almohads at the battle of Sitif in 1152, but instead of pushing the bedouin back east, the sultan began to recruit individual tribes into his service. Unlike his Berber forces, the Arabs had no political ambitions or regional loyalties. As nomads, they could be dispatched with ease to any province. Their ruthlessness and ferocity could be relied upon, and the sultans would set Arab tribes against a particular dissident Berber region and award them what grazing land or plunder they could seize.

The Merenids employed the Maql Arab confederacy during their border wars, but then adroitly directed these alarming and powerful allies south into the desert. In the Sahara the Maql (also known as the 'sons of Hassan') separated into their component tribal factions and established a predatory authority over the indigenous Berber tribes of the south. In the lawless desert their ferocious martial spirit was kept intact. It was common for an Arab tribe to refuse to brand their herds, on the principle that 'all animals are potentially ours'. These Arab tribes remained valuable military allies for any ruler who dared use them.

In the 16th century the Saadian sheiks recruited one of these Maql Arab tribes, the Rehamna, from their grazing grounds in northern Senegal. They placed them on the coastal plains in order to contain squadrons of Portuguese cavalry who had, in 1515, nearly captured Marrakech. The Rehamna disposed of this threat but increasingly converted the plain between Marrakech and the coast into their own domain. By the 17th century they refused any obedience or further service to the sultan. They were a proud nomadic tribe and scornfully rejected cultivation, for 'with the plough enters dishonour'. They concerned themselves with increasing their herds, escorting or plundering merchant convoys, and raiding their neighbours.

On the first sign of government weakness the Rehamna would revolt. In 1859, for instance, the defeat at Tetouan and the accession of a new sultan led to a Rehamna siege of Marrakech. All communication was cut, outlying rural souks were raided and the deserted crops efficiently harvested. The new Sultan Mohammed IV was quick to take up the challenge. He established a standing force of 600 cavalry at Marrakech to police the plains and invited Uld Billah, the *caid* of the Rehamna, to a magnificent banquet. The *caid* was detained at the end of the dinner and remained a hostage until the sultan's death in 1873. The Rehamna were dispersed and only spared the full extent of the sultan's revenge by the intercession of a revered holy man. The tribe's best lands, along the rivers Tensift and Nfiss, were confiscated and given to a coalition of rival Arab tribes.

However, the tribe was quick to reassert itself and in 1912 Al-Ayyadi, their *caid*, allied himself firmly with France. Rehamna cavalry fought alongside the French against the Blue Sultan, but the Rehamna landholdings were too central, extensive, and rich in phosphates for France to permit Caid Al-Ayyadi the feudal authority they allowed the Berber High Atlas *caids*. Instead they encouraged a rivalry between Al-Ayyadi and Thami el Glaoui that was fought out in the magnificence of their palaces and the prodigality of their entertainments. To fuel this duel of taste Al-Ayyadi recklessly sold tribal lands until his death in 1964. Pride had achieved what no sultan could—the destruction of the Rehamna.

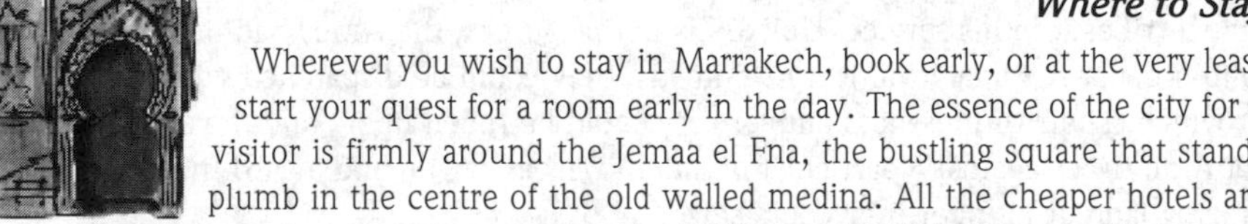

Where to Stay

Wherever you wish to stay in Marrakech, book early, or at the very least start your quest for a room early in the day. The essence of the city for a visitor is firmly around the Jemaa el Fna, the bustling square that stands plumb in the centre of the old walled medina. All the cheaper hotels are found here, and many of these, such as the **Gallia**, can hardly be bettered. If you want to go slightly upmarket and have the addition of bars and restaurants there are three good places still within the walls of the old town, the **Islane**, the faded **Foucauld** and the **Tazi**. In summer you may find that a hotel with a pool and a hint of a garden for sunbathing is more important than a view (and the surrounding noise and diesel fumes) of the Jemaa el Fna. In that case there are four hotels, the **Imilchil**, **Yasmine**, **Lalla Hasna** and **Moussafir** in the New Town which are small enough to have both some character and a pool. In the world of luxury hotels, the choice is between the well-decorated but out of town **Tichka**, the calm unpretentious atmosphere of the **Es Saadi** or the world-renowned glamour of the **Mamounia**.

luxury

It is impossible to talk about Marrakech hotels without first mentioning the **Mamounia**. This old palace (*see* above 'The Gardens of Marrakech') was converted into a fabulously elegant hotel in the colonial period. It was Winston Churchill's favourite haunt, and his suite is preserved with his books, bed and photographs of him painting in the garden. Since his day it has been almost entirely rebuilt, and turned into just another glamorous international hotel with over 200 bedrooms, a casino, conference centre and banqueting hall. The porters wear more gold braid than an admiral, and you are forced into a tie in the dining room, but the garden, its position in the city and its cooking remain superb. Off-the-street prices start at around $230 for a double room, though it is possible to pay much less by booking through an agency, or much, much more by taking your own suite or villa in the garden. It has four bars, four restaurants, eight boutiques, a good bookshop and shops, and is found on the edge of the medina along Av Bab Jedid, ✆ (04) 448981, @ 444660.

The **Es Saâdi Hôtel** on Av El Quadissa, ✆ (04) 448811, @ 447644, is beside the casino in the heart of the Hivernage quarter of the New Town. It also has a splendid garden, and delicious food with unusually attentive and charming staff. It has half as many rooms as the Mamounia, and is also about half the price.

The brittle international set that used to go to the Mamounia is increasingly using the **Tichka Hôtel**, ✆ (04) 448710, with structure by Charles Bocarra and an interior designed by the American Marrakechi socialite Bill Willis that has given it an undeniable cachet. It has also been discovered by the media and in an average week you can rely on seeing one passing film crew, two fashion shoots and three 'ideas-brokers' working their mobile phones poolside. Meals are served at the well dressed tables beside the pool, where the Sidi Bou Said birdcage canopy is illuminated in the evening. There are fires in the sitting room off the lovely entrance hallway in the winter, as well as a *hammam* in the basement and a Moroccan restaurant. It is however surrounded by other hotels (such as the Semiramis), and is situated in Semlalia, the uninteresting far northern edge of the New Town. To find it take the road for Casablanca, and watch out for a clutch of hotel signposts on the right.

expensive

Just west of the Koutoubia off Av Hoummane el Fetouaki and almost opposite the Mamounia is the well positioned but inconspicuous **Chems Hôtel**, ✆ (04) 444813. It is a functional motel-like place with its own car park, pool, bar and small garden. However both it and the similar **Les Almoravides**, ✆ (04) 445142, which is also within the walled old town north of the Ensemble Artisanal on Av Mohammed V at Arset Djenan Lakhdar, can be dominated by groups. This is also true of the large **Hotel Marrakech**, ✆ (04) 434351, @ 434980, although its central position on the Av Mohammed V (on the northern corner of Place de La Liberte) and its smart row of boutiques breath a bit of town life into the place.

moderate

In the New Town just west of the ramparts and south of Av Mohammed V is the comfortable **Le Grand Imilchil**, ✆ (04) 447653. It has a pool, bar, restaurant, a small garden and 90 bedrooms all with their own bathrooms.

In the same neighbourhood but dropping a notch in price there is the **Yasmine**, ✆ (04) 446142, which also has a pool and is also just outside the walls at the meeting of Rue Boualaka and Av des Remparts. It is usually a quiet place and has recently been restored, with the addition of a bar and restaurant.

The **Moussafir**, ✆ (04) 435929, ℻ 435936, just alongside the railway station on Av Hassan II is another part of this admirable chain which delivers a bar, restaurant, small pool and modern bedrooms at an affordable price. Although it is on the western edge of the New Town, this has its own logic if you are coming by train and there is never a shortage of taxis, which gather in the station forecourt.

The recently-opened **Lalla Hasna**, ✆ (04) 449972, ℻ 449994, stands right in the centre of the New Town at 247 Av Mohammed V. This individually-owned hotel (named after the proprietor's daughter) would seem to have everything going for it to attract the independent traveller: a café, two restaurants, a small but welcome pool and briskly clean bedrooms.

inexpensive

The **Hôtel Gallia**, ✆ (04) 445913, ℻ (04) 444853, is at 30 Rue de la Recette, a turning off Rue Bab Aguenaou which runs due south from the corner of the Jemaa el Fna. It is a discreet address, a calm, functional but very friendly hotel with resident turtles and just 20 rooms arranged around its two internal courtyards. It's extremely popular, and to have any hope of finding a room here you need to book at least two weeks in advance.

The **Hôtel De Foucauld**, ✆ (04) 445499, ℻ 441344, is on Av El Mouahidine, overlooking the triangular wooded park just to the west of the Jemaa el Fna. It has a pleasantly faded neo-Moorish interior, hip baths, a licensed restaurant on the ground floor, and a pleasant, warm character, like its manageress, the English-speaking Maria, who also rents out bicycles. If you are Californian it might be considered a bit worn but by English reckoning it is well above B&B standards.

The **Islane,** ✆ (04) 440083, ℻ 440085, at 279 Av Mohammed V is a valuable new addition to Marrakech's hotel stock. It stands within the walls, just outside the hassle area of the Jemaa el Fna but almost directly opposite the Koutoubia mosque. It has a licenced restuarant on its rooftop (no bar service without food) a popular local café on the street, just 23 well-appointed bedrooms upstairs and a small yard to park cars.

The **Grand Hôtel Tazi,** ✆ (04) 442452, is in the southern end of the medina on the corner of Rue Bab Aguenaou and Av Houmman el Fetouaki. It has 60 comfortable and well decorated rooms, a restaurant, a pool and an invaluable roof-terrace bar. If it's full you can try the clean but less characterful **Hôtel Minaret**, which has very recently opened behind the Tazi at 10 Rue Dispensaire.

cheap

All of the seven hotels listed below are characterful, safe and well established places that overlook, or are within a stone's throw of, the Jemaa el Fna.

The **Hôtel Ali**, ✆ (04) 44979, ℻ 433609, is on Rue Moulay Ismaïl, the street that runs beside the triangular garden square just west of the Jemaa el Fna. It is a popular backpackers' choice and has a busy central courtyard café-restaurant on the ground floor of the hotel. The rooms are scrupulously clean, although they can be a bit stuffy, while the international trekking clientele can be a bit earnest.

The **CTM,** © (04) 442325, has a superb position next to a café on the southern side of the Jemaa el Fna. It has a balconied roof terrace which overlooks the square, and a cool internal upstairs courtyard around which are the large comfortable bedrooms. Breakfast is served on the terrace, the maids Brika and Fatima take in washing, and there is a secure lock up garage in the old bus station next door.

The **Oukmaiden,** © (04) 441038, has been done up in the last few years and has a fine position overlooking the north side of Jemaa el Fna. Like the CTM it is one of the first budget hotels to get filled up.

Along or just off the Rue Riad ez Zitoun el Kedim (facing the CTM on the south side of Jemaa el Fna, this narrow arched alley is to your left) there are three good places to check out. At no. 197 there is the popular and friendly **Hôtel de France,** © (04) 443076. About 30m further down the street a right turn leads you to two of the best cheap places in town, the family-run, hospitable and much praised **Hotel Medina,** 1 Derb Sidi Bouloukat, © (04) 442927, and its almost as popular neighbour the **Essaouira** at no 3, © (04) 443805.

camping

The **Camping Municipal,** © (04) 431707, is on Av de France in the New Town. It is an unappealing site part-shaded by eucalyptus, with a café-restaurant and desultory pool patrolled by the more desperate hustlers. It's much better to try a cheap hotel.

Eating Out

In this city you can eat lavishly in magnificent surroundings, and eat cheap fresh local food in one of the world's great public spaces, but you can also just as easily be served a succession of dull, overpriced meals. It is a city that has been living off tourism for generations, and has developed a large range and variety of restaurants. All will be well if you go for extremes: eating either very cheaply or at the best that you can afford.

expensive—banquet restaurants in the medina

It is essential to book in advance for dinner in any of these three sublime restaurants, which combine some of the best traditional cooking in Morocco with a visual feast of furnishings, textiles and pictures in traditional town houses of an almost dream-like seclusion. For what they offer they are extremely good value (allow $50 a head for an almost embarrassingly opulent evening), but be aware that menus, if offered at all, are only for information or for selecting from the number of courses (anything between three and eight) that the house has prepared for all its guests that night. If you have the capacity for it, and have starved yourself beforehand, try them all.

Dar Yacout (La Maison de Saphir) © (04) 310104, is at 79 Sidi Ahmed Souissi. This well-established restaurant, founded by an American but now presided over by the Moroccan-British consul, is hidden away down a dark street off the Rue el Gza (which is 250m north of the Bab Doukkala, within the old walls). For your first visit you should take a taxi, which will be met at the end of the street by a lantern-bearing watchman. At the end of the evening coffee is served on a terrace that provides a serene view over the surrounding streets.

Dar M'jenna (also spelt Marjana, or known as La Maison), © (04) 445773. The master of the house, Chaaouqui, presides over aperitifs in the courtyard before you get so much as a whiff of the lavish feast of a meal that is served in the high, narrow old dining room, with a continuous supply of wine all included in the price.

Ksar Essaoussan, © (04) 440632, is at 3 Derb Chorfa El Messaoudyenne, off the Rue des Ksours alley, which is found by going through an archway off the Rue Fatima Zohra (from the Islane hotel café, turn left along Av Mohammed V, then first left onto Rue Fatima Zohra for 250m, with the arch appearing on your right at a road junction, after which the way is signposted). It is the newest of the three, established as a way of working-retirement by Parisian chef Jean-Laurent Graulhet (closed Sun).

An honourable choice if the others are booked up is a near neighbour of the Ksar Essaoussan, the **Stilia**, © (04) 443587, at 34 Rue Ksour.

expensive—lunch in the medina

If at lunch time you are looking for good traditional Moroccan cooking in an elegantly appointed restaurant with a drinks license there are three good addresses that spring to mind. They are also open in the evening, but can then tend to be dominated by floor shows with appetite-destroying audience participation.

The **Relais Al Baraka**, © (04) 442341, is tucked in the northwest corner of the Jemaa el Fna, beside the offices of the *Commissariat de Police.* Here you can eat in summer from a choice of three extensive menus, in the tranquil fountain court or in the two dining-room pavilions that flank it.

Le Restaurant Marrakechi at 52 Rue Banques, © (04) 443377, has a good kitchen and an extensive menu, and is large and easy to find on the northeastern corner of the Jemaa el Fna. It also has the essential midday asset of a roof terrace overlooking the street life in the square.

If you are in the southern half of the medina (maybe coming out of the Mellah, Dar Si Saïd, Badia or Bahia palaces) the **Douriya** Moroccan restaurant at 14 Derb Jedid Hay Essalame, © (04) 403030, is perfectly placed just north of Place des Ferbantiers off Av Houmman el Fetouaki. Ask for a table in one of the three private rooms off the upper terrace to avoid the big groups that may be fitted in on the ground floor.

expensive —fashionable restaurants

If you are hoping to mingle with the *haute monde de Marrakech* in the evening forget cocktails at the Mamounia and head for either of the following three restaurants. The **Villa Rossa**, © (04) 430832, at 64 Av Hassan II is a well-established meeting ground with an Italian, fish based menu, plus an associated boutique and jazz-bar. The equally highly-regarded**La Trattoria**, © (04) 432641, at 179 Rue Mohammed Beqal in the New Town, is also an Italian restaurant, decorated like the Tichka hotel by Bill Willis, and under the direction of Giancarlo (closed Mon).

The third, **Le Pavilion,**© (04) 391240 (closed Tues), is actually in the medina, in a traditional house at 47 Derb Zaouia, a little dead-end by the Bab Doukkala mosque. It is easily accessible by taxi, and the clientele and chef Didier's superb French cooking place it firmly within the fashionable category.

moderate —in the medina

The **Pizzeria Venetia** at 279 Av Mohammed V, © (04) 440081, is the roof-top restaurant of the Islane Hotel. It looks directly out at the Koutoubia, and has a number of classic Moroccan dishes on its menu as well as pizzas and the familiar Italian standards.

The restaurant at the **Hotel Foucauld,** © (04) 445499, on Av El Mouahidine offers a filling five-course set meal at reasonable prices as well as a mixed Moroccan-French and Italian menu (and has a drinks license). The cooking is sound if uninspired, but you get to eat and drink in a high-ceilinged Moorish dining room with a fine old whirring fan, and the almost-as-elderly waiters have great gravitas.

The **Grand Hôtel Tazi**, © (04) 442452, on Rue Bab Aguenaou is slightly further down the culinary pecking order, but the terraced bar tends to stay open longer. It is the sort of place where you order a *salade niçoise* to keep your wine company.

moderate—in the new town/Guéliz

Restaurant El Fassia, © (04) 434060, at 232 Av Mohammed V stands aside from the norm for restaurants anywhere in Morocco. It is an exceptional place, run by a staff of women who have achieved the rare balance of a committed approach to Moroccan cooking without degenerating into an Orientalist feast. Here you can order single dishes, not whole meals, from a well thought-out menu in a modern Islamic-style interior.

Le Jardin, © (04) 433839,on Rue Oum Rabia, near Place de L'Indépendence, is a small and convivial restaurant locally celebrated for its crêpes and grilled meats, eaten on wooden plates. Despite its name it has no garden, but meals are served in summer on a sun-dappled terrace.

Restaurant Le Jacaranda, © (04) 447215, is at the north end of the New Town at 32 Blvd Mohammed Zerqtouni, opposite the strategic tables of the Brasserie des Negociants on the busy Place Abdel Moumen ben Ali. It has a fire in winter, air conditioning in summer and a French menu that takes full advantage of the fish and shellfish available from the coast. (closed Tues and Wed lunch).

The **Café de la Paix,** © (04) 433118, is an attractive café at 68 Rue de Yougoslavie. It has a mixed French and Moroccan menu and tables placed outside in a shady garden, filled by the noise of a tinkling fountain. The cooking is not inspired, but it's a perfect place for a cold beer and a light, reasonably priced lunch such as a cheese omelette followed by a tagine and finished off with ice cream.

The **Bagatelle,** © (04) 430274 (closed Wed, and all September), nearby at 101 Rue de Yougoslavie, is a surviving relic from the colonial period, a calm and distinguished place with admirably poised waiters and an almost exclusively local clientele. An excellent venue for a long, slow lunch, starting with a bottle of chilled rosé and finishing with the house's renowned chocolate mousse.

Dropping a notch in price and style, **Le Petit Poucet**, © (04) 431188, at no 56 Av Mohammed V, on the corner of Rue Mohammed el Bequal, is another survivor from the colonial era.

cheap—in the medina

You will find in the evening that food can hardly taste more exotic than if you eat from the barrow grill-restaurants in the centre of the **Jemaa el Fna**. Wander around first, sniffing out the most extensive and succulent of the restaurants before you succumbing to the brilliant multilingual sales chatter and plonk yourself down on a bench. The portions are reasonably small, so you can easily justify trying a broad selection of daily offerings. It may be as well to check prices in advance, though most of the kiosks charge between 20–30dh for a meal if you appear to be reasonably in control of your mind.

If you are looking for a slightly more relaxing and longer meal you can use one of the terraced café-restaurants that overlook the northeast corner of the Jemaa el Fna. The **Café de France** and especially the newly overhauled **Restaurant Argana** are popular places—you may have to wait a bit for a table—that only charge about twice as much as the stalls on the square.

Otherwise, try any of the cafés along Rue Bani Marine or Rue Bab Aguenaou (the streets leading south from the Jemaa el Fna), particularly the **Café-Restaurant Oriental** at no. 33 Rue Bab Aguenaou, or the **Restaurant Etoile de Marrakech**, which serves dinner up until midnight.

At lunchtime, when there are fewer, if any, grill-stalls, you can still eat in the north-eastern corner of the Jemaa el Fna. **Chez Chegrouni** at no. 4–6 has a terrace that overlooks the Place where you can eat a nourishing meal of soup, salad, brochettes and sweetened yoghurts. The service is friendly and honest, if a little erratic.

If you find yourself in the southern Medina around lunchtime the rooftop **Café-Restaurant El Badi** (signposted on the street just west of Place des Ferblantiers) can also be enthusiastically recommended. Filling three course Moroccan meals are served almost on the same level as the storks' nests on the neighbouring walls of the El Badia palace

cheap—in the New Town/Guéliz

The **Agdal** café-restaurant at 86 Av Mohammed V stays open from breakfast to dinner, and can fulfil any need for a cheap meal in the New Town. It is just 30m from the Petit Poucet (see above) and also has a scattering of tables on the pavement.

cafés—in the medina

Overlooking the Place Jemaa el Fna the traditional choice to make is between the battered chairs on the terrace of the **Café de France** or those of the **Café Glacier**, beside the CTM, as your theatre from which to read, play cards, sip drinks, watch life on the square and eavesdrop on other foreigners. Alternatives include the first-floor terrace of the newly-restored **Argana** Café in the northwest corner of the Place (directly across the square from the Post Office.).

cafés —in the New Town/Guéliz

At the meeting point of Av Mohammed V and Blvd Mohammed Zerktouni the cane chairs of the **Café Renaissance** and **Brasserie des Negociants** look across the traffic at each other. The former has a lift up to a rooftop terrace, where non Muslims can be served drinks and enjoy a view of the sunset. Another nearby meeting place is the **Boule de Neige**, beside the **Pâtisserie Hilton** on Rue Yougoslavie, which is particularly popular with an elegant coterie of women. Other popular local haunts include the **Firdaous Café** on Av Mohammed V and the **Café-Pâtisserie Zohor** on Rue de la Liberté. For cakes, **Al Jawda** patisserie at 11 Rue de la Liberté, near the covered market, has been enthusiastcially recommended as the best in town.

bars

Apart from the other restaurants detailed above the only places for an affordable drink in the medina are the Tazi or Foucauld Hotels. If you are looking for some cocktails to be washed down to the tinkling of a piano, head for **Le Churchill** in the Mamounia Hotel, **Omar Khayoun** in the Pullman Mansour Eddahbi Hotel, or **Le Star's House** on Place de la Liberté. In the New Town there is a large number of bars outside of the big hotels. However, they are a male preserve, and can be unsettling for western men, let alone women. They chiefly serve half-litre bottles of beer in quick succession. The prophet Mohammed said that wine is both a great sin and a great advantage to man, but that the sin is greater than the advantage. Hangovers also seem particularly intense in the African sun. The **Haouz** is on Av Hassan II, the **Iceberg** on Av el Mouahadine, **L'Escale** on Rue Mauritania, the **Marché** at 44 Rue de la Liberté, the **Poste** on Rue el Imam Malik, the **Taverne** on Blvd Zerqtouni and **Tony Bar** on Rue Abou Bekr Esseddiq.

Shopping

The Marrakech souk has as extensive a range of **Moroccan crafts** as anywhere in the country. However, the bazaar merchants are also used to extracting some pretty fabulous sums from rich and careless visitors who have come straight off the aeroplane into this Aladdin's Cave. You may find that you will have to spend even more time and energy than normal bargaining things down to a decent price. Before going into the souk, check out the prices and quality in the Dar Si Saïd Museum and at the **Ensemble Artisanal**, on Av. Mohammed V inside the medina walls. If all you want to do is quickly gather together a hamper full of gifts, it's easiest to head straight for the covered market on Av Mohammed V in the New Town, which has good displays of reasonably priced fossils, minerals and pieces of Safi pottery in among the trays of dates and fresh fruit.

For antiques, fine craftwork, pictures and old books together with one or two fine pieces of embroidery and jewellery have a look at **L'Orientaliste**, run by Mme Amzallag, in the New Town at 15 Rue de la Liberte, © (04) 434074. Her husband Claude Amzallag also runs one of Marrakech's best leather-goods shops, **Place Vendome**, established since 1948 at 141 Av Mohammed V, © (04) 435263. They will make goods to order to your specific requirements. Also in the New Town you can find an interesting range of traditional and more modern decorative pieces at Isabelle Castagnet's interior design shop, **Maison d'Été** at 17 Rue de Yougoslavie, © (04) 436061.

In the Medina, Mustapha Blaoui at **Trésor des Nomades**, 128 Rue el Mouassine, ✆ (04) 445906, has an engaging stock of old doors, battered tables and lamps ancient and modern among a clutter of other decorative pieces. On the edge of the city on the Safi road there is a factory run by two Spanish brothers, **Roberto and Gerardo Ruiz**, who produce striking ironwork tables, chairs, shelves and beds. They also stock ceramics and will add a zellij mosaic top to the table of your choice, and can arrange shipment. Their address is Quartier Industriel, Sidi Ghranem, Route de Safi, Guéliz, ✆ (04) 492529.

For the carpets produced by the Arab tribes of the Plains have a look at the stock held in **Bazaar Chichoua** (chez Mustafa) at 5 Souk des Ksours, ✆ (04) 440713.

There is an English-language bookshop in town, the **American Bookstore** at 3 Impasse du Moulin, off Blvd Mohammed Zerqtouni, but for most purposes the elaborate but not overpriced kiosk in front of the Mamounia Hotel, and that beside the Tichka Hotel, have the best selection of **books, guides** and **newspapers**.

In order to assemble a **picnic**, or stock up on **wine**, go to the covered market in the heart of the New Town on Av Mohammed V. There are also several good grocery shops, which also stock local wine, on the other side of the Avenue, which also stay open after the market has closed.

Sports

go-karting

There is a Go-Kart track at the Kart Hotel, about 12km out of the city. There are 800m and 1360m tracks, open daily from 9am–midnight, call ✆ (04) 448163 for further details.

golf

There is the 18-hole Royal Golf course, ✆ (04) 443441, set in tranquil orchards some 4km out of town off the P31 road to Ouarzazate. It was first established by Thami el Glaoui and is open to non-members for a $30 green fee.

hill walking and mountain climbing

Marrakech is superbly located as an initial base for a walking holiday. Hill walkers can easily drive out in the morning to explore the lower valleys of the High Atlas passes or the Central High Atlas, or stay in hotels at Ourika, Asni, Oukaïmeden or Ouirgane. The more committed mountain climbers will want to be based in the series of mountain huts scattered in the Toubkal National Park (*see* pp.431–4).

riding

There are two riding schools just outside the city: **Club de l'Atlas**, ✆ (04) 431301, near the Menara gardens, and **Club Equipitage**, ✆ (04) 448529. There is also a polo club, ✆ (04) 435383, with a pitch about 4km out of town along the Beni-Mellal road. Also, the Roseraie Hotel at **Ouirgane** (a third of the way along the Tizi-n-Test pass into the High Atlas, *see* p.433) has a superb stable of Arab thoroughbreds which can be taken out for anything from a half-day to a week's camping in the hills.

skiing

This is possible but not predictable at Jbel Oukaïmeden in the High Atlas (*see* pp.442–3for details) anytime from Nov to Mar.

swimming

Much the best idea is to save up your swimming energy for a few days battling the Atlantic surf at the beaches and lagoons of Oualidia, Essaouira and El-Jadida, just a few hours away to the west. If your hotel doesn't have a pool of its own, there is a popular **municipal pool** in the Moulay Abdessalam garden, entered from Rue Abou El Abbes Sebti opposite the Ensemble Artisanal on Av Mohammed V. There is a small admission charge for this pool, and it's full of exuberant hordes of adolescent Marrekechi boys—which could be either a personal heaven or purgatory. For more tourists and tranquility you can also buy a day ticket and use the small pool at the **Grand Hotel Tazi** in the medina.

tennis

Aside from the three dozen or so courts and professional instructors found in the grounds of almost all the four and five star hotels, there is the **Royal Tennis Club**, ✆ (04) 431902, at Jnane El Harti, off Rue Oued el Makhazine.

Cultural Centres

The **French Cultural Centre** (*open Tue–Sun 8.30am–12pm, 2.30–6pm*) is on Rue de la Targa. They run a garden-café and a library, and arrange a full schedule of films, lectures and exhibitions.

The **American Language Centre** (*open Mon, Sat 9am–12 noon, 2.30–6.30pm; Tues–Fri 2.30–6pm only*) is at 3 Impasse du Moulin, off Blvd Zerqtouni. It has a small library, a bookshop and noticeboard and puts on a weekly film.

Nightlife

There are two fairly recent additions to Marrakech's nightlife which beneath a transatlantic shimmer have blurred the established division between the introverted world of the tourist complexes and the promenade cafés beloved by locals. The **Complexe Jet d'Eau** is on Place de la Liberté, and contains a restaurant, snack bar and **Le Star** disco. The **Palais des Congrès** on Av de France is an even more shocking piece of mall-glamour for the burgeoning world of the charge account. It contains seven restaurants, five café-bars, two night clubs and one luxury hotel for the *homme d'affaires.*

The two newest and best-equipped discos in Marrakech are the **Paradise** in the Pullman Mansour Eddahbi Hotel, ✆ (04) 448222, on Av de France (open 10pm–7am; 80dh adm) and the **Cotton Club**, ✆ (04) 433913, at the **Hôtel Tropicana**, Lotissement Semlalia (open 9pm–5am; 60dh adm). Other clubs include **Byblos** at **PLM N'Fis** on Av de France, ✆ (04) 448772, the **Charleston disco** at Place Abdelmoumen, ✆ (04) 431136, below the Grand Café Atlas, and **Le Diamant Noir** in Le Marrakech Hôtel on Place de la Liberté.

An alternative would be to hire your own **folklore troupe** for a moonlit picnic or dinner party. Try El Haj Allal at 96 Rue Mouassine, Eddibyn Mohammed at 160 Rue Mouassine or Haj Mohammed Baba at 36 Derb Dabachi.

casinos

Dress up a bit but don't overdo it; men wearing a dinner jacket will probably be mistaken for a croupier or a waiter. The **Mamounia Casino**, ✆ (04) 448981, is in the celebrated hotel on Av Bab Jedid. The other, older casino in Marrakech is run by the **Es Saadi** hotel and stands in the heart of the Hivernage district on Av Kadissa, ✆ (04) 448811/447010.

fantasias

Fantasia evenings are staged several times a week during most of the year and are bookable through the larger hotels or from the organizers. The three principal pitches include **El Bordj**, ✆ (04) 446376, **Zagora**, ✆ (04) 445237, and the renowned **Chez Ali**, ✆ (04) 448187, run by an Italian-Moroccan family with great style. Though they are arranged almost entirely for the benefit of tourists they are also one of the most popular events of local festivals. They are also undeniably well managed and impressive circus events that are seen at their best in the added romance of the night. Torch-lit entrances lead to caidal tents where traditional food is cooked before your eyes while skilled musicians and dancers entertain, leading to the finale of horse borne acrobatics, the spectacular *fantasia* charge of Arab horsemen, fireworks and swirling processions of musicians, all set amid illuminated towers and stirring martial music.

Festivals

The annual **National Folklore Festival** is held in the El Badia Palace for two weeks at some point during each summer. For all its orchestration it is perhaps the most rewarding festival in Morocco for a visitor to attend. It presents a fascinating opportunity to hear the distinctive varieties of Berber tribal music, and the chants and dances of the Sufi fraternities. Groups perform here who would not dream of any professional career. The festival takes place every evening from 9pm to midnight, and admission is just 50dh. At the same time the small pavilions to the north and southwest of the palace are opened, and you can see exhibitions as well as the permanent collection of excavated ceramics and an old minbar from the Koutoubia. There is, unfortunately, no way of predicting its dates, which can be any time between May and September.

The main **Fantasia Festival** is held outside the city walls at the end of July, the *moussem* of Sidi Abdel Kader ben Yassin is in September and the fair of contemporary arts is held in November.

South of Marrakech the *moussem* of Setti Fatma at the head of the Ourika Valley is held in August, the *moussem* of Sidi Boutamane in September, and the zaouia of Moulay Brahim holds its *moussem* after Mouloud.

The High Atlas

The highest and most dramatic range of mountains in North Africa, the High Atlas, rises immediately south of Marrakech. This jagged horizon of ethereal blue peaks is a lodestone that draws visitors out from the city. The two great sights of the region, the kasbah of Telouèt and the mosque of Tin-Mal are however more easily visited as you cross the mountains than as a day trip from Marrakech. The High Atlas can be crossed by only three mountain passes, of which only one, the Tizi-n-Babaou that links Marrakech to Agadir, is open all year round. The Tizi-n-Test that connects Marrakech to Taroudannt and the Tizi-n-Tichka to Ouarzazate are cut off by falls of snow and rocks for several weeks every year. As well as these crossings three other tarmac roads intrude into the mountainous region, allowing easy access to the Ourika Valley, Jbel Oukaïmeden and the village of Amizmiz. For a day or a weekend trip into the mountains, the Ourika valley with its selection of restaurants and small hotels, is the obvious, and continosly satisfying choice. The Ourika river sparkles and gurgles over rounded boulders and through the dappled shade of poplars, and even in the midsummer heat of Morocco the valley can appear like some image from an English pastoral poem. And yet, amid this tranquility it can reveal a darker nature. One night a few Augusts ago it was suddenly transformed into a raging torrent for a few murderous hours, when a thunderstorm up among the distant peaks of the High Atlas announced the unleashing of an

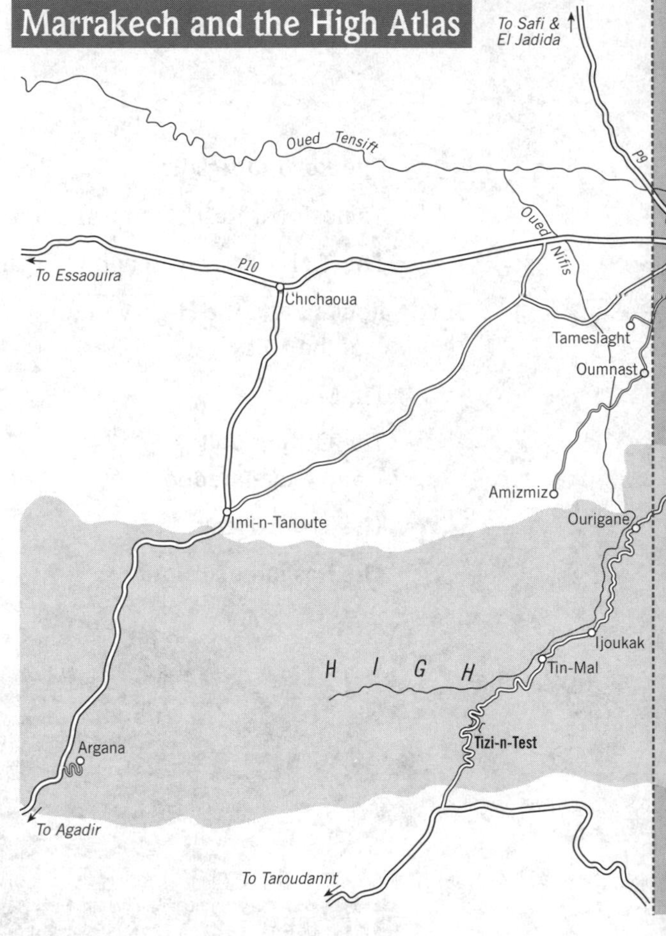

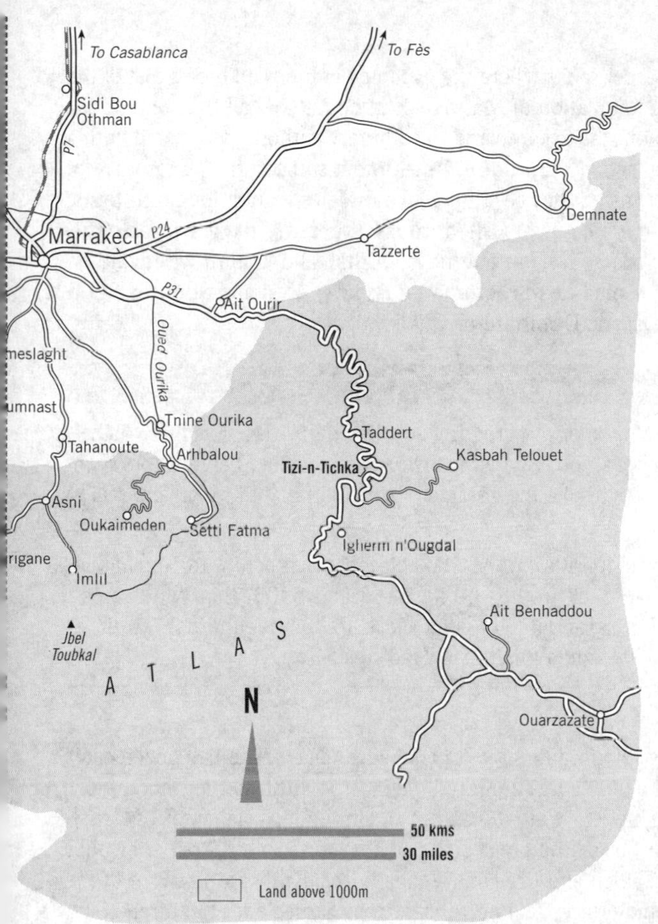

extraordinarily violent rainstorm that took the whole region by surprise. Roads, houses, bridges were swept aside in the confused hours of midnight, and when by morning the water had receded it left a residue of drowned animals and humans—rarely from the indigenous Berber communities, who had kept to the hillside dry-stone houses of their ancestors—mixed among uprooted trees and river-flung boulders. This is a land that has always demanded great hardiness from its inhabitants.

Long before Marrakech was founded the Berber tribes of the High Atlas region practised a seasonal migration. In the winter they brought their flocks down to the plains, planted crops during the brief spring, and then through the summer slowly worked their way back up to the cooler Alpine grazing of the highland peaks. The foundation of a strong central authority at Marrakech in the 11th century disturbed this pattern. The Almoravids with their desert technology improved the irrigation of the plain and established efficient gardens and a sedentary population on the most fertile tracts. Arab tribes who came to the region in the service of the sultans were rewarded with tracts of Berber tribal land below the foothills of the Atlas. By the 19th century most of the Berber tribes had been expelled from the plains by the fierce cavalry of these nomadic Arab tribes. The Berbers either stayed to work as sharecroppers on the plain for an alien landlord, or moved up into the mountains in order to remain free sedentary farmers. There they remain today.

Souks

There is a string of traditional Berber souks where the economy of the plain meets that of the High Atlas foothills. Before the foundation of Marrakech these fulfilled all the commercial requirements of the people without the expense and the arbitrary authority associated with a great city. The closest to Marrakech is **Tnine-de-l'Ourika**, but some of the atmosphere of this Monday souk has been lost since it has become a favourite destination for coach tours. **Aït-Ourir** and **Tazzerte** have much less visited souks the same day; **Tamesloght**, **Tahanaoute** and **Amizmiz** have souks on Tuesdays; **Azilal** and **Oulad-M'barek** on Thursdays, **Sidi-Rahhal** and **El-Kelaâ-des-Sraghana** on Fridays, **Asni** and **Souk-es-Sebt-des-Ouled-Nemâa** on Saturdays; and **Demnate** on Sundays.

The Road to Agadir

This is the fastest and least dramatic of the crossings of the High Atlas. Agadir, which is 275km southwest of Marrakech, can be reached in five hours' driving. Few visitors seem prepared to break their journey, so despite the volume of passing traffic this highland region remains surprisingly unspoilt.

A fast, busy road, the P10, leads due west of Marrakech for 74km across to Chichaoua. There is an older, slower tarmac track (routes 6028, 6453 and 6403) that winds cross-country from Marrakech to Imi-n-Tanoute, passing close to the Wednesday **souk at Guemassa** and (about 12km further on) a **kasbah** at **Had-des-Mjatt**.

Chichaoua

At the central crossroads of the town traffic stops to take advantage of the half-dozen cafés that serve *brochettes* and delicious, long-simmered *tagines*. A **souk** is held here every Thursday and Sunday while a craft centre attempts to maintain the high standards of carpet-making set by the Oulad Bou Sbaa, 'the sons of he of the lions'. This Arab tribe first established themselves in the Tafilalt and the Drâa Valley in the 13th century. Half of the tribe were recruited by a Merenid prince, Abou el Abbas, in his struggle for the throne, and were later posted on land between Marrakech and Essaouira in order to control the Berber tribes of Haha. Their carpets were much sought after in the 19th century, and in 1936 a cooperative was established at Chichaoua to maintain their quality. The other half of the tribe had stayed in the Drâa and remained there until the Berber Aït-Atta confederacy pushed them further south into the Western Sahara. There the Oulad Bou Sbaa carved out a new territory for themselves, but in 1910 they were destroyed in one of the last great tribal battles of Morocco when they literally resisted the Reguibat to the last man.

To the south of this dusty town there are beautifully calm garden estates ringed by cypress trees which stand tall and elegant, their dark green silhouettes piercing the horizon of low, bleak pink hills. Three km east of Chichaoua, by the dry riverbed, traces of a Saadian aqueduct and sugar refinery have been discovered. It is a sobering thought that despite the advances of the last 70 years this region is still far removed from the prosperity it enjoyed in the 16th century. About 25km west of Chichaoua on the road to Essaouira is the village of **Sidi-Mokhtar**, which has a market on Wednesdays where you can also find examples of the carpets of this region.

Imi-n-Tanoute

The town of Imi-n-Tanoute, 47km south of Chichaoua, is perched at the entrance to a High Atlas pass. It is built on the hard, dry land that rises above the cultivated valley and hosts a busy **souk** on Mondays. There is a choice of **cafés** in the central square where it is also possible to rent a basic room. By the riverbed, surrounded by olive groves, is a 19th-century **kasbah**, which with the **kasbah** of **Boubaoute**, 34km to the east, straddled the territory of the Enfifa and Demsira tribes, which were ruled by the M'Touggi, a dynasty of *caids*.

The M'Touggi *Caids*: A Foot in Both Camps

In the 1850s a M'Touggi *caid* had briefly extended his rule west over the neighbouring coastal province of Haha. His nephew who succeeded him, Abdel Malik M'Touggi, maintained a slave guard of 500 men who were all mounted on grey horses and distinguished by a silver ring in their ear.

Caid Abdel Malik M'Touggi's greatest hour was in 1911, when he was appointed Pacha of Marrakech by Sultan Moulay Hafid, and his men held all the kasbahs north of the High Atlas. The next year the new pacha was caught between the French army advancing from the north and the forces of the Blue Sultan from the south. His political manoeuvres were so quick and convoluted that in the words of Gavin Maxwell, 'the M'Touggi could scarcely be said even to have kept a foot in both camps'. His footwork was adroit and he survived with his feudal domain intact to become a lesser ally of the French.

The **Sembal Valley** to the east of Imi-n-Tanoute offers a possible approach into the mountainous hinterland. About 9km east of the town on the 6403 back road to Marrakech the village of **Bou Laouane** marks the junction with a 15km track that heads up the valley to the Thursday market held at **El-Khémis**. This is the limit for most vehicles, though the trek south further up the valley through the hamlet of **Lalla-Aziza** and up towards the **Tizi-n-Tabgourt** pass at 2666m makes for rewarding walking.

Through the Mountains

The most dramatic M'Touggi kasbah on the main road to Agadir is found above the hamlet of **Mintalous.** Perched on a hill of grey, slate-like stone, the ruined kasbah has a fine view over the terraced gardens and almond orchards of the valley below, and its deserted interior can be visited in a half-hour walk. It is a small traditional structure built from double layers of the surrounding grey stone; two water tanks still work and the heavy wooden gates remain in place, stamped with characteristic circular designs. The M'Touggi, men of the plains, were obliged continuously to master the highland tribes of the Bemsire and Ida-ou-Ziki in order to maintain their control of the whole of this strategic pass.

Thirty km south of Imi-n-Tanoute is the roadside **Café Populaire**, and just beyond it a seasonal waterfall. On your right in another 20km you should see a striking cliff-face of dried stalagmites left by a seasonal waterfall beneath, which a Berber village squats.

The turning to **Argana** is to the left, about 60km south of Imi-n-Tatoute. It straddles both banks of the river Aït Moussa. On the west bank are the ruins of a hill-top **agadir**, on the east a neat square little **fort** built by the French, below which a **souk** is held on Tuesdays—the

souk El Jemaa. A dirt track runs from here along the valley of the Aït Moussa, passing an impressive gorge before reaching the secluded villages of **Timesgadiouine** and **Aglagal**. From Argana a number of other tracks extend into the mountains. The most attractive of these climbs towards the summit of Jbel Aoulime (3555m), 25km due east of Argana as the crow flies. This mountain is well inside the territory of the Berber Seksawa tribe, who always remained quite independent of the authority of the M'Touggi *caids*.

Returning to the main road to Agadir you pass the villages of **Bigoudine** and **Tassademt**, before reaching the shores of the new **Tamzaourt Reservoir** and the cafés of **Ameskroud**, which are less than 50km from Agadir.

Tameslogh Kasbah and Amizmiz

The turning to the peaceful village of Tameslogh, surrounded by miles of olive and orange groves, is 15km south of Marrakech on the S507, the tarmac road to Amizmiz. Turn right here by a five-towered garden enclosure with an imposing white entrance tower, inhabited by a family and their donkey. In the garden there is an olive press, and the ruins of a pavilion and a koubba are just visible in the olive groves south of the town.

Arriving at the crossroads, take a left fork into the central souk area of the village, where you pick up a local guide for the short walk to the kasbah. Arcades line the fronts of three great pyramid-roofed **shrines** that hold the tombs of a saintly dynasty, and the **zaouia mosque** can be seen on your left. Beyond, long towering walls lead down to the dark gateway which guards the entrance to the old inner courtyard paved with rounded river cobble-stones, and the ruins of a succession of walled gardens. In the right-hand corner, knock on the old door to attract the attention of the venerable custodian. Providing he is feeling well disposed he will take you on a tour of the old apartments arranged around a rooftop courtyard. The gentle fading of the delicate floral paintwork and the carved plaster decoration, the rattle of locks and shutters, the fluttering of disturbed birds, all combine with the fine views over the old gardens to create a heady aura of melancholic decay. For those who follow Rose Macaulay and take pleasure in ruins the rambling mass of the **kasbah** is an ossified dream, though others may find it a time consuming expedition. The custodian likes to be tipped.

The Man of 366 Sciences

The Tameslogh Zaouia was founded in the 16th century by Abdallah ben Hossein el Hassani, a holy man famed for his miraculous powers and so knowledgeable that the superstitious referred to him as 'the man of 366 sciences'. By the 19th century the spiritual reputation of the zaouia had diminished, though its wealth remained. The sheik of the zaouia invested in the first machine-powered olive oil press in Morocco, but it was so efficient that the rival neighbouring mill owners organized a 'Luddite' riot against this foreign machine. The sheikh, increasingly isolated and alarmed for his wealth, arranged to be placed under British protection and received the British MP Cunninghame Graham in 1897. Graham left an account of 'its crenellated walls, flanking towers, and dome-shaped roofs. It had innumerable courts, a mosque, a women's wing, a granary, baths . . . a garden where water trickled in a thousand little rills; canes fluttered, rustling like feathers in the air . . . and over all the air of decadence, mixed with content.'

Amizmiz

The village of **Oumnast**, watched over by two kasbahs, is 10km south of Tamesloght, and 8km further there is a dam on the river Nfiss behind which a long lake stretches. This was the first dam built by the French in the region, finished in 1935, and it was named after the romantic ruins of the nearby kasbah of **Lalla-Takerkoust**. Amizmiz is 20km past the dam. The licensed but cheap **Hôtel de France** (recently reported to be closed) is on the way into town. It has half a dozen ground-floor bedrooms that open on to a pretty walled garden, partly covered by an extensive vine. Below the garden is the shell of a French chapel.

On the other side of the river, known as the Anougal or Amizmiz, lies the bulk of the village beside a ruined **kasbah** of deep red pisé. There are also some older ruins above the river gorge that have been empty and decaying since before the turn of the century. For it is recorded of them that 'the *caid* oppressed the people of the town and district beyond the powers of even Arabs and Berbers to endure; so they rebelled, and to the number of 12000 besieged the place, took it by storm and tore it all to pieces to search for money in the rose-pink walls' (Cunninghame Graham).

Amizmiz also has a **zaouia** founded by Sidi el Hossein ben Messoud, and an old ***mellah.*** There were Jewish communities in most of the lowland Atlas markets; they spoke ironically of the *caids* as their dear friends, in that they all owed money. One of the busiest and least tourist-visited **souks** of the area is held in Amizmiz every Tuesday; you are certain to find local Berber pottery for sale.

South of the town a dirt track leads up through attractive rough woodland for about 30km to the hamlet of **Medinet**, where a path approaches the summit of Jbel Erdouz (3578m).

The Tizi-n-Test: Asni, Ouirgane and Tin-Mal

The Tizi-n-Test pass crosses the High Atlas to link Marrakech and Taroudannt through 200km of mountain road. It can be closed by snow or made more dangerous by ice any time between December and March, and each year some portion is destroyed by falling rocks or a swollen mountain stream. Nevertheless, it is very worth venturing up here. You have the opportunity to climb the highest mountain in North Africa, one of only two mosques in Morocco (with the Hassan II in Casablanca) open to non-Muslims, and to admire a succession of ruined kasbahs. Or you might simply come for the clear air, to walk in the high valleys and stay in memorable hotels.

Getting Around

There are eight **buses** daily from Marrakech to Asni (90mins), which leave from Bab Doukkala bus station and call at the Bab er Rob stop on their way south. If you are heading further up the valley or wish to cross the pass there are three choices: the dawn departure (either 5 or 6am) for Taroundannt (7–8hrs away), the 2pm that arrives at Ijoukak village at around 4pm or the 6pm to Taliouine (a 7–8 hour journey).

A place in a ***grand taxi*** will get you to Asni or Zaouia-Moulay-Brahim in three-quarters of an hour for 12dh. Or you could bargain with a *grand taxi* and hire him for between 200 and 300dh for a whole day trip up to Idni.

Tahanaoute

Thirty-one km from Marrakech on the Taroudannt road, the S501, you pass the strikingly picturesque village of Tahanaoute on the far side of the riverbed. A cascade of pisé houses surrounds a great rock which shelters the **shrine** of Sidi Mohammed El Kebir, whose festival is celebrated at Mouloud. It was the subject of Winston Churchill's last painting in 1958. Tahanaoute proper is a kilometre further, an ancient marketplace on the border of the mountains and plains where a **souk** is held each Tuesday.

Zaouia-Moulay-Brahim

Beyond Tahanaoute the road twists up above the meandering course of the river as it flows past the five knuckles of black rock that protrude into Moulay Brahim Gorge. A cluster of **cafés** line the roadside and the riverbed just before the turning uphill to the village of Zaouia-Moulay-Brahim, and look out over a wooded hill on the other side of the river. This hillside **zaouia** is one of the most important centres of spiritual life in the region. A fortnight after Mouloud a great festival is held here. A camel is sacrificed at the gates of the town, and its head and skin are taken down to honour two nearby springs that are used for ritual washing by men and women. The 3hr trek to the koubba on the summit is an integral part of the pilgrimage. Gaily-caparisoned horses stand patiently on the banks of the riverbed beside mounting stools for the use of pilgrims in need of a photographic souvenir of themselves in the pose of a cavalier.

Even outside the festival, Moulay-Brahim remains a popular day-trip destination for Marrakechi families. The town is formed from a small maze of streets that extend in a confusion of levels, courts and paved passages around the central shrine. This has a distinctive green pyramid roof; a wooden bar has been placed below the minaret as a barrier to non-Muslims. The rest of the village with its cafés, pilgrim trinket stalls, two surviving potteries and hill views, is open and the population are pleasantly welcoming. You can stay in the centre of Zaouia-Moulay-Brahim in one of its several cheap and basic **hotels**, or at a new four-star hotel that has been in the process of construction on one side of the town, the **Hôtel Afoulaki**. To the west a dirt road passes through numerous very secluded hillside villages before reaching Amizmiz, 65km away.

Asni

This pleasant roadside village, 15km further south, is the local administrative centre and the destination for most *grands taxis* from the Bab er Rob in Marrakech. Apart from the opportunities for walking from the hotel here (Imlil, Zaouia-Moulay-Brahim and Ouirgane are all within easy reach), it could be worth a visit for the busy **souk** held here on Saturdays.

Where to Stay

The moderately-priced **Grand Hôtel du Toubkal**, © (04) 319203, in Asni is a calm, dignified establishment with a wonderful view of the mountains from its back terrace, an ornate Moorish hall lit by fires in winter, wonderful homemade bread, a pool, garden, a bar, a caged wild boar and only 25 bedrooms.

Toubkal National Park

From Asni a partly tarmacked road leads up to the hamlet of **Imlil**, which is the centre for hill walking in the Toubkal National Park. The park is named after the highest mountain in all North Africa and embraces some of the most striking and awesome highland scenery in Morocco. It does also attract about 75 per cent of the hill walkers who come to the country. Be warned that here you will not be the only foreigner in the mountains, while practically anywhere else in the country you will.

Imlil

The road to Imlil follows the right bank of the river Moulay Brahim, climbing from Asni at 1150m to Imlil at 1740m in 17km. On Saturday, for the **souk**, there is a regular truck-shuttle between Asni and Imlil. Other days of the week you will have to wait until the *grand taxi* is ready to do the trip. A seat in either usually costs 15dh/$1.50. Café meals are available in Imlil and some of the mountain villages, but prices can be high and rise steeply with the altitude. As there are kitchens in the hostels many walkers bring provisions from Marrakech and stock up on fresh vegetables, eggs and fruit at the Saturday morning souk in Asni.

The approach road passes low stone houses of the Berber Gheghaia tribe, farmers and herdsmen who have tenaciously created fertile garden terraces from a wilderness of stone. The dress of the High Atlas women compensates for a life of continual hard labour with a fantastic panoply of colour. Village life around the climbing centre of Imlil remains surprisingly undisturbed. It provides an insight into the reality of a highland culture and a lifestyle that has been consistently over-romanticized. The level of dirt is always surprising but the back-breaking daily labour—clearing stones from the fields, and hunting for firewood, grazing and water—is awesome.

The hamlet of Imlil is an initially disappointing cluster of cafés and shops centred on a hostel run by the Club Alpin Français. The ascent of Jbel Toubkal (4167m) is the primary objective of the visitors who come to Imlil. The village has a correspondingly hearty air, full of an international community of sports people with their well-meaning advice, backpacks and luminous bright cagoules.

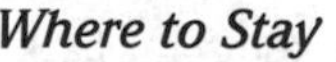

Where to Stay

A night in any of the Alpine Club hostels, including use of the kitchen and a tip to the guardian, will cost around 30dh. Escaping a little from the outward-bound atmosphere of the hostel there are meals and beds available from the cheap **Soleil**, **Aksoual** and **Toubkal** and various local lodgings signposted by the new Gîtes d'Etape organization.

Jbel Toubkal: Preparation

Climbing Jbel Toubkal between April and November requires no skills other than determination to scramble up innumerable scree slopes, while between December and March the snow and ice make the mountain face dangerous even for skilled climbers. You will need strong shoes or boots, a hat and dark glasses for daytime, and for night-time a sweater and sleeping bag, even in midsummer. Detailed local maps, guidebooks, experienced mountain guides and donkeys can all be found at Imlil. Mountain guides will cost about 150dh/$15 a day, and mules or donkeys about half that. Take added tiredness from the altitude and midday heat into account in your plans, and be sure to drink only bottled or well water. Most people find themselves resting overnight at the Louis Neltner hut before climbing to the summit in the morning.

Jbel Toubkal: The Climb

The hillside village of **Aremd/Around** is a good hour's walk from Imlil, but you can easily find it by following the river path uphill. It is the largest settlement of the valley and the Berber farmers are well used to creating a little income by renting out rooms and space for tents, and selling meals. Staying in a mountain village is in many ways preferable to Imlil and there is even a small but expensive grocery stall here.

From Aremd the trail zigzags up the valley. The path crosses over the stream about two hours later, just before the hamlet of **Sidi-Chamharouch** where soft sticky drinks, cooled by stream water, are sold. Just beyond the hamlet a concrete bridge crosses a gorge to the **koubba of Sidi Chamharouch**, a popular and venerated Berber shrine. As with many of the mountain cults, a Muslim saint has been created out of traditional beliefs in the spirit of the mountain and the guardian of the spring. It is offensive to local custom for a western tourist to even cross the bridge to approach the koubba. In 1840 a botanist ignored local advice and insisted on climbing Toubkal and was nearly lost in a fierce gale which suddenly arose. 'The Atlas tribesmen discouraged the expedition from ascending the mountain top, the sanctuary of the djinns. One of the Chleuh carried with him a live cock under his arm. In a state of utmost excitement he now proceeded to cut the animal's throat, in order thus to appease the wrath of our supernatural foes. But the storm, now almost a hurricane, raged with increasing violence.' (Hooker and Ball).

From Sidi-Chamharouch it is a three-hour climb up the zigzagging path to the Louis Neltner hut at 3207m, run by the Club Alpin Français. This is sited on the tree line beyond which stretch the completely barren boulder and scree faces of Jbel Toubkal. From Neltner the summit is another three-hour climb up a reasonably clear approach along the south corrie. It is crowned by a tripod, and the view south to Jbel Siroua and north to Marrakech is at its most magnificent in the clear, hazeless light of the morning.

Returning back to the Neltner hut you could consider a four-hour walk to **Lake Ifni**. This involves an hour's climb up to the **Tizi-n'Ouanouns** pass and a three-hour descent through scree slopes and stone fields to this deep, secretive mountain lake enclosed by shattered hills. In the summer the lakeside is an important watering point for sub-Saharan herds, and a seasonal hamlet of shepherd huts will often be found occupied. The lake can be fished for trout, and dried animal dung from the shores burnt to keep the flies and mosquitoes away.

East and West from Imlil

Having achieved the ascent of Jbel Toubkal you may want to tackle some of the less frequented tracks. East of Imlil is the village of **Tacheddirt**, which has another Alpine Club hut and is a mere four-hour walk away. From there you can ascend **Jbel Angour** (3616m), or walk to one of the hotels at Oukaïmeden or to Setti-Fatma at the head of the Ourika Valley. West from Imlil there are trails to the hotels at Ouirgane on the Tizi-n-Test pass.

These are all ambitious two- or three-day expeditions. They will require a guide, a mule to carry the luggage, and much earnest planning, map consulting and bargaining. But you may have already found that in Imlil it is difficult to bring conversation round to any other topic.

Ouirgane

Returning back to the main Tizi-n-Test road, the hamlet of Ouirgane lies 16km south of Asni. It mainly consists of two celebrated hotels, whose gardens face each other across a stream which drains the western face of Jbel Toubkal to merge with the river Nfiss just below the village. Four km south of Ouirgane there is the intriguing mass of drystone walls that forms the hilltop **agadir** at **Tagadirt-n-Bour**, to the right of the road. If you are staying overnight you will have time to walk upstream to the village of **Aneraz** and pay your respects (a coin to the custodian, or a lighted candle on the tomb) to three High Atlas Jewish mystics, the Rabbis Haim Ben Diouane, Mordechai Ben Hamou and Abraham Ben Hamou, who lie buried in a modern courtyard compound above the dense clutch of traditional village houses. Other strolls include the two-hour walk up to villages such as Tikhfist, or to a mountain waterfall in the company of local guides.

Where to Stay and Eating Out

expensive

The **Résidence La Roseraie**, © (04) 432094, is made up of some two dozen apartments scattered around an extensive riverside garden (a fusion of raw Morocco and bourgeois France) which also contains two swimming pools and a stunning mass of rose beds, all confined within a horizon of wooded mountains. There are a few cheaper rooms in the central buildings, which are otherwise occupied by the reception, a drawing room, restaurant and bar where a portrait of Caid Goudafa by E. Varley hangs. The original riverside **riding stables** were swept away in a horrific midsummer flood in 1996, but have been replaced by a new block safely uphill where the immaculately-groomed thoroughbreds and the stable donkey can be admired. A new health centre has also been established above the mineral stream, although the pseudo-medical nature of spa life compares unfavourably with the joys of walking or riding in the magnificent hinterland. The hotel is one of the best places from which to ride in Morocco, and can organise anything from an hour's tuition within the grounds of the estate or a week-long expedition into the mountains. Rooms in the hotel are only available on a full- or half-board basis, but the food is naturally excellent. It is deservedly popular, and often dominated by British guests, who tend to withdraw to the quieter upper pool or go out riding to avoid the passing lunch time-trade at weekends. There is a daily minibus in and out of Marrakech and a transfer service from the airport.

inexpensive

Le Sanglier Qui Fume, © (02) 121208, is one of Morocco's surviving colonial institutions, which Paul Bowles described in 1959: 'Lunch outside in the sun at Le Sanglier Qui Fume. Our table midway between a chained eagle and a chained monkey, both of which watched us distrustfully while we ate... Madame is

Hungarian and lives in the hope that people coming through Ouirgane will speak her language or at least know Budapest . . . obviously disappointed in us.' There are 16 bedrooms in the garden of this riverside hotel (directly opposite the Roseraie) which has a pool and a few pet boars and storks. The dining room is dominated by large dogs and a collection of kasbah oil paintings by Holbing, an ex-German professor in Marrakech.

In recent years the hotel has hit a patch of troubled water with the departure of Madame Thevenin-Frey and a legal dispute amongst the various heirs to the property. Even if the rooms may have deteriorated a little, though, the French cooking remains as good as ever.

Ijoukak and the High Valley of the Nfiss

From Ouirgane the road climbs through steep wooded hills beside the river to emerge 30km later into the high valley of the Nfiss. It is one of the most hauntingly beautiful places in Morocco, an archetypal vision of a secret valley surrounded by a jagged horizon of snow-capped mountains. Flowing through this upper valley is the river Nfiss: found in gentle aspect, a stream of slow-moving, cool, clear water full of darting trout, with orchards, terraced gardens and hillside hamlets lining its banks.

Walks Around Ijoukak

The roadside settlement of Ijoukak, 200m after you cross the Agoundis stream, is at the entrance to the valley. This hamlet is lined with four café-restaurants in a row: the last one, run by Brahim Aït Ougadir, serves delicious lentil and onion soup and *tagines* to order. You can ask for rooms to rent, and may find yourself in a splendid spartan bedroom equipped with candles, blankets and bottles of water for washing.

Just by the bridge a dirt road leads up the pretty Agoundis Valley through the villages of **Taghbart** and **El Maghzen**. It ends just past El Maghzen, about a three-hour walk from Ijoukak. A trail then continues the climb up the increasingly narrow and steep valley, punctuated by hamlets for another 8km until you reach the final edge of cultivable land at **Aït-Youb**.

Another good day's walk from Ijoukak is to take the right turn at Taghbart, cross the river and then climb up the side of Jbel Oucheddon (2840m).

The Goundafa Kasbah of Talat-n-Yâkoub

Just out of Ijoukak you pass a right turn that leads up to Talat-n-Yâkoub. It is a quiet, dusty administrative settlement but its two market courtyards, the arch below the mosque and the Café Tin-Mal can look pretty enough when filled for the Wednesday **souk**. From the souk you can look over the road down on to the kasbah of Talat-n-Yâkoub.

To the right of the road a small sculpted stone pavilion stands beside a water tank. An audible trickle of water descends to irrigate an orchard that stretches down to the Nfiss and the sprawling ruins of the Goundafa kasbah of Talat-n-Yâkoub. The kasbah is built of pisé and timber on stone foundations, and is at least the third to have stood on this site. The existing structure largely dates from after 1906, but it is already in a precarious state. Most of the stairways and upper storeys have fallen in, but if you are prepared to nose around among the ruins, the remains of the columned prayer-hall, reception room, great dark granaries, and the slim interior court overhung with balconies can still be made out.

Perched right beside the river and overlooked from the opposite bank by the Tisi Nemiri, the hill of stones, the kasbah is quite clearly unsuited to defence. It never served as a fortress, but as the palace and administrative court for two generations of Goundafa *caids* who ruled the Tizi-n-Test pass and the Nfiss Valley. It held an assorted population of 1200 servants and slaves and a harem of 300 women. A small ***mellah*** beside the kasbah held a Jewish community who provided vital skills such as pastry-making, silversmithing and financial services.

Si Taieb, a Caid of the High Atlas

Si Taieb succeeded his father as *caid* of the Goundafa tribe at the age of twenty. His father, after a lifetime of rebellion, had sued for peace with the government and sent a legendary gift to the palace at Marrakech: a hundred male slaves, each leading a horse and a camel; followed the next day by a hundred slave girls each leading a cow and a young calf. He also sent his son to join the army of Sultan Moulay Hassan; in 1883 he was confirmed as *caid* of the Goundafa and sent home. Once in power, the young *caid* launched a campaign of aggressive expansion. He had at his disposal a tribal force of 5000 men and his own slave guard of 500. By 1900 he had trebled the size of his domain, a fact which increasingly drove the rival High Atlas *caids*, the Glaoui and M'Touggi, into an alliance against him. In the words of the latter, 'He is a hill man who has discovered the plains. It will not be easy to get him out.' R. B. Cunninghame Graham has left a description of Si Taieb holding court in 1901: 'Forty years of age, thick set and dark complexioned...not noble in appearance but still looking as one accustomed to command; hands strong and muscular, voice rather harsh but low, and trained in the best school of Arab manners, so as to be hardly audible... His clothes white and of the finest wool...his secretaries never stopped opening and writing letters, now and then handing one to the caid...slave boys, in clothes perhaps worth eighteen pence, served coffee.'

In 1906 the rival *caids* seized their chance, for Si Taieb had been called to Fès. Their combined forces descended to plunder the Nfiss valley and burn the kasbah of Talat-n-Yâkoub. Si Taieb returned to find his homeland in desolation, and for six years never left the valley. Lyautey, the French Resident-General, was the only man who could entice the warrior *caid* from his mountain realm. In 1912 the lowland kasbahs of Amizmiz and Aguergour were returned to Si Taieb, and at a stroke he was restored to his pre-1906 position. He was also given arms and money for the conquest of the Sous Valley. After the capture of Taroudannt in 1913 he was honoured by being created *naib*, representative of the sultan in the south. In 1917 he was appointed pacha of Tiznit, and for seven years he remained in command of this frontier of the desert war. In 1924 he retired to his mountain kasbahs, where he died four years later, aged 65.

After his death his feudal authority was dismantled and replaced by the even rule of French officials, while his lands were divided between his son Lhassen and two nephews. A pleasant white house of spacious courtyards can be seen attached to the end of the kasbah of Talat-n-Yâkoub. This is the house of the *caid's* grandson, an electrical engineer from Casablanca.

Agadir-n-Gouf

Above the road on the left, about 2km south of Talat-n-Yâcoub, there is a hilltop agadir. This square castle commands excellent views over the valley and looks as ancient and as strong as the hills. It was built as a stronghold in 1907, the year after the Glaoui and M'Touggi had ravaged the valley. Fearing their return, Si Taieb kept what he treasured most—his horses—safe in the agadir, stabled around the enormous central court, which was built around a fissure in the hill. Large reception rooms were added later and traces of their elaborate carved plasterwork can still be seen. The agadir is now completely uninhabited. It is easier to walk up to it from the north, where a path winds down the valley.

Tin-Mal

Another 3km south the Almohad **mosque of Tin-Mal** emerges high up on the opposite bank of the river, a fortress of the faith with its high walls and strong towers. It is usually empty of tourists, yet must be considered one of the most memorable sites of Morocco, the sole survivor of the 12th-century city of Tin-Mal and one of only two mosques in Morocco that a non-Muslim may enter. Its striking position, deep in the High Atlas mountains, is only equalled by its extraordinary history.

It has been restored in the last decade and a small museum built to house various architectural fragments.The track from the road has also been repaired, and you no longer have to clamber across a broken bridge. Small boys lie in wait for visitors, and will enthusiastically lead you to the custodian Mohammed Filali, who may be in the company of his young son or one of his three hazel-eyed daughters. You might add a tip onto the price of your admission ticket. On Fridays the village of Tin-Mal uses the mosque and so it may be closed to tourists.

The Mosque

You enter through a small but sturdy door in the corner of the main tower which used to be reserved for the *imam*, the leader of the prayers, and the *khatib*, the pronouncer of the Friday sermon. The mosque is now roofless but this increases rather than diminishes the splendour of its interior. Deep shadows cast by the surviving brick columns and horseshoe arches contrast with an expanse of sunbaked wall which reflects the mountain sunlight to give the whole of the interior an enchanted roseate glow.

The central tower has been placed immediately above the mihrab, the arched niche which indicates the direction of Mecca. The dome above the

mihrab and the arches that link with the domes underneath the two corner towers were richly decorated to draw the worshipper's attention naturally in this direction. The central aisle would also have boasted more elaborate details. All the other aisles would have been supported by horseshoe arches, embellished by bas relief columns of which a few survive. At the opposite end to the mihrab is the *sahn*, the open-air court for worshippers to wash themselves, which has its own entrance arch and would have once contained an elaborate marble fountain. Either side of the *sahn* are two prayer-halls which, screened and provided with their own entrances, could be used by women. The old gates piled up against the outside walls are from the Koutoubia at Marrakech, rejected secondhand gifts from the sister mosque built by the Almohads.

In its prime the whole mosque would have been spotlessly white. During the recent restoration some excavations were carried out which unearthed not so much as a fragment of a green-glazed roof tile or a single piece of *zellij* mosaic, otherwise ubiquitous elements in any Moroccan shrine. Almohad Tin-Mal remained true to its puritanical origins, and was composed of just bricks, wood and white plaster. The three brick towers are an unusual feature in that they are built above the actual prayer-hall of the mosque. Most minarets are quite free-standing and rarely aligned with the mihrab. The corner minaret towers were crowned by lanterns, but the central one did not reach much higher than it does today. You can climb up its staircase and look south down the Nfiss valley to the Goundafa kasbah of Agadir-n-Gouf, which crowns the central hill. As testament to the restraint of the recent restoration programme a pair of owls have already started nesting in one of the domes.

Ibn Tumert and Tin-Mal

Ibn Tumert was a religious reformer who desired to enforce his puritanical doctrine over the Muslim community. A Chleuh Berber, he was born in one of the small villages on the northern slopes of the Anti-Atlas mountains and travelled east towards Mecca to study in the intellectual centres of the Islamic world. He was a well known and controversial figure before his return to Morocco, and by 1124 he had selected Tin-Mal to be the citadel of his theocratic state.

It became a place of total obedience where he trained the mountain tribes for war against all who would not accept his authority. Dancing, music and singing were

banned, art placed under his severe direction and codes of dress established which denied any ornamentation. Ibn Tumert lectured the Berber tribes in their own dialect, but taught them the Arabic Koran in a characteristically authoritarian manner. Long lines of warriors would each be given a word of the Koran as their name and by obediently calling out their new names in turn could learn whole *suras* of the Koran. As a capstone to his authority, Ibn Tumert gradually led his community to recognize that he was the *Mahdi*, the prophesied successor of Mohammed.

After two years at Tin-Mal he led a series of expeditions that enforced his authority in the valleys of the High Atlas, and consolidated these victories in 1128 by a bloody forty day purge of the tribes. In 1129 three Almoravid armies attempted a joint assault on Tin-Mal. Though these were beaten off, Ibn Tumert's own siege of Marrakech that same year ended in a costly defeat.

The death of Ibn Tumert in 1130 was kept a secret from his followers for three years while his chosen successor, Abdel Moumen, consolidated his authority. In 1148 he captured Marrakech, which became the administrative capital of the empire while Tin-Mal degenerated into the Almohad cult centre, secure treasury and favoured burial ground.

In 1154 Abdel Moumen subtly shifted the Almohads from a movement of religious reform to a dynasty invested in his own family. The great mosque of Tin-Mal was finished as a triumphant cult centre in the same year that Ibn Tumert's own children, grandchildren and cousins were quietly disposed of.

Tin-Mal Village

There is a ruined kasbah at the centre of the village, as well as a mosque, a Koranic school and an old water tank which produces a regular crop of edible frogs. Past the village (a kilometre north on the main road) the old city walls of Tin-Mal lead up from the riverbank to the heights above. Tin-Mal was both the first and the last bastion of the Almohads. It was finally stormed in 1276 by the Merenids who, though they respected the great mosque, left no house standing, no tomb undefiled, and no citizen of Tin-Mal alive. However, the historian Ibn Khaldoun, who visited Tin-Mal a generation later, found Koranic reciters had returned to the mosque. When they entered the valley in 1924 French administrators found the area around the mosque covered in old shrines of which there is now no trace.

An olive press stands on one side of the village square which was built from one family's savings accumulated in 16 years' emigrant labour in France. The owner is usually happy to show you the mill and explain the process, finishing off by selling you a litre or two of his Tin-Mal olive oil.

South of Tin-Mal

A few kilometres south of Tin-Mal, the village and ruined kasbah of **Mzouzite** is beside a school on the opposite bank of the river. A track passes through the village and up the valleys to the west, leading after about a seven-hour walk to the hamlet of **Arg**. This makes a convenient camping base for those wishing to climb the two mountains to the north and south, Jbel Erdouz (3575m) and Jbel Igdet (3615m).

The kasbah of **Tagoundaft**, 5km from Mzouzite, is perched high up on a pinnacle of rock at 1600m, overshadowed by a curtain wall of mountain. Tagoundaft has resisted all sieges and invaders but now its stone walls are being slowly dismantled and carted away for building rubble by the villagers. The remains of the great tower, aqueduct and overgrown water tank can be examined after a half-hour walk up a mule path. The real rewards for the climb are the view, and the sense of impregnable security you feel from the kasbah's position.

A *caid*'s daughter was placed in Tagoundaft Kasbah while there was fighting in the valley. The commander of the kasbah grew over-familiar with his charge. Rather than compromise her honour and that of her father she calmly walked out of the highest window of the tower.

The hamlet of **Idni** is 4km south of Tagoundaft at the foot of the long climb up the Tizi-n-Test pass. It is a traditional stopping place, a chance for one last calm glass of tea before tackling the hairpin bends of the pass. The **Hôtel Alpina** sadly remains closed after the death of its eccentric proprietor, Madame Gipolou, in 1985. The **Café Igdet** and the village store directly opposite have inherited the passing trade, providing snack meals and *tagines* to order. The café has a small open-air courtyard with three or four spartan rooms. If you stay here you will meet Bassin Mohammed, who trades in minerals and Berber jewellery.

Tizi-n-Test

From Idni the road climbs 18km to the summit of the Tizi-n-Test pass, at 2100 m. This route was opened by the French on 10 November 1928, with a convoy of 30 cars. Some of their initial sense of achievement can still be imagined when crossing the pass today. The road is narrow and often alarming, traversing long mountain slopes to twist suddenly in a tight hairpin bend and expose an unfenced vertical cliff face. The odd scarred relic of a fallen vehicle encourages all but the flashy local drivers to select a lower speed and gear. Crossing in the night, stabs of light can be seen on some improbably high and distant slope that warn you of the convoluted route to follow.

A kilometre before the summit of the pass, watch out for a turning to a TV relay station. This leads to a viewing platform which has easily the best view; both south over the Sous to the Anti-Atlas, and north to Jbel Toubkal. Beyond the actual summit there are a couple of cafés and the familiar mineral displays.

The descent south is possibly even more dramatic. The road drops 1600m to the Sous Valley in under 30km. As you descend, you pass wrecked vehicles and hamlets that cling to barren, steep-walled valleys, while the Sous Valley shimmers verdant in the distance—an exotic and mysterious land that beckons to the traveller. At the junction with the main P32 road Taroudannt is 51km west, Taliouine 67km to the east.

The Ourika Valley and Oukaïmeden

The Ourika is a narrow valley that cuts deep into the High Atlas. As you intrude south down the valley, the mountains rise ever more precipitously and the area of cultivation diminishes further. At the head of the valley constricted terraced gardens, their walls constructed from round river boulders, their bright crops shaded by slender almond trees, appear like some vision of the Promised Land. The gardens are productive throughout most of the year, since the Ourika stream which drains the northeast face of Jbel Toubkal seldom runs dry.

In the summer, when Marrakech can feel debilitatingly like a furnace, the Ourika Valley has a gentle trickle of cool, clear water, a breeze in the trees, trout in the river and oleanders that have just burst into flower. Small pottery workshops are found off the road and flour mills operate above the riverbed, fed by irrigation ditches that double as a source of power. For this constancy of supply the valley can pay an occasional but high price. Sudden fierce rainfall, especially in winter, carries a flood downstream which can rip out the sides of hills, bury houses in mud and boulders, and sweep all away in a great torrent of water.

In the past the people of the Ourika Valley were in a powerful position since they controlled the water supply to the city and gardens of Marrakech, for old Moroccan law did not acknowledge the rights of any user downstream. In practice this meant that no ruler of Marrakech could afford to have a hostile power in control of the valley and it has always been closely associated with the affairs of Marrakech. This is still true today, and the lower reaches of the valley are lined with the villas of the richer Marrakechis. It is a traditional place to relax, with a good selection of licensed restaurants and small hotels beside the road. You can camp at the head of the valley or just use it as a midday escape from the city. A fairly continuous stream of buses and *grands taxis* plies the road from the Bab er Rob in Marrakech to Ourika. A place in a *grand taxi* should cost 20dh/$2, though you might have difficulty in finding a taxi to Oukaïmeden in the summer months.

Twenty-eight km from Marrakech a dirt track to the left leads to the hamlet of **Aghmat**. This was, until the arrival of the Almoravids in the 11th century, the principal town of the region. There is little now to show of a city that until the 14th century boasted medersas and royal tombs. But because of its association with El Mutamid, the poet-prince of Seville who died here, exiled by the great Almoravid Sultan Youssef ben Tachfine, the shade of his koubba might make a romantic picnic spot.

At the entrance to the Ourika Valley, 33km from Marrakech, you pass through the Monday **souk of Tnine-de-l'Ourika** which has for that one day each week become a destination for coach tours, and for that reason alone is usually well worth missing. On the opposite side of the valley, across a bridge, is the settlement of **Dar-Caid-Ouriki**, the house of the *caid* of Ourika. The ruins of the kasbah and its garden are approached through the encroaching hamlet of farms. Dramatically placed below a geological fault, the ruins retain a certain aura. Abdallah, *caid* of the Ourika in the 19th century, was an early ally of the Glaoui, an alliance confirmed by his marriage to one of Madani's six daughters. This relationship did not, however, stop Madani's brother Si Thami el Glaoui, from removing Abdallah and appointing his own brother Mohammed El Arbi to the influential caidship.

The village of **Irhef** is 5km further up the valley. This used to be an entirely Jewish community, but only a few Jews remain and the Jewish charity school is now full of young Muslims.

Setti-Fatma

This hamlet, at 1500m and nearly 20km further, is the virtual edge of human habitation in the Ourika Valley. The last kilometre of road to Setti-Fatma takes the form of a washed bank of gravel, which is continually being swept away. Across the stream from the hamlet, a path crosses below a group of café-restaurants with rooms, beneath which you can camp, and continues up to a system of **seven waterfalls**. Getting up to the first fall with its plunge pool, sunbathing rocks and tiny café is a quarter-of-an-hour's stroll partly under the shade of walnut trees (raided by Barbary apes) but it does include the odd rock scramble. The other, higher falls demand some experience of rock climbing, or at least a good head for heights.

Following a path above the east bank of the main river you reach the green tiled **koubba** of Setti-Fatma (not accessible to non-Muslims), a popular burial ground as the tell-tale head- and foot-stones indicate. The window grilles of the shrine are covered in a web of cloth knots left by supplicants. This is the centre of a four-day *moussem* held in August which attracts Berber farmers and shepherds from all over the High Atlas.

For the adventurous there is a 10km walk up the valley to the hamlet of **Timichchi**, where paths branch off to Oukaïmeden, the CAF refuge at Tacheddirt, or the summit of Jbel Angour.

Where to Stay and Eating Out

Hotels get gradually seedier and accommodation cheaper as you proceed up the valley. All give Arhbalou as their address, but despite this they are easy to find, strung along the road.

First along the road, up a turning to the right, is the expensive **Ourika Hôtel**, © (02) 120999, which has a good view, a bar, a pool and good cooking but nevertheless a slightly soulless air. Then, not far after the Oukaïmeden turning, (which is on the right) you will come to the moderately priced **Auberge Marquis**. This is primarily a restaurant but also has a few rooms for rent. The bar can be lively and the tranquil licensed restaurant serves a reliably delicious *tagine*.

A few kilometres further up the main valley (km 49) there is a knot of places. The **Kasbah Restaurant** on the right has been established in an old Glaoui pavilion. It can be overrun with coach tours, but retains a certain chaotic style. Almost directly opposite is the **Hôtel Amnougar**, © (02) 110837 (reservations can also be made through its Marrakech office, © (04) 304502), which is a popular weekend base for Marrakechis. It has a bar, pool, dining room and is moderately priced. Also on the left is the expensive **Le Lion de l'Ourika** restaurant, © (04) 445322, which has a palatial dining room, uniformed waiters and elaborate set meals.

One of the last in this group, but by no means least, tucked away up a drive to the right of the road (at km 52) and in its own garden, is the moderate-priced **Auberge Ramuntchko**, © (02) 319102, which has just eight bedrooms, a bar, a fire-warmed dining room for winter and for summer lunches an elegant terrace shaded with white umbrellas, filled with the sound of the river and basking in a magnificent view of the mountains. Its near neighbour **Dar Piano**, © (02) 121073, is an equal in cuisine but more exclusive in terms of accommodation, with just three (expensive) rooms that often booked up weeks in advance.

The cheap places are all at Asgaour, where the tarmac road gives out. The best of these is the new **Tafoukt Hôtel**, though the village cafés such as the **Asgaour** are good for meals, basic rooms and roof space as well as advice on walks and introductions to possible mountain guides. In Setti-Fatma itself the **Café les Cascades** and its neighbours rent out basic bedrooms and prepare meals to order; or you can camp beside the café on shaded grass, listening to the music of the river.

Oukaïmeden

Getting to Oukaïmeden, 'the meeting place of the four winds', provides at least half of the excitement of the place. Ten kilometres south of Tnine-de-l'Ourika, at the village of **Arhbalou**, a right turn takes you, in 30 twisting kilometres, up to the foot of Jbel Oukaïmeden. The road mostly climbs within sight of a mountain stream, the Asif Aït Leqaq, which has cut a series of steep canyons and waterfalls in the side of the mountain. Along the way you pass a string of stone and pisé Berber hamlets, perched way up but still surrounded by carefully tended terraced gardens, bramble hedges and orchards, even above suicidal cliffs. As you climb up to Oukaïmeden, at 2600m, you pass through a whole series of altitude belts that gradually dispose of olive trees, almonds, henna and walnut, leaving you in a barren area of windswept rock. Providing there is no cloud cover there is a continual and magnificently changing view over the valleys of the High Atlas to the east and west or away to the north to Marrakech.

The settlement of Oukaïmeden itself is no more than a fairly ugly assortment of skiing chalets and associated huts and services sheltered by a rising platform of barren rock. The face of the mountain is scarred by the pylons that support the half-dozen ski lifts. As you arrive you pass a small reservoir lake well-stocked with fish, and a barrier at which you must pay an admission charge (currently 10dh) to enter the resort. In winter this provides the best skiing in the country, and in summer it makes a good, well-supplied base for walking in the high valleys. What is more, around it there is the most accessible collection of prehistoric rock carvings anywhere in Morocco. There is no view from Oukaïmeden, but a superb one from the Tizerag TV relay station, atop a peak at 2740m, which is at the end of a road that winds up for another 2km beyond the resort.

The Rock Carvings

There is a map in the Club Alpin Français (CAF) hut in Oukaïmeden that shows the location of the carvings, but the club is often locked up. Ask to be guided by any of the locals to the half-dozen sites. The French, in their efficient way, built protective shelters around them, which have all now rusted down to a few inches. You can, if you don't like being guided, look for these tell-tale signs just to the right of the road above the reservoir as you enter the town; there are also some near the Angour hotel. Among the rocks you will find a collection of images that includes representations of shafted stone knives, Aztec-like ritual knives, some circular or stellar–solar shapes with rings, snake–lightning bolts, a male hunter beside a small deer, and an elephant with mouse-like ears and a penis but no tusks. They all have been dated to the 9th century BC.

Where to Stay

Stay in the Ourika valley if you have the choice, although there are a number of places open in Oukaimeden, which tend to be filled with unbearably hearty mountain types and the smell of their boots and socks. For choice use the **Hotel L'Angour**, formerly and for many years known as the Hôtel Juju, © (04) 319005. It is a great wood-lined mock-Alpine thing, with a bar and restaurant and room rates set on a demi-pension basis.

skiing

The National Ski Centre at Oukaïmeden is open from November to March. The snow is variable and the best conditions are usually from February to March, and often coincide with an impassable road. The skiing is Scottish: icy in the morning, wet in the afternoon and with some potentially surprising patches of rock. There are half a dozen button lifts and a 1660m chair-lift. Day passes and ski-hire are available from the local shop.

walking

The most immediate objective for walkers is the sharp peak of **Jbel Oukaïmeden** (3273m), but to the southeast rises the higher and more distant peak of **Jbel Angour** (3616m). From Oukaïmeden you can walk southwest to Imlil and on down to the Tizi-n-Test road via the CAF refuge at Tacheddirt (*see* above pp.415–7). To get onto this route, climb to the end of the chair-lift, and then follow the track until a path leads off to the right. The Tacheddirt pass (2314m) is about two hours' walk away and from there you descend to the CAF hut.

The Tizi-n-Tichka

The Tizi-n-Tichka pass crosses the High Atlas from Marrakech to Ouarzazate, and like the Tizi-n-Test can be blocked any time between December and March. It is an exciting and memorable 200km journey, though on a perfectly safe road that climbs twisting up through forests to the treeless summits of the pass. Just beyond the summit is the turning for the **kasbah of Telouèt**, the chief attraction of the journey. Further south there is a sub-Saharan landscape of bleak twisted rock where permanent habitation is restricted to the oasis valleys that drain the Atlas slopes. Here you can stop and visit the surviving agadir at **Irherm** village, which makes a powerful contrast to Telouèt.

If you are driving allow half a day between your hotels in Marrakech and Ouarzazate, with a full day put aside if you are going to stop and have the time to see anything. Although this is a much travelled road few visitors stop overnight, but there is a hotel at **Aït-Ourir** and more basic accommodation available at **Taddert**, **Telouèt** and **Irherm-n-Ougdal**. If you are travelling by bus you'll have a better chance of finding a taxi for the drive to Telouèt at Irherm than north of the pass at Taddert.

To the Tizi-n-Tichka summit

Aït-Ourir, 30km southeast of Marrakech and off to the left of the main road, is one of the string of market towns that nestle at the foot of the High Atlas. Good farm land stretches below, and the Tuesday **souk** is usually busy and empty of tourists. A well-built Glaoui residence can be seen to the south of the town, but it is inaccessible as it now houses an orphanage. Aït-Ourir makes a tranquil and unusual base for exploring the region. You could stay or eat at the reasonably priced **Le Coq Hardi**, tel (04) 480056, a charming **motel** which has eight rooms, a garden and a licensed restaurant. It stands right beside the bridge over the river Zate, and can be filled at lunchtime with passing tour groups.

The ruins of the 12th-century Almoravid **fortress of Tasghimout** are 10km away south along the secondary road that links Aït-Ourir to Ourika, the 6702. A dirt track (marked by a signpost to Iguerfrouan) just after the village of **Amanouz** will lead you, after a two-hour walk south, up to a 150-acre table-top foothill. The stone foundations of the walls and a series of cisterns and ruined gatehouses can be clearly identified. Tasghimout was built by Sultan Ali ben Youssef in 1125 as a base from where his regiments of desert cavalry could control the spreading influence of the Almohad highlanders based in Tin-Mal. It was then known as the fortress of El Halal, and seems to have survived the Almohad victory since Ibn Khaldoun mentions Tasghimout as one of the towns founded by the Almohad Sultan Abdel Moumen.

Beyond Aït Ourir the road climbs quickly up into the foothills, passing in a few kilometres below the prominent **koubba of Sidi Lahoussine**. Just before the koubba a dirt track leads almost due south to the village of **Tidili-des-Mesfioua**. The Mesfioua, alone of the Berber tribes, succeeded in resisting the Arab tribes of the plains and held on to their area of the fertile plain of Haouz, centred on this village. They also preserved their traditions of tribal democracy and up to the 20th century suffered no autocratic *caid* to rule over them.

Twelve km east of Aït-Ourir a tarmac road turns right up the Zate Valley, passing through a series of Mesfioua villages where the timeless, tireless pace of subsistence farming continues undisturbed by tourism. The road ends at **Arba-Talatast**, overlooked to the southwest by the twin peaks of **Jbel Yagour** (2723m) and **Jbel Meltsene** (3588m). The slopes of Yagour have some of the best preserved prehistoric rock carvings in the area, while the summit of Meltsene is still rumoured to be used for the old Berber sacrifices celebrated on the equinox and solstices.

Back on the main road, the P31, you climb up through dramatic mountain scenery, the slopes covered in mixed woods of oak, pine and juniper. Perhaps the best **view** of these Mesfioua mountains is from the pass of **Tizi-n-Aït-Imguer**, at 1470m, where there is a particularly good view southeast to Jbel Tistouit, a summit looming up at 3224 m.

Taddert is a roadside village poised below the last 15km of twisting road that climbs to the Tizi-n-Tichka summit. Though unpromising at first sight, it makes a pleasant stop with its line of cramped cafés, the licensed but inexpensive **Auberge Les Noyers** can despite its road-side position make a pleasant stop with its terrace overlooking a mountain stream.. A number of paths lead away from the sound of grinding truck gears to pisé farmhouses placed idyllically beside the terraced banks of mountain streams.

The **summit of Tizi-n-Tichka**, 'the gate to the pastures', is 2260m high. From this central point in the High Atlas a windblown, desolate expanse extends in all directions, though the immediate environment is ringed by the now customary mineral stalls. Four km further on there is a left turn for the kasbah of Telouèt.

The Kasbah of Telouèt

Telouèt is 21km east from the main road on a tarmac lane that leads past stunted pines and mineral-stained soil which has given the ground a sanguinous hue in keeping with its reputation. Eventually you glimpse a minaret that rises from the low village of **El-Khémis Telouèt,** separated from the sprawling extent of the kasbah by the river Mellah. Above the kasbah, overlooking a prominent koubba in the centre of the cemetery, there is a simple hotel, the **Auberge Telouèt**, which provides meals and basic accommodation.

Three generations of *caids* of the Glaoui tribe built extravagant structures out of wood and pisé to form this kasbah. Most of Telouèt is consequently an area of leached and shapeless mud banks. Broken spars and wattle frames protrude like the bones of some decaying leviathan. This area of ruin is screened from immediate view by the most recent, stone-built, **White Kasbah**, with its layers of towers, buttresses, crenellations and curtain walls, built by *Caid Brahim*, Thami el Glaoui, between 1934 and 1955.

The Making of the Lords of the Atlas

The Glaoui first rose to fortune by aiding Sultan Moulay Hassan in completing a late crossing of the High Atlas in 1893. Moulay Hassan, the last of the great pre-colonial rulers of Morocco, rewarded them by a gift of munitions which was later followed by a position at his court. They prospered in the service of the sultans; Madani el Glaoui served Sultan Abdul Aziz as minister of war, before advancing to become grand vizier (prime minister) to Sultan Moulay Hafid, while his brother Thami was appointed pacha of Marrakech. The brothers used their new wealth and great position gradually to enlarge their influence over the Berber tribes of the High Atlas. The kasbah of Telouèt grew in stature with each new conquest of a village and submission of a tribe.

By 1907 the Glaoui had become key national figures, but their greatest hour came in 1912 when they became the sworn allies of the French. They undertook the expansion of French rule south of the High Atlas, and created an empire within an empire for themselves in the process. Thami succeeded his brother Madani in 1918 and inherited Telouèt on Hammou's death in 1934, and only the collapse of French power in 1956 toppled this aged but still avaricious warrior who at his peak had 600,000 souls under his care. Within a year of Independence the Glaoui chiefs were either dead, in prison, or in exile, their lands confiscated and their tribesmen disarmed. Each year their kasbah moves closer to its sentence of complete decay.

The road skirts the village to approach the kasbah from behind. Melted forms of old walls grow stronger where a few families squat with their chickens, dogs and children in the more weather-resistant corners. A gateway directs your approach through narrow walls that open into a large paved courtyard. Even the minaret of the kasbah mosque has been infected with the universal crumbling.

The amiable uniformed government custodian conducts tours of the main reception rooms of *Caid Brahim*'s White Kasbah (tips accepted). The haphazard evolution of the palace becomes apparent in the eccentric route to these rooms which affords tantalizing glimpses of dark corridors, subterranean staircases and obscure sun-baked terraces. The dusty long, echoing corridor to the reception rooms provides an astonishing contrast to the massive assertive confidence of these halls. The vulgarity of display mixes with detailed Moorish craftsmanship of the highest order to silence the visitor.

An ornate grille-window frames a significant view of the old kasbah of Telouèt, on the edge of the village with barely two of its walls left standing. The old kasbah is the size of a traditional fortress of a mountain *caid* and would have boasted little decoration beyond crenellated towers and motifs embossed into the pisé of the exterior walls. Inside, the rooms would most likely have been small, dark and infested. The halls of the White Kasbah of Telouèt are of another order, and though now empty of furniture the absence of rich cloth, carpets, worked metal and wood seems merely to enhance the grandeur of the interior. The roofs above are still secure and you are allowed up to enjoy the excellent view. They were once decorated with great expanses of green glazed tiles, but these now lie in shattered heaps at the foot of the outer walls.

On the way out the custodian may point out a large windowless room, the **cinema**. Edward G. Robinson was *Caid Brahim*'s brother-in-law. The screening of the latest fantasies from California seems bizarrely appropriate in this last outlandish product of feudal grandeur.

The rest of Telouèt is not officially accessible and for the pragmatically minded is securely locked up. Every year the buildings become more dangerous, but the custodians can sometimes be tactfully encouraged to take visitors around. For the brave, the route to the kitchens, Hammou's Kasbah and the harem runs through another delightful maze of passages. The kitchens are vast, and recognizable chiefly by their blackened walls. The mixture of soot, melting pisé and exposed beams is impressive only in its size and the imminent danger of final collapse. Telouèt was entirely staffed by slaves except for one salaried French chef. Over a thousand slaves fled overnight when the news of the death of Si Thami el Glaoui reached the kasbah.

At the heart of Telouèt, physically and emotionally, was **Hammou's Kasbah**, a stark, square keep formed from massive walls, dark and featureless inside. Hammou was the cousin and brother-in-law of Madani and Thami, but remained violently opposed to the French, who he would not permit to enter his feudal domain. He was the *caid* of Telouèt and ruler of the traditional mountain territory throughout the period of phenomenal growth in Glaoui power until his death in 1934. Stories of his occult powers blended with the grim truth of his violent, xenophobic and sadistic nature. *Sloghis*, hounds that could each kill a wild boar by themselves, trailed behind each guest who entered the kasbah like some canine thought police, while the final bloody resolution of a tribal feud too often ended at the hands of Hammou in his labyrinthine cellars. These have long since collapsed to bury the evidence of this grim underworld.

The **harem courtyard** is beyond Hammou's Kasbah and is approached through a number of rooms. The central courtyard was equipped with large pools of water which have now cracked and drained. The cool rooms that open from this internal space, thanks to a trick of design, are not overlooked by any battlemented tower. Two ornamental fruit trees survive and in spring still fill this breezeless space with the scent of cherry and apricot blossom. After the initial pleasure of discovery, the languid introspection and sterility of the harem creep back to repossess the spirit of the place.

Beyond these identifiable features you can wander freely among the curtain walls and acres of complete ruin. Banks of pisé now and then astonish you with their tremendous range in height, which hints at some past extravagant architectural form. Fragments of carved cedar, carved foliate arabesques and shattered tiles can be glimpsed buried deep in what appears at first to be nothing but bleached soil.

It may seem extraordinary that such a place as Telouèt should not be better preserved, but for a Moroccan Telouèt is a monument to treason on a vast scale. The Glaoui were totally identified with the most extreme French colonial ambitions right up to 1956. Si Thami el Glaoui was deeply involved in the deposition of Mohammed V, and his officials had extorted and stolen for years. Allied with the French, they had hunted down those who worked for independence and fought against the Liberation Army.

The Old Road South to Aït-Benhaddou

From Telouèt there is a road that continues east and south over a desolate, salt-stained stretch of grazing land. After about 11km you descend to the village of **Anemitèr**, which presides over the green, irrigated valley of the river Ounila. This valley is an oasis in the mountains, studded with a succession of hamlets largely composed of earth-built houses but with a number of decaying but still inhabited kasbahs. The tarmac road stops at Anemitèr; on the northern edge of the village, by the river crossing, there is a **café** where you can sleep rough, run by Elyazid Mohammed, a mountain guide. South from Anemitèr a rough, unsurfaced road follows this strikingly beautiful valley for 30 alarming kilometres. Only the condition and width of the track may stop you surrendering yourself to the magnificent austerity of the landscape. You return to the valleys and the tarmac at **Tamdaght**, just north of **Aït-Benhaddou**. A very fit walker could cover this in ten hours—ideally with a friendly car waiting at the broken bridge just south of Tamdaght.

The route has become increasingly popular four four-wheel-drive daytrips, which are gradually reopening an ancient trade route. This valley used to be the major artery that connected Marrakech to the Sahara. However, with the maddened xenophobic Hammou ruling over Telouèt the French decided to bypass his kasbah completely and so cut their new route further to the west through the Tizi-n-Tichka in 1928. Telouèt's ancient relevance astride the Atlas crossing was severed for ever; it decays in a cul-de-sac of its own making. It is as if history and geography are in tacit agreement over its destiny.

South from the Tizi-n-Tichka summit

The summit of the **Tizi-n-Lepsis** pass at 2125m is 8km south of the Tizi n Tichka.. Two kilometres below that is the village of **Aguelmous**, close to the head of the Asif Iminni stream which the road closely follows down to Ouarzazate.

The small settlement of **Irherm-n-Ougdal** is another 6km south. The communal fortified storehouse that stands at the heart of the village remains in an unusually good state of repair. It is visitable for 10dh to the old keeper. These structures, known as agadirs or *irherms*, were a distinctive feature of the village republics of the Berber mountain people. The **irherm** of the Ougdal is composed of a two-storey courtyard with a pillared balcony, around which are arranged a number of individual rooms. A few of the rooms have retained their original carved and painted details and there is a fine view of the valley from the flat roof. There is a basic hotel with a bar in the village, the **Chez Mimi**, which is a convenience for travellers that can become invaluable if you are caught by a sudden fall of snow. If you have come across the Tizi-n-Tichka by bus there is a much greater chance of finding a *grand taxi* for the trip to Telouèt in Irherm-n-Ougdal than at Taddert.

Franciscan friars established a craft cooperative at the village of **Agouim** (8km further south) to keep alive the old skills of carpet-making, blanket-weaving and embroidery. It is still functioning and selling its wares. Just before you enter the village a dirt track on the right, the 6849, leads in 30km to the much-praised **agadir of Sour**. For the more adventurous this provides a back route to Jbel Siroua and Jbel Toubkal. Another track from Agouim village leads up for 15km into the stonefields of the High Atlas wastes and to the tomb of Rabbi David O'Mouchy, one of the most esteemed of the Jewish saints of Morocco, who is venerated in an annual pilgrimmage at the end of October.

A tarmac turning across the Imini stream 25km south of Agouim leads to the manganese mines of **Imini**. This can be taken as a convenient border between the region of the High Atlas and the sub-Saharan world of the southern oasis valleys. **Tiseldei Kasbah**, which perches above its village in an attitude of feudal power is 6km north of the Imini mines, while 2km to south from here you reach **Iflilt**, the first ksar in the valley, occupied by the Aït-Zineb tribe. A scattering of ksour increasingly line the riverbed before you reach the road junction of **Amerzgane**, where a **souk** is held on Sundays.

Sites to the west of here are covered in 'Agadir, the Sous Valley and Anti-Atlas' (*see* pp.505–560).

About 2km beyond Amerzgane is the **ksar of El Mdint** and then that of **Tadoula**, two towered settlements surrounded by their palm groves that get a fraction of the tourists that flock to Aït-Benhaddou. The right turn to **Aït-Benhaddou** is 10km further east, but only a little further are the neglected **ksour of Tikirt and Tazenntoute**. This area and its distinctive history (and the town of Ouarzazate only some 15km further east) are described in 'Southern Oasis Valleys' (*see* pp.452–460).

The Southern Oasis Valleys

The numbing beauty of the sky is one of the great rewards of travelling through the sub-Saharan uplands of southeastern Morocco. The light at dawn and dusk is an explosion of fast-fading colours and shadows that more than compensates for the baking oppression of the day. A desert night awakes a child-like wonder at the stars. Palm trunks rear up like the pillars of a pantheistic temple to frame the endless configurations of the night sky.

The average annual rainfall in the area south of the High Atlas mountains is a mere 68mm. This is enough to support nomadic herding, but permanent agricultural settlements could not exist in this region without the handful of oasis valleys. These drain the upper slopes of the High Atlas and flow south to extend ribbons of vegetation to the threshold of the Sahara Desert. The effectiveness of this natural supply has been greatly extended by irrigation techniques which have developed over thousands of years.

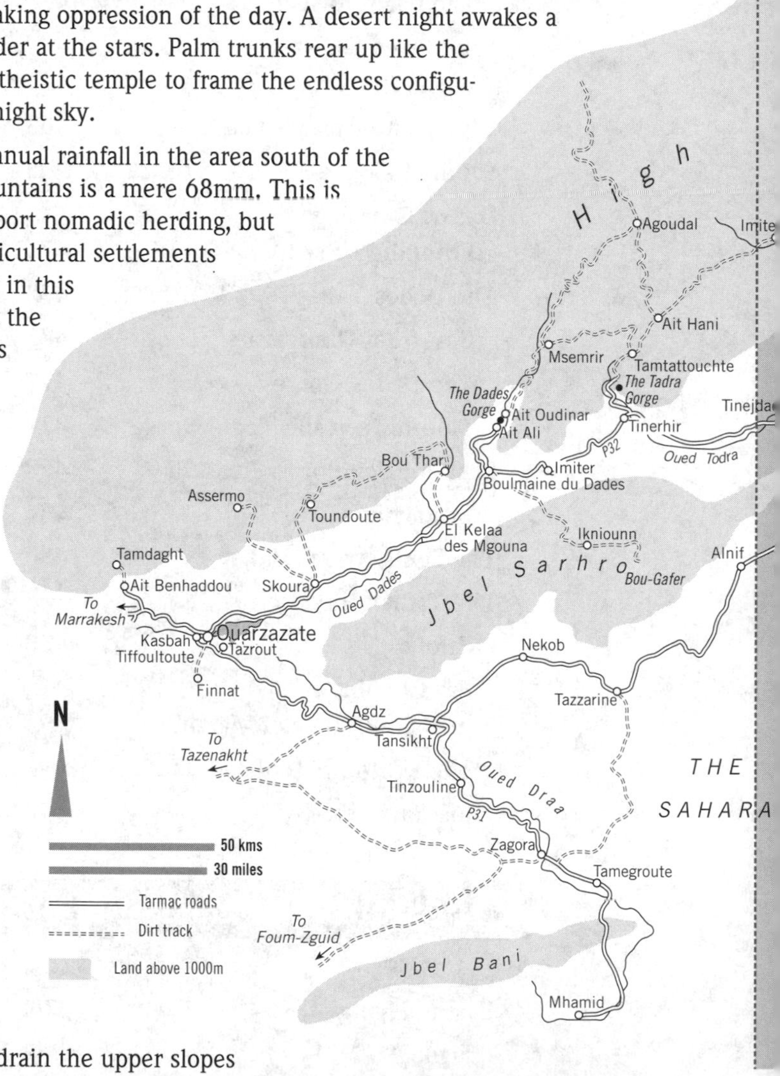

The five most important valleys of the region—the Drâa, Dadès, Todra, Rhéris and Ziz—produce a harvest that supports a considerable population. There are in addition hundreds of smaller settlements that cling to lesser streams, or are

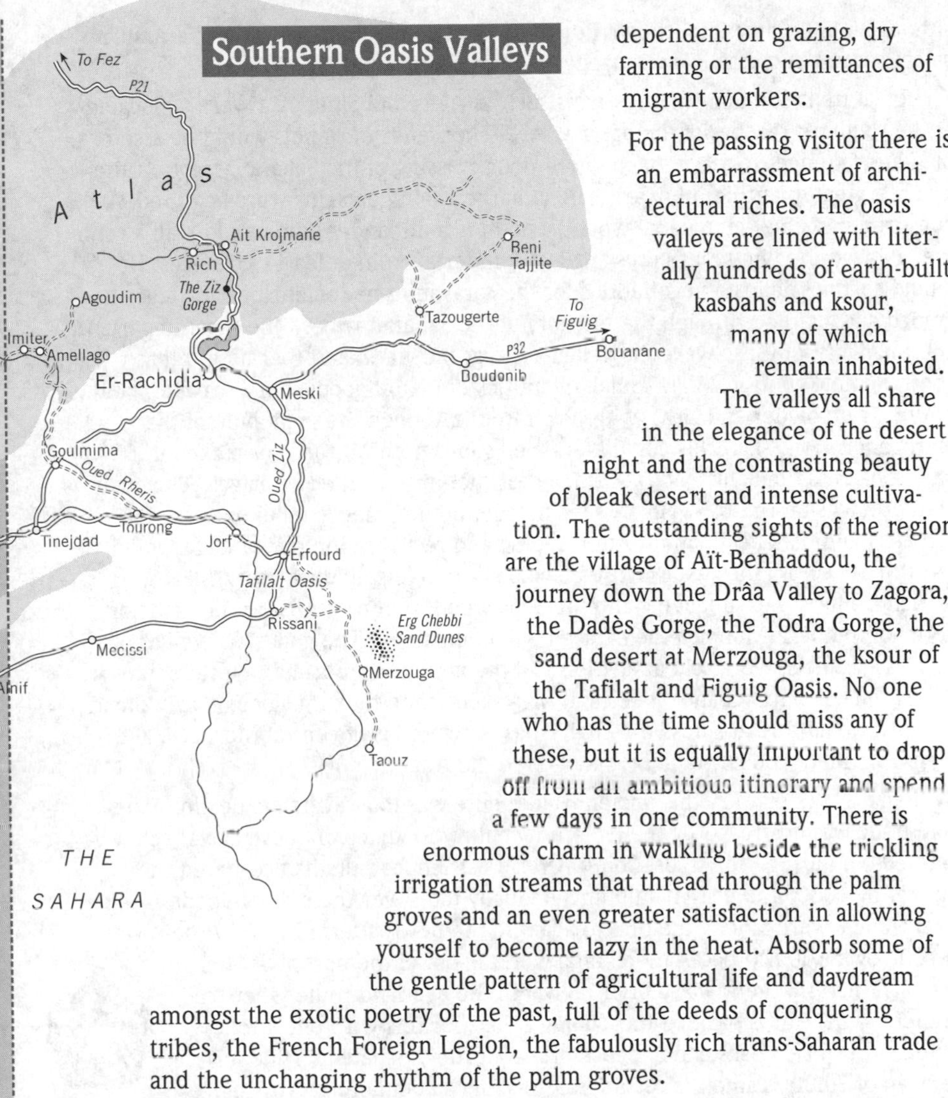

dependent on grazing, dry farming or the remittances of migrant workers.

For the passing visitor there is an embarrassment of architectural riches. The oasis valleys are lined with literally hundreds of earth-built kasbahs and ksour, many of which remain inhabited. The valleys all share in the elegance of the desert night and the contrasting beauty of bleak desert and intense cultivation. The outstanding sights of the region are the village of Aït-Benhaddou, the journey down the Drâa Valley to Zagora, the Dadès Gorge, the Todra Gorge, the sand desert at Merzouga, the ksour of the Tafilalt and Figuig Oasis. No one who has the time should miss any of these, but it is equally important to drop off from an ambitious itinerary and spend a few days in one community. There is enormous charm in walking beside the trickling irrigation streams that thread through the palm groves and an even greater satisfaction in allowing yourself to become lazy in the heat. Absorb some of the gentle pattern of agricultural life and daydream amongst the exotic poetry of the past, full of the deeds of conquering tribes, the French Foreign Legion, the fabulously rich trans-Saharan trade and the unchanging rhythm of the palm groves.

The Golden Trade of Morocco

The oasis valleys are isolated on the southeastern edge of Morocco, a comparatively poor region on the outer fringe of the national economy. This is a cruel and recent reversal, for only a century ago this region sat astride a vital link in world commerce. Cities such as Sijilmassa, in the Tafilalt Oasis, were the proud and opulent ports for the lucrative trans-Saharan trade routes. The profits of this trade run like a golden thread that connects the different periods of Moroccan history. It was an ancient trade route, known and described by Herodotus, although it only came into its own during the late Roman Empire, when the Arabian camel became successfully acclimatized to North Africa.

The great trans-Saharan trading towns such as Akka and Sijilmassa were all located at the southern reaches of the oasis valleys. Thousands of camels would be assembled and fattened up ready for the hazardous crossing of the Sahara Desert. At the markets great quantities of dates, barley, harness and goatskins were acquired. A consortium of chief merchants would appoint a commander who would plan a route that allowed the two-month crossing to be undertaken in at least two stages. He would conduct delicate negotiations for the caravan to be replenished, rested, guided and guarded through the territory of the Saharan tribes. The most important, and infamous, of these were the veiled Tuareg, the warlike Berber nation that controlled the central Sahara. Small quantities of luxury goods, horses, paper, cloth, swords, gunpowder and glass, were taken south, though the great bulk of the merchandise was salt. This could be carried south from Morocco or picked up halfway across the Sahara at Taodeni, a desolate mine worked by slaves. The great market towns on the river Niger, such as Gao, Bourem and Timbuktu, were the caravans' ultimate destination. After trading and recuperation the caravan would return back across the Sahara with a fabulous cargo of gold dust, ivory, slaves, ostrich feathers, rare unguents and precious woods. On returning to the 'Saharan ports' of southern Morocco the caravan would break up. The goods, as well as the surviving camels, were sold at auction and the various agents and investors took their profit. The merchants of Fès and Marrakech then took the goods north. Small convoys would thread across the High Atlas to the cities of central Morocco, and then from there goods would be taken on to the Atlantic ports.

By the late 19th century this ancient trade route was in irreversible decline. The gold trade was destroyed by the late 16th-century Saadian conquest, slavery slowly petered out during the 1870s, South African ostrich feathers had cornered the market by 1880, and coastal shipping gradually took over the bulkier goods. The local traders were among the first to adapt to the new pattern; by 1890 there were already over 100 Moroccan merchants working out of the port of St Louis in Senegal. In 1902 there was a brief revival in the overland route when the French Camel Corps pacified the Tuareg tribes, for this with one stroke reduced the major risks and expense of the journey. As late as 1908 a caravan of 20,000 camels is recorded as making a commercial crossing.

Ouarzazate and Taourirt Kasbah

Ouarzazate does not live up to the exotic elegance of its name. It is a modern-looking administrative centre for the half-million people who live in southeastern Morocco. It has recently been given a generous face-lift which has placed a number of opulent public squares, well-lit pavements and shady arcades along the central highway of the town. Ouarzazate is well placed to be a regional centre, for it has an airport and is on a strategic crossroads with trunk roads west to Agadir, north to Marrakech, south to Zagora and east to

Er Rachidia. It has also been invigorated by a burst of economic development based on those most ephemeral and deceptively glamorous of industries, film and tourism. Both have been attracted by the consistently dry, hot climate and the easy access to the stunning sub-Saharan landscape that surrounds the town.

Apart from the hundred-year-old Taourirt Kasbah, on the eastern edge of town, Ouarzazate itself contains little of interest. It is however a convenient shopping and transport centre, and its spacious cafés, large choice of hotels and easy street life can also appear attractive when compared to the hassle in other towns. You will in any case inevitably pass through the town several times while you are travelling in the south, and may well need to stay here.

History

The reservoir east of the town partly obscures the fact that Ouarzazate lies at the confluence of three important oasis valley systems, the Ouarzazate, Dadès and Drâa. It has always had strategic importance, and in order to control the vital trade routes along the southern valleys rulers have consistently garrisoned the low hills above this river junction. The Almohad sultans built a great kasbah which was known as Irherm-n-Ougelid, the fortress of the kings. Later dynasties continued to fortify the area, though almost nothing has survived from before this century. After Sultan Moulay Hassan's death in 1894 a three-year tribal war consumed the entire south. It was especially vicious and destructive, for the ancient economic structure of the region had decayed due to the collapse of the trans-Saharan trade. The war allowed a pair of government ministers, the Glaoui brothers Si Thami and Madani, to win control of Ouarzazate. It was a logical expansion of their influence, for their home base of Telouèt was due north of here, commanding the Tizi-n-Tichka across the High Atlas.

The Glaoui kasbah of Taourirt at Ouarzazate became the centre for the gradual expansion of their influence. Their authority was enormously increased in 1912 when they became the sworn allies and confidential agents of the French colonial regime. This partnership was confirmed in 1928 when the Foreign Legion established a fort on a hill just 300m west of Taourirt. It is still occupied by a military garrison, and it is from this army camp that the present modern town has grown. The burgeoning population, swollen by thousands of high school students, is mostly drawn from the surrounding oasis communities, especially Skoura.

Getting Around

Practically everything in Ouarzazate can be found along or just off Av Mohammed V, the main P32 Agadir to Er Rachidia highway as it passes through the town.

by air

Taourirt airport, © (04) 882345/882383 is just 3km northeast of the town centre, and served by *petits taxis*. Try and keep the cab fare down to 20dh. RAM run four flights a week to Marrakech and two to Agadir, from where there are numerous other connections. The local RAM office is on © (04) 882348/883236.

By bus

The CTM station is near the Tourist Office on Avenue Mohammed V; there are three departures daily for Marrakech (5hrs). Private lines such as SATAS operate from a terminal by Place du 3 Mars, off Avenue Mohammed V. There are two buses daily going east to Tinerhir (4hrs); two to the west through Tazenakht, Taliouine and Taroudannt to Inezgane-Agadir; and two that go south to Zagora.

by grand taxi

These leave from Place Mouhadine (40m north of the Hotel Royal on Avenue Mohammed V), with regular runs west to Tazenakht and east to Boumalne-Dadès for around 30dh a place in a six-person-packed taxi.

car, bicycle, mule and Land Rover hire

There is a small nest of firms on Place du 3 Mars (which fronts Av Mohammed V at the west end of town), including Hertz, ✆ (04) 882084, Europcar/InterRent, ✆ (04) 882035, @ 884077 and Dani Car, ✆ (04) 883063; Ksour Voyages rents out sturdy mountain bikes. Budget car hire has an office at Résidence El Warda, Av Mohammed V, ✆ (04) 882892, while the local Land Rover specialists Holiday Services, ✆ (04) 882997, are beside Hôtel La Gazelle on Av Mohammed V. Ask at the Hotel Belère at 22 Av Prince Moulay Rachid, ✆ (04) 882803, about hiring horses and mules. They also arrange riding trips around some local kasbahs.

Tourist Information

The **tourist office** (open Mon–Fri 8.30am–12 noon, 2.30–6.30pm; ✆ (04) 882485), is on Av Mohammed V in the eastern half of town, close to the CTM station and almost opposite the **Post Office** (open Mon–Sat 8.30am–12pm, 2.30–6.00pm; the international phone section keeps longer hours). The tourist office can help with advice on hotels, local souks and festivals. There are two tourist-oriented festivals a year, a craft fair in May and a *moussem* in September.

There is a string of **banks** along the north side of Av Mohammed V, including the BMCE, BCM and Banque Populaire, also at the east end of town near the tourist office and Post office. For health concerns visit the **Pharmacie de Nuit** on Av Mohammed V, ✆ (04) 882708.

Taourirt Kasbah

Open Mon–Fri 8.30am–12 noon, 3–6pm; Sat only 8.30am–12 noon; adm.

The hundred-year-old kasbah of Taourirt is Ouarzazate's only historical monument, which has been recently restored. It stands on the eastern edge of the town, overlooked by a cluster of cafés, bazaars and a state-run craft centre that form an ornamental square around its northern gateway, the main entrance. To the south, east and west sprawl a confusion of traditional houses that occupy some of the old courtyards, garden enclosures and wasteland that once surrounded the fortress. The resulting mass of walls, alleys and towers has gained in organic vitality but lost its old cruel exterior grandeur.

Restoration work has been concentrated on the old inner keep and private apartments of the Glaoui. From the square you pass through the entrance arch, in the shade of which shelter an amiable clutch of guides, to enter a paved courtyard. The ground floor apartments (on your left) are let out to craftsmen and often used to house exhibitions. In the corner of the courtyard stands a Krupp cannon, traditionally considered to be a gift to the Glaoui from Sultan Moulay Hassan in 1891. The cannon was instrumental in the rapid growth of Glaoui authority over the south, as it could, with a few shells, reduce the strongest tribal kasbah to ruin. In numerous tribal battles the heads of massacred defenders were heaped high up around the Krupp armament to almost obscure the barrel.

You are free to explore the kasbah interior, a labyrinth of stairs, rooms, passages, low doorways, light wells and small shuttered windows barred with ornate iron grills. The thick heavy walls, the structural beams and the simple but elegant scheme of red and white coloured limewash creates one of the most memorable interiors in southern Morocco. The three grandest rooms (with their wider room span provided by hardwood as opposed to palm wood beams) are known as the Dining Room, the Salon of the Favourite and the *Méchouar* balcony. They are decorated in the traditional style of a Moorish town house, with carved and painted plaster details and the exposed timber painted with arabesque themes. These rooms may seem small and meagre in comparison with the opulent palaces that the Glaoui were able to build after 1927. They do, however, summon up the medieval quality of that era, which has so many analogies with the war-torn and tower-studded Borders of Scotland. A centre of power in the period of Madani el Glaoui's authority, the kasbah inevitably declined after it was inherited by his eldest and idiot son, Muhammed al Arbi. Even in 1949, though, it still housed 1500 servants, slaves, employees and craftsmen.

If you plunge down the valley to the left of the official entrance of Taourirt you can wind your way through the lively village that still clusters at the foot of the kasbah walls. The streets and houses metamorphose out of the indeterminate crumbling earth circumference of the kasbah, which looks at its best viewed from the gravel bed of the river.

The Lake and Around the Town

The construction of the El Mansour Eddahbi Dam to control the irrigation of the river Drâa has formed a lake to the east of Ouarzazate. Even in this water-obsessed region, though, it is a surprisingly unimpressive site when viewed from any town rooftop. The water is brown, and ebbs and expands within a large bowl of washed gravel. However if you have a car there are magniifcent vistas of the lake some 10km east of town, with the stern surrounding hills and the imperishable blue skies reflected in the silent waters of the lake.

The ruined towers of the **Tazrout and Tihmasa Kasbah** (the stork fortress) can be seen to the south across the lake from Ouarzazate. It can be reached by walking east along the dry riverbed. Keep your eyes on the ground, for each year crystals and semi-precious stones are washed down from the mountains. The kasbah can also be approached along a track that turns off the road to Zagora.

About 3km to the west of Ouarzazate is the walled enclosure of **Atlas Studios**, where old props and a variety of film equipment can be viewed by the public from 8am–8pm. On the eastern edge of the town a small **zoological garden** has been established beside the municipal pool and Zat Hotel.

If you feel like a small trip into the countryside while staying in town the isolated oasis village of **Finnt** is a hospitable destination. A café-restaurant has recently opened which you can use as a day base from which to go walking in the small palm grove and surrounding hills. It lies about 10km south of town up a dirt track that turns off the Zagora road just west of the Ouarzazate junction.

Where to Stay

There has been a rapid growth in luxurious new hotels in Ouarzazate, which mostly stand in an imposing row of kasbah type silhouettes along the rising land just north of the main road. Completely self-contained and insulated from everything but the sun, they are closely tied in to the package tourist industry of Agadir and Marrakech.

expensive

Of the dozen hotels in this category the **Hotel Riad Salam**, ✆ (04) 882206, sign-posted just off Av Mohammed V between the town centre and Kasbah Taourirt, is much to be preferred. It is formed from two kasbah-like structures which frame a large fountain-fed pool and a small garden. It has a good position off the main street, just above the riverbed, and from there it is only a 200m walk east to Kasbah Taourirt. It also has the calmest domestic atmosphere, attracting individual guests staying for a few days rather then just fleets of passing coach-borne parties. If it is full make use of the motel-like **Le Zat**, ✆ (04) 882521, on the far eastern edge of town (about 600m east of Kasbah Taourirt beside the zoological garden), which has a fine view over the lake towards the Tazrout Kasbah.

moderate

La Gazelle, ✆ (04) 882151, is one of the town's oldest hotels. It is situated at the western end of town, on the north side of Av Mohammed V about 150m before you reach Place du 3 Mars. There is a small plunge pool above the car park and 30 bedrooms arranged around a neatly-labelled botanical courtyard. It has a restaurant, a popular bar and a tranquil, slightly shabby atmosphere.

inexpensive

Just over 2km due south of the town centre (beside the Zagora road and on the other side of the Ouarzazate riverbed), there are two hotels in the Hay Tabounte quarter of town. They are naturally well placed as stop-overs for anyone heading south in their own vehicles. The **Hôtel-Restaurant La Vallée**, ✆ (04) 882668, 📠 882810, has two categories of rooms, can serve wine in its restaurant (or its tent), is building its own pool and is well-kept under the eagle eye of Zaid, the *patron*. When it's full make use of the good but slightly more noisy **Saghro**, ✆ (04) 884305, which is found just another 500m to the south.

cheap

Two clean cheap hotels stand opposite each other on Avenue Mohammed V, plumb in the centre of the town. The **Es-Salam**, ✆ (04) 882512, has a three-storey catwalk interior to remind you of jug, while directly opposite at no. 24 is the slightly more upmarket **Royal**, where the rooms are arranged around a courtyard. If both are full (but not before) you could also make use of the small **Hôtel Atlas,** ✆ (04) 882307, at 13 Rue du Marché, behind the Royal

camping

On the eastern edge of town there is a well run campsite, ✆ (04) 882578, situated below the zoological gardens and beside the municipal pool. It is a welcoming place that has a good view south, and you can eat meals in the dining-room tent.

Eating Out

moderate

Despite the growth in hotels Ouarzazate is still dominated by two well-established restaurants: Tiffoultoute Kasbah and Chez Dimitri.

Chez Dimitri, ✆ (04) 882653 (closed Fridays), stands bang in the centre of town at 22 Avenue Mohammed V, opposite the Es-Salam hotel. It was established by one Dimitri, an ex-soldier of the French Foreign Legion, who set up shop here in 1928 directly below the fort. It is now a popular bar-brasserie with a few tables on the street terrace, and a moderately-priced French and Italian menu.

The old Glaoui **Kasbah of Tiffoultoute,** ✆ (04) 884636, is one of the most distinctive places to eat in the Moroccan south. It is 5km west of Ouarzazate, by the turning to Zagora. Wander through the massive gates and empty courtyard, and you will find yourself in an echoing hall surrounded by dining rooms. If there is a coach party eating you can avoid their cheerful noise by eating on the roof beside a crumbling storks' nest, and peering over the battlements at the bulk of the kasbah to the south. Copious set menus feature sugared melon or grapefruit, *tagines* and cinnamon *couscous* pudding, and the licensed restaurant is open for lunch and dinner.

cheap

In town the **Café-Restaurant Essalam,** ✆ (04) 882763, is the best of the half-dozen such places that cluster around the souk gates and bus station in the town centre. It is found on Av du Prince-Héritier Sidi Mohammed (a side road three blocks west of Chez Dimitri) and has a cool downstairs dining room, a sunbaked roof terrace and a functional European and Moroccan menu.

Up a notch in price is the café-restaurant **La Kasbah,** ✆ (04) 882033, which stands on the western corner of the sqaure facing Kasbah Taourirt. It has a delightful profusion of terraces, and small dining rooms with views that also catch a passing whiff of a breeze. It is unlicensed for alcohol, but happy to serve out any wine that you might bring prohibition-style in a plastic bag from the supermarket.

cafés, bars and nightlife

Aside from a drink at Chez Dimitri or the bar in La Gazelle hotel you can visit the café La Kasbah, with its splendid view of the illuminated Kasbah Taourirt. You could also could check out the three opulently designed kasbah-style hotels along Avenue Prince Moulay Rachid—the **Karam Palace, Belère** and **Azghor**. Their gardens, reception halls and pool-side bars are well worth visiting for the price of a drink.

There is also a new ***Fantasia*** ground, **El Farah**, established beside the tourist complex on the eastern edge of town, attached to the riding stables and associated **Le Ouarzazate** restaurant. Ask your hotel receptionist to find out times and prices.

Shopping

The supermarket next to the Es-Salam hotel on Avenue Mohammed V (directly opposite Chez Dimitri) offers the last opportunity to buy wine before heading anywhere south or east of Ouarzazate.

A side road to the left of Chez Dimitri leads directly to the souk arch, where you can stroll in the evening among the local shoppers. The tourist bazaars are mostly concentrated on the streets around Chez Dimitri on Av Mohammed V, and are not necessarily to be sneezed at. Penetrate beyond the first showroom, into ever smaller and more elaborate displays of goods, before asking to be shown the jewel chest. For textiles, the *hanbel*, carpets and colourful tent hangings (derived from the local Aït Ouaouzguite traditions of weaving and embroidery) that cover the walls just outside the Kasbah Taourirt indicate the greatest concentration of dealers.

Do not be put off either by the rather dusty and modern **Ensemble Artisanal**, opposite Kasbah Taourirt. It should be checked out carefully, as it contains a number of stalls filled by the work of resident craftsmen, mostly metalworkers and stonecarvers.

Aït-Benhaddou and Tamdaght Kasbah

The village of Aït-Benhaddou is one of the most memorable sites in the arid south. Its architectural celebrity has also made it the most visited village in Morocco. Hardly a month goes by without it being used as a dramatic backdrop for a fashion article, and it has notched up a number of film credits such as *Jesus of Nazareth.* The village is just a 28km drive or taxi-ride northwest of the hotels in Ouarzazate. About 18km out of town on the main P31 Marrakech road, turn north up a signposted tarmac road which takes you to Aït-Benhaddou in 10km.

The modern village stands on the west bank and enjoys a completely clear view across the gravel bed of the river to the stunning silhouette of the decaying old village. To get there, descend past the row of souvenir stalls to the riverbank, where mules sometimes wait to ferry visitors across the Mellah, the salt river. Striking small girls appear on the other side and forcefully adopt you. They will, for a tip, show you around their village, taking you into the interiors of the few inhabited kasbahs. Here you may be lucky enough to be offered mint tea and can watch the female-dominated life of the courtyard thick with chickens, rabbits, sheep and the odd cow.

Old Aït-Benhaddou is entirely composed of tightly-packed kasbahs, the deep red of their battlemented tapering towers and high decorated walls creating a marvellously rich and confusing array. The various kasbahs are quite separate from each other but their outbuildings and walled yards almost unite to create a common external wall. The formal gateway by the riverbank creates a misleading impression of the village, for these handsome gates were added by a film company.

Village life had its stresses and strains, as revealed in the writings of early travellers. The handsome towers on the four corners of the kasbahs were used as vantage points from which to snipe at your neighbour in long-drawn-out feuds. In times of danger the village would put aside its local squabbles and unite to create a common front. The earth-built kasbahs were vulnerable to a determined attacker, who would divert the river to sap at the foundations. Refuge could be taken in the *irherm* (a communal fortified storehouse), the circular stone outer wall of which perches on the summit of the golden coloured hill above the village.

Although Aït-Benhaddou is now a cul-de-sac the Mellah and Ounila valleys used to be one of the busiest trade routes across the High Atlas. The Glaoui-built **Tamdaght Kasbah**, just a few kilometres north of Aït Benhaddou, provides further evidence of its importance. The ruins of Tamdaght are a 20-minute walk up the tarmac road from the fallen bridge. It is perched above the strategic meeting point of the Mellah and Ounila rivers, which both provide possible approaches to the Glaoui stronghold of Telouèt Kasbah and the Tizi-n-Tichka pass (*see* pp.443–8). An orchard surrounds the kasbah walls, and in exchange for a tip the custodian will happily show you the view from the surviving portion of roof. An audience chamber with a ceiling of satin-blue cedar beams has a terrace that overlooks the high-walled and stone-paved courtyard. Here the privileged guests of the Glaoui *caids* were entertained by circles of dancing women.

Where to Stay and Eating Out

The café-restaurant **La Kasbah**, ✆ (04) 890302, 883787, the first such establishment in Aït Benhaddou, still dominates the local trade with its commanding position, wonderful views and undiminished standards of service and cooking. It also has twenty bedrooms, and a tent in the garden.

If you are looking for a quieter base you might like to stay in one of the dozen rooms of the French run **Auberge El Ouidane**, signposted at the entrance to the village (on the right aboout 200m before the Restaurant La Kasbah)

Kasbah Construction

The kasbahs of southern Morocco are primarily built to a rectangular plan that encloses an open courtyard, lined with narrow rooms, within high walls. Decoration is usually reserved for the upper walls and towers, built from sunbaked earth-bricks. These upper sections often bear a virtuoso display of geometric brickwork which makes skilful use of relief to enhance the strong contrasts between light and shade offered by the desert light. This dazzling honeycomb of lozenges, diamonds, arches and crosses is entirely in harmony with traditional crafts; merely the architectural aspect of designs seen elsewhere on carpets, metalwork, weaving and embroidery, though it is given an extra charm and interest by the melting fusion of the rain-bleached bricks. Originally this upper third would have been ornamented with a dazzling coat of whitewash, but all evidence of this tradition (short of the sketches of the first European travellers) has now disappeared.

If you look closely at the construction of the lower walls you will see that they are formed from giant bricks of sunbaked earth. These can be any size, but are typically about 3–4m long, 1–2m high and 1m wide. They were not manhandled into position, but are formed in situ from mobile box moulds, in a similar way to the modern use of concrete. These box moulds are made from plank boards held in place by rope-tied cross beams. A mixture of wet earth, clay, straw and gravel is then packed into the mould and rammed hard. After it has settled the box-mould is dismantled and moved along to create the next section. The characteristic scattering of holes left by box-moulds and cross-beams, and the cubular regularity of windows, doorways, gun slits and ventilation holes are a striking feature of this method of construction.

Long but narrow rooms are added along the sides of the internal courtyard, for roofing has always been a problem. Hardwood beams are a great luxury in the desert, and fibrous palm-tree trunks make weak beams. Room widths are traditionally determined by the comparatively short width that a palm beam could support. Above the beam, a cross-hatch of lesser branches and woven palm fronds supports a flat roof of earth. These leak in heavy rain, need constant repair and are the first thing to deteriorate when a kasbah is abandoned. Floors are of beaten earth, though courtyards, used for threshing, would be neatly flagged with stone. In the richest houses a plaster, partly made from burnt limestone and eggs, could be applied to the inside walls. This serves to repel insects, and can also bear carved and painted decoration.

South from Ouarzazate down the Drâa Valley to Zagora

The contrast of bare sun-baked rock and the lush fertility of palm groves, sharply defined beneath the achingly clear desert sky, is an astonishingly beautiful and powerful image.

The River Drâa drains the bleak eastern end of the Anti-Atlas and flows due south to Zagora to dwindle and dissipate in the desert beyond. In exceptional years the river will briefly flow the whole 1000km of its course to empty into the Atlantic. But in most years the Drâa scarcely provides enough water to sustain the 200km oasis valley that clings to its banks in an otherwise harsh desert landscape. The classical historian Polybius records that the Drâa was once infested with crocodiles. This is in part corroborated by a French hunter who shot the last Saharan crocodile in an isolated oasis in the Algerian desert in 1929.

The fertile, palm-shaded terraces of farmland in the Drâa valley are fed by a labyrinth of irrigation channels and neatly defined by earth walls. Apart from the odd bamboo screen in which to shelter from the midday heat there are no buildings. No plot of fertile irrigated land is wasted. All habitation is concentrated in ksour or groups of kasbahs. *Ksour* (*ksar* in the singular) are fortified villages, while *kasbahs* can be considered as fortified manorhouses. The ksour are drawn up at the edge of the palm groves and built on the desert wasteland: built on the desert and with the desert; for every wall has been formed from wet local earth pounded into compact shape between boards and then allowed to bake in the African sun. Walls rise up from the ground the same colour and texture as their surroundings, and when their period of use is over, melt back effortlessly into the landscape. None of the walls of the ksour in the Drâa is over a hundred years old, though the sites have probably been in continuous use for centuries. The walls and towers are astonishingly rich and varied in design. Arches, arcades, balustrades, battlements, crenellations and covered terraces are all used in a profuse and bewildering organic originality. The silhouettes seem to make reference to Gothic fortresses, to Edwardian border castles and to Nineveh, Tyre, Babylon and Egyptian Thebes. Maps, signposts and guidebooks list a bewildering variety of names for each village. Forget your Western desire to be sure of them and concentrate on the rewards of the architecture.

The Drâa has always been strongly influenced and interlinked with the destiny of the surrounding nomadic tribes. The sedentary population of the valley, currently around 80,000, speak both Berber and Arabic, although some villages proudly claim exclusive descent from only one of these groups. At the social summit stand the *shorfa*, clans who can proudly trace their lineage back to the family of the Prophet Mohammed. The shorfa of northern Morocco are usually of the Idrissid line, but here in the south descent from the Alaoui is much more likely. In earlier times there was a limited population of Jewish craftsmen and traders, who have now all gone, and a much larger and still resident population of *Haratine*, a black-skinned caste of cultivators descended from former slaves. Centuries of feuding has now been limited to a sartorial rivalry between the village women. The competing styles of dress are dominated by a choice between a black or dark blue *haik*, but this is picked out by highly individual assemblies of sequins, coins and poster bright embroidery. Note also the use made of contrasting red and purple stockings.

Sultans from the Drâa

In the medieval period the Drâa valley tended to be either under the control of Sijilmassa, the great trading city of the oasis of Tafilalt, or Sanhaja-speaking Berber nomad tribes from the Sahara. In the 13th century a coalition of Arab nomadic tribes, known as the Maql (*see* the 'Arab tribes of the Plain', p.411), brought Arabic speech to this Berber valley. These Arab tribes remained the dominant power for 300 years. The crisis of the 16th century, when Spain and Portugal seemed on the point of seizing control of the entire Moroccan coastline, produced an extraordinary burst of activity in the Drâa valley. Al-Qaim, who came from a saintly Arab family long resident in the ksar of Tagmadart in the Drâa, emerged as a local leader against the Christians. In 1510 he was acknowledged as leader of the entire south and set up a base on the Atlantic coast to harry the Portuguese, who held Agadir. A generation later the military victories of his sons firmly established his family as the ruling dynasty of Morocco. They are known to history as the Saadians, although during their time of power no one would have dared use that name. For 'Saadian' was a derogatory reference to the dynasty's descent from the Beni-Saad-Hawazin, a mere tribe of Bedouin Arabs, which made nonsense of their claim to be *shorfa*, directly descended from the Prophet Mohammed. In 1546, while the Saadians were busy fighting their way to power in the north of the country their Drâa homeland was devastated by an army of two thousand Tuareg warriors under the standard of the Sultan of Songhai, the Muslim monarch of Niger. The Saadians were able to exact their revenge 45 years later when they sent an army down to Zagora. This force succeeded in crossing the Sahara and then went on to plunder and conquer Songhai. The sacked capital of Timbuktu produced such fabulous booty that the ruling sultan in Marrakech was known as 'El Dehbi', the golden. The Drâa Valley became a rich conduit for this golden traffic, and a vital link to Morocco's distant province in West Africa. However the process of conquest, the feuds amongst the Moroccan military, and the exploitative rule of the pachas became so bloody and destructive that they, almost literally, killed the goose that laid the golden eggs. From the mid-17th century no more gold was ever to be brought north across the desert from the secluded swampland mines of the Upper Niger.

The Drâa soon fell back into its accustomed role. During times of weak government it fell under the domination of either the Tazeroualt dynasty of the Anti-Atlas mountains, or the Aït-Atta tribe of the Jbel Sarhro. When the French finally destroyed the power of the Aït-Atta in 1936 the valley passed under the control of Thami el Glaoui, before being reintegrated into the nation upon Independence in 1956. Only flickers of fighting from the Western Sahara or the odd border dispute with Algeria have disturbed the peace since.

Tizi-n-Tinififft

About 13km along the Zagora road from Ouarzazate a side road leads down to the El Mansour Eddahbi Dam, which controls the level of the lake to the east of Ouarzazate and the flow of the Drâa. At the moment a military post prohibits access to this impressive dam and the gorge cut through the mountains by the Drâa.

The main P31 road then climbs the deserted, denuded slopes of Jbel Tifernine, which stands at the western edge of the Sarhro mountain range. The oasis hamlet of **Aït-Saoun** lies in the arid valley between Jbel Tifernine and Jbel Anouart. The **Tizi-n-Tinififft** pass crosses the latter at a height of 1660m to provide a magnificent view: the Anti-Atlas to the west; the confused mass of Sarhro to the east; and the peaks of the High and Middle Atlas looming to the north. Meanwhile the surrounding slopes reveal weird patterns of violently twisted bonds of sedimentary rocks.

Agdz

The first view of the Drâa Valley with its sharply defined mass of palms comes only a few kilometres short of the administrative centre of Agdz, 68km south of Ouarzazate. The old military kasbah and the outlying keep-like office of the *caid* overlook the town square from a slight hill to the east. Groups of immaculately robed and turbaned farmers assemble in winter at the *caidat* to renew their leases, their braided cross-belts holding ceremonial daggers and embroidered leather purses.

The square is festooned with carpets which hang by day in a barrage of colour from the windows of the surrounding houses. There are several cafés, a few cheap hotels and some reasonably-priced bazaars clustered around it. The **souk** is held on Thursdays just south of the town in an enclosure beside the road, with a smaller affair on Sundays. To the north of the town the palm groves extend up past the Dar el Glaoui kasbah (1km away) towards the ksour of **Issafen** and **Rebat**, at the northern head of the valley. The river-filled gorge and Draa waterfall, some 20km out of Agdz, is the customary goal of local cross-country expeditions.

Where to Stay and Eating Out

The inexpensive **Hotel Kissane**, © (04) 843044, @ 843258, stands on the Ouarzazate edge of town and is a welcome new addition to Agdz, which has always been a good base for exploring the quieter and less visited northern half of the valley. It is efficiently run and has its own café, restaurant (no licence) and, more recently, a swimming pool. The latter is a vital resource, not least as a refuge from the coach parties off-loaded into the hotels' café and lavatories. In addition to this service the hotel runs Land Rover trips to the Drâa waterfall.

There are two cheap and basic hotels that overlook the town square: the **Hôtel des Palmiers**, © (04) 843127, and the **Hôtel du Drâa**. You can eat cheaply at the dining room in the du Drâa, or at the **Nadbah** café-restaurant.

There is also the well-established **Camping Kasbah de la Palmeraie**, © (04) 843080, signposted down a track 2km to the north of the town. It is a pleasant well-shaded site with a water tank, and which also organizes walking or jeep trips into the surrounding area.

Drâa Ksar between Agdz and Zagora

Just south of Agdz, but on the east bank of the Drâa, is the conspicous **ksar of Tamnougalt**, the old citadel of the Berber Mezguita tribe, who dominated this area of the valley. The Glaoui built **kasbah of Timiderte**, also known as the kasbah of Aït-Ali, is the next great building to appear further south, also on the east bank of the valley. It is the most striking and assertive fortress-like kasbah in the valley, standing in splendid golden isolation on a hill of friable grey schist. It was built in 1938 by Caid Brahim, eldest son and heir of Thami el Glaoui, the notorious pacha of Marrakech. You can wade across the Drâa in order to explore its empty passages and central arcaded courtyard, or take the track which fords the river by the '4km Agdz' milestone.

The **ksar of Tansikht**, 93km from Ouarzazate, marks the end of the old territory of the Mezguita. There is an all-weather bridge here, watched over by a café, which leads to the dirt road that bounces down to the relatively unvisited **ksour of Taakilt and Timaslâ** on the east side of the valley.

Back on the main road the attractive and easily approachable **ksar of Oulad-Atmane** is 14km south of the Tansikht bridge, dominated by the still-inhabited kasbah of Dar Caid Arabi. The use of a few lines of decorative green-glazed tile on this kasbah can be seen to echo the colour and shape of the palm-frond wattle used by traditional builders. A little further south at **Igdâoun** you get your first view of the high but truncated, almost pyramid-like, towers that are prevalent in the southern Drâa.

Tinezouline is the largest village between Agdz and Zagora, and with its roadside cafés and a busy souk on Mondays makes an attractive stop. The whole village is ringed with **kasbahs** in various forms of growth, decay and restoration. You could also ask in the cafés for a guide to show you the Libyo-Punic rock inscriptions found about 7km to the west. The Libyo-Punic language was created in the aftermath of the fall of Carthage, when skilled Punic officials escaped the rule of Rome and were employed by the Berber kings of North Africa.

The **Défilé de l'Azlag**, a small gorge through which the Drâa squeezes, lies just 25km north of Zagora. Azlag marks your entry into the palm groves of Ternata, the territory of the Arabic-speaking Oulad-Yahia and Roha tribes.

Zagora and Amazraou

The modern town of **Zagora** has been disappointing visitors for decades, and does so even more now that it is in the process of quadrupling its population and has been promoted into a new administrative centre. The arch across the road marks your entrance into the town centre, which is composed of two dusty but partly arcaded streets, Boulevard Mohammed V and Avenue Hassan II. These two streets join just before the fort-like office of the *caid*, where stands the town's most famous monument, the '52 days to Timbuktu' signpost. Beneath the *caidat* the road then swings down to cross over the Drâa riverbed into extensive palm groves. The grove on the east bank of the Drâa belongs to the village of **Amazraou**, whose traditional earth-brick houses stand just 1km south of ferro-concrete Zagora.

Once you have absorbed the initial disappointment you can relax and be grateful for Zagora–Amazraou, which has a good range of hotels in every price range and makes an ideal base from which to explore the surrounding palm groves and ksour, which are of such interest and charm that you become almost fond of the town itself. It is also considered, rather unfairly, to be a hassley sort of place. The fault is often with the visitor, blissfully unaware that the exceptionally hot and dry climate of the area distorts your character. Take things slowly, take a siesta and wake up in time to join the town paseo at dusk. Accept in advance that you are unlikely to leave without at least one child guide on your first walk through the Zagora palm groves, the Tamegroute Zaouia or Amazraou village. We all have to get by somehow. If you behave you might be given a gazelle or a hare made from folded palm leaves as a going-away present.

Getting Around

Three CTM **buses** leave for the 4–5hour trip to Ouarzazate daily (currently at 7am, 11am and 5pm) from the depot in the centre of the town by the souk on Boulevard Mohammed V. Private bus companies leave from the far northern end of the Boulevard, beyond the walled enclosure used by the souk.

Grands taxis operate from the same walled enclosure used by the private buses at the north end of town, just before the town gate. A place to Ouarzazate should cost around 40dh; negotiate to hire a taxi, at around 350dh for a day-trip, to take you south to Tamegroute, Tinfou and Mhamid. For **Landrover or truck taxis** *see* 'Desert Crossings from the Drâa', below.

Practically every hotel in town offers **camel trips**, from one hour to a morning or evening ride with meal, a 24-hour camping expedition, or a week-long tour. Prices are fairly uniform, but as most tours are actually run by the Hôtel La Fibule why not book directly from them. **Mountain bikes** can also be hired from Hôtel La Fibule.

Tourist Information

All the town cafés, the post office, the two petrol pumps, the two banks and all the cheap hotels and restaurants are on the main street, Boulevard Mohammed V.

The Town

The southern end of Boulevard Mohammed V culminates in the Cercle, the administrative offices of the super-*caid* of Zagora. In front of the guarded entrance to the Cercle is the intriguing and oft-photographed sign, 'Tombuktoo 52 jours', a journey which, due to an impassable frontier, has not been possible in the last 25 years. This crossing south from Zagora was the route taken by the Saadian expedition that conquered Timbuktu in 1591, although they took 135 days. This Saadian force was known as 'the army of the day' as it contained a large proportion of white-skinned European muskeeters who had converted to

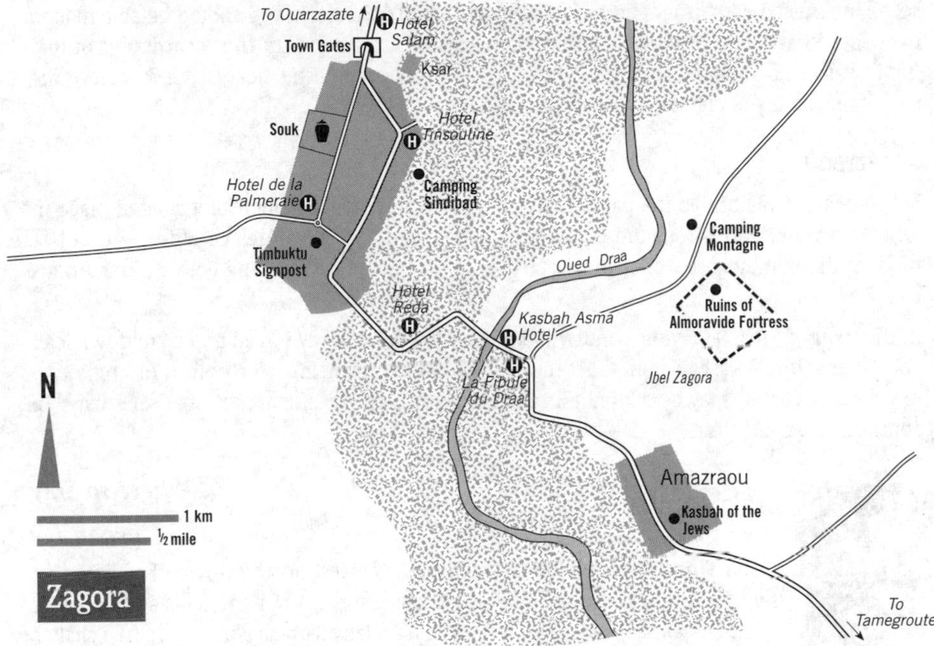

Islam. Their commander, Pacha Judar, had started life as a Catholic Spaniard but ended it as the Moroccan governor of Timbuktu.

The covered **souk** is busy practically everyday of the week in the morning and evening, but trading intensifies on Wednesdays and Sundays when the walled souk enclosure is filled by country traders. The dates of Zagora and the Drâa are excellent, and the date-sellers will allow you to taste from the many different qualities and varieties. Ask for *'boufeggous'*, which is renowned for both its sweetness and long storage life. The salt-miners of Taghaza, in the central Sahara, used to live off an exclusive diet of Drâa dates and corn, though they all starved when no caravan could reach the outpost for several years.

The Almoravid City

The present town of Zagora dates back to the 13th century, when it was founded by the Maql Arabs during their assertive migration into southern Morocco. The gaunt remains of an earlier Almoravid city can be explored on the side of **Jbel Zagora**, the extraordinary black sugar loaf hill standing just to the south. Once across the Drâa bridge, turn left along the dirt road, signposted to Camping La Montagne, which takes you directly to the foot of the ruins. The half-excavated walls and gates of this strictly rectangular city enclose a mound of building stone, ceramic sherds and the odd gaping entrance to a cistern. It was founded in the 11th century by the Almoravid Empire, whose strength was based on the Berber tribes of the Western Sahara. A stone citadel once stood on the summit of the mountain to watch and guard this walled town, built as a deliberate trading rival to the Tafilalt.

A military post on top of Jbel Zagora stops you climbing to the summit. But you can climb high enough to enjoy an excellent view of the green palm groves which snake north and south, encrusted with ksour and hemmed in by hills. To the north you should be able to look over Jbel Rhart to see the peaks of Jbel Sarhro, whilst to the south the escarpment of Jbel Bani rises out of an adjacent plain. Dusk or dawn allows you the clearest view, before the sun drains both you and the colour of the sky.

Amazraou

South of the Drâa bridge the palm groves of Amazraou offer a delightfully shaded place in which to walk. Paths from the Camping d'Amazraou and the Hôtel La Fibule fan out at random through the pisé-walled plots of barley and vegetables, overhung with arching fronds of strong palm.

In the **ksar** of Amazraou your hand will be charmingly but firmly seized and a child will lead you to the Jews' kasbah and the sand dunes before escorting you home for mint tea. Jewellery or carpets may be offered for sale, but with such graceful artistry that salesmanship approaches a court ritual.

Where to Stay

expensive

The **Tinsouline**, © (04) 847252, is the oldest hotel in town. The entrance is well-signposted, just off Boulevard Mohammed V. The hotel is a little faded, but fine if you are looking for something relatively peaceful, as the two slicker new hotels now draw off the bulk of the large tour groups. It has a pleasantly faded pink kasbah design, a pool, garden courtyards and rooms overlooking palm-filled gardens below. The hotel water tower provides an excellent view of Zagora.

The 100-room **Hotel Salam**, © (04) 847400, @ 847551, is just before the town gates and provides a perfectly acceptable alternative, though it will get even better when the young palm trees in the courtyard can spread a bit of shade and when the cooking improves. Another option is the slightly more expensive and opulent **Club Reda**, © (04) 847249/847012, with four pools contained within its central courtyard. The interior, in contrast, particularly the domed hall, is not a success. The entrance drive is about 150m before the Drâa bridge.

moderate

La Fibule du Drâa, © (04) 847318, @ 847271, is just 300m the other side of the Drâa bridge from Zagora, on your left amid the palm gardens. A few years ago it was just a small, cheap place, but it has now deservedly evolved into one of the social centres of the town. It remains a fine place to drop in for a drink or a meal, or to organize a camel ride, but as a hotel it's perhaps a bit cramped fully to justify its price (at the top of this range), unless you get one of the cheaper old rooms. It has a pool, but beware of the returning khaki-clad expeditioneers eager to communicate their desert experiences after one night under canvas in the Sahara.

On the other side of the road from La Fibule is the **Hôtel Kasbah Asmaa**, © (04) 847210, @ 847527, which has a mihrab-shaped pool, a fountain and tranquil garden, and is very busy for lunch, served in the courtyard restaurant or outside in carpet-strewn tents. Alcohol is only served at meals. On the first floor of the mock kasbah construction are the 17 hotel bedrooms, but this is only one more aspect of the Kasbah Asmaa, which, founded on the profits of a carpet bazaar, also has a thriving business organizing desert bivouacs and Saharan expeditions.

inexpensive

The **Hôtel Palmeraie**, ✆ (04) 847008, 📠 847878, stands at the far southern end of Boulevard Mohammed V. It has 16 rooms, a popular local bar, a licensed restaurant in a tent out the back, a reliable water supply and a brand new pool. Despite its name it stands nowhere near a palm tree, but enjoys the best view in Zagora of the sunset from its terrace. If the rooms are full you can also ask to sleep on the roof terrace.

cheap

Also along Boulevard Mohammed V there are a number of simple hotels. Try for one of the 14 rooms in the **Vallée Oued Drâa**, ✆ (04) 847210, first before trying its near neighbour the **Hôtel des Amis**.

camping

There are three good campsites: the **Sindibad** is close to the Tinsouline on Avenue Hassan II and has a café and a pleasantly shaded site; **Camping de la Montagne de Zagora** is situated 1km beyond the Draa bridge, first right, and the **Amezraou** is found just past the Hotel Fibule du Draa.

Eating Out

moderate

The licensed dining room in the **Tinsouline** is hung with the work of Fatima Hassani, one of the most celebrated contemporary naive artists in Morocco, and the four course *menu du jour* can make for a reasonably priced evening meal. The capacious dining room of the **Hotel La Fibule**, though, will provide a more exciting meal. Fresh bread is baked in the centre of the room, and though the service is famously erratic, somehow everybody yet manages to get fed the deliciously spiced *tagine* of their choice. On your way in, stop for a drink in the open-air bar shaded by palm trees, or the bar inside the hotel named after the poet Abou Noes.

Just beyond La Fibule hotel complex, on the right hand side of the road, stands the **Restaurant La Baraka**, ✆ (04) 847722, which has a short Moroccan menu, no garden and no alcohol, but good local cooking. The restaurant of the **Kasbah Asmaa** hotel is another reliable address which provides a small choice from its reasonaby priced *menu du jour*, and where you can eat on the garden terrace, in the kasbah courtyard or sprawled on banquettes desert-style in the hotel's capacious black tents.

cheap

Good cheap meals can be picked up in any of the café-restaurants along Boulevard Mohammed V. In particular, a table on the pavement outside the **Hotel des Amis** can be enthusiastically recommended for an evening meal combining good local food with plenty of people-watching.

Opposite the Hôtel Tinsouline there is the well stocked **Maison Berbère** bazaar, as well as some smaller jewellery stalls which sell the distinctive indigo dyed cotton cloth of the Tuareg 'blue men' and the bright embroidered black shawls of the women.

The *moussem* of Moulay Abdelkader Jilali is celebrated at Zagora at the same time as the feast of Mouloud, the prophet's birthday.

South of Zagora

Tamegroute

Twenty-two kilometres south of Zagora on pot-holed tarmac is the unpretentious-looking village and zaouia of Tamegroute. It was a celebrated centre of Islamic learning as early as the 11th century, part of the reforming impulse which further south into the Sahara would explode into the nucleus of the Almoravid Empire. It was revitalized in the 17th century when Abou Abdallah ben Mohammed Naceur founded a branch of the Naciri brotherhood here. The Naciri have always encouraged rigorous Koranic scholarship as the way to the true meaning of Islam. They have no truck with the musical and mystical enthusiasms of other Moroccan religious brotherhoods. In the early 19th century they functioned as a fundamentalist movement that was especially influential during the reign of Moulay Sliman, who was himself an adept of the Naciri. The brotherhood sent missionaries into the mountains in support of the sultan's military and political action against the Sharqawi brotherhood at Boujad in the Middle Atlas, the Derkawa at Tetouan and the Taibia at Ouezzane. This attack failed but the Naciri, unlike those other brotherhoods, still remain influential and an integral part of the national education system. The zaouia of Tamegroute contains a medersa for the education of theological students up to university level, a famous library, a mosque, and the hallowed tomb of its founder. The zaouia dispenses charity to the sick, old and mentally ill. The medieval mixture of scholarship and faith is here further reinforced by charity. A small crowd of poor and mad supplicants can often be seen around the founder's tomb where they patiently wait for a cure, or failing that subsistence and gifts from pilgrims and visitors.

It is rare to be allowed access to any building connected with Islam in Morocco but at Tamegroute non-Muslim visitors are welcome to look around the concrete modern **medersa**, the desiccated walled garden of the college, and the **library**. This is justly celebrated, for it contains a wonderful collection of Koranic commentaries, law books, astronomical guides, histories of Fès, dictionaries and tomes on mathematics. Some of the volumes are over 700 years old, while a few are written on gazelle vellum with rich and ornate gilding and generations of marginal notes and references in coloured inks. The wallet-like protective leather bindings are also distinctive Islamic features of this collection.

There is a **pottery** district in Tamegroute composed of a courtyard of sunken huts, coloured the pale grey of the local clay, and a modern open-air exhibition hall. The distinctive local products are mostly rough earthenware that is solid in shape and primitive in design. They are made attractive by a splendidly irregular glassy green glaze that suggests both palm trees and the banners of Islam. You may buy pieces from the hall, or at the weekly **souk** held on the edge of the village on Saturdays.

Tinfou Sand Dunes

Seven kilometres south of Tamegroute (25km from Zagora) on the east side of the road, lie the golden sand dunes of Tinfou. The dunes, reached down a dirt track just before the lone Auberge, are best climbed at dawn or dusk, or by moonlight. They are not comparable in extent with the Erg Chebbi at Merzouga, east of Erfoud, but are still entrancing.

Where to Stay and Eating Out

In **Tamegroute**, almost opposite the gateway to the Naciri medersa is the **Jnane Dar** (Chez Abdessadek Naciri) ✆ (04) 848622, a charming cafe-restaurant which occupies a pavilion in the centre of an old walled garden. Rooms are gradually being created in an old tower set against one wall, but meals, mint tea and impromptu musical sessions are already available.

Beside the road at **Tinfou** stands the **Auberge-Répos Sable Tinfou**, ✆ 848566 (postal booking address Chez el Farouj, BP 6, Tamegroute, Zagora). It is one of Morocco's most entrancing hotels—though if you dislike windblown sand and like your plumbing to cascade like Niagara you should certainly stay elsewhere. The Auberge is a modern kasbah built from traditional materials and to a traditional courtyard plan. You can sleep on the roof, in rooms off the courtyard, or in one of the more private rooms in a row outside. It is owned and run by the El Farouj family. Hassan el Farouj, whose family come from the Drâa, and his wife, Fatima Hassani of Tetouan, are two of Morocco's leading artists. Their work, which can be bought, is on show on the walls around the courtyard, and their four sons Hind, Moumen, Magid and Mourad run the hotel, make music, carve wood, create poems and organize camel trips, mainly out to the nearby dunes. Tea is available at all hours of the day; *tagines* should be ordered a bit in advance.

They have recently been joined by the **Porte du Sahara**, ✆ (04) 848562, 📠 847002, an efficiently run restaurant, moderately priced hotel and bivouac camp. Hassan and his German wife Helga specialize in arranging elegant encampments and al fresco dinners for groups (including a week-long traditional southern Moroccan wedding for a German couple and a hundred guests), though if you are looking for something a bit quieter you can sleep in one of the corner towers of the walled encampment.

Mhamid

South of Tinfou the road leaves the valley to use a pass across the Jbel Bani, which separates the southernmost reach of the Drâa from the rest of the oasis valley. The Jbel Bani is a long spur of baked black rock that runs west, like a natural rampart, for 250km all the way to Tata. A number of half-ruined towers, in occasional use by the military, guard the pass through the hills. The **ksour** of Nesrate and Beni-Hayoun are tucked in the great expanse of palms to the east of the road. **Tagounite** is a dusty modern settlement set in the hard-baked plateau, which comes alive for the **souk** on Mondays and Thursdays. Ask at the central café Essaada for Beckir Faiz, who can take you on a fascinating tour through the palm groves, ksour and kasbahs to the east, such as Zaouia Sidi Salah, Kebir, Regaba, El Blida, Hayoun, Rmal, Adafal and Beni Huit, the old Jewish settlement. Beyond Tagounite you climb a lesser spur of the Jbel Bani through the Tizi-Beni-Selmande pass, also watched over by ruined towers and an agadir. A track east on the north side of these hills leads to the ancient **Berber necropolis of Foum Eragene**, which dates back to 800 BC. Down in the Mhamid el Ghouzlane, the plain of gazelles, half way between Tagourite and Mhamid, there is a dirt track west towards the gorgeous golden crescents of the Erg Lihoudi sand dunes. Just a couple of kilometres before Mhamid the road passes through the immaculately maintained ksar of Oulad Driss, whose palm groves now boast two new roadside **Camping-Auberges** (the Auberge de Tuareg and Carrefour des Caravanes), which offer meals and beds under black tents or beneath the shade of palms.

With its Head in Fire and Feet in Water

It is said of the date palm that it requires its head to be in fire and its feet in water. The southern oasis valleys perfectly fulfil these requirements. The date palm is their one commercial crop, and it also provides vital shade beneath which all other plants are grown. Its roots hold the soil against erosion by the desert wind. A beam cut from a palm trunk is the basis for most pisé desert houses, and palm fronds provide the wattle for floors and walls and can be woven into baskets and mats. The palm also provides an aphrodisiac from its flowers, fibre from its trunk that can be woven into rope, kindling for fires, its hollowed trunk forms a bucket, and *mahyear*, a powerful and illicit spirit, can be distilled from sap wine.

There are four and a half million date palms in the southern oasis valleys which produce 95,000 tons of dates a year, of which at least a quarter is exported. The palm tree can remain productive for up to 150 years and starts to fruit after it is five. Between April and June they are mated. Pollen-bearing flowers from male trees are hung among the unfertilized clusters on female trees. The dates ripen in autumn, with the harvest stretching from November to February. This is the joyful culmination of the year, when you may see eager barefoot boys shinning up tattered trunks to slice off the tendrils of fruit with a blow of a machete, younger children catching the dates as they fall through the branches, women chanting as they shred the fallen fronds, and men, with a more serious demeanour, sorting, weighing and packing the dates.

Each region produces dates with different qualities: some are prized for their size, some for their sweetness, and some can stay fresh for years, while some are only good enough to be squashed to produce date honey, or fed to the goats. The best eating dates are found in Zagora.

Mhamid is the very last gasp of fertility in the Drâa. It used to be an important market for the nomadic tribes, and an oasis staging post for trans-Saharan trade. The Saadians kept a garrison of Christian renegades here at the Ksar Ksebt el Allouj as a support base for the Moroccan garrisons in the towns along the Niger river. Lektawa, a secret ksar south of Mhamid, was where the gold dust of Wangara was minted into Saadian dirhams. Its exact position is not known. In 1958 King Mohammed V made a speech here which reinstated Morocco's claim over the portion of the Sahara which the French administration had annexed to their colony of Algeria. Since then, though, the creation of closed national borders and the continuing tension between Morocco and Algeria has turned Mhamid into a dead end. In the new town built to sedentarize former nomads stand government offices,

three old courtyards for the rather meagre **Monday souk** and the cheap **Restaurant-Hotel Sahara and Iriqui** where Housine cooks meals and his partner Sbai runs the expeditions. Alternatively, head straight across the riverbed just to the east and follow signs to the cheap **Auberge El Khaima**, a delightful place with its own tent, mud house and palm-shaded garden. Using this as your base for either lunch or a week, you can explore the palm groves and ksour of Mhamid, which include Oulad Yussef, Zaouiat El Hna, Oulad M'Hiya (with a pair of picturesque koubbas), Zenaga and the Kasbah of the Shorfa. More ambitious expeditions, by jeep, donkey cart, camel or foot, can be taken to such distant objectives as the sand deserts of Erg Sedrat and Erg Smâr at Chegaga, the oasis of El Gloa or the Mel'alg hills.

Desert Crossings from the Drâa

If you are planning to drive it is wise to have two spare tyres, all official papers, something to dig with, sleeping bags, your own picnic supplies, candles and plenty of water. A compass and map may sound a little melodramatic when you are merely following a well-established dirt road, but sand storms can quickly obscure the tracks and leave you completely disorientated. Every year about half a dozen tourists die in the Moroccan and Tunisian Sahara. Curiously enough, drowning in desert flash floods is more common than death by dehydration.

The East Bank of the Drâa

A rough track suitable for Land Rovers starts just south of Jbel Zagora and continues north up the less visited eastern bank of the Drâa to rejoin the tarmac road at Tansikht bridge. Portions of this trip or the whole 100km can be arranged through hotels in Zagora such as La Fibule.

Agdz to Tazenakht

Take a turning to the west by the gates that stand on the Ouarzazate side of Agdz. For the first 55km you bounce slowly along through the still landscape of the Tamsift Valley, passing a few isolated palm groves and villages the largest of which, **Aït-Semgane-n-el-Grara**, has a café. Having stopped to fill your water bottles with the sweet water found at the shepherds' well, you will join the tarmac road about 11km west of the cobalt mine at Bou-Azzer. The mine workings are overlooked by a handsome goat-cave set into a dry tufa waterfall on the hillside to the north. West of the mine the road twists over two mountain passes and through a couple of slight gorges to reach Tazenakht, *see* p.533.

Zagora to Rissani via Tansikht

This route, once a gruelling ten-hour journey in a spine-jarring communal Land Rover-taxi, now runs entirely over tarmac roads.

Heading back north up the Drâa valley you hit the new road by the bridge over the Drâa at Tansikht, where the odd hitchhiker and a line of *grands taxis* can be seen sheltering beside the café La Gazelle. From there route 6956 heads northeast, slowly climbing up a dry valley flecked with the black tents of shepherds and the stark ruins of guard-post towers.

The palm-shrouded oasis of **Nekob** (40km from Tansikht) has a **souk** on Sundays and a few basic cafés. The town has a very diferent atmosphere to the Drâa, with its calm, well-ordered prosperity, neat kasbah-house walls, wind pumps and neatly turned out white-turbanned men sitting in the shade of the arcades. Nekob is a settlement of the Aït Atta, one of the proudest 'white' Berber tribes, who have traditionally remained aloof from the 'black' Berbers and Haratine of the Drâa ksour. If you are looking for a meal or a tea stop there is the **Camping Aït Atta**, in the shade of the palm grove on the east side of town. From Nekob there stretches a delicate string of hamlets, small palm groves and irrigated gardens defiantly cultivating this arid landscape beneath the great striding line of mountains to the south.

Tazzarine, perched beside a black stone gorge, marks the edge of this zone of cultivation. It is an old frontier town which boasts a military garrison, a petrol pump, a good hotel and a bivouac camp site. The **Hotel Bougafer** stands on the left of the road, overlooking the old cemetery and beneath the military kasbah. It serves a very good four-course lunch, has a drinks licence and over 40 bedrooms, and also runs the **Camping Bou Gafer** on the south bank of the river bed (tents, terraces, palm shade and a swimming pool promised). Long accused of negotiating room prices on a scale of need, the manager assures me that a double room costs only 150dh, and lunch just 80dh.

From Tazzarine it is 67km to the palm oasis of **Alnif**, which has petrol pumps, the simple **Gazelle du Sud** four-bedroom hotel and, opposite it, the **Restaurant Bougafer**. From there it is a relatively straight, unbroken 95km to join the main Erfoud–Rissani road in the Tafilalt.

West to Foum-Zguid

A lorry-taxi leaves Zagora at around noon on Wednesdays and Sundays for a bumpy five to eight-hour, 130km ride in order to arrive at the Thursday **souk** held at the oasis of **Foum-Zguid** or the Monday souk at the nearby ksar of **Smira**. There is a café by the petrol station at Foum-Zguid with very basic rooms. A further lorry-taxi connection runs west from there to Tata on Mondays and Thursdays, as well as more conventional buses, on Tuesdays, Thursdays and Saturdays, up to Tazenakht.

The Dadès Valley

The Dadès is known, by promotional brochures if no one else, as the valley of a thousand kasbahs. Pay no attention to petulant tourists who claim that once you've seen one kasbah you've seen them all. Each oasis valley has a distinctive character, but you cannot expect to appreciate this by merely staring through the windows of a passing car or bus. Be prepared to break your journey, taking it easy during the middle of the day and then walking along the riverbed during the perfect conditions of early morning and dusk.

The Dadès begins its life as a mountain stream in the peaks of the High Atlas. It cuts out a gorge in the foothills before flowing west across a high plateau. Here it is seen in a more tranquil mood, meandering through a broad river valley and ultimately adding its water to the lake at Ouarzazate, and thence to the Drâa. In the Dadès Valley settlement takes the pattern of family-based kasbahs scattered along the fertile bed of the river, rather than the fortified village ksour sited at regular intervals that you see elsewhere. A large proportion of the Dadès kasbahs are in an advanced state of ruin, but these can be compared with the few that have been kept in perfect condition and remain in active use. Increasingly, the population has moved from the valley floor and lives in modern villages beside the road. The new houses are just saved from box-like blandness by pleasant little decorative embellishments, odd cornices and battlements inherited from kasbah architecture.

A wider belt of cultivable land also robs the valley of the exotic constriction of the Ziz and the Drâa. The Dadès, apart from this greater feeling of space, is a busier and more commercially successful valley than the Drâa. It harbours a greater diversity of crops and employment, and has a steady population level of 80,000. This valley alone retains a geographical relevance as an east–west transport route, a role denied the other valleys since the closing of the Saharan border.

Of all the southern oasis valleys, the Dadès has the most undisturbed pattern of Berber settlement. The High Atlas slopes to the north were the grazing grounds of warlike Berber nomads, the Aït-Yafalman, who were never subdued. Neither the Maql Arabs, dominant in the region from the 13th to the 16th century, nor the Aït-Alouane section of the Aït-Atta super-tribe that became dominant in the 17th century could ever relax their guard. The valley women have a brightly coloured diversity of dress and ornament, but some of this may be hidden by the heavy dark blue cotton *haiks* of the region.

East from Ouarzazate

The 42km journey from Ouarzazate to Skoura skirts across an uninspiring sub-Saharan plain. The only break is a right turn 19km out of town that leads up to the **Restaurant du Lac**, which is open from May to September. It has a commanding view over the lake, and of a kasbah on the end of a peninsula occasionally marooned by the rising water.

Kasbahs around Skoura

About 3km west of Skoura the road passes conveniently close to the Dadès. This provides a good opportunity to stop for a walk (usually in the company of a young local guide—whether you like it or not) up through the palm groves to visit a series of magnificent piles. The kasbahs of Ben Moro and El Kabbaba stand about 200m apart just beside the road, while a stroll across the floor of the valley takes you toward the extravagant mass of the **kasbah of Amerhidil** on the north bank of the river. It and its neighbour, Dar-Aït-Sidi-El-Mati Kasbah, with their distinctive thin tapering towers, are some of the finest examples in the valley.

Skoura

Few people break their journey at Skoura, though it is conveniently placed on a loop just to the north of the main road. The modern town itself is of no interest but it offers a chance to wander along the maze of paths that thread among the earth walls of the palm groves to reach a number of fine **kasbahs**. Skoura was first established by the Almohad Sultan Yacoub el Mansour in the 12th century, when he built a government fortress between two tributary streams, just before they converge on the main valley bed. It has a **souk** on Mondays and just one cheap hotel, the **Nakhil**. This occupies the upstairs of the café beside the small paved square on the main street, and has lately tidied itself up a bit. The tables of the Nakhil Cafe are a good place to recruit a guide, who will be invaluable if you want to spend half a day walking through the palm grove paths and yet locate such local kasbahs as the Glaoui-built Dar-Aït-Sous and Dar Lahsoune, the splendid edifice of Aït-Ben-Abou and, on the edge of the palm groves, the maraboutic fortress of Sidi-Mbarek-ou-Ali.

Expeditions from Skoura

To the south of Skoura a dirt track, the 6834, climbs for 40km through the bleak twisted hills of the Jbel Sarhro massif to the mine of **Bou-Skour**. This is an arduous one-way journey that will take you deep into the original core territory of the Aït-Atta tribe. The track also provides an hour-long walk to **Sidi-Flah**, the central hamlet astride the Dadès riverbed.

To the north of Skoura there are two even more adventurous possibilities. A dirt track, the 6829, follows one of the most difficult of the old caravan crossings of the High Atlas—the **Tizi-n-Fedrhate**—between Skoura and Demnate. The ksar of **Aït-Sous** is just outside Skoura, but even a Land Rover will have difficulty in climbing the entrance to the pass 40km up the track, north of the mountain village of **Assermo**.

For an even more rewarding trip below the valleys and foothills of Ighil M'Goun (4071m), a 100km circuit on routes 6831 and 6903 will bring you back to the Dadès Valley at **El-Kelaâ-M'Gouna**. For this you would need a four-wheel-drive, but some indication of the country can be had by travelling the first and easiest 25km to look at the hilltop agadirs and kasbahs of the Aït-Yafalman around the villages of **Toundoute** and **Tabia-Aït-Zaghar**. The track is to the left just after Skoura, off the main road east to El-Kelaâ M'Gouna.

East of Skoura to El-Kelaâ M'Gouna

East of Skoura the P32 draws away from the Dadès to cross the Tizi-n-Taddert pass (1370m). After this there is a fine cluster of kasbahs around **Imassine**, 20km from Skoura. A further 22km of dull road follows before the **kasbah of Aït-Ridi**, which marks the entrance into the wide and fertile river beds of the Dadès and its tributary the M'Goun. The ksar **Aït-Ba-Ahmed** guards the bridge over the M'Goun, the banks of which are lined by terraced fields of vegetables and plots of barley shaded by almond trees and divided by low rambling hedges of rose bushes. Almonds supplant palms here for the valley, not much below 1500m here, is too high and cold in the winter for palms to be grown successfully.

Ten kilometres beyond the bridge you travel into the centre of the valley to approach the town of **El-Kelaâ M'Gouna**. It sits at the foot of a bluff of rock that separates the two verdant valley floors of Dadès and M'Goun. It makes a good base for opportunities to explore the dramatic hinterland of mountains and kasbahs, but is itself an uninspiring and inoffensive roadside settlement. A **souk** is held on Wednesdays, but you can buy the local rosewater at any time of the day or week from the shops, whose shelves are filled with little else.

Roses are grown as the hedgerows that divide up the gardens of the valley, and their flowers are harvested in May, when a celebratory harvest festival is held. Over 700 tons of petals are picked every year and then processed in the modern rosewater factory camouflaged as a kasbah, a disguise that is only spoiled by two chimneys that emerge on the right as you travel east from El-Kelaâ. Rosewater is exported as the basic stock for many scents, and prized as a formal handwash throughout the Islamic world.

Tours from El-Kelaâ M'Gouna

The **Roses du Dadès Hotel** organizes a number of tours: an hour-long circuit around some local kasbahs; a whole-day tour (from 9am–3.30pm; with a minimum of 6 people); or a two-day ride that visits numerous villages and kasbahs, and includes dinner, entertainments and a bed in the Kasbah Taourirt in Ouarzazate.

Directly opposite the Café Rendezvous des Amis on the main road is the **Bureau des Guides et Accompagnateurs**. The office is bedecked with maps and piles of equipment, and is run by a group of young Moroccans as a cooperative. They organize three basic expeditions. The **M'Goun Gorge tour**, north from El-Kelaâ, spends eight days in the mountains and walks an average of about 20km a day. The **Jbel Sarhro**, due south, is a seven-day expedition that is only attractive in the cooler season, between October and April. The **southern High Atlas** is the reverse, for it is only open in the summer, after the snow has melted, between March and September. These three trips are obviously best organized well in advance, but shorter, cheaper walks can be arranged at short notice. Their address is: Bureau des Guides, El-Kelaâ M'Gouna Centre, Ouarzazate.

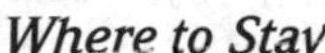

Where to Stay

expensive

The **Roses du Dadès**, ✆ (04) 883807, crowns the rocky bluff above the town, defiantly out of harmony with the rest of the valley. Its 1960s silhouette has not aged particularly well, but once inside the hotel its magnificent views, corral of elegant horses, sheltered swimming pool and bar rapidly win you over.

moderate

L'Auberge Pont d'Almou, ✆ (04) 836913, ℻ 836969, is an admirable new addition to the region. It stands 5km west of El-Kelaâ M'Gouna, with a terrace overlooking the edge of the valley beside the bridge of the same name. It has a traditional dining room, a tent and just a dozen modest rooms -

cheap

The grandly titled but inconspicuous **Hôtel du Grand Atlas**, ✆ (04) 883837, is on the main street. Run by the Aadhi family, it has its own restaurant and *hammam*.

Boumalne Dadès

New roadside villages predominate east of El-Kelaâ, though there are some wonderful old relics scattered along the valley floor. Notable are the **Kasbah El-Goumt** and the collection of kasbahs that overlook **Souk-El-Khémis-Zaouir-Er-Bir** (Souk-Khèmis-du-Dadès), although neither is accessible from the road without a scramble.

Boumalne Dadès is a small administrative town that overlooks the valley from the east bank. It lies just beyond the turning to the Dadès Gorge, with a pleasant yellow and white arcade to shade the row of shops and cafés at the town centre. In 1937 it consisted of just a fort, a café and a brothel. Only the Café Atlas, by the covered Wednesday souk, remains from that era, but a number of new hotels have sprung up along the crest of the hill, which looks out to the east over an arid steppe. It has a post office, a number of shops, *grands taxis* offering places to Ouarzazate and Tinerhir, but as yet no bank.

Boumalne might at first seem an unlikely holiday destination, but in recent years it has emerged as a centre for walking expeditions. It is well placed: to the north the Dadès Gorge offers an exciting entrance into the High Atlas, while to the south route 6907 heads to **Ikniouln**, the central market village of the Aït-Atta of Jbel Sarhro. Ikniouln is overlooked by a deserted French Foreign Legion fort and has a basic café-hotel beside its enclosed market square. You can ask here for a guide or muleteer if you wish to explore this fascinating region.

Where to Stay and Eating Out

All these Boumalne hotels have restaurants, though bear in mind that there are also a number of cheap and characterful places to stay and eat in the Dadès Gorge itself.

expensive

El Madayeq, ✆ (04) 830031, ℻ 882223, is a comfortable but unexceptional 100-bed hotel with a pool, bar and restaurant. It does however have a good view from its terrace over the sturdy but simple kasbahs on the valley floor.

moderate

Kasbah Tizzarouine, ✆ (04) 830690, ℻ 830256, has attracted a lot of favourable attention with its skilful employment of traditional architecture combined with efficient plumbing, exuberant internal décor and a suite of 'summer' rooms carved into the rock face—the perfect setting for a cool troglodytic siesta. The *patron*, Mohammed Lemnaouar, can also organise tours.

inexpensive

There are three small hotels to choose from, all admirably run by their owners. The **Soleil Blue**, ✆ (04) 830163, started life as a restaurant and is situated down a sign-posted track 300m to the north of the Madayeq, so that it shares the same fine view over the valley floor. It is run by Najim Lahcen, an enthusiastic ornithologist who prepares 'birding' walks and expeditions into the mountains.

The **Vallée des Oiseaux**, ✆ (04) 830764, is a functional 12-bedroom motel which stands behind the Shell petrol station on the road east of town. The manager Mohammed also organises expeditions and takes care of camper vans.

The **Chems**, ✆ (04) 830041, is also beside the road, on the edge of the palm groves. It has 15 rooms and a well regarded kitchen presided over by Abderrahmane Moubarik, and a fine view from its terrace.

cheap

The **Hôtel Adrar**, ✆ (04) 830355, stands right in the centre of Boumalne beside the bus station and the covered market. The rooms on the road-side have the better view.

The Dadès Gorge

This upper portion of the Dadès Valley has a relaxed air, with none of the daily hassle that you may have become used to. The few cheap hotels all serve good dishes from fresh local produce, and are locked in amicable competition with each other. In short, this could be a place to stay rather than just take in on a passing visit.

Getting Around

About 500m west of Boumalne, just before you cross the bridge over the Dadès river, there is a turning to the north signposted 'Mserhir'. This, the 6901, is the road to the gorge. If you are using public transport there is a daily mini-bus from Boumalne that goes up the gorge, leaving somewhere between 12 and 2pm, or you could charter a *grand taxi* or Land Rover taxi, or, once you are in the valley, thumb a lift.

The gorge itself lies 25km up from the turning, but the valley which leads to it is certainly as interesting. It has been described as a sabre cut in the High Atlas—a long verdant riverbed surrounded by scarlet scarred slopes. The brilliant range of red and carmine soils contrasts with a golden backdrop of denuded, treeless hills. It is too high for palm trees, but almond and walnut provide shade for the intensely worked gardens.

Six kilometres from the entrance of the valley you pass a ruined kasbah used by the Glaoui *caid* of the valley. The **Café Meguirne**, 14km along the road, run by Hassani Haddou and his young brother, marks the approach to the **Kasbah of the Rocks**. The landscape here is dominated by dark red eroded volcanic rocks which change their shape, form and character at different angles and distances. At first they are a great barrage of aggressive points angled menacingly at the sky in some cartoonist's image of massed arsenals of ballistic missiles. They alter as you dip down into the green valley floor, becoming increasingly phallic: a monstrous exhibition of lingam totems. These too melt before your eyes, dwindling to sprouting mushrooms before taking on the contours of a brain that finally suggests a placenta bed. It is a relief that the eroded golden limestone cliffs further up the valley are content to assume the form of sacred hawks and mother goddesses astride gaping caves.

The **kasbahs of the Aït-Atta** stand below the volcanic rocks and look fragile and impudent beneath such a powerful and massive natural formation. Their walls imitate perfectly the colours of the surrounding soil, topped with delicate towers lanced by double window frames, their summits crowned with corner battlements. It is a place of obsessive beauty and form, a place to plan picnics amongst the hanging rocks, to sketch and to dream.

The maraboutic **Aït-Ali ksar** lies 3km before the bridge over the Dadès at **Aït-Oudinar** which has a Sunday souk and marks the end of the tarmac, 23km up the valley. A little further up the road the river emerges from the gorge and a tributary joins the Dadès. The gorge's floor is taken up by the riverbed and makes for a delightful cool walk, wading upstream with the narrow walls of rock looming above and cutting out the fierce sun.

North of the Gorge

A good gravel road continues above the gorge for 5km to the hamlet of **Aït-Hammou**, which has a very basic, but welcome, café-hotel, the **Taghia**. The village of **Msemrir** is another

30km northeast along the track, and also has a café hotel which is used to putting up trekking tourists. Msemrir is at a junction of routes which without a trekking guide or a four-wheel-drive vehicle, you take at your own risk. To the east a 50km track, the 3444, crosses over the Tizi-n-Ugert-Zegzaoun pass to reach **Tamtattouchte** at the northern head of the Todra Gorge. To the north of Msemrir lorries use route 6905 which heads up over the Tizi-n-Ouano pass to reach **Agoudal** in 60km and, in another 45km, **Imilchil**. Imilchil has a souk on Saturdays, a number of cheap café-hotels and a fine kasbah, but is most famous as the site of the September marriage market of the Berber Aït-Haddidou tribe (*see* pp.350–1).

Where To Stay and Eating Out

All the hotels in this part of the valley are cheap, and used to serving lunch to passing visitors. In the evening you are much more likely to have the place to yourself and you should order your meal well in advance.

By the Kasbah of the Rocks is the **Tamlatte Hôtel**, which has the best view in the area and basic rooms. The **Hôtel Kasbah de la Vieille Tradition** is just 100m before the Tamlatte. It has a spacious hall, above which there is a balcony and a few clean simple rooms with cane ceilings.

At Aït-Oudinar, just by the bridge, is the **Auberge des Gorges du Dadès**, © (04) 831710, run by Haj Zahir Youssef. The food is excellent, and in season you may be served goat's cheese from the *patron*'s herd. Camping space is available beside the river, and guided mule trips can be arranged.

Right beside the gorge entrance there is a collection of even cheaper hotels. They are all fine but the **Hôtel La Kasbah de la Vallée**, © (04) 831717, which leans against the rock wall is the pick of the bunch. It is an especially friendly place, run by Saabi Hammou, who can also organize walking tours in the area.

From Boumalne Dadès to Tinerhir

The arid 50km-wide plain east from Boumalne Dadès to Tinerhir is broken by two oases. **Imiter** is the most appealing, dominated by a ksar of a thousand inhabitants and a separate group of outlying kasbahs. **Timadriouine**, 10km to the east, is an old ksar of the Aït-Atta.

The Aït-Atta: the Spartans of Jbel Sarhro

At the same time as the Saadians from the Drâa Valley were emerging as the new rulers of Morocco, an extraordinary martial society, the Aït-Atta, was being created. Dada Atta, a Berber chieftain from the bleak mountain slopes of the Jbel Sarhro, was the eponymous founder of this tribe of hardened warriors. Within a few decades the Aït Atta had overthrown the 300-year supremacy of the Maql Arabs and imposed their own rule. Like most of the larger tribal groups in Morocco, they expanded by the adoption of allies as well as conquest. There soon emerged five distinct *khums* or subdivisions, which included Berber and Arab speakers, though all agreed to recognize Dada Atta as their heroic ancestor. Of these *khums* the Aït-Alouane and the Aït-Khabbache were the most notorious. The Aït-Alouane became semi-nomadic, and the virtual overlords of the Drâa and the

Dadès valleys, which they claimed to protect. The Aït-Khabbache remained entirely nomadic and ranged the sub-Saharan steppes—merciless camel-borne raiders who left many a smouldering ksar in their wake.

Their power was not unopposed. The Berber tribes to the north of the Drâa formed a confederation, known as the Aït-Yafalman, to oppose any further expansion. To the east the defence of the Tafilalt oasis was organized in 1631 by Moulay Ali ech Cherif, the ancestor of the present ruling dynasty of Morocco. A number of the more forceful Alaouite sultans, Moulay Ismaïl in 1679 and Moulay Sliman and Moulay Hassan at the beginning and end of the 19th century, tried in vain to crush the Aït Atta.

They were the last of all the tribes in Morocco to submit to the French. The final battle came in 1934, some 25 years after the French army had first landed at Casablanca. Two brothers, Hammou and Hassou Ba Selam, led the Aït Atta defence of their mountain stronghold of Jbel Bou Gafer. For a whole month, 1,000 warriors resisted the assaults, bombardments and bombings from the air of the vastly superior French besieging force. At night the Aït Atta warriors would venture out from the mountain and murder the French sentries in order to steal bullets for the next day's battle. They were sometimes escorted by a powerful sorceress, whose spells were cast over the French army through the manipulation of livers that had to be torn from the living. The mountain finally fell to the Foreign Legion on 25 March 1934, and the bravery of the fallen tribal warriors is commemorated every year with an official celebration at Ouarzazate.

Tinerhir and the Todra Gorge

Tinerhir may at first seem just one of a string of dusty administrative centres, but it is an old and well established town, with a mixed population of farmers and craftsmen. It stands on a high bank of the Todra where the river leaves the protective folds of the High Atlas and flows out across the mountain plateau. Tinerhir overlooks magnificent dense palm groves. This band of vegetation hugs the riverbed and leads 12km north of Tinerhir to the celebrated canyon of the Todra Gorge. This dramatic geological rift in the mountains is the destination of most travellers, but the town and the palm groves have their own, more delicate charms.

Getting Around

Tinerhir is 169km from Ouarzazate and 141km from Er Rachidia. Buses and taxis all arrive and depart from the central arcaded garden square, Place Principale.

There are at least two **buses** a day west to Ouarzazate (5hrs), and two east to Er Rachidia (3hrs). ***Grands taxis*** run frequently west to Boumalne Dadès and east to Tinejdad, and places are easy to find. A taxi ride up into the Todra Gorge should be around 10dh per person. **Mules** can also be rented: ask at the hotels, and think in terms of 10dh an hour.

Tourist Information

Boulevard Mohammed V, the name the P32 assumes in town, has all the facilities you require; **banks**, a couple of pharmacies, telephone booths and shops. Around or just off the central garden square can be found the **Post Office**, buses, taxis, cheap hotels and café-restaurants. Tinerhir's weekly **souk** is held on Tuesdays in the walled compound about 2km out of town on the road to Ouarzazate.

Tinerhir

The ruined **Glaoui kasbah** still dominates the town from its hill to the west. Two great keeps are surrounded by outer yards and the whole wrapped up in a curtain wall. It was a deliberately palatial structure, built to intimidate and impress the hostile natives. Their behaviour to some extent mirrored the kasbah, and the Aït Atta tribe, when they finally succumbed to the French in 1934, asked only that they not be governed by the hated Glaoui. The unsafe structure of the kasbah is bricked up once a year, but local boys make a new entrance in order to use the sheltered courtyard for football; you may have to grub around a little to find their new hole. The view of the palm groves from the kasbah, or from the neighbouring Sarhro Hotel, is of one of the largest and richest oases of the Moroccan south.

Behind the Todra Hotel on the Place Principale, an animated network of **market streets** leads down to the riverbed. You pass the hiring corner where journeymen sit behind their trade tools, and descend downhill past booths of native jewellery. Tinerhir's most characteristic product is the small delicate wrought-iron grilles that decorate and protect local windows. Every stage of manufacture has a cluster of workshops with forges twisting, shaping and fixing before passing their work on to the framers and carpenters. As you descend, the town sheds its regularity to blend effortlessly into the confused patchwork of the palm groves and orchards.

Entering the **palm groves** from the heat, dust and light of a desert day you pass into a different environment. It is easy and pleasant to lose yourself amongst the paths, absorbing the different quality of colour and odour, and the flickering density of light. At dusk, the range of colour in the mud walls of the kasbahs and the renewed energy of the inhabitants creates a brief but glorious pageant.

The palm groves are populated by the clans of the Aït Atta. With few strong exterior threats, the domestic architecture celebrates the petty feuds of the area, symbolized by family-sized fortified kasbahs rather than ksour. Many of them are in good condition, and you can hire mules and guides in the town in order to explore them.

About 2km east of town the hamlet of Tidirine marks a 4km track that heads north to **Imarirene Kasbah**, up the east bank of the palm groves, past attractive settlements such as Aït Bujan and Taguntsa. Just west of town route 6906 heads southeast for 5km to rejoin the palm groves at the pretty hamlet of **Aït-Mohammed**. Taria, 2km further to the south, is where Hassou Ba Selam, the heroic chieftain of the Aït Atta's last stand at Jbel Sarhro, is buried. El-Harat, to the east of Aït-Mohammed (on the other bank of the Todra riverbed) has a working **pottery**. Following the track east you pass through Souk-el-Khemis on your way to rejoin the main P32 road just beyond Aït Aissa-Oubrahim.

North to the Todra Gorge

The turning to route 6902 is just east of Tinerhir. On the rough hills above the road there are a number of ruined agadirs which can be explored, though for ease of access the **kasbah of**

Amitane easily wins out. It is about 6km along the road from Tinerhir, and has some particularly good Berber brick-and-tile exterior decoration. Another 3km on you pass a nest of palm shaded campsites and cafés centred around a freshwater pool which has the melodious and romantic name of 'La Source des Poissons Sacrés'. About 12km north of Tinerhir the palm groves end at a village built around the **zaouia of Sidi Abdelali**. The water from a spring on the left, 500m beyond the zaouia, reputedly cures female infertility.

Shortly beyond this you enter the Todra Gorge, just past the Hôtel El Mansour, where the tarmac ends and a gravel track fords the Todra. The massive walls of the gorge rise steeply to cut off the sunlight from the gravel riverbed.

There are two hotels tucked in the deepest bit of the canyon, where the two facing cliffs soar and bulge 300m above them. The grandeur of the cliffs declines quite quickly beyond the hotels, but if you are lucky you can sometimes spot mountain goats and eagles by walking just a short way beyond. As late as 1950 the French Foreign Legion picketed the heights to discourage snipers from picking off tourists. In an attempt to maintain the atmosphere of rural menace and a slight state of suspense amongst walkers, rumours are enthusiastically circulated about panthers roaming the hills. A spring in front of the hotels flows all year, and harbours some very small shrimps. Try walking up the gorge at night: the contrast of pitch black looming mountain and the sliver of sparkling sky is peculiarly powerful.

North of the Gorge

It is possible in summer to drive across the High Atlas in a Land Rover, or be driven in an adventure tour, while more enterprising backpackers hitch a series of lifts in the lorry-taxis that connect the Berber markets along these routes. This journey places a useful initial test in your way as one of the worst sections is that immediately north of the Todra Gorge—it gets ploughed up every year by flash floods. Those looking for a milder, quieter adventure could follow the 16km track beyond the gorge to stay at one of the clutch of basic café-hotels in the village of **Tamtattouchte**. From here fit, serious walkers with a tent and a local guide might want to try the 50km mountainous track that connects the Todra and Dadès gorges.

Where To Stay

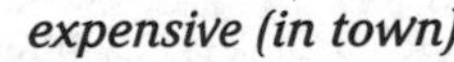

expensive (in town)

The **Sarhro**, ✆ (04) 834181, is conspicuously positioned beside the ruins of the hilltop kasbah. Its strong yellow outer walls marry pleasantly with the surrounding ruins. A covered passage leads to a separate enclosure containing its windproof open-air pool and surrounding rooms. The hotel has a restaurant, a bar and 62 rooms. Ask for a room in the older wing, as they have more character.

On the left as you enter Tinerhir stands the new kasbah-style **Hotel Kenzi Bougafer**, ✆ (04) 833200, fax 833282, which rivals the Sarhro in efficiency with its 70 bedrooms complete with brand new plumbing and air-conditioning. It also has a pool, vast restaurant and bar; the only thing it lacks is the Sarhro's splendid view.

moderate (in town)

The **Tomboctoo**, ✆ (04) 834604, fax 833505, is found down Av Bir-Anzarane (coming into town from the Ouarzazate road, turn right after passing a row of petrol stations and garages, as you reach the string of banks before the town square). It is an old kasbah converted by its Spanish owner into a 14-bedroom auberge. The restaurant follows the *patron*'s passions, ranging freely over the traditions of both Catalonia and southern Morocco (no drinks licence yet, but a pool under construction).

inexpensive (in town)

Hôtel Todra/Todgha, ✆ (04) 834249, is at 32 Avenue Hassan II on the Place Principale, and has 38 rooms, a restaurant, café and bar. It contains large, cool interior public rooms, and is decorated with a remarkable false wooden first-floor balcony overlooking the garden square. The plaster statuary scattered throughout the hotel was made by one Bucher, an Austrian who fell in love with a local girl.

Hôtel de l'Avenir, ✆ (04) 834604, @ 834599, is situated a block south of the Todra on the road leading down to the market district. It is run by another knowledgeable Spaniard who has settled in the town (marrying a local woman), who can also rent out bicycles and arrange guides and Land Rover excursions.

cheap (in town)

Hotel El Qods, on the Avenue Hassan side of the Place Principale, is one of the best cheap hotels in town, and has a good restaurant attached. If it is full try one of the others on the Place, such as the **Café-Hôtel Oasis**, ✆ (04) 833670, or the **Raha**.

cheap (in the palm groves) and camping

Though there are two well-equipped campsites on the edge of town, it's much better to head north into the palm groves. They are one of the most pleasant places to camp in the whole south. Gentle cool breezes come off the Atlas to rustle the palm leaves, olives and oleanders. The **Camping Atlas** is the tidiest of the sites, with raked gravel, a restaurant, two showers, a few rooms and three lavatories. The **Camping du Lac (Garden of Eden)** split off from **La Source des Poissons Sacrés Camping** about eighteen years ago, and has the best café-restaurant. 'The Sacred Fish Spring' is delightfully unorganized and contains secluded patches of beaten earth among the palms. The site borders the cool clear water of the Todra that issues from the gorge. It received its curious name in an attempt to protect the round tank of pet carp from possible poachers by giving them semi-divine attributes. The **Café-Restaurant Azlag**, just past the bridge, has excellent views from its few bedrooms.

cheap (in the gorge)

You can also stay in one of the three distinctive cheap hotels in the gorge. Whatever comfort you are used to, these places offer wonderful opportunities for star-gazing and evening strolls.

Hôtel El Mansour at the entrance to the gorge has two palm trees growing through the middle of it. It is the smallest and most basic place, but has its own kitchen and avoids the sometimes overcheerful tour groups that collect at the other two hotels.

The **Hôtel des Roches** and the **Hôtel Yasmina** (only one of the three with a telephone, ✆ (04) 833013), though both recently castellated and kasbah-ized, have been in their dramatic position since 1932. The towering rock walls that loom directly above and the spring of fresh water at their foot make them an enticing place to stay. The cleft of sky visible at night, hemmed in by the massive walls, appears as a crescent charged with a full field of stars. However, the generators and jovial tour groups tend to keep going until around 2am. Both hotels have bars, licenced restaurants and a variety of accommodation running from bedrooms with their own plumbing to a space on the roof. For 350dh you can take a day's horse-riding tour inland from the Gorge, and every year expensive Land Rover trips are organized by these hotels to the High Atlas *moussem* and marriage fair at Imilchil in September.

Eating Out

moderate

For a formal meal in the evening (with wine) you will have to go to either the **Sarhro** or **Kenzi Bougafer**, which both have bars and licenced restaurants. If you have your own supply of bottles you could dine at the **Tombuctoo**, with the evening devoted to gazpacho and paella to break the spell of *tagines*. Or (if you don't mind the presence of groups) have dinner in the mouth of the gorge in the tents or the dining rooms of **Des Roches** or the **Yasmina**, both of which serve alcohol.

cheap

There is a cluster of good restaurants attached to the hotels in and around the Place Principale, such as the **Qods**, **de l'Avenir** and the central **La Gazelle d'Or**. Aside from the café-restaurants in the market area there are also two other good places, the **Kasbah**, © (04) 834471, and **La Palmeraie** restaurants, which are situated along the north side of Avenue Mohammed V as it heads east to Er Rachidia.

East to Erfoud or Er Rachidia

Tinejdad, 40km east of Tinerhir, is the chief village in a scattering of ksour that occupy an area watered by the river Todra and known as the Ferkla palm groves. It has always remained free of Arab settlement, and is entirely occupied by Berbers and Haratine. The **Ksar Asrir** on the western edge of the palm grove is considered one of the finest. Very few people stay here, but if you want to explore these lesser-known palm groves try either the **Hôtel-Restaurant Tizgui** or the **Café Al Fath**.

The Road to Erfoud

From Tinejdad you can now drive directly to Erfoud in the Tafilalt Oasis on the all-tarmac 3451. A local bus leaves the town square at 9.30am for Erfoud and beyond, arriving in Rissani in the southern Tafilalt around 1pm.

The **ksar of Mellab**, 17km east of Tinejdad, marks the end of the Ferkla palm groves, and the landscape becomes considerably less interesting. **Tourong**, an isolated settlement 20km later, sits in the midst of a beautiful palm grove which has grown at the junction of the watercourses of the Todra and the Rhéris rivers. The bleak surrounding hills are studded with the ruins of two hill forts and a tower, all that remains of the endless border disputes between the rulers of the Dadès and the Tafilalt. Beside the road a koubba stands guard over a long graveyard of savage, rough black head and foot stones. After Tourong, small sand dunes drift across the road and whirls of desert dust prepare you for Erfoud. Long lines of *feggaguir/foggara*, subterranean tunnels collecting the moisture from the soil, seem like giant grey molehills in the arid plain.

Nineteen kilometres before Erfoud you pass through the palm groves of **Jorf** ; the village has a **souk** on Wednesdays. A black stone fort outside the village overlooks the ruins of a grey pisé palace with a picturesque chain of three Moorish arches. Just 11km from Erfoud three beautiful ksour lie beside the river Rhéris. The **oasis of Bouïa** on your right has a recently discovered Berber necropolis with a stone-built cairn.

The Road to Er Rachidia

Alternatively, you can continue the 83km to Er Rachidia along the P32. The first 24km to Goulmima is the bleakest passage, but east of there the line of the High Atlas and particularly the summit of Jbel Timetrout march with you to provide a changing view. As well as the area to be explored around Goulmima, the isolated **oasis hamlet of Tarda**, a right turn 23km before Er Rachidia, would make an interesting picnic spot.

Goulmima is a modern village that is the local centre for over twenty ksour that occupy the oasis palm groves known as **Gheris of Charis**. It's of much less interest than its hinterland but it does have a bank and the **Gheris**, ✆ (05) 783167, a cheap hotel with a restaurant.

The palm groves are watered by the river Rhéris, for long the fiercely held territory of the Aït-Morghad tribe. The ksar towers of this region are noticeably high and strong, a local architectural style that reflects the long struggle against raids by the Aït-Atta. The **ksar of Tilouine**, 15km downstream from Goulmima, is traditionally held by pure Arabs, an odd outpost left behind by the Maql Emirate in this otherwise Berber sea.

To the north in the steep valley cut in the High Atlas by the Rhéris are the beautiful but distant **kasbahs of Imiter and Agoudin**. The road north is passable for the first 20 km, to **Tadirhoust**, but gets increasingly rough after this. Imiter lies down a left turn at Amellago 35km later, and Agoudin is a further 23km up the right-hand track. This is, therefore, a mountain track foray only for the well-equipped and kasbah-obsessed.

Er Rachidia

Er Rachidia is a boring military and administrative centre. Its attraction to tourists is the transport it offers to the Ziz Valley and Gorge and to the Tafilalt Oasis and sand dunes to the south. Situated in the middle of the valley of the Ziz, the town first came to prominence as the forward base of the French Foreign Legion in their turn-of-the-century advance from Algeria. Their fortress was known as the Ksar es Souk, after its neighbouring market. To this day, Er Rachidia retains a strong military presence (as the home of numerous regimental headquarters, training academies and married quarter compounds), so don't think of taking any photographs. It is also reknowned for its loyalty to the ruling dynasty, and proportionately contributed more volunteers to the celebrated Green March into the Western Sahara than any other province. Though it has some elegant cafés this one-street town does not even compare favourably with Ouarzazate. Unless you are planning to head east towards Figuig on an early morning bus, there is no need to halt here.

Getting Around

The **bus station** is set back from Av Moulay Ali Cherif to form Place Principale, the central square of town life. There are four buses a day south to Erfoud/Rissani (allow 2–3hrs). Heading further east the daily Figuig bus (with a possible change at Bou Arfa) leaves at 5am on its 8hr trip. North to Midelt there are around 5 buses a day (3–4hrs) of which two continue to Fès and one to Meknès. Going west there are two buses to Tinerhir (3hrs) and a useful CTM service to Marrakech via Ouarzazate.

Grands taxis operate from outside the bus station, where you can pick up a place on the regular 2hr run south to Erfoud or west to Tinejdad. The town-restricted ***petits taxis*** have a rank outside the central market on Av Moulay Ali Cherif.

Tourist Information

The bus station, taxi ranks, central market and cafés are all on Avenue Moulay Ali Cherif, the central east–west avenue of the town. If you are heading further south or east, do make use of the efficient **banks** at Er Rachidia. The BCM is situated two blocks north of the bus station, while the BMCI and Crédit Agricole are opposite the **post office** on Avenue Mohammed V.

You can take a good walk north from the town towards the Atlas, through olive groves beside the river Ziz, passing the deserted ksour of Targa and Azzemour and the Hassan Addakhil Tirhiourine Dam, finished in 1971. At **Targa**, abandoned like most of the ksour after disastrous floods in the 1960s, a red-walled empty mosque looks out high over the steep bank of the river terrace. Throughout the decaying interior you find empty houses, broken pillars and olive presses. The site looks strangely similar to a classical ruin and feels suitably haunted, though many of its previous inhabitants now live in pisé or concrete houses just north of Er Rachidia. Ask at the Rissani or Oasis hotels to hire donkeys which allow you to explore the valley to the north or south, riding in summer along the dry riverbed of the Ziz.

The Er Rachidia **souk** is held on Sundays in a big enclosure on the western edge of town. There is a smaller affair on Thursdays. Since the town is not a tourist destination, the market is a pleasantly unspoilt rural affair, at its most animated in spring and autumn when the farmers have got something to sell.

If you are not already planning to take the road north you could drive up to take a look at the **Ziz Gorge**. Beyond the dammed lake, the Ziz has cut a majestic trench through the Atlas mountains. The cliff walls of the gorge rise serenely to enclose two beautiful oasis villages, **Amzrouf** and **Ifri**, and their kasbahs. Just to the north of these, through a tunnel built by the French Foreign Legion, is a wider mountain plateau landscape through which the Ziz flows more gently. For the route north to Midelt, *see* pp.365–8.

Where to Stay

expensive

The **Rissani**, ✆ (05) 572186, ✉ 572585 stands aloof from the town on the east bank of the Ziz. Given the nature of Er Rachidia its bar, pool, garden, restaurant and 60 recently overhauled rooms make it a tempting choice.

inexpensive

The **Oasis**, © (05) 572519, is at 4 Rue Sidi Abou Abdallah. It is a convenient, well-run place with a bar and a licenced restaurant. You'll find it two blocks north of Avenue Moulay Ali Cherif, just behind the cinema.

The **Meski**, © (05) 572065, is on the western edge of town, on your right as you enter Er Rachidia from the Tinerhir road. It has a slightly shabby air and a restaurant with no drinks licence but does boast a small swimming pool, and is sometimes full.

cheap

The **Hôtel Renaissance** at 19 Rue Moulay Youssef (the street due north of the bus station), © (05) 572633, is the best value in town. Showers work well, the café-restaurant serves great *couscous* and *tagines* and it remains balanced between local and tourist custom. If it's full there are two basic standbys overlooking Place Hassan II: the **Zitoun** (Oliviers), © (05) 572449, and **Royal**, © (05) 573068.

Eating Out

For a moderately-priced meal with wine, go to the **Rissani** or **Oasis** hotels. In the cheap range, the restaurant in the **Renaissance** is very good, but if you want just to stop for a light lunch as you pass through the main avenue there is the **Restaurant Terminus**, which offers a filling three-course menu in its garden, or the **Imilchil** beside the tourist information booth, with a shaded terrace. For watching morning and evening café society, when the main street of Er Rachidia comes alive, the **Pâtisserie Al Hamra** and the **Lipton** (open late into the night) are best.

The Southern Ziz Valley

The Ziz Valley is spectacular in a grand, natural manner. Thick green vegetation on the valley floor contrasts with the surrounding golden red hills. Sadly, the flood of 1965 swept the old buildings of the valley clean out from the river floor. Its diverse pattern of settlement, rambling ksour, and patchwork of irregular orchards and gardens were destroyed, 12,000 palms were uprooted and 25,000 people left homeless. As a result, the valley is now a pattern of regular terraced gardens with none of the complexities of generations of inheritance and subdivision. New villages are set in lines way above the edge of cultivable land.

The **Source Bleue de Meski campsite**, 22km south of Er Rachidia, is the traditional stopping point on the Ziz and an easy base from which to walk out and explore the valley floor. It is named after a spring of clear blue spring water which issues from a natural cave and from there flows into a large weathered concrete tank. It was built by the Foreign Legion, anxious to find a place in which to swim free from bilharzia and snipers. Carp of various sizes swim about with you in the tank, and can be hand fed. There is a snack café, a small line of shops and a plentiful supply of small children selling animals woven from palm fronds.The popularity of the spring has been rewarded by the steady spread of concrete pathing, and entrance to the pools is now controlled by an admission ticket. In the season it gets better when superbly tanned touts mix equably with a cheek-by-jowl encampment of temporary hippies escaping the grim realities of European office life.

On the opposite bank are the ruins of the **Meski Ksar**, reportedly destroyed in 1890. You can struggle across the streams through the oleanders to its walls, made from rounded river stones. The entrance spirals beneath higher walls, past wreckage of olive and grain mills.

Eleven kilometres south of Meski there is a spectacular panoramic view of the valley, where fossils are displayed for sale beside a parking place. The village of **Aoufouss**, also spelt Aulouz or Aufous, has three surviving ksour which you see as you enter, a zaouia and a Thursday **souk**. Further south and slightly off the road nearer the river are the less accessible ksour of **Zrigat**, **Zaouia-Jedida** and **Douira**. Douira marks the end of the Berber-occupied Ziz.

The Tafilalt Oasis

The Ziz flows south parallel to the Rhéris, and together they form the oasis of the Tafilalt, which has a quite distinct brooding, haunting atmosphere. The ksour here are memorable, mysterious places, and not particularly welcoming. The population of the Tafilalt is 80,000, and **Jorf**, largest ksar in the west of the region, houses 6000 people. More than anywhere else in the south, cultivating its 700,000 palm trees is the central occupation of its inhabitants.

Outlying palm groves thrive, but the central and southern belt is the last to receive water, and this has proved disastrous in the current long drought. On top of this the area has been harassed by Bayoud Palm Sickness. This used to be treated by magic, which proved to be at least as efficacious as the twenty-year inconclusive scientific study of this mysterious disease.

The Fruit of the Desert

The date palm has always attracted a near-mystical respect. In the 4th century AD the Roman author Ammianus Marcellinus wrote, 'It is said that the female trees produce fruit when impregnated by the seeds of the male trees, and even that they feel delight in their mutual love, and that this is clearly shown by the fact that they lean towards one another, and cannot be bent back by even the strongest winds. And if by any unusual accident a female tree is not impregnated by the male seed it produces nothing but imperfect fruit, and if they cannot find out what tree any female is in love with, they smear the trunk of some tree with the oil that proceeds from her, and then some other tree naturally conceives a fondness for the odour; and these proofs create some belief in the story of their copulation.'

The mystique of these vital trees is recognized by Islam, and saints' tombs are often placed in the densest groves. The Koran has a vigorous description of Christ's birth among the protecting palms: sura XIX describes Mary's labour, 'And the throes came upon her by the trunk of a palm. She cried: "Oh would that I died ere this, and had been a thing quite forgotten." And one [angel] cried to her from behind the palm tree: "Grieve thou not, thy Lord has provided a streamlet at thy feet, and shake the trunk of the palm tree toward thee it will drop fresh dates upon thee."'

Felling a date palm has always been regulated by religious traditions, and it used to be unlawful to sell a living tree, which was your family's sustenance. It was also forbidden to raise a mortgage from a living tree, though it was possible to raise money by selling a crop of dates in advance of the harvest. To this end the gathering of the harvest before the traditional date was also made an offence.

Erfoud

This small town of dusty red buildings was built beside the Ziz by the French in the 1930s as their administrative centre for the oasis. Windblown, dusty, partly planted with eucalyptus and tamarisk and fringed by palm groves to the north and west, it is both architecturally dull and yet powerfully marked by the surrounding desert. It is the central base for exploring the oasis ksour and for trips out to Erg Chebbi (the sand dunes of Merzouga), with a good range of hotels, a few bazaars, a pleasant souk courtyard, cafés and loquacious guide-salesmen.

The town preserves its military origins in its quadrilateral plan: two avenues run parallel toward the riverbed, where they lead into opposite sides of the main square. On the northern edge of this square is the entrance to Erfoud's courtyard souk, where you can find barrows of different varieties of dates, fossils and carved desert stones for sale. The date harvest begins in late September, and Erfoud celebrates in mid-October with a popular festival (telephone the big hotels a week or two in advance for a precise date, which depends on the moon).

From the square a bridge, the Bab el Oued, crosses the river and a track climbs a hill to **Borj-Est**, East Fort, the old French strongpoint, with magnificent views. It still has an army garrison, but they do not seem to mind tourists driving up to their front gate for the view.

The Red Man of Erfoud

Things were not always so peaceful in Erfoud. The French, advancing from the Algerian Sahara, first managed to place a garrison here in 1916. It was a position of some importance, held by a battalion of Senegalese soldiers and another from the Foreign Legion. Just before dawn on 9 August these battle-hardened troops were surprised and slaughtered in a massive uprising. Another Foreign Legion outpost fell in September when the river Ziz was cunningly diverted to sap away at its walls. It took the French two years of hard fighting to control the spread of this rebellion and reestablish a strong garrison at Erfoud.

For a dozen years this garrison was categorically forbidden to advance any further south in case they stirred up another tribal rising. By 1931 the French felt confident enough and marched south under the leadership of de Bournazel, who was known to the tribes as 'the Red Man'. De Bournazel always wore a distinctive scarlet uniform but seldom cared to carry a weapon. He led a charmed existence, untouched by any wound throughout his long and celebrated military career in North Africa. After the successful occupation of the Tafilalt he ruled the region as an enlightened and compassionate governor. His rule was cut short, for his first wound was also his last. He was shot in the stomach during the battle of Jbel Bou Gafer, the last engagement of the long-drawn-out French conquest. On a bare, sunbaked slope of the Jbel Sarhro in 1934, de Bournazel fulfilled his destiny. As he bled to death over his scarlet tunic, the French army subdued the last Moroccan tribe to resist their authority.

Getting Around

There are four **buses** a day between Er Rachidia and Erfoud (77km, about 2hrs), and four further south to Rissani (another 22km). Heading west there is a daily bus to Tinejdad, and one to Fès (11hrs). CTM coaches leave from Av Mohammed V, about

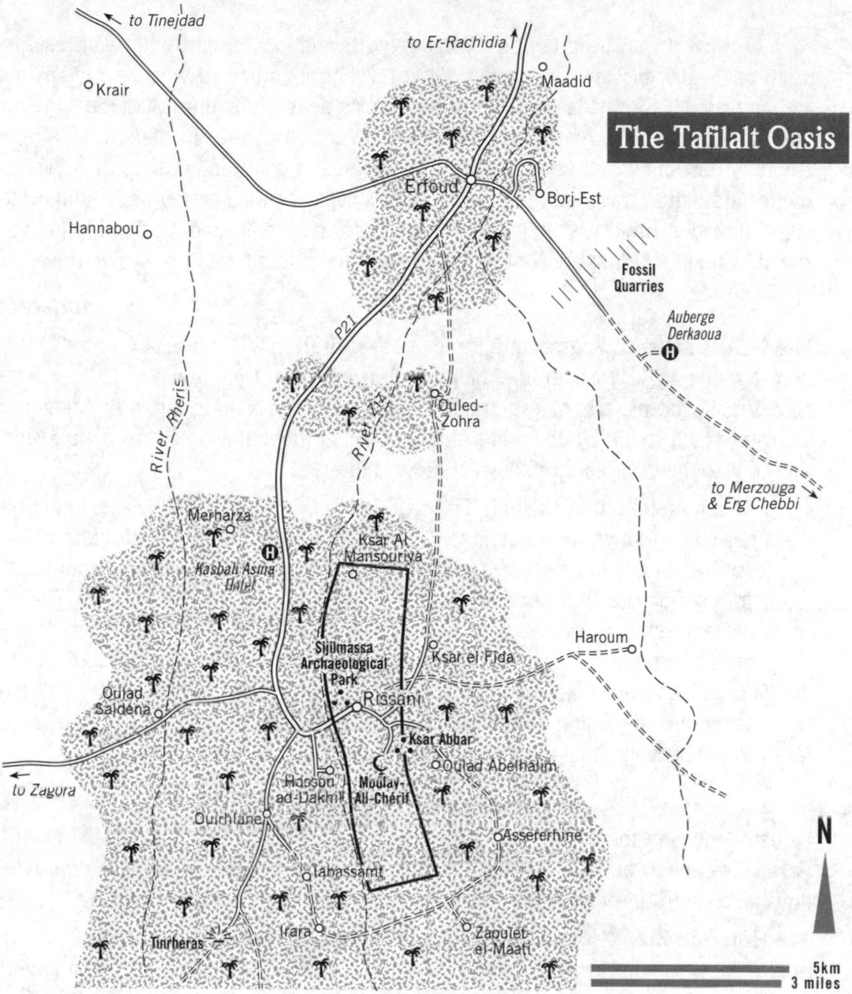

The Tafilalt Oasis

halfway between the main road and the Souk/Place des F.A.R. ***Grands taxis*** leave regularly for Er Rachidia, Tineghir and Rissani from the Place des FAR (main square).

Tourist Information

The **post office** and international phone office is at the crossroads of the main road and Av Mohammed V. Directly opposite is a branch of the **Banque Populaire** (though its slowness might drive you to use the change services of the larger hotels).

Where To Stay

expensive

The Sijilmassa, once the most attractive and secluded hotel in the Tafilalt, has passed into royal ownership. This leaves the **Salam**, © (05) 576425, @ 576426, which stands beside the Rissani/Tinejdad turning on the southern edge of town. It has been built in sympathy with the local ksour, with walls clad in traditional earth plaster. There is a pool in its central courtyard where young palms and bougainvillea provide shade and shelter for a delightfully enthusiastic dawn and dusk chorus of birds. As the only hotel of its grade for miles it tends to be either empty or bustling with tour groups or film crews. The charming staff do their best to shelter individual travellers, placing them in a separate Riad restaurant, though the buffet spread in the Oasis dining room for dinner and the aprés-dune breakfast are of enviable quality. Drinks are served in the bar of the fountain lobby or beside the pool.

moderate

The well established and recently renovated **Tafilalt**, ✆ (05) 576348, stands back from Avenue Moulay Ismaïl (the main road) near the centre of town. It has comfortable double rooms, a bar, restaurant, a small pool and a cool, big, airy octagonal lobby in which to loll around and drink tea.Like all the major hotels they run excursions out to the dunes at Merzouga at dawn and dusk..

The low silhouette of the **Kasbah Tizimi**, ✆ (05) 576179, 📠 577375, is found on the outer edge of town off the road to Tinerhir. It is a new but delightful place built and furnished in a high level of sympathy with traditional craftsmanship, from doors to the iron window grilles, carpet-strewn floors and the recurring use of cane. The 40 spacious bedrooms are arranged off cool corridor courtyards, with a pool dominating the central courtyard that is overlooked by a terrace from which you can look out to the palm groves as well as sun and star bathe. There are also several well-appointed reception rooms, including a bar. If this is to be the future face and scale of tourism in Morocco, there is nothing to be feared.

inexpensive

Directly opposite the Salam—on the Avenue Moulay Ismaïl crossroad—stands the **Farah Zouar Hôtel**, ✆ (05) 576146, 📠 576230. It's a pleasant, modern unpretentious place with thirty bedrooms, and an unlicenced restaurant.

The **Hôtel de Ziz**, ✆ (05) 576145, 📠 576811, is at 3 Avenue Mohammed V. It is a small, efficient, family-run place with its rooms (some of which are air conditioned) arranged around a courtyard. If it is full as a second choice try the **Sable d'Or**, ✆ (05) 576348, which is on the same street.

cheap and camping

The cheaper hotels can have varying supplies of electricity and water. Erfoud is not a place in which to test your tolerance to sanitation. If you are looking for budget accomodation with style, head out to the duneside auberge-cafés (*see* below). The most reliable and attractive of the half-dozen or so in the town are **Les Palmiers**, ✆ (05) 576033, at 36 Avenue Mohammed V, and **La Gazelle**, ✆ (05) 576028, at the other end of the avenue over the crossroads. The latter has the advantage of a coolish downstairs cellar where you can eat and lounge around with a mint tea.

The **campsite** is on hard stone ground on the easterly edge of Erfoud, and it also rents clean but empty rooms. There is a **municipal pool** directly opposite, which is open from June to September.

Eating Out

If you want a drink before dinner or a reasonably formal meal in the evening head for the **Salam**, Tafilalt or **Tizimi** hotels. For something cheaper, stroll down Av Mohammed V, which is lined with half a dozen good café-restaurants.

Shopping

There are several small **tourist bazaars** along Av Mohammed V and Av Moulay Ismail, though most of the more engaging shopkeepers are found on the right hand side of the souk compound.

Fossils come polished, unpolished or part-exposed in the dark 'Erfoud marble', which is exported around the world. Aside from baths, basins and tabletops it is also made into more portable objects such as eggs, plates, bowls and ashtrays. If you wish to buy direct the Erfoud marble factory (on the right hand side of the Tinerhir road before the Tizimi hotel) has a small showroom There is also a small **carpentry** industry making traditional arched shelves (which are placed high up on a wall in a Tafilalt house) from an attractive warm hue of wood.

No one should leave the town without buying something from the studio of the local resident expatriate artist, **Madeleine Laurent**, whose watercolours, prints or postcards can be viewed outside the entrance of the Salam hotel, or at 68 Rue el Wahda.

Last, but not least, there are **dates**. It is said that Christian missionaries cornered the date export market, and then encouraged them to be eaten around Christmas to boost their sales. It's a good conspiracy tale, which should not conflict with the reality of the October date harvest, or that fact that Moorish date-traders were a familiar feature in all the winter fairs of medieval Europe.

Erg Chebbi, the Sand Dunes of Merzouga

Fed on images of the desert that involve great crescents of sand, few visitors can resist the temptation of refuelling their fantasies by visiting the one giant patch of sand desert in the Moroccan south, the Erg Chebbi, in the south-east of the Tafilalt beyond Merzouga. The great massed piles of golden sand rising up from a bleak black desert plain is an impressive sight even in the crushing heat of midday.

The attractions of Merzouga have remained undiminished by the steady flow of romantics. In high summer the few rooms and even the roof space at the half dozen café-hotels at the foot of the dunes are often booked by 4pm. A dinner of *tagine* mopped up with fresh bread and eaten by gas- or candle-light and the expectations of the morning create an entertaining atmosphere. Half a night spent sleeping rough on the roof is a restless experience, for the clarity of the desert sky and the lack of any distracting urban light creates a quite dazzling display of stars, accompanied by the excited chatter of shooting-star spotting.

To climb up to one of the sand peaks just before dawn is the ideal. The shifting colours, rippling shadows from the crests of the dunes and the rapid change in temperature make all the preceding effort worthwhile. In spring, snow on the peaks of the Middle Atlas can be seen quite clearly from here.

The Road from Erfoud

The Hôtel Tafilalt in Erfoud runs Land Rover tours to Merzouga, varying from a cheap evening trip to a night spent at the Auberge Merzouga. If you have your own vehicle there is no need for a guide, as the route is quite straightforward from Erfoud (though if you want to be doubly secure there will be no difficulty in acquiring one). Do not, however, attempt it in a sandstorm or after rain. If you do not have transport, lifts can normally be arranged by chatting up fellow tourists. Allow two hours to get there, remembering that dawn is around 6am. Cross the bridge east of Erfoud's central square and pass below the hill conspicuously crowned by Borj-Est. Continue along this surfaced road and join the dirt track when the tarmac ends. If you follow the line of telegraph poles you cannot fail to reach Merzouga and the dunes. You pass a small settlement with a café and fossil stalls about 15km along the way, in the shadow of a crest of undulating hills that reach out into the surrounding plain in a broad crescent. Stop at the roadside or at any of the advertised tracks in order to be shown the seams of fossils embedded in the rock. The proprietors of the fossil stalls will be happy to show you the way, splashing the ancient lifeforms with well water to bring them briefly back to life and so create an almost irrestible urge to purchase from the onlookers. The gates of the Auberge Kasbah Derkaoua are passed about 9km later, and shortly after that a number of turnings lead off the main Merzouga track towards the individual café-hotels. Be prepared to dig or push yourself out, particularly as you approach the dunes and cafés.

The Road from Rissani

Take the road south of town and the first tarmac left turn should be signposted to Merzouga. After 1km take the first good dirt track road on your right, continue through palm groves and then cross the dry riverbed, where there is a café and a tent to eat in on the far bank. Then head for the line of Erfoud-to-Merzouga telegraph poles, and on a clear day the dunes should already be in view.

Where To Stay and Eating Out

The desert track runs west of the sand dunes on its way to Merzouga village. On the way you will pass a number of signposted drives leading to half a dozen auberges and café-hotels. These should be your objective, and are superior to a similar number of cheap hotels in Merzouga village itself.

moderate

Auberge Kasbah Derkaoua, ✆ and 📠 (05) 577140 (also known as Chez Michel after its fascinating proprietor), is easily the most elegant of the dune auberges, its pale green paintwork perfectly contrasting with the traditional adobe walls. In fact it is probably one of the most distinguished addresses in Morocco, not for any opulence but through the more delicate art of restraint. The dozen bedrooms are of monastic simplicity and scale. There is a small irrigation tank, filled with artesian water, in which to plunge, and shady benches on which to shelter from the sun with a book. Meals are served outside in the garden, in a tent or in a fire warmed dining room, according to season and the sandstorms. The staff achieve the rare combination of being attentive without becoming solicitous, and work almost as hard as the French-

Saharan and Moroccan management, who breed camels, cows and horses among other assorted livestock as well as planting hundreds of trees and nurturing their guests with almost as much devotion as the dogs and the grey parrot. At the back of the stables are the ruins of an old zaouia of the Derkaoua Sufi brotherhood, after-which the auberge is named. It is the first place you come across on the track from Erfoud (about 23km from the Ziz bridge). It is however too far from the dunes (10km) to contemplate a dawn or dusk stroll, and is closed in January, June and July.

cheap (beside the dunes)

Tucked into the sides of the dune are half a dozen romantically basic café-hotels. Taking them in geographical order from north to the south, they are the **Yasmina**, **Etoile de Sable**, **Du Sud**, **Dunes d'Or**, **Auberge Erg Chebbi** and **Oasis**. They are all friendly places, renting out a few rooms and roof space, preparing meals for the evening and selling soft drinks. Everybody has their favourite, which tends to be wherever they last slept and saw the sky dance with stars.

cheap (beside the dunes at Merzouga)

If everywhere else is full up there is a nest of three basic hotels just outside Merzouga: the **Auberge Merzouga**, **Hôtel Salaam** and **Hôtel Atlas Sahara**, while in the village itself there is the **Café des Amis** and on the other side of the river the **Hôtel des Palmiers**, below a water tower. The highest sand peak of the dunes, about 150m, is immediately above the Palmiers, and is favoured by sand skiers.

Merzouga

The village is not itself of interest unless you collect stickers, for its café-hotels are encrusted in a colourful assortment of logos from tour groups, guide books, safari expeditions, car rallies and sand skiers. Camel rides can be arranged from local hotels. A **souk** takes place on Saturday mornings, and this is by far the best day to get a place in a lorry or Land Rover taxi.

The **ksar of Taouz**,around which there are a number of cave rock-carvings and neolithic burial chambers, is 24km south of Merzouga on the left bank of the Ziz, and is as far as you are allowed to go. Beyond is the Algerian border, where the strategic road to Tindouf runs across an immense Saharan plateau, the Hammada du Guir, south of which stretches a vast sand desert, the Grand Erg Occidental. Fossils are a major trading item in the area, and if you are determined to find your own you should visit the **valley of the black rock** below a slight hill between Merzouga and Taouz, though you will need a guide to find the familiar spiral shaped goniatites which are reputed to proliferate here. On the way back from Taouz you could take a slightly different route and go by the **lead mines of Mfis**.

From November to March a brackish lake (Dayat Srji) sometimes forms just west of Merzouga and is visited by over 72 species of migrating birds, including pink flamingos.

The Southern Tafilalt

The wind, which gathered every particle of sand in the Erg Chebbi and deposited it to the east of the Tafilalt, is usually in evidence here. An intense and prolonged drought, and a long and rich history now come to nought combine with the wind to give the whole area a feeling

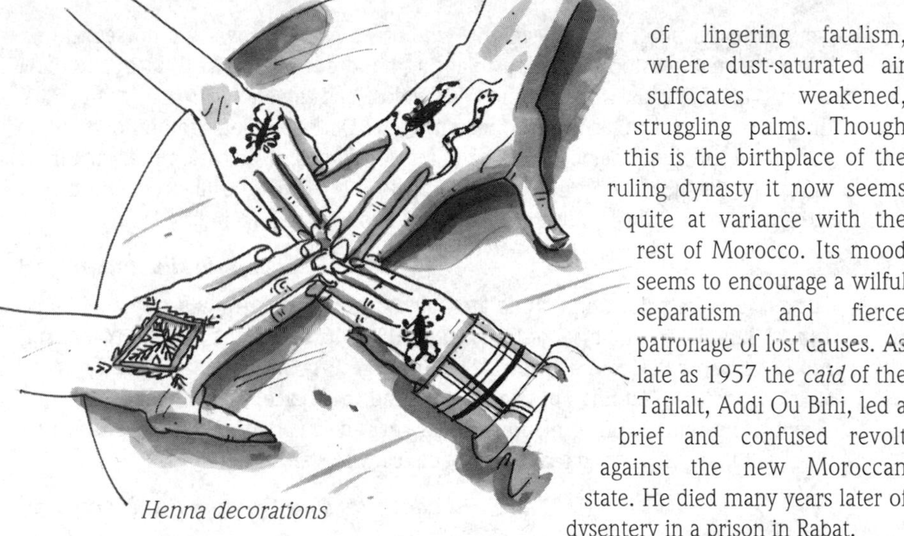
Henna decorations

of lingering fatalism, where dust-saturated air suffocates weakened, struggling palms. Though this is the birthplace of the ruling dynasty it now seems quite at variance with the rest of Morocco. Its mood seems to encourage a wilful separatism and fierce patronage of lost causes. As late as 1957 the *caid* of the Tafilalt, Addi Ou Bihi, led a brief and confused revolt against the new Moroccan state. He died many years later of dysentery in a prison in Rabat.

The brick-built upper third of the towers of the local ksour are decorated with a beehive complexity of chevrons, crosses, lines, bands of arches and holes with a profusion and artistry peculiar to this area. Theories on the origins of kasbah design abound and some mileage has been made out of the idea that the Tafilalt, where the first Arab city of Morocco was founded, was the area most similar to Mesopotamia, so that Muslim craftsmen from the east recreated the architecture of the Tigris and Euphrates on the banks of the Ziz and Rhéris. Kasbah design in North Africa does however predate Islam, as kasbahs are clearly portrayed in a famous Roman mosaic of the Nile in Palaestra, Italy. The local children seem to be among the most vociferous and aggressive in Morocco. Be warned but do not be put off, for the ksour are worth the effort and there has to be some price to pay for such easy access to medieval interiors of magical darkness and light.

Getting Around

Rissani is connected to Erfoud by ***grands taxis*** and four daily **buses**. The 10am bus will take you directly to Er Rachidia, and connects with the 1pm bus to Ouarzazate via Tinerhir. There are also periodic Land Rover taxis to Merzouga, and on Thursdays and Sundays places are available in the Land Rover that leaves from outside the El Filalia Hotel and cuts west across the arid plain in 10hrs to reach the Drâa valley, finishing at Zagora.

Rissani

The modern village of Rissani, heralded by a modern ornate triple arched gateway, grew around the old souk which was held outside the gates of two of the most important settlemnets in the Tafilalt oasis, the ancient ksar of Abou Aam and the government kasbah of El Zayani. It remains the market town and administrative centre of the southern Tafilalt. A selection of dust-blown contemporary buildings line the main road, where you will find the bank, two hotels, bus stop, a few craft shops and the entrance to the **souk**.

Before you find the souk, it will find you, for every visitor to Rissani will invariably be met by a local guide. The souk is much larger and busier than Erfoud's. Its long random lines of precarious-looking stalls, partly shaded by bamboo trellis, sell all manner of food and farmers' requirements on Sundays, Tuesdays and Thursdays. For a visitor the predominant images are the mass of dates, their bewildering variety, stern-looking turbanned farmers leading mule-loads of goods into the souk courtyard, and, above it all, the flies. No photographs of the Sahara ever seem to do sufficient justice to the flies.

Rissani: Ksar Abou Aam

As you sweep into Rissani's dusty square (usually dominated by parked coaches) the long imposing facade of Ksar Abou Aam appears on your right. It is a maze of dark, almost troglodyte passages and layers of small dwellings. Great towers, decorated at their summit by ornate brickwork, guard each corner and side of the long ksar wall. The impressive gates are picked out in green and white paint, or plaster and green-glazed tiles. Within, all is confusion for a stranger. Great lengths of dark passages lead into further blackness, and sudden hopeful pools of light offer three alternative dead ends. The original construction and layout of Abou Aam is impossible to date precisely. Few of the individual buildings are more than two hundred years old, yet its history of occupation stretches right back to the disintegration of the medieval city of Sijilmassa in the 14th century. As the population abandoned urban life for the security of the walled ksour (and their intense combination of clan and village loyalties), the ksar of Abou Aam, geographically the closest to the old city centre, inherited a position of prestige. It was named after its founder, Father Aam, a distinguished chief citizen of Sijilmassa, who had divided his life into thirds, dedicating a third to Islamic scholarship, a third to pilgrimage and the last third to the *jihad*, the struggle for the true religion. In this he followed the pattern of all the great Moroccan Muslim reformers, such as Ibn Yassin, the founder of the Almoaravids, and Ibn Tumert, founder of the Almohads. The ksar's local primacy was confirmed when Moulay Ali Cherif, the founder of the present Alaouite dynasty, used it as his headquarters when he united the Tafilalt in the early 17th century. He was later to be defeated in battle and kept a captive of the rival Tazeroualt dynasty of the Anti Atlas (though he was treated with the respect normally accorded to a honoured guest), but eventually regained his freedom and his homeland, and was later reverently buried outside Rissani. It was his son Moulay Rachid who was fated to unite Morocco, a process perfected during the long reign of his brother, Moulay Ismail.

Kasbah al Zayani

This kasbah is on your left as you enter Rissani. It was first built by Sultan Moulay Ismail as a centre of government, and named after the first *Caid* appointed to the region. The army still occupies the north-eastern section, but you are free to pass through the gateway to visit the Centre for Alaouite research. It contains archaeological finds from excavations into medieval Sijilmassa, which are being formed into a local museum. The curators are happy to show any interested visitor around during weekday office hours. Many of the pieces have not yet been published, and so photographs are not encouraged. There are fragments of imported wares from the wider Muslim world (Andalusia and Abbasid Iraq), as well as pieces that reveal the vanished Sijilmassa ceramic tradition, from the 11th to the 14th centuries, of dark brown calligraphy painted on a white field. There is also a fragment of carved wood from the

Kharijite Beni Midrar period (perhaps 8th century) found beneath the great mosque, as well as some plaster decoration with recognizably Mediterranean rather than Moorish motifs.

The Ruins of Sijilmassa

The medieval city of Sijilmassa (757-1395) occupied a 14km-long rectangle defined by walls and river-fed moats that stretched between the existing ksar of El Mansouriya and Tabassant. The former ksar (not accessible by tarmac road) contains a 14th-century gateway from the Merenid period which is the sole architectural survival from the medieval city. Modern Rissani stands halfway along the original length of the city, where the great mosque and the kasbah quarter are believed to have stood. This area has been registered as an archaeological park, and occupies a triangle of land bordered by the main road from Erfoud and the approach road to the Rissani town arch. The site is little more than an extensive mound of melted pisé, with odd fragments of ceramics and wood flashing out from the enveloping earth. These are the only remains of the first Arab and Islamic city in Morocco, for hundreds of years embellished with gardens and running water and fabulously rich from the products of trans-Saharan trade, ebony, gold, ivory, ostrich feathers and negro slaves, so that it rivalled Fès in the grandeur of its buildings. It remained one of the richest jewels of North Africa, passing like a sceptre through all the great Maghreb dynasties: the Shiite Fatimids of Tunisia, the Ommayads of Cordoba, the Almoravids and Almohads all ruled the city at some time, though the citizens of Sijilmassa constantly struggled to reestablish their old independence.

During the 14th century, in a process not yet fully understood by historians, this urban society imploded. The old city was abandoned, and the population moved out into self-governing ksour scattered like villages throughout the oasis. Although this was clearly a response to desperate political circumstances, the population (about 30,000) remained virtually unchanged. A series of succession struggles among rival Merenid princes leading to vicious sieges and counter-sieges of the city, and the immigration of the Maql, an Arabic-speaking nomadic confederation of tribes in the military service of the Merenid goverment, have all been sited as root causes. A local legend explains the fall of the city as being due to the actions of a tyrannical black Merenid pasha, who reorganized the water system in order to charge the population exorbitant water-rates. It has a curiously familiar ring,. but for whatever causes the once-fabulous city lay deserted by its citizens by 1395.

As you enter Rissani, turn left after the mosque down the track that passes the café-hotel Sijilmassa. If you continue along for about 300m and then walk uphill for another 200m you should approach some conspicuously high adobe walls that roughly frame two rectangular courtyards. These are the remains not of the medieval city but of the great mosque and medersa that Sultan Moulay Ismail had rebuilt over what was remembered as the site of the old great mosque. Recent excavations by joint American-Moroccan teams have been concerned to clarify this supposition with some trial trenches, now safely covered up again.

The Foundation of Sijilmassa, a Kharijite City-State

According to an ancient but dubious tradition the city was established on the site of a Roman marching camp known as *Sigilum Massae*. An alternative derivation could be from the Berber 'Sigil Oulmes', which can be translated as 'to guard' or 'look over' the 'always water'. Whatever the origins of the name, the oasis was certainly an important trading entrepôt before the Arab conquest of North Africa. When he planned the conquest of Morocco in the early 8th century the Arab general Musa ben Nasser had just two objectives. One was to seize Tangier, the gateway to Spain, the other was to seize the oasis of Tafilalt, the gateway to the trans-Saharan trade. Somewhere in the oasis, but not necessarily at Sijilmassa, the fortified garrison town of the Arab army of the caliphate was established in 707. The enormous profits of the trans-Saharan trade, coupled with slave raiding expeditions against unconverted Berber tribes and the discovery of rich silver mines, attracted a steady stream of merchants. Within a generation, though, the military garrison of the oasis was entirely composed of Islamicized Berbers recruited from local tribes.

In 740 this garrison followed the lead of their brothers in Tangier and overthrew the arrogant and exploitative rule of the Arab governors appointed by the Caliph. This revolution was an explosive reaction to bad government, but had also had been instigated by Arab missionaries of the Kharijite creed of Islam. The Kharijites (derived from *kharaja*, those who 'went out' of the community) taught a puritanical definition of Islam in which moral conduct, not mere protestation of belief, defined a Muslim. They also recognized no barriers of race or class within Islam. The creed made a direct appeal to the Islamicized Berber garrisons, and the revolt soon swept across the breadth of North Africa. The Caliph at Damascus despatched two Arab armies to subdue the Kharijite heresy, but after a catastrophic defeat (the 'Battle of the Nobles', fought beside the river Sebou) no further attempt was made to subdue Morocco.

In the first flush of victory the Kharijite army of the Tafilalt elected a black slave to be their first Imam (leader), in a dramatic proof of their principles. Leadership of the community would later devolve upon a tribal dynasty, the Beni Midrar, who had proved themselves efficient military commanders. It was the Beni Midrar Imams who decisively established the city of Sijilmassa, defined its boundaries, codified the irrigation system, cut new canals, sent out missionaries into the Sahara and West Africa and developed the system of camel caravans across the desert. Under their enlightened direction the city of Sijilmassa grew into one of the wealthiest communities of the Muslim world. Established states such as Ommayad Spain and Aghlabid Tunisia were forced to swallow their scruples so that they might share in the profits of the trans-Saharan trade.

The Shrine of Moulay Ali ech Cherif

The tomb of Moulay Ali ech Cherif is 2km out of Rissani to the southeast. Though revered as the founder of the Alaouite dynasty he achieved little political success in his own life. He was however greatly revered in the oasis, both for his holy lineage and as a teacher. He established three zaouia in the Tafilalt for the proper study of Islam, though none of them have survived the depredations of time. His own mausoleum was rebuilt after a flood in 1955 carried the older structure away. It is unmistakably a modern building, an unsuccessful exterior through which it is forbidden for non-Muslims to go. Walter Harris, who accompanied Sultan Moulay Hassan on his tour of the south in the late 19th century, suspected that the ailing sultan had in fact come to pray at the tomb of his ancestor rather than to exercise authority over the recalcitrant tribes. He describes the final approach to the shrine:

'Mounting on his great white horse, saddled and trapped in green and gold, with the canopy of crimson velvet over his head, rode the Sultan, while huge black slaves on either hand waved long scarfs to keep the flies from his sacred person.'

Ksar Abbar

500m before the shrine of Moulay Ali Cherif on the tarmac road from Rissani there is a fork in the road. Take the left fork, continue for 500m and stop at the dirt road beside an irrigation ditch. Follow the ditch to your right, which leads you towards the towers and gatehouse of this, one of the oldest surviving unrestored Alaouite ksour. It was built in 1830 by Sultan Moulay Abdal Rahman ben Hisham as a royal place suitably close to the tomb of his ancestor. Later it was used by redundant concubines and as a gilded cage for threatening royal children and passed-over princes, before falling into the hands of its current semi-licit inhabitants, a mixture of squatters and descendants of old slaves and trusted servants. It is now an empty, melancholic place, its gatehouse and corner towers alone in a good state of repair. You can go through the gates to visit the interior courtyard. The palace mosque stood just to the right of the gate, before which an ornate fountain once played. The main block in the centre once housed the *Dar el Kebira*, the principal apartments. When you are being besieged by children asking for presents remember that the population adds greatly to the mystique of the region. Imagine generations of impoverished Filali princes (the family name of the ruling Alaouite dynasty), existing with pride on their inheritance of a few palm trees, exiled to the heat and stagnant society of the Tafilalt. Strains of *shorfa*, Arab, Berber (both black and white), Haratine and Hara (freed black slaves) as well as Christian renegade soldiery have been bred into the population. The women are entirely covered in unadorned black, and hardly a crack shows in the envelope of material through which to catch even a glimpse of almond eyes.

The Kasbah of Oulad Abdelhalim

A further 2km along this same road brings you to the kasbah of Oulad Abdelhalim, a magnificent structure well worth visiting. It was built in 1900 by Moulay Hassan's elder brother, Moulay Rachid, who had been appointed governor of the Tafilalt. You enter through the side of one of the decorated corner towers and arrive in a large enclosed square to face the more impressive and ornate internal gateway. Two towers, still rich in plasterwork and capped with tiles, flank the gate, and on the left as you proceed through it is a small mosque. The third and final court is entered through an increasingly decayed and twisting passage, its large doors now stuck forever open. It has a cloister of horseshoe arches and four cool rooms leading off it in the traditional pattern. Delicate fragments of mosaic and plasterwork are picked over by the most obvious occupants—some busy chickens and an assertive cockerel.

Ksar Al-Fida

Just as you are leaving Rissani (on the road to Moulay Ali Cherif) you pass a school on your right opposite a fork in the road. Take the left turn here (past the Café Tombuctoo), and continue on the road, ignoring the turning to ksar El Beida (built by Sultan Moulay Sliman), and pass beside the large ksar of Ouled Youssef, surrounded by daughter settlements. A big prosperous ksar with an expanding population gives birth to a subsidiary community that slowly expands in the shadow of its parent. As the old ksar physically deteriorates the population progressively move into the new one. Eventually the old one falls into decay and is quarried for building materials, allowing the life of the community to continue unbroken. In this lies the confusion over dating, for any ksar can be considered both ancient or modern.

A kilometre further on this road you reach the royal ksar of **Al-Fida**, with its old isolated gateway defining the outer *méchouar*, the place of assembly, reserved for tents and horses. The ksar has been under restoration for a number of years and will soon be ready to be opened to the public. The secure outer gateway of the ksar leads into a labrythine world of corridors, cool arches, courtyards and apartments. In detail it is memorably confusing, but in plan very neat with all the service quarters—*hammam*, mosque, apartments for slaves, house of the women—arranged around the *Dar el Kebira*, the private courtyard apartment of the prince, which stands in the centre of the ksar with its own gatehouse.

It was first built by Sultan Moulay Ismail for one of his more favoured sons, Moulay Abdullah. Later it was totally destroyed, and then rebuilt by Sultan Sidi Mohammed ben Abder Rahman for his son Moulay Idriss, who did not succeed to the throne. The deed of gift from father to son is pleasingly exact, 'I give you the land, ksar, palm trees, property inside and out'. In 1854 it was given a facelift, and remained in the possession of the royal family until 1965, when it was given to the nation.

The Southern Ksour

From Oulad Abdelhalim a tarmac road, much deteriorated in parts, takes you on a circuitous tour of some of the larger ksour: Assererhine with its pool, Zaouïet-el-Maati, Irara, Tabassamt and Ouirhlane. From Ouirhlane route 3462 leads southwest to ksar Tinrheras, where a hillock provides a superb view of the surrounding palm groves and outer fringe of desert.

The Koubba of Hassan al Dakhil

Going back into Rissani from Ouirhlane or the main Erfoud road, just before the town arch, a narrow tarmac road turns off to the south by the petrol station. This leads past two ksar before bending left towards the isolated mausoleum of Hassan al Dakhil, which was restored this century. Hassan is the ancestor of all the Alaouite *shorfa* of Morocco.

In the middle of the 13th century the *ulema* of Sijilmassa were at their wits' end. The city, already racked by political disturbances, was yet faced with the even greater catastrophe of a five year drought. All their supplications had been in vain so they decided to send an embassy to Mecca in order to find a *shorfa*, a descendant of the prophet, who could appeal on behalf of the oasis on the propitious 29th night of Ramadan, when the heavens are opened to the supplications of the faithful. The Sijilmassa embassy was well received in Arabia, for the city's reputation for wealth travelled before it, and they presented their case to the sheikh of the *shorfa* who guarded the holy lineage of the Prophet. He looked favourably upon the Moroccan delegation, and though he would not command any of his children to go to the end of the world (Morocco was known as the land of the furthest west) he gave the ambassadors permission to approach his seven sons. Each was asked what he would do if called upon to be the Imam of Sijilmassa, and with ever-greater passion each successive son replied that they would rule over the oasis, lead a great army, build kasbahs, conquer many tribes, collect a vast treasure from taxation and so establish a great Islamic state. At last they approached Hassan al Dakhil, the seventh son, who replied that he would lead the people in prayer. They knew at once that here was a man whose piety matched his ancestry.

Where to Stay and Eating Out

moderate

The new **Kasbah Asmaâ** hotel-resturant, ✆ and ⊜ (05) 575494, stands alone among palms on the west side of the main Erfoud to Rissani road, about 4km before Rissani. At last there is a comfortable, and calm, base from which to explore this fascinating but undeniably exhausting area. The kasbah is the third in this admirable family-owned chain which delights in fusing traditional forms with contemporary Moroccan domestic taste to create opulent (if not delightfully over the top) interiors. It has a pool at the back, tents in the garden, a profusion of carpets, and bright 'damask' banquettes. Drinks are only served with meals.

cheap

There are two basic hotels in Rissani itself which both have restaurants. **El Filalia**, ✆ (05) 575096, stands in the centre of town by the bus stop and souk. It has lately been slightly upstaged by the newer, slightly more efficient and decorous **Sijilmassa**, ✆ (05) 575042.

Shopping

Do not waste your energy trying to ignore the young guides in Rissani; instead befriend them, suprise them by buying them a coffee or tea in the café, and then firmly establish your itinerary before promising a visit to any one of the towns three bazaars. They actually all work as freelance salesmen for either the **Maison Touareg** (on the road to Moulay Ali Cherif), the **Maison Berbère** (by the souk) or **La Maison Saharienne**, which occupies a fascinating old house in the heart of ksar Abou Aam. All the bazaars provide mint tea, or a glass of water, to their visitors without any obligation. You can therefore enjoy them as cool, well-decorated free cafés, with an option on some bargaining.

East to Figuig

For those seeking isolation, the day-long journey from Er Rachidia to Figuig, 405km to the east, can be recommended. The road runs between a continuous escarpment to the north and land draining away into a desert plain to the south. The route is scattered with bleak mining and military posts, but of more interest are the small oasis settlements along the course of the Guir and its tributary the Aït Aïssa, both of which, predictably, drain the southern slopes of the High Atlas. The bus breaks its journey whenever you imagine the landscape to be at its most desolate, where a tenacious Berber farmer and his wife cheerfully disembark with supplies of sugar, Omo and seed corn for their invisible home.

Herds of camels and goats around scatterings of tents betray the stronger nomadic influence on this desert borderland. Over this land too, the nomadic tribes of the Dounia Menia, the Oulad Djernir and the Aït-Atta fought for centuries. In 1908 a charismatic holy man, the Sherif Moulay Lahsin, secretly supported by Sultan Moulay Hafid, briefly united the tribes in resistance to the French, who were advancing west from their posts in Algeria, and the road passes through a number of battlegrounds where the conquest was resisted.

Er Rachidia to Bouârfa

For 70km east of Er Rachidia, the P32 follows below the bulk of Jbel Aguelmous (2113m). A rough track on the left, the 3466 follows the 3469 into the river Guir's breach through the mountains. The **kasbah of Tazouguerte** lies 10km north up this striking valley. From Tazougerte the track hugs the course of the Guir. Broken palm groves follow the riverbed for 30km, scattered with largely ruinous ksour, though 26,000 date palms are still cultivated.

Boudnib, 18km further east from the Tazouguerte turning, is a dusty military town with pleasant pink and white arcaded shops around its central garden square.

'Which is Nobler, the Owl or the Hawk?'

During the construction of the new fort a French cavalry regiment charged the Boudnib palm groves in an attempt to clear the area of snipers. In the confusion of the groves and walled gardens the enthusiasm of the charge was checked, and the troopers were overwhelmed by warriors who dropped from the trees. Boudnib was however eventually taken by the French, and you can still find Borj Sud, the 'south fort' built by them, to the south of the palm groves.

On 1 September 1908 a Moroccan force assembled by Sherif Moulay Lahsin attacked the new fort. Brave to the point of madness, thousands of warriors launched wave after wave of attacks on the fort through the day. Thousands more died on 7 September attacking French relief troops on the plain of Djorf, not before their veiled leader had delivered an unanswered and strangely prophetic challenge: 'Know that since your arrival in the Sahara, you have badly treated weak Muslims. You have made our country suffer intense harm, which tastes as galling to us as a bitter apple. Come out from behind your walls, you will judge which is nobler, the owl or the hawk'.

The next 150km or so are scattered with a few sights, if you feel like breaking your journey. The **ksour of Sahli**, east of Boudnib, is entirely populated by a clan of *shorfa*, descendants of the Prophet Mohammed. **Bouânane**, 57km east of Boudnib, an oasis town in the Aït Assa palm groves, marks the turnings to **Takoumit Kasbah**, 5km north, and the isolated **ksar of El-Hajoui**, 10km south. **Aïn-Ech-Chair**, another 67km further on, is a small pisé village at the foot of the crumbling walls of an almost empty ksar.

El Menabba, 18km past Aïn-Ech-Chair, is a small military post by the turning to the now-closed P19a border road. On 17 April 1908, the French force advancing to build Borj Sud camped here. As Douglas Porch describes in *The Conquest of Morocco*: 'A wave of several thousand Moroccan warriors, stripped naked and well oiled, had crept close to the French camp from the east. In the confusion of the light and without the tell-tale pair of trousers or jellaba it became difficult to distinguish friend from foe. It was like a riot in a nudist colony, though 19 soldiers were to die and another 101 would be wounded before breakfast.'

Bouârfa

The town is perched below the pass across Jbel Bouârfa, 50km from Mengoub and 287km from Er Rachidia. It is unassociated with any palm groves or oasis cultivation, for it is a modern foundation, the centre for this desert southeastern province which is still officially considered a military region. The better of the town's two basic hotels is the **Tamlatte**, on the left of the Oujda road beside the mosque. It occasionally wafts in the delicious odour of myrrh, which permeates from next door where, less exotically, they wash the dead. Food is best from the café-restaurants below the hotel next to where the buses park.

Bouârfa has a cottage industry of weaving durable carpet rugs from cloth scraps. The silvery kaleidoscope of colours and knotted texture is seen in many more Moroccan homes than the average tourist bazaar rugs. There are working looms throughout the town, and the one at 45 Boulevard Mohammed V sometimes has a small stock for sale.

From Bouârfa to Figuig there is nothing to impede your view of the 108km of desert between these two outposts.

Figuig

In the farthest southeastern corner of Morocco is the oasis of Figuig, an elliptical basin of palm groves surrounded by dark volcanic hills. Seven unequal and feuding Berber villages guarded the twenty springs and gardens from each other by a series of walls and towers. If there was a severe enough external threat they created a united front as Figuig city, 'the Berber island in an Arab sea'.

Figuig is a noticeably religious settlement with a gentle, practising piety. The chants from the various zaouia and mosques sound especially entrancing in a desert dusk when the sun, falling behind the surrounding wall of black mountains, lights up the white wall of a koubba with the last few minutes of its gently diffused and coloured light.

Getting Around and Tourist Information

There are four **buses** from Figuig to Bouârfa a day. The 6am meets the Er Rachidia connection, the 8am allows a long lunch in Bouârfa until the 2pm bus. There are four buses between Bouârfa and Oujda a day, another eight-hour journey, though you may be able to catch the weekly night freight train.

Buses arrive on the Boulevard Hassan II, which has all the cafés and hotels along it, a Banque Populaire and the pretty courtyard of the craft shop. Foreign currency, drink and picnic food, though, should all be procured before arriving in Figuig. It is 350km south of Oujda and 405km east of Er Rachidia, with little in the way of comfort along either route. Travelling by bus gives you a certain level of intimacy with the local population and plenty of time for sleep. Cars allow you to pursue the odd detour, picnic under some palms or travel through the cool and brilliance of the night. Road conditions are fine in both directions.

First impressions of Figuig are of a line of square, modern buildings ending at an administrative 'Cercle' and the army headquarters. Inevitably, behind the road the traditional pattern of adobe ksour reveals itself. The ksour are almost urban in style, and feature long outer perimeter walls embracing cultivated areas of the palm groves. These, where they still stand, are punctuated by conical perimeter towers, built with a stone base and a very narrow crawl entrance which allows access to an upper platform lined with a row of sniping holes. The oasis is a Berber Zenata stronghold, the same group that inhabits the Rif, and although none now survives in the north they also maintained bitter feuds up there from a similar system of

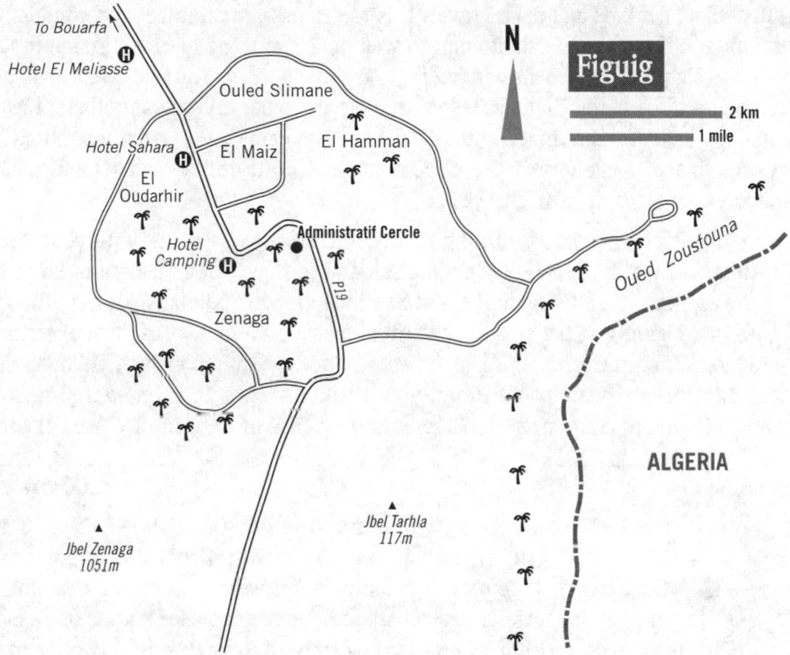

towers. Of the seven rival ksour, it is now only easy to distinguish four separate communities: El-Oudarhir, El-Maïz–Ouled-Slimane, El-Hammam and Zenaga.

El-Oudarhir, on the right as you enter the town, is in increasingly ruinous condition but if you like them it has some excellent dark subterranean passages to explore. Scattered throughout this ksar are over a dozen koubbas, one of which is next door to the oldest surviving mosque of the oasis, the minaret of which you may climb with the permission of the *caid.* There are two sources of water in the ksar, one a hot spring, the other salty.

The **ksar of El-Maïz** is on the left of the road, opposite, and is not easy to distinguish from the **ksar of Ouled-Slimane**. This is another satisfying warren of alleys and individual buildings. Perhaps the most amusing of the original ksour is **El-Hammam**, with its celebrated hot-water spring, where one can still bathe in the natural *hammams.* The women's *hammam* can be found by wandering through the palm grove of El-Hammam to the south. There is a maze of irrigation ditches and isolated shaded water tanks. Follow any watercourse upstream, along the network of levels and channels, and you should arrive at the outlet of the *hammam.* The men's *hammam* is further uphill and less easy to track down. A dark rock-cut staircase leads steeply down in a twisting subterranean passage to an echoing stone-vaulted pool in whose warm waters you can immerse yourself. There are reportedly over a hundred steps underground—I lost count when I crashed heavily into the wall, and a torch or a candle would be advisable. Above the *hammam* is the zaouia of Sidi Bou Amama, for long a centre of desert resistance to the French.

The most successful of the ksour is **Zenaga**, to the right of the road to the Algerian frontier. Since it lies at the bottom of the oasis depression, the recent lowering of the water-table has not affected its gardens and palm groves. It is the richest, most intact and confident of the communities of Figuig. You can attempt to walk to Zenaga, wandering through the baffling paths of the high walled gardens with their astonishing variety. You will catch small glimpses of the underground water channels where tunnels and pipes crisscross at different levels and flow in opposite directions. In the enthusiasm of Independence the government tried to regulate water rights in Figuig, but the inspectors gave up trying to understand the baffling complexity of the system after four years.

A kilometre before Zenaga, a turning to the left takes you to the **valley of the river Zousfana**. A string-like palm grove extends along the riverbed, a pleasant place to walk or picnic through the hot afternoon; there are various viewing points looking south. The hills that surround Figuig give the area an inward intensity, an almost urban feel of containment quite different from the sense of isolation and distance you might expect. To find a lingering view of the great expanses of the desert you would have to climb one of the surrounding hills, and it is well to clear any such climb with the police in this sensitive frontier town.

Where to Stay

The **Hôtel Camping Diamant Vert**, © (06) 699030, is off Boulevard Hassan II. It has an excellent view of the Zenaga palm grove from its terrace café. It rents out 5 simple rooms and space for camping in the grounds, and levies a small charge to non-residents for the use of the pool. If it is full try the **Hôtel Sahara** in the centre of town, where very basic rooms are rented out. The official *hammam*, 2dh entrance, is just outside the Sahara, and chants percolate upstairs from a nearby zaouia on Friday evenings. There is also the **Hôtel El Meliasse**, which is by the garage on the right as you enter Figuig from Bouârfa. It has cool, cavernous rooms, two small balconies and showers. Eating out in Figuig is a modest affair, either café- or hotel-based.

Algeria

The border with Algeria is currently completely closed due to the undeclared civil war in the country between the semi-military-government and the fundamentalist-inspired guerrilla opposition. It is unlikely that this situation will change in the immediate future. If, God Willing, there is a sudden peace, it is probably that the post-1989 procedure for border crossings will be reestablished. This required you first to get your passport stamped at the Figuig police station, which is open 8am–3pm. The actual Algerian–Moroccan border is 3km south of Figuig, but could be shut down for a three hour siesta after lunch. On the Algerian side you used to have to fill in at least three separate forms, make a declaration of your holdings of foreign currency (necessarily slightly fraudulent if you wished to make use of the black market) and change a certain amount (around $150/£100) at the highly disadvantageous government-fixed Algerian exchange rate. The border stands 3km north of the Algerian town of Beni-Ounif, which has banks (closed on Fridays and Saturdays) one hotel, and train and bus stations.

Agadir, the Sous Valley and the Anti-Atlas

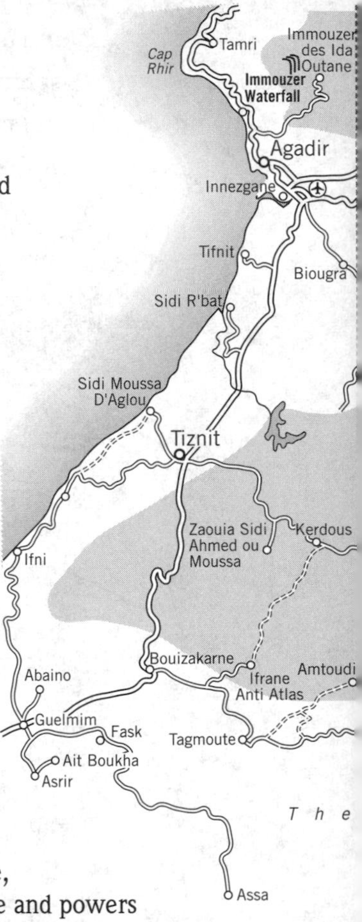

The Sous and the Anti-Atlas is the most distinctive and self-contained region of Morocco. It is an area of striking physical beauty, its landscape deeply imbued with both history and an older and abiding sense of spiritual mystery. The people are noticeably less aggressive to travellers than in some regions, and the climate is attractive throughout the year.

The semi-tropical Sous Valley is sealed to the north by the great peaks of the High Atlas and to the south by the Anti-Atlas mountains. To the east these two ranges meet to form the holy mountain of Jbel Siroua. Geographical isolation from the rest of Morocco has bred a strong regional identity. The people of the Sous and the Anti-Atlas have a tradition of dissidence and independence from central government that is continued today in support for the socialist opposition party, the UNFP. Though the accessible and fertile areas, like Agadir and Taroudannt, have a mixed population, the region is still dominated by the Chleuh group of tribes, who speak the Tachelait Berber dialect. Through accident or proud design the Chleuh have maintained a racial purity that has preserved characteristic features. A Chleuh is typically slight with a lithe, almost delicate frame, and great flexibility, grace and powers of endurance. Pronounced cheekbones give a broad look to the head and a slight impression of Central Asian or Native American ancestry.

The Chleuh are famous for their industry, which was originally directed to war and creating orchard gardens from the bleakest of landscapes. They evolved skilled specializations: the metalwork and weaponry of the Ida-ou-Kensous have been prized since the 11th century; the Akhassa specialized in building mosques; the Ammeln in shopkeeping; and Tazeroualt is the centre for Chleuh acrobats, who have dominated circuses throughout the world. The expansion of opportunities during the French Protectorate was quickly filled by the Anti-Atlas tribes: the Ida-ou-Gnidif became waiters, the Issendal chauffeurs and the Issagen cooks.

The transport hub of the region is the city of Agadir, which has an international airport, regular bus services and car hire firms. Apart from

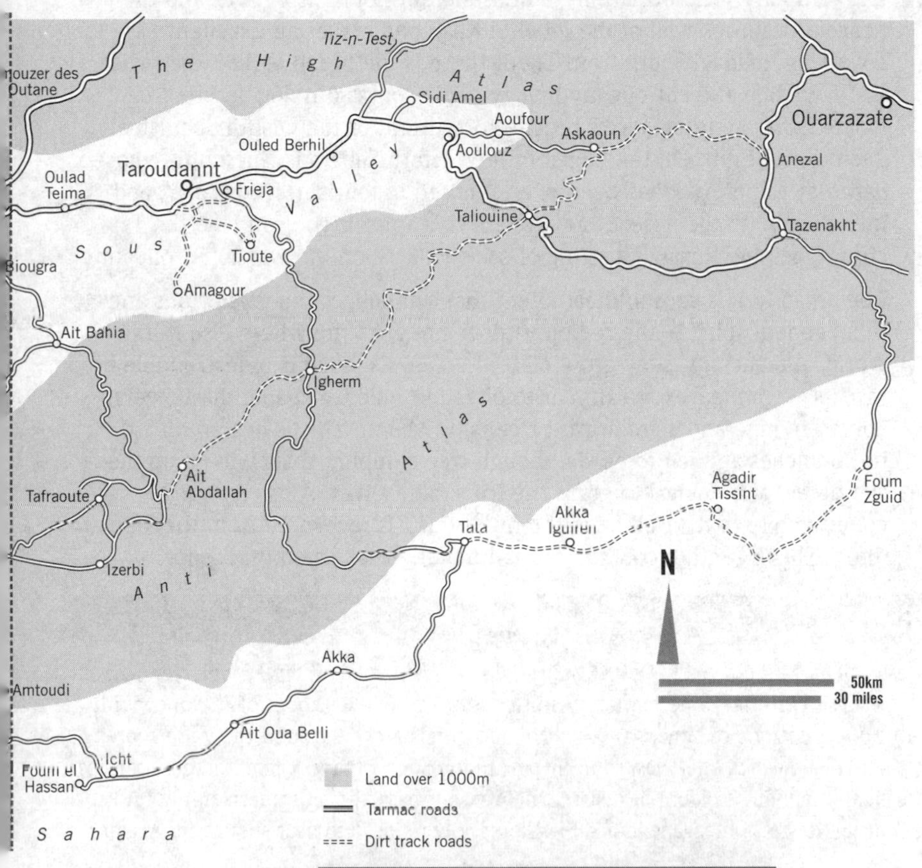

Agadir, the Sous and the Anti-Atlas

its magnificent beach the attraction of this modern resort city is slight, but out from Agadir stretches an unspoilt hinterland and coast. To the north are the celebrated long white sands of Tarhazoute and, inland, the mountain top village and mysterious waterfall of Imouzzèr-des-Ida-Outanane. To the east is Taroudannt, the ancient capital of the region, contained within an ancient circuit of ochre walls. Taroudannt has surprisingly few 'sights', but with its old hotels, fine cooking and busy, relaxed souk it is a city to stay for a while, rather than just visit.

The pink-walled city of Tiznit has a quite different aura, mixed from a recent but heady past of prostitutes, jewellers and blue sultans from the Sahara. It is also an excellent base from which to travel further south and east. The village of Tafraoute, perched high up in the centre of the Anti Atlas, is one of the great goals of travel in this region. It is surrounded by extraordinary rock formations, a dense pattern of oasis villages and the near-vertical rock wall of the Jebel El Kest, and makes an excellent base for a walking holiday. South from Tiznit there is the beach of Sidi Rbat, with all its wildlife and curious mythology; Sidi-Moussa-d'Aglou and its troglodyte fishermen; the seven beaches of Mirleft, or the wistful Spanish art deco town of Ifni. On the edge of the Western Sahara is Guelmim, whose Saturday camel souk has been over-exposed to tourism. It makes a good introduction to the desert, however. If this appeals you can take the Tata circuit, passing through a string of oasis villages on the way to Taroudannt.

The argan tree is an unofficial totem that symbolizes the mysterious and independent spirit of the region. It does not grow anywhere else in the world. A tenacious, slow-growing thorn tree, its wood is indestructible by insects. Argan leaves are similar to olive but fuller in shape; the flowers appear in June and a green fruit ripens by March. This is beaten off the branches and fed to herds, though tree-climbing goats will go up the slenderest of branches to graze the fruit themselves. A heavy orange-coloured oil is extracted from the nut, which is recovered from the animal dung. This is used in cooking, for lamp fuel, or is turned into soap.

Agadir

As a result of an earthquake in 1960, Agadir is a completely modern city, a well planned, all-season resort town that is permanently full of tourists. It is a model of its kind, with a concentric tourist zone of large, garden-shrouded hotels arched around the wide shores of its vast sandy bay, which stretches from the port to the Sous estuary. Inland there is a succession of neatly laid-out residential districts before you pass almost imperceptibly into the neighbouring towns of Inezgane and Aït-Melloul, now reduced to near suburbs of Agadir.

The centre of Agadir, dominated by its population of day-glow package tourists from Northern Europe, is undeniably drab. Compared to any other city in Morocco, the centre of Agadir is strangely calm and open, empty of mystery and verging on the bland. It is not for this desolate shopping mall that visitors fall in love with the place, but for the wonderful sandy bay below the town which offers some of the safest bathing on the Atlantic coast of Morocco. When this beach, overlooked by mountains to the north and stretching south for 10 empty kilometres to the Sous, begins to pall there are a series of undeveloped beaches and coves easily accessible off the coast road to the north of the city. Here the Atlantic is much stronger, and though more dangerous for weak swimmers it is near-perfect for surfers and windsurfers. If you are in search of a tan, a swim, a beach picnic or just another chance to watch the furious southern Sun set into the cool haze of the Atlantic horizon, you might yet end (despite yourself) falling slowly in love with this initially unlovely modern city.

Even if you hate sunbathing and loathe sand you will inevitably find yourself staying a night in two in Agadir if you are exploring the region. It is the capital of the south, the transport centre, where you can catch planes and buses, hire cars, cash cheques, make telephone calls and stock up with wine. In amongst these travellers' chores you can go and visit the ruined kasbah, walk around the fishing port and visit the Folk Art Museum before swimming off the magnificent beach. In the evening the beach front is transformed into an elegant Moroccan paseo that sways colourfully past the cafes, music bars and restaurants that line the promenade and look out over the stars and the moon reflected in the sea.

History

From a Tribal Granary to a Portuguese Fortress

The city is named after Agadir-n-Irir, the communal fortified granary of the Irir tribe that once stood on the site of the kasbah. In the 15th century European traders began to anchor in the calm and sheltered sandy bay that stood beneath the agadir. Here they could trade directly with Saharan caravans, and cut out the Fassi and Marrakechi middlemen. In 1505, a Portuguese merchant took advantage of the weakness of the central government and built a permanent fortified trading post beside the port. This, the castle of Santa Cruz de Capo Gere, he sold very profitably seven years later to the Portuguese king. The castle at Agadir rapidly became the largest and easily the most profitable Portuguese fortress in Morocco.

The Chief Port of the Saadians

The Portuguese governors' influence began to spread inland, but the Berber and Arab tribes buried their rivalries and united under the leadership of the Saadians, a holy family from the Drâa Valley. From 1515 they had the Portuguese castle under an intermittent form of siege. Once the Saadian sheikhs had sufficient resources to seize control of the hilltop *Agadir* and turn it into an artillery fortress, though, the castle was doomed. It fell to the Saadians in 1541, and the chain of Portuguese forts to the north was also abandoned as untenable. During the 120 years of Saadian rule the port of Agadir, overlooked by the artillery fortress (now known as the royal kasbah) enjoyed a golden period of prosperity, exporting locally produced sugar, cotton and saltpetre as well as the products of the Saharan trade.

Revolt and the Ruinous Revenge of the Sultans

The wheel of fortune was reversed under the Alaouites. In 1687 Sultan Moulay Ismaïl conquered the region, which had existed as a separate state for fifty years. The city was weakened under Moulay Ismaïl, but the fatal blow to Agadir was delivered in 1760. The city had joined in yet another regional revolt, and in revenge Sultan Sidi Mohammed determined to destroy the port. First he moved the all-important Jewish middlemen north to his new trading development at Essaouira, where he increasingly diverted all trade. Only then did he formally forbid any merchant to visit Agadir and close down the port. His plans were assisted by the fact that the slave-worked plantations of the West Indies had destroyed the demand for sugar from the Sous Valley, and by 1819 Agadir had shrivelled to a mere village.

A Powder Keg of the 20th Century

It remained a rural backwater until one of those petty incidents in the diplomatic poker game, the Agadir Crisis of July 1911, propelled it back into fame. By the end of the 19th century, France, Britain, Spain and Italy had divided North Africa into agreed areas of influence, deliberately excluding Germany from their plans. Under the pretence of helping the Moroccan sultan assert his independence, a German gunboat, the *Panther*, was dispatched to anchor off Agadir, which was then still unoccupied by France. The wheels of colonial diplomacy then spun into action, and German support for Moroccan independence was bought off with several million square miles of French West Africa.

The Earthquake and a New City

During the French Protectorate Agadir slowly grew back into a sizeable town, a pleasant unhurried place with a mixed international population of 35,000 by 1959. It had the misfortune to become world-famous again, though, when, thirteen minutes before midnight on 29 February 1960, Agadir was destroyed and half its inhabitants buried alive in an earthquake. It was impossible to extract most of the bodies from the rubble, and with cholera spreading among the survivors it was decided to bury the city and citizens in one mass grave. The burial mound, the Tell or 'Ancienne Talborjt', is to the north of the modern city, inland from the port. The new Agadir was rebuilt from scratch, and today there can be almost as many tourists in the town's 15,000 hotel beds as there were victims of that leap-year night disaster.

Getting Around

In former years there was a once-a-week ferry to Las Palmas in the Canary Isles, leaving on Saturday evening and arriving the next day at 5pm. This is no longer running, but may be revived. There is also an ambitious national plan to link Agadir and Laâyoune to the railway system via Marrakech and the Tizi-n-Test. Until these projects mature buses will remain the easiest means of land transport to Agadir.

by air

Agadir has a recently-built international airport, Al Massira, ✆ (08) 839122, which stands 35km to the east of the city. It receives a steady flow of charter and scheduled international flights, plus daily RAM flights to Casablanca and five connections a week to Tangier, one a week to Tan-Tan and two weekly flights to Laâyoune, Dakhla and Las Palmas in the Canary Isles. For tickets and information visit RAM on Av du Général Kettani, ✆ (08) 840793. The airport is best approached from the P32, the road to Taroudannt. There is a ***grand taxi*** rank at the airport (cabs should charge a flat 120dh by day, 150dh by night, and take anything from one to six passengers) as well as the much cheaper hourly **Supratours** bus, ✆ (08) 841207, to Place des Orangers near the city centre. On your way back out to the airport get your receptionist to call a taxi or dial ✆ (08) 822017 yourself.

by bus

All bus lines leave from the Talborjt station, which is just northeast of the café-lined Place Lahcen Tamri. The bus station remains happily outside Agadir's bland aura of efficiency: it is no more than a dusty square overlooked by the individual ticket offices, strung along Avenue Yacoub el Mansour. As ever, you should buy tickets as early as possible, having shopped around the various companies to check on the most convenient departure. Between the **CTM**, ✆ (08) 822077 and **SATAS**, ✆ (08) 842470 bus companies there are half a dozen departures a day to Casablanca (5hrs) or Marrakech (4hrs), five a day to Taroudannt (2–3hrs), four to Essaouira (3–4hrs), four to Tiznit (2hrs), four to Tafraoute (5hrs) and two a day south to Guelmim (4–5hrs) or southeast to Tata (9hrs, departing at 4am and 7am).

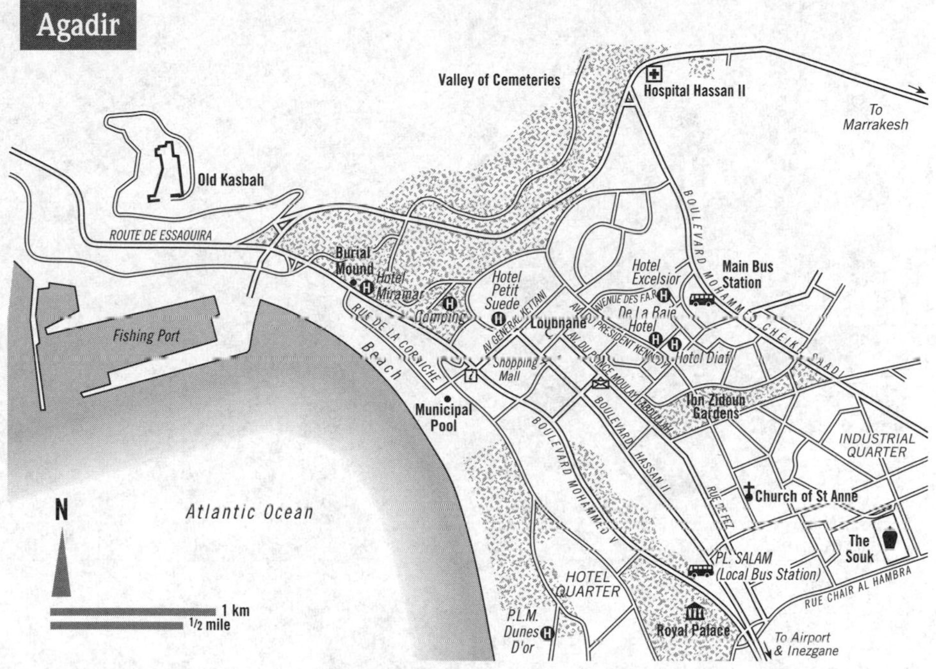

For greater comfort use the **ONCF** service, which leaves from Rue Ya'qub Al-Mansur to link up with the rail network at Marrakech in 4hrs. Buses leave at 4.50am, 10am, 2.26pm and 8pm, and at 7.30pm a coach heads south for the 12hr trip to Laâyoune.

Also bear in mind that **Inezgane** (just 13km south of Agadir) has its own bus station, near the central Place Al Massira, with a separate range of departures that include at least four daily buses to Marrakech, Taroudannt, Guelmim and Ouarzazate. It can be reached quickly by a 5dh place in a *grand taxi* from Place Salam in Agadir.

Local buses all depart from Place Salam (also known as Place de l'Abbatoir), which is at the southern end of Agadir's long Blvd Hassan II. Among the more useful local runs are no. **1** to the port, **5** and **6** to Inezgane, **12** to Tarhazoute and **14** to Tamri.

by taxi

Although ***grands taxis*** can often be found at the Talborjt bus station, Place Salam is the main centre for them in Agadir. From here there is a regular 2hr run to Taroudannt, with a change of cars halfway at Oulad-Teïma (also known as Kilometre 44, after its main monument). For a place in a *grand taxi* to Tiznit you will be better off going first to Inezgane (*see* above) and getting one from there.

Agadir's orange local ***petits taxis*** can carry three passengers and are useful for trips to the port, beach, kasbah and souk, but cannot operate beyond the city limits. Do not be mean with yourself: Agadir was designed with America in mind, its pavements are dull, and should be sped past in a taxi.

Central Agadir

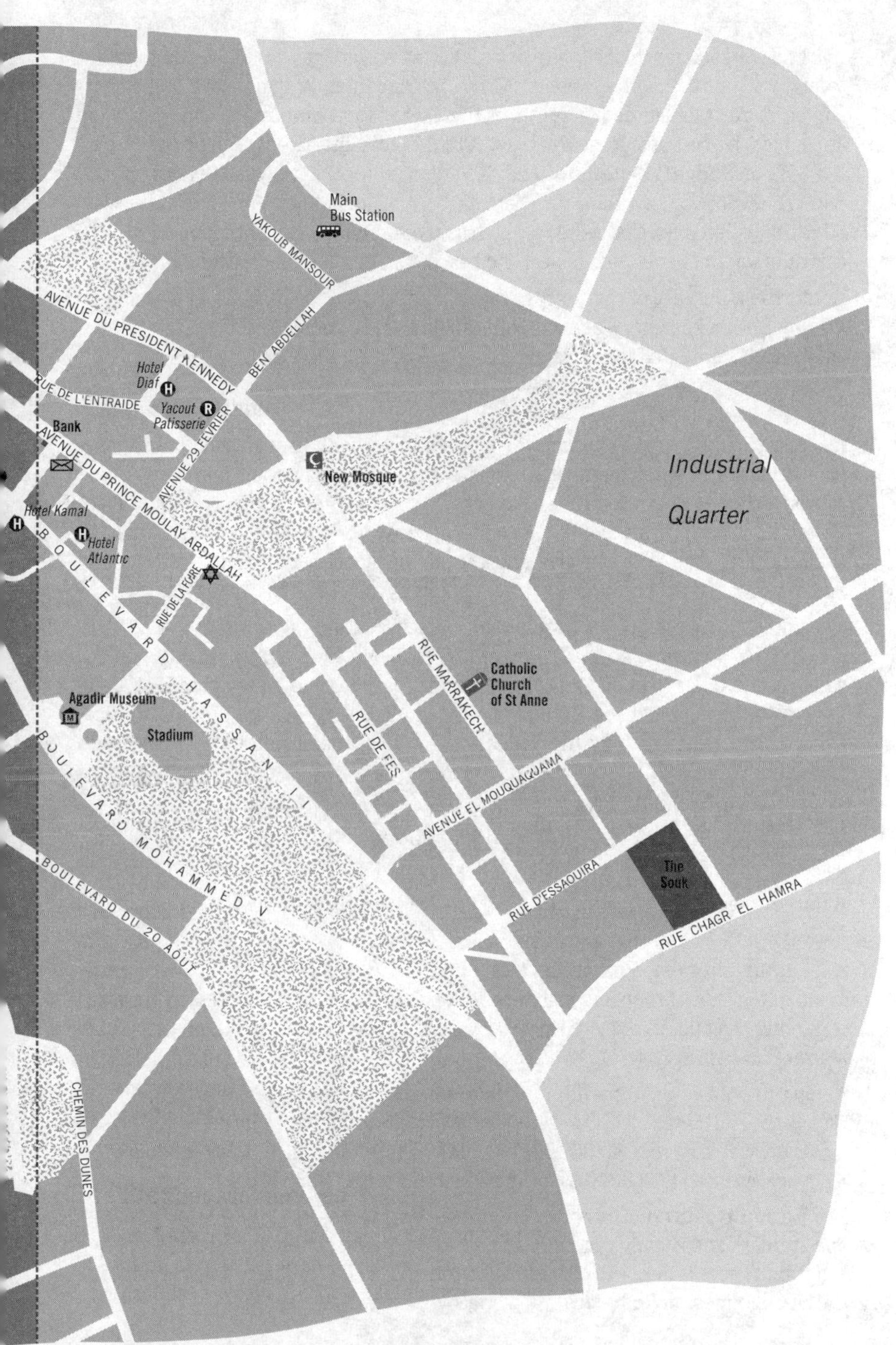
Main
Bus Station
YAKOUB MANSOUR
BEN ABDELLAH
AVENUE DU PRESIDENT KENNEDY
Hotel
Diaf
RUE DE L'ENTRAIDE
Yacout
Patisserie
Bank
AVENUE 29 FEVRIER
AVENUE DU PRINCE MOULAY ABDALLAH
New Mosque
Hotel Kamal
Hotel
Atlantic
BOULEVARD HASSAN II
RUE DE LA FOIRE
Industrial
Quarter
Catholic
Church
of St Anne
RUE MARRAKECH
RUE DE FES
Agadir Museum
Stadium
BOULEVARD MOHAMMED V
AVENUE EL MOUQAOUAMA
BOULEVARD DU 20 AOUT
RUE D'ESSAOUIRA
The
Souk
RUE CHAGR EL HAMRA
CHEMIN DES DUNES

by car/car hire

Agadir has a good range of car hire firms, and the bigger agencies allow you to return a car to any of their other depots. Most are conveniently bunched along a short stretch of Av Mohammed V south of the Oasis Hotel and town campsite. Shop around for the best deal from **Hertz**, ✆ (08) 840939; **InterRent/Europcar**, ✆ (08) 840337, or **Budget**, ✆ (08) 840762. A very good local agency is **Always**, ✆ (08) 846061, ✆ 845937, by the Hotel Marhaba on Av Mohammed V. Mopeds and small bikes can be hired from large hotels, such as the Almohades, and at around $15/£10 a day from a number of outlets near the beach, chiefly along Boulevard du 20 Août.

Agadir has a number of specialist **garages**: Renaults can be repaired at Castano on Avenue El Moukouama, Fiats and Fords at Auto-Hall, Rue de la Foire, and Citroëns and Peugeots are cared for at Garage Citroën, Rue du 3 Mars.

Tourist Information

It is easy to find your way around the modern town, with its wide avenues running parallel to the beach. The most striking feature is that there are no hasslers. The **tourist office** is in the southwestern corner of the central shopping mall on Place Hassan II, assisted by the Syndicat d'Initiative on Av Mohammed V. They hand out a colourful city map and can give suggestions on coach excursions, festivals and *Fantasias*. Actual tickets are bought from hotels or travel agents.

One of the most useful of the dozen **bank** branches in the city centre is the ABM, ✆ (08) 841567, which is normally open Mon–Fri 8.15–11.30am, 2.30–4.30pm, but which is also often open on Saturday morning. It is easto find on the corner of Av du Prince Sidi Mohammed and Av Prince Moulay Abdullah, opposite the **Post Office**. Other useful banks include the BMCE on Av du Général Kettani and Crédit du Maroc on Av des FAR.

The main hall of the post office is open Mon–Fri 9am–12 noon, 3–6pm, and Sat 9am–12 noon. You can make **international phone calls** from any number of independent telebooths or from an office at the side of the post office, open until 9pm.

Emergencies: for ambulance or fire, ✆ 15, for the police, in the station on Rue du 18 Novembre, ✆ 19.

A **24-hour chemist**, Pharmacie Municipalité d'Agadir, ✆ (08) 820349, can be found in the central shopping mall next to the town hall. For more pressing cases get your hotel receptionist to call a doctor or alert the Hospital Hassan out on the road to Marrakech, ✆ (08) 841477.

Among the dozen or so part-time **consulates** in the city there are no US, Dutch, Canadian, Australian, Irish or New Zealand representatives. Northern Europe is, however, well covered: ✆ (08) 827741/844343 for the British, ✆ (08) 823347 for the Norwegian, ✆ (08) 823048 for the Swedish, ✆ (08) 823821 for the Finnish.

The **Catholic church** of St Anne, on Rue de Marrakech, ✆ (08) 822251, has Mass on Saturdays at 6.30pm in French, and a more polyglot service on Sundays at 10am and 7pm. There is also a **Protestant church** at 2 Rue Chouhada in occasional use and **Synagogues** on Rue Afghanistan and Av Moulay Abdellah.

The Kasbah Ruins

The only real 'sight' of Agadir, the ruins of the old government kasbah, provide an excellent vantage point from which to view the whole town and the port. It is a long, steep but rewarding climb, though a road also allows for vehicle access. The kasbah was built by the Saadian Sultan Mohammed ech Cheikh as part of his prolonged jihad to remove the Portuguese from Morocco. Having fortified the site in 1540, he was able to expel the Portuguese from their precious castle-dominated harbour of Agadir once he moved in his heavy artillery the following year. Above the entrance gate is an inscription in Arabic and Dutch, inveighing you to fear God and honour the King: in 1746 Dutch merchants achieved a monopoly position in the Sous sugar trade, and helped rebuild the kasbah. Justifiably suspicious of both the tribes and the Europeans, in 1752 Sultan Moulay Abdullah placed a mixed garrison of Christian renegades and Turkish mercenaries in the kasbah.

In the anarchic years before the French Protectorate, the kasbah was no longer an official garrison and was lived in by the villagers of Agadir. Before the earthquake it held a warren of over 300 houses. You can easily discover the traces—twisted sheets of corrugated roofing, old electric cables and shattered reinforced concrete beams—within the ramparts. There are also several old water cisterns, which are well worth avoiding.

The Tell/Ancienne Talborjt

Below the kasbah, inland from Boulevard Mohammed V, is the site of Portuguese Agadir, and possibly that of Phoenician Rusadir. The 1960 burial mound of city and population now hides any traces. Trees have been planted on the mound, but the monument to the dead remains incomplete. It is visited by surviving relatives at sunset, and is a favourite practising ground for learner drivers. A small track from here crosses the main bypass to take you to a valley of cemeteries. Here, Christians, Jews and Muslims are buried in separate fields and cacti proliferate on the bleak slopes above.

The Town

The town centre itself is not a place of architectural elegance: its low, regular buildings, wide avenues and central pedestrian shopping zone faithfully echo a mid-Sixties automobile-dictated suburb somewhere in North America. It is almost absurdly out of place and out of touch with Moroccan traditions. Fortunately the more recently erected housing developments to the east of the city have found another way, and have integrated traditional themes (not least the welcome casting of shade) without any sacrifices to modernity. In the town centre, apart from the beach-front hotels, the only buildings with individuality are the town hall, the grand mosque, the law courts and the concrete bunker-like central post office, designed by the architect Zevaco.

The **Vallée des Oiseaux** (Valley of the Birds; *open Mon, Tues, 9.30am–12.30pm, Wed–Sun 9.30am–12.30pm, 2.30–6.30pm; adm*), a narrow strip of parkland embellished with zoo cages, aviaries, a children's playground, toy train rides and a cascade, has been created recently as part of the tourist furniture of Agadir. It makes happy use of a dry river valley to provide a pleasant walk down from the town centre (Boulevard Hassan II) to the beach-front square (Place al Amal) beside Boulevard 20 Aôut.

The Souk

A pink concrete kasbah has been built off the Rue Chayr el Hamra Mohammed ben Brahim, on the south side of the town centre, to house market stalls. It is surprisingly attractive, adorned with some impressive wooden gates. Some tourist bazaars have been fitted in on the north side, but the delightfully animated confusion of a Moroccan marketplace, usually at its busiest over the weekend, has already taken control.

Musée Municipal/Museum of Folk Art of Southern Morocco

Open Mon–Sat 9.30am–1pm, 2.30–6pm; closed Sun; adm., © (08) 840784

Beneath the concrete arcades of the town's open-air theatre (in the municipal park that stretches between Boulevard Hassan II and Boulevard Mohammed V) a small museum has been set up in the last few years with the assistance of Dutch anthropologist Bert Flint, whose textile-filled house in Marrakech, Maison Tiskiwin, is also open to the public (*see* p.404). The collection has been assembled over the last three decades, and though the pieces offer a timeless insight into traditional Berber culture of southern Morocco few are more than a hundred years old. Coming straight off the plane it might appear dusty and incomprehensible, but will be rewarding once you have walked through the mountain villages and oasis valleys. The two long halls contain a fine and varied display of the different weaving, ceramics, costume, leatherwork and jewellery of the tribes, from the nomads of the Sahara to the villagers of the snow-covered, forested heights of the Middle Atlas. Do not overlook the carved wood displayed in the first four salons: window frames, dowry chests, doors and slender columns from the prayer hall of a village mosque. The latter with their proto-Corinthian capitals seem to speak the same architectural language as ancient Assyria and Anatolia. Details from the wooden carvings are a treasury of traditional symbolism, evoking the duality between man and woman, bull and cow, sun and moon, opposites that must yet meet for the continuity of life. The swirling segments within a circle or near swastika-like patterns speak of the recurring cycle of seasons, a bull-head-like motif can be seen as a stylised woman giving birth, the frog posture (a flattened 'n' matched by its reflection) speaks again of birthing women, and the millennial attitude of prayer. A double zig-zag is the snake and the male principle, while the cross represents the opposites (man and woman, sun and moon) combined. You will also see representations of the double fibula (*tazerzit*) linked by a chain, worn by many Berber women. As well as a representation of portable wealth, status and a practical clothes pin, the triangle is a symbol of women and the fertility of the earth.

The Port

If you want to wander without shopping, the port is the most lively and intriguing area of Agadir. The fishing fleet, combined with that of Safi to the north, is the largest gatherer of sardines in the world, landing more than 160,000 tonnes a year. Outside the port gates there is a small square full of tables where fresh fish is served. Inside the gates is a massive fish market and a series of cafés for the fishermen. The Yacht Club is a restaurant and bar open to all, with a good view of some of the harbour's activity. In order to leave the central docks for the fishing fleet, a new harbour is being built for general trade in bulk agricultural goods, and a small yacht marina is under construction by the beach.

The Beach

The wide beach is magnificent, and one of the safest places to swim on the whole Atlantic coast. It does however still have a strong undertow and children, should be watched with care. The foothills of the Western High Atlas, at which you can gaze while floating leisurely in the sea, rise steeply north of the town. The kasbah-capped hilltop is inscribed with white-washed stones that trace out *Allah, Malik, Watan*—God, King and Country. Aside from the Place al Amal a slip road leads off Blvd Mohammed V to give access to the beach front by car. There are shaded car parks, and showers are available at a number of the café-bars on the promenade. Further south the beach is increasingly dominated by large hotels. Rows of sunbeds, camel rides, deck chairs, windsurfers and water-skiing instructors await their customers. Even further south the hotels give way to high sand dunes and miles of empty sand that stretch to the banks of the Sous estuary, a famous bird-watching spot.

Where to Stay

expensive

The **Sheraton**, ✆ (08) (08) 843232, ℻ 844379, has a near perfect situation, easily accessible by car on Blvd Mohammed V and just a short stroll from the beach. It is not the most elegant of buildings but undoubtedly has the calmest atmosphere of any of the major hotels, with a lawn around its large pool, just one restaurant, a big lobby in which to sip coffee as you watch the world go by and some stunning views from the bedrooms. The walk-in rates are at the top end of this price range, but you should be able to get better rates through a travel agent.

A drop below in calmness with a much more exuberant neo-Moorish style but an equally good location (off the side road opposite the open-air theatre on Blvd Mohammed V) is the **Melia al Medina Salam**, ✆ (08) 845353, ℻ 845308.

moderate

The **Miramar** , ✆ (08) 840770, is on Blvd Mohammed V at the very northern edge of town, directly east of the fishing harbour. It has a bar, a very good restaurant, just 12 rooms arranged around an open air courtyard on the upper floor, and is one of the few buildings to have survived the earthquake. It is perfectly placed as a stop over.

If it is full try the **Aferni**, ✆ (08) 840730, on Av du Général Kettani, a new, moderately sized (45-room) and unfussy place with a pool and restaurant.

Another useful address is the **Kamal**, a block from the Post Office on Blvd Hassan II, ✆ (08) 842817, ℻ 843940. Almost opposite is the 54-room **Atlantic Hotel**, ✆ (08) 843662, a simple functional place with car parking in the dead centre of the town.

The **Moussafir**, ✆ ℻ (consult tourist office for phone and fax), part of a well-run chain of moderate sized places with pool, restaurant and bar, is a new hotel away from the tourist-dominated beach strip, 500m before the 'souk' on Rue Oued Ziz.

moderate (in Inezgane and the Sous estuary)

When the old Inezgane-Agadir airport was in operation the older colonial hotels of Inezgane used to be perfectly placed as a stopover before heading south the next day. Now that the new airport is off the Taroudant road the Inezgane hotels have lost much of their original convenience, though they all remain pleasantly run down and louche escapes from the blandness of the package hotels of Agadir.

The **Provençal**, ✆ (08) 831208, has rooms arranged around an abundant courtyard garden with a pool. There is an adjoining busy local bar, a restaurant, and the hotel is littered with various hunting trophies. It is 9km out of Agadir on the right-hand side of the main road as you head south. The similar **Auberge La Pergola**, ✆ (08) 830841, has no pool, but French cooking under the direction of Mme Mirabel. It is situated 8km out of Agadir on the left-hand side of the road as you go south.

The **Pyramides**, ✆ (08) 830705, is found signposted off the Sous estuary road. This small hotel has a small pool and bar, and pyramid-roofed rooms arranged around two courtyards. You can rent horses from the neighbouring stables and ride in the company of a stable boy through the surrounding estuary, which teems with wildlife.

In addition the **PLM Dounia hotel**, ✆ (08) 835060, @ 835070, runs a secluded, quiet annexe on the edge of the Sous estuary called the **Hacienda Club**. This too has stables, with a regular itinerary of rides at 10am, 3pm and 5pm costing 200dh per person. There are several chalets arranged around the Club pool, popular with young German families. Speak to the director, Driss Namolsi, about a price.

inexpensive (in Agadir)

The **Petit Suède**, ✆ (08) 840779, is a calm place with just 16 rooms. It is inconspicuously tucked behind a bank off Boulevard Hassan II, and only 200m walk from the beach. **Les Palmiers**, ✆ (08) 843719, is another useful address. It has 28 rooms, a bar and restaurant, and is centrally placed on Av Prince Sidi Mohammed.

cheap (in Agadir)

All of these hotels are found in the 900m-wide grid of streets between Av Prince Moulay Abdullah and the bus station. They are fine, functional places, used almost as much by Moroccans as tourists and in an area full of cafés and cheap restaurants.

Hôtel Sindibad, ✆ (08) 823477, is perfectly sited on Place Lahcen Tamri and has a restaurant and bar. **Hôtel de Paris**, 57 Av Kennedy, ✆ (08) 822694, has 20 rooms around a courtyard; **Hôtel Diaf**, ✆ (08) 825852, on Av Allal ben Abdellah is clean with powerful showers, and seems to attract a good proportion of passing oddballs. **Hôtel El Bahia**, Rue Mehdi Ibn Tumert, ✆ (08) 822724, is a popular choice with English-speaking management. On the same street is the **Moderne**, ✆ (08) 823373.

camping

The well-organized, well-located campsite is on Av Mohammed V, ✆ (08) 840981. It is, though, tightly packed and dominated by camper-vans for most of the year.

Eating Out

expensive

For a traditional Moroccan dinner head for the **Johara**, ✆ (08) 845353, the entrance to which is hidden within the shopping mall on Blvd du 20 Août. You can choose a seven-course set feast, or pick your way through such delights as the chef's *briouates* or a bowl of *harira marrekchia aux dattes* followed by pigeons *kedra fassia* accompanied by a bottle of Cabernet Reservé and a glass of mint tea. Instead of bogus belly dancing we were treated to an unforgettable evening of traditional Andalusian music played on the oud by Driss Maloumi. The music of this moonlighting master, who teaches at a local academy, was alone worth the price of the meal.

moderate

Restaurant du Port, © (08) 843708, gets a mixed press. I have always found the fish a bit disappointing, but this observation has enraged some friends. It is certainly an interesting place to go for lunch with its view over the harbour, and a welcome escape from the masses. To find it go through the police gates at the harbour, straight ahead past the 25km speed limit sign, turn right, trundle on, and it's on the left.

In the evening you can eat well away from the madding crowd at the esteemed **Le Miramar**, © (08) 840770, at the hotel of the same name on Blvd Mohammed V. It has been refurbished by André Paccard (one of King Hassan's favourite designers) in a rare mood of restraint. They serve their own pasta, and, to order, fresh fish baked in salt. The dining room is kept in a ceaseless twirl of activity under the eagle eye of a *maître-d* who is a master of his craft. In season, book a table in advance.

cheap

The cheapest places to eat in Agadir are the café-restaurants in the bus stop area. Going slightly upmarket there is a row of four café-restaurants in Place Lahcen, the **Ibtissan**, **Coq d'Or**, **Maouid Echabab** and the **Sindibad**, which can produce good meals providing you stick to local dishes. For reasonably priced seafood wander along Rue des Orangiers, off Boulevard Hassan II. At no. 19 is **L'Amirauté**, which has a good reputation for fish, a large choice of Moroccan specialities and efficient, friendly service. There is also the **Daffy** at no. 2, where they serve hot prawn *pil-pil*, the **Ogill** at no. 86 and the **Tanalt**, © (08) 841257, at no. 98.

Shopping

The **Monoprix**, a fixed-price supermarket on the corner of Boulevard Hassan II and Avenue Prince-Héritier Sidi-Mohammed is an impersonal and colourless place to shop, but stock up here on all the **wine** you might need, for it has the best and the cheapest range of Moroccan wines in the entire south. For cut-price **scents**, sniff your way through the 99 styles stocked at **L'Artisan Perfumerie**, 5 Av Du Prince Moulay Abdullah; for **cakes**, croissants or for assembling a delicious **picnic** of four types of pastilla pies head straight to **Yacout**, **La Musée des Gouts**, on Av 29 Fevrier, © (08) 846587.

Foreign newspapers can be bought from kiosks along Blvd Hassan II, and there is a small range of **books** in **Débit Pilote** at no. 65. The **Crown English Bookshop**, near the tourist office on the mall walkway, has recently re-opened.

Sports

For **riding** in the Sous estuary, see the **Pyramides** hotel and **Hacienda Club** (*see* above). For information on local **fishing** and **shooting** possibilities, call **Agence Sport Evasion**, © (08) 840122.

There are two **golf** clubs in Agadir. The **Dunes**, © (08) 834690, is a 9-hole course (par 36) with a 340dh green fee. The **Royal Club de Golf**, © (08) 241278 is at Aït Melloul, 12km out of town off the main south road.

If you want to stray beyond hotel organised sport and find a local tennis partner try the **Royal Club de Tennis** on Av Hassan II, © (08) 821064.

Entertainment and Nightlife

All the big beachfront hotels have their own cabarets and discothèques. Designed to entertain block-booked holiday groups, they can be dreadful. The **Atlas Amadil**, © (08) 840620, on Route de Oued Sous and the **Sahara Hôtel**, © (08) 840660, on Blvd Mohammed V try to employ good resident bands, who generally play from 8–11pm, when the disco takes over. The **Byblos Disco**, in the PLM Dunes d'Or Hôtel, © (08) 820150, and **Black Jack Disco** in the Hôtel Agadir, © (08) 841525, are usually the most lively. Both open 9pm–5am and charge admission. There is also the **Central** in the Tagadirt complex on Blvd 20 Aout. Gamblers appreciate the **Casino Le Mirage**, in the Village Valtur beach complex, © (08) 840634, which is open for blackjack, gaming machines and roulette 9pm–4am daily.

Of quite a different order are the music bars and restaurants along the **beachfront promenade**. Start at Place Al Amal with its nut, sausage and brochette vendors, and walk on down past a long line of restaurants and bars. **Don Vito's**, © (08) 842225, **La Cote D'Or** and **D'Agadir**, © (08) 840610 all employ musicians from time to time. Halfway along the beach strip is the **Jour et Nuit**, © (08) 840248, the first such place on the beach and the only one that stays open throughout the night, gradually collecting all the sleepless souls. At the far, port end, the **Coréen** (Korean) **Jazzbar** with its distinctive atmosphere (and also open very late) marks the end of the strip. If you don't feel like spending a night in a hotel, these two places, facing the moonlit deserted beach, are a kind of preparation for a dawn bus departure.

For another type of entertainment again, **Sahara Tours**, © (08) 840634/840421, on Av du Général Kettani, organize ***Fantasia*** evenings, with cabaret turns, tented dinners and pyrotechnical cavalry charges, in a number of sites just outside the city.

North of Agadir

Tarhazoute

The **beach** at Tarhazoute/Taghagaut is a mere 16km north of Agadir. Its broad sweep of clear, pale sand in a sheltered bay is a justly celebrated alternative to hotel-dominated Agadir. At the centre of the bay, hardly visible from the road, is a **campsite**, the only accommodation—divided so that families stay on one side and other groups in a separate compound on another. Beyond it, on the beach front, there are a couple of café-restaurants and a grocery stall. The rock terrace on the north side of the bay is covered with the palm leaf umbrellas of the **Sables d'Or Restaurant** where, beer in hand, you can watch the sun descend.

Beyond is the **village**, a small, unpretentious roadside affair whose life is based around three cafés: the Florida, the de la Paix and the Café Gibraltar, the last of which is opposite the other two in one of the arches of the vegetable souk.

Tarhazoute has entered into hippie mythology as a centre for cheap winter living. The rocky coves of the coast provide camping sites and driftwood, whilst the surf provides exhilarating sport. The village is the social centre for this community, where meat, kif and vegetables are easily bought. The colony's busiest days have gone, though an obstinate rearguard of the acid revolution remains, mixing uneasily with the current generation of earnest European students. One or two genuine bums can normally be discovered in the mélange. The police have forbidden the renting of rooms in the village, and once in a while they clear the coast, driving herds of muttering free spirits into the restrictions of an official campsite. Their traditional camping grounds are north of the village, where the atmosphere of mild degeneracy ends at a rock bluff just north of the old anchor warehouse, the Almadraba Bou-Inden.

Another group of Europeans has drawn its camper vans up on the shore of Tarhazoute. The retired divide themselves into strict language and nationality compounds like some echo of the Crusades. They pickle themselves on spirits, sun and romantic fiction, adding a *frisson* to their adventure with the whispered tale of Germans hanged in Inezgane, a rumour that circulated as far back as the 1930s. Throughout the months of June, July and August, both these groups are swamped by Moroccan families escaping from the cities. They settle in one vast encampment by the seaside throughout the long summer holiday.

Amesnaz Beach, 11km north of Tarhazoute, is the last stretch of open sand and reasonably safe swimming before you reach **Cape Rhir** (or Ghir). This dramatic, wave-dashed headland 40km from Agadir is where the High Atlas meets the Atlantic, marked by a lighthouse. It also marks an ancient Berber tribal boundary. To the north are the lands of the Haha Confederation (*see* p..268), while east and south stretches the highland territory of the Ida-Outanane.

Imouzzèr-des-Ida-Outanane

To visit the hilltop village of Imouzzèr and its mesmerizing waterfall, take a right turn just before Tamrhakht, 12km out of Agadir on the P8 coast road. The journey is reward enough in itself, taking you up through a series of climatic belts from bananas and palms, then olives and grenadines that shade plots of winter barley and summer maize and past gnarled trunks of argan and thuja on the mountain slopes until you reach the neat trunks of almonds and apples in the mountains. A single-track tarmac mountain road, the 7002, twists through dramatic scenery for 50km to Imouzzèr, its turnings lined with banana stalls and quiet cafés. The banana plantations give the area its nickname—Banana Valley—but the most beautiful stretch comes when the plantations are replaced by palm trees, and the road runs beside the smooth river-polished rocks, limestone gorges and bathing pools of the Asif Tamrhakht. At the roadside, hollowed-out palm trunks are sold as curious but largely inadequate buckets and flower pots. Halfway through this area of palms is the **Café de la Palmeraie**, a delightfully relaxed hut surrounded by a clearing where you can eat a cheap rabbit *tagine* lunch.

The **Café-Restaurant-Hôtel Tifrit**, a few kilometres further on (about 40km from Agadir), is a more substantial place. The dining terrace is beside a pool and overlooks the stream and the lush valley floor. It is managed by Chez Zenid and family, who watch over the roadside shop, cook and look after their few guests, lodged in reasonably-priced rooms. The Tifrit marks the end of the palm gorge and the beginning of the long climb up to the mountain plateau and the village of Imouzzèr.

Imouzzèr-des-Ida-Outanane is a white mountain top administrative village which contrasts with the red stone and pisé hamlets that are scattered throughout the territory of the Ida-Outanane. A Berber tribal confederation, they have always occupied the western reaches of the High Atlas and have a reputation for industry, cultivating the most remote mountain valleys and grazing the highest slopes. Despite the fact that the Ida-Outanane were almost fully occupied by their own struggle against the environment, they still managed to throw some surplus energies into an intimate patchwork of local feuds. In all this they represent a typical, balanced Berber commonwealth, and enjoyed practical independence from governments and national history until the arrival of the French in the region in 1927.

The **souk** is held here on Thursdays, an absorbing, busy place in early summer, for Imouzzèr is celebrated for its honey. The bees, housed in natural hives made from great cane pods screened from the sun by bouquets of drying herbs, feed from an exotic range of mountain flowers. Honey made purely from marjoram or marijuana is greatly prized for its medicinal qualities, though aficionados relish the mixed aroma of a highland blend. A **honey festival** organised by the Agadir tourist office is held each year in the middle of August.

A left turn at the central *Caidat*, the dramatically sited office of the *caid* built on a cliff-edge stalagmite, takes you down a twisting narrow road 4km to the roomy **Café Restaurant le Miel**, surrounded by displays of cheap minerals and fossils. From here it is only a short walk through olive groves to the foot of the **waterfalls**. The Imouzzèr or Tinkert Falls are not dramatic for their volume of water, which never exceeds three healthy streams, but because of their rock formations, pools and heady air of mystery. The rich mineral content of the river has caused, over millennia, great blanket sheets of rock to be draped down over the mountains where the water has passed. Even living bushes and mosses can be seen encased in a stiffening layer of tufa deposit, and the viscous water appears to slide in reluctant waves rather than plummet. The blanket of deposited rock has been rent in places to reveal secretive dripping caves glistening with wet moss and fern. Strange, powerful, intriguing shapes are formed within the shadows.

The central fall of the three collects in a plunge pool before rushing down a natural rock-cut sluice to enter a perfect grotto. Here golden polished rocks with soft intricate curves loom up from the secretive depths through a deep pool of deathless blue water. This beautiful natural swimming pool is set in an enveloping bowl of oozing tufa rocks, greened by small growths of moss and hedged with dangling fig branches. It is an enchanting place, serene and mysterious when empty, but with a certain pagan charm even when full of sportive swimmers, high divers and bathers basking on the rocks. For sites further north, *see* pp.266–70.

Where to Stay

moderate

Imouzzèr has one hotel, the **Des Cascades**, ✆ (08) 842671, ℻ 821671, a delightful place perched on a natural mountain terrace (1170 metres high) which enjoys a magnificent view. On a clear day the sun can be watched as it declines through a cleft in the mountains to set in the Atlantic. The hotel is surrounded by a garden watered with chuckling rills and shaded with mature trees, with paths leading downhill past lilies and roses to the pool and tennis court and out to the natural rock pools of the river. The hotel is gradually expanding under the direction of its engaging local proprietor, Jamal Atbir Eddine. Breakfast, with home-baked breads and pancakes and half a dozen homemade jams and honeys, is served on the terrace. Lunch, which attracts a busy passing trade, is a buffet, while the calmer dinner is served in the dining room, with the tables littered with petals and warmed by fires in winter. Accomodation is only offered on half- or full-board rates: a double room for two at full board would work out at around 1400dh.

expeditions

The Des Cascades hotel also organises a number of walking expeditions into the fascinating hinterland. These can be simple day trips, or one- or two-night stopovers in local kasbahs and a converted shepherd's cottage in the highlands. Downstream destinations include the village of Tidili, the waterfall-fed rock pools by the koubba of Sidi Ali Izm, the Jebel Tanzourt circuit, the Tiskijji palm groves and the natural bridge just north of Assif el Had. The latter, lit by a sklight from a Piranesi print, planted with olive trees and beloved by nesting rock pigeons, is filled by the clear waters of a mountain stream. Heading further up-country from the hotel there is a highland walk along the Tarhrout and El Jrouf spur that passes through such villages as Tikki and apple-growing Imizer to reach Argana on one of the High Atlas roads to Marrakech. CLM or Best of Morocco can book you in for a week of walking broken by idle days recovering at the hotel. For a five-day expedition (meals, lodging, guides and mules inclusive) think in terms of 5700dh a person.

East of Agadir

Taroudannt is 80km from Agadir along the P32, the route used by all the bus companies. On Thursday you can break the journey halfway at **Oulad-Teïma** in order to visit the **souk.** Travelling by car you could also take a longer but more interesting journey along the Marrakech road, the P40, which climbs below the argan-covered foothills of Jbel Lgouz. After this stretch, a right turn onto the 7016 39km out of Agadir will take you onto the back road into Taroudannt. Near the village of **Sidi-Moussa** and visible from the road are the ruins of the ***caid's* garden**, an overgrown walled enclosure that makes an ideal picnic spot with its ruined towers, paths, tanks and wildlife.

Taroudannt

Taroudannt is enclosed by an enormous rectangle of golden battlemented walls, threaded with fortified towers. These walls are some of the best preserved in Morocco, and the chief architectural glory of the city. Olive and orange groves spread out in all directions from the very foot of the defences. High Atlas peaks rise up to the north behind the city, while the Anti-Atlas mountains to the south are often obscured by a vapour that rises from the verdant intensity of the Sous Valley.

Taroudannt has always been at the centre of the politics of the Sous Valley, and it enjoyed a brief period of national eminence in the 16th century. In 1510 Mohammed Al-Qaim, the first Saadian sheik and originally from the Drâa Valley, was invested as emir of the south. Taroudannt acted as his headquarters, though he and his two sons, who led armies in the

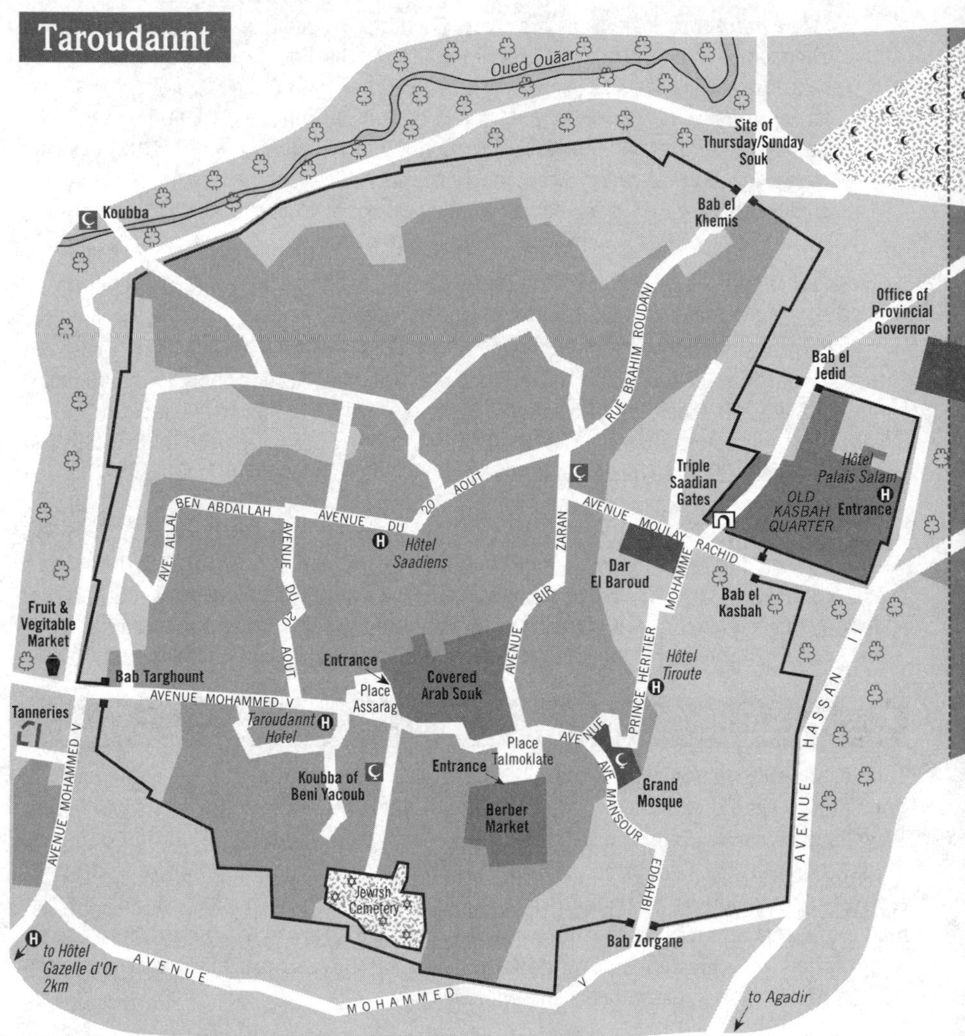

holy war against both the Portuguese and the corrupt regime in Fès, were seldom resident for long. The Saadian capture of Marrakech in 1524 and Agadir in 1541 shortly reduced Taroudannt to an honoured but secondary role.

Aside from this moment of glory it has played two unchanging roles: chief market town of the Sous, and a strategic citadel commanding the major trade routes. It has, even more than Marrakech, an African rather than Mediterranean identity. Its ancient walls contain not a venerable city of monuments but a market in a constant state of flux. The modern houses inside the spectacular walls are anti-climactic, but the central souk is one of the most enchanting and relaxing in Morocco. Taroudannt has the best cooking in the south and a number of excellent hotels. It has never appealed to the bulk of the tourist trade, and consequently there are comparatively few foreigners about. All the better.

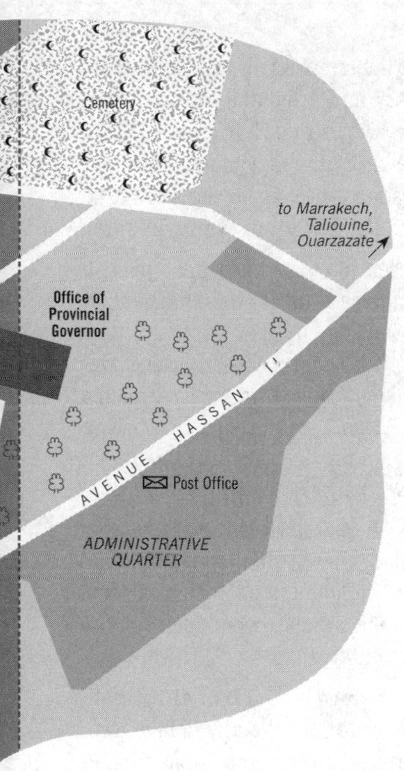

Getting Around

by bus

CTM buses leave from Place Assarag (their ticket office is in the Hôtel les Arcades) while most SATAS buses and those of other smaller companies usually leave from Place Talmoklate.

There are four CTM buses a day west to Agadir (currently at 5am, 10.30am, 2.30pm and 5.30pm) and five east to Taliouine (90mins) and on to Ouarzazate (3hrs). The quickest way to Marrakech (6hrs) is via the Agadir road on the 5am departure. The most dramatic way is on the 5am SATAS departure for Marrakech that goes over the magnificent Tizi-n-Test and arrives at around 1pm. On Wednesdays and Saturdays there is a SATAS 8am departure for Tata (about 8hrs), though this goes against the grain by departing from Place Assarag.

by grand taxi

These operate out of Place Talmoklate and Bab el Kasbah. There is an established system of linked places in taxis as you head east or west of the city. Heading west you will probably have to change at Oulad-Teïma for Agadir/Inezgane; heading east changes at Oulad-Berhil, Aoulouz, Taliouine and Tazenakht are possible before you arrive at Ouarzazate.

by bicycle

Cycles can be hired from the Hotel Palais Salaam, or from a shop in the western corner of Place Assarag, near the Hôtel Taroudannt.

Orientation

Taroudannt has hardly spilled beyond its ancient walls, and is not a difficult city to walk in. Roads into the town inevitably lead to one of the two central squares, Place Talmoklate and Place Assarag, which are just 250m apart. Blue *petits taxis* for local trips gather in Place Talmoklate, and the local souks open off it into a labyrinth of rough *fondouqs* and manufacturing stalls.

The main street of the town, lined with shops and cafés appealing largely to local custom, runs from the northwest corner of Place Talmoklate to Place Assarag. This square is the hub of travellers' Taroudannt, partly covered with café tables and lined by cheaper hotels and banks. The bar of the Hôtel Taroudannt, the entrance to the tourist souk, *grands taxis* and the SATAS bus depot are all to be found here.

The Ramparts

Horse-drawn carriages which can take you on a 5km tour of the ramparts, or just to the souk, can be found outside the gates of the Palais Salaam Hotel. Ask for Rachid and his sleek black horse Tixas, which pulls carriage no 4. Try and pay only 30dh a ride, but do not let the bargaining put you off taking as many journeys as possible, one of which should be by the light of the moon. On Thursdays and Sundays you can ask to be taken to the busy rural market that spills over the ground between the cemetery and Bab el Khemis (Thursday gate).

Taroudannt has few buildings of age or interest, for it has seen too many pillaging armies. It was last sacked as recently as 1913, though it was Sultan Moulay Ismaïl in the 17th century who was responsible for the destruction of the glittering Saadian city. For the first fifteen years of his reign he could not rest secure while his nephew, Ahmed ibn Mahrez, ruled over southern Morocco from Taroudannt. Ahmed was a skilful general and seems to have been a popular ruler, particularly when compared to his uncle. When Taroudannt finally fell to Moulay Ismaïl in 1687 he spared neither man, beast nor building. Only the walls were left standing, and the ruined, burned-out city was repopulated with a garrison of Riffi soldiers.

The great glory of Taroudannt is its walls. Their colour looks best at dusk, when the hues of gold, pink and orange contrast perfectly with the olive-green of the surrounding groves. The walls have been repaired whenever required, and substantially follow the original line as first laid out by the Almoravids. Small parts date from Merenid and Saadian rebuilding, but the major overhaul of the city's defences took place in the 18th century.

The indented, battlemented main entrance to Taroudannt, guarded by the **Bab el Kasbah**, is just south of the Palais Salaam hotel. The approach to the gate is flanked by orange trees which from March to April bathe the area with the rich perfume of orange blossom. A hundred yards on your right, having passed through Bab el Kasbah, is the surviving Saadian gatehouse. It is an elaborate version of a bayonet entrance, with three separate arches guarding two inner courtyards. Originally guards manned each of the four lockable gates, iron plated and riveted, which are now jammed open by time. An old fountain stands just to the left of the last arch within the old kasbah compound, now an indistinctive dusty residential quarter with some administrative buildings sited before the Bab el Jedid. The remains of the old governor's palace are now inextricably incorporated into the Palais Salaam.

Dominating the south side of Av Moulay Rachid is the imposing mass of the **Dar el Baroud** (the house of gunpowder). This old government building was last occupied by Moulay Abdullah, King Hassan's flamboyant, playboy younger brother, who used it to stage a number of his more memorable parties.

In the heyday of the Saadian Empire Sultan Mansour established in each regional centre of Morocco—Fès, Meknès, Taroudannt—as well as in his capital of Marrakech a gunpowder mill, an armoury and a foundry, where bronze cannon could be cast from a mixture of 80% copper and 20% tin. These metals of war, especially the tin, had to be imported. In exchange Morocco had vast supplies of saltpetre (potassium nitrate), and so dominated this vital trade that throughout the 16th century it was often known in Europe by the slang name of couscous. *Barud*, the Arabic name for gunpowder, seems to have been derived from *burada*, iron filings, and was being knowledgeably described by Moorish commentators such as Ibn Al Baytar in 1240. Although most historians belive that the first proper cannon were developed in the Middle East in the early 14th century, there is evidence of a simultaneous, if not earlier Moroccan invention. Ibn Khaldoun describes the Merenid siege of Sijilmassa in 1274 when 'the Sultan installed gunpowder engines whihc project small balls of iron. These balls are ejected from a chamber placed in front of a kindling fire of gunpowder'.

From the corner of the Dar el Baroud trot along Av Prince Heritier Sidi Mohammed towards the grand mosque, with glittering tiles in the Spanish rather than the Moroccan *zellij* tradition. From there the street sweeps past Place Tamoklate to Place Assarag and the souk. To the south of the Place a track leads towards a dusty square, sometimes filled in the evening with grill cafés and children's fairground rides, alongside the attractive old koubba of the Beni Yacoub saints. Passing beside the Taroudannt hotel, Av Mohammed V leads from Place Assarag to Bab Targhount, outside of which stands a vegetable market and the Tanneries.

The Souk

The entrance to the tourist or Arab souk is by the Banque Marocaine on Place Assarag. It is small compared to those of Fès and Marrakech, but is perhaps the most enjoyable to shop in. You can afford to wander aimlessly, for the size and temper of the town discourages hard hassle. Down the first turning on the left you can buy **incense**, **spices** and **dried roses**.

Taroudannt is the chief city of the Chleuh, with their long tradition of excellent craftsmanship. It is, along with Tiznit, one of the best places to buy or commission **native Berber jewellery**. The worked silver has a solidity and confidence of style which is not easy to find elsewhere. **Strap sandles**, like those worn by Roman legionaries, are made at souk stalls.

You will also see the usual incised grey marble 'African' **animal carvings**, but of much greater interest is the work of **Taroudannt sculptors** who prefer the warm colours of locally mined limestone. The linear and decorative obsession of Moorish art has been rejected in favour of firm, rotund figurative work. The studio workshops are well worth looking out for, and their prices are not extravagant. If you're keen on the local **cloaks**, whether the heavy ochre brown of a shepherd's burnous or the finer and lighter black wool ones complete with cavalier hoods and tassles, they can also be bargained for. Other things difficult to find elsewhere but perhaps a more specialized taste are the cured **skins** of wild Atlas **mountain foxes**, those of smaller predators and the usual **goat** and **sheep-skins**.

While in the souk ask to be shown the shop of **Lichir El Houssaine** at 36 and 37 Souk Smata, ✆ (08) 852145, 551680. It is a labryinth of rooms with as good a stock of antiques as you will find anywhere in Morocco. Before you start boasting of your connections and insider trading knowledge, have a glimpse at the visitors' book, filled with the names of august dealers from Bond Street and elsewhere in Europe.

On the southern edge of Place Talmoklate there is another smaller, cheaper covered market with a neat grid of alleys, and known locally as the **Marché Berbère**. This has its own fascination, though it is the people, the odd bolts of light, tatty beams and erratic sun screens that appeal rather as much as the goods, which are largely directed to the needs of local shoppers, interspersed with one or two tourist bazaars.

The Tanneries

The skins for sale at Taroudannt are cured just outside the city walls—turn left out of Bab Targhount (opposite the vegetable market) and right after 100m to reach the sign 'La Tannerie'. Though nothing like as impressive in scale and complexity as the ones in Fès or Marrakech, the distinctive vats, procedures and odours have a continual fascination. The morning is the best time to see them in action. Allow yourself to be led into the stalls that surround the dusty tannery courtyard, for the artisan-proprietors offer comparatively good prices on belts, sandles and the rather fetching leather satchels dyed the traditional babouche yellow. For those into skins, there are foxes, jackals, sheepskins, goats, cowhides and even whole camels, as well as fox wraps and fox hats.

Where to Stay

luxury

La Gazelle d'Or , ✆ (08) 852039, ℻ 852654, is the most exclusive hotel in Morocco. It was converted from a house built by a French baron just before World War II. It is 2km out of Taroudannt, first left at the petrol station on the road south to Amezgou. A semi-circle of ten cottages flank the central dining room, isolated in ten hectares of garden, with lawns still cut by hand. Breakfast is served on your porch, and a buffet lunch is prepared by the pool, surrounded by an orange grove and with a fine view of the High Atlas. There is a small stable of Arab horses for the use of guests, few of whom can drag themselves out of the grounds. Dinner is excellent, served by waiters dressed like acolytes for a sacred feast. Apart from price the major problem is that three-quarters of the guests are British. This can give this small, otherwise totally delightful hotel the atmosphere of an unfriendly house party, where all the guests give each other glacial smiles; if you're feeling murderous it would be the perfect setting for an Agatha Christie whodunnit. It is closed in July and August; telephone bookings are often refused; non-residents should dress up if they hope to be welcomed in for a meal or a drink.

expensive

The **Palais Salaam Hôtel**, ✆ (08) 852130, ℻ 852654, is another spectacular hotel, well-signposted and approached through its own gate in the city walls just off the road to Ouarzazate. The 19th-century palace of the pacha of Taroudannt, it is both the most interesting and accessible interior in Taroudannt and an outstanding hotel. Silhouetted battlements enclose the whole complex and overlook its main mihrab-shaped pool, surrounded by a luxuriant garden of high palms. The old rooms all open onto small verdant Moorish courtyards, and have an unusual split-level design with the sleeping area upstairs. The new rooms are designed to look like a medina street, and are larger and more expensive. The public rooms retain the original decoration of the palace, which is intimate rather than grandiose, and the dignified service and friendly environment attracts guests for weeks rather than just a passing night. During the daytime some of the more stuffy guests escape to the second pool in order to avoid the tour groups who are allowed in to look at this historic monument. In season you can eat at tables scattered around the terrapin pool and serpent fountain.

A variable price range on rooms means that this hotel can be either very expensive (if you stay in a suite in the new wing), or moderate if you opt for an old room.

moderate

The **Hôtel Saadiens**, © (08) 852589, @ 852118, on Bordj Oumansour has 57 rooms, a downstairs café, a terrace and licenced restaurant upstairs and a small pool round the back. It is a pleasant and clean place in the centre of town, and popular with adventure tours.

inexpensive

The **Hôtel Taroudannt,** © (08) 852416, is on the eastern corner of Place Assarag. It has 31 rooms that open onto a garden courtyard covered in masses of bougainvillea. Right in the middle of town, it has a street bar, a good licenced restaurant and a worn, relaxed, distinctive character, like its proprietor. A second address in this category is the **Hotel Tiout**, a clean new place on Av Prince Sidi Mohammed, © (08) 850341.

cheap

In Place Assarag, among others, there is the **Roudani** (ex de la Place), © (08) 852219. Ask for bedrooms 9, 10, 11 and 12, which open out onto a roof terrace where you can take breakfast overlooking the square. Another useful address is the **Hôtel les Arcades**, © (08) 852373, which has a restaurant downstairs. Place Talmoklate contains the small **Hôtel Mentaga**, © (08) 852383, and **Hôtel Restaurant El Warda**, © (08) 852763, which has balconies that overlook the square. You can eat a three-course menu in its animated first-floor café or on the terrace, and take breakfast out in the smart *pâtisserie* on the ground floor.

Eating Out

expensive

For those evenings when there is something to celebrate—like someone else paying—see if there is a table available at **La Gazelle d'Or**, © (08) 852039.

moderate

The licenced **Hôtel Taroudannt** will give you a delicious four-course meal from a Moroccan or French menu. The **Hôtel Saadiens** is also licenced and serves its Moroccan menu on a balcony overlooking the street. Eating in the evening at the **Palais Salaam** should start with a cocktail at the pool-side bar. You will usually need to have booked in the morning, and selected any of the more complicated dishes in advance. Avoid lunch, when the hotel can be swamped by the passing coach trade.

cheap

Taroudannt is renowned for its cooking, and you can eat well at any stall café in the city. On Sidi Mohammed, the street between the two squares, there are a number of hole-in-the-wall café-restaurants which produce plates of fried fish with spiced olives.

In Place Assarag among the places you can sit down for a meal are the **Roudani** and **Les Arcades**, with **El Warda** and **Restaurant Tout Va Bien** on Place Talmoklate. The latter serves particularly good *couscous*, and you can bring your own wine. The **Café Nada** on Rue Ferk Lahbab stays open at all hours serving *harira* and *tagine*.

Around Taroudannt

Kasbah de Freïja

To get to Freïja, drive 8km east of Taroudannt to Aït-Yazza and turn right for the Sous riverbed. The bridge has been down for years, but you should have no difficulty crossing the gravel bed. The kasbah has a spectacular position on the south bank overlooking the ford. It is now an inhabited farm building, but you can wander up a snaking path and descend through prickly pear hedges past a **koubba**. Below on the other side of the road are the ruins of an extensive palace, also inhabited, and which shelters within its walls a village school.

Tioute Oasis

The Tioute turning right off the Tata road is 18km on from the Freïja crossing of the Sous. About 9km of gravel track takes you to the half-dozen hamlets that comprise Tioute, enclosed by a verdant palm grove that is hemmed in by the surrounding hills. In this beautiful hidden valley are the ruins of the extensive ***caid's* kasbah**, on a promontory of high land just beyond the village. The kasbah was part of the extensive feudal holdings of the Glaoui Empire, and though it was damaged by the 1960 Agadir earthquake there are a few surviving rooms that retain their painted plaster decoration. North from the kasbah, the juxtaposition of a stone-paved threshing floor, a koubba set against a backdrop of palms, and the distant peaks of the High Atlas provides one of the most famous views of the Sous Valley. A large, modern **restaurant** has recently been built next to the kasbah. Be warned that though you can now have a meal or a coffee in Tioute you can also be joined by a coach tour out from Agadir. The ruins of the ***mellah***, the old Jewish quarter, are found a little further up the valley, beside a spring that is trapped to fill a tank. A venerated rabbi from this community is buried below the walls of a ruined agadir that crowns the nearby hill. The villagers identify this agadir as an old Portuguese fort, and though there are no records that support this it is odd to find bricks being used in this region.

Amagour Crater

Amagour is 40km south of Taroudannt, but only the first half of the journey is on tarmac, though in dry conditions it is accessible in a normal vehicle. Having packed a picnic, leave Taroudannt on the main road to Agadir. Directly after the crossing of the river Sous turn left on to route 7027 and then, almost immediately, turn right down a small tarmac road (the 7040) to Adouar and Souk-el-Arba-d'Assads. Keep straight on for 8km then turn left, at a large but illegible concrete signpost, on to the 7041. Then head towards the marble mine of **Assads**, which appears to be a white hill at this distance. At the mine fork left down a very rough track to Amagour, and park in the village centre behind the small mosque.

You will be met by an assortment of guides who will walk you up to the crater. It is a delightful place where mineral-rich water from undergound springs oozes up to fill pools beneath the natural bridges, tunnels, caverns and other weird rock formations of this extinct volcano. African hornbills nest in the craters, but you needn't be too worried about disturbing them. They seem to be used to the weekend visits of schoolchildren, and the government has appointed wardens to protect the rich wildlife of the surrounding foothills.

Taroudannt to Taliouine

A new road, the 7027, has been opened on the south side of the Sous Valley to provide the quickest way east from Taroudannt to Taliouine. If you have time, though, you might care to stay on the old P32 and admire some of the foothill villages on the way.

Ouled Aïssa, 26km east of Taroudannt, is a pleasant, verdant village with a kasbah, on the right-hand side of the road. The village of **Ouled Berhil** is another 9km east. Watch out for the signs to the historic house, **Riad Hida**, the old kasbah of the 19th century pasha Hida, which stands down a dirt road about 1km south of the town centre. It passed into the hands of a French *colonne* before being acquired by Kastberg Borge, a former officer of the Danish royal guard. He had retired to Morocco to cure his rheumatism, but once cured decided never to leave. On his death about seven years ago he left the kasbah to his Moroccan companion of many years, Lafici, a champion cyclist. He is now running the kasbah, complete with a wonderful courtyard garden, elegant Moorish rooms and pavilion as a moderately priced **hotel and restaurant**, ✆ (08) 531044. It would provide a delightful, slightly offbeat base for a holiday or walking north into the foothills of Jbel Tichka. The turning for the **Tizi-n-Test** is 53km from Taroudannt, and the start of one of the most spectacular roads in Morocco, leading you across the High Atlas to Marrakech (*see* pp.429–39).

The village and shrine of **Sidi Amel** is 6km before Aoulouz, along a short track leading up to the right. The white minaret of the mosque can be seen from the road. The guardian and the schoolteacher are humorous, welcoming men always ready to entertain the odd visitor with a glass of tea, and Sidi Amel is high enough to offer clear views back over the tropical-looking Sous Valley. The guardian will happily show you into the mosque's worn *sahn* with its well of fresh, cool water. The shrine of Sidi Amel is separate from the mosque, identifiable by an elegant koubba. The *moussem* held here in the last four days of the year is a survival from old Berber and Western European rites, when the new year was calculated on the European solar calendar rather than as it is now in Morocco, on the Islamic lunar cycle.

Aoulouz, on the south side of the river Sous, is a small but busy market town. The **souk** is on Sundays and Wednesdays, the market square and village centre being just to the east of the main road. There are beds available from the basic **Café-Restaurant Sous**. On the northern edge of town, just beside the bridge, is an inhabited four-towered **kasbah**, which has delicate exterior stalactite plasterwork on the upper towers. It is delightfully situated, with the Sous riverbed breaking through the mountain wall behind.

Taliouine

You will notice before you arrive at Taliouine that there are no longer any argan trees. This Soussi tree has its easternmost frontier at the kasbah of Iouzioua–Ounneïne. Taliouine, halfway between Taroudannt and Ouarzazate, is often ignored by travellers rushing to the dubious attractions of Ouarzazate. It is a beautiful steep-walled oasis valley full of almond trees, with agadirs, high villages and kasbahs perched on bleak hills echoing architectural details across to each other. The clean, cool mountain air makes it an exciting place to walk. If you have begun to fall for this stark, noble landscape you could consider booking yourself onto a five-day expedition up into the Jbel Siroua.

The **Glaoui kasbah** sits conspicuously on the valley floor just east of the village, a massive palace surrounded by carefully cultivated terraces shaded by thin almond trees. Four square towers feature shell motifs cut in plaster above the windows. The caretaker (a strange title for one who inhabits a disintegrating domain) lives in the tower, with his television aerial protruding. The surrounding courtyards and additional outbuildings are occupied by 25 families of ex-servants of the Glaoui, who are normally happy to talk and show you around the exterior. The small detached pavilion on the hill was used as an estate office, where rent was gathered in coin and kind.

Orientation

Taroudannt to Ouarzazate buses stop in the main village, where there is a football pitch, a big restaurant for hosting tour groups, a *hammam*, a simple café with rooms and a *grand taxi* stand offering places east to Tazenakht and west to Ouled Berhil.

Where To Stay and Eating Out

At the east end of Taliouine, by the kasbah, there are two contrasting hotels: the expensive Hôtel Ibn Tumert and the simple Auberge Souktana.

expensive

Hôtel Ibn Tumert, ✆ 30 through the post office, is a low, open, modern, red stucco building with a featureless interior. The view of the kasbah and the surrounding mountains is superb, and it has a large pool, a bar and a good restaurant. It has 106 rooms, but usually hardly any guests.

inexpensive

The **Auberge Souktana**, on the left of the main road below the kasbah, going east, is a delightful alternative. Get there early to make sure you get one of the four bedrooms, though in summer you can camp in the garden if not. The Auberge is run by Jadid Ahmed and his French wife Michelle, and has a relaxed and friendly atmosphere. Electricity and showers have recently replaced candles and shared barrels of water, but dinner is still served communally and at a leisurely pace.

The Jbel Siroua

The Jbel Siroua range of hills stretches to the north of Taliouine. The empty volcanic crater of the summit at 3304m is touched all year round with snow. It was a sacred mountain to the Masmuda Berbers, and is the junction of the two great ranges, the High Atlas and the Anti-Atlas. Bulls were once sacrificed every year at its summit, and pools of animal blood have still been seen recently near the crater. The mountain is the territory of the Aït-Ouaouzighte, a semi-nomadic tribe who move in the summer to the higher slopes for new crops and pasture. Their villages are austere dry-stone creations crowned by agadirs that are still used to store wool, cereals and carpets when the inhabitants seasonally migrate. At this time, a saint from the Tamegroute zaouia is invoked to protect the agadirs, and two guardians are left behind with a complete code of bye-laws for their administration. Well water and freshly baked bread are available from the villages. Some have a schoolmaster who will speak French, though he will be on holiday from June through August. Otherwise navigation and communication in this area can be difficult, and there are more tracks and villages with similar names than will appear on any map.

Jadid Ahmed of the Auberge Souktana in Taliouine organizes five-day expeditions to Jbel Siroua. These are usually planned well in advance for specific groups booked through travel agencies in the spring or autumn months. The usual route is to stay a night at the villages of Akhtamana, Tamgoute and Atougga for the climb to the summit, with a two-day return to the road by one of a number of local routes.

East to the Oasis Valleys

The road climbs out of Taliouine through the progressively bleaker hills of the Anti-Atlas, a cluster of mosques and koubbas at **Irhahi** (or Irhaki-Tinfat) the sole distraction. With a sufficiently robust vehicle you could, about 16km east of Taliouine, take the rough route 6837 south for 30km to visit the cliff-embedded **agadir of Ifri-n-Imadidene** outside the village of Agadir-Melloul. The Tizi-n-Taghatine pass at 1886m divides the watersheds of the Sous and the Drâa, though it seems to make no difference at all in this forbidding, waterless landscape.

Tazenakht is mostly enjoyed as a brief coffee stop, a passing refuge from the heat and savage landscape. It is however justly famous for its **carpets, rugs and kilims**, which are woven and knotted in the surrounding hill villages. If you are up early enough you can witness the local trade in the souk enclosure on Saturday mornings. Otherwise there are half a dozen dealers in town in addition to the roadside courtyard co-operative lined with over a dozen booths. Here you can sip tea and haggle over hard-wearing black-and-white-striped kilims, or the distinctive carpets of the Ouzguita women. The harsh geometric designs with vivid lozenges and diamonds are a hallmark of highland carpets, supposedly reflecting the dominating pattern of the mountains, their harsh silhouettes and bold forms.

Tazenakht is also a convenient base for a couple of desert crossings to the east. It has a reliable petrol station, a Banque Populaire and two cheap restaurants that also double as very basic hotels. You may want to stay over at either the **Hôtel Zenaga**, ✆ 32 through the post office, or the **Café-Restaurant Etoile**.

Routes from Tazenakht

East to Agdz (*see also* p.462): Follow the S510, a tarmac road which heads east for 38km to the mine at Bou-Azzer. About 9km further east take a left turn, which quickly deteriorates into a dirt track that follows the Tamsift Valley for about 48km to make a wonderful alternative approach to the village of Agdz in the Drâa Valley.

South to Foum-Zguid: About 22km out of Tazenakht on the S510 a turning leads south for 70km along a new road (the 6810) to the **oasis** of Foum-Zguid. This is now accessible by bus—one heads south from Tazenakht three times a week. Foum-Zguid is at its liveliest on Thursday mornings, for the **souk**. This is also the best time to catch a place in a lorry (*camionette*) taxi to Zagora (120km to the east) or Tata (142km west). If you have your own sturdy vehicle you can follow these truck-taxis as unofficial guides over the desert tracks.

If you do take either of these routes you will not have missed much. Apart from gathering small sheets of translucent mica that get blown on to thorn hedges there is little of interest on the **road to Ouarzazate**. Twenty-eight km north of Tazenakht a dirt track (the 6801) from the village of **Anezal** provides an opportunity for an adventurous trip to the villages and agadirs of the Ouzguita tribe on the slopes of Jbel Siroua. The riverbeds of the Tamgra and the Tamassint, just before Anezal, have small patches of palm and oleander to shade a picnic.

Fifty-three kilometres beyond Tazenakht the bridge over the Iriri was swept away by the full flood of the river in March 1988, taking a lorry with it. The previous November the Finnish ambassador and his wife were drowned east of Zagora in a similar flash flood. Water when it comes to the desert is as dangerous as when there is none. The bridge has been repaired, and here the P32 road east splits. For the Tizi-n-Tichka pass north to Marrakech, *see* pp.443–8; for Ouarzazate and Aït-Benhaddou, *see* pp.452–60.

South of Agadir

Beyond Inezgane and Aït Melloul, you leave the populated estuary of the Sous for the open road to Tiznit. The **forest of Ademine**, a belt of scrub wilderness which you pass through quickly on the edge of the Sous Valley, is the snake-charmers' favoured area for hunting for new twisting, rearing performers. The undulating coastal plain of the Sous is farmed by the Chtouka tribe of the Chleuh Berbers. This was once a dry grassland prairie, but the water from the Youssef ben Tachfine Dam on the river Massa now allows many more crops to be raised during the spring and autumn.

Tifnit

Thirty-three km out of Agadir, a turning to the west takes you 10km down a tarmac track, the 7048, to the beach at Tifnit. The village is a curious alternative community that attracts a drifting population of camper-vans, hippies, local soldiers and fishermen. An anarchy of low, grey, stone huts, it has been built on a sand spit that extends out to sea, and looks like a fledgling Phoenician colony. Low doors, wells, drifting sand dunes and the inherent complication of the pathways reassert the Moorish style after Agadir's international boulevards. A basic café exists amongst it all, with a sand terrace and floor threatened by every high tide. You can live off fresh water from the well, fresh fish and bread.

Sidi Rbat

Back on the road to Tiznit, look out for a right turn, 6km beyond the village of Tiferhal, signposted for Tassila. A deteriorating track at Tassila leads on for 8km to the small village of Massa and the divine isolation of **Sidi Rbat**. Massa, which is now just a line of farmers' plots leading down to the estuary, was in the 17th century a thriving port much visited by Genoese and Portuguese traders. There is a **ruined agadir** to explore which has recently been joined by a small but useful **hotel**, the **Tassila**.

The Massa flows down out of the Anti-Atlas mountains to this wide brackish estuary, sealed from the sea by a tidal sand bar and surrounded on both sides by dunes. It holds an astonishing wealth of **wildlife** and is a **sanctuary for migrating birds**. At dusk, flight after flight comes to the water, and geese congregate, silhouetted on the skyline of the southern dunes. The frogs too cannot be ignored, as their chorus becomes almost deafeningly vociferous.

The **Complexe et Balnéaire Sidi Rbat**, ✆ 94 through the post office, is one of the most glorious places to camp in the whole of Morocco. It is fortunately further on along the beach, out of earshot of the frogs, and a coastal breeze keeps the midges at bay. Rooms are also available around the open courtyard, which houses a café, bar and restaurant. Even after a week of walking along the empty beach exploring the cliff escarpments—where fishermen have carved shelters—and the protected dunes full of wildlife it is a difficult place to leave.

Men of Destiny

Sidi Rbat has earned itself a mythical place in the history books on several accounts. It is the beach where the Arab conqueror Uqba ben Nafi rode his horse into the sea to show Allah that there was no land further west for him to conquer for the true faith. The siting of an *r'bat* here, a fortified monastery for the propagation of the faith, shows that conversion was not immediate, and in fact Islam was not widespread in this area until after the 11th century. The beach is also believed to be where the prophet Jonah was disgorged by the whale. There is a more sinister tradition that states that the man of destiny, the Antichrist, will first be recognized at Sidi Rbat, rising naked and sublimely beautiful from the sea. Staying here, you begin to understand something of the nature of myth-making.

Returning back onto the Agadir to Tiznit road, an assortment of kasbahs and forts of every age guards the strategic crossing of the river Massa. Armed soldiers on the bridge give a sense of historical continuity.

Tiznit

On the arid edge of the Sous Plain, facing the foothills of the Anti-Atlas, stands the city of Tiznit. The approach road passes modern silos and pylons, but the heart of the city is still the medina, encased in a complete circuit of over five kilometres of massive pink-ochre walls.

Tiznit was founded by Sultan Moulay Hassan (1873–94) in the hope of creating a new centre of stability in the dissident south after he had destroyed the power of Tazeroualt. The sultan encased over a dozen existing kasbahs in the present walls and established the city's reputation for jewellery by settling Jewish craftsmen within them. Tiznit is now the provincial capital, with 45,000 people. Though only 5 per cent of the surrounding province is cultivated, chiefly with argan and almond trees, there are over 250,000 farmers in the hinterland.

Within its walls Tiznit is a delightful town to explore. At dawn or dusk the pink-brown walls of houses and the light blue of windows and doors flicker and glow in harmony with the heavens. Once you have survived, or good-naturedly surrendered to, the attempt to take you to a jewellery workshop (with shop attached) Tiznit is empty of student-guides and you can happily wander around getting lost in the old streets. Portions of the pre-city kasbahs jostle amid the street pattern in pleasant contrast to recently-built breeze-block houses.

Getting Around

Buses arrive and depart from the *Méchouar*, the rectangular square just within the city walls. There are two buses a day going east to Tata (7hrs) and two south to Ifni

(2hrs). At least half a dozen buses daily run north to Agadir/Inezgane and south to Guelmim (2–3hrs), including a cooler 5am departure. There are four buses to Tafraoute (3hrs) and a direct CTM coach to Casablanca, currently at 8am.

Grands taxis are found on Av Hassan II, in the central square about 100m from the main gates of the walled city. For the more established routes a *grand taxi* is almost as cheap as, and more convenient than, a bus. There are places available to Ifni, Guelmim (2hrs) and Inezgane/Agadir, and Land Rover taxis to Tafraoute.

Orientation

The *Méchouar* is at the heart of the medina through an entrance guarded by a splendid pair of tall towers pierced by three windows. The **Banque Populaire** and the best café-restaurants are all in the *Méchouar*, but the larger cafés lie on the Boulevard Hassan II outside the gate. Opposite the gate is the square where buses arrive and depart, and where you will also find the **post office** and CTM Hotel.

The Thursday **souk** is held just out of town on the Tafraoute road and is well worth attending in the growing season.

The Méchouar

Tiznit has a deserved reputation for craftsmanship, and particularly for metalwork and silver jewellery. Between the *Méchouar* and the outer wall is the **jewellers' souk** (*Souk des Bijoutiers*) where you will find a profusion of bracelets, necklaces, rings and brooches in both traditional Berber and contemporary Moroccan styles. The Soussi merchants entice you into their bejewelled lairs, plying you with mint tea and sales patter. The hand of Fatima, a symbol of good luck which wards off the evil eye, is a constant motif. It is an ancient symbol that was part of the regalia of the Assyrian kings and has been included into the Muslim heritage by being named after the chief lady of Islam, Fatima, the daughter of the Prophet.

The Grand Mosque and the Lalla Tiznit spring

From the *Méchouar* square head down the comparatively wide Rue de la Baine Maure alley, and when you reach an arcaded road (officially Tasoukt el Khemis) turn right. Walking along the arcade, lined with fruit salesmen (but hiding an old cemetery in the centre of the town), take the first left down a narrow road entirely fenced in by high walls, then continue straight ahead to reach the **Grand Mosque** on your right. The minaret of the mosque is studded with curious little perches. An odd tradition says that the souls of the dead rest here in order to gain virtue by their proximity to the prayers of the faithful. This is not at all in line with orthodox teaching, which dictates that souls wait for the Day of Judgement with no more sense of the passing centuries than a good night's sleep. However if you can discreetly linger during the evening and listen to the women chanting, it becomes understandable that the souls should wish to congregate here. Though the architecture is unusual in Morocco, 'perched mosques' are common south of the Sahara. There is a good example in Timbuktu.

Alongside the mosque, hidden behind the walls of one of the kasbahs that stood here before Sultan Moulay Hassan founded the city, but visited by women supplicants, lies the tomb of Lalla Tiznit; just to the west across the street is the spring that also bears her name, known as

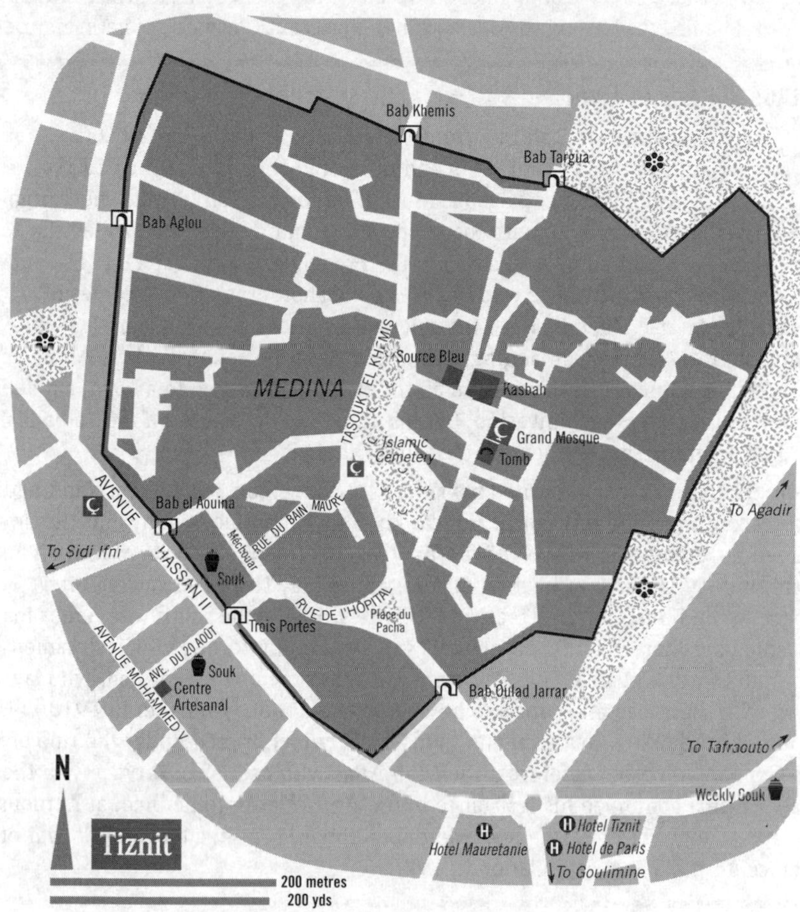

the ***Source Bleu***, where clear blue water once filled a natural basin. Lalla Tiznit was a Mary Magdalene type, a reformed prostitute who became strong in faith. She was martyred, but Allah recognized her holiness and marked her death by creating a cool refreshing spring. The pool is now more often than not a dismal shade of stagnant green emeshed in concrete. All over the world concrete seems to be the normal fate of any site associated with a miracle.

From the pool carry on, take a left and then a right in order to reappear on the main arcaded street. To your right there is a clear view down to a semi-circular recent opening in the walls by the Bab el Khemis. Both it and the next gate east, Bab Targua, have inside staircases that are still just about safe and roofs that provide a precarious view over part of the town and the decaying walls that once divided up the valuable and now dwindling olive groves outside.

Walking back up the main arcade of Tasoukt el Khemis you will pass on your right the entrance to Kasbah Idaoukknoun, another of the original pre-urban communities of Tiznit. Passing a new mosque with tall minaret you can continue up to the triangular garden known as Place du Pacha. There is nothing here to recall its turbulent history, when El Hiba was acclaimed sultan by the blue-robed Saharan tribes, the Tekna, Reguibat, Tidrarin and Delim.

The Blue Sultans of Tiznit

Among Moroccans Tiznit is strongly associated with the dynasty of Saharan warriors Ma el Ainin and his son El-Hiba (*see also* pp.573–6). Ma el Ainin was a courageous Muslim nationalist, an Idrissid sheik from the Western Sahara who with the support of Sultan Moulay Hassan led the desert tribes in fierce opposition to the French. From his capital at Es-Semara, he opposed the French advance into the Western Sahara from their colonies of Senegal and Algeria. When in 1910 the rulers of Morocco proved themselves incapable of opposing the French landings in the centre of the country, Ma el Ainin declared himself Sultan. He summoned all the tribes of Morocco to a *jihad*, a defensive holy war against the French invasion, but his army was destroyed on the Tadla Plain. He retired south to Tiznit, where he died that October.

His son El-Hiba, who had inherited his father's striking looks, intelligence and natural authority continued the resistance. He was known as the Blue Sultan, since he never discarded his *litham*, the indigo veil worn by Saharan men. He declared himself Sultan at Tiznit in May 1912, after hearing that Sultan Moulay Hafid had surrendered Morocco to the French in the Treaty of Fès. The whole of the south rose under his leadership, and Marrakech threw open its gates to his holy army, which streamed north from there to liberate Fès. The army was massacred by the French, who lay waiting with their machine guns and howitzers at Sidi-Bou-Othmane. In 1913 El-Hiba was ousted from first Taroudannt and then Tiznit, which passed under the rule of Si Taieb Gondaffi, a Berber chief from the High Atlas who had taken service with the French. El Hiba continued his resistance in the Anti-Atlas until he died, at Kerdous, in 1919. His younger brother, the poet Merebbi Rebbou, continued a guerrilla war of resistance until his final capitulation in 1926.

Where To Stay and Eating Out

moderate

The **Tiznit Hôtel**, ✆ (08) 862411, fax 862119, is just off the main crossroads on the road to Tafraoute, the Rue Bir Enzarn. Rooms face into an interior courtyard (cooler on the ground floor) thick with maze-like rosemary hedges around a low pool where there is a popular beer bar that serves snacks. You can eat in the large Moorish dining-room, looking west towards the walled town. In the evening you can watch the desert traffic; trucks filled up with the tents, goats and sheep of the nomad shepherds, packed coaches and military vehicles.

inexpensive

The **De Paris**, ✆ (08) 862865, is a new 20-room hotel that stands on the west side of the crossroads. It has a popular restaurant but no bar. The **Hôtel Mauritania**, ✆ (08) 862072, is on the left of the Guelmim road, close to the Tiznit Hotel. It has a restaurant, a raffish atmosphere, 16 bedrooms and the town's busiest bar.

cheap

The **CTM Hôtel**, © (08) 862211, is outside the town walls facing the post office on the large dusty bus square. It is clean, offers rooms with showers and has a good, cheerful little restaurant on the first floor.

Inside the walls there are a number of small pleasant hotels around the *Méchouar*. There is little to choose between them, but the **Hôtel Atlas**, © (08) 862060, is the most popular and vies with the **Restaurant Bon Accueil** for the best and most varied *tagines* in their pleasant ground-floor cafés. A second choice is the **Hôtel Belle Vue**, © (08) 862109, on Rue du Bain Maure northeast from the *Méchouar*.

Sport and Festivals

Tennis can be played at a court on the road to Mirhelt and you can pay to use the Tiznit Hotel **pool**, though the sea is close enough.

The ***moussem*** of Sidi-Abd-er-Rahmane is held in August in Tiznit. The ***moussem*** of Sidi Ahmed ou Moussa, six days in August, is the great festival for acrobats, and is held 35km east of Tiznit off the Tafraoute road.

Aglou-Plage (Sidi-Moussa-d'Aglou)

You can hitch a lift on the lorries that shuttle the 17km to pick up building sand from Aglou for Tiznit, though taxis are probably more convenient. At first, this coastal village (joined by a recent rash of bourgeois summer villas) appears to be dominated by electric cables, one of which is rather mysteriously connected to a distinctive, whitewashed **koubba**. Sidi Lahcen, the disciple of Sidi Ahmed ou Moussa, apparently requires electric light at his shrine alongside votive candles.

Facing the sea, the best **beach** is on your left, where the acrobats of Tiznit practise on the wet sand. To your right is a lagoon surrounded by curiously weathered rocks, beyond which a path leads to wavedashed shelves on which local fishermen perch. Houses with elaborate portals and doors have been tunnelled into the sandstone cliffs to make a **troglodyte village**.

Where to Stay

The long-established Motel Aglou has closed down, but just inland the new cafe-resturant-hotel **Amaragh**, © (08) 866196, is arising to take its place. Ask there for Lahcen Aguerten, a charming English-speaking mountain guide, if you would like to explore the nearby mountains and coast.

Route Choices from Tiznit

From Tiznit there are three equally enticing choices. The southern coastal route takes you through Ifni on the way to Guelmim, the gateway to the Western Sahara. The road due east leads inland to Tafraoute in the heart of the Anti-Atlas mountains and from there back to Agadir. Due south the Tata circuit can take you through a broad sweep of oasis settlements on the edge of the Sahara and the Anti-Atlas mountains to bring you round to Taroudannt through a much longer circuit.

The Coastal Route through Ifni to Guelmim

The 7064 leads southwest from Tiznit through the village of **Arba-Sahel** to the coast at Gourizim. The road twists violently, so that the Atlantic shifts constantly in and out of view.

Mirleft

This friendly, hospitable village (also spelt Mighleft and Mirhelt) is served by a dazzling array of beaches. It is set back nearly a kilometre from the shore and initially appears a rather unattractive jumble of block-like houses. A single yellow arcaded main street contains a string of cheap alternative hotels and a small covered vegetable market. Above the village crowning the hill is a **French fort** in an attractive-looking state of ruin. The view is worth the climb, but the interior consists only of a fairly recently deserted barracks and stables. Some interesting pornographic graffiti and drawings of mermaids can be seen in the far corner.

Staying in the relaxed atmosphere of Mirleft you have a choice of six **beaches**, known locally as Fish Beach, Camping Beach, Coquillage Beach, Hotel Aftas Beach (only open in high summer), Plage Sauvage and Marabout's Beach. The last, three km from the hotels, is the most dramatic, if a little awe-inspiring to swim and sunbathe on. The **koubba complex of Sidi-Mohamed-ou-Abdallah** sits in front of a massive upsurge of igneous rock, rising up through the middle of the sandy beach with outlying tendrils of natural rock that form arches and caves. It's a very potent place from which to watch the sun sink.

Mirleft's appeal is very strong, and many people spend weeks just living here. A typical day takes in the late morning social at a café, a little shopping for fruit and vegetables, a hot walk down to a beach, supper on Hotel Aftas Beach and music back in 'town' in the evening.

From Mirleft the road wiggles above the Atlantic shore for 31km before reaching Ifni. A rough outer suburb (a memory of the ethnic divisions of colonial days) is planted on the north side of the river Ifni before you reach the town itself.

Where to Stay and Eating Out

Food and accommodation in Mirleft is all in the cheap range. The **Tafkout** is possibly the best hotel in town, but if it's full try the **du Sud** or **Farah** before going to the **Aftas**. The Tafkout has a roof terrace full of tanning flesh, and the downstairs café provides some cool nooks and day beds as well as a good basic menu. Every evening local boys play a vast range of music, from Syrian love songs to Madonna impersonations. On the beach of Sidi Mohammed about 3km south of town, there is the four-bedroom **Hôtel de la Plage**, ✆ and ℻ (08) 719050. You might try and book a room here in advance, and also enquire about the expeditions (walks and jeep tours) that they organise.

Sidi Ifni

Sidi Ifni is a lugubrious town, a tranquil vacuum perched on sea cliffs in which to while away the time. It is a Spanish-built town surrounded by old military barracks and high hills that existed as a Spanish enclave, a bastion of imperial pretension, from 1934 to 1969. The political isolation from this period is still palpable in this geographically isolated town, where

Hispano-Berber colonial architecture gently decays in the midst of a time warp, swathed in the recurrent Atlantic sea mists.

The Spanish relationship with Ifni is based on two small periods of rule separated by four hundred years of absence—a pattern repeated at many of the anchorages along the Saharan coast of Morocco. The Spanish crown took over the fort of Santa Cruz de la Mar Pequeña, which had been built as a commercial venture by merchants from the Canary Islands, in 1476. For a generation this isolated tower above the beach served as a secure base for slave-raiding expeditions into the interior. It was swept away by the Saadian-led jihad in 1524.

Three hundred and fifty years later the Spanish were granted the right by the 1860 Treaty of Tetouan to build a fishing station on the coast of Morocco opposite the Canaries. However they did not take advantage of this until the region had been pacified by the French, and only arrived to build the town of Ifni in 1934. They refused to surrender Ifni to the newly-independent Morocco in 1957, which led to a little-known but violent desert war. The Moroccan Liberation Army supported by local tribes stormed the outlying Spanish forts, but the town itself was successfully defended by the *Tercio*, the Spanish Foreign Legion. The Moroccan government cut all land communication with the enclave, which was eventually ceded back to Morocco in 1969.

Ifni is also haunted by the memory of an ill-fated Scotsman, George Glas, who in 1764 chose the ruins of the Spanish fort as the site for a trading post. The venture failed, the ship that took him away mutinied, and the crew stole his goods and cast his murdered body into the sea.

Getting Around

There are two CTM **buses** a day to and from Tiznit, a 2½hr journey. These depart at 7am and 2pm from Av Mohammed V, about 150m north of the post office. Local buses also cover this route, stopping at Mirleft, as well as the road south to Guelmim, but leave from a street corner about 50m east, inland from the post office.

Whatever your map may show, there is a good tarmac road to Ifni in both directions from Tiznit or Guelmim. Given the frequency of buses the easiest way to get there is by taking a place in a ***grand taxi*** from Guelmim or Tiznit. To leave Sidi Ifni, *grands taxis* depart from a layby off the Guelmim road, in the north-west corner of the town's regular grid of streets.

Sidi Ifni Town

There are no remaining traces of the Spanish slaving tower or George Glas' trading post to be found. The 20th-century Spanish town, weathered art deco, is however full enough of quirky architectural surprises. Place Hassan II, the old Plaza España, has a mature Andalusian garden and is ringed by the major buildings of interest. A camouflaged, closed Catholic church and the large locked-up Spanish consulate sum up the state of limbo the whole town is in. They lead to a broad baroque sea-cliff stairway to the beach which is in a prime state of wistful decay. Lanterns on either side are truncated at varying and random heights, and one or two of the fat balustrades have exploded. The concrete prow of a building in the shape of a boat looms high above the shore to threaten the Hôtel Aït Bamrane. The empty pool beside the hotel and a sign warning against bathing complete the bizarre pattern of neglect.

An all-weather dock was vitally important to Spanish Ifni, since it was isolated by a Moroccan land blockade from 1957. To this end the most quixotic of all the remaining structures of Ifni was built, a concrete island constructed some 700m out into the sea. A cable car rusting beneath the connecting pylons still links this extraordinary grey fortress port with the shore, though it is no longer in use. Since recovering Ifni in 1969 the Moroccan government has totally ignored this device and has just finished building a brand new fishing harbour.

The airport must have been a more practical solution to the blockade, though pilots would have had to deal with both banks of sea mist and the clouds which lower themselves off the surrounding hills. The airfield is now overgrown and grazed by herds of goats. The surrounding plethora of official military buildings are guarded by bored but armed soldiers.

A vegetable market operates every day in the small central **souk** in the town. On Sundays the market for the Aït-Bamrane tribe assembles above the airport, and includes a collection of clowns and magicians. The women of Ifni seem particularly beautiful, and wear wind-torn tie-dyed indigo haiks, navy blue and black. The local *moussem* is held at the end of June.

Where to Stay

Sidi Ifni's hotels are in the inexpensive range. The **Hôtel Aït Bamrane**, © (08) 875267, is on the small area of beach, Avenue de la Plage, a tranquil, almost deserted place which also has a bar and restaurant. The **Hôtel Belle Vue**, © (08) 875072, is on Place Hassan II and has comfortable bedrooms with views over the sea and a bright orange stucco interior. There are two bars, and beer is also served on the terrace overlooking the central garden. The restaurant serves fish in the summer when available. When I last stayed there it had decidedly eccentric plumbing—neither shower nor basin produced any water, but the lavatory bowl had the rare luxury of being flushed with hot water. The **Hôtel Suerte Loca**, © (08) 875350, is on Rue Moulay Youssef, with a good view of the sea from its terrace. Once the evening haunt of the Spanish Legion, it has recently been restored and now offers some comfortable rooms and a friendly café-restaurant.

Eating Out

The three hotels listed above can all serve good meals, particularly if you give them time to put a slow-cooked fish *tagine* together. If you have just arrived or are passing through, use the restaurant **Atlantic**, ✆ (08) 875086, at the northern end of Av el Houria (the main road into town) which is German-run and correspondingly efficient. For a simpler lunch use the café-restaurant **Tamimt** on Av Hassan II, just south of the vegetable market area in the centre of town. The **Houria Hotel** on Av Mohammed V can also run up a plate of chops, chips and salad on a good day.

Guelmim

From Ifni it is about 60km to Guelmim, an attractive journey through the hills. About 20km from Ifni a weekly souk is held on Wednesdays at the village of **Mesti**. (About 15km before Guelmim you pass the turning to the baths of Abeïno, *see* below.)

There are two Guelmims. On Saturday mornings it is a much-hyped but ultimately disappointing tourist destination: streams of day-trip coaches leave Agadir for Guelmim, 'the gateway to the Sahara and the camel souk of the blue men'. Otherwise normal Moroccans dress up as 'blue men' in order to act as desert guides or jewellery salesmen. The rest of the week Guelmim is a quiet administrative and market town of 150,000 people on the border between the sedentary farming of the Anti-Atlas and the pastoral nomadism of the Western Sahara. A gentle, relaxed town, where visiting farmers and teachers are happy to talk to you about the realities of desert life—of waking up in the middle of a dark night with their new wife screaming with mysterious pain and not a doctor, a telephone or even a light anywhere in the wilderness for many miles. Its position has always been valued, since it commands the northern bank of the river Noun and a string of oasis settlements to the east, and was an important base for the Saharan caravan trade. Black hills overlook the town from the north where white stone emblems proclaim the three faiths: to God, King and Country.

The discovery of a trade route across the Sahara to the *Bilad as-Sudan*, the land of blacks, as it was known, was first made by the Berbers of the Draa and Noun rivers in the 8th century. Guelmim was the first centre of this profitable trade which swapped salt mined in the Sahara for West African gold, and it was a key link in the communications chain of the Almoravid Empire, which stretched in the 11th century from Spain to Ghana. Its position inevitably declined from these days of gold and glory. New Saharan trading routes were discovered, and the desert aristocracy of the Almoravid Empire was destroyed in 1147; nevertheless, even in the 19th century caravans were still being dispatched from Guelmim to Timbuktu. The abolition of the slave trade by the French in the 1930s destroyed the last remaining commodity of the Saharan trade. When the caravan trade had been active the Tekna and the Reguibat, the chief Berber tribes of this area of the Sahara—the 'blue men'— made a living by selling their 'protection' and their livestock to merchants at the great camel market of Guelmim. There was a continual demand for desert-reared camels, for even the most efficiently run caravan consumed a heavy toll of animals in a desert crossing.

Blue men have always excited much interest amongst tourists. It was a general description of all the tribes of Western and Central Sahara who had a penchant for wearing loose and long-flowing cotton robes dyed indigo. Their habitual use of turban and the *litham*, the desert veil worn by men, gave them a strikingly different appearance from the sedentary tribes of the Anti-Atlas. Even in the near-nakedness of the *hammam* they remain recognizably different and blue. The indigo dye is quite loosely fixed (wash separately if you buy your own desert veil) and easily leaks its colour on to sweaty flesh.

Getting Around

There are six **buses** a day to Tiznit (2½hrs) and three to Tan-Tan (3hrs). There are regular ***grand taxi*** connections north to Tiznit, with a possible change at Bouizakarne (2hrs). Heading south, Tan-Tan is a 2½hr taxi ride.

The Town Centre

Whichever direction you arrive from, north or south, you will find yourself in the central Place Bir Anzarane, a roundabout affair surrounded by the main cafés, the bank and the post office. Buses for Tiznit and Tan-Tan usually leave from here as well. Boulevard Mohammed V leads off downhill to the **souk**, otherwise known as Place Hassan II. This is overlooked by cafés with first-floor terraces. The entrance to the Café Khalima and the Café Ali Baba are off the passage to the souk. The shopping is remarkably low-key for such a celebrated market town. The meat market, with its joints of camel and hooves sold for stock, is worth a look.

From the souk, a climb up the slight rise to the **old kasbah**, an attractive pink pisé ruin, provides you with a good view of Guelmim and its surroundings. However, like many of Morocco's monuments, it suffers from being used as an outside lavatory.

The Guelmim Camel Market

No tourist brochure fails to mention the camel market. Where once the market of Guelmim must have been as full of deals as a secondhand car auction, camels as transportation died suddenly in the 1930s with the simultaneous ending of the slave trade and arrival of trucks in the region. Today they are raised purely for meat and status, and those that are paraded in front of tourists are not for a hard-working life in the desert, but for the butcher. In the last 20 years herds have been greatly depleted by long drought and the war in the Western Sahara. The much-visited Saturday market takes place between 7am and noon, just out of Guelmim on the road to Tan-Tan. In the growing season, from October to April, it is a bustling, lively affair. The upper compound is devoted to dry goods, the lower to livestock. Randy hobbled bulls rampage through corrals of sheep, goats and donkeys to get at beautiful cows. The farmers dress for the occasion, and spend most of the morning disparaging their neighbours' flocks. In high summer there is little happening in a Saharan agricultural market, but the camels are still paraded. Their eyelashes are a source of endless admiration and they earn a good income in photographic fees.

Sing to Your Camel

Camels came to the Sahara as weapons of war. The Persian Empire brought them from Asia in the 6th century BC, and Alexander the Great rode a camel across the Egyptian desert to visit the oracle of Zeus-Ammon at the oasis of Siwa. The first picture of a camel in Africa is that issued on a coin by Pompey's lieutenant, Lollius, in 64 BC. Camel breeding was only perfected in North Africa in the 5th century AD, and to this must go much of the credit for Islam's initial lightning advance. Arabian camels are not successful in a cold climate, which has been used partly to explain why the Berber tribes in the mountains effectively resisted Arab conquest, while those on the plains succumbed. Camels come in two shapes; the Bactrian two-humped, and the Arabian one-humped or dromedary. North African camels are all Arabian. There are an estimated 12 million in the world. They can live for 40 years, carry a 400lb cargo for 25 miles a day, and last 12 days without food and five without water, but can also drink a bathtub dry if given the opportunity. Sadly, with all these abilities improved by selective breeding, they are virtually incapable of sex without the assistance of man.

When camels appear fatigued on long journeys, they are sung to. There is a whole repertoire of such songs for a trio of voices, and 'it is worthy of observation how they renovate the camels, and the symphony and the time they keep surpasses what anyone would imagine'.

Exhibitions of Guedra Dancing

Guedra, the ancient dance of the women of the desert, is presented all over Guelmim for the benefit of tourists. The **Hôtel Salam** arranges dances on Saturday evening, and puts on daily lunch-time displays for coaches from Agadir in tents at the oasis of **Aït-Bekkou** (Aït-Boukha). On Saturdays at noon and 9pm there are performances at the **Mauritania** and **l'Ere Nouvelle** hotels. Though less reliable it is well worth checking the smaller and generally more intimate performances at the **Rendezvous des Hommes Bleus Café** on Friday night, and in high summer the hotel at Abeïno organizes the odd display on Saturdays. Guedra is performed on the knees, due to the low height of nomadic tents. It is a dance of the torso and arms and contains a traditional and extensive range of erotic references. The women of the desert were traditionally much freer than many of their Islamic sisters elsewhere. Tuareg women even had their own tents, where young warriors competed for their attention by reciting complimentary verses, performing heroic deeds and bestowing gifts of fresh meat. As a result Guedra was continually suppressed by Islamic reformers.

Accompanied by a deeply repetitive musical rhythm, in its natural habitat the dance has its own tantalizing pace, which requires all of the night and much of the following morning. The tourist performances are a mere introduction, and can seem a slightly depressing travesty when rows of slab-faced Europeans begin to look restless after half an hour, partly because the dancers are professional rather than inspired.

Where to Stay

If possible stay outside the town in one of a number of characterful places listed below; at Aït-Bekkou or Abeïno, or camp on Plage Blanche.

If you have to stay in town drop any idea of economy and go straight for the inexpensive **Hôtel Salam**, © (08) 872057, which overlooks the central crossroads of Av Hassan II and Route de Tan-Tan. It has about 20 bedrooms, a bar, restaurant and a fly-screened balcony. There are two functional but quite basic cheap hotels beside each other on Boulevard Mohammed V: **l'Ere Nouvelle**, © (08) 872119, and **La Jeunesse**, © (08) 872221.

Festivals

You could think about timing your arrival to coincide with one of the *moussems*: of Sidi Mohammed Ben Amar at Asrir at the end of May, and at Ksabi in mid-June; or that of Sid Laghazi at Guelmim at the end of June. There are, however, even larger concentrations of (other) tourists at the *moussems* than at the camel market.

Excursions from Guelmim

Guelmim only really comes alive as a destination once you leave it. There are several memorable trips to be made out from the town, to palm groves, a spa village with a hot spring, a beautiful deserted beach, and distant oases.

Asrir and Aït-Bekkou

A road leads 11km southeast of the town to the oasis village of Asrir, where the *moussem* of Sidi Mohammed Ben Amar takes place at the end of May. Asrir has always been an important desert centre, and a vestige of its old great July **camel market** is still held here every year, and attracts a great number of tourists. Traces of the pisé ksar walls are considered to be an 11th-century Almoravid foundation, for the core tribe of this dynasty were the Lemtuna, who then inhabited this region. Nearby is a watery pit where clay bricks are still shaped and left to bake out in the sun.

The road continues for 6km to Aït-Bekkou, a much larger oasis palm grove. Here you will probably be led by some charming child to have mint tea at home, and a look at some jewellery for sale. A baked track leads beyond the oasis upstream to a dam holding back an enchanting little lake. Campfires are made in the rock walls of the river terrace, where village boys come in the mornings to smoke the butts left behind by the camper-van tourists.

Abeïno

The **hot springs** of Abeïno are 15km north of Guelmim, up a right turn off the Ifni road. The spring by the koubba is now almost permanently dry, but the faithful still hang out fragments of sweat-stained cloth by the bush overhanging its dry cave.

The naturally-heated baths are well organized, however, and have two separate enclosures for men and women. A few dirhams lets you soak in a hot mineral pool while the sun bakes down on the corners of this open-air enclosure. Swimming trunks should be worn by men, and swimsuits or knickers by women. Black buckets are used for more personal washing. For a more direct experience of the holy water, you can lie naked in the steamy underground tunnel that issues from the baths.

Where to Stay

In Aït-Bekkou the moderately-priced **Tighmert**, © (08) 870353, is an impressive new hotel built in the style of a kasbah on the edge of the palm grove.

In Abeïno the inexpensive **Hôtel Abeïno** is pleasantly chaotic. It has two great thick-walled courtyards with rooms off them, areas to sit, a licensed restaurant and bar. You can **camp** in a small compound and get snacks from cafés in the village.

Bou-Jerif and Plage Blanche

Take the road from Guelmim to Ifni (the 7129) and about 4km later turn left on the 7101 to Tiséguenane, a good tarmac road. After the village there is about 20km of dirt road (passable in a normal car in dry weather) to the former **Foreign Legion fort** of Bou-Jerif (marked on maps as 'O.Noun') which sits on the south bank of the riverbed, known variously as the river Noun or the river Assaka. The fort has been converted into an **auberge** by an enterprising French couple, the Dreumonts, who offer meals, camping, simple accommodation and jeep expeditions. No phone, but postal bookings are possible: Bordj Bou-Jerif, BP 504, Guelmim.

From Bou-Jerif it is another 9km to the coast, where the **koubba of Foum-Assaka** watches over the estuary. This was the site of a rare example of Moroccan–Portuguese cooperation. In 1481 John II of Portugal accepted the sultan's invitation to build a fort here in order to evict the Castilians from the coast. To the south a completely empty coast, known as **Plage Blanche**, stretches for 80km between the estuaries of the Noun and the Drâa. Its emptiness is broken only by a remote fishing hamlet by the fort at Aoreora, and the odd group of campers.

If you follow the riverbed for about 9km southeast of Bou-Jerif you reach the river-cut limestone gorges of the Assaka (*see* below).

Assa

If you want to leave all traces of tourism and comfort behind, a tarmac road, the 7093, leads southeast for 108km from Guelmim to the total isolation of Assa, an ancient fortified Tekna camel and goat market. You pass through **Fask**, a s imple oasis community fringed by hills, where there is a café and petrol. You can also stop before Assa at **Targoumaït**, which is, in the words of an official posted there for two years, 'hot'. Bear in mind that there is no hotel anywhere along this route.

Tafraoute and the Anti-Atlas Mountains

The round trip to Tafraoute is one of the most classically beautiful journeys that you can make in Morocco. The astonishing grandeur of the Anti-Atlas mountains, the contrast between oasis greenery and bleak mountain slopes, and the extraordinary lunar landscape around Tafraoute are the major physical attractions. On the human side, the independence of the mountain Berbers, their dress and architecture and the welcoming tempo of their life woos you into a relaxing pace. This is an excellent opportunity to travel some out-of-the-way dirt roads if you have a car; if not, the walking around Tafraoute is a treat in itself.

Getting Around

There are a few hotels outside Tafraoute, but the town is the best base for any exploration of the Anti-Atlas. It is situated on a loop of road, route 7074, which runs from Tiznit to Agadir. It is 107km from Tiznit and 130km from Agadir.

There are four **buses** from Agadir to Tafraoute daily, and more on Wednesdays, when the **souk** is held. This direct journey takes about 5hrs. The approach from Tiznit is the most impressive route. Six buses leave Agadir for Tiznit a day (2hrs), and there are four from Tiznit to Tafraoute (3–6hrs). When leaving Tafraoute you have a choice of four buses to Agadir and three to Tiznit, daily.

Land Rover taxis occasionally make a run from Tiznit to Tafraoute and on to Irherm, which would make an exhilarating journey.

Tafraoute and the villages of the Ammeln

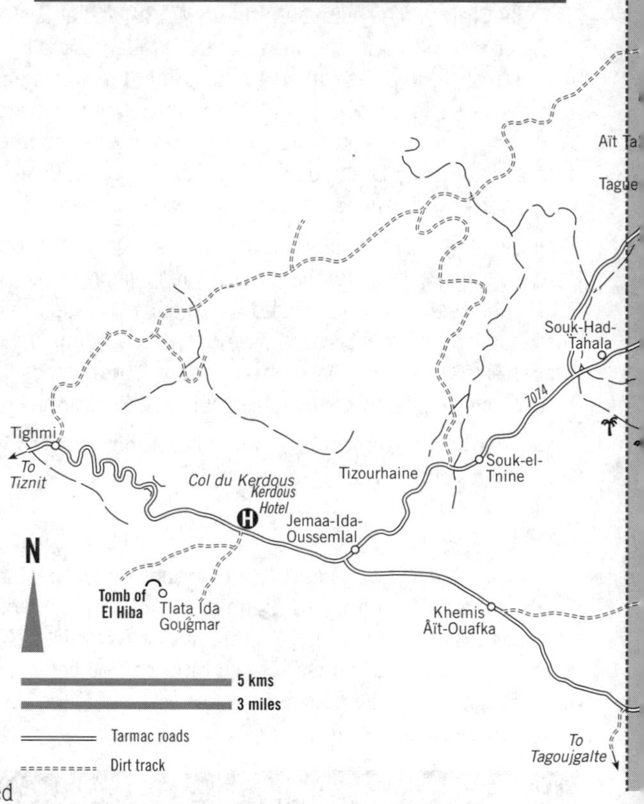

Into the Land of Tazeroualt

Twenty km east of Tiznit, where the coastal plain gives way to the foothills of the Anti-Atlas, is the village of **Assaka**. The road crosses the Tazeroualt river, which drains north into the Youssef ben Tachfine reservoir. Five **kasbahs** hug the fertile riverbed, and across the river a rough track leads 7km south to the **Souk-Sebt-d'Ouijjane**. Beyond Assaka the road penetrates into a steep gorge decorated with the strange twisting trunks of argan trees.

A right-hand turning 40km from Tiznit takes you 11km on a tarmac road to **Zaouia-Sidi-Ahmed-ou-Moussa**, a fascinating side-trip. Sidi Mohammed-ou-Moussa was an Idrissid marabout who founded the zaouia before his death in 1563. His son, Sidi Ali Bou Dmia, established the emirate of Tazeroualt, which in its heyday during the mid-17th century ruled over almost the entire south: the Sous, the Dadès and the Drâa. Sultan Moulay Hassan finally destroyed this principality in his campaign of 1882, founding Tiznit as the new bastion of central authority in the area. The kasbah of Illigh, the capital of Tazeroualt, was left in ruins, but the **zaouia** itself, only a few kilometres away, survives as a functioning religious centre.

The village has a small **souk** on Tuesdays, but is totally transformed for the ***moussem*** which starts on the third Thursday in August and lasts for six days. Acrobats in circuses all over the world come from this region, and Sidi Mohammed-ou-Moussa is their patron saint and protector. The *moussem* is their annual celebration. At other times of the year you can see them practising on nearby beaches, particularly at Aglou-Plage.

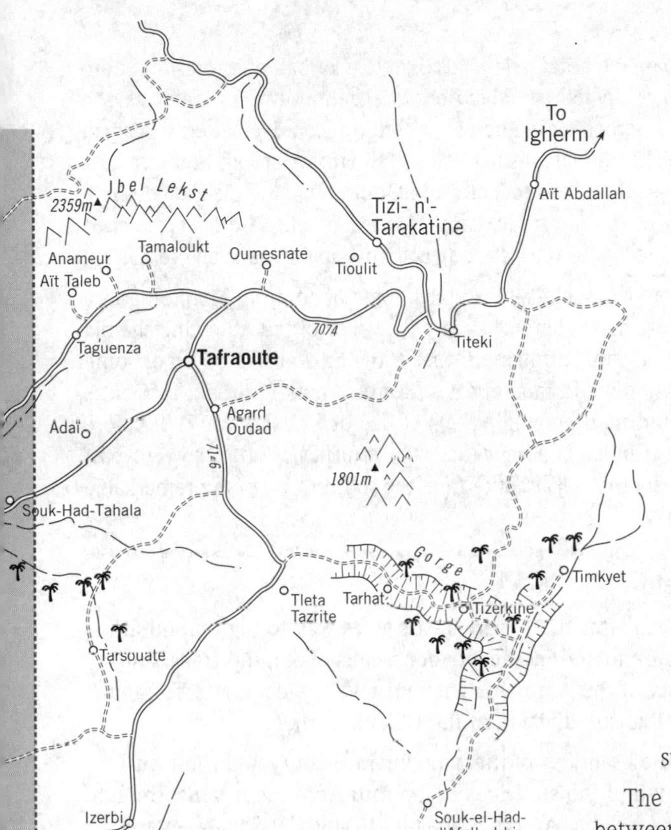

The village runs beside the dry bed of the stream, punctuated by deep stone wells from which women draw endless pitchers of water. The zaouia itself is the complex of whitewashed buildings that clusters around the mosque and its old tower. Sanctuary walls en close the burial hill above the village, and a gatehouse guards the approach to the green tiled pyramidal roof of the Sidi's tomb. A horse-shoe-arch arcade inside provides shade for the pilgrims, and a sacred way snakes up the hill past smaller stone tombs to the summit.

The large souk courtyard lies between this hill and the riverbed. Beside the river sits a pink café, just before two stone-arched bridges, one an attractive ruin, which indicate the rough track that in 6km leads to **Illigh** (or Anou-Illigh). Now largely abandoned, the site of the old capital of Tazeroualt is no more than hundreds of yards of decaying walls above the river bed. Scattered among the sleepy houses of the hamlet are the tombs of the various Idrissid marabout princes. To walk there, having crossed the river, turn left at the junction and then almost immediately right, up an unpromising track which climbs uphill over an arid goat-grazed steppe.

Kerdous

Tighmi, back on the main road, boasts the **Café Moderne**, a useful stop before advancing up the hairpin bends to the Col du Kerdous. This valley was the long-impregnable sanctuary of El-Hiba, the Blue Sultan, and his younger brother Merebbi Rebbou in their resistance to the French (*see* p.538). At the summit (1100m), the expensive **Kerdous Hotel**, ✆ (08) 862063, sits in an astonishing position with an eagle's-eye view over the valley. It has a small *mihrab*-shaped pool filled with river water, a good restaurant and a wonderfully tranquil feeling of isolation. It started life as a kasbah, then was an Islamic school until 1965, and opened in 1992 as a hotel. Ask for rooms 5 and 6, which have superb views.

A tarmac track turns right just past the hotel, and leads 3km to a kasbah of astonishing tranquillity. The wall above the heavy wooden studded door has been inset with green slate, a perfect example of the traditional Berber geometric and eyebrow decorative patterns. A small koubba and mosque lie to the right, the last resting place of **El-Hiba**. A rough track crosses over the stream bed and continues the 10km to **Tlata Ida Gougmar** (or Souk-Tleta-des-Ida-Gougmar). This used to be one of the old trading routes that led south from Taroudannt through the mountains to Ifrane-de-l'Anti-Atlas, starting point of Saharan caravan crossings.

Back on the main road the village of Jemaa-Ida-Oussemlal, some 65km from Tiznit, marks a junction of roads. Both provide dramatic approaches into the valley of the Ammeln. The old road, the 7074, passes through several Ammeln villages allowing you to stop off at some **local souks**. Souk el Tnine, 13km from Tafraoute, has a **Monday** market, Arba-n-Tafraoute, 4km further, has its souk on **Wednesdays** while Souk el Had de Tahala, just 7km before Tafraoute, buys and sells on **Sundays**. The new road, the resurfaced 7146, sweeps past Khmes aït Ouafka and Izerbi to approach Tafraoute from the south through the remarkable rock formations at Agard-Oudad.

The Territory of the Ammeln

As the mountain plateau after the Kerdous pass gives way to high mountain valleys, palm groves are joined by the slender trunks of almond trees, and you enter the territory of the Ammeln. The entire valley leading to Tafraoute is inhabited by this tribal sub-division of the Chleuh Berbers.

The Ammeln, thanks both to the grandeur of their mountain scenery and their business acumen, are the best known of the six tribes of the Anti-Atlas mountains, though the others—the Ida-ou-Gnidif, Aït-Baha, Aït-Mzal, Ida-ou-Ktir and Aït-Souab—were just as numerous. Until the 1920s they were habitually locked in furious inter village, clan and tribal feuds, although when faced by a common external threat they could field an army of 70,000 highlanders. All six of the tribes share a common mythology that recalls a golden past when they were but one prosperous, united people, made rich by the profits of the Tamdoult silver mine, near Akka. However, even then they were tight with their cash, and God punished their hard-heartedness with an earthquake. The silver mine was buried and they were forced into the barren hills to eke out a living in furious competition with each other.

Due to the especially limited resources of land and water in the area of the Jbel Lekst, the Ammeln developed a tradition of parsimony, discipline and emigration. They make outstanding grocers, and now run corner stores in practically every town and city in the country. They have the same proverbial financial caution and tenacious loyalty to their homeland that is elsewhere attributed to Scots and Jews. As a result, as you approach Tafraoute you will notice that the villages have a scattering of modern houses among the traditional pisé and stone architecture. They are often built by absent Tafraoutis, but are little used until retirement. Weddings and other family occasions are an excuse for week-long extravagant hospitality, and cosmopolitan reunions of Belgian miners, Tangier estate agents and wholesalers from Casablanca.

Tafraoute

In Tafraoute, due to expatriate prosperity, the pisé houses have been entirely replaced by large, modern, square red ones. The village of 1700 people is not, architecturally, very exciting. However, for several kilometres around Tafraoute you will have been aware of the bizarre and massive rock formations for which the area is so famous. From all over the village you can see, set off against the rich green of the oasis, glimpses of weird shapes in red and mauve granite, looking like meteorite showers on Mars. Soaring peaks and silhouetted rock fields, created in past millennia by slow cooling extrusions of igneous red lava, create illusions of gravity-defying rocks balanced precariously and improbably on thin summits. The ideal time to see this landscape is in mid-February, when the contrasting lush growth of barley and delicate almond blossom is at its peak.

You can effortlessly spend several days or weeks in Tafraoute, walking and exploring the surrounding souks, oasis villages, deserted hill top agadirs and mountain summits.

Dulcis and *Amara*

Almond trees are between four and ten metres high, with thin black sinuous branches, tight pink and white blossom and bright green, lance-shaped leaves. The fruit is green, drying into a leathery pouch with the familiar nut inside. It has two varieties: *dulcis*, the cultivated, edible variety, and *amara*, its wild sister, which grows tenaciously on high mountain slopes and produces a bitter narcotic oil spiced with poisonous prussic acid. The wood is reddish in colour and used for veneers. In mid-February you may be lucky enough to catch an almond blossom festival, the dates of which vary from year to year.

Orientation

Tafraoute is a small and totally relaxed town that is easy to stroll around. It has four hotels, a camp site, cafés, a *pâtisserie*, a *hammam*, a couple of bazaars, garages and a petrol station in its roughly triangular shape around the central square.

The **post office**, where you can make telephone calls, is on this square and is open Mon–Fri 8.30am–12 noon, 3–6.30pm. Behind it is a small but useful branch of the BMCE **bank**, which covers for the Wednesday-only service offered by the more conspicuous Banque Populaire. The weekly **souk**, on Wednesdays, is held out in a new roadside compound below the Hôtel les Amandiers.

The Villages of Jbel Lekst

The most celebrated area to walk in is the string of villages surrounded by spring-fed gardens nestling at the foot of the vast, towering, thousand-metre wall of Jbel Lekst (or El Kest). There are two dozen kasbahs, intricate braided irrigation ditches and walled terraced gardens with small orchards of fig, olive, almond and palm to explore. Though it does not matter enormously, perhaps the best place to start is at the village of **Oumesnat**, about 7km northeast of Tafraoute, approached along route 7147. Ask to be shown *La Maison Traditionelle*, a private museum which preserves an undisturbed traditional interior complete with all its objects. It is run by a young blind villager and his family (no admission, but tips expected). From Oumesnat you can wander on a network of paths through more than 27 villages. The new road, the 7148, now allows easy access to the west and east reaches of the valley. From the road you can follow individual tracks up to the **ksour of Tamalout**, **Anameur** where there is a natural spring-fed pool, **Tandelt**, **Tamaloukt** and **Aït-Taleb**, 14km from Oumesnat.

Rock Carvings

There are some fine prehistoric, and modern, rock carvings in the surrounding hills. The most easily accessible one, of a gazelle, is at the edge of the village of Tazka, a 2km walk southwest of Tafraoute on the road that leads past the souk and the Hotel les Amandiers. Another group is in the hamlet of Tirnmatmat, reached along a track northwest from Aït-Omar, itself on route 7148. Use local children in the villages to identify the carvings or book the services of a professional guide from the **Hôtel les Amandiers** or the **Hôtel Redouane**.

The Painted Rocks

Another trip, 4km south of Tafraoute on the new Tiznit road, is to the village of **Agard-Oudad** and the rock formation called 'Le Chapeau de Napoleon'. Considering that the French pacification of the Anti-Atlas in the 1930s was only achieved with a fair amount of indiscriminate aerial bombing it seems strange that the French should be so admired, though I have decided this particular name must be a joke (walk 500m south of the rock, and it looks just like a Barbary ape sucking its thumb). Continue another 2km or so on this road and you will pass a signpost to the **rock paintings** of the Belgian artist Jean Veran. They are a good 2km from the turning, but the walk acts like a slow musical movement, bringing you up to a terrace with a fine prospect over this bizarre, grandiloquent but satisfying gesture.

Tarhat Agadir and the Gorge

If you continue south beyond Agard-Oudad for another 3km and take the 7075 turning southeast, in 9km you will come to **Tlata Tasrite**, which has its market on Fridays. Leave your car or taxi on the rough track 4km east at the modern village of **Tarhat**, at the entrance of a striking and extensive gorge. The ruins of the old agadir are perched up on the mountain wall to the north of the village, and make a marvellous eyrie for a picnic. You can then continue walking along the floor of the gorge, turning back (if not before) when you reach the village of **Tizerkine**. Though this oasis valley now seems an isolated-enough corner of Morocco it was well placed in the past, for if you follow the valley down it leads eventually to Fam El Hisn (Foum el Hassan), one of the old entrepôts of the trans-Saharan trade.

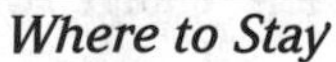

Where to Stay

The moderate-range **Hôtel les Amandiers**, ✆ (08) 800008, 📠 800343, is a mock kasbah which sits above the town with an undisturbed view of the fantastic surrounding rocks, and a varied garden. The rooms are spacious but simple, and there is a bar and restaurant, and a pool superbly located in a secluded rock garden.

The efficiently-run, inexpensive **Hôtel Tafraoute**, ✆ (08) 800121, on Place Moulay Rachid is a welcome new addition to the town. A little more upmarket is the **Salama** by the weekly souk, ✆ (08) 800026, 📠 800448. In the cheap range, there are two small, quite tatty hotels in the centre of town near the rich smells of the river bed which do, however, have quite decent restaurants. The **Tangier**, ✆ (08) 800033, is a bit tidier, and the **Redouane**, ✆ (08) 800006, cooler and slightly more spacious. Their showers usually work.

Eating Out

Tafraoute has a deserved reputation for careful and skilful cooking, and you can eat well throughout the town. A civilized three-course Moroccan menu with good service, wine and an unhurried atmosphere can be had for a moderate price at the **Hôtel les Amandiers.**

The **Restaurant l'Etoile du Sud** is cheap but has a certain intense style. It serves meals, after rosewater hand-baths, in a *caidal* tent in a garden littered with three broken old gramophones and other bits and pieces. **Café Atlas** at 2 Place du Marché is a less pretentious affair, though a band often drifts between tables. The house *hors d'oeuvre* is a delightful collection of indigenous flavours—three low bowls filled with local apricots, pure argan oil and *amallou*, a paste of argan oil and finely crushed almonds which you eat on bread. Otherwise they serve *harira*, vegetable *tagine* or chicken *tagines*. The **Tangier** and **Redouane** hotels also have good café-restaurants.

Northeast towards Igherm

Twenty km east of Tafraoute there is a turning to the right which leads you over the Tizi-n-Tarakatine pass at 1500m. The road is new and sweeps through the hills to the small village of **Aït-Abdallah**, where there is a **souk** on Wednesdays. A café is open all week but only prepares food on souk days. An old military kasbah fringed by wire defences sits above the village, but the skyline is dominated by the dramatic peaks of surrounding grey mountains.

The tarmac ends at the village, but a rough dirt track (the 7038), suitable for four-wheel drive, crosses the rounded red hills of the mountain plateau of the Iberkakene to **Igherm** (or Irherm), on the Tata–Taroudannt road. The mountain crests are crowned with crude, dry-stone agadirs, similar to the debased iron-age hill forts of Britain. A left-hand turning after Tiguermine leads you 3km to the fine **Agadir-Tasguent**, on the left before the village of **Et Tleta-des-Idouska**. Rejoining the main track you come upon an astonishing mountain panorama before **Azoura**, a village clinging to the side of a mountain and the centre for the Ida-ou-Zekri, a sedentary tribe who occupy over 75 ksour in the region. If you arrive at Igherm on a Friday, you will find the **souk** in progress (*see* below)

The Road to Agadir

The turning to Tizi-n-Tarakatine marks the end of the Tafraoute oasis, though the mountain scenery beyond remains dramatic. Argan trees cover the hills and small eminences are crowned with fortified farmhouses. These have an almost Apennine feel, whereas the stronger and more aloof agadirs have been compared to Greek mountain-top monasteries.

Thirty-six kilometres from Tafraoute a dirt road on the left will take a normal car to the **Thursday market** at Souk-Khemis-des-Ida-ou-Gnidif, whence a different track loops you back to the main road. The village of **Tioulit**, 46km from Tafraoute, is a spectacular example of the homeland of the Illalen, a confederation of 18 tribes who occupy the mountain plateau between Tafraoute and Aït-Baha. A **fortress** dominates the village from its magnificent position on an outcrop of rock. The agadirs of the Illalen are known to have contained as many as 300 compartments, in several storeys either side of a central aisle. Here families could safely store their valuables and grain. A custodian maintained propriety in the agadir, which was often used by the heads of families for council meetings and elections.

Aït-Baha, 82km from Tafraoute, is the old border between the Sous Plain and the rougher independent tribal lands of the Anti-Atlas. When Wyndham Lewis visited here in 1931 he remarked, 'A few kilometres further on was the ultimate frontier of Dissidence—that is to say the territory of the mountain cantons that have not made their submission to the French.' Aït-Baha has a **souk** on Wednesdays, and is served by two daily buses from Inezgane at 11am and 4pm. If you wish to stay here, the cheap and basic **Hôtel Café Tafraoute** has a pleasant, tranquil and cool interior.

Beyond is the territory of the Ikounda, one of the fifty fractions of the Achtouken who grazed the argan hills surrounding the Sous Valley. **Imi-Mqourn**, 'the great entrance', a key tariff-gathering spot on the old Saharan trading route, was theirs. They were pacified early by the French, allowing R. Montaigne, a Berber historian, to translate their rare written code for the management of communal agadirs. Every contingency was covered: 'He who fornicates with a she-ass inside the agadir, in view of the porter, or in view of any other witness, will pay a fine of 2 Dirkem to the Oumanas, and 3 *saas* of corn to the she-ass.' Few contemporary legal codes pay such respect to the outraged feelings of donkeys. **Biougra**, 33km from Agadir, is the centre of this steppe, and comes alive for the *moussem* of Sidi Said Cherif in May.

The Tata Circuit: Tiznit to Taroudannt

The Tata Circuit, a 520km journey from Tiznit to Taroudannt, has only been possible by regular bus since the opening of the Tata to Igherm stretch of road in 1988. It is a spectacular journey passing between the austere, scarred landscape of the Jbel Bani mountains and the edge of the Saharan plain, broken by a number of intriguing oasis settlements. This is a desert region, but it is a much more palatable introduction than heading south into the Western Sahara. The roads are good; they do not always follow exactly the routes shown on maps—of which no two are in total agreement—but on the main route there is no question of getting lost. The region has a freshness and charm as yet untouched by overfamiliarity with the ways of tourists, and a reputation for hospitality and interest in passing travellers. Though it is possible to stay at hotels or cafés in Bouizakarne, Ifrane-de-l'Anti-Atlas, Akka, Tata and Igherm, you may well find yourself invited to stay along the route by local people.

Tata is the principal oasis on the route, with a bank, a post office and some well-stocked shops. It also has the most comfortable hotel, the Renaissance, to use as a base for exploring the area, and the best food.

All the oasis settlements survive by tapping the underground drainage of the southern slopes of the Anti-Atlas. The oases occur at *khenegs*, breaches in the long wall of the Jbel Bani escarpment towards which the water flows. The escarpment runs from Tan-Tan to Zagora, dotted with settlements which used to form an important west–east trade route.

Getting Around

There is a twice daily **bus** service that connects Tiznit to Tata via Bouizakarne. These currently leave Tiznit at 4.30 and 11am, though the latter is hotter, and as it starts in Agadir may already be full. Onwards to Taroudannt (around 9hrs), there are buses from Tata on Thursdays and Mondays at 8am. In the other direction, there are buses from Taroudannt to Tata on Wednesdays and Sundays.

Grands taxis can be found to ferry you between Bouizakarne and Ifrane-de-l'Anti-Atlas, particularly on souk days, but otherwise they are thin on the ground. If you are hoping to hitch a lift or get a place in a *grand taxi* it is useful to remember that traffic will be going to Guelmim souk on Saturdays, to Bouizakarne and Igherm on Fridays and Ifrane-de-l'Anti-Atlas on Sundays. But more so than with many routes, the flexibility of a car (you can hire a Renault 4 in Agadir) greatly increases your options.

Tiznit to Bouizakarne

Fifteen kilometres out of Tiznit you reach the beautiful town of **Souk-el-Had-de-Reggada**, a collection of associated but rival ksour girt by strong exterior walls. A **koubba** is perfectly placed above the southern gateway, and a **souk** is held on Saturdays. Another fortified settlement, the village of **Talaïnt**, which has a **Wednesday souk**, lies left of the road 7km beyond El-Had. After Talaïnt you begin a steep climb to the pass of Tizi-Mighert at 1057m, where the twisted shapes of argan trees dominate the rough slopes. Beyond the pass a turning leads in 2km to the **Tuesday souk** at Tleta des Akhasass (or Souk-Tleta-des-Akhasass).

Bouizakarne

This town marks the foot of the southern slopes of the Anti-Atlas. By now palms have taken over from argan trees. The fortified exterior walls of this oasis have only recently been breached by the growth of the village, and it is strange to think that until as late as 1935 these walls served a vital purpose in protecting this agricultural village from the depradations of nomadic raiders. The palm groves are to the east of the village, an enchanting land where wheat, vegetables and cropped grass grow beneath the protective shade of palms. A few cafés are clustered around the Tata turning, from where a regular bus now operates to Ifrane-de-l'Anti-Atlas, 14km east. You can also catch taxis here. The **Friday souk** is easy to find, as loudspeakers now add to its bustle—it's at the south end of town beneath the town walls.

Where to Stay

The Café de la Poste used to have beds, but now directs you to the reasonably-priced **Hôtel Anti-Atlas**, © (08) 874134. This has a cool interior with card games in near continual progress, and looks out on to a sunbaked roadside terrace through three well-proportioned arches.

Ifrane-de-l'Anti-Atlas

Not marked on some maps, but just beneath Tabahnift, the village of Ifrane-de-l'Anti-Atlas is itself unexceptional. A long triple row of pink painted concrete and stone houses, it is a small, expanding administrative centre, whose *caid* governs a rural commune of 11,000 people. However, its setting is magnificent. Ifrane lies 10km north of the P30 road, 14km out from Bouizakarne, across a large bowl dotted with over 20 ksour that appear to be carved from the barren mountains. Above the village the exposed, twisting strata of the red and gold hills is matched by the colours of the strident exterior walls of the dozen ksour that exist in various states of decay just to the north of the new town. Verdant terraced plots, shaded by palms and olives, are ranged beside the white polished boulders of the riverbed.

Ifrane-de-l'Anti-Atlas is an ideal base for some leisurely exploration of desert life. East and west there are ksour, and a delightful **walled garden** stands to the east, below the red stones of a low volcanic hill. Knock repeatedly and the gardener should appear to show you around.

North of Ifrane, on the track to Tabahnift village you pass an old and increasingly ruined area of pisé **ksour**, surrounded in biblical juxtaposition by cemeteries and threshing grounds. Further along this road is a **Jewish necropolis**, visited once a year by the descendants of an ancient Jewish community now scattered in Tel Aviv, Casablanca, New York and Caracas. This track, the **old caravan route**, climbs for another 35km to the Kerdous pass (*see* above).

Ifrane's **souk** is on Sundays between 6am and noon, divided, as usual in Morocco, into areas of livestock, vegetables and dry goods. The chief attraction is not so much the wares on display as the immaculately dressed Berber farmers riding in from the surrounding country for this weekly social occasion. Hard-working farmers stroll hand in hand through the souk, their blue or white *gandouras* crossed by the shoulder strap of an embroidered satchel and a freshly laundered turban tightly bound around their heads. An air of ancient dignity, of grace, hospitality and tolerance hangs lightly over the population. A pair of exquisite men, their hats rakishly tilted and their eyes aggressively hennaed, wander through the agricultural market, nodding and greeting without a flicker of ridicule.

Where to Stay

There are a couple of very basic hotels in Ifrane. The **Café Restaurant de la Poste** is by the mosque at the top of the town and overlooks the river. The town's premier café is the **Café de la Paix**, where a number of bedrooms have been added above the first-floor tearoom.

Timoulaye, Tagmoute and Taghjicht

Back on the main road by the Ifrane turning, you pass **Timoulaye Ifla** (upstairs) and **Timoulaye Izder** (downstairs). The former is a minotaur's warren of ruined walls on the edge of an inhabited village, the latter a more fertile oasis palm grove guarded by a kasbah.

Twenty-six kilometres east of the Ifrane turning is the **oasis of Tagmoute**. The balcony of the **Café Bani**, beside the main road, provides the best opportunity this side of Tata for a lunch of omelette and salad, and accommodation is available in the **Hotel Taragno** on the outskirts of the village. A turning to the south off the main road leads through the palm grove, a tightly-packed ribbon of settlement sandwiched between twisted dark hills behind and wind-blown desiccation in front. You will find a few shops before the track continues to an outlying hamlet, which hosts a Sunday afternoon football match.

On the north side of the road is the long oasis of **Taghjicht**, its thin belt of palms and associated ksour largely hidden from view by mounds of baked clay and natural walls of mud.

Id-Aïssa, the Agadir of the Iznaguen

About 3km out of Tagmoute a left turn leads 10km through the **Taïnzert** palm grove to the Monday market of the Adaï tribe, **Souk-Tnine-d'Adaï** (there is a second, slightly shorter route some 15km later). The 12th-century **agadir of Iznaguen**, the fortified granary of the Aït-Assa, is a further 11km northeast at Id-Aïssa, or Amtoudi, along a dirt track through a palm-lined gorge. It occupies a prime strategic site, and its stone walls and gateway are in impressive condition considering this is probably one of the oldest surviving tribal forts in Morocco. The view is well worth the steep climb, or you can rent mules at the café below, where if you order a *tagine* it will wait simmering for your return. Be prepared to meet other tourists, as this is a popular excursion from Agadir. Further up the palm-shaded riverbed there is another agadir near a waterfall that fills natural swimming pools of polished rock.

Aït-Herbil

For those who have not strayed off the main road there is an opportunity about 55km east of Tagmoute for an exploratory walk to find the **prehistoric carvings** around Aït-Herbil. The turning to the village, 2km north, is beside the Ziz petrol station. Ask at this garage or the village café for a local guide. The two largest collections of rock carvings are on the east bank of the river Tamanart, one above the half-deserted hamlet at Eguire, the other about 400m due east of the old kasbah north of Aït-Herbil village. It is possible to follow the track north along the Tamanart to visit the **agadir** outside the next village, Aguerd, framed by dark hills.

Fam El Hisn

Icht is a small settlement 77km east of Tagmoute, where there is often a police checkpoint. Fam El Hisn (or Foum el Hassan), the larger, neighbouring settlement, lies 6km to the south. It first appears as a small dusty military post, the market square shuttered and lifeless, but by crossing the wide gravel bed of the river Tamanart you enter extensive and prosperous palm groves. The Aït-ou-Mribet tribe dominated this oasis from their ksar of Imi Ouagadir; they claim to be descended from Christian Berbers established here in the 13th century.

There are few architectural traces of the ksar left, and the farmers now live in low pisé houses above the palm groves. Wandering through the maze of paths that enclose walled oasis gardens, you will see palms shading crops from the savage sun, and the irrigation water which runs through the plots throughout the year. Each spring the irrigation canal that runs deep below the gravel bed of the Tamanart is dug out and cleaned, for without such constant attention these oasis settlements would wither away.

By following the irrigation stream you pass through a gorge, the Fam, eroded through the high peaks of the Jbel Bani. At the junction of the Tamanart and Tasseft there is a well and a grove of trees in which to rest. Along the lower banks of these rivers there are two prehistoric carvings etched into red stone—but be prepared for a half-hour search. The reward for finding them lies in their age and the hunt rather in the aesthetics of the carving.

Oua-Belli

From Icht, 40km of desert stretch between you and the twin villages of **Tisgui El Haratine** and **Aït Oua-Belli**, which bestride a breach in the wall of Jbel Bani. The **agadir** of Oua-Belli is perfectly positioned at the summit of the hill that guards the gorge. The exterior wall is in good condition and individual family storage chambers and the communal water basin can be seen. A half-hour climb to the summit is rewarded by the view: to the north, three dry riverbeds dotted with palm trees stretch into the distance; to the south are the irrigation works that feed the green pockets of this oasis, and the glimmering extent of the Sahara.

Akka

Following the main road another 40km you arrive at Akka, the chief village and military garrison for a group of half a dozen ksour which cultivate an extensive and rich oasis. Official dusty red buildings lining the road, armed guards, abandoned defensive sand walls and stone emplacements are at first inhibiting, but the village is worth exploring.

Behind the veneer of new buildings you will find old Akka, which still contains graceful pisé arches, elaborate metal grilles and well-built stone corrals. The **old souk** (in use on Thursdays and Sundays) straddles three arcaded courtyards of diminishing grandeur, of which the last has a central well. The products of Akka's orchards were celebrated, its rich sweet dates and dried and fresh fruit prized additions to the monotonous diet of a desert crossing.

From Akka you can walk northeast towards the **agadir** and **kasbah** found outside Azro, or alternatively drive 3km up route 7085 (the road to Imitek), passing by a couple of hamlets to arrive at **Aït Rahal**, which has a locally celebrated swimming hole shaded by palms.

Akka also has **prehistoric stone carvings** in its vicinity, but you will need to hire a local guide to find them. Ask in the roadside **Café Hôtel Tamdoult**, which also prepares meals and has basic rooms. The best carvings are all a fair way from the village, at Oum Alek about 7km southeast, or 5km north of Akka up the Targamnt riverbed by a deserted barracks.

Caravans from Akka

Akka was always a port of the trans-Saharan trade, but it gained a certain notoriety in the late 19th century when illicit slave caravans continued to use the Western Saharan route. The great merchants of Fès and Marrakech all kept agents at Akka. Two tracks leave Akka for Tindouf, now in Algeria, from where the caravans crossed the Sahara to Timbuktu. The whole journey could take 130 days, the camels often travelling seven hours a day for seven days without water. The trade was chiefly in salt, originally exchanged for gold, but later for slaves. The slave survivors of the return crossing would be rested at Akka and sold to waiting agents. Those too unfit to find a buyer were left to join the local Haratine community, who cultivated oasis orchards and gardens. The last slave caravan was seen skirting the Western Sahara in 1956, and Mauretania only officially abolished slavery in 1981.

Touzounine

Seventy kilometres out of Akka towards Tata you pass a few outlying settlements, the most notable of which is Touzounine, an unchanged and accessible oasis village. Here you can study the traditional building techniques—stone-based foundations, palm-trunk beams, cross-thatched with palm leaves and plastered with mud pisé create proportions consistent with the surrounding habitat, but with an astounding diversity of individual features. The community fights a continuous battle with the environment, and the ruins of a settlement to the north stand as a menacing warning of decay. The road on to Tata follows an escarpment, a natural wall of black rock grazed by goat and camel herds.

Tata

Tata is an attractive pink new town, laid out in a rigid grid of streets beside a riverbed and sheltered from desert winds and dust by a ring of hills. Opposite the Hôtel Renaissance are some stone steps that climb a hill, known as La Montagne, dominated by a pink administrative block. From here you get a good view of the extent of the town and can see the tarmac road east: it stops dead at the edge of town, and the dirt road to Foum-Zguid and Zagora takes over. Having been closed for security reasons for years, this is now open to regular traffic, though the police still mount several checkpoints. Locals travelling to the souks (at Tissinnt on Mondays and Foum-Zguid on Thursdays) use the lorry taxis that ply this route.

Tata is at the centre of a network of three riverbeds that drain the southern slopes of the Anti-Atlas. The beds are mined with irrigation canals, which feed the scattering of palm groves and gardens cultivated by the twenty or more surrounding ksour. The population is a roughly equal mix of Chleuh Berber and Haratine. The Haratine serfs have, since Independence, risen from their depressed status and now cultivate over half the available land for themselves. Both groups speak the Berber Tamazight dialect in preference to Arabic, and hold a **souk** on Thursdays and Sundays at El-Khemis, a series of walled enclosures about 6km out of town on the road to Akka. If you have missed or been excited by the lack of carpets at the souk some shopping therapy is in hand in the well stocked **Maison Nomade**.

The **ksour** of Tata have a distinctive look and identity that make them appear like a scattering of Mycenean acropolises. An indeterminate mix of walls and houses clusters tightly around a rise of barren rock. Dark, wide window portals, uncluttered by frames or grilles, stare out impassively over the surrounding patch of cultivation. **Tiiggane**, **Agarzagane** and **Taguent** are just a few of these striking sites that you can walk or drive out to and explore.

Orientation

Tata has a shaded central garden square, hotels, a campsite, a bank, a post office, some garages, and plenty of cafés along Av Mohammed V that serve a salads, soups, grilled meats and *tagines*. Buses leave from the main square, Place Marche Verte.

Where to Stay and Eating Out

The moderately-priced **Relais des Sables**, © (08) 802301, @ 802300 on Av des FAR provides the most comfortable accommodation, with 60 rooms arranged around a series of courtyards. It also has a pool, bar and restaurant.

The inexpensive **Hôtel de la Renaissance**, © (08) 802042, is also on Av des FAR, at no. 9, and with its new block straddles both sides of the road. It is slightly cheaper to stay in the older section, perched on the river terrace overlooking the dry bed towards a koubba. Bedrooms are comfortable, the water works, the cooking remains delicious and it now has a bar. Stay here. At the cheap end there's the **Hôtel Sahara**, © (08) 802161, at 81 Av Mohammed V, for basic accommodation.

From Tata to Taroudannt

From Tata a magnificent new road, the 7111, has been carved through the rock desert. It took six years to build, and two weeks after it opened in 1987 torrential rains tore out over a dozen bridges. It is an exhilarating route—geological strata are clearly visible in all their extraordinary convolutions, and you pass only one small settlement before reaching the cultivated Issafèn mountain valley, 52km from Tata, heralded by three decaying hilltop agadirs.

The Issafèn Valley

Issafèn is too high for palm trees: olive, almond, walnut and henna dominate the valley. Here, stone houses replace desert pisé, and the all-enveloping embroidered black cloak or *haik* of the oases gives way to the blue and purple smocks of Berber mountain women. They are contrasted by red edging or scarlet socks, and hair is swept back in a scarf fixed with a narrow striped fillet of material. The men of Issafèn used to be notorious raiders until the sheik of the Aït-Haroun placed the valley under a curse. Famine decimated the Issafèn, before its leaders agreed to solemnly renounce their careers of pillage before the sheik.

In the midst of the valley is the **kasbah of Tamghirt**, a stone-built keep in immaculate condition, a reminder of warlike days. Beyond is a gaunt, completely ruined and melting village, a Gomorrah-like vision of total destruction. A souk is held each Thursday at **Souk-Khemis-d'Issafèn** at the head of the valley.

Igherm

Igherm (or Irherm) is 38km north of the Issafèn Valley, over a bleak and twisting mountain road that crosses the Tizi-Touzlimt pass at 1692m. This small whitewashed village is set in the centre of a mountainous plateau 1700m above sea level. Low fruit trees grow in embattled, windswept orchards, but Igherm exists chiefly as a market for the highland hinterland. Mountain tracks fan out from the village, and it is possible to travel on them to Taliouine, Tafraoute and Amagour. Igherm hosts a busy vegetable market on Wednesdays and Fridays, and has a petrol station, four cafés and a number of mechanics who repair the damage done by mountain tracks. They follow a long tradition, for Igherm is the chief village of the Ida-ou-Kensous, craftsmen renowned in the past for their metalwork, especially swords, muskets and inlaid powder-horns. Now they concentrate on clutches and suspensions.

The **Café de la Jeunesse** has a few rooms to rent, which can be useful for anyone planning to hitch a lift on a truck or climb Adrar-n-Aklim, the 2531m summit 15km east of Igherm.

On to Taroudannt

The road to Taroudannt runs through broken hill country that does not compete with the earlier splendour of the route. Argan trees reappear as you approach their natural habitat, the Sous Valley. Nine kilometres out of Igherm there is a **Saturday market** at **Souk-es-Sebt-des-Indouzal**, a left turn off the road. A further 31km and there is a splendid **view** across the Sous to the High Atlas; a café has conveniently planted itself nearby. The road then makes a long twisting descent through rough foothills and wild argan groves.

A few kilometres before the main Taroudannt–Ouarzazate road there is a turning to **Tioute Kasbah** on the left, and the **Kasbah de Freïja** can be seen by the Sous crossing. These two Sous Valley kasbahs are described as day-trips out from Taroudannt, 8km west; *see* p.530.

The Western Sahara

Guelmim, once a great Saharan market town, marks the geographical frontier between the sedentary villages of the Anti-Atlas and the nomadic pastoralists of the Sahara. Although quite a number of tourists visit its somewhat dubious Saturday souk, very few venture further south into the heat, dust and bleak conditions of the Western Sahara. And there is certainly little of beauty to justify the great distances and discomfort involved. However, the disadvantages are a vital part of the attraction of this inhospitable terrain. It is a land of adventurous travel rather than tourism.

The desert of the Western Sahara is primarily *hammada*, a vast flat stony plain, an arid wasteland without prominent features. Travelling in the area involves very few choices. Due to the forbidding nature of the land and the recent war, in which the Algerian-backed Polisario fought Morocco for possession of the Western Sahara, it is important to keep to the main routes. There are many checkpoints, areas of interest may well be occupied by the military, monuments damaged and the population suspicious of your motives. In the last few years, however, areas have been opened up which you could never have visited before except at risk of your life. And now that a ceasefire is in operation and King Hassan II is speaking with the Polisario, the area is becoming still more accessible.

Getting Around

by air

There is an efficient grid of air connections throughout the Western Sahara based on well-established airports at Agadir, Tan-Tan, Laâyoune and Dakhla. Agadir is the main international airport and link to northern Morocco, and both it and Laâyoune have flights to Las Palmas in the nearby Canaries. A very useful connection if you are not driving is the flight from Dakhla to Agadir, as it allows you to return quickly from the region's southernmost town without having to retrace the route north.

by bus

Buses from Agadir to Laâyoune passes through Guelmim, Tan-Tan and Tarfaya. Beyond Laâyoune you must use Landrover taxis, *grands* and *petits taxis*, all of which are found at Laâyoune, Es-Semara and Dakhla, as well as in Guelmim and Tan-Tan.

by car

Driving through the desert yourself is an ideal experience, and cars can be hired at Agadir and Laâyoune. As an inducement to settlement petrol is greatly reduced in price in the region, just over half the usual, and there are now pumps at Dakhla, Boujdour, Es-Semara, Laâyoune and Tan-Tan.

Tourist Information

The climate is quite bearable from November to March. However, the heat of the summer brings on a recognized medical symptom of unreasonable anger. Villa Cisneros, as Dakhla was called by the Spanish, was known by its inhabitants as Villa Neurosis. The nights are cold throughout the year.

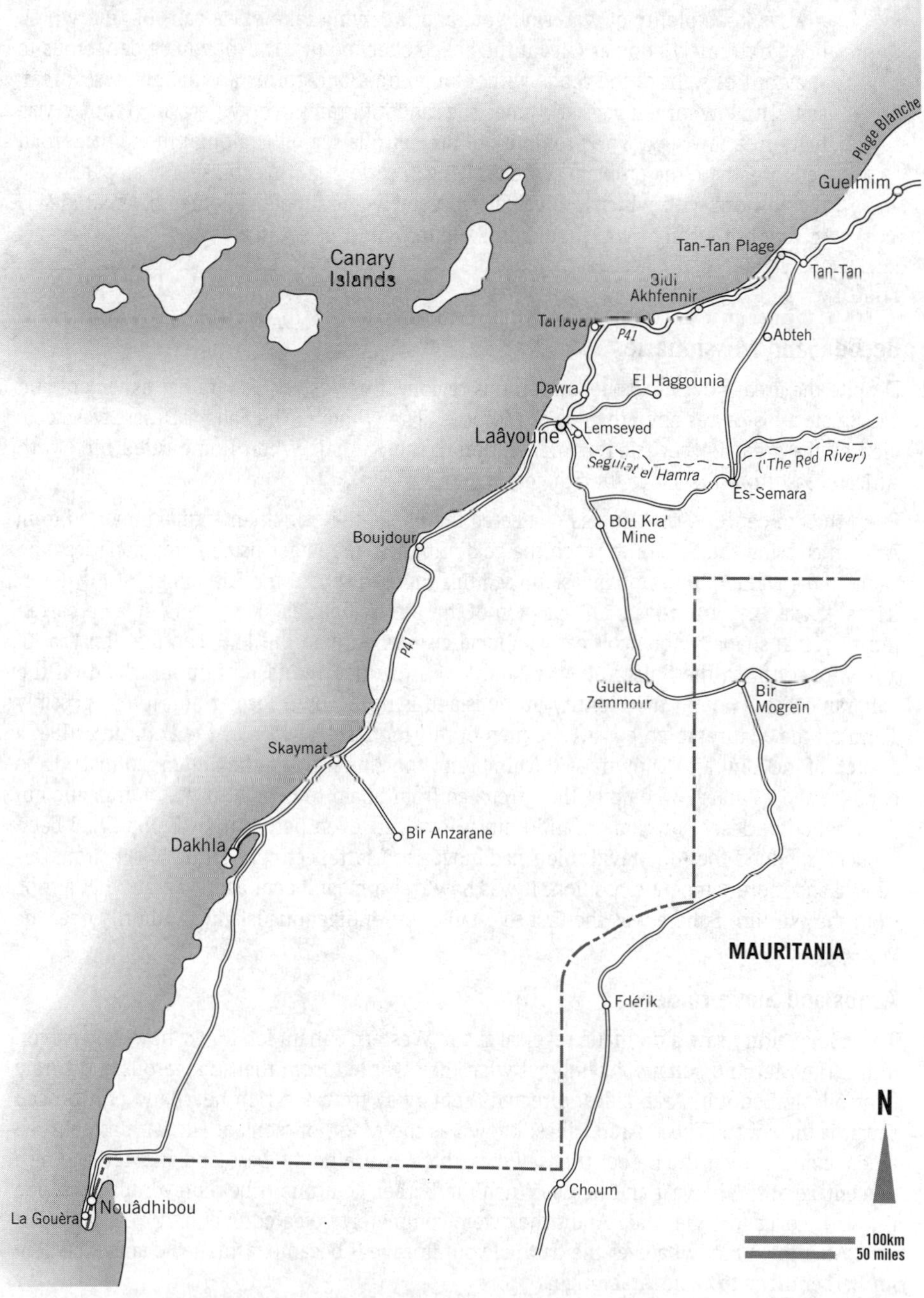
The Western Sahara
Plage Blanche
Guelmim
Tan-Tan Plage
Tan-Tan
Canary Islands
Sidi Akhfennir
Tarfaya
P41
Abteh
El Haggounia
Dawra
Laâyoune
Lemseyed
Seguiat el Hamra
('The Red River')
Es-Semara
Bou Kra' Mine
Boujdour
P41
Guelta Zemmour
Bir Mogreïn
Skaymat
Bir Anzarane
Dakhla
MAURITANIA
Fdérik
Choum
Nouâdhibou
La Gouèra
N
100km
50 miles

You might keep an eye out for snakes, rats and scorpions. Not that there is a lot that you can do if you are bitten, as most of the snakes you find in the Sahara, and even the bite of a palm rat, are deadly.

Always keep plenty of water on you, and if driving take extra cans of beer which make extremely popular gifts at the police checkpoints. It is of course dangerous to stray out of sight of the roads without a guide. Sandstorms are the greatest threat, and can blow for ten days at a time. The sand infiltrates everywhere and reduces visibility to a few feet. The proximity of precipitous sea cliffs along much of the road adds greatly to the problem. When driving in serious storms you should stop, and test the wisdom with which you calculated your water supplies. Remember that ideally in very hot weather you should drink up to 8 pints of liquid a day.

History

Berbers and Missionaries

Despite the great poverty of the land in this region, the Western Sahara has as violent and passionate a history as any province of Morocco. The whole of the Sahara Desert was occupied by the great Berber tribal confederation of the Sanhaja when Rome ruled the North African coast from the 1st to the 5th century AD.

From the 7th century, the Sanhaja pioneered the use of the camel, an animal imported from Asia, in crossing the Sahara to reach the gold mines on the Niger. Islamic missionaries who came in the wake of the Arab invasion used this route to spread the faith amongst the desert tribes. It was the enthusiasm and passion of these missionaries, converting in such barren territory, that shaped Morocco's early national history. Early in the 11th century, Ibn Yaasin, a missionary from the Sous Valley, established a fortified monastery on an island off the Saharan coast. Though the identity of the island is not known for certain, it was possibly Tidra off the Mauretanian coast. The men of this monastery were of the Lemtuna tribe, a branch of the Sanhaja. Known as Al-Murabitim, the Almoravids, they emerged in 1042 to conquer and establish an empire that stretched from Spain to Ghana. It was a dramatic but brief period of desert supremacy and unity. However, even before their Empire had been properly subdued the Almoravid rulers had moved to Marrakech, preferring to rule from this central and more temperate position. It was however a magnificent achievement that a tribe from the Western Sahara was the first to establish an indigenous Islamic authority over the whole of Morocco.

Arabs and Slave-raiders

The 13th century saw a dramatic reversal as the Western Sahara fell under new, fierce overlords. The Merenid sultans, having got what they wanted from their dangerous and barely controllable Bedouin Arab allies, directed them away from the rich heartland of Morocco towards the south. These Arab tribes, known as the Maql, or 'sons of Hassan', established feudal emirates over the Berber tribes of the Sahara, usurping the best land and demanding a percentage of the harvest and herds. When the Berber Lemtuna tribe did eventually reopen the struggle against the Maql Arabs they were completely defeated over a 30-year period of war. After this time, whatever the truth of your lineage it became fashionable and expedient for Berber tribes to claim Arab origins.

It was also in the 13th century the Spanish and Portuguese began to build towers along the Saharan Atlantic coast from which to raid the Maghrebi interior, although not a stone of these structures now survives. Their ploy was to catch Berbers or Arabs, and to hold them to ransom for a greater number of negro slaves. It was not until the Saadian-led *jihad* (holy war) of 1524 that these slave-raiding enclaves were decisively banished.

Spanish Rule

The end of the 19th century saw the Spanish returning to the Western Saharan coast after an absence of 600 years. The last remnants of the Spanish Empire, Cuba and the Philippines, had just been lost to the USA, and to make up for the indignity of having no colonial empire, the Spanish claimed control of a vast area of the Western Sahara. It became known as Rio de Oro or the Spanish Sahara, though in reality the Spanish only controlled two fortified and intermittently besieged posts, now known as La Gouèra and Ad-Dakhla.

From 1895 the actual ruler of the Western Sahara was Sheik Ma el Ainin, who presided over the nomadic tribes from his capital of Es-Semara. From here, with the support of the sultan, he organized resistance to the French, who were encroaching on Morocco from both the east and south. He, his sons (notably El Hiba) and other relations remained at the forefront of resistance right up until final French victory in 1934. Only after this were the Spanish able to impose their rule on the area inland from their two coastal forts, the last area in Africa to succumb to colonialism.

A period of armed colonial peace lasted 22 years. In 1957, after Morocco-proper had achieved independence from France, the Moroccan Liberation Army, supported by Tekna and Reguibat Berber tribes, launched a coordinated attack on Spanish positions in the Sahara. But, with the help of the French, the Spaniards were able to repel these the following year.

Saharan Nationalism and Moroccan Rule

The development of a Saharan national consciousness, separate from Morocco, was fostered by the Spanish in the following years through broadcasts and elected, though powerless, tribal assemblies. Added to this, the development of phosphate mines at Bou Kra gave the Saharans, for the first time, an economic base for a separate nation. while the 1963 Morocco–Algeria border war created a future sponsor for the Saharans in the neighbouring Algerian republic.

However, before they could become independent the Saharan nationalists, known as the Polisario Front, had to overthrow Spanish rule. In the 1970s they launched a guerrilla campaign against their overlords, and the Spanish, who in one week's fighting used up the equivalent of five years' phosphate profits, faced facts and prepared to quit the region. Meanwhile, in 1974, King Hassan II of Morocco had agreed with Mauritania to the south to divide the Western Sahara. In November 1975 he orchestrated 'The Green March', when 350,000 Moroccans crossed the border into the Spanish Sahara to reclaim the lost province. The Spanish government, in the midst of Franco's terminal illness, was caught unprepared. They surrendered sovereignty of the territory quickly, without even calling a referendum.

The Moroccan armed forces who had been protecting the green marchers (green, incidentally stood for Islam, not ecology) ended up fighting the Polisario movement by the end of the year. The figures are greatly disputed, but 10–30,000 Saharans subsequently left the area, objecting to Moroccan rule. They walked in a less publicized march to the Polisario-run refugee camps in Tindouf, Algeria, which were established and funded by the Algerian government. From these camps the enlarged Polisario waged a fast-moving, mobile campaign of hit and run raids. Mauritania, crippled by this guerrilla war, left its half of the Western Sahara in 1979. Morocco promptly occupied the entire territory.

The construction by the Moroccans of immense sand wall defences throughout the 1980s, now longer than the Great Wall of China, reversed the trend of the war in Morocco's favour. The Polisario were reduced to fighting a desultory perimeter war, unable to penetrate the wall into the centre of the province. In January 1989, the Polisario and King Hassan II met face to face for the first time in peace talks held at Marrakech, and a truce was declared in the desert. Both sides were pleasantly surprised by their adversaries, and under UN auspices a decision was made to hold a referendum. An agreement on the crucial aspect of who is eligible to vote—after years in which people from the rest of Morocco have been given incentives to settle in the south—has not been so easy to decide. Subsequent events, such as the defection of the Polisario foreign minister to the Moroccan camp and a split between Polisario and their Algerian patrons, seemed for several years to make a referendum even more unlikely. However, the 1996 appointment of former US Secretary of State James Baker as special envoy to the conflict by UN Secretary General Kofi Annan is an indication of renewed international interest in finding a solution to the dispute, and the Moroccan government has declared its willingness to respect the outcome of a referendum even if it is favourable to Saharan independence, and so it appears that—though as yet nothing is certain—after over two decades a settlement may finally be coming into sight.

The Moroccan government has invested millions in the Sahara, building roads, airports, fishing ports and the city of Laâyoune, not to mention their spending on the war itself. To a stranger, removed from the politics of rival nations, it seems extraordinary that anybody should ever have fought to possess so desolate a piece of land. That such a war has been so recently fought gives travel in the Sahara its piquant interest—the traveller as eyewitness to the strange passions of mankind.

From Guelmim to Tan-Tan

The road from Guelmim takes you through arid rolling hills for 80 km, and it is surprising to see how much of this low land is productive in the brief spring. In exceptional years, the Drâa river runs for a few days along its entire length from Ouarzazate. In the past it was a more substantial feature, which the classical historian Polybius recorded as infested with crocodiles.

Tan-Tan

For those travellers who find the Saturday tourist explosion in Guelmim disappointing, Tan-Tan provides a perfect and powerful antidote. The view as you descend on the town from the north is enticing, the great cluster of sand-yellow houses dominated by a military kasbah and overlooked by the bright green dome of the mosque of Sidi Mohammed Laghdal. Despite forming the major base for the 1975 Green March, Tan-Tan itself is, however, a completely unexploited, dry, dusty administrative town. Water and electricity supplies fluctuate, and the busiest aspect of Tan-Tan life is the sight of tractors pulling water tanks. They make up for their lack of brakes with free use of the horn.

The town is ranged off the long Avenue Mohammed V, which turns off the main road south to run parallel to the bed of the Ben Khlil, a tributary of the Drâa. The military kasbahs that surround the town are in use, and in this sensitive area they are closed to visitors. Walking along Avenue Mohammed V and up the hill to look at the exterior of the mosque is about the extent of the cultural tour of Tan-Tan. You can get into some fierce bargaining with a powerful and well-hennaed lady at no. 360 over vast stripey blankets and tie-dyed shawls. The **cinema** is open on Mondays, Wednesdays, Thursdays and Sundays, showing a mix of violent American and hopelessly romantic Indian films. Typically for this town, the annual *moussem* is particularly elusive, and tourists may be quoted dates in October, May, June and July. A parade of camels is promised.

Getting Around

From Av Mohammed V there are five **buses** that depart daily north for Agadir (7–8hrs) and Guelmim (3hrs), and three south to Laâyoune (7–8hrs). Of the latter the CTM night services currently leaving at 1am and 2am are the most convenient.

As well as the space for buses along the avenue there are small squares devoted to Land Rover **taxis**, *grands taxis* and *petits taxis*. There is a vast number and variety of taxis offering places on the regular shuttle to Guelmim (2–3hrs) or Laâyoune (5–6hrs).

Where to Stay

The major hotel in Tan-Tan is the **Royal**. It has the only bar and pool in town, but is currently forbidden to visitors as it is reserved for Moroccan army officers. At each square along Avenue Mohammed V there are clusters of small hotels and two one-star hotels, **L'Etoile du Sahara** , © (08) 877085, at 17 Rue Al Fida, and the **Amagala**, © (08) 877308. The well-advertised **Hôtel Dakhla**, © (08) 877308, at the bus square, has clean rooms, brightly painted balconies and is, for Tan-Tan, comparatively busy.

Eating Out

The shrub-shaded **Le Jardin** café-restaurant, on Avenue Mohammed V, is the centre of Tan-Tan's social life. You can sip tea and eat cakes here overlooked by a large concrete jaguar. For eating there are lots of small café-restaurants cooking *brochettes* along the avenue, but do not expect much activity before dusk. Next door to the Hôtel Dakhla there is a smart little ***pâtisserie***.

Tan-Tan-Plage

On the coast west of Tan-Tan, this is an uninspiring collection of bourgeois villas built on a grid pattern above a sandy and tranquil beach. Construction is still continuing, and a new mosque has been built. A dirt track is used by camper trailers and vans which park above the beach. The **Café d'Etoile de l'Océan** and immediately below it the combined **Café, Pâtisserie and Librairie de Fès** provide light lunches of salad, omelettes and very occasionally fresh fish from their terraces, both of which have views over the sea.

Just south of Tan-Tan-Plage a brand-new fishing port has been constructed as part of the great development plan to open up the Saharan seaboard to settlement.

South to Tarfaya

South of Tan-Tan the road crosses a section of the earth quite terrifying in its aridity and lifelessness. The desert is flat baked stone, and towards the horizon lies a complete, ugly and brutal wasteland rising some 50km inland in a series of cliff terraces. The ground is poisoned with salt, and rain, if it occurs, runs off to collect in stagnant depressions, quickly turning so saline that it is poisonous to everything but a very few, low, inedible shrubs.

From Tan-Tan-Plage onwards you are largely denied access to the sea by flaking sea cliffs. But there are three points at which it is accessible, at the rivers Chebeika, Fatima and el Aouina, where the road dips down to cross barren salt estuaries and their sheets of lifeless water. Here, though, it is possible to escape the desert and enter the refreshing but turbulent currents of the Atlantic.

Sidi Akhfennir is a hamlet which appears to consist of 16 identical café restaurants. In the few kilometres either side of this truck stop you will notice little shacks on the cliff edge belonging to line fishermen. They eke out an existence providing fish for the passing trade.

About 20km beyond Sidi Akhfennir the remains of the clifftop **koubba of Sidi Lemsid** can be seen. The shrine of the saint, traditional ancestor of the tribe of the Oulad-Tidrahin, has been badly damaged by the war. The Tidrahin are an indigenous Berber tribe of Sanhaja stock who lost their grazing grounds and hence their prestige to the Arab Delim. By the 18th century they had become a tributary to the Delim, but unlike other Berber groups their spiritual ancestry and powers earned their overlords' respect, and they remained desert herdsmen rather than take up the despised life of fishermen, last resort of the fallen in the Western Sahara. Below the cliffs and scattered stones of the koubba, the sea enters into a vast tidal estuary where great wet boulders appear dotted in the immensity like beached whales.

Rejoining the shore before Tarfaya, you come across the melancholy and outstanding feature of this section of the coast, 'the graveyard of sailors'. Wrecked hulks rising above the sea, continuous sand-flecked wind, and the knowledge of the endless pattern of violent sea death deprive this elegant stretch of long serene beach of some of its intrinsic appeal. It has, though, a lingering, impassive fascination.

Tarfaya

Two hundred and sixty kilometres south of Tan-Tan and 115km north of Laâyoune, the settlement of Tarfaya is composed of just a few bungalow cafés and stalls, partly obscured by banks of wind-blown sand. It does however have a basic hotel, unsignposted but easy to find opposite the two cafés. In all contexts, Tarfaya has been bypassed. The road runs straight past the town on to the south.

The ruins of Port Victoria, a conspicuous grey ruin on an old islet, and the rest of the Spanish-built barrack structures are still heavily guarded. The town was built to withstand constant sniping raids from the tribes of the region, who were among the last people in Africa to be pacified by Europeans.

History

Tarfaya has a curious history. It was built in 1878 by a British adventurer, Donald Mackenzie, who from 1867 had been an itinerant trader in the Sahara, the only European who was respected by the fierce, xenophobic tribes. He named it, of course, Port Victoria. In 1888 Mackenzie's manager at the trading post was murdered in a tribal raid. Sultan Moulay Hassan paid him compensation of £5000. By this time the French were increasingly dominating the Saharan market from their bases on the Senegal river, but Mackenzie continued trading. However, the British government put increasing pressure on him to sell his post, which he eventually did in 1895, selling out to the sultan for £50,000.

After that, Port Victoria was used by the sultan to supply the desert ruler Sheik Ma el Ainin with materials for building Es-Semara, and with a flow of arms for fighting the French in Mauritania. All this notwithstanding, the town had incidentally been ceded to Spain in the European carve-up of North Africa at the Conference of Berlin in 1885, although they did not colonize it and rename it Villa Bens until 1916, when the Spanish captured a German submarine unloading Turkish Korans and Krupp arms for El Hiba, Ma el Ainin's son.

The great source of wealth in the Sahara in the last 50 years has been the salaries and budgets of alien administrations, and for some time, Tarfaya, as Villa Bens, took its share. From 1920 to Independence in 1956 it was the Spanish headquarters for the Southern Protectorate of Morocco. After 1958 the Spanish administered the colony that they had retained, the Spanish Sahara, from Laâyoune, and the Moroccan government administered their southern frontiers from Tan-Tan. The newly named Tarfaya returned to obscurity.

The Road to Laâyoune

South of Tarfaya you pass through the central belt of sand desert, the Erg Lakhbayta, broken by two great salt basins, the **Sabkhat Tah** and the **Sabkhat Oum Dba** (or Sebkha Deboua). The Tah in particular was intensively mined for its salt deposits, the great currency of the desert. From 1958 to 1975 it was the border post between Morocco and the Spanish Sahara, and in November 1975 it was the starting point for the Green March. Further south beside the road is the oasis of **Dawra**, which was the stronghold of the Izarguin tribe. Dawra was famous for its productivity, and its crops were protected in the 19th century by two clay-walled and corner-towered forts.

Laâyoune

An extraordinary creation, Laâyoune is a city of 100,000 people, not yet 50 years old, set in the middle of the desert. It was first built by the Spanish after Tarfaya was returned to Morocco in 1956, and is now maintained almost purely by national will. Since 1976 Morocco has poured a billion dollars into the Saharan province, and Laâyoune appears to be largely composed of the offices and the machinery of government for the territory. The population is a mix of a minority of Saharan nomads and a larger proportion of Moroccans from the north, attracted by government-sponsored building projects, double wages, generous loans and access to tax-free imports.

Long-term economic survival for a settlement this size is however more difficult to envisage. The surrounding desert is beyond man's power to improve. The **Bou Kra mine**, southeast of town, holds only 2 per cent of Moroccan phosphate reserves and has been producing less than half what is needed to make it profitable. It is a fully automated process, and like the new fishing port at **Laâyoune-Plage**, 30km west of the town on the sea, it is not reliant on the town for survival. The only ancient and productive thing in Laâyoune is the lagoon on the riverbed to the west of town. Here, in defiance of nature, mullet somehow manage to cross drifting sand dunes to breed each year in the brackish water.

Laâyoune's most important function seems to be as a bulwark of Moroccan nationalism. Its population would easily dominate a territory-wide referendum on the future of the Sahara, to Morocco's advantage. The city exists as a powerful symbol of the forces of nationalism in Africa. Here the vocabulary of European imperialism is reworked, and so it is Morocco's historical destiny to bring culture and civilization to the south. There is no apparent awareness of how ironic this sounds coming from a nation that recovered its own independence only 40 years ago.

Getting Around

by air

The airport, to the east of town, has flights to Agadir (2 a week), Casablanca (daily), Dakhla (1 a week), Es-Semara (2 a week), Las Palmas (4 a week) and Tan-Tan (3 a week). For updated airport information, © (08) 893346, or the Royal Air Maroc offices at 7 Place Bir Anzarane, © (08) 894071.

by bus

Heading north use the CTM coaches which depart from outside their office at 20 Avenue de la Mecque. The even more comfortable ONCF service operates from Av Oum Saad (currently arriving at 2pm, departing north at 5.25pm) near the stadium. For less comfortable local services to Es-Semara, Tarfaya and Tan Tan go to the bus park by Place Dchira.

by car and taxi

Grands taxis for long hauls south and north leave in the evening from Place Lamkhakh, while the Landrover taxis for shorter local destinations use Av Mazouir. **Car hire** can be organized from the unusually helpful Tourist Office on Av de l'Islam (opposite the Parador) or Massira Tours on Av de la Mecque, © (08) 894229.

Tourist Information and Orientation

It is easy and intriguing to walk around Laâyoune. The original Spanish town runs along the western lagoon terrace. The new city monuments are uphill to the east and beyond these stretch the neat straight avenues of the Moroccan new town. The **banks** are the Banque Populaire on Av Mohammed V (ex Calle de Sol), BMCE on Rue Mohammed Zerktouni and Wafabank at 5 Av Mohammed V, © (08) 893598.

The Spanish settlement was built overlooking the riverbed of the As Saquia (or Seguiat) al Hamra. The terrace above the riverbed has become the depository for much of the town's rubbish and is constantly worked over by a few goats and rats. Above it stands the closed

Spanish cathedral, and some curiously shaped houses with white domed roofs which echo traditional designs in their attempt to create cool interior space. Walking uphill you pass the kasbah-like exterior of the Spanish-built **Parador** hotel which, with its small pool and gardens, has by far the most pleasant environment in the town.

Above the Parador and Al Massira hotels spreads the recent Moroccan development of the city, including a massive concrete football stadium, the airport to the south and the new central mosque, finished in 1983. From the mosque, the **lagoon** is seen enclosed by golden sand dunes, providing perhaps the single good view in Laâyoune, much reproduced on posters. However entrancing the lagoon may appear at first sight, do not swim in it. Near the mosque is an astonishing area, Place Méchouar. On one side of the square the view is dominated by a glittering modern glass pavilion, 'The Hall of the Green March', which contains a photographic exhibition of the great event. The rest of the space is designed for the Saharan tribes to congregate in to show their allegiance to the king when he comes on a tour of inspection. The slightly alarming portrait of him in dark glasses and black boots with a riding crop which you see on walls all over the country was taken here. The space is unashamedly theatrical and awe-inspiring.

Where to Stay

expensive

There are two extremely comfortable hotels which are either fully booked (often by the UN) or near empty. Of the two, the Spanish-built **Parador**, © (08) 894500, has the more tranquil atmosphere. **Al Massira Khadra**, © (08) 894225, was designed for tour groups from the Canaries, Agadir and passing cruise liners. Both have cool, tiled courtyards, well-watered gardens, small but delightfully welcome pools and a choice of restaurants, bars and public rooms. The Parador with its 33 rooms is on Rue Okbaa Iben Nafeh, the Al Massira Khadra with 75 rooms is on Rue de la Mecque.

moderate

The **Hôtel Nagjir**, © (08) 894168, is by Place Dchira. It offers a livelier alternative with its bar, nightclub, licensed restaurant and an interior dominated by an enthusiastic use of mirrors, red walls and black leather.

inexpensive

The **El Alia** at 1 Rue Kadi el Ghalaoui, © (08) 893133, is an indifferent place despite some interesting camel saddlery in its hall. You are better off in the uninspiring but functional **Hôtel Lakoura**, © (08) 893378, on Avenue Hassan II.

cheap

Hôtel Rif, just off Blvd 28 Fevrier, has an excellent position on the terrace edge below the cathedral and has reopened after a restoration programme. Your next choice would be the **Hôtel Marhaba**, © (08) 893249, which is directly opposite the Aghrab Cinema on Avenue de la Marine. Going towards the riverbed there is a large choice among very basic and exclusively local hotels such as the **Sidi Ifni**, the **Farah** and the **Sakia Elhamra**.

Eating Out and Nightlife

There are three good cheap Moroccan cafés below the **Aghrab Cinema**, which is incidentally open every day at 7dh a show. Otherwise, go to the **Parador** with its Moroccan restaurant, grills by the pool and its international dining room. The **Al Massira Khadra** also has its own restaurants, a night-club and glitzy interior bars. The **Nejjib**, in addition to its own restaurant, has a large downstairs disco and bar.

Laâyoune-Plage

The 20km road between the town and the beach is lined with devices erected to stop the sand dunes drifting on to the road. They are doomed to failure but are constantly assisted by busy mechanical diggers. Laâyoune-Plage is just north of the port complex, which has a separate phosphate jetty and terminal. There is a Club Med-run Maison de la Pêche, as well as an indifferent beach café-restaurant which can run up any mixture of eggs and tinned food. It seems slightly ridiculous to swim off Laâyoune beach, which is beside the one area of industrial and domestic effluent in a region otherwise largely devoid of human life. Safe sandy beaches are however rare enough in the Western Sahara.

Southeast from Laâyoune

Lemseyed's spring is one of the most reliable sources of water in the entire province and used to enjoy the holy status of a sanctuary, where feuds were forbidden, travellers could rest in safety and alliances could be negotiated. It lies about 19km east of Laâyoune, along a turning signposted **Lemseyed/Lemsid**, which is overlooked by a stone monument. Below is the small oasis of Lemseyed, surrounded by a few vegetable plots and date palms. Seldom is shade more welcome. Touring visitors are taken here and treated to mint tea and *brochettes* on the palm matting. Three brown tents have been pitched nearby to form a small theatre for musical entertainments in the evening.

Across the riverbed, in grim contrast, is the old camp and fortress of **Dchira**, a Spanish compound largely deserted but still forbidden to visitors. Here, in January 1958, the Moroccan Liberation Army and the Reguibat and Tekna tribesmen united in an attack which nearly liberated Spanish-held Laâyoune. However the Spanish, reinforced by French units from Mauritania, counter-attacked in February and advanced up the As Saquia al Hamra to retake Es-Semara, which they had lost.

If you want an entirely non-touristic diversion to feel the frail economic pulse of the Western Sahara, try the **phosphate mines of Bou Kra**. Along the road small tin huts can be seen guarding the depressions where barley is cultivated if there has been any rain. The cultivation and guarding of these precious fertile beds, seldom more than 50m in diameter, was the task of the Haratine serf caste, who are a mix of Sub-Saharan African and the original pre-Berber black inhabitants of the Sahara. They surrendered a large part of the crop to their nomadic overlords. Pylons and the phosphate conveyor also march parallel to the road. The conveyor runs over 100km to the port, the belts stretching 8km between 12 relay stations.

Bou Kra is literally a pit, or rather four pits. It is initially slightly disappointing to find that there are not hordes of swarthy miners glistening in the heat as they labour with picks. In fact, miners are rather hard to find. Everybody is a technician operating or trying to mend enormous trucks and diggers built in America.

The miners' compound is very hospitable, and houses two pools, a café, a kitchen and one of Morocco's greatest surprises. Even Casablanca doesn't have a zoo, but here in the Sahara you find one. Mostly with empty cages, admittedly, but there is an undeniable ape and a reclusive duck. The surrounding trees are fed with water pumped up from subterranean levels and attract a large number of migratory birds.

Beyond Bou Kra is a military zone. It is 140km from there to **Galtat Zemmour**, an old watering-point of the Reguibat, where there is a Spanish fort and what was the front line with the Polisario. Galtat (or Guelta) Zemmour is on the edge of the Tiris Desert, one of the driest areas in the whole of the Sahara and also one of the most hotly contested areas in the recent war. In 1981 it witnessed three distinct battles. In March it was besieged by 1500 Polisario. The attack was relaunched in October when the 2000-man Moroccan garrison was overwhelmed. In November a combined Moroccan ground and air assault stormed the post, only to evacuate it a few weeks later as the strategy of the sand-wall was enforced.

In good years the Galtat Zemmour water might be available for six months of the year. There are only 24 other waterholes (of lesser reliability) in the whole vast area to the south. The traditional importance of these is reflected in a precise local vocabulary. *Bir* means well, *sania* a well more than 20m deep, *hassyn* denotes a permanent supply, *metfia* a natural rock cistern, *ajdir* a rare natural well, *aïn* a spring and *daya* a lagoon.

Es-Semara

The grazing along the banks of the As Saquia al Hamra, which runs between Es-Semara and Laâyoune, is the richest in the whole of the Western Sahara. It was continually fought over, but by 1907 the Reguibat tribe had won control. They still possess the land, moving their herds in family groups of two or three tents. The tents are now bright white, to the great advantage of the inhabitants and of aerial surveillance. Passing through the control point you pass the ruins of **Sheik Ma el Ainin's palace** to the far left and the military barracks to your right. The town is chiefly composed of a broad main street of yellow-painted houses that climbs up a hill with a summit dominated by tall radar masts. Es-Semara has always been an area of hidden prestige, and it is ringed by the largest concentration of prehistoric rock carvings in the Western Sahara, cut into the dark Devonian stone.

The Desert Stronghold of Ma el Ainin

Es-Semara is indivisibly linked with one of the great heroes of the resistance against France, Sheik Ma el Ainin, literally 'water of the eyes'. His father was an Idrissid—a descendant of Morocco's first Islamic ruler, the chief of the Berber Galagnia tribe and the master of a Sufi brotherhood in the desert. By the age of seven Ma el Ainin already knew the whole of the Koran. As an adult he was widely respected for his miraculous powers as well as his 300 scholarly works. Based at first at the Bir Nazarin water-hole, he realized that a single focal point was needed to unite the tribes in resistance to the French and Spanish. In 1884 work began at Es-Semara, 'the rushes', where he moved in 1895 whilst organizing resistance to the French advance from the south. The help Ma el Ainin received from the sultan included skilled workmen from Fès, Tangier and Tetouan to help in the construction of his kasbah.

The settlement, now all but disappeared, was on the bank of the river Seluan and partially fortified. It was constructed with dry-stone walls, but the domes and some interiors were plastered and washed in white or ochre. The dominant building contained the domed central rooms where Ma el Ainin bathed and where he dispensed justice as the *khalifa* of the sultan. These were surrounded by the houses of his four official wives, and ranged beyond were storerooms, cisterns and enclosures for camels and tents. Only the great mosque partially survives. A triple line of bleak black stone arches represents the original interior area of 81 arcades, which was in fact never completed. Ma el Ainin also established a Koranic school for boys and a celebrated 450-volume library. Those few documents that survived were apparently removed by the departing Spanish in 1975.

Ma el Ainin died in 1911 in Tiznit where he is buried, his army having been defeated the previous year by the French at Kasba Tadla. The *jihad* was continued by his son El Hiba (known as the Blue Sultan), but he too suffered defeat at Sidi-Bou-Othmane near Marrakech in 1912. In 1913 a French force penetrated the Sahara to sack Es-Semara. The Spanish Legion arrived in 1934, building their barracks to the east of the ruins. Since then Es-Semara has remained a military focus, and was the centre of fiercely-fought battles in 1958 and 1979.

The Town

Surrounded by the desert of black stone, the town shows few traces of the 50 wells dug and the 200 Drâa palms planted at Es-Semara by Ma el Ainin. The skyline is dominated by a great red and white communications tower. Es-Semara is now almost entirely military, and any walk on the edge of the settlement is usually forbidden. The central yellow arcaded street is pleasant enough and enlivened by camouflaged jeeps, stacked with fuel cans and decorated with whip-cord wirelesses; veiled passengers nestle carbines in the back. I asked the police if the road east was closed for tourists. They answered, smiling, 'To everybody.'

The ruins are not easily accessible, as a military communications post has been established immediately behind them and a collection of damaged tanks and personnel carriers has been piled to one side. The army posts resolutely refused entry on the same day that the *Matin du Sahara* published a special two-page appreciation of the national importance of the site.

Below the ruins on the dry riverbed are the remains of a double cupola complex which gave access to the subterranean water flow. Both this and the **koubba** that presides over another well, with its photogenic weathered ancient thorn tree, are in the usual shocking shit-covered state. Their condition was rather unreasonably blamed on the Libyans.

Tea With the Reguibat

Es-Semara is the chief town of the province, and has schools and two shops which provide everything for the nomad's tent. Whatever the effects of Morocco's investments in the Sahara, the bulk of the indigenous population of this region lead an unchanged existence shepherding their herds of goats between the scant areas of pasture. To witness, even for the space of three cups of tea, the ritual of nomadic life is to be rewarded for the tedium of desert travel. Pick a group of tents beside the roads to Tan-Tan or Laâyoune at random, park and walk. The light can make the distance deceptive, but a long walk gives you time to recall the savage actions with which Paul Bowles accredits Reguibat bands.

The tradition of hospitality can usually be invoked by enthusiastic admiration of the herd, but it would be brash and indiscreet to approach too closely without first waiting for the almost inevitable invitation. The tents are called *khaima* and usually measure 4m by 12m. Their floors are generally of woven reed, but canvas is slowly replacing the patchwork of heavy brown cloth which constituted the fabric of the tents. Their interiors are often decorated with striped blankets, and a few carpets and ornate gilded leatherwork may be kept aside for special occasions. Tents are divided into two equal sections by a cotton screen, often of hanging clothes, restricting the view between the sexes but not the conversation. In spring, with the surplus of milk, butter fat, congealed inside the skin of a young calf, gently sways on a stick frame. Bowls of milk bobbing with clots of cream and steeped in sugar are offered to guests as well as the ubiquitous tea. Couscous, rice and millet is eaten with meat, but this latter is consumed surprisingly rarely.

To communicate with the Reguibat is to touch the history of the desert. They and the Tuareg are the only Berbers who still use the Tifinagh, an ancient alphabet derived from Phoenician and incorporating styles from Libyan script, though this is now only used for place names.

Where To Stay and Eating Out

cheap

All the town's hotels are very basic and stand next to each other in the central stretch of the main street, Avenue Hassan II. They have clean beds and passable water. In each of them this is stored in an old oil drum, which is topped up daily by a donkey cart that does a morning delivery from the modern pumping and desalination plant. Try first for a room at the **Chabab Sakia el Houra**, then at the **Erraha**, which has a first-floor sitting room with a view of the street through an ornate grille. The three other hotels, the **Maghrib El Arbi**, **Sable d'Or** and **Atlas**, are also perfectly adequate for a stop-over.

The two best **cafés** for eating are to the left of the central crossroads. There is a *hammam*, with male and female sections, nearby to the right of the football pitch, left at the crossroads. The arch visible on one side of the crossroads leads you to the market and eventually to the Place de l'Unité, where the fortress tower for the mosque interestingly contradicts the army camps, which are all decorated with false koubbas and minarets. A garden at the centre of the square is bordered by the **Pâtisserie de l'Arc en Ciel**, where pilots meet up in the evening and enjoy three sorts of fruit juice, and waitress service.

The Road from Es-Semara to Tan-Tan

Petrol for the whole of the journey north must be bought as you leave Es-Semara. The only permanent settlement on the 220km drive to Tan-Tan is **Abteh**, 140km out of Es-Semara, and there is no petrol there. Instead Abteh consists of four official bungalows, a decaying army fort on the red hills and a mosque with its graveyard. There is no longer a market there, but there are two cafés selling *tagines*.

South from Laâyoune through Boujdour to Dakhla

Boujdour lies 200km south, on a tarmac road with some surprisingly bumpy patches. Access to the sea is effectively prohibited by a continuous line of savage, crumbling cliffs on which cormorants nest unmolested. Only the sight of an occasional disintegrating shipwreck breaks the disturbing monotony of crossing the desert. Do not get excited by **Lemsid**, the main attraction marked on the map. It was once graced by the koubba of Sidi Mohammed Bou Gambour, but both the settlement and the shrine have been destroyed in recent fighting.

Boujdour

The most memorable feature of Boujdour is the **police checks**: one outside the town, one in the headquarters and one just as you leave. Do not attempt to speed up the process, even if you have to stop and wake up the friendly guards who manage to doze in huts amid a staggering density of flies. Your mother's maiden name and your whole holiday route may be requested, tea offered and the rival attractions of different Moroccan cities debated. Small gifts of cigarettes and canned drinks are cheerfully accepted in exchange for the tea, and make a welcome distraction from form-filling.

Boujdour's most prominent building is its **lighthouse**, around which cluster a nest of official white buildings and a large military compound of red buildings. The civil district starts through the arch. It consists of a single street, the Avenue Hassan II, which leads down to the fishing port. There are almost enough buildings along it to form a respectable village. Of these the **café** on the left as you walk down Hassan II, notable for its film posters, is the most sociable place from which to watch village life. Opposite on a street corner is **Rashida's Café**, where a line of cooking pots proffers delicious fish *tagine*, spiced onions with raisins and hot aromatic vegetable sauces. Accommodation is available at the **Boughraz Hotel**—no telephone and no water.

The **port area** marks another brave attempt to harness the natural resources of the Sahara to economic advantage. A fish market, freezing plant and desalination unit are all being built. The local fishermen are still using lines from small offshore boats and dare not venture too far from this one harbour, isolated as it is in an otherwise immense and vicious coast.

The **beach** looks promising but the sand in fact gives way at the shore edge to a rather sharp area of wave-cut rock platform—ideal for the amateur rock-pool naturalist but not for swimming. Along the shore European camper vans collect in the winter and form ghettos.

Beyond Boujdour

The road from Boujdour to Ad-Dakhla was completed in February 1988 and is now open for unescorted traffic. The opening of a petrol station at Boujdour was vital in making the road to Dakhla possible for all normal cars. The route runs through the same grindingly barren, flat *hammada* desert. About 147km out of Boujdour, you leave the coast to follow the valley of the river Assaq and climb out through some comparatively entertaining low canyons.

Skaymat, marked on maps and by a profusion of road signs, is eagerly awaited but an enormous disappointment, being no more than a dirt track turning to **Bir Anzarane** and the now disbanded road builders' encampment. The road returns to the coast after Skaymat and there are various adventurous opportunities to clamber down to the sea.

If you want a **swim**, the obvious place to stop is some 70km before Dakhla, where the Moroccan–Mauritanian frontier was for the three years from 1976 to 1979, before Mauritania gave up all interest in the Western Sahara. The old frontier post lies along a canyon, which is easy to walk down for the distance you need to travel.

Dakhla

Dakhla (or Ad-Dakhla, formerly Villa Cisneros) was founded by the Spanish in 1884, on the end of a long spit of land which runs parallel to the mainland and almost encloses a bay called the Rio de Oro. It is now as it was then, a military and administrative outpost. The military flavour of Dakhla first assails you at the checkpoint as you arrive at the neck of the land spit. Armed soldiers guard a system of pillboxes and shelters carved into yellowish white tufa rock. You are led into a crumbling yellow pisé hut set into a tufa hill from where trenches lead up to a command post. The shelter is decorated with recovered pieces of shrapnel and sturdy benches made from great sea-washed timber balks. The soldiers help to preserve the immediacy of the slightly intimidating atmosphere by strictly forbidding photographs, while talking of the beauty of Dakhla as they hand you mint tea. Your familiar details are all taken down, and by now you will have learned not to wince at the harsh French description *'célibataire'* if you are unmarried.

At this stage the peninsula is quite wide, and all the way down to the town itself the road follows the inland bay. Beyond the first checkpoint on your left the first of the four inland bays is dramatically revealed to you, a vast expanse of clear tide-washed glistening sand, whilst just to the north of the road moulder a string of largely abandoned stone barracks and hill forts. As well as the three further bays, the inland sea holds the intriguing 10km long basalt **island of Herne**, which used to be a flamingo colony. It is thought to be the 'Cerne Island' which Hanno, the Carthaginian admiral, used as a stopping point.

Shortly before you enter the town you pass **Fisherman's Cove**, an area where you can camp and park. There are no mussels to be gathered here, but plenty of winkles, which are best lightly steamed and eaten with pepper. Sole and red mullet are caught and local fishermen are free with advice. The peninsula ends at **Point Durnford**, named after a midshipman on a British marine survey ship which landed here in 1821. Sometimes you can see the masts of a World War I German merchant raider sunk off the point.

The town of Dakhla itself is completely dominated by the military. At the height of the war the airport was constantly buzzing with helicopters, ferrying troops out to isolated posts. The harbour and jetty, where patrol craft are moored, is under the control of the navy. The road into town, bedecked with an arch, passes two large military compounds decorated with stone turrets. The **souks**, to the left and then to the right of the main road are stocked with goods for 'garrison man': awesome quantities of aftershave, thermoses, pen-knives, trinkets, suitcases and tight fitting underpants. The **Spanish cathedral** is the only non-military structure of any size which it is safe to gaze upon and photograph.

Getting Around

Dakhla is as far as the casual visitor can go. Buses are unreliable, but there is a steady stream of lorries and *grands taxis* which cover the route north during the night. A place in one of them to Laâyoune costs around 200dh for the 540km.

Where to Stay

The moderately priced **Hotel Doums**, ✆ (08) 898045, ℻ 898045, is on Av El Walaa (on the left as you enter town) and has 30 rooms, a bar and restaurant, but is often filled up by a UN detachment, in which case you might try the inexpensive **Hotel Sahara** on Av Sidi Ahmed Laarousi (near the market), ✆ (08) 897773.

Facing the airfield there is a nest of cheap hotels, **Pension Atlas**, **Hôtel Oued Eddahab** and **Hôtel 14 Août**. The **Bahia**, behind Bar Juan on the coast road, has 4 or 5 beds to a room; newest and cleanest is the **Imlil**, to the right of the main road by the second souk area. These hotels are all full of soldiers on leave and have a barracks atmosphere, sustained by the heavy tread of boots and corridors full of lovat green.

Eating Out

There are pleasant cafés sprinkled throughout the town. Heavily spiced fresh fish *tagine*, if you like it, is the very best Dakhla has to offer. The **Café Terminus** on the road back out of town has a quieter, more civilian atmosphere than the town centre. Its tables are full of incessant card games. There is, however, no need to avoid the soldiers, who are generally charming and courteous. It is interesting to observe that the formal military salute serves as a mere token introduction to a more effusive system of fraternal greetings that seems to ignore rank completely. The **Bar Juan** has a notice forbidding the consumption of beer by Muslims. This only seems to apply to the premises, as there is a stream of camouflaged carry-outs.

Shopping

The constant odour of cloves is the most distinctive feature of Dakhla's shops. Or you could think about bargaining gently for tie-dyed cloth or long, striped blankets.

Bathing

Water is in short supply in the hotels, and the only practical places in which to wash are the *hammams*: **Le Bain de la Marche Verte** is in a reddish building, just behind a long white igloo hut off the souk streets, and the **Bath Sahara** beyond that. Both cost 5dh and admit women from 10am to 5pm, and men from 6 to 10pm.

South from Dakhla to Mauritania

Though the truce with the Polisario still holds, the area south of Dakhla remains a military zone with a lethal legacy of mines. The road is perfectly good but can only be taken in the company of the twice-weekly military convoy on Tuesdays and Fridays. All the paperwork of a border crossing (plus authorization from the provincial *caid* confirmed by Rabat) has to be performed at Dakhla. Permission to join the convoy is regularly given to the trucks run by trans-Saharan adventure holidays but is not so freely awarded to independent travellers.

The official border is 464km south of Dakhla at the old Spanish fishing village of La Gouèra/Lagouiria. In practice the Moroccan military tend to leave the convoy at the base of the peninsula, 20km before the Mauritanian frontier-post outside the regional capital of Nouâdhibou.

Abassids. The 2nd dynasty of caliphs who ruled the Muslim world from AD 750–1258.

Abd (sing.), **abid** (plural). A slave. By inference a negro, and used to distinguish the negro regiments from the tribal ones in the sultan's army.

Agadir. Principal city and port of southwestern Morocco. Literally the fortified communal hilltop granaries of the Berber tribes, also known as *ighrem*, *igherm* or *irherm*.

Aid. The holy day or feast, as in Aid es Seghir at the end of Ramadan.

Aïn. Spring or water hole. Plural **aïoun.**

Aït. Child of, as used in the creation of a tribal identity, such as Aït-Atta.

Aït-Atta. Berber tribe from Jbel Sarhro who dominated the south from the 16th century to 1934.

Akbar. 'The Great'—as in Allah Akbar.

Ali. Cousin and son-in-law of the Prophet through his marriage to Fatima, and father of Hassan and Hussein. Ali succeeded Othmann as 4th caliph in AD 656 but his reign was punctuated by disputes which split Islam into the Sunni, Shiite and Kharijite camps.

Almohad. 'The unitarians'. An Islamic reform movement founded by Ibn Tumert in the High Atlas which replaced Almoravid rule over Morocco. The Almohad Empire, AD 1147–1248, was a peak period of Moroccan history.

Almoravid. 'The warrior monks'. An Islamic reform movement founded by Ibn Yaasin in the Sahara, which under his successors Abu Bekr and Youssef ben Tachfine controlled an Empire that stretched from Spain to West Africa AD 1060–1147.

Alaouite. The present ruling dynasty of Morocco, who from their base in the Tafilalt oasis replaced the Saadian sultans in 1666.

Arabesque. General adjective describing the architecture and the calligraphic, floral and geometrical decoration of Islam.

Argan. Hard oil-producing thorn tree that only grows in southwestern Morocco.

Asif. River that flows throughout the year.

Averroes/Ibn Rushd. Muslim scholar born in Cordoba in 1126 who originally enjoyed the patronage of the Almohad sultans. His translation of Aristotle and philosophical works was of great influence to the Christian universities, though the orthodox of both Islam and Christendom condemned his rationalism.

Azrou. Rock, and the name of a town in the Middle Atlas.

Bab. Gate.

Beni. The sons of, often used in the description of a tribe, like the Beni-Merin.

Berghawata/Berghouata. Heretical Berber tribal group who occupied the coastal region from Salé to Casablanca until conquered in the 12th century by the Almohads.

Bit. Room.

Cadi. Judge of Muslim law.

Caftan/Kaftan. Formal outer garment, though it increasingly refers to an embroidered cotton robe.

Caid. Magistrate who in the lawless areas was often a tribal chief recognized by the sultan. Now the chief magistrate of a commune.

Islamic and Moroccan Terms

Caliph. The successor of the Prophet to the rule of the Muslim community.

Caravanserai. Defensive lodgings on a caravan route.

Chleuh. One of the three Berber tribal groupings who occupy the western High Atlas, the Sous and the Anti-Atlas. They are also known as Soussi or Masmuda and speak a dialect known as Tachelhait.

Cursive. The familiar style of flowing rounded Arabic script.

Dakhla. An entrance to a gorge and the name of a town of the Western Sahara, known under Spanish rule until 1976 as Villa Cisneros.

Dar. House, building or palace. City quarters are often named after the most distinctive house of the quarter, like Dar Sejene in Meknès.

Daya. Lake.

Dirham. The Ommayad caliphs based the first Muslim silver coinage on the Byzantine Drachmae. The name and style was in turn copied by Moroccan mints.

Drâa. Arm. The river Drâa flows south from Ouarzazate into the Sahara.

Emir. He who commands. Originally the military deputies of the caliph, and transformed into a title of sovereignty.

Erg. Dunes or region of dunes in a desert.

Fantasia. A display of horsemanship featuring small charges, dramatic halts and the firing of muskets.

Fassi. An inhabitant of Fès. It can also refer to the rich merchant class in Morocco.

Fatima. Only surviving daughter of the Prophet, wife of Ali and mother of Hassan and Hussein. The central female cult figure of Islam. The Hand of Fatima is an ancient good luck talisman.

Fiqh. The Islamic legal code. There are four traditional codes acknowledged by the orthodox Muslim: the Malekite, Hanefite, Chafiite and Hanbalite. The Malekite is favoured in Morocco.

Foggara/Khettara. Underground irrigation canal.

Fondouq/Fondouk. A courtyard surrounded by rooms which takes on a great range of functions.

Gandoura. Mostly worn by men, a simple cotton tunic with sleeves and plain collar.

Garum. Peculiar fish paste made of salt and mashed tuna intestines, beloved by the ancient Romans and manufactured for centuries on the Moroccan Atlantic coast.

Gnaoua/Gnawa/Gnaiwaya. Black religious brotherhood from West Africa and also the name of their spirit music.

Habous. Religious foundations.

Hadj. A pilgrimage to Mecca. The honorific title for those who have made the journey is Hadji.

Haik. Large cloth used by women to cover themselves in the street.

Hammada. Flat pebbly plateau of the Sahara.

Hammam. Steam or Turkish baths.

Haratine. Black serf caste in the south, having no tribal loyalties but often attached in a share-cropping arrangement to a nomadic warrior group.

Harmattan. Hot dry winds which blow from the Sahara.

Hassan II. King of Morocco, who succeeded his father Mohammed V to the throne in 1961. Born in 1929, he was educated in Rabat and Bordeaux, where he read law. He accompanied his father into exile from 1953 to 1955 and on Independence was put in command of the new royal army.

Hegira. The Islamic era which began with the flight of the Prophet from Mecca to Medina in July AD 622. The Muslim calendar is based on a lunar rather than a solar year, and each year is therefore 11 days shorter than each Gregorian year.

Hilali. A nomadic bedouin tribe that with the Sulaym left the Arabian peninsula in the 11th century to advance west along the North African coast.

Ibn Battuta. Travel writer who was born in Tangier in 1304 and died at Fès in 1377. Trained as a *cadi*, he travelled, worked and married throughout the Muslim world from Timbuktu to China.

Ibn Khaldoun. Celebrated historian and sociologist who was born in Tunis in 1332, his parents having fled from Andalusia. He obtained positions in a number of Muslim courts and lived in Fès before settling in Egypt as the Malekite Mufti of Cairo.

Idriss I/Moulay Idriss. Great-grandson of the Prophet and founder of the first Muslim kingdom of Morocco in AD 788. His tomb at Moulay Idriss is the pre-eminent national shrine.

Idriss II. Posthumous son of Idriss I. Creator of the city of Fès where his tomb is venerated. His descendants, the Idrissids, have been a numerous and influential clan throughout Moroccan history.

Ighrem. *See* **Agadir**.

Imam. Leader of prayers and by implication also a political leader.

Islam. Submission to God. Mohammed is the best-known and the last of a long line of prophets who taught submission to God, giving rules for the conduct of life and threatening unbelievers with divine punishment.

Istaqlal. Independence party founded by Allal al Fasi in 1934, which took a leading role in the civil resistance to the French Protectorate. It held a strong position in post-Independence government 1956–1962.

Jbel/Djebel. Mountain. The Djeballa are a specific group of Arabic-speaking tribes that occupy the western Rif. It is also a city dweller's label of contempt for the unsophisticated, the hill-billies.

Jdid/Djedid. New. As in Fès Jdid, new Fès, the 14th-century royal extension to the city.

Jellaba. Large cotton or wool outer garment with sleeves and a hood.

Jihad. Holy war against the enemies of Islam.

Kaaba. A meteorite venerated from antiquity in Mecca and situated on the spot where Abraham traditionally erected his altar. Muslims pray towards the Kaaba and circle it seven times before kissing it as the culmination of the Hadj.

Kasbah. The citadel of a town or a rural fortress.

Khaima. Grand tent of a tribal leader now much reproduced for use at fêtes and as restaurants.

Khettara. *See* **Foggara**.

Kilim. A woven carpet.

Kohl. Ground powder of the metallic-looking sulphur of antimony. Applied to the eyes, it stimulates an attractive watery sheen that is useful protection against soot and dust.

Koran. The word of God dictated to the Prophet Mohammed by the archangel Gabriel in Arabic.

Kouba. Women's room.

Koubba. Dome. By extension a koubba is the shrine of a saint's tomb which is usually covered by a small white cupola. They often form the object of a pilgrimage and are at the centre of female spiritual activity.

Ksar, pl. **ksour**. An Arabic noun derived from Caesar that describes a fortified village.

Kufic. Angular style of Arabic script, named after the city of Kufa in Iraq, which is chiefly used in stone and plaster carving.

Leo Africanus. Born in Granada in 1483, El Hassan ibn Mohammed el Fasi was enslaved by Christians, but when recognized as an intellectual was presented to the Pope. He was freed, baptized and awarded a pension by Pope Leo V, who encouraged him to write his famous description of North Africa. Having completed the great work he died a Muslim in Tunis in 1554.

Litham. Veil.

Lyautey, Marshal Hubert. One of the most important commanders of the French Colonial Army, he served in Madagascar and Indo-China before taking charge of the absorption of eastern Morocco from Algeria. As Resident-General from 1912 to 1926 he set the shape and objectives of the French Protectorate.

Maghreb. The land of the setting sun or furthest west, containing the three nations of Tunisia, Algeria and Morocco.

Makhzen. Government, or government district.

Maksoura/Maqsara. Wooden screens in a mosque that protect rulers from assassination.

Malekite. The most widely practised school of judicial practice and Koranic interpretation in North Africa. It was formulated by Malik ibn Anas, a judge from Medina who died in AD 795.

Marabout. Holy warrior, ascetic or the chief of a religious brotherhood who has won the respect of the people. His tomb may be covered by a dome.

Mauretania. The two Roman provinces of Mauretania Caesariensis and Mauretania Tingitania, whose boundaries approximate those of modern Morocco and Algeria. It now refers to the Saharan country south of Morocco on the Atlantic coast.

Mecca. Sacred town of the Muslims, 8km inland from the Red Sea, on the old caravan route from Syria to Yemen. Mosques are all oriented towards Mecca, 45° east and 12.5° south from Fès.

Méchouar. A square adjoining a palace in which the population can assemble to pay homage to the ruler.

Medersa. Residential schools for the study of the Koran and religious law. They were introduced into Morocco in the 12th century, though the earliest surviving buildings date from the 14th.

Medina. Walled city or old city, in distinction to the new European-style quarter. Named after the city that Mohammed fled to to avoid persecution in Mecca.

Mellah. The Jewish quarter. The name derives from the word *melh*, meaning salt, as the Jews used to perform the task of salting the severed heads of the sultan's enemies in order to preserve them.

Mendoub. Agent or representative of the sultan, as found in Tangier from 1927–56.

Merenids. Dynasty who originated from the Beni-Merin nomadic tribe who dominated the eastern plains of Morocco and replaced the Almohads in 1248.

Midha. Fountain for ritual washing before prayer.

Mihrab. A niche in a place of prayer which indicates the direction of Mecca.

Minaret. The tower of a mosque used for calling the faithful to prayer. The pinnacle is crowned with domes representing the daily prayers, and a blue or green flag flying indicates Friday, the Muslim sabbath.

Minbar. A pulpit-like staircase in mosques used for the noonday Friday sermon, the *khutba*.

Minzah. In a palace, a garden pavilion, especially one enjoying a fine view.

Mohammed. The Prophet, the last in the succession of Abraham, Noah, Moses and Jesus who have called man to worship the one God.

Mohammed V. The popular monarch who led the struggle for Moroccan Independence and was exiled by the French. After Independence in 1956 he initiated a new era by ruling as King Mohammed V.

Mosque. The place of prostration, the place of reunion, the place of prayer.

Moukarnas/muqarnas. Stalactite-like decorations chiefly of carved wood, stone or plaster.

Moulay. Honorific title, approximately 'lord'. Used in Morocco by the descendants of the Prophet.

Mouloud. The great feast day celebrating Mohammed's birthday on the 12th day of the Muslim month of Rabi at-Tani.

Moussem. Originally an annual popular pilgrimage to the tomb of a saint, but now by extension any festival or outdoor entertainment.

Msalla. Prayer area; open-air mosque.

Muezzin. The call to prayer, also the prayer caller.

Oasis. An island of life in the desert supported by a water gathering system.

Omayyads. The first dynasty of caliphs who ruled the Islamic world from AD 660–750 and were descended from Muawiya, the governor of Syria, who was proclaimed caliph after the assassination of Ali.

Oued. River.

Pacha. Provincial governor, or the governor of a city.

Pisé. Packed wet clay, naturally baked by the sun. Widely used throughout Morocco for the construction of walls, kasbahs and roads.

Protectorate. Period of French colonial rule of Morocco, 1912–56. Administered by the Resident-General under the pretence that the sultan had contracted his authority to France by the 1912 Treaty of Fès.

Rabat/R'bat. A R'bat is a fortified monastery. Rabat is a city founded by the Almohads on the site of an old R'bat which has been the capital of Morocco since 1912.

Ramadan. Muslim month of fasting in the ninth lunar month of the year. No food, drink or sex is allowed during the hours of daylight. Travellers, the sick, old, the pregnant and pre-pubescent children are exempt.

Reguibat. A desert Berber tribe, *see* pp.574–5 the Western Sahara

Rehamna. An Arab tribe that dominated the arid plains north of Marrakech from the 16th century.

Resident General. The French rulers of Morocco from 1912–56: Lyautey, Steeg, Saint, Ponsot, Peyrouton, Nogues, Puaux, Labonne, Juin, Lacoste, Grandval, Boyer de la Tour and Dubois.

Rharb/Gharb. West. The Rharb is the fertile coastal region between Larache and Kénitra.

Rogui. A pretender to the sultanate.

Roumi. Roman, Christian, foreigner.

Saadian. Moroccan dynasty which replaced the Wattasid sultans in the 15th century and repulsed the Portuguese. They originated as sheiks from the the Drâa Valley and established their first capital at Taroudannt.

Sabil. Public drinking fountain.

Sanhaja. One of the three great groupings of the Berber people occupying the Sahara and parts of the Middle and High Atlas. Their dialect is known as Tamazight.

Sebka. Decorative repetition of interlaced arches, as were often used on the stone gates and walls of the Almohads.

Sebkha. Lake or lagoon.

Seguia. Irrigation canal.

Sheik. Leader of a religious brotherhood.

Sherif/Shorfa. Descendant of the Prophet.

Sidi. Male honorific title, always used to denote a saint but also more widely used.

Souk. Market.

Sufi. General description for mystical Islamic brotherhoods.

Sultan. Ruler. A word of Turkish origin which implies a single, paramount ruler.

Sunni. The orthodox Muslims, and the prevalent Moroccan form of Islam. The dispute between the schismatic Shiites and Sunni has never been of importance in Morocco.

Taibia. Brotherhood.

Tagine. Traditional Moroccan stew.

Targui, pl. **Tuareg**. The Sanhajan Berber tribe that occupy the central Sahara and dominated the caravan routes. They alone have retained a Berber alphabet, known as Tifinagh and speak a Berber dialect known as Temajegh.

Tizi. A mountain pass.

Ulema. The council of professors of Islamic law who since the 12th century have been consulted by sultans for the approval of new laws. They must also formally approve the accession of each new ruler.

Vizier. Chief minister of an Islamic ruler.

Wadi. Dry riverbed.

Wahabbi. Puritanical reforming Muslim sect from Arabia who were active from the 18th century.

Wattasid. Cousins of the Merenid sultans who first became hereditary Viziers and from 1472 ruled directly until replaced in 1554 by the Saadians.

Zaouia/Zawiya, pl. **Zouawi**. The sanctuary or college of students that often collects around the tomb or sanctuary of a marabout.

Zellij. Geometrical mosaic pattern usually seen on the lower portion of a wall made from chipped glazed tiles.

Zenata. One of the three great divisions of the Berber people, whose homeland is the northeast, the Rif and the eastern plains. Their dialect is known as Riffi or Tarifit.

Language

The official language of Morocco is Arabic, though 40 per cent of the population speak one of the three Berber dialects as their first language. Moroccans have a natural linguistic ability, and in the cities they will typically speak Arabic, possibly know one of the Berber dialects, learn French or Spanish at school and also juggle with a little English, Dutch or German. In all but the most rural areas you will be understood speaking French. Despite an official Arabicization policy, French remains the language of higher education, technology, government and big business. Spanish is understood and spoken in Spain's old colonial possessions in the far north and south, the Rif and the Western Sahara. Hotel porters, guides and hustlers can usually be relied on to know some English. In short it is easy to travel and communicate in Morocco without learning Arabic. However, if you can learn a few phrases or greetings you will not only give great pleasure but will also earn goodwill useful in any transaction or relationship.

Moroccan Arabic Pronunciation: Classical Arabic and modern Arabic as spoken in Cairo or Mecca are very different from the official language of Morocco—Moghrebi Arabic. It is a very guttural language, but this does not mean that it should be hard sounding. As a general rule, hard consonants should be pronounced as far back in the throat as possible, thereby softening them slightly. In particular:

'q' should be quite like a 'k', softened by being vocalized from further back in the throat
'gh' should sound like a purring 'gr', again from the back of the throat, a hardened French 'r'
'kh' like a Gaelic 'ch', pronounced from the back of the throat, as in the Scottish 'loch'
'j' again a softer sound, like the French pronunciation of the letter, as in 'Frère Jacques'
'ai' should sound like the letter 'i' as you would pronounce it when reciting the alphabet
'ay' should sound like the letter 'a' as in the recited alphabet

English	*French*	*Arabic*
Basic		
Yes, No	*Oui, Non*	*Eeyeh/Waha, La*
Please	*S'il vous plaît*	*Minfadlik*
Thank you	*Merci*	*Shokran/Barakalayfik*
Good, Bad	*Bon, Mauvais*	*Mizeyen, Meshee mizeyen*
Meetings, Greetings, Conversation		
Sir, Madam	*Monsieur, Madame*	*Si/Sidi, Lalla*
Hello	*Bonjour*	*Labes (informal), Salam Alaykoom*
How are you?	*Comment allez-vous?*	*Ooach khbar'ek?*
Fine	*Ça va bien*	*Labes*
Good morning	*Bonjour*	*Sbah l'khir*
Good evening	*Bonsoir*	*Msa l'khir*
Goodbye	*Au revoir*	*B'slemah*
Good night	*Bonne nuit*	*Leela saieeda*
My name is ...	*Je m'appelle ...*	*Ismee ...*
How do you say ... in Arabic?	*Comment dit-on ... en Arabe?*	*Keef tkoobal ... Arbia?*
I don't understand	*Je ne comprends pas*	*Ma fhemshi*
I don't know	*Je ne sais pas*	*Ma arafshi*
Help!	*Au secours!*	*Ateqq!*
Excuse me, Sorry	*Excusez-moi, Pardon*	*Smeh lee, Asif*
Never mind/such is life	*C'est la vie*	*Maalesh*
No problem	*Pas de problème*	*Mush mushkillah*
Travelling and Directions		
Train	*train*	*tren*
Bus	*autobus*	*l'kar/tobis*
Car	*voiture*	*tomobeel, sayara*
When is the first/ last/next ...?	*A quelle heure part le premier/dernier/prochain...?*	*Waqtash ... loowel/l'akher/lee minbad?*

Where is …?	*Où se trouve …?*	*Fayn kayn …?*
… a hotel	*… un hôtel*	*… otel/fondouk*
… a campsite	*… un camping*	*… mookhaiyem*
… a restaurant	*… un restaurant*	*… restaurant*
… a lavatory	*… un W.C.*	*… vaysay*
… the bus station	*… la gare d'autobus*	*… mahata d'lkeeran*
… the train station	*… la gare*	*… mahata d'ltren*
… a bank	*… une banque*	*… bank*
… a post office	*… une poste*	*… bousta/barid*
ticket	*billet*	*bitaka/beeyay*
left, right	*à gauche, à droite*	*al leeser, al leemin*

At a Hotel

I want a room	*Je voudrais une chambre*	*B'gheet beet*
Do you have a room?	*Est-ce que vous avez une chambre?*	*Wesh andik wahid beet?*
Can I look at it?	*Est-ce qu'on peut la voir?*	*Wesh yimkin nshoof?*

At a Restaurant

What do you have to eat?/to drink?	*Qu'est ce que vous avez à manger?/à boire?*	*Ashnoo kane f'l-makla? /f'l musharoubat?*
What is this?	*Qu'est ce que c'est?*	*Shnoo hada?*
big, small	*grand, petit*	*kbir, sghrir*
glass, plate	*verre, assiette*	*kess, t'b-sil*
knife, fork, spoon	*couteau, fourchette, cuillère*	*moos, forsheta, malka*
bread, eggs	*pain, œufs*	*l'hobs, beda*
salt, pepper	*sel, poivre*	*l'melha, lebzar*
sugar	*sucre*	*azoukar*
The bill please	*L'addition, s'il vous plaît*	*L'h'seb minfadlik*

Vegetables/Salads — *Legumes/Salades* — *lkhoudra/chalada*

olives, rice	*olives, riz*	*zitoun, rouz*
potatoes (chips)	*pommes de terre (frites)*	*btata (btata mklya)*
tomatoes, onions	*tomates, oignons*	*matesha, l'basla*
mixed salad	*salade Marocaine*	*chalada*

Meat/Poultry/Fish/Fruit — *Viande/Volaille/Poisson/Fruits* — *L'hem/L'hout/Fekiha*

beef, mutton	*bœuf, mouton*	*l'habra, l'houli/kabch*
chicken	*poulet*	*djaj*
fish	*poisson*	*l'hout*
sardines	*sardines*	*sardile*
oranges, grapes, bananas	*oranges, raisins, bananes*	*leetcheen, l'a'arib, banane*
peaches, apricots	*pêches, abricots*	*l'khoukh, mishmash*
almonds, dates, figs	*amandes, dattes, figues*	*louze, tmer, kermus*

Numbers — *Nombres*

1, 2, 3, 4, 5,	*un, deux, trois, quatre, cinq*	*wahed, jooj, tlata, arba, khamsa*
6, 7, 8, 9,	*six, sept, huit, neuf*	*setta, seba, tmenia, tse'ud*
10, 20, 50	*dix, vingt, cinquante*	*achra, achrin, khamsin*
100, 1000	*cent, mille*	*mia, alef*

Buying and Bargaining

How much is that?	*C'est combien?*	*Bsh hal hadeek?*
Too expensive	*trop cher*	*Ghalee bzef*
Do you have …?	*Est-ce que vous avez des …?*	*Wesh andik …?*
I want …	*Je cherche …*	*Bgheet …*
larger, smaller, cheaper	*plus grand, plus petit, moins cher*	*kebira, seghira, rkhaysa*
This is no good	*Ça ne va pas*	*Hadee meshee mizeyen*
I don't want any	*Je n'en veux pas*	*Mabgheet shee*
Okay!	*Okay!*	*Wakha!*

Further Reading

Travelling Companions

Bidwell, Margaret and Robin, *Morocco, The Travellers' Companion*, (IB Tauris, 1992), a wide-ranging anthology of travel writing; **Rabinow**, Paul, *Reflections on Fieldwork in Morocco*, an almost painfully honest account of an anthropologist's attempt to find a Moroccan friend he can trust; **Rogerson**, Barnaby *The Traveller's History of North Africa*, (Windrush Press, 1998), the only one-volume history in English of the Maghreb from the Stone Age to the 20th century.

History

Abun-Nasr, Jamil M, *History of the Maghrib in the Islamic Period* (Cambridge, 1987); **Africanus**, Leo, *A Description of Africa, 1600*; **Barbour**, Nevill, *Morocco* (London, 1965); **Blunt**, Wilfrid, *Black Sunrise, The Life and Times of Moulai Ismail, Emperor of Morocco, 1646-1727* (Methuen, 1950); **Bovill**, EV, *The Golden Trade of the Moors* (OUP); **Dunn**, Ross E, *Resistance in the Desert, 1881–1912* (Croom Helm, 1977); **Forbes**, Rosita, *El Raisuni, The Sultan of the Mountains* (Thornton Butterworth, 1924); **Hodges**, Tony, *Western Sahara, Roots of a Desert War* (Croom Helm, 1983); **Ibn Battuta**, *Travels in Africa and Asia, 1324–54* (RKP); **El Idrisi**, *Description of Africa and Spain* (1866); **Julien**, CE, *History of North Africa* (London 1970); **Le Tourneau**, R, *Fez in the Age of the Merenids* (Norman, Okla 1961); **Lewis**, Bernard, *The Jews of Islam* (Princeton, 1984); **Maxwell**, Gavin, *Lords of the Atlas, The Rise and Fall of the House of Glaoui 1893–1956* (Longmans, 1966, rep Century, 1983); **Meakin**, Budget, *The Moorish Empire, The Land of the Moors* and *The Moors* (London 1899, 1901, 1902); **Montagne**, R, *The Berbers* (London, 1973); **Perkins**, KJ, *Quaids, Captains and Colons in the Maghrib* (New York, 1981); **Porch**, Douglas, *The Conquest of Morocco* (Cape, 1983), and *The Conquest of the Sahara* (Cape, 1985); **Thompson**, V, and **Adloff**, R, *The Western Saharans, Background to Conflict* (Croom Helm, 1980); **Woolman**, David, *Rebels in the Rif* (OUP).

Anthropology

Chimenti, Elisa, *Tales and Legends of Morocco* (New York, 1943)—folk tales collected by the daughter of a royal surgeon; **Crapanzo**, Vincent, *Tuhami, a Portrait of a Moroccan* (Univ. of Chicago)—an academic study of an illiterate artisan; **Deshen**, Shlomo, *The Mellah Society* (Univ. of Chicago, 1989)—pre-colonial life in Jewish communities; **Dwyer**, Kevin, *Moroccan Dialogues* (Johns Hopkins, 1982)—interviews from the Sous valley; **Gellner**, Ernest, *Saints of the Atlas* (Weidenfeld & Nicolson, 1969)—celebrated study of a holy dynasty in the High Atlas; **Mernissi**, Fatima, *Doing Daily Battle: Interviews with Moroccan Women* (Women's Press, 1988); *Beyond the Veil: Male-Female Dynamics in Modern Muslim Society* (Al Saqi, 1985); and *Islam and Democracy: Fear of the Modern World* (Virago, 1993)—a hard-hitting assault on Muslim political culture in the wake of the Gulf war; **Munson**, Henry, *The House of Si Abd Allah*—conversations with a family (his wife's) outside Tangier; **Peets**, Leonara, *Women of Marrakesh, 1930–79* (Hurst)—acute social observations by a long-resident Estonian doctor; **Waterbury**, John, *North for the Trade* (Berkeley 1972); **Westermarck**, Edward, *Ritual and Belief in Morocco* (London, 2 vols, 1926), and *Wit and Wisdom in Morocco* (London, 1930).

Travel Writing

Bowles, Paul, *Their Heads Are Green* and *Points in Time* (Peter Owen); **Canetti**, Elias, *The Voices of Marrakesh* (M. Boyars); if you read just one book, make it this one; **Cunnighame Graham**, RB, *Moghreb el Acksa* (London, 1898, rep Century); **Harris**, Walter, *Morocco That*

Was (London, 1921, rep Eland Books). Other books by Harris, *The Land of an African Sultan* (London 1889) and *Tafilet* (Blackwood, Edinburgh 1895), remain out of print; **Landau**, Ron, *Kasbahs of Southern Morocco* (Faber & Faber, 1969); **Lewis**, Wyndham, *Journey into Barbary*, first published as *Filibusters in Barbary* (London, 1932, rep Penguin); **Saint-Exupéry**, Antoine de, *Wind, Sand and Stars* (Heinemann 1939, rep Penguin)—the pioneer poet of flight flying mail across the Sahara; **Wharton**, Edith, *Morocco* (Travellers Library, 1927, rep Century).

Moroccan Fiction Translated into English

Maghrebi fiction is at its best in novella or short story form. It is distinguished by its fast narrative and plots, its violence and recurring theme of betrayal by friends and lovers. *Five Eyes* (Black Sparrow Press) is a collection of short stories by Mohammed Mrabet, Mohammed Choukri, Larbi Layachi, Ahmed Yacoubi and Abdesalam Boulaich, translated by Paul Bowles.

Ben Jalloun, Tahar, *The Sand Child* (H. Hamilton), *Sacred Night* (Quartet), *With Downcast Eyes* (Little, Brown, USA), three novels by one of Morocco's most fêted and literate of novelists, a long-time resident of Paris; **Choukri**, Mohammed, *For Bread Alone, an Autobiography* (Peter Owen, 1973)—a celebrated description of a harrowing childhood on the outer edge of society; **Chraibi**, Driss, *Heirs To The Past* (Heinemann), *Mother Comes of Age* (Three Continents Press), *The Butts* (Forest Books), three novels, of which the first is a classic not matched by its successors; **Layachi**, Larbi, *A Life Full Of Holes* (Grove Press, under Driss Charhadi pename), *Yesterday and Today* (Black Sparrow Press, 1985) *The Jealous Lover* (Tombouctou Books, California, 1986); **Mrabet**, Mohammed, *Love With a Few Hairs* (Arena, 1986), *M'Hashish* (Peter Owen, 1988), *The Beach Café* and *The Voice* (Black Sparrow Press, USA, 1980), *The Chest* (Tombouctou Books, California, 1983), *Marriage With Papers* (Tombouctou Books, California, 1988), *Look and Move On* (Peter Owen, 1989)—all translated by Paul Bowles. Start with the 1960s collection of ten tales *M'Hashish*, which could be translated as 'bombed out of your mind'; **Serhane**, Abselhake, *Messaouda* (Carcanet)—rites of passage for a young boy growing up in Azrou and for Morocco shedding the paternalism of the French Protectorate.

Western Fiction Set in Morocco

Barea, Arturo, *The Forging of a Rebel* (Flamingo, 3 vols; vol 2, *The Track*, deals with the Rif war); **Bowles**, Paul, *The Sheltering Sky* (Granada), set in the Algerian Sahara, *Let It Come Down* (Arena, 1985), on Tangier, *The Spider's House* (Arena), and *Collected Stories, 1939-1976* (Black Sparrow Press, USA 1986)—the most complete collection, though there is a host of rivals such as *The Delicate Prey* (1950), *A Hundred Camels in the Courtyard* (1962), *The Time of Friendship* (1967), *Things Gone and Things Still Here* (1977), *A Little Stone* (1950), *Call at Corazon* (1980); **Burgess**, Anthony, *Enderby* (Penguin)—scenes from Tangier clublife; **Burroughs**, William, *Naked Lunch* (Paladin)—to those who know them the silhouettes of Tangier and Gibraltar emerge through the dazzling, distorted static of this fantasy; **Busi**, Aldo, *Sodomies in Eleven Point* (Faber, 1992)—in the words of the blurb, 'a journey of the heart and soul through Literature, Life and Homosexuality'. Morocco and its men on pp 37–129; **Chirbes**, Rafael, *Mimoun* (Serpent's Tail, 1992)—the tale of the breakdown of a young Spaniard in Sefrou, in which every object, each moment is rendered mysterious; **Freud**, Esther, *Hideous Kinky* (Hamish Hamilton, 1992/Penguin, 1993)—a warm evocation of the joys of Morocco, as seen in the life of an English hippy mother by her 5-year old daughter; **Gray**, Pat, *Mr Narrator* (Dedalus 1989)—an unpublicized modern classic that 'portrays with documentary accuracy a Morocco... colonized by surrealism'; **Grenier**, Richard, *The Marrakesh One-Two* (Macdonald, 1984)—a comic adventure that takes its humour from the clash between Western and Muslim culture; **Gysin**, Brian, *The Process* (Abacus)—fabulous kif-induced adventures in sixties Tangier and the Sahara; **Hughes**, Richard, *In the Lap of the Atlas* (Chatto)—set in a fictional Telouèt; **Malouf**, Amin, *Leo the African* (Quartet)—historical novel on the 15th-century life of Leo Africanus; **Maugham**, Robin, *The Wrong People* (David Griffin 1967)—gay adventures among the smart British expatriate set of Tangier.

Journals, Letters, Diaries from Tangier

Bowles, Paul, *Without Stopping*, Paul (Peter Owen, 1972)—an autobiography nicknamed *Without Telling*, a failing not much corrected in the unauthorized biography by C. Sawyer-Lauccano, *An Invisible Spectator* (Bloomsbury, 1989). Other Bowles-iana include *Paul Bowles by His Friends*, ed. G Pulsifer (Peter Owen), Bowles's slim *A Tangier Journal, 1987-89* (Peter Owen, 1990) and Jane Bowles' *In and Out in the World, Letters 1935-70* (Black Sparrow 1985). The Tangier scene has been well covered in: **Green**, Michelle, *The Dream at the End of the World: Paul Bowles and the Literary Renegades of Tangier* (Bloomsbury), and **Finlayson**, Ian, *Tangier, City of the Dream* (HarperCollins 1992). Entertaining memoirs include **Croft-Cooke**, Rupert, *The Caves of Hercules* (London 1974); **Edge**, David, *Harem*; **Herbert**, David, *Second Son* (Peter Owen, 1972) and *Engaging Eccentrics* (Peter Owen, 1990); **Stewart**, Angus, *Tangier, a Writer's Notebook* (London 1977); and *Joe Orton's Diaries* (London 1986).

Art and Architecture

Besancot, Jean, *Costumes et Types du Maroc* (Paris 1942) and *Bijoux Arabes et Berbères du Maroc* (Casablanca 1954), rep KPI, London; **Burkhardt**, Titus, *Art of Islam, Language and Meaning* and *Moorish Culture in Spain*; **Damluji**, Salma, *Zillij: the Art of Moroccan Ceramics* (Garnet, UK)—expensive but definitive examination of the Ceramic tradition; **Dennis**, Lisl and Landt, *Living In Morocco* (Thames and Hudson)—illustrated handbook on using traditional crafts in modern interiors; **Hurbert**, Claude, *Islamic Ornamental design* (Faber & Faber, 1980); **Jacques-Meunie**, DJ, *Greniers Citadelles au Maroc* (Paris 1951), *Architectures et Habitats du Dadès* (Paris 1962), *Sites et Forteresses de L'Atlas*, (Paris 1951); **Khatabi**, A, and **Sigilmassa**, M, *The Splendours of Islamic Calligraphy* (Thames & Hudson, 1976); *Matisse in Morocco: the Paintings and Drawings, 1912-13* (Nat. Gallery of Art, Washington DC); **Parker**, RB, *Islamic Monuments in Morocco* (Baraka Press, USA); **Wade**, D, *Pattern in Islamic Art* (London, 1976).

Islam

The Koran, trans. NJ Dawood (Penguin, 1956), or *The Koran* (OUP) are the most easily available of the various rival texts; **Burkhardt**, Titus, *An Introduction to Sufi Doctrine*; **Guillaume**, Alfred, *Islam* (Penguin); **Nigosian**, Solomon, *Islam: the Way of Submission* (Crucible 1987).

Flowers, Birds and Animals

Bergier, P & F, *A Birdwatcher's Guide to Morocco* (Prion Press, UK)—a practical site guide for the committed birder; **Heinzel, Fitter & Parslow**, *The Birds of Britain & Europe with North Africa and the Middle East* (Collins).

Cooking

Benkirane, Fettouma, *Secrets of Moroccan Cooking* and *Moroccan Cooking—the Best Recipes* (Sochepress); **Carrier**, Robert, *Taste of Morocco* (Arrow, London)—an illustrated labour of love concentrating on the palace traditions; **Guinaudeau**, Z, *Fez, Traditional Moroccan Cooking* (Rabat, 1957); **Wolfert**, Paula, *Good Food from Morocco* (John Murray, 1962)—all the secrets of traditional home cooking.

Index

Note: Page numbers in *italics* indicate maps. **Bold** references indicate main references.